The Complete Works Of Thomas Brooks

Volume 5
of
6 Volume Set

Sovereign Grace Publishers, Inc.
P.O. Box 4998
Lafayette, IN 47903

Printed In the United States of America
By Lightning Source, Inc.

THE COMPLETE WORKS

OF

THOMAS BROOKS.

Edited, with Memoir,

BY THE REV. ALEXANDER BALLOCH GROSART,

LIVERPOOL.

VOL. V.

CONTAINING:

THE GOLDEN KEY TO OPEN HIDDEN TREASURES ;

PARADISE OPENED ;

AND

A WORD IN SEASON.

EDINBURGH : JAMES NICHOL.

LONDON : JAMES NISBET AND CO.   DUBLIN : G. HERBERT.

M.DCCC.LXVII.

CONTENTS.

THE

GOLDEN KEY

TO

OPEN HIDDEN TREASURES.

NOTE.

The 'Golden Key' forms Part I. of, spiritually, the richest and most nurturing of Brooks's larger treatises. Part II. follows in this volume. The title-page of the former will be found below.* It is interesting to compare Brooks's 'Golden Key' with the earlier work of Francis Dillingham, entitled 'A Golden Keye opening the Locke to eternall Happiness : containing seven most sweete and comfortable directions to a Christian life,' 1609, 12mo.—G.

* GOLDEN KEY

TO OPEN

Hidden Treasures,

OR

Several great Points, that refer to the Saints present blessedness, and their future happiness, with the resolution of several important questions.

Here you have also

The Active and Passive Obedience of Christ vindicated and improved, against men of corrupt minds, &c. Who boldly, in Pulpit and Press, contend against those glorious Truths of the Gospel.

You have farther

Eleven serious singular Pleas, that all sincere Christians may safely and groundedly make, to those ten Scriptures in the Old and New Testament, that speak of the general Judgment, and of that particular Judgment, that must certainly pass upon them all immediately after death,

The Godhead and Manhood of Christ, is here largely proved, and improved against all Gainsayers, by what names and titles soever they are distinguished and known among us. Several things concerning Hell, and hellish torments, opened, cleared and improved against all Atheists, and all others that boldly assert, that there is no Hell, but what is in us. Some other points of importance are here cleared and opened, which other Authors (so far as the Author hath read) have passed over them in great silence, all tending to the confirmation of the strong, and support, peace, comfort, settlement and satisfaction of poor, weak, doubting, trembling, staggering Christians.

By *Tho. Brooks* late Preacher of the Gospel, at *Margarets-New-Fish-street.*

LONDON,

Printed for *Dorman Newman,* at the King's-Arms in the *Poultrey;* and at the Ship and Anchor, at the Bridg-foot, on *Southwark* side, 1675.

[4to.—G.]

THE EPISTLE DEDICATORY.

To his much honoured and worthily esteemed friend, Sir NATHANIEL
HERNE, Knight, Sheriff of London, and Governor of the East
India Company.[1]

Grace, mercy, and peace be multiplied upon you and yours.

SIR,—Much might be said, were it necessary, for the dedication of
books unto persons of worth, interest, service, and honour, this having
been the constant practice of the best and wisest of men in all the
ages of the world; and therefore I need not make any farther apology
for my present practice.

What is written is permanent, *litera scripta manet,*[2] and spreads
itself farther by far, for time, place, and persons, than the voice can
reach. Augustine, writing to Volusian, saith, ' That which is written is always at hand to be read when the reader is at leisure.'[3]
There are those that think—and, as they conceive, from Scripture
grounds too—that the glory of the saints in heaven receives additions
and increases daily, as their holy walk and faithful service when here on
earth doth, after they are gone, bring forth fruit to the praise of God
amongst those that are left behind them. If this be so, what greater
encouragement can there be to write, print, preach, and to walk holily
in this world?

I must also confess that that general acceptation that my former
labours have found, both in the nation and in foreign parts, and that
singular blessing that has attended them from on High, hath been
none of the least encouragements to me once more to cast in my mite
into the common treasury.[4] Besides, I am not unsensible of your
candid esteem of some former endeavours of mine in this kind, neither.
do I know any way wherein I am more capacitated to serve the glory
of God, the interest of Christ, the public good, reproached truths, and
the interest of the churches, in my generation, than this, as my case
and condition is circumstanced; and I am very well satisfied that
there is nothing in this treatise but what tends to the advantage, com-

---

[1] Cf. Herbert, as before.—G.
[2] Supposed to be a portion of a mediæval pentameter hymn.—G.
[3] Aug., Epist. i., ad Volus.
[4] It was a saying of Phidias, concerning his first portraiture, If it be liked, I will
draw more besides this, if loathed, none but this.

fort, support, settlement, and encouragement of those whose concernment lies in peace and truth, in holiness and righteousness, throughout the nations.

Sir, the points here insisted on are of the greatest use, worth, weight, necessity, excellency, and utility imaginable; they are such wherein our present blessedness and our future happiness, yea, wherein our very all, both as to this and that other world, is wrapped up. It will be your life, honour, and happiness to read them, digest them, experience them, and to exemplify them in a suitable conversation, Deut. xxx. 15, 19, and xxxii. 47, which, that you may, let your immortal soul lie always open to the warm, powerful, and hourly influences of heaven.

Let it be the top of your ambition, and the height of all your designs, to glorify God,[1] to secure your interest in Christ, to serve your generation, to provide for eternity, to walk with God, to be tender of all that have *aliquid Christi*, anything of Christ, shining in them, and so to steer your course in this world as that you may give up your account at last with joy, Mat. xxv. 21, *seq.* All other ambition is base and low. Ambition, saith one, [Bernard,] is a gilded misery, a secret poison, a hidden plague, the engineer of deceit, the mother of hypocrisy, the parent of envy, the original of vices, the moth of holiness, the blinder of hearts, turning medicines into maladies, and remedies into diseases.[2] In the enthronisation of the pope, before he is set in his chair and puts on his triple crown, a piece of tow or wad of straw is set on fire before him, and one appointed to say *Sic transit gloria mundi*, The glory of this world is but a blaze.[3] St Luke calls Agrippa's pomp μετὰ πολλῆς φαντασίας, a fantasy or vain show, Acts xxv. 23; and indeed all worldly pomp and state is but a fantasy or vain show. St Matthew calls all the world's glory Δόξαν, an opinion, Mat. iv. 8; and St Paul calls it Σχῆμα, a mathematical figure, 1 Cor. vii. 31, which is a mere notion, and nothing in substance. The word here used intimateth that there is nothing of any firmness or solid consistency in the creature; it is but a surface, outside, empty thing; all the beauty of it is but skin deep. Mollerus,[4] upon that Ps. lxxiii. 20, concludeth, 'that men's earthly dignities are but as idle dreams, their splendid braveries but lucid fantasies.'[5] High seats are never but uneasy, and crowns are always stuffed with thorns, which made one say of his crown, 'O crown, more noble than happy.' Shall the Spirit of God, the grace of God, the power of God, the presence of God, arm you against all other sins, evils, snares, and temptations, as you are by a good hand of heaven armed against worldly ambition and worldly glory?

Sir, you know he was a Saul that said, 'Honour me before the people,' 1 Sam. xv. 30; and he was a Jehu that said, 'Come, see my

---

[1] 2 Cor. v. 9, φιλοτιμούμεθα. We ambitiously labour, we count it our highest honour and glory to be accepted of God.

[2] Cardinal Bourbon would not lose his part in Paris for his part in paradise. [Foxe] Act. and Mon., fol. 899. [As before.—G.]

[3] Cf. Sibbes, vol. iv. pp. 58, 305. 'Wad' is a little bundle.—G.

[4] Geneva, 1591, folio.—G.

[5] The Romans built Virtue's and Honour's temples close together, to shew that the way to true honour was by virtue.—*Augustine.*

zeal for the Lord of Hosts,' 2 Kings x. 16; and they were[1] three Irish kings that rebelled in Henry the Second's days, being derided for their rude habits and fashions; and they were some of the worst of cardinals that, when they were like to die, would give great sums of money for a cardinal's hat, that they might be so styled upon their tombs;[2] and they were the Romans and other barbarous nations that were most ambitious of worldly honour and glory; and he was a Julius Cæsar whose excessive desire of honour made him to be mortally hated by the senators and all others. God grants no man a patent for honour *durante vita*, but *durante bene-placito*, as the lawyers speak, during his life, but during his own good pleasure. All worldly honour and glory is subject to mutability. Honours, riches, and pleasures are the three deities that in these days a world of men adore, and to whom they sacrifice, morning and evening, their best thoughts; and these, for their unparalleled vanity, may well be called the vanity of vanities, Eccles. i. 2. Worldly honours are but a mere conceit, a shadow, a vapour, a feather in the cap, without substance or subsistence, and yet the most powerful charm of Satan, whereby he lulls men to sleep in the paradise of fools; to cast them, when they are awake, into the bottomless pit of eternal woe. For had not Satan held them to be the strongest of all temptations, he had not reserved them for his last battery against the constancy of our blessed Saviour, as he did, Mat. iv. 8, 9. And although this roaring cannon of his could not prevail against Christ, the rock of ages, Mat. xvi. 18, yet how many thousands in these days are captivated and deluded by the glorious glistering of worldly honours! Men of great honour and worldly glory stand but in slippery places. Adonibezek, a mighty prince, was made fellow-commoner with the dogs, Judges i. 7; and Nebuchadnezzar, a mighty conqueror, was turned a-grazing among the oxen, Dan. iv. 28; and Herod was reduced from a conceited[3] god to the most loathsome of men, a living carrion, arrested by the vilest creatures, upon the suit of his affronted Creator, Acts xii. 23. The lice did fully confute his auditory, and triumph over his throne. A great Haman is feasted with the king one day, and made a feast for crows the next, Esth. vii. 10. In all the ages of the world God hath taken a delight to stain the pride of all the glory of this lower world, Isa. xxiii. 9. See it in a few instances:—

Valerian, the Roman emperor, fell from being an emperor to be a footstool to Sapor, king of Persia, as often as he took horse.[4]

Bibulus the consul, riding in his triumphant chariot, by the fall of a tile-stone from a house was made a sacrifice before he could reach the capitol, to offer up there the bulls and garlands he had prepared.

Aurelianus, the Roman emperor, brought Tetricus his opposite, and the brave Queen Zenobia of Palmyra, in triumph to Rome in golden chains.[5]

Sejanus, that prodigious favourite, on the same day that he was attended by the senate, on the same day he was torn in pieces by the

---

[1] Qu. ' there were?'—G.   [2] Erasmus writes that he knew some such cardinals.
[3] ' Imagined.'—G.   [4] Trebell. Poll. Fragm. Vit. Valerian; Eckhel, vii. 307.—G.
[5] Tetricus: cf. De Boze in Mémoires de l'Academie de Sciences et Belles Lettres, vol. xxiii.: Zenobia, as before.—G.

people. Seneca, speaking of him, saith, that he who in the morning was swollen with titles, ere night there remained not so much as a mammock [1] of flesh for the hangman to fasten his hook in.[2]

Belisarius, a most famous general under Justinian the emperor, after all the great and famous services that he had done, he had his eyes put out in his old age by the Empress Theodora; and at the temple of St Sophia forced to beg: *Date panem Belisario*, &c., Give a crust to old blind Belisarius, whom virtue advanced, but envy hath brought into this great misery.[3]

Henry the Fourth, emperor, in sixty-two battles, for the most part, he became victorious; yet he was deposed, and driven to that misery that he desired only a clerk's place in a house at Spires, of his own building, which the bishop of that place denied him: whereupon he brake forth into that speech of Job: ' *Miseremini mei, amici; quia manus Dei tetigit me*, Have pity upon me, oh my friends, for the hand of God hath touched me,' Job xix. 21. He died of grief and want.[4]

Bajazet, a proud emperor of the Turks, whom Tamerlane a Tartarian took prisoner, and bound him in chains of gold, and used him for a footstool when he took horse; when he was at table he made him gather crumbs and scraps under his table, and eat them for his food.[5]

Dionysius, king of Sicily, was such a cruel tyrant that his people banished him. After his banishment he went to Corinth, where he lived a base and contemptible life. At last he became a schoolmaster; so that, when he could not tyrannise any longer over men he might over boys.[6]

Pythias was pined to death for want of bread, who once was able to entertain and maintain Xerxes his mighty army.[7]

Great Pompey had not so much as room to be buried in; and William the Conqueror's corpse lay three days unburied, his interment being hindered by one that claimed the ground to be his.

Caesar having bathed his sword in the blood of the senate and his own countrymen, is, after a while, miserably murdered in the senate by his own friends, Cassius and Brutus.

King Guillimet, a potent king of the Vandals, was brought so low as to entreat his friend to send him a sponge, a loaf of bread, and a harp; a sponge to dry up his tears, a loaf of bread to maintain his life, and a harp to solace himself in his misery.[8]

A Duke of Exeter, who, though he had married Edward the Fourth's sister, yet was seen begging barefoot in the Low Countries.[9]

The Emperor Nero promoted Tigelenus to the greatest dignities of the Roman empire, but it was because he had been the private agent to his base and lascivious delights, for which he was justly deprived of his honours and life by Otho the emperor.[10]

---

[1] 'Morsel,' a Shakesperian word: Coriolanus, i. 3.—G.
[2] Seneca, De Tranquillitate, cap. 11.—G.
[3] Cf. Lord Mahon's ' Belisarius.'—G.
[4] As before.—G.
[5] As before.—G.
[6] *Ibid.*—G.
[7] Turk. History, p. 220. [Knolles.]
[8] Procopius reports this of him.
[9] Philip de Comines saw him thus beg.
[10] See Tacitus in Otho's Life. [Annals, xv. 37–40, and 61. Juvenal, i. 155. Tacitus Hist., i. 72, and Plutarch *Galb.*, 2, 13, 17, 19, 23, 29. Otho the Second.—G.]

By all these instances, and many more that might be produced, it is most evident that worldly glory is but a breath, a vapour, a froth, a phantasm, a shadow, a reflection, an apparition, a very nothing. Like the incubus or nightmare in a dream, you imagine it a substance, a weight; you grasp at it and awake, and it is nothing. Pleasure and wealth will abide a sense or two—the one a touch or taste, the other a sight of the eyes; but this of glory can neither be felt, seen, or understood. The philosophers are at strife among themselves where to fix it in any being or existence, whether *in honorante,* or *in honorato,* the giver or the taker. The inconstancy and slipperiness of it is discernible in the instances last cited. It hath raised some, but hath ruined more; and those commonly whom it hath most raised, it hath most ruined. Sir, if there be anything glorious in the world, it is a mind that divinely contemns that glory; and such a mind I judge and hope God hath given you. I have hinted a little at the vanity of worldly glory, because happily this treatise, passing up and down the world, may fall into the hands of such as may be troubled with that itch; and if so, who can tell but that that little that I have said may prove a sovereign salve to cure that Egyptian botch: and if so, I have my end.

Sir, let nothing lie so near your heart in all the world as these eight things: 1. Your sins, to humble you and abase you at the foot of God. 2. Free and rich and sovereign grace, to soften and melt you down into the will of God. 3. The Lord Jesus Christ, to assist, help, strengthen, and influence you to all the duties and services that are incumbent upon you. 4. The blessed Scriptures, to guide you and lead you, ' and to be a lamp unto your feet, and a light unto your paths.'[1] 5. The afflictions of Joseph, to draw out your charity, mercy, pity, sympathy, and compassion to men in misery. 6. The glory and happiness of another world, to arm you and steel you against all the sins, snares, and temptations that your high places, offices, and circumstances may lay you open to. 7. The grand points in this treatise, which, being laid upon your heart by the warm hand of the Spirit, are able to make you wise unto salvation, and to secure your precious and immortal soul against those pernicious and most dangerous, may I not say damnable, errors and opinions, that are preached, printed, and cried up in this vain world, 2 Pet. ii. 1. 8. The interest of Christ and his people, which will be your honour whilst you live, your joy and comfort when you come to die, and your crown of rejoicing in the great day of our Lord, 1 Thes. i. 19, 20.

Sir, I shall not so far disgust you as to tell the world how many several score pounds of your money hath passed through my hands towards the relief, refreshment, support, and preservation of such who, for their piety and extreme poverty and necessity, were proper objects of your charity; but shall take this opportunity to tell you, and all others into whose hands this treatise may fall, that of all the duties of religion there are none, 1. More commanded than this of charity, pity, compassion, and mercy to men in misery, especially to those of ' the household of faith;' 2. There is no one duty more highly com-

[1] Col. i. 10–13; Phil. iv. 12–14; Gal. ii. 20; 1 Cor. xv. 10; 2 Cor. xii. 10; Ps. cxix. 105; Amos vi. 3–6; Neh. i. 1–5.

mended and extolled than this; 3. There is no one duty that hath more choice and precious promises annexed to it than this; 4. There is no one duty that hath greater rewards attending it than this.[1] Evagrius, a rich man, being importuned by Synesius, a bishop, to give something to charitable uses, he yielded at last to give three hundred pounds; but first took bond of the bishop that it should be repaid him in another world, according to the promise of our Saviour, with a hundredfold advantage, Mat. xix. 29. Before he had been one day dead, he is said to have appeared to the bishop, delivering in the bond cancelled, as thereby acknowledging that what was promised was made good. It is certain, that one day's being in heaven will make a sufficient recompense for whatsoever a man has given on earth.

Neither shall I acquaint the world with those particular favours and respects which you have shewed to myself, but treasure them up in an awakened breast, and be your remembrancer at the throne of grace. Only I must let the world know that I owe you more than an epistle; and if you please to accept of this mite in part of payment, and improve it for your soul's advantage, you will put a farther obligation upon me, to study how I may farther serve the interest of your immortal soul.

Let the lustre of your prudence, wisdom, charity, fidelity, generosity, and humility of spirit shine gloriously through all your places, offices, abilities, riches, employments, and enjoyments; for this is the height of all true excellency. And that it may be so, remember for ever that the eyes of God, of Christ, of angels, of devils, of sinners, of saints, of good, of bad, are always fixed upon you. God is all ear to hear, all hand to punish, all power to protect, all wisdom to direct, all goodness to relieve, all grace to pardon, and he is *totus oculus*, all eye, to observe the thoughts, hearts, words, ways, and walkings of the children of men.[2] As the eyes of a well-drawn picture are fastened on us, which way soever we turn, so are the eyes of the Lord. Zeno, a wise heathen, affirmeth, that God beheld even the very thoughts of men. Athenodorus, another heathen, saith that all men ought to be careful of the actions of their life, because God was everywhere, and beheld all that was done. Of all men on earth, magistrates and ministers had need pray with David, 'Teach us thy way, O Lord, and lead us in a plain path, because of our enemies,' Ps. xxvii. 11; or, nearer the Hebrew, 'because of our observers.' In all the ages of the world there have been Sauls and Doegs, who have looked upon God's Davids with an evil eye, and watched for their halting, Jer. xx. 10. There are multitudes that will be still eyeing and prying into the practices, offices, carriages, and conversations of magistrates and ministers, the more it concerns them to watch, pray, act, and walk like so many earthly angels in the midst of a crooked, perverse, and froward generation, Phil. ii. 15.

Wise and prudent governors are an unspeakable mercy to a kingdom or commonwealth, which Jethro well understood when he gave Moses

---

[1] Prov. iii. 9, 10; Eccles. xi. 1, 2; Gal. vi. 10; 2 Cor. viii. 3-5, and ix. 1, 2; Isa. lviii. 7-13, [ponder upon it;] Mat. xxv. 34-41.

[2] Jer. xvi. 17; Job xxxiv. 21; Prov. v. 21; Jer. xxxii. 19; Heb. iv. 13. It is a saying of the schoolmen, *Quicquid est in Deo est ipse Deus.*

that good counsel, to make choice out of the people of grave and able men, ' such as feared God, men of truth, hating covetousness; and to make them rulers over thousands, and rulers over hundreds, over fifties, and over tens.'[1] But in the nations round, how rare is it to find magistrates qualified, suitable to Jethro's counsel! Alphonsus, king of Spain, coming very young to the crown, some advised that seven counsellors might be joined to govern with him, who should be men fearing God, lovers of justice, free from filthy lusts, and such as would not take bribes; to which Alphonsus replied, If you can find seven such men, nay, bring me but one so qualified, and I will not only admit him to govern with me, but shall willingly resign the kingdom itself to him. Wicked policies are ever destructive to their authors; as you may see in Pharaoh, in Ahithophel, in Haman, &c., Exod. i. 10, 22; 2 Sam. xvi. and xxiii. 23; Esth. vii. 10. As long as the Roman civil magistrates, senators, and commanders of armies were chosen into places of honour and trust for their noble descent, their prudence and valour, their state did flourish, and did enlarge its dominions more in one century of years than it did in three after these places of honour came to be venal, and purchased by concession.[2] For then men of no parts were for money promoted to highest dignities; whereupon civil contentions were fomented, factions increased, and continual bloody intestine wars maintained; by which the ancient liberties of that state were suppressed, and the last government of it changed into an imperial monarchy. As long as the chief offices of the crown of France, and the places of judicature of the realm, were given by Charles the Fifth, surnamed the Wise, to men of learning, of wisdom, and valour in recompense of their loyalty, virtue, and merits, that kingdom did flourish, with peace, honour, and prosperity;[3] and the courts of parliaments of France had the honour, for their justice and equity, to be the arbitrators and umpires of all the differences that happened in those days between the greatest princes of Christendom. But when these places of honour and trust were made venal, in the reigns of Francis the Second, Charles the Ninth, and Henry the Third, and sold for ready money to such as gave most for them, then was justice and equity banished, and that flourishing kingdom reduced to the brim of ruin and desolation by variety of factions and a bloody civil war. The wicked counsel given by the Cardinal de Lorraine, and the Duke of Guise his brother, to Charles the Ninth, king of France, to allure all the Protestants to Paris, under colour of the marriage of Henry de Bourbon with Margaret de Valois, the king's sister, to have them all as in a trap, for to cut their throats in their beds, as they did for the greatest part, proved fatal to the king, to the cardinal, and the duke; for the king, by the just judgment of God, died shortly after by an issue of blood, which came out of his mouth, ears, and nostrils, and could never be stopped; and the cardinal and the duke were both slain by the commandment of Henry the Third in the castle of Blois.[4] The barbarous policy of Philip the Second, king of Spain, to banish two or three hundred thousand Moors, with their wives and children, under

---

[1] Exod. xviii. 21, 22. *Magistratus virum indicat,* is a maxim as true as old.
[2] See Livius, Decades. [3] See the History of France.
[4] See the Massacre of Paris in the Inventory of France.

colour of religion, on purpose to confiscate all their land, and to appropriate the same to his demesnes, was fatal to him and to all the Spanish nation; for by the just judgment of God he was eaten up of lice, and the Spanish nation never thrived since, &c.[1] Were it not for exceeding the bounds of an epistle, I might shew, in all the ages of the world, how destructive the wicked policies of rulers and governors have been to themselves and the states and nations under them, &c.; but from such policies God has, and I hope will for ever, deliver your soul. Sir, the best policy in the world is to know God savingly, to serve him sincerely, to do the work of your generation throughly, and to secure your future happiness and blessedness effectually, &c.

Sir, I do not offer you that which cost me nothing, or little, Mal. i. 13, 14. God best knows the pains, the prayers, and the study that the travailing of this treatise into the world hath cost me, in the midst of trials, troubles, temptations, afflictions, and my frequent labours in the ministry. The truths that I offer for your serious consideration in this treatise are not such as I have formerly preached, in one place or another, at one time or another, but such as, at several times, the Lord has brought to hand; and, I hope, in order to the service and saving of many, many souls.[2] And should you redeem time from your many and weighty occasions, and live to read it as often over as there be leaves in it, I am apt to think you would never repent of your pains when you come to die and make up your account with God. Sir, I must and shall say, because I love and honour you, and would have you happy to eternity, that it is your greatest wisdom, and should be your greatest care, to redeem time from your worldly business to acquaint yourself more and more with the great and main points of religion, to serve your God, to be useful in your day, and to make sure and safe work for your soul to escape hell and to get heaven, Eph.- v. 15, 16; Col. iv. 5; Eccles. ix. 10. Sir Thomas More, one of the great wits of that day, would commonly say, There is a devil called *negotium*, business, that carries more souls to hell than all the devils in hell beside. Many men have so many irons in the fire, and are cumbered about so many things, Luke x. 40–42, that upon the matter they wholly neglect the one thing necessary, though I hope better things of you.[3] The stars which have the least circuit are nearest the pole, and men that are least perplexed with a crowd of worldly business are commonly nearest to God. Sir, as you love God, as you love your soul, as you love eternity, as you would be found at Christ's right hand at last, and as you would meet me with joy in the great day of the Lord, make much conscience of redeeming time daily from your secular affairs, to be with God in your closet, in your family, to read the Scriptures, to study the Scriptures, and such men's writings that are sound in the faith, and that treat of the great things of the gospel. It is dangerous crying, *Cras, cras,* to-morrow, to-morrow. Manna must be gathered in the morning; the orient pearl is generated by the

---

[1] See the Spanish History in Philip the Second's life.

[2] Commonly men preach those points first that afterwards they print; but not knowing how long the door of liberty may be open, I have sent this treatise into the world.

[3] When one presented Antipater, king of Macedonia, with a book treating of happiness, his answer was *ou scholazo,* I am not at leisure. The Duke of Alva had so much to do on earth, that he had no time to look up to heaven.

morning dew. There is nothing puts a more serious frame into a man's spirit than to know the worth and preciousness of time. Time, saith one [Bernard], were a good commodity in hell, and the traffic of it most gainful; where, for one day, a man would give ten thousand worlds if he had them. One called his friends thieves, because they stole time from him. And certainly there are no worse thieves than those that rob us of our praying seasons, our hearing seasons, our mourning seasons, &c. There was an eminent minister who would often say, that he could eat the flesh off his arm in indignation against himself for his lost hours.[1]

It was good counsel that an ancient Christian, that is now triumphing in glory, gave to another, who is still alive, Be either like Christ or Mary: the first was always doing good, the latter was still a-receiving good. This is the way to be strong in grace, and to be soon ripe for glory. Certainly time is infinitely precious in regard of what depends upon it. What more necessary than repentance? yet that depends upon time: Rev. ii. 21, 'I gave her space to repent of her fornications.' What more desirable than the favour of God? This depends upon time, and is therefore called 'the acceptable time,' Isa. xlix. 8. What more excellent than salvation? this likewise depends upon time: 2 Cor. vi. 4, 'Now is the accepted time, now is the day of salvation.' Pythagoras saith that time is *anima cœli*, the soul of heaven. But to draw to a close, what can there be of more worth, and weight, and moment, than eternity? it is the heaven of heaven, and the very hell of hell; without which neither would heaven be so desirable nor hell so formidable. Now this depends upon time. Time is the prologue to eternity. The great weight of eternity hangs upon the small wire of time.[2] Whether our time here be longer or shorter, upon the spending of this depends either the bliss or the bane of body and soul to all eternity. This is our seed-time, eternity is the harvest. Whatsoever seed we sow, whether of sin or grace, it cometh up in eternity; 'Whatsoever a man soweth, the same shall he reap,' Gal. vi. 7, 8; 2 Cor. ix. 6. This is our market-time, in which, if we be wise merchants, we may make a happy exchange of earth for heaven, of a valley of tears for a paradise of delights. This is our working time: 'I must work the works of him that sent me; the night cometh, when no man can work,' John ix. 4. According as the work is we do now, such will be our wages in eternity. Though time itself lasts not, yet whatsoever is everlasting, dependeth upon it; and therefore should be carefully improved to the best advantage for our souls, and for the making sure of such things as will go with us beyond the grave.

Shall your lady live to be an honour to God, to be wise for eternity, to be a pattern of piety, humility, modesty, &c., to others, to be a joyful mother of many children, and to bring them up in the nurture and admonition of the Lord? Shall you both live to see Christ formed up

---

[1] Blessed Hooper was spare of diet, sparer of words, and sparest of time. And Bradford counted that hour lost wherein he did not some good by his tongue, pen, or purse. A heathen could say he lived no day without a line—that is, he did something remarkable every day. Cato was wont to say that there were three things which he abhorred: 1. To commit secrets to a woman; 2. To go by water when he might go by land; 3. To spend one day idle.—*Plutarch*.

[2] A favourite emblem: as before.—G.

in your offspring, and to see their souls flourish in grace and holiness, and God bestowing himself as a portion upon them? Shall you all round be blessed with 'all spiritual blessings in heavenly places in Christ,' and shall you all round be crowned with the highest glory, happiness, and blessedness in the world to come? Shall you all live in the sense of divine love and die in the sense of divine favour?[1] Now, to the everlasting arms of divine protection, and to the constant influences of free, rich, and sovereign grace and mercy, he commends you all, Gal. v. 22, 23; who is,

Sir,

Your much obliged friend and soul's servant,

THOMAS BROOKS.

[1] 1 Pet. iii. 3–5; 1 Tim. ii. 9, 10; Eph. vi. 4; Prov. xxxi. 1–3; Gal. iv. 19; 1 Tim. i. 5, 6; Isa. xliv. 3, 4, and lix. 21; Ps. cxii. 1, 2; Eph. i. 3.

TO THE READER.

CHRISTIAN READER!—Some preachers in our days are like Heraclitus, who was called the dark doctor,[1] because he affected dark speeches; so they affect sublime notions, obscure expressions, uncouth phrases: making plain truths difficult, and easy truths hard, &c. They 'darken counsel by words without knowledge,' Job xxxviii. 2. Men of abstract conceits and wise speculations are but wise fools: like the lark that soareth up on high, peering and peering, but at last falleth into the net of the fowler. Such persons commonly are as censorious as they are curious, and do Christ and his church but very, very little service in this world.

The heathenish priests had their mythologies and strange canting expressions, of their imaginary unaccessible deities, to amaze and amuse[2] their blind superstitious followers; and thereby to hold up their Popish and apish idolatries in greater veneration. The prudent reader can tell how to make application.

If thou affectest high strains of wit, or larded, pompous, and high-flown expressions, or eloquent trappings, or fine new notions, or such things that thou mayst rather wonder at than understand, I shall not encourage thee to the perusal of this treatise. But,

First, If thou wouldst be furnished with sovereign antidotes against the most dangerous errors that are rampant in these days, then seriously peruse this treatise: 2 Pet. iii. 16; 1 John iv. 1-3; 2 John 7-11.

Secondly, If thou wouldst be established, strengthened, settled, and confirmed in the grand points of the gospel, then seriously peruse this treatise: 1 Pet. v. 10. But,

Thirdly, If thou wouldst know what that faith is that gives thee an interest in Christ and in all that fundamental good that comes by Christ, then seriously peruse this treatise: John i. 12, iii. 16, and v. 24. But,

Fourthly, If thou wouldst have thy judgment rightly informed in some great truths, about which several men of note have been mistaken, then seriously peruse this treatise: 1 Cor. ii. 6, 7; Ps. cxix. 18. But,

---

[1] Heraclitus was a philosopher of Ephesus; he was surnamed Σκοτεινὸς, *Obscurus*, because he affected dark speeches.　　　　[2] As before: see Glossary, *s. v.*—G.

Fifthly, If thou wouldst know what safe and excellent pleas to make to those ten scriptures that refer to the general judgment, and to thy particular day of judgment, then seriously peruse this treatise: 2 Cor. v. 10; Heb. ix. 27. But,

Sixthly, If thou wouldst have thy heart brought and kept in a humble, broken, bleeding, melting, tender frame, then seriously peruse this treatise: Ps. xxxiv. 18; Isa. lvii. 15; 2 Chron. xxxiv. 27. But,

Seventhly, If thou wouldst always come to the Lord's table with such a frame of spirit, as Christ may take a delight to meet thee, to bless thee, to bid thee welcome, and to seal up his love and thy pardon to thee, then seriously peruse this treatise, especially that part of it where the dreadful and amazing sufferings of our Lord Jesus Christ, both in body and soul, are at large set forth: Mat. xxvi. 26–28; Luke xxii. 19, 20; 1 Cor. xi. 23–30. But,

Eighthly, If thou wouldst have a clear sight of the length, and breadth, and depth, and height of the love of Christ, then seriously peruse this treatise: Eph. iii. 18; Ps. cxlvi. 8. But,

Ninthly, If thou wouldst have thy love to Christ tried, raised, acted, inflamed, discovered, and augmented, &c., then seriously peruse this treatise: Cant. i. 7, and viii. 5–7. But,

Tenthly, If thou art a strong man in Christ Jesus, and wouldst have thy head and heart exercised in the great things of God, and in the deep things of God, and in the mysterious things of God, then seriously peruse this treatise: 2 Tim. ii. 1; Heb. v. 14; 1 Cor. ii. 6, 7; 1 John ii. 14. But,

Eleventhly, If thou art but a weak Christian, a babe, a little child, a shrub, a dwarf in grace, holiness, and communion with God, and in thy spiritual attainments, enjoyments, and experiences, then seriously peruse this treatise, especially the first part of it: 1 Cor. iii. 1; Heb. v. 13; 1 Pet. ii. 2; 1 John ii. 1, 12, 13. But,

Twelfthly, If thou wouldst know whether thou art an indulger of sin, and if thou wouldst be stocked with singular remedies against thy special sins, then seriously peruse the former part of this treatise: Job xx. 11–14; Micah vi. 6, 7; Rom. xiii. 14; James iv. 3. But,

Thirteenthly, If thou wouldst be rooted, grounded, strengthened, and settled in those two grand points of the gospel, viz., the active and passive obedience of Christ, and be daily refreshed with those pleasant streams, with those waters of life that flow from thence, then seriously peruse this treatise: 1 Pet. v. 10; Isa. liii.; Heb. x. 10, 12, 14; Gal. iv. 4, 5; Rom. viii. 3, 4; 2 Cor. v. 21. But,

Fourteenthly, If thou wouldst be throughly acquainted with the sufferings of Christ, in his body and soul, with their greatness and grievousness, &c., and if thou wouldst understand the mighty advantages we have by his sufferings, then seriously peruse this treatise: Isa. liii. and lxiii. 2; 1 Pet. ii. 21–24; John x. 11, 15, 17, 18. But,

Fifteenthly, If thou wouldst be able strongly to prove, against the Socinians and the high atheists of the day, and such as make so great a noise about a light within them, that there is a hell, a place of torment, provided and prepared for all wicked and ungodly persons, then seriously peruse this treatise: Mat. xxv. 41; Ps. ix. 17; Prov. v. 5. But,

Sixteenthly, If thou wouldst, in a scripture-glass, see the torments of hell, and know how to avoid them, and what divine improvements to make of them, and be resolved in several questions concerning hell and hellish torments, then seriously peruse this treatise. But,

Seventeenthly, If thou wouldst be able strenuously to maintain and defend Christ's eternal deity and manhood against all corrupt teachers and gainsayers, then seriously peruse this treatise: 1 John i. 2, 14; 1 Tim. ii. 5. But,

Eighteenthly, If thou wouldst be rooted and grounded in that great doctrine of the imputed righteousness of Christ, and be warmed, refreshed, cheered, comforted, and delighted with those choice and singular consolations that flow from thence, then seriously peruse this treatise: Jer. xxiii. 6; Isa. xlv. 24, and lxi. 10; 1 Cor. i. 30. But,

Nineteenthly, If thou wouldst be set at liberty from many fears and doubts and disputes that often arise in thy soul about thy internal and eternal estate, then seriously peruse this treatise: Ps. xlii. 5, 11, and lv. 5; 2 Cor. vii. 5. But,

Twentiethly, If thou wouldst have all grace to flourish and abound in thy soul, if thou wouldst be eminently serviceable in thy generation, if thou wouldst be ripe for sufferings, for death, for heaven, if thou wouldst be temptation-proof, if thou wouldst be weaned from this world and triumph in Christ Jesus when the world triumphs over thee, then seriously peruse this treatise: Ps. xcii. 12–14; Rom. xv. 13; Acts xiii. 36; 2 Cor. xii. 9, 10; Rev. xii. 1; 2 Cor. ii. 14.

Reader, if thou wouldst make any earnings of thy reading this treatise, then thou must—1. Read, and believe what thou readest. 2. Thou must read, and meditate on what thou readest. 3. Thou must read, and pray over what thou readest. 4. Thou must read, and try what thou readest by the touchstone of the word. 5. Thou must read, and apply what thou readest; that plaster will never heal that is not applied, &c. 6. Thou must read, and make conscience of living up to what thou readest, and of living out what thou readest.[1] This is the way to honour thy God, to gain profit by this treatise, to credit religion, to stop foul mouths, to strengthen weak hands, to better a bad head, to mend a bad heart, to rectify a disorderly life, and to make sure work for thy soul, for heaven, for eternity.

Reader, in a fountain sealed and treasures hid, there is little profit or comfort. No fountain to that which flows for common good, no treasures to those that lie open for public service. If thou gettest any good by reading this treatise, give God alone the glory; and remember the author when thou art in the mount with God. His prayers for thee are, that thou mayest be a knowing Christian, a sincere Christian, a growing Christian, a rooted Christian, a resolute Christian, an untainted Christian, an exemplary Christian, a humble Christian, and then he knows thou wilt be a saved Christian in the day of Christ; so he rests, who is thy cordial friend and soul's servant,

THOMAS BROOKS.

[1] Acts xviii. 8, and xxiv. 14; Ps. i. 2, and cxix. 5, 18; Acts xvii. 11; Ps. cxix. 9; John xiii. 17; Ps. cxix. 105, 106.

SERIOUS AND WEIGHTY QUESTIONS CLEARLY AND SATISFACTORILY ANSWERED.

THE first question or case is this:—

1st Quest. What are the special remedies, means, or helps against cherishing or keeping up of any special or peculiar sin, either in heart or life, against the Lord, or against the light and conviction of a man's own conscience?

Before I come to the resolution of this question, I shall premise a few things that may clear my way.

1. First, *When men's hearts are sincere with God;* when they don't indulge, cherish, or keep up any known transgression in their hearts or lives against the Lord, they may on very good grounds plead an interest in God, in Christ, and in the covenant of grace, though their corruptions prevail against them, and too frequently worst them and lead them captive, as is most evident in these special scriptures, 2 Sam. xxiii. 5 ; Ps. lxv. 3 ; Rom. vii. 23, 25 ; Isa. lxiii. 16, 17, 19 ; Jer. xiv. 7–9 ; Hosea xiv. 1–4, 8.

But now, when any man's heart doth condemn him for dealing deceitfully and guilefully with God in this or that or the other particular, or for connivings or winking at any known transgression that is kept up, either in his heart or life against the Lord, and against the light of his own conscience, which he will not let go, nor in good earnest use the means whereby it should be subdued and mortified ; it is not to be expected that such a person can come to any clearness or satisfaction about their interest in Christ and the covenant of grace and their right to the great things of that other world. When a person will dally with sin, and will be playing with snares and baits, and allow a secret liberty in his heart to sin, conniving at many workings of it, and not setting upon mortification with earnest endeavours ; though they are convinced, yet they are not persuaded to arise with all their might against the Lord's enemies, but do his work negligently, which is an accursed thing ; and for this, God casts such a person into sore straits, and lets him wander in the dark, without any sight, sense, or assurance of their gracious estate or interest in Christ, &c. The Israelites should perfectly have rooted out the Canaanites, but because they did it but by halves, and did not engage all their power and strength against them, therefore God left them to be as 'thorns in their eyes, and as goads in their sides.' So when men have taken Christ's press-money and are engaged to fight with all their might against those rebels that war against him in their hearts, ways, and walkings, and to pursue the victory to the utmost, till their spiritual enemies lie dead at their feet, and yet they do but trifle and make slender opposition against their sins; this provokes God to stand afar off, and to hide his reconciled face from them.

It is true, when men are really in Christ, they ought not to question their state in him, but yet a guilty conscience will be clamorous and full of objections, and God will not speak peace unto it till it be humbled at his foot. God will make his dearest children know that it is a bitter thing to be bold with sin. Now, before I lay down the remedies, give me leave to shew you what it is to indulge sin, or when a man may be said to indulge or cherish, or keep up any known transgression in his soul against the Lord. Now, for a clear understanding of me in this particular, take me thus:—

[1.] First, *To indulge sin or to cherish it, it is to make daily provision for it*, Rom. xiii. 14. It is to give the breast to it, and to feed it and nourish it, as fond parents do feed and humour the sick child, the darling child; it must have what it will, and do what it will, it must not be crossed. Now, when men ordinarily, habitually, commonly, are studious and laborious to make provision for sin, then sin is indulged by them. But,

[2.] Secondly, *When sin is commonly, habitually, sweet and pleasant to the soul*, when a man takes a daily pleasure and delight in sin, then sin is indulged. 2 Thes. ii. 12 you read of them that had 'pleasure in unrighteousness;' Isa. lxvi. 3, 'And their soul delighteth in their abominations;' Prov. ii. 14, 'Who rejoice to do evil,' &c.

[3.] Thirdly, *When men commonly, habitually, side with sin, and take up arms in the defence of sin*, and in defiance of the commands of God, the motions of the Spirit, the checks of conscience, and the reproofs of others, then sin is indulged. But,

[4.] Fourthly, *When men ordinarily, habitually, do yield a quiet, free, willing, and total subjection to the authority and commands of sin*, then sin is indulged. That man that is wholly addicted and devoted to the service of sin, that man indulges sin. Now in none of these senses does any godly man indulge any one sin in his soul. Though sin lives in him, yet he doth not live in sin. Every man that hath drink in him is not in drink. A child of God may slip into a sin, as a sheep may slip into the mire, but he does not, nor cannot wallow in sin as the swine does in the mire, nor yet keep on in a road of sin, as sinners do: Ps. cxxxix. 24, 'See if there be any way of wickedness in me.' A course, a trade of sin is not consistent with the truth or state of grace: Job x. 7, 'Thou knowest that I am not wicked.' He doth not say, Thou knowest that I am not a sinner, or thou knowest that I have not sinned. No! for the best of saints are sinners, though the worst and weakest of saints are not wicked. Every real Christian is a renewed Christian, and every renewed Christian takes his denomination from his renovation, and not from the remainders of corruptions in him; and therefore such a one may well look God in the face and say, 'Lord thou knowest that I am not wicked;' weaknesses are chargeable upon me, but wickednesses are not chargeable upon me. And certainly that man gives a strong demonstration of his own uprightness, who dares appeal to God himself that he is not wicked.

That no godly man does, or can indulge himself in any course or way or trade of sin, may be thus made evident.

[1.] First, *He sins not with allowance.* When he does evil, he disallows of the evil he does: Rom. vii. 15, 'For that which I do, I allow not.' A Christian is sometimes wherried[1] and whirled away by sin before he is aware, or hath time to consider of it. See Ps. cxix. 1, 3; 1 John iii. 9; Prov. xvi. 12.

[2.] Secondly, A godly man *hates all known sin:* Ps. cxix. 128, 'I hate every false way.' True hatred is πρὸς τὰ γένη, against the whole kind. That contrariety to sin which is in a real Christian, springs from an inward gracious nature or principle, and so is to the whole species or kind of sin, and is irreconcileable to any sin whatsoever. As contrarieties of nature are to the whole kind, as light is contrary to all darkness, and fire to all water; so this contrariety to all sin arising from the inward man, is universal to all sin. He who hates a toad because it is a toad, hates every toad; and he who hates a godly man because he is godly, he hates every godly man; and so he who hates sin because it is sin, he hates every sin: Rom. vii. 15, 'What I hate, that do I.'

[3.] Thirdly, Every godly man would *fain have his sins not only pardoned but destroyed.* His heart is alienated from his sins, and therefore nothing will serve him or satisfy him but the blood and death of his sins, Isa. ii. 20, and xxx. 22; Hosea xiv. 8; Rom. viii. 24. Saul hated David, and sought his life; and Haman hated Mordecai, and sought his destruction; and Absalom hated Amnon, and killed him; Julian the apostate hated the Christians, and put many thousands of them to death. The great thing that a Christian has in his eye, in all the duties he performs, and in all the ordinances that he attends, is the blood and death and ruin of his sins.

[4.] Fourthly, Every godly man *groans under the burden of sin:* 2 Cor. v. 4, 'For we that are in this tabernacle do groan, being burdened.' Never did any porter groan more to be delivered from his heavy burden, than a Christian groans to be delivered from the burden of sin. The burden of affliction, the burden of temptation, the burden of desertion, the burden of opposition, the burden of persecution, the burden of scorn and contempt, is nothing to the burden of sin. Ponder upon that Ps. xxxviii. 4, and xl. 12; Rom. vii. 24.

[5.] Fifthly, Every godly man *combats and conflicts with all known sin.* In every gracious soul there is a constant and perpetual conflict. 'The flesh will be still a-lusting against the spirit, and the spirit against the flesh,' Gal. v. 17; Rom. vii. 22, 23; 1 Kings xiv. 30, 31. Though sin and grace were not born together, and though sin and grace shall never die together, yet whiles a believer lives in this world, they must ive together; and whilst sin and grace do cohabit together, they will still be opposing and conflicting one with another.

---

[1] 'Tossed' as in a 'wherry.'—G.

[6.] Sixthly, Every gracious heart is .still *a-crying out against his sins.* He cries out to God to subdue them; he cries out to Christ to crucify them; he cries out to the Spirit to mortify them; he cries out to faithful ministers to arm him against them; and he cries out to sincere Christians, that they would pray hard that he may be made victorious over them. Now certainly it is a most sure sign that sin has not gained a man's heart, a man's love, nor his consent, but committed a rape upon his soul, when he cries out bitterly against his sin. It is observable, that if the ravished virgin, under the law, cried out, she was guiltless, Deut. xxii. 25–27. Certainly such as cry out of their sins, and that would not for all the world indulge themselves in a way of sin, such are guiltless before the Lord. That which a Christian does not indulge himself in, that he does not do in divine account. But,

[7.] Seventhly, *The fixed purposes and designs* of a godly man, *is not to sin:* Ps. xvii. 3, ' I am purposed that my mouth shall not transgress,' that is, I have laid my design so as not to sin. Though I may have many particular failings, yet my general purpose is not to sin: Ps. xxxix. 1, ' I said, I will take heed to my ways, that I sin not with my tongue; I will keep my mouth with a bridle, while the wicked is before me.' Whenever a godly man sins, he sins against the general purpose of his soul. David laid a law upon his tongue. He uses three words in the first and second verses to the same purpose, which is as if he should say in plain English, ' I was silent, I was silent, I was silent;' and all this to express how he kept in his passion, that he might not offend with his tongue. Though a godly man sins, yet he doth not purpose to sin, for his purposes are fixed against sin. Holiness is his highway; and as sin is itself a byway, so it is besides his way. The honest traveller purposes to keep straight on his way; so that if at any time he miss his way, he misses his purpose. Though Peter denied Christ, yet he did not purpose to deny Christ; yea, the settled purpose of his soul was rather to die with Christ than to deny Christ: Mat. xxvi. 35, ' Peter said unto him, Though I should die with thee, yet will I not deny thee.' Interpreters agree that Peter meant as he speaks. But,

[8.] Eighthly, The settled resolutions of a gracious heart is not to sin: Ps. cxix. 106, ' I have sworn, and I will perform it, that I will keep thy righteous judgments;' Neh. x. 28–31, dwell on it; Job xxxi. 1, &c.; Micah iv. 5, ' For all people will walk, every one in the name of his god, and we walk in the name of the Lord our God for ever and ever.' So Daniel and the three children.

Blessed Hooper resolves rather to be discharged of his bishopric than yield to certain ceremonies.

Jerome writes of a brave woman, who, being upon the rack, bid her persecutors do their worst, for she was resolved that she would rather die than lie.

The Prince of Conde being taken prisoner by Charles the Ninth of France, and put to his choice—first, whether he would go to mass; or second, be put to death; or thirdly, suffer perpetual imprisonment, answered, ' As for the first, I will never do, by the assistance of God's grace; and as for the other two, let the king do with me what he pleaseth, for I am very well assured that God will turn all to the best.'

'The heavens shall as soon fall,' said William Flower to the bishop that persuaded him to save his life by retracting, 'as I will forsake the opinion and faith I am in, God assisting of me.'

So Marcus Arethusius chose rather to suffer a most cruel death than to give one halfpenny towards the building of an idol temple.

So Cyprian, when the emperor, in the way to his execution, said, 'Now I give thee space to consider whether thou wilt obey me in casting a grain of frankincense into the fire, or be thus miserably slain.' 'Nay,' saith he, 'there needs no deliberation in the case.' There are many thousands of such instances scattered up and down in history.

[9.] Ninthly, *There is a real willingness* in every gracious soul *to be rid of all sin*, Rom. vii. 24; Hosea xiv. 2, 8; Job vii. 21. Saving grace makes a Christian as willing to leave his sin as a slave is willing to leave his galley, or a prisoner his dungeon, or a thief his bolts, or a beggar his rags. 'Many a day have I sought death with tears,' saith blessed Cooper, 'not out of impatience, distrust, or perturbation, but because I am weary of sin, and fearful of falling into it.' Look, as the daughters of Heth even made Rebekah weary of her life, (Gen. xxvii. 46;) so corruptions within makes a gracious soul even weary of his life. A gracious soul looks upon sin with as evil and as envious an eye as Saul looked on David when the evil spirit was upon him. 'Oh,' saith Saul, 'that I was but once well rid of this David;' and oh, saith a gracious soul, that I was but once well rid of 'this proud heart, this hard heart, this unbelieving heart, this unclean heart, this earthly heart, this froward heart of mine.'

[10.] Tenthly, Every godly man *complains of his known sins, and mourns over his known sins*, and would be fain rid of his known sins, as might be made evident out of many scores of scripture, Job vii. 21; Ps. li. 14; Hosea ii.

[11.] Eleventhly, Every gracious soul *sets himself mostly, resolutely, valiantly, and habitually against his special sins, his constitution sins, his most prevalent sins*: Ps. xviii. 23, 'I was also upright before him, and I kept myself from mine iniquity.' Certainly that which is the special sin of a godly man, is his special burden; it is not delighted in, but lamented. There is no sin which costs him so much sorrow as that to which either the temper of his body or the occasions of his life leads him. That sin which he finds his heart most set upon, he sets his heart, his whole soul, most against. The Scripture gives much evidence that David, though a man after God's own heart, was very apt to fall into the sin of lying; he used many unlawful shifts. We read of his often faltering in that kind, when he was in straits and hard put to it, 1 Sam. xxi. 2, 8, and xxvii. 8, 10, &c., but it is as clear in Scripture that his heart was set against lying, and that it was the grief and daily burden of his soul. Certainly that sin is a man's greatest burden and grief which he prays most to be delivered from. Oh, how earnestly did David pray to be delivered from the sin of lying: Ps. cxix. 29, 'Keep me from the way of lying.' And as he prayed earnestly against lying, so he as earnestly detested it: ver. 163, 'I hate and abhor lying.' Though lying was David's special sin, yet he hated and abhorred it as he did hell itself. And he tells us how he was affected, or afflicted rather, with that sin, whatsoever it was, which was his iniquity: Ps. xxxi. 10, ' My life is spent with grief, and my years with sighings; my strength faileth, and my bones are consumed,' or moth-eaten, as the Hebrew has it. Here are deep expressions of a troubled spirit; and why all this? Mark, he gives you the reason of it in the same verse, ' because of mine iniquity:' as if he had said, there is a base corruption which so haunts and dogs me, that my life is spent with grief, and my years with sighing. He found, it seems, his heart running out to some sin or other, which yet was so far from being a beloved sin, a bosom sin, a darling sin, that it was the breaking of his heart and the consumption of his bones. So Ps. xxxviii. 18, ' I will declare mine iniquity, I will be sorry for my sin.' There is no sin that a gracious heart is more perfectly set against than against his special sin; for by this sin God first has been most dishonoured; and secondly, Christ most crucified; and thirdly, the Spirit most grieved; and fourthly, conscience most wounded; and fifthly, Satan most advantaged; and sixthly, mercies most embittered; and seventhly, duties most hindered; and eighthly, fears and doubts most raised and increased; and ninthly, afflictions most multiplied; and tenthly, death made most formidable and terrible; and therefore he breaks out against this sin with the greatest detestation and abhorrency. Ephraim's special sin was idolatry, Hosea iv. 17; he thought the choicest gold and silver in the world hardly good enough to frame his idols of. But when it was the day of the Lord's gracious power upon Ephraim, then he thought no place bad enough to cast his choicest idols into, as you may see by comparing of these scriptures together, Hosea xiv. 8; Isa. ii. 20, and xxx. 22. True grace will make a man stand stoutly and steadfastly on God's side, and work the heart to take part with him against a man's special sins, though they be as right hands or right eyes. True grace will lay hands upon a man's special sins, and cry out to heaven, ' Lord, crucify them, crucify them; down with them, down with them, even to the ground: Lord, do justice, do speedy justice, do signal justice, do exemplary justice upon these special sins of mine: Lord, hew down root and branch; let the very stumps of this Dagon be broken all in pieces: Lord, curse this wild fig-tree, that never more fruit may grow thereon.' But,

[12.] Twelfthly, *There is no time wherein a gracious soul cannot sincerely say with the apostle in that* Heb. xiii. 18, ' *Pray for us, for we trust we have a good conscience, in all things willingly to live honestly.'* Gracious hearts affect that which they cannot effect. So Acts xxiv. 16, 'And herein do I exercise myself, to have always a conscience void of offence towards God, and towards men;' in all cases, in all places, by all means, and at all times. A sincere Christian labours to have a good conscience, void of offence towards God and towards men: Prov. xvi. 17, ' The highway of the upright is to depart from evil,' that is, it is the ordinary, usual, constant course of an upright man to depart from evil. An honest traveller may step out of the king's highway into a house, a wood, a close; but his work, his business, is to go on in the king's highway; so the business, the work, of an upright man is to depart from evil. It is possible for an upright man to step into a sinful path, or to touch upon sinful facts; but his main way, his principal work and business, is to depart from iniquity; as a bee may light upon a thistle, but her work is to be gathering at flowers; or as a sheep may slip into the dirt, but its work is to be grazing upon the mountains or in the meadows. But,

[13.] Thirteenthly and lastly, *Jesus Christ is the real Christian's only beloved ; he is the saint's only darling :* Cant. ii. 3, ' As the apple-tree among the trees of the wood, so is my beloved among the sons;' ver. 8, ' The voice of my beloved, behold, he cometh leaping upon the mountains, and skipping upon the hills;' ver. 9, ' My beloved is like a roe, or a young hart;' ver. 10, 'My beloved spake, and said unto me, Rise up, my love, my fair one, and come away;' ver. 17, ' Turn, my beloved, and be thou like a roe or a young hart upon the mountains of Bether;' Cant. iv. 16, ' Let my beloved come into his garden, and eat his pleasant fruits.' Seven times Christ is called ' the beloved of his spouse' in the fifth of Canticles, and twice in the sixth chapter, and four times in the seventh chapter, and once in the eighth chapter. In this book of Solomon's Song, Christ is called the church's beloved just twenty times. I might turn you to many other scriptures, but in the mouth of twenty witnesses you may be very clearly and fully satisfied that Jesus Christ is the saints' beloved.

1. When the Dutch martyr was asked whether he did not love his wife and children, he answered, ' Were all the world a lump of gold, and in my hand to dispose of, I would give it to live with my wife and children in a prison, but Christ is dearer to me than all.' 2. Saith Jerome, ' If my father should stand before me, and if my mother should hang upon me, and my brethren should press about me, I would break through my brethren, throw down my mother, and tread under foot my father, that I might cleave the faster and closer unto Jesus Christ.' 3. That blessed virgin in Basil, being condemned for Christianity to the fire, and having her estate and life offered her if she would worship idols, cried out, ' Let money perish and life vanish, Christ is better than all.' 4. Love made Jerome to say, ' Oh, my Saviour, didst thou die for love of me, a love more dolorous than death, but to me a death more lovely than love itself. I cannot live, love thee, and be longer from thee.' 5. Henry Voes said, ' If I had ten heads, they should all off for Christ.' 6. John Ardley, martyr, said, ' If every hair of my head were a man, they should all suffer for the faith of Christ.' 7. Ignatius said, ' Let fire, racks, pulleys, yea, and all the torments of hell, come on me, so I may win Christ.' 8. George Carpenter, being asked whether he loved not his wife and children, when they all wept before them, answered, ' My wife and children are dearer to me than all Bavaria, yet for the love of Christ I know them not.' 9. ' O Lord Jesus,' said Bernard, ' I love thee more than all my goods, and I love thee more than all my friends, yea, I love thee more

than my very self.' 10. Austin saith he would willingly go through hell to Christ. 11. Another saith, ' He had rather be in his chimney-corner with Christ than in heaven without him.' 12. Another cries out, ' I had rather have one Christ than a thousand worlds;' by all which it is most evident that Jesus Christ is the saint's best beloved, and not this or that sin.

Now by these thirteen arguments it is most clear that no gracious Christian does or can indulge himself in any trade, course, or way of sin.

Yea, by these thirteen arguments it is most evident that no godly man has, or can have, any one beloved sin, any one bosom, darling sin, though many worthy ministers, both in their preaching and writings, make a great noise about the saints' beloved sins, about their bosom, darling sins. I readily grant that all unregenerate persons have their beloved sins, their bosom sins, their darling sins; but that no such sins are chargeable upon the regenerate is sufficiently demonstrated by the thirteen arguments last cited; and oh that this were wisely and seriously considered of, both by ministers and Christians! There is no known sin that a godly man is not troubled at, and that he would not be rid of. There is as much difference between sin in a regenerate person and in an unregenerate person, as there is between poison in a man and poison in a serpent. Poison in a man's body is most offensive and burdensome, and he readily uses all arts and anti-dotes to expel it and get rid; but poison in a serpent, is in its natural place, and is most pleasing and delightful: so sin in a regenerate man is most offensive and burdensome, and he readily uses all holy means and antidotes to expel it and to get rid of it. But sin in an unre-generate man is most pleasing and delightful, it being in its natural place. A godly man still enters his protest against sin. A gracious soul, while he commits sin, hates the sin he commits.

O sirs! there is a vast difference between a special and a beloved sin, a darling sin, a bosom sin. Noah had a sin, and Lot had a sin, and Jacob had a sin, and Job had a sin, and David had a sin, which was his special sin; but neither of these had any sin which was their beloved sin, their bosom sin, their darling sin. That passage in Job xxxi. 33 is observable, ' If I covered my transgression as Adam, by hiding mine iniquity in my bosom.' Mark, in this text, while Job calleth some sin or other his iniquity, he denieth that he had any beloved sin; for saith he, 'Did I hide it in my bosom? did I shew it any favour? did I cherish it or nourish it, or keep it warm in my bosom? Oh, no; I did not.' A godly man may have many sins, yet he hath not one beloved sin, one bosom sin, one darling sin; he may have some particular sin, to which the unregenerate part of his will may strongly incline, and to which his unmortified affections may run out with violence to; yet he hath no sin he bears any good-will to, or doth really or cordially affect. Mark, that may be called a man's particular way of sinning, which yet we cannot, we may not call his beloved sin, his bosom sin, his darling sin; for it may be his greatest grief and torment, and may cost him more sorrow and tears than all the rest of his sins; it may be a tyrant usurping power over him, when it is not the delight and pleasure of his soul. A godly man may be more prone to fall into some one sin rather than another; it may be passion, or pride, or slavish fear, or worldliness, or hypocrisy, or this, or that, or t'other vanity; yet are not these his beloved sins, his bosom sins, his darling sins; for these are the enemies he hates and abhors; these are the grand enemies that he prays against, and complains of, and mourns over; these are the potent rebels that his soul cries out most against, and by which his soul suffers the greatest violence. Mark, no sin, but Christ, is the dearly beloved of a Christian's soul; Christ, and not this sin or that, is 'the chiefest of ten thousand' to a gracious soul; and yet some particular corruption or other may more frequently worst a believer and lead him captive; but then the believer cries out most against that particular sin. Oh, saith he, this is mine iniquity; this is the Saul, the Pharaoh that is always a-pursuing after the blood of my soul. Lord! let this Saul fall by the sword of thy Spirit; let this Pharaoh be drowned in the Red Sea of thy son's blood. O sirs, it is a point of very great importance for gracious souls to understand the vast difference that there is between a beloved sin and this or that particular sin, violently tyrannising over them; for this is most certain, whosoever giveth up himself freely, willingly, cheerfully, habitually, to the service of any one particular lust or sin, he is in the state of nature, under wrath, and in the way to eternal ruin.

Now a little to shew the vanity, folly, and falsehood of that opinion that is received and commonly avowed by ministers and Christians— viz., that every godly person hath his beloved sin, his bosom sin, his darling sin—seriously and frequently consider with me of these following particulars:—

[1.] First, That this opinion is not *bottomed or founded upon any clear scripture or scriptures, either in the Old or New Testament.*

[2.] Secondly, This opinion that is now under consideration runs *counter-cross to all those thirteen arguments but now alleged,* and to all those scores of plain scriptures by which those arguments are confirmed.

[3.] Thirdly, This opinion that is now under consideration *has a great tendency to harden and strengthen wicked men in their sins;* for when they shall hear and read that the saints, the dearly beloved of God, have their beloved sins, their bosom sins, their darling sins, what inferences will they not be ready to make! What are these they call saints? wherein are they better than us? Have we our beloved sins? so have they. Have we our bosom sins? so have they. Have we our darling sins? so have they. They have their beloved sins, and yet are beloved of God; and why not we—why not we? Saints have their beloved sins, and yet God is kind to them; and why then not to us, why not to us also? Saints have their beloved sins, and yet God will save them; and why then should we believe that God will damn us? Saints have their beloved sins, their bosom sins, their darling sins, and therefore certainly they are not to be so dearly loved, and highly prized, and greatly honoured as ministers would make us believe. Saints have their beloved sins, their bosom sins, their darling sins, and therefore what iniquity is it to account and call them hypocrites, deceivers, dissemblers, that pretend they have a great deal of love to God, and love to Christ, and love to his word, and love to his ways? and yet for all this they have their beloved sins, their bosom sins, their darling sins. Surely these men's hearts are not right with God: with much more to the same purpose.

[4.] Fourthly, *If Christ be really the saints' beloved, then sin is not their beloved.* But Christ is the saints' beloved, as I have formerly clearly proved; and therefore sin is not the beloved. A man may as well serve two masters, as have two beloveds—viz., a beloved Christ and a beloved lust.

[5.] Fifthly, *Those supernatural graces or those divine qualities that are infused into the soul at first conversion, are contrary to all sin, and opposite to all sin, and engages the heart against all sin;* and therefore a converted person can have no beloved sin, no bosom sin, no darling sin. Seriously weigh this argument.

[6.] Sixthly, This opinion may *fill many weak Christians with many needless fears, doubts, and jealousies about their spiritual and eternal conditions.* Weak Christians are very apt to reason thus: Surely my conversion is not sound; my spiritual estate is not good; my heart is not right with God; a saving work has never yet passed upon me in power; I fear I have not the root of the matter in me; I fear I have never had a thorough change; I fear I have never yet been effectually called out of darkness into his marvellous light; I fear I have never yet been espoused to Christ; I fear the Spirit of God hath never taken up my heart for his habitation; I fear that after all my high profession I shall at last be found a hypocrite; I fear the execution of that dreadful sentence, Mat. xxv. 41, 'Go ye cursed,' &c. And why all this? O poor soul answer [not][1] because I carry about with me my beloved sins, my bosom sins, my darling sins. Ministers had need be very wary in their preaching and writing, that they don't bring forth fuel to feed the fears and doubts of weak Christians, it being a great part of their work to arm weak Christians against their fears and faintings. But,

[7.] Seventhly, This opinion that is now under consideration, is an opinion that is *very repugnant to sound and sincere repentance ;* for sound, sincere repentance includes and takes in a divorce, an aliena-tion, a detestation, a separation, and a turning from all sin, without exception or reservation. One of the first works of the Spirit upon the soul, is the dividing between all known sin and the soul; it is a making an utter breach betwixt all sin and the soul; it is a dissolving of that old league that has been between a sinner and his sins, yea, between a sinner and his beloved lusts. One of the first works of the Spirit is to make a man to look upon all his sins as enemies, yea, as his greatest enemies, and to deal with his sins as enemies, and to hate and loathe them as enemies, and to fear them as enemies, and to arm against them as enemies. Seriously ponder upon these scriptures, Ezek. xviii. 28, 30, 31; Ezek. vi.; 2 Cor. vii. 1; Ps. cxix. 101, 104,

---

[1] The 'not,' which I place in parenthesis, seems to have been dropped out, inasmuch as Brooks is arguing against any such answer.—G.

128. True repentance is a turning from all sin, without any reservation or exception. He never truly repented of any sin, whose heart is not turned against every sin. The true penitent casts off all the rags of old Adam; he is for throwing down every stone of the old building; he will not leave a horn nor a hoof behind. The reasons of turning from sin are universally binding to a penitent soul. There are the same reasons and grounds for a penitent man's turning from every sin, as there is for his turning from any one sin. Do you turn from this or that sin because the Lord has forbid it? Why! upon the same ground you must turn from every sin; for God has forbid every sin as well as this or that particular sin. There is the same authority forbidding or commanding in all; and if the authority of God awes a man from one sin, it will awe him from all. He that turns from any one sin, because it is a transgression of the holy and righteous law of God, he will turn from every sin upon the same account. He that turns from any one sin because it is a dishonour to God, a reproach to Christ, a grief to the Spirit, a wound to religion, &c., will upon the same grounds turn from every sin.

Quest. But wherein does a true penitential turning from all sin consist? Ans. In these six things:—

First, In the alienation and inward aversation and drawing off of the soul from the love and liking of all sin, and from all free and voluntary subjection unto sin, the heart being filled with a loathing and detestation of all sin, [Ps. cxix. 104, 128,] as that which is most contrary to all goodness and happiness.

Secondly, In the will's detestation and hatred of all sin. When the very bent and inclination of the will is set against all sin, and opposes and crosses all sin, and is set upon the ruin and destruction of all sin, then the penitent is turned from all sin, Rom. vii. 15, 19, 21, 23; Isa. xxx. 22; Hosea xiv. 8. When the will stands upon such terms of defiance with all sin, as that it will never enter into a league of friendship with any sin, then is the soul turned from every sin.

Thirdly, In the judgment's turning away from all sin, by disapproving, disallowing, and condemning all sin, Rom. vii. 15. Oh! saith the judgment of a Christian, sin is the greatest evil in all the world; it is the only thing God abhors, and that brought Jesus Christ to the cross, that damns souls, that shuts heaven, and that has laid the foundations of hell! Oh! it is the pricking thorn in my eye, the deadly arrow in my side, the two-edged sword that hath wounded my conscience, and slain my comforts, and separated between God and my soul. Oh! sin is that which hath hindered my prayers, and imbittered my mercies, and put a sting into all my crosses; and therefore I can't but disapprove of it, and disallow of it, and condemn it to death, yea, to hell, from whence it came.

Fourthly, In the purpose and resolution of the soul; the soul sincerely purposing and resolving never willingly, wilfully, or wickedly to transgress any more, Ps. xvii. 3. The general purpose and resolution of my heart is not to transgress. Though particular failings may attend me, yet my resolutions and purposes are firmly set against doing evil, Ps. xxxix. 1. The true penitent holds up his purposes and resolutions to keep off from sin, and to keep close with God, though he be not able in everything and at all times to make good his purposes and resolutions, &c. But,

Fi,thly, In the earnest and unfeigned desires, and careful endeavours of the soul to abandon all sin, to forsake all sin, and to be rid of all sin, Rom. vii. 22, 23. You know when a prudent, tender, indulgent father sees his child to fail and come short in that which he enjoins him to do; yet knowing that his desires and endeavours is to please him, and serve him, he will not be harsh, rigid, sour, or severe towards him, but will spare him, and exercise much tenderness and indulgence towards him; and will God, will God whose mercies reach above the heavens, and whose compassions are infinite, and whose love is like himself, carry it worse towards his children than men do carry it towards theirs? Surely no. God's fatherly indulgence accepts of the will for the work, Heb. xiii. 18; 2 Cor. viii. 12. Certainly, a sick man is not more desirous to be rid of all his diseases, nor a prisoner to be freed from all his bolts and chains, than the true penitent is desirous to be rid of all his sins.

Sixthly and lastly, *In the common and ordinary declining, shunning, and avoiding of all known occasions of sin, yea, and all temptations, provocations, inducements, and enticements to sin,* &c. That royal law, 1 Thes. v. 22, ' Abstain from all appearance of evil,' is a law that is very precious in a penitent man's eye, and commonly lies warm upon a penitent man's heart; so that take him in his ordinary course, and you shall find him very ready to shun and be shy of the very appearance of sin, of the very shows and shadows of sin. Job made ' a covenant with his eyes,' Job xxxi. 1; and Joseph would not hearken to his bold tempting mistress, ' to lie by her, or to be with her,' Gen. xxxix. 10; and David when himself, would not ' sit with vain persons,' Ps. xxvi. 3–5. Now a true penitential turning from all sins lies in these six things: and therefore you had need look about you; for if there be any one way of wickedness wherein you walk, and which you are resolved you will not forsake, you are no true penitents, and you will certainly lose your souls, and be miserable for ever.

[8.] This opinion that is now under consideration, is an opinion that *will exceedingly deject many precious Christians, and cause them greatly to hang down their heads, especially in four days.* 1. In the day of common calamity; 2. In the day of personal affliction; 3. In the day of death; 4. In the great day of account.

First, In a day of common calamity, when the sword is drunk with the blood of the slain, or when the raging pestilence lays thousands in heap upon heap, or when fevers, agues, gripes, and other diseases carry hundreds every week to their long homes. Oh, now the remembrance of a man's beloved sins, his bosom sins, his darling sins— if a saint had any such sins—will be very apt to fill his soul with fears, dreads, and perplexities. Surely now God will meet with me, now God will avenge himself on me for my beloved sins, my bosom sins, my darling sins! Oh, how righteous a thing is it with God, because of my beloved lusts, to sweep me away by these sweeping judgments that are abroad in the earth! On the contrary, how sweet and comfortable a thing is it, when in a day of common calamity a Christian can appeal to God, and appeal to conscience, that though he has many weaknesses and infirmities that hang upon him, that yet he has no beloved sin, no bosom sin, no darling sin, that either God or conscience can charge upon him. Oh, such a consideration as this may be as life from the dead to a gracious Christian, in the midst of all the common calamities that does surround him and that hourly threaten him.

Secondly, In the day of personal afflictions, when the smarting rod is upon him, and God writes bitter things against him ; when the hand of the Almighty has touched him in his name, estate, relations, &c. Oh, now the remembrance of a man's beloved sins, his bosom sins, his darling sins—if a saint had any such sins—will be as 'the handwriting upon the wall,' Dan v. 5, 6, 'that will make his countenance to be changed, his thoughts to be troubled, his joints to be loosed, and his knees to be dashed one against another.' Oh, now a Christian will be ready to conclude, Oh, it is my beloved sins, my bosom sins, my darling sins that has caused God to put this bitter cup into my hand, and that has provoked him to 'give me gall and wormwood to drink,' Lam. iii. 19. Whereas on the contrary, when a man under all his personal trials, though they are many and great, yet can lift up his head and appeal to God and conscience, that though he has many sinful weaknesses and infirmities hanging upon him, yet neither God nor conscience can charge upon him any beloved sins, any bosom sins, any darling sins. Oh, such a consideration as this will help a man to bear up bravely, sweetly, cheerfully, patiently, and contentedly, under the heaviest hand of God, as is evident in that great instance of Job. Who so sorely afflicted as Job? and yet no beloved sin, no bosom sin, no darling sin being chargeable upon him by God or conscience, [Job x. 7, and xxxi. 33,] how bravely, sweetly, and Christianly does Job bear up under those sad changes and dreadful providences that would have broke a thousand of such men's hearts, upon whom God and conscience could charge beloved sins, bosom sins, darling sins ! But,

Thirdly, In the day of death; Death is the king of terrors, as Job speaks ; and the 'terror of kings,' as the philosopher speaks.[1] Oh how terrible will this king of terrors be to that man upon whom God and conscience can charge beloved sins, bosom sins, darling sins. This is certain, when a wicked man comes to die, all the sins that ever he committed don't so grieve him and terrify him, so sad him and sink him, and raise such horrors and terrors in him, and put him into such a hell on this side hell, as his beloved sins, his bosom sins, his darling sins ; and had saints their beloved sins, their bosom sins, their darling sins, ah, what a hell of horror and terror would these sins raise in their souls, when they come to lie upon a dying bed ! But now when a child of God shall lie upon a dying bed, and shall be able to say, ' Lord, thou knowest, and conscience thou knowest, that though I have had many and great failings, yet there are no beloved sins, no bosom sins, no darling sins, that are chargeable upon me ! Lord, thou knowest, and conscience thou knowest: 1. That there is no known sin that I don't hate and abhor. 2. That there is no known sin that I

---

[1] Aristotle: cf. Sibbes, vol. iv. note *e*, p. 78, and vii. 603, where the original is given —G.

don't combat and conflict with. 3. That there is no known sin that I don't grieve and mourn over. 4. That there is no known sin that I would not presently, freely, willingly, and heartily be rid of. 5. That there is no known sin that I don't in some weak measure endeavour in the use of holy means to be delivered from. 6. That there is no known sin, the effectual subduing and mortifying of which would not administer matter of the greatest joy and comfort to me!' Now, when God and conscience shall acquit a man upon a dying bed of beloved sins, of bosom sins, of darling sins, who can express the joy, the comfort, the peace, the support that such an acquittance will fill a man with?

Fourthly, In the day of account, the very thoughts of which day, to many, is more terrible than death itself. Such Christians as are captivated under the power of this opinion, viz., that the saints have their beloved sins, their bosom sins, their darling sins, such cannot but greatly fear and tremble to appear before the tribunal of God. Oh, saith such poor hearts, how shall we be able to answer for our beloved sins, our bosom sins, our darling sins. As for infirmities, weaknesses, and follies that has attended us, we can plead with God, and tell him, Lord! when grace has been weak, corruptions strong, temptations great, and thy Spirit withdrawn, and we off from our watch, we have been worsted and captivated! But what shall we say as to our beloved sins, our bosom sins, our darling sins? Oh, these fill us with terror and horror, and how shall we be able to hold up our heads before the Lord, when he shall reckon with us for these sins! But now when a poor child of God thinks of the day of account, and is able, through grace, to say, 'Lord, though we cannot clear ourselves of infirmities, and many sinful weaknesses, yet we can comfortably appeal to thee and our consciences that we have no beloved sins, no bosom sins, no darling sins!' Oh, with what comfort, confidence, and boldness will such poor hearts hold up their heads in the day of account, when a Christian can plead those six things before a judgment-seat, that he pleaded in the third particular, when he lay upon a dying bed! how will his fears vanish, and how will his hopes and heart revive, and how comfortably and boldly will he stand before a judgment-seat! But,

[9.] Ninthly, This opinion that is now under consideration, *has a very great tendency to discourage and deaden the hearts of Christians to the most noble and spiritual duties of religion*—viz., 1. Praising of God; 2. Delighting in God; 3. Rejoicing in God; 4. Admiring of God; 5. Taking full content and satisfaction in God; 6. Witnessing for God, his truth, his ordinances, and ways; 7. To self-trial and self-examination; 8. To the making of their calling and election sure. I cannot see with what comfort, confidence, or courage such souls can apply themselves to the eight duties last mentioned, who lie under the power of this opinion, viz., that saints have their beloved sins, their bosom sins, their darling sins. But now when a Christian is clear, and he can clear himself, as every sincere Christian can, of beloved sins, of bosom sins, of darling sins, how is he upon the advantage ground to fall in roundly with all the eight duties last mentioned! But,

[10.] Tenthly and lastly, This opinion that is now under consideration, has a very great tendency *to discourage multitudes of Christians from coming to the Lord's table.* I would willingly know with what comfort, with what confidence, with what hope, with what expectation of good from God, or of good from the ordinance, can such souls draw near to the Lord's table, who lie under the power of this opinion or persuasion, that they carry about with them their bosom sins, their beloved sins, their darling sins. How can such souls expect that God should meet with them in the ordinance, and bless the ordinance to them? How can such souls expect that God should make that great ordinance to be strengthening, comforting, refreshing, establishing, and enriching unto them? How can such souls expect, that in that ordinance God should seal up to them his eternal loves, their interest in Christ, their right to the covenant, their title to heaven, and the remission of their sins, who bring to his table their beloved sins, their bosom sins, their darling sins? But now when the people of God draw near to the table of the Lord, and can appeal to God, that though they have many sinful failings and infirmities hanging upon them, yet they have no beloved sins, no bosom sins, no darling sins that they carry about with them; how comfortably and confidently may they expect that God will make that great ordinance a blessing to them, and that in time all those glorious ends for which that ordinance was appointed shall be accomplished in them, and upon them!

Now, by these ten arguments, you may see the weakness and falseness, yea, the dangerous nature of that opinion that many worthy men have so long preached, maintained, and printed to the world, viz., That the saints have their beloved sins, their bosom sins, their darling sins; neither do I wonder that they should be so sadly out in this particular, when I consider how apt men are to receive things by tradition, without bringing of things to a strict examination; and when I consider what strange definitions of faith many famous, worthy men have given, both in their writings and preachings; and when I consider what a mighty noise many famous men have made about legal preparations, before men presume to close with Christ, or to give up themselves in a marriage covenant to Christ, most of them requiring men to be better Christians before they come to Christ, than commonly they prove after they are implanted into Christ, &c.

Now, though I have said enough, I suppose, to lay that opinion asleep that has been last under consideration, viz., That the saints have their beloved sins, their bosom sins, their darling sins, yet for a close of this discourse, premise with me these five things:

[1.] First, *That all unconverted persons have their beloved sins, their bosom sins, their darling sins.* The beloved, the bosom, the darling sin of the Jews was idolatry. The beloved, the bosom, the darling sin of the Corinthians was uncleanness, wantonness, 1 Cor. vi. 15, 20. The beloved, the bosom, the darling sin of the Cretans was lying, Titus ii. 12. Jeroboam's beloved sin was idolatry, and Cain's beloved sin was envy, and Korah's beloved sin was gainsaying, and Esau's beloved sin was profaneness, and Ishmael's beloved sin was scoffing, and Balaam's beloved sin was ambition; Simeon and Levi's beloved sin was treachery, Manasseh's beloved sin was cruelty, and

Nebuchadnezzar's beloved sin was pride, and Herod's beloved sin was uncleanness, and Judas his beloved sin was covetousness, and the young man's beloved sin in that 19th of Matthew was worldly-mindedness, &c.

[2.] Secondly, Premise this with me, *that the elect of God, before their conversion, had their beloved sins.* Manasseh's beloved sin was cruelty; and Ephraim's beloved sin, before conversion, was idolatry, Hosea iv. 17; and Zaccheus his beloved sin before conversion was worldly-mindedness and defrauding of others; and Paul's beloved sin, before conversion, was persecution; and the jailer's beloved sin, before conversion, was cruelty; and Mary Magdalene's beloved sin, before conversion, was wantonness and uncleanness, &c.

[3.] Thirdly, Premise this with me, viz., *that after conversion there is no sin that the heart of a Christian is more seriously, more frequently, more resolutely, and more perfectly set against than that which was once his beloved lust.* The hatred, detestation, and indignation of a converted person breaks out and discovers itself most against that sin which was once a beloved sin, a bosom sin, a darling sin; his care, his fear, his jealousy, his watchfulness is most exercised against that sin which was once the darling of his soul. The converted person eyes this sin as an old enemy; he looks upon this sin as the sin by which God has been most dishonoured, and his own conscience most enslaved, and his immortal soul most endangered, and Satan most advantaged, and accordingly his spirit rises against it, Hosea xiv. 8; Isa. ii. 20, and xxx. 22. And all Christians' experience confirms this truth; but of this more before.

[4.] Fourthly, *After conversion, a Christian endeavours to be most eminent in that particular grace which is most contrary and opposite to that sin which was once his beloved sin, his bosom sin, his darling sin.* Zaccheus his beloved sin was worldliness and defrauding, but, being converted, he labours to excel in restitution and liberality; the jailer's beloved sin was severity and cruelty, but, being converted, he labours to excel in pity and courtesy; Paul's beloved sin was persecution, but, being converted, how mightily does he bestir himself to convert souls, and to edify souls, and to build up souls, and to strengthen souls, and to establish souls, and to encourage souls in the ways of the Lord—he gives it you under his own hand, ' That he laboured more abundantly than they all,' 2 Cor. xi. 23; Austin's beloved sin, his bosom sin, his darling sin, before his conversion, was wantonness and uncleanness; but, when he was converted, he was most careful and watchful to arm against that sin, and to avoid all temptations and occasions that might lead him to it afterwards. If a man's beloved sin, before conversion, has been worldliness, then after conversion he will labour above all to excel in heavenly-mindedness; or if his sin, his beloved sin, has been pride, then he will labour above all to excel in humility; or if his beloved sin has been intemperance, then he will labour above all to excel in temperance and sobriety; or if his beloved sin has been wantonness and uncleanness, then he will labour above all to excel in all chastity and purity; or if his beloved sin has been oppressing of others, then he will labour above all to excel in piety and compassion towards others; or if his beloved sin has been hypocrisy, then he will labour above all to excel in sincerity, &c. But,

[5.] Fifthly, Though no godly man, though no sincere gracious Christian hath any beloved sin, and bosom, darling sin, *yet there is no godly man, there is no sincere gracious soul, but has some sin or other to which they are more prone than to others.* Every real Christian hath his inclination to one kind of sin rather than another, which may be called his special sin, his peculiar sin, or his own iniquity, as David speaks in Ps. xviii. 23. Now the main power of grace and of uprightness is mainly seen and exercised in a man's keeping of himself from his iniquity. Now that special, that peculiar sin, to which a gracious soul may be most prone and addicted to may arise—1. From the temperament and constitution of his body. The complexion and constitution of a man's body may be a more prepared instrument for one vice rather than another; or, 2. It may arise from his particular calling. Christians have distinct and particular callings that incline them to particular sins. For instance, the soldier's calling puts him upon rapine and violence: Luke iii. 14, 'Do violence to no man, neither accuse any falsely, and be content with your wages.' And the tradesman's calling puts him upon lying, deceiving, defrauding, and overreaching his brother. And the minister's calling puts him upon flattering of the gallants and great ones of his parish, and upon pleasing the rest by speaking of smooth things, Isa. xxx. 10, 'and by sewing of pillows under their elbows,' Ezek. xiii. 18, 20. And the magistrates', judges', and justices' employments lays them open to oppression, bribery, injustice, &c. If Christians are not very much upon their watch, their very callings and offices may prove a very great snare to their souls; or, 3. It may arise from his outward state and condition in this world, whether his state be a state of prosperity or a state of adversity, or whether he be in a marriage state or in a single state. Many times a man's outward state and condition in this world hath a strong influence upon him to incline him to this or that particular sin as best suiting with his condition; or, 4. It may arise from distinct and peculiar ages; for it is certain that distinct and peculiar ages do strongly incline persons to distinct and peculiar sins. Youth inclines to wantonness and prodigality; and manhood to pride and ambition; and old age to covetousness and frowardness. Common experience tells us that many times wantonness is the sinner's darling in the time of his youth, and worldliness his darling in the time of his age; and without controversy, Christians' distinct and peculiar ages may more strongly incline them to this or that sin rather than any other; or, 5. It may arise from that distinct and particular way of breeding and education which he has had. Now to arm such Christians against their special sins, their peculiar sins—whose sins are advantaged against them, either by their constitutions and complexion, or else by their particular calling, or else by their outward state and condition, or else by their distinct and peculiar ages, or else by their particular way of breeding and education—is my present work and business; for though the reigning power of this or that special peculiar sin be broken in a man's conversion, yet the remaining life and strength that is still left in those corruptions, will by Satan be improved against the growth, peace, comfort, and assurance of the soul. Satan will strive to enter in at the same door; and by the same Delilah, by which he hath betrayed and wounded the soul, he will do all he can to do the soul a further mischief. Satan will be still a-reminding of the soul of those former sweets, pleasures, profits, delights, and contents that have come in upon the old score, so that it will be a hard thing, even for a godly man, to keep himself from his iniquity, from his special or peculiar sin, which the fathers commonly call, though not truly, *peccatum in deliciis*, a man's special darling and beloved sin. Well, Christians, remember this once for all, viz., that sound conversion includes a noble and serious revenge upon that sin which was once a man's beloved, bosom, darling sin: 2 Cor. vii. 11, ' Yea, what clearing of yourselves, yea, what indignation, yea, what fear, yea, what vehement desire, yea, what zeal, yea, what revenge.' You see this in Cranmer, who when he had subscribed with his right hand to that which was against his conscience, he afterwards, as a holy revenge, put that right hand into the flames; so Mary Magdalene takes that hair of hers. Of all sins, saith the sound convert, I am resolved to be avenged on my once beloved, bosom, darling sins, by which I have most dishonoured God, and wronged my own precious and immortal soul, and by which I have most endangered my everlasting estate.

Having thus cleared up my way, I shall now endeavour to lay before you some special remedies, means, or helps against cherishing or keeping up of any special or peculiar sin, either in heart or life, against the Lord, or against the light and conviction of a man's own conscience.

1. First, Cherishing or keeping up of any special or peculiar sin, either in heart or life, against the Lord, or against the light and conviction of a man's own conscience, will *hinder assurance* these several ways:—

[1.] First, *It will abate the degrees of our graces, and so make them more undiscernible.* Now grace rather in its degrees than in its sincerity, or simple being only, is that which gives the clearest evidence of a gracious estate, or of a man's interest in Christ. Sin, lived in, is like a vermin to the tree, which destroys the fruit. Grace cannot thrive in a sinful heart. In some soil, plants will not grow. The cherishing of sin is the withering of grace. The casting of a favourable eye on any one special sin hinders the growth of grace. If a man has a choice plant or flower in his garden, and it withers and shrivels and is dying, he opens the ground and looks at the root, and there finds a worm gnawing the root; and this is the cause of the flower's fading: the application is easy.

[2.] Secondly, The cherishing of any special peculiar sin, or the keeping up of any known transgression against the Lord, and against the light of a man's own conscience, *will hinder the lively actings and exercise of grace;* it will keep grace at an under, so that it will hardly be seen to stir or act; yea, it will keep grace so down that it will hardly be heard to speak. When a special or peculiar sin is entertained, it will exceedingly mar the vigorous exercises of those graces which are the evidences of a lively faith, and of a gracious state, and of a man's interest in Christ. Grace is never apparent and sensible to the soul, but while it is in action; therefore want of action must needs cause want of assurance. Habits are not felt immediately but by the freeness and facility of their acts; of the very being of the soul itself, nothing is felt or perceived, but only its acts. The fire that lieth still in the flint, is neither seen nor felt; but when you smite it and force it into act, it is easily discernible. For the most part, so long as a Christian hath his graces in lively action, so long he is assured of them. He that would be assured that this sacred fire of grace is in his heart, he must blow it up and get it into a flame. But,

[3.] Thirdly, The cherishing of any special sin, or the keeping up of any known transgression in heart or life against the Lord and against the light of a man's own conscience, *so blears, dims, and darkens the eye of the soul, that it cannot see its own condition, nor have any clear knowledge of its gracious state, or of its interest in Christ,* &c. Sometimes men in riding raise such a dust that they can neither see themselves nor their dearest friends, so as to distinguish one from another: the application is easy. The room sometimes is so full of smoke that a man cannot see the jewels, the treasures that lie before him; so it is here. But,

[4.] Fourthly, Cherishing of any special or peculiar sin, or the keeping up of any known transgression against the Lord or against the light of a man's own conscience, *provokes the Lord to withdraw himself, his comforts, and the gracious presence and assistance of his blessed Spirit;* without which presence and assistance the soul may search and seek long enough for assurance, comfort, and a sight of a man's interest in Christ, before it will enjoy the one or see the other. If by keeping up of any known transgression against the Lord, you set the Holy Spirit a-mourning, which alone can comfort you, and assure you of your interest in Christ, you may walk long enough without comfort and assurance, Lam i. 16. 'The Comforter that should relieve my soul, is far from me;' so in that 1 John iii. 21, it is supposed that a self-condemning heart makes void a man's confidence before God. The precious jewel of faith can be holden in no other place, but in a pure conscience; that is the only royal palace wherein it must and will dwell: 1 Tim. i. 19, 'Holding faith and a good conscience:' Heb. x. 22, 'Let us draw near with a true heart, in full assurance of faith, having our hearts sprinkled from an evil conscience.' He that comes to God with a true, honest, upright heart, being sprinkled from an evil conscience, may draw near to God in full assurance of faith; whereas guilt clouds, clogs, and distracts the soul, that it can never be with God, either as it would or as it should. *Conscientia pura semper secura,* a good conscience hath sure confidence. Conscience is *mille testes,* a thousand witnesses for or against a man. Conscience is God's preacher in the bosom. It is better, with Evagrius, to lie secure on a bed of straw, than to have a turbulent conscience on a bed of down. It was a divine saying of Seneca, a heathen, viz., 'That if there were no God to punish him, no devil to torment him, no hell to burn him, no man to see him; yet would he not sin, for the ugliness of sin, and the grief of his own conscience.' But,

[5.] Fifthly, Cherishing of any special or peculiar sin, or the keeping up of any known transgression, in heart or life, against the Lord, and against the light of a man's own conscience, will greatly hinder his *high esteem and reputation of Jesus Christ, and so it will keep him from comfort, assurance, and sight of his interest in him,* so that sometimes his dearest children are constrained to cry out, ' God is departed from me, and he answereth me not, neither by dream nor vision, neither this way nor that,' 1 Sam. xxviii. 15. But,

[6.] Sixthly, The greatest and most common cause of the want of assurance, comfort, and peace, is *some unmortified lust, some secret, special, peculiar sin, unto which men give entertainment, or at least, which they do not so vigorously oppose, and heartily renounce as they should and might.* Hinc illæ lachrymæ, and this is that which casts them on sore straits and difficulties. And how should it be otherwise, seeing God, who is infinitely wise, holy, and righteous, either cannot or will not reveal the secrets of his love to those who harbour his known enemies in their bosoms? The great God either cannot or will not regard the whinings and complainings of those who play or dally with that very sin which galls their consciences, and connive and wink at the stirrings and workings of that very lust for which he hides his face from them, and writes ' bitter things against them.' Mark, all fears and doubts and scruples are begotten upon sin, either real or imaginary. Now, if the sin be but imaginary, an enlightened rectified judgment may easily and quickly scatter such fears, doubts, and scruples, as the sun doth mists and clouds, when it shines in its brightness; but if the sin be real, then there is no possibility of curing those fears, doubts, and scruples arising from thence, but by an unfeigned repentance and returning from that sin. Now, if I should produce all the scriptures and instances that stand ready pressed to prove this, I must transcribe a good part of the Bible; but this would be labour in vain, seeing it seemeth to have been a notion engraven even on natural conscience, viz., that sin so defiles persons, that till they be washed from it, neither they nor their services can be accepted; from whence arose that custom of setting water-pots at their entrance into their temples or places of worship. Let him that wants assurance, comfort, peace, and a sight of his interest in Christ, cast out every known sin, and set upon a universal course of reformation; for God will not give his cordials to those that have a foul stomach. Those that, against light and checks of conscience, dally and tamper with this sin or that, those God will have no commerce, no communion with; on such God will not lift up the light of his countenance: Rev. ii. 17, ' To him that overcometh will I give to eat of the hidden manna, and I will give him a white stone, and in that stone, a new name written.' These are all metaphorical expressions, which, being put together, do amount to as much as assurance; but mark, these are promised, τῷ νικῶντι, 'to him that overcometh,' to him that rides on conquering and to conquer. Oh that Christians would seriously remember this! The dearer it cost any one to part with his sins, the more sweet and comfortable will it be to call to mind the victory that through the Spirit of grace he has got over his sins. There is no comfort, joy, or peace to that which arises from the conquests of sin, especially of special sins. When Goliath was slain, what joy and triumph was there in the camp! So here.

[7.] Seventhly, Cherishing of any special or peculiar sin, or the keeping up of any known transgression, either in heart or life, against the Lord, and against the light of a man's own conscience, will hinder the soul from that *warm, lively, fervent, frequent, seasonable, sincere, and constant way of duty, as contributes most to the increase of grace, peace, comfort, and assurance*, &c.

[8.] Eighthly, *Seriously consider of the several assertions and concurrent judgments of our best and most famous divines in the present case.* I shall give you a taste of some of their sayings.[1]

First, 'A man,' saith one, 'can have no peace in his conscience that favoureth and retaineth any one sin in himself against his conscience.'

Secondly, Another saith, 'A man is in a damnable state, whatsoever good deeds seem to be in him, if he yield not to the work of the Holy Ghost for the leaving but of any one known sin which fighteth against peace of conscience.' But,

Thirdly, 'So long,' saith another, 'as the power of mortification destroyeth thy sinful affections, and so long as thou art unfeignedly displeased with all sin, and dost mortify the deeds of the body by the Spirit, thy case is the case of salvation.' But,

Fourthly, Another saith, 'A good conscience stands not with a purpose of sinning, no, not with irresolution against sin.' This must be understood of habitual purposes, and of a constant irresolution against sin.

Fifthly, 'The rich and precious box of a good conscience,' saith another, 'is polluted and made impure, if but one dead fly be suffered in it. One sin being quietly permitted, and suffered to live in the soul without being disturbed, resisted, resolved against, or lamented over, will certainly mar the peace of a good conscience.'

Sixthly, 'Where there is but any one sin,' saith another, 'nourished and fostered, all other our graces are not only blemished, but abolished; they are no graces.[2]

Seventhly, Most true is that saying of Aquinas, 'That all sins are coupled together, though not in regard of conversion to temporal good, for some look to the good of gain, some of glory, some of pleasure, yet in regard of aversion from eternal good, that is God; so that he that looks but towards one sin is as much averted and turned back from God as if he looked to all; in which respect St James says, "He that offendeth in one is guilty of all,"' James ii. 10. Now, that ye may not mistake Aquinas, nor the scripture he cites, you must remember that the whole law is but one copulative, Exod. xvi. 18; Ezek. xviii. 10–13. Mark, he that breaketh one command habitually, breaketh all; not so actually. Such as are truly godly in respect of the habitual desires, purposes, bents, biases, inclinations, resolutions, and endeavours of their souls, do keep those very commands that actually they daily break. But a dispensatory conscience keeps not any one commandment of God. He that willingly and wilfully and habitually gives himself liberty to break any one commandment, is guilty of all; that is, 1. Either he breaks the chain of duties, and so breaks all the

---

[1] Most of these quotations, with many more of like sort, will be found in Spencer's fine folio of 'Things New and Old,' (1658.) Cf. under 'conscience' and 'sin.'—G.

[2] Dyke, 'Of the deceitfulness of the heart,' c. 16.

law, being copulative; or, 2. With the same disposition of heart, that he willingly, wilfully, habitually breaks one, with the same disposition of heart he is ready pressed to break all. The apostle's meaning in that James ii. 10, is certainly this, viz., that suppose a man should keep the whole law for substance, except in some one particular, yet by allowing of himself in this particular, thereby he manifests that he kept no precept of the law in obedience and conscience unto God; for if he did, then he would be careful to keep every precept. Thus much the words following import, and hereby he manifests that he is guilty of all. Some others conceive that therefore such a one may be said to be guilty of all, because by allowing of himself in any one sin, thereby he lies under that curse which is threatened against the transgressors of the law, Deut. xxvii. 26.

Eighthly, 'Every Christian should carry in his heart,' saith another, 'a constant and resolute purpose not to sin in anything; for faith and the purpose of sinning can never stand together.' This must be understood of a habitual, not actual; of a constant, not transient purpose.˙ But,

Ninthly, 'One flaw in a diamond,' saith another, 'takes away the lustre and the price.' One puddle, if we wallow in it, will defile us. One man, in law, may keep possession. One piece of ward-land makes the heir liable to the king. So one sin lived in, and allowed, may make a man miserable for ever. But,

Tenthly, One turn may bring a man quite out of the way. One act of treason makes a traitor. Gideon had seventy sons, but one bastard, and yet that one bastard destroyed all the rest, Judg. viii. 31. 'One sin,' as well as one sinner, 'lived in and allowed, may destroy much good,' saith another.

Eleventhly, 'He that favoureth one sin, though he forego many, does but as Benhadad, recover of one disease and die of another; yea, he doth but take pains to go to hell,' saith another.

Twelfthly, 'Satan, by one lie to our first parents, made fruitless what God himself had preached to them immediately before,' saith another.

Thirteenthly, A man may, by one short act of sin, bring a long curse upon himself and his posterity, as Ham did when he saw his father Noah drunk: Gen. ix. 24, 25, 'And Noah awoke from his wine, and knew what his younger son had done unto him, and he said, Cursed is Canaan, a servant of servants shall he be unto his brethren.' Canaan was Ham's son. Noah, as God's mouth, prophesied a curse upon the son for his father's sin. Here Ham is cursed in his son Canaan, and the curse entailed not only to Canaan, but to his posterity. Noah prophesies a long series and chain of curses upon Canaan and his children. He makes the curse hereditary to the name and nation of the Canaanites: 'A servant of servants shall he be unto his brethren,' that is, the vilest and basest servant; for the Hebrews express the superlative degree by such a duplication as 'vanity of vanities;' that is, most vain: 'a song of songs;' that is, a most excellent song. So here, 'a servant of servants;' that is, the vilest, the basest servant. Ah, heavy and prodigious curse, upon the account of one sin! But,

Fourteenthly, Satan can be content that men should yield to God in many things, provided that they will be but true to him in some one thing; for he knows very well, that as one dram of poison may poison a man, and one stab at the heart may kill a man; so one sin unrepented of, one sin allowed, retained, cherished, and practised, will certainly damn a man. But,

Fifteenthly, Though all the parts of a man's body be sound, save only one, that one diseased and ulcerous part may be deadly to thee; for all the sound members cannot preserve thy life, but that one diseased and ulcerous member will hasten thy death; so one sin allowed, indulged, and lived in, will prove killing and damning to thee.

Sixteenthly, 'Observe,' saith another, 'that an unmortified sin allowed and wilfully retained will eat out all appearance of virtue and piety. Herod's high esteem of John and his ministry, and his reverencing of him and observing of him, and his forward performance of many good things, are all given over and laid aside at the instance and command of his master-sin, his reigning sin. John's head must go for it, if he won't let Herod enjoy his Herodias quietly.' But,

Seventeenthly, Some will leave all their sins but one; Jacob would let all his sons go but Benjamin. Satan can hold a man fast enough by one sin that he allows and lives in, as the fowler can hold the bird fast enough by one wing or by one claw.

Eighteenthly, Holy Polycarp, in the time of the fourth persecution, when he was commanded but to swear one oath, he made this answer: " Four-score and six years have I endeavoured to do God service, and all this while he never hurt me; how then can I speak evil of so good a Lord and Master who hath thus long preserved me! I am a Christian, and cannot swear; let heathens and infidels swear if they will, I cannot do it, were it to the saving of my life.'

Ninteenthly, A willing and a wilful keeping up, either in heart or life, any known transgression against the Lord, is a breach of the holy law of God; it is a fighting against the honour and glory of God, and is a reproach to the eye of God, the omnipresence of God.

Twentiethly, The keeping up of any known transgression against the Lord may endanger the souls of others, and may be found a fighting against all the cries, prayers, tears, promises, vows, and covenants that thou hast made to God, when thou hast been upon a sick-bed, or in eminent dangers, or near death; or else when thou hast been in solemn seeking of the Lord, either alone or with others. These things should be frequently and seriously thought of by such poor fools as are entangled by any lust.

Twenty-firstly, The keeping up of any known transgression against the Lord, either in heart or life, is a high tempting of Satan to tempt the soul; it will also greatly unfit the soul for all sorts of duties and services that he either owes to God, to himself, or others; it will also put a sting into all a man's troubles, afflictions, and distresses; it will also lay a foundation for despair; and it will make death, which is the king of terrors, and the terror of kings, to be very terrible to the soul.

Twenty-secondly, The keeping up of any known transgression against the Lord, either in heart or life, will fight against all those patterns and examples in Holy Writ, that in duty and honour we are bound to imitate and follow. Pray, where do you find in any of the blessed Scriptures, that any of the patriarchs, prophets, apostles, or saints are ever charged with a willing or a wilful keeping up, either in their hearts or lives, any known transgression against the Lord?

Twenty-thirdly, The keeping up of any known transgression against the Lord will highly make against all clear, sweet, and standing communion with God. Parents use not to smile, nor be familiar with their children, nor to keep up any intimate communion with them, in their neglects and disobedience. It is so here.

Twenty-fourthly, The keeping up, either in heart or life, of any known transgression against the Lord, will fight against the standing joy, peace, comfort, and assurance of the soul. Joy in the Holy Ghost will make its nest nowhere but in a holy soul. So far as the Spirit is grieved he will suspend his consolations, Lam. i. 16. A man will have no more comfort from God than he makes conscience of sinning against God. A conscience good in point of integrity will be good also in point of tranquillity. If our hearts condemn us not, 'then have we confidence towards God'—and I may say also towards men, Acts xxiv. 16—oh, what comfort and solace hath a clear conscience! he hath something within to answer accusations without. I shall conclude this particular with a notable saying of one of the ancients. The joys of a good conscience are the paradise of souls, the delight of angels, the garden of delights, the field of blessing, the temple of Solomon, the court of God, the habitation of the Spirit. [Bernard.]

Twenty-fifthly, The keeping up of any known transgression, either in heart or life, against the Lord, is a high contempt of the all-seeing eye of God, of the omnipresence of God. It is well known what Ahasuerus, that great monarch, said concerning Haman, when coming in, he found him cast upon the queen's bed on which she sat; 'What,' saith he, 'will he force the queen before me, in the house?' Esther vii. 8. There was the killing emphasis in the words, 'before me;' 'will he force the queen before me?' What! will he dare to commit such a villany, and I stand and look on? O sirs! to do wickedly in the sight of God is a thing that he looks upon as the greatest affront and indignity that can possibly be done unto him. What, saith he, wilt thou be drunk before me, and swear and blaspheme before me, and be wanton and unclean before me, and break my laws before my eyes! This, then, is the killing aggravation of all sin that is done before the face of God, in the presence of God; whereas, the very consideration of God's omnipresence, that he stands and looks on, should be as a bar, a remora, to stop the proceedings of all wicked intendments, a dissuasive rather from sin than the least encouragement thereunto. It was an excellent saying of Ambrose, 'If thou canst not hide thyself from the sun, which is God's minister of light, how impossible will it be to hide thyself from him whose eyes are ten thousand times brighter than the sun.' [1] God's eye is the best marshal to keep the soul in a comely order. Let thine eye be ever on him whose eye is ever on thee. 'The eyes of

---

[1] Offic. l. i., c. 14.

the Lord are in every place, beholding the evil and the good,' Prov. xv. 9. There is no drawing of a curtain between God and thee. God is *totus oculus*, all eye; he seeth all things, in all places, and at all times. When thou art in secret, consider conscience is present, which is more than a thousand witnesses; and God is present, which is more than a thousand consciences. It was a pretty fancy of one that would have his chamber painted full of eyes, that which way soever he looked he might still have some eyes upon him; and he fancying, according to the moralist's advice, always under the eye of a keeper, might be the more careful of his carriage. O sirs! if the eyes of men make even the vilest to forbear their beloved lusts for a while, that the adulterer watcheth for the twilight, and 'they that are drunken are drunken in the night,' how powerful will the eye and presence of God be with those that fear his anger and know the sweetness of his favour! The thought of this omnipresence of God will affrighten thee from sin. Gehazi durst not ask or receive any part of Naaman's presents in his master's presence, but when he had got out of Elisha's sight, then he tells his lie, and gives way to his lusts. Men never sin more freely than when they presume upon secrecy; 'They break in pieces thy people, O Lord, and afflict thy heritage. They slay the widow and stranger, and murder the fatherless,' yet they say, 'The Lord doth not see, neither shall the God of Jacob regard it,' Ps. xciv. 5–7. They who abounded in abominations said, 'The Lord seeth us not, the Lord hath forsaken the earth,' Ezek. viii. 9, 12. The wise man dissuadeth from wickedness upon the consideration of God's eye and omniscience. 'And why wilt thou, my son, be ravished with a strange woman, and embrace the bosom of a stranger; for the ways of man are before the eyes of the Lord, and he pondereth all his goings,' Prov. v. 20, 21. Joseph saw God in the room, and therefore durst not yield; but his mistress saw none but Joseph, and so was impudently alluring and tempting him to folly. I have read of two religious men that took contrary courses with two lewd women whom they were desirous to reclaim from their vicious course of life. One of the men told one of the women that he was desirous to enjoy her company, so it might be with secrecy, and when she had brought him into a close room, that none could pry into, he told her, 'All the bars and bolts here cannot keep God out.' The other desired the other woman to company with him, openly in the streets, which when she rejected as a mad request, he told her, 'It was better to do it in the eyes of a multitude, than in the eyes of God.' Oh, why shall not the presence of that God who hates sin, and who is resolved to punish it with hell-flames, make us ashamed or afraid to sin, and dare him to his face!

Twenty-sixthly, There have been many a prodigal, who, by one cast of the dice, have lost a fair inheritance. A man may be killed with one stab of a pen-knife, and one hole in a ship may sink it, and one thief may rob a man of all he has in the world. A man may escape many gross sins, and yet, by living in the allowance of some one sin, be deprived of the glory of heaven for ever. Moses came within the sight of Canaan, but for one sin—not sanctifying God's name—he was shut out. And no less will it be to any man that, for living in any one sin, shall be for ever shut out of the kingdom of heaven; not but that there may be some remainders of sin, and yet the heart taken off from every sin; but if there be any secret closing with any one way of sin, all the profession of godliness and leaving all other sins will be to no purpose, nor ever bring a man to happiness.

Twenty-seventhly, As the philosopher saith, a cup or some such thing that hath a hole in it is no cup; it will hold nothing, and therefore cannot perform the use of a cup, though it have but one hole in it. So if the heart have but one hole in it, if it retain the devil but in one thing, if it make choice but of any one sin to lie and wallow in, and tumble in, it doth evacuate all the other good, by the entertainment of that one sin. The whole box of ointment will be spoiled by the dropping of that one fly into it. By the laws of our kingdom, a man can never have a true possession till he have voided all. And in the state of grace, no man can have a full interest in Christ till all sin, that is, all reigning, domineering sin be rooted out.

Thus you see the concurrent judgments of our most famous divines, against men's allowing, indulging, or retaining any one known sin against their light and consciences; but that these sayings of theirs may lie in more weight and power upon every poor soul that is entangled with any base lusts, be pleased seriously and frequently to consider of these following particulars:—

[1.] First, *It is to no purpose for a man to turn from some sins, if he does not turn from all his sins,* James i. 26. 'If any man among you seem to be religious, and bridle not his tongue, but deceiveth his own heart, this man's religion is in vain.' This, at first sight, may seem to be a hard saying, that for one fault, for one fault in the tongue, all a man's religion should be counted vain; and yet this, you see, the Holy Ghost does peremptorily conclude. Let a man make never so glorious a profession of religion, yet, if he gives himself liberty to live in the practice of any known sin, yea, though it be but in a sin of the tongue, his religion is in vain, and that one sin will separate him from God for ever. If a wife be never so officious [1] to her husband in many things, yet if she entertains any other lover into his bed besides himself, it will for ever alienate his affections from her, and make an everlasting separation between them. The application is easy. To turn from one sin to another is but to be tossed from one hand of the devil to another, it is but, with Benhadad, to recover of one disease and die of another; it is but to take pains to go to hell. If a ship spring three leaks, and only two be stopped, the third will sink the ship; or if a man have two grievous wounds in his body, and takes order only to cure one, that which is neglected will certainly kill him. It is so here. Herod, Judas, and Saul, with the scribes and Pharisees, have for many hundred years experienced this truth. But,

[2.] Secondly, *Partial obedience is indeed no obedience; it is only universal obedience that is true obedience:* Exod. xxiv. 7, 'All that the Lord hath said will we do, and be obedient.' They only are indeed obedient who have a care to do all that is commanded; for to obey is to do that which is commanded because it is commanded. Though the thing done be commanded, yet if it be not therefore done because it is commanded, it is no obedience. Now if this be the nature of obedience,

[1] As before : see Glossary.—G.

then where obedience is indeed, it is not partial, but universal; for he that doth any one thing that is commanded because it is commanded, he will be careful to do everything that is commanded, there being the same reason for all.   They that are only for a partial obedience, they do break asunder the bond and reason of all obedience; for all obedience is to be founded upon the authority and will of God, because God, who hath authority over all his creatures, doth will and command us to obey his voice, to walk in his statutes.   For this very reason do we stand bound to obey him; and if we do obey him upon this reason, then must we walk in all his statutes, for so hath he commanded us. And if we will not come up to this, but will walk in what statutes of his we please, then do we renounce his will as the obliging reason of our obedience, and do set up our own liking and pleasure as the reason thereof.   God has so connexed the duties of his law one to another, that if there be not a conscientious care to walk according to all that the law requires, a man becomes a transgressor of the whole law; according to that of St James, chap. ii. 10, 'Whosoever shall keep the whole law, and yet offend in one point, is guilty of all.'   The bond of all is broken, the authority of all is slighted, and that evil disposition, that sinful frame of heart, that works a man to venture upon the breach of one command, would make him venture upon the breach of any command, were it not for some infirmity of nature, or because his purse will not hold out to maintain it, or for shame, or loss, or because of the eyes of friends, or the sword of the magistrate, or for some other sinister respects.   He that gives himself liberty to live in the breach of any one command of God, is qualified with a disposition of heart to break them all.   Every single sin contains virtually all sin in it.   He that allows himself a liberty to live in the breach of any one particular law of God, he casts contempt and scorn upon the authority that made the whole law, and upon this account breaks it all.   And the apostle gives the reason of it in verse 11; for he that said, 'Do not commit adultery,' said also, 'Do not kill.'   Now, if thou commit no adultery, yet if thou kill, thou art become a transgressor of the law; not that he is guilty of all distributively, but collectively; for the law is copulative, there is a chain of duties, and these are all so linked one to another, that you cannot break one link of the chain, but you break the whole chain.   No man can live in the breach of any known command of God, but he wrongs every command of God.   He hath no real regard to any of the commandments of God, that hath not a regard to all the command- ments of God.   There is one and the same lawgiver in respect of all the commandments; he that gave one command gave also another. Therefore he that observes one commandment in obedience unto God, whose commandment it is, he will observe all, because all are his com- mandments ; and he that slights one commandment is guilty of all, because he doth contemn the authority of him that gave them all. Even in those commandments which he doth observe, he hath no respect to the will and authority of him that gave them ; therefore, as Calvin doth well observe upon James ii. 10, 11, 'That there is no obedience towards God, where there is not a uniform endeavour to please God, as well in one thing as in another.'

    [3.] Thirdly, Partial obedience tends *to plain atheism;* for by the same reason that you slight the will of God in any commandment, by the same reason you may despise his will in every commandment; for every commandment of God is his will, and it is ' holy, spiritual, just, and good,' Rom. vii. 12, 14, and contrary to our sinful lusts. And if this be the reason why such and such commandments of God won't down with you, then by the same reason none of them must be of authority with you.

[4.] Fourthly, God requires *universal obedience:* Deut. v. 33, &c., and x. 12, and xi. 21, 22, &c.; and Jer. vii. 23, 'Walk ye in all the ways that I have commanded you, that it may be well unto you;' Mat. xxviii. 20, 'Teaching them to observe all things that I have commanded you,' &c.

[5.] Fifthly, Partial obedience is *an audacious charge against God himself, as to his wisdom, or power, or goodness;* for those statutes of God which you will not come up unto, either they are as righteous as the rest, and as holy as the rest, and as spiritual as the rest, and as good as the rest, or they are not. If they be as holy, spiritual, just, righteous, and good as the rest, why should you not walk in them as well as in the rest? To say they are not as holy, spiritual, righteous, &c., as the rest, Oh what a blasphemous charge is this against God himself, in prescribing unto him anything that is not righteous and good, &c., and likewise in making his will, which is the rule of all' righteousness and goodness, to be partly righteous and partly unrighteous, to be partly good and partly bad.

[6.] Sixthly, *God delights in universal obedience, and in those that perform it:* Deut. v. 29, 'O that there were such a heart in them, that they would fear me, and keep all my commandments always.' Upon this account Abraham is called the friend of God in Scripture three times, Isa. xli. 8; 2 Chron. xx. 7; James ii. 3. And upon the very same account God called David ' a man after his own heart:' Acts xiii. 22, ' I have found David the son of Jesse, a man after mine own heart, which shall fulfil all my will,'—πάντα τα θελήματα, all my wills, to note the universality and sincerity of his obedience.

[7.] Seventhly, *There is not any one statute of God but it is good and for our good; ergo,* we should walk in all his statutes: Deut. v. 25, 'Ye shall walk in all the ways which the Lord your God hath commanded you, that you may live, and that it may be well with you.' What one path hath the Lord commanded us to walk in, but as it concerns his own glory, so likewise it concerns our good?

Is it not good for us to love the Lord, and to set him up as the object of our fear, and to act faith on him, and to worship him in spirit and in truth, and to be tender of his glory, and to sanctify his day, and to keep off from sin, and to keep close to his ways? But,

[8.] Eighthly, Universal obedience is *the condition upon which the promise of mercy and salvation runs:* Ezek. xviii. 21, 'If the wicked will turn from all his sins that he hath committed, and keep all his statutes, and do that which is lawful and right, he shall surely live, he shall not die.'

[9.] Ninthly, *Our hearts must be perfect with the Lord our God:* Deut. xviii. 13, 'Thou shalt be perfect with the Lord thy God;' and Gen. xvii. 1, ' Walk before me, and be thou perfect.' Now, how can our hearts be said to be perfect with God if we do prevaricate with him; if in some things we obey him and in other things we will not obey him, if we walk in some of his statutes but will not walk in all his statutes, if in some part we will be his servants and in other part of our lives we will be the servants of sin. But,

[10.] Tenthly, *If the heart be sound and upright, it will yield entire and universal obedience:* Ps. cxix. 80, 'Let my heart be sound in thy statutes, that I may not be ashamed;' and verse 6, 'Then shall I not be ashamed when I have respect to all thy commandments.' By these verses, compared together, it appears that then the heart is sound and sincere, when a man has respect unto all God's commandments. Without a universal obedience, a man can never have that 'hope which maketh not ashamed.' But,

[11.] Eleventhly, *Either we must endeavour to walk in all the statutes of God, or else we must find some dispensation or toleration from God to free us, and excuse us and hold us indemnified, though we do not walk in all of them.* Now, what one commandment is there from obedience whereunto, God excuseth any man, or will not punish him for the neglect of obedience unto it? The apostle saith, 'That whosoever shall keep the whole law, and yet offend in one point, he is guilty of all,' James ii. 10. If he prevaricates with God, as to any one particular commandment of his, his heart is naught; he is guilty of all, he hath really no regard of any of the rest of God's laws. But,

[12.] Twelfthly, *The precious saints and servants of God, whose examples are recorded, and set forth for our imitation, they have been very careful to perform universal obedience.* Will you see it in Abraham, who was ready to comply with God in all his royal commands? When God commanded him to leave his country, and his father's house, he did it, Gen. xii. When God commanded him to be circumcised, though it were both shameful and painful, he submitted unto it, Gen. xvii. When God commanded him to send away his son Ishmael, though when Sarah spake to him about it, the thing seemed very grievous unto him, yet as soon as he saw it to be the will of God, he was obedient unto it, Gen. xxi. When God commanded him to sacrifice his son Isaac, his only son, the son of his old age, the son of the promise, the son of his delight; yea, that son from whom was to proceed that Jesus in whom all the nations of the earth should be blessed; and though all this might seem to cross both nature and grace, both reason and religion, yet Abraham was willing to obey God in this also, and to do what he commanded, Gen. xxii. So David was 'a man after God's own heart,' which fulfilled all his wills, as the original runs in Acts xiii. 22. And it is said of Zacharias and Elizabeth, that they walked in all the commandments and ordinances of the Lord, &c., Luke i. 6; 1 Thes. ii. 10, 'Ye are witnesses, and God also, how holily, and justly, and unblamably we behaved ourselves among you that believe.'

[13.] Thirteenthly, Universal obedience speaks out *the strength of our love to Christ, and the reality of our friendship with Christ,* John xv. 14, 'Ye are my friends, if ye do whatsoever I command you.' That child shews most love to his father, that observes all his pecepts; and that servant shews most love to his master, that observes all his master's commands, and that wife shews most love to her husband, that observes all he requires in the Lord. So here, &c.

[14.] Fourteenthly, Universal obedience will give *most peace, rest, quiet, and comfort to the conscience.* Such a Christian will be as an eye that hath no mote to trouble it; as a kingdom that hath no rebel to annoy·it; as a ship that hath no leak to disturb it: Ps. cxix. 165, ' Great peace have they which love thy law, and nothing shall offend them.' But,

[15.] Fifteenthly, *Man's holiness must be conformable to God's holiness:* Eph. v. 1, 2, ' Be ye followers of God as dear children ;' Mat. v. 48, ' Be ye perfect, as your heavenly Father is perfect.' Now ' God is righteous in all his ways, and holy in all his works,' and so ought all to desire and endeavour to be, that would be saved : 1 Pet. i. 15, ' As he who hath called you is holy, so be ye also holy in all manner of conversation; ver. 16, because it is written, Be ye holy, for I am holy.' But,

[16.] Sixteenthly, *The holiness of a Christian must be conformable to the holiness of Christ,* ' Be ye followers of me, as I am of Christ,' 1 Cor. xi. 1. Now Christ was holy in all things. ' It behoveth us,' said he, ' to fulfil all righteousness.' And this should be the care of every one that professeth himself to be Christ's, to endeavour ' to be holy as Christ was holy:' 1 John ii. 6, ' He that saith he abideth in him, ought himself to walk even as he walked.' But,

[17.] Seventeenthly, *Servants must obey their earthly masters, not in some things only, but in all things, to wit, that are just and lawful:* Titus ii. 9, ' Exhort servants to be obedient to their own masters, and to please them well in all things.' What master will be content that his servant should choose how far forth he will observe and do those things which he doth require of him ? much less may we think that such arbitrary and partial performances will please that God who is our heavenly Master.

[18.] Eighteenthly, *The promises of mercy, both spiritual and temporal, are made over to universal obedience,* 1 Kings vi. 12, 13; Deut. xxviii. 1–3; Ezek. xviii. 21, 22, 27, 28. Turn to all these promises and dilate on them, &c.

[19.] Nineteenthly, *One sin never goes alone, as you may see in the falls of Adam and Eve, Lot, Abraham, Noah, Jacob, Joseph, Job, David, Solomon, Peter, Ahab, Judas, Jeroboam.* One sin will make way for more; as one little thief can open the door to let in many great ones. Satan will be sure to nest himself, to lodge himself in the least sins, as birds nest and lodge themselves in the smallest branches of the tree, and there he will do all he can to hatch all manner of wickedness. A little wedge makes way for a greater; and so do little sins make way for greater.

[20.] Twentiethly, *The reasons of turning from sin are universally binding to a gracious soul.* ` There are the same reasons and grounds for a penitent man's turning from every sin as there is for his turning from any one sin. Do you turn from this or that sin because the Lord hath forbid it ? why! upon the same ground you must turn from every sin; for God has forbid every sin as well as this or that particular sin. There is the same authority forbidding or commanding in all; and if the authority of God awes a man from one sin, it will awe him from all, &c. But,

[21.] Twenty-firstly, *One sin allowed and lived in will keep Christ and the soul asunder.* As one rebel, one traitor, hid and kept in the house, will keep a prince and his subjects asunder; or as one stone in the pipe will keep the water and the cistern asunder; so here. But,

[22.] Twenty-secondly, *One sin allowed and lived in will unfit a person for suffering;* as one cut or shot in the shoulder may hinder a man from bearing a burden. Will he ever lay down his life for Christ, that can't, that won't lay down a lust for Christ? But,

[23.] Twenty-thirdly, *One sin allowed and lived in is sufficient to deprive a man for ever of the greatest good.* One sin allowed and wallowed in will as certainly deprive a man of the blessed vision of God, and of all the treasures, pleasures, and delights that be at God's right hand, as a thousand. One sin stripped the fallen angels of all their glory; and one sin stripped our first parents of all their dignity and excellency, Gen. iii. 4, 5. One fly in the box of precious ointment spoils the whole box; one thief may rob a man of all his treasure; one disease may deprive a man of all his health; and one drop of poison will spoil the whole glass of wine: and so one sin allowed and lived in will make a man miserable for ever. One millstone will sink a man to the bottom of the sea, as well as a hundred. It is so here. But,

[24.] Twenty-fourthly, *One sin allowed and lived in will eat out all peace of conscience.* As one string that jars will spoil the sweetest music; so one sin countenanced and lived in will spoil the music of conscience. One pirate may rob a man of all he has in this world. But,

[25.] Twenty-fifthly and lastly, *The sinner would have God to forgive him, not only some of his sins, but all his sins; and therefore it is but just and equal that he should turn from all his sins.* If God be so faithful and just to forgive us all our sins, we must be so faithful and just as to turn from all our sins. The plaster must be as broad as the sore, and the tent[1] as long and as deep as the wound. It argues horrid hypocrisy, damnable folly, and wonderful impudency for a man to beg the pardon of those very sins that he is resolved never to forsake, &c.

Objection. But it is impossible for any man on earth to walk in all God's statutes, to obey all his commands, to do his will in all things, to walk according to the full breadth of God's royal law.

Solution. I answer, there is a twofold walking in all the statutes of God; there is a twofold obedience to all the royal commands of God.

(1.) First, *One is legal, when all is done that God requireth;* and all is done as God requireth, when there is not one path of duty, but we do walk in it perfectly and continually. Thus no man on earth doth or can walk in all God's statutes, or fully do what he commandeth. 'For in many things we offend all,' James iii. 2. So Eccles. vii. 20, 'There is not a just man upon the earth, that doeth good, and sinneth not.' 1 Kings viii. 46, 'For there is no man that sinneth not.'

---

[1] 'A roll of lint used in searching or cleansing a deep wound.'—G.

Prov. xx. 9, 'Who can say, I have made my heart clean, I am pure from my sin?' Job xiv. 4, 'Who can bring a clean thing out of an unclean? not one.' 1 John i. 8, ' If we say we have no sin, we deceive ourselves, and the truth is not in us.'

(2.) *Secondly, Another is evangelical, which is such a walking in all the statutes of God, and such a keeping of all the commands of God, as is in Christ accepted of, and accounted of, as if we did keep them all.* This walking in all God's statutes, and keeping of all his commandments, and doing of them all, is not only possible, but it is also actual in every believer, in every sincere Christian, and it consists in these particulars :—

[1.] First, *In the approbation of all the statutes and commandments of God.* Rom. vii. 12, 'The commandment is holy, and just, and good.' Ver. 16, 'I consent unto the law that it is good.' There is both assent and consent. Ps. cxix. 128, ' I esteem all thy precepts concerning all things to be right.' A sincere Christian approves of all divine commands, though he cannot perfectly keep all divine commands. But,

[2.] Secondly, It consists *in a conscientious submission unto the authority of all the statutes of God.* Every command of God hath an authority within his heart, and over his heart. Ps. cxix. 161, ' My heart standeth in awe of thy word.' A sincere Christian stands in awe of every known command of God, and hath a spiritual regard unto them all. Ps. cxix. 6, 'I have respect unto all thy commandments.' But,

[3.] Thirdly, It consists *in a cordial willingness and a cordial desire to walk in all the statutes of God, and to obey all the commands of God.* Rom. vii. 18, ' For to will is present with me.' Ps. cxix. 5, 'O that my ways were directed to keep thy statutes !' Ver. 8, ' I will keep thy statutes.' But,

[4.] Fourthly, It consists *in a sweet complacency in all God's commands.* Ps. cxix. 47, ' I will delight myself in thy commandment which I have loved.' Rom. vii. 22, ' I delight in the law of God after the inward man.' But,

[5.] Fifthly, *He who obeys sincerely obeys universally.* Though not in regard of practice, which is impossible, yet in regard of affection, he loves all the commands of God, yea, he dearly loves those very commands of God that he cannot obey, by reason of the infirmity of the flesh, by reason of that body of sin and death that he bears about with him. Ponder upon that : Ps. cxix. 97, ' O how I love thy law!' Such a pang of love he felt, as could not otherwise be vented, but by this pathetical exclamation, ' O how I love thy law,' vers. 113, 163, 127, 159, 167. Ponder upon all these verses. But,

[6.] Sixthly, A sincere Christian obeys all the commands of God ; he is universal in his obedience, *in respect of valuation or esteem.* He highly values all the commands of God ; he highly prizes all the commands of· God ; as you may clearly see by comparing these scriptures together, Ps. cxix. 72, 127, 128, xix. 8–11 ; Job xxiii. 12. But,

[7.] Seventhly, A sincere Christian is universal in his obedience, *in respect of his purpose and resolution ;* he purposes and resolves, by divine assistance, to obey all, to keep all. Ps. cxix. 106, ' I have sworn, and will perform it, that I will keep thy righteous judgments.' Ps. xvii. 3, ' I am purposed that my mouth shall not transgress. But,

[8.] Eighthly, A sincere Christian is universal in his obedience, *in respect of his inclination ;* he has an habitual inclination in him to keep all the commands of God, 1 Kings viii. 57, 58 ; 2 Chron. xxx. 17–20 ; Ps. cxix. 112, ' I have inclined my heart to perform thy statutes always, even to the end.' But,

[9.] Ninthly and lastly, Their evangelical keeping of all the commands of God consists *in their sincere endeavour to keep them all ;* they put out themselves in all the ways and parts of obedience ; they do not willingly and wittingly slight or neglect any commandment, but are striving to conform themselves thereunto. As a dutiful son doth all his father's commands, at least in point of endeavour, so your sincere Christians make conscience of keeping all the commands of God in respect of endeavours. Ps. cxix. 59, ' I turned my feet unto thy testimonies.' God esteems of evangelical obedience as perfect obedience. Zacharias had his failings, he did hesitate through unbelief, for which he was struck dumb ; yet the text tells you, ' That he walked in all the commandments of the Lord blameless,' Luke i. 6, because he did cordially desire and endeavour to obey God in all things. Evangelical obedience is true for the essence, though not perfect for the degree. A child of God obeys all the commands of God, in respect of all his sincere desires, purposes, resolutions, and endeavours ; and this God accepts in Christ for perfect and complete obedience. This is the glory of the covenant of grace, that God accepts and esteems of sincere obedience as perfect obedience. Such who sincerely endeavour to keep the whole law of God, they do keep the whole law of God in an evangelical sense, though not in a legal sense. A sincere Christian is for the first table as well as the second, and the second as well as the first ; he doth not adhere to the first and neglect the second, as hypocrites do ; neither doth he adhere to the second and contemn the first, as profane men do. O Christians, for your support and comfort, know that when your desires and endeavours are to do the will of God entirely, as well in one thing as another, God will graciously pardon your failings, and pass by your imperfections. ' He will spare you as a man spareth his son that serveth him,' Mal. iii. 17. Though a father see his son to fail, and come short in many things which he enjoins him to do, yet knowing that his desires and endeavours are to serve him, and please him to the full, he will not be rigid and severe with him, but will be indulgent to him, and will spare him, and pity him, and shew all love and kindness to him. The application is easy, &c.

The second question or case is this, viz., *What is that faith that gives a man an interest in Christ, and in all those blessed benefits and favours that come by Christ?* or *whether that person that experiences the following particulars, may not safely, groundedly, and comfortably conclude that his faith is a true, justifying, saving faith, the faith of God's elect, and such a faith as clearly evidences a gracious estate, and will certainly bring the soul to heaven?* Now, in answer to this important question, we may suppose the poor believer is ready to express himself thus:—

[1.] First, Upon search and sad experience, I find myself *a poor, lost, miserable, and undone creature*, as the Scriptures everywhere do evidence, Eph. ii. 1, 2, 5, 12; Col. ii. 13; Rom. viii. 7; Luke xix. 10.

[2.] Secondly, *I am convinced that it is not in myself to deliver myself out of this lost, miserable, and forlorn estate.* Could I make as many prayers as might be piled up between heaven and earth, and weep as much blood as there is water in the sea, yet all this could not procure the pardon of one sin, nor one smile from God, &c.

[3.] Thirdly, I am convinced that it is not *in angels or men to deliver me out of my lost, miserable, and undone condition.* I know provoked justice must be satisfied, divine wrath pacified, my sins pardoned, my heart renewed, my state changed, &c., or my soul can never be saved; and I know it is not in angels or men to do any of these things for me.

[4.] Fourthly, I find that I *stand in absolute need of a Saviour to save me from wrath to come*, 1 Thes. i. 10, 'to save me from the curse of the law,' Gal. iii. 10, 13, 'and to save me from infernal flames,' Isa. xxxiii. 14; so that I may well cry out with those in Acts ii. 37, 'Men and brethren, what shall we do?' and with the jailer, Acts xvi. 36, 'Sirs, what shall I do to be saved?'

[5.] Fifthly, *I see and know, through grace, that there is an utter impossibility of obtaining salvation by anything, or by any person, but by Christ alone*, according to that of the apostle: Acts iv. 12, 'Neither is there salvation in any other, for there is no other name' that is, no other person, 'under heaven, given among men, by which we must be saved.' I know there is no saviour that can deliver me from eternal death, and bring me to eternal life and glory, but that Jesus, of whom it is said, 'that he shall save his people from their sins,' Luke i. 21; and therefore I must conclude that there is an utter impossibility of obtaining salvation by any other person or things, &c. But,

[6.] Sixthly, *I see and know, through grace, that Jesus Christ is an all-sufficient Saviour, that he is a mighty, yea, an almighty Saviour, a Saviour that is able to save to the utmost all them that come to him*, as the Scripture speaks, Ps. lxxxix. 19, 'I have laid help upon one that is mighty;' Isa. lxiii. 1, 'I that speak in righteousness, mighty to save;' Heb. vii. 25, 'Wherefore he is able also to save them to the uttermost, that come unto God by him, seeing he ever liveth to make intercession for them.' I know that the Lord Jesus is mighty to save me from that wrath, and from that curse, and from that hell, and from that damnation that is due to me, by reason of my sins; and that he is mighty to justify me, and mighty to pardon me, and mighty to reconcile me to God the Father, and mighty to bring me to glory, as the Scripture does everywhere testify. But,

[7.] Seventhly, *I know, through grace, that Jesus Christ is the only person anointed, appointed, fitted, and furnished by the Father, for that great and blessed work or office, of saving sinners' souls ;* as these scriptures, amongst others, do clearly testify, Isa. lxi. 1–4 ; Luke iv. 18–21 ; Mat. i. 20, 21 ; John vi. 27. Certainly were Jesus Christ never so able and mighty to save, yet if he were not anointed, appointed, fitted, and furnished by the Father for that great office of saving poor lost sinners, I know no reason why I should expect salvation by him. But,

[8.] Eighthly, *I know through grace that the Lord Jesus Christ hath sufficiently satisfied, as mediator, the justice of God, and pacified his wrath, and fulfilled all righteousness, and procured the favour of God and the pardon of sin, &c., for all them that close with him, that accept of him, as he is offered in the gospel of grace,* Gal. iii. 19, 20 ; 1 Tim. ii. 5 ; Heb. viii. 6 ; Heb. ix. 14, 15, and xii. 24 ; Heb. x. 12, 14 ; Mat. iii. 15 ; Rom. viii. 1–4, 33, 34, and v. 8–10 ; Acts xiii. 39.

[9.] Ninthly, *I find that Jesus Christ is freely offered in the gospel to poor, lost, undone sinners, such as I am.* I find that the ministers of the gospel are commanded by Christ to proclaim in his name a general pardon, and to make a general offer of him to all to whom they preach the everlasting gospel, without excluding any: Mark xvi. 15, 'And he said unto them, Go ye into all the world, and preach the gospel unto every creature.' And what is it to preach the gospel unto every creature, but to say unto them, as the angels did to the shepherds, Luke x. 11, 'I bring you good tidings of great joy, which shall be to all people; for unto you is born this day, in the city of David, a Saviour, which is Christ the Lord' ? &c.

[10.] Tenthly, *I know, through grace, that all sorts of sinners are invited to come to Christ, to receive Christ, to accept of Christ, and to close with Christ,* Isa. lv. 1, 2 ; Mat. xi. 28, 29 ; John vii. 37 ; Rev. iii. 20, and xxii. 17, &c. But,

[11.] Eleventhly, *Through grace, I do in my understanding really assent to that blessed record and report that God the Father, in the blessed Scriptures, has given concerning Christ,* 1 John v. 10–12. The report that God the Father has made concerning the person of Christ, and concerning the offices of Christ, and concerning the work of redemption by Christ, I do really and cordially assent unto, as most true and certain, upon the authority of God's testimony, who is truth itself, and cannot lie. Now, though this assent alone is not enough to make a saving reception of Christ, yet it is in saving faith, and that without which it is impossible that there should be any saving faith. But,

[12.] Twelfthly, *I can say, through grace, that in my judgment I do approve of the Lord Jesus Christ, not only as a good, but as the greatest good, as a universal good, as a matchless good, as an incomparable good, as an infinite good, as an eternal good, and as the most suitable good in heaven and earth to my poor soul ;* as these scriptures do evidence, Ps. lxxiii. 25, 26 ; Cant. v. 10, 45 ; Ps. i. 2 ; Phil. iii. 7–10 ; 1 Tim. i. 15. I know there is everything in Christ that may suit the state, case, necessities, and wants of my poor soul. There is mercy in him to pardon me, and power in him to save me, and wisdom in him to counsel me, and grace in him to enrich me, and righteousness in him to clothe me, &c., and therefore I cannot but approve of the Lord Jesus, as such a good as exceeds all the good that is to be found in angels and men. The good that I see in Christ doth not only counterpoise, but also excel all that real or imaginary good that ever I have met with in anything below Christ. Christ must come into the will, he must be received there, else he is never savingly received. Now before the will will receive him, the will must be certainly informed that he is good, yea, the best and greatest good, or else he shall never be admitted there. Let the understanding assent never so much to all propositions concerning Christ as true, if the judgment doth not approve of them as good, yea, as the best good, Christ will never be truly received. God in his working maintains the faculties of the soul in their actings, as he made them.

[13.] Thirteenthly, *So far as I know my own heart, I am sincerely willing to receive the Lord Jesus Christ in a matrimonial covenant;* according to these scriptures, Hos. ii. 19, 20; 2 Cor. xi. 2; Isa. liv. 5; Isa. lxi. 10; Isa. lxii. 5; Cant. iii. 11, &c. Through grace I am,

First, Sincerely willing to take the Lord Jesus Christ for my Saviour and sovereign Lord. So far as I know my own heart, I do through mercy give my hearty consent, that Christ, and Christ alone, shall be my saviour and Redeemer. It is true, I do duties, but the desire of my soul is to do them out of love to Christ, and in obedience to his royal law and pleasure. I know my best righteousnesses are but ' as filthy rags,' Isa. lxiv. 6. And woe would be to me, had I no other shelter, or saviour, or resting-place for my poor soul, than rags, than filthy rags. And so far as I know my own heart, I am sincerely willing to give up myself to the guidance and government of Jesus Christ, as my sovereign Lord and king, desiring nothing more in this world, than to live and die under the guidance and government of his Spirit, word, and grace. But,

Secondly, I am willing, through grace, to give a bill of divorce to all other lovers, without exception or reservation. So far as I know my own heart, I desire nothing more in this world, than that God would pull out right-eye sins, and cut off right-hand sins. I am very desirous, through grace, to have all sins brought under by the power, Spirit, and grace of Christ; but especially my special sins, my head corruptions. I would have Christ alone to rule and reign in the haven[1] of my heart, without any competitor. But,

Thirdly, I am sincerely willing, through grace, to take the Lord Jesus Christ for better, for worse, for richer, for poorer, in sickness and in health, and in his strength I would go with him through fire and water, resolving, through his grace, that nothing shall divide betwixt Christ and my soul. So far as I know my own heart, I would have Christ, though I beg with him, though I go to prison with him, though in agonies in the garden with him, though to the cross with him. But,

Fourthly, So far as I know my own heart, I am sincerely willing,

1 Qu. ' heaven ' ?—G,

First, *to receive the Lord Jesus Christ presently*, John i. 12. Secondly, *to receive him in all his offices*, as king, prophet, and priest, Col. ii. 6; Acts v. 31. Thirdly, *To receive him into every room of my soul;* to receive him into my understanding, mind, will, affections, &c. Fourthly, *To receive him upon his own terms*, of denying myself, taking up his cross and following of him wherever he goes, Mat. xvi. 21; Rev. xiv. 4, &c.

Fifthly and lastly, *So far as I know my own heart, I do freely consent*, 1. To be really Christ's; 2. To be presently Christ's; 3. To be wholly Christ's; 4. To be only Christ's; 5. To be eminently Christ's; 6. To be for ever Christ's, &c.

Certainly that Christian that has and does experience the particulars last mentioned under the second question, that Christian may safely, groundedly, boldly, and comfortably conclude that his faith is a true, justifying, saving faith, the faith of God's elect, and such a faith as clearly evidences a gracious estate, and will never leave his soul short of heaven.

Now how many thousand Christians are there, that have this faith that is here described, which is doubtless a true, justifying, saving faith, that gives a man an interest in the person of Christ, and in all the blessings and benefits that comes by Christ, who yet question whether they have true faith or no, partly from weakness, partly from temptations, and partly from the various definitions that are given of faith by Protestants, both in their preachings and writings; and it is and must be for a lamentation, that in a point of so great moment the trumpet should give such an uncertain sound.

The third question, or case is this, viz., *Whether in the great day of the Lord, the day of general judgment, or in the particular judgment that will pass upon every soul immediately after death, which is the stating of the soul in an eternal estate or condition, either of happiness or misery; whether the sins of the saints, the follies and vanities of believers, the infirmities and enormities of sincere Christians shall be brought into the judgment of discussion and discovery, or no? Whether the Lord will either in the great day of account, or in a man's particular day of account or judgment, publicly manifest, proclaim, and make mention of the sins of his people, or no?* This question is bottomed upon the ten scriptures in the margin,[1] which I desire the Christian reader to consult; and upon the sad and daily complaints of many dear sincere Christians, who frequently cry out, ' Oh, we can never answer for one evil thought of ten thousand, nor we can never answer for one idle word of twenty thousand; nor we can never answer for one evil action of a hundred thousand; and how then shall we stand in judgment? how shall we look the judge in the face? how shall we be ever able to answer for all our omissions, and for all our commissions; for all our sins of ignorance, and sins against light and knowledge; for all our sins against the law, and for all our sins against

[1] Eccles. xi. 9, and xii. 14; Mat. xii. 36, and xviii. 23; Luke xvi. 2; Rom. xiv. 10, 12; 2 Cor. v. 10; Heb. ix. 27, and xiii. 17; 1 Peter iv. 5.

the gospel, and for all our sins against sovereign grace, and for all our sins against the remedy, against the Lord Jesus, and for all the sins of our infancy, of our youth, and of old age? Job. ix. 3 ; Ps. xix. 12, and clxiii. 2 ; Ezra xix. 6, &c. What account shall we be able to give up, when we come to our particular day of judgment, immediately after our death, or in the great and general day of account, when angels, devils, and men shall stand before the Lord Jesus, Heb. ix. 27, whom God the Father hath ordained to be the judge of quick and dead, Acts xvii. 31?

Now to this great question I answer, *that the sins of the saints, the infirmities and enormities of believers, shall never be brought into the judgment of discussion and discovery ; they shall never be objected against them, either in their particular day of judgment, or in the great day of their account.* Now this truth I shall make good by an induction of particulars ; thus,—

[1.] First, *Our Lord Jesus Christ, in his judicial proceedings in the last day, which is set down clearly and largely in* Mat. xxv. 34–42, *doth only enumerate the good works they have done, but takes not the least notice of the spots and blemishes, of the infirmities or enormities, of the weaknesses or wickednesses, of his people.* God has sealed up the sins of his people, never to be remembered or looked upon more, Deut. xxxii. 4–6 ; Dan. ix. 24. In the great day the book of God's remembrance shall be opened and publicly read, that all the good things that the saints have done for God, for Christ, for saints, for their own souls, for sinners ; and that all the great things that they have suffered for Christ's sake, and the gospel's sake, may be mentioned to their everlasting praise, to their eternal honour. And though the choicest and chiefest saints on earth have, 1. Sin dwelling in them ; 2. Operating and working in them ; 3. Vexing and molesting of them, being as so many goads in their sides and thorns in their eyes ; 4. Captivating and prevailing over them, Rom. vii. 23, 24 ; Gal. v. 17 ; yet in that large recital which shall then be read of the saints' lives, Mat. xxv., there is not the least mention made either of sins of omission or commission ; nor the least mention made either of great sins or of small sins ; nor the least mention made either of sins before conversion or after conversion. Here in this world the best of saints have had their *buts*, their spots, their blots, their specks, as the fairest day hath its clouds, the finest linen its spots, and the richest jewels their specks ; but now in the judicial process of this last and universal assizes there is not found in all the books that shall then be opened, so much as one unsavoury ' but' to blemish the fair characters of the saints. Surely he that sees no iniquity in Jacob, nor perverseness in Israel, Num. xxiii. 21, to impute it to them whilst they live, he will never charge iniquity or perverseness upon them in the great day, Rev. xx. 12 ; Dan. vii. 10. Surely he who has fully satisfied his Father's justice for his people's sins, and who hath by his own blood balanced and made up all reckonings and accounts between God and their souls, he will never charge upon them their faults and follies in the great day. Surely he who hath spoken so much for his saints whilst he was on earth, and who hath continually interceded for them since he went to heaven, John xvii. ; Heb. vii. 25 ; he won't, though he hath cause to blame them for many things, speak anything against them in the great day. Surely Jesus Christ, the saints' paymaster, who hath discharged their whole debt at once, who hath paid down upon the nail the ten thousand talents which we owed, and took in the bond and nailed it to the cross, Heb. x. 10, 12, 14; Mat. xviii. 24; Col. ii. 14; leaving no back reckonings unpaid, to bring his poor children, which are the travail of his soul, Isa. liii. 11, afterward into any danger from the hands of divine justice; he will never mention the sins of his people, he will never charge the sins of his people upon them in the great day. Our dear Lord Jesus, who is the righteous judge of heaven and earth in the great day of account, he will bring in *omnia bene* in his presentment, all fair and well, and accordingly will make proclamation in that high court of justice, before God, angels, devils, saints, and sinners, &c. Christ will not charge his children with the least unkindness, he will not charge his spouse with the least unfaithfulness in the great day; yea, he will represent them before God, angels, and men, as complete in him, as all fair and spotless, as without spot or wrinkle, as without fault before the throne of God, as holy and unblamable and unreprovable in his sight, as immaculate as the angels themselves who kept their first estate, Col. ii. 10; Cant. iv. 7; Eph. v. 27; Rev. xiv. 5. This honour shall have all the saints, and thus shall Christ be glorified in his saints, and admired in all them that believe, 1 Thes. ii. 10. The greatest part of the saints by far will have passed their particular judgment long before the general judgment, Heb. ix. 27, and being therein acquitted and discharged from all their sins by God the Judge of the quick and dead, 2 Tim. iv. 1, and admitted into heaven upon the credit of Christ's blood, righteous satisfaction, and their free and full justification, it cannot be imagined that Jesus Christ, in the great day, will bring in any new charge against his children when they have been cleared and absolved already. Certainly when once the saints are freely and fully absolved from all their sins by a divine sentence, then their sins shall never be remembered, they shall never be objected against them any more; for one divine sentence cannot cross and rescind another. The Judge of all the world had long since cast all their sins behind his back, Isa. xxxviii. 17; and will he now set them before his face, and before the faces of all the world? Surely no. He has long since cast all their sins into the depths of the sea, Micah vii. 19,—bottomless depths of everlasting oblivion—that they might never be buoyed up any more! He has not only forgiven their sins, but he has also forgotten their sins, Jer. xxxi. 34; and will he remember them and declare them in the great day? Surely no. God has long since blotted out the transgressions of his people, Isa. xliii. 25. This metaphor is taken from creditors, who, when they purpose never to exact a debt, will blot it out of their books. Now after that a debt is struck out of a bill, bond, or book, it cannot be exacted, the evidence cannot be pleaded. Christ having crossed the debt-book with the red lines of his blood, Col. ii. 14; if now he should call the sins of his people to remembrance, and charge them upon them, he should cross the great design of his cross. Upon this foundation stands the absolute impossibility that any sin, that the least sin, yea, that the least circumstance of sin, or the least aggravation of sin, should be so much as mentioned by the righteous Judge of heaven and earth in the process of that judicial trial in the great day, except it be in a way of absolution in order to the magnifying of their pardon. God has long since blotted out as a thick cloud the transgressions of his people, and as a cloud their sins, Isa. xliv. 22. Now we know that the clouds which are driven away by the winds appear no more; nor the mist which is dried by the sun appears no more; other clouds and other mists may arise, but not they which are driven away and dried up. Thus the sins of the saints being forgiven, they shall no more return upon them, they shall never more be objected against them.

[2.] Further, *The Lord saith, 'Though your sins be as scarlet, they shall be white as snow; though they be red like crimson, they shall be as wool,'* Isa. i. 18. Pardon makes such a clear riddance of sin, that it is as if it had never been. The scarlet sinner is as white as snow, snow newly fallen from the sky, which was never sullied. The crimson sinner is as wool, wool which never received the least tincture in the dye-fat. You know scarlet and crimson are double and deep dyes, dyes in grain; yet if the cloth dyed therewith be as the wool before it was dyed, and if it be as white as snow, what is become of those dyes? Are they any more? Is not the cloth as if it had not been dyed at all? Even so; though our sins, by reiterating them, by long lying in them, have made deep impressions upon us, yet, by God's discharge of them, we are as if we had never commited them.

[3.] Again, *The psalmist pronounceth him 'blessed whose sin is covered,'* Ps. xxxii. 1. A thing covered is not seen; so sin forgiven is before God as not seen. The same psalmist pronounceth him ' blessed to whom the Lord imputeth not sin,' Ps. xxxii. 2.

Now a sin not imputed is as not committed. The prophet Jeremiah tells us that ' the iniquity of Israel shall be sought for, and there shall be none; and the sins of Judah, and they shall not be found,' Jer. l. 20. Now is not that fully discharged which shall never be found, never appear, never be remembered, never be mentioned?

Thus, by the many metaphors used in Scripture to set out forgiveness of sin, pardon of sin, you plainly and evidently see that God's discharge is free and full, and therefore he will never charge their sins upon them in the great day, Jer. xxxi. 34; Ezek. xviii. 22. But

Some may object and say, *That the Scripture saith, that 'God shall bring every work into judgment, with every secret thing, whether it be good, or whether it be evil,'* Eccles. xii. 14. How then can this be, that the sins of the saints shall not be mentioned, nor charged upon them in the great day?

I answer, *This scripture is to be understood respectivè, &c.*, with a just respect to the two great parties which are to be judged, Mat. xxv. 32, 33. Sheep and goats, saints and sinners, sons and slaves, elect and reprobate, holy and profane, pious and impious, faithful and unfaithful; that is to say, all the grace, the holiness, the godliness, the good of those that are good, shall be brought into the judgment of mercy, that it may be freely, graciously, and nobly rewarded, and all the wickedness of the wicked shall be brought into the judgment of condemnation, that it may be righteously and everlastingly punished in this great day of the Lord. All sincerity shall be discovered and rewarded; and all hypocrisy shall be disclosed and revenged. In this great day all the works of the saints shall follow them into heaven; and in this great day all the evil works of the wicked shall hunt and pursue them into hell.[1] In this great day all the hearts, thoughts, secrets, words, ways, works, and walkings of wicked men shall be discovered and laid open before all the world, to their everlasting shame and sorrow, to their eternal amazement and astonishment. And in this great day the Lord will make mention, in the ears of all the world, of every prayer that the saints have made, and of every sermon that they have heard, and of every tear that they have shed, and of every fast that they have kept, and of every sigh and groan that ever they have fetched, and of all the good words that ever they have spoke, and of all the good works that ever they have done, and of all the great things that ever they have suffered; yea, in this great day they shall reap the fruit of many good services which themselves had forgot. 'Lord, when saw we thee hungry, and fed thee; or thirsty, and gave thee drink; or naked, and clothed thee; or sick or in prison, and visited thee?' Mat. xxv. 34–41. They had done many good works, and forgot them; but Christ records them, remembers them, and rewards them before all the world. In this great day a bit of bread, a cup of cold water shall not pass without a reward, Eccles. xi. 1, 6. In this great day the saints shall reap a plentiful and glorious crop, as the fruit of that good seed, that for a time hath seemed to be buried and lost. In this great day of the Lord the saints shall find that bread which long before was cast upon the waters. But my

Second reason is taken from *Christ's vehement protestations, that they shall not come into judgment:* John v. 24, 'Verily, verily, I say unto you, he that heareth my word, and believeth on him that sent me, hath everlasting life, and shall not come into condemnation, but is passed from death unto life.'[2] Those words, 'shall not come into condemnation,' are not rightly translated. The original is εἰς κρίσιν, 'shall not come into judgment,' not into damnation, as you read it in all your English books. I will not say what should put men upon this exposition rather than a true translation of the original word. Further, it is very observable that no evangelist useth this double asseveration but St John, and he never useth it but in matters of greatest weight and importance, and to show the earnestness of his spirit, and to stir us up to better attention, and to put the thing asserted out of all question and beyond all contradiction; as when we would put a thing for ever out of all question, we do it by a double asseveration—verily, verily, it is so, &c., John i. 51, iii. 3, 11, and vi, 26, 32, 47, 53, &c.'

Thirdly, Because his not bringing their sins into judgment *doth most and best agree with many precious and glorious expressions*

---

[1] See Wisdom, c. ii. throughout, and chap. v., from the first verse to the tenth.
[2] *Vide* Aquin. 87; Suppl. est. in l. 4; Ser. dist., 47.

that we find scattered, as so many shining, sparkling pearls, up and down in Scripture; as,

First, With those of God's blotting out the sins of his people: 'I, even I, am he that blotteth out thy transgressions for my own sake, and will not remember thy sins. I have blotted out, as a thick cloud, thy transgressions, and, as a cloud, thy sins,' Isa. xliii. 25, and xliv. 22.

Who is this that blots out transgressions? He that hath the keys of heaven and hell at his girdle; that opens, and no man shuts; that shuts, and no man opens; he that hath the power of life and death, of condemning and absolving, of killing and making alive; he it is that blotteth out transgressions. If an under officer should blot out an indictment, that perhaps might do a man no good; a man might, for all that, be at last cast by the judge; but when the judge or king shall blot out the indictment with their own hand, then the indictment cannot return. Now this is every believer's case and happiness.

Secondly, To those glorious expressions of God's not remembering of their sins any more, Jer. xxxi. 34; Isa. xliii. 25. 'And I will not remember thy sins: and they shall teach no more every man his neighbour, and every man his brother, saying, Know ye the Lord, for they shall all know me, from the least of them to the greatest of them, saith the Lord, for I will forgive their iniquity, and I will remember their sin no more.' So the apostle, 'For I will be merciful to their unrighteousness, and their sins and their iniquities will I remember no more,' Heb. viii. 12.

And again, the same apostle saith, 'This is the covenant that I will make with them after those days, saith the Lord, I will put my laws into their hearts, and in their minds will I write them, and their sins and iniquities will I remember no more,' Heb. x. 17.[1]

The meaning is, their iniquities shall be quite forgotten: I will never mention them more, I will never take notice of them more, they shall never hear more of them from me. Though God hath an iron memory to remember the sins of the wicked, yet he hath no memory to remember the sins of the righteous.

*Thirdly, His not bringing their sins into judgment doth most and best agree with those blessed expressions of *his casting their sins into the depth of the sea, and of his casting them behind his back*. 'He will turn again, he will have compassion upon us, he will subdue our iniquities, and thou wilt cast all their sins into the depths of the sea,' Mic. vii. 19. Where sin is once pardoned, the remission stands never to be repealed. Pardoned sin shall never come in account against the pardoned man before God any more; for so much doth this borrowed speech import. If a thing were cast into a river, it might be brought up again; or if it were cast upon the sea, it might be discerned and taken up again; but when it is cast into the depths, the bottom of the sea, it can never be buoyed up again.

By the metaphor in the text, the Lord would have us to know that sins pardoned shall rise no more, they shall never be seen

---

[1] That which Cicero said flatteringly of Cæsar, is truly affirmed of God, *Nihil obliviasci solet præter injurias,* he forgetteth nothing but the wrongs that daily are done him by his.

more, they shall never come on the account more. He will so drown their sins that they shall never come up before him the second time.

And so much that other scripture imports, 'Behold, for peace I had great bitterness; but thou hast in love to my soul delivered it from the pit of corruption; for thou hast cast all my sins behind thy back,' Isa. xxxviii. 17. These last words are a borrowed speech, taken from the manner of men, who are wont to cast behind their backs such things as they have no mind to see, regard, or remember. A gracious soul hath always his sins before his face, 'I acknowledge my transgressions, and my sin is ever before me,' Ps. li. 3, and therefore no wonder if the Lord cast them behind his back. The father soon forgets, and casts behind his back those faults that the child remembers, and hath always in his eyes; so doth the Father of spirits.

Fourthly, His not bringing their sins into judgment doth best agree with that *sweet and choice expression of God's pardoning the sins of his people.*

'And I will cleanse them from all their iniquity, whereby they have sinned against me; and I will pardon all their iniquities, whereby they have sinned, and whereby they have transgressed against me,' Jer. xxxiii. 8. So in Micah, 'Who is a God like unto thee, that pardoneth iniquity, and passeth by the transgressions of the remnant of his heritage?'—as though he would not see it, but wink at it—'he retaineth not his anger for ever, because he delighteth in mercy,' Mic. vii. 18. The Hebrew word—*nose* from *nasa*—that is here rendered *pardoneth*, signifies a taking away. When God pardons sin, he takes it sheer away; that if it should be sought for, yet it could not be found, as the prophet speaks, Jer. l. 20, 'In those days, and in that time, saith the Lord, the iniquity of Israel shall be sought for, and there shall be none; and the sins of Judah, and they shall not be found, for I will pardon them whom I reserve;' and these words, 'and passeth by,' in the afore-cited seventh of Micah and the 18th verse, according to the Hebrew *Vignober Gnal* is, 'and passeth over,' 'God passeth over the transgression of his heritage,' that is, he takes no notice of it; as a man in a deep muse, or as one that hath haste of business, seeth not things before him, his mind being busied about other matters, he neglects all to mind his business.

As David, when he saw in Mephibosheth the feature of his friend Jonathan, took no notice of his lameness, or any other defect or deformity; so God, beholding in his people the glorious image of his Son, winks at all their faults and deformities, Isa. xl. 1, 2, which made Luther say, 'Do with me what thou wilt, since thou hast pardoned my sin;' and what is it to pardon sin, but not to mention sin?

Fifthly, His not bringing their sins into the judgment of discussion and discovery doth best agree to those *expressions of forgiving and covering*, 'Blessed is he whose transgression is forgiven, whose sin is covered,' Ps. xxxii. 1. In the original, it is in the plural, blessednesses; so here is a plurality of blessings, a chain of pearls.

The like expression you have in the 85th Psalm and the 2d verse, 'Thou hast forgiven the iniquity of thy people, thou hast covered all their sin. Selah.' For the understanding of these scriptures aright, take notice that to cover is a metaphorical expression. Covering is such an action which is opposed to disclosure; to be covered, it is to be so hid and closed as not to appear.[1] Some make the metaphor from filthy loathsome objects which are covered from our eyes as dead carcasses are buried under the ground; some from garments, that are put upon us to cover our nakedness; others from the Egyptians that were drowned in the Red Sea, and so covered with water; others from a great gulf in the earth, that is filled up and covered with earth injected into it; and others make it, in the last place, an allusive expression to the mercy-seat, over which was a covering.

Now all these metaphors in the general tend to shew this, that the Lord will not look, he will not see, he will not take notice of the sins he hath pardoned, to call them any more to a judicial account.

. As when a prince reads over many treasons and rebellions, and meets with such and such which he hath pardoned, he reads on, he passeth by, he taketh no notice of them, the pardoned person shall never hear more of them, he will never call him to account for those sins more; so here, &c. When Cæsar was painted, he puts his finger upon his scar, his wart. God puts his fingers upon all his people's scars and warts, upon all their weaknesses and infirmities, that nothing can be seen but what is fair and lovely: ' Thou art all fair, my love, and there is no spot in thee,' Cant. iv. 7.

Sixthly, It best agrees to that expression *of not imputing of sin.* 'Blessed is the man to whom the Lord imputeth not iniquity, and in whose spirit there is no guile,' Ps. xxxii. 2. So the apostle in that Rom. iv. 6–8. Now not to impute iniquity, is not to charge iniquity, not to set iniquity upon his score who is blessed and pardoned, &c.

Seventhly, and lastly, It best agrees *with that expression that you have in the 113th Psalm and the 11th and 12th verses,* ' For as the heaven is high above the earth, so great is his mercy towards them that fear him; as far as the east is from the west, so far hath he removed our transgressions from us.' What a vast distance is there betwixt the east and west! of all visible latitudes, this is the greatest; and thus much for the third argument. The

[4.] Fourth argument that prevails with me to judge that Jesus Christ will not bring the sins of the saints into the judgment of discussion and discovery in the great day is, because *it seems unsuitable to three considerable things for Jesus Christ to proclaim the infirmities and miscarriages of his people to all the world.*

First, It seems to be unsuitable *to the glory and solemnity of that day,* which to the saints will be a day of refreshing, a day of restitution, a day of redemption, a day of coronation, as hath been already proved. Now how suitable to this great day of solemnity the proclamation of the saints' sins will be, I leave the reader to judge.

Secondly, It seems unsuitable *to all those near and dear relations that Jesus Christ stands in towards his.* He stands in the relation of

[1] Sic velantur, ut in judicio non revelentur.

a Father, a Brother, a Head, a Husband, a Friend, an Advocate.[1] Now, are not all these by the law of relation, bound rather to hide, and keep secret, at least from the world, the weaknesses, and infirmities of their near and dear relations; and is not Christ, is not Christ much more, by how much 'he is more a Father, a Brother, a Head, a Husband, &c., in a spiritual way, than any others can be in a natural way? &c.

Thirdly, It seems very unsuitable *to what the Lord Jesus requires of his in this world.* The Lord requires that his people should cast a mantle of love, of wisdom, of silence, and secrecy over one another's weaknesses and infirmities, &c.

Hatred stirreth up strifes, but love covereth all sins—love's mantle is very large. Love will find a hand, a plaster to clap upon every sore, Prov. x. 12, and 1 Pet. iv. 8. Flavius Vespasianus, the emperor, was very ready to conceal his friends' vices, and as ready to reveal their virtues. So is divine love in the hearts of the saints, ' If thy brother offend thee, go and tell him his fault between him and thee alone; if he shall hear thee, thou hast gained thy brother,' Mat. xviii. 15. As the pills of reprehension are to be gilded and sugared over with much gentleness and softness, so they are to be given in secret. Tell him between him and thee alone. Tale-bearers and tale-hearers are alike abominable. Heaven is too hot, and too holy a place for them, Ps. xv. 3. Now will Jesus Christ have us carry it thus towards offending Christians, and will he himself act otherwise? Nay, is it an evil in us to lay open the weaknesses and infirmities of the saints to the world? and will it be an excellency, a glory, a virtue in Christ, to do it in the great day? &c.

[5.] A *fifth* argument is this, *It is the glory of a man to pass over a transgression.* ' The discretion of a man deferreth his anger, and it is his glory to pass over a transgression,' Prov. xix. 11. Or to pass by it, as we do by persons or things we know not, or would take no notice of. Now, ' Is it the glory of a man to pass over a transgression?' and will it not much more be the glory of Christ, silently to pass over the transgressions of his people in that great day?[2] The greater the treasons and rebellions are that a prince passes over, and takes no notice of, the more is his honour and glory; and so doubtless it will be Christ's in that great day, to pass over all the treasons and rebellions of his people, to take no notice of them, to forget them as well as to forgive them.

The heathens have long since observed, that in nothing man came nearer to the glory and perfection of God himself than in goodness and clemency. Surely, if it be such an honour to man, ' to pass over a transgression,' it cannot be a dishonour to Christ, to pass over the transgressions of his people, he having already buried them in the sea of his blood. Again, saith Solomon, ' It is the glory of God to conceal a thing,' Prov. xxv. 2. And why it should not make for the glory of divine love, to conceal the sins of the saints in that great day, I know not. And whether the concealing the sins of the saints in the great day, will not make most for their joy and wicked men's sorrows, for

---

[1] Isa. ix. 6; Heb. ii. 11, 12; Eph. i. 21, 22; Rev. xix. 7; John xv. 1; ii. 1, 2.
[2] *Non amo quenquam nisi offendam,* said a heathen.

their comfort and wicked men's terror and torment, I will leave you to judge, and time and experience to decide ; and thus much for the resolution of that great question.

I. Now, from what has been said, in answer to this third question, a sincere Christian may form up this first plea as to the ten scriptures in the margin,[1] that refer either to the general judgment, or to the particular judgment that will pass upon every Christian immediately after death. *O blessed God, Jesus Christ has by his own blood balanced and made up all reckonings and accounts that were between thee and me; and thou hast vehemently protested, that thou wilt not bring me into judgment; that thou wilt blot out my transgressions as a thick cloud, and that thou wilt remember my sins no more; and that thou wilt cast them behind thy back, and hurl them into the depth of the sea; and that thou wilt forgive them, and cover them, and not impute them to me,* &c. This is my plea, O Lord, and by this plea I shall stand. Well, saith the Judge of quick and dead, ' I own this plea, I accept of this plea, I have nothing to say against this plea ; the plea is just, safe, honourable, and righteous, enter thou into the joy of thy Lord.'

Secondly, Every sinner at his first believing and closing with Christ, *is justified in the court of glory from all his sins, both guilt and punishment,* Acts xiii. 39. Justification doth not increase or decrease, but all sin is pardoned at the first act of believing. All who are justified are justified alike. There is no difference amongst believers, as to their justification ; one is not more justified than another, for every justified person hath a plenary remission of his sins, and the same righteousness of Christ imputed ; but in sanctification there is difference amongst believers. Every one is not sanctified alike, for some are stronger and higher, and others are weaker and lower in grace. As soon as any are made believers in Christ, all the sins which they have committed in time past, and all the sins which they are guilty of, as to the time present, they are actually pardoned unto them in general, and in particular, 1 Cor. xii. 12–14 ; 1 John ii. 1, 12–14. Now, that all the sins of a believer are pardoned at once, and actually unto them, may be thus demonstrated.

[1.] First, *All phrases in Scripture imply thus much.* Isa. xliii. 25, ' I, even I, am he which blotteth out thy transgressions for mine own sake, and will not remember thy sins.' Jer. xxxi. 34, ' I will forgive their iniquity, and I will remember their sin no more.' Jer. xxxiii. 8, ' And I will pardon all their iniquities whereby they have sinned, and whereby they have transgressed against me.' Ezek. xviii. 22, ' All his transgressions that he hath committed, they shall not be mentioned unto him.' Heb. viii. 12, ' I will be merciful unto their unrighteousness, and their sins and their iniquities I will remember no more ;' *ergo,* all is pardoned at once. But,

[2.] Secondly, *That remission of sins that leaves no condemnation to the party offending, is the remission of all sins;* for if there were any sin remaining, a man is still in the state of condemnation ; but justification leaves no condemnation. Rom. viii. 1, ' There is no condemna-

---

[1] Eccles. xi. 9, and xii. 14 ; Mat. xii. 36, and xviii. 23 ; Luke xvi. 2 ; Rom. xiv. 10, 12 ; 2 Cor. v. 10 ; Heb. ix. 27, and xiii. 17 ; 1 Pet. iv. 5.

tion to them that are in Christ Jesus,' and ver. 33, ' Who shall lay anything to the charge of God's elect? It is God that justifieth;' and ver. 38, 39, ' Nor things present, nor things to come, shall be able to separate us from the love of God, which is in Christ Jesus our Lord;' and John v. 24, ' He that heareth my word, and believeth on him that sent me, hath everlasting life, and shall not come into condemnation, but is passed from death to life;' *ergo*, all sins are pardoned at once, or else they were in a state of condemnation, &c.[1] Thus you see it evident that there is no condemnation to them that are in Christ Jesus. Therefore there is full remission of all sins to the soul at the first act of believing. But,

[3.] Thirdly, *A believer, even when he sinneth, is still united to Christ*, John xv. 1, 6, xvii. 21-23; 1 Cor. vi. 17, ' And he is still clothed with the righteousness of Christ which covers all his sins, and dischargeth him from them, so that no guile can redound to him,' Isa. lxi. 10; Jer. xxiii. 6; 1 Cor. i. 30; Phil. iii. 9, &c. But,

[4.] Fourthly, *A believer is not to fear curse or hell at all*, which yet he might do if all his sins were not pardoned at once; but some of his new sins were for a while unpardoned, &c. But,

[5.] Fifthly, *Our Lord Jesus Christ, by once suffering, suffered for all the sins of the elect, past, present, and to come.* The infinite wrath of God the Father fell on him for all the sins of the chosen of God, Isa. liii. 9; Heb. xii. 14, and x. 9, 10, 12, 14. If Christ had suffered for ten thousand worlds, he could have suffered no more than he did; for he suffered the whole infinite wrath of God the Father. The wrath of God was infinite wrath, and the sufferings of Christ were infinite sufferings; *ergo*, Look, as Adam's sin was enough to infect a thousand worlds, so our Saviour's merits are sufficient to save a thousand worlds. Those sufferings that he suffered for sins past, are sufficient to satisfy for sins present and to come. That all the sins of God's people, in their absolute number, from first to last, were laid upon Christ, who in the days of his sufferings did meritoriously purchase perfect remission of all their sins, to be applied in future times to them, and by them, is most certain, Isa. liv. 5, 6. But,

[6.] Sixthly, *Repentance is not at all required for our justification—where our pardon is only to be found—but only faith;* therefore pardon of sin is not suspended until we repent of our sins. But,

[7.] Seventhly, *If the remission of all sins be not at once, it is either because my faith cannot lay hold on it, or because there is some hindrances in the way: but a man by the hand of faith may lay hold on all the merits of Christ, and the word reveals the pardon of all; and the sacrament of the Lord's Supper seals and confirms the pardon of all;* and there is no danger nor inconvenience that attends this assertion, for it puts the highest obligation imaginable upon the soul, as to fear and obedience: Ps. cxxx. 3, ' If thou, Lord, shouldest mark iniquities, O Lord, who shall stand?' ver. 4, ' But there is

---

[1] At a sinner's first conversion his sins are truly and perfectly pardoned. 1. All as to sin already past; 2. All as to the state of remission. They had a perfect right to the pardon of all their sins, past, present, and to come, though not an equal investure.

forgiveness with thee, that thou mayest be feared.' Forgiveness makes not a Christian bold with sin, but fearful of sin, and careful to obey, as Christians find in their daily experience. By this argument it appears clear, that the forgiveness of all sins is made to the soul at once, at the first act of believing. But,

[8.] Eighthly, If *new sins were not pardoned until you do repent, then we should be left to an uncertainty whiles our sins be pardoned, or when they will be pardoned;* for it may be long ere we repent, as you see in David, who lay long under the guilt of murder and adultery before he repented, and you know Solomon lay long under many high sins before he repented, &c., and it may be more long ere we do, or can know that we do truly repent of our sins. But,

[9.] Ninthly, If all sins were not forgiven at once, *then justification is not perfect at once, but is more and more increased and perfected as more and more sins are pardoned, which cannot consist with the true doctrine of justification.* Certainly as to the state of justification, there is a full and perfect remission of all sins—considered under the differences of time past, present, and to come. As in the state of condemnation there is not any one sin pardoned, so in the estate of justification, there is not any one sin but is pardoned; for the state of justification is opposite to all condemnation and curse and wrath. But,

[10.] Tenthly, *All agree that as to God's eternal decree or purpose of forgiveness, all the sins of his people are forgiven.* God did not intend to forgive some of their sins and not the rest, but a universal and full and complete forgiveness was fixedly purposed and resolved on by God. Forgiveness of sins is a gracious act, or work of God for Christ's sake, discharging and absolving believing and repenting persons from the guilt and punishment of all their sins, so that God is no longer displeased with them, nor will he ever remember them any more, nor call them to an account for them, nor condemn them for their sins, but will look on them, and deal with them as if they had never sinned, never offended him.

Thirdly, Consider, *that at the very moment of a believer's dissolution, all his sins are perfectly and fully forgiven.* All their sins are so fully and finally forgiven them, that at the very moment of their souls going out from the body, there is not one sin of omission or commission, nor any aggravation or least circumstance left standing in the book of God's remembrance; and this is the true reason why there shall not be the least mention made of their sins in their trial at Christ's tribunal, because they were all pardoned fully and finally at the hour of their death. All debts were then discharged, all scores were then crossed, so that in the great day, when the books shall be opened and perused, there shall not one sin be found, but all blotted out, and all reckonings made even in the blood of Christ.

Indeed, if God should pardon some sins, and not others, he would at the same time be a friend and an enemy, and we should be at once both happy and miserable, which are manifest contradictions. Besides, God doth nothing in vain; but it would be in vain for God to pardon some sins but not all, for as one leak in a ship unstopped will sink the ship, and as one sore or one disease, not healed nor cured, will kill the body, so one sin unpardoned will destroy the soul.

Fourthly, God looks not upon those as sinners, whose sins are pardoned: Luke vii. 37, 'And behold a woman in the city which was a sinner.' A notorious sinner, a branded sinner. Mark, it is not said, behold a woman which is a sinner, but 'behold a woman which *was* a sinner;' to note that sinners converted and pardoned are no longer reputed sinners, 'Behold a woman which was a sinner.' Look, as a man, when he is cleansed from filth, is as if he had never been defiled; so when a sinner is pardoned, he is in God's account as if he had never sinned. Hence those phrases in Cant. 4. 7, 'Thou art all fair, my love, and there is no spot in thee:' Col. ii. 10, 'And ye are complete in him, who is the head of all principality and power,' as though he had said, because in himself he hath the well-head of glory and majesty, the which becometh ours; in that he is also the head of his church: Col. i. 21, 'And you that were sometime alienated, and enemies in your mind, by wicked works, yet now hath he reconciled;' ver. 22, 'In the body of his flesh, through death, to present you holy and unblamable, and unreprovable in his sight;' that is, by his righteousness imputed and imparted: Eph. v. 27, 'that he might present it to himself a glorious church, not having spot or wrinkle, or any such thing, but that it should be holy and without blemish.' The word 'present' is taken from the custom of solemnizing a marriage; first the spouse was wooed, and then set before her husband adorned with his jewels, as Rebekah was with Isaac's: Rev. xiv. 5, 'And in their mouth was found no guile, for they are without fault before the throne of God.' 1. They are without fault by imputation. 2. By inchoation. Hence Job is said to be a perfect man, Job ii., and David to be 'a man after God's own heart,' Acts xiii. 22. The forgiven party is now looked upon and received with that love and favour, as if he had never offended God, and as if God had never been offended by him, Hosea xiv. 1, 2, 4; Isa. liv. 7–10; Jer. xxxi. 33, 34, 36, 37; Luke xv. 19–23. Here the sins of the prodigal are pardoned, and his father receives him with such expressions of love and familiarity as if he had never sinned against him; his father never so much as objects any one of all his high sinnings against him. Hence it is that you read of such sweet, kind, tender, loving, comfortable expressions of God towards those whose sins he had pardoned: Jer. xxxi. 16, 'Refrain thy voice from weeping, and thine eyes from tears;' ver. 20, 'Is Ephraim my dear son, is he a pleasant child?' Mat. ix. 2, 'Son, be of good cheer, thy sins are forgiven thee.' The schools say that the remission of sins is not only *ablativa mali,* but *collativa boni,* a remotion of guilt, but a collation of good. Look, as he that is legally acquitted of theft or murder, is no more reputed a thief or murderer, so here, Jer. l. 20, 'In those days, and in that time, saith the Lord, the iniquity of Israel shall be sought for, and there shall be none; and the sins of Judah, and they shall not be found; for I will pardon them whom I reserve.' Pardoned sin is in God's account no sin, and the pardoned sinner in God's account is no sinner, as the pardoned debtor is no debtor. Where God hath pardoned a man, there he never looks upon that man

as a sinner, but as a just man. Pardon of sin is an utter abolition of
it, as it doth reflect upon the person, making him guilty, and obliging
him actually to condemnation; in this respect the pardoned man is as
free as if he had never sinned. Therefore the believer, the penitent
person, hath infinite cause of rejoicing, that God hath perfectly pardoned
his sins, and that he looks upon him no more [as] a sinner, but as a just
and righteous person. O sirs! what can the great God do more for
your comfort and consolation? and therefore, never entertain any hard
thoughts of God, as if he were like those men who say they forgive
with all their hearts, and yet retain their secret hate and inward malice
as much as ever; but for ever live in the faith of this truth, viz., that
when God doth pardon sin, he takes it so away, as that the party
acquitted is no more looked upon as a sinner. Now upon this consideration, what a glorious plea hath every sincere Christian to make
in the day of account! But,

*Fifthly, Forgiveness takes off our obligation to suffer eternal pun-
ishment;* so that, look, as a forgiven debtor is freed from whatsoever
penalty his debt did render him liable to, so is the forgiven sinner from
the punishment itself. In this respect Aristotle saith, ' To forgive sin
is not to punish it.' And Austin saith, ' To forgive sin is not to inflict the punishment due unto it.' And the schools say, 'To remit the
sin is not to impute the punishment.' When a king pardons a thief,
his theft now shall not prejudice him. The guilt obliging is that
whereby the sinner is actually bound to undergo the punishment due
to him by the law, and passed on him by the judge for the breach of
it; this is that which by the schools is called the extrinsecal guilt of
sin, to distinguish it from the intrinsecal, which is included in the
deordination[1] of the act, and which is inseparable from the sin. And
if you would know wherein the nature of forgiveness immediately and
primarily consists, it is in the taking off this obligation, and discharging the sinner from it. Hence it is that the pardoned sinner is said
not to be under the law: Rom. vi. 14, and not to be under the
curse; Gal. iii. 13, and not to be under the sentence of condemnation. And according to this notion, all Scripture phrases are to be
construed by which forgiveness is expressed, Rom. viii. 1. God, when
he forgives sin, he is said to cover them, Ps. xxxii. 1, lxxxv. 2; Rom.
iv. 7; ' to remember them no more,' Isa. xliii. 25; Jer. xxxi. 34; Heb.
viii. 12; ' to cast them behind his back,' Isa. xxxviii. 17; ' to throw
them into the depth of the sea,' Micah vii. 19; ' to blot them out as a
cloud,' Isa. xliv. 22; ' and to turn away his face from them,' Ps. li. 9.
By all which expressions we are not to think that God doth not know
sin, or that God doth not see sin, or that God is not displeased with
sin, or that God is not displeased with believers for their sins; but
that he will not so take notice of them as to enter into judgment with
the persons for them. So that the forgiven sinner is free from obligation of the punishment, as truly, as surely, as fully, and as perfectly
as if he had never committed the sin, but were altogether innocent.
In every sin there are two things considerable: first, the offence which
is done to God, whereby he is displeased; secondly, the obligation of
the man so offending him to eternal condemnation. Now, remission

---

[1] ' Disorder,' = unlawfulness.—G.

of sin doth wholly lie in the removing of these two; so that when God doth will neither to punish or to be offended with the person, then he is said to forgive. ' It is true there remains paternal and medicinal chastisements after sin is forgiven, but no offence or punishment strictly so taken. And is not this a noble plea for a believer to make in the day of account? But,

Sixthly, Consider *that all the sins of believers were laid upon Christ their surety*, Heb. vii. 21, 22. What is that? That is, he became bound to God, he became responsible to him for all their sins, for all that God in justice could charge upon them, and demand for satisfaction: Isa. liii. 5, 6, 'Our salvation was laid upon one that is mighty; Ps. lxxxix. 19; Isa. lxiii. 1. As Judah became a surety to Jacob for Benjamin, he engaged himself to his father: 'I will be surety for him, of my hand shalt thou require him; if I bring him not unto thee, and set him before thee, then let me bear the blame for ever,' Gen. xliii. 9; herein he was a type of Christ, that came of him, who is both our surety to God for the discharge of our debt and duty, and God's surety to us for the performance of his promises. 'Father,' saith Christ, 'I will take upon me all the sins of thy[1] people; I will be bound to answer for them; I will sacrifice myself for them; at my hands do thou require satisfaction for their sins, and a full compensation unto thy justice; 1 will die, I will lay down my life, I will make my soul an offering for sins; I will become a curse, I will endure thy wrath.' Oh, what unspeakable comfort is this, that there is a Christ to answer for that which we could never answer! Christ is a surety in way of satisfaction, undertaking for the debts, the trespasses, the sins of his elect. In this respect it is that Christ is most properly called a surety, in regard of his taking upon him the sins of his elect, and undertaking to answer and make satisfaction unto the justice of God for them. Christ interposeth himself betwixt the wrath of God and his people, undertaking to satisfy their debts, and so to reconcile them unto God. Christ had nothing of his own to be condemned for, nothing of his own to be acquitted from. He was condemned to pay your debt, as your surety, and therefore you cannot be condemned too. He was acquitted from it, being paid, as your surety, and therefore you cannot but be acquitted too. He appeared the first time with your sin to his condemnation, he shall appear the second time without your sin unto your salvation, Heb. ix. 28. God the Father says to Christ, 'Son, if you would have poor sinners pardoned, you must take their debts upon yourself, you must be their surety, and you must enter into bonds to pay every farthing of that debt poor sinners owe; you must pay all if you will undertake for them, for I will never come upon them for it, but on you.' Certainly these were some of those transactions that were between God the Father and God the Son from all eternity about the pardoning of poor sinners. If ever thy sins be pardoned, Christ must take thy debts upon himself, and be thy surety; 2 Cor. v. 21, 'He made him to be sin for us, who knew no sin.' Christ was made sin for us—1, by way of imputation, 'for our sins were made to meet upon him,' as that evangelical prophet hath it, Isa. liii. 6; and, secondly, by reputation, 'for he was reckoned among malefactors,'

[1] Qu. 'my'?—G.

ver. 12. The way of pardon is by a translation of all our sins upon Christ, it is by charging them all upon Christ's score. That is a great expression of Nathan to David, 'The Lord hath put away thy sin;' but the original runs thus, 'The Lord hath made thy sins to pass over;' that is, to pass over from thee to his Son; he hath laid them to his charge.

Now Christ hath discharged all his people's debts and bonds. There is a twofold debt which lay upon us. One was the debt of obedience unto the law, and this Christ did pay by 'fulfilling all righteousness,' Mat. iii. 15. The other was the debt of punishment for our transgressions, and this debt Christ discharged by his death on the cross, Isa. liii. 4, 10, 12; 'And by being made a curse for us, to redeem us from the curse,' Gal. iii. 13. Hence it is that we are said to be 'bought with a price,' 1 Cor. vi. 20, and vii. 23; and that Christ is called our 'Ransom,' λυτρον, Mat. xx. 28, and ἀντίλυτρον, 1 Tim. ii. 6. The words do signify a valuable price laid down for another's ransom. The blood of Christ, the Son of God, was a valuable price, a sufficient price; it was as much as would take off all enmities, and take away all sin, and to satisfy divine justice, and indeed so it did; and therefore you read that 'in his blood we have redemption, even the forgiveness of our sins,' Eph. i. 7; Col. i. 14, 20; and his death was such a full compensation to divine justice, that the apostle makes a challenge to all: Rom. viii. 33, 'Who shall lay anything to the charge of God's elect?' and ver. 34, 'Who is he that condemneth? it is Christ that died.' As if he had said, Christ hath satisfied and discharged all. The Greek word ἀντίλυτρον is of special emphasis. The Vulgar Latin renders it *redemptionem*, redemption; Beza, *redemptionis pretium*, a price of redemption; but neither of them fully expressing the force of the word, which properly signifieth a counter-price, when one doth undergo in the room of another that which he should have undergone in his own person, as when one yields himself a captive for the redeeming of another out of captivity, or giveth his own life for the saving of another's. There were such sureties among the Greeks as gave life for life, body for body; and in this sense the apostle is to be understood, when he saith that Christ gave himself ἀντίλυτρον, a ransom, a counter-price, paying a price for his people. Christ hath laid down a price for all believers, they are his 'dear bought ones,' they are his 'choice redeemed ones,' Isa. li. 11. Christ gave himself ἀντίλυτρον, a counter-price, a ransom, submitting himself to the like punishment that his redeemed ones should have undergone. Christ, to deliver his elect from the curse of the law, did subject himself to that same curse of the law under which all mankind lay. Jesus Christ was a true surety, one that gave his life for the life of others. As the apostle saith of Castor and Pollux, that the one redeemed the other's life with his own death,[1] so did the Lord Jesus; he became such a surety for his elect, giving himself an ἀντίλυτρον, a ransom for them, John vi. 51; Tit. ii. 14; 1 Pet. i. 18; Rev. i. 51, and v. 9. Oh,

---

[1] The only reference in the New Testament to Castor and Pollux is found in Acts xxviii. 11, so that for 'apostle,' we must here read 'the poet,' or the like. For the old Greek myth of Castor and Pollux, see any of the classical dictionaries, under Dioscori or Polydeuces.—G.

what comfort is this unto us to have such a Jesus, who himself bare our sins, even all our sins, left not one unsatisfied for, laid down a full ransom, a full price, such an expiatory sacrifice as that now we are out of the hands of justice, and wrath, and death, and curse, and hell, and are reconciled and made near by the blood of the everlasting covenant! The blood of Christ, as the Scripture speaks, is 'the blood of God,' Acts xx. 28, so that there is not only satisfaction, but merit in his blood. There is more in Christ's blood than mere payment or satisfaction. There was merit also in it, to acquire and procure and purchase all spiritual good, and all eternal good for the people of God; not only immunities from sin, death, wrath, curse, hell, &c., but privileges and dignities of sons and heirs; yea, all grace, and all love, and all peace, and all glory, even that glorious inheritance purchased by his blood, Eph. i. 14.

Remember this once for all, that in justification our debts are charged upon Christ, they go upon his accounts. You know that in sin there is the vicious and staining quality of it, and there is the resulting guilt of it, which is the obligation of a sinner over to the judgment-seat of God to answer for it. Now this guilt, in which lies our debt, this is charged upon Christ. Therefore, saith the apostle, 'God was in Christ, reconciling the world to himself, not imputing their trespasses unto them,' 2 Cor. v. 19; 'And hath made him to be sin for us, who knew no sin,' ver. 21. You know in law the wife's debts are charged upon the husband; and if the debtor be disabled, then the creditor sues the surety. *Fide-jussor*, or surety and debtor, in law are reputed as one person. Now Christ is our *fide-jussor*. 'He is made sin for us,' saith the apostle; 'for us'—that is, in our stead—a surety for us, one who puts our scores on his accounts, our burden on his shoulders. So saith that princely prophet Isaiah: Isa. liii. 4, 5, 'He hath borne our griefs, and carried our sorrows.' How so? 'He was wounded for our transgressions; he was bruised for our iniquities;' that is, he stood in our stead, he took upon him the answering of our sins, the satisfying of our debts, the clearing of our guilt; and therefore was it that he was so bruised, &c.

You remember the scape-goat; upon his head all the iniquities of the children of Israel, and all their transgressions in all their sins were confessed and put: 'And the goat did bear upon him all their iniquities,' Lev. xvi. 21, 22. What is the meaning of this? Surely Jesus Christ, upon whom our sins were laid, and who alone died for the ungodly, Rom. v. 6, 'and bore our burdens away.' Therefore the believer in the sense of guilt should run unto Christ, and offer up his blood unto the Father, and say, 'Lord, it is true, I owe thee so much; yet, Father, forgive me; remember that thine own Son was my ransom, his blood was the price; he was my surety, and undertook to answer for my sins. I beseech thee, accept of his atonement, for he is my surety, my redemption. Thou must be satisfied! but Christ hath satisfied thee, not for himself—what sins had he of his own?—but for me. They were my debts which he satisfied for; and look over thy book, and thou shalt find it so; for thou hast said, "He was made sin for us, and that he was wounded for our transgressions."' Now, what a singular support, what an admirable comfort is this, that we ourselves are not to make up our accounts and reckonings; but that Christ hath cleared all accounts and reckonings between God and us. Therefore it is said that 'in his blood we have redemption, even the forgiveness of sins,' Eph. i. 7.

Quest. *Whether it were not against the justice of God that Christ, who was in himself innocent,—without all sin, a Lamb without a spot,—should bear and endure all these punishments for us who were the offending and guilty and obnoxious persons only?* Or if you please thus,

Whether God was not unjust to give his Son Jesus Christ to be our surety and mediator and redeemer and saviour, forasmuch as Christ could not be any one of these for and unto us but by a willing susception of our sins upon himself, to be for them responsible unto the justice of God, in suffering those punishments which were due for our sins?

I shall speak a few words to this main question. I say, then, that it is not always and in all cases unjust, but it is sometimes and in some cases very just, to punish one who is himself innocent, for him or those who are the nocent and guilty. Grotius in his book, *De Satisfactione*, gives divers instances; but I shall mention only two.

First, In the case of conjunction, where the innocent party and the nocent party do become legally one party; and therefore if a man marries a woman indebted, he thereupon becomes obnoxious to pay her debts, although, absolutely considered, he was not obnoxious thereunto. But,

Secondly, In case of suretyship, where a person, knowing the weak and insufficient condition of another, doth yet voluntarily put forth himself, and will be bound to the creditor for him as his surety to answer for him, by reason of which suretyship the creditor may come upon him, and deal with him as he might have dealt with the principal debtor himself; and this course we do ordinarily take with sureties for the recovery of our right, without any violation of justice. Now, both these are exactly applicable to the business in hand; for Jesus Christ was pleased to marry our nature unto himself; he did partake of our flesh and blood, and became man, and one with us. And besides that, he did, both by the will of his Father and his own free consent, become our surety, and was content to stand in our stead or room, so as to be made sin and curse for us—that is, to have all our debts and sorrows, all our sins and punishments laid upon him, and did engage himself to satisfy God by bearing and suffering what we should have borne and suffered. And therefore although Jesus Christ, absolutely considered in himself, was innocent and had no sin inherent in himself, which therefore might make him liable to death and wrath and curse, yet by becoming one with us, and sustaining the office of our surety, our sins were laid on him, and our sins being laid upon him, he made himself therefore obnoxious, and that justly, to all those punishments which he did suffer for our sins. I do confess, that had Christ been unwilling and forced into this suretyship, or had any detriment or prejudice risen to any party concerned in this transaction, then some complaint might have been made concerning the justice of God. But,

[1.] First, *There was a willingness on all sides for the passive work of Christ.* First, God the Father, who was the offended party, he was willing, which Christ assures us of when he said, ' Thy will be done,' Mat. xxvi. 42; Acts iv. 25–28. *Secondly,* We poor sinners, who are the offending party, are willing. We accept of this gracious and wonderful redemption, and bless the Lord who ' so loved us as to give his Son for us.' And, *thirdly,* Jesus Christ was willing to suffer for us: ' Behold I come,' Ps. xl. 7: 'And shall I not drink of the cup which my Father hath given me to drink?' John xviii. 11 : ' I have a baptism to be baptized with, and how am I straitened till it be accomplished?' Luke xii. 50. He calls the death of his cross a baptism, partly because it was a certain immersion into extreme calamities into which he was cast, and partly because in the cross he was so to be sprinkled in his own blood as if he had been drowned and baptized in it. The Greek word, συνέχομαι, that is here rendered straitened, signifies to be pained, pressed, or pent up, not with such a grief as made him unwilling to come to it, but with such as made him desire that it were once over. ' There seems,' saith Grotius, ' to be a similitude implied in the original word, taken from a woman with child, which is so afraid of her bringing forth that yet she would fain be eased of her burden.' John x. 11, ' I am the good Shepherd. The good Shepherd giveth his life for the sheep.' Christ is that good Shepherd by an excellency, that held not his life dear for his sheep's safety: ver 15, ' I lay down my life for the sheep': ver. 17, ' Therefore doth my Father love me, because I lay down my life:' ver. 18, ' No man taketh it from me, but I lay it down of myself.' A necessity there was of our Saviour's death; but it was a necessity of immutability— because God had decreed it, Acts ii. 23—not of coaction. He laid down his life freely, he died willingly. But,

[2.] Secondly, *No parties whatsoever were prejudiced, or lost by it.* We lost nothing by it, for we are saved by his death, and reconciled by his death; and Christ lost nothing by it: ' Ought not Christ to have suffered these things, and enter into his glory?' Luke xxiv. 26. ' The Captain of our salvation is made perfect through sufferings,' Heb. ii. 10. You may see Christ's glorious rewards for his sufferings in that Isa. liii. 10–12. And God the Father lost nothing by it, for he is glorified by it: ' I have glorified thee on earth, I have finished the work which thou gavest me to do,' John xvii. 4. Yea, he is fully satisfied and repaired again in all the honour which he lost by our sinning—I say he is now fully repaired again by the sufferings of Christ, in which he found a price sufficient, and a ransom, and enough to make peace for ever. In the day of account, a Christian's great plea is, that Christ has been his surety, and paid his debts, and made up his accounts for him.

II. Now, from what has been said last, a Christian may form up this second plea to the ten scriptures in the margin;[1] that refer either to the general judgment or to the particular judgment that will pass upon every Christian immediately after death. *O blessed Lord! upon my first believing and closing with Jesus Christ, thou didst justify me in the*

---

[1] Eccles. xi. 9, and xii. 14; Mat. xii. 36, and xviii. 23 ; Luke xvi. 2 ; Rom. xiv. 10, 12 ; 2 Cor. v. 10; Heb. ix. 27, and xiii. 17; 1 Pet. iv. 5.

court of glory from all my sins, both as to guilt and punishment. Upon my first act of believing, thou didst pardon all my sins, thou didst forgive all my iniquities, thou didst blot out all my transgressions; and as upon my first believing thou didst give me the remission of all my sins, so upon my first believing thou didst free me from a state of condemnation, and interest me in the great salvation. Upon my first believing, I was united to Jesus Christ, and I was clothed with the righteousness of Christ, which covered all my sins and discharged me from all my transgressions, Rom. viii. 10; Heb. ii. 3; *and remember, O Lord, that at the very moment of my dissolution thou didst really, perfectly, universally, and finally forgive all my sins. Every debt that moment was discharged, and every score that moment was crossed, and every bill and bond that moment was cancelled, so that there was not left in the book of thy remembrance one sin, no, not the least sin, standing upon record against my soul; and besides all this, thou knowest, O Lord, that all my sins were laid upon Christ my surety,* Heb. vii. 21, 22, *and that he became responsible for them all. He did die, he did lay down his life, he did make his soul an offering for my sins, he did become a curse, he did endure thy infinite wrath, he did give complete satisfaction, and a full compensation unto thy justice for all my sins, debts, trespasses.* This is my plea, O Lord! and by this plea I shall stand. 'Well,' saith the Lord, 'I allow of this plea, I accept of this plea as just, honourable, and righteous. Enter thou into the joy of thy Lord.' But,

Seventhly, Consider, *that whatever we are bound to do, or to suffer by the law of God, all that did Christ do and suffer for us, as being our surety and mediator.* Now the law of God hath a double challenge or demand upon us; one is of active obedience, in fulfilling what it requires; the other is of passive obedience, in suffering that punishment which lies upon us, for the transgression of it, in doing what it forbids. For as we are created by God, we did owe unto him all obedience which he required; and as we sinned against God, we did owe unto him a suffering of all that punishment which he threatened, and we being fallen by transgression, can neither pay the one debt, nor yet the other; we cannot do all that the law requires, nay of ourselves we can do nothing; neither can we so suffer as to satisfy God in his justice wronged by us, or to recover ourselves into life and favour again; and therefore Jesus Christ, who was God, made man, did become our surety, and stood in our stead or room; and he did perform what we should but could not perform; and he did bear our sins and our sorrows. He did suffer and bear for us what we ourselves should have borne and suffered, whereby he did fully satisfy the justice of God, and made our peace, and purchased life and happiness for us. Let me a little more clearly and fully open this great truth in these few particulars.

(1.) *First, Jesus Christ did perform that active obedience unto the law of God, which we should, but, by reason of sin, could not perform;* in which respect he is said, Gal. iv. 4, ' to be made under the law, that he might redeem them that were under the law.' So far was Christ under the law, as to redeem them that were under the law. But redeem them that were under the law he could not, unless by discharging the bonds of the law in force upon us ; and all those bonds could not be, and were not discharged, unless a perfect righteousness had been presented on our behalf, who were under the law, to fulfil the law.   Now there is a twofold righteousness necessary to the actual fulfilling of the law : one is an internal righteousness of the nature of man ; the other is an external righteousness of the life or works of man : both of these do the law require.   The former, ' Thou shalt love the Lord thy God with all thy heart,' &c., which is the sum of the first table ; ' And thou shalt love thy neighbour as thyself,' which is the sum of the second table : the latter, ' Do this and live,' Lev. xviii. 5, ' He that continueth not in all things, which are written in the book of the law, to do them, is cursed,' Gal. iii. 10.   Now both these righteousnesses were found in Christ.   First, the internal : Heb. vii. 26, ' He was holy, harmless, undefiled, separated from sinners ; Heb. ix. 14, ' And offered himself without spot to God ;' 2 Cor. v. 21, ' He knew no sin.'   Secondly, external : 1 Peter ii. 22, ' He did no sin, neither was guile found in his mouth ;' John xvii. 4, ' I have finished the work which thou gavest me to do ;' Mat. iii. 15, ' He must fulfil all righteousness,' Rom. x. 4 ; ' Christ is the end of the law for righteousness to every one that believeth.'   Now concerning Christ's active obedience to the law of God, these things are considerable in it.

[1.] First, *The universality of it :* he did whatsoever his Father required, and left nothing of his Father's will undone.   He kept the whole law, and offended not in one point.   Whatever was required of us, by virtue of any law, that he did, and fulfilled.   Hence he is said to be made under the law, Gal. iv. 4, subject or obnoxious to it, to all the precepts or commands of it.   Christ was so made under the law, as those were under the law whom he was to redeem.   Now we were under the law, not only as obnoxious to its penalties, but as bound to all the duties of it.   That this is our being under the law, is evident by that of the apostle : Gal. iv. 21, ' Tell me, ye that desire to be under the law.'   Surely it was not the penalty of the law they desired to be under, but to be under it in respect of obedience.   So Mat. iii. 15. Here Christ tells you, that ' it became him to fulfil all righteousness,' πᾶσαν δικαιοσύνην, all manner of righteousness whatsoever ; that is, everything that God required, as is evident from the application of that general axiom to the baptism of John.   But,

[2.] Secondly, *The exactness and perfection of it.*   He kept the whole law exactly.   As he was not wanting in matter, so he did not fail in the manner of performing his Father's will.   There was no defects, nothing lacking in his obedience ; he did all things well. What we are pressing towards, and reaching forth unto, he attained ; he was perfect in every good work, and stood complete in the whole will of his Father.   And hence it is, that it is recorded of him, that he was without sin, knew no sin, did no sin, which could not be if he had failed in anything.   But,

[3.] Thirdly, *The constancy of it.*   Christ did not obey by fits, but constantly.   Though we cannot, yet he ' continued in all things which are written in the book of the law, to do them.'   This righteous one held on his way, he did not fail, nor was he discouraged ; yea, when persecution and tribulation did arise against him, because of his doing the will of his Father, he was not offended, but did always do the things which pleased his Father, as he told the Jews, John viii. 29.

[4.] Fourthly, *The delight that he took* ' in doing the will of his Father:' Ps. xl. 8, ' I delight to do thy will, O my God; yea, thy law is within my heart,' or in the midst of my bowels, as the Hebrew runs. By the law of God we are to understand all the commandments of God. There is not one command which Christ did not delight to do. Christ's obedience was without murmuring or grudging; his Father's commandments were not grievous to him; he tells his disciples, that it was his ' meat to do the will of him that sent him, and to finish his work,' John iv. 34. But,

[5.] Fifthly, *The virtue and efficacy of it;* for his obedience, his righteousness never returns to him void, but it always ' accomplishes that which he pleases, and prospers in the thing whereto he ordains it,' and that is the making others righteous, according to that of the apostle: Rom. v. 19, ' For as by one man's disobedience many were made sinners, so by the disobedience of one shall many be made righteous;' 2 Cor. v. 21, ' God made him to be sin for us, who knew no sin, that we might be made the righteousness of God in him;' and accordingly we are, ' for of God he is made unto us righteousness,' 1 Cor. i. 30.

The perfect complete obedience of Christ to the law is certainly reckoned to us. That is an everlasting truth, ' If thou wilt enter into life, keep the commandments,' Mat. xix. 17. The commandments must be kept either by ourselves, or by our surety, or there is no entering into life; Christ did obey the law, not for himself but for us, and in our stead: Rom. v. 18, 19, ' By the righteousness of one, the free gift came upon all men unto justification of life; by the obedience of one, many shall be made righteous.' By his obedience to the law, we are made righteous. Christ's obedience is reckoned to us for righteousness. Christ, by his obedience to the royal law, is made righteousness to us, 1 Cor. i. 30. We are saved by that perfect obedience, which Christ, when he was in this world, yielded to the blessed law of God. Mark, whatever Christ did as mediator, he did it for those whose mediator he was, or in whose stead and for whose good he executed the office of a mediator before God. This the Holy Ghost witnesseth: Rom. viii. 3, 4, ' What the law could not do, in that it was weak through the flesh, God sending his own Son in the likeness of sinful flesh, and for sin, condemned sin in the flesh, that the righteousness of the law might be fulfilled in us.' The word ' likeness,' is not simply to be referred to flesh, but to sinful flesh, as Basil well observes; for Christ was like unto us in all things, sin only excepted. If with our justification from sin, there be joined that active obedience of Christ, which is imputed to us, we are just before God, according to that perfect form which the law requireth. Because we could not, in this condition of weakness whereinto we are cast by sin, come to God, and be freed from condemnation by the law, God sent Christ as a mediator to do and suffer whatever the law required at our hands for that end and purpose, that we might not be condemned, but accepted of God. It was all to this end, that the righteousness of the law might be fulfilled in us; that is, which the law required of us, consisting in duties of obedience. This Christ performed for us. This expression of the apostle, 'God sending his own Son in the likeness of sinful flesh, and for sin, condemned sin in the flesh,' if you will add to it that of Gal. iv. 4—'that he was so sent forth, as that he was γενόμενον ὑπὸ νομον, 'made under the law;' that is, obnoxious to it, to yield all the obedience that it doth require,—compares[1] the whole of what Christ did or suffered; and all this, the Holy Ghost tells us was for us, ver. 5, He that made the law as God, was made under the law as God-man, whereby both the obligations of the law fell upon him: 1. Penal; 2. Preceptive. First, The penal obligation to undergo the curse, and so to satisfy divine justice. Secondly, The preceptive obligation, to fulfil all righteousness, Mat. iii. 15. This obligation he fulfilled by doing, the other by dying. Mark, this double obligation could not have befallen the Lord Jesus Christ upon any natural account of his own, but upon his mediatory account only, as he voluntarily became the surety of this new and better covenant, Heb. vii. 22; so that the fruit and benefit of Christ's voluntary subjection to the law, redoundeth not at all to himself, 'but unto the persons which were given him of the Father,' John xvii., whose sponsor he became. For their sakes he underwent the penal obligation of the law, that it might do them no harm, 'He being made a curse for us," Gal. iii. 13; and for their sakes he fulfilled the preceptive obligation of the law, 'do this,' that so the law might do them good. This the evangelical apostle clearly asserts, 'Christ is the end of the law for righteousness, to every one that believeth,' Rom. x. 4, 'Christ is the end of the law,' τέλος. What end? why finis perfectivus, the perfection and accomplishment of the law; he is the end of the law for righteousness, that is, to the end that by Christ his active obedience, God might have his perfect law perfectly kept, that so there might be a righteousness extant in the human nature, every way adequate to the perfection of the law. And who must wear this garment of righteousness, when Christ hath finished it? Surely the believer who wanted a righteousness of his own; for so it follows, 'for righteousness to every one that believeth,' that is, that every poor naked sinner, believing in Jesus Christ, might have a righteousness, wherein being found, he might appear at God's tribunal, but his nakedness not appear; but as Jacob in the garment of his elder brother Esau, so the believer in the garment of his elder brother Jesus, might inherit the blessing, even the great blessing of justification.

The only matter of man's righteousness, since the fall of Adam, wherein he can appear with comfort before the justice of God, and consequently, whereby alone he can be justified in his sight, is the obedience and sufferings of Jesus Christ, the righteousness of the mediator. There is not any other way imaginable, how the justice of God may be satisfied, and we may have our sins pardoned in a way of justice, but by the righteousness of the Son of God, and therefore is his name Jehovah, צדקנו, 'The Lord our righteousness,' Jer. xxiii. 6. This is his name; that is, this is the prerogative of the Lord Jesus, a matter that appertains to him alone, to be able to bring in 'an everlasting righteousness, and to make reconciliation for iniquity,' Dan. ix. 24.

[1] Qu. 'comprises'?—G.

It is by Christ alone, that they who ' believe are justified from all things, from which they cannot be justified by the law of Moses,' Acts xiii. 39.

III. Now from the active obedience of Christ, a sincere Christian may form up this third plea as to the ten scriptures in the margin,[1] that refer either to the general judgment, or to the particular judgment that will pass upon every Christian immediately after death. *O blessed God, thou knowest that Jesus Christ, as my surety, did perform all that active obedience unto thy holy and righteous law that I should have performed, but by reason of the indwelling power of sin, and of the vexing and molesting power of sin, and of the captivating power of sin, could not.* There was in Christ an habitual righteousness, a conformity of his nature to the holiness of the law: 1 Pet. i. 19, ' For he is a lamb without spot and blemish.' The law could never have required so much righteousness as is to be found in him ; and as for practical righteousness, there was never any aberration in his thoughts, words, or deeds, Heb. vii. 25 ; ' The prince of this world cometh, and hath nothing in me,' John xiv. 30. The apostle tells us, that ' we are made the righteousness of God in him,' 2 Cor. v. 21. He doth emphatically add that clause, ἐν αὐτῷ, *in him*, that he may take away all conceit of inherence in us, and establish the doctrine of imputation. As Christ is made sin in us by imputation, so we are made righteousness in him by the same way. Augustine's place which Beza cites is a most full commentary, ' God the Father,' saith he, ' made him to be sin, who knew no sin, that we might be the righteousness of God, not our own; and in him, that is in Christ, not in ourselves; and being thus justified, we are so righteous, as if we were righteousness itself.' Oh, holy God, Christ my surety hath universally kept thy royal law, he hath not offended in any one point ; yea, he hath exactly and perfectly kept the whole law of God, he stood complete in the whole will of the Father; his active obedience was so full, so perfect, and so adequate to all the law's demands, that the law could not but say, ' I have enough, I am fully satisfied; I have found a ransom, I can ask no more.' Neither was the obedience of Christ fickle or transient, but permanent and constant; it was his delight, his meat and drink, yea, his heaven, to be still a-doing the will of his Father, John iv. 33, 34. Assuredly, whilst our Lord Jesus Christ was in this world, he did in his own person fully obey the law ; he did in his own person perfectly conform to all the holy, just, and righteous commands of the law. Now this his most perfect and complete obedience to the law is made over to all his members, to all believers, to all sincere Christians ; it is reckoned to them, it is imputed to them, as if they themselves, in their own persons, had performed it. All sound believers being in Christ, as their head and surety, the law's righteousness is fulfilled in them legally and imputively, though it be not fulfilled in them formally, subjectively, inherently, or personally; suitable to that of the apostle, that ' the righteousness of the law might be fulfilled in us,' Rom. viii. 4. Mark, not by us, but in us; for Christ in our nature hath fulfilled the right of the law, and therefore in us, because of our communion

[1] Eccles. xi. 9, and xii. 14 ; Mat. xii. 36, and xviii. 23 ; Luke xvi. 2 ; Rom. xiv. 10, 12 ; 2 Cor. v. 10 ; Heb. ix. 27, and xiii. 17 ; 1 Pet. iv. 5.

with him, and our ingrafting into him.[1] God hath condemned sin in the flesh of his Son, that all that which the law by right could require of us might be performed by him for us, so as if we ourselves had in our own persons performed the same. The law must have its right before a sinner can be saved ; we cannot of ourselves fulfil the right of it. But here is the comfort, Christ our surety hath fulfilled it in us, and we have fulfilled it in him. Certainly, whatsoever Christ did concerning the law is ours by imputation so fully, as if ourselves had done it. Does the law require obedience? saith Christ, ' I will give it,' Mat. iii. 15. Does the law threaten curses? says Christ, ' They shall be borne,' Mat. v. 17, 18. The precept of the law, saith Christ, shall be kept, and the promises received, and the punishments endured, that poor sinners may be saved. Our righteousness and title to eternal life do indispensably depend upon the imputation of Christ's active obedience to us. There must be a perfect obeying of the law, as the condition of life, either by the sinner himself or by his surety, or else no life; which doth sufficiently evince the absolute necessity of the imputation of Christ's active obedience to us. The sinner himself being altogether unable to fulfil the law, that he may stand righteous before the great and glorious God, Christ's fulfilling of it must necessarily be imputed to him in order to righteousness. There are two great things which Jesus Christ did undertake for his redeemed ones ; the one was to make full satisfaction to divine justice for all their sins. Now this he did by his blood and death. The other was to yield most absolute conformity to the law of God, both in nature and life. By the one he has freed all his redeemed ones from hell, and by the other he has qualified all the redeemed ones for heaven. This is my plea, O Lord, and by this plea I shall stand. ' Well,' saith the Lord, ' I accept of this plea as honourable, just, and righteous; Enter thou into the joy of thy Lord.'

(2.) Secondly, As Jesus Christ did for us perform all that active obedience which the law of God required; so he did also *suffer all those punishments which we had deserved by the transgression of the law of God*, in which respect he is said, 2 Cor. ii. 22, ' To be made sin for us;' 1 Pet. ii. 24, ' Himself to bear our sins in his own body on the tree;' 1 Pet. iii. 18, ' For Christ also hath once suffered for sin, the just for the unjust, that he might bring us to God;' Phil. ii. 8, ' To humble himself and to become obedient unto death, even the death of the cross;' Gal. iii. 13, ' To be made a curse, an execration for us;' Eph. v. 2, ' To give himself for us an offering and sacrifice unto God;' Heb. ix. 15, ' And for this cause he is the mediator of the new testament, that by means of death, for the redemption of the transgressions that were under the first testament, they which were called might receive the promise of eternal inheritance.' Now concerning the passive obedience, or suffering of Christ, I would present unto you these conclusions.

[1.] First, That the sufferings of Jesus Christ were *free and voluntary, and not constrained or forced*. Austin saith, that Christ did suffer *quia voluit, et quando voluit, et quomodo voluit:* John x. 17,

---

[r] [1] δικαιωμα, which Beza well renders, *Ut jus legis,* that the right of the law might be fulfilled in us.

'I lay down my life;' ver. 18, 'No man taketh it from me, but I lay it down of myself; I have power to lay it down, and I have power to take it again;' Gal. ii. 20, 'Who gave himself for me.' Christ's sufferings did rise out of obedience to his Father: John x. 18, 'This commandment have I received of my Father;' and John xviii. 11, 'The cup which my Father hath given me, shall I not drink it?' And Christ's sufferings did spring and rise out of his love to us, 'who loved me, and gave himself for me,' Gal. ii. 20; so Eph. v. 25, 'As Christ loved the church, and gave himself for it.' And indeed, had Christ's sufferings been involuntary, they could not have been a part of his obedience, much less could they have mounted to anything of merit for us. Christ was very free and willing to undertake the work of man's redemption. When he cometh into the world, he saith, 'Sacrifice and offerings thou wouldest not, but a body hast thou prepared me; then said I, Lo, I come to do thy will, O God,' Heb. x. 5. It is the expression of one overjoyed to do the will of God. So Luke xii. 50, 'I have a baptism to be baptized with, and how am I straitened till it be accomplished.' There was no power, no force to compel Christ to lay down his life, therefore it is called the offering of the body of Jesus, Heb. x. 10. Nothing could fasten Christ to the cross, but the golden link of his free love. Christ was big of love, and therefore he freely opens all the pores of his body, that his blood may flow out from every part, as a precious balsam to cure our wounds. The heart of Christ was so full of love that it could not hold, but must needs burst out through every part and member of his body into a bloody sweat, Luke xxii. 44. At this time it is most certain that there was no manner of violence offered to the body of Christ; no man touched him, or came near him with whips, or thorns, or spears, or lances. Though the night was cold, and the air cold, and the earth on which he kneeled cold, yet such a burning love he had in his breasts to his people as cast him into a bloody sweat. It is certain that Christ never repented of his sufferings: Isa. liii. 11, 'He shall see of the travail of his soul, and shall be satisfied.' It is a metaphor that alludes to a mother, who though she hath had hard labour, yet doth not repent of it, when she sees a child brought forth. So though Christ had hard travail upon the cross, yet he doth not repent of it, but thinks all his sweat and blood well bestowed, because he sees the manchild of redemption is brought forth into the world. He shall be satisfied: the Hebrew word, יִשְׂבַּע, signifies such a satiating as a man hath at some sweet repast or banquet. And what does this speak out, but his freeness in suffering?

Obj. But here some may object, and say, *that the Lord Jesus, when the hour of his sufferings drew nigh, did repent of his suretyship; and in a deep passion prayed to his Father to be released from his sufferings:* 'Father, if it be possible, let this cup pass from me;' and that three times over, Mat. xxvi. 39, 42, 44.

Ans. Now to this objection I shall answer, first more generally, and secondly more particularly.

[1.] *First,* in the general, I say that this earnest prayer of his doth not denote absolutely his unwillingness, but rather sets out the greatness of his willingness; for although Christ as a man was of the same natural affections with us, and desires, and abhorrences of what was destructive to nature, and therefore did fear and deprecate that bitter cup which he was ready to drink; yet as our mediator and surety, and knowing it would be a cup of salvation to us, though of exceeding bitterness to himself, he did yield and lay aside his natural reluctances as man, and willingly obeyed his Father's will to drink it, as our loving mediator, as if he should say, 'O Father, whatsoever becometh of me, of my natural fear or desire, I am content to submit to the drinking of this cup; thy will be done.' But,

[2.] *Secondly*, and more particularly, I answer, that in these words of our Lord there is a twofold voice. 1. There is *vox naturæ*, the voice of nature; 'Let this cup pass from me.' 2. There is *vox officii*, the voice of his mediatory office; 'Nevertheless, not as I will, but as thou wilt.' The first voice, 'Let this cup pass,' intimates the velleity of the inferior part of his soul, the sensitive part, proceeding from unnatural[1] abhorrency of death as he was a creature. The latter voice, 'Nevertheless, not as I will, but as thou wilt,' expresseth the full and free consent of his will, complying with the will of his Father in that grand everlasting design of 'bringing many sons unto glory, by making the captain of their salvation perfect through sufferings,' Heb. ii. 10.

It was an argument of the truth of Christ his human nature, that he naturally dreaded a dissolution. He owed it to himself as a creature to desire the conservation of his being, and he could not become unnatural to himself, 'For no man ever yet hated his own flesh,' Eph. v. 29: Phil. ii. 8, 'But being a son, he learned submission, and became obedient to the death, even the death of the cross;' that shameful, cruel, cursed death of the cross, the suffering whereof he owed to that solemn astipulation, which from everlasting passed between his Father and himself, the third person in the blessed Trinity, the Holy Ghost being witness. And therefore, though the cup was the bitterest cup that ever was given man to drink, as wherein there was not death only, but wrath and curse: yet seeing there was no other way left of satisfying the justice of his Father, and of saving sinners, most willingly he took the cup, and having given thanks, as it were, in those words, 'The cup which my Father hath given me, shall I not drink it?' never did bridegroom go with more cheerfulness to be married to his bride, than our Lord Jesus went to his cross, Luke xii. 20.

Though the cup that God the Father put into Christ's hand was bitter, very bitter, yea, the bitterest that ever was put into any hand, yet he found it sweetened with three ingredients. 1. It was but a cup, it was not a sea; 2. It was his Father, and not Satan, that mingled it, and that put in all the bitter ingredients that were in it; 3. It was a gift, not a curse, as to himself: 'The cup which my Father *giveth me.*' He drank it, I say, and drank it up every drop, leaving nothing behind for his redeemed but large draughts of love and salvation, in the sacramental cup of his own institution, saying, 'This cup is the new testament in my blood, for the remission of sins; this do ye in remembrance of me,' 1 Cor. xi. 25; Mat. xxvi. 28. Thus, my friends, look upon Christ as mediator, in which capacity only he covenanted with his Father for the salvation of mankind; and there was not so

---

[1] 'Qu. 'a natural'?—ED.

much as a shadow of any receding from or repenting of what he had
undertaken. But,

Ans. 2. Secondly, As the sufferings of Jesus Christ were very free
and voluntary, so they were *very great and heinous.* What agony,
what torment was our Saviour racked with! how deep were his
wounds! how weighty his burden! how full of trembling his cup,
when he lay under the mountains of the guilt of all the elect! How
bitter were his tears! how painful his sweat! how sharp his encoun-
ters! how dreadful his death! who can compute[1] how many vials of
God's inexpressible, insupportable wrath Christ drank off? In that
53d of Isaiah you may read of despising, rejected, stripes, smitings,
wounds, sorrows, bruising, chastisement, oppression, affliction, cutting
off, putting to grief, and pouring out of his soul to death; all these
put together speaks out Christ to be a very great sufferer. He was a
man of sorrows, as if he were a man made up of sorrows: as the man
of sin, as if he were made up of sin, as if he were nothing else. He
knew more sorrows than any man, yea, than all men ever did; for the
iniquity, and consequently the sorrows, of all men met in him as if he
had been their centre; and he was acquainted with griefs; he had
little acquaintance else, grief was his familiar acquaintance, he had
no acquaintance with laughter. We read not that he laughed at all,
when he was in the world. His other acquaintance stood afar off, but
grief followed him to the cross. From his birth to his death, from his
cradle to the cross, from the womb to the tomb, he was a man of sorrows, and never were sorrows like his; he might say, Never grief or
sorrow like mine. It is indeed impossible to express the sufferings and
sorrows of Christ; and the Greek Christians used to beg of God, δι'
ἀγνωστων κοπων, that for the unknown sufferings of Christ he would
have mercy upon them! Though Christ's sufferings are abundantly
made known, yet they are but little known; eye hath not seen, nor
ear heard, nor hath it or can it enter into the heart of man to conceive
what Christ suffered; 'who hath known the power of God's wrath?'
Christ Jesus knew it, for he underwent it; his whole life was made
up of suffering. He was no sooner born, but sufferings came troop-
ing in upon him. He was born in an inn, yea, in a stable, and had
but a manger for his cradle. As soon as his birth was noised abroad,
Herod, under a pretence of worshipping of him, had a design to murder him, so that his supposed father was fain to fly into Egypt to
secure his life. He was persecuted before he could, after the manner
of men, be sensible of persecution; and as he grew up in years, so his
sufferings grew up with him. Hunger and thirst, travel and weariness, scorns and reproaches, false accusations and contradictions still
waited on him, and he had not where to lay his head: 1 Pet. iii. 18,
' For Christ also hath once suffered for sins.' This is the wonderment
of angels, the happiness of fallen man, and the torment of devils, &c.,
that Christ hath suffered. The apostle's words look like a riddle,
' Christ hath suffered;' as if he should say, read thou if thou canst
what he hath suffered; as for my part they are so many, that in this
short epistle I have no mind to record them; and they are so grievous, that my passionate love won't suffer me to repeat them, and

---

[1] Misprinted 'impute.'—G.

therefore I content myself thus abruptly to deliver them, 'Christ hath suffered.' Christ's sufferings were unspeakable, his sufferings were unutterable; and therefore the apostle satisfies himself with this imperfect, broken speech, 'Christ hath suffered.' Oh, what woes and lamentations, what cries and exclamations, what complaints and sorrows, what wringing of hands, what knocking of breasts, what weeping of eyes, what wailing of tongues belong to the speaking and hearing of this doleful tragedy! Even in the prologue I tremble, and at the first entrance I am as at a *non-plus*, that I know not with what woeful gesture to act it, with what moanful voice to pronounce it, with what mournful words, with what pathetical speeches, with what emphatical phrases, with what interrupted accents, with what passionate compassionate plaints to express it. The multiplicity of the plot, and the variety of the acts and scenes is so intricate, that my memory fails to comprise it; the matter so important, and the story so excellent, that my tongue fails to declare it; the cruelty so savage, and the massacre so barbarous, that my heart even fails to consider it. Wherefore I must needs content myself, with the apostle here, to speak but imperfectly of it, and thinks this enough to say, 'Christ hath suffered;' and well may I think this enough, for behold what perfection there is in this seeming imperfect speech. For,

First, To say indefinitely, he 'suffered' without any limitation of time, what is it but to say that he always suffered without exception of time? And so indeed the prophet speaks of him, namely, 'That he was a man of sorrows,' Isa. liii. 3. His whole life was filled up with sufferings. But,

Secondly, To say only he 'suffered,' and nothing else, what is it but to say that he patiently suffered; he never resisted, never rebelled, never opposed? 'He was led as a sheep to the slaughter; and as a lamb dumb before the shearer, so opened he not his mouth,' Acts viii. 32; Isa. liii. 7. 'And when he was reviled, he reviled not again; when he suffered, he threatened not,' 1 Pet. ii. 23. But,

Thirdly, To say precisely he 'suffered,' and no more, what is it but to say that he freely suffered, that he voluntarily suffered? Christ was under no force, no compulsion, but freely suffered himself to suffer, and voluntarily suffered the Jews to make him suffer, having power to quit himself from suffering if he had pleased. 'I lay down my life, no man taketh it from me, but I lay it down of myself: I have power to lay it down, and I have power to take it again,' John x. 17. But of this before.

Fourthly, To say plainly he 'suffered,' what is it but to say that he innocently suffered, that he wrongfully suffered? For had he been a malefactor, or an offender, it should have been said that he was punished, or that he was executed; but he was full of innocency, he was holy and harmless; and so it follows in that 1 Pet. iii. 18, 'The just for the unjust.' But,

Fifthly, To say peremptorily he 'suffered,' what is it but to say that he principally suffered, that he excessively suffered? To say he 'suffered,' what is it but to say he was the chief sufferer, the arch-sufferer? and that not only in respect of the manner of his sufferings, that he suffered absolutely so as never did any, but also in respect of the measure of his sufferings, that he suffered excessively beyond what ever any did. And thus we may well understand and take those words, 'He suffered.' That lamentation of the prophet, Lam. i. 12, is very applicable to Christ, ' Behold, and see if there be any sorrows like unto my sorrow, which is done unto me, wherewith the Lord hath afflicted me in the day of his fierce anger.' Now, is it not enough for the apostle to say that ' Christ has suffered ;' but will you yet ask what ? But pray, friends, be satisfied, and rather of the two ask what not ? For what sufferings can you think of that Christ did not suffer ? Christ suffered in his birth, and he suffered in his life, and he suffered in his death ; he suffered in his body, for he was diversely tormented ; he suffered in his soul, for his soul was heavy unto death ; he suffered in his estate, they parted his raiment, and he had not where to rest his head ; he suffered in his good name, for he was counted a Samaritan, a devilish sorcerer, a wine-bibber, an enemy to Cæsar, &c. He suffered from heaven, when he cried out, ' My God, my God, why hast thou forsaken me ?' He suffered from the earth, when, being hungry, the fig-tree proved fruitless to him. He suffered from hell, Satan assaulting and encountering of him with his most black and horrid temptations. He began his life meanly and basely, and was sharply persecuted. He continued his life poorly and distressedly, and was cruelly hated. He ended his life woefully and miserably, and was most grievously tormented with whips, thorns, nails, and, above all, with the terrors of his Father's wrath and horrors of hellish agonies.

Ego sum qui peccavi: ' I am the man that have sinned ; but these sheep, what have they done ?' said David, when he saw the angel destroying his people, 2 Sam. xxiv. 17. And the same speech may every one of us take up for ourselves and apply to Christ, and say, ' I have sinned, I have done wickedly ; but this sheep, what hath he done ?' Yea, much more cause have we than David had to take up this complaint. For,

First, David saw them die, whom he knew to be sinners ; but we see him die, who, we know, ' knew no sin,' 2 Cor. v. 21. But,

Secondly, David saw them die a quick, speedy death ; we see him die with lingering torments. He was a-dying from six to nine, Mat. xxvii. 45, 46. Now in this three hours' darkness, he was set upon by all the powers of darkness with utmost might and malice ; but he foiled and spoiled them all, and made an open show of them, as the Roman conquerors used to do, triumphing over them on his cross as on his chariot of state, Col. ii. 15, attended by his vanquished enemies, with their hands bound behind them, Eph. iv. 8. But,

Thirdly, David saw them die, who, by their own confession, was worth ten thousand of them ; we see him die for us, whose worth admitteth no comparison. But,

Fourthly, David saw the Lord of glory destroying mortal men, and we see mortal men destroying the Lord of glory, 1 Cor. ii. 8. Oh, how much more cause have we then to say as David, ' I have sinned, I have done wickedly ; but this innocent Lamb, the Lord Jesus, what hath he done? what hath he deserved that he should be thus greatly tormented ?' Tully, though a great orator, yet when he comes to speak of the death of the cross, he wants words to express it,—*Quid dicam, in crucem tollere?* What shall I say of this death? saith he. But,

Ans. 3. Thirdly, As the sufferings of Christ were very great, so *the punishments which Christ did suffer for our sins, these were in their kinds and parts and degrees and proportion all those punishments which were due unto us by reason of our sins, and which we ourselves should otherwise have suffered.* Whatsoever we should have suffered as sinners, all that did Christ suffer as our surety and mediator, always excepting those punishments which could not be endured without a pollution and guilt of sin: 'The chastisement of our peace was upon him,' Isa. liii. 5; and including the punishments common to the nature of man, not the personal, arising out of imperfection and defect and distemper. Now, the punishments due to us for sin were corporal and spiritual. And again, they were the punishments of loss and of sense; and all these did Christ suffer for us, which I shall evidence by an induction of particulars.

I. First, *That Christ suffered corporal punishments is most clear in Scripture.* You read of the injuries to his person, of the crown of thorns on his head, of the smiting of his cheeks, of spitting on his face, of the scourging of his body, of the cross on his back, of the vinegar in his mouth, of the nails in his hands and feet, of the spear in his side, and of his crucifying and dying on the cross: 1 Pet. ii. 24, 'Who himself in his own body on the tree bare our sins;' 1 Cor. xv. 3, 'Christ died for our sins, according to the Scriptures;' Rev. i. 5, 'And washed us from our sins in his own blood;' Col. i. 14, 'In whom we have redemption through his blood, even the forgiveness of sins;' Mat. xxvi. 28, 'For this is my blood of the New Testament, which is shed for many for the remission of sins.' Christ suffered derision in every one of his offices.

First, In his kingly office. They put a sceptre in his hand, a crown on his head, and bowed their knees, saying, 'Hail, king of the Jews!' Mat. xxvii. 29.

Secondly, In his priestly office. 'They put upon him a gorgeous white robe,' such as the priests wore, Luke xxiii. 11.[1]

Thirdly, In his prophetical office. 'When they had blindfolded him, Prophesy, say they, who it is that smiteth thee,' Luke xxii. 64. Sometimes they said, 'Thou art a Samaritan, and hast a devil,' John viii. 48; and sometimes they said, 'He is beside himself, why hear ye him?' Mark iii. 21.

And as Christ suffered in every one of his offices, so he suffered in every member of his body: in his hearing, by their reproaches, and crying, 'Crucify him, crucify him;' in his sight, by their scoffings and scornful gestures; in his smell, in his being in that noisome place Golgotha, Mat. xxvii. 33; in his taste, by his tasting of vinegar mingled with gall, which they gave him to drink, Mat. xxvii. 33; in his feeling, by the thorns on his head, blows on his cheeks, spittle on his face, the spear in his side,[2] and the nails in his hands. He suffered in all parts and members of his body from head to foot. His head, which deserved a better crown than the best in the world, was crowned

---

[1] Cf. Sibbes, vol. vii., p. 603, on note *s*, vol. ii., p. 195.—G.

[2] An oversight, as the Saviour was dead before his side was pierced, John xix. 34.—G.

with thorns, and they smote him on the head. Osorius, writing of the sufferings of Christ, saith, ' That the crown of thorns bored his head with seventy-two wounds.' To see that head, before which angels cast down themselves and worshipped, as I may say, crowned with thorns, might well amaze us; to see those eyes, that were purer than the sun, put out by the darkness of death; to see those ears which hear nothing to speak to capacity, but halleluiahs of saints and angels, to hear the blasphemies of the multitude; to see that face which was fairer than the sons of men,—for being born and conceived without sin, he was freed from the contagious effects of it, deformity, and was most perfectly beautiful, Ps. xlv. 2; Cant. v. 10—to be spit on by those beastly, wretched Jews; to see that mouth and tongue, that ' spake as never man spake,' accused for false doctrines, nay blasphemy; to see those hands, which freely swayed the sceptre of heaven, nailed to the cross; to see those feet, ' like unto fine brass,' Rev. i. 15, nailed to the cross for man's sins; who can behold Christ thus suffering in all the members of his body, and not be struck with astonishment? Who can sum up the horrible abuses that were put upon Christ by his base attendants? The evangelist tells us that they spit in his face and buffeted him, and that others smote him with the palms of their hands, saying, ' Prophesy unto us, thou Christ, who is he that smote thee?' Mat. xxvi. 67, 68; and, as Luke adds, ' many other things blasphemously spake they against him,' Luke xxii. 65. What those many other things were is not discovered; only some ancient writers say, ' That Christ in that night suffered so many and such hideous things, that the whole knowledge of them is reserved only for the last day of judgment.' Mallonius[1] writes thus, ' After Caiaphas and the priests had sentenced Christ worthy of death, they committed him to their ministers, warily to keep till day, and they immediately threw him into the dungeon in Caiaphas's house; there they bound him to a stony pillar, with his hands bound on his back, and then they fell upon him with their palms and fists.' Others add that the soldiers, not yet content, they threw him into a filthy, dirty puddle, where he abode for the remainder of that night; of which the psalmist seems to speak, ' Thou hast laid me in the lowest pit, in darkness, and in the deeps, and I sink in the deep mire, where there is no standing,' Ps. lxxxviii. 6, and lxix. 2. But that you may clearly see what horrible abuses were put upon Christ by his attendants, consider seriously of these particulars:—

[1.] First, ' They spit in his face,' Mat. xxvi. 67. Now, this was accounted among the Jews a matter of great infamy and reproach: Num. xii. 14, ' And the Lord said to Moses, If her father had spit in her face, should she not be ashamed seven days?' Spitting in the face among the Jews was a sign of anger, shame, and contempt: Job xxx. 10, ' They abhor me, they flee far from me, and spare not to spit in my face.' The face is the table of beauty or comeliness, and when it is spit upon, it is made the seat of shame. Spitting in the face was a sign of the greatest disgrace that could be put upon a person; and therefore it could not but be very bitter to Job to see base beggars spit in that face that was wont to be honoured by princes. But this we are not to wonder at, for there is no indignity so base and ignominious but the choicest saints may meet with it in and from this evil world. Afflicted persons are sacred things, and by the laws of nature and nations should not be misused and trampled upon, but rather pitied and lamented over; but barbarous miscreants, when they have an opportunity, they will not spare to exercise any kind of cruelty, as you see by their spitting in the very face of Christ himself: 'I hid not my face,' saith Christ, 'from shame and spitting,' Isa. l. 6, 2. Though 'I was fairer than the children of men,' Ps. xlv. 2, yet I used no mask to keep me fair; though 'I was white and ruddy,' 'the chiefest among ten thousand,' Cant. v. 10, yet I preserved not my beauty from their nasty spittle. Oh, that that sweet and blessed face of Jesus Christ, that is so much honoured and adored in heaven, should ever be spit upon by beastly wretches in this world!

[2.] Secondly, 'They struck him:' John xviii. 22, 'One of the officers which stood by struck Jesus with the palm of his hand, saying, Answerest thou the high priest so?' Because our Saviour gave not the high priest his usual titles, but dealt freely with him, this impious apparitor, or sergeant, to curry favour with his master, strikes him with his hand, with his rod, say some, with his stick, say others; like master like man. Oh, that that holy face which was designed to be the object of heaven, in the beholding of which much of the celestial glory doth consist—that that face which the angels stare upon with wonder, like infants at a bright sunbeam—should ever be smitten by a base varlet in the presence of a judge! Among all the sufferings of Christ, one would think that there was no great matter in this, that a vain officer did strike him with the palm of his hand; and yet if the Scriptures are consulted, you will find that the Holy Ghost lays a great stress upon it. Thus Jeremiah: 'He giveth his cheek to him that smiteth him; he is filled full with reproach,' Lam. iii. 30. Christ did patiently and willingly take the stripes that vain men did injuriously lay upon him; he sustained all kinds of vexations from the hands of all kinds of ungodly ones. Thus Micah, speaking of Christ, saith, 'They shall smite the Judge of Israel with a rod upon the cheek,' Micah v. 1. Hugo, by this Judge of Israel, understandeth our Lord Jesus Christ, who was indeed at his passion contumeliously 'buffeted and smitten with rods upon the cheek,' Mat. xxvi. 67. By smiting the Judge of Israel with a rod upon the cheek, they express their scorn and contempt of Christ. Smiting upon the face the apostle makes a sign of great reproach: 2 Cor. xi. 20, 'If a man smite you on the face.' 'There is nothing more disgraceful,' saith Chrysostom, 'than to be smitten on the cheek.'[1] And the diverse reading of the original word does fully evidence it: 'He struck him with a rod,' or 'he struck him with the palm of his hand,' ἔδωκε ῥάπισμα. Now, the word ῥάπισμα, say some, refers to his being struck with a rod, or club, or shoe, or plantofle;[2] others say it refers to his being struck with the palm of men's hands. Now, of the two, it is generally judged more disgraceful to be struck with the palm of the hand than to be struck with either a rod or a shoe; and therefore we read the text

[1] Homil. 82 in John c. 18.
[2] 'Plant,'=foot: plantofle=covering of foot, or a slipper.

thus, 'He struck Jesus with the palm of his hand,' that is, with open hand, or with his hand stretched out.

Some of the ancients, commenting on this cuff, say, Let the heavens be afraid, and let the earth tremble, at Christ's patience and his servant's impudence! O ye angels! how were ye silent? how could you contain your hands when you saw his hand striking at God?[1] 'If we consider him,' saith another,[2] 'who took the blow, was not he that struck him worthy to be consumed of fire, or to be swallowed up of earth, or to be given up to Satan, and thrown down into hell.' Bernard saith, 'That his hand that struck Christ was armed with an iron glove.'[3] And Vincentius affirms, 'That by the blow Christ was felled to the earth.'[4] And Ludovicus adds, 'That blood gushed out of his mouth; and that the impression of the varlet's fingers remained on Christ's cheek with a tumour and wan colour.'[5] If a subject should but lift up his hand against a sovereign, would he not be severely punished? But should he strike him, would it not be present death? Oh, what desperate madness and wickedness was it then to strike the King of kings and Lord of lords, whom not only men, but the cherubims and seraphims, and all the celestial powers above, adore and worship? Rev. xvii. 16; Heb. i. 6. Those monsters in that Mat. xxvi. 67 did not only strike Christ with the palm of their hands, but they buffeted him also. Now, some of the learned observe this difference betwixt ῥάπισμα and κολαφος; the one is given with the open hand, the other with the fist shut up; and thus they used him at this time. They struck him with their fists, and so the stroke was greater and more offensive; for by this means they made his face to swell, and to become full of bunches all over. One gives it in thus: By these blows of their fists his whole head was swollen, his face became black and blue, and his teeth ready to fall out of his jaws. Very probable it is that, with the violence of their strokes, they made him reel and stagger, they made his mouth, and nose, and face to bleed, and his eyes to startle in his head.

Now, concerning Christ's sufferings on the cross, I shall only hint a few things, and so close up this particular concerning Christ's corporeal sufferings. Take me thus,

1. *First*, The death of Christ on the cross, it was *a bitter death, a sorrowful death, a bloody death.* The bitter thoughts of his sufferings put him into a most dreadful agony: Luke xxii. 44, 'Being in an agony, he prayed more earnestly, and his sweat was as great drops of blood falling to the ground.' The Greek word that is here used, Ἀγωνία, signifies a striving or wrestling against, as two combatants or wrestlers do strive each against other. The things which our Saviour strove against was not only the terror of death, as other men are wont to do—for then many Christians and martyrs might have seemed more constant and courageous than he—but with the terrible justice of God, pouring out his high anger and indignation upon him on the account of all the sins of his chosen that were laid upon him, than which nothing could be more dreadful, Isa. liii. 4–6. Christ was

---

[1] Chrysostom, Hom. 81 in John c. 18.
[3] Bernard, Ser. de Pas. Vinc. Serm. de Pas.
[4] Comment. in Ep. ad Ebrœos. 1634, folio.—G.

[2] Augustine in Trall. 13.
[5] Ludov. de *Vita Christi*.

in a vehement conflict in his soul, through the deepest sense of his Father's wrath against sinners, for whom he now stood as a surety and Redeemer, 2 Cor. v. 21. And for a close of this particular, let me say that God's justice which we have provoked, being fully satisfied by the inestimable merit of Christ's passion, is the surest and highest ground of consolation that we have in this world; but for the more full opening[1] of this blessed scripture, let us take notice of these following particulars:—

(1.) First, '*His sweat was as it were blood.*' Some of the ancients look upon these words only as a similitude or figurative hyperbole, it being a usual kind of speech to call a vehement sweat a bloody sweat, as he that weeps bitterly is said to weep tears of blood; but the most and best of the ancients understand the words in a literal sense, and believe it was truly and properly a bloody sweat, and with them I close. But some will object, and say it was *sicut guttæ sanguinis*, as it were drops of blood. Now to this I answer, *first*, if the Holy Ghost had only intended that *sicut* for a similitude or hyperbole, he would rather have expressed it as it were drops of water,[2] than 'as it were drops of blood;' for we all know that sweat is more like to water than to blood. But, *secondly*, I answer that *sicut*, as in Scripture phrase, doth not always denote a similitude, but sometimes the very thing itself, according to the verity of it. Take an instance or two instead of many: 'We beheld his glory, as the glory of the only begotten of the Father;' and 'their words seemed to them as it were idle tales, and they believed them not;' the words in the original, ὡς, ὡσεί, are the same. Certainly Christ's sweat in the garden was a wonderful sweat, not a sweat of water, but of red gore-blood. But,

(2.) Secondly, He sweat *great drops of blood, clotty blood*, issuing through flesh and skin in great abundance, θρόμβοι αἵματος, clotted or congealed blood. There is a thin faint sweat, and there is a thick clotted sweat. In this sweat of Christ blood came not from him in small dews, but in great drops, they were drops, and great drops of blood, crassy[3] and thick drops. Some read it droppings down of blood; that is, blood distilling in greater and grosser drops; and hence it is concluded as preternatural; for though much may be said for sweating blood in a course of nature, according to what Aristotle affirms, and Austin saith that he knew a man that could sweat blood, even when he pleased; and it is granted on all hands that in faint bodies a subtle thin blood like sweat may pass through the pores of the skin; but that through the same pores crassy, thick, and great drops of blood should issue out,—it was not, it could not be without a miracle.[4] Certainly the drops of blood that fell from Christ's body were great, very great; yea, so great as if they had started through his skin to outrun the streams and rivers of his cross. But,

(3.) Thirdly, These great drops of blood did not only *distillare*,[5] drop out, but *decurrere*, run down like a stream, so fast, as if they had issued out of most deadly wounds. They were 'great drops of blood falling down to the ground'! Here is magnitude and multitude; great drops,

---

[1] Misprinted 'opinion.'—G.　　[2] Misprinted 'nature.'—G.　　[3] 'Thick,' 'fat.'—G.
[4] Arist. lib. iii., de Hist. Animal, c. 29; August. lib. 14, de Civit. Dei., c. 24.
[5] Misprinted 'dillare.'—G.

and those so many, so plenteous, as that they went through his apparel, and all streamed down to the ground; and now was the time that his garments were dyed with crimson red. That of the prophet, though spoken in another sense, yet in some respect may be applied to this, 'Wherefore art thou red in thy apparel, and thy garments like him that treadeth the wine-fat?' Isa. lxiii. 2. Oh, what a sight was here! His head and members are all on a bloody sweat, and this sweat trickles down, and bedecks his garments, which stood like a new firmament, studded with stars, portending an approaching storm; nor stays it there, but it falls down to the ground. Oh, happy garden that was watered with such tears of blood! Oh, how much better are these rivers than Abana and Pharpar,' rivers of Damascus, yea, than all the waters of Israel; yea, than all those rivers that water the garden of Eden![1] So great was Scanderbeg's ardour in battle,[2] that the blood burst out of his lips; but from our champion's, not lips only, but whole body, burst out a bloody sweat. Not his eyes only were fountains of tears, or his head waters, as Jeremiah wished, Jer. ix. 1, but his whole body was turned, as it were, into rivers of blood. A sweet comfort to such as are cast down for that that their sorrow for sin is not so deep and soaking as they could desire.

Christ's blood is put in Scripture by a synecdoche of the part, for all the sufferings which he underwent for all the sins of the elect, especially his bloody death with all its concomitants, so called. *First*, because death, especially when it is violent, is joined with the effusion of blood: 'If we had lived in the days of our fathers, we would not have been partakers with them in the blood of the prophets,' Mat. xxiii. 30. And so again, Pilate said, 'I am innocent of the blood of this just person,' that is, of his death, Mat. xxvii. 24. *Secondly*, Herein respect is had to all the sacrifices of the law, whose blood was poured out when they were offered up. 'Almost all things are by the law purged with blood, and without shedding of blood there is no remission,' Heb. ix. 22; so that the blood of Christ is the antitype aimed at in the blood of those sacrifices that were slain for sinners' sins. But,

2. *Secondly*, as the death of Christ on the cross, was a bitter death, a bloody death, so the death of Christ on the cross was *a lingering death*. It was more for Christ to suffer one hour than for us to have suffered for ever; but his death was lengthened out, he hung three hours on the cross, he died many deaths before he could die one: 'from the sixth till the ninth hour'—that is, from twelve till three in the afternoon—'there was darkness over all the land,' Mat. xxvii. 45. About twelve, when the sun is usually brightest, it began now to darken, and this darkness was so great that it spread over all the land of Jewry; yea, some think over all the world. So we translate it in Luke, 'And there was darkness over all the earth,' Luke xxiii. 44, to show God's dislike of their horrid cruelty. He would not have the sun give light to so horrid an act. The sun as it were, hid his face that he might not see the Sun of righteousness so unworthily, so wickedly handled. It was dark: 1. To show the blindness, darkness, and ignorance of the Jews in crucifying the Lord of glory; 2. To show the detestation of the fact; 3. To show the vileness of our sins. This darkness was not a natural eclipse of the sun; for, first, it cannot be so total, so general;

[1] Bernard.   [2] Bucholcer.

nor secondly, it could not be so long, for the interposed moon goeth swiftly away. Certainly this was no ordinary eclipse of the sun, seeing the passover was kept at the full moon, when the moon stands right opposite to the sun on the other side of the heaven, and for this cause cannot hinder the light of the sun, but a supernatural work of God coming to pass by miracle, 'like as the darkness in Egypt,' Exod. x. 22. The moon being now in the full, it being in the midst of the lunar month when the passover was killed, and so of necessity the body of the moon—which useth to eclipse the sun by its interposition, and being between us and the sun—must be opposite to and distant from the sun the diametrical breadth of the hemisphere, the full moon ever rising at the sun's setting, and therefore this eclipse could never be a natural eclipse. Many Gentiles besides Jews observed this darkness as a great miracle. Dionysius the Areopagite, as Suidas relates, could say at first sight of it, 'Either the world is ending, or the God of nature is suffering of this darkness.[1] Amos long before had prophesied: 'And it shall come to pass in that day, that I will cause the sun to go down at noon, and I will darken the earth in the clear day,' Amos viii. 9. The opinion of authors concerning the cause of this darkness are various. Some think that the sun by divine power, withdrew and held back its beams; others say that the obscurity was caused by some thick clouds which were miraculously produced in the air, and spread themselves over all the earth; others say that this darkness was by a wonderful interposition of the moon, which at that time was at full, but by a miracle interposed itself betwixt the earth and sun. Whatsoever was the cause of this darkness, it is certain that it continued for the space of three hours as dark as the darkest winter nights.

About three, which the Jews call the ninth hour, Mat. xxvii. 46, the sun now beginning to receive his light, Jesus cried with a loud voice, 'Eli, Eli, lama sabachthani, My God, my God, why hast thou forsaken me?' And then, that the Scripture might be fulfilled, he said 'I thirst;' and when he had received the vinegar, he said, 'It is finished,' John xix. 28, 30; and at last, crying with a loud voice, he said, 'Father, into thy hands I commend my spirit;' and having said thus, 'he gave up the ghost,' Luke xxiii. 46. Christ's words were ever gracious, but never more gracious than at this time. You cannot find in all the books and writings of men, in all the annals and records of time, either such sufferings or such sayings as were these last words and wounds, sayings and sufferings of Jesus Christ. 'And having said thus, he gave up the ghost;' or as John relates it, 'He bowed his head and gave up the ghost,' John xix. 30. Christ would not off the cross till all was done that was here to be done.[2] Christ bowed not because he was dead, but first he bowed and then died; that is, he died freely and willingly without constraint, and he died cheerfully and comfortably without murmuring or repining. Oh, what a wonder of love is this, that Jesus Christ, who is the author of life, the fountain of life, the lord of life, that he should so freely, so readily, so cheerfully lay down his life for us! &c.

About four in the afternoon he was pierced with a spear, and there issued out of his side both blood and water: 'and one of the soldiers with a spear pierced his side, and forthwith came there-out blood and

---

[1] Suidas in vita Dion.   [1] Emisit, non amisit.—Ambrose.

water,' John xix. 34. Out of the side of Christ, being now dead, there issues water and blood, signifying that he is both our justification and sanctification.

Thus was fulfilled that which was long before foretold: ' They shall look upon me whom they have pierced,' Zech. xii. 10; thus ' came Jesus by water and by blood,' 1 John v. 6; thus was there ' a fountain opened to the house of David, and the inhabitants of Jerusalem,' even to all the elect, 'for sin and for uncleanness,' Zech. xiii. 1. The soldier's malice lived when Christ was dead. The water and blood forthwith issuing out as soon as it was pierced with a spear, did evidently show that he was truly dead. The Syriac paraphrase saith he pierced his rib, that is, the fifth rib, where the *pericardium* lay. It is very likely that the very *pericardium* was pierced. Now the *pericardium* is a film or skin, like unto a purse, wherein is contained clear water to cool the heat of the heart.[1] The blood, saith one,[2] signifies the perfect expiation of the sins of the Church, and the water, the daily washing and purging of it from the remainder of her corruption. ' Water and blood issued out of Christ's side,' saith another, ' to teach us that Christ justifieth none by his merit, but such whom he sanctifieth by his Spirit.' Christ was pierced with a spear, and water and blood presently issued out of his side, that his enemies might not object that he rose again because he was but half dead on the cross, and being so taken down he revived. To testify the contrary truth, John so seriously affirmeth the certainty of his death, he being an eye-witness of the streaming out of Christ's blood as he stood by Christ's cross. O gates of heaven! O windows of paradise! O palace of refuge! O tower of strength! O sanctuary of the just! O flourishing bed of the spouse of Solomon! Methinks I see water and blood running out of his side more freshly than these golden streams which ran out of the garden of Eden and watered the whole world. But here I may not dwell, &c.

But to shut up this particular, about five, which the Jews call the eleventh and the last hour of the day, Christ was taken down and buried by Joseph and Nicodemus. But,

3. *Thirdly*, As the death of Christ on the cross was a lingering death, so the death of Christ was *a painful death*. This appears several ways.

[1.] *First*, His legs and hands were violently racked and pulled out to the places fitted for his fastenings, and then pierced through with nails. His hands and feet were nailed, which parts being full of sinews, and therefore very tender, his pains could not but be very acute and sharp.

[2.] *Secondly*, By this means he wanted the use both of his hands and feet, and so he was forced to hang immovable upon the cross, as being unable to turn any way for his ease, and therefore he could not but be under very dolorous pains.

[3.] *Thirdly*, The longer he lived, the more he endured; for by the weight of his body his wounds were opened and enlarged, his nerves and veins were rent and torn asunder, and his blood gushed out more

---

[1] The whole subject is conclusively discussed by Dr Stroud in his ' Physical Cause of Christ's Death,' 1 vol. 8vo. 1847. And cf. the interesting correspondence of eminent medical men in Appendix to Dr Hanna's ' Last Day of our Lord's Passion.' 1862. —G.

[2] Ambrose on Luke.

and more abundantly still. Now the envenomed arrows of God's wrath shot to his heart. This was the direful catastrophe, and caused that vociferation and outcry upon the cross, 'My God, my God, why hast thou forsaken me?' The justice of God was now inflamed and heightened to its full ἀκμή: Rom. viii. 32, 'God spared not his Son;' God would not abate one farthing of the debt. But,

[4.] *Fourthly*, He died by piece-meals, he died by little and little, he died not all at once. He that died on the cross was long a-dying. Christ was kept a great while upon the rack; it was full three hours betwixt his affixion and expiration; and certainly it would have been longer if he had not freely and willingly given up the ghost. I have read that Andrew the apostle was two whole days on the cross before he died; and so long might Christ have been a-dying, if God had not supernaturally heightened the degrees of his torment. Doubtless when Christ was on the cross he felt the very pains of hell, though not locally, yet equivalently. But,

4. *Fourthly*, As the death of Christ on the cross was a painful death, so the death of Christ on the cross was *a shameful death.* Christ was *in medio positus*, he hung between two thieves, as if he had been the principal malefactor, Mark xxvii. 38. Here they placed him to make the world believe that he was the great ringleader of such men. Christ was crucified in the midst as the chief of sinners that we might have place in the midst of heavenly angels; the one of these thieves went railing to hell, the other went repenting forth right to heaven, living long in a little time, Zech. iii. 7.

If you ask me the names of these two thieves who were crucified with Christ, I must answer, that although the Scripture nominates them not, yet some writers give them these names, Dismas and Gesmas; Dismas the happy, and Gesmas the miserable thief, according to the poet—

that is,
> Gesmas damnatur, Dismas ad astra levatur:

> When Gesmas died, to Dives he was sent;
> When Dismas died, to Abraham up he went.[1]

Well might the lamp of heaven withdraw its light and mask itself with darkness, as blushing to behold the Sun of righteousness hanging between two thieves! He shall be an Apollo to me that can tell me which was the greater, the blood of the cross, or the shame of the cross, Heb. xii. 2. It was a mighty shame that Saul's sons were hanged on a tree, 2 Sam. xxi. 6. Oh, what a shameful death was it for Christ to hang on a tree between two notorious thieves! But,

5. *Fifthly* and lastly, As the death of Christ was a shameful death, so the death of Christ was a cursed death; 'Cursed is every one that hangeth on a tree,' Deut. xxi. 23. The death on the tree was accursed above all kinds of death; 'as the serpent was accursed above all beasts of the field,' Gen. iii. 14, both for the first transgression, whereof the serpent was the instrument, the tree the occasion. Since the death of any malefactor might be a monument of God's curse for sin, it may be questioned, why this brand is peculiarly set

---

[1] Rather Demas, and Gestas, *not* Gesmas. Evangel. Nicod. i. 10; Narrat. Joseph, c. 3.—G.

upon this kind of punishment; that he that is hanged is accursed of God. To which I answer, that the reason of this was, because this was esteemed the most shameful, the most dishonourable and infamous of all kinds of death, and was usually therefore the punishment of those that had by some notorious wickedness provoked God to pour out his wrath upon the whole land, and so were hanged up to appease his wrath, as we may see in the hanging of those princes that were guilty of committing whoredom with the daughters of Moab, Num. xxv. 4; and in the hanging of those sons of Saul in the days of David, when there was a famine in the land, because of Saul's perfidious oppressing of the Gibeonites, 2 Sam. xxi. 6. Nor was it without cause that this kind of death was both by the Israelites and other nations esteemed the most shameful and accursed; because the very manner of the death did intimate that such men as were thus executed were such execrable and accursed wretches, that they did defile the earth with treading upon it, and would pollute the earth if they should die upon it; and therefore were so trussed up in the air as not fit to live amongst men; and that others might look upon them as men made spectacles of God's indignation and curse, because of the wickedness they had committed, which was not done in other kinds of death. And hence it was that the Lord God would have his Son, the Lord Christ, to suffer this kind of death, that even hence it might be the more evident, that in his death he bare the curse due to our sins, according to that of the apostle: 'Christ hath redeemed us from the curse of the law, being made a curse for us; for it is written, Cursed is every one that hangeth on a tree,' Gal. iii. 13. The Chaldee translateth, 'For because he sinned before the Lord he is hanged.' The tree whereon a man was hanged, the stone wherewith he was stoned, the sword wherewith he was beheaded, and the napkin wherewith he was strangled, they were all buried, that there might be no evil memorial of such a one, to say, This was the tree, sword, stone, napkin, wherewith such a one was executed. This kind of death was so execrable that Constantine made a law that no Christian should die upon the cross; he abolished this kind of death out of his empire. When this kind of death was in use among the Jews, it was chiefly inflicted upon slaves, that either falsely accused, or treacherously conspired their master's death. But on whomsoever it was inflicted, this death in all ages among the Jews had been branded with a special kind of ignominy; and so much the apostle signifies when he saith, 'He abased himself to the death, even to the death of the cross,' Phil. ii. 2. I know Moses' law speaks nothing in particular of crucifying, yet he doth include the same under the general of hanging on a tree; and some conceive that Moses, in speaking of that curse, foresaw what manner of death the Lord Jesus should die. And let thus much suffice concerning Christ's sufferings on the cross, or concerning his corporeal sufferings.

II. I shall now, in the second place, speak concerning Christ's *spiritual sufferings*, his sufferings in his soul, which were exceeding high and great. Now here I shall endeavour to do two things: First, To prove that Christ suffered in his soul, and so much the rather because that the papists say and write, that Christ did not truly and properly and immediately suffer in his soul, but only by way of sympathy and compassion with his body to the mystical body; and that his bare bodily sufferings were sufficient for man's redemption. Second, That the sufferings of Christ in his soul were exceeding high and great. For the first, that Christ suffered in his soul, I shall thus demonstrate.

(1.) First, *Express Scriptures do evidence this:* Isa. liii. 10, 'When thou shalt make his soul an offering for sin, he shall see his seed,' &c.; John xii. 27, 'Now is my soul troubled; and what shall I say? Father, save me from this hour: but for this cause came I unto this hour;' Mat. xxvi. 37, 38, 'He began to be sorrowful and very heavy.' These were but the beginnings of sorrow: he began, &c. Sorrow is a thing that drinks up our spirits, and he was heavy, as feeling a heavy load upon him; ver. 38, 'My soul is exceeding sorrowful, even unto death.' Christ was as full of sorrow as his heart could hold. Every word is emphatical, 'My soul;' his sorrow pierced his heaven-born soul. As the soul was the first agent in transgression, so it is here the first patient in affliction. The sufferings of his body were but the body of his sufferings; the soul of his sufferings were the sufferings of his soul, which was now beset with sorrows, and heavy as heart could hold.[1] Christ was sorrowful, his soul was sorrowful, his soul was exceeding sorrowful, his soul was exceeding sorrowful unto death. Christ's soul was in such extremity of sorrow, that it made him cry out, 'Father, if it be possible, let this cup pass;' and this was with 'strong cryings and tears,' Heb. v. 7. To cry, and to cry with a loud voice, argues great extremity of sufferings: Mark xiv. 33, Mark saith, 'And he began to be amazed, and to be very heavy;' or we may more fully express it thus, according to the original, καὶ ἤρξατο ἐκθαμβεῖσθαι, καὶ ἀδημονεῖν, 'He begun to be gastred[2] with wonderful astonishment, and to be satiated, filled brimful with heaviness: a very sad condition! All the sins of the elect, like a huge army, meeting upon Christ, made a dreadful onset on his soul: Luke xxii. 43, 44, it is said 'He was in an agony.' That is a conflict in which a poor creature wrestles with deadly pangs, with all his might, mustering up all his faculties and force to grapple with them and withstand them. Thus did Christ struggle with the indignation of the Lord, praying once and again with more intense fervency, 'Oh, that this cup may pass away; if it be possible, let this cup pass away!' Luke xxii. 42, 43; while yet an angel strengthened his outward man from utter sinking in the conflict. Now, if this weight that Christ did bear had been laid on the shoulders of all the angels in heaven, it would have sunk them down to the lowest hell; it would have cracked the axle-tree of heaven and earth. It made his blood startle out of his body in congealed cloddered[3] heaps. The heat of God's fiery indignation made his blood to boil up till it ran over; yea, divine wrath affrighted it out of its wonted channel. The creation of the world cost him but a word; he spake and the world was made; but the redemption of souls cost him bloody sweats and soul-distraction. What conflicts, what strugglings with the wrath of God! the powers of darkness! what weights! what burdens! what wrath did he undergo when his soul was heavy unto death! 'beset with terrors,' as

---

[1] Christ's soul was beleaguered, or compassed round, round with sorrow, as that word περίλυπος sounds.   [2] 'Terrified.'—G.   [3] 'Coagulated.'—G.

the word implies, when he drank that bitter cup, that cup of bitterness, that cup mingled with curses, which made him sweat drops of blood ! which, if men or angels had but sipped of, it would have made them reel, stagger, and tumble into hell. The soul of Christ was overcast with a cloud of God's displeasure. The Greek Church, speaking of the sufferings of Christ, calls them ἀγνωστα παθηματα, ' unknown sufferings.' Ah Christians ! who can speak out this sorrow ? ' The spirit of a man will sustain his infirmity; but a wounded spirit who can bear ?' Prov. xviii. 14. Christ's soul is sorrowful ; but give me that word again, his soul is exceeding sorrowful ; but if that word be yet too low, then I must tell you that ' his soul was exceeding sorrowful, even unto death:' not only extensively, such as must continue for the space of seventeen or eighteen hours, even until death itself should finish it, but also intensively such, and so great as that which is used to be at the very point of death, and such as were able to bring death itself, had not Christ been reserved to a greater and heavier punishment. Of this sorrow is that especially spoken, ' Behold and see if there be any sorrow like unto my sorrow which is done unto me, wherewith the Lord hath afflicted me in the day of his fierce anger,' Lam. i. 12. Many a sad and sorrowful soul hath, no question, been in the world ; but the like sorrow to this was never since the creation. The very terms or phrases used by the evangelists speak no less. He was ' sorrowful and heavy,' saith one; ' amazed, and very heavy,' saith another; ' in an agony,' saith a third; ' in a soul-trouble,' saith a fourth. Certainly, the bodily torments of the cross were much inferior to the agony of his soul. The pain of the body is the body of pain. Oh, but the very soul of sorrow is the soul's sorrow, and the very soul of pain is the soul's pain.

(2.) Secondly, *That which Christ assumed or took of our nature, he assumed to this end, to suffer in it; and by suffering, to save and redeem it.* But he took the whole nature of man, both body and soul ; *ergo*, he suffered in both. First, the assumption is evident, and needs no proof ; that Christ took upon him both our soul and body, the apostle assures us, where he saith, ' That in all things it became him to be like unto us,' Heb. ii. 17 ; therefore he had both body and soul as we have. Secondly, concerning the proposition, viz., That what Christ took of our nature, he took it by suffering in it properly and immediately to redeem us. Now this is evident by that blessed word, where the apostle saith, ' Christ took part with them that he might destroy, through death, him that had the power of death, that is, the devil,' ver. 14, 15 ; ' and deliver them, who through fear of death were all their lifetime subject to bondage.' Hence I reason thus, that wherein Christ delivered us, he took part with us in ; but he delivered us from fear of death ; *ergo*, he did therein communicate with us. Now mark, this fear was the proper and immediate passion of the soul, namely, the fear of death and God's anger. And the text giveth this sense, Because the fear of this death kept them in bondage, but the fear only of the bodily death doth not bring us into such bondage ; witness that Song of Zacharias ; ' That we, being delivered from the hands of our enemies, should serve him without fear,' Luke i. 74. This then is a spiritual fear, from the which Christ did deliver us ;

ergo, He did communicate with us in this fear; for the apostle saith, 'In that wherein he suffered, and was tempted, he is able to succour them that are tempted,' Heb. ii. 18. Certainly that fear which fell on Christ was a real fear, and it was in his soul, and did not arise from the mere contemplation of bodily torments only, for the very martyrs in the encountering with them have feared little. Assuredly there was some great matter that lay upon the very soul of Christ, which made him so heavy, and sorrowful, and so afraid, and in such an agony.

But if you please, take this second argument in another form of words, thus: *what Christ took of ours, that he in suffering offered up for us*, for his assuming of our nature, was for this end, to suffer for us in our nature; but he took our nature in body and in soul, and he delivered our souls as well as our bodies; and the sins of our souls did need his sacrifice as well as the sins of our bodies; and our souls were crucified with Christ as well as our bodies. *Mens mea in Christo crucifixa est*, saith Ambrose. Surely if our whole man was lost, then our whole man did need the benefit and help of a whole Saviour; and if Christ had assumed only our flesh, our body, then our souls adjudged, adjudged to punishment, had remained under transgression without hope of pardon. Several sayings of the ancients doth further strengthen this argument. Take a taste of some. *Si totus homo periit, totus beneficio salvatoris indiguit*, &c. If the whole man perished, the whole man needed a Saviour.[1] Christ therefore took the whole man, body and soul. If he had taken only flesh, the soul should remain addict to punishment of the first transgression, without hope of pardon. By the same reason, Christ must also suffer properly in soul, because not by taking our soul, but by satisfying in his soul, our soul is delivered.

'*Suscepit animam meam, suscepit corpus meum*,' [saith] Ambrose, 'He took all our passions, or affections, to sanctify them all in himself; but Christ was sanctified and consecrated by his death, and so doth he consecrate us,' [saith] Damascene. 'For by one offering, he hath perfected for ever them that are sanctified, Heb. x. 14; *ergo*, by his offering of our soul, and suffering in our soul, hath he consecrated our soul and affections.

Suscepit affectum meum, ut emendaret, He took my affection to amend it, &c. Now he hath amended it, in that he consecrated it by his offering, Heb. x. 14; *Illud pro nobis suscepit, quod in nobis amplius periclitabatur*. He hath taken that for us, which was most in danger for us, &c., that is, our soul as he expoundeth it: [Damascene] *de Incarnatione*, c. 7. But Christ hath not otherwise delivered us from the danger, but by entering into the danger for us; this danger of the soul is the fear and feeling of God's wrath.

(3.) Thirdly, *Christ bore our sorrows*, Isa. liii. 4. Now what sorrows should we bear, but the sorrows due unto us for our sins; and surely these were not corporal only, but spiritual also, and those did Christ bear in his soul. The same prophet saith, ver. 10, 'He shall make his soul an offering for sin;' *ergo*, Christ offered his soul as well as his body. Again, our Saviour himself saith, 'My soul is very heavy unto death,' Mat. xxvi. 38. Certainly it was not the bodily death which Christ feared, for then he should have been weaker than

---

[1] Augustine Conf.: Felician., c. 13.

many martyrs, yea, than many of the Romans, who made no more of dying, than of dining; therefore Christ's soul was verily and properly stricken with heaviness, and not with the beholding of bodily torments only, as some dream. But,

(4.) Fourthly, *That whereby Adam and we ever since, do most properly commit sin, by the same hath Christ, the second Adam, made satisfaction properly for our sin;* but Adam did, and we all do properly commit sin in our souls, our bodies being but the instruments; *ergo,* Christ by, and in his soul, hath properly made satisfaction.

[1.] First, *The truth of the proposition is confirmed by the apostle,* 'As by one man's disobedience we are made sinners, so by the obedience of one many shall be made righteous,' Rom. v. 19. Christ then satisfied for us by the same wherein Adam disobeyed. Now Adam's soul was in the transgression as well as his body, and accordingly was Christ's very soul in his sufferings and satisfaction, and Christ obeyed, that is, in his soul; for obedience belongeth to the soul, as one observeth upon those words of the apostle: Phil. ii. 8, ' He became obedient unto death, even the death of the cross: who doth not understand,' saith the same author, 'that obedience doth belong to the human will?'[1]

That there is a kind of dying in the soul when it is pierced with grief, besides the death of the soul, either by sin or damnation, is not disagreeing to the Scripture. Simeon saith to Mary, ' A sword shall pierce through thy soul,' Luke ii. 35. Look as then the body dieth, being pierced with a sword, so the soul may be said to die or languish, when it is pierced with grief. What else is crucifying but dying? Now, the soul is said to be crucified, as is evident by that passage of the apostle, ' I am crucified to the world,' Gal. vi. 14, when as yet his body was alive. So Ambrose doubts not to say, *Mens mea in Christo crucifixa est,* My soul was crucified in Christ, that is, Christ in his soul was crucified, which he calleth our soul, because he did assume our soul and body;[2] or else where he saith, *Mea est voluntas, quam suam dixit,* &c. It is my will, which he calleth his; it is my heaviness, which he took with my affections; yet was it properly and personally Christ's soul and will, but ours by community of nature.[3]

[2.] Secondly, *For the assumption.* 1. Howsoever it be admitted that the body is the instrument of the soul, both in sinning and suffering, yet the conclusion is this, that because sin is committed in the soul principally and properly, therefore the satisfaction must be made in the soul principally and properly. If this conclusion be granted, we have that we would; for the bodily pains affecting the soul are not the proper passions of the soul, neither is the soul said to suffer properly, when the body suffereth, but by way of compassion and consent. 2. We grant that in the proper and immediate sufferings of the soul the body also is affected: as when Christ was in his agony in the garden, his whole body was therewith stirred and moved, and that it did sweat drops of blood. But it is one thing when the grief beginneth immediately in the soul and so affecteth the body, and when the pain is first inflicted upon the body and so worketh upon the soul,

[1] Agatho Epist. ad Constantin. upon Phil. ii. 8.
[2] Ambrose, lib. v. in Luc.   [3] Ambrose, lib. ii., de sid. c. 3.

there the soul suffereth properly and principally; of which sufferings we speak here neither properly nor principally, which is not the thing in question. 3. It is not the reasonable soul that is affected with the body, for it is a ground in philosophy that the soul suffereth not, but only the sensitive part. But the grief that we speak of, that is satisfactory for sin, must be in the very reasonable soul where sin took the beginning, and so Ambrose saith[1] upon those words of Christ, ' My soul is heavy to death,' *Ad rationabilis assumptionem animæ,* &c., *naturæ humanæ refertur affectum,* It is referred to the assumption of the reasonable soul, and human affection.

Pride, ambition, infidelity began in Adam's soul, and had their determination there. In the committing of those sins the body had no part. Indeed with the ear they heard the suggestion of Satan; but it was no sin till in their minds they had consented unto it. Wherefore seeing the first sin committed was properly and wholly in the soul, for the same the soul must properly and wholly satisfy.

Because sin took beginning from Adam's soul, the satisfaction also must begin in Christ's soul, as Ambrose saith,[2] *Incipio in Christo vincere, unde in Adam victus sum,* I begin there to win in Christ, where in Adam I was overcome. Then it followeth that the sufferings of Christ's soul took beginning there, and were not derived by sympathy from the stripes and pain of the body. We infer, then, that therefore Christ's soul had proper and immediate sufferings, besides those which proceeded from sympathy with his body, and all Christ's sufferings were satisfactory: *ergo,* Christ did satisfy for our sins properly and immediately in his soul.

But if you please, take this fourth argument in another form of words, thus, *The punishment which was pronounced against the first Adam, our first surety, and in him against us, that same did Christ, the second Adam, our next and best surety, bear for us, or else it must still lie upon us to suffer it. But the punishment threatened and denounced against Adam for transgression, was not only corporal, respecting our bodies, but spiritual also, respecting our souls.* There was a spiritual malediction due unto our souls, as well as a corporal, &c.

Look, as God put a sanction on the law and covenant of works made with all of us in Adam, that he and his should be liable to death, both of body and soul, which covenant being broken by sin, all sinners became obnoxious to the death both of body and soul, so it was necessary that the redeemed should be delivered from the death of both by the Redeemer's tasting of death in both kinds, as much as should be sufficient for their redemption. O sirs, as sin infected the whole man, soul and body, and the curse following on sin left no part nor power of the man's soul free; so justice required that the Redeemer, coming in the room of the persons redeemed, should feel the force of the curse both in body and soul. But,

(5.) Fifthly, ' He shall see of the travail *of his soul,*' Isa. liii. 11. Here the soul is taken properly, and the travail of Christ's soul is his sufferings; for it follows, ' and he shall bear their iniquities.' But,

(6.) Sixthly, Christ gave himself for his people's sins: ' Who gave

---

[1] Ambrose de Incarnat., cap. 7.   [2] Ambrose, lib. iv. in Luc.

himself for our sins,' Tit. ii. 14; 'Who gave himself for us, that he might redeem us from all iniquities,' &c., Eph. v. 25; 1 Tim. ii. 6. But the body only is not himself; *ergo*, the apostle saith, Phil. ii. 7, *Christus ἐκένωσε, exinanivit*, Christ did empty or evacuate himself; or, as Tertullian expounds it,[1] *exhausit;* he drew out himself, or was exhaust, which agrees with the prophecy of Daniel, chap. ix. 26, ' Messias shall have nothing, being brought to nothing by his death, without life, strength, esteem, honour,' &c. Hence we conclude that if Christ were exhaust upon the cross, if nothing was left him, that he suffered in body and soul, that there was no part within or without free from the cross, but all was emptied and poured out for our redemption.

Again, we read that Christ, 'through the eternal Spirit, offered himself to God,' Heb. ix. 14. Whatsoever was in Christ did either offer or was offered; his eternal Spirit only did offer; *ergo*, his whole human nature, both body and soul, was offered. Thus Origen witnesseth in these words, *Vide quomodo verus pontifex Jesus Christus, adsumpto batillo carnis humanœ*, &c.[2]—See how our true priest, Jesus Christ, taking the censer of his human flesh, putting to the fire of the altar— that is, his magnificent soul, wherewith he was born in the flesh—and adding incense—that is, an immaculate spirit—stood in the midst between the living and the dead. Thus you see that he makes Christ's soul a part in the sacrifice.

(7.) Seventhly and lastly, *Christ's love unto man, in suffering for him, was in the highest degree and greatest measure that could be;* as the Lord saith, ' What could I have done any more for my vineyard that I have not done unto it ?' But if Christ had given his body only, and not his soul for us, he had not done for us all he could, and so his love should have been greatly impaired and diminished; *ergo*, he gave his soul also, together with his body, to be the full price of our redemption. And certainly the travail and labour of Christ's soul was most acceptable unto God: ' Therefore I will give him a portion with the great, because he hath poured out his soul unto death,' &c., ' and bare the sins of many,' Isa. liii. 12. Doubtless the sufferings of Christ in his soul, together with his body, doth most fully and amply commend and set forth God's great love to poor sinners. Before I close up this particular, take a few testimonies of the fathers, which do witness with us for the sufferings of Christ, both in soul and body.

Christ hath taken off[3] us that which he should offer as proper for us, to redeem us; and whatsoever Christ took off[3] us, he offered; *ergo*, he offered body and soul, for he took both.[4]

Another upon these words, ' My soul is heavy,' saith, '*Anima passionibus obnoxia, divinitas libera,*' His soul was subject to passions, his divinity was free, &c.[5] If nothing were free but his divine nature, then his soul was subject to the proper and immediate passions thereof.

Perspicuum est, sicut corpus flagellatum, ita animam verè doluisse, &c.[6]—It is evident that as his body was whipped, so his soul was verily

---

[1] Tertullian, Contra Marcian., lib. v.   [2] Origen, Hom. 9 in Levit.
[3] Qu. ' of '?—ED.   [4] Ambrose de Incarnat., c. 6.
[5] Concil. Hispalens., ii. c. 13.   [6] Jerome in 53d cap. Isaiah.

and truly grieved, lest some part of Christ's suffering should be true, some part false; *ergo,* Christ's soul as properly and truly suffered as his body. The soul had her proper grief, as the body had whipping; the whipping, then, of the body was not the proper grief of the soul. Whole Christ gave himself, and whole Christ offered himself; *ergo,* he offered his soul, not only to suffer by way of compassion with his body, as it may be answered, but he offered it as a sacrifice, and suffered all passions whatsoever incident to the soul. The same author expounds himself further thus: 'Because this God took whole man, therefore he shewed in truth in himself the passions of whole man; and having a reasonable soul, what infirmities soever of the soul without sin he took and bare.[1] If Christ, then, did take and bear all the passions of the soul without sin, then the proper and immediate grief and anguish thereof, and not the compassion only with the body. To these let me add the consent of the Reformed churches:[2] 'Christ did suffer both in body and soul, and was made like unto us in all things, sin only excepted.'

Thomas [Aquinas] granteth that Christ, *secundum genus, passus est omnem passionem humanam,* in general, suffered all human sufferings, as in his soul heaviness, fear, &c.[3]

Now the testimonies of the fathers, and the consent of the Reformed churches, affirming the same, that Christ was crucified in his soul, and that he gave his soul a price of redemption for our souls. . . . . Who can then doubt of this, but that Christ verily, properly, immediately suffered in his soul, in all the proper passions thereof, as he endured pains and torments in his flesh; and if you please, this may go for an eighth argument to prove that Christ suffered in his soul.

2. Secondly, That the sufferings of Christ in his soul were *very high, and great, and wonderful, both as to the punishment of loss, and as to the punishment of sense;* all which I shall make evident in these four particulars:

[1.] First, *That Jesus Christ did suffer dereliction of God really; that he was indeed deserted and forsaken of God is most evident:* Mat. xxvii. 46, 'My God, my God, why hast thou forsaken me?' But to prevent mistakes in this high point, seriously consider, 1. That I do not mean that there was any such desertion of Christ by God as did dissolve the union of the natures in the person of Christ.[4] For Christ in all his sufferings still remained God and man. Nor, 2, do I mean an absolute desertion in respect of the presence of God. For God was still present with Christ in all his sufferings, and the Godhead did support his humanity in and under his sufferings. But that which I mean is this—that as to the sensible and comforting manifestations of God's presence, thus he was for a time left and forsaken of God. God for a time had taken away all sensible consolation and felt joy from Christ's human soul, that so divine justice might in his sufferings be the more fully satisfied. In this desertion, Christ is not to be looked upon simply as he is in his own person, the Son of

---

[1] Fulgentius ad Thrasimund., lib. iii.   [2] French Confess. Harm., p. 99, § 6.
[3] 3 par., qu. 46, artic. 5.
[4] Forsaken, 1. By denying of protection; 2. By withdrawing of solace: *Non solvit unionem, sed subtraxit visionem,* The union was not dissolved, but the beams, the influence was restrained.—*Leo.*

the Father, Mat. iii. 17, in whom he is always well pleased, Mark i. 11, but as he standeth in the room of sinners, surety and cautioner, paying their debt; in which respect it concerned Christ to be dealt with as one standing in our stead, as one guilty, and paying the debt of being forsaken of God, which we were bound to suffer fully and for ever, if he had not interposed for us. There is between Christ and God, 1. An eternal union natural of the person; 2. Of the Godhead and manhood; 3. Of grace and protection. In this last sense, he means forsaken according to his feeling. Hence he said not, My Father, my Father, but, My God, my God; which words are not words of complaining, but words expressing his grief and sorrow. Our Lord Christ was forsaken, not only of all creature comforts, but that which was worse than all, of his Father's favour, to his present apprehension, left forlorn and destitute for a time, that we might be received for ever. Christ was for a time left and forsaken of God, as David, who in this particular was a type of Christ's suffering, cried out, Ps. xxii. 1, ' My God, my God, why hast thou forsaken me? why art thou so far from my help?' He was indeed really forsaken of God; God did indeed leave him in respect of his sense and feeling.[1] So was Christ truly and really forsaken of God, and not in colour or show, as some affirm. Athanasius, speaking of God's forsaking of Christ, saith, ' All things were done naturally and in truth, not in opinion or show.' [2] Though God did still continue a God to David, yet in David's apprehension and feeling he was forsaken of God. Though God was still a God to Christ, yet as to his feeling he was left of God, to wrestle with God, and to bear the wrath of God, due unto us. Look, as Christ was scourged, that we might not be scourged, so Christ was forsaken, that we might not be forsaken. Christ was forsaken for a time, that we might not be forsaken for ever [Ambrose].

Fevardentius absolutely denies that Christ did truly complain upon the cross that he was forsaken of God; and therefore he thus object-eth and reasoneth: ' If Christ were truly forsaken of God, it would follow that the hypostatical union was dissolved, and that Christ was personally separated from God, for otherwise he could not be forsaken.' [3]

To what he objects we thus reply, *first*, If Christ had been totally and eternally forsaken, the personal union must have been dissolved; but upon this temporal and partial rejection or dereliction there followeth not a personal dissolution, or general dereliction. But *secondly*, As the body of Christ, being without life, was still hypostatically united to the Godhead, so was the soul of Christ, though for a time without feeling of his favour. The dereliction of the one doth no more dissolve the hypostatical union than the death of the other. If life went from the body, and yet the deity was not separated in the personal conse-cration, but only suspended in operation, so the feeling of God's favour, which is the life of the soul, might be intermitted in Christ, and yet the divine union not dissolved. *Thirdly*, Augustine doth well shew

---

[1] ' My God, my God, why hast thou forsaken me.' Christ spake these words that thereby he might draw the Jews to a serious consideration and animadversion of his death and passion, which he underwent, not for his own but for our sins.—*Pet. Gal.*, lib. viii. c. 18, p. 343. [Pet. Galesinus.—G.]

[2] Relinquit Deus dum non relinquit, saith Tertullian.

[3] Fevarden., p. 473, confut 1. [Franciscus Fevardentius.—G.]

how this may be when he saith, *Passio Christi dulcis fuit divinitatis somnus*,[1]—That the passion of Christ was the sweet sleep of his divinity; like as when in sleep the soul is not departed, though the operation thereof be deferred ; so in Christ's sleep upon the cross the Godhead was not separated, though the working power thereof were for a time sequestered.   Look, as the elect members of Christ may be forsaken, though not totally or finally, but *ex parte*, in part and for a time, and yet their election remain firm still ; the same may be the case of our head, that he was *ex parte derelictus*, only in part forsaken, and for a time, always beloved for his own innocency, but for us and in our person, as our pledge and surety, deserted.

There are two kinds of dereliction or forsaking ; one is for a time and in part; so the elect may be, and so Christ was forsaken upon the cross : another which is total, final, and general ; and so neither Christ nor his members never was nor never shall be forsaken.   Christ, in the deepest anguish of his soul, is upheld and sustained by his faith, 'My God, my God,' whereby he sheweth his singular confidence and trust in God, notwithstanding the present sense of his wrath.

Quest. But how can Christ be forsaken of God, himself being God ; for the Father, Son, and Holy Ghost are all three but one and the same God ?   Yea, how can he be forsaken of God, seeing he is the Son of God ? and if the Lord leave not his children, which hope and trust in him, how can he forsake Christ, his only-begotten Son, who depended upon him and his mighty power ?

Ans. 1. First, By God here we are to understand God the Father, the first person of the blessed Trinity.   According to the vulgar and common rule, when God is compared with the Son or Holy Ghost, then the Father is meant by this title God ; not that the Father is more God than the Son—for in dignity all the three persons are equal —but they are distinguished in order only ; and thus the Father is the first person, the Son the second, and the Holy Ghost the third.

Ans. 2. Secondly, Our Saviour's complaint, that he was forsaken, must be understood in regard of his human nature, and not of his Godhead ; although the Godhead and manhood were never severed from the first time of his incarnation ; but the Godhead of Christ, and so the Godhead of the Father, did not shew forth his power in his manhood, but did as it were lie asleep for a time, that the manhood might suffer.

Ans. 3. Thirdly, Christ was not indeed utterly forsaken of God in regard of his human nature, but only as it were forsaken—that is, although there were some few minutes and moments in which he received no sensible consolations from the Deity, yet that he was not utterly forsaken is most clear from this place, where he flees unto the Lord as unto his God, 'My God, my God,' as also from his resurrection the third day.

Ans. 4. Fourthly, Divines say that there are six kinds of dereliction or forsakings :—1. By disunion of person ; and 2. By loss of grace ; and 3. By diminution and weakenings of grace ; and 4. By want of assurance of future deliverance and present support ; and 5. By denial of protection ; and 6. By withdrawing of all solace and

---

[1] August., lib de essen. divin.

comfort. Now it is foolish and impious to think that Christ was forsaken any of the first four ways, for the unity of his person was never dissolved, his graces were never either taken away or diminished, neither was it possible that he should want assurance of future deliverance and present support that was eternal God and Lord of life; but the two last ways he may rightly be said to have been forsaken, in that his Father denied to protect and keep him out of the hands of his cruel, bloody, and merciless enemies, no ways restraining them, but suffering them to do the uttermost that their wicked hearts could imagine, and left him to endure the extremity of their fury and malice; and, that nothing might be wanting to make his sorrows beyond measure sorrowful, withdrew from him that solace and comfort that he was wont to find in God, and removed far from him all things for a little time that might any way lessen and assuage the extremity of his pain.

[2.] Secondly, *That Jesus Christ did feel and suffer the wrath of God which was due unto us for our sins.* The prophet Isaiah, chap. liii. 4, saith, ' That he was plagued and smitten of God'; and ver. 5, ' The chastisement of our peace was upon him.' To be plagued and smitten of God is to feel and suffer the stroke of his wrath; and so to be chastised of God, as to make peace with God or to appease him, is so to suffer the wrath of God as to satisfy God and to remove it. And truly how Christ should possibly escape the feeling of the wrath of God incensed against our sins, he standing as a surety for us with our sins laid upon him, and for them fully to satisfy the justice of God, is not Christianly or rationally imaginable.

And whereas some do object that Christ was always the beloved of his Father, and therefore could never be the object of God's wrath:

I answer, By distinguishing of the person of Christ, whom his Father always loved, and as sustaining our sins, and in our room standing to satisfy the justice of God; and as so the wrath of God fell upon him and he bore it, and so satisfied the justice of God, that we thereby are now delivered from wrath through him. So the apostle, Rom. v. 9, ' Much more, being justified by his blood, we shall be saved from wrath by him;' 1 Thes. i. 10, ' And to wait for his Son from heaven, whom he raised from the dead, even Jesus, which delivered us from the wrath to come.'

It is a groundless conceit of some learned heads, who deny the cause of Christ's agony to be the drinking of that cup of wrath that was given to him by his Father, John xviii. 11, saying that the sight of it only, and of the peril he saw we were in, was the cause of his agony; for the cup was not only shewed unto him, and the great wrath due to our sins set before him, that he should see it and tremble at the apprehension of the danger we were in, but it was poured not only on him, but into him, that he for the sins of his redeemed ones should suffer it sensibly, and drink it, that the bitterness thereof might affect all the powers of his soul and body; for the Scripture does sufficiently testify that not only upon the sight and apprehension of this wrath and curse coming on him the holy human nature did holily abhor it, but also that he submitted to receive it upon the consideration of the divine decree and agreement made upon the price to be paid by him, and that upon the feeling of this wrath, this agony in his soul, the bloody sweat of his body was brought on.[1]

Quest. But how could the pourings forth of the Father's wrath upon his innocent and dear Son consist with his Fatherly love to him ? &c.

Ans. Even as the innocency and holiness of Christ could well consist with his taking upon him the punishment of our sins ; for even the wrath of a just man, inflicting capital punishment on a condemned person, put case it be his own child, can well consist with fatherly affection towards his child suffering punishment. Did you never see a father weep over such a son that he has corrected most severely ? Did you never see a judge shed tears for those very persons that he has condemned ? There is no doubt but wrath and love can well consist in God, in whom affections do not war one with another, nor fight with reason, as it often falls among men ; for the affections ascribed unto God are effects rather of his holy will towards us, than properly called affections in him ; and these effects of God's will about us do always tend to our happiness and blessedness at last, however they are diverse one from another in themselves.

[3.] Thirdly, That Jesus Christ did feel and suffer *the very torments of hell, though not after a hellish manner.* I readily grant that Jesus Christ did not locally descend into hell, to suffer there amongst the damned, neither did he suffer hellish darkness, nor the flames of hell, nor the worm that never dies, nor final despair, nor guilt of conscience, nor gnashing of teeth, nor impatient indignation, nor eternal separation from God. These things were absolutely inconsistent with the holiness, purity, and dignity of his person, and with the office of a mediator and redeemer. But yet I say that our Lord Jesus Christ did suffer in his soul for our sins such pain, horror, terror, agony, and consternation, as amounted unto *cruciatus infernales*, and are in Scripture called ' The sorrows of hell.' ' The sorrows of hell did compass me about,' Ps. xviii. 5, or the cords of hell did compass me about, such as wherewith they bind malefactors when they are led forth to execution. Now these sorrows, these cords of hell, were the things that extorted from him that passionate expostulation, ' My God, my God, why hast thou forsaken me ?' Mat. xxvii. 46. Christ's sufferings were unspeakable, and somewhat answerable to the pains of hell. Hence the Greek Litany, ' By thine unknown sufferings, good Lord deliver us,' Διὰ ἀγνώστων σοῦ παθηματων. Funinus, an Italian martyr, being asked by one why he was so merry at his death, sith Christ himself was so sorrowful ; ' Christ,' said he, ' sustained in his soul all the sorrows and conflicts with hell and death due to us ;' by whose sufferings we are delivered from sorrow and the fear of them all.[2] It was a great saying of a very learned man, that setting iniquity and eternity of punishment aside, which Christ might not sustain, Christ did more vehemently and sharply feel the wrath of God than ever any man did or shall, no not any person reprobated and damned excepted ; and certainly the reason annexed to prove this expression is very weighty, because all the wrath that was due for all the sins of the elect, all whose sins

[1] Heb. v. 7; Mat. xxvi. 38, 39, 42, 44; 1 Cor. vi. 20, and vii. 23.
[2] [Foxe] Acts and Mon., fol. 853.

were laid on Christ, Isa. liii. 6, was greater than the wrath which belonged to any one sinner, though damned for his personal sinning: and besides this, if you do seriously consider those sufferings of Christ in his agony in the garden, you may by them conjecture what hellish torments Christ did suffer for us. In that agony of his, he was afraid and amazed, and fell flat on the ground, Mat. xiv. 33, 34. He began to be sore amazed, and to be very heavy; and saith unto them, ' My soul is exceeding sorrowful unto death,' Luke xxii. 44; and his sweat was as it were great drops of blood falling down to the ground. He did sweat clotted blood to such abundance, that it streamed through his apparel, and did wet the ground ; which dreadful agony of Christ, how it could arise from any other cause than the sense of the wrath of God, parallel to that in hell, I know not.

Orthodox divines do generally take Christ's sufferings in his soul, and the detaining his body in the grave, put in as the close and last part of Christ's sufferings, as the true meaning of that expression, 'He descended into hell,' not only because these pains which Christ suffered both in body and soul were due to us in full measure, but also because that which Christ in point of torment and vexation suffered was in some respect of the same kind with the torment of the damned. For the clearing of this, consider, that in the punishment of the damned there are these three things: 1. The perverse disposition of the mind of the damned in their sufferings; 2. The duration and perpetuity of their punishment; and 3. The punishment itself, tormenting soul and body. Of these three, the first two could have no place in Christ : not the first, because he willingly offered himself a sacrifice for our sins, and upon agreement paid the ransom fully, Heb. ix. 14, and x. 5-8 ; not the second, because he could no longer be held under sorrows and sufferings than he had satisfied divine justice, and paid the price that he was to lay down, Acts ii. 24. And his infinite excellency and glory made his short sufferings to be of infinite worth, and equivalent to our everlasting sufferings, 1 Pet. ii. 24 ; 1 Cor. vi. 20. The third, then, only remaineth, which was the real and sensible torments of his soul and body, which he did really feel and experience when he was upon the cross. O sirs! what need you question Christ's undergoing of hellish pains, when all the pains, torments, curse, and wrath which was due to the elect did fall on Christ, and lie on Christ till divine justice was fully satisfied. Though Christ did not suffer eternal death for sinners, yet he suffered that which was equivalent, and therefore the justice of God is by his death wholly appeased.

It is good seriously to ponder upon these scriptures : Ps. xviii. 51, ' The sorrows of hell did compass me about;' Ps. lxxxviii. 31, 'My soul is filled with evil, and my life draweth near to hell ;' Ps. lxxxvi. 13, ' Thou hast delivered my soul from the nethermost hell.' In these places the prophet speaks in the person of Christ, and the Papists themselves do confess that the Hebrew word *sheol*, that is here used, is taken for hell properly, and not for the grave ; therefore these places do strongly conclude for the hellish sorrows or sufferings of Christ. So Acts ii. 27, ' Thou wilt not leave my soul in hell.' If Christ's soul be not left or forsaken in hell, yet it follows it was in hell; not that Christ did feel the sorrows of hell after death, but that he did feel the very sorrows of hell in his soul while he lived. Certainly the whole punishment of body and soul which was due unto us, Christ our Redeemer was in general to suffer and satisfy for in his own person; but the torments and terrors of hell, and the vehement sense of God's wrath, are that punishment which did belong to the soul; *ergo*, Christ did suffer the torments and terrors of hell. By the whole punishment you are to understand the whole kind or substance of the punishment, not all the circumstances, and the very same manner. The whole punishment then is the whole kind of punishment—that is, in body and soul—which Christ ought to have suffered, though not in the same manner and circumstance. 1. Neither for the place of hell locally; nor 2. For the time eternally; nor 3. For the manner sinfully. When we say Christ was to suffer our whole punishment, all such punishments as cannot be suffered without sin, as desperation [and] final reprobation, are manifestly excepted. Christ did bear all our punishment, though not as we should have borne it; that is, 1. Sinfully; 2. Eternally; 3. Hellishly. But he did so bear all our punishment as to finish all upon the cross; and in such sort as God's justice was satisfied, his person not disgraced, nor his holiness defiled, and yet man's salvation fully perfected, Col. ii. 14, 15; Heb. ix. 14, and x. 15. We constantly affirm that Christ did suffer the pains of hell in his soul, with these three restrictions:—1. That there be neither indignity offered to his royal person; 2. Nor injury to his holy nature; 3. Nor impossibility to his glorious work. All such pains of hell then as Christ might have suffered:—1. His person not dishonoured; 2. His nature with sin not defiled; 3. His work of our redemption not hindered, we do steadfastly believe were sustained by our blessed Saviour. Consider a few things.

First, Consider *the adjuncts of hell*, which are these four: 1. The place, which is infernal; 2. The time, which is perpetual; 3. The darkness, which is unspeakable; 4. The ministers and tormentors—the spirits and devils, which are irreconcilable. Now these adjuncts of hell Christ is freed from. For the dignity of his person, it was not fit that the Son of God, the heir of heaven, should be shut up in hell, or that he should for ever be tormented, who is never from God's presence sequestered, or that the light of the world should be closed up in darkness, or that he who bindeth the evil spirits should be bound by them, &c.

Secondly, Consider *the effects, or rather the defects, of hell*, which are chiefly these two: First, The deprivation of all virtue, grace, holiness; Secondly, The real possession of all vice, impiety, blasphemy, &c. Now the necessity of the work of Christ doth exempt him from these effects; for if he had been either void of grace, or possessed with vice, he could not have been the Redeemer of poor lost souls; for the want of virtue he could not have redeemed others; for the presence of sin he should have been redeemed himself; and from fretting indignation and fearful desperation, the piety and sanctity of his nature doth preserve him, who, being without sin, could neither by indignation displease his Father, nor by desperation destroy himself. So that, if you consider either the adjuncts of hell or the effects, then I say we do remove all them as far off from the holy soul of Christ as heaven is from hell, or the east from the west, or darkness from light, &c.

Thirdly, Consider *the punishment itself.* Now, concerning this, we say that our blessed Saviour, as in himself he bare all the sins of the elect: so he also suffered the whole punishment of body and soul in general that was due unto us, for the same which we should have endured if he had not satisfied for it; and so consequently we affirm that he felt the anguish of soul and horror of God's wrath, and so in soul entered into the torments of hell for us, sustained them and vanquished them. One speaking in honour of Christ's passion, saith, *Cum iram Dei sibi propositum videret,* When he saw the wrath of God set before him, presenting himself before God's tribunal loaden with the sins of the whole world, it was necessary for him to fear the deep bottomless pit of death.[1] Again saith the same author,[2] *Cum species Christo objecta est,* &c., Such an object being offered to Christ's view, as though God being set against him, he were appointed to destruction; he was with horror affrighted, which was able a hundred times to have swallowed up all mortal creatures, but he, by the wonderful power of his Spirit, escaped with victory. ' What dishonour was it to our Saviour Christ,' saith another,[3] ' to suffer that which was necessary for our redemption,'—namely, that torment of hell which we had deserved, and which the justice of God required that he should endure for our redemption; or rather, what is more to the honour of Christ, than that he vouchsafed to descend into hell for us, and to abide that bitter pain which we had deserved to suffer eternally; and what may rather be called hell than the anguish of soul which he suffered, when, he being yet God, complained that he was forsaken of God? O sirs, this we need not fear to confess, that Christ, bearing our sins in himself upon the cross, did feel himself during that combat as rejected and forsaken of God and accursed for us, and the flames of his Father's wrath burning within him; so that to the honour of Christ's passion we confess that our blessed Redeemer refused no part of our punishment, but endured the very pains of hell, so far as they tended not neither to the derogation of his person, deprivation of his nature, destruction of his office, &c.

Here it may be queried whether the Lord Jesus Christ underwent the *idem*, the very self-same punishment that we should have undergone, or only the *tantundem*, that which did amount and was equivalent thereunto? To which I answer, that in different respects both may be affirmed. The punishment which Christ endured, if it be considered in its substance, kind, or nature, so it was the same with that the sinner himself should have undergone; but if it be considered with respect to certain circumstances, adjuncts, or accidents which attend that punishment, as inflicted upon the sinner, so it was but equivalent, and not the same. The punishment due to the sinner was death, the curse of the law, upon the breach of the first covenant. Now this Christ underwent, for 'he was made a curse for us,' Gal. iii. 13. The adjuncts attending this death were the eternity of it, desperation going along with it, &c. These Christ was freed from, the dignity of his person supplying the former, the sanctity of his person securing him against the latter; therefore in reference unto these, and to some

---

[1] Calvin, in Mat. xxvi. 39.   [2] Calvin, in Mat. xxvii. 46.
[3] Fulk. in Act. ii. sec. 11. [Fulke or Fulkius or Fulcones.—G.]

other things already mentioned, it was but the *tantundem*, not the *idem ;* but suppose there had been nothing of sameness, nothing beyond equivalency in what Christ suffered, yet that was enough, for it was not required that Christ should suffer every kind of curse which is the effect of sin, but in the general accursed death. Look, as in his fulfilling of the law for us, it was not necessary that he should perform every holy duty that the law requireth ; for he could not perform that obedience which magistrates or married persons are bound to do—it is enough that there was a fulfilling of it in the general for us : so here it was not necessary that Jesus Christ should undergo in every respect the same punishment which the offender himself was liable unto ; but if he shall undergo so much as may satisfy the law's threatenings, and vindicate the lawgiver in his truth, justice, and righteous government, that was enough. Now that was unquestionably done by Christ.

Object. 1. But some may object and say, How could Christ suffer the pains of the second death without disunion of the Godhead from the manhood ? For the Godhead could not die. Or what interest had Christ's Godhead in his human sufferings, to make them both so short and so precious and satisfactory to divine justice for the sins of so many sinners, especially when we consider that God cannot suffer ?

Ans. 1. I answer, It followeth not that because Christ is united into one person with God, that therefore he did not suffer the pains of hell; for by the same reason he should not have suffered in his body, for the union of his person could have preserved him from sufferings in the one as well as in the other, and neither God, angels, nor men compelled him to undertake this difficult and bloody work, but his own free and unspeakable love to mankind, as himself declares, John x. 17, ' Therefore my Father loves me, because I lay down my life;' ver. 18, ' No man taketh it from me, but I lay it down of myself.' If Christ had been constrained to suffer, then both men and angels might fear and tremble; but as one [Bernard] saith well, *Voluntas sponte morientis placuit Deo,* The willingness of him that died pleased God, who offered himself to be the Redeemer of fallen man, Isa. liii. 12 ; Ps. xl. 7, 8 ; Heb. x. 9, 10.

Ans. 2. But secondly, I answer from 1 John iii. 16, ' Hereby perceive we the love of God, because he laid down his life for us.' The person dying was God, else his person could have done us no good. The person suffering must be God as well as man, but the Godhead suffered not. As if you shoot off a cannon in the bright air, the air suffers, but the light of it suffers not. Actions and passions belong to persons. Nothing less than that person who is God-man could bear the brunt of the day, satisfy divine justice, pacify divine wrath, bring in an everlasting righteousness, and make us happy for ever. But,

Ans. 3. Thirdly, I answer thus, Albeit the passion of the human nature could not so far reach the Godhead of Christ, that it should in a physical sense suffer, which, indeed, is impossible, yet these sufferings did so affect the person, that it may truly be said that God suffered, and by his blood bought his people to himself; for albeit the proper and formal subject of physical sufferings be only the human nature, yet the principal subject of sufferings, both in a physical and moral sense, is Christ's person, God and man, from the dignity whereof the worth and excellency of all sorts of sufferings, the merit and the satisfactory sufficiency of the price did flow, Acts xx. 28; 1 Pet. i. 18–20; 1 Cor. vi. 20, and vii. 23.

O sirs! you must seriously consider, that though Christ as God in his Godhead could not suffer in a physical sense, yet in a moral sense he might suffer and did suffer. For he being 'in the form of God, thought it not robbery to be equal with God, but made himself of no reputation, and took upon him the form of a servant, and was made in the likeness of men; and being found in fashion as a man, he humbled himself, and became obedient unto death, even the death of the cross,' Phil. ii. 6–8. Oh, who can sum up the contradictions, the railings, the revilings, the contempts, the despisings and calumnies that Christ met with from sinners, yea, from the worst of sinners!

Object. 2. But how could so low a debasing of the Son of man, or of the human nature assumed by Christ, consist with the majesty of the person of the Son of God?

Ans. We must distinguish those things in Christ, which are proper to either of the two natures, from those things which are ascribed to his person in respect of either of the natures or both the natures; for infirmity, physical suffering, or mortality are proper to the human nature. The glory of power, and grace, and mercy, and super-excellent majesty, and such like, are proper to the Deity; but the sufferings of the human nature are so far from diminishing the glory of the divine nature, that they do manifest the same, and make it appear more clearly and gloriously; for by how much the human nature was weakened, depressed, and despised for our sins, for our sakes, by so much the more the love of Christ, God and man in one person toward man, and his mercy, and power, and grace to man, do shine in the eyes of all that judiciously do look upon him.

Object. 3. How could Christ endure hell fire without grievous sins, as blasphemy and despair, &c.?

Ans. 1. I answer, That we may walk safely and without offence, these things must be premised: First, That the sorrows and sufferings of hell be no otherwise attributed to Christ, than as they may stand with the dignity and worthiness of his person, the holiness of his nature, and the performance of the office and work of our redemption.

[1.] First, then, For the soul of Christ to suffer in the local place of hell, to remain in the darkness thereof, and to be tormented with the material flames there, and eternally to be damned, was not for the dignity of his person, to whom for his excellency and worthiness both the place, manner, and time of those torments were dispensed with.

[2.] Secondly, Final rejection and desperation, blasphemy, and the worm of conscience, agreeth not with the holiness of his nature, 'Who was a lamb without a spot,' Heb. ix. 14; 1 Pet. i. 19, and therefore we do not, we dare not ascribe them to him. But,

[3.] Thirdly, Destruction of body and soul, which is the second death, could not fall upon Christ; for this were to have destroyed the work of our redemption, if he had been subject to destruction. But,

[4.] Fourthly and lastly, Blasphemy and despair are no parts of the pains of the damned, but the consequents, and follow the sense of God's wrath in a sinful creature that is overcome by it. But Christ had no sin of his own, neither was he overcome of wrath, and therefore he always held fast his integrity and innocency, Rev. xvi. 9, 11. Despair is an unavoidable companion, attending the pains of the second death, as all reprobates do experience. Desperation is an utter hopelessness of any good, and a certain expectation and waiting on the worst that can befall; and this is the lot and portion of the damned in hell. The wretched sinner in hell, seeing the sentence passed against him, God's purpose fulfilled, never to be reversed, the gates of hell made fast upon him, and a great gulf fixed betwixt hell and heaven, which renders his escape impossible; he now gives up all, and reckons on nothing but uttermost misery, Luke xvi. 26. Now mark, this despair is not an essential part of the second death, but only a consequent, or, at the most, an effect occasioned by the sinner's view of his irremediless, woeful condition. But this neither did nor could possibly befall the Lord Jesus. He was able, by the power of his Godhead, both to suffer and to satisfy and to overcome; therefore he expected a good issue, and knew that the end should be happy, and that he should not be ashamed, Isa. l. 6, 7, &c.; Ps. xvi. 9, 10; Acts ii. 26, 28, 31. Though a very shallow stream would easily drown a little child, there being no hope of escape for it unless one or another should step in seasonably to prevent it, yet a man that is grown up may groundedly hope to escape out of a far more deep and dangerous place, because by reason of his stature, strength, and skill he could wade or swim out. Surely the wrath of the Almighty, manifested in hell, is like the vast ocean, or some broad, deep river; and therefore when the sinful sons and daughters of Adam, which are without strength, Rom. v. 6, are hurled into the midst of it, they must needs lie down in their confusion, as altogether hopeless of deliverance or escaping. But this despair could not seize upon Jesus Christ, because, although his Father took him and cast him into the sea of his wrath, so that all the billows of it went over him, Isa. lxiii. 1–3, seq., yet being the mighty God, with whom nothing is impossible, he was very able to pass through that sea of wrath and sorrow, which would have drowned all the world, and come safe to shore.

Object. 4. But when did Christ suffer hellish torments? They are inflicted after death, not usually before it; but Christ's soul went straight after death into paradise. How else could he say to the penitent thief, ' This day shalt thou be with me in paradise' ? Now, to this objection I shall give these following answers:

Ans. 1. First, *That Christ's soul, after his passion upon the cross, did not really and locally descend into the place of the damned, may be thus made evident:*

[1.] First, All the evangelists, and so Luke among the rest, intending to make an exact narrative of the life and death of Christ, hath set down at large his passion, death, burial, resurrection, and ascension; and besides, they make rehearsal of very small circumstances; therefore we may safely conclude, that they would never have omitted Christ's local descent into the place of the damned, if there had been any such thing. Besides, the great end why they penned this history was, that we might believe that 'Jesus Christ is the Son of God; and that thus believing we might have life everlasting,' John xx. 31. Now there could not have been a greater matter for the confirmation of our faith than this, that Jesus, the son of Mary, who went down to the place of the damned, returned thence to live in all happiness and blessedness for ever. But,

[2.] Secondly, If Christ did go into the place of the damned, then he went either in soul, or in body, or in his Godhead. Not in his Godhead, for that could not descend, because it is everywhere, and his body was in the grave; and as for his soul, it went not to hell, but immediately after his death it went to paradise—that is, the third heaven, a place of joy and happiness: 'This day shalt thou be with me in paradise,' Luke xxiii. 43; which words of Christ must be understood of his manhood or soul, and not of his Godhead; for they are an answer to a demand, and therefore unto it they must be suitable. The thief makes his request, 'Lord, remember me when thou comest into thy kingdom,' ver. 42; to which Christ answers, 'Verily I say unto thee, To-day shalt thou be with me in paradise.' 'I shall,' saith Christ, 'this day enter into paradise, and there shalt thou be with me.' Now, there is no entrance but in regard of his soul or manhood, for the Godhead, which is at all times in all places, cannot be properly said to enter into a place, Ps. cxxxix. 7, 13; Jer. xxiii. 23, 24. But,

[3.] Thirdly, When Christ saith, 'To-day shalt thou be with me in paradise,' he doth intimate, as some observe, a resemblance which is between the first and second Adam. The first Adam quickly sinned against God, and was as quickly cast out of paradise by God. Christ, the second Adam, having made a perfect and complete satisfaction to the justice of God, and the law of God, for man's sin, must immediately enter into paradise, Heb. ix. 26, 28, and x. 14. Now to say that Christ, in soul, descended locally into hell, is to abolish this analogy between the first and second Adam. But,

Ans. 2. Secondly, *It is not impossible that the pains of the second death should be suffered in this life.* Time and place are but circumstances. The main substance of the second death is the bearing of God's fierce wrath and indignation. Divine favour shining upon a man in hell, would turn hell into a heaven. All sober, seeing, serious Christians will grant, that the true, though not the full joys of heaven may be felt and experienced in this life: 1 Pet. i. 8, 'Whom having not seen, ye love; in whom, though now ye see him not, yet believing, ye rejoice with joy unspeakable and full of glory,' or glorious; either because this their rejoicing was a taste of their future glory, or because it made them glorious in the eyes of men. The original word, δεδο-ξαμένη, is glorified already; a piece of God's kingdom and heaven's happiness aforehand. Ah, how many precious saints, both living and dying, have cried out, Oh the joy! the joy! the inexpressible joy that I find in my soul! Eph. ii. 6, 'He hath made us sit together in heavenly places, in Christ Jesus.' What is this else, but even while we live, by faith to possess the very joys of heaven on this side heaven! Now look, as the true joys of heaven may be felt on this side heaven, so the true, though not the full pains of hell, may be felt on this side hell ; and doubtless Cain, Judas, Julian, Spira, and others have found it so.   That father hit the mark, who said, *Judicis in mente tua sedes; ibi Deus adest, accusator conscientia, tortor timor*, The judge's tribunal-seat is in thy soul, God sitteth there as judge, thy conscience is the accuser, and fear is the tormentor.[1]   Now if there be in the soul a judge, an accuser, and a tormentor, then certainly there is a true taste of the torments of hell on this side hell.

Ans. 3. Thirdly, *The place hell is no part of the payment.* The laying down of the price makes the satisfaction. This is all that is spoken and threatened to Adam, ' Thou shalt die the death,' Gen. ii. 17; and this may be suffered here. The wicked go to hell as their prison, because they can never pay their debts, otherwise the debt may as well be paid in the market as the jail.[2]   Now Christ did discharge all his people's debts in the days of his flesh, when he offered up strong cries and tears, Heb. v. 7, and not after death. Look, as a king entering into prison to loose the prisoners' chains, and to pay their debts, is said to have been in prison ; so our Lord Jesus Christ, by his soul's sufferings, which is the hell he entered into, hath released us of our pains and chains, and paid our debts, and in this sense he may be said to have entered into hell, though he never actually entered into the local place of the damned, which is properly called hell ; for in that place there is neither virtue nor goodness, holiness nor happiness, and therefore the holiness of Christ's person would never suffer him to descend into such a place. In the local place of heaven and hell, it is not possible for any neither to be at once, nor yet at sundry times successively, for there is no passing from heaven to hell, or from hell to heaven, Luke xvi. 26. The place of suffering is but a circumstance in the business. Hell, the place of the damned, is no part of the debt, therefore neither is suffering there locally any part of the payment of it, no more than a prison is any part of an earthly debt, or of the payment of it. The surety may satisfy the creditor in the place appointed for payment, or in the open court, which being done, the debtor and surety both are acquitted, that they need not go to prison. If either of them go to prison, it is because they do not or cannot pay the debt ; for all that justice requires is to satisfy the debt, to the which the prison is merely extrinsecal. Even so the justice of God cannot be satisfied for the transgression of the law, but by the death of the sinner ; but it doth not require that this should be done in the place of the damned. The wicked go to prison because they do not, they cannot, make satisfaction ; otherwise Christ, having fully discharged the debt, needed not go to prison.

Object. 5. But the pains and torments that are due to man's sins are to be everlasting, and how then can Christ's short sufferings countervail them ?

Ans. 1. That Christ's sufferings in his soul and body were equivalent to it ; although, to speak properly, eternity is not of the essence

---

[1] Augustine in Ps. lvii.

[2] Peter saith, the devils are cast down to hell, and kept in chains of darkness, 2 Pet. ii. 4.   And Paul calls the devil the prince that ruleth in the air, Eph. ii. 2.   The air then is the devil's hell.   Well, then, seeing this air is the devil's present hell, we may safely conclude that hell may be in this present world ; and therefore it is neither impossible nor improbable that the cross was Christ's hell.

of death, which is the reward of sin and threatened by God; but it is accidental, because man thus dying is never able to satisfy God, therefore, seeing he cannot pay the last farthing, he is for ever kept in prison, Mat. xviii. 28, 35. Look, as eternal death hath in it eternity and despair necessarily in all those that so die, so Christ could not suffer, but what was wanting in duration was supplied—1. By the immensity of his sorrows conflicting with the sense of God's wrath, because of our sins imputed to him, so that he suffered more grief than if the sorrows of all men were put together. Christ's hell-sorrows on the cross were meritorious and fully satisfactory for our everlasting punishment, and therefore in greatness were to exceed all other men's sorrows, as being answerable to God's justice. 2. By the dignity and worth of him that did suffer. Therefore the Scripture calls it the blood of God. The damned must bear the wrath of God to all eternity, because they can never satisfy the justice of God for sin. Therefore they must lie by it world without end. But Christ hath made an infinite satisfaction in a finite time, by undergoing that fierce battle with the wrath of God, and getting the victory in a few hours, which is equivalent to the creatures bearing it and grappling with it everlastingly. This length or shortness of durance is but a circumstance, not of any necessary consideration in this case. Suppose a man indebted £100, and likely to lie in prison till he shall pay it, yet utterly unable, if another man comes and lays down the money on two hours' warning, is not this as well or better done ? that which may be done to as good or better purpose in a short time, what need is there to draw it out at length ? The justice of the law did not require that either the sinner or his surety should suffer the eternity of hell's torments, but only their extremity. It doth abundantly counterpoise the eternity of the punishment, that the person which suffered was the eternal God. Besides, it was impossible that he should be detained under the sorrows of death, Acts ii. 24. And if he had been so detained, then he had not 'spoiled principalities and powers, nor triumphed over them,' Col. ii. 15, but had been overcome, and so had not attained his end. But,

Ans. 2. Secondly, The pains of hell which Christ suffered, though they were not infinite in time, yet were they of an infinite price and value for the dignity of the person that suffered them. Christ's temporal enduring of hellish sorrows was as effectual and meritorious as if they had been perpetual. The dignity of Christ's person did bear him out in that which was not meet for him to suffer, nor fit in respect of our redemption; for if he should have suffered eternally, our redemption could never have been accomplished. But for him to suffer in soul as he did in body, was neither derogatory to his person nor prejudicial to his work. Infinitely in time Christ was not to suffer. As one well observes,[1] Christ died *secundum tempus*, in time, or according to time. *Tempora in mundo sunt*, &c., Times are in the world where the sun riseth and setteth. Unto this time he died. But where there is no time, there he was found, not only living, but conquering. Christ, God-man, suffered punishment in measure infinite, and therefore there is no ground why he should endure it

[1] Ambrose in 5 ad Rom. vi.

eternally; and indeed it was impossible that Christ should be holden of death, Acts ii. 24, because he was both the Lord of life and the Lord's Holy One, 1 Cor. ii. 8; Acts ii. 27. But,

Ans. 3. Thirdly, If the measure of a man's punishment were infinite, the duration needs not be infinite. Sinful man's measure of punishment is finite, and therefore the duration of his punishment must be infinite, because the punishment must be answerable to the infinite evil of sin committed against an infinite God. O sirs, continual imprisonment in hell arises from man's not being able to pay the price; for could he pay the debt in one year, he needs not lie two years in prison. Now the debt is the first and second death; and because sinful man cannot pay it in any time, he must endure it eternally. But now Christ has laid down ready pay upon the nail to the full for all his chosen ones, and therefore it is not required of him that he should suffer for ever, neither can it stand with the holiness or justice of God to hold him under the second death, he having paid the debt to the utmost farthing. Now that he hath fully paid the debt himself, witnesseth John, chap. xix. 30, saying 'when he had received the vinegar, It is finished;' so ver. 28, 'After this, Jesus knowing that all things were accomplished.' Though there are many interpretations given of this place by Augustine, Chrysostom, Jansenius, and others, yet doubtless this alone will hold water—viz., that the heavy wrath of the Lord which did pursue Christ, and the second death which filled him with grievous terrors, is now over and past, and man's redemption finished. He speaketh here of that which presently should be, and in the yielding up his ghost was accomplished.

And thus you see that Jesus Christ did feel and suffer the very torments of hell, though not after a hellish manner; and you see also that Christ did not locally descend into hell. Shall we make a few inferences from hence:

1. First, then, Oh, how should these sad sufferings of Christ for us endear Christ to us! Oh, what precious thoughts should we have of him! Ps. cxxxvi. 17, 18. Oh, how should we prize him! how should we honour him! how should we love him! and how should we be swallowed up in the admiration of him! As his love to us has been matchless, so his sufferings for us has been matchless. I have read of Nero, that he had a shirt made of a salamander's skin, so that if he did walk through the fire in it, it would keep him from burning. So Christ is the true salamander's skin that will keep the soul from everlasting burnings, Isa. xxxiii. 14; and therefore well may Christians cry out with that martyr, [Lambert], 'None but Christ, none but Christ.' Tigranes, in Xenophon, coming to redeem his father and friends, with his wife, that were taken prisoners by Cyrus, was asked among other things, what ransom he would give for his wife. He answered, 'He would redeem her liberty with his own life;' but having prevailed, as they returned together, every one commended Cyrus for a goodly man; and Tigranes would needs know of his wife, 'What she thought of him.' 'Truly,' said she, 'I cannot tell, for I did not so much as look on him, or see him.' 'Whom then,' said he, wondering, 'did you look upon?' 'Whom should I look upon,' replied she, 'but him that would have redeemed my liberty

with his own life?' So every believer should esteem nothing worth a looking on, but that Jesus who hath redeemed him with his own blood, 1 Cor. vi. 20; Acts xx. 28; 1 Pet. i. 18, 19. Plutarch tells us,[1] ' That when Titus Flaminius had freed the poor Grecians from the bondage with which they had been long ground by their oppressions, and the herald was to proclaim in their audience the articles of peace he had concluded for them, they so pressed upon him, not being half of them able to hear, that he was in great danger to have lost his life in the press; at last, reading them a second time, when they came to understand distinctly how that their case stood, they so shouted for joy, crying σώτηρ, σώτηρ, a saviour, a saviour, that they made the very heavens ring again with their acclamations, and the very birds fall down astonished.' And all that night the poor Grecians, with instruments of music, and songs of praise, danced and sang about his tent, extolling him as a god that had delivered them. But oh, then, what infinite cause have we to exalt and cry up our dear Lord Jesus, who by the hellish sorrows that he suffered for us, hath freed us from that more dreadful bondage of sin, Satan, and wrath that we lay under! Oh, prize that Jesus! Oh, exalt that Christ! Oh, extol that Saviour, who has saved you from that eternal wrath that all the angels in heaven, and all the men on earth could never have saved you from! The name of Jesus, saith one, [Chrysostom,] hath a thousand treasures of joy and comfort in it, and is therefore used by Paul five hundred times, as some have observed. The name of a Saviour, saith another, [Bernard,] ' is honey in the mouth, and music in the ears, and a jubilee in the heart,' *Dulce nomen Christi.* Were Christ in your bosom as a flower of delight, for he is a whole paradise of delight, saith one, [Justin Martyr.] ' I had rather,' saith another, [Luther,] ' be in hell with Christ, than in heaven without him, for Christ is the crown of crowns, the glory of glories, and the heaven of heaven.' One saith, [Austin,] ' that he would willingly go through hell to Christ.' Another saith, [Bernard,] ' he had rather be in his chimney-corner with Christ, than in heaven without him.' One cried out, ' I had rather have one Christ than a thousand worlds.' Jesus, in the China tongue, signifies the rising sun, and such a rising sun was he to Julius Palmer, that when all concluded that he was dead, being turned as black as a coal in the fire, at last he moved his scorched lips, and was heard to say, ' Sweet Jesus,' Mal. iv. 2. It was an excellent answer of one of the martyrs, when he was offered riches and honours if he would recant: ' Do but,' said he, ' offer me somewhat that is better than my Lord Jesus Christ, and you shall see what I will say to you.' Now, oh that the hellish sorrows and sufferings of Christ for us, might raise in all our hearts such a high estimation, and such a deep admiration, as hath been raised in those worthies last mentioned! It was a sweet prayer of him who thus prayed, ' Lord, make thy Son dear, very dear, exceeding dear, and only dear and precious to me.' Whenever we seriously think of the great and sore sufferings of Christ, it will be good to pray as he prayed. But,

2. Secondly, If Jesus Christ did feel and suffer the very torments of hell, though not after a hellish manner, then let me infer that certainly

[1] Plutarch in vita Tit. Flam.

there is a hell, a place of torment provided and prepared for all wicked and ungodly persons.[1] Danæus reckons up no less than nineteen several sorts of heretics that denied it; and are there not many erroneous and deluded persons that stoutly and daily assert that there is no hell but what men feel in their own consciences? Ah, how many are there that rejoice to do evil, and delight in their abominations, and take pleasure in unrighteousness![2] But could men do thus, durst men do thus, did they really believe that hell was prepared and fitted for them, and that the fiery lake was but a little before' them? Heaven is a place where all is joyful, and hell is a place where all is doleful. In heaven there is nothing but happiness, and in hell there is nothing but heaviness, nothing but endless, easeless, and remediless torments. Did men believe this, how could they go so merrily on in the way to hell? Cato once said to Cæsar, *Credo quæ de inferis dicuntur falsa esse existimas*, I believe that thou thinkest all that is said of hell to be false and fabulous. So I may say to many in this day, Surely you think that all that is spoken and written of hell is but a story. Don't you look upon the people of God to be of all men the most miserable, and yourselves of all men the most happy? Yes! Oh, but how can this be, did you really believe that there was a heaven for the righteous and a hell for the wicked? It is an Italian proverb, *Qui Venetias non vidit, non credit*, &c., He who hath not seen Venice will not believe; and he who hath not lived some time there doth not understand what a city it is. This in a sense is true of hell. But now for the *Quod sit*, that there is a hell, that there is such a place of misery prepared and appointed for the wicked, I shall briefly demonstrate against the high atheists and Socinians of this day, and therefore thus,

[1.] First, *God created angels and men after his own image.* Man must be so much honoured as to be made like God; and no creature must be so much honoured as to be made like man. The pattern after which man was made is sometimes called image alone. So 'God created man in his own image, in the image of God created he him,' Gen. i. 27. Sometimes likeness alone: Gen. v. 1, 'In the day that God created man, in the likeness of God made he him.' Sometimes both: Gen. i. 26, ' Let us make man in our image, after our likeness;' which makes a prudent interpreter think that when they are joined it is by hendiadys, and that the Holy Ghost meaneth an image most like his own.[3] It is exceeding much for man's honour that he is an epitome of the world, an abridgment of other creatures, partaking with the stones in being, with the stars in motion, with the plants in growing, with the beasts in sense, and with angels in science. But his being made after God's image is far more. You know, when great men erect a stately building, they cause their own picture to be hung upon it, that spectators may know who was the chief founder of it. So when God had created the fabric of this world, the last thing

[1] All the hell Socinians grant is annihilation, by reason it is said, they shall be destroyed, *vide* Socinus, Racov[ian] Cat[echism], Crellius, Biddle, Richardson, &c.
[2] Jer. xi. 15; Prov. ii. 14; Isa. lxv. 3; 2 Thes. ii. 11; Mat. xxv. 41; Isa. xxx. 33.
[3] Andr. Rivet, in Gen. Exercit. 4. *Nihil est in mæcrocosmo magnum præter microcosmum*, There is nothing in the vast world of creatures truly great, except the little world of man.—*Favorinus.* [It takes another form—There is nothing great on earth but man, and there is nothing great in man but mind.—G.]

he did was the setting up his own picture in it, creating man after his own image. When the great Creator went about that noble work, that prime piece of making of man, he doth, as it were, call a solemn council of the sacred persons in the Trinity: 'And God said, Let us make man in our image,' &c., Gen. i. 26. Man before his fall was the best of creatures, but since his fall he is become the worst of creatures.[1] He that was once the image of God, the glory of Paradise, the world's lord, and the Lord's darling, is now become an abomination to God, a burden to heaven, a plague to the world, and a slave to Satan. When man first came out of God's mint he did shine most gloriously, as being bespangled with holiness and clad with the royal robe of righteousness; his understanding was filled with knowledge; his will with uprightness; his affections with holiness, &c. But yet, being a mutable creature, and subject to temptations, Satan quickly stripped him of his happiness, and cheated and cozened him of his imperial crown—as we use to do children—with an apple. If God had created angels and men immutable, he had created them gods and not creatures; but being made mutable we know they did fall from their primitive purity and glory; and we know that out of the whole host of angels he kept some from falling; and when all mankind was fallen he redeemed some by his Son. Now mark, as he shews mercy upon some in their salvation, so it is meet that he should glorify his justice upon others in their condemnation, Rom. vii. 21-23. And because there must be distinct places for the exercise of the one and for the execution of the other, which are in God equally infinite by an irrecoverable [2] decree from the foundation of the world, a glorious habitation was prepared for the one, and a most hideous dungeon for the other. 'These shall go into everlasting punishment, and the righteous into life eternal,' Mat. xxv. 46; yea, so certain are both these places that they were of old prepared for that very purpose. 'Inherit the kingdom prepared for you from the foundation of the world;' and so, 'Depart, ye cursed, into everlasting fire prepared for the devil and his angels,' ver. 41. Look, as God foresaw the different estates and conditions of men and angels, so he provided for them distinct and different places. Doubtless, hell was constituted before angels or men fell. Hell was framed before sin was hatched, as heaven was formed and fitted before any of the inhabitants were produced. But,

[2.] Secondly, That there is a hell, *both the Old and New Testament doth clearly and fully testify.* Take some instances: Ps. ix. 17, 'The wicked shall be turned into hell, and all the nations that forget God.' In the Hebrew there are two 'intos,' 'into, into' hell; that is, 'The wicked shall certainly be turned into the nethermost hell;' yea, they shall forcibly be turned into the lowest and darkest place in hell.[3] God will, as it were, with both hands thrust him into hell. If Sheol here signify the grave only, what punishment is here threatened to the wicked, which the righteous is not equally liable to? Doubtless, Sheol here is to be taken for that prison or place of torment where

---

[1] Man, saith one, in his creation is angelic; in his corruption diabolical; in his renovation theological; in his translation majestical; an angel in Eden, a devil in the world, a saint in the church, a king in heaven.

[2] = irreversible.—G.

[3] Sheol is often put for the grave, Ps. xvi. 10, but not always.

divine justice detains all those in hold that have all their days rebelled against him, scorned his Son, despised the means of grace, and died in open rebellion against him.[1] The psalmist, saith my author, [Mollerus,] declares the miserable condition of all those who live and die in their sins: '*Æternis punientur pœnis*,' They shall be everlastingly punished. And Musculus reads the place thus: '*Animi impiorum cruciatibus debitis apud inferos punientur*,' The souls of the ungodly shall be punished in hell with deserved torments. Certainly, the very place in which the wicked shall lodge and be tormented to all eternity—viz., hell, the bottomless pit, a dungeon of darkness, a lake of fire and brimstone, a fiery furnace,—will extremely aggravate the dolefulness of their condition.[2] O sirs, were all the water in the sea ink, and every pile of grass a pen, and every hair on all the men's heads in the world the hand of a ready writer, all would be too short graphically to delineate the nature of this dungeon, where all lost souls must lodge for ever. Where is the man who, to gain a world, would lodge one night in a room that is haunted with devils; and is it nothing to dwell in hell with them for ever? So Solomon, Prov. v. 5, saith of the harlot, ' that her feet go down to death, her steps take hold on hell.' Here Sheol is translated hell, and in the judgment of Lavater is well translated too: *Foveam vel infernum passus ejus tenebunt;* which, saith he, is spoken not so much of natural death as of spiritual, and that eternal destruction which followeth thereupon; and he gives this for a reason why we should understand the place so, because whoredom being an abominable sin, defiling the members of the body of Christ, dissolving and making void the covenant between God and man, must needs be accompanied with an equivalent judgment, even excluding those that are guilty thereof, without repentance, the kingdom of heaven, into which pure and undefiled place no unclean thing can enter.[3] And mark those words of the apostle, ' Whoremongers and adulterers God will judge.' If men will not judge them, God himself will, and give them a portion of misery answerable to their transgression.[4] Though the magistrate be negligent in punishing them, yet God will judge them. Sometimes he judges them in this life, by pouring forth of his wrath upon their bodies, souls, consciences, names, and estates; but if he do not thus judge them in this life, yet he will be sure to judge them in the life to come; which Bishop Latimer well understood when he presented to Henry the Eighth, for a New-year's gift, a New Testament, with a napkin, having this posie about it, ' Whoremongers and adulterers God will judge;'[5] yea, he has already adjudged them ' to the lake that burneth with fire and brimstone, which is the second death,' Rev. xxi. 8. ' Nothing,' saith one, ' hath so much enriched hell as beautiful faces.' The Germans have a proverb that ' the pavement of hell is made of the skulls of shaved priests and the glorious crests of gallants.'

---

[1] In tenebras ex tenebris; infeliciter exclusi, infelicius excludendi.—*Augustine*.
[2] *Vide* Bellarmine de Eter. Fœlic.
[3] By death and hell is in this place meant not only temporal death and the visible grave, but also eternal death and hell itself, even the place of the damned.—*The Dutch Annotations*.
[4] 1 Cor. vi. 9, 10; Gal. v. 19–21; Rev. xxi. 27; Heb. xiii. 4.
[5] [Foxe] Act. and Mon., 1594.

Their meaning is, that these sorts of persons being most given up to fleshly lusts and pleasures, they shall be sure to have the lowest place in hell. The harlot's feet go down to death, and her steps take hold on hell.[1] Wantonness brings men to hell. 'Whoremongers shall have their part in the lake which burneth with fire and brimstone,' Rev. xxi. 8. 'For fornication and uncleanness the wrath of God cometh on the children of disobedience,' Col. iii. 5, 6. The adulterer herself goes thither; and is it not fit that her companions in sin should be her companions in misery? 'I will cast her into a bed, and them that commit adultery with her into great tribulation,' Rev. ii. 22. She hastens with sails and oars to hell, and draws her lovers with her. All her courses tend towards hell. Strumpets are the foundations and upholders of hell ; they are the devil's best customers. Oh, the thousands of men and women that are sent to hell for wantonness! Hell would be very thin and empty were it not for these. Other sins are toilsome and troublesome, but wantonness is pleasant, and sends men and women merrily to hell. I have read a story, that one asking the devil which were the greatest sins? he answered, 'Covetousness and lust.' The other asking again, whether perjury and blasphemy were not greater sins? the devil replied, that in the schools of divinity they were the greater sins, but for the increase of his revenues the other were the greater. Bede,[2] therefore, styleth lust, *Filiam diaboli*, 'the daughter of the devil, which bringeth forth many children to him.' Oh that all wantons would take that counsel of Bernard,[3] '*Ardor gehennæ extinguat in te ardorem luxuriæ, major ardor minorem superet;*' let the fire of hell extinguish the fire of lust in thee ; let the greater burning overcome the lesser, 1 Tim. v. 6. Ponder upon that Prov. ix. 18, 'But he knoweth not that the dead are there, and that her guests are in the depths of hell.' To wit, those that are spiritually dead, and that are in the high way to be cut off, either by filthy diseases, or by the rage of the jealous husband, or by the sword of the magistrate, or by some quarrels arising amongst those that are rivals in the harlot's love, and are as sure to be damned as if they were in hell already. A metaphor from a dungeon. He knoweth not that the dead are there, and that her guests are in the depths of hell. Aben Ezra will have the original word םש *ibi*, 'there,' to be referred to hell ;[4] and the meaning of the whole verse to be more plainly thus, He knoweth not that her guests being dead are in the depth of hell. But the Hebrew word here used and translated dead, is *Rephaim*, which word, *Rephaim*, properly signifies giants, and to that sense is always rendered by the seventy γίγαντες. The meaning of this place seems to be no other, but that the strange woman will bring them who are her guests to hell, to keep the apostate giants company,—those mighty men of renown of the old world, whose wickedness was so great in the earth, that it repented and grieved God that he had made man, Gen. vi. 4, 5 ; and to take vengeance on whom he brought the general deluge upon the earth, and destroyed both man

---

[1] This is a *catachrestical* metaphor : they are sure to bring her thither, as a man hath that in possession on which with much delight he takes fast hold.
[2] Bede, in Prov. xxx.   [3] Bern. Serm. 23, ad soror.
[4] Aben Ezra, in hunc vers.

and beast from the face thereof. These giants are called in Hebrew
Nephilim, such as, being fallen from God, fell upon men, and by force
and violence made others fall before them, even as the beasts of the
field do fall before the roaring lions. These great oppressors were first
drowned, and then damned, and sent to that accursed place which was
appointed for them. Now to that place and condition, in which they
are, the harlot will bring all her wanton lovers. Take one scripture
more: Prov. xv. 11, 'Hell and destruction are before the Lord ; how
much more then the hearts of the children of men.'¹ Some think the
latter is exegetical of the former ; some by *Sheol* understand the grave,
and by *Abaddon* hell. There is nothing so deep, or secret, that can
be hid from the eyes of God. He knows the souls in hell, and the
bodies in the grave, and much more men's thoughts here in this place,
Prov. xv. 11. The Jews take the word *Abaddon*, which we render
destruction, for *Gehenna*, that is, elliptically for *Beth-Abaddon*, the
house of destruction. Though we know not where hell is, nor what is
done there—though we know not what is become of those that are
destroyed, nor what they suffer, yet God doth ; and if the secrets of
hell and devils are known to him, then much more the secrets of the
hearts of the children of men. The devil, who is the great executioner
of the wrath of God, is expressed by this word ; as hell is called
destruction in the abstract, so the devil is called a destroyer in the
concrete. 'And they had a king over them, which is the angel of the
bottomless pit, or hell, whose name in the Hebrew tongue is Abaddon,
but in the Greek tongue hath his name Apollyon,' Rev. ix. 11. Both
the one and the other, the Hebrew and the Greek, signify the same
thing—a destroyer. The devil, who is the jailer of hell, is called a
destroyer, as hell itself is called destruction. Oh, sirs ! hell is destruction ; they that are once there are lost, yea, lost for ever, Rev. xiv. 11.
The reason why hell is called destruction, is because they that are cast
to hell are undone to all eternity. ' If hell,' said one, ' were to be
endured a thousand years, methinks I could bear it, but for ever, that
amazeth me.' Bellarmine, out of Barocius,² tells us of a learned man,
who after his death appeared to his friend, complaining that he was
adjudged to hell-torments, which, saith he, were they to last but a
thousand thousand years, I should think it tolerable, but alas ! they
are eternal. The fire in hell is like that stone in Arcadia I have read
of, which being once kindled, could not be quenched.³ There is no
estate on earth so miserable, but a man may be delivered out of it;
but out of hell there is no deliverance. It is not the prayer, no, not of
a Gregory, though never so great, whatever they fable, that can rescue
any that is once become hell's prisoner. I might add other scriptures
out of the Old Testament, but let these suffice.

That there is such a place as hell is, prepared for the torment of the
bodies and souls of wicked and impenitent sinners, is most clear and
evident in the New Testament as well as in the Old. Amongst the
many that might be produced, take these for a taste: Mat. v. 22,
' But I say unto you, that whosoever is angry with his brother without
a cause'—rashly, vainly, and unreasonably—' shall be in danger of the

¹ Destruction is put as an adjunct or epithet of hell.
² De arte bene moriendi. [Qu., 'Baronius' ?—G.]   ³ As before, 'asbestos.'— G.

judgment; and whosoever shall say to his brother, Raca, shall be in danger of the council; but whosoever shall say, Thou fool, shall be in danger of hell fire,'—*Gr.*, to, or in the Gehenna of fire.

In this scripture our Lord Jesus doth allude to the custom of punishing offenders used among the Jews. Now there were three degrees of punishments that were used among the Jews.

First, In every town where there were a hundred and twenty inhabitants, there was a little council of three, which judged smaller matters, for which whipping or some pecuniary mulct was imposed.

Secondly, There was a council consisting of three-and-twenty; seven of these were judges, fourteen assessors, who were mostly of the Levites; and to these were added two supernumeraries, which made the twenty-three, which the Hebrews generally say was the number that made up the second council. Now this council sat in the gates of the city, and did judge of civil matters, having also power of life and death, [Josephus.]

Thirdly, There was the great synedrion, or high court of judicatory, which consisted of seventy-and-two, six chosen of every tribe. Now this council sat in the court of the temple, and had all matters of greatest moment brought before them, as heresy, idolatry, apostasy. Sometimes they convented before them the high priest, and sometimes false prophets, yea, sometimes a whole tribe, as my reverend author thinks, [Beza.] Now look, as there is a gradation of sin, so there is a gradation of punishment pointed at in this scripture; for the opening of which, consider you have here three degrees of secret murder, or of inward heart murder. And,

[1.] The first is rash anger. Now this brings a man in danger of the judgment. By the judgment he means not the judgment of the three, who judged of money matters, but by judgment he means the council of the three-and-twenty men. Now they are called 'the judgment,' because they judged of murders, and inflicted death, &c. Now he that shall rashly, vainly, causelessly, unseasonably be angry with his brother, he shall be liable to the punishments that are to be inflicted by the judges. Look, what punishments they in the Sanhedrim inflicted upon actual and apparent murderers, the same were they liable to, and did deserve at the hands of God, who were guilty of this secret kind of murder, viz., rash anger. From the different degrees of punishments among the Jews, Christ would shew the degrees of punisment in another world, according to the greatness of men's sins. As if he should say: Look, as among you Jews there are different offences—some are judged in your little council of three, and others are judged in your council of three-and-twenty, and others in your great Sanhedrim—so in the high court of heaven, some sins, as rash anger, are less punished, and others are more sorely punished, as when your rash anger shall break forth into railings, &c. In these words, 'Whosoever is angry with his brother without a cause, shall be in danger of judgment,' you may see that Christ gives as much to rash anger as the Jews did to murder; as if he should have said, 'You Pharisees exceed all measure and bounds in your anger, and, with a malicious heart, you rail upon the most innocent persons, upon me and my disciples; but I would have you take heed of rash anger, for you shall have greater torments in hell for your rash anger than those that murderers suffer by your council of three-and-twenty.' But these words, 'he shall be in danger of judgment,' do contain the reward and punishment of unlawful anger; as if our Saviour had said, 'Rash anger shall not escape just punishment, but shall be arraigned and summoned before God's tribunal at the dreadful day of judgment, when the angry man shall not be able to answer one word of a thousand.'

[2.] The second kind of secret murder is to say to our brother, Raca, that is, say some, 'O vain man'! Others say, it signifies a brainless fellow; and the learned Tremellius saith, it signifies one void of judgment, reason, and brains. Some will have this word Raca come of the Greek ῥάκως, *Racos*, cloth, as though one should call a man a base patch, or piece of cloth, or beggarly.[1] Raca signifies an idle head, a light brain; for so *Rik* in the Hebrew, to which the Syriac word *Racha* agreeth both in sound and sense, signifieth light or vain. Racha is a Syriac word, and signifies, say some, these three things:—1. Empty, as empty of wealth, or poor; or as some, empty of brains or wit; or, as others, a light-head or cock-brain, wide[2] and empty of wisdom or understanding. 2. It signifies spittle or spit upon; to signify that they esteemed one another no better than the spittle they spat out of their mouths. 3. It signifies contemned, vile, despised, abject, and in this signification one, in his proem of the Syriac Grammar, [Michael Maronita,] thinks it to be taken. The Ethiopian expounds *Racha* thus, ' He that shall say to his brother, Be poor by contempt, and of torn garments, shall be guilty of the council;' such a one, saith our Saviour, ' shall be in danger of the council,' that is, contract as great guilt unto himself, and is subject to as severe a judgment in the court of heaven, as any capital crime that is censured in the Sanhedrim or high-court of the Jews. But,

[3.] The third kind of secret murder is an open reviling and reproaching of a brother in these words, 'But whosoever shall say, Thou fool, shall be in danger of hell-fire.' 'Thou fool,' this is a word of greater disgrace than the former. μωρέ signifies unsavoury, or without relish; a fool here is, by a metaphor, called insipid, Hebrew שוטה *Sote*, which we call *Sot*, ' shall be in danger of hell-fire,' or to be cast into Gehenna. Gehenna comes from the Hebrew word *Gettinnom*, that is, the valley of Hinnom, lying near the city of Jerusalem; in which valley, in former times, the idolatrous Jews caused their children to be burned alive between the glowing arms of the brazen image of Moloch, imitating the abominations of the heathen, Josh. xv. 8. And hence the Scripture often makes use of that word to signify the place of eternal punishment, where the damned must abide under the wrath of God for ever, 2 Kings xxiii. 10; Jer. vii. 31, xxxii. 35, and xix. 4, 5, 6. There were four kinds of punishments exercised among the Jews,—1. Stranglings; 2. The sword; 3. Stoning; 4. The fire. Now this last they always judged the worst, as Beza affirms upon this very place. In these words, ' shall be in danger of hell-fire,' Christ alludes

---

[1] Whether the word Raca be Hebrew, or as some say Syriac, or as others say Chaldee, it matters not; for all agree in this, that it is a word that notes scorn and contempt, &c.—*Vide* Lapide, Weemes, &c., on the Judicial Law of Moses, and Dr Field, 'Of the Church.'

[2] Query, ' void'?—ED.

to the great Sanhedrim, and the highest degree of punishment that was inflicted by them, namely, to be burned in the valley of Hinnom, which, by a known metaphor, is transferred to hell itself, and the inexpressible torments thereof. For as those poor wretches being inclosed in a brazen idol, heat with fire, were miserably tormented in this valley of Hinnom; so the wicked being cast into hell, the prison of the damned, shall be eternally tormented in unquenchable fire. This valley of Hinnom, by reason of the pollution of it with slaughter, blood, and stench of carcasses, did become so execrable, that hell itself did afterwards inherit the same name, and was called Gehenna of this very place. And that, 1. In respect of the hollowness and depth thereof, being a low and deep valley. 2. This valley of Hinnom was a place of misery, in regard of those many slaughters that were committed in it through their barbarous idolatry; so hell is a place of misery and infelicity, wherein there is nothing but sorrow. 3. Thirdly, by the bitter and lamentable cries of poor infants in this valley, is shadowed out the cries and lamentable torments of the damned in hell. 4. In this valley of Hinnom was another fire which was kept continually burning for the consuming of dead carcasses, and filth, and the garbage [1] that came out of the city. Now our Saviour, by the fire of Gehenna, in this Mat. v. 22, hath reference principally to this fire, signifying hereby the perpetuity and everlastingness of hellish pains. To this last judgment of the Sanhedrim, viz., burning, doth Christ appropriate that kind of murder, which is by open reviling of a brother, that he might notify the heinousness of that sin. Mark, in this scripture, judgment, council, and hell-fire do but signify three degrees of the same punishment, &c.

See also Mat. v. 29, 30, ' And if thy right eye offend thee, pluck it out, and cast it from thee; for it is profitable for thee that one of thy members should perish, and not that thy whole body should be cast into hell. And if thy right hand offend thee, cut it off, and cast it from thee; for it is profitable for thee that one of thy members should perish, and not that thy whole body should be cast into hell-fire.' Julian, taking these commands literally, mocked at [the] Christian religion, as foolish, cruel, and vain, because they require men to maim their members. He mocked at Christians because no man did it; and he mocked at Christ because no man obeyed him. But this apostate might have seen from the scope that these words were not to be taken literally, but figuratively. Some of the ancients, by the right hand, and the right eye, do understand relations, friends, or any other dear enjoyments which draws the heart from God. Others of them, by the right eye, and the right hand, do understand such darling sins that are as dear to men as their right eyes or right hands. That this hell here spoken of is not meant of the grave, into which the body shall be laid, is most evident, because those Christians who do pull out their right eyes, and cut off their right hands—that is, mortify those special sins which are as dear and near to them as the very members of their bodies—shall be secured and delivered from this hell, whereas none shall be exempt from the grave, though they are the choicest persons on earth for grace and holiness. Death, like the Duke of Parma's

---

[1] Spelled ' garbidge.'—G.

sword, knows no difference betwixt robes and rags, betwixt prince and peasant. 'All flesh is grass,' Isa. xl. 6. The flesh of princes, nobles, counsellors, generals, &c., is grass, as well as the flesh of the meanest beggar that walks the streets. 'The mortal scythe,' saith one, 'is master of the royal sceptre, it mows down the lilies of the crown, as well as the grass of the field.[1] Never was there orator so eloquent, nor monarch so potent, that could either persuade or withstand the stroke of death when it came. Death's motto is, *Nulli cedo*. It is one of Solomon's sacred aphorisms, 'The rich and the poor meet together,' Prov. xxii. 2, sometimes in the same bed, sometimes at the same board, and sometimes in the same grave. Death is the common inn of all mankind. 'There is no defence against the stroke of death, nor no discharge in that war,' Heb. ix. 27; Eccles. viii. 8. Death is that only king against whom there is no rising up, Prov. xxx. 31. If your houses be fired, by good help they may be quenched; if the sea break out, by art and industry it may be repaired; if princes invade by power and policy, they may be repulsed; if devils from hell shall tempt, by assistance from heaven they may be resisted. But death comes into royal palaces, and into the meanest cottages, and there is not a man to be found that can make resistance against this king of terrors and terror of kings. Death's motto is, *Nemini parco*, I spare none. Thus you see that by hell in Mat. v. 29, 30, you may not, you cannot, understand the grave; and therefore by it you must understand the place of the damned. But if you please you may cast your eye upon another scripture, viz., Mat. x. 28, 'Fear not them which kill the body, but are not able to kill the soul; but rather fear him which is able to destroy both soul and body in hell.' The word 'rather' is not a comparative, but an adversative. We should not fear man at all when he stands in competition with God. So Victorian, the proconsul of Carthage, being solicited to Arianism by the ambassadors of King Hunnerick, answered thus,[2] 'Being assured of God and my Lord Christ, I tell you, what you may tell the king, Let him burn me, let him drive me to the beasts, let him torment me with all kinds of torments, I shall never consent to be an Arian;' and though the tyrant afterwards did torture him with very great tortures, yet he could never work him over to Arianism. The best remedy against the slavish fear of tyrants, is to set that great God up as the object of our fear, who is able to destroy both soul and body in hell. Mark, he doth not say to destroy soul and body simply or absolutely, so that they should be no more—for that many that love their lusts, and prize the world above a Saviour, would be contented withal, rather than to run the hazard of a fierce, hot persecution—but to punish them eternally in hell, where the worm never dieth, nor the fire never goeth out. Now by hell in this Mat. x. 28, the grave cannot be meant, because the soul is not destroyed with the body in the grave, as they both shall be, if the person be wicked, after the morning of the resurrection, in hell, Eccles. xii. 7, and Phil. i. 3. From the immortality of the soul, we may infer the eternity of man's future condition. The soul being immortal, it must be immortally happy or

[1] Horat. l. 1, Ode 28. [Qu. rather l. 1, Ode 4?—G.]
[2] Victor. Uticens. l. 3. Wandal. Persecut. [Clarke, as before.—G.]

immortally miserable. It was Luther's complaint of old, 'We more fear the pope, with his purgatory, than God, with his hell; and we trust more in the absolution of the pope from purgatory, than in the true absolution of God from hell.' And is it not so with many this day, who bear their heads high in the land, and who look and long for nothing more than to see Rome[1] flourishing in the midst of us?

Take one scripture more, viz., 1 Pet. iii. 19, 20, 'By which also he went and preached unto the spirits in prison; which sometimes were disobedient, when once the long-suffering of God waited in the days of Noah.'[2] That is, Christ by his Spirit, in the ministry of Noah, did preach to the men of the old world who are now in hell. In Noah's time they were on earth, but in Peter's time they were in hell. Mark, Christ did not preach by his Spirit, in his ministry, or any other way, to spirits who were in prison or in hell while he preached to them. There are no sermons in hell, nor any salvation there. The loving-kindness of God is abundantly declared on earth, but it shall never be declared in hell. Look, as there is nothing felt in hell but destruction, so there is nothing found in hell of the offers of salvation. One offer of Christ in hell would turn hell into a heaven. One of the ancients hath reported the opinion of some in his time who thought, that though there be destruction in hell, yet not eternal destruction, but that sinners should be punished, some a lesser, others a longer time, and that, at last, all shall be freed. 'And yet,' saith he, 'Origen was more merciful in that point than these men, for he held that the devil himself should be saved at last.' Of this opinion I shall say no more in this place, than this one thing which he there said. These men will be found to err by so much the more foully, and against the right words of God so much the more perversely, by how much they seem to themselves to judge more mercifully; for indeed the justice of God in punishing of sinners is as much above the reach of man's thoughts as his mercies in pardoning them are, Isa. lv. 7–9. Oh, let not such who have neglected the great salvation when they were on earth, Heb. ii. 3, ever expect to have an offer of salvation made to them when they are in hell! Consult these scriptures, Mat. xxv. 30, xiii. 41, 42; Rev. ix. 2, xiv. 19, 20, xx. 1–3, 7. I must make haste, and therefore may not stand upon the opening of these scriptures, having said enough already to prove both out of the Old and New Testament that there is a hell, a place of torment, provided and prepared for all wicked and ungodly men. But the third argument to prove that there is a hell, is this,—

[3.] *The beams of natural light in some of the heathens have made such impressions on the heart of natural conscience, that several of them have had confused notions of a hell, as well as of a judgment to come.* Though the poor blind heathens were ignorant of Christ

---

[1] Spelled 'Room,' and thereby showing the pronunciation of the day; on which, as illustrated by this word, see various communications in 'Notes and Queries' for 1866.—G.

[2] Spirits, that is, the souls departed, not men, but spirits, to keep an analogy to the 18th ver., 'Christ suffered, being made dead in the flesh, and made alive by the Spirit; in which Spirit he had gone and preached to them that are now spirits in prison, because they disobeyed, when the time was, when the patience of God once waited in the days of Noah.—*Broughton*, in his Epistle to the Nobility of England. *Augustine*, lib. i. de civ. dei. cap. 17.

and the gospel, and the great work of redemption, &c., yet by the light of nature, and reasonings from thence, they did attain to the understanding of a deity, who was both just and good ; as also, that the soul was immortal, and that both rewards and punishments were prepared for the souls of men after this life, according as they were found either virtuous or vicious. Profound Bradwardine, and several others, have produced many proofs concerning their apprehensions of this truth.[1] What made the heathen Emperor Adrian when he lay a-dying, cry out, ' *O animula vagula blandula,*' &c. O my little wretched wandering soul, whither art thou now hastening? &c. Oh, what will become of me ! live I cannot, die I dare not ! but some discoveries of hell, of wrath to come ? Look, as these poor heathens did feign such a place as the Elysian fields, where the virtuous should spend an eternity in pleasures ; so also they did feign a place called Tartarum, or hell, where the vicious should be eternally tormented. Tertullian, and after him Chrysostom, affirmeth that poets and philosophers, and all sorts of men, speaking of a future retribution, have said that many are punished in hell. Plato is very plain, that whoever are not expiated, but profane, shall go into hell to be tormented for their wickednesses, with the greatest, most bitter and terrible punishments, for ever in that prison in, hell. And Jupiter, speaking to the other gods concerning the Grecians and Trojans, saith,—

> If any shall so hardy be,
> To aid each part in spite of me ;
> Him will I tumble down to hell,
> In that infernal place to dwell.[2]

So Horace, speaking concerning Jove's thunderbolts, says,—

> Quo bruta tellus et vaga flumina,
> Quo Styx, et invisi horrida Tænari sedes, &c.
>
> With which earth, seas, the Stygian lake,
> And hell with all her furies quake.[3]

And Trismegistus affirms concerning the soul's going out of the body defiled, that it is tossed to and fro with eternal punishments.[4] Nor was Virgil ignorant thereof when he said,—

> Dent ocyus omnes,
> Quas meruere pati—sic stat sententia—pœnas.
>
> They all shall pack,
> Sentence once past, to their deserved rack.[5]

The horror of which place he acknowledgeth he could not express,

> Non mihi si linguæ centum sint, oraque centum, ...
> Omnia pænarum percurrere nomina possim.
>
> No heart of man can think, no tongue can tell,
> The direful pains ordained and felt in hell.[6]

It was the common opinion among the poor heathen that the wicked were held in chains by Pluto—so they called the prince of devils—in

---

[1] Bradw. *de causa dei.* i. 1, cap. 1, &c.   [2] Iliad, viii. 10–13.—G.

[3] Odes 1, 34, 10.—G.

[4] One of the many opinions ascribed to Trismegistus, who, like Socrates, left no writings.—G.

[5] *Not* Virgil, but Ovid, Met. viii. 3.—G.   [6] Virgil—Æneid, vi. 625.—G.

chains which cannot be loosed. To conclude, the very Turks speak of the house of perdition, and affirm that they who have turned the grace of God into impiety, shall abide eternally in the fire of hell, and there be eternally tormented.[1] I might have spent much more time upon this head, but that I do not judge it expedient, considering the persons for whose sakes and satisfaction I have sent this piece into the world. But,

[4.] Fourthly, *The secret checks, gripes, stings, and the amazing horrors and terrors of conscience, that do sometimes astonish, affright, and even distract sinful wretches, do clearly and abundantly evidence that there is a hell, that there is a place of torment prepared and appointed for ungodly sinners.*[2] Doubtless, it was not merely the dissolution of nature, but the sad consequent, that so startled and terrified Belshazzar when he saw the handwriting on the wall, Dan. v. 5, 6. Guilty man, when conscience is awakened, fears an after-reckoning, when he shall be paid the wages of his crying sins proportionable to his demerits.

Wolfius[3] tells you of one John Hufmeister that fell sick in his inn as he was travelling towards Augsburg in Germany, and grew to that horror that they were fain to bind him in his bed with chains, where he cried out that ' he was for ever cast off from before the face of God, and should perish for ever, he having greatly wounded his conscience by sin,' &c.

James Abyes, who suffered martyrdom for Christ's sake and the gospel's, as he was going along to execution he gave all his money and his clothes away to one and another to his shirt, upon which one of the sheriff's attendants scoffingly said that ' he was a madman and a heretic;' but as soon as the good man was executed this wretch was struck mad, and threw away his clothes, and cried out that ' James Abyes was a good man, and gone to heaven, but he was a wicked man, and was damned;' and thus he continued crying out until his death.[4]

Dionysius was so troubled with fear and horror of conscience, that, not daring to trust his best friends with a razor, he used to singe his beard with burning coals, [Cicero.]

Bessus having slain his father, and being afterwards banqueting with several nobles, arose from the table and beat down a swallow's nest which was in the chimney, saying they lied ' to say that he slew his father,' for his guilty conscience made him think that the swallows, when they chattered, proclaimed his parricide to the world.[5]

Theodoricus the king having slain Boetius and Symmachus, and being afterwards at dinner, began to change countenance, his guilty conscience so blinding his eyes that he thought the head of a fish which stood before him to have been the head of his cousin Symmachus, who bit his lip at him and threatened him, the horror whereof did so amaze him that he presently died.[6]

---

[1] Alcoran, Mahom. c. 14, p. 160, and c. 20, p. 198.
[2] *Suæ quemque exagitant furiæ,* Every man is tormented with his own fury, that is, his conscience, saith the philosopher.
[3] Wolf. Lectiones, Memor. tom. 2, &c.   [4] Foxe, as before.—G.
[5] Plut. *de sera* [*numinis*] *vindicata.* [Misprinted ' Bossus,' cf. Plutarch, *Alexander,* 42, 43, &c.—G.]   [6] Sigonius de occid. Imper.

Nero, that monster of nature, having once slain his mother, had never more any peace within, but was astonished with horrors, fears, visions, and clamours which his guilty conscience set before him and suggested unto him. *Imo latens in prædio, familiares suspectos habuit, vocem humanam horruit, ad catuli latratum, galli cantum, rami ex vento motum, terrebatur ; loqui non ausus, ne audiretur:* He suspected his nearest and dearest friends and favourites, he trembled at the barking of a puppy, and the crowing of a cock, yea, the wagging of a leaf, and neither durst speak unto others nor could endure others to speak to him, when he was retired into a private house, lest the noise should be heard by some who lay in wait for his life.[1]

Now were there not a hell, were there not a place of torment where God will certainly inflict unspeakable miseries and intolerable torments upon wicked and ungodly men, why should their consciences thus amaze, torture, and torment them? Yea, the very heathen had so much light in their natural consciences, as made such a discovery of that place of darkness, that some of them have been terrified with their own inventions concerning it, and distracted with the very sense of those very torments which their own persons have described. As Pygmalion doted on his own picture, so were they amazed with their own comments. The very flashes of hell-fire which sinners do daily experience in their own consciences in this world, may be an argument sufficient to satisfy them that there is a hell, a place of torment provided for them in another world.

[5.] Fifthly, *Those matchless, easeless, and endless torments that God will certainly inflict upon the bodies and souls of all wicked and ungodly men, after the resurrection, does sufficiently evidence that there is a hell, that there is a place of torment provided, prepared, and fitted by God,* wherein he will, ' pour forth all the vials of his wrath upon wicked and ungodly men:' Isa. xxx. 33, ' For Tophet is ordained of old, yea, for the king it is prepared; he hath made it deep and large, the pile thereof is fire and much wood, the breath of the Lord like a stream of brimstone doth kindle it.' This place that was so famous for judgment and vengeance is used to express the torments of hell, the place of the damned. Tophet was a place in the valley of Hinnom; it was the place where the angel of the Lord destroyed the host of Sennacherib, king of Assyria, Isa. xxx. 31, 33; and this was the place where the idolatrous Jews were slain and massacred by the Babylonian armies, when their city was taken and their carcasses left, for want of room for burial, for meat to the fowls of heaven and beasts of the field, according to the word of the Lord by the prophet Jeremiah, Jer. vii. 31–33, and xix. 4–6. And this was the place where the children of Israel committed that abominable idolatry in making their children pass through the fire to Moloch; that is, burnt them to the devil, 2 Kings xxiii. 10; 2 Chron. xxxiii. 6; for an eternal destruction whereof king Josiah polluted it, and made it a place execrable, ordaining it to be the place whither dead carcasses, garbage, and other unclean things should be cast out. For consuming whereof, to prevent annoyance, a continual fire was there burning, 2 Kings xxxiii. 8. Now this place, being so many ways execrable for what had been

---

[1] Xiphil. in Nerone, &c. [Xipilinus of Trapezus, abridgment of Dion. Cassius.—G.]

done therein, especially having been as it were the gate to eternal destruction, by so remarkable judgments and vengeance of God there executed for sin, it came to be translated to signify the place of the damned, as the most accursed, execrable, and abominable place of all places. The Spirit of God, in Scripture, by metaphors of all sorts of things that are dreadful unto sense, sets forth the condition of the damned, and the torments that he has reserved for them in the life to come. Hell's punishments do infinitely exceed all other punishments; no pain so extreme as that of the damned. Look, as there are no joys to the joys of heaven, so there are no pains to the pains of hell, Ps. cxvi. 3. All the cruelties in the world cannot possibly make up any horror comparable to the horrors of hell. The brick-kilns of Egypt, the furnace of Babel,[1] are but as the glowing sparkle, or as the blaze of a brush-faggot, to this tormenting Tophet that has been prepared of old to punish the bodies and souls of sinners with. Hanging, racking, burning, scourging, stoning, sawing asunder, flaying of the skin, &c., are not to be named in the day wherein the tortures of hell are spoken of. If all the pains, sorrows, miseries, and calamities that have been inflicted upon all the sons of men, since Adam fell in Paradise, should meet together and centre in one man, they would not so much as amount to one of the least of the pains of hell. Who can sum up the diversity of torments that are in hell! In hell there is, 1. Darkness; hell is a dark region. 2. In hell there are sorrows. 3. In hell there are bonds and chains. 4. In hell there is pains and pangs. 5. In hell there is the worm that never dies. 6. In hell there is a lake of fire. 7. In hell there is a furnace of fire. 8. In hell there is the devil and his angels; and oh, how dreadful must it be to be shut up for ever with those roaring lions! 9. In hell there is weeping and gnashing of teeth.[2] Certainly, did men believe the torments of hell, that weeping for extremity of heat, and that gnashing of teeth that is there for extremity of cold, they would never offer to fetch profits or pleasures out of those flames.[3] 10. In hell there is unquenchable fire, Mat. iii. 12, 'He will burn the chaff with unquenchable fire;' in hell there is 'everlasting burnings,' Isa. xxxiii. 14. ' The sinners in Zion are afraid, fearfulness hath surprised the hypocrites; who among us shall dwell with the devouring fire? who among us shall dwell with everlasting burnings?' Wicked men, who are now the only jolly fellows of the time, shall one day go from burning to burning; from burning in sin to burning in hell; from burning in flames of lusts to burning in flames of torment, except there be found true repentance on their sides, and pardoning grace on God's.[4] O sirs! in this devouring fire, in these everlasting burnings, Cain shall find no cities to build, nor his posterity shall have no instruments of music to invent there; none shall take up the timbrel or harp, or rejoice at the sound of the organ. There Belshazzar

[1] Babylon.—G.

[2] Jude 13; Ps. cxvi. 3; 2 Pet. ii. 4; Jude 6; Mark ix. 44; Rev. xx. 15; Mat. xiii. 41, 42, xxv. 41, xxiv. 51, xxv. 30, xiii. 42.

[3] Who would give, saith Bernard, to my eyes a fountain of tears, that by my weeping here I may prevent weeping and gnashing of teeth hereafter. Some devout personages have caused this scripture to be writ in letters of gold upon their chimney-pieces.— Bishop of Belly in France in his ' Draught of Eternity.' [Camus, as before.—G.]

[4] Gen. iv. 17; Amos vi. 7; Job xxi. 12; Dan. v. 21; Amos vi. 4.

cannot drink wines in bowls, nor eat the lambs out of the flocks, nor the calves out of the midst of the stall. In everlasting burnings there will be no merry company to pass time away, nor no dice nor cards to pass care away; nor no cellars of wine wherein to drown the sinner's grief. By fire in the scriptures last cited, is meant, as I conceive, all the positive part of the torments of hell; and because they are not only upon the soul but also upon the body. As in heaven there shall be all bodily perfection, so there shall be also in hell all bodily miseries. Whatsoever may make a man perfectly miserable shall be in hell; therefore the wrath of God and all the positive effects of this wrath is here meant by fire.

I have read of Pope Clement the Fifth, that when a nephew of his, whom he had loved sensually and sinfully, died, he sent his chaplain to a necromancer to learn how it fared with him in the other world. The conjuror shewed him the chaplain lying in a fiery bed in hell; which when it was told the Pope, he never joyed more after it, but, within a short time after, died also.[1] Out of this fiery bed there is no deliverance. When a sinner is in hell, shall another Christ be found to die for him, or will the same Christ be crucified again? Oh, no!

O sirs, the torments of hell will be exceeding great and terrible, such as will make the stoutest sinners to quake and tremble! If the handwriting upon the wall, *Mene, Mene, Tekel, Upharsin,* made Belshazzar's ' countenance to change, his thoughts to be troubled, and his joints to be loosed, and his knees to be dashed one against another,' Dan. v. 5, vi. 25; oh, how terrible will the torments of hell be to the damned! The torments of hell will be universal torments. All torments meet together in that place of torment. Hell is the centre of all punishments, of all sorrows, of all pains, of all wrath, and of all vengeance, &c. One of the ancients saith, [Bernard,] that the least punishment in hell is more grievous than if a child-bearing woman should continue in the most violent pangs and throes a thousand years together, without the least ease or intermission.

An ancient writer mentioned by Discipulus, *de tempore,* goeth much further, affirming that if all the men which have been from Adam's time till this day, and which shall be to the end of the world; and all the piles of grass in the world were turned into so many men to augment the number; and that punishment inflicted in hell upon any one, were to be divided amongst all these, so as to every one might befall an equal part of that punishment; yet that which would be the portion of one man would be far more grievous than all the cruel deaths and exquisite tortures which have been inflicted upon men ever since the world began.[2] A heathen poet, speaking of the multitude of the pains and torments of the wicked in hell, affirmed,

---

[1] Jac. Reu. Hist. Pontif, Rom. 199 [*sic :* but Query, ' Platina Historia de Vitis Pontificum Romanorum. Colon : 1626, 4o '?—G.]

[2] *Tytius* his vulture, though feeding on his liver, is but a flea-biting to the gnawing worm that is in hell [Qu. ' Prometheus the *Titan* '?—G.]—Ixion his wheel is a place of rest, if compared with those billows of wrath, and that wheel of justice which is in hell brought upon the ungodly [Cf. Schol. *ad Hom.;* Od. xxi. 303; Serv. ad Virgil, Æn. vi. 601; Georg. iii. 38, iv. 484.—G.]—The lash of Danaüs his daughters is but a sport compared to the torture of the damned in hell [Pindar. Nem. x. 7 ; Ovid : Met. iv. 462 ; Horat. Carm. iii. 11, &c.—G.]

'that although he had a hundred mouths, and as many tongues, with a voice as strong as iron, yet were they not able to express the names of them.' But this poet spoke more like a prophet than a poet. The poets tell you of a place called *Tartarum*, or hell, where the impious shall be eternally tormented. This *Tartarum* the poets did set forth with many fictions to affright people from vicious practices, such as of the four lakes of Acheron, Styx, Phlegethon, and Cocytus;[1] over which Charon, in his boat, did waft over the departed souls; of the three judges, Æacus, Minos, and Rhadamanthus,[2] who were to call the souls to an account, and judge them to their state; of the three furies, Tisophone, Megæra, and Alecto, who lashed guilty souls to extort confession from them;[3] of Cerberus, the dog of hell, with three heads, which would let none come out when once they were in; and of several sorts of punishments inflicted, as iron chains, horrid stripes, gnawing of vultures, wheels, rolling great stones, and the like. In the chapel of *Ticam*, the China Pluto, the pains of hell were so deciphered that could not but strike terror into the beholders,—some roasted in iron beds, some fried in scalding oil, some cut in pieces, or divided in the middle, or torn of dogs, &c. In another part of the chapel were painted the dungeons of hell, with horrible serpents, flames, devils, &c.[4]

' In hell,' saith Mahomet, [Alcoran,'&c.,] ' there is the floor of brimstone, smoky, pitchy, with stinking flames, deep pits of scalding pitch, and sulphurous flames wherein the damned are punished daily.' There the wicked shall be fed with the tree *Ezecum*, which shall burn in their bellies like fire; there they shall drink fire, and be holden in chains of seventy cubits. In the midst of hell, they say, is a tree full of fruit, every apple being like to the head of a devil, which groweth green in the midst of all those flames, called *Zoaccum Agacci*, or the tree of bitterness; and the souls that shall eat thereof, thinking to refresh themselves, shall so find them, and by them and their pains in hell, they shall grow mad, and the devils shall bind them with chains of fire, and shall drag them up and down in hell; with much more which I am not free to transcribe. Now, although most of those things which you may find among many poets, heathens, and Turks, concerning the torments of hell, are fictions of their own brains; yet that there is such a place as hell, and that there are diversity of torments there, the very light of nature doth witness, and hath forced many to confess, &c.

And as there are diversity of torments in hell, so the torments of hell are everlasting. Mark, everything that is conducible to the torments of the damned is eternal. 1. God himself that damns them is eternal, Deut. xxxiii. 27; 1 Tim. i. 17. 2. The fire that torments them is eternal, Isa. xxx. 33, and lxvi. 24; Jude 7. 3. The prison and chains that hold them are eternal, Jude 6, 7, 13; 2 Pet. ii. 17. 4.

---

[1] Homer: Od. x. 513; cf. Paus. i. 17, sec. 5. Rather Pyriphlegeton.—G.

[2] *Æacus:* Ovid, Met. xiii. 25; Horat, Carm. ii. 13, 22; Plato, Gorg. and Apolog.— *Minos:* Homer, Il. xiii. 450, xiv. 322; Od. xi. 321, 567, xvii. 523, xix. 178.—*Rhadamanthus:* Apollod. iii. 1, sec. 2, ii. 4, sec. 11; Hom. Od. iv. 564, vii. 323; Pindar. ol. ii. 137.—G.

[3] Rather Tisiphone: Orph. Arg. 966. Megæra and Alecto; Orph. Hymn 68; Virg. Æn. xii. 845; Cerberus: Hom. Il. viii. 368; Od. xi. 623.—G.

[4] Purchas his Pilgrims, 3d vol., pp. 407, 408.

The worm that gnaws them is eternal, Mark ix. 44. 5. The sentence that shall be passed upon them shall be eternal, Mat. xxv. 41, ' Depart from me, ye cursed, into everlasting fire.' You know that fire is the most tormenting element.[1] Oh, the most dreadful impression that it makes upon the flesh, everlasting fire! There is the vengeance and continuance of it, You shall go into fire, into everlasting fire, that shall never consume itself, nor consume you. Eternity of eternity is the hell of hell. The fire in hell is like that stone in Arcadia, which being once kindled could never be quenched: If all the fires that ever were, or shall be in the world, were contracted into one fire, how terrible would it be! Yet such a fire would be but as a painted fire upon the wall, to the fire of hell. For to be tormented without end, this is that which goes beyond all the bounds of desperation. Grievous is the torment of the damned, for the bitterness of the punishments, but it is more grievous for the diversity of the punishments, but most grievous for the eternity of the punishments.[2] If, after so many millions of years as there be drops in the ocean, there might be a deliverance out of hell, this would yield a little ease, a little comfort to the damned. Oh, but this word *eternity, eternity, eternity;* this word *everlasting, everlasting, everlasting;* this word *for ever, for ever, for ever,* will even break the hearts of the damned in ten thousand pieces! Oh, that word *never,* said a poor despairing creature on his death-bed, breaks my heart. ' The reprobate shall have punishment without pity; misery without mercy, sorrow without succour, crying without compassion, mischief without measure, and torment without end,' [Drexelius.] Plato could say, ' That whoever are not expiated, but profane, shall go into hell, to be tormented for their wickedness, with the greatest, the most bitter and terrible punishments for ever in that prison of hell.' And Trismegistus could say, ' That souls going out of the body defiled, were tossed to and fro with eternal punishments.' Yea, the very Turks, speaking of the house of perdition, do affirm, ' That they who have turned God's grace into wantonness, shall abide eternally in the fire of hell, and there be eternally tormented.'[3] A certain religious man going to visit Olympius, who lived cloistered up in a dark cell, which he thought uninhabitable, by reason of heat, and swarms of gnats and flies, and asking him how he could endure to live in such a place, he answered, ' All this is but a light matter, that I may escape eternal torments: I can endure the stinging of gnats, that I might not endure the stinging of conscience, and the gnawing of that worm that never dies; this heat thou thinkest grievous, I can easily endure, when I think of the eternal fire of hell; these sufferings are but short, but the sufferings of hell are eternal.'[4] Certainly, infernal fire is neither tolerable nor terminable. Impenitent sinners in hell shall have end without end, death without death, night without day, mourning without mirth, sorrow without solace, and bondage without liberty. The damned shall live as long in hell as God himself shall live in heaven.

---

[1] Melanchthon calls it a hellish fury. Of this fire, see more in my ' London's Lamentation on the late Fiery Dispensation,' part ii. page 105–131. [Vol. vi.—G.]

[2] Dionys. in 18. Apocalyps. fol. 301.

[3] Alcoran Mahom. c. xiv. p. 160, &c.; c. xx. p. 198, &c.

[4] There is no Christian which doth not believe the fire of hell to be everlasting. Dr Jackson on the Creed, lib. xi. c. 23.

Their imprisonment in that land of darkness, in that bottomless pit, is not an imprisonment during the king's pleasure, but an imprisonment during the everlasting displeasure of the King of kings. Suppose, say some, that the whole world were turned to a mountain of sand, and that a little wren should come every thousand year and carry away from that heap one grain of sand, what an infinite number of years, not to be numbered by all finite beings, would be spent and expired, before this supposed mountain could be fetched away! Now if a man should lie in everlasting burnings so long a time, and then have an end of his woe, it would administer some ease, refreshment, and comfort to him; but when that immortal bird shall have carried away this supposed mountain, a thousand times over and over, alas, alas, sinful man shall be as far from the end of his anguish and torment as ever he was; he shall be no nearer a-coming out of hell, than he was the very first moment that he entered into hell.[1] If the fire of hell were terminable, it might be tolerable; but being endless, it must needs be easeless, and remediless. We may well say of it, as one doth, Oh, killing life! oh, immortal death![2]

Suppose, say others, that a man were to endure the torments of hell as many years, and no more, as there be sands on the sea-shore, drops of water in the sea, stars in heaven, leaves on trees, piles of grass on the ground, hairs on his head, yea, upon the heads of all the sons of Adam that ever were or are, or shall be in the world, from the beginning of it to the end of it, yet he would comfort himself with this poor thought, Well, there will come a day when my misery and torment shall certainly have an end. But woe and alas, this word, 'never, never, never,' will fill the hearts of the damned with the greatest horror and terror, wrath and rage, amazement, and astonishment.

Suppose, say others, that the torments of hell were to end, after a little bird should have emptied the sea, and only carry out her bill-full once in a thousand years. Suppose, say others, that the whole world, from the lowest earth to the highest heavens, were filled with grains of sand, and once in a thousand years an angel should fetch away one grain, and so continue till the whole heap were spent. Suppose, say others, if one of the damned in hell, should weep after this manner, viz., that he should only let fall one tear in a thousand years, and these should be kept together, till such time as they should equal the drops of water in the sea; how many millions of ages would pass, before they could make up one river, much more a whole; and when that were done, should he weep again after the same manner, till he had filled a second, a third, and a fourth sea. If then there should be an end of their miseries, there would be some hope, some comfort, that they would end at last; but that they shall never, never, never end, this is that which sinks them under the most tormenting terrors and horrors.

You know that the extremity and eternity of hellish torments is set forth by the worm that never dies; and it is observable that Christ, at the close of his sermon, makes a threefold repetition of this worm:

---

[1] An often recurring illustration with the Mediæval preachers; as are also those that follow.—G.

[2] Bellar. de arte moriendi, lib. ii. c. 3.

Mark ix. 44, 'where their worm dieth not;' and again, ver. 46, 'where their worm dieth not;' and again, ver. 48, 'where their worm dieth not, and their fire goeth not out.' Certainly, those punishments are beyond all conception and expression, which our Lord Jesus doth so often inculcate within so small a space.

Now if there be such a diversity, extremity, and eternity of hellish pains and torments, which the great God will certainly inflict upon the bodies and souls of all impenitent persons, after the day of judgment; then there must certainly be some hell, some place of torment, wherein the wrath of God shall be executed upon wicked and ungodly men. But,

[6.] Sixthly, *The greatest part of wicked and ungodly men escape unpunished in this world.* The greatest number of men do spend their days in pride, ease, pleasures, and delights, in lust and luxury, in voluptuousness and wantonness: 'They take the timbrel and harp, and rejoice to the sound of the organ;' 'They chant to the sound of the viol, and invent to themselves instruments of music;' 'They drink wine in bowls;' 'They lie upon beds of ivory, and stretch themselves upon their couches, and eat the lambs out of the flock, and the calves out of the midst of the stall;' and therefore there will be a time when these shall be punished in another world, Ps. lxxiii. 3–13; Job xxi. 12; Amos v. 6.

God doth not punish all here, that he may make way for the displaying of his mercy and goodness, his patience and forbearance. Nor doth he forbear all here, that he may manifest his justice and righteousness, lest the world should turn atheist, and deny his providence, Rom. ii. 4, 5; 2 Pet. iii. 9–15. He spares that he may punish, and he punisheth that he may spare. God smites some sinners in the very acting of their sins, as he did Korah, Dathan, and Abiram, and others, Num. xvi.; not till they have filled up the measure of their sins, as you see in the men of the old world, Gen. vi. 5–7. But the greatest number of sinners God reserves for the great day of his wrath, Mat. vii. 13. There is a sure punishment, though not always a present punishment, for every sinner, Eccles. viii. 12, 13. Those wicked persons which God suffers to go uncorrected here, he reserves to be punished for ever hereafter, 2 Thes. i. 7–10. Sinners, know your doom,—you must either smart for your sins in this world, or in the world to come. That ancient hit the mark that said, 'Many sins are punished in this world, that the providence of God might be more apparent; and many, yea, most, reserved to be punished in the world to come, that we might know that there is yet judgment behind.'[1]

Sir James Hamilton, having been murdered by the Scottish king's means, he appeared to the king in a vision, with a naked sword drawn, and strikes off both his arms, with these words, 'Take this, before thou receivest a final payment for all thy impieties;' and within twenty-four hours two of the king's sons died.[2] If the glutton in that historical parable being in hell, Luke xvi. 22–24, only in part, to wit, in soul, yet cried out that he 'was horribly tormented in that flame,' what think ye shall that torment be when body and soul come to be united

---

[1] Augustine, Epist. 54.
[2] Mr Knox in his History of Scotland. [See Laing's 'Works' of Knox, *s. n.*—G.]

for torture! It being just with God, that as they have been, like Simeon and Levi, brethren in iniquity, and have sinned together desperately and impenitently, so they should suffer together jointly, eternally, Gen. xlix. 5. The Hebrew doctors have a pretty parable to this purpose: A man planted an orchard, and going from home, was careful to leave such watchmen as both might keep it from strangers and not deceive him themselves; therefore he appointed one blind, but strong of his limbs, and the other seeing, but a cripple. These two, in their master's absence, conspired together; and the blind took the lame on his shoulders, and so gathered the fruit. Their master returning, and finding out this subtlety, punished them both together. So shall it be with those two sinful yoke-fellows, the soul and the body, in the great day; they have sinned together, and they shall suffer at last together, 2 Cor. v. 10, 11. But now in this world the greatest number of transgressors do commonly escape all sorts of punishments; and therefore we may safely conclude that there is another world, wherein the righteous God will revenge upon the bodies and souls of sinners the high dishonours that have been done to his name by them. But,

[7.] Seventhly, *In all things natural, and supernatural, there is an opposition and contrariety.* There is good, and there is evil; there is light and darkness, joy and sorrow. Now as there are two several ways, so there are two distinct ends: Heaven, a place of admirable and inexpressible happiness, whither the good angels convoy the souls of the saints who have, by a holy conversation, glorified God, and adorned their profession, Luke xvi. 22; and hell, a place of horror and confusion, whither the evil angels do hurry the souls of wicked, incorrigible, and impenitent wretches, when they are once separated from their bodies. ' The rich man also died and was buried; and in hell he lifted up his eyes, being in torments,' ver. 22, 23; ' and these shall go away into everlasting punishment, and the righteous into life eternal,' Mat. xxv. 46. In these words we have described the different estate of the wicked and the righteous after judgment, ' They shall go away into everlasting punishment, but these into life eternal.' After the sentence is past, the wicked go into everlasting punishment, and the righteous into life eternal. Everlasting punishment, the end thereof is not known, its duration is undetermined. Hell is a bottomless pit, and therefore shall never be fathomed. It is an unquenchable fire, and therefore the smoke of their torments doth ascend for ever and ever, Rev. xiv. 11. Hell is a prison from whence is no freedom, because there is no ransom to be paid. No price will be accepted for one in that estate. And as there is no end of the punishments of hell, into which the wicked must enter, so there is no end of the joys of heaven, into which the saints must enter. ' In thy presence is fulness of joy, and at thy right hand there are pleasures for evermore,' Ps. xvi. 11. Here is as much said as can be said, for quality, there is in heaven joy and pleasures; for quantity, a fulness, a torrent; for constancy, it is at God's right hand; and for perpetuity, it is for evermore. The joys of heaven are without measure, mixture, or end. Thus you see that there are two distinct ends, two distinct places, to which the wicked and the righteous go. And, indeed, if this were not so, then Nero would be as good a man as Paul, and Esau as happy a man as Jacob, and Cain as blessed a man as Abel. Then as believers say, ' If in this life only we have hope in Christ, we are of all men most miserable,' 1 Cor. xv. 19; because none out of hell ever suffered more, if so much, as the saints have done; so might the wicked say, ' If in this life only we were miserable, we were then of all men most happy.' But,

[8.] Eighthly, and lastly, *You know that all the princes of the world, for their greater grandeur and state, as they have their royal palaces for themselves, their nobles and attendants, so they have their jails, prisons, and dark dungeons for rogues and robbers, for malefactors and traitors.* And shall not he who is the King of kings and Lord of lords, Rev. xix. 16; he who is the Prince of the kings of the earth, Rev. i. 5; he who removeth kings and setteth up kings, Dan. ii. 21; shall not he have his royal palace, a glorious heaven, where he and all his noble attendants, angels, and saints shall live for ever? Shall not the great king have his royal and magnificent court in that upper world, as poor petty princes have theirs in this lower world? Surely he shall, as you may see by comparing the scriptures in the margin together.[1] And shall not the same great King have his hell, his prison, his dungeon, to secure and punish impenitent sinners in? Surely yes. And doubtless, the least glimpse of this hell, of this place of torment, would strike the proudest, and the stoutest sinners dead with horror. O sirs! they that have seen the flames, and heard the roarings of Ætna, the flashing of Vesuvius, the thundering and burning flakes evaporating from those marine rocks, have not yet seen, no, not so much as the very glimmering of hell. A painted fire is a better shadow of these, than these can be of hell torments, and the miseries of the damned therein. Now these eight arguments are sufficient to demonstrate that there is a hell, a place of torment, to which the wicked shall be sent at last. Now certainly, Socinians, atheists, and all others that are men of corrupt minds, and that believe that there is no hell, but what they carry about with them in their own consciences; these are worse than those poor Indians that hold that there are thirteen hells,[2] according to the differing demerits of men's sins; yea, they are worse than devils, for they believe and tremble, James ii. 19. φρίσσουσι; this Greek word signifies to roar as the sea; from thence, saith Eustatius, it is translated to the hideous clashing of armour in the battle. The original word seemeth to imply an extreme fear, which causeth not only tremblings, but also a roaring and shrieking out. Their hearts ache and quake within them, they quiver and shake as men do when their teeth chatter in their heads in extreme cold weather, Mark vi. 49, and Acts xvi. 29. The devils acknowledge four articles of our faith: Mat. viii. 29, ' And behold, they cried out, saying, What have we do with thee, Jesus, thou son of God? Art thou come hither to torment us before the time.' 1. They acknowledge God; 2. Christ; 3. The day of judgment; 4. That they shall be tormented then. They who scorn the day of judgment are worse than devils; and they who deny the deity of Christ are worse than devils,

[1] Eph. ii. 3; John xiv. 1-4 Luke xii. 32; Neh. ix. 6; 1 Kings viii. 27; Heb. viii. 1; Rev. iii. 21.   [2] Purchas his Pilgrimage.

[Piscator.] The devils are, as it were, for a time respited and re-prieved, in respect of full torment, and they are suffered as free prisoners to flutter in the air, and to course about the earth till the great day of the Lord, which they tremble to think on; and which they that mock at, or make light of, are worse than devils. The devils knew that torments were prepared for them, and a time when these torments should be fully and fatally inflicted on them, and loath they were to suffer before that time. Ah, sirs, shall not men tremble to deny what the devils are forced to confess! Shall I now make a few short inferences from what has been said, and so conclude this head?

1. First, then, *Oh labour to set up God as the great object of your fear.* This grand lesson Christ commands us to take out, ' Fear not them which kill the body, but are not able to kill the soul; but rather fear him which is able to destroy both soul and body in hell; yea, I say unto you, fear him,' Mat. x. 28. Christ doubles the precept, that it might stick with more life and power upon us, Luke xii. 5. As one fire, so one fear, drives out another. Both the punishment of loss and the punishment of sense may be the objects of a filial fear, the fear of a son, of a saint, of a soul that is espoused and married to Christ. The fear of God, and the fear of sin, will drive out the fear of death, and the fear of hell, 2 Cor. xi. 2; Hos. ii. 19, 20. O sirs, will you not fear that God that hath the keys of hell and death in his own hand, that can speak you into hell at pleasure, that can by a word of command bring you to dwell with a devouring fire, yea, to dwell with everlasting burnings? Rev. i. 18.

Ah, friends, will you fear a burning fever, and will you not fear a burning in hell? Will you fear when the house you live in is on fire, and when the bed you lie on is on fire, though it may be quenched, and will you not fear that fire that is unquenchable? Isa. xxxiii. 14. When men run through the streets and cry, Fire, fire, fire! how do your hearts quake and tremble in you; and will you not fear the fire of hell? will you not fear everlasting fire? Mat. iii. 12, xxv. 41. Sir Francis Bacon, in his history of Henry the Seventh,[1] relates how it was a by-word of the Lord Cordes, who was a profane, popish, atheistical French lord, that he could be content to lie seven years in hell, so he might win Calais from the English; but had this popish lord lain but seven minutes under unsupportable torments, he would quickly have re-pented of his mad bargain. It was good counsel that one of the ancients gave, *Descendamus in infernum viventes, ne descendamus morientes*, Let us go into hell while we are alive, by a serious medita-tion and holy consideration, that we may not go into it when we be dead, by real miseries, [Bernard.] God can kill, and more than that, he can cast into hell. Here is both temporal and eternal destruction, both rods and scorpions. He can kill the body, and then damn both body and soul, and cast them into hell; and therefore it becomes every one to set up God as the great object of their fear. Yea, I say unto you, fear him; yea, I say unto you, fear him. This redoubling of the speech adds a greater enforcement to the admonition. It is like the last stroke of the hammer, that rivets and drives up all to the head. Thus David uses this ingemination, ' Thou, even thou, art to be feared,

[1] As before. See Index sub nomine.—G.

and who may stand in thy sight; when thou art angry, thou canst look them to death, yea, to hell,' Ps. lxxvi. 7. And it is worth the observing, that this ingemination and reinforcement here annexed is to the affirmative clause, not to the negative. Our Saviour saith not, ' Yea, I say unto you, fear not them;' but he places the reduplication upon the affirmative precept, ' I say unto you, fear him.' O sirs, temporal judgments are but the smoke of his anger, but in hell there are the flames of his anger. That fire burns fiercely, and there is no quenching of it. Excuse me, saith the father, thou breakest [1] bonds and imprisonments, O emperor, but God's threatenings are much more terrible. He threatens hell torments and everlasting damnation; and certainly, where there is the greatest danger, there it is fit that there should be the greatest dread. But,

2. Secondly, Then *flee from the wrath to come*, Mat. iii. 7.[2] O sirs, that you would seriously and frequently dwell upon those short hints!

[1.] Wrath to come is *the greatest wrath, it is the greatest evil that can befall a soul.* ' Who knows the power of thy wrath?' Ps. xix. 11. Wrath to come is such wrath as no man can either avoid or abide, and yet such is most men's stupidity, that they will not believe it till they feel it. As God is a great God, so his wrath is a great wrath. I may allude to that which Zebah and Zalmunna said to Gideon, ' As the man is, so is his strength,' Judges viii. 21. So may I say, as the Lord is, so is his wrath. The wrath of an earthly king is compared to the roaring of a lion, Prov. xix. 12; *Heb.*, of a young lion, which, being in his prime, roars most terribly. He roars with such a force that he amazes the creatures whom he hunts, so as that they have no power to fly from him. Now if the wrath of a king be so terrible, oh how dreadful must the wrath of the King of kings then be! The greater the evil is, the more cause we have to flee from it. Now wrath to come is the greatest evil, and therefore the more it concerns us to flee from it, Rev. xvii. 14. But,

[2.] Secondly, Wrath to come is *treasured-up wrath.* Sinners are still ' a-treasuring up wrath against the day of wrath,' Rom. ii. 5. In treasuring there is, 1. Laying in; 2. Lying hid; 3. Bringing out again as there is occasion.

Whilst wicked men are following their own lusts, they think that they are still adding to their own happiness; but alas, they do but add wrath to wrath, they do but heap up judgment upon judgment, punishment upon punishment. Look, as men are daily adding to their treasure more and more, so impenitent sinners are daily increasing the treasures of wrath against their own souls. Now, who would not flee from treasures of wrath? But,

[3.] Thirdly, Wrath to come is *pure wrath.* It is ' judgment without mercy,' James ii. 13. The cup of wrath which God will put into sinners' hands at last will be a cup of pure wrath, all wrath, nothing but wrath, Rev. xiv. 10, ' The same shall drink of the wine of the wrath of God, which is poured out without mixture into the cup of his indignation; and he shall be tormented with fire and brimstone

---

[1] Query, ' threatenest '?—ED.

[2] Though destruction by the Romans is not here excluded, yet the principal thing that he means by wrath to come is hell-fire, Mat. xxiii. 33.

in the presence of the holy angels, and in the presence of the lamb.'[1] Look, as there is nothing but the pure glory of God that can make a man perfectly and fully happy, so there is nothing but the pure wrath of God that can make a man fully and perfectly miserable. Reprobates shall not only sip of the top of God's cup, but they shall drink the dregs of his cup. They shall not have at last one drop of mercy, nor one crumb of comfort. They have filled up their lifetime with sin, and God will fill up their eternity with torments. But,

[4.] Fourthly and lastly, As wrath to come is pure wrath, so wrath to come is *everlasting wrath :* Rev. xiv. 11, 'And the smoke of their torment ascendeth up for ever and ever.' ' Would to God,' saith one, [Chrysostom,] ' men would everywhere think and talk more of hell, and of that eternity of extremity, that they shall never else be able to avoid, or to abide.' See the scriptures in the margin.[2] ' The damned,' saith Gregory, ' shall suffer an end without end, a death without death, a decay without decay ; for their death ever liveth, their end ever beginneth, their decay never ceaseth, they are ever healed to be new wounded, and always repaired to be new devoured ; they are ever dying and never dead, eternally broiling and never burnt up, ever roaring in the pangs of death, and never rid of those pangs ; for they shall have punishment without pity, misery without mercy, sorrow without succour, crying without comfort, mischief without measure, and torment without ease, " where the worm dieth not, and the fire is never quenched."' The torments of the damned shall continue as many worlds as there be stars in the firmament, as there be grains of sand on the sea-shore, and as there be drops of water found in the sea ; and when these worlds are ended, the pains and torments of hell shall not cease, but begin afresh, and thus this wheel shall turn round without end.

Oh the folly and vanity, the madness and baseness of poor wretched sinners who expose themselves to everlasting torments for a few fleshly momentary pleasures ! O sirs ! who can stand before his indignation, and who can abide in the fierceness of his anger ? ' His fury is poured out like fire, and the rocks are thrown down by him,' Nahum i. 6. Now how should these things work poor sinners to flee from wrath to come by fleeing to Christ, ' who alone is able to save them from wrath to come,' 1 Thes. i. 10. Themistocles, understanding that King Admetus was highly displeased with him, he took up the king's young son in his arms, and so treated with the father, holding his darling in his bosom, and by that means pacified his wrath.[3] Ah sinners, sinners, the King of kings is highly offended with you, and there is no way to appease his wrath, but by taking up Christ in your arms, and so present your suits to him. But,

3. Thirdly, If there be a hell, then don't *let fly so fiercely against those faithful ministers who seriously and conscientiously do all they can to prevent your dropping into hell,* 2 Cor. v. 20, xii. 15. Don't call them legal preachers who tell you that there is a hell, and that

---

[1] This drinking of the wine of the wrath of God, without mixture, notes *summam pœnæ severitatem.*

[2] 2 Thes. i. 8 ; Jude 6, 7 ; Mat. xxv. 46 ; Isa. xxxiii. 14, &c.

[3] Plutarch *in vita.*

there is no torments to hellish torments, if either you consider their extremity or eternity. Be not so hot nor so angry with those ambassadors of Christ who are willing to spend and be spent that they may keep you from running headlong to hell. 'To think of hell,' saith one,[1] 'preserves a man from falling into it;' and, saith the same author, *Utinam ubique de gehenna dissereretur,* I could wish men would discourse much and oft of hell. It was a saying of Gregory Nyssen, who lived about thirteen hundred years ago, 'He that does but hear of hell is, without any further labour or study, taken off from sinful pleasures.' But what minister can say so now? Surely men's hearts are grown worse since, for how do most men run headlong to hell, and take a pleasure to dance hoodwinked into everlasting burnings![2] Oh, had but the desperate sinners of this day who swear and curse, drink and drab, and drown themselves in fleshly pleasures, but one sight of this hell, how would it charm their mouths, appal their spirits, and strike fear and astonishment into their hearts!

I cannot think that the high transgressors of this day durst be so highly wicked as they are, did they but either see or foresee what they shall one day certainly feel, except there be sound and serious repentance on their sides, and pardoning grace on God's. Bellarmine was of opinion that one glimpse of hell were enough to make a man, not only turn Christian and sober, but monk too: to live after the strictest rule that may be. And yet, he tells us of a certain advocate of the court of Rome, who being, at the point of death, stirred up by them that were about him to repent and call upon God for mercy, he, with a constant countenance, and without sign of any fear, turned his speech to God, and said, Lord, I have longed much to speak to thee, not for myself, but for my wife and children; for I am hasting to hell, I am now a-going to dwell with devils, neither is there anything that I would have thee to do for me; and this he spoke, saith Bellarmine, who was then present and heard it, *Animo tam tranquillo ac si de itinere ad villam loqueretur,* with as placate, serene and tranquil a mind, as if he had been speaking of going to the next town or village. Ah, who can read or write such a relation without horror and terror![3] But,

4. Fourthly, If there be a hell, then *do not fret, do not envy the prosperity and flourishing estate and condition of wicked and ungodly men;* for God has given it under his hand, that they shall be turned into hell: 'The wicked shall be turned into hell, and all the nations that forget God,' Ps. xxxvii. 1, 2, lxxiii. 21; Prov. iii. 31; Ps. ix. 17. It was a wise saying of Marius to those that envy great men their honour, Let them, saith he, envy them their burdens. I have read a story of a Roman, who was by a court-martial condemned to die for breaking his rank to steal a bunch of grapes; and as he was going to execution, some of the soldiers envied him, that he had grapes, and they had none. Saith he, Do you envy me my grapes, I must pay dear for

---

[1] Chrysostom, hom. xliv. in Mat.

[2] Look, as he said that nothing but the eloquence of Tully could sufficiently set forth Tully's eloquence, so none can express these everlasting torments but he that is from everlasting to everlasting. Millions of years multiplied by millions, make not up one minute to this eternity; but who considers it, who believes it? &c.

[3] Bellar. de arte moriendi, lib. ii. cap. 10.

them! Ah sirs! do not envy wicked men's grapes, do not envy their riches, their honours, their greatness, their offices, their dignities; for they shall one day pay dear for their things. High seats to many are uneasy, and the downfall terrible: 'How art thou fallen from heaven, O Lucifer, son of the morning!' Isa. xiv. 12. It is spoken of the Chaldean monarch, who, though high, yet had a sudden change befell him. It is not a matter of so great joy to have been high and honourable, as it is of grief, anguish, and vexation to be afterwards despicable and contemptible: 'Come down, and sit in the dust,' Isa. xlvii. 1. Babylon was the lady of kingdoms; but, saith God, 'sit in the dust; take the mill-stones, and grind,' ver. 2; 'The Lord of hosts hath purposed to stain (Heb., to pollute) the pride of all glory, and to bring into contempt all the honourable of the earth,' Isa. xxiii. 9; 'He shall bring down their pride together,' Isa. xxv. 11; 'Woe to the crown of pride: the crown of pride shall be trodden under feet,' Isa. xxviii. 1, 3. God will bring down the crown of pride to the dust, to ashes, yea, to hell; and, therefore, do not envy the crown of pride. Crœsus was so puffed up with his crown of pride, with his great riches and worldly glory, that he boasted himself to be the happiest man that lived; but Solon told him that no man was to be accounted happy before death. Crœsus little regarded what Solon had said unto him, until he came, by miserable experience, to find the uncertainty of his riches, and all worldly glory, which before he would not believe. For when he was taken by King Cyrus, and condemned to be burned, and saw the fire preparing for him, then he cried out, O Solon, Solon! Cyrus asking him the cause of the outcry, he answered, that now he remembered what Solon had told him in his prosperity— nemo ante obitum felix— that no man was to be accounted happy before death. Who can sum up those crowns of pride that in Scripture and history God has brought down to the dust, yea, to the dunghill! Have not some wished, when they have been breathing out their last, that they had never been kings, nor queens, nor lords, nor ladies? &c. Where is there one of ten thousand who is advanced, and thereby anything bettered? Solus imperatorum Vespasianus in melius mutatus. Few men believe what vexations lie under the pillows of princes. You look upon my crown and my purple robes, saith Artaxerxes; but did you know how they were lined with thorns, you would not stoop to take them up. Damocles highly extolled Dionysius his condition. Dionysius, to convince him of his mistake, provides a royal feast, invites him to it, commands his servants to attend him. No meat, no mirth, no music is wanting; but withal caused a sharp sword to be hung overhead by a horse hair, which made Damocles tremble, and to forbear both meat and mirth. Such, even such, saith Dionysius the Sicilian tyrant, is my life, which thou deemest so pleasant and happy. O sirs! there is a sword of wrath which hangs over every sinner's head, even when he is surrounded with all the gay and gallant things of this world.

Outward prosperity is commonly given in wrath, as you may see by comparing the scriptures in the margin together.[1] Prosperity kills and damns more than adversity. The Germans have this proverb,

[1] Hos. xiii. 11; Ps. lxxiii. and lxxviii. 30, 31; Prov. i. 32; Luke xii. 16–22; Eccles. v. 12, 13.

That the pavement of hell is made of the glorious crests of gallants. It had been infinitely better for the great men of this world that they had never been so great, for their horrid abuse of God's mercy and bounty will but increase their misery and damnation at last. That ancient hit it, [Augustine,] who said, Because they have tasted so liberally of God's kindness, and have employed it only against God's glory, their felicity shall be short, but their misery shall be endless; and therefore to see the wicked prosper and flourish in this world is matter rather of pity than envy, it is all the heaven they must have.[1] These are as terrible texts as any in the whole Book of God: Mat. vi. 2, ' Verily I say unto you, they have their reward;' Luke vi. 24, 'Woe to you that are rich, for you have received your consolation;' James v. 1–3, ' Go to, now, ye rich men, weep and howl for your miseries that shall come upon you. Your riches are corrupted, and your garments are moth-eaten. Your gold and silver is cankered: and the rust of them shall be a witness against you, and shall eat your flesh as it were fire.' Gregory, being advanced to places of great preferment, professed that there was no scripture that went so near his heart, and that struck such a trembling into his spirit, as that speech of Abraham to Dives, Luke xvi. 25, ' Son, remember thou in thy lifetime receivedst thy good things.' They that have their heaven here, are in danger to miss it hereafter. It is not God's usual way, saith one, [Jerome,] to remove *a deliciis ad delicias,* from delights to delights—to bestow two heavens, one here and another hereafter; and doubtless hence it was that David made it his solemn prayer, ' Deliver me from the wicked, from men of the world, which have their portion in this life, and whose belly thou fillest with thy hid treasure,' Ps. xvii. 14. It is a very hard thing to have earth and heaven too. God did not turn man out of one paradise that he should here provide himself of another. Many men with the prodigal cry out, ' Give me the portion that belongs to me,' Luke xv. 12—give me riches, and give me honour, and give me preferment, &c., and God gives them their desires, but it is with a vengeance; as the Israelites had quails to choke them, and afterwards a king to vex them, and a table to be a snare unto them, Ps. lxxviii. 24–32. When the Israelites had eaten of their dainty dishes, justice sent in a sad reckoning which spoiled all. Ah friends, there is no reason why we should envy the prosperity of wicked men. Suppose, saith one, [Chrysostom,] that a man one night should have a pleasant dream that for the time might much delight him, and for the pleasure of such a dream should be tormented a thousand years together with exquisite torments, would any man desire to have such a dream upon such conditions? All the contentments of this life are not so much to eternity as a dream is to a thousand years. And, oh, how little is that man's condition to be envied, who for these short pleasures of sin must endure an eternity of torments! O sirs! do wicked men purchase their present pleasures at so dear a rate as eternal torments? and do we envy their enjoyment of them so short a time? Would any envy a man going to execution, because he saw him in prison nobly feasted and

---

[1] The whole Turkish empire is nothing else but a crust cast by our Father to his dogs, and it is all they are likely to have, let them make them merry with it, said Luther.

nobly attended and bravely courted? or because he saw him go up the ladder with a gold chain about his neck and a scarlet gown upon his back? or because he saw him walk to execution through pleasant fields or delightsome gardens? or because there went before him drums beating, colours flying, and trumpets sounding, &c.? Surely no. Oh, no more should we envy the grandeur of the men of the day, for every step they take is but a step to an eternal execution! The sinner is cursed, and all his blessings are cursed; and who in their wits would envy a man under a curse? Oh, how much more worthy of our pity than envy is that man's condition who hath all his happiness confined to the narrow compass of this life, but his misery extended to the uttermost bounds of an everlasting duration! Mal. ii. 2. But,

5. Fifthly, If there be a hell, then, Christians, *spend your days in admiring and in being greatly affected with the transcendent love of Christ, in undergoing hellish punishments in our steads.* Oh pray, pray hard that you ' may be able to comprehend with all saints what is the breadth, and length, and depth, and height of that love of Christ which passeth knowledge,' Eph. iii. 18, 19,—of that love of Christ that put him upon these corporeal and spiritual sufferings which were so exceeding great, acute, extreme, universal and continual, and all to save us from wrath to come, 1 Thes. i. 10. Christ's outward and inward miseries, sorrows, and sufferings are not to be paralleled, and therefore Christians have the more cause to lose themselves in the contemplation of his matchless love. Oh, bless Christ! oh, kiss Christ! oh, embrace Christ! oh, welcome Christ! oh, cleave to Christ! oh, follow Christ! oh, walk with Christ! oh, long for Christ! who for your sakes hath undergone insupportable wrath and most hellish torments, as I have evidenced at large before, and therefore a touch here may suffice.[1] Oh, look up to dear Jesus, and say, O blessed Jesus, thou wast accursed that I might be blessed, Gal. iii. 13; thou wast condemned that I might be justified, Isa. liii.; thou didst for a time undergo the very torments of hell, that I might for ever enjoy the pleasures of heaven, Rom. viii. 30, 34; Ps. xvi. 11; and therefore I cannot but dearly love thee, and highly esteem thee, and greatly honour thee, and earnestly long after thee; and this is all I shall say by way of inference.

But, for a close, you will say, *ubi sit?* where is hell? where is this place of torment? where is that very place that is so frequently called hell in the Scripture? That there is a hell, you have sufficiently proved; but, pray, where is it? where is it? Now, to this I answer,

[1.] First, That it becomes all sober, serious Christians to rest satisfied and contented with those scriptural arguments that do undeniably prove that there is a hell, a place appointed where the wicked, the damned, shall be tormented for ever and ever, though they do not know, nor for the present cannot understand, where this hell is. But,

[1] Ps. ciii. 1, 2, and ii. 12; Cant. iii. 4; Rev. xiv. 4, 5; Isa. lxiii. 8; Gen. vi. 9; Cant. viii. 14.

[2.] Secondly, I answer, Curiosity is one of the most dangerous engines that the devil uses to undo souls withal. When Satan observes that men do in good earnest set themselves to the obtaining of knowledge, then he strives to turn them to vain inquiries and curious speculations; that so, if they will be knowing, he may keep them busied about unprofitable curiosities.[1] The way to make us mere fools is to affect to know more than God would have us. Adam's tree of knowledge made him and his posterity fools, Gen. iii. 5, 6. Curiosity was the bait whereby the devil caught our first parents, and undid us all. Curiosity is the spiritual adultery of the soul.[2] Curiosity is spiritual drunkenness. So that, look, as the drunkard, be the cup never so deep, he is not satisfied unless he see the bottom of it; so the curious searcher into the depths of God, he is unsatisfied till he comes to the bottom of them, and by this means they come to be mere fools, as the apostle saith, Rom. i. 22. Adam had a mind to know as much of God as God himself; and by this means he came to know nothing. Curiosity is that green-sickness of the soul, whereby it longs for novelties, and loathes sound and wholesome truths; it is the epidemical distemper of this age. Ah! how many are there who spend their precious time in nice and curious questions![3] As, what did Christ dispute of among the doctors? Where did Paradise stand? In what part of the world is local hell? What fruit was it that Adam ate, and ruined us all? What became of Moses his body? How many orders and degrees of elect angels are there? &c. Oh that we could learn contentedly to be ignorant where God would not have us knowing, and let us not account it any disparagement to acknowledge some depths in God's counsels, purposes, decrees, and judgments, which our shallow reason cannot fathom, Rom. xi. 33. It is sad when men will be wise above what is written, and love to pry into God's secrets, and scan the mysteries of religion by carnal reason, Rom. xii. 3, and 1 Cor. iv. 6. God often plagues such pride and curiosity by leaving that sort of men to strange and fearful falls. When a curious inquisitor asked Austin what God did before he created the world, Austin told him he was making hell for such busy questionists, for such curious inquirers into God's secrets. Such handsome jerks are the best answers to men of curious minds. But,

[3.] Thirdly, I answer, It concerns us but little to know whether hell be in the air, or in the concave of the earth, or of what longitude, latitude, or profundity it is.[4] Let hell be where it hath pleased God in his secret counsel to place it, to men unknown, whether in the north or in the south, under the frozen zone, or under the burning zone, or in a pit or a gulf. Our great care should be to avoid it, to escape it, and not to be curiously inquisitive about that place, which

---

[1] Curious inquirers have always lain under the lash of Christ, as you may see by comparing these scriptures together : Job xxi. 22; Acts i. 6, 7 ; Luke xiii. 22, 24.

[2] August. Epist. 77.

[3] Basil saith divers questions may be made about a very fly, which no philosopher is ever able to answer; how much rather about heaven, hell, or the work of grace?

[4] Let us not be inquisitive where hell is, but rather let our care be to escape it, saith Chrysostom.

the Lord in his infinite wisdom hath not thought fit clearly to reveal or make known to the sons of men.

> In hell there's nothing heard but yells and cries;
> In hell the fire never slacks, nor worm never dies.
> But where is this hell placed? My muse, stop there:
> Lord, shew me what it is, but never where!
>
> To worm and fire, to torments there,
> No term he gave, they cannot wear.[1]

Look, as there are many that please themselves with discourses of the degrees of glory, whilst others make sure their interest in glory; so many please themselves with discourses of the degrees of the torments of hell, whilst others make sure their escaping those torments; and look, as many take pleasure to be discoursing about the place where hell is, so some take pleasure to make sure their escaping of that place; and certainly they are the best and wisest of men who spend most thoughts, and time, and pains how to keep out of it, than to exercise themselves with disputes about it.[2] But,

[4.] Fourthly, I answer, That it has been the common opinion of the fathers, that hell is in the bowels of the earth; yea, Christ and the blessed Scriptures, which are the highest authority, do strongly seem to favour this opinion, by speaking of a descent unto hell, in opposition unto heaven; and, therefore, we may as well doubt whether heaven be above us, as doubt of hell being beneath us.[3] Among other scriptures ponder upon these: Ps. cxl. 10, 'Let them be cast into the deep pits, that they rise not up again. Bring them down into the pit of destruction;' Prov. ix. 18, 'Her guests are in the depths of hell;' Prov. xv. 24, 'The way of life is above to the wise, that he may depart from hell beneath.' Sheol is sometimes taken for a pit, sometimes for the grave, and sometimes, and that significantly too, for hell, all downwards. One saith[4] that Sheol generally signifies all places under the earth; whence some conclude that hell is in the heart of the earth, or under the earth. Without doubt it is below, because it is everywhere opposed to heaven, which is above. It is therefore called *Abyssus*, a deep pit, a vast gulf; such a pit as, by reason of the depth thereof, may be said to have no bottom. The devils entreated Christ that he would not send them to this place, Luke viii. 31, *in Abyssum*, which is, saith one, *Immensæ profunditatis vorago, quasi absque fundo*: A gulf of immeasurable depth, &c.[5] The apostle, 2 Pet. ii. 4, speaking of the angels that sinned, saith, 'God cast them down into hell.' So Beza, in his Annotations, telleth us the Greeks called that place which was ordained for the prison and torment of the damned. And reason itself doth teach us that it must needs be opposite and contrary to that place in which the spirits of just men made perfect, Heb. xii. 23, do reside, which, on all hands, is granted to be above; and hell therefore must needs be below, in

---

[1] A Pentelogia, dolor inferni.—Prudentius the poet.
[2] As in heaven one is more glorious than another, so in hell one shall be more miserable than another.—*Augustine.*
[3] Infernum est locus subterraneus, Tertul. lib. 3. de Anim.
[4] Mercerus upon Gen. xxxvii. [Comment. on Genesis, 1598, folio.—G.]
[5] Beza upon Mat.

the centre of the earth, say some, which is from the superficies three thousand five hundred miles, as some judge. Hesiod saith, hell is as far under the earth as heaven is above it. Some have been of opinion that the pit spoken of, into which Korah, Dathan, and Abiram went down alive, when the earth clave asunder and swallowed them up, was the pit of hell, into which both their souls and bodies were immediately conveyed, Num. xvi. 33. As we know little in respect of the height of heaven, so we know as little in respect of the lowness of hell. Some of the upper part of the earth is to us yet *terra incognita*, an unknown land ; but all of the lowest parts of hell is to us an unknown land. Many thousands have travelled thither, but none have returned thence, to make reports or write books of their travels. That piece of geography is very imperfect. Heaven and hell are the greatest opposites, or remotest extremes: ' Thou, Capernaum, which art exalted unto heaven, shalt be brought down to hell !' Mat. xi. 23. Heaven and hell are at farthest natural distance, and are therefore the everlasting receptacles of those who are at the farthest moral distance—believers and unbelievers, saints and impenitents. And it is observable, that as the height of heaven, so the depth of hell, is ascribed to wisdom, to shew the unsearchableness of it. ' Oh the depth,' as well as ' Oh the height,' ' of the wisdom of God! how unsearchable are his judgments, and his ways past finding out !' Rom. xi. 33. Certainly God's depths, and Satan's depths, and hell's depths, lie far out of our view, and are hard to be found out, 1 Cor. ii. 10, and Rev. ii. 24. Though I ought religiously to reverence the wonderful wisdom of God, and to wonder at his unsearchable judgments, yet I ought not curiously and profanely to search beyond the compass of that which God hath revealed to us in his word. The Romans had a certain lake, the depth whereof they knew not; this lake they dedicated to victory. Doubtless hell is such a lake, the depth whereof no man knows; it is such a bottomless pit that no mortal can sound. But,

[5.] Fifthly and lastly, I answer, Some of the learned are of opinion, that hell is without this visible world, which will pass away at the last day, 2 Pet. iii. 10–13, and removed at the greatest distance from the *sedes beatorum*, the place where the righteous shall for ever inhabit: Mat. viii. 12, ' But the children of the kingdom shall be cast out into outer darkness.' Mat. xxii. 30, ' Then said the king to his servants, Bind him hand and foot, and take him away, and cast him into outer darkness.' Mat. xxv. 30, ' And cast ye the unprofitable servant into outer darkness.' Into a darkness beyond a darkness, into a dungeon beyond and beneath the prison.[1] The darkness of hell is compared to the darkness of those prisons, which were oftentimes out of the city,[2] 2 Pet. ii. 4; Jude 6; Acts xii. 10. By outer darkness, the Holy Ghost would signify to us that the wicked should be in a state most remote from

---

[1] In tenebras ex tenebris, infeliciter exclusi, infelicius excludendi.—*Augustine.*

[2] This prison was without the gate, near mount Calvary, and it was the loathsomest and vilest prison of all, for in it the thieves who were carried to Calvary to be executed were kept; and Christ alludeth to this prison in that Mat. viii. 12, and that Mat. xxii. 13, and that Mat. xxv. 30, ' Cast him into utter darkness;' which allusion could not be understood, unless there had been a dark prison without the city, where was utter darkness.

all heavenly happiness and blessedness ; and that they should be expulsed out of the blessed presence of God, who is *mentium lumen*. It is usual among the Greeks by a comparative to set forth the superlative degree. By outer darkness we are to understand the greatest darkness that is, as in a place most remote from all light. They shall be cast into outer darkness, that is, they shall be cast into the corporal and palpable darkness of the infernal prison ; immediately after death sinners' souls shall be cast into the infernal prison, and in the day of judgment both their souls and their bodies shall be cast into outer darkness. Darkness is no other thing than a privation of light.

Now light is twofold, viz.—1. Spiritual, as wisdom, grace, truth. Now the privation of this light is internal darkness, and ignorance in the spirit and inward man. 2. There is a sensible and corporal light, whose privation is outer darkness ; and this is the darkness spoken of in the three scriptures last cited. For although there be fire in hell, yet it is a dark and smoky fire, and not clear, except only so as the damned may see one another, for the greater increase of their misery, as some write. Now I shall leave the ingenuous reader to conclude as he pleases concerning the place where hell is, desiring and hoping that he will make it the greatest business of his life to escape hell, and to get to heaven, &c.

6. Sixthly, *If Jesus Christ did feel and suffer the very torments of hell, though not after a hellish manner, then let me infer that certainly the papists are greatly out, they are greatly mistaken, and do greatly err, who boldly and confidently assert that Christ's soul in substance went really and locally into hell.* Bellarmine takes a great deal of pains to make good this assertion,[1] but this great champion of the Romish church may easily be confuted. First, Because that *limbus patrum*, and Christ's fetching the fathers from the skirts of hell, about which he makes so great a noise, is a mere fable, and not bottomed upon any solid grounds of Scripture. Secondly, Because upon Christ's dying, and satisfying for our sins, his soul went that very day into paradise—as Adam sinning was that very day cast out of paradise—and his soul could not be in two places at once. Thirdly, Because this descent of Christ's soul into hell was altogether needless, and to no end. What need was there of it, or to what end did he descend ? Not to suffer in hell, for that was finished on the cross ; not to redeem or rescue the fathers out of hell, for the elect were never there, and redemption from hell was wrought by Christ's death, as the Scriptures do clearly evidence ; not to triumph there over the devils, &c.,[2] for Christ triumphed over them when he was on the cross.[3] Christ, in the day of his solemn inauguration into his heavenly kingdom, triumphed over sin, death, devils, and hell. When Christ was on the cross, he made the devils a public spectacle of scorn and derision ; as Tamerlane did Bajazet the great Turk, whom he shut up in an iron cage made like a grate, in such

[1] Bellar. de Christ. anima. lib. iv. cap. 10-16, tom. 1. *Vide* Calvin in Institut. lib. ii. cap. 16, sect. 9.
[2] Luke xxiii. 43; Gen. iii. 23, 24; John xviii. 30; Heb. ix. 12; 1 Thes. i. 10; Eph. iv. 8; Heb. ii. 14, 15; Col. ii. 14, 15.
[3] It is a plain allusion to the Roman triumphs, where the victor ascended to the Capitol in a chariot of state, the prisoners following on foot with their hands bound behind them, &c.

sort as that he might on every side be seen, and so carried him up and down all Asia, to be scorned and derided by his own people.[1]   By these few hints you may see the vanity and folly of the papists, who tell you that Christ's soul and substance went really and locally into hell.   I might make other inferences, but let these suffice at this time.

7. Seventhly, *As Jesus Christ did feel and suffer the very torments of hell, though not after a hellish manner, so Jesus Christ was really, certainly made a curse for us.*   Jesus Christ did in his soul and body bear that curse of the law, which by reason of transgression was due to us.   'Christ hath redeemed us from the curse of the law, being made a curse for us; for it is written, Cursed is every one that hangeth on a tree,' Gal. iii. 13.   He saith not Christ was *cursed*, but *a curse*, which is more: it shows that the curse of all did lie upon him.   The death on the tree was accursed above all kinds of deaths, as the serpent was accursed above all the beasts of the field, Gen. iii. 14.   This scripture refers to Deut. xxi. 33, 'His body shall not remain all night upon the tree; but thou shalt in any wise bury him that day, for he that is hanged is accursed of God.'[2]   The holy and wise God appointed this kind of punishment, as being the most cruel and reproachful, for a type of the punishment which his Son must suffer to deliver us from the curse.   Hanging on a tree was accounted the most shameful, the most dishonourable, the most odious and infamous, and accursed, of all kinds of death, both by the Israelites and other nations, because the very manner of the death did intimate that such men as were thus executed were such execrable, base, vile, and accursed wretches, that they did defile the earth with treading on it, and would pollute the earth if they should die upon it, and therefore were hanged up in the air, as persons not fit to converse amongst men, or touch the surface of the ground any more.   But what should be the reason why the ceremonial law affixed the curse to this death rather than any other death?   I answer, first, because this was reckoned the most shameful and dishonourable of all deaths, and was usually therefore the punishment of those that had by some notorious wickedness provoked God to pour out his wrath upon the whole land, and so were hanged up to appease his wrath; as you may see in the hanging of those princes that were guilty of committing whoredom with the daughters of Moab, Num. xxv. 4; and in the hanging of Saul's seven sons in the days of David, when there was a famine in the land because of Saul's perfidious oppressing of the Gibeonites, 2 Sam. xxi. 6–9; and in Joshua's hanging of the five kings of the Amorites, Josh. xvi. 26.   But, secondly and mainly, it was with respect to the death Christ was to die.   God would have his Son, the Lord Jesus, to suffer this kind of death, that hence it might be the more evident that in his death he bare the curse due to our sins, according to that of the apostle, Gal. iii. 13.   Christ was certainly made that curse which he redeemed us from, otherwise the apostle does not reason either soundly or fairly, when he tells us we

---

[1] [Knolles,] Turk Hist. 220.

[2] Not that all that are hanged should be damned, for the contrary appears in that Luke xxiii. 43.   Neither is hanging in itself, or by the law of nature, or by civil law, more execrable than any other death.

are redeemed from the curse because Christ was made a curse for us; he remitteth that curse to us which he received in himself. That father hit the mark who saith,[1] *Christus supplicium nostrum sine reatu suscepit, ut solveret reatum, et finiret supplicium*, Christ hath taken our punishment without guilt, to loose the guilt and end the punishment. We were subject to the curse, because we had transgressed the law; Christ was not subject, because he had fulfilled it. *Eam ergo execrationem suscepit, cui obnoxius non erat, quum suspensus fuit in ligno, ut execrationem solveret, quæ adversus nos erat*, He therefore took that curse, to the which he was not subject, when he hanged upon the tree, to loose the curse which was against us.[2] Such a curse or execration was Christ made for us. as was that from which he redeemed us; and that curse from which he redeemed us was no other than the curse of the law, and that the curse of the law included all the punishment which sinners were to bear or suffer for transgression of the law, of which his hanging on the cross was a sign and symbol; and this curse was Christ made for us, that is, he did bear and suffer it to redeem us from it. Christ was verily made a curse for us, and did bear both in his body and soul that curse, which by reason of the transgression of the law was due to us; and therefore I may well conclude this head with that saying of Jerome, *Injuria Domini, nostra gloria*, The Lord's injury is our glory.[3] The more we ascribe to Christ's suffering, the less remaineth of ours; the more painfully that he suffered, the more fully are we redeemed; the greater his sorrow was, the greater our solace; his dissolution is our consolation, his cross our comfort; his annoy our endless joy; his distress in soul our release, his calamity our comfort; his misery our mercy, his adversity our felicity, his hell our heaven. Christ is not only accursed, but a curse; and this expression is used both for more significancy and usefulness, to note out the truth and realness of the thing, and also to shew the order and way he took for bringing us back unto that blessedness which we had lost. The law was our righteousness in our innocent condition, and so it was our blessedness; but the first Adam, falling away from God by his first transgression, plunged himself into all unrighteousness, and so inwrapped himself in the curse, James i. 24. Now Christ the second Adam, that he may restore the lost man into an estate of blessedness, he becomes that for them which the law is unto them, namely, a curse; beginning where the law ends, and so going backward to satisfy the demands of the law to the uttermost, he becomes first a curse for them and then their righteousness, and so their blessedness, Rom. x. 24. Now Christ's becoming a curse for us stands in this, that whereas we are all accursed by the sentence of the law because of sin, he now comes in our room, and stands under the stroke of that curse which of right belongs to us; so that it lies not now any longer on the backs of poor sinners, but on him for them and in their stead; therefore he is called a surety, Heb. vii. 22. The surety stands in the room of a debtor, malefactor, or him that is any way obnoxious to the law. Such is Adam and all his posterity. We are by the doom of the law evil-doers, transgressors, and upon that score we stand indebted to the justice of God, and lie under the stroke of his wrath. Now the

---

[1] Bede in Gal. iii. [2] Œcumenius in Gal. iii. [3] Jerome in Gal. iii.

Lord Jesus, seeing us in this condition, he steps in and stands between us and the blow; yea, he takes this wrath and curse off from us unto himself. He stands not only or merely after the manner of a surety among men, in the case of debt; for here the surety indeed enters bond with the principal for the payment of the debt; but yet he expects that the debtor should not put him to it, but that he should discharge the debt himself: he only stands as a good security. No, Christ Jesus doth not expect that we should pay the debt ourselves, but he takes it wholly to himself. As a surety for a murderer or traitor, or some other notorious malefactor, that hath broken prison and is run away, he lies by it body for body, state for state, and undergoes whatsoever the male-factor is chargeable withal for satisfying the law; even so, the Lord Jesus Christ stands surety for us runagate malefactors, making him-self liable to all that curse which belongs to us, that he might both answer the law fully and bring us back again to God. As the first Adam stood in the room of all mankind fallen; so Christ the second Adam stands in the room of all mankind which is to be restored; he sustains the person of all those which do spiritually descend from him, and unto whom he bears the relation of a head, Eph. i. 22, 23. Christ did actually undergo and suffer the wrath of God, and the fearful effects thereof, in the punishments threatened in the law. As he became a debtor, and was so accounted, even so he became payment thereof; he was made a sacrifice for sin, and bare to the full all that ever divine justice did or could require, even the uttermost extent of the curse of the law of God. He must thus undergo the curse, because he had taken upon him our sin. The justice of the most high God, revealed in the law, looks upon the Lord Jesus as a sinner, because he hath un-dertaken for us, and seizeth upon him accordingly, pouring down on his head the whole curse, and all those dreadful punishments which are threatened in it against sin; for the curse followeth sin as the shadow the body, whether it be sin inherent or sin imputed; even as the bless-ing follows righteousness, whether it be righteousness inherent or righteousness imputed. But,

8. Eighthly, He that did feel and suffer the very torments of hell, though not after a hellish manner, was *God man.* Christ participates of both natures, being Θεάνθρωπος, God and man, God-man. Such a mediator sinners needed. No mediator but such a one who hath in-terest in both parties, could serve their turns or save their souls, and such a one is the Lord Jesus; he hath an interest in both parties, and he has an interest in both natures, the Godhead and the manhood. The blessed Scriptures are so express and clear in these points, that they must shut their eyes with a witness against the light, that cannot see Christ to be God-man, to be God and man. I shall first speak something of Christ, as he is God. Now here are fathomless depths and bottomless bottoms, if I may so speak; here are stupendous and amazing mysteries, astonishing and confounding excellencies, such as the holy angels themselves desire to pry into.[1] God is φῶς οἰκῶν ἀπρόσιτον, dwelling in inaccessible light: 1 Tim. vi. 16. Here are such beauties and perfections that had I, as the poet speaks, a hundred

---

[1] 1 Pet. i. 12, παρακύψαι. The word signifies to look wishly and intently, as the cherubims of old looked into the mercy-seat, Exod. xxv. 18, 19. It signifies prying into

tongues, a hundred mouths, and a voice of steel, yet I could not sufficiently describe them. Nevertheless give me leave to say something concerning our Lord Jesus Christ, who is one eternal God with the Father, and with the Holy Ghost. I might produce a cloud of witnesses in the case, but it is enough that we have the authority of the sacred Scriptures, both in the Old and New Testament, confirming of it; and therefore I shall lay down some proofs or demonstrations of the eternal godhead of Christ, which I shall draw out of the blessed Scripture. This is a point of high concernment, that Christ is God; so high as whosoever buildeth not upon this buildeth upon the sands. This is the rock of our salvation, ' The Word was God,' John i. 1. Concerning this important point, consider—

1. First, *That the godhead of Christ is clearly asserted, and manifested both in the Old and New Testament.* Take a taste of some of those many scriptures which may be cited: Isa. xliii. 10–12, ' That ye may know and believe, and understand that I am he, I, even I am Jehovah, and besides me there is no Saviour:' and Isa. xli. 21–25, ' There is no God else besides me: a just God and Saviour, there is none besides me. Look unto me and be ye saved, all the ends of the earth, for I am God, and there is none else. To me every knee shall bow. . . . . In Jehovah have I righteousness. . . . In Jehovah shall the seed of Israel be justified.' [1] Compare this with Rom. xiv. 10, 11. And the Socinians may as safely conclude, that there is no other God but Jesus Christ, as they may conclude that there is no God but God the Father, from the 17th of John. But they and we ought to conclude from these scriptures, that Jesus Christ is not a different God from the Father, but is one and the same God with him. So he is called ' The mighty God, the everlasting Father,' Isa. ix. 6. Take a few clear places out of the New Testament, as that in Rom. ix. 5, ' Of whom as concerning the flesh Christ came, who is over all, God blessed for evermore.' Christ is here himself called God blessed for ever. So Titus ii. 13, ' Looking for that hope, and the glorious appearance of the great God, and our Saviour Jesus Christ.' Who is it that shall appear at the last day in the clouds, but Christ? who is called the great God and our Saviour? ' God blessed for ever,' saith Paul to the Romans; ' The great God,' saith Paul to Titus: 1 John v. 20, ' And we know that the Son of God is come, and hath given us an understanding, that we may know him that is true ; and we are in him that is true, even in his Son Jesus Christ. This is the true God, and eternal life:' Phil. ii. 6, ' He was in the form of God, and thought it no robbery to be equal with God:' and Col. ii. 9, ' In him dwelleth the fulness of the Godhead bodily:' John xx. 28, ' My Lord, and my God:' 1 Tim. iii. 16, ' God manifested in the flesh :' ' To which of the saints or angels did God say at any time, Thou art my Son ?' Heb. i. 1. ' The heir of all things, the illustrious brightness of my glory, and lively character of my person.' ' Thy throne, O God, is for ever and ever, and all the angels of God shall worship thee.' Certainly he

a thing overveiled and hidden from sight, to look, as we say, wishly, [' wistfully '—G.] at it, as if we would look even through it.
[1] Compare these scriptures of the Old Testament with these in the New. Heb. i. 2, 3; 1 John i. 7; Acts iv. 12; Eph. iv. 8; Rom. ix. 30; [and also] Jer. xxxiii. 23; Ps. vi., lxviii. 18–20.

who is God's own proper, natural, consubstantial, co-essential, only-begotten Son, he is God; wherever this sonship is, there is the deity or the divine essence. Now Christ is thus God's Son, therefore he is God. What the Father is as to his nature, that the Son must also be; now the first person, the Father of Christ, is God; whereupon he too who is the Son must be God also. A son always participates of his father's essence, there is betwixt them evermore an identity and oneness of nature. If therefore Christ be God's Son, as is most evident throughout the Scripture he is, then he must needs have that very nature and essence which God the Father hath, insomuch that if the second person be not really a God, the first person is but equivocally a Father. These scriptures out of the Old and New Testament are so evident and pregnant to prove the godhead of Christ, that they need no illustration; yea, they speak so fully for the divinity of Christ, that all the Arians and Socinians in the world do but in vain go about to elude them. But,

2. Secondly, *Let us ponder seriously upon these scriptures:* John iii. 13, 'And no man hath ascended up to heaven, but he that came down from heaven, even the Son of man, which is in heaven;' ver. 31, 'He that cometh from above is above all: he that cometh from heaven is above all;' John viii. 23, 'Ye are from beneath, I am from above;' John xvi. 28, 'I came forth from the Father, and am come into the world; and again I leave the world, and go to the Father.' Now from these blessed scriptures we may thus argue: he who was in heaven before he was on the earth, and who was also in heaven whilst he was on the earth, is certainly the eternal God; but all this doth Jesus Christ strongly assert concerning himself, as is evident in the scriptures last cited; therefore he is the eternal God, blessed for ever. But,

3. Thirdly, Christ's eternal deity, co-equality, and consubstantiality with the Father, may be demonstrated from *his divine names and titles.* As,

(1.) First, *Jehovah* is one of the incommunicable names of God, which signifies his eternal essence.

The Jews observe that in God's name Jehovah, the Trinity is implied. *Je* signifies the present tense, *ho* the preterperfect tense, *vah* the future. The Jews also observe that in his name Jehovah all the Hebrew letters are *literæ quiescentes*, that denote rest, implying that in God and from God is all our rest. Every gracious soul is like Noah's dove, he can find no rest nor satisfaction but in God. God alone is the godly man's ark of rest and safety. Jehovah is the incommunicable name of God, and is never attributed to any but God: Ps. lxxxiii. 19, 'Thou whose name alone is Jehovah.' Jehovah is a name so full of divine mysteries, that the Jews hold it unlawful to pronounce it.[1] Jehovah signifies three things:—

[1.] That God is an eternal, independent being of himself.
[2.] That he gives being to all creatures, Acts xvii. 28.
[3.] That he doth, and will give, being to his promises. God tells

---

[1] Exod. xv. 3; Gen. ii. 4. The Jews called it *nomen Dei ineffabile.* But this name Jehovah is not unspeakable in regard of the name, but in regard of the essence of God, set forth by it, as Zanchy [Zanchius] noteth. This name was always thrice repeated when the priest blessed the people, Num. vi. 24–26.

Moses, Exod. vi. 3, that he 'appeared unto Abraham, unto Isaac, and unto Jacob by the name of *El Shaddai*, God Almighty, but by my name Jehovah was I not known to them.' The name Jehovah was known to Abraham, Isaac, and Jacob, but not *mysterium nominis*, the mystery of the name.[1] This was revealed to Moses from God, and from Moses to the people. It is meant of the performances of his great promises made to Abraham. God did promise to give the land of Canaan to Abraham's seed for an inheritance, which promise was not performed to him, but to his seed after him; so that this is the meaning, God appeared to Abraham, Isaac, and Jacob, *El Shaddai*, God Almighty, in protecting, delivering, and rewarding of them, but by his name Jehovah he was not known to them. God did not perform his promise made to Abraham, Isaac, and Jacob, but unto their seed and posterity after them. This name Jehovah is the proper and peculiar name of the one, only true God, a name as far significant of his nature and being as possibly we are enabled to understand; so that this is taken for granted on all hands, that he whose name is Jehovah is the only true God. Whenever that name is used properly, without a trope or figure, it is used of God only.

Now this glorious name Jehovah, that is so full of mysteries, is frequently ascribed to Christ: Isa. vi. 1, he is called Jehovah, for there Isaiah is said to see 'Jehovah sitting upon a throne,' &c. And, John xii. 41, this is expressly by the holy evangelist applied to Christ, of whom he saith, that 'Isaiah saw his glory, and spake of him.' Exod. xvii. 1, the people are said to 'tempt Jehovah;' and the apostle saith, 1 Cor. x. 9, 'Let us not tempt Christ, as some of them also tempted, and were destroyed of serpents.' It is said of Jehovah, 'Of old hast thou laid the foundation of the earth, and the heavens are the works of thy hands; they shall perish, but thou shalt endure,' &c., Ps. cii. 25, 26; and the apostle clearly testifies, Heb. i. 10, that these words are spoken of Christ. So Jehovah rained fire and brimstone from Jehovah out of heaven, Gen. xix. 24; that is, Jehovah, the Son of God, that stayed with Abraham, Gen. xviii., rained fire and brimstone from Jehovah the Father; and Christ is called *Jehovah-Tsidkenu*, the Lord our righteousness; and in that Zech. xiii. 7, Christ is called the Father's fellow. The Lord Christ is that Jehovah, to whom every knee must bow, as appears by comparing Isa. xlv. 21–25 with Rom. xiv. 9–12 and Phil. ii. 6, 9–11. I might further insist upon this argument, and shew that the title of Lord, so often given to Christ in the New Testament, doth answer to the title of Jehovah in the Old Testament. And, as some learned men conceive, the apostles did purposely use the title of Lord, that they might not offend the Jews with frequent pronouncing of the word Jehovah: 'Thou shalt fear Jehovah thy God.' Deut. vi. 13 and x. 20 is rendered by the apostle, 'Thou shalt worship the Lord thy God;' and so Deut. vi. 5, 'Thou shalt love Jehovah thy God,' is rendered, Mat. xxii. 37, 'Thou shalt love the Lord thy God.' Thus you see that in several precious scriptures

---

[1] Gen. xx. 14, 'Abraham called the name of the place Jehovah-Jireh, the Lord will see, or provide.' Besides, the fathers of old are said not to have known God by his name Jehovah, in comparison of that which their posterity knew afterwards; for to them God made himself more clearly and plenarily known.

Jesus Christ is called Jehovah; and therefore we may very safely and confidently conclude that Jesus Christ is very God, God blessed for ever. But,

(2.) The second name or title which denotes the essence of God is *Ehieh*, 'I am that I am,' or, I will be what I will be, Exod. iii. 14.[1] It hath the same root with Jehovah, and signifies that God is an eternal, unchangeable being. Some make this name to be God's extraordinary name. Damascene saith this name containeth all things in it, like a vast and infinite ocean without bounds. This glorious name of God, I AM THAT I AM, implies these six things. [1.] God's *incomprehensibleness*: as we use to say of anything we would not have others pry into, it is what it is, so God saith here to Moses, I AM WHAT I AM. [2.] It implies God's *immensity*, that his being is without any limits. Angels and men have their beings, but then they are bounded and limited within such a compass; but God is an immense being that cannot be included within any bounds. [3.] It implies that God is *of himself*, and hath not a being dependent upon any other. 'I am,' that is, by and from and of myself. [4.] It implies God's *eternal and unchangeable* being in himself. It implies God's everlastingness. 'I am before anything was, and shall for ever be.' There never was nor shall be time wherein God could not say of himself, 'I am.' [5.] It implies that there is *no succession of time with God*. And, [6.] It implies that he is a God that *gives being to all things*.[2] In short, the reason why God nameth himself, 'I AM THAT I AM,' or will be that I will be, is because he is the Being of beings, subsisting by himself; as if he should say, I am my being, I am my essence; my existence differeth not from my essence, because I am that I am, and as I am, so will I be to all eternity,' 'the same yesterday, to-day, and for ever.' 'There is no shadow of change, no variableness at all in me.'

Now this glorious name is given to Jesus Christ: Rev. i. 8, 'I am Alpha and Omega, the beginning and the ending, saith the Lord, which is, and which was, and which is to come, the Almighty.'[3] This kind of speaking is taken from the Greek alphabet, in which language John wrote this book. *A*, called *Alpha* by them, being their first letter, and *Ω*, which they call *Omega*, the last. The sense is, I was before all creatures, and shall abide for ever, though all creatures should perish; or I am he from whom all creatures had their beginning, and to whom they are referred, as their uttermost end. Christ, in calling of himself Alpha and Omega, the beginning and the end, and that absolutely, doth therein assume unto himself absolute perfection, power, dominion, eternity, and divinity, which is, and which was, and which is to come. Christ assumeth all those epithets here to himself by which John, ver. 4, described God; and what wonder is it if Christ, who is God, doth take to himself whatever is due to God? The Almighty: this is another epithet proper to God, which Christ also

---

[1] The Hebrew Ehieh, after Ehieh, properly signifies, 'I will be that I will be.' The Septuagint renders it 'Εγώ ειμι ὁ ὢν, I am he that is; and in that Rev. xvi. 5, God is called, He that is, and that was, and that will be.

[2] Every creature is temporary and mutable. No creature can say, *Ero qui ero*, I will be that I will be.

[3] In this verse you have a clear and pregnant proof of Christ's deity.

taketh to himself, shewing that he is the true, eternal, and omnipotent God, in all things equal and co-essential with the Father and the Holy Ghost. This being the seventh argument which John makes use of to prove the deity of Christ, is three times repeated. He is the first and the last, which is, was, and is to come, and the Almighty, and therefore he is, without a peradventure, God eternal; for so Jehovah saith of himself, ' I the Lord, the first and the last, I am he ; I am the first, and I am the last, and besides me there is no God ; I am God Almighty.[1] But Christ doth challenge, as due to himself, all these divine attributes ; therefore he is Jehovah, that one, eternal, and omnipotent God with the Father and the Holy Ghost. Oh, the stateliness and majesty of our Lord Jesus Christ ! What an excellent and stately person is he, there being not a property attributed to God but is agreeable to Christ ! Every word in this Rev. i. 8, is a proper attribute of God. He is infinite in power, sovereign in dominion, and not bounded as creatures are. And that this is clearly spoken of Christ is most evident, not only from the scope, John being to set out Christ, from whom he had this revelation, but also from the 11th and 17th verses following, where he gives him the same titles over again, or rather, if you please, Christ, speaking of himself, taketh and repeateth the same titles.[2] Heb. xiii. 8, ' Jesus Christ, the same yesterday, and to-day, and for ever.' ' Yesterday,' that is, the time past, before his coming in the flesh ; ' to-day,' while in the flesh ; ' and for ever,' that is, after. The same afore time, in time, and after time. ' Jesus Christ the same,' that is, unchangeable in his essence, promises, and doctrine. Jesus Christ was always the same, and is still the same, and will abide for ever the same, as being one selfsame God, and one selfsame Mediator, as well in the Old as in the New Testament. John viii. 58, ' Jesus said unto them, Verily, verily, I say unto you, before Abraham was, I am.' According to my divine nature, which is from everlasting, before Abraham was, I am. I who, according to my humanity, am not above fifty years old, according to my divine nature am eternal, and so before Abraham and all the creatures, Micah v. 1, 2. I have a being from all eternity, and so before Abraham was born ; and therefore, as young as you take me to be in respect of my age here, I may well have seen and known Abraham, though he died above two thousand years since. But,

(3.) The third name or title which denotes the essence of God is *Elohim*, which signifies the persons in the essence. It is a name of the plural number, expressing the trinity of persons in the unity of essence ; and, therefore, it is observed by the learned that the Holy Ghost beginneth the story of the creation with this plural name of God, joined with a verb of the singular number, as *Elohim Bara, Dii creavit*, the mighty Gods, or all the three persons in the godhead, created, Gen. i. 1, 2. So Gen. iii. 22, ' And Jehovah Elohim said, Behold, the man is become as one of us.' It is a holy irrision of man's vain affectation of the deity. God upbraids our first parents for their vain affectation of being like unto him in that ironical expression, ' Behold, the man is become as one of us, to know good and evil ;'

[1] Isa. xli. 4, xliv. 6, and Gen. xvii. 1.
[2] See Rev. xxi. 6, and xxii. 13.

meaning, that by his sin he was become most unlike him. This name Elohim, by which God expresseth his nature, denotes the power and strength of God ; to shew us that God is strong and powerful, and that he can do great things for his people, and bring great desolations and destructions upon his and his people's enemies. O sirs, God is too strong for his strongest enemies, and too powerful for all the powers of hell ! Though Jacob, a worm in his own eyes, and in his enemies' eyes, yet Jacob need never fear ; for Elohim, the strong and powerful God, will stand by him, and help him, Isa. xli. 10, 13, 14.

Now this name is also attributed unto Christ : Ps. xlv. 6, ' Thy throne, O God, is for ever and ever : the sceptre of thy kingdom is a right sceptre.' ' Thy throne, O God,' Hebrew אלהים gods—' Thy throne, O Gods,' Elohim. It signifies the trinity of persons in the unity of essence, as I have before noted. The prophet directs his speech, not to Solomon but to Christ, as is most evident by the clear and unquestionable testimony of the Holy Ghost : Heb. i. 8, ' But unto the Son he saith, Thy throne, O God, is for ever and ever : a sceptre of righteousness is the sceptre of thy kingdom.' Christ is called God, not by an excellency only as the angels are, nor by office and title only as magistrates are called gods, nor catachrestically and ironically as the heathen gods are called, nor a diminutive God, inferior to the Father, as Arius held, but God by nature every way, co-essential, co-eternal, and co-equal with the Father and the Holy Ghost.[1] Hold fast all truth, but, above all, hold fast this glorious truth, that Jesus Christ is God blessed for ever.

(4.) The fourth name or title which denotes the essence of God is *El Gibbor*, the strong and mighty God. God is not only strong in his own essence, but he is also strong in the defence of his people, and it is he that giveth all strength and power to all other creatures, 2 Chron. xvi. 9. There are no men, no powers, that are a match for the strong God.

Now this title is also attributed to Christ : Isa. ix. 6, ' El Gibbor, the strong God, the mighty God.' The word אל, signifying God, doth also signify strong. He is so strong that he is almighty, he is one to whom nothing is impossible. Christ's name is God, for he is the same essence with God the Father. This title, ' the mighty God,' fitteth well to Christ, who hath all the names of the deity given to him in Scripture ; and who, by the strength and power of his godhead, did satisfy the justice of God, and pacify the wrath of God, and make peace, and purchase pardon and eternal life for all his elect.

(5.) The fifth name or title which denotes the essence of God is *El Shaddai*, God omnipotent or all-sufficient, Gen. xvii. 1. He wanteth nothing, but is infinitely blessed with the infinite perfection of his glorious being. By this name God makes himself known to be self-sufficient, all-sufficient, absolutely perfect. Certainly that man can want nothing who hath an all-sufficient God for his God. He that loseth his all for God, shall find all in an all-sufficient God, Mat. xix. 29. Esau had much, but Jacob had all, because he had the God of all, Gen. xxxiii. 9–11. *Habet omnia, qui habet habentem omnia.* What are riches, honours, pleasures, profits, lands, friends, yea, millions

---

[1] Ps. viii. 5, compared with Heb. ii. 6–8, and Ps. lxxxii. 16.

of worlds, to one Shaddai, God Almighty, God All-sufficient? [Augustine.] [1] This glorious name Shaddai, was a noble bottom for Abraham to act his faith upon, though in things above nature or against it, &c. He that is El Shaddai is perfectly able to defend his servants from all evil, and to bless them with all spiritual and temporal blessings, and to perform all his promises which concern both this life and that which is to come.

Now this name, this title Shaddai, is attributed to Christ, as you may clearly see by comparing Gen. xxxv. 6, 9–11, and xxxii. 24–30, with Hosea xii. 3-5.[2] That angel that appeared to Jacob was Christ, the angel of the covenant. Mark, you shall never find either God the Father or the Holy Ghost called an angel in Scripture; nor was this a created angel, for then Jacob would never have made supplication to him; but he was an uncreated angel, even the Lord of hosts, the Almighty God, who spake with Jacob in Bethel. He that in this divine story is said to be a man, was the Son of God in human shape, as is most evident by the whole narration. The angel in the text is the same angel that conducted the Israelites in the wilderness, and fought their battles for them, Exod. iii. 2; Acts vii. 30; 1 Cor. x. 4, 5, 9, even Jesus Christ, who is styled once and again the Almighty, Rev. i. 8, and iv. 8. In this last scripture is acknowledged Christ's holiness, power, and godhead. Ah Christians! when will you once learn to set one Almighty Christ against all the mighty ones of the world, that you may bear up bravely and stoutly against their rage and wrath, and go on cheerfully and resolutely in the way of your duty.

(6.) The sixth name or title is *Adonai*, my Lord. Though this name Adonai be given sometimes analogically to creatures, yet properly it belongs to God above.[3] This name is often used in the Old Testament; and, in Mal. i. 6, it is used in the plural number to note the mystery of the holy Trinity, ' If I be *Adonim*, Lords, where is my fear?' Some derive the word Adonai from a word in the Hebrew [אָדַן] that signifies *judicare*, to judge, because God is the Judge of the world; others derive it from a word which signifies *basis*, a foundation, intimating that God is the upholder of all things, as the foundation of a house is the support of the whole building.

Now this name is given to Christ: Dan. ix. 17, ' Cause thy face to shine upon thy sanctuary that is desolate, for Adonai, the Lord Christ, sake.' Daniel pleads here no merits of their own, but the merits and mediation of the Messias, whom God hath made both Lord and Christ. So Ps. cx. 1, ' The Lord said unto my Lord, Sit thou at my right hand until I make thine enemies thy footstool.'[4] Christ applies these words to himself, as you may see in that Mat. xxii. 24, ' Jehovah said,' that is, God the Father said, לַאדֹנִי *La-adoni*, ' unto my Lord,' that is, to Christ; ' sit thou at my right hand,' sit thou with me in my throne. It notes the advancement of Christ, as he was both God and man in

---

[1] This name Shaddai belongeth only to the godhead, and to no creature; no, not to the humanity of Christ.

[2] See my treatise on closet-prayer, opening that Gen. xxxii., and that Hosea xii., pp. 48–51, where you have four arguments to prove that Jesus Christ is the angel, the man, that is there spoken of, &c. [Vol. ii., pp. 139, *seq.* ' The Privy Key of Heaven.'—G.]

[3] Query, ' alone'?—G.   [4] Acts ii. ; Luke i. 43, and ii. 11, 12 ; Heb. i. 13.

one person, to the supremest place of power and authority, of honour
and heavenly glory, Mat. xxviii. 18; John iii. 35. God's right hand
notes a place of equal power and authority with God, even that he
should be advanced far above all principality, and power, and might,
and dominion, Eph. i. 21; Heb. i. 3; Luke xxii. 69. Christ's reign
over the whole world is sometimes called 'the right hand of the
majesty,' and sometimes the 'right hand of the power of God.' 'Until I
make thine enemies thy footstool.' This implies, [1.] That Jesus
Christ hath ever had, and will have enemies, even to the end of the
world. [2.] Victory, a perfect conquest over them. Conquerors used
to make their enemies their footstool. Those proud enemies of Christ,
who now set up their crests, face the heavens, and strut it out against
him, even those shall be brought under his feet. [3.] It implies
ignominy, the lowest subjection. Sapores, King of Persia, overcoming
the Emperor Valerian in battle, used his back for a stirrup when he
got upon his horse; and so Tamerlane served Bajazet. [4.] The footstool is a piece of state, and both raiseth and easeth him that sits on
the throne; so Christ will both raise himself and ease himself by that
vengeance that he will take on his enemies, &c.

Now from these divine names and titles which are given to Jesus
Christ, we may thus argue, He to whom the incommunicable titles of
the most high God are attributed, he is the most high God; but the
incommunicable titles of the most high God are attributed unto Christ,
ergo, he is the most high God. But,

4. Fourthly, Christ's eternal deity, co-equality, and consubstantiality
with the Father may be demonstrated from his *divine properties and
attributes*. I shall shew you for the opening of this that the glorious
attributes of God are ascribed to the Lord Jesus. I shall begin,—

(1.) First, with *the eternity of God*. God is an eternal God. 'From
everlasting to everlasting thou art God,' Ps. xc. 2; 'The eternal God
is thy refuge,' Deut. xxxiii. 27; 'He inhabits eternity,' Isa. lvii. 15.
He is called 'the ancient of days,' Dan. vii. 9; and he is said to be
'everlasting,' and to be 'king of old,' Ps. lxxiv. 12. This sheweth
he had no beginning. In respect of his eternity, after time, he is called
'the everlasting God,' Rom. xvi. 26; 'An everlasting king,' 1 Tim.
i. 17. That there is no succession or priority or posteri[ori]ty in God,
but that he is from everlasting to everlasting the same, we may see Ps.
cii. 26, 27, 'The heavens shall perish, but thou shalt endure; yea, all
of them shall wax old like a garment, and as a vesture shalt thou
change them, and they shall be changed; but thou art the same, and
thy years shall have no end.' There is no succession or variation in
God, but he is eternally the same. Eternity is an interminable being
and duration before any time, and beyond all time; it is a fixed duration, without beginning or ending.[1] The eternity of God is beyond
all possible conception of measure or time. God ever was, ever is, and
ever shall be. Though the manifestations of himself unto the crea-

---

[1] Eternity is taken three ways. [1.] *Proprie, properly*, so it noteth to be without
beginning and end, so God only is eternal; [2.] *Improprie, improperly*, so it noteth to
have a beginning but no ending; so angels, so the souls of men are eternal; [3.] *Abusive*,
so some things are said to be eternal which have had a beginning, and shall also have
an end. They are called eternal in respect of their long continuance and duration; so
circumcision and other Mosaical ceremonies were called eternal or everlasting.

tures are in time, yet his essence or being never did nor shall be bound up by time. Look backward or forward, God from eternity to eternity, is a most self-sufficient, infinite, perfect, blessed being, the first cause of our being, and without any cause of his own being; an eternal infinite fulness, and possession to himself and of himself. What God is, he was from eternity, and what God is, he will be so to eternity. Oh, this glorious attribute drops mirth[1] and mercy, oil and honey !

Now this attribute of eternity is ascribed to Jesus Christ: John i. 1, ' In the beginning was the Word ;' ' was ' notes some former duration, and therefore we conclude that he was before the beginning, before any creation or creatures, for it is said he was God in the beginning, and his divine nature whereby he works is eternal, Heb. ix. 14. He is ' the first and last,' Rev. i. 17. Hence it is that he is called ' the firstborn of every creature,' because he who created all, and upholds all, hath power to command and dispose of all, as the firstborn had power to command the family or kingdom, Col. i. 15–17 ; compare Isa. lxvi. 6, with Rev. xxii. 13. John xvii. 5, ' Father glorify thou me with thine own self, with the glory I had with thee before the world was.' Such glory had the Lord Christ with his Father, viz., in the heavens, and that before the world was. This he had not only in regard of destination, being predestinated to it by God his Father, as Grotius would evade it, but in regard of actual possession. ' The Lord possessed me in the beginning of his way,' saith Christ the Son of God, Prov. viii. 22. And as his Father possessed him, so he was possessed of the selfsame glory with his Father before the world was, from eternity. ' His goings forth have been from of old, from everlasting,' from the days of eternity, saith the prophet Micah, speaking of the Messiah, Micah v. 2. See the eternity of Christ further confirmed by the scriptures in the margin.[2] But,

(2.) Secondly, As the attribute of eternity is ascribed to Christ, so the attribute of *omniscience* is ascribed to Christ ; and this speaks out the godhead of Christ. He knows all things: John xxi. 17, ' Lord, thou knowest all things,' τὰ παρόντα καὶ τὰ μέλλοντα, all things present and future; what I now am, and what I shall be, saith one, [Chrysostom] on the words: John ii. 25, ' He needed not that any should testify of man, for he knew what was in man.' Shall artificers know the nature and properties of their works, and shall not Christ know the hearts of men, which are the work of his own hands? Rev. ii. 23, ' And all the churches shall know that I am he which searcheth the reins and hearts.' Now of all a man's inwards, the heart and the reins are the most inward. Christ is nearer to us than we are to ourselves. The Greek word ἐρευνῶν, that is here rendered *searcheth*, signifies to search with the greatest seriousness, exactness, and diligence that can be ; the word is metaphorically taken from such as use to search in mines for silver and gold. He is also frequently said to know the thoughts of men, and that before they bewrayed themselves

---

[1] Spelled 'myrth': query, 'myrrh'?—G.

[2] John viii. 58, and xvii. 24 ; Rev. i. 8, 17 ; Heb. i. 10–12, and vii. 3 ; Isa. ix. 6, &c. Christ is without beginning of days or end of time, and without all bounds of precession or succession.

by any outward expressions.[1] Now this is confessedly God's peculiar, 'God which knoweth the hearts.' He is the wisdom of the Father, 1 Cor. i. 24. He knows the Father, and doth, according to his will, reveal the secrets of his Father's bosom. The bosom is the seat of love and secrecy, John i. 18. Men admit those into their bosoms, with whom they impart all their secrets; the breast is the place of counsels; that is, Christ revealeth the secret and mysterious counsels, and the tender and compassionate affections of the Father to the world. Being in the bosom implieth communication of secrets: the bosom is a place for them. It is a speech of Tully to a friend that had betrusted him with a secret, *crede mihi*, &c., Believe me, saith he, what thou hast committed to me, it is in my bosom still, I am not ungirt to let it slip out. But Scripture addeth this hint too, where it speaketh of the bosom as the place of secrets: Prov. xvii. 23, 'A wicked man taketh a gift out of the bosom, to pervert the ways of judgment,' speaking of a bribe: Prov. xxi. 14, 'A gift in secret pacifieth anger, and a reward in the bosom expiateth wrath.' Here is 'secret' and 'bosom' all one, as gift and reward are one. So Christ lieth in the Father's bosom; this intimateth his being conscious to all the Father's secrets. But,

(3.) Thirdly, As the attribute of God's omniscience is ascribed to Christ, so the attribute of God's *omnipresence* is ascribed to Christ; Mat. xviii. 20, 'Where two or three are gathered together in my name, there am I in the midst of them;' and chap. xxviii. 29, 'I am with you alway, even to the end of the world.' He is not contained in any place, who was before there was any place, Prov. viii. 22, and John i. 1, 3, and did create all places by his own power. Whilst Christ was on earth in respect of his bodily presence, he was in the bosom of his Father, which must be understood of his divine nature and person. He did come down from heaven, and yet remained in heaven.[2] Christ is universally present, he is present at all times and all places, and among all persons; he is repletively everywhere, inclusively nowhere. Diana's temple was burnt down when she was busy at Alexander's birth, and could not be at two places together; but Christ is present both in paradise and in the wilderness at the same time, *ubi non est per gratiam, adest per vindictam*, where he is not by his gracious influence, there he is by his vindictive power.[3] Empedocles could say that God is a circle, whose centre is everywhere, whose circumference is nowhere. The poor blind heathens could say that God is the soul of the world; and thus, as the soul is *tota in toto*, and *tota in qualibet parte*, so is he, that his eye is in every corner, &c. To which purpose they so portrayed their goddess Minerva, that which way soever one cast his eye, she always beheld him. But,

(4.) Fourthly, As the attribute of God's omnipresence is ascribed to Christ, so the attribute of God's *omnipotency* is ascribed to Christ, and this speaks out the Godhead of Christ, 'All power is given unto

---

[1] Mat. ix. 24, and xii. 25; Luke v. 22, vi. 18, xi. 17, and xxiv. 38, &c.
[2] John i. 18, iii. 13; Ps. cxxxix. 7-11.
[3] Greg. in Ezek. Hom. 8, Aug. medit. c. 29, where two are sitting together, and conversing about the law, there is Shechinah, the divine majesty, among them. Grotius on Mat. xviii. 20.

me, in heaven and in earth,' Mat. xxviii. 18; John v. 19. 'What things soever the Father doth, these also doth the Son,' Phil. iii. 21. He is called by a metonymy 'the power of God,' 1 Cor. i. 24. 'He is the Almighty,' Rev. i. 8. 'He made all things,' John i. 3. 'He upholds all things,' Heb. i. 3. 'He shall change our vile body,' saith the apostle, 'that it may be like unto his glorious body, according to the mighty working whereby he is able to subdue all things to himself,' Phil. iii. 21. Now from what has been said we may thus argue, He to whom the incommunicable properties of the most high God are attributed, he is the most high God; but the incommunicable properties of the most high God are attributed to Christ, *ergo*, Christ is the most high God.[1] But,

5. Fifthly, Christ's eternal deity, co-equality, and consubstantiality with the Father, may be demonstrated from his *divine works*. The same works which are peculiar to God are ascribed to Christ. Such proper and peculiar, such divine and supernatural works as none but God can perform, Christ did perform. As, [1.] *Election.* The elect are called his elect, Mat. xxiv. 31; John xiii. 18. ' I know whom I have chosen,' John xv. 16. ' I have chosen you, and ordained you, that you should go and bring forth fruit, and that your fruit should remain;' ver. 19, 'But I have chosen you out of the world, therefore the world hateth you.' [2.] *Redemption.* O sirs, none but the great God could save us from wrath to come, none but God blessed for ever could deliver us from the curse of the law, the dominion of sin, the damnatory power of sin, the rule of Satan, and the flames of hell.[2] Ah, friends, these enemies were too potent, strong, and mighty for any mere creature, yea, for all mere creatures, to conquer and overcome. None but the most high God could everlastingly secure us against such high enemies. [3.] *Remission of sins.* Mat. ix. 6, ' The Son of man hath power to forgive sins.' Christ here positively proves that he had power on earth to forgive sins, because miraculously, by a word of his mouth, he causes the palsy man to walk, so that he arose and departed to his house immediately. Christ he forgives sin authoritatively. Preachers forgive only declaratively, John xx. 23, as Nathan to David, 'The Lord hath put away thine iniquity,' 2 Sam. xii. 7. I have read of a man that could remove mountains, but none but the man Christ Jesus could ever remit sin. All the persons in the Trinity forgive sins, yet not in the same manner. The Father bestows forgiveness, the Son merits forgiveness, and the Holy Ghost seals up forgiveness, and applies forgiveness. [4.] The bestowing of *eternal life*. John x. 28, ' My sheep hear my voice, and I give unto them eternal life.' Christ is the prince and principle of life, and therefore all out of him are dead whilst they live, Col. iii. 3, 4. Eternal life is too great a gift for any to give but a God. [5.] *Creation.* John i. 3, 'All things are made by him;' and ver. 10, 'The world was made by him.' Col. i. 16, ' By him were all things created that are in heaven, and that are in the earth, visible and invisible.' Now the apostle telleth you ' he that built all things is God;' Christ built all things, *ergo*, Christ is God.[3]

---

[1] See Col. i. 16, 17, Ps. cii. 26, compared with Heb. i. 8, 10, John i. 10.
[2] 1 Thes. i. 10; Gal. iii. 13; Rom. vi. 14, and viii. 1; Luke i. 68-80.
[3] Justin Martyr quoteth two Greek verses out of Pythagoras to prove there is but one

The argument lieth fair and undeniable. The all things that were created by Christ, Paul reduceth to two heads, visible and invisible; but Zanchius addeth a third branch to this distinction, and maketh it more plain by saying that all things that were made are either visible or invisible, or mixed—visible, as the stars and fowls and clouds of heaven, the fish in the sea, and beasts upon the earth; invisible things, as the angels, they also were made; then there is a third sort of creatures which are of a mixed nature, partly visible in regard of their bodies, and partly invisible in regard of their souls, and those are men: Eph. ii. 9, ' Who created all things by Jesus Christ;' Heb. i. 2, ' He hath, in these last days, spoken to us by his Son, whom he hath appointed heir of all things; by whom also he made the worlds.' This may seem somewhat difficult, because he speaketh of worlds, whereas we acknowledge but one; but this seeming difficulty you may easily get over if you please but to consider the persons to whom he writes, which were Hebrews, whose custom it was to style God *Rabboni, dominus mundorum*, the Lord of the worlds. They were wont to speak of three worlds—the lower world, the higher world, and the middle world; the lower world containeth the elements, earth and water and air and fire; the higher world that containeth the heaven of the blessed; and the middle world that containeth the starry heaven. They now being acquainted with this language, and the apostle writing to them, he saith that God by Christ made the worlds—those worlds which they were wont to speak so frequently of. And whereas one scruple might arise from that expression in the Ephesians, ' God created all things " *by* " Jesus Christ,' and this to the Hebrews, ' *by* whom he made the worlds,' as if Christ were only an instrument in the creation and not the principal efficient; therefore another place in this chapter will clear it, which speaketh of Christ as the principal efficient of all things: Heb. i., compare the 8th and 10th verses together, ' To the Son he saith, Thy throne, O God, is for ever and ever;' then Christ is God. Then, ' And, Thou, Lord,' ver. 10, ' hast laid the foundation of the earth; and the heavens are the works of thy hands.' Namely ' thine,' that is, the Son, which he spake of before. Christ is the principal efficient of the creation; and in this sense it is said, ' By him were all things made,' not as by an instrument, but as by the chief efficient. [6.] *The preservation and sustentation of all things:* Col. i. 17, ' By him all things consist.' They would soon fall asunder had not Christ undertaken to uphold the shattered condition thereof by the word of his power. All creatures that are made are preserved by him in being, life, and motion: Heb. i. 3, ' He upholdeth all things by the word of his power.' Both in respect of being, excellencies, and operations, sin had hurled confusion over the world, which would have fallen about Adam's ears had not Christ undertaken the shattered condition thereof, to uphold it. He keeps the world together, saith one, as the hoops do the barrel. Christ bears up all

God : ει ἐψμι θεὸς, &c., saith Pythagoras, If any will assume to himself and say, I am God, except only one, let him lay such a world as this is to stake, and say, This world is mine; then I will believe him, not otherwise, Heb. i. 2, Διʼ ὃν, not *propter quem*, as Grotius would evade the text ' for ' whom he made the worlds, but *per* quem, by whom; so the apostle, to put it out of all doubt, putteth them together: Col. i. 16, ' All things were created by him and for him,' δἰ αὐτόν και εἰς αὐτόν.

things, continuing to the several creatures their being, ordering and governing them, and this he doth by the word of his power. By this word he made the world. ' He spake, and it was done.' And by this word he governeth the world, by his own mighty word, the word of his power. Both these are divine actions, and being ascribed unto Christ, evidence him to be no less than God. Now from what has been said we may thus argue, he to whom those actions are ascribed, which are proper to the most high God, he is the most high God; but such actions or works are ascribed to Christ, *ergo*, he is the most high God. But,

6. Sixthly, Christ's eternal deity may be demonstrated from that *divine honour and worship that is due to him, and by angels and saints given unto him.* The apostle sheweth, Gal. iv. 8, that religious worship ought to be performed to none but to him that is God by nature; and that they are ignorant of the true God who religiously worship them that are no gods by nature; and therefore, if Christ were not God by nature, and consubstantial with the Father, we ought not to perform religious worship to him.[1] Divine worship is due to the second person of this co essential Trinity, to Jesus Christ our Lord and God. There is but one immediate, formal, proper, adequate, and fundamental reason of divine worship or adorability, as the schools speak, and that is the sovereign, supreme, singular majesty, independent and infinite excellency of the eternal Godhead; for by divine worship we do acknowledge and declare the infinite majesty, truth, wisdom, goodness, and glory of our blessed God. We do not esteem anything worthy of divine honour and worship which hath but a finite and created glory, because divine honour is proper and peculiar to the only true God, who will not give his glory to any other who is not God. God alone is the adequate object of divine faith, hope, love, and worship, because these graces are all exercised, and this worship performed, in acknowledgment of his infinite perfection and independent excellency; and therefore no such worship can be due to any creature or thing below God. There is not one kind of divine honour due to the Father and another to the Son, nor one degree of honour due to the Father and another to the Son; for there can be no degrees imaginable in one and the same excellency, which is single because infinite; and what is infinite doth excel and transcend all degrees and bounds. And if there be no degrees in the ground and adequate reason of divine worship, there can be no reason or ground of a difference of degrees in the worship itself. The Father and the Son are one, John x. 30,—one in power, excellency, nature,—one God, and therefore to be honoured with the same worship, 'that all men should honour the Son even as they honour the Father,' John v. 23. Every tongue must confess that Jesus Christ, who is man, is God also, and therefore equal to his Father, Phil. ii. 6, 11, 12; and it can be no robbery, no derogation to the Father's honour, for us to give equal honour to him and his co-equal Son, who subsists in the form of God, in the nature of God. Thus

---

[1] This is a clear and full evidence that Jesus Christ is, and must be more than ψίλος ἄνθρωπος, mere man, or yet a divine man, as Dr Lushington styles him in Heb. vii. 22. [In his anonymous ' Expiation of a Sinner, in a Commentary upon the Epistle to the Hebrews.' 1646. Folio.—G.]

you see the divine nature, the infinite excellency of Jesus Christ, is an undeniable ground of this co-equal honour ; and therefore the worship due to Christ as God, the same God with his Father, is the very same worship, both for kind and degree, which is due to the Father. But, for the further and clearer opening of this, consider,

(1.) First, that all *inward worship is due to Christ.* As,

[1.] *Believing on him.* Faith is a worship which belongs only to God, enjoined in the first commandment, and against trusting in man there is a curse denounced, Jer. xvii. 5, 6. But Christ commands us to believe in him, John i. xii. John xiv. 1, ' Ye believe in God, believe also in me.' John iii. 16, ' For God so loved the world, that he gave his only-begotten Son, that whosoever believeth in him should not perish, but have everlasting life.' Ver. 36, ' He that believeth in the Son hath everlasting life, and he that believeth not the Son, shall not see life, but the wrath of God abideth on him.' John vi. 47, ' Verily, verily, I say unto you, he that believeth on me hath everlasting life.' The same respect that Christians give unto God the Father, they must also give unto the Son, believing on him ; which is an honour due only to God. Other creatures, men and angels, may be believed, but not believed on, rested on. This were to make them gods ; this were no less than idolatry.

[2.] Secondly, *Loving of Jesus Christ with all the heart,* commanded above the love, nay, even to the hatred, of father, mother, wife, children, yea, and our own lives, Luke xiv. 26. He who is not disposed, where these loves are incompatible, to hate father and all other relations, for the love of Christ, can be none of his. I ought dearly and tenderly to love father and mother—the law of God and nature requiring it of me,—but to prefer dear Jesus, who is God blessed for ever, before all, and above all, as Paul and the primitive Christians and martyrs have done before me. Your house, home, and goods, your life, and all that ever you have, saith that martyr,[1] God hath given you as love-tokens, to admonish you of his love, to win your love to him again. Now will he try your love, whether you set more by him or by his tokens, &c. When relations or life stand in competition with Christ and his gospel, they are to be abandoned, hated, &c. But,

(2.) Secondly, *All outward worship is due to Christ.* As,

[1.] First, *Dedication in baptism is in his name.* Mat. xxviii. 19, ' Baptizing them in the name of the Father, and of the Son, and of the Holy Ghost :' εἰς τὸ ὄνομα, into the name, by that rite initiating them, and receiving of them into the profession of the service of one God in three persons, and of depending on Christ alone for salvation. Baptizing them into the name of the Father, and of the Son, and of the Holy Ghost, is the consecrating of them unto the sincere service of the sacred Trinity.

[2.] Secondly, *Divine invocation is given to Jesus Christ.* Acts vii. 59, ' Stephen calls upon the Lord Jesus to receive his spirit.' 1 Cor. i. 2, ' All that in every place call upon the name of Jesus Christ our Lord.' 1 Thes. iii. 11, ' God himself and our Father, and our Lord Jesus Christ, direct our way unto you.' Eph. i. 2, ' Grace

---

[1] Master Brad[ford], Acts and Mon., fol. 1492. Phil. iii. 7, 8.

be to you, and peace from God our Father, and from our Lord Jesus Christ.' It is the saints' character that they are such as call on the Lord Jesus, Acts ii. 21; Acts ix. 14.[1] But,

[3.] Thirdly, *Praises are offered to our Lord Jesus Christ:* Rev. v. 9, 'And they sung a new song, saying, Thou art worthy to take the book, and to open the seals thereof; for thou wast slain, and hast redeemed us to God by thy blood, out of every kindred, and tongue, and people, and nation.' Ver. 11, 'And I beheld, and I heard the voice of many angels round about the throne, and the beasts, and the elders; and the number of them was ten thousand times ten thousand, and thousands of thousands.'[2] Ver. 12, 'Saying with a loud voice, Worthy is the Lamb that was slain to receive power, and riches, and wisdom, and strength, and honour, and glory, and blessing.' Ver. 13, 'And every creature which is in heaven, and on the earth, and under the earth, and such as are in the sea, and all that are in them, heard I saying, Blessing, and honour, and glory, and power, be unto him that sitteth upon the throne, and unto the Lamb, for ever and ever.' Here you have a catholic confession of Christ's divine nature and power. All the creatures, both reasonable and unreasonable, do in some sort set forth the praises of Christ, because in some sort they serve to illustrate and set forth his glory. Here you see that Christ is adored with religious worship by all creatures, which doth evidently prove that he is God. Since all the creatures worship him with religious worship, we may safely and boldly conclude upon his deity. Here are three parties that bear a part in this new song: 1. The redeemed of the Lord; and they sing in the last part of the 8th verse, and in the 9th and 10th verses. Then, 2, the angels follow, verses 11th and 12th. In the third place, all creatures are brought in, joining in this new song, ver. 13. That noble company of the church triumphant and church militant, sounding out the praises of the Lamb, may sufficiently satisfy us concerning the divinity of the Lamb. But,

[4.] Fourthly, *Divine adoration is also given to him:* Mat. viii. 2, 'A leper worshipped him.' Mark saith he kneeled down, and Luke saith he fell upon his face, Mark i. 40; Luke v. 12. He shewed reverence in his gesture. 'Lord, if thou wilt thou canst make me clean.'[3] He acknowledged a divine power in Christ, in that he saith he could make him clean if he would. This poor leper lay at Christ's feet, imploring and beseeching him, as a dog at his master's feet, as Zanchy [*de Red.*] renders the word, which shews that this leper looked upon Christ as more than a prophet or a holy man; and that believing he was God, and so able to heal him if he would, he gave him religious worship. He doth not say to Christ, Lord, if thou wilt pray to God, or to thy Father for me, I shall be whole; but 'Lord, if thou wilt I

[1] Ponder upon these scriptures: 2 Cor. xii. 8, 9; 1 Thes. i. 1; 2 Thes. i. 1, 2; 2 Cor. i. 2.

[2] This is taken out of Daniel, chap. vii. 10, whereby the glory and power of God and Christ is held forth, they being attended with innumerable millions of angels, which stood before the fiery throne of God, &c.

[3] So that he touched Christ his feet, as the word γονυπετων signifies; not kneeled, as the word is translated, Mark i. 40. This leper came to know Christ was God, 1. By inspiration; 2. By the miracles which Christ did.

shall be whole.' He acknowledges the leprosy curable by Christ, which he and all men knew was incurable by others, which was a plain argument of his faith; for though the *psora* or scabbedness may be cured, yet that which is called *lepra* physicians acknowledge incurable; for if a particular cancer cannot be cured, much less can a universal cancer. As Avicenna [1] observes: Mat. ii. 11, ' Though the wise men of the east, who saw Herod in all his royalty and glory, worshipped him not, yet they fell down before Christ.' No doubt but that by divine instinct they knew the divinity of Christ, hence they worshipped him, not only with civil worship, as one born king of the Jews, but with divine worship; which was, it is like, the outward gesture of reverence, and kneeling, and falling down, for so the Greek words signify. Is it probable that they would worship a young babe, that by reason of his infancy understands nothing, except they did believe some divine thing to be in him? and therefore not the childhood, but the divinity in the child, was worshipped by them, [Chrysostom.] Certainly if Christ had been no more than a natural child, they would never have undertaken so long, so tedious, and so perilous a journey to have found him out; principally, considering, as some conceive, they themselves were little inferior to the kings of the Jews. It is uncertain what these wise men, who were Gentiles, knew particularly concerning the mystery of the Messiah; but certainly they knew that he was something more than a man, by the internal revelation of the Spirit of God, who by faith taught them to believe that he was a king though in a cottage, and a God though in a cradle; and therefore as unto a God they fell down and worshipped him, &c. But,

[5.] Fifthly, *When Jesus Christ was declared to the world, God did command even the most glorious angels to worship him, as his natural and co-essential Son, who was begotten from the days of eternity, in the unity of the Godhead;* for, when he brought in his first-begotten and only-begotten Son into the world, he said, ' And let all the angels of God worship him,' Heb. i. 6,—the glorious angels who refuse divine honour to be given to themselves : ' See thou do it not,' saith the angel to John, when John fell at his feet to worship him, ' I am thy fellow-servant,' &c., Rev. xix. 10, and xxii. 9; yet they give, and must give, divine honour unto Christ, Phil. ii. 9. The manhood of itself could not be thus adored, because it is a creature, but as it is received into unity of person with the Deity, and hath a partner agency therewith, according to its measure in the work of redemption and mediation. All the honour due to Christ, according to his divine nature, was due from all eternity; and there is no divine honour due to him from and by reason of his human nature, or any perfection which doth truly and properly belong to Christ as man. He who was born of Mary is to be adored with divine worship; but not for that reason, because he was born of Mary, but because he is God, the co-essential and eternal Son of God. From what has been said we may thus argue, He to whom religious worship is truly exhibited, is the most high God. But religious worship is truly exhibited unto Christ, *ergo*, Christ is the most high God. But,

7. Seventhly, Christ's eternal deity may be demonstrated from *Christ's*

[1] Or Ibn-Sina.—G.

oneness with the Father, and from that claim that Jesus Christ doth lay to all that belongs to the Father, as God.[1] Now, certainly, if Jesus Christ were not very God, he would never have laid claim to all that is the Father's, as God. The ancients insist much upon that : John xvi. 15, ' All things that the Father hath,' as God, ' are mine.' The Father hath an eternal godhead, and that is mine ; the Father hath infinite power and wisdom, and that is mine ; the Father hath infinite majesty and glory, and that is mine ; the Father hath infinite happiness and blessedness in himself, and that is mine, saith Christ. The words are very emphatical, having in them a double universality. [1.] ' All things :' there is one note of universality ; [2.] ' Whatsoever :' there is another note of universality. Well, saith Christ, there is nothing in the Father, as God, but is mine, ' All that the Father hath is mine ;' the Father is God, and I am God ; the Father is life, and I am life ; for whatsoever the Father hath is mine : John x. 30, ' I and my Father are one ;' we are one eternal God, we are one in consent, will, essence, nature, power, dominion, glory, &c., ' I and my Father are one ;' two persons, but one God. He speaketh this as he is God, one in substance, being, and deity, &c. As God, he saith, ' I and my Father are one ;' but, *secundum formam servi*, in respect of the form of a servant, his assumed humanity, he saith, John xiv. 28, ' My Father is greater than I :' John x. 37, ' If I do not the works of my Father, believe me not :' ver. 38, ' But if I do, though ye believe not me, believe the works,' &c. The argument of itself is plain. No man can of himself, and by his own power, do divine works, unless he be truly God ; I do divine works by my own power, yea, ' I do the works of my Father ;' not only the like and equal, but the same with the Father. Therefore I am truly God ; neither deserve I to be called a blasphemer, because I said I was one with the Father : 1 John v. 7, ' And these three are one,' one in nature and essence, one in power and will, and one in the act of producing all such actions, as without themselves any of them is said to perform. Look, as three lamps are lighted in one chamber, albeit the lamps be divers. yet the lights cannot be severed ; so in the godhead, as there is a distinction of persons, so a simplicity of nature. From the scriptures last cited we may safely and confidently conclude that Christ hath the same divine nature and godhead with the Father, that they both have the same divine and essential titles and attributes, and perform the same inward operations in reference to all creatures whatsoever. To make it yet more plain, compare John xvii. 10 with John xvi. 15. ' All things that the Father hath are mine,' John xvi. 15 ; ' Father, all mine are thine, and thine are mine,' John xvii. 10. That is, whatsoever doth belong to the Father, as God, doth belong to Christ ; for we speak not of personal but essential properties. Christ doth lay claim to all that is natural, to all that belongs to the Father, as God, not to anything which belongs to him as the Father, as the first person of the

---

[1] Never did any mere creature challenge to himself the honour due to God, but miscarried and were confounded. Witness the angels that God cast out of heaven, 2 Pet. ii. 4 ; and Adam that he cast out of paradise, Gen. iii. 22–24 ; and Herod, whom the angel smote with a fatal blow, Acts xii. 23 ; and those several Popes that we read of in ecclesiastical stories ; and therefore had Jesus Christ been but a mere creature, divine justice would have confounded him for making himself a God.

blessed Trinity. 'All things that the Father hath are mine.' This he speaketh in the person of the mediator, 'Because of his fulness we all receive grace for grace,' John i. 16; and herein sheweth the unity of essence in the holy Trinity, and community of power, wisdom, sanctity, truth, eternity, glory, majesty. Such is the strict union of the persons of the blessed Trinity, that there is among them a perfect communion in all things, for 'all things that the Father hath are mine.' And let thus much suffice for the proof of the godhead of Christ.

Concerning the manhood of Christ, let me say, that as he is very God, so he is very man: 1 Tim. ii. 5, 'the man Christ Jesus.' Christ is true man, but not mere man; *verus, sed non merus.* The word is not to be taken exclusively, as denying the divine nature. Christ is Θεάνθρωπος, both God and man; sometimes denominated from the one nature, and sometimes from the other; sometimes called God, and sometimes man; yet so as he is truly both, and in that respect fitly said to be a mediator betwixt God and men, having an interest in and participating of both natures. This title, 'the Son of man,' is given to Christ in the New Testament four score and eight times, the design being not only to express a man, according to the Syrian dialect then used, בר נשא, *bar nosho;* nor only to express Christ's humanity, who was truly man, in all things like unto us, sin only excepted; nor only to intimate his humility, by calling himself so often by this humble name; but also to tell us to what a high honour God hath raised our nature in him, and to confute their imaginations who denied him to be very man, flesh, blood, and bones, as we truly are; and who held, that whatever he was, and whatever he did, and whatever he suffered, was only seeming and in appearance, and not real; and to lead us to that original promise, the first that was made to mankind, 'The seed of the woman shall bruise the serpent's head,' Gen. iii. 15, that so he might intimate, saith Epiphanius, that himself was the party meant, intended, and foretold of by all the prophets, who was to come into the world, to all nations in the world. Jews and Gentiles originally alike descended of the woman, who both had a like interest in the woman and her seed, though the Jews did and might challenge greater propriety in the seed of Abraham than the Gentiles could, Rom. iii. 1, 2; but they having been a long time, as it were, God's favourites, a selected people, a chosen nation, did wholly appropriate the Messias to themselves, and would endure no co-partners, Exod. xix. 6; 1 Pet. ii. 9; nor that any should have any right, title, or interest in him but themselves; and therefore they would never talk otherwise than of the Messias, the King of Israel, the son of David, never naming him once the light of the Gentiles, the expectation of the Gentiles, the hope and desire of the eternal hills, the hope of all the ends of the earth, the seed of the woman, the Son of man, as descending from Eve, extracted from Adam, and allied unto all mankind.[1] And it is observable that the evangelist Luke, at the story of Christ's baptism, when he was to be installed into his ministry, and had that glorious testimony from heaven, deriveth his pedigree up to the first Adam, the better to draw all men's eyes to that first promise concerning the seed of the woman, and to cause them to own him for that seed there promised, and for that

---

[1] Isa. xlii. 6; Hab. iii. 6; Ps. lxv. 5; Gen. iii. 15; Luke iii. 23, to the end.

effect that is there mentioned of dissolving the works of Satan. And as that evangelist giveth that hint when he is now entering this quarrel with Satan, even in the entrance of his ministry, so doth he very frequently and commonly by this very phrase give the same intimation for the same purpose. No sooner had Nathanael proclaimed him the Son of God: John i. 49, ' Nathanael answered, and said unto him, Rabbi, thou art the Son of God, thou art the King of Israel:' but he instantly titles himself the Son of man, ver. 51 ; not only to shew his humanity, for that Nathanael was assured of by the words of Philip, who calls him Jesus of Nazareth, the son of Joseph, ver. 45; but also to draw the thoughts of the hearers to the first promise, and to work them to look for a full recovery of all that by the second Adam which was lost in the first. Though the gates of heaven were shut against the first Adam by reason of his fall, yet were they open to the second Adam : ver. 51, ' And he saith unto him, Verily, verily, I say unto you'—this double asseveration, ' Verily, verily,' puts the matter beyond all doubt and controversy—' hereafter you shall see heaven open, and the angels of God ascending and descending upon the Son of man,'—the Jacob's ladder, the bridge that joineth heaven and earth together, as Gregory hath it.[1] This 51st verse doth greatly illustrate Christ's glory, and further confirm believers' faith, that Christ is Lord of angels even in his state of humiliation, and hath them ready at his call, as he or his people shall need their service, to move from earth to heaven, and from heaven to earth. This title, ' the Son of man,' shews that the Son of God was also the Son of man ; and that he delighted to be so, and therefore doth so often take this title to himself, ' the Son of man.'

Now concerning the manhood of Christ, the prophet plainly speaks : Isa. ix. 6, ' Unto us a child is born, and unto us a son was given.' *Parvulus*, a child, that noteth his humanity ; *Filius*, a Son, that noteth his deity. *Parvulus*, a child, even man of the substance of his mother, born in the world, Mat. i. 25 ; *Filius*, a Son, even God of the substance of his Father, begotten before the world, Prov. viii. 22 to the end. *Parvulus*, a child : behold his humility, ' she brought forth her first-born son, and wrapped him in swaddling clothes, and laid him in a manger,' Luke ii. 7 ; *Filius*, a Son: behold his dignity; ' when he bringeth his first-begotten Son into the world, he saith, And let all the angels of God worship him,' Heb. i. 6 ; to prove that he was man, it is enough to say, that he was born, he lived, he died. God became man by a wonderful, unspeakable, and inconceivable union. Behold God is offended by man's affecting and coveting his wisdom and his glory—for that was the devil's temptation to our first parents, ' Ye shall be as gods,' Gen. iii. 5 ; and man is redeemed by God's assuming and taking his frailty and his infirmity. Man would be as God, and so offended him ; and therefore God becomes man, and so redeemeth him. Christ, as man, came of the race of kings ; as man he shall judge the world, Acts xvii. 31 ; as man, he was wonderfully born of a virgin, Mat. i. 23 ; Isa. vii. 14 ; called therefore by a peculiar name, *Shiloh*, which signifies a secundine or after-birth, Gen. xlix. 19. The word comes of שׁלה, which signifies *tranquillum esse*, intimating that Christ is he who has

---

[1] He alludes to Jacob's ladder, Gen. **xxviii. 12.**

brought us peace and tranquillity; and that he might be our peace-maker, it was necessary that he should be *Shiloh*, born of the sanctified seed of a woman without the seed of man. The apostle expounds the name where he saith of Christ that he was 'made of a woman,' not of a man and woman both, but of a woman alone without a man, Gal. iv. 4. Christ as man was foretold of by the prophets, and by sundry types. Christ as man was attended upon at his birth by holy angels, and a peculiar star was created for him, Luke ii. 13, 14; Mat. ii. 1, 2. Christ as man was our sacrifice and expiation; he was our ἀντίλυτρον, *a counterprice*, such as we could never have paid, but must have remained, and even rotted in the prison of hell for ever. Christ as man was conceived of the Holy Ghost, Mat. i. 18. Christ as man is ascended into heaven, Acts i. 9, 10. Christ as man sits at the right hand of God, Col. iii. 1. Now what do all these things import, but that Jesus Christ is a very precious and most excellent person, and that even according to his manhood? Christ had the true pro-perties, affections, and actions of man. He was conceived, born, cir-cumcised; he did hunger, thirst; he was clothed; he did eat, drink, sleep, hear, see, touch, speak, sigh, groan, weep, and grow in wisdom and stature, &c., as all the four evangelists do abundantly testify. But because this is a point of grand importance, especially in these days, wherein there are risen up so many deceivers in the midst of us, it may not be amiss to consider of these following particulars,—

(1.) First, Of these special scriptures that speak out the certainty and verity of *Christ's body* : John i. 14, 'And the Word was made flesh;' 1 Tim. iii. 16, ' Without controversy, great is the mystery of godliness, God manifested in the flesh.' Christ is one and the same, begotten of the Father without time, the Son of God without mother; and born of the Virgin in time, the Son of man without father; the natural and consubstantial son of both; and, oh! what a great mystery is this! Heb. ii. 14, 16, ' Forasmuch then as the children are partakers of flesh and blood, he also himself likewise took part of the same, that through death he might destroy him that had the power of death, that is, the devil: for verily he took not on him the nature of angels: but he took on him the seed of Abraham:' according to the Greek ἐπιλαμ-βάνεται, He assumed, caught, laid hold on, as the angels did on Lot, Gen. xix. 16; or as Christ did on Peter, Mat. xiv. 31; or as men use to do upon a thing they are glad they have got, and are loath to let go again. O sirs! this is a main pillar of our comfort, that Christ took our flesh, for if he had not taken our flesh, we could never have been saved by him : Rom. i. 3, ' Concerning his Son Jesus Christ our Lord, who was made of the seed of David according to the flesh:' Rom, ix. 5, ' Whose are the fathers, and of whom, as concerning the flesh, Christ came, who is over all, God blessed for ever. Amen.' This is a greater honour to all mankind, than if the greatest king in the world should marry into some poor family of his subjects. Christ saith, 'My flesh is meat indeed,' and I say his flesh was flesh indeed; as true, real, proper, very flesh as that which any of us carry about with us: Col. i. 22, ' In the body of his flesh through death;' Heb. x. 5, ' Wherefore when he cometh into the world he saith, Sacrifice and offer-ing thou wouldst not, but a body hast thou prepared me.' Κατηρτίσω:

It is a metaphor taken from mechanics, who do artificially,[1] fit one part of their work to another, and so finish the whole; God fitted his Son's body to be joined with the deity, and to be an expiatory sacrifice for sin: 1 Pet. ii. 24, ' Who his own self bare our sins in his own body on the tree,' &c. The word αὐτὸς, himself, hath a great emphasis, and therefore that evangelical prophet Isaiah mentions it no less than five times in that Isa. liii. 4, 5, 7, 11, 12. Christ had none to help or uphold him under the heavy burden of our sins and his Father's wrath, Isa. lxiii. 3. It is most certain, that in the work of man's redemption Christ had no coadjutor. He who did bear our sins, that is, the punishments that were due to our sins, in his own body on the tree; he did assume flesh, cast into the very mould and form of our bodies, having the same several parts, members, lineaments, the same proportion which they have. Christ's body was no spectrum or phantasm, no putative body, as if it had no being but what was in appearance and from imagination—as the Marcionites, Manichees, and other heretics of old affirmed, and as some men of corrupt minds do assert in our days—but as real, as solid a body as ever any was. And therefore the apostle calls it a body of flesh, Col. i. 22—a body, to shew the organisation of it, and a body of flesh, to shew the reality of it, in opposition to all aerial and imaginary bodies. Christ's body had all the essential properties of a true body ; such as are organicalness, extension, local presence, confinement, circumscription, penetrability, visibility, palpability, &c., as all the evangelists do abundantly witness. Take a few instances for all : Luke xxiv. 39, ' Behold my hands and my feet, that it is I myself, handle me and see, for a spirit hath not flesh and bones as ye see me have.' Christ here admits of the testimony of their own senses to assure them that it was no vision or spirit, but a true and real body risen from the dead, which they now saw. Certainly whatever is essential to a true glorified body, that is yet in Christ's body. Those stamps of dishonour that the Jews had set upon Christ by wicked hands, those he retained after his resurrection, partly for the confirmation of his apostles, and partly to work us to a willingness and resoluteness to suffer for him when we are called to it : 1 John i. 1, ' That which was from the beginning, which we have heard, which we have seen with our eyes, which we have looked upon, and our hands have handled, of the word of life.' He alludes to the sermons which he and the other apostles heard from Christ's own mouth, and also to the glorious testimony which the Father gave once and again from heaven to Christ. He alludes also to the miracles that were wrought by Christ, and to that sight that they had of his glory in the mount, and to his resurrection and visible ascension into the highest heaven, Mat. xvii., Acts i. He alludes to the familiar conversation which the apostles had with Christ for about three years, and also to that touching, when after the resurrection Christ offered himself to the apostles that believed not in him to touch him, Luke xxiv. The truth of these things were confirmed to them by three senses—hearing, seeing, handling, the latter still surer than the former ; and this proves Christ to be a true man, as his being from the beginning sets

[1] Artfully = skilfully.—G.

out his deity. Christ had also those natural affections, passions, infirmities, which are proper to a body, as hunger: Mat. iv. 2, ' When
he had fasted forty days and forty nights, he was afterwards an hun-
gered.' All Christ's actions are for our instruction, not all for our
imitation. Matthew expressly makes mention of nights, lest it should
be thought to be such a fast as that of the Jews, who fasted in the day,
and did eat at the evening and in the night, [Chemnitius.] He would
not extend his fast above the term of Moses and Elias, lest he should
have seemed to have appeared only, and not to have been, a true man.
He was hungry, not because his fasting wrought upon him, but because God left man to his own nature, [Hilary.]. It seems Christ felt
no hunger till the forty days and forty nights were expired, but was
kept by the power of the Deity, as the three children, or rather champions, from feeling the heat of the fire, Dan. iii. 27. Christ fasted
forty days and forty nights, and not longer, lest he might be thought
not to have a true human body; for Moses and Elias had fasted thus
long before, but never did any man fast longer. When Christ began
to be hungry the tempter came to him, not when he was fasting. The
devil is cunning, and will take all the advantage he can upon us.
During the forty days and forty nights the devil stood doubtful, and
durst not assault the Lord Jesus, partly because of that voice he heard
from heaven, ' This is my beloved Son, in whom I am well pleased,'
Mat. iii. 17, and partly because his forty days and forty nights' fast did
portend some great thing; but now, seeing Christ to be hungry, he
impudently assaults him. Christ was not hungry all the forty days;
but after, he was hungry, to shew he was man. Some think that
Christ by his hunger did objectively allure Satan to tempt him, that
so he might overcome him, as soldiers sometimes feign a running
away, that they may the better allure their enemies closely to pursue
them, that so they may cut them off, either by an ambush or by an
orderly facing about: so the devil tempted Christ as man, not knowing
him to be God; or if he did know him to be God, Christ did as it
were encourage his cowardly enemy, that durst not set upon him as
God, shewing himself to be man. And as Christ was hungry, so
Christ was thirsty: John iv. 7, ' There came a woman of Samaria to
draw water: Jesus saith unto her, Give me drink.' Here you see that
he that is rich and Lord of all became poor for us, that he might make
us rich, 2 Cor. viii. 9; and he that gives to all the creatures their
meat in due season, Ps. civ. 27, he begs water of a poor tankard-bearer
to refresh himself in his weariness and thirst: John xix. 28, ' Jesus
saith, I thirst.' Bleeding breeds thirsting. Sleeping: Mat. viii. 24,
he was asleep, to shew the truth of the human nature, and the weakness of his disciples' faith. Christ was in a fast and dead sleep, for so
much the Greek word, ἐκάθευδε, signifies: his senses were well and
fast bound, as if he had no operation of life, and therefore the disciples
are said to raise him, as it were from the dead. The same Greek word
is used in many places where mention is made of the resurrection, as
you may see by comparing the scriptures in the margin together.[1] He
was asleep, [1.] By reason of his labour in preaching and journey he
slept; [2.] To shew forth the truth of his human nature. Some think

---

[1] John ii. 19; Mat. xxvii. 52; 1 Cor. xv. 12.

the devil stirred up the storm, hoping thereby to drown Christ and his disciples, as he had destroyed Job's children in a tempest before, Job i. 18, 19; but though Satan had malice and will enough to do it, yet he had not power; yea, though Christ slept in his human nature, yet was he awake in his deity, that the disciples being in danger might cry unto him more fervently, and be saved more remarkably. And as Jesus slept, so he was also weary: John iv. 6, 'Now Jacob's well was there; Jesus therefore, being wearied with his journey, sat thus on the well: and it was about the sixth hour,' about noon. In the heat of the day Christ was weary. Christ took on him not only our nature, but the common infirmities thereof, and he is to be as seriously eyed in his humanity as in the glory of his godhead. Therefore it is re-corded that he was weary with his journey ere half the day was spent; and that through weariness 'he sat thus on the well;' that is, even as the seat offered, or as weary men use to sit, &c. But, in a word, he was conceived, retained so long in the virgin's womb, born, circumcised, lived about thirty years on earth, conversed all that time with men, suffered, died, and was crucified, buried, rose again, ascended, and sat down with his body at the right hand of God, and with it will come again to judge the world. Now what do all these things speak out, but that Christ hath a true body? and who in their wits will assert that all this could be done in, and upon, and by, an imaginary body? But,

(2.) Secondly, *The several denominations that are given to Jesus Christ in Scripture* do clearly evidence the verity and reality of his human nature. He is called (1.) The son of the virgin, Isa. vii. 14: (2.) Her first-born son, Luke ii. 7: (3.) The branch, Zech. iii. 8, and vi. 12: (4.) The branch of righteousness, Jer. xxxiii. 15, and xxiii. 5: (5.) A rod out of the stem of Jesse, and a branch out of his roots, Isa. xi. 1: (6.) The seed of the woman, Gen. iii. 15: (7.) The seed of Abraham, Gen. xxii. 18: (8.) The fruit of David's loins, Ps. lxxx. 36, and cxxxii. 11; Acts ii. 30: (9.) Of the seed of David according to the flesh, Rom. i. 3; 2 Sam. vii. 2: (10.) The lion of the tribe of Judah, Rev. v. 5: (11.) The seed of Jacob, Gen. xxviii. 14: (12.) The seed of Isaac, Gen. xxvi. 4: (13.) A son born to us, a child given to us, Isa. ix. 6: (14.) The son of man, Mat. viii. 20, and xvii. 13; Rev. i. 13; Dan. vii. 13; John iii. 13: (15.) He is called the man Christ Jesus, 1 Tim. ii. 5; 1 Cor. xv. 21, 'Since by man came death, by man came also the resurrection of the dead.' God's justice would be satisfied in the same nature that had sinned: (16.) God's Son made of a woman, Gal. iv. 4: (17.) Man, 1 Tim. ii. 5; the man Christ Jesus: (18.) The son of David, Mat. i. 1; Mark xii. 35. 'How say the scribes, that Christ is the son of David?' In that the scribes and Pharisees knew and acknowledged, according to the Scripture, that Christ should be the son of David—that is, should be born and descend of the stock and posterity of David according to the flesh, —hence we may easily gather the truth of Christ's human nature, that he was ordained of God to be true man as well as God, in one and the same person; for else he could not be the son of David. Now, that he must be the son of David, even the scribes and the Pharisees knew and acknowledged, as we see here; and this was a truth which they had learned out of the Scriptures; and not only they, but even the common sort of Jews in our Saviour's time: John vii. 42, some of the common people spake thus, 'Hath not the Scripture said that Christ cometh of the seed of David?' And the Messiah was then commonly called the son of David, Rom. i. 3. So then, Christ being of the seed of David after the flesh, he must needs be true man as well as God; for which cause he was incarnate in the due time appointed of God; that is to say, he being the Son of God from everlasting, did in time become man, taking our nature upon him, together with the infirmities of our nature, sin only excepted, John i. 14. Now thus you see that the eighteen denominations that are given to Christ in the blessed Scriptures do abundantly demonstrate the certainty of Christ's human nature. But,

(3.) Thirdly, *Christ took the whole human nature.* He was truly and completely man, consisting of flesh and spirit, body and soul; yea, that he assumed the entire human nature, with whatever is proper to it. Christ took to himself the whole human nature, in both the essential parts of man, soul and body. The two essential and constitutive parts of man are soul and body; where these two are, there is the true man. Now Christ had both, and therefore he was true man.

[1.] First, Christ had a true human and reasonable soul. The reasonable soul is the highest and noblest part of man. This is that which principally makes the man, and hath the greatest influence into his being and essence. If, therefore, Jesus Christ had only a human body without a human soul, he had wanted that part which is most essential to man, and so he could not have been looked upon as true and perfect man. O sirs! Christ redeemed and saved nothing but what he assumed. The redemption and salvation reach no further than the assumption. Our soul then would have been never the better for Christ, had he not taken that as well as our body. Hence said Augustine,[1] Therefore he took the whole man without sin, that he might heal the whole of which man consists, of the plague of sin. And Fulgentius, to the same purpose:[2] As the devil smote by deceiving the whole man, so God saves by assuming the whole man. If he will save the whole man from sin, he will assume the whole man without sin, saith Nazianzen. The Scriptures do clearly evidence that Christ had a real human soul: Mat. xxvi. 38, 'My soul is exceeding sorrowful, even unto death.' Every word is emphatical: 'My *soul;*' his sorrows pierced his soul, and 'sorrowful round about,' even to death, περίλυπός—that is, 'heavy round about,' Ps. xxii. 16. Look, as the soul was the first agent in transgression, so it is here the first patient in affliction. 'To death;' that is, this sorrow will never be finished or intermitted but by death. 'My soul is *exceeding sorrowful.*' Then Christ had a true human soul; neither was his deity to him for a soul, as, of old, men of corrupt minds have fancied; for then our bodies only had been redeemed by him, and not our souls, if he had not suffered in soul as well as in body. The sufferings of his body were but the body of his sufferings; the soul of his suffer-

---

[1] Aug. de civ. Dei, lib. x. c. 27, p. 586.
[2] Fulgent. ad Thrasymund, lib. i. p. 251.

ings were the sufferings of his soul, which was now beset with sorrows, and heavy as heart could hold: John xii. 27, 'Now is my soul troubled, and what shall I say?' The Greek word signifies a vehement commotion and perturbation; as Herod's mind was troubled when he heard that a new king was born, Mat. ii. 3; or as the disciples were troubled when they thought they saw a spirit walking on the sea, and cried out for fear, Mat. xiv. 26; or as Zacharias, Luke i. 12, was troubled at the sudden sight of the angel. The rise and cause of Christ's soul-trouble was this: the Godhead hiding itself from the humanity's sense; and the Father letting out, not only an apprehension of his sufferings to come, but a present taste of the horror of his wrath, due to man for sin. He is amazed, overwhelmed, and perplexed with it in his humanity; and no wonder, since he had the sins of all the elect, laid upon him by imputation, to suffer for. And so this wrath is not let out against his person, but against their sins which were laid on him. Now though Christ was here troubled, or jumbled and puzzled, as the word imports, yet we are not to conceive that there was any sin in this exercise of his, for he was like clean water in a clean vessel, which, being never so often stirred and shaken, yet still keeps clean and clear. Neither are we to think it strange that the Son of God should be put to such perplexities in this trouble as not to know what to say; for considering him as man, encompassed with our sinless infirmities, and that this heavy weight of wrath did light upon him on a sudden, it is no wonder that it did confound all his thoughts as man. O sirs! look, that as sin has infected both the souls and bodies of the elect, and chiefly their souls, where it hath its chief seat, so Christ, to expiate this sin, did suffer unspeakable sorrows and trouble in his soul, as well as torture in his body; 'for my soul is troubled,' saith he. Though some sufferings of the body be very exquisite and painful, and Christ's in particular were such, yet sad trouble of mind is far more grievous than any bodily distress, as Christ also found, who silently bare all his outward troubles, but yet could not but cry out of his inward trouble, 'Now is my soul troubled.' Isa. liii. 10, 'Thou shalt make his soul an offering for sin,' Isa. liii. 7; 1 Pet. ii. 24. When Christ suffered for us, our sins were laid upon him, ver. 5, 6, as by the law of sacrificing of old, the sinner was to lay his hands upon the head of the beast, confessing his sins, and then the beast was slain, and offered for expiation, Lev. viii. 14, 18, 22; thus having the man's sins as it were taken and put upon it, and hereby the sinner is made righteous. The sinner could never be pardoned, nor the guilt of sin removed, but by Christ's making his soul an offering for sin. What did Christ in special recommend to God, when he was breathing out his last gasp, but his soul? Luke xxiii. 46, 'When Jesus had cried out with a loud voice, he said, Father, into thy hands I commend my spirit; and having said thus, he gave up the ghost;' that is, To thy safe custody and blessed tuition I commend my soul, as a special treasure or jewel, most charily and tenderly to be preserved and kept: Luke ii. 52, 'He increased in wisdom and stature;' here is stature for his body, and wisdom for his soul. His growth in that speaks the truth of the former, and his growth in this the truth of the latter: his body properly could not grow in wisdom, nor his soul in stature, therefore he must have both. There are two essential parts which make up one of his natures, his manhood, viz., soul and body, but both of these two of old have been denied. Marcion divests Christ of a body, and Apollinaris of a soul; and the Arians held that Christ had no soul, but that the deity was to him instead of a soul, and supplied the office thereof, that what the soul is to us, and doth in our bodies, all that the divine nature was to Christ, and did in his body; and are there not some among us, that make a great noise about a light in them, that dash upon the same rock? But the choice scriptures last cited may serve sufficiently to confute all such brain-sick men. But,

[2.] Secondly, As Christ had a true human and reasonable soul, so Christ had *a perfect, entire, complete body, and everything which is proper to a body;* for instance, (1.) He had blood: Heb. ii. 14, ' He also took part of the same,' that is, of flesh and blood. Christ had in him the blood of a man. Shedding of blood there must be, for without it there is no remission of sin, Heb. ix. 22. The blood of brute creatures could not wash away the blots of reasonable creatures, Heb. x. 4, 5, 10; wherefore Christ took our nature, that he might have our blood to shed for our sins. There is an emphasis put upon Christ as man, in the great business of man's salvation, ' The man Christ Jesus,' 1 Tim. ii. 5; the remedy carrying in it a suitableness to the malady, the sufferings of a man to expiate the sin of man. (2.) He had bones as well as flesh: Luke xxiv. 39, ' A spirit hath not flesh and bones, as ye see me have.' (3.) Christ had in him the bowels of a man, Phil. ii. 8, which bowels he fully expressed when he was on earth, Mat. xii. 18–20; nay, he retaineth those bowels now he is in heaven; in glory he hath a fellow-feeling of his people's miseries: Acts ix. 4, ' Saul, Saul, why persecutest thou me?' See Mat. xxv. 35, to the end of that chapter. Though Christ in his glorified state be freed from that state of frailty, passibility, mortality, yet he still retains his wonted pity. (4.) He had in him the familiarity of a man; how familiarly did Christ converse with all sorts of persons in this world, all the evangelists do sufficiently testify. Man is a sociable and familiar creature; Christ became man that he might be a merciful high priest, Heb. ii. 17; not that his becoming man made him more merciful, as though the mercies of a man were more than the mercies of God, but because by this means mercy is conveyed more suitably and familiarly to man. But,

(4.) Fourthly and lastly, Our Lord Jesus Christ *took our infirmities upon him.* When Christ was in this world he submitted to the common accidents, adjuncts, infirmities, miseries, calamities, which are incident to human nature. For the opening of this, remember there are three sorts of infirmities; (1.) There are sinful infirmities: James v. 7; Ps. lxxvii. 10. The best of men are but men at the best. Witness Abraham's unbelief, David's security, Job's cursing, Jonah his passion, Thomas his unbelief, Peter's lying, &c. Now these infirmities Jesus Christ took not upon him; for though he was made like unto us in all things, yet without sin, Heb. iv. 15. (2.) There are personal infirmities, which from some particular causes befall this or that person; as leprosy, blindness, dumbness, palsy, dropsy, epilepsy, stone, gout, sickness. Christ was never sick. Sickness arises from the unfit or unequal temperature of the humours, or from intemperance of labour, study, &c., but none of these were in Christ. He had no sin, and therefore no sickness. Christ took not the passions or infirmities which were proper to this or that man. (3.) There are natural infirmities which belong to all mankind since the fall; as hunger, thirst, wearisomeness, sorrowfulness, sweating, bleeding, wounds, death, burial. Now these natural infirmities that are common to the whole nature, these Jesus Christ took upon him, as all the evangelists do abundantly testify. Our dear Lord Jesus he lay so many weeks and months in the Virgin's womb; he received nourishment and growth in the ordinary way; he was brought forth and bred up just as common infants are; he had his life sustained by common food, as ours is; he was poor, afflicted, reproached, persecuted, tempted, deserted, falsely accused, &c.; he lived an afflicted life, and died an accursed death; his whole life, from the cradle to the cross, was made up of nothing but sorrows and sufferings; and thus you see that Jesus Christ did put himself under those infirmities which properly belong to the common nature of man, though he did not take upon him the particular infirmities of individuals.[1] Now what do all these things speak out, but the certainty and reality of Christ's manhood?

Quest. But *why must Christ partake of both natures? was it absolutely necessary that he should so do?* *Ans.* Yea, it was absolutely necessary that Christ should partake of both natures; and that both in respect of God, and in respect of us: (1.) First, in respect of us: and that,

[1.] First, *Because man had sinned, and therefore man must be punished.* By man came death, therefore by man must come the resurrection of the dead, 1 Cor. xv. 21. Man was the offender, therefore man must be the satisfier; man had been the sinner, and therefore man must be the sufferer. It is but justice to punish sin in that nature, in which it had been committed. By man we fell from God, and by man we must be brought back to God. By the first Adam we were ruined, by the second Adam we must be repaired, Rom. v. 12. The human nature was to be redeemed, therefore it was necessary that the human nature should be assumed. The law was given to man, and the law was broken by man, and therefore it was necessary that the law should be fulfilled by man. But,

[2.] Secondly, That *by this means the justice of God might be satisfied in the same nature which had sinned, which was the nature of man.* Angels could not satisfy divine justice, because they had no bodies to suffer. The brutish sensible creatures could not satisfy the justice of God, because they had no souls to suffer. The sensible creatures could not satisfy divine justice, because they had no sense to suffer. Therefore man, having body, soul, and sense, must do it; for he had sinned in all, and he could suffer in all.

(2.) Secondly, There are reasons both *in respect of God and* in respect of ourselves, why Jesus Christ should be God, and God-man also; and they are these five:—

[1.] First, That he might be a *meet mediator between God and*

---

[1] Printed curiously 'individuums,' the Latinised and transition form.—G.

man. Christ's office, as mediator, was to deal with God for man, and to deal for God with man. Now that he might be fit for both these transactions, for both parts of this office, he must partake of both natures. That he might effectually deal with God for man, he must be God, ' If a man sin against the Lord, who shall entreat for him ?' saith Eli to his sons, 1 Sam. ii. 25. And that he might deal for God with man, he must be man. He must be God, that he may be fit to transact, treat, and negotiate with God ; and he must be man, that he may be fit to transact, treat, and negotiate with man. When God spake unto Israel at Mount Sinai at the giving of the law, the people were not able to abide that voice or presence, and therefore they desired an *Internuncius,* a man like themselves, who might be as a mediator to go betwixt God and them, Exod. xx. 18, 19. Now upon this very ground, besides many others that might be mentioned, it was very requisite that Jesus Christ should be both God and man, that he might be a meet mediator to deal betwixt God and man, Heb. xii. 18. Jesus Christ was the fittest person, either in that upper or in this lower world, to mediate between God and us. There was none fit to umpire the business between God and man, but he that was God-man. Job hit the nail when he said, ' Neither is there any days-man betwixt us, that might lay his hand upon us both,' Job ix. 33. There was a double use of the days-man, and his laying his hand upon them : (1.) To keep the dissenting parties asunder, lest they should fall out and strike one another ; (2.) To keep them together, and compose all differences, that they might not depart from each other. The application is easy. Man is not fit to mediate, because man is the person offending ; angels are not fit to mediate, for they cannot satisfy divine justice, nor pacify divine wrath, nor procure our pardon, nor make our peace, nor bring in an everlasting righteousness upon us. God, the Father, was not fit for this work, for he was the person offended ; and he was as much too high to deal with man, as man was too low to deal with God. The Holy Ghost was not fit for this work, for it is his work to apply this mediation, and to clear up the believer's interest in this mediation. So then there is no other person fit for this office but Jesus Christ, who was a middle person, betwixt both, that he might deal with both. Christ could never have been fit to be the mediator in respect of his office, if he had not first been a middle person in respect of his natures ; for, saith the apostle, Gal. iii. 20, ' Now a mediator is not a mediator of one ; but God is one.' ' A mediator is not a mediator of one,' that is, of one party, but is always of two differing parties to unite them ; ' not of one ;' that is, (1.) Not of one person, because mediation implies more persons than one ; it necessarily supposes different parties betwixt whom he doth mediate. Christ, to speak after the manner of men, lays his hand upon God, the Father, and saith, O blessed Father, wilt thou be at peace with these poor sinners ? wilt thou pardon them ? and wilt thou lift up the light of thy countenance upon them ? If thou wilt, then I will undertake to satisfy thy justice, and to pacify thy wrath, and to fulfil thy royal law, and to make good all the wrong they have done against thee. And then he layeth his hand upon the poor sinner, and saith, Sinner, art thou willing to be changed and renewed ? art thou willing to come under the bond of the covenant ? art thou willing to give up thy heart and life to the guidance and government of the Spirit ? Then be not discouraged, for thou shalt certainly be justified and saved. (2.) Not of one nature—the mediator must necessarily have more natures than one—he must have the divine and human nature united in his single person, or else he could never suffer what he was to suffer, nor never satisfy what he was to satisfy, nor never bring poor sinners into a state of reconciliation with God ; and it is further observable that the text last cited saith, ' God is one,' 1 Tim. ii. 5 ; viz., as he is essentially considered, and therefore as so he cannot be the mediator ; but Christ, as personally considered, he ' is not of one,' that is, not of one nature, for he is God and man too, and therefore he is the only person that is fitted and qualified to be the mediator ; and it is observable that, when Christ is spoken of as mediator, his manhood is brought in, that nature being so necessary to that office : 1 Tim. ii. 5, ' For there is one God, and one mediator between God and man, the man Christ Jesus.' Jesus Christ was God and man ; as man he ought to satisfy, but could not ; as God he could satisfy, but ought not. But consider him as God and man, and so he both could satisfy and ought to satisfy, and accordingly he did satisfy, according to what was prophesied of him : Dan. ix. 24, ' He did make reconciliation for iniquity, and brought in everlasting righteousness.' He did not begin to do something and then faint and leave his work imperfect, but he finished it, and that to the glory of his Father : John xvii. 4, ' I have glorified thee on the earth, I have finished the work which thou gavest me to do.' And it is good to observe the singularity and oneness of the person mediating ; not many, not a few, not two, but one mediator between God and man. There was none with him in his difficult work of mediatorship, but he carried it on alone. Though there are many mediators among men, yet there is but εἶς μεσίτης, one only mediator betwixt God and men : and it is as high folly and madness to make more mediators than one, as it is to make more Gods than one, Isa. lxiii. 3. ' There is one God, and one mediator betwixt God and men ;' for look, as one husband satisfies the wife, as one father satisfies the child, as one lord satisfies the servant, and one sun satisfies the world, so one mediator is enough to satisfy all the world, that desire a mediator, or that have an interest in a mediator.[1] The true sense and import of this word μεσίτης, a mediator, is a middle person, or one that interposes betwixt two parties at variance, to make peace betwixt them. Though μεσίτης, a mediator, be rendered variously, sometimes an umpire or arbitrator, sometimes a messenger betwixt two persons, sometimes an interpreter imparting the mind of one to another, sometimes a reconciler or peace-maker ; yet this word, μεσίτης, doth most properly signify a mediator or a middler, because Jesus Christ is both a middle person, and a middle officer betwixt God and man, to reconcile and reunite God and man. This of all others is the most proper and genuine

[1] I confess the word μεσίτης is given to Moses, in that Gal. iii. 19, but Moses was but a typical mediator, and you never find that Moses is called a mediator in a way of redemption, or satisfaction, or paying a ransom ; for so dear Jesus is the only mediator : so the word μεσίτης is used in that 1 Tim. ii. 5 ; Heb. viii. 6–8, ix. 14, 15, and xii. 22–24.

signification of this name μεσίτης, Jesus Christ is the middle, that is, the second person in the Trinity, betwixt the Father and the Holy Ghost. He is the only middle person betwixt God and man, being in one person God-man; and his being a middle person fits and capacitates him to stand in the midst between God and us. And as he is the middle person, so he is the middle officer, intervening or interposing or coming between God and man by office, satisfying God's justice to the full for man's sins by his sufferings and death, and maintaining our constant peace in heaven by his meritorious intercession. Hence, as one observes, [Gerhard,] Jesus Christ is a true mediator, is still found *in medio*, in the middle. He was born, as some think, from Wisd. xviii. 14, about the middle of the night; he suffered, Heb. xiii. 12, in the middle of the world, that is, at Jerusalem, seated in the middle of the earth: he was crucified in the midst, between the two thieves, John xix. 18: he died in the air on the cross, in the midst between heaven and earth: he stood after his resurrection in the midst of his disciples, John xx. 19; and he has promised, that where two or three are gathered together in his name, he will be in the midst of them, Mat. xviii. 20: and he walks in the midst of the seven golden candlesticks, Rev. ii. 1, that is, the churches: and he as the heart in the midst of the body, distributes spirits and virtue to all the parts of his mystical body, Eph. iv. 15, 16. Thus Jesus Christ is the mediator betwixt God and man; middle in person and middle in office. And thus you have seen at large what a meet mediator Jesus Christ is, considered in both his natures, considered as God-man. But,

[2.] Secondly, *If Jesus Christ be not God, then there is no spiritual nor eternal good to be expected or enjoyed.* If Christ be not God, our preaching is in vain, and your hearing is in vain, and your praying is in vain, and your believing is in vain, and your hope of pardon and forgiveness by Jesus Christ is in vain; for none can forgive sins but a God. Christ hath promised that 'believers shall never perish;' he hath promised them 'eternal life,' and that he will 'raise them up at the last day,' he has promised 'a crown of righteousness,' he has promised 'a crown of life,' he has promised 'a crown of glory,' he has promised that conquering Christians shall 'sit down with him in his throne, as he is set down with his Father in his throne:' he has promised that they shall not be hurt of 'the second death.'[1] And a thousand other good things Jesus Christ has promised; but if Jesus Christ be not God, how shall these promises be made good? If a man that hath never a foot of land in England, nor yet worth one groat in all the world, shall make his will, and bequeath to thee such and such houses, and lands, and lordships in such a county or such a county; and shall by will, give thee so much in plate, and so much in jewels, and so much in ready money; whereas he is not, upon any account, worth one penny in all the world; certainly such legacies will never make a man the richer nor the happier. None of those great and precious promises, which are hinted at above, will signify anything, if Christ be not God; for they can neither refresh us, nor cheer us in

[1] Mark ii. 7; John iii. 16; John x. 28; 2 Tim. iv. 8; James i. 12; 1 Pet. v. 4; Rev. iii. 21, and ii. 11.

this world, nor make us happy in that other world. If Christ be not God, how can he purchase our pardon, procure our peace, pacify divine wrath, and satisfy infinite justice? A man may satisfy the justice of man, but who but a God can satisfy the justice of God? 'Will God accept of thousands of rams, or ten thousands of rivers of oil, or the firstborn of thy body for the sin of thy soul?' Micah vi. 7. Oh, no! he will not, he cannot. That scripture is worthy to be written in letters of gold: Acts xx. 28, 'Take heed therefore unto yourselves, and to all the flock, over the which the Holy Ghost hath made you overseers; to feed the church of God, which he hath purchased with his own blood.' This must needs relate to Christ, and Christ is here called God, and Christ's blood is called the blood of God; and without a peradventure Christ could never have gone through with the purchase of the church, if the blood he shed had not been the blood of God. This blood is called God's own blood, because the Son of God, being and remaining true God, assumed human flesh and blood in unity of person. By this phrase, that which appertaineth to the humanity of Christ is attributed to his divinity, because of the union of the two natures in one person, and communion of properties. The church is to Christ a bloody spouse, an Aceldama or field of blood: for she could not be redeemed with silver and gold, but with the blood of God, 1 Pet. i. 18, 19: so it is called by a communication of properties, to set forth the incomparable value and virtue thereof. But,

[3.] Thirdly, *If Christ be not God, yea, God-man, then we shall never be able to answer all the challenges that either divine justice or Satan can make upon us.* Whatsoever the justice of God can exact, that the blood of God can discharge. Now the blood of Christ is the blood of God, as I have evidenced in the second reason. By reason of the hypostatical union, the human nature being united to the divine, the human nature did suffer, the divine did satisfy. Christ's godhead did give both majesty and efficacy to his sufferings. Christ was sacrifice, priest, and altar. He was sacrifice as he was man, priest as he was God and man, and altar as he was God. It is the property of the altar to sanctify the thing offered on it, Mat. xxiii. 19; so the altar of Christ's divine nature sanctified the sacrifice of his death, and made it meritorious. Man sinned, and therefore man must satisfy. Therefore the human nature must be assumed by a surety, for man cannot do it. If an angel should have assumed human nature, it would have polluted him. Human nature was so defiled by sin that it could not be assumed by any but God. Now Christ being God, the divine nature purified the human nature which he took, and so it was a sufficient sacrifice, the person offered in sacrifice being God as well as man. This is a most noble ground upon which a believer may challenge Satan to say his worst and to do his worst. Let him present God as terrible, yea, as a consuming fire, Heb. xii. 29; let him present me as odious and abominable in the sight of God, as once he did Joshua, Zech. iii. 2, 3; let him present me before the Lord as vile and mercenary, as once he did Job, chap. i. 9–11; let him aggravate the height of God's displeasure, and the height and depth and length and breadth of my sins, I shall readily grant all, and against all this I will set the infinite satisfaction of dear Jesus. This I know, that though the justice of God cannot be avoided nor bribed, yet it may be satisfied. Here is a proportionable satisfaction, here is God answering God. It is a very noble plea of the apostle, 'Who is he that condemneth? It is Christ that died,' Rom. viii. 34. Let Satan urge the justice of God as much as he can, I am sure that the justice of God makes me sure of salvation; and the reason is evident, because his justice obligeth him to accept of an adequate satisfaction of his own appointing, 1 John i. 7-9. The justice of God maketh me sure of mine own happiness, because if God be just, that satisfaction should be had, when that satisfaction is made, justice requireth that the person for whom it is made shall be received into favour. I confess that unless God had obliged himself by promise, there were no pressing his justice thus far, because *noxa sequitur caput.* There was mercy in the promise of sending Christ, out of mercy to undertake for us, otherwise we cannot say that God was bound in justice to accept of satisfaction, unless he had first in mercy been pleased to appoint the way of a surety, Gen. ii. 15.[1] Justice indeed required satisfaction, but it required it of the person that sinneth: Gen. ii. 17, ' But of the tree of the knowledge of good and evil, thou shalt not eat of it; for in the day thou eatest thereof thou shalt surely die '—or dying thou shalt die; or, as others read the words, thou shalt surely and shortly or suddenly die; and, without controversy, every man should die the same day he is born. ' The wages of sin is death,' Rom. vi. 23; and this wages should be presently paid, did not Christ, as a boon, beg poor sinners' lives for a season: for which cause he is called the Saviour of all men, 1 Tim. iv. 10—not of eternal preservation, but of temporal reservation. It was free and noble mercy to all mankind, that dear Jesus was promised and provided, sealed and sent into the world, John vi. 27, that some might be eternally saved, and the rest preserved from wrath for a time. Here cometh in mercy, that a surety shall be accepted; and what he doth is as if the person that offended should have done it himself. Here is mercy and salvation surely bottomed upon both. Ah, what sweet and transcendent comfort flows from this very consideration, that Christ is God! But,

[4.] Fourthly, *The great and glorious majesty of God required it, that Christ should be God.* God the Father being a God of infinite holiness, purity, justice, and righteousness, none but he who was very God, who was essentially one with the Father, could or durst interpose between God and fallen man, John x. 30, and xiv. 9-11, &c. The angels, though they are glorious creatures, yet they are but creatures; and could these satisfy divine justice, and bear infinite wrath, and purchase divine favour, and reconcile us to God, and procure our pardon, and change our hearts, and renew our natures, and adorn our souls with grace? and yet all these things must be done, or we undone, and that for ever! Now if this were a work too high for angels, then we may safely conclude that it was a work too hard for fallen man. Man was once the mirror of all understanding, the hieroglyphic of wisdom, but now *quantum mutatus ab illo,* there is a great alteration; for poor sorry man is now sent to school to learn wisdom and instruc-

---

[1] Had not Christ stepped in between man's sin and God's wrath, the world had fallen about Adam's ears.

tion of the beasts, birds, and creeping things, he is sent to the pismire to learn providence, Prov. vi. 6, to the stork and to the swallow to learn to make a right use of time, Jer. viii. 7, to the ox and the ass to learn knowledge, Isa. i. 3, and to the fowls of the air to learn confidence, Mat. vi. Man that was once a master of knowledge, a wonder of understanding, perfect in the science of all things, is now grown blockish, sottish, and senseless, and therefore altogether unfit and unable to make his peace with God, to reconcile himself to God, &c. But,

[5.] Fifthly and lastly, *That Christ's sufferings and merits might be sufficient, it was absolutely necessary that he should be God.* The sin of man was infinite, I mean infinitely punishable; if not infinite in number, yet infinite in nature, every offence being infinite, it being committed against an infinite God. No creature could therefore satisfy for it, but the sufferer must be God, that so his infiniteness might be answerable to the infiniteness of men's offences. There was an absolute necessity of Christ's sufferings, partly because he was pleased to substitute himself in the sinner's stead, and partly because his sufferings only could be satisfactory. Now, unless he had been man, how could he suffer? and unless he had been God, how could he satisfy offended justice? Look, as he must be more than man, that he may be able to suffer, that his sufferings may be meritorious, so he must be man, that he may be in a capacity to suffer, die, and obey; for these are no work for one who is only God. A God only cannot suffer, a man only cannot merit; God cannot obey, man is bound to obey; wherefore Christ, that he might obey and suffer, he was man; and that he might merit by his obedience and suffering, he was God-man; just such a person did the work of redemption call for. That Christ's merits might be sufficient, he must be God; for sufficient merit for mankind could not be in the person of any mere man, no, not in Christ himself, considered only as man; for so all the grace he had he did receive it, and all the good he did he was bound to do it; for he ' was made of a woman, and made under the law,' Gal. iv. 4—not only under the ceremonial law as he was a Jew, but under the moral as a man, for it is under that law under which we were, and from which we are redeemed, Gal. iii. 13—therefore in fulfilling it he did no more than that which was his duty to do; he could not merit by it, no, not for himself, much less for others, considered only as man; therefore he must also be God, that the dignity of his person might add dignity, and virtue, and value to his works. In a word, *Deus potuit, sed non debuit; homo debuit, sed non potuit*—God could, but he should not; man should, but he could not make satisfaction; therefore he that would do it must be both God and man. *Torris erutus ab igne?* as the prophet speaketh; ' Is not this a firebrand taken out of the fire?' Zech. iii. 2. You know that in a firebrand taken out of the fire, there is fire and wood inseparably mixed, and in Christ there is God and man wonderfully united. He was God, else neither his sufferings nor his merits could have been sufficient; and if his could not, much less any man's else; for all other men are both conceived and born in original sin, and also much and often defiled with actual sin, and therefore we ought for ever to abhor all such Popish doctrines, prayers, and masses for the dead, which exalt man's merits, man's satisfaction: 'For no man can by any means redeem his brother, nor give to God a ransom for him; for the redemption of their soul is precious, and it ceaseth for ever,' Ps. xlix. 7, 8. And therefore all the money that hath been given for masses, dirges, trentals,[1] &c., hath been cast away; for Jesus Christ, who is God-man, is the only Redeemer, and in the other world money beareth no mastery. Let me make a few inferences from what has been said; and therefore,

1. First, Is it so, that Christ is God-man, that he is God and man? Then *let this raise our faith, and strengthen our faith, in our Lord Jesus Christ.* Faith is built on God, 1 Pet. i. 21. Now, Jesus Christ is very God, and therefore the fittest foundation in the world for us to build our faith upon. 'God manifest in the flesh' is a firm basis for faith and comfort. 'He is able to save to the uttermost,' Heb. vii. 25. Christ is a thorough Saviour, he saves perfectly, and he saves perpetually; he never carries on redemption work by halves.[2] Christ being God as well as man, is able, by the power of his godhead, to vanquish death, devils, hell, and all the enemies of our salvation; and by the power of his godhead is able to merit pardon of sin, the favour of God, the heavenly inheritance, and all the glory of the other world; for this dignity of his person addeth virtue and efficacy to his death and sufferings, in that he that suffered and died was very God; therefore God is said to have 'purchased the church with his own blood,' Acts xx. 28. Christ having suffered in our nature, which he took upon him, that is, in his human soul and body, the wrath of God, the curse, and all the punishments which were due to our sins, hath paid the price of our redemption, pacified divine wrath, and satisfied divine justice, in the very same nature in which we have sinned and provoked the Holy One of Israel, so that now all believers may triumphingly say, 'There is no condemnation to us that are in Christ Jesus,' Rom. viii. 1. Christ having, in our nature, suffered the whole curse and punishment due to our sins, God cannot in justice but accept of his sufferings as a full and complete satisfaction for all our sins, 1 John i. 7, 9; so that now there remaineth no more curse or punishment properly so called for us to suffer, either in our souls or bodies, either in this life or in the life to come, but we are certainly and fully delivered from all; not only from the eternal curse, and all the punishments and torments of hell, but also from the curse and sting of bodily death, and from all afflictions as they are curses and punishments of sin, 1 Cor. xv. 55, 56. That Jesus, who is God-man, hath changed the nature of them to us, so that of bitter curses and heavy punishments, they are become fatherly chastisements, the fruits of divine love, and the promoters of the internal and eternal good of our souls, Heb. xii. 5–7, and Rev. iii. 19. Oh, how should these things strengthen our faith in dear Jesus, and work us to lean and stay our weary souls wholly and only upon him who is God-man, 'and who of God is made unto us wisdom, righteousness, sanctification, and redemption,' 1 Cor. i. 30. Among the evangelists we find that Christ had a threefold entertainment among the sons of men: some received him into house, not into heart, as Simon the Pharisee, who gave him no kiss nor water to his feet,

---

[1] 'Thirty masses.'—G.   [2] *Ad plenum,* saith Erasmus; *ad perfectum,* say others.

Luke vii. 44; some neither into heart nor house, as the graceless, swinish Gergesites, Mat. viii. 34, who had neither civility nor honesty; some both into house and heart, as Lazarus, Mary, Martha, &c., John xi. 16. Certainly that Jesus who is God-man deserves the best room in all our souls, and the uppermost seat in all our hearts. But,

2. Secondly, If Jesus Christ be God-man, very God and very man, then *what high cause have we to observe, admire, wonder, and even stand amazed at the transcendent love of Christ in becoming man!* Oh! the firstness, the freeness, the unchangeableness, the greatness, the matchlessness of Christ's love to fallen man in becoming man! Men many times shew their love to one another, by hanging up one another's pictures in their families; but, ah, what love did Christ shew when he took our nature upon him! Heb. ii. 16, ' For verily he took not on him the nature of angels, but he took on him the seed of Abraham;' 'Ἐπιλαμβάνεται, he assumed, apprehended, caught, laid hold on the seed of Abraham, as the angel did on Lot, Gen. xix. 16, as Christ did on Peter, Mat. xiv. 31, or as men do upon a thing they are glad they have got and are loath to let go again. O sirs! it is a main ground and pillar of our comfort and confidence, that Jesus Christ took our flesh; for if he had not took our flesh upon him, we could never have been saved by him. Christ took not a part, but the whole nature of man, that is, a true human soul and body, together with all the essential properties and faculties of both; that in man's nature he might die, and suffer the wrath of God, and whole curse due to our sins, which otherwise, being God only, he could never have done; and that he might satisfy divine justice for sin, in the same nature that had sinned, and indeed it was most meet and fit, that the mediator, who was to reconcile God and man, should partake in the natures of both parties to be reconciled, Heb. ii. 14. Oh, what matchless love was this, that made our dear Lord Jesus to lay by for a time all that ' glory that he had with the Father before the world was,' John xvii. 5, and to assume our nature, and to be ' found in fashion as a man,' Phil. ii. 8. To see the great God in the form of a servant, or hanging upon the cross, how wonderful and astonishing was it to all that believed him to be God-man! God ' manifested in our flesh' is an amazing mystery, 1 Tim. iii. 16, a mystery fit for the speculation of angels, 1 Pet. i. 11, that the eternal God should become the man Christ Jesus, 1 Tim. ii. 5; that a most glorious creator should become a poor creature; that the ancient of days, Dan. vii. 9, 13, 22, should become an infant of days, Mat. ii. 11; that the most high should stoop so low as to dwell in a body of flesh—is a glorious mystery, that transcends all human understanding. It would have seemed a high blasphemy for us to have thought of such a thing, or to have desired such a thing, or to have spoken of such a thing, if God, in his everlasting gospel, had not revealed such a thing to us. Among the Romish priests, friars, Jesuits, they count it a great demonstration of love, a high honour that is done to any of their orders, when any nobleman or great prince, who is weary of the world, and the world weary of him, comes among them, and takes any of their habits upon him, and lives and dies in their habits. Oh, what a demonstration of Christ's love is it! and what a mighty honour hath Jesus Christ put upon mankind, in that he took our nature

upon him, in that he lived in our nature and died in our nature, and
rose in our nature, and ascended in our nature, and now sits at his
Father's right hand in our nature! Acts i. 10, 11. Though Jacob's
love to Rachel, and Jonathan's love to David, and David's love to
Absalom, and the primitive Christians' love to one another was strong,
very strong; yet Christ's love in taking our human nature upon him
does infinitely transcend all their loves. I think, saith one speaking
of Christ,[1] he 'cannot despise me, who is bone of my bone, and flesh of
my flesh; for if he neglect me as a brother, yet he will love me as a husband; that is my comfort.' ' O my Saviour,' saith one, [Jerome,] 'didst
thou die for love for me? a love more dolorous than death, but to me
a death more lovely than love itself; I cannot live, love, and be longer
from thee.' I read in Josephus,[2] that when Herod Antipater was accused to Julius (?) Cæsar as no good friend of his, he made no other
apology, but stripping himself stark naked, shewed Cæsar his wounds
and said, let me hold my tongue, these wounds will speak for me how
I have loved Cæsar. Ah, my friends, Christ's wounds in our nature
speak out the admirable love of Jesus Christ to us; and oh, how
should this love of his draw out our love to Christ, and inflame our
love to that Jesus who is God-man blessed for ever. Mr Welch, a
Suffolkshire minister, weeping at table, being asked the reason, said, it
was because he could love Christ no more.[3] Ah, what reason have we
to weep, and weep again and again, that we can love that Jesus no
more, who hath shewed such unparalleled love to us in assuming of
the human nature! *Et ipsam animam odio haberem, si non diligeret
meum Jesum,* I must hate my very soul, if it should not love my
Jesus, saith Bernard. Ah, what cause have we even to hate ourselves,
because we love that dear Jesus no more, who is very God and very
man. But,

3. Thirdly, Is Jesus Christ God-man? is he very God and very
man? Then *we may very safely and roundly assert that the work of
redemption was a very great work.*[4] The redemption of souls is a
mighty work, a costly work. To redeem poor souls from sin, from
wrath, from the power of Satan, from the curse, from hell, from the
condemnation, was a mighty work. Wherefore was Christ born,
wherefore did he live, sweat, groan, bleed, die, rise, ascend? Was it
not to 'deliverance to the captives, and the opening of the
prison to them that are bound'? Was it not to 'make an end of sin,
to finish transgression, and to bring in everlasting righteousness,' and
'to destroy the works of the devil,' and to 'abolish death,' and to
'bring life and immortality to light,' and to 'redeem us from all iniquity, and to purify us to himself, and to make us a peculiar people,
zealous of good works'? Certainly the work of redemption was no
ordinary or common thing; God-man must engage in it, or poor
fallen man is undone for ever. The greater the person is that is
engaged in any work, the greater is that work. The great monarchs
of the world do not use to engage their sons in poor, low, mean, and

---

[1] Bernard sup. Cant. ser. 20.   [2] Jos. Bel. Jud. l. 1, c. 8.   [3] As before, 'Welsh.'—G.
[4] Consult these scriptures, Isa. lxi. 1; Dan. ix. 24; 1 John iii. 8; Luke i. 74, 75;
Tit. ii. 14; 1 Pet. i. 4.

petty services, but in such services as are high and honourable, noble and weighty; and will you imagine that ever the great and glorious God would have sent his Son, his own Son, his only-begotten Son, his bosom Son, his Son in whom his soul delighted before the foundations of the earth was laid, to redeem poor sinners' souls, if this had not been a great work, a high work, and a most glorious work in his eye? John i. 18, and Prov. viii. 22-33. The creation of the world did but cost God a word of his mouth, ' Let there be light, and there was light,' Gen. i. 3; but the redemption of souls cost him his dearest Son. There is a divine greatness stamped upon the works of providence, but what are the works of providence to the work of redemption? What are all providential works to Christ's coming from heaven, to his being incarnate, to his doings, sufferings, and dying; and all this to ransom poor souls from the curse, hell, wrath, and eternal death? Souls are dear and costly things, and of great price in the sight of God. Amongst the Romans, those their proper goods and estates which men had gotten in the wars with hazard of their lives, were called *Peculium Castrense*, of a field purchase. Oh, how much more may the precious and immortal souls of men be called Christ's *Peculium Castrense*, his purchase, gotten, not only by the jeopardy of his life, but with the loss of his life and blood! ' Ye know,' saith the apostle, ' that ye were not redeemed with corruptible things, as with silver and gold, from your vain conversation, received by tradition, but with the precious blood of the Son of God, as of a lamb without a spot,' 1 Pet. i. 18, 19. Christ, that only went to the price of souls, hath told us that one soul is more worth than all the world, Mat. xvi. 26. Christ left his Father's bosom, and all the glory of heaven, for the good of souls; he assumed the nature of man for the happiness of the soul of man; he trod the wine-press of his Father's wrath for souls; he wept for souls, he sweat for souls, he prayed for souls, he paid for souls, and he bled out his heart blood for the redemption of souls. The soul is the breath of God, the beauty of man, the wonder of angels, and the envy of devils. It is of an angelical nature, it is a heavenly spark, a celestial plant, and of a divine offspring. It is capable of the knowledge of God, of union with God, of communion with God, and of an eternal fruition of God, John xiv. 8, and Ps. xvii. 15. There is nothing that can suit the soul below God, there is nothing that can satisfy the soul without God. The soul is so high and so noble a piece that it scorns all the world. What are all the riches of the East or West Indies, what are rocks of diamonds, or mountains of gold, or the price of Cleopatra's draught, to the price that Christ laid down for souls? It is only the blood of him that is God-man that is an equivalent price for the redemption of souls. Silver and gold hath redeemed many thousands out of Turkish bondage, but all the silver and gold in the world could never redeem one poor soul from hellish bondage, from hellish torments. Souls are a dear commodity. He that bought them found them so; and yet at how cheap a rate do some sinners sell their immortal souls! Callenuceus tells us of a nobleman of Naples that was wont profanely to say that he had two souls in his body, one for God, and another for who-

186

soever would buy it;[1] but if he hath one soul in hell, I believe he will never find another for heaven. A person of quality, who is still alive, told me a few years since, that in discourse with one of his servants he asked him what he thought would become of his soul if he lived and died in his ignorance and emnity against God, &c. He most profanely and atheistically answered that when he died, he would hang his soul on a hedge, and say, Run God, run devil, and he that can run fastest let him take my soul.[2] I have read[3] of a most blasphemous wretch that, on a time being with his companions in a common inn, carousing and making merry, asked them if they thought a man had a soul or no; whereunto when they replied that the souls of men are immortal, and that some of them after death lived in hell and others in heaven—for so the writings of the prophets and apostles instructed them—he answered and swore that he thought it nothing so, but rather that there was no soul in man to survive the body, but that heaven and hell were mere fables and inventions of priests to get gain; and for himself, he was ready to sell his soul to any that would buy it. Then one of his companions took up a cup of wine, and said, sell me thy soul for this cup of wine; which he receiving, bade him take his soul, and drank up the wine. Now Satan himself being there in man's shape, bought it again of the other at the same price, and by and by bade him give him his soul, the whole company affirming it was meet he should have it, since he had bought it, not perceiving the devil; but presently, he laying hold of this soul-seller, carried him into the air before them all, to the great astonishment and amazement of the beholders; and from that day to this he was never heard of, but hath now found by experience that men have souls, and that hell is no fable![4] Ah, for what a thing of nought do many thousands sell their souls to Satan every day! How many thousands are there who swear, curse, lie, cheat, deceive, &c., for a little gain every day! I have read that there was a time when the Romans did wear jewels on their shoes. Oh that in these days men did not worse! Oh that they did not trample under feet that matchless jewel, their precious and immortal souls! O sirs, there is nothing below heaven so precious and noble as your souls, and therefore do not play the courtiers with your poor souls. Now the courtier does all things late. He rises late, and dines late, and sups late, and goes to bed late, and repents late. Christ made himself an offering for sin, that souls might not be undone by sin; the Lord died that slaves might live; the Son dies that servants might live; the natural Son dies that adopted sons may live; the only-begotten Son dies that bastards might live; yea, the judge dies that malefactors may live. Ah, friends, as there was never sorrow like Christ's, so there was never love like Christ's love; and of all his love, none to that of soul love. Christ, who is God-man, did

---

[1] As before.—G.   [2] This pious gentleman was with me in May 1673, at my house.
[3] Discipulus de temp. Serm., 132.
[4] We laugh at little children to see them part with rich jewels for silly trifles, and yet daily experience tells us that multitudes are so childish as to part with such rich and precious jewels as their immortal souls for a lust, or for base and unworthy trifles; of whom it may be truly said, as Augustus Cæsar said in another case, they are like a man that fishes with a golden hook; the gain can never recompense the loss that may be sustained.

take upon him thy nature, and bare thy sins, and suffered death, and encountered the cross, and was made a sacrifice and a curse, and all to bring about thy redemption; and therefore thou mayest safely conclude that the work of redemption is a great work. But,

4. Fourthly, Is Jesus Christ God-man? is he very God and very man? Then *let this encourage poor sinners to come to Christ, to close with Christ, to accept of Christ, to match with Christ, and to enter into a marriage union and communion with Christ.* The great work of gospel ministers is like that of Eliezer, Abraham's servant, to seek a match for our Master's Son. Now our way to win you to him, is not only to tell you what he has, but what he is. Now he is ' God-man in one person.' He is man, that you may not be afraid of him; and he is God, that he may be able to save you to the uttermost; he is ' the Prince of the kings of the earth;' he is ' Lord of lords and King of kings;' he is the ' Heir of all things;' he is ' fairer than the children of men;' he is ' the chiefest of ten thousand;' he is ' altogether lovely.'[1] There is everything in Jesus, who is God-man, to encourage you to come to him. If you look upon his names, if you look upon his natures, if you look upon his offices, if you look upon his dignities, if you look upon his personal excellencies, if you look upon his mighty conquests, if you look upon his royal attendance,—all these things call aloud upon you to come to Christ, to close with Christ. If you look upon the great things that he has done for sinners, and the hard things that he has suffered for sinners, and the glorious things that he has prepared and laid up for sinners, how can you but readily accept of him, and sweetly embrace him? Though thou hast no loveliness nor comeliness, no beauty nor glory, Ezek. xvi. 4, 5, and Isa. lv. 1, 2; though thou hast not one penny in thy purse, nor a rag to hang on thy back, yet if thou art but really and heartily willing to be divorced from all thy sinful lovers, and accept of Christ for thy sovereign Lord, he is willing that the match should be made up between thee and him, Hos. iii. 3, and Rev. xxii. 17. Now shall Christ woo you himself, shall he declare his willingness to take you with nothing, shall he engage himself to protect you, to maintain you, and at last, as a dowry, to bestow heaven upon you, and will you refuse him, will you turn your backs upon him? O sirs! what could Christ have done that he has not done to do you good, and to make you happy for ever? Lo! he has laid aside his glorious robes, and he has put on your rags; he has clothed himself with your flesh; he came off from his royal throne, he humbled himself to the death of the cross, and has brought life, immortality, and glory to your very doors; and will you yet stand out against him? Oh, ' how shall such escape who neglect so great salvation,' Heb. ii. 3; who say, ' This man shall not rule over us,' Luke xix. 14; who ' tread under foot the Son of God'? Heb. x. 28. Oh, what wrath, what great wrath, what pure wrath, what infinite wrath, what everlasting wrath, is reserved for such persons! John iii. 36. Doubtless, Turks, Jews, and Pagans will have a cooler and a lighter hell than the despisers and rejecters of Christ, John v. 40, and Mat. xxiii. 13, 14. The great damnation is for those that might have

[1] Heb. vii. 25 ; Rev. i. 5, and xvii. 14 ; Heb. i. 3 ; Ps. xlv. 1 ; Cant. v. 10, 16.

Christ, but would not. And no wonder! for the sin of rejecting Christ is not chargeable upon the devils. Ah sinners, sinners! that you would labour to understand more, and dwell more upon, the pre-eminent excellencies of Christ! for till the soul can discern a better, a greater excellency in Christ than in any other thing, it will never yield to match with Christ. Oh, labour every day more and more to take the height and depth and breadth of the excellency of Christ. He is the chiefest and the choicest of all, both in that upper and in this lower world. The godhead dwells bodily in him; he is full of grace; he is the heir of glory; the holy one of God; the brightness of his Father's image; the fountain of life, the well of salvation, and the wonder of heaven. Oh, when will you so understand the super-lative excellency of Christ as to fall in love with him, as to cry out with the martyr, ' Oh, none but Christ; oh, none to Christ!'[1] It is your wisdom, it is your duty, it is your safety, it is your glory, it is your salvation, it is your all to accept of Christ, to close with Christ, and to bestow yourselves, your souls, your all on Christ. If you embrace him, you are made for ever; but if you reject him, you perish for ever. Bernard calls Christ, *Sponsus sanguinum*, the Bridegroom of Bloods, because he espoused his church to himself upon the bed of his cross, his head begirt with a pillow of thorns, his body drenched in a bath of his own blood. To turn your backs upon this bridegroom of bloods will certainly cost you the blood of your souls; and there-fore look to it. But,

5. Fifthly, Is Jesus Christ God-man? is he very God and very man? Oh, then, *honour him above all*. Oh, let him have the pre-eminence, exalt him as high as God the Father hath exalted him. It is the absolute will of the Father that ' all should honour his Son, even as they honour himself:'[2] for he having the same nature and essence with the Father, the Father will have him have the same honour which he himself hath; which whosoever denies to him reflects dishonour upon the Father, who will not bear anything derogatory to the glory of his Son. Certainly there is due to Christ, as he is God-man, the highest respect, reverence, and veneration, which angels and men can possibly give unto him. Oh, look upon the Lord Jesus as God; and according to that honour that is due to him as God, so must you honour him. The apostle speaks of some who, ' when they knew God, they did not glorify him as God,' Rom. i. 21; so several pretend to give some glory to Christ, but they do not glorify him as God. O sirs, this is that which you must come up to, viz., to honour Christ in such a manner as may be suitable to his natures, and as he is the infinite, blessed, and eternal God; and ah! what honour can be high enough for such a person? Christ's honour was very dear to him, who said, Lord, use me for thy shield to keep off those wounds of dishonour, which else would fall on thee, [Bernard.] Luther, in an epistle to Spalatinus, saith, ' They call me a devil, but be it so, so long as Christ is magnified, I am well a-payed.' The inanimate creatures are so compliant with his pleasure, that they will thwart their own

---

[1] Lambert, as before.—G.

[2] Col. i. 18; Phil. ii. 6–10; John v. 23. This text looks sourly on Jews, Turks, Papists, Socinians, and others.

nature to serve his honour; fire will descend, as on Sodom and Gomorrah, Gen. xix.; and water, though a fluid body, stand up like a solid wall, as in the Red Sea, Exod. xiv. 22; if he do but speak the word. Oh, let not the inanimate creatures one day rise in judgment against us for not giving Christ his due honour. If we honour Christ we shall have honour, that is a bargain of Christ's own making; but if we dishonour him, he will put dishonour upon us, as Scripture and history in all ages do sufficiently evidence, 1 Sam. ii. 30. In history we read of an impostor that gave it out that he was that star which Balaam prophesied of, which was a prophecy of Christ, Num. xxiv. 17; this fellow called himself *Ben-chomar*, the son of a star. This man professed himself to be Christ, but he was slain with thunder and lightning from heaven, and then the Jews called him *Ben-cosmar*, which signifieth the son of a lie.[1] Learned Buxtorf tells us that the Jews call Christ *Bar-chozabb*, the son of a lie, a bastard; and his gospel *Aven-gelaion*, the volume of lies, or the volume of iniquity; and hath not God been a-revenging this upon them for above this sixteen hundred years? Rabbi Samuel, who long since writ a tract in form of an epistle to Rabbi Isaac, master of the synagogue of the Jews; wherein he doth excellently discuss the cause of their long captivity and extreme misery, and after that he had proved it was inflicted for some grievous sin, he sheweth that sin to be the same which Amos speaks of. ' For three trangressions of Israel, and for four, I will not turn away the punishment thereof; because they sold the righteous for silver, and the poor for a pair of shoes,' Amos ii. 6. The selling of Joseph he makes the first sin, the worshipping the calf in Horeb the second sin, the abusing and killing God's prophets the third sin, and the selling of Jesus Christ the fourth sin. For the first they served four hundred years in Egypt, for the second they wandered forty years in the wilderness, for the third they were captives seventy years in Babylon, and for the fourth they are held in pitiful captivity, even to this very day. Oh, how severely has God revenged the wrongs and indignities done to Christ the Lord, by this miserable people, to this very hour! and yet, oh, the several ways, wherein this poor people do every day express their malice and hatred against the Lord Jesus! Oh, pray, pray hard, that the veil may be taken away that has been so long before their eyes. Herod imprisons Peter, and killeth James with the sword, Acts xii. 1–4; this God puts up, but when he comes to usurp the honour due to Christ, he must die for it, ver. 23. Herod might more safely take away the liberty of one, and the life of another, than the glory due to Christ. Long before his death, being in chains, he met with a strange omen; for, as he stood bound before the palace, leaning dejectedly upon a tree, among many others that were prisoners with him, an owl came and sat down in that tree to which he leaned; which a German seeing, being one of those that stood there bound, he asked who he was that was in the purple, and leaned there; and understanding who he was, he told him of his enlargement, promotion to honour, and prosperity; and that when he should see that bird again he should die within five days after.[2] Now when Herod

---

[1] Synag. Judaica, cap. 5 and 36.

[2] Josephus of the Antiquities of the Jews, lib. xviii. pp. 475, 476, and 510, 511. [More

had imprisoned Peter, and slain James with the sword, he went down to Cæsarea, and there he made sports and shows in honour of Cæsar; and, on the second day, being most gorgeously apparelled, and the sun shining very bright upon his robe of silver, his flatterers saluted him for a god, and cried out to him, 'Be merciful unto us! hitherto have we feared thee as a man, but, henceforward, we will acknowledge thee to be of a nature more excellent than mortal frailty can attain to.' The wretched king reproved not this abominable flattery, but was well pleased with it; and, not long after, he espied the owl which the German had foretold to be the omen of his death. And suddenly he was seized with miserable gripings in his belly, which came upon him with vehement extremity; whereupon, turning himself towards his friends, saith, Lo, he whom you esteem for a god is doomed to die, and destiny shall evidently confute you, in those flattering and false speeches which you lately used concerning me; for I, who have been adored by you as one immortal, am now under the hands of death; and his griefs and torments increasing, his death drew on apace; whereupon he was removed into the palace, and all the people put on sackcloth, and lay on the ground, praying for him; which he, beholding, could not refrain from tears; and so after five days he gave up the ghost.[1] Thus you see how dearly they have paid for it that have not given Christ his due glory; and let these instances of his wrath alarm all your hearts so, that we may make more conscience than ever, of setting the crown of honour only upon Christ's head, 'for he only is worthy of all honour, glory, and praise,' Rev. xiv. 10, 11. But,

6. Sixthly, Is Jesus Christ God-man? is he very God and very man? Then *from hence as in a glass you may see the true reasons why the death and sufferings of Christ, though short, very short, yet have a sufficient power and virtue in them to satisfy God's justice, to pacify his wrath, to procure our pardon, and to save our immortal souls—viz., because of the dignity of his person that died and suffered for us, the Son of God, yea, God himself.* There was an infinite virtue and value in all his sufferings; hence his blood is called 'precious blood,' yea, 'the blood of God.'[2] Did man transgress the royal law of God? behold God himself is become a man to make up that breach, and to satisfy divine justice to the uttermost farthing, Rom. viii. 2–4. For the man Christ Jesus to stand before the bar of the law, and to make full and complete reparation to it, was the highest honour that ever was done to the law of God. This is infinitely more pleasing and delightful to divine justice than if all the curses of the law had been poured out upon fallen man, and than if the law had built up its honour upon the destruction of the whole creation. To see one sun clouded is much more than to see the moon and all the stars in heaven overcast. Christ considered as God-man was great, very great; and the greater his person was, the greater were his sorrows, his sufferings, his humiliation, his compassion, his satisfaction to divine justice. Had

---

accurately xix. 8, 2: cf. 2 Mac. ix. 9, and Jortin, Eccles. Hist. ii. 320, with a note of Gibbon, c. xiv.: Tertullian ad Scap. c. iii., §. 20. Michælis i. 65.—G.]
[1] All as quaintly told by Clarke in his 'Life' of Herod.— G.
[2] Heb. ix. 14; 1 Pet. i. 19; Acts xx. 28; Gal. iv. 4–6.

not Christ been God-man, he could never have been an able surety, Heb. vii. 25—he could never have paid our debts, he could never have satisfied divine justice, he could never have brought in an everlasting righteousness, Dan. ix. 24, he could never have 'spoiled principalities and powers, and made a show of them openly, triumphing over them on the cross,' Col. ii. 15—a plain allusion to the Roman triumphs, where the victor ascending up to the capitol in a chariot of state, all the prisoners following him on foot with their hands bound behind them, and the victor commonly threw certain pieces of coin abroad to be picked up by the common people. So Christ, in the day of his solemn inauguration into his heavenly kingdom, triumphed over sin, death, devils, and hell, 'and gave gifts to men.' And had he not been God-man, he could never have merited for us a glorious reward. If we consider Christ himself as a mere man, setting aside his godhead, Eph. iv. 8, he could not merit by his sufferings; for, 1. Christ as he was man only, was a creature. Now a mere creature can merit nothing from the Creator. 2. Christ's sufferings, as he was man only, were finite, and therefore could not merit infinite glory. Indeed, as he was God, his sufferings were meritorious; but, consider him purely as man, they were not. This is wisely to be observed against the papists, who make so great a noise of men's merits; for if Christ's sufferings, as he was mere man, could not merit the least favour from God, then what mortal man is able to merit, at the hand of God, the least of mercies by his greatest sufferings? But,

7. Seventhly, Is Jesus Christ God-man? is he very God and very man? Then from hence *we may see the greatest pattern of humility and self-denial that ever was or will be in this world.* That he who was the Lord of glory, that he who was equal with God, that he should leave the bosom of his Father, Phil. ii. 6; John i. 18, which was a bosom of the sweetest loves and the most ineffable delights, that he should put off all that glory that he had with the Father before the foundation of the world was laid, John xvii. 5, that he should so far abase himself as to become man, by taking on him our base, vile nature, so that in this our nature he might die, suffer, satisfy, and bring many sons to glory, Heb. ii. 10,—oh, here is the greatest humility and abasement that ever was! And oh that all sincere Christians would endeavour to imitate this matchless example of humility and self-denial! Oh the admirable condescensions of dear Jesus, that he should take our nature, and make us partakers of his divine nature! 2 Pet. i. 4, that he should put on our rags, and put upon us his royal robes! Rev. xix. 7, 8, that he should make himself poor that we might be rich! 2 Cor. viii. 9, low that we might be high! accursed that we might be blessed! Gal. iii. 10, 13. Oh wonderful love! oh grace unsearchable! Ah, Christians, did Christ stoop low, and will you be stout, proud, and high? Was he content to be accounted a worm, a wine-bibber, an enemy to Cæsar, a friend of publicans and sinners, a devil, and must you be all in a flame when vain men make little account of you? Was he willing to be a curse, a reproach for you, and will you shrug, and shrink, and faint, and fret when you are reproached for his name? Did Jesus Christ stoop so low as to wash his disciples' feet, John xiii. 14, and are you so stout

and sturdy that you cannot hear together, nor pray together, nor sit at the table of the Lord together, though you all hope at last to sit down with Abraham, Isaac, and Jacob, in the kingdom of heaven? Mat. viii. 11.   Shall one heaven hold you at last; and shall not one house, one bed, one table, one church, hold you here? Oh, that ever worms should swell with such intolerable pride and stoutness!   He who was God-man, was lowly, meek, self-denying, and of a most condescending spirit; and oh that all you, who hope for salvation by him, would labour to write after so fair a copy.   Bernard calls humility a self-annihilation.   The same author saith that humility is *conservatrix virtutum*.   'Thou wilt save the humble,' saith Job, chap. xxii. 29; in the Hebrew it is, 'him that is of low eyes,' וישׁח עינים. A humble Christian hath lower thoughts of himself than others can have of him.   Abraham is 'dust and ashes' in his own eyes, Gen. xviii., Jacob is 'less than the least of all mercies,' Gen. xxxii. 10; David, though a great king, yet looks upon himself as a worm; 'I am a worm, and no man,' Ps. xxii. 6.   The word in the original, *Tolugnath*, signifieth a very little worm, which breedeth in scarlet; a worm that is so little, that a man can hardly see it or perceive it.   Oh, how little, how very little was David in his own eyes; and Paul, who was the greatest among the apostles, yet, in his own eyes, he was 'less than the least of all saints.'[1]   *Non sum dignus dici minimus*, saith Ignatius, 'I am not worthy to be called the least.'   'Lord! I am hell, but thou art heaven,' said blessed Cooper: 'I am a most hypocritical wretch, not worthy that the earth should bear me,' said holy Bradford: Luther, in humility, speaks thus of himself; 'I have no other name than sinner; sinner is my name, sinner is my surname; this is the name by which I shall be always known; I have sinned, I do sin, I shall sin, *in infinitum*.'   Ah, how can proud, stout spirits read these instances and not blush!   Certainly the sincere humble Christian is like the violet, which grows low, hangs the head down, and hides itself with its own leaves; and were it not that the frequent smell of his many virtues discovers him to the world, he would choose to live and die in his self-contenting secrecy.   But,

8. Eighthly, Is Jesus Christ God-man? is he very God and very man?   Then hence we may see *how to have access to God; namely, by means of Christ's human nature, which he hath taken upon him, to that very end, that he might in it die and suffer for our sins, and so reconcile us to God, and give us access to him*, Rom. v. 1, 2; Eph. iii. 12, and ii. 18.   'By him we have access to the Father.'   The word is προσαγωγὴν, 'a leading by the hand,' an introduction, an adduction: it is an allusion, saith Estius, to the customs of princes, to whom there is no passage, unless we are brought in by one of their favourites, Esth. i.   Though the Persian kings held it a piece of their silly glory to hold off their best friends, who might not come near them, but upon special licence; yet the great King of heaven and earth counts it his glory to give us free access at all times, in all places, and upon all occasions, by the man Christ Jesus: 1 Tim. ii. 5, 'There is one mediator between God and us, even the man Christ

[1] Eph. iii. 8.   See my 'Unsearchable Riches of Christ' upon that text.   [Vol. iii. pp. 1–232.—G.]

Jesus.' Christ was made true man, that in our nature he might reconcile us to God, and give us access to God, which he could never have done, had he not been very God and very man. Without the human nature of Christ, we could never have had access to God, or fellowship with God; being by nature enemies to God, and estranged from God, and dead in trespasses and sins, Rom. v. 10, it is only by the mediation of Christ incarnate that we come to be reconciled to God, Eph. ii. 1, 12–14, to have access to him, and acceptance with him. In Christ's human nature God and we meet together, and have fellowship together, 1 John i. 1–3. It could never stand with the unspotted holiness and justice of God, who is 'a consuming fire,' Heb. xii. 29, to honour us with one cast of his countenance, or one hour's communion with himself, were it not upon the account of the man Christ Jesus. The least serious thought of God out of Christ will breed nothing in the soul but horror and amazement; which made Luther say, *Nolo Deum absolutum*, let me have nothing to do with an absolute God. Believers have free and blessed access to God, but still it is upon the credit of the man Christ Jesus, Heb. iv. 15, 16. ' Let us come boldly to the throne of grace,' saith the apostle, speaking of Christ, ' that we may obtain mercy, and find grace to help in time of need.' The apostle's phrase is μετὰ παρρησίας, a word which signifies liberty of speech, and boldness of face; as when a man with a bold and undaunted spirit, utters his mind before the great ones of the world without blushing, without weakness of heart, without shaking of his voice, without imperfection and faltering in speech, when neither majesty nor authority can take off his courage, so as to stop his mouth, and make him afraid to speak. With such heroic and undaunted spirits would the apostle have us to come to the throne of grace; and all upon the credit of Christ our high priest, who is God-man. But,

9. Ninthly, Is Jesus Christ God-man? is he very God and very man? Then *you may be very confident of his sympathising with you in all your afflictions*, Ezek. xxxv. 10–13; Isa. xxxvii. 23, 24; *then this may serve as a foundation to support you under all your troubles, and as a cordial to comfort you under all your afflictions, in that Christ partaking of the same nature, and having had experience of the infirmities of it, he is the more able and willing to help and succour us* Heb. ii. 17, ' Wherefore in all things it behoveth him to be like his brethren, that he might be a merciful and faithful high priest in things pertaining to God, to make reconciliation for the sins of the people:' so Heb. iv. 15. If one come to visit a man that is sick of a grievous disease, who hath himself been formerly troubled with the same disease, he will sympathise more, and shew more compassion than twenty others, who have not felt the like:[1] so here, from Christ's sufferings in his human nature we may safely gather that he will shew himself a merciful high priest to us in our sufferings, and one that will be ready to help and succour us in all our afflictions and miseries, which we suffer in this life, inasmuch as himself had experience of suffering the like in our nature; ' for in that he himself hath suffered, being tempted, he is able to succour them that are tempted:' and this

---

[1] As the brazen serpent was like the fiery serpent, but had no sting.

should be a staff to support us, and a cordial to comfort us in all our sorrows and miseries. It is between Christ and his church as it is between two lute strings that are tuned one to another; no sooner is one struck but the other trembles:[1] Isa. lxiii. 9, 'In all their afflictions he was afflicted.' These words may be read interrogatively thus: was he in all their afflictions afflicted? Christ took to heart the afflictions of his church, he was himself grieved for them and with them. The Lord, the better to allure and draw his people to himself, speaks after the manner of men, attributing to himself all the affection, love, and fatherly compassion that can possibly be in them to men in misery. Christ did so sympathise with his people in all their afflictions and sufferings, as if he himself had felt the weight, the smart, the pain of them all. 'He was in all things made like unto his brethren,' not only in nature, but also in infirmities and sufferings, and by all manner of temptations, that thereby 'he might be able,' experimentally, 'to succour them that are tempted.' He that toucheth them toucheth not only his eye but the apple of his eye, which is the tenderest piece of the tenderest part,[2] to express the inexpressible tenderness of Christ's compassion towards them. Let persecutors take heed how they meddle with God's eyes, for he will retaliate eye for eye, Exod. xxi. 24: he is wise in heart and mighty in strength, and sinners shall one day pay dear for touching the apple of his eye. Christ counts himself persecuted when his church is persecuted; 'Saul, Saul, why persecutest thou me?' Acts ix. 4. And he looks upon himself as hungry, thirsty, naked, and in prison, when his members are so, Mat. xxv. 35, 36; so greatly does he sympathise with them. Hence the afflictions of Christians are called ὑστερήματα, 'the remainders of the afflictions of Christ,' Col. i. 24: such as Christ, by his fellow-feeling, suffereth in his members, and as they by correspondency are to fill up, as exercises and trials of their faith and patience. Christ gave many evidences of his sympathy or fellow-feeling of our infirmities when he was on earth, as he groaned in his spirit and was troubled, John xi. 33; when he saw those that wept for Lazarus he wept also, ver. 35; as he did over Jerusalem also, Luke xix. 41. It is often observed in the Gospel that Christ was moved with compassion; and that he frequently put forth acts of pity, mercy, and succour to those that were in any distress, either in body or soul. Christ retaineth this sympathy and fellow-feeling with us now he is in heaven; and does so far commiserate our distresses as may stand with a glorified condition. Jesus Christ grieves for the afflictions of his people; 'the angel of the Lord answered and said, O Lord of hosts, how long wilt thou not have mercy on Jerusalem,' Zech. i. 12. The angel here is that Jesus who is our advocate with the Father, 1 John ii. 1, 2. He speaks as one intimately affected with the state and condition of poor Jerusalem. Christ plays the advocate for his suffering people, and feelingly pleads for them; he being afflicted in all their afflictions, it moved him to observe that God's enemies were in a better case than his people; and this put him upon that passionate

---

[1] If we perish, Christ perisheth with us.—*Luther.*

[2] Zech. ii. 8, *Ishon* of *Ish*, it is here called *Bath*, the daughter of the eye, because it is as dear to a man as his only daughter.

expostulation, 'O Lord of hosts, how long wilt thou not have mercy on Jerusalem!' Alexander the Great applied his crown to the soldier's forehead that had received a wound for him; and Constantine the Great kissed the hollow of Paphnutius's eye that he had lost for Christ. What an honour was it to the soldier and to Paphnutius that these great men should have fellow-feeling of their sufferings, and sympathise with them in their sorrows! but, oh then! what an honour is it to such poor worms as we are, that Jesus Christ, who is God-man, who is the Prince of the kings of the earth, that he should have a fellow-feeling of all our miseries, and sympathise with us in all our troubles! Rev. i. 5. But,

10. Tenthly, Is Jesus Christ God-man? is he very God and very man? Then from hence you may see *the excellency of Christ above man, above all other men, yea, above Adam in innocency.* Christ, as man, was perfect in all graces: Isa. xi. 1, 2, 'And there shall come forth a rod out of the stem of Jesse, and a branch shall grow out of his roots; and the Spirit of the Lord shall rest upon him, the Spirit of wisdom and understanding, the Spirit of counsel and might, the Spirit of knowledge, and of the fear of the Lord.' God gave the Spirit of wisdom to him not by measure; and therefore, at twelve years of age, you find him in the Sanhedrim disputing with the doctors, and asking them questions, John iii. 34; Luke ii. 46, 47; John i. 16, 'And of his fulness have all we received grace for grace;' Col. i. 19, 'For it pleased the Father that in him should all fulness dwell;' ii. 3, 'In whom are hid all the treasures of wisdom and knowledge.' The state of innocency was an excellent estate, it was an estate of perfect holiness and righteousness, Gen. i. 27. By his holiness he was carried out to know the Lord, to love the Lord, to delight in the Lord, to fear the Lord, and to take him as his chiefest good, Eph. iv. 22–24. A legal holiness consists in an exact, perfect, and complete conformity in heart and life to the whole revealed will of God; and this was the holiness that Adam had in his innocency, and this holiness was immediately derived from God, and was perfect. Adam's holiness was as co-natural to him as unholiness is now to us. Adam's holiness was as natural, and as pleasing, and as delightful to him as any way of unholiness can be natural, pleasing, and delightful to us. The estate of innocency was an estate of perfect wisdom, knowledge, and under-standing. Witness the names that Adam gave to all the creatures, suitable and apposite to their natures, Gen. ii. 20. The estate of innocency was an estate of great honour and dignity. David brings in Adam in his innocent estate with a crown upon his head, and that crown was a crown of glory and honour: 'Thou hast crowned him with glory and honour,' his place was 'a little lower than the angels,' but far above all other creatures, Ps. viii. 5. The estate of innocency, it was an estate of great dominion and authority, man being made the sovereign lord of the whole creation, Ps. viii. 6–8. We need not stand to enlarge upon one parcel of his demesnes, namely, that which they call paradise, sith the whole both of sea and land, and all the creatures in both, were his possession, his paradise. Certainly man's first estate was a state of perfect and complete happiness, there being nothing within him but what was desirable, nothing without him but what was

amiable, and nothing about him but what was serviceable and comfortable; and yet Jesus Christ, who is God-man, is infinitely more glorious and excellent than ever Adam was; for Adam was set in a mutable condition, but Christ is the Rock of ages. He is steadfast and abiding for ever; he is 'yesterday, and to-day, and the same for ever,' Heb. xiii. 8. He is the same afore time, in time, and after time; he is the same, that is unchangeable, in his essence, promises, and doctrine. Christ is the same in respect of virtue, and the faith of believers; even his manhood, before it was in being, was clothed with perfection of grace, and so continueth for ever. And again, Adam was a mere man, and alone by himself; but in Christ the human nature was hypostatically united unto the divine; and hence it comes to pass that Christ, even as man, had a greater measure of knowledge and revelation of grace and heavenly gifts than ever Adam had. The apostle tells us that in 'Christ dwells all the fulness of the Godhead,' σωματικῶς, bodily, that is, essentially; that is, not by a naked and bare communicating of virtue, as God is said to dwell in his saints, but by a substantial union of the two natures, divine and human, the eternal Word and the man, consisting of soul and body, whereby they become one, ὑφιστάμενον, one person, one subsistence. Now from this admirable and wonderful union of the two natures in Christ, there flows to the manhood of Christ a plenitude and fulness of all spiritual wisdom and grace, such as was never found in any mere man, no, not in Adam whilst he stood in his integrity and uprightness. But,

11. Eleventhly, Is Jesus Christ God-man? is he very God and very man? Then *this truth looks very sourly and frowningly upon all such as deny the godhead of Christ;* as Arians, Turks, Jews. How many be there in this city, in this nation, who stiffly deny the divinity of Christ, and dispute against it, and write against it, and blaspheme that great truth, without which, I think, a man may safely say, there is no possibility of salvation. In ancient times, near unto the age of the apostles, this doctrine of Christ's godhead, and eternal generation from the Father, was greatly opposed by sundry wicked and blasphemous heretics, as Ebion, Cerinthus, Arius, &c., who stirred up great troubles, and bloody persecutions against the church, for maintaining this great truth of Christ's godhead. They asserted that Christ had no true flesh; it was only the likeness of flesh which he appeared in, and that his body was only a fantastic imaginary body; but had the body of Christ been only such a body, then his conception, nativity, death, resurrection, are all too but imaginary things; and then his sufferings and crucifixion are but mere fancies too; and if so, then what would become of us, what would become of our salvation? then our faith would be in vain, and our hope would be in vain, and our hearing, preaching, praying, and receiving, would all be in vain; yea, then all our religion would vanish into a mere fancy also. When a man's conscience is awakened to see his sin and misery, and he shall find guilt to lay like a load upon his soul, and when he shall see that divine justice is to be satisfied, and divine wrath to be pacified, and the curse to be borne, and the law to be fulfilled, and his nature to be renewed, his heart to be changed, and his sins to be pardoned, or

else his soul can never be saved: how can such a person venture his soul, his all, upon one that is but a mere creature? Certainly, a mere man is no rock, no city of refuge, and no sure foundation for a man to build his faith and hope upon. Woe to that man, that ever he was born, that has no Jesus, but a Socinian's Jesus to rest upon! Oh, it is sad trusting to one, who is man, but not God; flesh, but not spirit. As you love the eternal safety of your precious souls, and would be happy for ever; as you would escape hell, and get to heaven, lean on none, rest on none, but that Jesus who is God-man, who is very God and very man. Apollinaris held that Christ took not the whole nature of man, but a human body only, without a soul, and that the Godhead was instead of a soul to the manhood. Also Eutyches, who confounded the two natures of Christ, and their properties, &c. Also Apelles and the Manichees, who denied the true human body, and held him to have an aerial or imaginary body. Though the popular sort deified Alexander the Great;[1] yet, having got a clap with an arrow, he said, ye style me Jupiter's son, as if immortal; *sed hoc vulnus clamat esse hominem;* this blood that issues from the wound proves me in the issue a man: this is ἁῖμα τοῦ ἀνθρώπου, the blood of man, not of God, and smelling the stench of his own flesh, he asked his flatterers if the gods yielded such a scent. So may it be said of Jesus Christ our Saviour, though myriads of angels and saints acclaim he is a God, *ergo,* immortal; and a crew of heretics disclaim him to be man, as the Marcionites averred that he had a fantastical body, and Apelles who conceived that he had a sidereal substance, yet the streams of blood following the arrow of death that struck him, makes it good that he was perfect man; of a reasonable soul and human flesh subsisting. And as this truth looks sourly upon the above-mentioned persons, so it looks sourly upon the papists, who, by their doctrine of the real presence of Christ's body in the sacrament, do overthrow one of the properties of his human nature, which is to be but in one place present at once. This truth also looks sourly upon the Lutherans or Ubiquitaries, who teach that Christ's human nature is in all places by virtue of their personal union, &c. I wonder that of all the old errors, swept down into this latter age, as into a sink of time, this of the Socinians and Arians should be held forth among the rest. O sirs, beware of their doctrines, shun their meetings, and persons that come to you with the denial of the divinity of Christ in their mouths. This was John's doctrine and practice. Irenæus saith, that after he was returned from his banishment, and came to Ephesus, he came to bathe himself, and in the bath he found Cerinthus, that said, Christ had no being till he received it from the Virgin Mary; upon the sight of whom, John skipped out of the bath, and called his companions from thence; saying, let us go from this place, lest the bath should fall down upon us, because Cerinthus is in it, that is so great an enemy to God.[2] Ye see his doctrine, see his words too: 2 John 10, 11, 'If any come to you, having not this doctrine, receive him not into your house, neither bid him God speed: for he that biddeth him God speed, is partaker of his evil deeds.' What that doctrine was, if you cast your eye upon the scripture, you shall find it to be the doctrine of the divinity of Christ.

[1] Plutarch, *in vita.*   [2] As before.—G.

Shew no love where you owe nothing but hatred: ' I hate every false
way,' saith David, Ps. cxix. 118.   And I shall look upon Auxentius as
upon a devil, so long as he is an Arian, said Hilarius.   We must shew
no countenance, nor give no encouragement to such as deny either the
divinity or humanity of Christ.

I have been the longer upon the divinity and humanity of Christ,
1. Because the times we live in require it.   2. That poor, weak, staggering Christians may be strengthened, established, and settled in the
truth, as it is in Jesus.   3. That I may give in my testimony and
witness against all those who are poisoned and corrupted with Socinian
and Arian principles, which destroy the souls of men.   4. That those
in whose hands this book may fall may be the better furnished to
make head against men of corrupt minds; who, ' by sleight-of-hand
and cunning craftiness, lie in wait to deceive,' Eph. iv. 14.

[6.] Sixthly, As he that did feel and suffer the very torments of hell,
though not after a hellish manner, was God-man, so *the punishments*
that Christ did sustain for us must be referred only to the substance,
and not unto the circumstances of punishment.   The punishment
which Christ endured, if it be considered in its substance, kind, or
nature, so it was the same with what the sinner himself should have
undergone.   Now the punishment due to the sinner was death, the
curse of the law, &c.   Now this Christ underwent, for ' he was made
a curse for us,' Gal. iii. 13.   But if you consider the punishment
which Christ endured, with respect to certain circumstances, adjuncts,
and accidents, as the eternity of it, desperation going along with
it, &c., then, I say, it was not the same, but equivalent.[1]   And the
reason is, because, though the enduring of the punishments, as to the
substance of them, could, and did agree with him as a surety, yet the
circumstances of those punishments could not have befallen him unless
he had been a sinner ; and therefore every inordination in suffering
was far from Christ, and a perpetual duration of suffering could not
befall him, for the first of these had been contrary to the holiness and
dignity of his person, and the other had made void the end of his
suretyship and mediatorship, which was so to suffer, as yet to conquer
and to deliver, and therefore, though he did suffer death for us in the
substance of it, yet he neither did nor could suffer death in the circumstances of it, so as for ever to be held by death; for then, in suffering death,
he should not have conquered death, nor delivered us from death.   Neither was it necessary to Christ's substitution that he should undergo in
every respect the same punishment which the offender himself was liable
unto ; but if he underwent so much punishment as did satisfy the law,
and vindicate the lawgiver in his holiness, truth, justice, and righteousness, that was enough.   Now that was unquestionably done by Christ,
as the Scriptures do abundantly testify.   It must be readily granted
that Christ was to suffer the whole punishment due unto sin, so far as
it became the dignity of his person and the necessity of the work ; but
if he had suffered eternally, the work of redemption could never have
been accomplished ; and besides, he should have suffered that which

---

[1] Whether the work of man's redemption could have been wrought without the sufferings and humiliation of Christ is not determinable by men; but that it was the most
admirable way which wisdom, justice, and mercy could require, cannot be denied.

could noways beseem him. And therefore the apostle saith, Heb. ii. 10, ' It became him to be consecrated through sufferings.' Christ was only to pass through such sufferings as became him who was ordained to be the prince and captain of our salvation. It became him to be man, and it became him in our human nature to suffer death, and it became him to sustain for us the substance of those punishments that we should have undergone ; and accordingly he did. What our sins did deserve, and what justice might lay upon us for those sins, all that did Christ certainly suffer or bear. Jesus Christ did so suffer for our sins, as that his sufferings were fully answerable to the demerit of our sins. And I think I may safely say that God, in justice, could not require any more, or lay on any one more punishment than Jesus Christ did suffer for our sins ; and my reason is this, because Christ bare all our sins, and all our sorrows, and was obedient unto the death, and made a curse for us, Isa. liii., and Gal. iii. 13 ; and more than this the law of God could not require. And if Christ did suffer all that the law of God required, then certainly he suffered so much as did satisfy the justice of God, viz., as much punishment as was commensurated with sin. But,

[7.] Seventhly and lastly, *The meritorious cause, the main end, and the special occasion of all the sufferings of Christ were the sins of his people.*[1] Christ was our surety, and he could not satisfy for our sins, nor reconcile us to God without suffering : Isa. liii. 5, ' But he was wounded for our transgressions.' The Hebrew word for wounded, מחלל, hath a double emphasis : either it may signify that he was pierced through as with a dart, or that he was tormented or pained, as women or other creatures are wont to be that bring forth with pain and torment, at the time of their travail; for the word in the text last cited comes regularly from a root that signifies properly to be in pain, as women are when they bring forth. It was our transgressions that gave Christ his deadly wounds ; it was our sins that smote him, and bruised him. Look, as Zipporah said to Moses, Exod. iv. 25, ' Surely a bloody husband art thou to me,' so may Christ say to his church, Surely a bloody spouse hast thou been to me. Christ's spouse may look upon him and say, It was I that have been that Judas that have betrayed thee ! It was I that was the soldiers that murdered thee ! It was my sins that brought all sorrows and sufferings, all mischiefs and evils upon thee ! -I have sinned, and thou hast suffered ! I have eaten the sour grapes, and thy teeth were set on edge ! I have sinned, and thou hast died ! I have wounded thee, and thou hast healed me ! It is the wisdom, and oh that it might be more and more the work of every believer to look upon a humble Christ with a humble heart, a broken Christ with a broken heart, a bleeding Christ with a bleeding heart, a wounded Christ with a wounded heart; according to that, Zech. xii. 10, Christ was wounded, bruised, and cut off for sinners' sins. When Christ was taken by the soldiers, he said, ' If ye seek me, let these go their way :' Christ was willing that the hurt which sinners

[1] Isa. liii. 4, 5. There were other subordinate ends of his sufferings ; as, (1.) To sanctify sufferings to us. (2.) To sweeten sufferings to us. (3.) To succour us experimentally under all our sufferings, Heb. ii. 17, 18. (4.) That he might be prepared to enter into his glory, Luke xxiv. 26. (5.) That he might be a conqueror over sufferings, which was one piece of his greatest glory, &c.

had done to God, and the debt which they owed to him, should be set
upon his score, and put upon his account; and the apostle mentions it
as a remarkable thing, ' that Christ died for the ungodly,' Rom. v. 8;
' the just for the unjust,' 1 Pet. iii. 18. Our sins were the meritorious
cause of Christ's sufferings, Heb. iv. 15, and vii. 26. Christ did not
suffer for himself, ' for he was without sin, neither was guile found in
his mouth.' The grand design, errand, and business about which
Christ came into the world, was to save sinners, 1 Tim. i. 15. He
had his name Jesus, because he was to save his people from their sins,
Mat. i. 21. He died for our sins; not only for our good, as the final
cause, but for our sins, as the procuring cause of his death. 'He was
delivered for our offences,' 'Christ died for our sins according to the
Scriptures,' Rom. iv. 25, and 1 Cor. xv. 3; that is, according to what
was typified, prophesied, and promised in the blessed Scriptures: Gal.
i. 4, ' He gave himself for our sins;' 1 Pet. ii. 24, 'Who his own self
bare our sins in his own body upon the tree;'. . . by whose stripes ye
were healed, οὐ τῷ μώλωπι αὐτου ἰάθητε. The whole Testament hath
not the like two relatives at once in the original, as if I should say, by
whose stripes of his we are healed. Peter, saith Estius, alludes to the
stripes that servants receive from their cruel masters; therefore he returns to the second person, ' ye are healed.' Here you see that the
physician's blood became the sick man's salve. We can hardly believe the power of sword salve! But here is a mystery, that only the
gospel can assure us of, that the wounding of one should be the cure
of another. Oh, what an odious thing is sin to God, that he will
pardon none without blood, yea, without the blood of his dearest Son!
Heb. ix. 22, and 1 Pet. i. 18, 19. Oh, what a hell of wickedness
must there be in sin, that nothing can expiate it but the best, the
purest, the noblest blood that ever run in veins! Oh, what a transcendent evil must sin be, that nothing can purge it away but death,
but the death of the cross, no death but an accursed death! Oh, what
a leprosy is sin, that it must have blood, yea, the blood of God, to take
it away!

Now thus you have seen, (1.) That the sufferings of Christ have
been free and voluntary, and not constrained or forced. (2.) That
they have been very great and heinous. (3.) That the punishments
which Christ did suffer for our sins, were, in their parts, and kinds,
and degrees, and proportion, all those punishments which were due
unto us by reason of our sins; and which we ourselves would otherwise
have suffered. (4.) That Jesus Christ did feel and suffer the very torments of hell, though not after a hellish manner. (5.) That he that did
feel and suffer the torments of hell, though not after a hellish manner, was
God-man. (6.) That the punishments that Christ did sustain for us,
must be referred only to the substance, and not to the circumstances
of punishment. (7.) That the meritorious cause of all the sufferings
of Christ, were the sins of his people.

IV. Now to that great question of giving up your account at last,
according to the import of those ten scriptures in the margin,[1] you
may, in the fourth place, make this safe, noble, and happy plea. 'O

[1] Eccles. xi. 12, 14; Mat. xii. 14, and xviii. 23; Luke xvi. 3; Rom. xiv. 10; 2 Cor.
v. 10; Heb. ix. 27, and xiii. 17; 1 Pet. iv. 7.

blessed God, Jesus Christ hath suffered all those things that were due unto me for my sin; he hath suffered even to the worst and uttermost; for all that the law threatened was a curse, and Christ was made a curse for me, Gal. iii. 13 ; *he knew no sin, but was made sin for me,* 2 Cor. v. 21 ; *and what Christ suffered he suffered as my surety, and in my stead; and therefore, what he suffered for me, is as if I had suffered all that myself; and his sufferings hath appeased thy wrath, and satisfied thy justice, and reconciled thee to myself.* For, 2 Cor. v. 19, ' God was in Christ, reconciling the world to himself, not imputing their trespasses unto them.' ' *And he hath reconciled both Jews and Gentiles unto God, in one body, on the cross ; having slain enmity thereby.*' Jesus Christ took upon him all my sins, they were all of them laid upon him, and he bare or suffered all the wrath and punishment due for them, and he suffered all as my surety, in my stead, and for my good; and thou didst design him for all this, and accepted of it as sufficient and effectual on my behalf. Oh, with what comfort, courage, and confidence, may a believer, upon these considerations, hold up his head in the great day of his account. Let me now make a few inferences from the consideration of all the great and grievous sufferings of our Lord Jesus Christ: and therefore,

1. First, *Let us stand still, and admire and wonder at the love of Jesus Christ to poor sinners; that Christ should rather die for us, than the angels.* They were creatures of a more noble extract, and in all probability might have brought greater revenues of glory to God : yet that Christ should pass by those golden vessels, and make us vessels of glory,—oh, what amazing and astonishing love is this ! [1] The angels were more honourable and excellent creatures than we. They were celestial spirits ; we earthly bodies, dust and ashes : they were immediate attendants upon God, they were, as I may say, of his privy chamber ; we servants of his in the lower house of this world, farther remote from his glorious presence : their office was to sing hallelujahs, songs of praise to God in the heavenly paradise ; ours to dress the garden of Eden, which was but an earthly paradise : they sinned but once, and but in thought, as is commonly thought; but Adam sinned in thought by lusting, in deed by tasting, and in word by excusing. Why did not Christ suffer for their sins, as well as for ours ? or if for any, why not for theirs rather than ours? ' Even so, O Father, for so it pleased thee,' Mat. xi. 26. We move this question, not as being curious to search thy secret counsels, O Lord, but that we may be the more swallowed up in the admiration of the ' breadth, and length, and depth, and height of the love of Christ, which passeth knowledge.' The apostle, being in a holy admiration of Christ's love, affirms it to pass knowledge, Eph. iii. 18, 19 ; that God, who is the eternal Being, should love man when he had scarce a being, Prov. viii. 30, 31, that he should be enamoured with deformity, that he should love us when in our blood, Ezek. xvi., that he should pity us when no eye pitied us, no, not our own. Oh, such was Christ's transcendent love, that man's extreme misery could not abate it. The deploredness of man's condition did but heighten the holy flame of Christ's love. It is as high as heaven, who can reach it? It is as

[1] This is the envy of devils, and the admiration of angels and saints.

low as hell, who can understand it? Heaven, through its glory, could not contain him, man being miserable, nor hell's torments make him refrain, such was his perfect matchless love to fallen man. That Christ's love should extend to the ungodly, to sinners, to enemies that were in arms of rebellion against him, Rom. v. 6, 8, 10; yea, not only so, but that he should hug them in his arms, lodge them in his bosom, dandle them upon his knees, and lay them to his breasts, that they may suck and be satisfied, is the highest improvement of love, Isa. lxvi. 11–13. That Christ should come from the eternal bosom of his Father, to a region of sorrow and death, John i. 18; that God should be manifested in the flesh, the Creator made a creature, Isa. liii. 4; that he that was clothed with glory, should be wrapped with rags of flesh, 1 Tim. iii. 16; that he that filled heaven, should be cradled in a manger, John xvii. 5; that the God of Israel should fly into Egypt, Mat. ii. 14; that the God of strength should be weary; that the judge of all flesh should be condemned; that the God of life should be put to death, John xix. 41; that he that is one with his Father, should cry out of misery, 'O my Father, if it be possible, let this cup pass from me!' Mat. xxvi. 39: that he that had the keys of hell and death, Rev. i. 18, should lie imprisoned in the sepulchre of another, having, in his lifetime, nowhere to lay his head; nor after death, to lay his body, John xix. 41, 42; and all this for man, for fallen man, for miserable man, for worthless man, is beyond the thoughts of created natures. The sharp, the universal and continual sufferings of our Lord Jesus Christ, from the cradle to the cross, does above all other things speak out the transcendent love of Jesus Christ to poor sinners. That wrath, that great wrath, that fierce wrath, that pure wrath, that infinite wrath, that matchless wrath of an angry God, that was so terribly impressed upon the soul of Christ, quickly spent his natural strength, and turned his moisture into the drought of summer, Ps. xxxii. 4; and yet all this wrath he patiently underwent, that sinners might be saved, and that 'he might bring many sons unto glory,' Heb. ii. 10. Oh wonder of love! Love is passive, it enables to suffer. The Curtii laid down their lives for the Romans, because they loved them; so it was love that made our dear Lord Jesus lay down his life, to save us from hell and to bring us to heaven. As the pelican, out of her love to her young ones, when they are bitten with serpents, feeds them with her own blood to recover them again; so when we were bitten by the old serpent, and our wound incurable, and we in danger of eternal death, then did our dear Lord Jesus, that he might recover us and heal us, feed us with his own blood, Gen. iii. 15; John vi. 53–56. Oh love unspeakable! This made one cry out, 'Lord, thou hast loved me more than thyself; for thou hast laid down thy life for me.'[1] It was only the golden link of love that fastened Christ to the cross, John x. 17, and that made him die freely for us, and that made him willing 'to be numbered among transgressors,' Isa. liii. 12, that we might be numbered among [the] 'general assembly and church of the firstborn, which are written in heaven,' Heb. xii. 23. If Jonathan's love to David was wonderful, 2 Sam. i. 26, how wonderful must the love of Christ be to us, which led him by the hand to make him-

---

[1] Dilexisti me Domine magis quàm teipsum.—*Bernard.*

self an offering for us, Heb. x. 10, which Jonathan never did for David: for though Jonathan loved David's life and safety well, yet he loved his own better; for when his father cast a javelin at him to smite him, he flies for it, and would not abide his father's fury, being very willing to sleep in a whole skin, notwithstanding his wonderful love to David, 1 Sam. xx. 33–35; making good the philosopher's notion, that man is a life-lover. Christ's love is like his name, and that is Wonderful, Isa. ix. 6; yea, it is so wonderful, that it is *supra omnem creaturam, ultra omnem mensuram, contra omnem naturam,* above all creatures, beyond all measure, contrary to all nature. It is above all creatures, for it is above the angels, and therefore above all others. It is beyond all measure, for time did not begin it, and time shall never end it; place doth not bound it, sin doth not exceed it, no estate, no age, no sex is denied it, tongues cannot express it, understandings cannot conceive it: and it is contrary to all nature; for what nature can love where it is hated? what nature can forgive where it is provoked? what nature can offer reconcilement where it receiveth wrong? what nature can heap up kindness upon contempt, favour upon ingratitude, mercy upon sin? and yet Christ's love hath led him to all this; so that well may we spend all our days in admiring and adoring of this wonderful love, and be always ravished with the thoughts of it. But,

2. Secondly, Then look that *ye love the Lord Jesus Christ with a superlative love, with an overtopping love.* There are none have suffered so much for you as Christ; there are none that can suffer so much for you as Christ. The least measure of that wrath that Christ hath sustained for you, would have broke the hearts, necks, and backs of all created beings. O my friends! there is no love but a superlative love that is any ways suitable to the transcendent sufferings of dear Jesus. Oh, love him above your lusts, love him above your relations, love him above the world, love him above all your outward contentments and enjoyments; yea, love him above your very lives; for thus the patriarchs, prophets, apostles, saints, primitive Christians, and the martyrs of old, have loved our Lord Jesus Christ with an overtopping love: Rev. xii. 11, ' They loved not their lives unto the death;' that is, they slighted, contemned, yea, despised their lives, exposing them to hazard and loss, out of love to the Lamb, ' who had washed them in his blood.'[1] I have read of one Kilian, a Dutch schoolmaster, who being asked whether he did not love his wife and children, answered, Were all the world a lump of gold, and in my hands to dispose of, I would leave it at my enemies' feet to live with them in a prison; but my soul and my Saviour are dearer to me than all. If my father, saith Jerome,[2] should stand before me, and my mother hang upon, and my brethren should press about me, I would break through my brethren, throw down my father, and tread underfoot my mother, to cleave to Jesus Christ. Had I ten heads, said Henry Voes, they should all off for Christ. If every hair of my head, said John Ardley, martyr, were a man, they should all suffer for the faith of Christ. Let fire, racks, pulleys, said Ignatius, and all the

[1] Acts xx. 24, and xxi. 12, 13; 2 Cor. i. 8–10, iv. 11, and xi. 23; Heb. xi. 36–39.
[2] Jerome ad Heliodor, epist. 1.

torments of hell come upon me, so I may win Christ. Love made Jerome to say, O my Saviour, didst thou die for love of me?—a love more dolorous than death ; but to me a death more lovely than love itself. I cannot live, love thee, and be longer from thee.[1] George Carpenter, being asked whether he did not love his wife and children, which stood weeping before him, answered, My wife and children!— my wife and children! are dearer to me than all Bavaria ; yet, for the love of Christ, I know them not. That blessed virgin in Basil, being condemned for Christianity to the fire, and having her estate and life offered her if she would worship idols, cried out, ' Let money perish, and life vanish, Christ is better than all.' Sufferings for Christ are the saints' greatest glory ; they are those things wherein they have most gloried: *Crudelitas vestra, gloria nostra*, your cruelty is our glory, saith Tertullian. It is reported of Babylas, that when he was to die for Christ, he desired this favour, that his chains might be buried with him, as the ensigns of his honour.[2] Thus you see with what a superlative love, with what an overtopping love, former saints have loved our Lord Jesus ; and can you, Christians, who are cold and low in your love to Christ, read over these instances, and not blush ? Certainly the more Christ hath suffered for us, the more dear Christ should be unto us ; the more bitter his sufferings have been for us, the more sweet his love should be to us, and the more eminent should be our love to him. Oh, let a suffering Christ lie nearest your hearts ; let him be your manna, your tree of life, your morning star. It is better to part with all than with this pearl of price. Christ is that golden pipe through which the golden oil of salvation runs ; and oh, how should this inflame our love to Christ ! Oh that our hearts were more affected with the sufferings of Christ ! Who can tread upon these hot coals, and his heart not burn in love to Christ, and cry out with Ignatius, Christ my love is crucified ? Cant. viii. 7, 8. If a friend should die for us, how would our hearts be affected with his kindness! and shall the God of glory lay down his life for us, and shall we not be affected with his goodness ? John x. 17, 18. Shall Saul be affected with David's kindness in sparing his life, 1 Sam. xxiv. 16, and shall not we be affected with Christ's kindness, who, to save our life, lost his own ? Oh, the infinite love of Christ, that he should leave his Father's bosom, John i. 18, and come down from heaven, that he might carry you up to heaven, John xiv. 1–4 ; that he that was a Son should take upon him the form of a servant, Phil. ii. 5–8 ; that you of slaves should be made sons, of enemies should be made friends, of heirs of wrath should be made heirs of God and joint-heirs with Christ, Rom. viii. 17 ; that to save us from everlasting ruin, Christ should stick at nothing, but be willing to be made flesh, to lie in a manger, to be tempted, deserted, persecuted, and to die upon a cross ! Oh what flames of love should these things kindle in all our hearts to Christ ! Love is compared to

---

[1] *Certè non amant illi Christum, qui aliquid plus quàm Christum amant:* They do not love Christ, who love anything more than Christ.—*Augustine de Resurrect.*—The more Christ hath suffered for us, the dearer Christ should be unto us ; the greater and the bitterer Christ's sufferings have been for us, the greater and the sweeter should our love be to him.

[2] For all above names, see Foxe and Clarke, as before.—G.

fire; in heaping love upon our enemy, we heap coals of fire upon his head, Rom. xii. 19, 20; Prov. xxvi. 21. Now the property of fire is to turn all it meets with into its own nature: fire maketh all things fire; the coal maketh burning coals; and is it not a wonder then that Christ, having heaped abundance of the fiery coals of his love upon our heads, we should yet be but key-cold in our love to him. Ah! what sad metal are we made of, that Christ's fiery love cannot inflame our love to Christ! Moses wondered why the bush consumed not, when he sees it all on fire, Exod. iii. 3; but if you please but to look into your own hearts, you shall see a greater wonder; for you shall see that, though you walk like those three children in the fiery furnace, Dan. iii., even in the midst of Christ's fiery love flaming round about you; yet there is but little, very little, true smell of that sweet fire of love to be felt or found upon you or in you. Oh, when shall the sufferings of a dear and tender-hearted Saviour kindle such a flame of love in all our hearts, as shall still be a-breaking forth in our lips and lives, in our words and ways, to the praise and glory of free grace? Oh that the sufferings of a loving Jesus might at last make us all sick of love! Cant. ii. v. Oh let him for ever lie betwixt our breasts, Cant. i. 13, who hath left his Father's bosom for a time, that he might be embosomed by us for ever. But,

3. Thirdly, Then in the sufferings of Christ, as in a gospel-glass, you may see *the odious nature of sin, and accordingly learn to hate it, arm against it, turn from it, and subdue it.* Sin never appears so odious as when we behold it in the red glass of Christ's sufferings, Ps. cxix., civ., cxiii., cxxviii., and Rom. vii. 15, and xii. 9. Can we look upon sin as the occasion of all Christ's sufferings, can we look upon sin as that which made Christ a curse, and that made him forsaken of his Father, and that made him live such a miserable life, and that brought him to die such a shameful, painful, and cruel death, and our hearts not rise against it? Shall our sins be grievous unto Christ, and shall they not be odious unto us? shall he die for our sins, and shall not we die to our sins? did not he therefore suffer for sin, that we might cease from sin? did not he 'bear our sins in his own body on the tree, that we being dead to sin, should live to righteousness'? 1 Pet. iv. 1, and ii. 24. If one should kill our father, would we hug and embrace him as our father? no, we would be revenged on him. Sin hath killed our Saviour, and shall we not be revenged on it. Can a man look upon that snake that hath stung his dearly-beloved spouse to death, and preserve it alive, warm it at the fire, and hug it in his bosom, and not rather stab it with a thousand wounds? It is sin that hath stung our dear Jesus to death, that has crucified our Lord, clouded his glory, and shed his precious blood, and oh, how should this stir up our indignation against it. Ah, how can a Christian make much of those sins that killed his dearest Lord! how can he cherish those sins that betrayed Christ, and apprehended Christ, and bound Christ, and condemned Christ, and scourged Christ, and that violently drew him to the cross, and there murdered him! It was neither Judas, nor Pilate, nor the Jews, nor the soldiers that could have done our Lord Jesus the least hurt, had not our sins, like so many butchers and hangmen, come in to their assistance. After Julius Cæsar was

treacherously murdered in the senate-house, Antonius brought forth his coat, all bloody, cut and mangled, and laying it open to the view of the people, said, Look, here is your emperor's coat; and as the bloody conspirators have dealt by it, so have they dealt with Cæsar's body; whereupon the people were all in an uproar, and nothing would satisfy them but the death of the murderers, and they ran to the houses of the conspirators and burnt them down to the ground. But what was Cæsar's coat and Cæsar's body to the body of our dear Lord Jesus, which was all bloody, rent, and torn for our sins? Ah, how should this provoke us to be revenged on our sins! how should we for ever loathe and abhor them! how should our fury be whetted against them! how should we labour with all our might to be the death of those sins that have been the death of so great a Lord, and will, if not prevented, be the death of our souls to all eternity! To see God thrust the sword of his pure, infinite, and incensed wrath through the very heart of his dearest Son, notwithstanding all his supplications, prayers, tears, and strong cries, Heb. v. 7, is the highest discovery of the Lord's hatred and indignation of sin that ever was or will be. It is true God discovered his great hatred against sin by turning Adam out of paradise, and by casting the angels down to hell, by drowning the old world, and by raining hell out of heaven upon Sodom and Gomorrah, and by the various and dreadful judgments that he has been a-pouring forth upon the world in all ages; but all this hatred is but the picture of hatred, to that hatred which God manifested against sin in causing the whole curse to meet upon our crucified Lord, as all streams meet in the sea. It is true God discovers his hatred of sin by those endless, easeless, and remediless torments that he inflicts upon devils and damned spirits; but this is no hatred to that hatred against sin which God discovered when he opened all the floodgates of his envenomed wrath upon his Son, his own Son, his only Son, his Son that always pleased him, his Son that never offended him, Isa. liii. 5, 6, and Prov. viii. 30, 31, and Mat. iii. 17. Should you see a father that had but one son, and he such a son in whom he always delighted, and by whom he had never been provoked; a son that always made it his business, his work, his heaven to promote the honour and glory of his father, John viii. 49, 50, and ix. 4; a son who was always most at ease when most engaged in his father's service; a son who counted it his meat and drink to do his father's will, John iv. 34: now should you see the father of such a son inflicting the most exquisite pains and punishments, tortures and torments, calamities and miseries upon this his dearest son, you would readily conclude that certainly the sins, the offences that have put the father upon exercising such amazing, such matchless severity, fury and cruelty upon his only son, are infinitely hateful, odious, and abominable to him.[1] Now, if you please but to cast your eye upon the actings of God the Father towards Jesus Christ, you will find that he hath inflicted more torments and greater torments upon the Son of his dearest love, than all mortals ever have or could inflict upon their only sons: Isa. liii. 6, ' The Lord hath laid

---

[1] Jer. xliv. 4, and Zech. viii. 17. The Rabbins, to scare their scholars from sin, used to tell them that sin made God's head ache; but I may say sin hath made Christ's head ache, and his heart ache too.

upon him the iniquity of us all,' *Heb.*, hath made the iniquities of us all to meet on him, or to light or fall on him rather. God made all the penalties and sufferings that were due to us to fall upon Jesus Christ, as a man is wont to fall with all his might, in a hostile manner, upon his enemy. God himself inflicted upon dear Jesus whatsoever was requisite to the satisfying of his justice, to the obtaining of pardon, and to the saving of all his elect: ver. 10, 'It pleased the Lord to bruise him, he hath put him to grief.' All the devils in hell, nor all the men upon earth, could never have bruised or put to grief our Lord Jesus. If it had not pleased the Lord to bruise him and put him to grief, he had never been bruised or put to grief. Oh, how should this work us to look upon sin with indignation !

Suppose a man should come to a table, and there should be a knife laid at his trencher, and it should be told him, This is the very knife that cut the throat of your child or father; if this person should use this knife as any other knife, would not every one say, Surely this man had but very little love to his father or his child, who can use this bloody knife as any other knife. So when you meet with any temptation to sin, oh, then say, This is the very knife that cut the throat of Jesus Christ, and pierced his sides, that was the cause of his sufferings, and that made Christ to be a curse; and accordingly let your hearts rise against it. Ah, how well doth it become Christians to look upon sin as that accursed thing that made Christ a curse, and accordingly to abhor it ! Oh, with what detestation should a man fling away such a knife ! and with the like detestation should every Christian fling away his sins, as Ephraim did his idols : 'Get you hence ; what have I any more to do with you ?' Hosea xiv. 8. Sin, thou hast slain my Lord ; thou hast been the only cause of the death of my Saviour, Isa. ii. 20, and xxx. 22. Let us say as David, 'Is not this the blood of the men that went in jeopardy of their lives ?' 2 Sam. xxiii. 17. So is not this the sin that poured out Christ's blood ? Oh, how should this enrage our hearts against sin, because it cost the Captain of our salvation, Heb. ii. 10, not the hazard, but the very loss of his life ! God shewed Moses a tree wherewith he might make the bitter waters sweet, Exod. xv. 25 ; but, lo ! here is a tree wherewith ye may make the sweet waters of sin to become bitter. Look upon the tree on which Christ was crucified, remember his cross, and the pains he suffered thereon, and the seeming sweetness that is in sin will quickly vanish. When you are solicited to sin, cast your eye upon Christ's cross, remember his astonishing sufferings for sin, and it will soon grow distasteful to your souls ; for how can that choose but be hateful to us, if we seriously consider how hurtful it was to Jesus Christ ? Who can look upon the cross of Christ and excuse his sin, as Adam did, saying, 'The woman which thou gavest me, she gave me of the tree, and I did eat' ? Gen. iii. 12. Who can look upon the cross of Christ and colour his sin, as Judas did, saying, 'Hail, Master' ? Mat. xxvi. 49. Who can look upon the cross of Christ and deny his sin, as Gehazi did, saying, 'Thy servant went no whither' ? 2 Kings v. 25. Who can look upon the cross of Christ and defend his sin, as Jonah did, saying, 'I do well to be angry' ? Jonah iv. 9. O sirs ! where is that hatred of sin that used to be in the saints of old ? David could say, 'I hate vain thoughts, and

I hate every false way,' Ps. cxix. 104, 113, 128. And Paul could say, 'What I hate that do I,' Rom. vii. 15. It is better, saith one, to be in hell with Christ, than to be in heaven with sin. Oh, how odious was sin in the saints' eye! The primitive Christians chose rather to be cast to lions without than to be left to lusts within, so great was their hatred of sin.[1] 'I had rather,' saith Anselm, 'go to hell pure from sin, than to heaven polluted with that guilt.' 'I will rather,' saith another, 'leap into a bonfire, than wilfully to sin against God.' Under the law, if an ox gored a man that he died, the ox was to be killed, Exod. xxi. 28; sin hath gored and pierced our dear Lord Jesus, oh, let it die for it! oh, avenge yourselves upon it, as Samson did avenge himself upon the Philistines for his two eyes! Judg. xvi. 28. Plutarch reports of Marcus Cato, that he never declared his opinion in any matter in the senate, but he would close it with this passage, 'Methinks still Carthage should be destroyed;' so a Christian should never cast his eye upon the cross of Christ, the sufferings of Christ, nor upon his sins, but his heart should say, Methinks pride should be destroyed, and unbelief should be destroyed, and hypocrisy should be destroyed, and earthly-mindedness should be destroyed, and self-love should be destroyed, and vain-glory should be destroyed, &c. The Jews would not have the pieces of silver which Judas cast down in the temple put in the treasury, because they were the price of blood, Mat. xxvii. 5, 6. Oh, lodge not any one sin in the treasury of your hearts, for they are all the price of blood. But,

4. Fourthly, Let the sufferings of our Lord Jesus *raise in all our hearts a high estimation of Christ.* Oh, let us prize a suffering Christ above all our duties, and above all our graces, and above all our privileges, and above all our outward contentments, and above all our spiritual enjoyments! Mat. x. 37; Luke xiv. 26. A suffering Christ is a commodity of greater value than all the riches of the Indies, yea, than all the wealth of the whole world. 'He is better than rubies,' saith Solomon, 'and all the things thou canst desire are not to be compared to him,' Prov. viii. 11. He is that pearl of price which the wise merchant purchased with all that ever he had, Mat. xiii. 46; no man can buy such gold too dear. Joseph,—a type of the Lord Jesus,—then a precious jewel of the world, was far more precious, had the Ishmaelitish merchants known so much, than all the balms and myrrhs that they transported, Gen. xxvii. 37; and so is a suffering Christ, as all will grant that really know him, and that have experienced the sweet of union and communion with him. Christ went through heaven and hell, life and death, sorrow and suffering, misery and cruelty, and all to bring us to glory, and shall we not prize him? When in a storm the nobles of Xerxes were to lighten the ship to preserve their king's life, they did their obeisance, and leaped into the sea; but our Lord Jesus Christ, to preserve our lives, our souls, he leaps into a sea of wrath, Col. i. 18. Oh, how should this work us to set up Christ above all! What a deal ado has there been in the world about Alexander the Great, and Constantine the Great, and Pompey the Great, because of their civil power and authority; but what was all their greatness and grandeur to that greatness and grandeur that God

---

[1] *Ad leonem magis quàm lenonem,* saith Tertullian.

the Father put upon our Lord Jesus Christ when he gave all power in heaven and in earth unto him, and set him down at his own right hand? Mat. xxviii. 13; Heb. i. 13; Eph. i. 20. O sirs! will you value men according to their titles, and will you not highly value our Lord Jesus Christ, who has the most magnificent titles given him? He is called King of kings and Lord of lords, Rev. xvii. 14, and xix. 16. It is observed by learned Drusius, that those titles were usually given to the great kings of Persia, than which there was none assumed more to themselves than they did; yet the Holy Ghost attributes these great titles to Christ, to let us know that, as God hath exalted Christ above all earthly powers, so we should magnify and exalt him accordingly. Paul, casting his eye upon a suffering Christ, tells us that he esteems of τὰ πάντα, 'all things,' Phil. iii. 8, as nothing in comparison of Christ. 'All things' is the greatest account that can be cast up, for it includeth all prizes, all sums; it taketh in heaven, it taketh in the vast and huge globe and circle of the capacious world, and all excellencies, within its bosom. 'All things' includes all nations, all angels, all gold, all jewels, all honours, all delights, and everything else besides; and yet the apostle looks upon all these things but as σκύβαλα, 'dung,' dogs' dung, as some interpret the word, or dogs' meat, coarse and contemptible, in comparison of dear Jesus.[1] Galeacius, [Carraciolus,] that noble Italian marquis, was of the same mind and metal with Paul, for when he was strongly tempted, and solicited with great sums of money and preferments, to return to the Romish church, he gave this heroic answer, Cursed be he that prefers all the wealth of the world to one day's communion with Christ. What if a man had large domains, stately buildings, and ten thousand rivers of oil! What if all the mountains of the world were pearl, the mighty rocks rubies, and the whole globe a shining chrysolite! yet all this were not to be named in the same day wherein there is mention made of a suffering Christ. Look, as one ocean hath more waters than all the rivers in the world, and as one sun hath more light than all the luminaries in heaven, so one suffering Christ is more 'all' to a poor soul than if it had the *all* of the whole world a thousand times over and over. O sirs! if you cast but your eye upon a suffering Christ, a crucified Jesus, there you shall find righteousness in him to cover all your sins, and plenty enough in him to supply all your wants, and grace enough in him to subdue all your lusts, and wisdom enough in him to resolve all your doubts, and power enough in him to vanquish all your enemies, and virtue enough in him to heal all your diseases, and fulness enough in him both to satisfy you and save you, and that to the utmost,[2] Heb. vii. 25. All the good things that can be reckoned up here below have only a finite and limited benignity. Some can clothe but cannot feed, others can nourish but they cannot heal, others

---

[1] σκύβαλα, quasi κυσίβαλα, micæ quæ canibus.—Vide a-Lapide: vide Bezam. The original word notes the filth that comes out of the entrails of beasts, or offal cast to dogs.

[2] I have read of a Roman servant, who knowing his master was sought for by officers to be put to death, he put himself into his master's clothes, that he might be taken for him; and so he was, and was put to death for him; whereupon his master, in memory of his thankfulness to him and honour of him, erected a brazen statue; but what a statue of gold should we set up in our hearts to the eternal honour and exaltation of that Jesus, who not in our clothes but in our very nature, hath laid down his life for us!

can enrich but they cannot secure, others can adorn but cannot advance, all do serve but none do satisfy. They are like a beggar's coat, made up of many pieces, not all enough either to beautify, defend, or satisfy; but there is enough in a suffering Christ to fill us and satisfy us to the full. Christ has the greatest worth and wealth in him. Look, as the worth and value of many pieces of silver is to be found in one piece of gold, so all the petty excellencies that are scattered abroad in the creatures are to be found in a bleeding, dying Christ; yea, all the whole volume of perfections which is spread through heaven and earth is epitomised in him that suffered on the cross—*Nec Christus, nec cœlum patitur hyperbolen*, A man cannot hyperbolise in speaking of Christ and heaven, but must entreat his hearers, as Tully doth his readers concerning the worth of L. Crassus—*Ut majus quiddam de iis quam quæ scripta sunt suspicarentur*, That they would conceive much more than he was able to express.[1] Certainly it is as easy to compass the heavens with a span, and contain the sea in a nut-shell, as to relate fully a suffering Christ's excellencies, or heaven's happiness. O sirs! there is in a crucified Jesus something proportionable to all the straits, wants, necessities, and desires of his poor people.[2] He is bread to nourish them, and a garment to cover and adorn them, a physician to heal them, a counseller to advise them, a captain to defend them, a prince to rule, a prophet to teach, and a priest to make atonement for them; a husband to protect, a father to provide, a brother to relieve, a foundation to support, a root to quicken, a head to guide, a treasure to enrich, a sun to enlighten, and a fountain to cleanse. Now what can any Christian desire more to satisfy him and save him, to make him holy and happy in both worlds? Shall the Romans and other nations highly value those that have but ventured to lay down their lives for their country, and shall not we highly value the Lord Jesus Christ, who hath actually laid down his life for his sheep? John x. 11, 15, 17. I have read of one who, walking in the fields by himself, of a sudden fell into loud cries and weeping, and being asked by one that passed by and overheard him the cause of his lamentation,—I weep, saith he, to think that the Lord Jesus Christ should do so much for us men, and yet not one man of a thousand so much as mind him or think of him. Oh what a bitter lamentation have we cause to take up, that the Lord Jesus Christ has suffered so many great and grievous things for poor sinners, and that there are so few that sincerely love him, or that highly value him; most men preferring their lusts, or else the toys and trifles of this world, above him. But,

5. Fifthly, Let the sufferings of our Lord Jesus Christ *work us all into a gracious willingness to embrace sufferings for his sake, and cheerfully and resolutely to take up his cross and follow him*, Mat. xvi. 24. Did Christ suffer, who knew no sin; and shall we think it strange to suffer, who know nothing but sin? Shall he lie sweltering under his Father's wrath, and shall we cry out of men's anger? Was he crowned with thorns, and must we be crowned with rose-buds?[3] Was his whole

---

[1] De Oratore, 3.

[2] John vi. 5, 6, 37; Rev. xiii. 14; Mat. ix. 12; Isa. ix. 6; Heb. ii. 10; Acts v. 31, and vii. 37, 38; Heb. ii. 17, 18, and iv. 15, 16; 2 Cor. xi. 2; Isa. ix. 6, 7; John xx. 17; Isa. xxviii. 16; Rev. xxii. 16; Eph. i. 22, 23.

[3] Godfrey of Bouillon, first king of Jerusalem, refused to be crowned with a crown of

life, from the cradle to the cross, made up of nothing but sorrows and sufferings; and must our lives, from the cradle to the grave, be filled up with nothing but pleasures and delights? Was he despised, and must we be admired? Was he debased, and must we be exalted? Was he poor, and must we be rich? Was he low, and must we be high? Did he drink of a bitter cup, a bloody cup; and will no cups serve our turns but cups of consolation? Let us not think anything too much to do for Christ, nor anything too great to suffer for Christ, nor anything too dear to part with for such a Christ, such a Saviour, that thought nothing too much to do, or too grievous to suffer, that so he might accomplish the work of our redemption. He left heaven for us; and shall not we let go this world for him? He left his Father's bosom for us, John i. 18; and shall not we leave the bosoms of our dearest relations for him? Ps. xlv. 10, 11; Mat. x. 37. He underwent all sorts of sufferings for us, let us as readily encounter with all sorts of sufferings for him. Paul was so inured to sufferings for Christ, that he could rejoice in his sufferings, he gloried most in his chains, and he looked upon his scars, buffetings, scourgings, stonings for Christ, as his greatest triumphs, 2 Cor. xii. 10, and xi. 23–28. And how ambitious were the primitive Christians of martyrdom in the cause of Christ: and of late, in the times of the Marian persecution, how many hundreds cheerfully and willingly laid down their lives—mounting Elijah-like to heaven in fiery chariots! And oh, how will Christ own and honour such Christians at last, as have not set on others, but exposed themselves to hazards, losses, and sufferings for his sake! Rev. iii. 21, as those brave souls, who loved not their lives unto the death, Rev. xii. 11; that is, they despised their lives in comparison of Christ; they exposed their bodies to horrible and painful deaths, their temporal estates to the spoil, and their persons to all manner of shame and contempt, for the cause of Christ, Heb. xi. 33–39, and x. 34. In the days of that bloody persecutor Dioclesian, the Christians shewed as glorious power in the faith of martyrdom as in the faith of miracles, the valour of the patients, and the savageness of the persecutors, striving together; till both, exceeding nature and belief, bred wonder and astonishment in beholders and readers.[1] In all ages and generations, they that have been born after the flesh have persecuted them that have been born after the Spirit, Gal. iv. 29; and the seed of the serpent have been still a-multiplying of troubles upon the seed of the woman. Would any man take the church's picture, saith Luther, then let him paint a poor silly maid, sitting in a wilderness, compassed about with hungry lions, wolves, boars, and bears, and with all manner of other cruel hurtful beasts; and in the midst of a great many furious men, assaulting her every moment and minute. And why should we wonder at this, when we consider that the whole life of Christ was filled up with all sorts and kinds of sufferings? Oh, where is that brave spirit that has been upon the saints of old? Blessed Bradford looked upon his sufferings for Christ as an evidence to him that he was in the right way. 'It is better for me to be a martyr

gold, saying that it became not a Christian to wear a crown of gold, where Christ, for our salvation, had worn a crown of thorns.

[1] Certatim gloriosa in certamina ruebatur, &c.—*Sulpicius.*

than a monarch,' said Ignatius when he was to suffer.[1] Happy is that soul, and to be equalled with angels, who is willing to suffer, if it were possible, as great things for Christ, as Christ hath suffered for it, saith Jerome. Sufferings are the ensigns of heavenly nobility, saith Calvin. Modestus, lieutenant to Julian the emperor, said to Julian, While they suffer they deride us, saith he, and the torments are more fearful to them that stand by than to the tormented. Luther reports of Vincentius, that he laughed at those that slew him, saying, that to Christians tortures and death were but sports, and he gloried when he went upon hot burning coals, as if he trod upon roses. It was a notable saying of a French martyr, when the rope was about his fellow, Give me that golden chain, and dub me a knight of that noble order. Paul rattled his chain, which he bore for the gospel, and was as proud of it as a woman of her ornaments, saith Chrysostom. Do your worst, do your worst, said Justin Martyr to his persecutors ; but this I will tell you, that you may put all that you are like to gain by the bargain into your eye and weep it out again. Basil will tell you, that the most cruel martyrdom is but a trick to escape death, to pass from life to life, as he speaks, for it can be but a day's journey between the cross and paradise. Their names that are written in red letters of blood in the church's calendar, are written in golden letters in Christ's register, in the book of life, saith Prudentius. Though the cross be bitter, yet it is but short. A little storm, as one said of Julian's persecution, and an eternal calm follows. Methinks, said one, I tread upon pearls, when he trod upon hot burning coals, and I feel no more pain than if I lay in a bed of down, and yet he lay in flames of fire. ' I am heartily angry,' saith Luther, ' with those that speak of my sufferings, which, if compared to that which Christ suffered for me, are not once to be mentioned in the same day.' Paul greatly rejoiced in his sufferings for Christ ; and therefore oftentimes sings it out : ' I Paul a prisoner,' as you may see by the scriptures in the margin,[2] not ' I Paul an apostle,' nor ' I Paul rapt up in the third heaven.' Christ shewed his love to him, in rapping him up in the third heaven ; and he shews his love to Christ in suffering for him. During the cruel persecutions of the heathen emperors, the Christian faith was spread through all places of the empire, because the oftener they were mowed down, saith Tertullian, the more they grew. ' I am in prison till I am in prison,' said one of the martyrs. ' I am the unmeetest man for this high office of suffering for Christ that ever was appointed to it,' said blessed Sanders. Austin observed, that though there were many thousand Christians put to death for professing Christ, yet they were never the fewer for being slain. Cyprian, speaking of the Christians and martyrs in his time, said, *Occidi poterant, sed vinci non poterant*, They may kill them, but they cannot overcome them.[3] ' The more we are cut down by the sword of persecution, the more we increase,' saith Tertullian.

---

[1] If one man did suffer all the sorrows of all the saints in the world, yet they are not worth one hour's glory in heaven.—*Chrysostom*.

[2] See Acts xxviii. 17 ; Eph. iii. 1, and iv. 1 ; 2 Tim. i. 8 ; Phil. 1, 9 : 2 Cor. xi. 23 ; Rom. xvi. 7 ; Col. iv. 10 ; Phil. 23.

[3] Lodde la Corda computeth forty-four several kinds of torment, wherewith the primitive Christians were tried.—Adv. Sacr., cap. 128.

Eusebius tells us of one that writ to his friend from a stinking dungeon, and dates his letter from ' My delicate orchard.' ' Burn my foot if you will,' said that noble martyr in Basil, ' that it may dance everlastingly with the blessed angels in heaven.' The young child in Josephus, who, when his flesh was pulled in pieces with pincers, by the command of Antiochus, said with a smiling countenance, ' Tyrant, thou losest time; where are those smarting pains with which thou threatenest me? Make me to shrink and cry out if thou canst:' and Bainam, an English martyr, when the fire was flaming about him, said, You Papists talk of miracles, behold here a miracle, I feel no more pain than if I were in a bed of down; it is as sweet to me as a bed of roses. Lawrence, when his body was roasted upon a burning gridiron, cried out, ' This side is roasted enough, turn the other side.' Marcus of Arethusa, when his body was cut and mangled, and anointed with honey, and hung up aloft in a basket, to be stung to death by wasps and bees, looked down, saying, .' I am advanced, despising you that are below.' Henry Voes kissed the stake. Hawks clapped his hands in the flames when they were half consumed. John Noys blessed God that ever he was born to see that day; and Bishop Ridley called his execution day his wedding day. Thus you see a ' cloud of witnesses' to raise and inflame your hearts into a free, ready, willing, cheerful, and resolute suffering for that Jesus who has suffered so much for you. O sirs, when we see all sorts and sexes of Christians, divinely to defy and scorn their torments and tormentors, when we see them conquering in the midst of hideous sufferings, when we hear them expressing their greatest joy in the midst of their greatest sufferings, we cannot but conclude that there was something more than ordinary that did thus raise, cheer, and encourage their spirits in their sufferings ; and doubtless this was it, ' the recompense of reward' on the one hand, and the matchless sufferings of Jesus Christ for them on the other hand, Heb. xi. 24–26, and xii. 2. The cordial wherewith Peter is said, by Clemens, to comfort his wife when he saw her led to martyrdom, was this, ' Remember the Lord, whose disciples if we be, we must not think to speed better than our master.'

It is said of Antiochus that, being to fight with Judas, captain of the host of the Jews, he showed unto his elephants the blood of the grapes and mulberries, to provoke them the better to fight, 1 Mac. vi. 3, 4 : so the Holy Ghost hath set before us the wounds, the blood, the sufferings, the dying of our dear Lord Jesus, to encourage us to suffer, with all readiness and resoluteness, whatsoever calamities or miseries may attend us for Christ's sake, or the gospel's sake. Ah, what a shame would it be if we should not be always ready to suffer anything for his sake, who hath suffered so much for our sins as is beyond all conception, all expression ! Never was Jacob more gracious and acceptable to his father Isaac, than when he stood before him clothed in the garments of his rough brother Esau. Then the father, smelling the savour of the elder brother's garments, said, ' Behold, the smell of my son is as the smell of a field which the Lord hath blessed,' Gen. xxvii. 27. And never are we more gracious and acceptable to our heavenly Father, than when we stand before him clothed in the rough garments of Christ's afflictions and sufferings. O Christians, all your sufferings for Christ, they are but inlets to your glorious reigning with Christ. Justin Martyr saith that when the Romans did immortalise their emperors, as they called it, they brought one to swear that he saw him go to heaven out of the fire; but we may see, by an eye of faith, the blessed souls of martyrs fly to heaven, like Elias in his fiery chariot, or like the angel that appeared to Manoah, in the flames. By the consent of the schoolmen, all martyrs shall appear in the church triumphant, bearing the signs of their Christian wounds about them, as so many speaking testimonies of their holy courage, that what here they endured in the behalf of their Saviour may be there an addition to their glory. But,

6. Sixthly, Hath Jesus Christ suffered such great and grievous things for you? Oh then, *in all your fears, doubts, and conflicts with enemies, within or without, fly to the sufferings of Christ as your city of refuge.* Did Christ endure a most ignominious death for thee? Did he take on him thy sinful person, and bear thy sin and death and cross, and was made a sacrifice and curse for thee? Oh then, in all thy inward and outward distresses, shelter thyself under the wings of a suffering Christ, Ps. xc. 1, and xci. 1, 4, 9. I have read of Nero, that he had a shirt made of a salamander's skin, so that if he went through the fire in it, it would keep him from burning. O sirs, a suffering Christ is this salamander's skin, that will keep the saints from burning in the midst of burning, from suffering in the midst of sufferings, from drowning in the midst of drowning, Dan. iii. 24, 29, and Isa. xliii. 2. In all the storms that beat upon your inward or your outward man, eye the sufferings of Christ, lean upon the sufferings of Christ, plead the sufferings of Christ, and triumph in the sufferings of Christ, Zech. xii. 10; Cant. viii. 5; 2 Cor. ii. 14; Eph. vi. 14. It is storied of a martyr,[1] that, writing to his wife, where she might find him when he was fled from home, 'Oh, my dear,' said he, 'if thou desirest to see me, seek me in the side of Christ, in the cleft of the rock, in the hollow of his wounds; for there I have made my nest, there will I dwell, there shalt thou find me, and nowhere else but there.' In every temptation let us look up to a crucified Christ, who is fitted and qualified to succour tempted souls, Heb. ii. 17, 18, and iv. 15, 16. Oh my soul, whenever thou art assaulted, let the wounds of Christ be thy city of refuge whither thou mayest fly and live! Let us learn in every tentation which presseth us, whether it be sin, or death, or curse, or any other evil, to translate it from ourselves to Christ; and all the good in Christ, let us learn to translate it from Christ to ourselves. Look, as the burgess of a town or corporation, sitting in the Parliament-house, beareth the persons of that whole town or place, and what he saith the whole town saith, and what is done to him is done to the whole town; even so Christ upon the cross stood in our place, and bare our sins, Isa. liii. 4–6; and whatsoever he suffered we suffered; and when he died all the faithful died with him and in him. I have read of a gracious woman who, being by Satan strongly tempted, replied, Satan, if thou hast anything to say to me, say it to my Christ, say it to my surety, who has under-

---

[1] Surius, in vita sancti Elzearii.

taken all for me,' who hath paid all my debts, and satisfied divine justice, and set all reckonings even between God and my soul.[1] Do your sins terrify you? Oh then, look up to a crucified Saviour, who bare your sins in his own body on the tree, 1 Pet. ii. 24. When sin stares you in the face, oh then turn your face to a dying Jesus, and behold him with a spear in his side, with thorns in his head, with nails in his feet, and a pardon in his hands.[2] Hast thou wounded thy conscience by any great fall or falls? Oh then, remember that there is nothing in heaven or earth more efficacious to cure the wounds of conscience than a frequent and serious meditation on the wounds of Christ.[3] Doth death, that rides upon the pale horse, Rev. vi. 8, look gashly[4] and deadly upon thee? Oh then, remember that Christ died for you, Rom. v. 6, 8, and that by his death he hath swallowed up death in victory, 1 Cor. xv. 55–57. Oh, remember that a crucified Christ hath stripped death of his sting, and disarmed it of all its destroying power. Death may buzz about our ears, but it can never sting our souls. Look, as a crucified Christ hath taken away the guilt of sin, though he hath not taken away sin itself, so he hath taken away the sting of death, though he hath not taken away death itself. He spake excellently that said, ' That is not death, but life, which joins the dying man to Christ; and that is not life, but death, which separates the living man from Christ.'[5] Austin longed to die, that he might see that head that was crowned with thorns. ' Did Christ die for me,' saith one, ' that I might live with him? I will not, therefore, desire to live long from him.' All men go willingly to see him whom they love, and shall I be unwilling to die that I may see him whom my soul loves? Bernard would have us never to let go out of our minds the thoughts of a crucified Christ. Let these, says he, be meat and drink unto you, let them be your sweetness and consolation, your honey and your desire, your reading and your meditation, your contemplation, your life, death, and resurrection. Certainly he that shall live up to this counsel will look upon the king of terrors as the king of desires. Are you apt to tremble when you eye the curse threatened in the law? Oh then, look up to a crucified Christ, and remember that ' he hath redeemed you from the curse of the law, being made a curse for you,' Gal. iii. 13. Doth the wrath of God amaze you? Oh then, look up to a crucified Christ, and remember that Christ hath trod the winepress of his Father's wrath alone, Isa. lxiii. 3, that he might deliver you from wrath to come, 1 Thes. i. 10. Is the face of God clouded?—doth he that should comfort you stand afar off? oh then, look up to a crucified Christ, and remember that he was forsaken for a time, that you might not be forsaken for ever. Are you sometimes afraid of condemnation? Oh then, look upon a crucified Christ, who was condemned that you might be justified, Lam. i. 16. ' Who shall lay anything to the charge of God's elect? It is God that justifieth. Who is he that condemneth? It is Christ that died.' Rom. viii. 33, 34. Ah, Christians, that you would at last, under all your temptations,

---

[1] As before.—G.
[2] The strongest antidote against sin is to look upon sin in the red glass of Christ's blood.—*Austin*.　[3] Bern. Ser. 61, in Cant.　[4] ' Ghastly.'—G.
[5] Ambrose, in 1 Tim. v. 6. Death will blow the bud of grace into the flower of glory.

afflictions, fears, doubts, conflicts, and disputes, be persuaded to keep a
fixed eye upon crucified Jesus ; and remember that all he did he did
for you, and that all he suffered he suffered for you ; and this will be
a strong cordial to keep you from fainting under all your inward
and outward distresses, according to that saying of one of the ancients,
Turbabor, sed non perturbabor, quia vulnerum Christi recordabor, I
may be troubled, but I shall not be overwhelmed, because I remember
the print of the nails and of the spear in the hands and side of Jesus
Christ, [Augustine.] Oh that Christians would labour, under all their
soul-troubles, to keep a fixed eye upon a bleeding Christ ; for there
is nothing that will ease them, quiet them, settle them, and satisfy
them like this. Many, may I not say most, Christians are more apt
to eye their sins, their sorrows, their prayers, their tears, their resolves,
their complaints, than they are to eye a suffering Christ ; and from
hence springs their greatest woes, wounds, miseries, and dejection
of spirit. Oh that a crucified Christ might be for ever in your eye,
and always upon your hearts ! But,

7. Seventhly and lastly, Hath Jesus Christ suffered such great and
grievous things ? Then this truth *looks sadly and sourly upon the
papists.* In this red glass of Christ's blood, you may see how vain
and wicked, how ridiculous and superstitious the devices of the papists
are, who for pacifying of God's wrath, and for the allaying of his
anger, and for satisfying his justice, and for the obtaining of pardon,
&c., have appointed penances and pilgrimages, and self-scourgings and
soul-masses, and purgatory, and several other suchlike abominations,
which the Scripture nowhere commands, but everywhere forbids ;
which inventions and abominations of theirs tend only to derogate
from the dignity and sufficiency of Christ's sufferings, and to reflect
dishonour and disgrace upon that full and perfect price that Christ
hath paid for our ransom, and to set up other saviours in the room of
our blessed Redeemer.[1] Certainly all Popish pardons, penances,
pilgrimages, masses, whippings, scourgings, &c., they unavoidably fall
before the sufferings of our Lord Jesus Christ, as Dagon fell before the
ark, Goliath before David, Haman before Mordecai, and as the darkness
falls before the morning light ; and as for their purgatory, they do not
know certainly where it is, nor how long it will last, nor what sort
of fire is there ; neither can they shew us how corporeal fire should
work upon the souls in purgatory, they being spiritual and incorporeal ;
they cannot tell us whether the pains of purgatory be at all times
alike, neither can they tell us whether the good or evil angels are the
tormentors of the souls in purgatory ; and as for the whipping, scalding, freezing of souls in purgatory, they are but ' old wives' fables,' and
the brain-sick fancies of some deceitful persons, to cheat poor ignorant
people of their money, under a blind pretence of praying their souls
out of purgatory. Christ offered himself ' once for all,' Heb. x. 10,
but the Romish priests offer him up daily in the mass, an unbloody
sacrifice ; and so they do what lies in them to ' tread under foot the

---

[1] Surely that religion that loves to lap blood, and that is propagated and maintained by
blood, and that prefers their own inventions and abominations before the blood and
sufferings of Christ, that religion is not of God but such is the Romish religion—*ergo*
their religion is not of God.

blood of God, the blood of the covenant,' Acts xx. 28 ; Heb. x. 29. To be short, Popery in effect is nothing else but an underhand, close witness-bearing against Christ in all his offices, and against all that he hath done and suffered for the redemption and salvation of sinners, as might be made abundantly evident, but that I may not now launch out into that ocean. I only give this brief touch by the way, that I might raise up in all your hearts a greater detestation of Popery, in this day wherein many are so warm for it, as if it were their only Diana. And let thus much suffice concerning the sufferings of our Lord Jesus Christ, and the improvement that we should make of them.

Thus you may clearly see, by what I have said concerning the active and passive obedience of our Lord Jesus Christ, that whatsoever we are bound to do or suffer by the law of God, all that did Christ do and suffer for us, as being our surety and mediator.[1] Now the law of God hath a double challenge or demand upon us ; one is of active obedience, in fulfilling what it requires ; the other is of passive obedience, in suffering that punishment which is due to us for the transgression of it, in doing what it forbids : for as we were created by God, we did owe unto him all obedience which he required ; and as we sinned against God, we did owe unto him a suffering of all that punishment which he threatened ; and we being fallen by transgression, can neither pay the one debt, nor yet the other. Of ourselves we can do nothing that the law requires ; neither can we so suffer as to satisfy God in his justice wronged by us, or to recover ourselves into life and favour again. And therefore Jesus Christ, who was God-man, did become our surety, and stood in our stead or room, and he did perform what we should but could not perform, and he did bear our sins and our sorrows, he did suffer and bear for us what we ourselves should have borne and suffered, whereby he did fully satisfy the justice of God, and made our peace, and purchased pardon and life for us. Christ did fully answer to all the demands of the law, he did come up to perfect and universal conformity to it. He did whatever the law enjoins, and he suffered whatever the law threatens. Christ, by his active and passive obedience, hath fulfilled the law most exactly and completely, Gal. iii. 13. As he was perfectly holy, he did what the law commanded, and as he was made a curse, he underwent what the law threatened ; and all this he did and suffered in our steads and as our surety. Whatever Christ did as our surety, he made it good to the full ; so that neither the righteous God, nor yet the righteous law, could ever tax him with the least defect. And this must be our great plea, our choice, our sweet, our safe, our comfortable, our acceptable plea, both in the day of our particular accounts when we die, and in the great day of our account, when a crucified Saviour shall judge the world. Although sin, as an act, be transient, yet in the guilt of it, it lies in the Lord's high court of justice, filed upon record against the sinner, and calling aloud for deserved punishment, saying, Man hath sinned, and man must suffer for sin ! But now Christ has suffered, that plea is taken off. Lo here, saith the Lord, the same nature that sinned, suffereth ; mine own

[1] A Christian's plea from the passive obedience of Christ. God did insist on it, that our surety should pay down the whole debt at once, and accordingly he did, Heb. x. 10, 12.

Son, being made flesh, hath suffered death for sin in the flesh; the thing is done, the law is satisfied, and so nonsuits the action, and casts it out of the court as unjust. Thus whereas sin would have condemned us, Christ hath condemned sin; he hath weakened, yea, nullified and taken away sin, in the guilt and condemning power of it, by that abundant satisfaction that he hath given to the justice of God by his active and passive obedience: so that, ' there is no condemnation to them that are in Christ Jesus,' Rom. viii. 1, 3; for the blood of the mediator outcries the clamour of sin; and this must be a Christian's joy and triumph and plea in the great day of our Lord Jesus. As Christ was ' made sin for us,' 2 Cor. v. 21, so the Lord doth impute the sufferings of Christ to us—that is, he accepts of them on our behalf, and puts them upon our account; as if the Lord should say unto every particular believer, My Son was thy surety and stood in thy stead, and suffered and satisfied and took away thy sins by his blood, and that for thee: in his blood I find a ransom for thy soul; I do acknowledge myself satisfied for thee, and satisfied towards thee, and thou art delivered and discharged; I forgive thee thy sins, and am reconciled unto thee, and will save thee and glorify thee for my Son's sake; in his blood thou hast redemption, the forgiveness of thy sins. As when a surety satisfies the creditor for a debt, this is accounted to the debtor, and reckoned as a discharge to him in particular. I am paid and you are discharged, saith the creditor; so it is in this case; I am paid, saith God, and you are discharged, and I have no more to say to you but this, ' Enter into the joy of your Lord,' Mat. xxv. 21.

V. The fifth plea that you are to make in order to the ten scriptures in the margin,[1] that respects the account that you are to give up in the great day of the Lord, is drawn from the imputed righteousness of Christ to us. The justification of a sinner in the sight of God, upon the account of Christ's righteousness imputed to him, whereby the guilt of sin is removed, and the person of the sinner is accepted as righteous with the God of heaven, is that which I shall open to you distinctly in these following branches:—

1. First, *That the grace of justification in the sight of God is made up of two parts*—1. There is forgiveness of the offences committed against the Lord; 2. Acceptation of the person offending, pronouncing him a righteous person, and receiving him into favour again, as if he had never offended. This is most clear and evident in the blessed Scriptures.

[1.] First, *There is an act of absolution and acquittal from the guilt of sin, and freedom from the condemnation deserved by sin.* The desert of sin is an inseparable accident or concomitant of it, that can never be removed. It may be truly said of the sins of a justified person, that they deserve everlasting destruction; but justification is the freeing of a sinner from the guilt of his iniquity, whereby he was actually bound over to condemnation.[2] As soon as any man doth sin, there is a guilt

---

[1] Eccles. xi. 9, and xii. 14; Mat. xii. 14, and xviii. 23; Luke xvi. 3; Rom. xiv. 10; 2 Cor. v. 10; Heb. ix. 27, and xiii. 17; 1 Pet. iv. 5.

[2] Rom. viii. 1. κατάκριμα: It is a forensic word, relating to what is in use amongst men in their courts of judicature to condemn. It is the sentence of a judge decreeing a mulct or penalty to be inflicted upon the guilty person.

upon him, by which he is bound over to the wrath and curse of God; and this guilt or obligation is inseparable from sin; the sin doth deserve no less than everlasting damnation. Now, forgiveness of sin hath a peculiar respect to the guilt of sin, and removal of that. When the Lord forgives a man, he doth discharge him of that obligation by which he was bound over to wrath and condemnation: Rom. viii. 1, 'There is no condemnation to them that are in Christ Jesus;' ver. 33, 'Who shall lay anything to the charge of God's elect? It is God that justifieth;' ver. 34, 'Who is he that condemneth? It is Christ that died.' Beloved, the Lord is a holy and just God; and he 'reveals his wrath from heaven against all unrighteousness,' Rom. i. 18; and there is a curse threatened to every transgression of the law, Gal. iii. 10; and when any man sinneth, he is obnoxious unto the curse, and God may inflict the same upon him, Rom. i. 32; but when God forgives sins, he therein doth interpose, as it were, between the sin and the curse, and between the obligation and the condemnation, Rom. vi. 23. When the sinner sins, God might say unto him, Sinner, by your sinning you are now fallen into my hands of justice; and for your sins I may, according to my righteous law, condemn and curse you for ever; but such is my free, my rich, my sovereign grace, that for Christ's sake I will spare you and pardon you, and that curse and condemnation which you have deserved shall never fall upon you. Oh, my bowels, my bowels, are yearning towards you, Jer. xxxi. 20; and therefore I will have mercy, mercy upon you, and will deliver your souls from going down into the pit, Job xxxiii. 13, 24, 28, 30. When the poor sinner is indicted and arraigned at God's bar, and process is made against him, and he found guilty of the violation of God's holy law, and accordingly judged guilty by God, and adjudged to everlasting death, then mercy steps in and pleads, I have found a ransom, Job xxxiii. 24; the sinner shall not die, but live. When the law saith, Ah, sinner, sinner! thus and thus hast thou transgressed, all sorts of duties thou hast omitted, and all sorts of sins thou hast committed, and all sorts of mercies thou hast abused, and all sorts of means thou hast neglected, and all sorts of offers thou hast slighted; then God steps in and saith, Ah, sinner, sinner! what dost thou say, what canst thou say, to this heavy charge? Is it true or false?—wilt thou grant it or deny it?—what defence or plea canst thou make for thyself? Alas! the poor sinner is speechless: Mat. xxii. 12, ἐφιμώθη, he was muzzled or haltered up, that is, he held his peace as though he had a bridle or a halter in his mouth. This is the import of the Greek word here used: he hath not one word to say for himself; he can neither deny, nor excuse, or extenuate what is charged upon him. Why now, saith God, I must and do pronounce thee to be guilty; and as I am a just and righteous God, I cannot but adjudge thee to die eternally. But such is the riches of my mercy, that I will freely justify thee through the righteousness of my Son; I will forgive thy sins, and discharge thee of that obligation by which thou wast bound over to wrath, and curse, and condemnation; so that the justified person may triumphingly say, 'Who is he that condemneth?' He may read over the most dreadful passages of the law without being terrified or amazed, as knowing that the curse is removed, and that all his sins, that brought him under the curse, are pardoned, and are, in point of condemnation, as if they had never been. This is to be justified, to have the sin pardoned and the penalty remitted: Rom. iv. 5-8, ' But to him that worketh not, but believeth on him that justifieth the ungodly, his faith is counted for righteousness. Even as David also describeth the blessedness of the man, to whom God imputeth righteousness without works; saying, Blessed are they whose iniquities are forgiven, and whose sins are covered. Blessed is the man to whom the Lord will not impute sin.' It is observable that what David calleth forgiveness of sin, and not imputing of iniquity, St Paul styles a being justified. But,

[2.] Secondly, As the first part of justification consists in the pardon of sin, so the second part of justification consists *in the acceptation of the sinner's person as perfectly righteous in God's sight*, pronouncing him such, and dealing with him as such, and by bringing of him under the shadow of that divine favour which he had formerly lost by his transgressions: Cant. iv. 7, ' Thou art all fair, my love, and there is no spot in thee;' that is, none in my account, nor no such spots as the wicked are full of, Deut. xxxii. 5. Look, as David saw nothing in lame Mephibosheth but what was lovely, because he saw in him the features of his friend Jonathan, 2 Sam. ix. 3, 4, 13, 14, so God, beholding his people in the face of his Son, sees nothing amiss in them. They are all ' glorious within and without,' Ps. xlv. 13. Look, as Absalom had no blemish from head to foot, so they are irreprehensible and ' without blemish before the throne of God,' Rev. xiv. 5. The pardoned sinner, in respect of divine acceptation, is ' without spot, or wrinkle, or any such thing,' Eph. v. 26, 27. God accepts the pardoned sinner as complete in him who is the head of all principality and power, Col. ii. 10. Christ makes us comely through his beauty; he gives us white raiment to stand before the Lord. Christ is all in all in regard of divine acceptance: Eph. i. 6, ' He hath made us accepted in the beloved;' ἐχαρίτωσεν ἡμᾶς, ' he hath made us favourites,' so Chrysostom and Theophylact render it; ' God hath ingratiated us,' he hath made us gracious in the Son of his love. Through the blood of Christ we look of a sanguine complexion, ruddy and beautiful in God's eyes: Isa. lxii. 4, ' Thou shalt no more be termed forsaken, but thou shalt be called Hephzibah; for the Lord delighteth in thee.' [1] The acceptation of our persons with God takes in six things: (1.) God's honouring of us; (2.) His delight in us; (3.) His being well pleased with us; (4.) His extending love and favour to us; (5.) His high estimation of us; (6.) His giving us free access to himself. It is the observation of Ambrose, that though Jacob was not by birth the first-born, yet, hiding himself under his brother's clothes, and having put on his coat, which smelled most fragrantly, he came into his father's presence, and got away the blessing from his elder brother, Gen. xxvii. 36; so it is very necessary, in order to our acceptation with God, that we lie hid under the precious robe of Christ, our elder brother; that, having the sweet savour of his garments upon us, our sins may be covered with his perfections, and our unrighteousness with the robes of his righteousness,

---

[1] All persons out of Christ are cursed enemies, objects of God's wrath and justice, displeasing, offending, and provoking creatures; and therefore God cannot but loathe them and abhor them.

2 Cor. ii. 15; that so we may offer up ourselves unto God 'a living and acceptable sacrifice,' Rom. xii. 1; 'not having our own righteousness, which are but as filthy rags,' Isa. lxiv. 6; but that which is 'through the faith of Christ, the righteousness which is of God by faith,' Phil. iii. 9.

Thus you see that justification, for the nature of it, lies in the gracious pardon of the sinner's transgressions, and in the acceptation of his person as righteous in God's sight. But,

2. Secondly, In order to the partaking of this grace, of the forgiveness of our sins and the acceptation of our persons, *we must be able to produce a perfect righteousness before the Lord, and to present it and tender it unto him ;* and the reason is evident from the very nature of God, who is 'of purer eyes than to behold iniquity,' Hab. i. 13, that is, with patience or pleasure, or without punishing it.[1] There are four things that God cannot do: (1.) He cannot lie; (2.) He cannot die; (3.) He cannot deny himself; (4.) He cannot behold iniquity with approbation and delight: Josh. xxiv. 19, 'And Joshua said unto the people, Ye cannot serve the Lord, for he is an holy God, he is a jealous God, he will not forgive your transgressions nor your sins:' such is the holiness of God's nature that he cannot behold sin, that he cannot but punish sin wherever he finds it, Ps. v. 4–6. God is infinitely, immutably, and inexorably just, as well as he is incomprehensibly gracious. Now, in the justification of a sinner God doth act as a God of justice, as well as a God of compassion. God is infinite in all his attributes, in his justice as well as in his mercy: these two cannot interfere. As justice cannot intrench upon mercy, so neither may mercy encroach upon justice; the glory of both must be maintained. Now, by the breach of the law the justice of God is wronged; so that although mercy be apt to pardon, yet justice requires satisfaction, and calls for vengeance on sinners. 'Every transgression must receive just recompense,' Heb. ii. 2, and God will not in any case absolve the guilty, Exod. xxxiv. 7: till this be done, the hands of mercy are tied that she cannot act. And seeing satisfaction could not be made to an infinite Majesty, but by an equal person and price; therefore the Son of God must become a curse for us, by taking our nature and pouring out his soul to the death; and by this means justice and mercy are reconciled and kiss each other, and mercy now being set at liberty, hath her free course to save poor sinners. God will have his justice satisfied to the full, and therefore Christ must bear all the punishment due to our sins; or else God cannot set us free, for he cannot go against his own just will. Observe the force of that phrase, 'Christ ought to suffer,' and 'thus it behoved Christ to suffer,' Luke xxiv. 26; Mat. xxvi. 54, 'Thus it must be.' Why must? but because it was, (1.) So decreed by God; (2.) Foretold by the prophets. Every particular of Christ's sufferings were foretold by the prophets, even to their very spitting in his face. (3.) Prefigured in the daily morning and evening sacrifice; this Lamb of God was sacrificed from the beginning of the world. A necessity then there was of our Saviour's sufferings; not a necessity of co-action, for he died freely and voluntarily, but of immutability and infallibility, for the former reasons mentioned, John

---

[1] *Heb.*, 'And to look on iniquity thou canst not do it.'

x. 11, 14, 17, 18. An earthly prince that is just, holds himself bound to inflict punishment impartially upon the malefactor or his surety. It stands upon his honour; he saith, It must be so, I cannot do otherwise. This is true much more of God, who is justice itself. God, 'who is great in counsel and excellent in working,' had store of means at hand whereby to set free and recover lost mankind; yet he was pleased, in his infinite wisdom, to pitch upon this way of satisfaction, as being most agreeable to his holy nature, and most suitable to his high and sovereign ends—viz., man's salvation and his own glory: and that God doth stand upon full satisfaction, and will not forgive one sin without it, may be thus made evident.

[1.] First, From *the nature of sin, which is that 'abominable thing which God hates,'* Jer. xliv. 4.[1] The sinner deserves to die for his sins: Rom. vi. 23, 'The wages of sin is death.' Every sinner is worthy of death; 'they which commit such things are worthy of death,' Rom. i. 32. Now God is just and righteous. 'It is a righteous thing with God to recompense tribulation to them that trouble you,' 2 Thes. i. 6; yea, and God did, therefore, 'set forth Christ to be a propitiation through faith in his blood,' Rom. iii. 25; 'to declare his righteousness, that he might be just,' ver. 26. Now, if God be a just and righteous God, then sin cannot absolutely escape unpunished; for it is just with God to punish the sinner who is worthy of punishment; and certainly God must deny himself if he will not be just, 2 Tim. ii. 13; but this he can never do. Sin is of an infinite guilt, and hath an infinite evil in the nature of it; and therefore no person in heaven or earth, but that person our Lord Jesus, who is God-man, and who had an infinite dignity, could either procure the pardon of it, or make satisfaction for it. No prayers, no cries, no tears, no humblings, no repentings, no resolutions, no reformations, &c., can stop the course of justice, or procure the guilty sinner's pardon. It is Christ alone that can dissolve all obligations to punishment, and break all bonds and chains of guilt, and hand a pardon to us through his own blood, Eph. i. 7. We are set free by the blood of Christ. 'By the blood of thy covenant I have sent forth thy prisoners out of the pit,' Zech. ix. 11: it is by his blood that we are justified and saved from wrath: Rom. v. 9, 'Much more being justified by his blood, we shall be saved from wrath by him.' Pray tell me what is it to be justified but to be pardoned; and what is it to be saved from wrath but to be delivered from all punishment? and both these depend upon the blood of Christ, Eph. ii. 13; Col. i. 20. But,

[2.] *The veracity of God requires it.* Look, as God cannot but be just, so he cannot but be true; and if he cannot but be true, then he will make good the threatenings that are gone out his mouth: Gen. ii. 17, 'In the day that thou eatest thereof thou shalt surely die:' Heb. 'In dying, thou shalt die.' Death is a fall that came in by a fall, and without all peradventure every man should die the same day he was born, for 'the wages of sin is death,' and this wages should be presently paid, did not Christ reprieve poor sinners' lives for a season,[2]

---

[1] God could not, *salvo jure*, pass over the sin of man, so as absolutely to let it go unpunished.

[2] Under the name of death are comprehended all other calamities, miseries, and sorrows.

upon which account he is said to be the Saviour of all men, 1 Tim. iv. 10; not of eternal preservation, but of a temporal reservation. ' He will by no means clear the guilty,' Exod. xxxiv. 7. ' The soul that sinneth, it shall die ; ' ' The wickedness of the wicked shall be upon him,' Ezek. xviii. 20. 'He will render to every man according to his deeds,' Rom. ii. 6. O sirs, God can never so far yield as to abrogate his own law, and quietly to sit down with injury and loss to his own justice, himself having established a law, &c. The law pronounces him cursed that ' continues not in all things that are written therein, to do them,' Gal. iii. 10. Now, though the threatenings of men are frequently vain and frivolous, yet the threatenings of the great God shall certainly take place and have their accomplishment; though many ten thousand millions of sinners perish, not one tittle of the dreadful threatenings of God shall fail till all be fulfilled, Mat. v. 18. Josephus saith that from that very time that old Eli heard those terrible threatenings, that made their ears tingle and hearts tremble that heard them, Eli never ceased weeping, 1 Sam. iii. 11-14. Ah, who can look upon the dreadful threatenings that are pointed against sinners all over the book of God, and not tremble and weep ! God cannot but in justice punish sinners ; neither is it in his choice or freedom whether he will damn the obstinate impenitent sinner or no. Look, as God cannot but love holiness wherever he sees it, so he cannot but loathe and punish wickedness wherever he beholds it ; neither will it stand with the infinite wisdom of God to admit of a dispensation or relaxation of the threatenings without satisfaction. God had passed a peremptory doom, and made a solemn declaration of it in his word, that ' he that sinneth, shall die the death ;' and he will not, he cannot break his word. You know he had foreordained Jesus Christ, and set him forth to take upon himself this burden, to become a propitiation for sin through his blood, Rom. iii. 25 ; 1 Pet. i. 20, and made known his mind concerning it in his written word plainly, Isa. liii. 7. If we read the words, ' it is exacted or strictly required,' meaning the iniquity or punishment of us all, ver. 6.[1] It is required at his hands, he must answer it in our stead, and so he is afflicted, and this affliction reacheth even to the cutting him off, ver. 8. Therefore when Christ puts this work upon an *ought* and *must be*, he lays the weight of all on the Scriptures, ' Thus it is written,' as you may see in the texts lately cited ; as if he should say, God hath spoken it, and his truth engageth him to see it done ; so God hath threatened to punish sin, and his truth engageth him to see it done. O sirs, there is no standing before that God that is ' a consuming fire,' a just judge, a holy God, except I have one to ' undertake for me,' Heb. xii. 29, that is ' mighty to save,' Isa. lxiii. 1, and mighty to satisfy divine justice, and mighty to pacify divine wrath, and mighty to bear the threatenings, and mighty to forgive sin. When God forgives sin, he does it in a way of righteousness, Isa. xix. 20. 1 John i. 9, ' He is faithful and just to forgive us our sins, and to cleanse us from all unrighteousness.' He doth not say he is merciful, but '*just*, to forgive us our sins ;' because they are satisfied for, and God's justice will not let him demand the same debt twice, of the surety and of the debtor too. It

---

[1] Exigitur, as Junius and some others read it.

will never stand with the unspotted justice and righteousness of God to require such debts of us, which Christ, by shedding his most precious blood, hath discharged for us, Rom. iii. 25. Mark, the maledictory sentence of death, denounced by the law against sinners, was inflicted by God upon Christ. This is that which the prophet Isaiah positively asserts, where he saith, 'The chastisement,' that is, the punishment (called a chastisement, because inflicted by a father, and only for a time,) ' of our peace was upon him.' And again, 'He was oppressed, and he was afflicted,' Isa. liii. 5, 7 ; which, according to the genuine sense of the original, is better rendered, ' It was exacted'— to wit, the punishment of our sin ; and he was afflicted, or he answered—to wit, to the demand of the penalty. The curse to which we are subject, saith Theodorus,[1] he assumed upon himself of his own accord. 'The death that was not due to him he underwent, that we might not undergo that death which was due to us,' saith Gregory.[2] 'He made himself a debtor for us, who were debtors ; and therefore the creditor exacts it from him,' saith Arnoldus.[3] Now God's justice being satisfied for our offences, it cannot but remit those offences to us. As the creditor cannot demand that of the debtor which the surety hath already paid, so neither can God exact the punishment of us which Christ hath suffered ; and therefore ' it is just with God to forgive us our sins.' It will be altogether needless to inquire whether it had been injustice in God to forgive without satisfaction. St Austin's determination is very solid : There wanted not to God another possible way, and if it were unjust, it were impossible ; but this of satisfaction was most agreeable to divine wisdom.[4] Before God did decree this way, it might be free to have used it or not; but in decreeing, this seemed most convenient, and after, it became necessary, so that there can be no remission without it ; and however it might not have been unjust with God to have forgiven without it, yet we are sure it is most just with him to forgive upon satisfaction.[5] Indeed, the debt being paid by Christ, God's very justice, as I may say with reverence, would trouble him if he should not give in the bond, and give out an acquittance. The believing penitent sinner may, in a humble confidence, sue out his pardon, not only at the throne of grace, but at the bar of justice, in these or the like expressions : Lord, thou hast punished my sins in thy Son, wilt thou punish them in me ? Thou hast accepted that suffering of thy Son as the punishment of my sin, therefore thou canst not in justice exact it of me, for this were to punish twice for one offence, which thy justice cannot but abhor. O sirs ! God doth not pronounce men righteous when they are not; but first he makes them so, and then he pronounces them to be such ; so that if a man will be justified, he must be able to produce such a complete righteousness wherewith he may stand before the justice of God. Ah sinners ! the Lord is infinitely just, as well

---

[1] Theod. disp., l. xv. c. 5.   [2] Gregory Moral., l. iii. c. 13.
[3] Arnold. de sep. verb, Tr. i.   [4] Aug. de Trinit., l. xiii. c. 10.
[5] When you are forgiven, you are then released, and for ever acquitted from any after-reckonings with the justice of God. Divine justice hath no more to say or do against you, for *remissa culpa, remittitur pœna*, If the fault be forgiven, then also is the punishment forgiven ; nay, let me speak with a holy and humble reverence, God cannot in his justice punish when he hath pardoned.

as merciful; and if ever your sins be pardoned, it must be by an admirable contemperament, or mixture of mercy and justice together. It was one of the great ends of the gospel dispensation that God might exalt his justice in the justification of a sinner: Rom. iii. 26, 'To declare, I say, at this time his righteousness, that he might be just, and the justifier of him that believeth in Jesus.' But,

3. Thirdly, The only matter of man's righteousness, since the fall of Adam, wherein he can appear with comfort before the justice of God, and consequently whereby alone he can be justified in his sight, is *the obedience and suffering of Jesus Christ, the righteousness of the mediator.* There is not any other way imaginable, how the justice of God may be satisfied, and we may have our sins pardoned in a way of justice, but by the righteousness of the Son of God; and therefore this is his name, 'Jehovah-Tsidkenu, the Lord our Righteousness,' Jer. xxiii. 6. 'This is his name,' that is, this is the prerogative of the Lord Jesus, a matter that appertaineth to him alone, to be able to 'bring in everlasting righteousness, and to make reconciliation for iniquity,' Dan. ix. 24. The costly cloak of Alcisthenes, which Dionysius sold to the Carthaginians for an hundred talents, was indeed a mean and beggarly rag to that embroidered mantle of Christ's righteousness that he puts upon us: Isa. lxi. 10, 'I will greatly rejoice in the Lord, my soul shall be joyful in my God; for he hath clothed me with the garments of salvation, he hath covered me with the robe of righteousness, as a bridegroom decketh himself with ornaments, and a bride adorneth herself with her jewels.'[1] Christ's righteousness is that garment of wrought gold, that we all need, to cover all our imperfections, and to render us perfectly beautiful and glorious in the sight of God.[2] In this robe of righteousness we are complete, we are without spot or wrinkle, we are without fault before the throne of God. Through the imputation of Christ's righteousness, we are made righteous in the sight of God. God looking upon us, as invested with the righteousness of his Son, accounts us righteous. All believers have a righteousness in Christ as full and complete as if they had fulfilled the law. 'Christ being the end of the law for righteousness to believers,' Rom. viii. 3, 4, invests believers with a righteousness every way as complete, as the personal obedience of the law would have invested them withal. When men had violated God's holy law, God in justice resolved that his law should be satisfied before man should be saved. Now this was done by Christ, who was the end of the law; he fulfilled it actively and passively, and so the injury offered to the law is recompensed. God had rather that all men should be destroyed, than that his law should not be satisfied. No man can perfectly be justified in the sight of God without a perfect righteousness, every way commensurable to God's holy law, which is the rule of righteousness, 'Do this and live:' neither can any person have any choice, spiritual, lively communion with a righteous God, till he be clothed with the righteousness of Jesus Christ. All Christ's active and passive obedience was either for himself, or in our stead and behalf; but it was not for himself, but

---

[1] It is a sign of great favour from the Great Turk, when a rich garment is cast upon any that come into his presence.—*Knolles Hist.* The application is easy.

[2] Ps. xlv. 13; Rom. v. 19; Col. ii. 10; Eph. v. 27; Rev. xiv. 5; Rom. iii. 21, 22, 25, 26.

for us, that he suffered and obeyed.   Whatsoever Christ did or suffered in the whole course of his life, he did it and suffered it as our
surety, and in our steads: for as God would not dispense with the
penalty of the law without satisfaction, so he would not dispense with
the commands of the law without perfect obedience.   Remember, once
for all, that the actions and sufferings of Christ make but up one
entire and perfect obedience to the whole law ; nor had Christ been a
perfect and complete Saviour, if he had not performed what the law
required, as well as suffered the penalty which the law inflicted.   The
imputation of Christ's righteousness to us is a gracious act of God the
Father, according to his good will and pleasure, whereby as a judge
he accounts believers' sins unto the surety, as if he had committed the
same ; and the righteousness of Christ unto the believer, as if he had
performed the same, the same obedience that Christ did in his own
person : so that Christ's imputed righteousness is as effectual to the
full, for the acceptance of the believing sinner, as if he had yielded
such obedience to the Lord himself.   Hence his righteousness is called
' our righteousness,' Jer. xxiii. 6.   Now without this righteousness
there is no standing before the justice of God.   But,

   4. Fourthly, As this great design of Christ's redeeming sinners by
his blood and sufferings, and by his being made a curse for them, doth
sound aloud the glory of divine justice, and the glory of God's veracity,
so it sounds forth *the glory of his wisdom; for hereby he maintains
the authority of his righteous law.*[1]   When a law is solemnly enacted,
with a penalty in case of transgression, all those whom it concerns may
conclude for certain, that the lawgiver will proceed accordingly; and
it is a rule in policy, that laws once established and published, should
be vigorously preserved.   If the Lord should have wholly waived the
execution of the law upon sinners or their surety, it might have tended
greatly to the weakening of its authority, and the diminishing of the
reverence of his sovereignty in the hearts of the sons of men.   How
often does God use that oath, ' As I live,' for the fulfilling of his
threatenings as well as of his promises, Jer. xxii. 24, and Ezek. v.
9–11.   The Lord Jehovah is as true, faithful, and constant in his
threatenings as in his promises.   What he hath threatened shall
undoubtedly come to pass; he will be made known by his name
Jehovah in the full execution of all his threatenings.   The old world
found it so, and Jerusalem found it so ; yea, the whole nation of the
Jews have found it so to this very day, see Ezek. v. 13, 15.   Look, as
all the saints in heaven will readily put to their seals, that God is true
and faithful in all his promises ; so all the damned in hell will readily
put to their seals, that God is faithful in all his threatenings.   Men
frequently deride the laws and threatenings of great men, when they
are not put into execution.   It is the execution of laws that is the very
life and soul of good laws, Eccles. viii. 11.   Should God pardon sin,
without exacting the penalty of the law, how would sinners be hardened,
and emboldened to say, with those men, or rather monsters, in Malachi,
' Where is the God of judgment ?' chap. ii. 17, *i.e.,* nowhere ; either

---

[1] Solon, that wise lawmaker, could never find out a law to put all other good laws in
execution ; but such as are living laws, will make the laws to live : and will not the wise
and living God make his laws and threatenings to live ?   Surely he will.

there is no God, or at least not a God of that exact, precise, and impartial judgment, as some men say and as others teach.[1] But now when God lets sinners see that he will not pardon sin without exacting the penalty of the law, either of the sinner or of his surety, then the sinner cries out, ' O the depth of the riches, both of the wisdom and knowledge of God!' Rom. xi. 33. God stood so much upon the complete satisfaction and accomplishment of his law, that he was willing that Christ should be a sacrifice, that the law might be satisfied in its penalty, and that Christ in his own person should fulfil the righteousness of the law, that it might be satisfied in its commands, Rom. viii. 3-5. Now in this plenary satisfaction made to the law, the wisdom of God does gloriously shine. The heart of God was so set upon a full satisfaction to his law, that rather than it should not be done, his own Son must come from heaven and put on flesh, and be himself made under the law, Gal. iv. 4, 5 ; he must live a holy life, and die a cursed death, and all to satisfy the law, and to keep up the authority of it. But,

5. Fifthly, God doth stand upon full satisfaction, and will not forgive one sin without it, that *he might hereby cut off all occasions, which the devil, his arch-enemy, might take to calumniate and traduce him ;* for if God did not stand upon full satisfaction, the devil might accuse him (1.) of inconstancy and changeableness, that having threatened death to transgressors, he did quite forget himself, in waiving the threatening, and dispensing wholly with his law, by granting them free remission ; yea, (2.) of partiality and respect of persons, that he should be so easy and forbearing, as to let them pass without any punishment at all ; having been formerly so severe and rigid against himself, in casting him and his angels down to hell, and keeping them in everlasting flames and chains of darkness, without the least hope of recovery, 2 Pet. ii. 4 ; Jude 6. Satan might say, Lord, thou mightest have spared me as well as man. But the Lord can now answer, Man hath made satisfaction, he hath borne the curse, and thereby fully discharged all the demands of the law ; if he had not, I would no more have spared him than thee. Ambrose brings in the devil boasting against Christ, and challenging Judas as his own ; he is not thine, Lord Jesus, he is mine, his thoughts beat for me ; he eats with thee, but is fed by me ; he takes bread from thee, but money from me ; he drinks with thee, but sells thy blood to me. Had God pardoned sin without satisfaction, ah how would Satan have boasted and triumphed over God himself ! But,

6. Sixthly, God's standing upon full satisfaction, and his not forgiving one sin without it, bears *a visible character of his goodness and loving-kindness,* as well as it sounds out aloud the glory of divine justice. ' The great and the holy God, whose name is holy,' Exod. xv. 1, 11, might have rigorously exacted the penalty of the law on the persons of sinners themselves ; but he hath so far dispensed with his own law, as to admit of a surety, by whom the end of the law, that is, the manifestation of his justice and hatred of sin, might be fulfilled, and yet a considerable part of mankind might be preserved from the jaws of the second death, which otherwise must unavoidably have

---

[1] Such an emphasis there is in the Hebrew, as Corn. à Lapide observes.

perished to all eternity, Rev. xx. 6. God seems to speak at such a rate as this; I may not, I will not, suffer this high affront of Adam and his posterity against my 'holy and righteous law,' Rom. vii. 12, 14, whereby the honour both of my justice and truth is in danger to be trampled underfoot; and yet if I should let out all my wrath upon them, they were never able to stand under it, but ' their spirits would fail before me, and the souls that I have made,' Ps. lxxviii. 38; Isa. lvii. 16. I will therefore let out all my wrath upon their surety, and he shall bear it for them, that they may be delivered; and thus the Lord ' in wrath remembers mercy,' Hab. iii. 2. But,

7. Seventhly, We can receive no benefit by the righteousness of Christ for justification in the sight of God, nor can we be pardoned and accepted thereupon, *until that righteousness become ours, and be made over unto us.* How can we plead this righteousness before God, except we have an interest in this righteousness? Isa. xlv. 24, 25. How can we rejoice and triumph in this righteousness, if this righteousness be not made ours? How can we have peace with God, and boldness at the throne of grace, through this righteousness, except we can lay claim to this righteousness? How can we conclude that we are happy and blessed upon the account of this righteousness, except it be made over to us?[1] There is none of us that have such an inherent righteousness in ourselves that we dare plead before the bar of God; and though God hath provided such a glorious robe of righteousness for poor sinners, as is the wonder and amazement of angels, yet what would all this avail the poor sinner, if this righteousness be not made over to him? O sirs! remember this, Christ's righteousness must be yours, it must be made over to you, or else it will never stand you in stead: Rom. v. 17, ' For if by one man's offence, death reigned by one; much more they which receive abundance of grace, and of the gift of righteousness, shall reign in glory by one, Jesus Christ.' Except they receive the righteousness of Christ, it is nothing to them. Christ's righteousness is in itself white raiment, and beautiful and glorious apparel; but it will never cover our nakedness, except it be put on, and we are clothed with it. It must be made over to us, or we can never be justified by it: 1 Cor. i. 30, ' He of God is made to us righteousness;' if he be not made to us righteousness, we shall never be righteous. Though man hath lost a righteousness to be justified by, yet there is an absolute necessity of having one. God cannot love nor delight in anything but righteousness. God is a holy God, a righteous God, and therefore can only love and take pleasure in those that are righteous, both by a righteousness imputed, and a righteousness imparted: Isa. xlv. 24, ' Surely, shall one say, in the Lord have I righteousness and strength;' ver. 25, ' In the Lord shall all the seed of Israel be justified, and shall glory:' Isa. liv. 17, ' Their righteousness is of me, saith the Lord:' Ps. lxxi. 16, ' I will make mention of thy righteousness, even of thine only.' Look, as no man can be made rich by another man's riches, except they are made his; so no man

---

[1] 2 Cor. ii. 14; Gal. vi. 14; Rom. v. 1; Heb. iv. 15, 16; Ps. xxxii. 1, 2; Rom. iv. 7-11; Rom. iv. 3. If Christ's obedience be imputed to us, it must be so imputed as to be our righteousness before God; no imputation below this will serve our turns, cheer our hearts, and save our souls. Rev. xiv. 8; Isa. lxiii. 1; Rev. iii. 18.

can be made righteous by the righteousness of Christ, except his righteousness be made over to him; hence he is called, ' The Lord our Righteousness,' Jer. xxiii. 6; and hence we are said to be ' the righteousness of God in him,' 2 Cor. v. 21; hence we are said ' by his obedience to be made righteous,' 2 Cor. v. 21.

8. Eighthly and lastly, The way whereby this righteousness of God's providing is conveyed and made over to us, that we may receive the benefit thereof, and be justified thereby, *it is by way of imputation.* The meaning is this: God doth reckon the righteousness of Christ unto his people, as if it were their own; he doth count unto them Christ's sufferings and satisfaction, and makes them partakers of the virtue thereof, as if themselves had suffered and satisfied. This is the genuine and proper import of the word *imputation,* when that which is personally done by one, is accounted and reckoned to another, and laid upon his score, as if he had done it.[1] Thus it is in this very case; we sinned and fell short of the glory of God, and became obnoxious to the vindictive justice of God; and the Lord Jesus Christ, by his obedience and death, hath given full content and satisfaction to divine justice on our behalf. Now when God doth pardon and accept us hereupon, he doth put it upon our account, he doth reckon or impute it unto us as fully, in respect of the benefit thereof, as if we ourselves had performed it in our own persons; and this is the way wherein the Holy Ghost frequently expresseth it: Rom. iv. 6, ' Even as David also describeth the blessedness of the man unto whom God imputeth righteousness without works;' and ver. 11, ' That righteousness might be imputed to them also;' and therefore it highly concerns us to mind this scripture rule, that in order to the satisfaction of the justice of God, the sins of God's people were imputed and reckoned unto Christ; and in order to our partaking of the benefit of that satisfaction, or deliverance thereby, Christ's righteousness must be imputed and reckoned unto us. The first branch of this rule you have, Isa. liii. 5, 6, ' He was wounded for our transgressions, he was bruised for our iniquities,' &c., and ' the Lord hath laid on him the iniquity of us all;' and for the other branch of the rule, see Rom. v. 19, ' As by one man's disobedience many were made sinners, so by the obedience of one shall many be made righteous;' ver. 17, ' As by one man's offence death reigned by one, much more they which receive abundance of grace, and of the gift of righteousness, shall reign in life by one, Jesus Christ.' From the comparison between the first and second Adam, it is evident that as Adam's transgression of the law of God is imputed to all his posterity, and that in respect thereof they are reputed sinners, and accursed and liable to eternal death; so also Christ's obedience, whereby he fulfilled the law, is so imputed to the members of his mystical body, that in regard of God, they stand as innocent, justified and accepted to eternal life. Look, as Adam was the common root of all mankind, and so his sin is imputed to all his posterity, so Jesus Christ is the common root of all the faithful, and his obedience is imputed to them all; for

[1] Rom. iii. 21, and Isa. liii. Imputed righteousness seems to be prefigured by the skins wherewith the Lord, after the fall, clothed our first parents. The bodies of the beasts were for sacrifice, and the skins, to put them in mind that their own righteousness was like the fig leaves, imperfect, and that therefore they must be justified another way.

it were ridiculous to say that Adam's sin had more power to condemn, than Christ's righteousness hath to save ; and who but fools in folio will say that God doth not impute Christ's righteousness, as well as Adam's sin ? The apostle's parallel between the two Adams does clearly evidence that as the guilt of Adam's disobedience is really imputed to us, insomuch that in his sinning we all sin ; so the obedience of Christ is as really imputed unto us, insomuch that in his obeying, reputatively and legally we obey also. How did Adam's sin become ours ? Why, by way of imputation. He transgressed the covenant, and did eat the forbidden fruit, and it was justly reckoned unto us. It was personally the sinful act of our first parent, but it is imputed to all of us who come out of his loins ; for we were in him not only naturally, as he was the root of mankind, but also legally, as he was the great representative of mankind.[1] In the covenant of works, and the transactions thereof, Adam stood in the stead, and acted in the behalf, not only of himself, but of all his posterity, and therefore his sin is reckoned unto them ; even so, saith the apostle, after the same manner, the obedience and righteousness of Christ is made over to many for justification. I cannot understand the analogy betwixt the two Adams, wherein the apostle is so clear and full, unless this imputation, as here stated, be granted. Look, as Christ was made sin for us only by imputation, so we are made righteous only by the imputation of his righteousness to us, as the Scripture everywhere evidences, 1 Pet. ii. 22 ; 2 Cor. v. 21, ' He hath made him to be sin for us who knew no sin, that we might be made the righteousness of God in him.' How was Christ made sin for us ? Not sin inherent, for he had no sin in him ; he was ' holy, harmless, and undefiled, separate from sinners, and made higher than the heavens,' Heb. vii. 26 ; but by imputation. Christ's righteousness is imputed to us in that way wherein our sin was imputed to him. Now our sin was imputed to Christ, not only in the bitter effects of it, but he took the guilt of them upon himself, as I have in this treatise already evidenced ; so, then, his righteousness or active obedience itself must be proportionably imputed to us, and not only in the effects thereof. The mediatory righteousness of Christ can no way become the believer's, but as the first Adam's disobedience became his posterity's, who never had the least actual share in his transgression ; that is, by an act of imputation from God as a judge. The Lord Jesus having fulfilled the law as a second Adam, God the Father imputeth it to the believing soul, as if he had done it in his own person. I do not say that God the Father doth account the sinner to have done it, but I say that God the Father doth impute it to the believing sinner, as if he had done it, unto all saving intents and purposes. Hence Christ is called ' the Lord our Righteousness,' Jer. xxiii. 6. An awakened soul, that is truly sensible of his own baseness and unrighteousness, would not have this golden sentence, ' The Lord our Righteousness,' blotted out by a hand of heaven out of the Bible, for as many worlds as there are men in the world. So is that text to a believer, living and dying, a strong cordial, viz., 1 Cor. i. 30, ' Christ Jesus is made unto

---

[1] Gen. iii. 6, 11, 12. As imitation of Adam only made us not sinners, so imitation of Christ only makes us not righteous, but the imputation,—Down[ame]—of Justification.

us of God wisdom, righteousness,' &c.[1]   And pray how is Christ made
righteousness to the believer?   Not by infusion, but imputation; not
by putting righteousness into him, but by putting a righteousness upon
him, even his own righteousness, by the imputing his merits, his satisfaction, his obedience unto them, through which they are accepted as
righteous unto eternal life, Rom. v. 19.   Christ's righteousness is
his in respect of inhesion, but it is ours in respect of imputation;
his righteousness is his personally, but ours meritoriously; we are
justified by another's righteousness, and that only, and therefore by
imputed righteousness; for another's righteousness can no other way
be made ours, but only by imputation: Rom. v. 18, ' By the righteousness of one the free gift came upon all men to justification.'   Were it
any other than imputed righteousness, it would be as manifold a
righteousness as there are persons justified; but it is said to be 'the
righteousness of one, that comes upon all men for justification of life.'
That is a choice word that you have in Rev. xix. 8, ' And to her,' that
is, Christ's spouse, ' was granted that she should be arrayed in fine
linen, clean and white; for the fine linen is the righteousness of the
saints.'   The Greek word here is δικαιώματα, ' righteousnesses ' or
' justifications.'   This, say some, signifieth a double righteousness
given to us—(1.) The righteousness of justification, whereby we are
justified before God; (2.) The righteousness of sanctification, by which
we evidence our justification to men.   But others say it is a Hebrew-
ism rather, by the plural righteousnesses noting the most absolute,
complete, and perfect righteousness which we have in Christ.[2]   Now
though I would not exclude inherent righteousness, yet I judge that
imputed righteousness is the righteousness here meant; and that,
(1.) Because this clothing is that which is the righteousness of all
saints, by which they stand recti in curia before God.   Now there is
no standing before God in our inherent righteousness; for though,
next to Christ, our graces are our best jewels, yet they are but weak
and imperfect, they have their specks and spots, they are like the
moon, which, when it shines brightest, yet has her black spots.[3]
(2.) Christ's righteousness is the only pure, clean, white, spotless
righteousness.   There is no speck or spot to be found upon Christ's
righteousness; but ' we are all as an unclean thing, and all our
righteousnesses are as filthy rags,' as that evangelical prophet speaks,
Isa. lxiv. 6, 3.   The word here is plural, δικαιώματα, ' righteousnesses.'
Christ hath many righteousnesses—first, He hath his · essential and
personal righteousness as God.   Now this essential personal righteousness of Christ cannot be imputed to us.   Osiander was of opinion that
men were justified by the essential righteousness of Christ as God,
which was a most dangerous opinion, and learnedly and largely confuted by Calvin in his Institutions,[4] and by others since; secondly,

---

[1] In this 1 Cor. i. 30, the apostle (1.) distinguisheth righteousness from sanctification,
imputed righteousness from inherent righteousness; (2.) he saith that Christ's righteousness is made ours of God. See Rom. iv. 6; Ps. lxxi. 16.
[2] So the Hebrew word is used, Isa. xlv. 24.
[3] Ps. lxxvi. 7, and cxliii. 2; Job ix. 15, xxii. 2-4, and xxxv. 7.   The saints are said
(Rev. vii. 15) to be clothed in white robes, not because they had merited, or adorned themselves with good works, but because they had washed and made white their robes in the
blood of the Lamb.   [4] i. 15, 3, 5.   ii. 12, 5-7.   iii. 11, 5.—G.

There is the mediatory righteousness of Christ. Now this is that righteousness which he wrought for us as mediator, whereby he did subject himself to the precepts, to the penalties, commands and curses, answering both God's vindictive and rewarding justice. There is Christ's active righteousness, and there is Christ's passive righteousness, &c. Of these I have spoken already in this treatise, and therefore a hint here is enough; but, *thirdly*, There are some expressions in the text that is under consideration that do best agree with the righteousness of Christ; as *first* that, that 'she is arrayed in fine linen, clean and white.'[1] This clearly points at imputed righteousness, which Christ puts upon his bride as a royal robe. That which makes Christ's bride beautiful, yea, whiter than the snow, and more glorious than the sun in his eyes, is not any beauty of her own, nor any inherent righteousness in herself, but the white robe of Christ's own righteousness that he puts upon her; *second*, that expression in the text, 'to her it was granted, that she should be arrayed in fine linen,' &c. 'It was granted to her,' to shew that this fine linen was none of her own spinning, it was a free gift of Christ unto her. Saints have no other righteousness, to make them comely and lovely in the eyes of God, but the robe of Christ's righteousness, which is that fine white linen that Christ gives them, and that he puts upon them; *lastly*, observe the confirmation and ratification that is given to these words in the 9th verse, 'Write, these are the true sayings of God.' These are not my sayings, nor the sayings of angels, but they are the sayings of that God that is truth itself, that cannot die, nor lie, nor deny himself, nor deceive the sons of God; and therefore you may safely rest upon these sayings of God, both in the 8th and 9th verses, as most sure and certain. Surely the righteousness the believer hath is imputed; it is an accounted or reckoned righteousness to him; it is not that which he hath inherently in himself, but God through Christ doth esteem of him as if he had it, and so deals with him as wholly righteous— (1.) It stands with reason that that satisfaction should be imputed to me, which my surety hath made for my debt. Now Christ was our surety, as the apostle calls him, Heb. vii. 22. (2.) Adam's sin was justly imputed by God to all his posterity, though it was not their own inherently and actually, as the apostle tells us, Rom. v. 14; and the sins of all the elect were imputed unto Christ, though they were not his own inherently and actually. ' He made him to be sin for us, who knew no sin,' saith the apostle, 2 Cor. v. 21; and 'upon him was laid the iniquity of us all,'[2] Isa. liii. 6. All the sins of all the believers in the world, from the first creation to the last judgment, were laid on him. How laid on him but by imputation? Surely there was in Christ no fundamental guilt! No, no; but he was made sin by imputation and law-account; he was our surety, and so our sins were laid on him in order to punishment. And to prefigure this, all the

[1] How can it stand with reason that the Papists by the Pope's indulgences should be made partakers of the merits and good works one of another, and yet be against reason that we by the ordinance of God should be made partakers of the merits and righteousness of Jesus Christ?

[2] This must be Luther's meaning when he saith, Christ was the greatest sinner; he was Manasseh that idolater, David that adulterer, Peter that denier of his Master, &c., to wit, by imputation only, he being made sin for them, as the apostle speaks.

iniquities of God's people were imputed to their sacrifice, though they were not inherently his own, as we read, Lev. xvi. 21, 22, ' Aaron shall put all the iniquities of all the children of Israel, and all their transgressions, and all their sins, upon the head of the goat; and the goat shall bear upon him all their iniquities.' And why then should it seem strange that the perfect righteousness of our sacrifice and surety, though it be not our own inherently, should be imputed to us by the Lord and made ours ?[1]

Frequently and seriously consider that the word answering this imputing is in the Hebrew *Chashab*, and in the Greek λογίζεσθαι, of which the sum, as the learned say, comes to this, that though the words in the general signify to think, to reason, to imagine, &c., yet very frequently they are used to signify to account or reckon, by way of computation, as arithmeticians use to do, so that it is, as it were, a judgment passed upon a thing when all reasons and arguments are cast together. And from this it is applied to signify any kind of accounting or reckoning; and in this sense imputation is taken here for God's esteeming and accounting of us righteous; חשׁב, signifies to reckon or account. It is taken by a borrowed speech from merchants' reckonings and accounts, who have their debt-books, wherein they set down how their reckonings stand in the particulars they deal in. Now, in such debt-books merchants use to set down whatever payments are only made, either by the debtors themselves, or by others in the behalf of them; an example whereof we have in the Epistle of Philemon, ver. 18, where Paul undertakes to Philemon for Onesimus, ' If he hath wronged thee, or oweth thee anything, put that on my account;' that is, account Onesimus his debt to Paul, and Paul's satisfaction or payment to Onesimus, which answers the double imputation in point of justification; that is, of our sins to Christ, and of Christ's satisfaction to us, Ps. xxxii. 1, 2; both which are implied, 2 Cor. v. 21, ' He made him to be sin for us;' that is, our sins were imputed to him, ' that we might be the righteousness of God in him;' that is, that his righteousness might be imputed to us. The language of Jesus Christ to his Father seems to be this, O holy Father, I have freely and willingly taken all the debts and all the sins of all the believers in the world upon me; I have undertaken to be their paymaster, to satisfy thy justice, to pacify thy wrath, to fulfil thy law, &c., and therefore, lo, here I am, ready to do whatever thou commandest, and ready to suffer whatsoever thou pleasest; I am willing to be reckoned a sinner, that they may be reckoned righteous; I am willing to be accounted cursed, that they may be for ever blessed; I am willing to pay all their debts, that they may be set at liberty; I am willing to lay down my life, that they may escape the second death; I am willing that my soul should be exercised with the most hideous agonies, that their souls may be possessed of heaven's happinesses, Ps. xl. 6–8; Heb. x. 4–9; John x. 11, 15, 17, 18; Rev. xx. 6. Oh, what wonderful wisdom, grace, and love is here manifested! that when we were neither able to satisfy the penalty of the law, or to bring a con-

[1] To impute in the general, is to acknowledge that to be another's which is not indeed his; and it is used either in a good or bad sense, so that it is no more than to account or reckon. It is the righteousness of Christ imputed to us, and accepted for us, by which we are judged righteous.

formity to it, that then Christ should interpose, and become both redemption and righteousness for us !

Now, from the imputed righteousness of Christ, a believer may form up this fifth plea, as to all the ten scriptures in the margin, that refer to the great day of account:[1] *O blessed God, thou hast given me to understand that the mediatory righteousness of Christ includes, first, the habitual holiness of his person, in the absence of all sin, and in the rich and plentiful presence of all holy and requisite qualities ;* secondly, *the actual holiness of his life and death by obedience. By his active obedience he perfectly fulfilled the commands of the law, and by his passive obedience, his voluntary sufferings, he satisfied the penalty and commination of the law for transgressions, that perfect satisfaction to divine justice, in whatsoever it requires, either in way of punishing for sin, or obedience to the law, made by the Lord Jesus Christ, God and man, the mediator of the new covenant, as a common head, repre-senting all those whom the Father hath given to him, and made over unto them that believe in him; this is that righteousness that is im-puted to all believers in their justification, and this imputed righteous-ness of thy dear Son and my dear Saviour is now my plea before thy bar of justice.* Imputed righteousness is the same materially with that which the law requireth. It is obedience to the law of God, exactly and punctually performed, to the very utmost *iota* and tittle thereof. Without the least abatement, Christ hath paid the utter-most farthing. He is the fulfilling of the law for righteousness, and he hath fulfilled the law in the human nature, to the intent that it might be fulfilled in the same nature to which it was at first given; and all this he hath expressly done in all their names, and on all their behalfs, that believe in him, 'that the righteousness of the law might be fulfilled in them,' Rom. viii. 3, 4.[2] It is as if our dear Lord Jesus had said, O blessed Father, this I suffer, and this I do, to the use and in the stead and room of all those that have ventured their souls upon me, that they may have a righteousness which they may truly call their own, and on which they may safely rest, and in which they may for ever glory, Isa. xlv. 24, 25. Now it will never stand with the unspotted holiness, justice, and righteousness of God, to reject this righteousness of his Son, or that plea that is bottomed upon it. Oh, the matchless happiness of believers, who have so fair, so full, and so noble a plea to make in the great day of our Lord Jesus!

Quest. But some may say, *What blessed fruit grows upon this glorious tree of paradise*—viz., the righteousness of Jesus Christ, that is imputed to all believers? *What strong consolations flows from this fountain,* the imputed righteousness of our Lord Jesus Christ? I answer, there are these nine choice consolations, that flow in upon all believers, through the righteousness of Christ imputed to them:—

1. First, Let all believers know for their comfort, that in this im-puted righteousness of Christ *there is enough to satisfy the justice of*

---

[1] Eccles. xi. 9, and xii. 14; Mat. xii. 14, and xviii. 23; Luke xvi. 3; Rom. xiv. 10; 2 Cor. v. 10; Heb. ix. 27, and xiii. 17; 1 Pet. iv. 5.

[2] The righteousness which the law requireth, upon pain of damnation, is a perfect obedience and conformity to the whole law of God, performed by every son and daugh-ter of Adam in his own person. Now imputed righteousness is the same materially with that which the law requireth.

God to the uttermost farthing, and to take off all his judicial anger and fury. The mediatory righteousness of Christ is so perfect, so full, so exact, so complete, and so fully satisfactory to the justice of God, as that divine justice cries out, I have enough, and I require no more; I have found a ransom, and I am fully pacified towards you, Ezek. xvi. 61–63; Heb. x. 10–12, 14; Isa. liii. 4–6. It is certain that Christ was truly and properly a sacrifice for sin; and it is as certain that our sins were the meritorious cause of his sufferings. He did put himself into poor sinners' stead, he took their guilt upon him, and did undergo that punishment which they should have undergone; he did die, and shed his blood, that he might thereby atone God and expiate sin, Rom. v. 6–12; and therefore we may safely and boldly conclude, that Jesus Christ hath satisfied the justice of God to the uttermost; so that now the believing sinner may rejoice and triumph in the justice as well as 'in the mercy of God, Heb. vii. 25 ; for doubt-less the mediatory righteousness of Christ was infinitely more satis-factory and pleasing to God, than all the sins of believers could be displeasing to him. God took more pleasure and delight in the bruis-ing of his Son, in the humiliation of his Son, and he smelt a sweeter savour in his sacrifice, than all our sins could possibly offend him or provoke him, 1sa. liii. 10. When a believer casts his eyes upon his many thousand sinful commissions and omissions, no wonder if he fears and trembles; but then, when he looks upon Christ's satisfac-tion, he may see himself acquitted, and rejoice; for if there be no charge, no accusation against the Lord Jesus, there can be none against the believer, Rom. viii. 33–37. Christ's expiatory sacrifice hath fully satisfied divine justice; and upon that very ground every believer hath cause to triumph in Christ Jesus, and in that righteous-ness of his by which he stands justified before the throne of God, 2 Cor. ii. 14; Rev. xiv. 4, 5. Christ is a person of infinite, transcen-dent worth and excellency, and it makes highly for his honour to justify believers, in the most ample and glorious way imaginable, &c. ; and what way is that, but by working out for [them], and then investing them with, a righteousness adequate to the law of God; a righteousness that should be every way commensurate to the miserable estate of fallen man, and to the holy design of the glorious God. It is the high honour of the second Adam that he hath restored to fallen man a more glorious righteousness than that he lost in the first Adam; and it would be high blasphemy, in the eyes of angels and men, for any mortal to assert that the second Adam, our Lord Jesus Christ, was less powerful to save, than the first Adam was to destroy. The second Adam is 'able to save to the uttermost all such as come to God through him,' Heb. vii. 25. The second Adam is able to save to all ends and purposes perfectly, saith Beza; perpetually, or for ever, saith Tremellius; *in æternum*, saith Syrus; *in perpetuum*, saith the Vulg.; *ad plenum*, saith Erasmus; *ad perfectum*, saith Stapul-ensis.[1] He is able to save to the uttermost obligation of the law, preceptive, as well as penal; and to bring in perfect righteousness, as well as perfect innocency. He is able to save to the uttermost demand of divine justice, by that perfect satisfaction that he has given to

[1] εἰς τὸ παντελὲς, 'to the uttermost' of time, at all times, and for ever, &c.

divine justice. ' Christ is mighty to save,' Isa. lxiii. 1; and as he is mighty to save, so he loves to save poor sinners, in such a way wherein he may most magnify his own might; and therefore he will purchase their pardon with his blood, 1 Pet. i. 18, 19, and make reparation to divine justice for all the wrongs and injuries which fallen man had done to his Creator and his royal law; and bestow upon him a better righteousness than that which Adam lost; and bring him into a more safe, high, honourable, and durable estate than that which Adam fell from when he was in his created perfection. All the attributes of God do acquiesce in the imputed righteousness of Christ, so that a believer may look upon the holiness, justice, and righteousness of God, and rejoice, and lay himself down in peace, Ps. iv. 8. I have read in story, that Pilate being called to Rome, to give an account unto the emperor for some misgovernment and mal-administration, he put on the seamless coat of Christ; and all the time that he had that coat upon his back, Cæsar's fury was abated. Christ has put his coat, his robe of righteousness, upon every believer, Isa. lxi. 10; upon which account all the judicial anger, wrath, and fury of God towards believers ceaseth : Isa. liv. 9, ' For this is as the waters of Noah unto me: for as I have sworn that the waters of Noah should no more go over the earth; so have I sworn that I would not be wroth with thee, nor rebuke thee.' Ver. 10, ' For the mountains shall depart, and the hills be removed; but my kindness shall not depart from thee, neither shall the covenant of my peace be removed, saith the Lord that hath mercy on thee.' But,

2. Secondly, Know for your comfort, that this imputed, this media-tory righteousness of Christ *takes away all your unrighteousness*. It cancels every bond; it takes away all iniquity, and answers for all your sins, Isa. liii. 5–7; Col. ii. 12–15. Lord, here are my sins of omission, and here are my sins of commission; but the righteousness of Christ hath answered for them all. Here are my sins against the law, and here are my sins against the gospel, and here are my sins against the offers of grace, the tenders of grace, the strivings of grace, the bowels of grace; but the righteousness of Christ hath answered for them all. I have read that when a cordial was offered to a godly man that was sick, Oh, said he, the cordial of cordials which I daily take is, ' that the blood of Jesus Christ cleanseth us from all our sins,' 1 John i. 7. O sirs ! it would be high blasphemy for any to imagine that there should be more demerit in any sin, yea, in all sin, to condemn a believer, than there is merit in Christ's righteous-ness to absolve him, to justify him, Rom. viii. 1, 33–35. The right-eousness of Christ was shadowed out by the glorious robes and apparel of the high priest, Exod. xxx. That attire in which the high priest appeared before God, what was it else but a type of Christ's righteous-ness ? The filthy garments of Joshua, who represented the church, were not only taken off from him, thereby signifying the removal of our sins, Zech. iii. 4, 5; but also a new, fair garment was put upon him, to signify our being clothed with the wedding-garment of Christ's righteousness. If any shall say, How is it possible that a soul that is defiled with the worst of sins should be whiter than the snow, yea, beautiful and glorious in the eyes of God ? Ps. li. 7. The answer is

at hand, because to whomsoever the Lord doth give the pardon of his sins, which is the first part of our justification, to them he doth also impute the righteousness of Christ, which is the second part of our justification before God. Thus David describeth, saith the apostle, 'the blessedness of the man to whom the Lord imputeth righteousness without works; saying, Blessed are they whose iniquities are forgiven, and whose sins are covered,' Rom. iv. 6, 7. Now to that man whose sins the Lord forgives, to him he doth impute righteousness also: 'Take away the filthy garments from him,' saith the Lord of Joshua; 'and he said unto him, Behold, I have caused thine iniquity to pass from thee, and I will clothe thee with change of raiment,' Zech. iii. 4. And what was that change of raiment? Surely the perfect obedience and righteousness of the Lord Jesus, which God doth impute unto us; in which respect also we are said, by justifying faith, to put on the Lord Jesus, Rom. xiii. 14; and to be clothed with him as with a garment, Gal. iii. 27. And no marvel if, being so apparelled, we appear beautiful and glorious in the sight of God: 'To her,' that is, Christ's bride, 'was granted that she should be arryed in fine linen, clean and white, for the fine linen is the righteousness of saints,' Rev. xix. 8. This perfect righteousness of Christ, which the Lord imputeth to us, and wherewith, as with a garment, he clotheth us, is the only righteousness which the saints have to stand before God with; and having that robe of righteousness on, they may stand with great boldness and comfort before the judgment-seat of God. But,

3. Thirdly, Know for your comfort, that this righteousness of Christ *presents us perfectly righteous in the sight of God.* 'He is made to us righteousness,' 1 Cor. i. 30. The robe of innocency, like the veil of the temple, is rent asunder; our righteousness is a ragged righteousness, our righteousnesses are as filthy rags, Isa. lxiv. 4. Look, as under rags the naked body is seen, so under the rags of our righteousnesses the body of death is seen. Christ is all in all in regard of righteousness: Christ is 'the end of the law for righteousness to them that believe,'[1] Rom. x. 4.

That is, through Christ we are as righteous as if we had satisfied the law in our own persons. The end of the law is to justify and save those which fulfil it. Christ subjected himself thereto; he perfectly fulfilled it for us, and his perfect righteousness is imputed to us. Christ fulfilled the moral law, not for himself, but for us; therefore Christ doing it for believers, they fulfil the law in Christ. And so Christ by doing, and they believing in him that doth it, do fulfil the law; or Christ may be said to be the end of the law, because the end of the law is perfect righteousness, that a man may be justified thereby, which end we cannot attain of ourselves, through the frailty of our flesh; but by Christ we attain it, who hath fulfilled the law for us. Christ hath perfectly fulfilled the decalogue for us, and that three ways: (1.) In his pure conception; (2.) In his godly life; (3.) in his holy and obedient sufferings; and all for us. For whatsoever the law required that we should be, do, or suffer, he hath performed in our behalf. Therefore one wittily saith, (Aretius,) that Christ is τέλος, the end or tribute; and we by his payment ἀτελεῖς, tribute-free. We

---

[1] Finis perficiens, non interficiens.—*Augustine.*

are discharged by him before God. Christ, in respect of the integrity and purity of his nature, being conceived without sin, Mat. i. 18; and in respect of his life and actions, being wholly conformed to the absolute righteousness of the law, Luke i. 35; and in respect of the punishment which he suffered, to make satisfaction unto God's justice for the breach of the law, 2 Cor. v. 21; Col. i. 20,—in these respects Christ is the perfection of the law, and 'the end of the law for righteousness to them that believe.' Jacob got the blessing in the garment of his elder brother; so in the garment of Christ's righteousness, who is our elder brother, we obtain the blessing; yea, 'all spiritual blessings in heavenly places,' Eph. i. 4. We are made 'the righteousness of God in him,' 2 Cor. v. 21. The church, saith Marorate, which puts on Christ, and his righteousness, is more illustrious than the air is by the sun. The infinite wisdom and power of dear Jesus in reconciling the law and the gospel, in this great mystery of justification, is greatly to be magnified. In the blessed Scriptures we find the righteousness of justification to take its various denominations. In respect of the material cause, it is called the righteousness of the law, Rom. v. 17; in respect of the efficient cause, it is called the righteousness of Christ, 1 Cor. i. 30; in respect of the formal, it is called the righteousness of God, he imputing of it, Rom. iii. 22; in respect of the instrumental cause, it is called the righteousness of faith, Phil. iii. 9; and in respect of the moving and final cause, we are said to be justified freely by grace, Rom. iii. 24; Titus iii. 7. The law, as it was a covenant of works, required exact and perfect obedience, in men's proper persons; this was legal justification. But in the new covenant, God is contented to accept this righteousness in the hand of a surety, and this is evangelical justification. This righteousness presents us in the sight of God as 'all fair,' Cant. iv. 7; as 'complete,' Col. ii. 10; as 'without spot or wrinkle,' Eph. v. 27; as 'without fault before the throne of God,' Rev. xiv. 5; as 'holy, and unblamable, and unreprovable in his sight,' Col. i. 22. Oh, the happiness and blessedness, the safety and glory, of those precious souls, who, in the righteousness of Jesus Christ, stand perfectly righteous in the sight of God! But,

4. Fourthly, Know for your comfort, that this imputed righteousness of Christ *will answer to all the fears, doubts, and objections of your souls.* How shall I look up to God? The answer is, in the righteousness of Jesus Christ. How shall I have any communion with a holy God in this world? The answer is, in the righteousness of Christ. How shall I find acceptance with God? The answer is, in the righteousness of Christ. How shall I die? The answer is, in the righteousness of Christ. How shall I stand before the judgment-seat? The answer is, in the righteousness of Jesus Christ. Your sure and only way, under all temptations, fears, conflicts, doubts, and disputes, is, by faith, to remember Christ, and the sufferings of Christ, as your mediator and surety; and say, O Christ, thou art my sin, in being made sin for me, 2 Cor. v. 21; and thou art my curse, being made a curse for me, Gal. iii. 13; or rather, I am thy sin, and thou art my righteousness; I am thy curse, and thou art my blessing; I am thy death, and thou art my life; I am the wrath of God to thee, and thou art the love of God to me; I am thy hell, and thou art my heaven.

O sirs! if you think of your sins, and of God's wrath; if you think of your guiltiness, and of God's justice, your hearts will faint and fail, they will fear and tremble and sink into despair, if you do not think of Christ, if you do not stay and rest your souls upon the mediatory righteousness of Christ, the imputed righteousness of Christ. The imputed righteousness of Christ answers all cavils and objections, though there were millions of them, that can be made against the good estate of a believer. This is a precious truth, more worth than a world, that all our sins are pardoned, not only in a way of truth and mercy, but in a way of justice. Satan and our own consciences will object many things against our souls, if we plead only the mercy and the truth of God; and will be ready to say, Oh, but where is then the justice of God? can mercy pardon without the consent of his justice? But now, whilst we rest upon the satisfaction of Christ, 'justice and mercy kiss each other,' Ps. lxxxv. 10; yea, justice saith, I am pleased. In a day of temptation, many things will be cast in our dish, about the multitude of our sins, and the greatness of our sins, and the grievousness of our sins, and about the circumstances and aggravations of our sins; but that good word, ' Christ hath redeemed us from all iniquities,' he hath paid the full price that justice could exact or require; and that good word, ' Mercy rejoiceth against judgment,' James ii. 13, may support, comfort, and bear us up under all. The infinite worth of Christ's obedience, did arise from the dignity of his person, who was God-man; so that all the obedience of angels and men, if put together, could not amount to the excellency of Christ's satisfaction. The righteousness of Christ, is often called the righteousness of God, because it is a righteousness of God's providing, and a righteousness that God is fully satisfied with; and therefore, no fears, no doubts, no cavils, no objections, no disputes, can stand before this blessed and glorious righteousness of Jesus Christ, that is imputed to us. But,

5. Fifthly, Know for your comfort, that the imputed righteousness of Christ is *the best title that you have to shew for* ' a kingdom that shakes not, for riches that corrupt not, for an inheritance that fadeth not away, and for an house not made with hands, but one eternal in the heavens,' Heb. xii. 28; 1 Pet. i. 3-5; 2 Cor. v. 1-4. It is the fairest certificate that you have to shew for all that happiness and blessedness that you look for in that other world. The righteousness of Christ is your life, your joy, your comfort, your crown, your confidence, your heaven, your all. Oh that you were still so wise as to keep a fixed eye and an awakened heart upon the mediatory righteousness of Christ; for that is the righteousness by which you may safely and comfortably live, and by which you may happily and quietly die. It was a very sweet and golden confession, which Bernard made, when he thought himself to be at the point of death.[1] I confess, said he, I am not worthy, I have no merits of mine own to obtain heaven by, but my Lord had a double right thereunto; an hereditary right as a Son, and a meritorious right as a sacrifice; he was contented with the one right himself, the other right he hath given unto me; by the virtue of which gift I do rightly lay claim unto it, and am not confounded. Ah, that believers would dwell much upon this, that they

Guliel. Abbas, in vita Bern., lib. i. cap. 12.

have a righteousness in Christ, that is as full, perfect, and complete, as if they had fulfilled the law. ' Christ being the end of the law for righteousness to believers,' invests believers with a righteousness, every way as complete as the personal obedience of the law would have invested them withal, Rom. viii. 3, 4; yea, the righteousness that believers have by Christ is, in some respect, better than that they should have had by Adam: (1.) Because of the dignity of Christ's person, he being the Son of God, his righteousness is more glorious than Adam's was; his righteousness is called ' The righteousness of God;' and we are made the ' righteousness of God in him,' 2 Cor. v. 21. The first Adam was a mere man, the second Adam is God and man. (2.) Because the righteousness is perpetual. Adam was a mutable person, he lost his righteousness in one day, say some, and all that glory which his posterity should have possessed, had he stood fast in innocency; but the righteousness of Christ cannot be lost. His righteousness is like himself, from everlasting to everlasting. It is an everlasting righteousness, Dan. ix. 24. When once this white raiment is put upon a believer, it can never fall off, it can never be taken off. This splendid glorious righteousness of Jesus Christ's, is as really a believer's, as if he had wrought it himself, Rev. xix. 8. A believer is no loser, but a gainer, by Adam's fall. By the loss of Adam's righteousness is brought to light a more glorious and durable righteousness than ever Adam's was; and upon the account of an interest in this righteousness a believer may challenge all the glory of that upper world. But,

6. Sixthly, Know for your comfort, that this imputed righteousness of Christ *is the only true basis, bottom, and ground, for a believer to build his happiness upon, his joy and comfort upon, and the true peace and quiet of his conscience upon.* What though Satan, or thy own heart, or the world, condemns thee; yet in this thou mayest rejoice, that God justifies thee. You see what a bold challenge Paul makes, Rom. viii. 33, ' Who shall lay anything to the charge of God's elect? it is God that justifieth;' some read it question-wise, thus, ' Shall God that justifieth?' no such matter.[1] And if the judge acquit the prisoner at the bar, he cares not though the jailer or his fellow-prisoners condemn him; so here there are no accusers that a believer needs to fear, seeing that it is God himself, who is the supreme judge, that absolves him as just. God absolves, and therefore it is to no purpose for Satan to accuse us, Rev. xii. 10; nor for the law of Moses to accuse us, John v. 45; nor for our own consciences to accuse us, Rom. ii. 25; nor for the world to accuse us. God is the highest judge, and his tribunal-seat is the supreme judgment-seat; therefore from thence there is no appealing. As amongst men, persons accused or condemned, may appeal, till they come to the highest court; but if in the highest, they are absolved and discharged, then they are free, and safe and well: so the believer being absolved before God's tribunal-seat, there is no further accusations to be feared, all appeals from thence being void

---

[1] Rom. viii. 33. ἐγκαλέσει, signifies *in jus vocare*, or call unto the law. It is a law-custom to clear men by proclamation. If one hath been indicted at the Assizes, and no bill brought in against him, there is an ' Oh yes ' made, if any have anything to say against the prisoner at the bar, let him come forth, since he stands upon his freedom. The application is easy.

and of no force. The consideration of which should arm us and comfort us and strengthen us against all terrors of conscience, guilt of sin, accusation of the law, and cruelty of Satan; inasmuch as these either dare not appear before God to accuse us or charge us; or if they do, it is but lost labour. Ambrose gives the sense thus, None can or dare retract the judgment of God; for he confidently provoketh all adversaries, if they dare come forth to accuse; not that there is no cause, but because God hath justified. ' It is God that justifieth,' therefore it is in vain to accuse them; and ' it is God that justifieth them :' if God doth it none can reverse it, for there are none that are equal with God. Let all the accusations, which shall come in against thee, from one hand or another, be true or false, they shall never hurt thee; for he from whom there is no appeal, hath fully acquitted thee, and therefore no accusation can endanger thy peace. Ah! what a strong cordial would this be to all the people of God, if they would but live in the power of this glorious truth, that it is ' God that justifies them,' and that there lies no accusations in the court of heaven against them! The great reason why many poor Christians are under so many dejections, despondencies, and perplexities, is because they drink no more of this water of life, ' It is God that justifieth.' Did Christians live more upon this breast, ' It is God that justifieth,' they would be no more like Pharaoh's lean kine, but would be fat and flourishing, Gen. xli. 1-3. Did they but draw more out of this well of salvation, ' It is God that justifieth,' how would their spirits revive, and a new life rise up in them, as did in the dead child, by the prophet Elisha's applying himself to it, 2 Kings iv. 34-37. The imputed righteousness of Christ is a real, sure, and solid foundation, upon which a believer may safely build his peace, joy, and everlasting rest; yea, it will help him to glory in tribulations, and to triumph over all adversities; Rom. v. 1-3; Isa. xlv. 24, ' Surely, shall one say, in the Lord I have righteousness and strength.' That which is the greatest terror in the world to unbelievers, is the strongest ground of comfort to believers; that is the justice and wrath of God against sin. Look how it was when the angel appeared at the resurrection of our Saviour Jesus Christ, ' The keepers were affrighted, and became as dead men ;' but it was said to the women, ' Fear not ye, for ye seek Jesus of Nazareth, that was crucified,' Mat. xxviii. 4, 5: so it is much more in this case. When God's justice is powerfully manifested, the sinners of Sion and the world are afraid and terrified, Isa. xxxiii. 14. But yet, poor believers, seek for Christ who was crucified; ye need not fear anything; yea, you may be wonderfully cheered at this, and it is your greatest comfort that you have to deal with this just God, who hath already received satisfaction for your sins. It is observable that the saints triumph in the justice and judgments of God, that are most terrible to the enemies of God, in that which is the substance of the song of Moses and the Lamb, Rev. xv. 3-5: so in that, Luke xxi. 28, where the day of judgment is described, say some, and that in it, ' there shall be distress of nations, and men's hearts failing them for fear'—viz., of the justice and wrath of God. Why so? It is for ' looking after those things that are to come upon the earth; for the powers of the earth shall be shaken,' &c. ' But when these things begin to come to pass, then look up, and lift up your heads; for your redemption draweth near.' This day is the most dreadful day that ever was in the world to all the ungodly; but the just and faithful then shall be able to lift up their heads, to see all the world on a-light fire about them, and all the elements in terrible confusion. But how dare a poor creature lift up his head in such a case as this? 'They shall see the Son of man, coming in a cloud, with power and great glory.' Here is enough to comfort the poor members of Christ,—to see Christ, on whom they have believed, and who hath satisfied God's justice for them, and imputed his own righteousness to them: to see him set upon his judgment-seat, cannot but be matter of joy and rejoicing to them. Now they shall find the power of that word upon their souls: Isa. xl. 1, 'Comfort ye, comfort ye my people, saith the Lord; speak ye comfortably to Jerusalem, and say unto her that her warfare is accomplished, that her iniquity is pardoned; for she hath received at the Lord's hand double for her sins;' i.e., their conflict with the wrath of God is at an end, the punishment of their iniquity is accepted, they have received in their head and surety, Christ Jesus, double for their sins; i.e., justice hath passed upon them, in their head, Christ Jesus; and they are sure that the judge of all the earth will do right, and will not punish their sins twice. The exactness of God's justice cannot do this: Job xxxiv. 10, 'Far be it from God that he should do wickedness, and from the Almighty that he should commit iniquity;' ver. 12, 'Yea, surely God will not do wickedly, neither will the Almighty pervert judgment.' It would be high injustice in a magistrate to punish the same offence twice; and it would be high blasphemy for any to assert that ever God should be guilty of such injustice. Whilst Christians set up a righteousness of their own, and build not upon the righteousness of Christ, how unsettled are they! Rom. x. 3; how miserably are they tossed up and down, sometimes fearing and sometimes hoping, sometimes supposing themselves in a good condition, and anon seeing themselves upon the very brink of hell! but now all is quiet and serene with that soul that builds upon the righteousness of Christ; for, he being 'justified by faith, hath peace with God,' Rom. v. 1. Observe that noble description of Christ in that Isa. xxxii. 2, 'And a man,' that is, the man Christ Jesus, 'shall be as a hiding-place from the wind, and a covert from the tempest, as rivers of water in a dry place, as the shadow of a great rock in a weary land.' When a man is clothed with the righteousness of Christ, who is God-man, it is neither wind nor tempest, it is neither drought nor weariness, that can disturb the peace of his soul; for Christ and his righteousness will be a hiding-place, a covert, and rivers of water, and the shadow of a great rock unto him; for, being at perfect peace with God, he may well say with the psalmist, 'I will lay me down in peace,' Ps. iv. 6–8. The peace and comfort of an awakened sinner can never stand firm and stable, but upon the basis of a positive righteousness. When a sensible sinner casts his eye upon his own righteousness, holiness, fastings, prayers, tears, humblings, meltings, he can find no place for the sole of his foot to rest firmly upon, by reason of the spots, and blots, and blemishes, that cleaves both to his graces and duties. He knows that his prayers need pardon, and that his tears need washing in the blood of the Lamb, and that his very righteousness needs another's righteousness to secure him from condemnation. 'If thou, Lord, shouldst mark iniquity, O Lord, who shall stand?' Ps. cxxx. 3, and i. 5; that is, *rectus in curia*, 'stand,' that is, in judgment. Extremity of justice he deprecateth; he would not be dealt with in rigour and rage. The best man's life is fuller of sins than the firmament is of stars, or the furnace of sparks; and therefore who can stand in judgment, and not fall under the weight of thy just wrath, which burneth as low as hell itself? *i.e.*, none can stand. Were the faults of the best man alive but written in his forehead, he was never able to stand in judgment. When a man comes to the law for justification, it convinceth him of sin; when he pleads his innocence, that he is not so great a sinner as others are, when he pleads his righteousness, his duties, his good meanings, and his good desires, the law tells him that they are all weighed in the balance of the sanctuary, and found too light, Dan. v. 27; the law tells him that the best of his duties will not save him, and that the least of his sins will damn him; the law tells him that his own righteousnesses are as filthy rags, do but defile him, and that his best services do but witness against him; the law looks for perfect and personal obedience, and because the sinner cannot come up to it, it pronounceth him accursed, Gal. iii. 10; and though the sinner sues hard for mercy, yet the law will shew him none, no, though he seeks it carefully with tears, Heb. xii. 17. But now, when the believing sinner casts his eye upon the righteousness of Christ, he sees that righteousness to be a perfect and exact righteousness, as perfect and exact as that of the law; yea, it is the very righteousness of the law, though not performed by him, yet by his surety, 'The Lord his righteousness;' and upon this foundation he stands firm, and 'rejoices with joy unspeakable, and full of glory.' The saints of old have always placed their happiness, peace, and comfort, in their perfect and complete justification, rather than in their imperfect and incomplete sanctification, as you may see by the scriptures in the margin, with many others that are scattered up and down in the blessed book of God.[1] That text is worthy to be written in letters of gold: Isa. lxi. 10, 'I will greatly rejoice in the Lord,' saith the sound believer, 'my soul shall be joyful in my God; for he hath clothed me with the garments of salvation.' He hath imputed and given unto me the perfect holiness and obedience of my blessed Saviour, and made it mine. 'He hath covered me (all over, from top to toe) with the robe of righteousness, as a bridegroom decketh himself with ornaments, and as a bride adorneth herself with her jewels.' Though a Christian's inherent righteousness be weak and imperfect, maimed and stained, blotted and blurred, as it is, yet it affords much comfort, peace, joy, and rejoicing, as you may see by comparing the scriptures in the margin together.[2] Job was much taken with his inherent righteousness:

[1] Jer. xxiii. 6; 1 Peter i. 8; Luke vii. 48, 50; Rom. iv. 6, 8, and v. 1, 3; Isa. xxxviii. 16, 17, and xlv. 24, 25; Phil. iv. 7.

[2] 1 Chron. xxix. 9; Job xxvii. 4–6; Neh. xiii. 14, 22, 3; Isa. xxxviii. 31; Prov. xxi. 14; 2 Cor. i. 12; 1 Pet. iii. 3, 4, and v. 4.

Job xxix. 14, ‘I put on righteousness, and it clothed me ; my judgment was as a robe and a diadem unto me.’   Look, as sober, modest, comely apparel doth much set forth and adorn the body in the eyes of men, so doth inherent grace, inherent holiness, inherent righteousness, when it sparkles in the faces, lips, lives, and good works of the saints, much more beautify and adorn them in the eyes both of God and man.   Now if this garment of inherent righteousness, that hath so many spots and rents in it, will adorn us, and joy us so much, what a beauty and glory is that which the Lord our God hath put upon us, in clothing us with the robe of his Son's righteousness ; for by this means we shall recover more by Christ than we lost by Adam.   The robe of righteousness which we have gotten by Christ, the second Adam, is far more glorious than that which we were deprived of by the first Adam.   But,

7. Seventhly, Then know for your comfort, that you have *the highest reason in the world to rejoice and triumph in Christ Jesus*, Gal. vi. 14: Phil. iii. 3, ‘For we are the circumcision, which worship God in the spirit, and rejoice in Christ Jesus.’   We rejoice in the person of Christ, and we rejoice in the righteousness of Christ: 2 Cor. ii. 14, ‘Now thanks be to God, which always causeth us to triumph in Christ.’   *Deo gratias* was ever in Paul's mouth, and ever in Austin's mouth, and should be ever in a Christian's mouth, when his eye is fixed upon the righteousness of Christ.   Every believer is in a more blessed and happy estate, by means of the righteousness of Christ, than Adam was in innocency.   And that upon a threefold account ; all which are just and noble grounds for every Christian to rejoice and triumph in Christ Jesus.

(1.) That righteousness which Adam had was *uncertain, and such as it was possible for him to lose*, Gen. iii. ; yea, he did lose it, and that in a very short time, Ps. viii. 5.   God gave him power and freedom of will either to hold it or lose it ; and we know soon after, upon choice, he proved a bankrupt ; but the righteousness that we have by Jesus Christ is made more firm and sure to us.   It is that good part, that noble portion, that shall never be taken from us, as Christ said to Mary, Luke x. 42.   Adam sinned away his righteousness, but a believer cannot sin away the righteousness of Jesus Christ.   It is not possible for the elect of God so to sin as to lose Christ, or to strip themselves of that robe of righteousness which Christ hath put upon them, 1 John iii. 9 ; Rom. viii. 35, 39.   The gates of hell shall never be able to prevail against that soul that is interested in Christ, that is clothed with the righteousness of Christ, Mat. xvi. 18.   Now what higher ground of joy and triumph in Christ Jesus can there be than this?   But,

(2.) The righteousness that Adam had was *in his own keeping;* the spring and root of it was founded in himself, and that was the cause why he lost it so soon.   Adam, like the prodigal son, Luke xv. 12, 13, had all his portion, his happiness, his holiness, his blessedness, his righteousness, in his own hands, in his own keeping ; and so quickly lost stock and block, as some speak.   Oh but now, that blessed righteousness that we have by Jesus Christ, is not in our own keeping, but in our Father's keeping.   Look, as our persons, graces, and inherent righteousness are kept, as in a garrison,[1] by the power of God unto salvation, 1 Pet. i. 5; so that righteousness that we have by Jesus Christ is kept for us by the mighty power of God unto salvation. God the Father is the Lord Keeper, not only of our inherent righteousness, but also of the imputed righteousness of Jesus Christ unto us. 'My sheep shall never perish,' saith our Saviour, John x. 28, 29, 'neither shall any pluck them out of my hand; my Father that gave them me is greater than all, and none is able to pluck them out of my Father's hands.' Though the saints may meet with many shakings and tossings in their various conditions in this world, yet their final perseverance, till they come to full possession of eternal life, is certain. God is so unchangeable in his purposes of love, and so invincible in his power, that neither Satan, nor the world, nor their own flesh, shall ever be able to separate them from 'a crown of righteousness,' 2 Tim. iv. 7, 8; 'a crown of life,' Rev. ii. 10; 'a crown of glory,' 1 Pet. v. 4. The power of God is so far above all created opposition, that it will certainly maintain the saints in a state of grace. Now what a bottom and ground for rejoicing and triumphing in Christ Jesus is here! But,

(3.) Admit, that the righteousness that Adam had in his creation had been unchangeable, and that he could never have lost it; yet, it had been but *the righteousness of a man, of a mere creature;* and what a poor, low righteousness would that have been, to that high and glorious righteousness that we have by Jesus Christ, which is the righteousness of such a person as was God as well as man; yea, that righteousness that we have by Jesus Christ is a higher righteousness, and a more excellent, transcendent righteousness than that of the angels. Though the righteousness of the angels be perfect and complete in its kind, yet it is but the righteousness of mere creatures; but the righteousness of the saints, in which they stand clothed before the throne of God, is the righteousness of that person which is both God and man. Look, as the second Adam was a far more excellent person than the first Adam was: 'The first man was of the earth, earthy,' as the apostle speaks; 'the second was the Lord from heaven,' 1 Cor. xv. 47; not for the matter of his body, for he was made of a woman, but for the original and dignity of his person; whereof you may see a lively and lofty description in Heb. i. 2, 3;[2] so his righteousness also must needs be far more excellent, absolute, glorious, and every way all-sufficient to satisfy the infinite justice of God, and the exact perfection of his holy law, than ever Adam's righteousness could possibly have done. Remember, sirs, that that righteousness that we have by Jesus Christ is called the righteousness of God: 'He made him to be sin for us, who knew no sin, that we might be made the righteousness of God in him,' saith the apostle in 2 Cor. v. 21. Now that righteousness that we have by Jesus Christ, is called the righteousness of God: (1.) Because it is such a righteousness as God requires; (2.) As he approves of and accepts; (3.) As he takes infinite pleasure and delight and

---

[1] φρονουμένους. The original is a military word, and signifies safe keeping; kept as with a guard, or in a garrison, that is, well fenced with walls and works, and so is made impregnable.

[2] Look, as Adam conveys his guilt to all his children, so Christ conveys his righteousness to all his: he was *caput cum fœdere*, as well as the first Adam.

satisfaction in. The righteousness the apostle speaks of in that scripture last mentioned, is not to be understood of the essential righteousness of Christ, which is infinite, and no ways communicable to the creature, unless we will make a creature a god; but we are to understand it, of that righteousness of Christ that is imputed to believers, as their sin is imputed to him. Now what a well of salvation is here! What three noble grounds and what matchless bottoms are here for a Christian's joy and triumph in Christ Jesus, who hath put so glorious a robe as his own righteousness upon them! Ah, Christians, let not the consolations of God be small in your eyes, Job xv. 11; why take you no more comfort and delight in Christ Jesus? why rejoice you no more in him? Not to rejoice in Christ Jesus is a plain breach of that gospel command, 'Rejoice in the Lord alway,' that is, rejoice in Christ, 'and again I say, rejoice,' saith the apostle, Phil. iv. 4. He doubleth the mandate, to shew the necessity and excellency of the duty: so Phil. iii. 1, 'Finally, my brethren, rejoice in the Lord.' Now, in some respects, the breach of the commands of the gospel are greater than the breach of the commands of the moral law; for the breach of the commands of the gospel carrieth in it a contempt and light esteem of Jesus Christ, see Heb. ii. 2, 3, viii. 6, and x. 28, 29. Men's not rejoicing in Christ Jesus must flow from some dangerous humour, and base corruption or other, that highly distempers their precious souls. If all created excellencies, if all the privileges of God's people, if all the kingdoms of the earth, and the glory of them, were to be presented at one view, they would all appear as nothing and emptiness, in comparison of the excellency and fulness that is to be found in Christ Jesus: and therefore the greater is their sin, who rejoice not in Christ Jesus. Do you ask me where be my jewels? my jewels are my husband and his triumphs, said Phocion's wife.[1] Do you ask me where be my ornaments? my ornaments are my two sons brought up in virtue and learning, said the mother of the Gracchi. Do you ask me where be my treasures? my treasures are my friends, said Constantius, the father of Constantine. But now, if you ask a child of God, when he is not clouded, tempted, deserted, dejected, where be his jewels, his treasures, his ornaments, his comfort, his joy, his delight; he will answer with that martyr, none but Christ, none but Christ. Oh! none to Christ, none to Christ! 'Christ is all in all unto me,' Col. iii. 11. *Æterna erit exultatio, quæ bono lætatur æterno:* That joy lasts for ever, whose object remains for ever. Such an object is our Lord Jesus Christ, and therefore the joy of the saints should still be exercised upon our Lord Jesus Christ. Shall the worldling rejoice in his barns, the rich man in his bags, the ambitious man in his honours, the voluptuous man in his pleasures, and the wanton in his Delilahs; and shall not a Christian rejoice in Christ Jesus, and in that robe of righteousness, and in those garments of salvation, with which Christ hath covered him? Isa. lxi. 10. The joy of that Christian that keeps a fixed eye upon Christ and his righteousness cannot be expressed, it cannot be painted. No man can paint the sweetness of the honeycomb, nor the sweetness of a cluster of Canaan, nor the fragrancy of the rose of Sharon. As the being of

[1] Plutarch in Phocione.

things cannot be painted, so the sweetness of things cannot be painted. The joy of the Holy Ghost cannot be painted, nor that joy that arises in a Christian's heart, who keeps up a daily converse with Christ and his righteousness, cannot be painted, it cannot be expressed. Who can look upon the glorious body of our Lord Jesus Christ, and seriously consider, that even every vein of that blessed body did bleed to bring him to heaven, and not rejoice in Christ Jesus? who can look upon the glorious righteousness of Christ, imputed to him, and not be filled with an exuberancy of spiritual joy in God his Saviour? There is not the pardon of the least sin, nor the least degree of grace, nor the least drop of mercy, but cost Christ dear, for he must die, and he must be made a sacrifice, and he must be accursed, that pardon may be thine, and grace thine, and mercy thine: and oh, how should this draw out thy heart to rejoice and triumph in Christ Jesus! The work of redemption sets both angels and saints a-rejoicing and triumphing in Christ Jesus, Rev. v. 11-14; and why not we, why not we also, who have received infinite more benefit by the work of redemption, than ever the angels have? Rev. i. 5, 6, and v. 8-10. A beautiful face is at all times pleasing to the eye; but then especially, when there is joy manifested in the countenance. Joy in the face puts a new beauty upon a person, and makes that which before was beautiful, to be exceeding beautiful, it puts a lustre upon beauty; so does holy joy and rejoicing in Christ Jesus, put, as it were, a new beauty and lustre upon Christ. Though the Romans punished one that feasted, and looked out at a window with a garland on his head, in the second Punic war;[1] yet, you may be sure, that God will never punish you for rejoicing and triumphing in Christ Jesus, let the times be never so sad or bad, in respect of war, blood, or misery. But,

8. Eighthly, The imputed righteousness of Christ may serve *to comfort, support, and bear up the hearts of the people of God, from fainting and sinking under the sense of the weakness and imperfection of their inherent righteousness.* The church of old have lamentingly said, 'We are all as an unclean thing, and all our righteousness is as filthy rags,' Isa. lxiv. 6. When a Christian keeps a serious eye upon the spots, blots, blemishes, infirmities, and follies, that cleaves to his inherent righteousness, fears and tremblings arise, to the saddening and sinking of his soul; but when he casts a fixed eye upon the righteousness of Christ imputed to him, then his comforts revive, and his heart bears up; for, though he hath no righteousness of his own, by which his soul may stand accepted before God, yet he hath God's righteousness, which infinitely transcends his own, and such as, in God's account, goes for his, as if he had exactly fulfilled the righteousness which the law requires; according to that of the apostle, Rom. ix. 30, 'What shall we say then? the Gentiles which followed not after righteousness, have attained to righteousness, even the righteousness which is of faith.' Faith wraps itself in the righteousness of Christ, and so justifieth us. The Gentiles, sought righteousness, not in themselves but in Christ, which they apprehending by faith, were by it justified in the sight of God; and the Jews, seeking it in themselves, and thinking, by the goodness of their own works, to attain to the righteousness

[1] Pliny, i. c. 7.

of the law, missed of it; it being in no man's power perfectly to fulfil the same, only Christ hath exactly fulfilled it for all that by faith close savingly with him. O sirs! none can be justified in the sight of God, by a righteousness of their own making: but whosoever will be justified, must be justified by the righteousness of Christ through faith, Rom. iii. 20, 28, and x. 3; Gal. ii. 16; Tit. iii. 5. The Gentiles by faith attain the righteousness of the law, therefore the righteousness of the law and of faith are all one; viz., in respect of matter and form; the difference is only in the worker. The law requires it to be done by ourselves; the gospel mitigates the rigour of the law, and offers the righteousness of Christ, who performed the law, even to a hair's-breadth. The right way to righteousness for justification is by Christ, who is the way, the door, the truth, and the life. Because we want a righteousness of our own, God hath assigned us the righteousness of Christ, which is infinitely better than our own, yea, better than our very lives—may I not say, yea, better than our very souls? 'The branch,' Christ Jesus is called, 'Jehovah Tsidkenu, the Lord our righteousness:' Jer. xxiii. 6, 'And this is his name whereby he shall be called, THE LORD OUR RIGHTEOUSNESS.' Where note, *first*, to be called by this name is to be so really, for Christ is never called what he is not; and so he is to the same purpose elsewhere called 'Immanuel, God with us,' Mat. i. 23; that is, he shall be so indeed, 'God with us,' so here he shall be called, 'the Lord our righteousness;' that is, he shall be so indeed. *Secondly*, observe this is one of his glorious names; that is, one of his attributes, which he accounts his excellency and his glory. Now all the attributes of Christ are unchangeable, so that he can as easily change his nature as his name. Now remember that this imputed righteousness of Christ procures acceptance for our inherent righteousness. When a sincere Christian casts his eye upon the weaknesses, infirmities, and imperfections that daily attend his best services, he sighs and mourns; but if he looks upward to the imputed righteousness of Jesus Christ, that shall bring forth his infirm, weak, and sinful performances perfect, spotless, and sinless, and approved according to the tenor of the gospel, so that they become spiritual sacrifices, he cannot but rejoice, 1 Pet. ii. 5. For as there is an imputation of righteousness to the persons of believers, so there is also an imputation to their services and actions. As the fact of Phinehas was imputed to him for righteousness, Ps. cvi. 31, so the imperfect good works that are done by believers are accounted righteousness, or, as Calvin speaks, 'are accounted for righteousness, they being dipped in the blood of Christ,' *tincta sanguine Christi, i.e.*, they are accounted righteous actions; and so sincere Christians shall be judged according to their good works, though not saved for them, Rev. xi. 18, and xx. 12; Mat. xxv. 34-37. And it is observable, in that famous process of the last judgment, that the supreme judge makes mention of the bounty and liberality of the saints, and so bestows the crown of life and the eternal inheritance upon them; so that, though the Lord's faithful ones have eminent cause to be humbled and afflicted for the many weaknesses that cleaves to their best duties, yet, on the other hand, they have wonderful cause to rejoice and triumph that they are made perfect through Jesus Christ, and that the Lord looks at them, through the righteousness of Christ, as fruits of his own Spirit, Heb. xiii. 20, 21 ; 1 Cor. vi. 11. The Sun of Righteousness hath healing enough in his wings for all our spiritual maladies, Mal. iv. 2. The saints' prayers, being perfumed with Christ's odours, are highly accepted in heaven, Rev. viii. 3, 4. Upon this bottom of imputed righteousness believers may have exceeding strong consolation, and good hope through grace, that both their persons and services do find singular acceptation with God, as having no spot or blemish at all in them. Surely righteousness imputed must be the top of our happiness and blessedness, Rom. iv. 5, 6. But,

9. Ninthly and lastly, Know for your comfort, that imputed righteousness will give you *the greatest boldness before God's judgment-seat*. There is an absolute and indispensable necessity of a perfect righteousness wherewith to appear before God. The holiness of God's nature, the righteousness of his government, the severity of his law, and the terror of wrath, calls aloud upon the sinner for a complete righteousness, without which there is no standing in judgment, Ps. i. 5. That righteousness only is able to justify us before God which is perfect, and that hath no defect nor blemish in it, such as may abide the trial before his judgment-seat, such as may fitly satisfy his justice, and make our peace with him; and consequently, such as whereby the law of God is fulfilled. Therefore it is called the righteousness of God; such a righteousness as he requires, as will stand before him, and satisfy his justice, Rom. x. 3. So the apostle saith, ' The righteousness of the law must be fulfilled in us,' Rom. viii. 4. Now there is no other righteousness under heaven whereby the law of God was ever perfectly fulfilled, but by the righteousness of Christ alone. No righteousness below the righteousness of Christ was ever able to abide the trial at God's judgment-seat, and fully to satisfy his justice, and pacify his wrath. A gracious soul triumphs more in the righteousness of Christ imputed, than he would have done if he could have stood in the righteousness in which he was created. This is the crowning comfort to a sensible and understanding soul, that he stands righteous before a judgment-seat, in that full, exact, perfect, complete, matchless, spotless, peerless, and most acceptable righteousness of Christ imputed to him. The righteousness of Christ is therefore called the righteousness of God, because it is it which God hath assigned, and which God doth accept for us in our justification, and for and in which he doth acquit and pronounce us righteous before his seat of justice, Rom. iii. 21, 22, and x. 3 ; Phil. iii. 9. There is an indispensable necessity that lies upon the sinner to have such a righteousness to his justification as may render his appearance safe and comfortable in the day of judgment. Now there is no righteousness that can abide that day of fiery trial, but the righteousness of Christ imputed to us. Paul, that great apostle, had as fair and as full a certificate to shew for a legal justification as any person under heaven had, Phil. iii. 4–6; Acts xxiii. 6; 2 Cor. xi. 22; but yet he durst not stand by that righteousness, he durst not plead that righteousness, he durst not appear in that righteousness before the dreadful judgment-seat. But oh, how earnest, how importunate is he, that he may be found, in that great day of the Lord, in the mediatory righteousness of Christ, and not in his own personal righteous-

ness, which he looked upon as filthy rags, as dross, dung, dogs' meat, Phil. iii. 9, 10. The great thing that he most strongly insists upon is, that he might be clothed with the robe of Christ's righteousness; for then he knew that the law could not say black was his eye, and that the judge upon the bench would pronounce him righteous, and bid him enter into the joy of his Lord, Mat. xxv. 21, 23, 24; a joy too great to enter into him, and therefore he must enter into that. When the match is made up between Christ and the soul, that soul bears her sovereign's name. The spouse of the first Adam and her husband had both one name, ' God called their name Adam, in the day that he made them,' Gen. v. 2; so the spouse of the second Adam, in the change of her condition, from a single to a married estate with Christ the Lamb, had a change of her name. The head is called, ' the Lord our righteousness,' Jer. xxiii. 6; and so is the church: Jer. xxxiii. 16, ' In those days shall Judah be saved, and Jerusalem shall dwell safely: and this is the name wherewith she shall be called, the Lord our righteousness.' Here is a sameness of name.[1] As Christ is called, ' the Lord our righteousness,' so his spouse is called, ' the Lord our righteousness.' Oh, happy transnomination! Christ's bride being one with himself, and having his righteousness imputed to her, is called, ' the Lord our righteousness;' and therefore they may, with the greatest cheerfulness and boldness, bear up, in the great day of account, who have the perfect righteousness of Christ imputed to them, especially if you consider, (1.) That this righteousness is of infinite value and worth; (2.) That it is an everlasting righteousness, a righteousness that can never be lost, Dan. ix. 24; (3.) That it is an unchangeable righteousness. Though times change, and men change, and friends change, and providences change, and the moon change, yet the Sun of Righteousness never changes, 'in him is no variableness, neither shadow of turning,' Mal. iv. 2; James i. 17; (4.) That it is a complete and unspotted righteousness, an unblamable righteousness, and unblemished righteousness; and therefore God can neither in justice except or object against it. In this righteousness the believer lives, in this righteousness the believer dies; and in this righteousness believers shall arise, and appear before the judgment-seat of Christ, to the deep admiration of all the elect angels, and to the transcendent terror and horror of all reprobates, and to the matchless joy and triumph of all on Christ's right hand, who shall then shout and sing, Isa. lxi. 10, ' I will greatly rejoice in the Lord, my soul shall be joyful in my God; for he hath clothed me with the garments of salvation, he hath covered me with the robe of righteousness, as a bridegroom decketh himself with ornaments, and as a bride adorneth herself with jewels.' Oh, how will Christ, in this great day, be admired and glorified in all his saints, 2 Thes. i. 10, when every saint, wrapped up in this fine linen, in this white robe of Christ's righteousness, shall shine more gloriously than ten thousand suns! In the great day of the Lord, when the saints shall stand before the

---

[1] Christ and Christians are namesakes. *Caput et corpus, unus est Christus.—Aug.* The head is called Christ, and the members are called Christ, 1 Cor. xii. 12. Christ is called Solomon, Cant. i. 1, and iii. 11, in Hebrew, *Shelomah* of peace, and the church is called Shulamite, by her bridegroom's name, Cant. vi. 13.

tribunal of God, clothed in the perfect righteousness of Jesus Christ, they shall then stand, *rectus in curiâ ;* they shall then be pronounced righteous, even in the court of divine justice, which sentence will fill their souls with comfort, and the souls of sinners with astonishment, Rev. xx. 12, and xii. 10. Suppose we saw the believing sinner, holding up his hand at God's bar ; the books opened, the accuser of the brethren present, the witnesses ready, and the judge on the bench thus bespeaking the sinner at the bar, Rom. vii. 12, 14, 16, and Gal. iii. 10. O sinner, sinner, thou standest here indicted before me, for many millions of sins of commission, and for many millions of sins of omission ; thou hast broken my holy, just, and righteous laws beyond all human conception or expression, and hereof thou art proved guilty; what hast thou now to say for thyself why thou shouldst not be eternally cast? Upon this, the sinner pleads guilty ; but withal he earnestly desires that he may have time and liberty to plead for himself, and to offer his reasons why that dreadful sentence, Go, you cursed, &c., Mat. xxv. 41, should not be passed upon him. The liberty desired being granted by the judge, the sinner pleads that his surety, Jesus Christ, hath, by his blood and sufferings, given full and complete satisfaction to divine justice, and that he hath paid down upon the nail the whole debt at once, and that it can never stand with the holiness and unspotted justice of God to demand satisfaction twice, Heb. x. 10, 14. If the judge shall further object, Ay, but sinner, sinner, the law requireth an exact and perfect righteousness in the personal fulfilling of it; now, sinner, where is thy exact and perfect righteousness? Gal. iii. 10 ; Isa. xlv. 24. Upon which the believing sinner very readily, cheerfully, humbly, and boldly replies, My righteousness is upon the bench, ' in the Lord have I righteousness.' Christ, my surety, hath fulfilled the law on my behalf. The law's righteousness consists in two things, (1.) In its requiring perfect conformity to its commands ; (2.) In its demanding satisfaction, or the undergoing of its penalty, upon the violation of it. Now Christ, by his active and passive obedience, hath fulfilled the law for righteousness, and this active and passive obedience of Jesus Christ is imputed to me. His obeying the law to the full, his perfect conforming to its commands, his doing, as well as his dying obedience, is by grace made over and reckoned to me, in order to my justification and salvation ; and this is my plea, by which I will stand before the judge of all the world. Upon this the sinner's plea is accepted as good in law, and accordingly he is pronounced righteous ; and goes away, glorying and rejoicing, triumphing and shouting it out, Righteous, righteous, righteous, righteous ; ' In the Lord shall all the seed of Israel be justified, and shall glory,' Isa. xlv. 25. And thus you see that there are nine springs of strong consolation that flow into your souls, through the imputation of Christ's righteousness unto you. But,

VI. The sixth plea that a believer may form up as to the ten scriptures in the margin[1] that refer to the great day of account, or to a man's particular account, may be drawn from the consideration

[1] Eccles. xi. 9, and xii. 14; Mat. xii. 14, and xviii. 23; Luke xvi. 3; Rom. xiv. 10; 2 Cor. v. 10; Heb. ix. 27, and xii. 17; 1 Pet. iv. 5.

of Christ as a common person, a representative head, one that represents another man's person, and acts the part of another, according to the appointment of the law, the acceptation of the judge; so that what is done by him, the person is said to do whose person he doth represent. And so was Adam a common person, and that by an act of God's sovereignty appointing him, in making a covenant with him so to be, and he did represent all mankind, Rom. v. 15-19. And hence it comes to pass that his sin is imputed unto us, and made ours;[1] so in our law an attorney appears in the behalf of his client, and so Christ is said to be gone to heaven as our attorney, to appear in the presence of God for us, Heb. ix. 24. ἐμφανισθῆναι, To appear as a lawyer appears for his client, opens the cause, pleads the cause, and carries it. The word *appear* is *verbum forense*, an expression borrowed from the custom of human courts; for in them, when the plaintiff or defendant is called, their attorney appeareth in their behalf; so 1 John ii. 1. You know that the Levitical priest was wont to appear before God in the people's name. Now he was but a figure; in Christ is the solid truth, and full effect of the figure. Or as taking possession, livery, and seizing[2] by an attorney is all one as if done by the person himself who is represented, and is valid; so the Lord Jesus, he is a common person by an act of God's sovereignty, representing the persons of all the elect of God, being designed and appointed by God to be a second Adam. And as the first Adam did represent all in him, so the second Adam does represent all in him also; and therefore as judgment came upon all in the first Adam, so righteousness comes upon all in the second Adam. We all transgressed the royal law in Adam, we were all in Adam's loins; what he was, we were; what he did, we did. Although we did not in our own persons either talk with the serpent, or put forth our hands to take the fruit, yet we did eat the forbidden fruit as well as he, and so broke the holy law, and turned aside in him; for he was not a single person, standing for himself alone, but a public person, standing in the room of all mankind; therefore his sin, being not merely the sin of his person, but of the whole nature of man, is justly imputed to us all. If Adam had stood fast in his uprightness, in his primitive purity, glory and excellency, we should all have shared in his happiness and blessedness, Eccles. vii. 29; but he falling and forfeiting all, we must all share with him in his loss and misery. Ponder upon Rom. v. 12, ' In whom all have sinned.' As the murrain infects the whole flock, so sin and the curse seizeth upon all the whole world, as well as upon Adam and Eve. And ver. 19, ' By one man's disobedience many are made sinners.' ' Many' is here put for ' all,' as ' all' elsewhere is put for ' many,' 1 Tim. ii. 3. All sinners are tainted with Adam's guilt and filth. Adam was the head, all his posterity the members. If the head plot and practise treason against the state, is not this judged the act of the whole body? He was the tree, we the branches; when the tree falls, all the branches fall with it. When Christ died on the cross, he did stand in our room, and

---

[1] We were all in Adam, as the whole country [county] is in a parliament-man; and although we chose not, yet God chose for us.

[2] ' Livery'=delivery ; ' seizing'=taking possession. Law terms in use still.—G.

place, and stead; for he did lay down his life for us as a ransom. Now when one dies for another in way of ransom, he does not only die for the benefit and profit of the ransomed, but in the place, and room, and stead of the ransomed; and thus Christ died for us, as himself testifies: ' The son of man came to give himself a ransom for many,' Mark x. 45. λύτρον ἀντὶ πολλῶν. Christ rose as a common person, representing all his elect; and Christ was sanctified as a common person, representing all his elect; and Christ was justified as a common person, representing all his elect. Look, as we were condemned in Adam, as he was a common person, so we are justified by Christ, as in a common person also; so that every believer may well look upon himself as acquitted, in his justification, from the guilt of his sins, they being laid upon the head of his surety, Heb. ix. 28. It is a very great part of a Christian's wisdom to be often looking upon Christ as a representative-head, as one in whom he died, in whom he rose, in whom he is sanctified, and in whom he is justified, Eph. ii. 6. How would such a daily eyeing of Christ scatter a Christian's fears, arm him against temptations, support him under afflictions, weaken his sins, strengthen his graces, cheer his soul, and mend his life!

It is very observable, that in the Levitical expiatory sacrifices there was the substitution of them in the place and stead of the offenders themselves. The people's sin, and the punishment due to them thereupon, was laid upon the poor beasts that died for them. I might multiply scriptures to evidence this, but I shall only hint at one or two plain, pregnant texts to clear it. Take that, Lev. xvii. 11, ' For the life of the flesh is in the blood; and I have given it to you upon the altar, to make an atonement for your souls: for it is the blood that maketh atonement for the soul.'[1] Mark here, the blood is to make atonement for the souls of the people of Israel—that is, in the room and stead of their souls, and accordingly it did make atonement for their souls; so that in the blood sacrificed, which was a type of the blood of Christ, there was soul for soul, life for life; the soul and life of the sacrifice for the precious soul and life of the sinner. Now here you see substitution of the one in the room of the other. The transferring of the guilt and punishment of the people's sins over to their sacrifices in those days, was the reason why the sacrifices were said to bear the iniquities of the people, Lev. xvi. 22, and x. 17, &c. And it is observable that at the great expiation Aaron was to lay both his hands upon the head of the live goat, and to confess over him all the sins of the children of Israel, &c., Lev. xvi. 21. By this ceremony of imposition of hands, is signified the transferring of their sins upon the goat, herein to type out Christ, upon whom God ' did lay the iniquity of us all,' Isa. liii. 6. Certainly the main thing that is held forth by this rite,—viz., Aaron's laying both his hands upon the head of the live goat, is the translation of the sinner's guilt to the sacrifice, and the substitution of it in his stead. Typically, the very sins of the people were imposed upon the goat, who herein was a type of Christ which did himself bear our sins. Yea, the Hebrews [Maimonides]

---

[1] Justin Martyr observes the great mercy of God to mankind in that, *loco hominis*, instead of man, he caused beasts to be sacrificed.

themselves hold that the scapegoat made atonement for all their sins, lighter and greater, presumptuously and ignorantly committed. Certainly the scapegoat.was a most lively type of our blessed Saviour— (1.) In that ' the Lord laid upon him the iniquity of us all,' as the sins of Israel were laid upon the head of the goat. (2.) As the goat was carried away, so Christ was ' cut off from the land of the living, his life was taken from off the earth,' Isa. iv. 3, and liii. 8. (3.) As this goat was not killed, so ' Christ through the eternal Spirit offered up himself,' whereby he was made alive after death, Acts ix. 33; Heb. ix. 14; 1 Pet. iii. 18. Though Christ Jesus died for our sins according to his humanity, yet death could not detain him nor overcome him, nor keep him prisoner, Hosea xiii. 14, but, by virtue of his impassible deity, he rises again and triumphs over death and the grave, and over principalities and powers, Col. ii. 15. (4.) As this goat went into an inhabitable place,[1] so Christ went into heaven—' whither I go ye cannot come,' John xiii. 33. Christ speaks this not to exclude his disciples out of heaven, but only to shew that their entrance was put off for a time, ver. 36. Saints must not expect to go to heaven and rest with Christ till they have ' fought the good fight of faith, finished their course, run their race,' and ' served their generation.' [2] Christ's own children, by all their studies, prayers, tears, and endeavours, cannot get to heaven unless Christ come and fetches them thither. Christ's own servants cannot get to heaven presently nor of themselves, no more than the Jews could do. Now if you please to cast your eye upon the Lord Jesus, you will find an exact correspondency between the type and the antitype, the one fully answering to the other. Did they carry substitution in them? that eminently was in Christ. He indeed substituted himself in the sinner's room; he took our guilt upon him, and put himself in our place, and died in our stead; he died that we might not die. Whatever we should have undergone, that he underwent in his body and soul; he did bear as our $\dot{a}\nu\tau\acute{\iota}$ $\psi\nu\chi o\varsigma$ all the punishments and torments that were due to us. Christ's suffering, dying, satisfying in our stead, is the great article of a Christian's faith, and the main prop and foundation of the believer's hope. It is bottomed, as an eternal and unmovable truth, upon the sure basis of the blessed word. Substitution, in the case of the old sacrifices, is not so evidently held forth in the law, but substitution with respect to Christ and his sacrifice is more evidently set forth in the gospel. Ponder seriously upon these texts: Rom. v. 6, ' For when we were yet without strength, in due time Christ died for the ungodly;' ver. 8, ' For God commendeth his love towards us, in that while we were yet sinners Christ died for us.' Herein God lays naked to us the tenderest bowels of his Fatherly compassions, as in an anatomy.[3] There was an absolute necessity of Christ's dying for sinners, for, (1.) God's justice had decreed it; (2.) His word had foretold it;

---

[1] The Elizabethan writers used *inhabitable* as the opposite of *habitable.*—G.

[2] 2 Tim. iv. 7, 8; Heb. xii. 1; 1 Cor. ix. 24; Acts xiii. 36; John xiv. 1–3.

[3] This shews us the greatness of man's sin and of Christ's love, of Satan's malice and of God's justice; and it shews us the madness and blindness of the popish religion, which tells us that some sins are so light and venial as that the sprinkling of holy water and ashes will purge them away.

(3.) The sacrifices in the law had prefigured it; (4.) The foulness of man's sin had deserved it; (5.) The redemption of man called for it; (6.) The glory of God was greatly exalted by it. So 1 Pet. iii. 18, 'For Christ also hath once suffered for sins, the just for the unjust.' To see Christ the just suffer in the stead of the unjust, is the wonderment of angels and the torment of devils: 1 Pet. iv. 1, 'Forasmuch then as Christ hath suffered for us in the flesh,' &c., that is, in the human nature, for the expiation and taking away of our sins; 1 Pet. ii. 21, 'Because Christ also suffered for us;' John x. 11, 'I lay down my life for the sheep.' This good shepherd lays down life for life, his own dear life for the life of his sheep: John xi. 50, 'Nor consider that it is expedient for us, that one man should die for the people, and that the whole nation perish not,' that is, rather than the whole nation should perish. Caiaphas took it for granted, that either Christ or their nation must perish, and, as he foolishly thought, that of two evils he designed the least to be chosen, that is, that Christ should rather perish than their nation; but God so guided his tongue that he unwittingly, by the powerful instinct of the Spirit, prophesied of the fruit of Christ's death for the reconciliation and salvation of the elect of God. Heb. ii. 9, 'That he by the grace of God should taste death for every man,' ὑπὲρ παντὸς, or for every creature. Who all these be, the context sheweth—(1.) Sons that must be led unto glory, ver. 10; (2.) Christ's brethren, ver. 11; (3.) Such children as are given by God unto Christ, ver. 13. In all which scriptures the preposition ὑπὲρ is used, which most commonly notes substitution, the doing or suffering of something by one in the stead and place of others, and so it is all along here to be taken. But there is another preposition, ἀντὶ, that proves the thing I am upon undeniably: Mat. xx. 28, 'Even as the Son of man came not to be ministered unto, but to minister, and to give his life a ransom for many,' λύτρον ἀντὶ πολλῶν. Λύτρον signifies a redemptory price, a valuable rate; for it was the blood of God wherewith the church was purchased, Acts xx. 28: 1 Tim. ii. 6, 'Who gave himself a ransom,' ἀντίλυτρον, 'for all.' The Greek word signifies a counterprice, such as we could never have paid, but must have remained everlasting prisoners to the wrath and justice of God. O sirs! Christ did not barely deliver poor captive souls, but he delivered them in the way of a ransom, which ransom he paid down upon the nail. When their ransom was ten thousand talents, and they had not one farthing to lay down, Christ stands up in their room and pays the whole ransom, Mat. xviii. 24. Every one knows that ἀντὶ, in composition, signifies but two things, either opposition and contrariety, or substitution and commutation, Mat. v. 38; so that the matter will thus issue, that either we must carry it thus, that Christ 'gave himself a ransom against sinners,' than which nothing can be more absurd and false, or else thus, that he 'gave himself a ransom in the room and stead of sinners,' which is as true as truth itself, John ii. 28, 29. Certainly no head can invent, no heart can conceive, nor no tongue can express more clear, plain, pregnant, and apposite words and phrases for the setting forth of Christ's substitution, than is to be found in that golden chapter of Isaiah liii.

In this chapter, as in a holy armoury, we may find, had I time to go through it, many pointed daggers, and two-edged swords, and shields of brass, to arm us against the corrupt notions and opinions of the blinded and deluded Socinians, who fight with all their might against the doctrine of Christ's substitution. Ver. 4, 'Surely he hath borne our griefs, and carried our sorrows,' &c.; ver. 5, 'The chastisement of our peace was upon him, and with his stripes we are healed;' ver. 6, 'The Lord hath laid on him the iniquities of us all;' or, 'the Lord hath made the iniquity of us all to meet on him;' ver. 7, 'He was oppressed and he was afflicted,' &c.; or, as the words are rendered by some, 'It was exacted and he answered;' ver. 8, 'For the transgression of my people he was stricken;' ver. 11, 'For he shall bear their iniquities;' ver. 12, 'And he bare the sin of many.' All men of worth and weight conclude that all this is spoken of the Lord Jesus Christ. Now what more clear and evident proofs can there be of Christ's susception, of the sinner's guilt, and of his bearing the punishment due for it? The priests of old, you know, are said to bear the iniquity of the people: Lev. x. 17, 'God hath given it you to bear the iniquity of the congregation, to make atonement for them before the Lord.' The sinner bears his iniquity subjectively, the priest typically, and the Lord Christ really: Exod. xxviii. 38, 'That Aaron may bear the iniquity of the holy things.' Herein the high priest was a type of Christ; answerable to which the prophet Isaiah tells us that Christ, our high priest, had the iniquities of all believers laid upon him, and that he bare them in his own person, Heb. iv. 14, 15; so the apostle, Heb. ix. 28, 'So Christ was once offered to bear the sins of many,' &c., ἀνενεγκεῖν ἁμαρτίας. It is an allusion to the priests who carried up the sacrifice, and with it the sins of the people, to the altar. Christ our priest did carry up the sins of his people upon the cross, and there made satisfaction for them, in their room or stead, by the sacrifice of himself; and that scripture is more worth than the Indies—viz., 1 Pet. ii. 24, 'Who his own self bare our sins in his own body on the tree,' ἀνήνεγκεν, 'he bare them aloft'—viz., when he climbed up his cross, and nailed them thereunto, Col. ii. 13–15. Christ in the human nature, when he was upon the cross, did suffer all the punishments and torments that were due to our sins; he cancelled all bonds, annihilated the curse; in which respects he is said 'to bear our sins in his own body on the tree.' But to prevent prolixity I shall produce no more scriptures, though many more might have been produced, to prove Christ a common person, a representative head of all his elect; and that he did really substitute himself in their room, and took upon himself their guilt, and put himself in their place, and did undergo whatever they should have undergone.

Now from all these considerations, a child of God may form up this sixth plea as to the ten scriptures in the margin,[1] that refer to the great day of account, or to a man's particular account. *O blessed God, Jesus Christ was a common person, a representative head: I am to be considered in him, who is my surety, and therefore he is bound to pay all my debts: and as he is a common person and stood in my*

---

[1] Eccles. xi. 9, and xii. 14; Mat. xii. 14, and xviii. 23; Luke xvi. 3; Rom. iv. 10; 2 Cor. v. 10; Heb. ix. 27, and xiii. 17, and 1 Pet. iv. 5.

stead, so the satisfaction that is made unto thy justice by him, is in law to be accounted mine, as really as if my attorney should pay a debt for me: and therefore, I must rest satisfied that the debt is paid, and in law shall never be exacted of me ; though it was not paid by myself in person, but by another who did personate me in that act, and did it for me and in my behalf. Christ was a common person, personating as a second Adam, the first Adam and all his posterity; offering the same nature for sin, which fell by sin from the pattern of perfection, God himself. ' By man came death, and by man came the resurrection from the dead,' 1 Cor. xv. 21 ; man for man, person for person, nature for nature, and name for name. There are two roots out of which life and death springs. (1.) As all that die receive their death-wounds by the disobedience of the first Adam; so all that live receive life from the obedience of the second Adam. (2.) As all die who are the sons of the first Adam by natural generation ; so all live, who are the sons of the second Adam through spiritual regeneration. O holy and blessed God, thou hast set up Jesus Christ as a common person, as the representative head of all thy elect, and I am to be considered in that common head ; and all that he has done as my head, and in my stead and room, is to be reckoned to me, as if I had done it in my own person, and by this plea I will stand, rejoice, and triumph. Upon this God accepts of the plea, as sound and good, and saith to him that pleads it, ' enter thou into the joy of thy Lord,' Mat. xxv. 21.

VII. The seventh plea that a believer may form up, as to the ten scriptures formerly cited, that refer to the great day of account, or to a man's particular account, may be drawn from the consideration of Christ's suretyship. Christ is called a surety: Heb. vii. 22, ' By so much was Jesus made a surety of a better testament.' The Greek word Ἔγγυος, *sponsor, fidejussor, præs,* a surety, a pledger, is very significative, being derived, as some think, from γυιον, an hand, as it were ἐν γυιοῖς, in hands, because the security or pledge is given in hand.[1] A surety is properly one that willingly promiseth and undertakes to pay and discharge the debt, if the debtor fail, and be not able to make satisfaction himself. Thus Paul willingly and spontaneously, from the love he had to his new convert Onesimus, promised and undertook to make satisfaction to Philemon, for any wrong that Onesimus had done him: Philem. 18, 19, ' If he hath wronged thee, or oweth thee aught, put it upon mine account; I Paul have written it with mine own hand, I will repay it,' *i.e.,* account Onesimus his debt to Paul, and Paul's satisfaction or payment to Onesimus ; which answers the double imputation in point of justification, that is, of our sins or debts to Christ, and of Christ's satisfaction to us. Consider Christ as a surety, and so he hath fully paid all our debts, and set us perfectly free for ever. A surety is one that enters into bond, and engages himself for the debt of another ; and so Christ is become our surety. Therefore he was bound by our bond, and engageth himself for the

[1] Our English translation hath it, ' Of a better testament,' but not so fitly, because properly, a testament, neither useth nor needeth to have a surety, as a covenant doth. Beza therefore justly blameth both Erasmus and the Vulgar translation, for rendering it ' testament;' for that a surety is not added in testaments ; and it should be added, how can the same be both a testator and a surety ! So that this word ' surety,' hath reference properly to a covenant, and not to a testament.

debt of another. For our debt he was made under the law, and so as a sacrifice, he stood in the stead of a sinner, and the sacrifice was to be offered for the man; and so some expound that place, ' He was made sin for us,' 2 Cor. v. 21, that is, a sin-offering; therefore he doth take our sins upon him as his own, Isa. liii.; and so the Lord doth impute them and lay them upon him as his own: ver. 6, ' He did make to meet upon him the iniquities of us all.' The original word here used comes from פגע pagang, which word in its native propriety intends a kind of force or violence, *impetum fecit*, they met with all their violence upon him, and therefore 'he was made sin for us,' that is, as a surety in our stead, ' he did bear our sins in his body upon the tree; he was delivered for our transgressions.' Our surety hath paid all our debts. ' The chastisement of our peace was upon him, and it pleased the Father to bruise him,' Isa. liii. 5, 10. The original word signifies to break him to pieces as in a mortar. By the great things that our surety has done for us, and the great things that he hath suffered for us, he hath given most perfect and complete satisfaction both to his Father's law, and to his Father's justice; and this pleased the Father. Weigh well that, Col. ii. 14, ' He blotted out the handwriting of ordinances that was against us, that was contrary unto us, and took it out of the way, nailing it to his cross.'[1] Christ hath crossed out the black lines of our sin with the red lines of his own blood. The Greek word χειρόγραφον, i.e., the handwriting, some do take here for a writing written with God's own hand in tables of stone, as the law of the ten commandments were, Exod. xxxiv. 1; and this is by them understood of the moral law, or of the ten commandments, which are said to be against us, in respect of their strict requiring of perfect obedience, or in default thereof, by reason of its curse, which Christ as our surety hath borne for us on the cross, and delivered us from it, Gal. iii. 10, 13. But others by this handwriting do understand the law of the ceremonies of the Old Testament. In the general, it was something that God had against us; to shew or convince, or prove, that we had sinned against him, and were his debtors. I suppose that this handwriting was principally the moral law, obliging us unto perfect obedience, and condemning us for the defect of the same, and likewise those ceremonial rites, which, as Beza observes, were a kind of public confession of our debts. Now these were against, and contrary unto us, inasmuch as they did argue us guilty of sin and condemnation, which the moral law threatened and sentenced, &c., but saith the apostle, ' Christ hath blotted out the handwriting, and hath taken it out of the way and nailed it to his cross,' that is, Jesus Christ hath not only abrogated the ceremonial law, but also the damnatory power of the moral law, as our surety, by performing an act of obedience which the law did require, and by undergoing the punishment which the law did exact from the transgressors of it; and so Christ doing and suffering, what we were bound to do and to suffer, he did thereby blot out the handwriting, and cancelled it; and therefore we may safely con-

[1] Some by the handwriting do understand the covenant of God with Adam. Beza and Calvin do understand it of the ceremonial law. But, saith Chrysostom, 'It is meant not only of the ceremonial law, but also of the moral law, as a covenant of works.' Œcumenius, Jerome, and others, are of the same opinion. But, saith Zanchy, ' This is spoken to comfort the Colossians, who were never under the ceremonial law.'

clude, that the creditor is fully satisfied, when he gives in his bond to be cancelled. There are two ways of cancelling a bond, *laceratione et liturâ.* Here it is blotted out, and can be read no more than if it had never been; the obligatory power of the law as a covenant is taken away. God delivered his people from Pharaoh by force, and from Babylon by favour; but that deliverance that Christ, as our surety, hands out to us, from sin, from wrath, from hell, from the curse, and from the moral law as it is a covenant of works, is obtained *justo pretio soluto,* by paying a full price; by which one becomes satisfied, and another thereupon delivered: Heb. ix. 26, 'He hath appeared to put away sin by the sacrifice of himself;' to put away sin, Dan. ix. 24, is to abolish or make void the guilt or obligation of sin, whereby it binds over unbelievers to condemnation; to put away sin is to abrogate it, it is to bind it up in a bundle, to seal it up in a bag, to cast it behind him, as cancelled obligations, Isa. xxxviii. 17; Micah vii. 19; it is to blot out the black handwriting with the red lines of his blood drawn over it; so that sin has no force, no power to accuse or condemn, or shut such poor souls out of heaven, who have that Jesus for their surety, that made himself a sacrifice to put away sin. Christ as our surety laid down a satisfactory price, not only for our good, but also in our stead or room: 1 Pet. iii. 18, 'Christ also hath suffered for sin, the just for the unjust, that he might bring us to God.' What the unjust sinner should have suffered, that the just Christ suffered for him: 1 Cor. v. 21, ' He was made sin for us;' that is, an offering, a sacrifice in our stead, for the expiation of our sins: 'Christ was made a curse for us,'Gal. iii. 13. Now Christ's becoming a curse for us stands in this, that whereas we are all accursed by the sentence of the law because of sin, he now comes into our room, and stands under the stroke of that curse which of right belongs to us; so that it lies not now any longer on the backs of poor sinners, but on him for them and in their stead; therefore he is called a surety, Heb. vii. 22. The surety stands in the room of a debtor, malefactor, or him that is any way obnoxious to the law. Such is Adam and all his posterity. We are, by the doom of the law, evil-doers, transgressors; and upon that score we stand indebted to the justice of God, and lie under the stroke of his wrath. Now the Lord Jesus Christ seeing us in this condition, he steps in and stands between us and the blow; yea, he takes this wrath and curse off from us unto himself; he stands not only or merely after the manner of a surety among men in the case of debt, for here the surety enters bond with the principal for the payment of the debt, but yet expects that the debtor should not put him to it, but that he should discharge the debt himself, he only stands as a good security for the debtor: no, Christ Jesus doth not expect that we should pay the debt ourselves, but he takes it wholly upon himself. As a surety for a murderer or traitor, or some other notorious malefactor that hath broken prison and is run away, he lies by it body for body, state for state, and undergoes whatsoever the malefactor is chargeable withal for satisfying the law; even so the Lord Jesus stands surety for us runagate malefactors, making himself liable to all that curse that belongs to us, that he might both answer the law fully, and bring us back again to God. As the first Adam stood in the room of all mankind fallen, so Christ, the second

Adam, stands in the room of all mankind that are to be restored; he sustains the person of all those which do spiritually descend from him, and unto whom he bears the relation of a head. When God appointed his dearest Son to be a surety for us, and charged all our debts upon him, and required an exact satisfaction to his law and justice, insomuch that he would not abate the Son of his love one farthing-token of the debt, he did demonstrate a greater love to justice than if he had damned as many worlds as there are men in the world. Oh, let us never cast an eye upon Christ's suretyship, but let us stand and wonder, yea, let us be swallowed up in a deep admiration of Christ's love, and of his Father's impartial justice! Ah, what transcendent wisdom also does here appear in reconciling the riches of mercy and infinite justice both in one by the means of a surety! If all the angels in heaven, and all the men on earth, had been put to answer these questions, How shall sin be pardoned? How shall the sinner be reconciled and saved? How shall the wrath of God be pacified? How shall the justice of God be satisfied? How shall the redemption of man be brought about, in such a way whereby God may be most eminently glorified? they could never have answered the questions. But God, in his infinite wisdom, hath found out a way to save sinners, not only in a way of mercy and grace, but in a way of justice and righteousness; and all this by the means of Christ's suretyship, as hath been already declared.

Now, from the consideration of Christ's suretyship, a believer may form up this seventh, safe, comfortable, and blessed plea as to the ten scriptures formerly cited, that refer to the great day of account, or to a man's particular account: *O blessed Father, remember that thine own Son was my ransom, his blood was the price; he was my surety, and undertook to answer for my sins. I know, O blessed God, that thou must be satisfied, but remember my surety hath satisfied thee; not for himself, for he was holy and harmless, a lamb without a spot; but for me. They were my debts he satisfied for; and look over thy books, and thou shalt find that he hath cleared all accounts and reckonings between thee and me.*[1] *The guilt of all my sins have been imputed to my surety, who did present himself in my stead, to make full payment and satisfaction to thy justice.* As Paul said to Philemon, ver. 18, concerning his servant Onesimus, ' If he hath wronged thee, or oweth thee anything, put it upon my account,' so saith Christ to the penitent and believing soul, If thou hast any guilt, any debt to be answered for unto God, put them all upon my account. If thou hast wronged my Father, I will make satisfaction to the uttermost: for I was made sin for thee, Isa. liii. 12; 2 Cor. v. 21. I poured out my soul for thy transgressions. It cost me my heart's blood to reconcile thee to my Father, and to slay all enmity, Acts xx. 28. And as Rebekah said to Jacob in another case, ' Upon me, my son, be the curse,' Gen. xxvii. 13, so saith Christ to the believing soul, Why, thy sins did expose thee unto the curse of the law, but I was made a curse for thee, Gal. iii. 13. I did bear that burden myself upon the cross, and upon my shoulders were all thy griefs and sorrows borne; I was wounded

[1] When a man marries a woman, with her person he takes her debts and satisfaction too; so does Christ when he takes us to be his, he takes our sins also to be his.

for thy transgressions, and I was bruised for thy iniquities, Isa. liii. 4–8, 10; and therefore we are said to have 'redemption and remission of sins in his blood,' Eph. i. 7. O blessed God! thou knowest that a surety doth not pay the debt only for the debtor's good, but as standing in the debtor's stead, and so his payment is reckoned to the debtor. And thus the case stands between Christ and my soul; for, as my surety, he hath paid all my debts, and that very payment that he hath made, in honour and justice, thou art obliged to accept of as made in my stead. O dearest Father! that Jesus, who is God-man, as my surety, he hath done all that the law requireth of me, and thereby he hath freed me from wrath to come, and from the curse that was due to me for my sins, 1 Thes. i. 10. This is my plea, O holy God, and by this plea I shall stand. Hereupon God declares, This plea I accept as just and good, and therefore 'enter thou into the joy of thy Lord.'

Christian reader, I have gone as far in the opening and clearing up of those grand points of the gospel that have fallen under our consideration as I judge meet at this time. By the title-page thou mayest safely conclude, that I have promised much more than in this treatise I have performed; but be but a little patient, and by divine assistance, I shall make sure and full payment. The covenant of grace, and the covenant of redemption, with some other points of high importance, I shall present to thee in the second part, which will be the last part. In this first part I don't offer thee that which cost me nothing. I desire that all the interest thou hast in heaven may be so fully and duly improved, that this first part may be so blest from on high, as that saints and sinners may have cause to bless God to all eternity, for what is brought to hand; and beg hard, that the other part, which is drawn up and fitted for the press, may also be crowned with many blessings. Hereby thou wilt put a high obligation upon the author, to do all he can, to be yet a little further serviceable to thy soul and others', to thy salvation and others', before he goes hence and shall be seen no more.[1]

---

[1] Appended here is a list of Errata, all of which have been carefully attended to—The note may be given :—' There are sundry other mistakes in pointings, changes, and transpositions of letters, misfiguring of pages, &c., besides. Some are omitted, because they do not much disturb the sense, others because they will not easily escape thy notice. Share the faults between the author's absence and the printer's negligence: and then correct before thou readest.'—We have endeavoured to make all the 'corrections' thus generally indicated.—G.

THE

GOLDEN KEY

TO

PARADISE OPENED

THE EPISTLE DEDICATORY.

To his honoured friends, Sir JOHN MORE, Knight and Alderman of the City of London ; and to his good Lady, MARY MORE, his most affectionate Consort.[1]

The Father of all mercies, and the God of all blessings, bless you both with grace and peace here, and glory hereafter.

Honoured Friends,—Christian friendship makes such a knot, that great Alexander cannot cut. It was well observed by Sir Francis Bacon,[2] ' That old wood is best to burn, and old books best to read, and old friends best to trust. It was a witty saying of the Duke of Buckingham to Bishop Morton,[3] in Richard the III. his time, ' Faithful friends,' saith he, ' are in this age for the most part gone all in pilgrimage, and their return is uncertain.' ' They seem to take away the sun out of the world,' said the heathen orator,[4] ' who take away friendship from the life of men, and we do not more need fire and water than true friendship.[5] In this epistle I shall endeavour so to acquit myself as becomes a real friend, a cordial friend, a faithful friend, and a soul-friend, as to your great and everlasting concernments, that it may go well with you for ever and ever.

Sir, The points that are handled in this following treatise, and in the first part, are of as high, choice, necessary, noble, useful, and comfortable a nature, as any that can be treated on by mortal man. The

---

[1] More, or Moore, was elected Alderman of Walbrook in 1671; served the office of Sheriff in 1672, and that of Lord Mayor in 1682. See Northoack's ' History of London,' (1778.) He was of the Grocers' Company. Buried in St Dunstan's-in-the-East, Thames Street.—Herbert's ' History of the Twelve Companies of London,' i. 330.—G.

[2] Bacon's Works, by Spedding, vii. 139. Apophthegms, No. 97 of edition of 1625, and 75 of those printed in the *Resuscitatio*. Brooks quotes evidently from memory. The following is the passage :—' Alonso of Arragon was wont to say in commendation of age, that age appeared to be best in four things : old wood best to burn ; old wine to drink ; old friends to trust ; and old authors to read.'—G.

[3] Misprinted ' Monton.' A full account of Morton is to be found in Godwin *de Præsulibus*,' (ed. : Richardson, p. 130.) He was John Morton, then Bishop of Ely, but afterwards Archbishop of Canterbury : and the above saying was probably uttered while the bishop was under Buckingham's wardship at Brecon, by command of Richard III. See Foss's 'Judges of England,' v. 59.—G.　　　　[4] Cicero : de Amicitiâ.—G.

[5] It is the saying of Euripides, ' That a faithful friend is better than a calm sea to a weather-beaten mariner.' [Orestes 717 chorus, ed. Porson ; cf. also .two passages of the Andromache, 748, 749, and in 891.—G.]

four things which God minds most and loves most are, (1.) His honour. (2.) His worship. (3.) His people. (4.) His truth. Surely their souls must needs be of a very sad complexion who can read the great truths that are here opened and applied, and not (1.) dearly love them, (2.) highly prize them, (3.) cordially bless God for them, (4.) seriously ponder and meditate upon them, (5.) and not frequently and diligently study them, and make a gracious and daily improvement of them.

The covenant of grace, and the covenant of redemption, are a rich armoury, out of which you may furnish yourselves with all sorts of spiritual weapons, wherewith you may encounter Satan's temptations, wiles, devices, methods, depths, stratagems. Nothing of Satan's can stand before the covenant of grace and the covenant of redemption, well understood and well applied, Eph. vi. 11; 2 Cor. ii. 11; Rev. ii. 24.

In the covenant of grace and the covenant of redemption that is passed betwixt God the Father and our Lord Jesus Christ,[1] you will find many rich and rare cordials, which have a strong tendency to preserve all gracious souls from desponding and fainting: (1.) in times of afflictions; (2.) in times of temptations; (3.) in times of desertion; (4.) in times of sufferings for Christ's sake and the gospel's sake; (5.) in times of opposition; (6.) and at the time of death and dissolution. There are no comforts nor cordials that can reach the souls of Christians in their deep distresses, but such as flow from these two covenants. The more it concerns all such Christians to study these two covenants, and to be well acquainted with them, that so they may the more readily have recourse to such cordials as their present estate and condition calls for.

In these two covenants you will find much matter which has a strong tendency (1.) to inflame your love to God and Christ, and all in the covenant of grace; (2.) to strengthen your faith; (3.) to raise your hopes; (4.) to cheer your souls; (5.) to quiet and satisfy your consciences; (6.) to engage you to a close and holy walking with God; (7.) to provoke you to triumph in free grace, and in the Lord Jesus Christ; (8.) to sit loose from this world.[2] The riches and treasures that are wrapt up in both these covenants are so great, so sure, so durable, and so suitable to all believers, as may well deaden their hearts to all the riches and glories of this lower world, Rev. xii. 1.

In these two covenants every sincere Christian will find (1.) a special salve for every spiritual sore; (2.) a special remedy against every spiritual malady; (3.) a special plaster against every spiritual wound; (4.) a spiritual magazine to supply all their spiritual wants; and (5.) a spiritual shelter under every spiritual storm. In these two covenants you will find food to nourish you, a staff to support you, a guide to lead you, a fire to warm you, and springs of life to cheer and refresh you.

In this covenant of grace and the covenant of redemption, you may clearly see the wisdom, counsel, love, and transactions between the Father and the Son sparkling and shining, there being nothing under

[1] 2 Sam. xxiii. 5; Isa. liv. 9, 10; Jer. xxxii. 38–41; Zech. ix. 11; Heb. xiii. 20.

[2] Ps. cxvi. 1–9, 16, and iii.; 2 Sam. xxiii. 5; Ps. ciii. 17, 18, and cxi. 5, 9, 17; 2 Cor. ii. 14; Gal. vi. 14.

heaven that contributes more to the peace, comfort, assurance, settlement, and satisfaction of sincere Christians than such a sight. [1] The main reason why so many gracious souls are so full of fears, doubts, darkness, and disputes about their internal and eternal estates, is because they have no more clear and full understanding of these two covenants; and if such Christians would but more seriously buckle to the study of those two covenants, as they are opened and applied in the following treatise, their fears and doubts, &c., would quickly vanish; and they would have their triumphant songs: their mourning would soon be turned into rejoicing, and their complaints into hallelujahs. Neither do I know anything in all this world that would contribute more to seriousness, spiritualness, heavenliness, humbleness, holiness, and fruitfulness, than a right understanding of these two covenants, and a divine improvement of them. There are many choice Christians who have always either tears in their eyes, complaints in their mouths, or sighs in their breasts; and oh that these, above all all others, would make these two covenants their daily companions! Let these few hints[2] suffice concerning the following treatise.

Now, Sir John, I shall crave leave to put you and your lady a little in mind of your deceased and glorified father.[3] 'He is a true friend,' saith the Smyrnean poet of old, 'who continueth the memory of his deceased friend.'[4] When a friend of Austin's died, he professed he was put into a great strait, whether he himself should be willing to live or willing to die: he was unwilling to live, because one half of himself was dead; yet he was not willing to die, because his friend did partly live in him, though he was dead. Let you and I make the application as we see cause: your glorified father's name and memory remains to this day as fresh and fragrant as the Rose of Sharon— Cant. ii. 1—among all those that fear the Lord, and had the happiness of inward acquaintance with him. 'The memory of the just is blessed, but the name of the wicked shall rot,' Prov. x. 7. In the original it is, 'The memory of the just לברכה in benedictionem, shall be for a blessing;' the very remembering of them shall bring a bless· ing to such as do remember them.[5] The moralists say of fame, or of a man's good name—

> Omnia si perdas famam servare memento,
> Quà semel amissâ postea nullus eris;[6]

i.e, Whatsoever commodity you lose, be sure yet to preserve that jewel of a good name.[7] This jewel, among others, your honoured father

---

[1] It was the saying of an eminent saint, on his death-bed, that he had much peace and quietness, not so much from a greater measure of grace than other Christians had, or from any immediate witness of the Spirit, but because he had a more clear understanding of the covenant of grace than many others, having studied it and preached it so many years as he had done. [Qu. William Strong?— G.]

[2] Misprinted 'kinds.'—G.

[3] Ponder upon that Deut. xiii. 6 : Thy friend which is as thine own soul.

[4] Qu. Homer? Smyrna was one of the seven cities which claimed him. Strabo, l. c. Cicero, Arch. 8.—G.

[5] Memoria justi erit celebris, So Barn. [Qu. Bernard?—G.] Ego si bonam famam serv asso, sat dives ero. If I may but keep a good name, I have wealth enough, saith the heathen—Plautus.   [6] Claudian, De. Cons. Mall. Theod. v. 3.—G.

[7] Heb. xi. 13, 39. A good renown is better than a golden girdle, saith the French proverb.

carried with him to the grave—yea, to heaven. There is nothing raises a man's name and fame in the world like holiness. The seven deacons that the church chose were ' holy men,' Acts vi. 5 ; and they were men of ' good report,' ver. 3. They were men well witnessed unto, well testified of, as the Greek word imports.[1] Cornelius was a 'holy man,' Acts x. 1–4 ; and he was a man of ' good report' among all the nation of the Jews, ver. 22. Ananias was a ' holy man,' Acts ix. 10, 20 ; and he was a man of a ' good report,' Acts xxii. 12. Caius and Demetrius were both ' holy men,' and of a ' good report ;' witness that Third Epistle of John. The patriarchs and prophets were ' holy men,' and they were men of a ' good report,' Heb. xi. 1, 2—' For by it the elders obtained a good report ;' their holiness did eternalise their names. The apostles were ' holy men,' 1 Thes. ii. 10 ; and they were men of ' good report,' 2 Cor. vi. 8. Now certainly it is none of the least of mercies to be well reputed and reported of. Next to a good God and a good conscience, a good report, a good name, is the noblest blessing. It is no great matter, if a man be great and rich in the world, to obtain a great report ; but without holiness you can never obtain a good report. Holiness, uprightness, righteousness, will embalm your names ; it will make them immortal : Ps. cxii. 6, ' The righteous shall be in everlasting remembrance.' Wicked men many times outlive their names, but the names of the righteous outlive them. Holy Abel hath been dead above this five thousand years, and yet his name is as fresh and fragrant as it was the first day he was made a martyr, 1 John iii. 12. When a sincere Christian dies, he leaves his name as a sweet and as a lasting scent behind him ; his fame shall live when he is dead. This is verified in your precious father, who is now 'asleep in Jesus,' 1 Thes. iv. 14.

Now you both very well know that there was no Christian friend that had so great a room in his heart, in his affections, as I had, and you can easily guess at the reasons of it. Neither can you forget how frequently, both in his health, sickness, and before his death, he would be pressing of me to be a soul-friend to you, and to improve all the interest I had in heaven for your internal and eternal good, that he might meet you both in that upper world, Mat. xxv. 33, and that you might both be found with him at the right hand of Christ in the great day of the Lord. I know that your glorified father, whilst he was on earth, did lay up many a prayer for you in heaven. My desire and prayer is, that those prayers of his may return in mighty power upon both your hearts ; and having a fair opportunity now before me, I shall endeavour to improve it for the everlasting advantage of both your souls ; and therefore let my following counsel be not only accepted, but carefully, faithfully, and diligently followed by you, that so you may be happy here and blessed hereafter.

1. The first word of counsel is this : Let it be the principal care of both of you *to look after the welfare of your precious and immortal souls.* If your souls are safe, all is safe ; if they are well, all is well ;

---

[1] The Persians seldom write their king's name but in characters of gold. Throughout the Old and New Testaments God has written the names of just men in golden characters, as I may speak.

but if they are lost, all is lost, and you lost and undone in both worlds.[1] Christ, that only went to the price of souls, hath told us that one soul is more worth than all the world. Chrysostom well observeth, 'that whereas God hath given us many other things double—viz., two eyes to see with, two ears to hear with, two hands to work with, and two feet to walk with, to the intent that the failing of the one might be supplied with the other—he hath given us but one soul; if that be lost, hast thou,' saith he, 'another soul to give in recompense for it?' Ah, friends! Christ left his Father's bosom and all the glory of heaven for the good of souls; he assumed the nature of men for the happiness of the soul of man; he trod the wine-press of his Father's wrath for souls; he prayed for souls; he paid for souls, and he bled out his heart-blood for souls.[2] The soul is the breath of God, the beauty of man, the wonder of angels, and the envy of devils. It is of an angelical nature; it is a heavenly spark, a celestial plant, and of a divine offspring, 1 Pet. v. 8. Again, weigh well τὸ λύτρον, 'the incomparable price,' which Christ paid for the redemption of the soul, 1 Pet. i. 18, 19. What are the riches of the East or West Indies, the spoil of the richest nations, rocks of diamonds, mountains of gold, or the price of Cleopatra's draught, to the price that Christ laid down for souls! 1 John i. 4, 12, and Heb. xxii. 23. The soul is a spiritual substance, capable of the knowledge of God, of union with God, of communion with God, and of an eternal fruition of God. There is nothing can suit the soul below God, nor nothing that can satisfy the soul without God, nor nothing that can save the soul but God. The soul is so choice, so high, and so noble a piece, that it divinely scorns all the world in point of acceptation, justification, satisfaction, delectation, and salvation. Christ made himself an offering for sin, that souls might not be undone by sin. The Lord died that slaves might live; the Son died that servants might live; the natural Son died that adopted sons might live; the only-begotten Son died that bastards might live; yea, the judge died that malefactors might live, Heb. ix. 11-14, and x. 10, 14; Gal. iv. 4-6; Heb. ii. 8. Ah, friends! as there was never sorrow like Christ's sorrow, so there was never love like Christ's love, and of all his love none to that of soul-love, Isa. liii. 3, and Gal. ii. 20. To say much in a little room, the spiritual enemies which daily war against the soul, the glorious angels which hourly guard the soul, and the precious ordinances which God hath appointed as means both to convert and nourish the soul, [shew forth that love,] Eph. vi. 11, 12; 1 Pet. ii. 11; Rom. x. 17; 1 Cor. xi. 23-27. The soul is capable of 'a crown of life,' Rev. ii. 10; of 'a crown of glory,' 1 Pet. v. 4; of 'a crown of righteousness,' 2 Tim. iv. 8; of 'an incorruptible crown,' 1 Cor. ix. 25. The crowns of earthly princes stand as a sophister's[3] cap, on one side of the head. Many may say of their crowns as that king said of his, O crown, more noble than happy![4] In the time of Galienus the emperor, Anno Christo 260, there were thirty competi-

---

[1] Mat. xvi. 26. The soul is a greater miracle in man than all the miracles wrought amongst men, saith Augustine.

[2] Isa. lxiii. 3; John xvii.; Luke xxiii. 34; Mat. xxvi. 28.

[3] 'Sophister,' a 'pretender to wisdom,' but here probably a University term for an undergraduate of a given (early) standing.—G.

[4] Queen Elizabeth was said to swim to her crown through a sea of sorrow.

tors on foot for the Roman crown and throne, who confounded and destroyed one another. A princely crown is oftentimes the mark for envy and ambition to shoot at. Henry the Sixth was honoured with the crowns of two kingdoms, France and England ; the first was lost through the faction of his nobles, the other was twice plucked from his head. Earthly crowns have so many cares, fears, vexations, and dangers that daily attend them, that oftentimes they make the heads and hearts of monarchs ache, which made Cyrus say, ' You look upon my crown and my purple robes, but did you but know how they were lined with thorns, you would not stoop to take them up.'¹ But the crowns that immortal souls are capable of are crowns without crosses ; they are not attended with care of keeping or fear of losing ; there are no evil persons nor evil spirits that haunt those crowns. Darius, that great monarch, fleeing from his enemies, he threw away the crown of gold from his head that he might run the faster ; but a sincere Christian is in no danger of losing his crown, 2 Tim. iv. 8. His crown is laid up in a safe hand, in an omnipotent hand, 1 Pet. i. 5. Now what do all these things speak out but the preciousness and excellency of the soul ? Once more, the excellency of the case or cabinet—viz., the body—intimates a more than ordinary excellency of this jewel. The body is of all materials the most excellent. How does David admire the rare texture and workmanship of his body ! ' I am wonderfully made ; I was curiously wrought in the lowest parts of the earth,' Ps. cxxxix. 13, 15. When curious workmen have some choice piece in hand, they perfect it in private, and then bring it forth to the light for men to gaze at. So here, the greatest miracle in the world is man, in whose very body—how much more in his soul !—are miracles enough, betwixt head and feet, to fill a volume. One complains that men much wonder at the high mountains of the earth, the huge waves of the sea, the deep falls of rivers, the vastness of the ocean, and at the motions of the stars, &c., but wonder not at all at their wonderful selves.² Galen, a profane physician and a great atheist, writing of the excellent parts of man's body, he could not choose but sing an hymn to that God, whosoever he were, that was the author of so excellent and admirable a piece of work ; he could not but cry out, ' Now I adore the God of nature.'³ Now if the cabinet be so curiously wrought, what is the jewel that is contained in it ! Oh, how richly and gloriously is the soul embroidered ! How divinely inlaid and enamelled is that ! Princes impress their images or effigies upon the choicest metals, viz., gold and silver. God hath engraven his own image with his own hand upon angels and men, Gen. i. 26, [Damascene.] The soul is the glory of the creation, a beam of God, a spark of celestial brightness, a vessel of honour, a bird of paradise, a habitation for God. The soul is spiritual in its essence ; God breathed it in ; God hath invested it with many noble endowments ; he hath made it a mirror of beauty, and printed upon it a surpassing excellency. The soul is

¹ Prov. xxvii. 4, ' Doth the crown endure to all generations'—*Heb.*, to generation and generation !'
² Austin. The Stoic thought it was better to be a fool in the form of a man than wise in the shape of a beast.

spiritual in its object; it contemplates God and heaven. God is the orb and centre where the soul doth fix.[1] God is the *terminus ad quem*, the soul moves to him as to his rest, ' Return to thy rest, O my soul.' This dove can find no rest but in this heavenly ark.[2] Nothing can fill the soul but God, nothing can quiet the soul but God, nothing can satisfy the soul but God, nothing can secure the soul but God, nothing can save the soul but God. The soul being spiritual, God only can be the adequate object of it. The soul is spiritual in its operations. It being immaterial, doth not depend upon the body in its working. The rich and rare endowments, and the noble operations of the soul, speak out the excellency of the soul. The soul, saith one, [Aristotle.] hath a nature distinct from the body; it moves and operates of itself, though the body be dead, and hath no dependence upon, or co-existence with, the body. The soul hath an intrinsecal principle of life and motion, though it be separate from the body. And doth not the immortality of the soul speak out the excellency of the soul, against that dangerous notion of the soul's mortality? Consult the scriptures in the margin,[3] and seriously and frequently think of this one argument, among a multitude of arguments that might be produced to prove the immortality of the soul. That which is not capable of killing is not capable of dying; but the soul is not capable of killing, *ergo.* Our Lord Jesus proves the minor proposition, that it is not capable of killing: Luke xii. 4, ' Fear not them that kill the body, and after that have no more that they can do.' Therefore the soul, not being capable of killing, is not in a possibility of dying. The essence of the soul is metaphysical: it hath a beginning, but no end; it is eternal *à parte post;* it runs parallel with eternity. The soul doth not wax old; it lives for ever, which we cannot affirm of any sublunary created glory. To conclude this first word of counsel, what Job saith of wisdom, I may fitly apply to the soul, ' Man knows not the price thereof; it cannot be valued with the gold of Ophir, with the precious onyx, or the sapphire, the gold and crystal cannot equal it, and the exchange of it shall not be for jewels of fine gold,' Job xxviii. 13, 16, 17. O my friends, it is the greatest wisdom, policy, equity, and justice, to provide for your precious souls, to secure your precious souls; for they are jewels of more worth than ten thousand worlds. All the honours, riches, greatness, and glory of this world are but chips, toys, and pebbles to these glorious pearls. But,

2. The second word of counsel is this, as you would be safe here, and saved in the great day of the Lord, as you would be happy here, and blessed hereafter, *take up in nothing below a gracious acquaintance with Christ, a choice acceptation of Christ, a holy reliance upon Christ, a full resignation of yourselves to Christ, and a real and glorious union with Christ,* Acts ii. 20; Job xxii. 21; 1 Tim. i. 15; Job xiii. 15; 2 Cor. ii. 11. If you do, you are lost and undone in both worlds.

[1.] First, *Some take up in a name to live when they are dead,* Rev.

---

[1] Gen. ii. 7; Heb. xii. 9; Eccles. xii. 7; Zech. xii. 1; Ps. cxvi. 7; John xiv. 8; Ps. xvii. 16.

[2] ' Lord,' saith Austin, ' thou hast made us for thyself, and our heart is unquiet till it comes unto thyself.' [Confessions, as before.—G.]

[3] Luke xxiii. 43; 1 Thes. iv. 17, 18; Phil. i. 23; Acts vii. 59.

iii. 1, dead in trespasses and sins, Eph. ii. 1, dead Godwards, and dead Christwards, and dead heavenwards, and dead holinesswards. The Sadducees derive their name from Zeduchim or Zadducæus, a just man. But the worst men, saith the historian, got the best names. The Alcoran of the Turks hath its name from brightness, *Al*,[1] in the Arabic, being as much as *Kazan* in the Hebrew, ' to shine' or ' cast forth in brightness,' when it is full of darkness, and fraught with false-hoods. It will be but a poor comfort to any for the world to com-mend them as gracious, if God condemn them as graceless; for the world to commend them as pious, if God condemn them as impious; for the world to commend them as sincere, if God condemn them as hypocrites. But,

[2.] Secondly, Some take up *in a form of godliness when they are strangers to the power*, 2 Tim. iii. 5; *when they deny, yea, when they oppose and persecute, the power.* Such monsters this age hath abounded with; but their seeming goodness is but a religious cheat, Acts xiii. 45, 50.

[3.] Thirdly, There are some that take up *in their religious duties and services ;* in their praying, fasting, prophesying, hearing, receiving; they make a God, a Christ, a Saviour of their own duties and services. This was the undoing and damning sin of the Scribes and Pharisees, and is the undoing and damning sin of many thousands in our days, Mat. vii. 22; Luke xviii. 12, xiii. 26, and xvi. 15; Ezek. xxxiii. 31, 32.

[4.] Fourthly, There are many that take up *in their common gifts and parts ;* in a gift of knowledge, and in a gift of teaching, and in a gift of utterance, and in a gift of memory, and in a gift of prayer, and this proves ruinous and destructive to them, Mat. vii. 22; Rom. ii. 17–24; 1 Cor. xii. ; Heb. vi. 4, 5.

[5.] Fifthly, There are many that take up *in their riches, pro-sperity, and worldly grandeur and glory:* Prov. xviii. 11, 'The rich man's wealth is his strong city.' It is hard to have wealth, and not trust to it, Mat. xix. 24. Wealth was never true to those that trusted it. There is an utter uncertainty in riches, 1 Tim. vi. 17; a nonentity, Prov. xxiii. 5, 6; an impotency to help in an evil day, Zeph. i. 18; an impossibility to stretch to eternity, unless it be to destroy the owner for ever,[2] Prov. x. 15; Ps. lxxiii. 19; Mat. xx. 26. There is nothing more clear in Scripture and history than that riches, prosperity, and worldly glory hath been commonly their portion who never have had a God for their portion, Luke xvi. 25. It was an excellent saying of Lewis of Bavaria, emperor of Germany: *Hujus-modi comparandæ sunt opes, quæ cum naufragio simul enatent,* Such goods are worth getting and owning as will not sink or wash away if a shipwreck happen.[3] *Solus sapiens dives,* Only the wise man is the rich man, saith the philosopher. Another saith, [Augustine,] *Divitiæ corporales paupertatis plenæ sunt,* That earthly riches are full of poverty, they cannot enrich the soul; for oftentimes under silken apparel there is a threadbare soul.

---

[1] Query, '*Koran*'? *Al* is simply the definite article, *the*.—ED.

[2] *Divitibus ideo pietas deest, quia nihil deest,* Rich men's wealth proves an hin-drance to their happiness, Eccles. v. 13; James v. 1, 2.

[3] Riches are called thick clay, Hab. ii. 6, which will sooner break the back than lighten the heart.

He that is rich in conscience sleeps more soundly than he that is richly clothed in purple.

No man is rich which cannot carry hence that which he hath; that which we must leave behind us is not ours but some other's, [Ambrose, lib. 8, ep. 10.]

The shortest cut to riches is by their contempt. It is great riches not to desire riches, and he hath most that covets least. If there were any happiness in riches, the gods would not want them, saith the same author, [Seneca.]

When one was a-commending the riches and wealth of merchants: I do not love that wealth, said a poor heathen, which hangs upon ropes; for if they break, the ship miscarrieth, and then where is the merchant's riches?

If I had an enemy, saith one, whom it was lawful to wish evil unto, I would chiefly wish him great store of riches, for then he should never enjoy quiet, [Latimer.]

The historian [Tacitus] observes, that the riches of Cyprus invited the Romans to hazard many dangerous fights for the conquering of it.

Earthly riches, saith one, [Augustine,] are an evil master, a treacherous servant, fathers of flattery, sons of grief, a cause of fear to those that have them, and a cause of sorrow to those that want them.

I have read a famous story of Zelimus, emperor of Constantinople, that after he had taken Egypt, he found a great deal of treasure there; and the soldiers coming to him, and asking of him what they should do with the citizens of Egypt, for that they had found great treasure among them, and had taken their riches? Oh, saith the emperor, hang them all up, for they are too rich to be made slaves; and this was all the thanks they had for the riches they were spoiled of.[1] What more contemptible than a rich fool, a golden beast, as Caligula called his father-in-law Syllanius?[2] Not but that some are great and gracious, rich and righteous, as Abraham, Lot, Job, David, Hezekiah, &c.

It is said of Shusa in Persia, saith Cassiodorus, that it was so rich that the stones were joined together with gold; and that in it Alexander found seventy thousand talents of gold. If you can take this city, saith Aristagorus[3] to his soldiers, you may vie with Jove himself for riches. The riches of Shusa did but make the soldiers the more desperate in their attempt to take it.

By these short hints you may see the folly and vanity of those men who take up in their riches. But,

[6.] Sixthly, Many there are that take up *in their own righteousness, which at best is but as filthy rags,* Isa. lxiv. 6. This was the damning sin of the Jews, and of the scribes and Pharisees; and is the undoing sin of many of the professors of this age, Rom. x. 2, 3; Mat. v. 20.

---

[1] [Knolles] The Turkish History. The poets feigned Pluto to be the god of riches and hell, as if they were inseparable.—*Homer.*

[2] Rather 'Silanus:' Dion Cass, lviii. 25.—G.

[3] Rather 'Aristagoras' Herod:' iv. 138, v. 37, 38: for Shusa rather 'Susa.'—G.

[7.] Seventhly, Many there are that take up *in their external church privileges*, crying out, 'The temple of the Lord, the temple of the Lord,' Jer. vii. 4, 8–11, when they have no union nor communion with the Lord of the temple. These forget that there will come a day, when the 'children of the kingdom shall be cast out,' Mat. viii. 12. It would be very good for such persons to make these five scriptures their daily companions, Mat. xxii. 10, 12–14; Luke xiii. 25–28; Rom. ii. 28, 29; Gal. vi. 15; Jer. ix. 25, 26. That they may never dare to take up in their outward church privileges, which can neither secure them from hell, nor secure them of heaven. But,

[8.] Eighthly, Many there be that take up *in common convictions*. Judas had mighty convictions of his sin, but they issued in desperation, Mat. xxvii. 4, 5. Balaam was mightily enlightened and convinced, insomuch that he desired to die the death of the righteous; but under all his convictions he died Christless and graceless, Num. xxiii. and xxiv. Nebuchadnezzar had great convictions, Dan. iv. 31, 32, yet we do not read that ever he was converted before he was driven from the society of men, to be a companion with the beasts of the field, Dan. iv. 31, 32. He had strong convictions, (1.) by Daniel's interpreting of his dream, Dan. ii. 47. (2.) He told Daniel, that 'his God was the God of gods, and a Lord of kings, and a revealer of secrets;' and yet presently he fell into gross idolatry, Dan. iii., and strictly commanded to worship the golden image that he had set up; and as if he had lost all his former convictions, he was so swelled up with pride and impudence, as to say to the three children, when they divinely scorned to worship the image he had set up, 'What God is there that can deliver you out of my hand?' ver. 15. Saul had great convictions, 'I have sinned, return, my son David, I will no more do thee harm,' &c. And Saul lifted up his voice and wept; and he said unto David, 'Thou art more righteous than I, for thou hast rewarded me good, whereas I have rewarded thee evil,' 1 Sam. xxvi. 21, 25, and xxiv. 16–19. But these convictions issued in no saving change, for after these he lived and died in the height of his sins. Pharaoh had great convictions: 'And Pharaoh sent, and called for Moses and Aaron, and said unto them, I have sinned this time: the Lord is righteous, and I and my people are wicked.' And again, 'Then Pharaoh called for Moses and Aaron in haste; and he said, I have sinned against the Lord your God, and against you,' Exod. ix. 27, and x. 16. But these convictions issued in no reformation, in no sound conversion, and therefore drowning and damning followed. Cain was under convictions, but went and built a city, and lost his convictions in a crowd of worldly business, Gen. iv. Herod and Felix were under convictions, but they went off, and never issued in any saving work upon their souls, Mark vi. 20; Acts xxiv. 25. Oh, how many men and women have fallen under such deep convictions, that they have day and night cried out of their sins, and of their lost and undone estates, and that they should certainly go to hell and be damned for ever, so that many good people have hoped that these were the pangs of the new birth; and yet either merry company, or carnal pleasures and delights, or much worldly business, or else length of time, have wrought off all their convictions, and they have grown more profane and wicked than ever they were before. As water heated, if taken off the fire, will soon return to its natural coldness, yea, becomes colder after heating than before, [Aristotle,] this hath been the case of many under convictions. I shall forbear giving of particular instances. But,

[9.] Ninthly, Many take up *in an outward change and reformation;* they have left some old courses and sinful practices which formerly they walked in, &c., and therefore they conclude and hope that their condition is good, and that all is well, and shall be for ever well with them. They were wont to swear, whore, be drunk, profane Sabbaths, reproach saints, &c.; but now they have left all these practices, and therefore the main work is done, and they are made for ever. I confess sin is that abominable thing which God hates, Jer. xliv. 4, and therefore it is a very great mercy to turn from it. To leave one sin is a greater mercy than to win the whole world, Mat. xvi. 26; and it is certain that he that doth not outwardly reform shall never go to heaven, Job xxii. 23, 26. He that doth not leave his sins, he can never be happy here nor blessed hereafter; and yet it is possible for a man, with Herod, to reform many things, and yet be a lost and undone man for ever, as he was, Mark vi. 20. Judas was a very reformed man, but he was never inwardly changed nor throughout sanctified, Mat. xxvi. 20–22; 1 Thes. v. 23. The scribes and Pharisees were outwardly reformed, but they were not inwardly renewed. A man may be another man than what once he was, and yet not be a new man, a new creature. When a sinner is sermon-sick, oh, then he will leave his sins; but when that sickness is off, he returns with the dog to his vomit, and with the sow to her wallowing in the mire, 2 Cor. v. 17; 2 Pet. ii. 20, 22. Sometimes conscience is like the handwriting upon the wall, Dan. v. 5–8: it makes the sinner's countenance to change, and his thoughts to be troubled, and the joints of his loins to be loosed, and his knees to smite one against another. And now the sinner is all for reforming, and turning over a new leaf; but when these agonies of conscience are over, the sinner returns to his old courses again, and oftentimes is twofold more a child of hell than before, Mat. xxiii. 15. There was a man in this city who was given up to the highest wickednesses; on his sick-bed conscience made an arrest of him, and he was filled with such wonderful horror and terror, that he cried out day and night that he was damned, he was damned, he was damned; and when he had some small intervals, oh, what large promises did he make! what a new man, a reformed man, he would be! but when in time his terrors and sickness wrought off, he was sevenfold worse than before. Sometimes the awakened sinner parts with some sins to make room for others, and sometimes the sinner seems to give a bill of divorce to this sin and that, but it is only because his bodily strength fails him, or because he wants an opportunity, or because there is a more strict eye and watch upon him, or because the sword of the magistrate is more sharpened against him, or because he wants fuel, James iv. 3; he wants a purse to bear it out, or because some company, or some relations, or some friends lie between him and his sins, so that he must either tread over them, or else keep from his sins; or because he has deeply smarted for this sin, and that his name has been blotted, his credit and reputation stained, his trade decayed, his health impaired, his body wasted, &c., Prov. vi. 32–35. By these short hints it is evident that men may attain to some outward reformation, whose states and hearts were never changed, and who were never taken into marriage union with Christ. But,

[10.] Tenthly and lastly, Many take up *in a party.* As of old some cried up Paul as the only deep preacher, and others cried up Apollos as the only eloquent preacher, and many cried up Cephas as the most zealous preacher, 1 Cor. i. 10–13. We are for the Church of England, say some; we are for the Baptized people, say others; we are for the Presbyterian government, cry some; we are for the Congregational way, cry others. I have so much ingenuity and charity, as to judge that some of all these several parties and persuasions are really holy and will be eternally happy, are gracious and will be glorious, are sanctified and will be saved, are now governed by Christ and will be hereafter glorified with Christ. Judas was one of Christ's party, if I may so speak, and yet he had no part nor portion in Christ, Mat. xxvi. 20–26. Demas was one of Paul's party, and yet he played the apostate, and turned an idolatrous priest at Thessalonica, as Dorotheus saith, 2 Tim. iv. 10.[1] And Phygellus and Hermogenes were of Paul's party, but were only famous for their recidivation[2] and apostasy, 2 Tim. i. 15. Hymeneus and Alexander were of Paul's party, but they made shipwreck of faith and a good conscience, 1 Tim. i. 19, 20. The five foolish virgins were in society with the wise, and were accounted as members of their association, and yet the door of heaven was shut against them, Mat. xxv. 1, 2, 12. Many light, slight, and vain persons went with the children of Israel out of the land of Egypt, even a mixed multitude that embarked in the same bottom with them, and yet never arrived at the land of promise, Exod. xii. 38; Num. xi. 4. O my friends, it is not a man's being of this party or that, this church or that, this way or that, this society or that, that will bring him to heaven, without a spiritual conjunction with Christ, 1 Pet. i. 4; Heb. i. 2. He that would enjoy the heavenly inheritance must be espoused to Christ, the heir of all things: 'For he that hath the Son hath life, and he that hath not the Son hath not life,' 1 John v. 12. This marriage-union between Christ and the soul is set forth to the life throughout the book of Solomon's Song, Cant. ii. 16. Though the marriage-union between Christ and the soul be imperceptible to the eye of reason, yet it is real, 1 Cor. vi. 17. Things in nature often work insensibly, yet really. We do not see the hand move on the dial, yet it moves. The sun exhales and draws up the vapours of the earth insensibly, yet really, Eccles. xi. 6. Now this marriage-union between Christ and the soul includes and takes in these following particulars:—

First, This marriage-union between Christ and the soul does include and take in *the soul's giving a present bill of divorce to all other lovers;* sin, the world, and Satan.[3] Are you seriously and sincerely willing for ever to renounce these, and be divorced from these? There is no compounding betwixt Christ and them. Sin and your souls

[1] As before, see foot-note and Index *sub nomine.*—G.
[2] 'Relapse'=backsliding.—G.
[3] Consult these scriptures: Hosea xiv. 8; Isa. ii. 20, and xxx. 22; Ps. xlv. 10; Exod. xii. 33; Isa. lix. 20.

must part, or Christ and your souls can never meet; sin and your souls must be two, or Christ and your souls can never be one; you must in good earnest fall out with sins, or else you can never in good earnest fall in with a Saviour; the heart must be separated from all other lovers, before Christ will take the soul into his bed of loves. Christ takes none into marriage-union with himself, but such as are cordially willing that all old former leagues with sin and the world shall be for ever broken and dissolved. Your cordial willingness to part with sin, is your parting with sin in divine account. . You may as soon bring east and west together, light and darkness together, heaven and hell together, as bring Christ to espouse himself to such a soul, as has no mind, no will, no heart to be divorced from his former lovers. It is a foolish thing for any to think of keeping both Christ and their lusts too. It is a vain thing for any to think of saving the life of his sins, and the life of his soul too. If sin escape, your soul cannot escape; if thou art not the death of thy sins, they will be the death and ruin of thy soul. Marriage is a knot or tie, wherein persons are mutually limited and bound each to other, in a way of conjugal separation from all others, and this in Scripture is called a covenant, Prov. ii. 7. So when any one marries Christ, he doth therein discharge himself in affection and subjection from all that is contrary unto Christ, and solemnly covenants and binds himself to Christ alone; he will have no Saviour and no Lord but Christ, and to him will he cleave for ever, Ps. lxiii. 8; Acts xi. 23. But,

Secondly, This marriage-union with Christ doth include and take in *a hearty willingness, to take, to receive the Lord Jesus Christ for your Saviour and sovereign.*[1] Are you willing to consent to the match.? It is not enough that Christ is willing to enter into a marriage-union with us, but we must be willing also to enter into a marriage-union with him.[2] God will never force a Christ, nor force salvation upon us, whether we will or no. Many approve of Christ, and cry up Christ, who yet are not willing to give their consent, that he, and he alone shall be their Prince and Saviour. Though knowledge of persons be necessary and fit, yet it is not sufficient to marriage, without consent, for marriage ought to be a voluntary transaction of persons. In marriage we do in a sort give away ourselves, and elect and make choice for ourselves, and therefore consent is a necessary concurrence to marriage. Now this consent is nothing else but a free and plain act of the will, accepting of Jesus Christ before all others to be its head and Lord, and in the soul's choice of him to be its Saviour and sovereign. Then a man is married to Christ, when he doth freely and absolutely and presently receive the Lord Jesus; not, I would have Christ if it did not prejudice my worldly estate, ease, friends, relations, &c., or hereafter, I will accept of him when I come to die, and be in distress, but now when salvation is offered, now while Christ tenders himself, I now yield up my heart and life unto him. But,

Thirdly, This marriage-union with Christ includes and takes in

---

[1] John i. 12; Acts v. 31; Col. ii. 6: weigh well these scriptures: Ps. cxii. 3, and xxv. 5; Hosea ii. 7.

[2] Many can choose Christ as a refuge to hide them from danger, and as a friend to help them in their need, who yet refuse him as a husband.

a universal and perpetual consent for all time and in all states and conditions. There is, you know, a great difference between a wife and a strumpet; a wife takes her husband upon all terms, to have and to hold, for better and for worse, for richer and for poorer, in sickness and in health, whereas a strumpet is only for hire and lust. When the purse is emptied, or the body wasted and strength consumed, the harlot's love is at an end: so here. That acceptance and consent which ties the marriage-knot between Christ and the soul, must be an unlimited and indefinite acceptance and consent, when we take the Lord Jesus Christ wholly and entirely, without any secret reservations or exceptions. That soul that will have Christ, must have all Christ or no Christ, 'for Christ is not divided,' 1 Cor. i. 13. That soul must entertain him to all purposes and intents, he must follow the Lamb wheresoever he goeth, Rev. xiv. 4, though it should be through fire and water, over mountains and hills. He must take him with his cup of affliction as well as his cup of consolation, Ps. lxvi. 12, with his shameful cross as well as his glorious crown, with his great sufferings as well as his great salvation, Heb. ii. 3, with his grace as well as his mercy, with his Spirit to lead and govern them, as well as his blood to redeem and justify them, to suffer for him as well as to reign with him, to die for him as well as to live to him, 2 Tim. ii. 12; Acts xxi. 13; Rom. xiv. 7, 8. Christianity, like the wind *Cæcias*, doth ever draw clouds and afflictions after it.[1] 'All that will live godly in Christ Jesus shall suffer persecution,' 2 Tim. iii. 12. A man may have many faint wishes and cold desires after godliness, and yet escape persecution, yea, he may make some essays and attempts, as if he would be godly, and yet escape persecution; but when a man is thoroughly resolved to be godly, and sets himself in good earnest upon pursuing after holiness, and living a life of godliness, then he must expect to meet with afflictions and persecutions. Whoever escapes, the godly man shall not escape persecution in one kind or another, in one degree or another.[2] He that is peremptorily resolved to live up to holy rules, and to live out holy principles, must prepare for sufferings. All the roses of holiness are surrounded with pricking briars. The history of the Ten Persecutions, and that little Book of Martyrs, the 11th of the Hebrews, and Mr Foxe his Acts and Monuments, with many other treatises that are extant, do abundantly evidence that from age to age, and from one generation to another, they that have been born after the flesh have persecuted them that hath been born after the spirit, and that the seed of the serpent have been still a-multiplying of troubles upon the seed of the woman, Gal. iv. 29; but a believer's future glory and pleasure will abundantly recompense him for his present pain and ignominy. But such as will have Christ for their Saviour and sovereign, but still with some proviso or other—viz., that they may keep such a beloved lust, or enjoy such carnal pleasures and delights, or raise such an estate for them and theirs, or comply with the times, and such and such great men's humours, or that they may follow the Lamb only

---

[1] The north-east wind, (καικίας,) Pl. 2, 46, 47; Vitr. 1, 6; Sen. Q. N. 5, 16.—G.

[2] The common cry of persecutors have been, *Christianos ad Leones :* within the first three hundred years after Christ, upon the matter all that made a profession of the apostle's doctrine, were cruelly murdered.

in sunshine weather, &c., these are still Satan's bond-slaves, and such as Christ can take no pleasure nor delight to espouse himself unto. But,

3. The third word of advice and counsel is this, viz.—' *Put off the old man, and put on the new,*' Col. iii. 9, 10. Consult the scriptures in the margin.[1] You must be new creatures, or else it had been better you had been any creatures than what you are: 2 Cor. v. 17, ' If any man be in Christ he is a new creature, old things are passed away, behold all things are become new.' The new creature includes a new light, a new sight, a new understanding. Now the soul sees sin to be the greatest evil, and Christ and holiness to be the chiefest good, Ps. xxxviii. 4, and Cant. v. 10. When a man is a new creature he has a new judgment and opinion, he looks upon God as his only happiness, and Christ as his all in all, Col. iii. 11, and upon the ways of God as ways of pleasantness, Prov. iii. 17. The new man has new cares, new requests, new desires. Oh that my soul may be saved! Acts ii. 37, and xvi. 30; Oh that my interest in Christ may be cleared! Oh that my heart may be adorned with grace! Oh that my whole man may be secured from wrath to come! 1 Thes. i. 10. The new man is a man of new principles. If you make a serious inspection into his soul, you shall find a principle of faith, of repentance, of holiness, of love, of contentment, of patience, &c.[2] There is not any one spiritual and heavenly principle respecting salvation, but may be found in the new creature. The new man experiences a new combat and conflict in his soul. ' The flesh lusteth against the spirit, and the spirit lusteth against the flesh.' ' I see another law in my members warring against the law of my mind,' Gal. v. 17, and Rom. vii. 23. The new man experiences a combat in every faculty. Here is the judgment against the judgment, and the will against the will, and the affections against the affections. And the reason is this; because there is flesh and spirit, sin and grace co-existent and cohabiting in every faculty of the soul; renewing grace is in every faculty, and remaining corruption is also in every faculty, like Jacob and Esau struggling in the same womb, or like heat and cold in the same water, and in every part of it. The new man also combats with all sorts of known sins, whether they be great or small, inward or outward, whether they be the sins of the heart or the sins of the life; and besides, the conflict in the new man is a daily conflict, a constant conflict. The new creature can never, the new creature will never, be at peace with sin; sin and the new creature will fight it out to the death. The new creature will never be brought into a league of friendship with sin. The new man is a man of a new life and conversation. Always a new life attends a new heart. You see it in Paul, Mary Magdalene, Zaccheus, the jailor, and all the others that are upon Scripture record.[3] The new man has new society, new company: Ps. cxix. 63, ' I am a companion of all them that fear thee, and of them that keep thy precepts.' Ps. xvi. 3, ' My goodness extends not to thee, but to the saints that are in the earth, and to the excellent, in whom is all my delight.' Holy society is the only society for persons of holy hearts, and in that society can no man delight until God renew

---

[1] Eph. iv. 22–24; Gal. vi. 15; 1 Pet. ii. 2.
[2] Phil. i. 29; Acts xi. 18; 1 Thes. iv. 9; Phil. iv. 11; 1 Cor. iv. 12.
[3] See 1 John iii. 14; 2 Cor. vi. 14; Ps. cxx. 5, cxxxix. 21, and xlii. 4.

his heart by grace. Many men be as the planet Mercury, good in conjunction with those that are good, and bad with those that are bad; these are they that do *Virtutis stragulam pudefacere*, Put honesty to an open shame.[1] Clothes and company do oftentimes tell tales in a mute but significant language. Tell me with whom thou goest, and I will tell thee what thou art, saith the Spanish proverb. Algerius, an Italian martyr, had rather be in prison with Cato than with Cæsar in the senate-house.[2] But to conclude this word of counsel, the new man walks by a new rule. As soon as ever God has made a man a new creature, he presently sets up a new rule of life to walk by, and that is no other but that which God himself sets up for his people to walk by, and that is his written word: Isa. viii. 20, 'To the law and to the testimony;' Ps. cxix. 105, 'Thy word is a lamp unto my feet, and a light unto my path;' ver. 133, 'Order my steps in thy word;' Gal. vi. 16, 'And as many as walk according to this rule, peace be on them and mercy, and upon the Israel of God.' This rule he sets up for all matters of faith, and for all matters of fact. The word is like the stone *Garamantides*, that hath drops of gold within itself, enriching of every soul that makes it his rule to walk by. Alexander kept Homer's Iliads in a cabinet, embroidered with gold and pearls;[3] and shall not we keep the word in the cabinet of our hearts, that it may be always ready at hand as a rule for us to walk by? Well, friends, whatever you do forget, be sure that for ever you remember this—viz., that none can or shall be glorious creatures, but such as by grace are made new creatures. But,

4. The fourth word of advice and counsel is this, *Labour to be more inwardly sincere than outwardly glorious.* 'The king's daughter is all glorious within,' Ps. xlv. 13. Oh labour rather to be good than to be thought to be good, to live than to have a name to live, Rev. iii. 1, 15-17. Whatever you let go, be sure you hold fast your integrity. A man were better to let friends go, relations go, estate go, liberty go, and all go, than let his integrity go. 'God forbid that I should justify you; till I die I will not remove my integrity from me; my righteousness I will hold fast, and I will not let it go: my heart shall not reproach me so long as I live,' Job xxvii. 5, 6. Job is highly and fully resolved to keep his integrity close against all assaults of enemies or suspicions of friends. Job's integrity was the best jewel he had in all the world, and this jewel he was resolved to keep to his dying day. It was neither good men, nor bad men, nor devils that should baffle Job out of his integrity; and though they all pulled, and pulled hard, at his integrity, yet he would not let it go, he would hold fast this pearl of price whatever it cost him. The sincere Christian, like John Baptist, will hold his integrity though he lose his head for it, Mark vi. The very heathens loved a candid and sincere spirit, as he that wished that there was a glass in his breast, that all the world might see what was in his heart. Integrity will be a sword to defend you, a staff to support you, a star to guide you, and a cordial to cheer you; and therefore, above all gettings get sincerity, and above all keepings keep sincerity, as your crown, your comfort, your life. But,

[1] Cicero had rather have no companion than a bad one.
[2] Clarke, as before, p. 187.—G.
[3] As before.—G.

5. The fifth word of comfort and counsel is this, *Be true to the light of your consciences, and maintain and keep up a constant tenderness.in your consciences.* A tender conscience is a mercy more worth than a world. Conscience is God's spy in our bosoms: keep this clear and tender, and then all is well, Acts xxiv. 16 ; 2 Cor. i. 12. Act nothing against the dictates of conscience, rebel not against the light of conscience. You were better that all the world should upbraid you and reproach you, than that your consciences should upbraid you and reproach you, Job xxvii. 5, 6. Beware of stifling conscience, and of suppressing the warnings of conscience, lest a warning conscience prove a gnawing conscience, a tormenting conscience. The blind man in the Gospel, Mark viii., newly recovering his sight, imagined trees to be men: and the Burgundians, as Comines reports, expecting a battle, supposed long thistles to be lances. Thus men under guilt are apt to conceit every thistle a tree, and every tree a man, and every man a devil. Take heed of tongue-tied consciences ; for when God shall untie these strings, and unmuzzle your consciences, conscience will then be heard, and ten concerts of music shall not drown her clamorous cries. Hearken to the voice of conscience, obey the voice of conscience, and when conscience shall whisper you in the ear, and tell you there is this and that amiss in the house, in the habit, in the heart, in the life, in the closet ; don't say to conscience, Conscience be quiet, be still, make no noise now, I will hear thee in a more convenient season, Acts xxiv. 24, 25. The heathen orator could say, *A recta conscientia ne latum quidem unguem discedendum,* A man may not depart a hair's-breadth all his life long from the dictates of a good conscience.[1] Will not this heathen one day rise in judgment against those who daily crucify the light of their own consciences ? But,

6. The sixth word of advice and counsel is this, *Make it the great business of your lives to make sure such things as will go with you beyond the grave.*[2] Riches and honours and offices, and all worldly grandeur, won't go with us beyond the grave. Saladin, a Turkish emperor—he was the first of that nation that conquered Jerusalem—lying at the point of death, after many glorious victories, commanded that a white sheet should be borne before him to his grave, upon the point of a spear, with this proclamation: ' These are the rich spoils which Saladin carrieth away with him, of all his triumphs and victories, of all his riches and realms that he had ; now nothing at all is left for him to carry with him but this sheet.' It is with us in this world as it was in the Jewish fields and vineyards, pluck and eat they might what they would while they were there, but they might not pocket nor put up aught to carry with them, Deut. xxiii. 24, 25. Death, as a porter, stands at the gate, and strips men of all their worldly wealth and glory. Athenæus speaks of one that, at the hour of death, devoured many pieces of gold, and sewed the rest in his coat, commanding that they should be buried with him. Hermocrates, being loath that any man should enjoy his goods after him, made himself by will heir of his own goods. These muck-worms would fain live

---

[1] Cicero : in Offic.

[2] See my Treatise on Assurance, and there you will find how you may secure something that will go with you beyond the grave.—[Vol. ii., p. 301, *seq.*—G.]

still on this side Jordan; having made their gold their god, they cannot think of parting with it. They would, if possible, carry the world out of the world. But what saith the apostle? 'We brought nothing with us into this world, and it is certain'—see how he assevereth and assureth it, as if some rich wretches made question of it—'we can carry nothing out,' nothing but a winding-sheet, 1 Tim. vi. 7. Oh, how should this alarm us to make sure our calling and election,[1] to make sure our interest in Christ, to make sure our covenant-relation, to make sure a work of grace in power upon our souls, to make sure the testimony of a good conscience, Gal. iv. 5-7, to make sure our sonship, our saintship, our heirship, &c., Rom. viii. 15, 16; for these are the only things that will go with us into another world. In the Marian persecution there was a woman who, being convened before Bonner, then Bishop of London,[2] upon the trial of religion, he threatened her that he would take away her husband from her. Saith she, Christ is my husband. I will take away thy child. Christ, saith she, is better to me than ten sons. I will strip thee, saith he, of all thy outward comfort. Yea, but Christ is mine, saith she, and you cannot strip me of him. Assurance that Christ was hers, and that he would go with her beyond the grave, bore her heart up above the threats of being spoiled of all, Heb. x. 34. When a great lord had shewed a sober, serious, knowing Christian his riches, his stately habitation, his pleasant gardens, his delightful walks, his rich grounds, and his various sorts of pleasure, the serious Christian, turning himself to this great lord, said: My lord, you had need to make sure Christ and heaven, you had need make sure something that will go with you beyond the grave, for else when you die you will be a very great loser. O my friends, I must tell you, it highly concerns you to make sure something that will go with you beyond the grave, or else you will be very great losers when you come to die, God having given you an abundance of the good things and of the great things of this world, beyond what he has given to many thousands of others. But,

7. The seventh word of advice and counsel is this, *Look upon all the things of this world, and value all the things of this world now, as you will certainly look upon them and value them when you come to lie upon a sick-bed, a dying-bed,* 1 Cor. vii. 29–31. When a man is sick in good earnest, and when death knocks at the door in good earnest, oh, with what a disdainful eye, with what a weaned eye, with what a scornful eye does a man then look upon the honours, riches, dignities, and glories of this world! If men could but thus look upon them now, it would keep them from being fond of them, from trusting in them, from doting upon them, from being proud of them, and from venturing a damning either in getting or in keeping of them. But,

8. The eighth word of advice and counsel is this, *In all places and companies carry your soul-preservatives still about you*—viz., a holy care, a holy fear, a holy jealousy, a holy watchfulness over your own thoughts, hearts, words, and ways, Prov. iv. 23, and xxviii. 14; Gen. vi. 9, and xxxix. 9, 10; Ps. xvii. 4, xviii. 23, and xxxix. 1, &c. You

---

[1] 2 Pet. i. 10; 2 Cor. v. 17; 2 Sam. xxiii. 5; 1 Thes. v. 23; 2 Cor. i. 12.
[2] Foxe's Acts and Monuments.

know that in infectious times men and women carry their several pre-
servatives about them, that they may be kept from the infection of
the times. Never were there more infectious times than now. Oh
the snares, the baits, the infections that attend us at all times, in all
places, in all companies, in all employments, and in all enjoyments,
so that if we do not carry our soul-preservatives about us, we shall
be in imminent danger of being infected with the pride, ill customs,
and vanities of the times wherein we live. But,

9. The ninth word of advice and counsel is this, *Live not at uncer-
tainties as to your spiritual and eternal estates.*[1] There are none so
miserable as those that are strangers to the state of their own souls.
It is good for a man to know the state of his flock, the state of his
family, the state of the nation, the state of his body; but above all to
know the state and condition of his own soul. How many thousands
are there that can give a better account of their lands, their lordships,
their riches, their crops, their shops, their trades, their merchandise,
yea, of their hawks, their hounds, their misses, than they can of the
estate of their own souls! O my friends, your souls are more worth
than ten thousand worlds, Mat. xvi. 26, and therefore it must be the
greatest prudence, and the choicest policy in the world, to secure their
everlasting welfare, and to know how things stands between God and
your souls, what you are worth for eternity, and how it is like to go
with you in that other world. Whilst a Christian lives at uncer-
tainties as to his spiritual and everlasting estate, as whether he has
grace or no grace, or whether his grace be true or counterfeit, whether
he has an interest in Christ or not, a work in power upon his soul or
not, or whether God loves him or loathes him, whether he will bring
him to heaven or throw him to hell—how can any Christian who
lives at so great an uncertainty delight in God, rejoice evermore,
triumph in Christ Jesus, be ready to suffer, and desirous to die? Job
xxvii. 10; Phil. iv. 4; 2 Cor. ii. 14; Phil. i. 23. All men love to be
at a certainty in all their outward concernments; and yet how many
thousands are there that are at a marvellous uncertainty as to the
present and future state of their precious and immortal souls! But,

10. The tenth word of advice and counsel is this, *Set the highest
Scripture examples and patterns before you, of grace and holiness, for
your imitation,* 1 Cor. iv. 16. In the point of faith and obedience set
an Abraham before you, Gen. xii. and xxii.; in the point of meekness set a Moses before you, Num. xii. 3; in the point of courage set
a Joshua before you, Josh. i.; in the point of uprightness set a David
before you, Ps. xviii. 23; in the point of zeal set a Phinehas before
you; and in the point of patience set a Job before you. Make Christ
your main pattern, 'Be ye followers of me, as I am of Christ,' James
v. 11, 12, and 1 Cor. xi. 1. And next to him set the patterns of the
choicest saints before you for your imitation.[2] The nearer you come
to those blessed copies that they have set before you, the more will be
your joy and comfort, and the more God will be honoured, Christ

---

[1] See my ' Box of Precious Ointment.' In that glass you may read the state of your
souls.—[Vol. iii. p. 233, *seq.*—G.]

[2] *Præcepta docent, exempla movent,* Precepts may instruct, but examples do persuade.—[As before.—G.]

exalted, the Spirit pleased, religion adorned, the mouths of sinners stopped, and the hearts of saints rejoiced. He that shooteth at the sun, though he shoot far short, yet will shoot higher than he that aimeth at a shrub. It is safest, it is best, to eye the highest and worthiest examples. Examples are, (1.) More awakening than precepts; (2.) More convincing than precepts; (3.) More encouraging than precepts, Heb. xi. 8; and that because in them we see that the exercise of godliness, though difficult, yet is possible; when we see men subject to like passions with ourselves to be so and so mortified, self-denying, humble, holy, &c.; what should hinder but that it may be so with us also? Such as begin to work with the needle, look much on their sampler and pattern: it is so in learning to write, and indeed in learning to live also. Observe the gracious conversations and carriages of the choicest saints, keep a fixed eye upon the wise, prudent, humble, holy, and heavenly deportment; write after the fairest copy you can find, labour to imitate those Christians that are most eminent in grace. I shall conclude this head with that of the heathen: *Optimum est majorum sequi vestigia, si rectè præcesserint,* It is best to tread in the steps of those who are gone in a safe and good way before us, [Seneca.] But,

11. The eleventh word of advice and counsel is this, *Be much in the most spiritual exercises of religion.* There are external exercises, such as hearing, praying, singing, receiving, holy conference, &c., Isa. i. 11–14, and 1 Tim. iv. 8, and Mat. vi. Now custom, conviction, education, and a hundred other external considerations, may lead persons to these external exercises: but then there are the more spiritual exercises of religion, such as loving of God, delighting in God, prizing of Christ, compliance with the motions, counsels, and dictates of the Spirit, living in an exercise of grace, triumphing in Christ Jesus, setting our affections upon things above, meditation, self-examination, self-judging, &c. Now the more you live in the exercise of these more spiritual duties of religion, the more you glorify God—the more you evidence the power of grace, and the in-dwellings of the Spirit—and the more you difference and distinguish yourselves from hypocrites and all unsound professors, and the better foundation you lay for a bright, strong, and growing assurance. But,

12. The twelfth and last word of advice and counsel I shall give you is, *To make a wise, a seasonable, a sincere, a daily, and a thorough improvement of all the talents that God has intrusted you with.* There is a talent of time, of power, of riches, of honour, of greatness, that some are more intrusted with than others are. The improvement of these is your great wisdom, and should be your daily works, 1 Cor iv. 1, 2. You know you are but stewards, and that you must shortly give an account of your stewardship, Luke xvi. 1–4. And oh that you may make such a faithful and full improvement of all the great talents that God has intrusted you with, that you may give up your account at last with joy, and not with grief! Some princes have wished upon their beds that they had never reigned, because they have not improved their power for God and his people, but against God and his people; and some rich men have wished that they had never been rich, because they have not improved their riches for the glory of God, nor for the

succour and relief of his suffering saints. A beggar upon the way asked something of an honourable lady : she gave him sixpence, saying, This is more than ever God gave me. Oh ! says the beggar, Madam, you have abundance, and God hath given you all that you have ; say not so, good madam. Well, says she, I speak the truth, for God hath not given but lent unto me what I have, that I may bestow it upon such as thou art. And it is very true, indeed, that poor Christians are Christ's alms-men, and the rich are but his stewards, into whose hands God hath put his moneys, to distribute to them as their necessities require. It is credibly reported of Mr Thomas Sutton, the sole founder of that eminent hospital commonly known by his name, that he used often to repair into a private garden, where he poured forth his prayers unto God, and, amongst other passages, was frequently overheard to use this expression : Lord, thou hast given me a liberal and large estate, give me also a heart to make good use of it ; which was granted to him accordingly.[1] Riches are a great blessing, but a heart to use them aright is a far greater blessing. Every rich man is not so much a treasurer as a steward, whose praise is more how to lay out well than to have received much. I know I have transgressed the bounds of an epistle, but love to your souls, and theirs into whose hands this treatise may fall, must be my apology.

Sir, if you and your lady were both my own children, and my only children, I could not give you better nor more faithful counsel than what I have given you in this epistle ; and all out of a sincere, serious, and cordial desire and design, that both of you may be happy here, and found at Christ's right hand in the great day of account, Mat. xxv. 33, 34.

Now the God of all grace fill both your hearts with all the fruits of righteousness and holiness, and greatly bless you both with all spiritual blessings in heavenly places, and make you meet-helps to each other heaven-ward, and at last crown you both with ineffable glory in the life to come. 1 Pet. v. 1 ; Gal. v. 22, 23 ; Eph. i. 3.

So I take leave, and rest your assured friend, and soul's servant,

THOMAS BROOKS.

---

[1] Fuller's Church History of Britain. [The founder of the Charter-house, London.—G.]

THE COVENANT OF GRACE PROVED
AND OPENED.

BELOVED IN OUR LORD,—In the first part of my Golden Key, I have shewed you seven several pleas, that all sincere Christians may form up, as to those several scriptures in the Old and New Testament, that refer either to the great day of account, or to their particular days of account. In this second part, I shall go on where I left, and shew you several other choice pleas, that all believers may make in the present case.

VIII. The eighth plea that a believer may form up as to the ten scriptures in the margin,[1] that refer to the great day of account, or to a man's particular account, may be drawn up from *the consideration of the covenant of grace, or the new covenant that all believers are under*. It is of high concernment to understand the tenure of the covenant of grace, or the new covenant, which is the law you must judge of your estates by, for if you mistake in that you will err in the conclusion. That person is very unfit to make a judge, who is ignorant of the law, by which himself and others must be tried. For the clearing of my way, let me premise these six things:—

1. First, Premise this with me, that *God hath commonly dealt with man in the way of a covenant;* that being a way that is most suitable to man, and most honourable for man, and the most amicable and friendly way of dealing with man. No sooner was man made, but God entered into covenant with him, ' In the day thou eatest thereof, thou shalt die the death,' Gen. ii. 17; and after this, he made a covenant with the world, by Noah, Gen. ix. 11–15, and vi. 18; and after this, he made a covenant with Abraham, Gen. xvii. 1, 2; and after this, he made a covenant with the Jews at Mount Sinai, Exod. xix. Thus you see that God has commonly dealt with man in the way of a covenant. But,

2. Secondly, Premise this with me, *All men are under some covenant or other;* they are either under a covenant of works, or they are under a covenant of grace. All persons that live and die without an interest in Christ, they live and die under a covenant of works; such as live and die with an interest in Christ, they live and die under a

---

[1] Eccles. xi. 9, and xii. 14; Mat. xii. 14, and xviii. 23; Luke xvi. 2; Rom. xiv. 10; 2 Cor. v. 10; Heb. ix. 27, and xiii. 17; 1 Pet. iv. 5.

covenant of grace. There is but a twofold standing taken notice of in the blessed Scriptures ; the one is under the law, the other is under grace. Now he that is not under grace, is under the law, Rom vi. 14. It is true, in the Scripture you do not read, *in totidem syllabis*, of the covenant of works and the covenant of grace ; but that of the apostle comes near it : Rom. iii. 27, 'Where is boasting then ? It is excluded. By what law ? of works ? Nay, but by the law of faith.' [1] Here you have the law of works, opposed to the law of faith ; which holds out as much as the covenant of works and the covenant of grace. The apostle sets forth this twofold condition of men, by a very pertinent resemblance, namely, by that of marriage, Rom. vii. 1-3. All Adam's seed are married to one of these two husbands; either to the law, or to Christ. He that is not spiritually married to Christ, and so brought under his covenant, is still under the law as a covenant of works ; even as a wife is under the law of her husband while he is yet alive. Certainly there were never any but two covenants made with man, the one legal, the other evangelical ; the one of works, the other of grace ; the first in innocency, the other after the fall : ponder upon Rom. iv. 13. But,

3. Thirdly, Let me premise this, that *the covenant of grace was so legally dispensed to the Jews, that it seems to be nothing else but the repetition of the covenant of works ;* in respect of which legal dispensations of it, the same covenant, under the law, is called a covenant of works ; under the gospel, in regard of the clearer manifestation of it, it is called a covenant of grace : but these were not two distinct covenants, but one and the same covenant diversely dispensed. The covenant of grace is the same for substance now to us since Christ was exhibited, as it was to the Jews before he was exhibited ; but the manner of administration of it is different, because it is :—(1.) Now clearer : things were declared then in types and shadows, heaven was then typed out by the land of Canaan, but now we have things more plainly manifested, 2 Cor. iii. 12 ; Heb. vii. 22. In this respect it is called ' a better testament or covenant,' Heb. viii. 6 ; not in substance, but in the manner of revealing it ; and the promises are said to be ' better promises' upon the same account, Acts x. 35. (2.) The covenant of grace, is now more largely extended ; then it extended only to the Jews, but now to all that know the Lord, and that choose him, fear him, love him, and serve him in all nations, Col. iii. 11 ; Neh. vii. 2 ; Job i. 1, 8 ; Acts xiii. 22, *seq. ;* Rom. iv. 18-20. (3.) There is more abundance of the Spirit, of grace, of light, of knowledge, of holiness, poured out generally upon the people of God now, than there was in those times. Though then some few eminent saints had much of the Spirit, and much of grace and holiness, both in their hearts and lives ; but now the generality of the saints have more of the Spirit, and more grace and holiness, than the generality of the saints had in those times. But,

4. Fourthly, Premise this with me, that *a right notion of the covenant, according to the originals of the Old and New Testament, will*

---

[1] I am not of Cameron's mind, that there were three covenants ; but of the apostle's mind, who expressly tells us that there are two testaments, and no more, in that Gal. iv. 24.

conduce much to a right understanding of God's covenant.[1] The derivation of the Hebrew word, and of the Greek, may give us great light, and is of special use to shew the nature of the covenant which they principally signify, and what special things are therein required. (1.) The Hebrew word, בְּרִית, *Berith*, a covenant, is by learned men derived from several roots :

[1.] First, Some derive it from בָּרַר, *Barar*, to purify, make clear, and to purge out dross, chaff, and all uncleanness; and to select, and choose out, and separate the pure from the impure, the gold and silver from the dross, and the pure wheat from the chaff. The reasons of this derivation are these two :—(1.) Because by covenants open and clear amity is confirmed, and faithfulness is plainly and clearly declared and ratified, without deceit or sophistication, betwixt covenanters ; and things are made plain and clear betwixt them in every point and article. (2.) Because God, in the covenant of works, did choose out man especially, with whom he made the covenant; and because in the covenant of grace he chooseth out of the multitude his elect, even his church and faithful people, whom he did separate by predestination and election from all eternity, to be a holy people to himself in Christ, Eph. i. 4. (3.) Some derive it from בָּרָה, and verily, the Lord, when he makes a covenant with any, he doth separate them from others, he looks on them, and takes them, and owns them for his 'peculiar people,' 1 Pet. ii. 9, for his 'peculiar treasure,' Exod. xix. 5, and agrees with them as the chosen and choicest of all others. The first staff in Zech. xi. 10, is called 'Beauty,' and this was the covenant; and certainly it must be a high honour for a people to be in covenant with God ; for by this means God becomes ours, and we are made nigh unto him, Jer. xxxi. 38, 40, 41. He is ours, and we are his, in a very peculiar way of relation ; and by this means God opens his love and all his treasures of grace unto us. In his covenant he tells us of his special care, love, kindness, and great intentions of good to us ; and by this means his faithfulness comes to be obliged to make good all his covenant relations and engagements to us, Deut. vii. 9. Now in all this God puts a great favour and honour upon his people. Hence, when the Lord told Abraham that he would make a covenant with him, Abraham fell upon his face ; he was amazed at so great a love and honour, Gen. xvii. 2, 3.

[2.] Secondly, Some derive the word from בָּרָה, *Barah*, *comedit*, to eat, because usually they had a feast at the making of covenants. In the Eastern countries they commonly established their covenants by eating and drinking together. Herodotus tells us that the Persians were wont to contract leagues and friendship, *inter vinum et epulas*, in a full feast, whereat their wives, children, and friends, were present. The like, Tacitus reports of the Germans. Amongst the Greeks and other nations, the covenanters ate bread and salt together. The Emperor of Russia, at this day, when he would shew extraordinary

---

[1] The word *covenant* in our English tongue, signifies, as we all know, a mutual promise, bargain, and obligation, between two persons ; and so likewise doth the Hebrew *Berith*, and the Greek διαθήκη. A covenant is a solemn compact or agreement between two chosen parties, or more ; whereby, with mutual, free, and full consent, they bind and oblige themselves one to another. A covenant is *Amicus status inter fœderatos* : so Martin [Luther?] ' A friendly state between allies.'

grace and favour unto any, sends him bread and salt from his
table; and when he invited Baron Sigismund, the Emperor Ferdin-
and's ambassador, he did it in this form: *Sigismunde, comedes sal
et panem nostrum nobiscum:* Sigismund, you shall eat our bread
and salt with us.   Hence that symbol of Pythagoras, Ἄρτον μὴ
καταγνύειν, 'break no bread,' is interpreted by Erasmus and others to
mean, 'break no friendship.'[1]   Moreover, the Egyptians, Thracians,
and Lybians in special, are said to have used to make leagues, and
contract friendship, by presenting a cup of wine one to another; which
custom we find still in use amongst our western nations.   It has been
the universal custom of mankind, and still remains in use, to contract
covenants, and make leagues and friendship, by eating and drinking
together.   When Isaac made a covenant with Abimelech, the king of
Gerar, the text saith, ' He made him, and those that were with him,
a feast; and they did eat and drink, and rose up betimes in the morning, and sware one to another,' Gen. xxvi. 30, 31.   When Jacob
made a covenant with Laban, after they had sworn together, he
made him a feast, ' and called his brethren to eat bread,' saith the
text, Gen. xxxi. 54.   When David made a league with Abner, upon
his promise of bringing all Israel unto him, David made ' Abner and
the men that were with him a feast,' saith the text, 2 Sam. iii. 20.
Hence, in the Hebrew tongue a covenant is called בְּרִית, *Berith*, of
ברה, *Barah*, to eat, as if they should say an eating; which derivation
is so natural, that it deserves, say some, to be preferred before that,
from the other signification of the same verb, which is to choose; of
which before.   Now they that derive *Berith* from *Barah*, which signifies to eat and refresh one's self with meat, they give this reason for
that derivation, viz., because the old covenant of God, made with man
in the creation, was a covenant wherein the condition or law was about
eating; that man should eat of all the trees and fruits, except of the
tree of knowledge of good and evil, Gen. ii. 16, 17; and in the solemn
making and sealing of the covenant of grace in Christ, the blessed
seed, the public ceremony was slaying and sacrificing of beasts, and
eating some part of them, after the fat and the choice parts were
offered up and burned on the altar.   For God, by virtue of that covenant, gave man leave to eat the flesh of beasts, Deut. xii. 27, which
he might not do in the state of innocency, Gen. i. 29, being limited to
fruits of trees, and herbs bearing seed, for his meat.   So, also, in
solemn covenants between men, the parties were wont to eat together,
Gen. xxxi. 46.

[3.] Thirdly, Others derive the word *Berith* from ברא, *Bara*, or
ברה, *Barah*, to smite, strike, cut, or divide, as both these words signify.
The word also signifies to elect or choose; and the reasons they give
for this derivation, are these two:—*First*, Because covenants are not
made, but by choice persons, chosen out one by another, and about
choice matters, and upon choice conditions, chosen out, and agreed
upon by both parties. *Secondly*, Because, in making of covenants,
commonly sacrifices were stricken and slain, for confirmation and
solemnity.   Of old, God sealed his covenants by sacrifices of beasts
slain, divided, and cut asunder, and the choice fat, and other parts,

---

[1] Vide Turcium ritum opud Busbequium, epist. i. 11.

offered upon the altar. And in making of great and solemn covenants, men, in old time, were wont to kill and cut asunder sacrificed beasts; and to pass between the parts divided, for a solemn testimony, or for the confirmation of the covenants that they had made, Gen. xv. 9, 10, 17.[1] And as, learned men have long since observed, that the very heathen, in their covenanting, used sacrifices, and divided them, passing between the parts; and this they did, as some conjecture, in imitation of God's people. This third is the common opinion, about the original of this name; and therefore preferred before all other. So this word בְּרִית, *Berith*, covenant, seems to sound as much as כָּרִית, *Kerith*, a smiting or striking, because of sacrifices slain in covenanting. Hence the word covenant is often joined with כָּרַת, *Karath*, which signifies striking of covenant. An example of this beyond all exception, saith my author,[2] is in that sacrifice, wherein God by Moses, made a covenant with all the people of Israel, and bound them to obey his law: the description of it is in Exod. xxiv. 4–8, ' And Moses wrote all the words of the Lord, and rose up early in the morning and builded an altar under the hill, and twelve pillars, according to the twelve tribes of Israel. And he sent young men of the children of Israel, which offered burnt-offerings, and sacrificed peace-offerings of oxen unto the Lord. And Moses took half of the blood, and put it in basins; and half of the blood he sprinkled on the altar. And he took the book of the covenant and read it in the audience of the people; and they said, All that the Lord hath said will we do, and be obedient. And Moses took the blood, and sprinkled it on the people, and said, Behold the blood of the covenant, which the Lord hath made with you concerning all these words.'[3] I shall not trouble my reader with that mystical and too curious a sense, that some of the ancients put upon these words:[4] the historical sense is here more fit: for in this ceremony of dividing the blood in two parts, and so besprinkling the altar with the one half, which represented God; and the people with the other, between whom the covenant was confirmed, the old use in striking of covenants is observed. For the ancient custom was, that they which made a league or covenant, divided some beasts, and put the parts asunder, walking in the midst; signifying that as the beast was divided, so they should be which brake the covenant. So when Saul went against the Ammonites, coming out of the field, he hewed two oxen, and sent them into all the coasts of Israel, 1 Sam. xi. 7; expressing the like signification, that so should his oxen be served that came not forth after Saul and Samuel. After the same manner, when God made a covenant with Abraham, Gen. xv. 12–19, and he had divided certain beasts, as God had commanded him, and laid one part against another, a smoking firebrand went between, representing God, signifying, that so he should be divided, which violated the covenant. So in this place, not much unlike; the blood is parted in twain, shewing that so should his blood be shed, which kept not the covenant.

---

[1] Jer. xxxiv. 18–20, and Lev. xxvi. 25. Weigh well these two scriptures. Covenant breakers may well look upon them as flaming swords, as terrible thunderbolts.
[2] And. Rivetus in Gen. xxxi; Exercitat 135. [Misprinted ' Riven.'—G.]
[3] Anciently covenants were made with blood, to betoken constancy in the covenant, even to the shedding of blood, and loss of life.
[4] Rupertus, Ambrose, Cajetan, &c.

[4.] Fourthly, Some derive the word *Berith* from ברא, *Bara*, to create ; and the reason they give for this derivation is this, because the first state of creation was confirmed by the covenant which God made with man, and all creatures were to be upheld by means of observing of the law and condition of the covenant ; and that covenant being broken by man, the world, made subject to ruin, is upheld, yea, and as it were created anew, by the covenant of grace in Christ.

[5.] Fifthly, Some derive the word *Berith* from ברת, *Berath*, which signfies firmness, sureness, because covenants are firm and sure, and all things agreed on are confirmed and made sure by them. God's covenant is a sure covenant: Deut. vii. 9, ' The Lord thy God, he is the faithful God,' or the God of Amen, ' which keepeth covenant with them that love him:' Ps. lxxxix. 34, ' My covenant will I not break'—Hebrew, ' I will not profane,' ' nor alter the thing that is gone out of my lips.'[1] All God's precepts, all God's predictions, all God's menaces, and all God's promises, are the issue of a most just, faithful, and righteous will. There are three things that God cannot do:—(1.) He cannot die. (2.) He cannot lie: Titus i. 2, ' In hope of eternal life, which God, that cannot lie, promised before the world began.' (3.) He cannot deny himself. Now the derivation of *Berith*, from the several roots specified, and not from one only, doth give much light to the point under consideration ; and doth reconcile in one, all the several opinions of the learned, and justifies their several derivations, without rejecting or offering any wrong or disgrace to any.

(2.) Secondly, The Greek name Διαθήκη, *Diatheke*, a covenant or a testament. By this Greek word the Septuagint, in their Greek translation, do commonly express the Hebrew word *Berith ;* and it is observable that this is the only word by which the Hebrew word *Berith* is rendered in the New Testament. This Greek word, Διαθήκη, is translated *covenant* in the New Testament about twenty times ; and the same word is translated *testament* in the New Testament about twelve times.[2] Wherever you find the word *covenant* in the New Testament, there you shall find *Diatheke ;* and wherever you find the word *testament* in the New Testament, there you shall find *Diatheke ;* so that it is of importance for us to understand this word aright. Now this Greek word, Διαθήκη, is derived from Διατίθημι, *Diatithemi*, which hath divers of the significations of the Hebrew words of which *Berith* is derived ; for it signifies to set things in order and frame, to appoint orders, and make laws, to pacify and make satisfaction, and to dispose things by one's last will and testament. Now to compose and set things in order is to uphold the creation ; to walk by orders and laws made and appointed is to walk by rule, and to live, to deal plainly and faithfully without deceit. To pacify and make satisfaction includes sacrifices and sin-offerings. To dispose by will and testament implies choice of persons and gifts ; for men do commonly by will give their best and most choice things to their most dear and most choice friends. Thus the Greek which the apostles use in the New Testament to signify a covenant, to express the Hebrew

---

[1] Jer. xxxi. 31, 33, 35–37 ; Ps. xix. 7 ; Rev. iii. 14 ; Isa. liv. 10.
[2] Heb. viii. 6–10, and i. 4 ; Luke i. 72 ; Rom. ix. 4, &c. ; Mat. xxvi. 28 ; Luke xxii. 20, &c.

word *Berith*, which is used in the law and the prophets, doth confirm our derivation of it from all the words before named. And this derivation of the Hebrew and Greek names of a covenant being thus laid down, and confirmed by the reasons formerly cited, is of great use. The various acceptation and use of these two names in the Old and New Testament is very considerable for the opening of the covenant : *First*, To shew unto us the full signification of the word *covenant*, and what the nature of a covenant is in general. *Second*, To justify the divers acceptations of the word, and to shew the nature of every word in particular, and so to make way for the knowledge of the agreement and difference between the old and new covenant. Here, as in a crystal glass, you may see that this word *Berith*, and this word *Diatheke*, signify all covenants in general, whether they are religious or civil ; for there is nothing in any true covenant which is not comprised in the signification of these words, being expounded according to the former derivations. Here also we may see what is the nature of a covenant in general, and what things are thereunto required ; as, *first*, every true covenant presupposeth a division or separation ; *secondly*, it comprehends in it a mutual promising and binding between two distinct parties ; *thirdly*, there must be faithful dealing, without fraud, or dissembling on both sides ; *fourthly*, this must be between choice persons ; ·*fifthly*, it must be about choice matters and upon choice conditions, agreed upon by both ; *sixthly* and lastly, it must tend to the well-ordering and composing of things between them. Now all these are manifest by the several significations of the words from which *Berith* and *Diatheke* are derived. And thus much for the word *covenant* according to the originals of the Old and New Testament.

5. Fifthly, Premise this with me, that there was *a covenant of works, or a reciprocal covenant, betwixt God and Adam, together with all his posterity.* Before Adam fell from his primitive holiness, beauty, glory, and excellency, God made a covenant with Adam as a public person, which represented all mankind. The covenant of works was made with all men in Adam, who was made and stood as a public person, head and root, in a common and comprehensive capacity. I say, it was made with him as such, and we all in him ; he and all stood and fell together. (1.) Witness the imputation of Adam's sin to all mankind: Rom. v. 12, ' In whom,' or forasmuch as, ' all have sinned ;' they sinned not all in themselves, therefore in Adam ; see ver. 14, ' In him all died.' (2.) Witness the curse of the covenant that all mankind are directly under ; consult the scriptures in the margin.[1] Those on whom the curse of the covenant comes, those are under the bond and precept of the covenant. But all mankind are under the curse of the covenant, and therefore all mankind are under the bond and precept of the covenant. Adam did understand the terms of the covenant, and did consent to the terms of the covenant ; for God dealt with him in a rational way, and expected from him a reasonable service. The end of this covenant was the upholding of the creation, and of all the creatures in their pure natural estate, for the comfort of man continually, and for the special manifestation of God's free grace ;

[1] 1 Cor. xv. 47; Deut. xxix. 21; Rom. viii. 20, 21; Gal. iii. 10, 13.

and that he might put the greater obligation upon Adam to obey his Creator and to sweeten his authority to man; and that he might draw out Adam to an exercise of his faith, love, and hope in his Creator; and that he might leave Adam the more inexcusable in case he should sin; and that so a clear way might be made for God's justification and man's conviction.   Upon these grounds God dealt with Adam, not only in a way of sovereignty, but in a way of covenant.

Quest. But how may it be evidenced that God entered into a covenant of works with the first Adam before his fall, there being no mention of such a covenant in the Scripture that we read of ?

Ans. Though the name be not in the Scripture, yet the thing is in the Scripture, as will evidently appear by comparing scripture with scripture.[1]   Though it be not positively and plainly said in the blessed Scripture that God made a covenant of works with Adam before his fall, yet, upon sundry scripture grounds and considerations, it may be sufficiently evidenced that God did make such a covenant with Adam before his fall; and therefore it is a nice cavil, and a foolish vanity, for any to make such a noise about the word covenant, and for want of the word covenant, boldly to conclude that there was no such covenant made with Adam, when the thing is lively set down in other words, though the word covenant be not expressed; and this I shall make evident by an induction of particulars, thus :—

[1.] First, God, to declare his sovereignty and man's subjection, gave Adam, though innocent, *a law.*   God's express prescription of a positive law unto Adam in his innocent state, is clearly and fully laid down in that Gen. ii. 16, 17, 'And the Lord God commanded the man, saying, Of every tree of the garden thou mayest freely eat; but of the tree of the knowledge of good and evil, thou shalt not eat of it: for in the day that thou eatest thereof thou shalt surely die;' Hebrew, 'dying thou shalt die.'   Mark how God bounds man's obedience with a double fence: *first*, He fenced him with a free indulgence to eat of every tree in the garden but one, the less cause he had to be liquorish after forbidden fruit; but 'stolen waters are sweet.'   *Secondly*, By an exploratory[2] prohibition, upon pain of death.   By the first, the Lord woos him by love; by the second, he frights him by the terror of his justice, and bids him touch and taste if he durst.   The *fœderati* were God and Adam; God the Creator, and man, the creature, made 'after God's image and likeness;' and so not contrary to God, nor at enmity with him, but like unto God, though far different and inferior to God in nature and substance.   Here are also terms agreed on, and matters covenanted reciprocally, by these parties.   Adam, on his part, was to be obedient to God, in forbearing to eat of the tree of knowledge only. God's charge to our first parents was only negative, not to eat of the tree of knowledge; the other, to eat of the trees, was left unto their

---

[1] Socinians call for the word ' Satisfaction,' others call for the word ' Sacrament,' others call for the word ' Trinity,' and others call for the word ' Sabbath,' for Lord's day, &c. ; and thence conclude against Satisfaction, Sacraments, Trinity, Sabbath, for want of express words, when the things themselves are plainly and lively set down, in other words, in the blessed Scriptures; so it is in this case of God's covenant with Adam.   The vanity and folly of such ways of reasoning is sufficiently demonstrated by all writers upon those subjects that are sound in the faith, &c.

[2] Qu. 'explanatory'?—G.

choice. Eve confesseth that God spake unto them both, and said, ' Ye shall not eat of it,' Gen. iii. 2; and God speaks unto both of them together in these words, ' Behold, I have given unto you every herb, and every tree,' &c., Gen. i. 19. At which time also it is very like that he gave them the other prohibition of not eating of that one tree ; for if God had ˉmade that exception before, he would not have given a general permission after ; or if this general grant had gone before, the exception coming should seem to abrogate the former grant. The Septuagint seem to be of this mind, that this precept was given both to Adam and Eve, reading thus in the plural number, ' In what day ye shall eat thereof ye shall die.' [1] And though, in the original, the precept be given in the name of Adam only, that is only (1.) Because Adam was the more principal, and he had the charge of the woman ; and (2.) Because that the greatest danger was in his transgression, which was the cause of the ruin of his posterity ; (3.) Because, as Mercerus well observes, Adam was the common name both of the man and woman, Gen. v. 2, and so is taken, ver. 15. And God, on his part, for the present, permits Adam to eat of all other trees of the garden ; and for the future, in his explicit threatening of death in case of disobedience, implicitly promiseth life in case of obedience herein.

[2.] Secondly, *The promises of this covenant on God's part were very glorious*—*First*, That heaven, and earth, and all creatures should continue in their natural course and order wherein God had created and placed them, serving always for man's use, and that man should have the benefit and lordship of them all. *Secondly*, As for natural life, in respect of the body, Adam should have had perfection without defect, beauty without deformity, labour without weariness. *Thirdly*, As for spiritual life, Adam should never have known what it was to be under terrors and horrors of conscience, nor what a wounded spirit means, Prov. xviii. 14 ; he should never have found ' the arrows of the Almighty sticking fast in him, nor the poison thereof drinking up his spirits, nor the terrors of God to set themselves in array against him,' Job vi. 4 ; nor he should never have tasted of death. Death is a fall that came in by a fall. Had Adam never sinned, Adam had never died ; had Adam stood fast in innocency, he should have been translated to glory without dissolution. Death came in by sin, and sin goeth out by death. As the worm kills the worm that bred it, so death kills sin that bred it. Now where there are parties covenanting, promising, and agreeing upon terms, and terms mutually agreed upon by those parties, as here, there is the substance of an express covenant, though it be not formally and in express words called a covenant. This was the first covenant which God made with man, and this is called by the name *Berith*, Jer. xxxiii. 20, where God saith, ' If you can break my covenant of the day and night, and that there shall not be day and night in their season,' ver. 21, ' then may also my covenant with David be broken.' In these words he speaks plainly of the promise in the creation, that day and night should keep their course, and the sun, moon, and stars, and all creatures, should serve for man's use, Gen. i. 14–16. Now though man did break the covenant on his part, yet God, being immutable, could not break covenant

[1] So doth Gregory read as the Septuagint does.—*Greg. Moral.* lib. xxxv. cap. 10.

on his part, neither did he suffer his promise to fail; but, by virtue of Christ promised to man in the new covenant, he will keep touch with man so long as mankind hath a being on the earth.   In this first covenant, God promised unto man life and happiness, lordship over all the creatures, liberty to use them, and all other blessings which his heart could desire, to keep him in that happy estate wherein he was created.   And man was bound to God to walk in perfect righteousness, to observe and keep God's commandments, and to obey his will in all things which were within the reach of his nature, and so far as was revealed to him.   In the first covenant, God revealed himself to man as one God, Creator, and Governor of all things, infinite in power, wisdom, goodness, nature, and substance.   God was man's good Lord, and man was God's good servant; God dearly loved man, and man greatly loved God with all his heart.   There was not the least shadow or occasion of hatred or enmity between them; there was nothing but mutual love, mutual delight, mutual content, and mutual satisfaction between God and man.   Man, in his primitive glory, needed no mediator to come between God and him.   Man was perfect, pure, upright, and good, created after God's own image; and the nearer he came to God, the greater was his joy and comfort.   God's presence now was man's great delight, and it was man's heaven on earth to walk with God.   But,

[3.] Thirdly, Consider *the intention and use of the two eminent trees in the garden, that are mentioned in a more peculiar manner*—viz., the tree of life and the tree of knowledge.   The intended use of these two trees in paradise was sacramental.   Hence they are called *symbolical* trees, and *sacramental* trees, by learned writers, both ancient and modern.   By these the Lord did signify and seal to our first parents that they should always enjoy that happy state of life in which they were made, upon condition of obedience to his commandments; *i.e.*, in eating of the tree of life, and not eating of the tree of knowledge.[1] The tree of life is so called, not because of any native property and peculiar virtue it had in itself to convey life, but symbolically, morally, and sacramentally.   It was a sign and obligation to them of life, natural and spiritual, to be continued to them as long as they continued in obedience to God.   The seal of the first covenant was the tree of life, which if Adam had received by taking and eating of it, whilst he stood in the state of innocency before his fall, he had certainly been established in that estate for ever; and the covenant being sealed and confirmed between God and him on both parts, he could not have been seduced and supplanted by Satan, as some learned men do think, and as God's own words seem to imply, Gen. iii. 22, 'And now, lest he put forth his hand, and take also of the tree of life, and eat, and live for ever.'   'The tree of knowledge of good and evil' was spoken from the sad event and experience they had of it, as Samson had of God's departing from him when he lost his Nazaritish hair by Delilah.   'The tree of life' was a sacrament of life; 'the tree of knowledge' a sacrament of death.   'The tree of life' was for confirmation of man's obe-

---

[1] The tree of life was the sign and seal which God gave to man for confirmation of this first covenant; and it was to man a sacrament and pledge of eternal life on earth and of all blessings needful to keep man in life.

dience, and 'the tree of knowledge' was for caution against disobedience. Now if those two trees were two sacraments, the one assuring of life in case of obedience, the other assuring of death in case of disobedience, then hence we may collect that God not only entered into a covenant of works with the first Adam, but also gave him this covenant under sacramental signs and seals. But,

[4.] Fourthly, Seriously consider that *a covenant of works lay clear, in that commandment*, Gen. ii. 16, 17, which may thus be made evident:—(1.) Because that was the condition of man's standing and life, as it was expressly declared; (2.) Because, in the breach of that commandment given him, he lost all, and we in him. God made the covenant of works primarily with Adam, and with us in him, as our head, inclusively; so that when he did fall we did fall, when he lost all we lost all. There are five things we lost in our fall:—(1.) Our holy image, and so became vile; (2.) Our sonship, and so became slaves; (3.) Our friendship, and so became enemies; (4.) Our communion with God, and so became strangers; (5.) Our glory, and so became miserable. Sin and death came into the world by Adam's fall. In Adam's sinning we all sinned, and in Adam's dying we all died; as you may see, by comparing the scriptures in the margin together.[1] In Adam's first sin, we all became sinners by imputation: Adam being a universal person, and all mankind one in him, by God's covenant of works with him. *Omnes ille unus homo fuerunt*, All were that one man, [Augustine,] viz., by federal consociation. God covenanted with Adam, and in him with all his posterity; and therefore Adam's breach of covenant fell not only upon him, but upon all his posterity. But,

[5.] Fifthly and lastly, We read of *a second covenant*, Heb. x. 9; Rom. ix. 4; Gal. iv. 24; Eph. ii. 12, and we read of a 'new covenant:' Jer. xxxi. 31, 'Behold the days come, saith the Lord, that I will make a new covenant with the house of Israel, and with the house of Judah.' So Heb. viii. 8, 'I will make a new covenant,' &c.; ver. 13, 'In that he saith a new covenant, he hath made the first old,' &c.; chap. xii. 24, 'And to Jesus the mediator of the new covenant,' &c. Now if there be a 'second covenant,' then we may safely conclude there was a 'first;' and if there be a 'new covenant,' then we may boldly conclude that there was an 'old covenant.' A covenant of grace always supposeth a covenant of works, Heb. viii. 7-9. I know there is a repetition of the covenant of works with Adam, in the law of Moses; as in that of the apostle to the Galatians, 'The law is not of faith, but the man that doth these things, shall live in them,' Gal. iii. 10-12. The law requires works, and promiseth no life to those that will be justified by faith. In the first covenant, three things are observable:—(1.) The precept, that ' continueth not in all things;' the precept requires perfect, personal, and perpetual obedience; (2.) The promise, 'live;' 'the man that doth them shall live;' live happily, blessedly, cheerfully, everlastingly; (3.) The curse in case of transgression, 'Cursed is every one that continueth not in all things which are written in the book of the law, to do them.' One sin, and that but in thought, broke the angels' covenant, and hath brought them into everlasting chains,

[1] 1 Cor. xv. 22; Rom. v. 12 to the end, &c.

Jude 6. So the same apostle to the Romans further tells us, that 'Moses describeth the righteousness which is of the law, that the man that doth those things shall live by them,' Rom. x. 5. Thus it was with Adam, principally and properly, therefore he was under a covenant of works, when God gave him that command, Gen. ii. 16, 17. This first covenant is called a covenant of works, because this covenant required working on our part as the condition of it, for justification and happiness, 'The man that doth these things shall live.' Under this covenant God left man to stand upon his own bottom, and to live upon his own stock, and by his own industry. God made him perfect and upright, and gave him power and ability to stand, and laid no necessity at all upon him to fall. In this first covenant of works, man had no need of a mediator, God did then stipulate with Adam immediately; for seeing he had not made God his enemy by sin, he needed no daysman to make friendly intercession for him, Job ix. 33.

Adam was invested and endowed with righteousness and holiness in his first glorious estate; with righteousness, that he might carry it fairly, justly, evenly, and righteously towards man; and with holiness, that he might carry it wisely, lovingly, reverentially, and holily towards God, and that he might take up in God as his chiefest good, as in his great all.[1] I shall not now stand upon the discovery of Adam's beauty, authority, dominion, dignity, honour, and glory, with which he was adorned, invested, and crowned in innocency. Let this satisfy, that Adam's first estate was a state of perfect knowledge, wisdom, and understanding; it was a perfect state of holiness, righteousness, and happiness. There was nothing within him but what was desirable and delectable; there was nothing without him but what was amiable and commendable; nor nothing about him but what was serviceable and comfortable. Adam, in his innocent estate, was the wonder of all understanding, the mirror of wisdom and knowledge, the image of God, the delight of heaven, the glory of the creation, the world's great lord, and the Lord's great darling. Upon all these accounts, he had no need of a mediator. And let thus much suffice to have spoken concerning the first covenant of works, that was between God and Adam in innocency. But,

6. Sixthly, Premise this with me—viz., that there is *a new covenant, a second covenant, or a covenant of grace betwixt God and his people*, Heb. viii. 6-13. Express scriptures prove this: Deut. vii. 9, 'Know therefore, that the Lord thy God, he is God; the faithful God, which keepeth covenant and mercy with them that love him, and keep his commandments, to a thousand generations;' 2 Sam. xxiii. 5, 'Although my house be not so with God, yet he hath made with me an everlasting covenant, ordered in all things, and sure: for this is all my salvation, and all my desire; although he make it not to grow;'[2] Neh. i. 5, 'I beseech thee, O Lord God of heaven, the great and terrible God; that keepeth covenant and mercy for them that love him, and keep his commandments;' Isa. liv. 10, 'For the mountains shall depart, and the hills be removed; but my kindness shall not

---

[1] Eph. iv. 22-24. In this scripture, the apostle speaks plainly of the renovation of that knowledge, holiness, and righteousness that Adam sometimes had, but lost it by his fall, Ps. viii. 4-6; Gen. ii. 20.

[2] See this, 2 Sam. xxiii. 5, opened in my 'Box of Precious Ointments,' pp. 369-374. [Vol. iii. p. 491, *seq.*—G.]

depart from thee, neither shall the covenant of my peace be removed, saith the Lord, that hath mercy on thee;' Jer. xxxii. 40, 'And I will make an everlasting covenant with them, that I will not turn away from them, to do them good; but I will put my fear in their hearts, that they shall not depart from me;' Ezek. xx. 37, 'And I will cause you to pass under the rod, and I will bring you into the bond of the covenant;' Deut. xxix. 12, 'That thou shouldest enter into covenant with the Lord thy God; and into his oath, which the Lord thy God maketh with thee to-day.' Consult the scriptures in the margin also, for they cannot be applied to Christ, but to us.[1] But for the further evidencing of that covenant that is between the Lord and his people —now that there is a covenant betwixt God and his people may be further evinced by unanswerable arguments—let me point at some among many.

[1.] First, *Christ is said to be 'the mediator of this covenant:'* Heb. ix. 15, 'And for this cause he is the mediator of the new testament, that by means of death, for the redemption of the transgressions that were under the first testament, they which are called might receive the promise of eternal inheritance.' Certainly that covenant, of which Christ is the testator, must needs be a covenant made with us; for else, if the covenant were made only with Christ, as some would have it, then it will roundly follow that Jesus Christ is both testator and the party to whom the testaments and legacies are bequeathed; which sounds harsh, yea, which to assert is very absurd. Since the creation of the world, was it ever known that ever any man did bequeath a testament and legacies to himself? Surely no. Christ is the testator of the new covenant, and therefore we may safely conclude that the new covenant is made with us. The office of mediator, you know, is to stand betwixt two at variance. The two at variance were God and man. Man had offended and incensed God against him. God's wrath was an insupportable burden, and a consuming fire; no creature was able to stand under it, or before it. Therefore Christ, to rescue and redeem man, becomes a mediator. Christ, undertaking to be a mediator, both procured a covenant to pass betwixt God and man, and also engaged himself for the performance thereof on both parts; and to assure man of partaking of the benefit of God's covenant, Christ turns the covenant into a testament, that the conditions of the covenant, on God's part, might be as so many legacies, which, being confirmed by the death of the testator, none might disannul: Heb. viii. 6, 'He is the mediator of a better covenant, which was established upon better promises.' The promises of the new covenant are said to be better in these six respects:—(1.) All the promises of the law were conditional; 'Do this, and thou shalt live.' The promises of the new covenant are absolute, of grace, as well as to grace. (2.) In this better covenant God promiseth higher things. Here God promiseth Himself, his Son, his Spirit, a higher righteousness and a higher sonship. (3.) Because of their stability; those of the old covenant were 'swallowed up in the curse.' These are the 'sure mercies of David.' (4.) They are all bottomed upon faith, they

---

[1] Deut. iv. 23; Isa. lv. 1-3; Jer. xxiv. 7, xxx. 22, xxxi. 31, 33, and xxxii. 38; Heb. viii. 8-10.

all depend upon faith.[1]   (5.) They are all promised upon our interest in Christ. This makes the promises sweet, because they lead us to Christ, the fountain of them, whose mouth is most sweet, and in whose person all the sweets of all created beings do centre.   (6.) Because God hath promised to pour out a greater measure of his Spirit, under the new covenant, than he did under the old covenant: Heb. xii. 24, 'And to Jesus, the mediator of the new covenant.' Thus you see that Christ is called 'the mediator of the covenant' three several times.   Now he could not be the mediator of that covenant that is betwixt God and himself, of which more shortly, but of that covenant that is betwixt God and his people.   But,

[2.] Secondly, *The people of God have pleaded the covenant that is betwixt God and them:* 'Remember thy covenant.'   Now how could they plead the covenant betwixt God and them if there were no such covenant ?   See the scriptures in the margin.[2]   But,

[3.] Thirdly, *God is often said to remember his covenant:*[3] Gen. ix. 15, 'I will remember my covenant, which is between you and me ;' Exod. vi. 5, 'I have remembered my covenant ;' Lev. xxvi. 42, 'I remember my covenant with Jacob, and also my covenant with Isaac, and also my covenant with Abraham will I remember ;' Ezek. xvi. 60, 'I will remember my covenant with thee, and I will establish unto thee an everlasting covenant.'   Now how can God be said to remember his covenant with his people, if there were no covenant betwixt God and them ?   But,

[4.] Fourthly, *The temporal and spiritual deliverances that you have by the covenant do clearly evidence that there is a covenant betwixt God and you:* Zech. ix. 11, 'As for thee also, by the blood of thy covenant, I have sent forth thy prisoners out of the pit, wherein there was no water.'[4]   These words include both temporal and spiritual deliverances.   So that now, if there be not a covenant betwixt God and you, what deliverances can you expect, seeing they all flow in upon the creature by virtue of the covenant, and according to the covenant ? By the blood of the covenant believers are delivered from the infernal pit, where there is not so much water as might cool Dives his tongue, Luke xvi. 24, 25 ; and by the blood of the covenant they are delivered from those deaths and dangers that do surround them, 2 Cor. i. 8–10. When sincere Christians fall into desperate distresses and most deadly dangers, yet they are prisoners of hope, and may look for deliverance by the blood of the covenant.   This does sufficiently evince a covenant betwixt God and his people.   But,

[5.] Fifthly, *God has threatened severely to avenge and punish the quarrel of his covenant:* Lev. xxvi. 25, 'And I will bring a sword upon you, that shall avenge the quarrel of my covenant ;' or which shall avenge the vengeance of the covenant, &c.   Consult the scriptures in the margin.[5]   Breach of covenant betwixt God and man, breaks

---

[1] Rom. iv. 15, 16 ; Gal. iii. 16, 17 ; 2 Cor. i. 20 ; Cant. v. 16 ; Col. i. 19, and ii. 3 ; Isa. xliv. 3 ; Joel ii. 28 ; Acts ii. 16, 17 ; Gal. iii. 2.

[2] Jer. xiv. 21; Luke i. 72 ; Ps. xxv. 6.

[3] Ponder upon these scriptures, Ps. cv. 8, cvi. 45, and cxi. 5.

[4] Gen. ix. 11 ; Isa. liv. 9;, Ps. cxi. 9 ; Isa. lix. 21.

[5] Deut. xxix. 20, 21, 24, 25, and xxxi. 20, 21 ; Josh. vii. 11, 12, 15, and xxiii. 15, 16 Judges ii. 20 ; 2 Kings xviii. 9–12.

the peace, and breeds a quarrel betwixt them ; in which he will take vengeance of man's revolt, except there be repentance on man's side, and pardoning grace on his. For breach of covenant, Jerusalem is long since laid waste, and the seven golden candlesticks broken in pieces ; and many others, this day, lie a-bleeding in the nations who have made no more of breaking covenant with the great God than if therein they had to do with poor mortals, with dust and ashes like themselves. Now how can there be such a sin as breach of covenant, for which God will be avenged, if there were no covenant betwixt God and his people ? But,

[6.] Sixthly, *The seals of the covenant are given to God's people.* Now to those to whom the seals of the covenant are given, with them is the covenant made ; for the seals of the covenant, and the covenant, go to the same persons : but the seals of the covenant are given to believers. 'Abraham receives the sign of circumcision, a seal of the righteousness of faith,' Rom. iv. 11, *ergo*, the covenant is made with believers. Circumcision is a sign, in regard of the thing signified, and a seal, in regard of the covenant made betwixt God and man. Seal is a borrowed word, taken from kings and princes, who add their broad seal, or privy-seal, to ratify and confirm the leagues, edicts, grants, covenants, charters, that are made with their subjects or confederates. God had made a covenant with Abraham, and by circumcision signs and seals up that covenant.[1] But,

[7.] Seventhly, *The people of God are said sometimes to keep covenant with God :* Ps. xxv. 10, ' All the paths of the Lord are mercy and truth unto such as keep his covenant and his testimonies.' Mercies flowing in upon us, through the covenant, are of all mercies the most soul-satisfying, soul-refreshing, soul-cheering mercies ; yea, they are the very cream of mercy. Oh, how well is it with that saint that can look upon every mercy as a present sent him from heaven by virtue of the covenant ! Oh, this sweetens every drop, and sip, and crust, and crumb of mercy that a Christian enjoys, that all flows in upon him through the covenant ! The promise last cited is a very sweet, choice, precious promise, a promise more worth than all the riches of the Indies. Mark, ' all the paths of the Lord' to his people, they are not only ' mercy,' but they are ' mercy and truth ;' that is, they are sure mercies that stream in upon them, through the covenant. Solomon's dinner of green herbs, Prov. xv. 17 ; Daniel's pulse, Dan. i. 12 ; barley loaves and a few fishes, John vi. 9 ; swimming in upon a Christian, through the new covenant, are far better, greater and sweeter mercies, than all those great things are that flow in upon the great men of the world, through that general providence that feeds the birds of the air, and the beasts of the field : Ps. xliv. 17, ' Yet have we not forgotten thee, neither have we dealt falsely in thy covenant ;' that is, we have kept covenant with thee, by endeavouring to the uttermost of our power to keep off from the breach of thy covenant, and to live up to the duties of thy covenant, suitable to that of the prophet Micah, ' We will walk in the name of the Lord our God for

---

[1] In reason, the covenant and the seals must go together. Were it not a fond and foolish thing in any man to make a covenant with one, and to give the seals to another ? In equity and justice, the covenant and the seals must go to the same persons.

ever and ever,' Micah iv. 5. Persons in covenant with God will not only take a turn or two in his ways, as temporaries and hypocrites do, who are hot at hand, but soon tire and give in, but they will hold on in a course of holiness, and not fail to follow the Lamb, whithersoever he goes: Rev. xiv. 4, and xvii. 14 ; Ps. ciii. 17, ' The mercy of the Lord is from everlasting to everlasting :' ver. 18, ' To such as keep his covenant,' &c. All sincere Christians they keep covenant with God :—(1.) In respect of their cordial desires to keep covenant with God ; (2.) In respect of their habitual purposes and resolutions to keep covenant with God ; (3.) In respect of their habitual and constant endeavours to keep covenant with God, Neh. i. 11 ; Ps. cxix. 133, and xxxix. 1, 2. This is an evangelical and incomplete keeping covenant with God, which in Christ God owns and accepts, and is as well pleased with it as he was with Adam's keeping of covenant with him before his fall. From what has been said, we may thus argue : Those that keep covenant with God, those are in covenant with God, those have made a covenant with God ; but all sincere Christians they do keep covenant with God, *ergo.* But,

[8.] Eighthly and lastly, *The Lord hath, by many choice, precious, and pathetical promises, engaged himself to make good that blessed covenant that he has made with his people, yea, with his choice and chosen ones,* 2 Pet. i. 4. Take a few instances, ' If ye hearken to these judgments,'[1] saith God to Israel, ' and keep and do them, the Lord thy God shall keep unto thee the covenant and the mercy which he sware unto thy fathers,' Deut. vii. 12. This blessed covenant is grounded upon God's free grace ; and therefore in recompensing their obedience God hath a respect to his own mercy, and not to their merits. So Judges ii. 1, ' I made you to go up out of Egypt, and have brought you into the land which I sware unto your fathers ; and I said, I will never break my covenant with you.' God is a God of mercy, and his covenant with his people is a covenant of mercy ; and therefore he will be sure to keep touch with them. So Ps. lxxxix. 34, ' My covenant will I not break, nor alter the thing that is gone out of my mouth ;' as if he should have said, Though they break my statutes, yet will I not break my covenant ; for this seems to have reference to the 31st verse, ' If they break my statutes,' &c. Though they had profaned God's statutes, yet God would not profane his covenant, as the Hebrew runs, ' My covenant will I not break ;' that is, I will stand steadfastly to the performance of it, and to every part and branch of it, I will never be inconstant, I will never be off and on with my people, I will never change my purpose, nor eat my words, nor unsay what I have said. So Jer. xxxiii. 20, ' Thus saith the Lord, If ye can break my covenant of the day, and my covenant of the night,[2] and that there shall not be day and night in their season ;' ver. 21, ' Then may also my covenant be broken with my servant David,' &c. It is impossible for any created power to break off the intercourse of night and day, so it is impossible for me to break the covenant that

---

[1] Under the name judgments, the commandments and statutes of God are contained.

[2] That is, the order that I have set upon the courses and the revolutions of day and night.

I have made with David, my servant ; the day and night shall as soon
fail as my covenant shall fail.   So Isa. liv. 10, ' The mountains shall
depart, and the hills be removed ; but my kindness shall not depart
from thee, neither shall the covenant of my peace be removed, saith
the Lord that hath mercy on thee.'   Though great and huge mountains
should remove, yea, though heaven and earth should meet, Ps. xlvi. 2,
yet the covenant of God with his people shall stand unmovable.
The covenant of God, the mercy of God, and the loving-kindness
of God to his people, shall last for ever, and remain constant and immutable, though all things in the world should be turned upside
down.   So Ps. cxi. 4, ' The Lord is gracious, and full of compassion ;'
ver. 5, ' He will ever be mindful of his covenant.'   God looks not
at his people's sins, but at his own promise ; he will pass by their
infirmities, and supply all their necessities.   God will never break his
covenant, he will never alter his covenant, he will still keep it, he will
for ever be mindful of it.   The covenant of God with his people shall
be as inviolable as the course and revolution of day and night, and
more immovable than the very hills and mountains.   From what has
been said, we may thus argue : If God hath, by many choice, precious,
and pathetical promises, engaged himself to make good that blessed
covenant that he has made with his people, then certainly there is a
covenant between God and his people ; but God hath, by many choice,
precious, and pathetical promises, engaged himself to make good his
covenant to his people.   *Ergo.* . . .

I might have laid down several other unanswerable arguments to
have evinced this blessed truth, that there is a covenant betwixt God
and his people ; but let these eight suffice for the present.

7. Seventhly and lastly, Premise this with me—viz., *that it is a
matter of high importance and of great concernment, for all mortals to
have a clear and a right understanding of that covenant under which
they are,* 2 Sam. xxiii. 3, 4.   God deals with all men according to
the covenant under which they stand.   We shall never come to understand our spiritual estate and condition, till we come to know under
what covenant we are, Ps. cv. 8, cxi. 5 ; 1 Cor. xi. 28 ; Gal. iv. 23–25.
If we are under a covenant of works, our state is misérable ; if we are
under a covenant of grace, our state is happy ; if we die under a
covenant of works, we shall be certainly damned ; if we die under a
covenant of grace, we shall be certainly saved.   Until we come to
understand under what covenant we are, we shall never be able to put
a right construction, a right interpretation, upon any of God's actions,
dealings, or dispensations towards us.   When we come to understand
that we are under the covenant of grace, then we shall be able to put
a sweet, a loving, and a favourable construction upon the most sharp,
smart, severe, and terrible dispensations of God, knowing that all
flows from love, and shall work for our external, internal, and eternal
good, and for the advancement of God's honour and glory in the
world.[1]   When we come to understand that we are under a covenant
of works, then we shall know that there is wrath, and curses, and
woes wrapped up in the most favourable dispensations, and in the

---

[1] Rev. iii. 19 ; Job i. 21 ; Jer. xxiv. 4, 5 ; Rom. viii. 28 ; Heb. xii. 10, 11 ; 2 Cor.
iv. 15–18.

greatest outward mercies and blessings that Christ confers upon us.[1] If a man be under a covenant of grace, and doth not know it, how can he rejoice in the Lord? How can he sing out the high praises of God? How can he delight himself in the Almighty? How can he triumph in Christ Jesus? How can he cheerfully run the race that is before him? How can he bear up bravely and resolutely in his sufferings for the cause of Christ? How can he besiege the throne of grace with boldness? How can he be temptation-proof? How can he be dead to this world? How can he long to be with Christ in that other world? And if a man be under a covenant of works, and doth not know it, how can he lament and bewail his sad condition? How can he be earnest with God to bring him under the bond of the new covenant? How can he make out after Christ? How can he choose the things that please God? How can he cease from doing evil, and learn to do well? How can he lay hold on eternal life? How can he be saved from wrath to come? &c. If we are under a covenant of grace, and do not know it, how can we manage our duties and services with that life, love, seriousness, holiness, spiritualness, and uprightness, as becomes us?[2] &c. If we are under a covenant of works,[3] and do not know it, how rare shall we be in religious duties! How weary shall we be of religious duties, and how ready shall we be to cast off religious duties! By these few things I have been hinting at, you may easily discern how greatly it concerns all sorts of persons to know what covenant they are under; whether they are under the first or second covenant; whether they are under a covenant of works or a covenant of grace. Now having premised these seven things, my way is clear to that I would be at, which is this—viz., 1. *That there are but two famous covenants that we must abide by.* In one of them, all men and women in the world must of necessity be found—either in the covenant of grace or in the covenant of works. The covenant of works is a witness of God's holiness and perfection; the covenant of grace is a witness of God's goodness and commiseration. The covenant of works is a standing evidence of man's guiltiness; the covenant of grace is the standing evidence of God's righteousness. The covenant of works is the lasting monument of man's impotency and changeableness; the covenant of grace is the everlasting monument of God's omnipotency and immutability. Now no man can be under both these covenants at once. If he be under a covenant of works, he is not under a covenant of grace; and if he be under a covenant of grace, he cannot be under a covenant of works. Such as are under a covenant of works, they have the breach of that covenant to count for, they being the serpentine brood of a transgressing stock; but such as are under a covenant of grace shall never be tried by the law of works, because Christ, their surety, hath fulfilled it for them, Acts xiii. 38, 39; Rom. viii. 2-4; Gal. iv. 4-6. But let me open myself more fully thus :—

That all unbelievers, all Christless, graceless persons, are under a covenant of works, which they are never able safely to live under.

---

[1] Prov. i. 32; Mal. ii. 2; Deut. xxviii. 15-20; Lev. xxvi. 14-24; 2 Cor. ii. 14; Heb. xii. 1.

[2] Ps. xvi. 4; Amos viii. 5; Mal. i. 13; Hosea vi. 4, and iv. 10; Ps. xxxvi. 3.

[3] Query, 'grace?'—Ed.

Should they live and die under a covenant of works, they were surely lost and destroyed for ever; for the covenant of works condemns and curses the sinner: Gal. iii. 10, 'Cursed is every one that continueth not in all things which are written in the book of the law to do them.' Neither hath the sinner any way to escape that curse of the law, nor the wrath of God revealed against all unrighteousness and ungodliness, but in the covenant of grace, Rom. i. 18. This covenant of works the apostle calls 'the law of works,' Rom. iii. 27. This is the covenant which God made with man in the state of innocency before the fall, Gen. ii. 16, 17. In this covenant God promised to Adam, for himself and his posterity, life and happiness, upon the condition of perfect, personal, and perpetual obedience; and it is summed up by the apostle, 'Do this and live,' Gal. iii. 12. God having created man upright, after his own image, Eccles. vii. 29; Gen. i. 26, 27, and so having furnished him with all abilities sufficient for obedience, thereupon he made a covenant with him for life upon the condition of obedience; I say, he made such a covenant with Adam, as a public person, as the head of the covenant; and as he promised life to him and his posterity in case of obedience, so he threatened death and a curse unto him and his posterity in case of disobedience: 'In the day thou eatest thereof thou shalt surely die;' or, 'dying thou shalt die,' Gen. ii. 17.[1] God, in this covenant of works, did deal with Adam and his posterity in a way of supremacy and righteousness, and therefore there is mention made only of the threatenings: 'In the day thou eatest thereof thou shalt die the death.' And it is further observable, that in this covenant that God made with Adam and his posterity, he did promise unto them eternal life and happiness in heaven, and not eternal life in this world only, as some would have it; for hell was threatened in these words, 'In the day thou eatest thereof thou shalt die the death;' and therefore heaven and happiness, salvation and glory, was promised on the contrary. We must necessarily conclude that the promise was as ample, large, and full as the threatening was; yet this must be remembered, that when God did at first enter into covenant with us, and did promise us heaven and salvation, it was upon condition of our personal, perfect, and perpetual obedience, and therefore called a covenant of works. 'Do this and live' was not only a command, but a covenant, with a promise of eternal happiness upon perfect and perpetual obedience. All that are under a covenant of works, are under the curse of the covenant, and they are all bound over unto eternal wrath; but the Lord Christ has put an end to this covenant, and abolished it unto all that are in him, being himself made under it; and satisfying the precept and the curse of it, and so he did cancel it, 'as a handwriting against us, nailing it unto his cross,' Col. ii. 14. So that all they that are in Christ are freed from the law as a covenant; but unto all other men it remains a covenant still, and they remain under the curse of it for ever, and the wrath of God abides upon them, John iii. 36. Though the covenant of works, as it is a

---

[1] Gal. iii. 10. Not only the covenant of grace, but the covenant of works also, is an eternal covenant; and therefore the curse of the covenant remains upon men unto eternity. There is an eternal obligation upon the creature, he being bound to God by an eternal law; and the transgression of that law carries with it an eternal guilt, which eternal guilt brings sinners under an eternal curse.

covenant for life, ceaseth unto believers, yet it stands in force against all unbelievers.

Now, oh how sad is it for a man to be under a covenant of works! For,

First, The covenant of works, in the nature of it, requires perfect, personal, and perpetual obedience, under pain of the curse and death, according to that of the apostle, 'As many as are of the works of the law, are under the curse,' Gal. iii. 10—presupposing man's fall, and, consequently, his inability to keep it—'For it is written, Cursed is every one that continueth not in all things that are written in the book of the law to do them,' Deut. xxvii. 26. The covenant of works, therefore, affords no mercy to the transgressors of it, but inflicts death and curse for the least delinquency: 'For whosoever shall keep the whole law, and yet offend in one point, he is guilty of all,' James ii. 10. The whole law is but one copulative; he that breaketh one commandment habitually, breaketh all. A dispensatory conscience keeps not any commandment. When the disposition of the heart is qualified to break every command, then a man breaks every command in the account of God. Every one sin contains virtually all sin in it. He that dares contemn the lawgiver in any one command, he dares contemn the lawgiver in every command. He that allows himself in any one known sin, in any course, way, or trade of sin, he lays himself under that curse which is threatened against the transgressors of the law.

They that are under this covenant of works must of necessity perish. The case stands thus: Adam did break this covenant, and so brought the curse of it both upon himself and all his seed to the end of the world; in his sin all men sinned, Rom. v. 12. Now if we consider all men as involved in the first transgression of the covenant, they must all needs perish without a Saviour. This is the miserable condition that all mortals are in that are under a covenant of works. But,

Secondly, Such as are under a covenant of works, their best and choicest duties are rejected and abhorred, for the least miscarriages or blemishes that do attend them or cleave to them. Observe the dreadful language of that covenant of works, 'Cursed is he that continueth not in all things that are written in the law of God to do them,' Gal. iii. 10. Hence it is that the best duties of all unregenerate persons are loathed and abhorred by God; as you may clearly see by comparing the scriptures in the margin together.[1] The most glorious duties and the most splendid performances of those that are under a covenant of works, are loathsome to God, for the least mistake that doth accompany them. The covenant of works deals with men according to the exactest terms of strict justice. It doth not make nor allow any favourable or gracious interpretation as the covenant of grace doth; the very least failure exposes the soul to wrath, to great wrath, to everlasting wrath. This covenant is not a covenant of mercy, but of pure justice. But,

Thirdly, This covenant admits of no mediator. There was no daysman betwixt God and man, none to stand between them, neither was there any need of a mediator; for God and man were at no dis-

[1] Isa. i. 11-15; Jer. vi. 20; Isa. lxvi. 3; Amos v. 21; Micah vi. 6; Mal. i. 10.

tance, at no variance.[1] Man was then righteous, perfectly righteous.
Now the proper work of a mediator is to make peace and reconciliation between God and us. At the first, in the state of innocency, there
was peace and friendship between God and man, there was no enmity
in God's heart towards man, nor no enmity in man's heart towards
God: but upon the fall a breach and separation was made between
God and man; so that man flies from God, and hides from God, and
trembles at the voice of God, Gen. iii. 8–10. Fallen man is now
turned rebel, and is become a desperate enemy to God; yea, his heart
is full of enmity against God. 'The wisdom of the flesh is enmity
against God,' Rom. viii. 7; not an 'enemy,' as the Vulgar Latin read-
eth it, but 'enmity,' in the abstract; noting an excess of enmity: as
when we see a proud man, we say, There goes pride, so here is enmity.[2]
Nothing can be said more; for an 'enemy' may be reconciled, but
'enmity' can never; a vicious man may become virtuous, but vice
cannot. There are natural antipathies between some creatures, as
between the lion and the cock, the elephant and the boar, the camel
and the horse, the eagle and the dragon, &c. But what are all these
antipathies to that antipathy and enmity that is in the hearts of all
carnal men against God? Now whilst men stand under a covenant
of works, there is none to interpose by way of mediation, but fallen
man lies open to the wrath of God, and to all the curses that are
written in this book. When breaches are made between God and
man, under the covenant of grace, there is a mediator to interpose and
to make up all such breaches; but under the covenant of works there
is no mediator to interpose between God and fallen man. These three
things I have hinted a little at, on purpose to work my reader, if under
a covenant of works, to be restless till he be got from under that covenant, into the covenant of grace, where alone lies man's safety, felicity,
happiness, and comfort. Now this consideration leads me by the
hand to tell you,

2. Secondly, *That there is a covenant of grace, that all believers,
all sincere Christians, all real saints are under;* for under these two
covenants all mankind fall. The apostle calls this covenant of grace,
'the law of faith,' Rom. iii. 17. Now, first, this covenant of grace is
sometimes styled an 'everlasting covenant:' Isa. lv. 3, 'And I will
make an everlasting covenant with you, even the sure mercies of
David.' You need not question my security, in respect of the great
things that I have propounded and promised in my word, for the encouragement of your faith and hope; for I will give you my bond for
all I have spoken, which shall be as surely made good to you as the
mercies that I have performed to my servant David, 2 Sam. xxiii. 5.
The word *everlasting* hath two acceptations; it doth denote, (1.)
Sometimes a long duration; in which respect the old covenant, clothed
with figures and ceremonies, is called everlasting, because it was to
endure, and did endure, a long time, Ps. cv. 9, 10; (2.) Sometimes it
denotes a perpetual duration, a duration which shall last for ever, Heb.
xiii. 20, &c. In this respect the covenant of grace is everlasting; it

---

[1] Hence this covenant is called by some, *Pactum amicitiæ*, a covenant of friendship.

[2] The word signifies the act of a carnal mind, comprehending thoughts, desire, discourse, &c. *Vide* Pareus, on the words.

shall never cease, never be broken, nor never be altered. Now the covenant of grace is an everlasting covenant in a twofold respect.

First, Ex parte fœderantis, in respect of God, who will never break covenant with his people; but is their God, and will be their God, for ever and ever, Titus i. 2; Ps. xc. 2, and xlviii. 14, 'For this God is our God, for ever and ever; he will be our God even unto death;' ay, and after death too: for this is not to be taken exclusively; oh no! for 'he will never, never leave them, nor forsake them,' Heb. xiii. 5. There are five negatives in the Greek, to assure God's people that he will never forsake them. According to the Greek it may be rendered thus, 'I will not, not leave thee, neither will I not, not forsake thee.'[1] Leave us! God may, to our thinking, leave us; but forsake us he will not. So Ps. lxxxix. 34, 'My covenant will I not break'— *Heb.*, I will not profane my covenant—'nor alter the thing that is gone out of my mouth'—*Heb.*, the issue of my lips I will not alter. Though God's people should profane his statutes, ver. 31, yet God will not profane his covenant; though his people often break with him, yet he will never break with them; though they may be inconstant, yet God will be constant to his covenant: Isa. liv. 10, 'For the mountains shall depart, and the hills be removed; but my kindness shall not depart from thee, neither shall the covenant of my peace be removed, saith the Lord that hath mercy on thee.' Though huge mountains should remove, which is not probable, or though heaven and earth should meet, which is not likely, yet his covenant shall stand immovable; and his mercy and kindness to his people shall be immutable. This new covenant of grace is like the new heavens and new earth, which will never wax old or vanish away, Isa. lxvi. 22. But,

Secondly, The covenant of grace is called an everlasting covenant: *Ex parte confœderatorum;* in respect of the people of God, who are brought into covenant, and shall continue in covenant for ever and ever, Mal. iii. 6; Hosea ii. 19; Gen. xvii. 7. You have both these expressed in that excellent scripture, Jer. xxxii. 40, 'I will make an everlasting covenant with them'—*Heb.*, I will cut out with them a covenant of perpetuity—'that I will not turn away from them, to do them good; but'—*Heb.*, and—'I will put my fear into their hearts, that they shall not depart from me.' Seriously dwell upon the place; it shews that the covenant is everlasting on God's part, and also on our part.[2] On God's part, 'I will never turn away from them to do them good;' and on our part, 'they shall never depart from me.' How so? 'I will put my fear into their hearts, that they shall not depart from me.' That they may continue constant with me, and not constrain me, by their apostasy, to break again with them : I will so deeply rivet a reverent dread of myself in their souls, as shall cause them to cling, and cleave, and keep close to me for ever. In the covenant of grace, God undertakes for both parts; for his own, that he 'will be their God'—*i.e.*, that all he is, and all he has, shall be employed for their external, internal, and eternal good;

---

[1] Five times in Scripture is this precious promise renewed : Josh. i. 5; Deut. xxxi. 8; 1 Kings viii. 57; Gen. xxviii. 15, that we may be still a-pressing of it till we have pressed all the sweetness out of it, Isa. lxvi. 11.

[2] God will never surcease to pursue and follow his covenant-people with favours and blessings incessantly.

and for ours, that we ' shall be his people'—*i. e.*, that we shall believe, love, fear, repent, obey, serve him, and walk with him, as he requires, Jer. xxxii. 38 ; Ezek. xxxvi. 26, 27 ; and thus the covenant of grace becomes an ' everlasting covenant ;' yea, such a covenant as hath the sure or unfailable mercies of David wrapped up in it. The covenant of grace is a new compact or agreement, which God hath made with sinful man, out of his mere mercy and grace, wherein he undertakes, both for himself and for fallen man, and wherein he engages himself to make fallen man everlastingly happy. In the covenant of grace there are two things considerable : *first*, the covenant that God makes for himself to us, which consists mainly of these branches : (1.) That he will be our God ; that is as if he said, You shall have as true an interest in all my attributes for your good, as they are mine for my own glory, Jer. xxxi. 38 ; Ps. cxliv. 15 ; 2 Cor. vi. 16–18. My grace, saith God, shall be yours to pardon you, and my power shall be yours to protect you, and my wisdom shall be yours to direct you, and my goodness shall be yours to relieve you, and my mercy shall be yours to supply you, and my glory shall be yours to crown you. This is a comprehensive promise, for God to be our God : it includes all, *Deus meus et omnia*, said Luther. (2.) That he ' will give us his Spirit.' Hence the Spirit is called ' the Holy Spirit of promise.' The giving of the Holy Ghost is the great promise which Christ, from the Father, hath made unto us. It is the Spirit that reveals the promises, that applies the promises, and that helps the soul to live upon the promises, and to draw marrow and fatness out of the promises. The great promise of the Old Testament was the promise of Christ, Gen. iii. 16, and the great promise of the New Testament is the promise of the Spirit, as you may see by the scriptures in the margin.[1] That in this last age of the world there may be a more clear and full discovery of Christ, of the great things of the gospel, of Antichrist, and of the glorious conquests that are in the last days to be made upon him, the giving of the Spirit is promised as the most excellent gift. (3.) That he ' will take away the heart of stone, and give a heart of flesh,' *i.e.*, a soft and tender heart, Ezek. xxxvi. 26. (4.) That he ' will not turn away his face from us, from doing of us good ;' and that ' he will put his fear into our hearts,' Jer. xxxii. 40. (5.) That he ' will cleanse 'us from all our filthiness, and from all our idols,' Ezek. xxxvi. 25. (6.) That he ' will rejoice over us, to do us good,' Jer. xxxiii. 9, 10, and xxxii. 41. The *second* thing considerable in the covenant of grace is the covenant which God doth make for us to himself, which consists mainly in these things : (1.) That we ' shall be his people.' (2.) That we ' shall fear him for ever.' (3.) That we ' shall walk in his statutes, keep his judgments, and do them.' (4.) That we ' shall never depart from him.' (5.) That we ' shall persevere, and hold out to the end.' (6.) That we ' shall grow, and flourish in grace.' (7.) A true right to the creatures. (8.) That all providences, changes, and conditions shall work for our good. (9.) Union and communion with Christ. (10.) That we shall have a kingdom, a crown, and glory at last. And what

[1] Isa. xliv. 3 ; Jer. xxxi. 33 ; Joel ii. 28 ; John xiv. 16, 20 ; Acts ii. 23 ; Luke xxiv. 49 ; John xv. 26, and xvi. 7.

would we have more?[1] By these short hints it is most evident that the covenant of grace is an entire covenant, an everlasting covenant, made by God both for himself and for us. O sirs! this is the glory of the covenant of grace, that whatsoever God requires of us, that he stands engaged to give unto us. Whatever in the covenant of grace God requires on man's part, that he undertakes to perform for man. That this covenant of grace is an 'everlasting covenant' may be made further clear,

[1.] First, *From God's denomination, who hath often styled it an 'everlasting covenant.'* In the Old Testament he frequently calls it, in Heb., ברית עלם, *Bereth Gnolam*, a covenant of eternity. In the New Testament he calls it, in Greek, Διαθήκη αἰώνιος, the eternal covenant, or the everlasting covenant. And those whom God has taken into covenant with himself, they have frequently acknowledged it to be an everlasting covenant, as is evident up and down the Scripture. The covenant of works was not everlasting, it was soon overthrown by Adam's sin; but the covenant of grace is everlasting. The joy that is wrapped up in the covenant is an everlasting joy, Isa. xxxv. 10; and the righteousness that is wrapped up in the covenant is an everlasting righteousness, Dan. ix. 24; and the life that is wrapped up in the covenant is an everlasting life, John iii. 16; and all the happiness, and glory, and salvation that is wrapped up in the covenant is everlasting, John xii. 2; Mat. xix. 29; 1 Pet. v. 4; Isa. xlv. 17. The covenant-relation that is betwixt God and his people is everlasting; and the mediator of the covenant is everlasting—viz., 'Jesus Christ, yesterday, and to-day, and the same for ever,' Heb. xiii. 8. Though the covenant, in respect of our own personal entering into it, is made with us now in time, and hath a beginning; yet for continuance it is everlasting and without end; it shall remain for ever and ever. But,

[2.] Secondly, This covenant of grace, under which the saints stand, is sometimes styled *a covenant of life*: Mal. ii. 5, 'My covenant was with him of life and peace.' Life is restored, and life is promised, and life is settled by the covenant. There is no safe life, no comfortable life, no easy life, no happy life, no honourable life, no glorious life, for any sinner that is not under the bond of this covenant.[2] All mankind had been eternally lost, and God had lost all the glory of his mercy for ever, had he not, of his own free grace and mercy, made a covenant of life with poor sinners. A man, in the covenant of grace, hath three degrees of life: the first in this life, when Christ lives in him; the second, when his 'body returns to the earth, and his soul to God that gave it;' the third, at the end of the world, when body and soul re-united shall enjoy heaven.

[3.] Thirdly, This covenant of grace, under which the saints or faithful people of Christ stand, is sometimes styled *a holy covenant.* Daniel, describing the wickedness of Antiochus Epiphanes, saith, 'His

---

[1] Jer. xxxii. 38, 40; Ezek. xxxvi. 27; Job xvii. 9; Prov. iv. 18; Ps. i. 3; Hosea xiv. 5–7; Zech. xii. 18; Mal. iv. 2; Jer. xxiv. 5; Rom. viii. 28; Luke xii. 32; Rev. ii. 10; Ps. lxxxiv. 11; John x. 28. See the truth of this fully evidenced in twelve particulars, in my 'Box of Precious Ointment,' pp. 364–367.—[Vol. iii., p. 487, *seq.*—G.]

[2] *Omnis vita est propter delectationem.* Philosophers say that a fly is more excellent than the heavens, because the fly has life, which the heavens have not.

heart shall be against the holy covenant,' Dan. xi. 28, 30 ; he shall
have indignation against the holy covenant, and have intelligence with
them that forsake the holy covenant. So the psalmist, ' For he remembered his holy promise, and Abraham his servant,' Ps. cv. 42, 43 ; [1]
promise here being put for covenant by a synecdoche; Luke i. 72, ' To
perform the mercy promised to our fathers, and to remember his holy
covenant.' The parties interested in this covenant are holy. Here you
have a holy God and a holy people in covenant together. Holiness is
one of the principal things that is promised in the covenant. The
covenant commands holiness, and encourages to holiness, and works
souls up to a higher degree of holiness, and fences and arms gracious
souls against all external and internal unholiness.[2] The author of
this covenant is holy ; the mediator of this covenant is holy ; the great
blessings contained in this covenant are holy blessings ; and the people
taken into this covenant are sometimes styled holy brethren, holy men,
holy women. ' An holy temple, an holy priesthood, an holy nation,
an holy people,' as you may see by comparing the scriptures in the
margin together.[3] Whenever God brings a poor soul under the bond
of the covenant, he makes him holy, and he makes him love holiness,
and prize holiness, and delight in holiness, and press and follow hard
after holiness. A holy God will not take an unholy person by the
hand, as Job speaks, chap. viii. ; neither will he allow of such to take
his covenant into their mouths, as the psalmist speaks, Ps. xx. 6.

[4.] Fourthly, This covenant of grace, under which the saints stand,
is sometimes styled *a covenant of peace:* Num. xxv. 12, ' Behold, I
give unto him my covenant of peace.' Peace is the comprehension of
all blessings and prosperity. All sorts of peace, viz., peace with God,
and peace with conscience, and peace with the creatures, flows from the
covenant of grace, Mal. ii. 5. There is (1.) An external peace, and
that is with men ; (2.) There is a supernatural peace, and that is
with God ; (3.) There is an internal peace, and that is with conscience ;
(4.) There is an eternal peace, and that is in heaven. Now all these
sorts of peace flow in upon us through the covenant of grace. The
Hebrew word for peace comes from a root which denotes perfection.
The end of the upright man is perfection of happiness, Ps. xxxvii. 37.[4]
Hence the Rabbins say, that ' the holy blessed God finds not any
vessel that will contain enough of blessings for Israel, but the vessel of
peace.' Peace is a very comprehensive word. It carries in the womb
of it all outward blessings. It was the common greeting of the Jews,
' Peace be unto you:' and thus David, by his proxy, salutes Nabal,
' Peace be to thee, and thy house.' The ancients were wont to paint
peace in the form of a woman, with a horn of plenty in her hand.
The covenant of grace is that hand, by which God gives out all sorts
of peace unto us: Isa. liv. 10, ' Neither shall the covenant of my peace

---

[1] *Heb.*, The word of his holiness, that is, his sacred and gracious covenant that he had
made with Abraham and his posterity.

[2] See my Treatise of Holiness. [Vol. iv.—G.]

[3] Ps. l. 5 ; Heb. iii. 1 ; 1 Thes. v. 27 ; 2 Peter i. 21 ; 1 Peter iii. 5 ; 1 Cor. iii. 17 ; 1
Peter ii. 9, &c.

[4] This covenant is styled a covenant of peace, because it breeds, settles, quiets, and
establisheth our hearts in perfect peace, it stills all fears and doubts and thoughts of
heart.

be removed, saith the Lord that hath mercy on thee.' The covenant is here called the covenant of peace, because the Lord therein offers us all those things that may make us completely happy; for under this word peace the Hebrews comprehend all happiness and felicity: Ezek. xxxiv. 25, 'And I will make with them a covenant of peace;' the Hebrew is, 'I will cut with them a covenant of peace.' This expression of cutting a covenant is taken from the custom of the Jews in their making of covenants. The manner of this ceremony or solemnity, Jeremiah declares, saying, 'I will give the men that have transgressed my covenant, which have not performed the words of the covenant which they had struck before me, when they cut the calf in twain, and passed between the parts thereof,' Jer. xxxiv. 18. Their manner was to kill sacrifices, to cut these sacrifices in twain, to lay the two parts thus divided in the midst, piece against piece, exactly one over against another, to answer each other: then the parties covenanting passed betwixt the parts of the sacrifices so slit in twain, and laid answerably to one another: the meaning of which ceremonies and solemnities is conceived to be this—viz., as part answered to part, so there was a harmonious correspondency and answerableness of their minds and hearts that struck covenant: and as part was severed from part, so the covenanters implied, if not expressed, an imprecation or curse; wishing the like dissection and destruction to the parties covenanting, as most deserved, if they should break the covenant, or deal falsely therein.[1] To this custom God alludes, when he saith, 'I will cut with them a covenant of peace,' Isa. xlii. 6; and this he did by making Christ a sacrifice, by shedding his blood, and dividing his soul and body, who is said to be given for a covenant of the people, that is, to be the mediator of the covenant between God and his people. So Ezek. xxxvii. 26, 'Moreover, I will make a covenant of peace with them; it shall be an everlasting covenant with them,' &c. The word for peace is *Shalom*, by which the Hebrews understand not only outward quietness, but all kind of outward happiness. Others, by the covenant of peace here, do understand the gospel, wherein we see Christ hath pacified all things by the blood of his cross. And Lavater saith, it is called a covenant of peace, *Quia Christi merito, pax inter Deum et nos constituta est.* Not only outward, but inward peace, between God and us, is merited by our Lord Jesus Christ, Col. i. 20. But,

[5.] Fifthly, This covenant of grace, under which the saints stand, is sometimes styled a *new covenant*: Jer. xxxi. 31, 'Behold, the days come, saith the Lord, that I will make a new covenant with the house of Israel, and with the house of Judah:' Heb. xii. 24, 'And to Jesus, the mediator of the new covenant,' &c., Heb. viii. 8, 13, and ix. 15. Now the covenant of grace is styled a new covenant in several respects. (1.) In opposition to the former covenant, that was old, and being old, vanished away, Heb. viii. 13. It is called a new covenant in opposition to the covenant that was made with Adam in the state of innocency, and in opposition to the covenant that was made with the Jews in the time of the Old Testament. (2.) To shew the excellency of the covenant of grace. New things are rare and excellent things.

---

[1] This ceremony or solemnity of covenanting, the Romans and other nations used. Some judge the heathens borrowed this custom from the Jews. But of this before.

In the blessed Scriptures excellent things are frequently called 'new;' as a 'new testament,' a 'new Jerusalem,' 'new heavens,' and 'new earth;' 'a new name,' that is, an excellent name; a 'new commandment,' that is, an excellent commandment; a 'new way,' that is, an excellent way; a 'new heart,' is an excellent heart; a 'new spirit,' is an excellent spirit; and a 'new song,' is an excellent song.[1] (3.) In regard of the succession of it in the room of the former. (4.) In regard of the dilation and enlargement of it, it being in the days of old confined to the Jewish nation and state, and some few proselytes that adjoined themselves thereunto; whereas now it is propounded and extended, without respect of persons or places, unto all indifferently, of all people and nations that shall embrace the faith of Christ. (5.) Sometimes that is styled new, which is diverse from what it was before: 2 Cor. v. 17, 'If any man be in Christ, he is a new creature,' that is, he is not such a man as he was before; a man must be either a new man or no man in Christ.[2] The substance of the soul is not changed, but the qualities and operations of it are altered; in regeneration our natures are changed, not destroyed. This word 'new,' in Scripture, signifieth as much as 'another;' not that it is essentially new, but new only in regard of qualities. A new creature is a changed creature: 2 Cor. iii. 18, 'But we all, with open face beholding as in a glass the glory of the Lord, are changed into the same image, from glory to glory,' that is, from grace to grace. In this respect also, is the covenant styled new, not only because it is diverse from the covenant of works, but also because it is diverse from itself in respect of the administration of it, after that Christ was manifested in the flesh, and died and rose again. From the different administration it is called old and new. This new covenant hath not those seals of circumcision and the passover; nor those manifold sacrifices, ceremonies, types, and shadows, &c., to the observation whereof the Jews were strictly obliged; but now all these things are taken away upon the coming of Christ, and a service of God, much more spiritual, substituted in the room of them; upon which accounts the covenant of grace is called a 'new covenant.' (6.) It is styled new, because it is fresh, and green, and flourishing, it is like unto Aaron's rod, which continued new, fresh, and flourishing, Num. xvii. 8.[3] All the choice blessings, all the great blessings, all the internal and all the eternal blessings of the new covenant, are as new, fresh, and flourishing, as they were when God brought your souls first under the bond of the new covenant. But, (7.) Such things are sometimes styled new which are strange, rare, wonderful, marvellous, and unusual, the like not heard of before. So Jer. xxxi. 22, 'The Lord hath created a new thing in the earth, a woman shall compass a man;' as the nut encloseth the kernel, not receiving aught from without, but conceiving and breeding of herself, by the power of

---

[1] Mat. xxvi. 28; Rev. xxi. 2; 2 Pet. iii. 13; Rev. ii. 17; John xiii. 34; Ezek. xxxvi. 26, 27; Ps. xl. 3.

[2] A new creature has a new light, a new judgment, a new will, new affections, new thoughts, new company, new choice, new Lord, new law, new way, new work, &c. A new creature is a changed creature throughout, 1 Thes. v. 23.

[3] Austin, and others, think that the commandment of love is called a new commandment, because it is always fresh, and green, and flourishing; and why may not the covenant of grace be called a new covenant upon the same account?

the Almighty, from within. That a virgin should conceive and bring forth a man-child, this was indeed a new thing, a strange thing, a wonderful thing, a thing that was never thought of, never heard of, never read of, from the creation of the world to that very day. So Isa. xliii. 19, ' Behold, I will do a new thing, I will make a way in the wilderness, and rivers in the desert.'[1] This was a new work, that is, a wonderful and unusual work; for God to make a plain or free way in the wilderness, where the ways are wont to be uneven, with hills and dales, and obstructed with thickets, and overgrown with brambles and briars, is a strange and marvellous work indeed. In this respect also, the covenant of grace is styled new, that is, it is a wonderful covenant. O sirs! what a wonder is this, that the great God, who was so transcendently dishonoured, despised, provoked, incensed, and injured by poor base sinners, should yet so freely, so readily, so graciously, condescend to vile forlorn sinners, as to treat with them, as to own them, as to love them, and as to enter into a covenant of grace and mercy with them! This may well be the wonder of angels, and the astonishment of men. (8.) and lastly, It is called a new covenant, because it is never to be antiquated, as the apostle explains himself, Heb. viii. 13. But,

[6.] Sixthly, This covenant of grace, under which the saints stand, is sometimes styled a *covenant of salt*: Lev. ii. 13, ' Neither shalt thou suffer the salt of the covenant of thy God to be lacking from the meat-offering,' &c.[2] The salt of the covenant signifies that covenant that God hath made with us in Christ, who seasoneth us, and makes all our services savoury. The meaning of the words, say some, is this, The salt shall put thee in mind of my covenant, whereby thou standest engaged to endeavour always for an untainted and uncorrupted life and conversation. By this salting, say others, was signified the covenant of grace in Christ, which we by faith apprehend unto incorruption, wherefore our unregenerate estate is likened to a child new born and not salted, Ezek. xvi. 4. Others say it signifies the eternal and perpetual holiness of the covenant between God and man ; and some there be that say that this salt of the covenant signifies the grace of God, whereby they are guided and sanctified that belong unto the covenant of grace. So Num. xviii. 19, ' It is a covenant of salt for ever before the Lord, unto thee, and to thy seed with thee.' A covenant of salt is used for an inviolable, incorruptible, and perpetual covenant. This covenant which the Lord made with the priests is called a covenant of salt, because, as salt keepeth from corruption, so that covenant was perpetual, authentical, and inviolable[3]—as anciently the most solemn ceremony that was used in covenants was to take and eat of the same salt, and it was esteemed more sacred and firm than to eat at the same table and drink of the same cup. This covenant, in regard of its perpetuity, is here called a ' covenant of salt,' that is, a sure and

[1] The word 'new' doth intimate some more excellent mercies than God had formerly conferred upon his people.

[2] Salt they were bound as by a covenant to use in all sacrifices, or it meaneth a sure and pure covenant. Some, by the salt of the covenant, do mystically understand the grace of the New Testament.

[3] Of old, amity and friendship was symbolised by salt, for its consolidating and conserving property, saith Pierius.

stable, a firm and incorruptible covenant.   So 2 Chron. xiii. 5, ' Ought
you not to know that the Lord God of Israel gave the kingdom over
Israel to David for ever, even to him and to his sons by a covenant of
salt?'—*i. e.*, perpetual and inviolable, solemn and sure.   By this
metaphor of salt, a perpetuity is set forth, for salt makes things last.[1]
The covenant therefore here intended is by this metaphor declared to
be a perpetual covenant, that was not to be abrogated or nulled.   In
this respect these two phrases, ' a covenant of salt,' and ' for ever,' are
joined together.   Some take this metaphor of salt to be used in relation to their manner of making their covenant with a sacrifice, on which
salt was always sprinkled, and thereby is implied that it was a most
solemn covenant not to be violated.[2]   But,

[7.]   Seventhly, The covenant of grace, under which the saints stand,
is sometimes styled *a sure covenant, a firm covenant, a covenant that
God will punctually and accurately perform.*   In this regard, the covenant of grace is in the Old Testament styled שמרה, *Shemurah*, that is,
kept, observed, performed.   The word imports care, diligence, and
solicitude lest anything be let go, let slip, &c.   God is ever mindful of
his covenant, and will have that singular care and that constant and
due regard to it, that not the least branch of it shall ever fail, as you
may clearly see by consulting the special scriptures in the margin.[3]
Hence it is called the mercy and the truth: Mic. vii. 20, ' Thou wilt
perform the truth to Jacob'—*Heb.*, ' thou wilt give,' for all is of free
gift—' and the mercy to Abraham.'   The covenant is called mercy,
because mercy only drew this covenant; it was free mercy, it was
mere mercy, it was only mercy which moved God to enter into covenant with us.   And it is called truth, because the great God who has
made this covenant will assuredly make good all that mercy and all
that grace and all that favour that is wrapped up in it.   God having
made himself a voluntary debtor to his people, he will come off fairly
with them, and not be worse than his word.   Hence Christ is said to
have a rainbow upon his head, to shew that he is faithful and constant
in his covenant, Rev. x. 1.   God hath hitherto kept promise with
nights and days, that one shall succeed the other, Isa. liv. 9, 10; therefore much more will he keep promise with his people, Jer. xxxiii. 20,
25.[4]   Hence also the covenant is called the oath: Luke i. 73, ' The
oath which he sware unto our father Abraham.'   You never read of
God's oath in a covenant of works.   In that first covenant you read
not of a mediator nor of an oath.; but in the covenant of grace you
read both of a mediator and of an oath, the more effectually to confirm
us as touching the immutability of his will and purpose, for the accomplishment of all the good and the great things that are mentioned in the
covenant of grace.   The covenant of grace is incomparably more firm,
sure, immutable, and irrevocable than all other covenants in the world.

---

[1] Zanchy's [Zanchius] exposition of the place is strange and farfetched.
[2] Num. xviii. 19, but now opened, Lev. ii. 13.
[3] 2 Sam. xxiii. 5; Deut. vii. 9; 2 Chron. vi. 14; Ps. xix. 7, and lxxxix. 28; Titus i.
2; Ps. cxxxii. 11; Isa. liv. 10.   See my ' Box of Precious Ointment,' pp. 367, 368,
371-373.   [Vol. iii., as before.—G.]
[4] The stability of God's covenant is compared to the unvariable course of the day and
the night, and to the firmness and unmovableness of the mighty mountains, Isa. liv.
9, 10.

Therefore it is said, Heb. vi. 17, 18, ' God willing more abundantly to shew unto the heirs of promise the immutability of his counsel, confirmed it by an oath; that by two immutable things, in which it was impossible for God to lie, we might have strong consolation,'[1] ἰσχυραν παρακλησιν, that is, a valiant, strong, prevailing consolation, such as swalloweth up all worldly griefs, as Moses his serpent did the sorcerers' serpents, or as the fire doth the fuel. God's word, his promise, his covenant, is sufficient to assure us of all the good that he has engaged to bestow upon us; yet God, considering of our infirmity, hath bound his word with an oath. His word cannot be made more true, but yet it may be made more credible. Now two things make a thing more credible: (1.) The quality of the person speaking; (2.) The manner of the speech. If God doth not simply speak, but solemnly swear, we have the highest cause imaginable to rest assured and abundantly satisfied in the word and oath of God. An oath amongst men is the strongest, surest, most sacred, and inviolable bond; ' For men verily swear by the greater, and an oath for confirmation is to them an end of all strife,' Heb. vi. 16. The end of an oath among men is to help the truth in necessity, and to clear men's innocency, Exod. xxii. 11. O sirs! God doth not only make his covenant, but swears his covenant; ' My covenant,' saith the psalmist, ' will I not break, nor alter the thing that is gone out of my lips; once have I sworn by my holiness that I will not lie unto David,' Ps. lxxxix. 34, 35. This is as great and deep an oath as God could take; for his holiness is himself, who is most holy, and the foundation of all holiness.[2] God is essentially holy, unmixedly holy, universally holy, transcendently holy, originally holy, independently holy, constantly holy, and exemplarily holy. Now for so holy a God to swear once for all by his holiness that he will keep covenant, that he will keep touch with his people, how abundantly should it settle and satisfy them! Ah! my friends, hath God said it, and will he not do it? Yea, hath he sworn it, and will he not bring it to pass? Dare we trust an honest man upon his bare word, much more upon his oath; and shall we not much more trust a holy, wise, and faithful God upon his word, upon his covenant, when confirmed by an oath? The covenant of grace is sure in itself; it is a firm covenant, an unalterable covenant, an everlasting covenant, a ratified covenant; so that heaven and earth may sooner pass away, than the least branch or word of his covenant should pass away unfulfilled, Mat. v. 18.

(1.) *Let us but cast our eyes upon the several springs from whence the covenant of grace flows*, and then we cannot but strongly conclude that the covenant of grace is a sure covenant. Now if you cast your eye aright, you shall see that the covenant of grace flows from these three springs.

First, From *the free grace and favour of God*. There was nothing in fallen man to invite God to enter into covenant with him; yea, there was everything in fallen man that might justly provoke God to abandon man, to abhor man, to revenge himself upon man. It was mere

---

[1] Who shall doubt when God doth swear, who cannot possibly deny himself or forswear himself?

[2] See my Treatise of Holiness, p. 585 to p. 595. [Vol. iv., as before.— G.]

grace that made the covenant, and it is mere grace that makes good the covenant. Now that which springs from mere grace must needs be unexceptionably sure. The love of God is unchangeable ; 'whom he loves he loves to the end,' John xiii. 3 ; whom God loves once he loves for ever. He is not as man, soon in and soon off again, Mal. iii. 6 ; James i. 17 ; soon in, and as soon out, as Joab's dagger was ! Oh no ! his love is like himself, lasting, yea, everlasting: 'I have loved thee with an everlasting love,' Jer. xxxi. 3. Though we break off with him, yet he abides faithful, 2 Tim. ii. 13. Now what can be more sure than that which springs from free love, from everlasting love ? Rom. iv. 16. Hence the covenant must be sure. The former covenant was not sure, because it was of works ; but this covenant is sure, because it is of grace, and rests not on any sufficiency in us, but only on grace.

Secondly, The covenant of grace springs from *the immutable counsel of God:* Heb. vi. 17, ' God, willing more abundantly to shew unto the heirs of promise the immutability of his counsel, confirmed it by an oath.' Times are mutable, and all sorts of men are mutable, and the love and favour of the creature is mutable ; but the counsel of God, from which the covenant of grace flows, is immutable, and therefore it must needs be sure, Isa. xl. 6 ; Ps. cxlvi. 3, 4 ; Jer. xxxiii. 14. The manifestation of the immutability of God's counsel is here brought in, as one end of God's oath. God swears, that it might evidently appear that what he had purposed, counselled, determined, and promised to Abraham and his seed should assuredly be accomplished ; there should be, there could be, no alteration thereof. His counsel was more firm than the laws of the Medes and Persians, which altereth not, Dan. vi. 13. Certainly God's counsel is inviolable : ' My counsel shall stand,' Isa. xlvi. 10 ; Ps. xxxiii. 11, ' The counsel of the Lord standeth for ever, the thoughts of his heart to all generations ;' Prov. xix. 21, ' Nevertheless the counsel of the Lord, that shall stand.' The immutability of God's counsel springs from the unchangeableness of his essence, the perfection of his wisdom, the infiniteness of his goodness, the absoluteness of his sovereignty, the omnipotency of his power. God in his essence being unchangeable, his counsel also must needs be so. Can darkness flow out of light, or fulness out of emptiness, or heaven out of hell ? No ! no more can changeable counsels flow from an immutable nature. Now the covenant of grace flows from the immutable counsel of God, which is most firm and inviolable, and therefore it must needs be a sure covenant. But,

Thirdly, The covenant of grace springs from *the purpose of God, resolving and intending everlasting good unto us.* Now this purpose of God is sure ; so the apostle, 2 Tim. ii. 19, ' The foundation of God standeth sure.'[1] That foundation of God is his election, which is compared to a foundation ; because it is that upon which all our good and happiness is built, and because as a foundation it abides firm and sure. The gracious purpose of God is the fountain-head of all our spiritual blessings. It is the impulsive cause of our vocation,

---

[1] Our graces are imperfect, our comforts ebb and flow ; but God's foundation stands sure.

justification, glorification; it is the highest link in the golden chain of salvation. What is the reason that God has entered into a covenant with fallen man? it is from his eternal purpose. What is the reason that one man is brought under the bond of the covenant and not another? it is from the eternal purpose of God, Ezek. xx. 37. In all the great concerns of the covenant of grace, the purpose of God gives the casting voice. The purpose of God is the sovereign cause of all that good that is in man, and of all that external, internal, and eternal good that comes to man. Not works past, for men are chosen from everlasting; not works present, for Jacob was loved and chosen before he was born; nor works foreseen, for men were all corrupt in Adam. All a believer's present happiness, and all his future happiness, springs from the eternal purpose of God; as you may see, by comparing the scriptures in the margin together.[1] This purpose of God speaks our stability and certainty of salvation by Christ, God's eternal purpose never changes, never alters; 'Surely, as I have thought, so shall it come to pass, and as I have purposed,' saith God, 'so shall it stand.' God's purposes are immutable, so is his covenant. God's purposes are sure, very sure, so is his covenant. The covenant of grace that flows from the eternal purpose of God, is as sure as God is sure; for God can neither deceive nor be deceived. That covenant that is built upon this rock of God's eternal purpose, must needs be sure; and therefore all that are in covenant with God need never fear falling away. There is no man, no power, no devil, no violent temptation, that shall ever be able to overturn those that God has brought under the bond of the covenant, John x. 28–31; 1 Pet. i. 5. But,

(2.) Secondly, Consider that the covenant of grace *is confirmed and made sure by the blood of Jesus Christ*, which is called ' the blood of the everlasting covenant,' Heb. xiii. 20. Christ, by his irrevocable death, hath made sure the covenant to us, Heb. ix. 16, 17. The covenant of grace is to be considered under the notion of a testament; and Christ, as the testator of this will and testament.[2] Now look, as a man's will and testament is irrevocably confirmed by the testator's death;—' For where a testament is, there must also, of necessity, be the death of the testator; for a testament is of force, after men are dead; otherwise, it is of no strength at all whilst the testator liveth;'— these two verses are added as a proof of the necessity of Christ's manner of confirming the new testament as he did, namely, by his death. The argument is taken from the common use and equity of confirming testaments, which is by the death of the testator. A testament is only and wholly at his pleasure that maketh it, so that he may alter it, or disannul it while he liveth, as he seeth good; but when he is dead, he not remaining to alter it, none else can do it. In the seventeenth verse, the apostle declareth the inviolableness of a man's last will, being ratified as before by the testator's death. This he sheweth two ways: (1.) Affirmatively; in these words, ' A testa-

[1] Rom. viii. 28, and ix. 11; Eph. i. 11, and iii. 11; 2 Tim. i. 9.
[2] The main point which the apostle intended, by setting down the inviolableness of men's last wills after their death, is to prove that Christ's death was very requisite for ratifying of the New Testament: consult the scriptures, Mat. xvi. 21; Luke xxiv. 26; Heb. ii. 10, 17.

ment is of force after men are dead.' (2.) Negatively, in these words,
'Otherwise it is of no strength.' Now from the affirmative and the
negative, it plainly appears that a testament is made inviolable by the
testator's death ; so Jesus Christ hath unalterably confirmed this will
and testament—viz., the new covenant, by his blood and death, ' that
by means of death, for the redemption of the transgressions that 'were
under the first testament, they which are called might receive the
promise of eternal inheritance,' Heb. ix. 15. Christ died to purchase
an eternal inheritance ; and on this ground eternal life is called an
eternal inheritance ; for we come to it as heirs, through the good-
will, grace, and favour of this purchaser thereof, manifested by the
last will and testament. Hence you read, ' This is my blood of the
new testament, which is shed for many, for the remission of sins,' Mat.
xxvi. 28. Again, ' This cup is the new testament in my blood, which
is shed for you,' Luke xxii. 20 ; 1 Cor. xi. 25. The covenant is called
both a covenant and a testament, because his covenant and testament
is founded, established, ratified, and immutably sealed up, in and by
his blood. Christ is the faithful and true witness, yea, truth itself ;
his word shall not pass away, Rev. iii. 14 ; John xiv. 6 ; Mark xiii.
31. If the word of Christ be sure, if his promise be sure, if his covenant be sure, then surely his last will and testament, which is ratified
and confirmed by his death, must needs be very sure. Christ's blood
is too precious a thing to be spilt in vain ; but in vain is it spilt if
his testament, his covenant, ratified thereby, be altered. If the
covenant of grace be not a sure covenant, 1 Cor. xv. 14, then
Christ died in vain, and our preaching is in vain, and your hearing,
and receiving, and believing is all in vain. Christ's death is a declaration and evidence of the eternal counsel of his Father, which is most
stable and immutable in itself. But how much more it is so when it is
ratified by the death of his dearest Son, ' In whom all the promises are
yea and amen,' 2 Cor. i. 20 ; that is, in Christ they are made, performed, and ratified. By all this we may safely conclude that the
covenant of grace is a most sure covenant. There can be no addition
to it, detraction from it, or alteration of it, unless the death of Jesus
Christ, whereby it is confirmed, be frustrated and overthrown. Certainly the covenant is as sure as Christ's death is sure. The sureness
and certainty of the covenant is the ground and bottom of bottoms for
our faith, hope, joy, patience, peace, &c. Take this corner, this foundation-stone away, and all will tumble. Were the covenant uncertain,
a Christian could never have a good day all his days, his whole life
would be filled up with tears, doubts, disputes, distractions, &c. ; and
he would be still a-crying out, Oh, I can never be sure that God will
be mine, or that Christ will be mine, or that mercy will be mine, or that
pardon of sin will be mine, or that heaven will be mine ! Oh, I can
never be sure that I shall escape ' the great damnation, the worm that
never dies, the fire that never goes out, or an eternal separation from
the presence of the Lord and from the glory of his power,' 2 Thes. i. 9.
The great glory of the covenant is the certainty of the covenant ; and
this is the top of God's glory, and of a Christian's comfort, that all the
mercies that are in the covenant of grace are ' the sure mercies of
David,' and that all the grace that is in the covenant is sure grace,

and that all the glory that is in the covenant is sure glory, and that all the external, internal, and eternal blessings of the covenant are sure blessings.

I might further argue the sureness of the covenant of grace from all the attributes of God, which are deeply engaged to make it good, as his wisdom, love, power, justice, holiness, faithfulness, righteousness, &c. ; and I might further argue the certainty of the covenant of grace from the seals which God hath annexed to it.   You know what was sealed by the king's ring could not be altered, Esth. viii. 8.   God hath set his seals to this covenant: his broad seal in the sacraments, and his privy seal in the witness of his Spirit; and therefore the covenant of grace is sure, and can never be reversed.   But upon several accounts I may not now insist on these things.   And therefore,

[8.] Eighthly and lastly, The covenant of grace is styled *a well-ordered covenant:* 2 Sam. xxiii. 5, 'He hath made with me an ever-lasting covenant, ordered in all things, and sure.'   Oh, the admirable counsel, wisdom, love, care, and tenderness of the blessed God, that sparkles and shines in the well-ordering of the covenant of grace![1] Oh, how comely and beautiful, with what symmetry and proportion, are all things in this covenant ordered and prepared!   Oh, what head can conceive, or what tongue can express, that infinite understanding that God has manifested in ordering the covenant of grace, so as it may most and best suit to all the wants, and straits, and necessities, and miseries, and desires, and longings of poor sinners' souls!   Here are fit and full supplies for all our spiritual wants, so excellently and orderly hath God composed and constituted the covenant of grace.   In the covenant of grace every poor sinner may find a suit-able help, a suitable remedy, a suitable succour, a suitable support, a suitable supply, Jer. xxxiii. 8; Ezek. xxxvi. 25; Ps. xciv. 19. The covenant of grace is so well ordered by the unsearchable wisdom of God, that you may find in it remedies to cure all your spiritual diseases, and cordials to comfort you under all your soul-faintings, and a spiritual armoury to arm you against all sorts of sins, and all sorts of snares, and all sorts of temptations, and all sorts of oppositions, and all sorts of enemies, whether inward or outward, open or secret, subtle or silly, Eph. vi. 10–18.   Dost thou, O distressed sinner, want a loving God, a compassionate God, a reconciled God, a sin-pardoning God, a tender-hearted God?   Here thou mayest find him in the covenant of grace, Exod. xxxiv. 5-7.   Dost thou, O sinner, want a Christ, to counsel thee by his wisdom, and to clothe thee with his righteousness, and to enrich thee with his grace, and to enlighten thee with his eyesalve, and to justify thee from thy sins, and to recon-cile thee to God, and to secure thee from wrath to come, and after all, to bring thee to heaven? Rev. iii. 17, 18; Acts xiii. 39; 1 Thes. i. 10; John x. 28–31.   Here thou mayest find him in a covenant of grace.   Dost thou, O sinner! want the Holy Spirit to awaken thee, and to convince thee of sin, of righteousness, and of judgment? or to enlighten thee, and teach thee, and lead thee, and guide thee in the way everlasting? or to cleanse thee, or comfort thee, or to seal thee

[1] Rom. xi. 33–36; 1 Cor. ii. 7; Eph. i. 8, and iii. 10; Ps. cxlvii. 5; Isa. xl. 28; Rev. vii. 12.

up to the day of redemption? Ezek. xxxvi. 25-27; Luke xi. 13; Eph. i. 13. Here thou mayest find him in the covenant of grace. Dost thou, O sinner! want grace, all grace, great grace, abundance of grace, multiplied grace? Here thou mayest find it in the covenant of grace? Dost thou, O sinner! want peace, or ease, or rest, or quiet in thy conscience? Here thou mayest find it in the covenant of grace. Dost thou want, O sinner! joy, or comfort, or content, or satisfaction? Here thou mayest have it in a covenant of grace. O sinner, sinner! whatever thy bodily wants are, or whatever thy soul wants are, they may all be supplied out of the covenant of grace. God, in his infinite wisdom and love, has laid into the covenant of grace, as into a common store, all those good things, and all those great things, and all those suitable things, that either sinners or saints can either beg or need. Now the adequate suitableness of the covenant of grace to all a sinner's wants, straits, necessities, miseries, and desires, does sufficiently demonstrate the covenant of grace to be a well-ordered covenant. Look, as that is a well-ordered commonwealth, where there are no wholesome laws wanting to govern a people, and where there are no wholesome remedies wanting to relieve a people, and where there are no defences wanting to secure a people; so that must needs be a well-ordered covenant, where there is nothing wanting to govern poor souls, or to secure poor souls, or to save poor souls; and such a covenant is the covenant of grace. I might easily lay down other arguments to evince the covenant of grace to be a well-ordered covenant. As for the right placing of all persons and things in the covenant of grace, and from the outward dispensation of it, God revealed it but gradually. First, he discovered it more darkly, remotely, and imperfectly, as we see things a great way off; but afterwards the Lord did more clearly, fully, immediately, frequently, and completely discover it, as we discern things at hand. God did not at once open all the riches and rarities of the covenant to his people, but in the opening of those treasures that were there laid up, God had a respect to the non-age and full-age of his people; and from God's dispensing and giving out all the good and all the great things of the covenant in their fittest time, in a right and proper season, when his people most need them, and when they can live no longer without them. But I must hasten to a closing up of this particular. Thus you see in these eight particulars how gloriously the covenant of grace, under which the saints stand, is set out in the blessed Scriptures.

Concerning the covenant of grace, or the new covenant, that all sincere Christians are under, and by which at last they shall be judged, let me further say, besides what I have already said, *All mankind had been eternally lost, and God had lost all the glory of his mercy for ever, had he not, of his own free grace and mercy, made a new covenant with sinful man.* The fountain from whence this new covenant flows is the grace of God: Gen. xvii. 22, 'I will make' (*Heb.*, 'I will') 'my covenant.' This covenant is called a covenant of grace, because it flows from the mere grace and mercy of God. There was nothing out of God, nor nothing in God, but his mere mercy and grace, that moved him to enter into covenant with poor sinners, who were miserable, who were loathsome, and polluted in their blood, and who had broken the covenant of their God, and were actually in arms against him.[1] This must needs be of mere favour and love, for God to enter into covenant with man, when he lay wallowing in his blood, and no eye pitied him, no, not his own. As there was nothing in fallen man to draw God's favour or affection towards him, so there was everything in fallen man that might justly provoke God's wrath and indignation against him; and therefore it must be a very high act of favour and grace, for the great, the glorious, the holy, the wise, and the all-sufficient God, to enter into covenant with such a forlorn creature as fallen man was. Nothing but free grace was the foundation of the covenant of grace with poor sinners. Now let us seriously mind how this covenant of grace, or this new covenant, runs both in the Old and in the New Testament:[2] Jer. xxxi. 31, 'Behold, the days come, saith the Lord, that I will make a new covenant with the house of Israel, and with the house of Judah;' ver. 32, 'Not according to the covenant that I made with their fathers, in the day that I took them by the hand to bring them out of the land of Egypt; which my covenant they brake, although I was an husband unto them, saith the Lord;' ver. 33, 'But this shall be the covenant that I will make with the house of Israel; After those days, saith the Lord, I will put my law in their inward parts, and write it in their hearts, and will be their God, and they shall be my people;' ver. 34, 'And they shall teach no more every man his neighbour, and every man his brother, saying, Know the Lord; for they shall all know me, from the least of them unto the greatest of them, saith the Lord: for I will forgive their iniquities, and I will remember their sin no more.' Now let us see how Paul doth exegetically explain this new covenant in that Heb. viii. 6, 'But now hath he obtained a more excellent ministry, by how much also he is the mediator of a better covenant, which was established upon better promises;' ver. 7, 'For if that first covenant had been faultless, then should no place have been sought for the second; but finding fault with them, he saith,' ver. 8, 'Behold, the days come, saith the Lord, when I will make a new covenant with the house of Israel, and the house of Judah': ver. 9, 'Not according to the covenant that I made with their fathers, in the day when I took them by the hand to lead them out of the land of Egypt; because they continued not in my covenant, and I regarded them not, saith the Lord;' ver. 10, 'But this is the covenant that I will make with the house of Israel, after those days, saith the Lord; I will put my laws into their mind, and write them in their hearts: and I will be to them a God, and they shall be to me a people;' ver. 11, 'And they shall not teach every man his neighbour, and every man his brother, saying, Know the Lord: for all shall know me, from the least to the greatest;' ver. 12, 'For I will be merciful

---

[1] Isa. xli. 1, 2; Eph. i. 5-7, and ii. 5, 7, 8; 2 Sam. vii. 21; Rom. ix. 18, 23; Jer. xxxii. 38-41; Ezek. xxxvi. 25-27, and xvi. 1-10. Surely if a woman commit adultery, it is a mere act of favour if her husband accept of her again, Jer. iii. 7. The application is easy.

[2] Though the covenant of redemption made to the fathers, and this which was given after, seem diverse, yet they are all one, and grounded on Jesus Christ, save that this is called 'new;' because of the manifestations of Christ, and the abundant graces of the Holy Ghost, given to his church under the gospel, 2 Cor. iii. 1-3.

to their unrighteousness, and their sins and their iniquities will I re-member no more;' ver. 13, 'In that he saith, A new covenant, he hath made the first old. Now that which decayeth and waxeth old is ready to vanish away.' This is the substance of the new covenant; and thus the Lord did fore-promise it by Jeremiah, and afterwards expounded it by Paul. Some small difference there is in their words, but the sense is one and the same. Now this covenant is styled the new covenant, because it is to continue new, and never to wax old or wear away, so long as this world shall continue. Neither doth the Holy Scriptures anywhere reveal another covenant, which shall suc-ceed this covenant.[1] If any covenant should succeed this, it must be either a covenant of works, or a covenant of grace; not a covenant of works, for that would bring us all under a curse, and make our condi-tion utterly desperate; not a covenant of grace, because more grace cannot be shewn in any other covenant than in this; here is all grace and all mercy, here is Jesus Christ with all his righteousness, mediator-ship, merits, purchase. This covenant is so full, so ample, so large, so perfect, so complete, and is every way so accommodated to the condition of lost sinners, that nothing can be altered, nor added, nor mended: and therefore it must needs be the last covenant, that ever God will make with man. So Heb. x. 16, 'This is the covenant that I will make with them, after those days, saith the Lord; I will put my laws into their hearts, and in their minds will I write them;' ver. 17, 'And their sins and iniquities will I remember no more.' Rom. xi. 26, 'There shall come out of Zion the Deliverer, and shall turn away ungodliness from Jacob.' The person delivering is Christ, described here by his office and by his original; his office, the deliverer; the original word ῥυόμενος, which Paul useth, signifies delivering by a strong hand, to rescue by force, as David delivered the lamb out of the lion's paw; ver. 27, 'For this is my covenant unto them, when I shall take away their sin.' This covenant concerning the pardon of believers' sins, and their deliverance by Christ, God will certainly make good to his people.

Now from the covenant of grace, or the new covenant that God has made with sincere Christians, a believer may form up this eighth plea to the ten scriptures cited in the margin,[2] that refer to the great day of account, or to a man's particular account, viz., *O blessed God, thou hast, in the covenant of grace, by which I must be tried, freely and fully engaged thyself that thou wilt pardon mine iniquities, and remember my sins no more;* so runs the new covenant: Jer. xxxi. 34, 'I will forgive their iniquity, and I will remember their sin no more;' so again, Heb. viii. 12, 'I will be merciful to their unright-eousness, and their sins and their iniquities will I remember no more;' so Heb. x. 17, 'Their sins and iniquities will I remember no more;' Isa. xliii. 25, 'I, even I, am he that blotteth out thy transgressions

---

[1] Where then is the fire of purgatory, and that popish distinction of the fault and the punishment? As for the fiction of purgatory, it deserves rather to be hissed at, than by arguments refuted. And to punish sin in purgatory, as popish doctors teach, what is this, but to call sin to mind and memory, to view and sight, to reckoning and account? which is contrary to the doctrine of the new covenant.

[2] Eccles. xi. 9, and xii. 14; Mat. xii. 14, and xviii. 23; Luke xvi. 2; Rom. xiv. 10 2 Cor. v. 10; Heb. ix. 27, and xiii. 17; 1 Pet. iv. 5.

for mine own sake, and will not remember thy sins;' Ezek. xviii. 22, 'All his transgressions that he hath committed, they shall not be mentioned unto him;' Jer. l. 20, 'In those days, saith the Lord, the iniquity of Israel shall be sought for, and there shall be none; and the sins of Judah, and they shall not be found; for I will pardon them whom I reserve.' *Now, O holy God, I cannot but observe that in the new covenant thou hast made such necessary, choice, absolute, and blessed provision for thy poor people, that no sin can disannul the covenant, or make a final separation between thee and thy covenant-people.*[1] Breaches made in the first covenant were irreparable, but breaches made in the new covenant are not so, because this new covenant is established in Christ. Christ lies at the bottom of the covenant. The new covenant is an everlasting covenant; and all the breaches that we make upon that covenant are repaired and made up by the blood and intercession of dear Jesus. Every jar doth not break the marriage covenant between husband and wife; no more doth every sin break the new covenant that is between God and our souls. Every breach of peace with God is not a breach of covenant with God. That free, that rich, that infinite, that sovereign, and that glorious grace of God that shines in that covenant of grace, tells us that our eternal estates shall never be judged by a covenant of works; and that the want of an absolute perfection shall never damn a believing soul; and that the obedience that God requires at our hands is not a legal, but an evangelical obedience. So long as a Christian doth not renounce his covenant with God, so long as he doth not wilfully, wickedly, and habitually break the bond of the covenant, the main, the substance, of the covenant is not yet broken, though some articles of the covenant may be violated; as among men, there be some trespasses against some particular clauses in covenants, which, though they be violated, yet the whole covenant is not forfeited; it is so here between God and his people.

And, O blessed God, I cannot but observe that in the new covenant thou hast engaged thyself to pardon all my sins: 'I will be merciful to their unrighteousness, and their sins and their iniquities will I remember no more,' Heb. viii. 12; Jer. xxxi. 34.[2] Here are two things worthy of our notice: (1.) The reconciliation of God with his people, 'I will be merciful to their unrighteousness;' he will be merciful or propitious, appeased and pacified towards them; which hath respect to the ransom and satisfaction of Christ. (2.) That God will pardon the sins of his people fully, completely, perfectly. Here are three words, 'unrighteousness,' 'sins,' and 'iniquities,' to shew that he will forgive all sorts, kinds, and degrees of sins. The three original words here expressed are all in the plural number; 1. Ἀδικίαις, *unrighteousnesses.* This word is by some appropriated to the wrongs and injuries that are done against men; 2. Ἁμαρτιῶν, *sins,* is a general word, and according to the notation of the Greek, may imply a not following of that which is set before us; for he sinneth that followeth not the rule

---

[1] The new covenant can never be broken. 2 Chron. xiii. 5; Ps. lxxxix. 34; Isa. l. 7
[2] 2 Sam. xxiii. 5; Heb. vii. 25; 1 John ii. 1, 2; Isa. liv. 10.
[2] He is a forgiving God, Neh. ix. 31. None like him for that, Micah vii. 18. He forgives naturally, Exod. ii. 2; abundantly, Isa. lv. 7, 3; constantly, Ps. cxxx. 4; Mal. iii. 6.

that is set before him by God. The third word, Ανομιῶν, *iniquities,*
according to the notation of the Greek, signifies in general, transgressions of the law. This word is by some appropriated to sins against
God. The Greek word Ἀνομία, that is frequently translated ' iniquity,'
is a general word, which signifieth a transgression of the law, and so
it is translated, 1 John iii. 4. The word iniquity is of as large an extent as the word unrighteousness, and implieth an unequal dealing,
which is contrary to the rule or law of God. And all this heap of
words is to intimate to us that it is neither the several sorts of sins,
nor degrees of sin, nor aggravations of sin, nor yet the multitude of
sins, that shall ever prejudice those souls that are in covenant with
God. God hath mercy enough, and pardons enough, for all his covenant-people's sins, whether original or actual, whether against the law
or against the gospel, whether against the light of nature or the rule
of grace, whether against mercies or judgments, whether against great
means of grace or small means of grace. The covenant remedy against
all sorts and degrees of sin, doth infinitely transcend and surpass all
our infirmities and enormities, our weaknesses and wickednesses, our
follies and unworthinesses, &c. What is our unrighteousness to Christ's
righteousness, our debts to Christ's pardons, our unholiness to Christ's
holiness, our emptiness to Christ's fulness, our weakness to Christ's
strength, our poverty to Christ's riches, our wounds to that healing
that is under the wings of the Sun of Righteousness! 1 Cor. i. 30;
Ps. i. 3, 9, 10; Mal. iv. 2. Parallel to this, Heb. viii. 12, is that noble
description that Moses gives of God in that Book of Exodus: chap.
iii. 4, 6, 7, ' The Lord, the Lord merciful and gracious; forgiving iniquity, transgression, and sin.' Some, by these three words, do understand such sins as are committed against our neighbour, against God,
or against ourselves. A merciful God, a gracious God will pardon all
sorts of sinners, and all sorts and degrees of sin, by what names or
titles soever they may be styled or distinguished. Some by *iniquity*
do understand sins of infirmity; and by *transgression* they understand
sins of malice; and by *sin* they understand sins of ignorance. God is
said to keep mercy, and to forgive all sorts of sins, as if his mercy were
kept on purpose for pardoning all sorts of sinners and all sorts of sins.
The Hebrew word עָוֹן, *Gnavon,* that is here translated *iniquity,* signifies that which is unright, unequal, crooked or perverse; it notes the
vitiosity or crookedness of nature; it notes crooked offences, such as
flow from malice, hatred, and are committed on purpose. Secondly,
the Hebrew word וָפֶשַׁע, from פֶּשַׁע, *Pashang,* that is here translated
transgression, signifies to deal unfaithfully; it notes such sins as are
treacherously committed against God, such sins as flow from pride
and contempt of God. Thirdly, the Hebrew word וַחֲטָאָה, *Chataah,*
generally signifieth sin, but is more especially here taken for sins of
ignorance and infirmity. Oh, what singular mercy, what rich grace
is here: that God will not only pardon our light, our small offences,
but our great and mighty sins! &c.

And I cannot, O dear Father, but further observe that in the new
covenant thou hast frequently and deeply engaged thyself, that thou
wilt remember the sins of thy people no more! O my God, thou
hast told me six several times in thy word, that thou wilt remember

my sins no more. In the new covenant thou hast engaged thyself not only to forgive but also to forget, and that thou wilt cross thy debt-book, and never question or call me to an account for my sins; that thou wilt pass an eternal act of oblivion upon them, and utterly bury them in the grave of oblivion, as if they had never been. The sins that are forgiven by God are forgotten by God, the sins that God remits he removes from his remembrance, Heb. x. 13–19, and 1–15. Christ hath so fully satisfied the justice of God for the sins of all his seed, by the price of his own blood and death, that there needs no more expiatory sacrifices to be offered for their sins for ever. Christ hath, by the sacrifice of himself, blotted out the remembrance of his people's sins with God for ever. The new covenant runs thus, 'And their sinful error,' לא אזכר־עוד, *Lo escar guhod*, 'I will not remember any more,' Jer. xxxi. 34; but the Greek runs thus, 'And their sinful errors and their unrighteousnesses, I will not remember again, or any more,' Heb. viii. 12; οὐ μὴ μνησθῶ ἔτι. Here are two negatives, which do more vehemently deny, according to the propriety of the Greek language; that is, I will never remember them again, I will in no case remember them any more, I will so forgive as to forget: not that in propriety of phrase, God either remembers or forgets, for all things are present to him; he knows all things, he beholds, he sees, he observes all things, by one eternal and simple act of his knowledge, which is no way capable of change, as now knowing and anon forgetting; but it is an allusion to the manner of men, who, when they forgive injuries fully and heartily, do also forget them, blot them out of mind; or rather, as some think, it is an allusion to the manner of the old covenant's administration in the sacrifices, where there was a remembrance again of sins every year, there was a fresh indictment and arraignment of the people for sin continually, Heb. x. 1–3, &c.; but under this new covenant our Lord Jesus Christ hath, 'by one offering, perfected for ever them that are sanctified,' [see from ver. 5 to ver. 20;] Christ hath, for ever, taken away the sins of the elect; there needs no more expiatory sacrifice for them; they that are sprinkled with the blood of this sacrifice shall never have their sins remembered any more against them. God's not remembering or forgetting a thing is not simply to be taken of his essential knowledge, but respectively of his judicial knowledge, to bring the same into judgment. Not to remember a thing that was once known, and was in mind and memory, is to forget it; but this properly is not incident to God, it is an infirmity. To him all things past and future are as present.' What he once knoweth he always knoweth. His memory is his very essence, neither can anything that hath once been in it slip out of it. For God to remit sin is not to remember it; and not to remember it is to remit it. These are two reciprocal propositions, therefore they are thus joined together. 'I will forgive their iniquity, and I will remember their sin no more: I, even I, am he that blotteth out thy transgressions for mine own sake, and will not remember thy sins,' Jer. xxxi. 34; Isa. xliii. 25. To remember implieth a fourfold act; (1.) To lay up in the mind what is conceived thereby; (2.) To hold it fast; (3.) To call it to mind again; (4.) Oft to think of it. Now in that God saith, 'I will remember their iniquities no more;' he implieth that he will neither lay them up in his mind, nor there hold them, nor call them again to mind, nor think on them, but that they shall be to him as if they had never been committed. God's discharge of their sins shall be a full discharge. Such sinners shall never be called to account for them. Both the guilt and the punishment of them shall be fully and everlastingly removed. Let the sins of a believer be what they will for nature, and never so many for number, they shall all be blotted out, they shall never be mentioned more; [1] (1.) God will never remember, he will never mention their sins, so as to impute them or charge them upon his people; (2.) God will never remember, he will never mention their sins any more, so as to upbraid his people with their follies or miscarriages. He will never hit them in the teeth with their sins, he will never cast their weaknesses into their dish. When persons are justified, their sins shall be as if they had not been; God will bid them welcome into his presence, and embrace them in his arms, and will never object to them their former unkindness, unfruitfulness, unthankfulness, vileness, stubbornness, wickedness, as you may plainly see in the return of the prodigal, and his father's deportment towards him: Luke xv. 20–23, 'When he was a great way off.' The prodigal was but conceiving a purpose to return, and God met him. The very intention, and secret motions, and close purposes of our hearts, are known to God. The old father sees a great way off. Dim eyes can see a great way when the son is the object; 'his father saw him, and had compassion.' His bowels roll within him. The father not only sees, but commiserates and compassionates the returning prodigal, as he did Ephraim of old, ' My bowels are troubled for him, I will surely have mercy on him;' or, as the Hebrew runs, ' I will, having mercy, have mercy, have mercy on him, or I will abundantly have mercy on him,' Jer. xxxi. 20. Look, saith God, here is a poor prodigal returning to me, the poor child is come back, he hath smarted enough, he hath suffered enough. I will bid him welcome, I will forgive him all his high offences, and will never hit him in the teeth with his former vanities. 'And ran.' The feet of mercy are swift to meet a returning sinner. It had been sufficient for him to have stood, being old, and a father; but the father runs to the son. ' And fell on his neck.' He cannot stay and embrace him, or take him by the hand; but he falls upon him, and incorporates himself into him. How open are the arms of mercy to embrace the returning sinner, and lay him in the bosom of love! ' And kissed him.' Free, rich, and sovereign mercy hath not only feet to meet us, and arms to clasp us, but also lips to kiss us. One would have thought that he should rather have kicked him or killed him, than have kissed him. But God is *Pater miserationum*, he is all bowels. All this while the father speaks not one word. His joy was too great to be uttered. He ran, he fell on his neck, and kissed him, and so sealed up to him mercy and peace, love and reconciliation, with the kisses of his lips. And the son said

---

[1] Mat. xii. 31 ; Isa. lv. 7 ; Jer. xxxi. 12 ; Ezek. xviii. 22 ; Ps. xxxii. 2 ; Rom. iv. 8. Now if God will not remember nor mention his people's sins, then we may safely and roundly infer that either there is no purgatory, or else that God severely punishes those sins in purgatory which he remembers not.

unto him, 'Father, I have sinned against heaven, and in thy sight.' Sincerely confess, and the mends[1] is made; acknowledge but the debt, and he will cross the book. 'And am no more worthy to be called thy son.' *Infernus sum, Domine,* said that blessed martyr,[2] 'Lord, I am hell, but thou art heaven; I am soil and a sink of sin, but thou art a gracious God,' &c. But the father said to his servants, 'Bring forth the best robe, and put it on him, and put a ring on his hands, and shoes on his feet. And bring hither the fatted calf, and kill it, and let us eat and be merry.' Here you have, (1.) The best robe; (2.) The precious ring;[3] (3.) The comely shoes; and (4.) The fatted calf. The returning prodigal hath garments, and ornaments, and necessaries, and comfortables. Some understand by the robe the royalty which Adam lost; and by the ring they understand the seal of God's Holy Spirit; and by the shoes the preparation of the gospel of peace; and by the fatted calf they understand Christ, who was slain from the beginning. Christ is that fatted calf, saith Mr Tyndale the martyr, slain to make penitent sinners good cheer withal, and his righteousness is the goodly raiment to cover the naked deformities of their sins.[4] The great things intended in this parable is to set forth the riches of grace, and God's infinite goodness, and the returning sinner's happiness. When once the sinner returns in good earnest to God, God will supply all his wants, and bestow upon him more than ever he lost, and set him in a safer and happier estate than that from which he did fall in Adam; and will never hit him in the teeth with his former enormities, nor never cast in his dish his old wickednesses. You see plainly in this parable that the father of the prodigal does not so much as mention or object the former pleasures, lusts, or vanities wherein his prodigal son had formerly lived. All old scores are quit, and the returning prodigal embraced and welcomed, as if he had never offended. And now, O Lord, I must humbly take leave to tell thee further that thou hast confirmed the new covenant by thy word, and by thy oath, and by the seals that thou hast annexed to it, and by the death of thy Son, and therefore thou canst not but make good every tittle, word, branch, and article of it. Now this new covenant is my plea, O holy God, and by this plea I shall stand. Hereupon God declares, this plea, I accept as holy, just, and good. I have nothing to say against thee; enter thou into the joy of thy Lord.

IX. The ninth plea that a believer may form up as to the ten scriptures that are in the margin,[5] that refer to the great day of account, or to a man's particular account, may be drawn up from the consideration of that *evangelical obedience that God requires, and that the believer yields to God.* There is a legal, and there is an evangelical account. Now the saints, in the great day, shall not be put to give up a legal account; the account they shall be put to give up is an evangelical account. In the covenant of works, God required perfect obedience in our own persons; but in the covenant of grace God

[1] 'Amends.'—G.   [2] Mr Hooper, at his death.—[Foxe,] Act. and Mon., 1374.
[3] Among the Romans the ring was an ensign of virtue, honour, and especially nobility, whereby they were distinguished from the common people.
[4] [Foxe,] Act. and Mon., fol. 986.
[5] Eccles. xi. 9, and xii. 14; Mat. xii. 14, and xviii. 23; Luke xvi. 2; Rom. xiv. 10; 2 Cor. v. 10; Heb. ix. 27, and xiii. 17; 1 Pet. iv. 5.

will be content if there be but uprightness in us, if there be but sincere desires to obey, if there be faithful endeavours to obey, if there be a hearty willingness to obey. Well, saith God, though I stood upon perfect obedience in the covenant of works, 2 Cor. viii. 12; yet now I will be satisfied with the will for the deed; if there be but uprightness of heart, though that be attended with many weaknesses and infirmities, yet I will be satisfied and contented with that. God, under the covenant of grace, will for Christ's sake accept of less than he requires in the covenant of works. He requires perfection of degrees, but he will accept of perfection of parts; he requires us to live without sin, but he will accept of our sincere endeavours to do it. Though a believer, in his own person, cannot perform all that God commands, yet Jesus Christ, as his surety and in his stead, hath fulfilled the law for him. So that Christ's perfect righteousness is a complete cover for a believer's imperfect righteousness. Hence the believer flies from the covenant of works to the covenant of grace; from his own unrighteousness to the righteousness of Christ.[1] If we consider the law in a high and rigid notion, so no believer can fulfil it; but if we consider the law in a soft and mild notion, so every believer does fulfil it: Acts xiii. 22, ' I have found David the son of Jesse, a man after mine own heart, which shall fulfil all my will;' πάντα τὰ θελήματα, ' All my wills,' to note the universality and sincerity of his obedience. David had many slips and falls, he often transgressed the royal law; but being sincere in the main bent and frame of his heart, and in the course of his life, God looked upon his sincere obedience as perfect obedience. A sincere Christian's obedience is an entire obedience to all the commands of God, though not in respect of practice, which is impossible, but in disposition and affection.[2] A sincere obedience is a universal obedience. It is universal in respect of the subject, the whole man; it is universal in respect of the object, the whole law; and it is universal in respect of durance, the whole life; he who obeys sincerely obeys universally. There is no man that serves God truly that doth not endeavour to serve God fully: sincerity turns upon the hinges of universality; he who obeys sincerely endeavours to obey thoroughly, Num. xiv. 24. A sincere Christian does not only love the law, and like the law, and approve of the law, and delight in the law, and consent to the law, that it is holy, just, and good, but he obeys it in part, Rom. vii. 12, 16, 22; which, though it be but in part, yet he being sincere therein, pressing towards the mark, and desiring and endeavouring to arrive at what is perfect, Phil. iii. 13, 14, God accepts of such a soul, and is as well pleased with such a soul, as if he had perfectly fulfilled the law. Where the heart is sincerely resolved to obey, there it does obey. A heart to obey, is our obeying; a heart to do, is our doing; a heart to believe, is our believing; a heart to repent, is our repenting; a heart to wait, is our waiting; a heart to suffer, is our suffering; a heart to pray, is our praying; a heart to hear, is our hearing; a heart to give, feed, clothe, visit, is our giving, feeding,

---

[1] Luke i. 5, 6; Mat. xxviii. 20; Acts xxiv. 16; 1 Pet. i. 14, 15; Heb. xiii. 18. *Lex data est ut gratia quæreretur; gratia data est ut lex impleretur.*—Augustine.
[2] Ps. cxix. 6. Heb., When my eye is to all thy commandments.

clothing, visiting; a heart to walk circumspectly, is our walking circumspectly; a heart to work righteousness, is our working righteousness; a heart to shew mercy, is our shewing mercy; a heart to sympathise with others, is our sympathising with others. He that sincerely desires and resolves to keep the commandments of God, he does keep the commandments of God, and he that truly desires and resolves to walk in the statutes of God, he does walk in the statutes of God. In God's account and God's acceptation, every believer, every sincere Christian, is as wise, holy, humble, heavenly, spiritual, watchful, faithful, fruitful, useful, thankful, joyful, &c., as he desires to be, as he resolves to be, and as he endeavours to be; and this is the glory of the new covenant, and the happiness that we gain by dear Jesus. And, my friends, it is remarkable that our inchoate, partial and very imperfect obedience is frequently set forth in the blessed Scriptures by our fulfilling of the law, Luke x. 25–27. Take a few places for a taste: Rom. ii. 27, ' And shall not uncircumcision, which is by nature, if it fulfil the law, judge thee?' &c.; Rom. xiii. 8, 'He that loveth another, hath fulfilled the law;' ver. 10, ' Love is the fulfilling of the law.' Not to love is to do ill and to break the law, but love is the fulfilling of it; *Non potest peccari per illam, quœ legis est perfectio;* we cannot do ill by that which is the perfection and the fulfilling of the law.[1] Love is the sum of the law, love is the perfection of the law; and were love perfect in us, it would make us perfect keepers of the law. Love works the saints to keep the law in desires and endeavours, with care and study to observe it in perfection of parts, though not in perfection of degrees: Gal. v. 14, ' All the law is fulfilled in one word, even in this, Thou shalt love thy neighbour as thyself;' Gal. vi. 2, ' Bear ye one another's burdens, and so fulfil the law of Christ.' Now in this sense that is under consideration, the saints in themselves, even in this life, do keep the royal law. Now, from what has been said, a believer may form up this plea:—

O blessed God, in Christ my head I have perfectly and completely kept thy royal law; and in my own person I have evangelically kept thy royal law, in respect of my sincere desires, purposes, resolutions, and endeavours to keep it: and this evangelical keeping in Christ, and in the new covenant, thou art pleased to accept of, and art well satisfied with it. I know that breaches made in the first covenant were irreparable, but breaches made in the covenant of grace are not so; because this covenant is established in Christ; who is still a-making up all breaches. Now this is my plea, O holy God, and by this plea I shall stand. Well, saith God, I cannot in honour or justice but accept of this plea, and therefore enter thou into the joy of thy Lord.

X. The tenth plea that a believer may form up, as to the ten scriptures that are in the margin,[2] that refer to the great day of account, or to a man's particular account, may be drawn up from the consideration of that *compact, covenant, and agreement, that was solemnly made between God and Christ, touching the whole business of man's salvation*

---

[1] Ambrose, *in loco.*
[2] Eccles. xi. 9, and xii. 14; Mat. xii. 14, and xviii. 23; Luke xvi. 2; Rom. xiv. 10; 2 Cor. v. 10; Heb. ix. 27, and xiii. 17; 1 Pet. iv. 5.

or redemption. We may present it to our understanding in this form : God the Father saith to Christ the mediator, I look upon Adam and his posterity as a degenerate seed, ' a generation of vipers,' of apostates and backsliders, yea, traitors and rebels ; liable to all temporal, spiritual, and eternal judgments ; yet I cannot find in my heart to damn them all ; ' Mine heart is turned within me, my repentings are kindled together ; I will not execute the fierceness of mine anger : for I am God, and not man,' Hosea xi. 8, 9 : and therefore I have determined to shew mercy upon many millions of them, and save them from wrath to come, and to bring them to glory, Rev. vii. 9, 10 ; but this I must do with a salvo to my law, justice, and honour. If, therefore, thou wilt undertake for them, and become a curse for their sakes, Gal. iii. 10, 13, and so make satisfaction to my justice for their sins ; I will give them unto thee, John xvii. 2, 6, 11, to take care of them, and to bring them up to my kingdom, for the manifestation of the glory of my grace. Well, saith Christ, I am content, I will do all thou requirest with all my heart, and so the agreement is made between thee and me. This may be gathered from the scriptures in the margin.[1] Christ the Son speaks in both places. In the first he publisheth the decree or ordinance of heaven, touching himself, and bringeth in the Father, installing him into the priesthood or office of mediator ; for so the apostle applieth that text, Heb. v. 5, ' Thou art my son,' &c., and also avoucheth this covenant and agreement in the two main parts of it.

1. First, *The condition which he will have performed on Christ's part, as mediator ; or what Christ must do, as mediator,* ' He must ask of God ;' that is, not only verbally, by prayers and supplications, beg mercy, pardon, righteousness, and salvation for poor lost sinners ; but also really, by fulfilling the righteousness of the law, both in doing and suffering ; and so by satisfaction and merit, purchasing acceptation for them at his hands.[2] The Father engaged so and so to Christ, and Christ reciprocally engaged so and so to the Father ; a considerable part of the terms and matter of which covenant is set down : Isa. liii. 10, ' When thou shalt make his soul an offering for sin, he shall see his seed,' &c. The Father covenants to do thus and thus for fallen man ; but first in order thereunto the Son must covenant to take man's nature, therein to satisfy offended justice, to repair and vindicate his Father's honour, &c. Well, he submits, assents to these demands, indents and covenants to make all good ; and this was the substance of the covenant of redemption. But,

2. Secondly, Let us consider *the promise which the Father engageth to perform on his part ;* the Son must ask, and the Father will give : ' He will give him the heathen for his inheritance, and the uttermost parts of the earth for his possession,' Ps. ii. 8. An allusion to great princes, when they would shew great affection to their favourites, they bid them ask what they will, as Ahasuerus did, and as Herod did ; that is, he shall both be the Lord's salvation to the ends of the earth, and ' have all power given him in heaven and earth ;

---

[1] Ps. ii. 7–9, and xl. 6–8.

[2] Consider Christ in the capacity of a mediator, for so only he covenanted with the Father, for the salvation of mankind.

so that all knees shall bow to him, and every tongue shall confess him to be Lord.'[1] In the other text before mentioned, Ps. xl., Christ declares his compliance to the agreement, and his subscribing the covenant on his part, when he came into the world, as the apostle explains it, Heb. x. 5, &c.; ' Mine ears,' saith he, ' hast thou digged or pierced : Lo, I come to do thy will ;' as if he had said, O Father, thou dost engage me to be thy servant in this great work of saving sinners. Lo, I come to do the work, I here covenant and agree to yield up myself to thy disposing, and to serve thee for ever. It seems to be an allusion to the master's ' boring through the servant's ear,' Exod. xxi. 6. Among the Jews only one ear was bored, but in this Ps. xl. 6, here are ears in the plural number, a token of that perfect and desirable subjection, which Christ, as mediator, was in to his Father. But for a more clear, distinct, and full opening of the covenant of redemption, or that blessed compact between God the Father and Jesus Christ, which is a matter of grand importance to all our souls ; and considering that it is a point that I have never yet treated of in pulpit or press, I shall therefore take the liberty at this time to open myself as clearly and as fully as I can. And therefore thus :—

Quest. If you ask me, What this covenant of redemption is ?

Ans. 1. I answer, in the general, that a covenant is a mutual agreement between parties, upon articles or propositions on both sides, so that each party is tied and bound to perform his own conditions. This description holds the general nature of a covenant, and is common to all covenants, public and private, divine or human. But,

Ans. 2. Secondly, and more particularly, I answer, the covenant of redemption is that federal transaction or mutual stipulation that was betwixt God and Christ from everlasting, for the accomplishment of the work of our redemption, by the mediation of Jesus Christ, to the eternal honour, and unspeakable praise, of the glorious grace of God. Or, if you please, take it in another form of words, thus :—

It is a compact, bargain, and agreement between God the Father and God the Son, designed mediator, concerning the conversion, sanctification, and salvation of the elect, through the death, satisfaction, and obedience of Jesus Christ, which in due time was to be given to the Father. But for the making good the definition I have laid down, I must take leave to tell you that there are many choice scriptures which give clear intimation of such a federal transaction between God the Father and Jesus Christ, in order to the recovery, and everlasting happiness, and salvation of his elect. I shall instance in the most considerable of them :—

(1.) The first is this, Gen. iii. 15, ' And I will put enmity between thee and the woman, and between thy seed and her seed ; it shall bruise thy head, and thou shalt bruise his heel.' Here begins the book of the Lord's wars, God's battles.[2] This is spoken of that holy enmity that is between Christ and the devil, and of Christ's destroying the kingdom and power of Satan : ' Forasmuch then as the children are partakers of flesh and blood, he also himself likewise took part of the same ; that through death he might destroy him that had the power of death, that

---

[1] Esth. v. 3 ; Mark vi. 23 ; Isa. xlix. 6 ; Mat. xxviii. 18 ; Phil. ii. 10, 11 ; Ps. xl. 6-8.
[2] The Scriptures are called the Book of the Battles of the Lord, Num. xxi.—*Rupertus.*

is, the devil,' Heb. ii. 14. God, by way of threatening, told Satan that the seed of the deceived woman should overmatch him at last, and should break in pieces his power and crafty plots. He gives Satan leave to do his worst, and proclaims an open and an utter enmity between Christ and him. From this scripture some conclude that Christ covenanted from eternity to take upon him the seed of the woman, and the sinless infirmities of our true human nature; and under those infirmities to enter the lists with Satan, and to continue obedient through all his afflictions, temptations, and trials, to the death, even to the death of the cross, Phil. ii. 8, 9. And that God the Father had covenanted with Christ, that in case Christ did continue obedient through all his sufferings, temptations, and trials, that then his obedience to the death should be accounted as full satisfaction to divine justice for all those wrongs and injuries that were done to God by the sins of man. Christ must die, or else he could not have been the mediator of the new covenant through death, Heb. ix. 15, 16. But,

(2.) The second scripture is that, Isa. xlii. 6, 'The Lord hath called thee in righteousness, and will hold thine hand, and will keep thee, and give thee for a covenant of the people, for a light of the Gentiles.' Thus God speaks of Christ. In this chapter we have a glorious prophecy of Christ our Redeemer. Here are four things prophesied of him: (1.) The divine call, whereby he was appointed to the work of our redemption: ver. 1, 'Behold my servant whom I uphold, mine elect in whom my soul delighteth; I have put my Spirit upon him: he shall bring forth judgment to the Gentiles.' Jesus Christ would not. yea, he could not, he durst not, thrust himself upon this great work, or engage in this great work, till he had a clear call from heaven. (2.) Here you have the gracious carriage and deportment of Christ, in the work to which he was called; this is fully set down, vers. 2–4, 'He shall not cry, nor lift up, nor cause his voice to be heard in the street.' He shall come clothed with majesty and glory, and yet full of meekness: 'a bruised reed shall he not break, and the smoking flax shall he not quench; he shall bring forth judgment unto truth.' In the words there is a *meiosis*,[1] 'he will not break,' that is, he will bind up the bruised reed, he will comfort the bruised reed, he will strengthen the bruised reed. Christ will acknowledge and encourage the least degrees of grace; he will turn a spark of grace into a flame, a drop into a sea, &c.: 'He shall not fail, nor be discouraged.' These words shew his kingly courage and magnanimity. Though he should meet with opposition from all hands, yet nothing should daunt him, nothing should dismay him; no afflictions, no temptations, no sufferings should in the least abate his courage and valour. (3.) The divine assistance he should have from him that called him. This is set down in two expressions: ver. 6, 'I will hold thy hand, I will keep thee.' Divine assistance doth usually concur with a divine call. When God sets his servants on work, he uses to defend and uphold them in the work. (4.) The work itself to which Christ was called. This is expressed under divers phrases: ver. 6, 7, 'To be a light to the Gentiles, to open the blind eyes, to bring out the prisoners from the prison, and to be a covenant to the people.' In these last words you have two things

---

[1] Same as *litotes*, as before.—G.

observable; the first is one special part of Christ's office: 'He was given for a covenant.' Second, The persons in reference to whom this office was designed: 'a covenant of the people.' One end why God the Father gave Christ out of his bosom, was, that he might be a covenant to his people. Christ is given for a covenant both to the believing Jews and Gentiles. As he is 'the glory of the people of Israel,' so he is 'a light to lighten the Gentiles.' In this scripture last cited, you have the Father's designation and sealing of Christ to the mediatorial employment, promising him much upon his undertaking it, and his acceptation of this office, and voluntary submission to the will of the Father in it: 'Lo, I come to do thy will,' Heb. v. 4, 5; Ps. xl. 7, 8; John x. 17, 18. And these together amount to the making up of a covenant between God the Father and his Son; for what more can be necessary to the making up of a covenant than is here expressed? But,

(3.) The third scripture is that, Isa. xlix. 1, 'Listen, O isles, unto me; and hearken, ye people, from far; The Lord God hath called me from the womb; from the bowels of my mother hath he made mention of my name.'[1] These words are spoken in the person of Christ; he tells us how he is called by his Father to be a mediator and Saviour of his people. Jesus Christ would not take one step in the work of our redemption till he was called and commissionated by his Father to that work. God the Father, who from eternity had fore-assigned Christ to this office of a mediator, a Redeemer, did, both while he was in the womb, and as soon as he was come out of it, manifest and make known this his purpose concerning Christ both to men and angels. Christ did not thrust himself, he did not intrude himself at random into the office of a Redeemer: 'No man takes this honour to himself, but he that is called of God, as was Aaron,' Heb. v. 4, 5. So Christ took not upon himself the office of a mediator, a Saviour, but upon a call and a commission from God. The sum is, that Christ took up the office of a Redeemer by the ordinance of his Father, that he might fulfil the work of our redemption unto which he was destinated. Ver. 2, 'And he made my mouth like a sharp sword; in the shadow of his hand hath he hid me, and made me a polished shaft; in his quiver hath he hid me.' Christ having avouched his Father's calling of him to the work of man's redemption, he gives you a relation in this verse of God's fitting and furnishing of him with abilities sufficient for so important a work, together with his sustaining and supporting of him in the performance of the same. Here are two similitudes or comparisons: (1.) That of a 'sharp sword;' that of a bright and 'sharp arrow,' to shew the efficacy of Christ's doctrine.[2] The word of Christ is a sword of great power and efficacy for the subduing of the souls of men to the obedience of it, and for the cutting off of whomsoever or whatsoever shall oppose or withstand it. Christ was not sent of the Father to conquer by force of arms, as earthly princes do; but he conquers all sorts of sinners, even the proudest and stoutest of them,

---

[1] This prophecy is applied to Christ, Luke ii. 32; Acts xiii. 47; Gal. iii. 16; Heb. v. 4, 5. And many of the Jews do confess that this place is to be understood of Christ only, Mat. i. 21, 22; Luke ii. 10, 11; Heb. i. 6.

[2] See Eph. vi. 17; Heb. iv. 12; Rev. i. 16, and vi. 2.

by the sword of the Spirit, which is the word of God, as you may see
by comparing the scriptures in the margin together.[1] Having spoken
of the efficacy of Christ's doctrine, he tells us that he will take care
of the security of his person : ' In the shadow of his hand hath he hid
me, and in his quiver hath he hid me.' God the Father undertakes
to protect the Lord Jesus Christ against all sorts of adversaries that
should band themselves against him, and to maintain his doctrine
against all enemies that should conspire to suppress it.[2] God so protected his dear Son against all the might and malice of his most
capital enemies that they neither could lay hold on him, or do aught,
before the time by God fore-designed was come. Christ was sheltered
under the wing of God's protection till that voluntarily he went to
his passion ; neither could they keep him under when that time was
once over, though they endeavoured with all their might to do it.
Now in the third verse, God the Father tells Jesus Christ what a
glorious reward he should have for undertaking the great work of
redemption : ' And said unto me, Thou art my servant, O Israel, in
whom I will be glorified.'[3] God having called Christ, set him apart,
sanctified him, and sent him into the world for the execution of
the office of a Redeemer, he doth in this third verse encourage him
to set upon it, and to go on cheerfully, resolutely, and constantly in it,
with assurance of good and comfortable success, notwithstanding all
the plots, designs, and oppositions that Satan and his imps might
make against him. Ver. 4, ' Then I said, I have laboured in vain,
I have spent my strength for nought, and in vain'; yet surely my
judgment is with the Lord, and my work with my God.' In these
words Jesus Christ complains to his Father of the incredulity, wickedness, and obstinate rebellion of the greatest part of the Jews against
that blessed word which he had clearly and faithfully made known
to them. When Christ looked upon the paucity and small number of
those that his ministry had any saving and powerful work upon, he
pours out his complaints before the Father : not that Christ's pains in
his ministry among the Jews were wholly in vain, either in regard of
God that sent him, or in regard of the persons unto whom he was
sent, as if not any at all were converted. Oh no ! for some were
called, converted, and sanctified, as you may see by the scriptures in
the margin.[4] Or in regard of himself, as if any loss or prejudice
should thereby redound unto him. Oh no ! but in regard of the small,
the slender effect, that his great labours had hitherto found. ' Yet
surely my judgment is with the Lord.' Christ, for the better support
and re-encouraging of himself to persist in his employment, opposeth
unto the want of the chiefly desired success of his labours with men,
the gracious acceptance of them with God. It is as if Christ had said,
Although my labour hath not produced such fruits and effects as I

---

[1] Acts ii. 37, 41, iv. 1-4, and xvi. 29-35 ; 2 Cor. x. 4, 6.

[2] John vii. 30, 44 ; Luke xxii. 53 ; Mat. xxvii. 62-66, and 2-6 ; Acts ii. 23, 24.

[3] Or, as some render the words, Thou art my servant to Israel, or for Israel ; that is,
for Israel's good, for my people's behoof.—Few, saith Sasbont, to this day do consider
Christ's labour in preaching, prayer, fasting, and suffering a cruel death for us ; for if
they did, they would be more affected with love towards him that loved them so dearly.
[By ' Sasbont' is probably intended Adam Sasbouth, or Sasbouthius. See his Commentarius in Isaiam. 1563 : 8vo.—G.]

[4] Isa. vi. 13, and viii. 18, &c.

indeed desired, yet I do comfort and bear up my heart with this, that my heavenly Father knows that in the office and place wherein he hath set me, I have faithfully done all that could be done for the salvation of poor sinners' souls, and for the securing of them from wrath to come: 'And my work,' or reward, 'with my God;' that is, the reward of my work, or my wages for my work, which God will render unto me, not according to the issue or success of my labours, but according to my pains therein taken, and the faithful discharge of my office and duty therein. What, saith Christ, though the Jews believe not, repent not, return not to the Most High, yet my labour is not lost, for my God will really, he will signally reward me. Upon this, God the Father comes off more freely and roundly, and opens his heart more abundantly to Jesus Christ, and tells him in the fifth and sixth verses following, that he will give him full, complete, and honourable satisfaction for all his pains and labours in preaching, in doing, in suffering, in dying, that he might bring many sons to glory. Ver. 5, 'And now, saith the Lord, that formed me from the womb to be his servant, to bring Jacob again to him, Though Israel is not gathered, yet shall I be glorious in the eyes of the Lord, and my God shall be my strength.' In this verse you have a further encouragement to our Lord Jesus Christ, God the Father engaging himself not only to support him and protect him in the work of his ministry, but of making him glorious in it and by it also; and that though his work should not prove so successful among his own people as he desired, yet his ministry should become very glorious and efficacious upon the Gentiles, far and near, throughout the whole world.[1] Jesus Christ is very confident of his being high in the esteem of his Father for the faithful discharge of his duty; and that, notwithstanding all the hard measure that he met with from the body of the Jews, that yet his Father would crown him with honour and glory, and that he would enable him to go through the work that is incumbent upon him, and that he would protect him and defend him in his work, against all might and malice, all power and policy, that should make head against him. Ver. 6, 'And he said, It is a light thing that thou shouldest be my servant, to raise up the tribes of Jacob, and to restore the preserved of Israel; I will also give thee for a light to the Gentiles, that thou mayest be my salvation to the ends of the earth.' Thus you see that God the Father still goes on to shew that the labours of Christ should be very glorious, not only in the eyes of God, but in the eyes of all the world. You know elsewhere Christ is called 'the way, the truth, and the life,' John xiv. 6; and here he is called the light and salvation of the Gentiles. God the Father, speaking to Jesus Christ, tells him that it was but a small matter, a mean thing—*Heb.*, it is too light—for him to have such happy and ample success as to reduce and win the Jews, in comparison of that further work that he intended to effect by him, even the salvation of the Gentiles unto the ends of the earth. God the Father seems to say thus to Jesus Christ, The dignity and worthiness of thy person, thou being the eternal and only Son of God, as also the high office whereunto I have called thee, requireth more excellent things than that thou shouldest only raise up and restore the people of Israel

[1] John v. 20, 23, x. 15, 17, and xvii. 1, 5; Phil. ii. 9.

to their right; I have also appointed and ordained thee for a Saviour to the Gentiles, even to the ends of the earth; therefore though the greatest part among the Jews will not receive thee nor submit unto thee, yet the Gentiles they shall own thee and honour thee, they shall embrace thee and give themselves up unto thee. I shall be briefer in the remaining proofs; and therefore,

(4.) The fourth scripture is that, Isa. lii. 13, 14, 'Behold, my servant shall deal prudently, he shall be exalted and extolled, and be very high.'[1] The three last verses of this chapter, with the next chapter, do jointly make up an entire prophecy concerning Christ his person, parentage, condition, manner of life, sufferings, humiliation, exaltation, &c., with the noble benefits that redound to us, and the great honour that redounds to himself. In these two verses you have—(1.) The two parties contracting, viz., God the Father, and Jesus Christ: 'Behold my servant,' saith God the Father. This title is several times given by the Father to Jesus Christ, because he did the Father great service in the work of man's redemption, freeing fallen man from the thraldom of sin and Satan. (2.) Both parties are very sure and confident of the event of the paction, and of the accomplishment of the whole work of redemption: 'Behold, my servant shall deal prudently, he shall be exalted and extolled, and be very high.' Here are divers terms heaped up to express in part the transcendent and unexpressible advancement of Jesus Christ. When men are raised from a mean and low estate to some honourable condition, when men are furnished with such parts and endowments of prudence, wisdom, and understanding as makes them admirable in the eyes of others, and when they are enabled to do and suffer great things whereby they become famous and renowned far and near, then we say they are highly exalted. Now in all these respects our Lord Jesus Christ was most eminently exalted above all creatures in heaven and earth, as is most evident throughout the Scriptures. (3.) He tells you of the price which Jesus Christ should pay for the redemption of his people, agreed upon by paction, viz., the humbling of himself to the death of the cross, as you may see in ver. 14: 'As many were astonished at thee; his visage was so marred, more than any man's, and his form more than the sons of men.' This is the speech of the Father to Jesus Christ; his visage was so marred that the Jews were ashamed to own him for their King and Messiah. The astonishment here spoken of is such an astonishment as ariseth from the contemplation of some strange, uncouth, and rueful spectacle of desolation, deformity, and misery. And no wonder if many were astonished at the sight of our Saviour's condition, in regard of those base, disgraceful, and despiteful usages that were offered and done to him in the time of his humiliation here on earth, when his own followers were so amazed at the relation of them when they were foretold of them, Mat. x. 32–34. O sirs! the words last cited are not so to be understood as if our blessed Saviour had, in regard of his bodily person or presence, been some strange, deformed, or misshapen creature, Isa. liii. 3, but in regard of his outward estate, coming of mean and obscure parents,

[1] The Chaldee paraphrast, and some of [the] Jewish doctors, expound this place of the Messiah, Isa. xlii. 1, and liii. 11, &c.

living in a low, despicable condition, exposed to scorn and contempt, and to much affliction, through the whole course of his life, and more especially yet in regard of what he was also in his personal appearance, through the base and scornful usages that he sustained at the hands of his malicious and mischievous adversaries, when they had gotten him into their power; besides his watchings, draggings to and fro from place to place, buffetings, scourgings, carrying his cross, and other base usages, could not but much alter the state of his body, and impair, yea, deface all the sightliness of it. And yet all this he suffered, to make good the compact and agreement that he had made with his Father about the redemption of his elect. But,

(5.) The fifth scripture is that 53d of Isaiah. This scripture, among many others, gives us very clear intimations of a federal trans-action between God the Father and Jesus Christ, in order to the re-covery and everlasting happiness of poor sinners. The glorious gospel seems to be epitomized in this chapter. The subject-matter of it is the grievous sufferings and dolorous death of Christ, and the happy and glorious issue thereof. Of all the prophets, this prophet Isaiah was the most evangelical prophet, and of all the prophecies of this prophet, that which you have in this chapter is the most evangelical prophecy.[1] In this chapter you have a most plain, lively, and full description and representation of the humiliation, death, and passion of Jesus Christ; which indeed is so exact, and so consonant to what hath fallen out since, that Isaiah seems here rather to pen a history than a prophecy.[2] The matter contained in this chapter is so convic-tive, from that clear light that goes along with it, that several of the Jews, in reading of this chapter, have been converted, as not being able to stand any longer out against the shining light and evidence of it. Out of this chapter, which is more worth than all the gold of Ophir, yea, than ten thousand worlds, observe with me these eight things:

[1.] First, Observe that *God and Christ are sweetly agreed, and in-finitely pleased in the conversion of the elect:* ver. 10, 'He shall see his seed,' that is, he shall see them called, converted, changed, and sanctified: 'he shall see his seed,' that is, an innumerable company shall be converted to him by his word and Spirit, in all countries and nations, through the mighty workings of the Spirit, and the incorrupt-ible seed of the word, Ps. cx. 3; 1 Pet. i. 23; infinite numbers of poor souls should be brought in to Jesus Christ, which he should see to his full content and infinite satisfaction, Rev. vii. 9; Heb. ii. 10, 13. 'He shall see his seed,' that is, he shall see them increase and multiply; he shall see believers brought in to him from all corners and quarters, and he shall see them greatly increase and grow by the preaching of the everlasting gospel, especially after his ascension into heaven, and a more glorious pouring forth of the Holy Ghost upon his apostles and others, Acts ii. 37, 41, iv. 1–4, and viii. No accountants on earth can count or reckon up Christ's spiritual seed and issue. But,

---

[1] Jerome calls him Isaiah the evangelist.
[2] In this chapter you have the compact and agreement between God the Father and Jesus Christ plainly asserted and proved.

[2.] Secondly, Observe with me, that *in the persons redeemed by Jesus Christ there was neither weight nor worth, neither portion nor proportion, neither inward nor outward excellencies or beauties, for which the punishment due to them should be transferred upon dear Jesus*, Ezek. xvi. 1–10; for if you look upon them in their sins, in their guilt, you shall find them despisers and rejecters of Christ: ver. 4, 'Surely he hath borne our griefs, and carried our sorrows; yet we did esteem him stricken, smitten of God, and afflicted.' Christ took upon him not our nature alone, but the infirmities also of it, and became liable to such sorrows, and afflictions, and pains, and griefs, as man's sinful nature is exposed and subject unto. They are called ours because they were procured to him by our sins, and sustained by him for the discharge of our sins; unto the guilt whereof, out of love to us undertaken by him, they were deservedly due, Rom. viii. 3; Heb. iv. 15. Christ, for our sakes, hath taken all our spiritual maladies, that is, all our sins, upon him, to make satisfaction for them; and as our surety, to pay the debt that we had run into. Christ, in the quality of a pledge for his elect, hath given full satisfaction for all their sins, bearing all the punishments due for them, in torments and extreme griefs, both of body and soul.[1] The reason why they so much disesteemed of Christ was, because they made no other account, but that all those afflictions that befell him were by God inflicted upon him for his own evil deserts. They accounted him to be one out of grace and favour with God, yea, to be one pursued by him with all those evils, for his sins. When the Jews saw what grievous things Christ suffered, they wickedly and impiously judged that he was thus handled by God, in way of vengeance for his sins. By all which, you may see, that in the persons redeemed by Christ, there was nothing of worth or honour to be found, for which the punishment, due to them, should be transferred upon our Lord Jesus Christ. But,

[3.] Thirdly, Observe with me, that *no sin, nor meritorious cause of punishment, is found in Jesus Christ, our blessed Redeemer, for which he should be stricken, smitten, and afflicted by God:* ver. 5, 9, 'He was wounded for our transgressions, he was bruised for our iniquities; the chastisement of our peace was upon him, and with his stripes we are healed. He had done no violence, neither was any deceit in his mouth.' Sin had cast God and us at infinite distance. Now Christ is punished that our sins may be pardoned; he is chastised that God and we may be reconciled. Guilt stuck close upon us, but Christ, by the price of his blood, hath discharged that guilt, pacified divine wrath, and made God and us friends.[2] God the Father laid upon dear Jesus all the punishments that were due to the elect, for whom he was a pledge; and by this means they come to be acquitted, and to obtain peace with God. 'Christ was holy, harmless, and undefiled.' No man could convince him of sin; yea, the devil himself could find nothing amiss in him, either as to word or deed. Christ was without original blemish or actual blot.[3] All

---

[1] You know they traduced him as a notorious deceiver, a drunkard, a friend of publicans and sinners, and one that wrought by the devil.

[2] 1 Pet. i. 18, 19; Rom. iii. 25, and v. 1, 10; 2 Cor. v. 19, 21; Col. i. 19, 20.

[3] Heb. vii. 26; John viii. 46, and xiv. 30; 1 John iii. 5.

Christ's words and works were upright, just, and sincere. Christ's innocency is sufficiently vindicated, ver. 9. It is true, Christ suffered great and grievous things, but not for his own sins; ' For he had done no violence, neither was any deceit found in his mouth ;' but for ours. Christ had now put himself in the sinner's stead, and was become his surety, and so obnoxious to whatever the sinner had deserved in his own person; and upon this account, and no other, was he wounded, bruised, and chastised. The Lord Jesus had no sin in him by *inhesion*, but he had a great deal of sin upon him by *imputation :* ' He was made sin that knew no sin, that we might be made the righteousness of God in him,' 2 Cor. v. 21. It pleased our Lord Jesus Christ to put himself under our guilt, and therefore it pleased the Father to wound him, bruise him, and chastise him. But,

[4.] Fourthly, Observe with me, that *peace and reconciliation with God, and the healing of all our sinful maladies, and our deliverance from wrath to come, are all such noble favours as are purchased for us by the blood of Christ :*[1] ver. 5, ' The chastisement of our peace was upon him, and with his stripes we are healed.' Christ was chastised to procure our peace, by removal of our sins, that set God and us asunder ; the guilt thereof being discharged with the price of his blood, and we reconciled to God by the same price. Christ was punished that we by him might obtain perfect peace with God, who was at enmity with us by reason of our sins. By Christ's stripes we are freed both from sin and punishment. Now because some produce this scripture to justify that corrupt doctrine of universal redemption, give me leave to argue thus from it. That chastisement for sin that was laid upon the person of Jesus Christ procured peace for them for whom he was so chastised, Isa. lvii. 21 ; Eph. ii. 14 ; but there was no peace procured for the reprobates, or those who should never believe, *ergo.* . . . Further, ' By his stripes we are healed.' Whence I reason thus : the stripes inflicted upon Christ are intended, and do become healing medicines for them for whom they are inflicted ; but they never become healing medicines for reprobates or unbelievers : Nahum iii. 9, ' There is no healing of their bruise.' *Ergo.* . . But,

[5.] Fifthly, Observe with me, that *the great and the grievous sufferings that were inflicted upon Jesus Christ he did endure freely, willingly, meekly, patiently, according to the covenant and agreement that was made between the Father and himself :* ver. 7, ' He was oppressed and he was afflicted, yet he opened not his mouth : he is brought as a lamb to the slaughter, and as a sheep before her shearers is dumb, so he opened not his mouth.' This is a very pregnant place to prove the satisfaction made by Christ's sufferings for our sins ; if we look upon the words as they run in the original, for thus they run ; ' It was exacted, and he answered ;' that is, the penalty due to God's justice for our sins was exacted of Christ, and he sustained the same for us. The prophet doth not speak of one and the same party or parties, both sinning and suffering or sustaining penalties for their own defaults ; but as one suffering, for the sins of another, and sustaining grievous penalties for faults made and faults committed by

[1] 1 Thes. i. 10; 1 Pet. i. 18, 19; Rom. iii. 25, and v. 1, 16; 2 Cor. v. 19, 21.

other persons. The words, rightly read and understood, do sufficiently confirm the doctrine of satisfaction, made to God's justice by Christ's sufferings, for our sins. The penalty due to us was, in rigour of justice, exacted of him, and he became a sponsor or surety for us, by undertaking in our behalf the discharge of it. Christ did voluntarily undertake and engage himself unto God his Father in our behalf, as a surety for the payment of all our debts. They were exacted of him, and he answered for them all; that is, he not only undertook them, but he also discharged us of them. So we use the word commonly in our English tongue; to answer a debt, for to discharge it; and this is most true of our dear Lord Jesus, for he answered our debt, and caused our bond to be cancelled, that it might never come to be put in suit against us, either in this or that other world, John xix. 30; Rom. iv. 25; Col. ii. 14. 'Yet he opened not his mouth:' this has respect to his patience; for the oppressions and afflictions that he sustained for others, and that in regard of those by whom he suffered them unjustly, yet was he silent. He neither murmured or repined at God's disposal of things in that manner, nor used any railing or reviling speeches against those that dealt so despitefully with him, but carried himself calmly and quietly under them; Christ having an eye to his voluntary obedience and submission to the will of his Father, and agreement thereunto, Mat. xxvi. 39, 42; Mark xiv. 36; John xviii. 23; 1 Pet. ii. 23. He undertook willingly what his Father required of him, and as willingly, when the time came, underwent it; neither hanging back or opposing aught in way of contradiction thereunto, when it was by his Father propounded to him at first; nor afterward seeking to shift it off, when he was to perform what he had engaged himself unto, by pleading aught for himself, and the releasement of him from their most unjust proceedings in whose hands he then was. 'He opened not his mouth' to confute the slanders and false accusations of his enemies; neither did he utter anything to the prejudice of them that put him to death, but prayed for them that crucified him, Luke xxiii. 34; Mat. xxvi. 63, and xxvii. 12, 14. 'He was led as a lamb to the slaughter,'—properly, as a ewe-lamb, or she-lamb; the ewe is mentioned as the quieter of that kind, because the rams are sometimes more unruly,—'and as a sheep that is dumb before the face of her shearers.' A lamb doth not bite nor push him that is going about to kill it, but goeth as quietly to the shambles or the slaughter-house as if it were going to the fold wherein it is usually lodged, or the field where it is wont to feed. But,

[6.] Sixthly, Observe with me, that *the original cause of this compact or covenant between the Father and the Son, by virtue of which God the Father demands a price, and Jesus Christ pays the price according to God's demands, is only from the free grace and favour of God:* ver. 10, ' It pleased the Lord to bruise him, he hath put him to grief.' God the Father looks upon Jesus Christ as sustaining our person and cause; he looks upon all our sins as laid upon him, and to be punished in him. Sin could not be abolished, the justice of God could not be satisfied, the wrath of God could not be appeased, the terrible curse could not be removed, but by the death of Christ; and therefore God the Father took a pleasure to bruise him, and to put him to grief, according to the agreement between him and his Son. It must be readily granted that God did not incite or instigate the wicked Jews to those vile and cruel courses and carriages of theirs to Jesus Christ. But yet that his sufferings were by God predetermined for the salvation of mankind is most evident by the scriptures in the margin ;[1] and, accordingly, it pleased the Lord to bruise him, and to put him to grief. The singular pleasure that God the Father takes in the work of our redemption is a wonderful demonstration of his love and affection to us.

[7.] Seventhly, Observe with me, that *it is agreed between the Father and the Son that our sins should be imputed unto him, and that his righteousness should be imputed unto us, and that all the redeemed should believe in him, and so be justified:* ver. 11, ' He shall see of the travail of his soul, and shall be satisfied : by his knowledge (or faith in him) shall my righteous servant justify many ; for he shall bear their iniquities ;' or, as some render it, ' He shall see the fruit of the travail of his soul, and shall be satisfied'—that is, Jesus Christ shall receive and enjoy that, as the effect and issue of all the great pains that he hath taken, and of all the grievous things that he hath suffered, as shall give him full content and satisfaction. When Christ hath accomplished the work of redemption, he shall receive a full reward for all his sufferings. Christ takes a singular pleasure in the work of our redemption, and doth herein, as it were, refresh himself, as with the fruits, of his own labours. God the Father engages to Jesus Christ that he should not travail in vain, but that he should survive to see with great joy a numerous issue of faithful souls begotten unto God. You know when women, after sore, sharp, hard labour, are delivered, they are so greatly refreshed, delighted, gladded, and satisfied, that they forget their former pains and sorrow, ' for joy that a man-child is born into the world,' John xvi. 21. God the Father undertakes that Jesus Christ should have such a holy seed, such a blessed issue, as the main fruit and effect of his passion, as should joy him, please him, and as he should rest satisfied in. Certainly there could be no such joy and satisfaction to Christ as for him to see poor souls reconciled, justified, and saved by his sufferings and satisfaction ; as it is the highest joy of a faithful minister to see souls won over to Christ, and to see souls built up in Christ. 1 Thes. ii. 19, 20 ; Gal. iv. 19. Christ did bear the guilt of his people's sins, and thereby he made full satisfaction ; and therefore he is said here ' to justify many ;' not all promiscuously, but those only whose sins he undertook to discharge, and for whom he laid down his life.[2] Christ's justifying of many is his discharging of many from the guilt of sin, by making satisfaction to God for the same. But,

[8.] Eighthly, Observe with me, that *it is agreed between the Father and the Son, that for those persons for whom Jesus Christ should lay down his life, he should stand intercessor for them also, that so they may be brought to the possession of all those noble favours and blessings that he has purchased with his dearest blood:* ver. 12, ' He bare the sins of many, and made intercession for the trans-

---

[1] Acts ii. 23, and iv. 28.
[2] Besides the elect, he intercedes for none, John xvii. 9, 10.

gressors,' saying, 'Father, forgive them; for they know not what they do,' Luke xxiii. 34. For those very transgressors, by whom he suffered, he does intercede; for the article here is emphatical, and seems to point unto that special act, and those particular persons. Not but that these words have relation also to Christ's intercession for all those sinners that belong to him, and that have an interest in him; which intercession continues still, and shall do to the end of the world, Heb. vii. 25. But,

(6.) The sixth scripture is that, Isa. lix. 20, 21, 'And the Redeemer shall come to Zion, and unto them that turn from transgression in Jacob, saith the Lord. As for me, this is my covenant with them, saith the Lord; My spirit that is upon thee, and my words which I have put in thy mouth, shall not depart out of thy mouth, nor out of the mouth of thy seed, nor out of the mouth of thy seed's seed, saith the Lord, from henceforth, and for ever.' Out of this blessed scripture you may observe these following things: *First*, The parties covenanting and agreeing, and they are God the Father and Jesus Christ: God the Father in those words, 'Saith the Lord;' and Jesus Christ in those words, 'The Redeemer shall come to Zion.' *Secondly*, You have God the Father, first covenanting with Jesus Christ, and then with his seed, as is evident in the 21st verse. *Thirdly*, You have the persons described, that shall be sharers in redemption mercies, and they are the Zionites, the people of God, the citizens of Zion. But lest any should think that all Zion should be saved, it is added by way of explication, that only such of Zion 'as turn from transgression in Jacob,' shall have benefit by the Redeemer. The true citizens of Zion, the right Jacobs, the sincere Israelites, in whom there is no guile, Rom. xi. 26, are they and only they that turn from their sins. None have interest in Christ, none have redemption by Christ. but converts, but such as cast away their transgressions, as Ephraim did his idols, saying, 'What have I any more to do with you?' Hosea xiv. 8. *Fourthly*, You have the way and manner of the elect's delivery, and that is, not only by paying down upon the nail, the price agreed on, but also by a strong and powerful hand, as the original imports in the scriptures cited in the margin.[1] The Greek word that is used by Paul, and the Hebrew word that is used by Isaiah, do both signify delivering 'by strong hand,' to rescue by force, as David delivered the lamb out of the lion's paw. *Fifthly*, You have the special blessings that are to be conferred upon the elect—viz., redemption, conversion, faith, repentance, reconciliation, turning from their iniquity; all comprehended under that term 'the redeemed.' *Sixthly*, You have the Lord Jesus Christ considered as the head of the church, from whom all spiritual gifts—sanctification, salvation and perseverance do flow and run, as a precious balsam, upon the members of his body: 'My Spirit that is in me,' saith God the Father, to Christ the Redeemer, 'and my word which I have put into thy mouth, shall not depart out of thy mouth; nor out of the mouth of thy seed,' &c. In these words, God the Father engages, that his Spirit and word should continue with his church to direct and instruct it, and the children of it, in all necessaries, throughout all ages successively, even unto the world's end. But,

[1] Rom. xi. 26; Isa. lix. 20.

(7.) The seventh scripture is that, Zech. vi. 12, 13, ' And speak unto him, saying, Thus speaketh the Lord of hosts, saying, Behold the man whose name is the Branch; and he shall grow up out of his place, and he shall build the temple of the Lord: even he shall build the temple of the Lord; and he shall bear the glory, and shall sit and rule upon his throne; and he shall be a priest upon his throne: and the counsel of peace shall be between them both.' Now that the business of man's redemption was transacted betwixt the Father and the Son, is very clear from this text, ' And the counsel of peace shall be between them both,' that is, the two persons spoken of—viz., the Lord Jehovah, who speaks, and the man, whose name is the Branch, Jesus Christ. This counsel was primarily about the reconciliation of the riches of God's grace, and the glory of his justice. The design and counsel, both of the Father and the Son, was our peace.[1] The counsel of reconciliation, how man, that is now an enemy to God, may be reconciled to God, and God to him; this counsel or consultation shall be ' betwixt them both,' that is Jehovah and the Branch. There were blessed transactions between the Father and the Son, in order to the making of peace between an angry God and sinful men. I know several learned men interpret it of Christ's offices—viz., of his kingly and priestly office; for both conspire to make peace betwixt God and man. Now if you will thus understand the text, yet it will roundly follow, that there was a consultation at the council-board in heaven, concerning the reconciliation of fallen man to God; which reconciliation Christ, as king and priest, was to bring about. Look, as there was a counsel taken, touching the creation of mankind, between the persons in the blessed Trinity, ' Let us make man after our image,' Gen. i. 26; Col. iii. 19; Eph. iv. 24; so there was a consultation held concerning the restoration of mankind out of their lapsed condition: ' The counsel of peace shall be between them both.' Certainly there was a covenant of redemption made with Christ; upon the terms whereof he is constituted to be a reconciler and a redeemer, to say to the prisoners, ' Go forth, to bring deliverance to the captives, and to proclaim the year of release or jubilee, the acceptable year of the Lord,' as it is, Isa. lxi. 1, 2. But,

(8.) The eighth scripture is that, Ps. xl. 6–8, ' Sacrifice and offering thou didst not desire; mine ears hast thou opened: burnt-offering and sin-offering hast thou not required. Then said I, Lo, I come: in the volume of the book it is written of me, I delight to do thy will, O my God; yea, thy law is within my heart'—*Heb.*, ' in the midst of my bowels.' Compared with that, Heb. x. 5–7, ' Wherefore, when he cometh into the world, he saith, Sacrifice and offering thou wouldest not, but a body hast thou prepared for me: in burnt-offerings and sacrifices for sin thou hast had no pleasure: then said I, Lo, I come, in the volume of the book it is written of me, to do thy will, O God.' In these two scriptures, two things are concluded:—(1.) The impotency of legal sacrifices, ver. 5, 6; (2.) The all-sufficiency of Christ's sacrifice, ver. 7. There is some difference in words and phrases betwixt the apostle and the prophet, but both agree in sense, as we shall

[1] Whatever Socinians say, it is most certain that reconciliation is not only on the sinner's part, but on God's also.

endeavour to demonstrate. Penmen of the New Testament were not translators of the Old, but only quoted them for proof of the point in hand, so as they were not tied to syllables and letters, but to the sense. That which the prophet speaketh of himself, the apostle applieth to Christ, say some. This may be readily granted ; for David being a special type of Christ, that may in history and type be spoken of David, which, in mystery and truth, is understood of Christ. But that which David uttered in the aforesaid text, is questionless, uttered by the way of prophecy, concerning Christ, as is evident by these reasons.

First, In David's time, God required sacrifices and burnt-offerings, and took delight therein, 1 Chron. xxi. 26 ; 1 Sam. xxvi. 19 ; for God answered David from heaven by fire, upon the altar of burnt-offering ; and David himself advised Saul to offer a burnt-offering that God might accept of it.

Secondly, David was not able so ' to do the will of God,' as by doing it, to make all sacrifices void ; therefore this must be taken as a prophecy of Christ.

Thirdly, In the verse before, namely, Ps. xl. 5, such an admiration of God's goodness is premised, as cannot fitly be applied to any other evidence, than of his goodness in giving Christ ; in reference to whom, it may be truly said, ' That eye hath not seen, nor ear heard, neither have entered into the heart of man, the things which God hath prepared for them that love him,' 1 Cor. ii. 9.

Fourthly, These words used by the apostle, ' when he cometh into the world, he saith,' are meant of Christ ; which argue that that which followeth was an express prophecy of Christ. These things being premised, out of the texts last cited we may observe these following particulars that make to our purpose.

[1.] First, *That the Holy Spirit opens and expounds the covenant of redemption, bringing in the Father and the Son, as conferring and agreeing together about the terms of it ;* and the first thing agreed on between them is the price ; and the price that God the Father stands upon is ' blood ;' and that not ' the blood of bulls and goats, but the blood of his Son ;' which was the best, the purest, and the noblest blood, that ever ran in veins.[1]   Now Christ, to bring about the redemption of fallen man, is willing to come up to the demands of his Father, and to lay down his blood. The scripture calls the blood of Christ, τίμιον αἷμα, precious blood. Oh, the virtue in it, the value of it !   Through this red sea we must pass to heaven ; *Sanguis Christi clavis cœli*, Christ's blood is heaven's key. ' Precious in the sight of the Lord is the blood of the saints,' Ps. cxvi. 15, and truly ' precious in the sight of the saints is the blood of Christ.' *Una guttula plus valet quam cœlum et terra*, One little drop is more worth than heaven and earth, [Luther.] Christ's blood is ' precious blood,' in regard of the dignity of his person. It is ' the blood of God himself,' Acts xx. 28, it is the blood of that person, who is very God as well as very man. Christ's blood was noble blood, and therefore precious. He came of the race of kings, as touching his manhood ; but being withal the Son of God. This renders his nobility matchless and peerless. It was

[1] Heb. x. 4, and ix. 22 ; John x. 11, 15, 17, 18, and i. 29 ; 1 Pet. i. 18, 19.

Pharaoh's brag that he was the son of ancient kings, Isa. xix. 11. Who can lay claim to this more than Christ? Who can challenge this honour before him? He is the Son of the ancientest king in the world, he was begot a king from all eternity, Dan. vii. 9, 13, 27; and the blood of good kings is precious; 'Thou are worth ten thousand of us,' said David's subjects to him, 2 Sam. xviii. 3; and therefore they would not suffer him to hazard himself in the battle. The nobleness of his person did set a high rate upon his blood. And whom doth this argument more commend unto us than Christ? And the blood of Christ is precious blood in regard of the virtues of it. By this blood, God and man are reconciled; by this blood, the chosen of God are redeemed. It was an excellent saying of Leo, 'The effusion of Christ's blood is so rich and available, that if the whole multitude of captive sinners would believe in their Redeemer, not one of them should be detained in the tyrant's chains.'[1] This precious blood justifies our persons in the sight of God, it frees us from the guilt of sin, and it frees us from the reign and dominion of sin, and it frees us from the punishments that are due to sin, it saves us, ἀπὸ τῆς ὀργῆς τῆς ἐρχομένης, 'from that wrath that is to come,' Acts xiii. 38, 39; Rom. iii. 24, 25; 1 John i. 7; 1 Thes. i. 10. Now were not Christ's blood of infinite value and virtue, it could never have produced such glorious effects. The blood of Christ is precious, beyond all account; and yet our Lord Jesus did not think it too dear a price to pay down for his saints. God the Father would be satisfied with no other price; and therefore God the Son comes up to his Father's price, that our redemption might be sure. But,

[2.] Secondly, Observe that *God rejects all ways of satisfaction by men.* Could men make as many prayers as there be stars in heaven and drops in the sea, and could they weep as much blood as there is water in the ocean, and should they 'give all their goods to the poor, and their bodies to be burned,' 1 Cor. xiii. 3, as some have done, yet all this would not satisfy for the least sin, not for an idle word, not for a vain thought: Heb. x. 5, 'Sacrifice and offering thou wouldest not;' that is, thou wilt not accept of them for an expiation and satisfaction for sin, as the Jews imagined. The apostle shews the impotency and insufficiency of legal sacrifices by God's rejecting of them. The things here set down not to be regarded by God—as sacrifices, offerings, burnt-offerings, and sacrifices for sin, together with other legal ordinances comprised under them—do evidently demonstrate that God regards none of those things in a way of satisfaction; they are no current price, they are no such pay that will be accepted of in the court of heaven. Remission of sin could never be obtained by sacrifices and offerings, nor by prayers, tears, humblings, meltings, watchings, fastings, penances, pilgrimages, &c. Remission of sins cost Christ dear, though it cost us nothing. Remission of sins drops down from God to us through Christ's wounds, and swims to us in Christ's blood. It was well said by one of the ancients: 'I have not whence I may glory in my own works, I have not whence I may boast myself, and therefore I will glory in Christ; I will not glory that I am righteous, but I will glory that I am redeemed; I will glory, not

---

[1] Leo de pas., serm. xii. c. 4.

because I am without sin, but because my sins are forgiven; I will not glory because I have profited, or because any hath profited me, but because Christ is an advocate with the Father for me, but because the blood of Christ is shed for me.'[1] Certainly the popish doctrine of man's own satisfaction in part for his sins is most derogatory to the blood, and to the plenary and complete satisfaction, of Jesus Christ. But,

[3.] Thirdly, Observe that *nothing below the obedience and sufferings of Christ, our mediator, could satisfy divine justice:* Heb. x. 5, 'But a body hast thou prepared me.' The Hebrew text, Ps. xl. 7, saith, 'Thou hast bored through mine ears;' but the apostle follows the Greek translation, seeing the same sense is contained in both. Christ having declared what his Father delighteth not in, he further sheweth affirmatively what it was wherein he rested well pleased, in these words, 'But a body hast thou prepared me.' In this phrase, 'A body hast thou prepared me,' Christ is brought in, speaking to his Father. By body is meant the human nature of Christ. Body is synecdochically put for the whole human nature, consisting of body and soul; the body was the visible part of Christ's human nature. A body is fit for a sacrifice, fit to be slain, fit to have blood shed out of it, fit to be offered up, fit to be made a price, and a ransom for our sins, and fit to answer the types under the law. Pertinently therefore, to this purpose, is it said of Christ, 'He himself bare our sins in his own body,' 1 Pet. ii. 24; and those infirmities wherein he was 'made like unto us,' Heb. ii. 9, 14, 17, were most conspicuously evidenced in his body; and hereby Christ was manifested to be a true man: he had a body like ours, a body subject to manifold infirmities, yea, to death itself. That body which Christ had is said to be 'prepared by God;' the Greek word, κατηρτίσω, which is translated *prepared*, is a metaphor from mechanics, who do artificially fit one part of their work to another, and so finish the whole. God fitted his Son's body to be joined with the deity, and to be an expiatory sacrifice for sin. The word 'prepared' implies that God the Father ordained, formed, and made fit and able, Christ's human nature to undergo, suffer, and fulfil that for which he was sent into the world. God the Father is here said to have prepared Christ a body; because Christ having received of his Father the human nature out of the flesh and blood of the Virgin Mary by the power of the Holy Ghost, Mat. i. 20; Luke i. 31, 35, here gives up the same unto the service of his Father, to do, to suffer, to die, that he might be a sacrifice of expiation for our sins. As for the words of the psalmist, Ps. xl. 6, 'Mine ear hast thou opened,'—*Heb.*, 'digged open,' it is a proverbial manner of speech, whereby there is implied the qualifying or fitting a man unto obedience in service—the ear, or the opening of the ear, being an emblem, or symbol, or a metaphorical sign of obedience, Isa. lv. 5; Job xxxiii. 16. Now St Paul, following the translation of the Septuagint, and being directed by the Spirit of God, expounds this of God's sanctifying and fitting a body unto Christ, wherein he was obedient, even unto the shameful death of the cross. These words, 'Thou hast bored through mine ears,' do import that Christ, now becoming man, gives up himself to

[1] Ambrose de Jacob, et Vita beat. lib. i. cap. vi. pp. 290, 291.

be a willing servant of his Father, to obey him unto the death of the cross. And it is a similitude taken from the servants of the Hebrews, who, after that they had served their masters six years, would not depart out of their masters' service the seventh year, but abide in it continually until death; for a testimony whereof their ear was bored through on the posts of the door, as may be seen, Exod. xxi. 6. It is therefore as much as if he should say, Thou hast given me a body that is willing and ready in thy service, even unto death. But to conclude this head, the apostle speaking of disannulling the sacrifice of the law, he uses this word *body* to set out a sacrifice which should come instead of the legal sacrifices, to effect that which the legal sacrifices could not effect. But,

[4.] Fourthly, Observe that *Christ, our mediator, freely and readily offers himself to be our pledge and surety.* ' Then said I, Lo, I come,' to wit, as surety, to pay the ransom, and to do thy will, O God. Every word carrieth a special emphasis as, (1.) The time, ' then,' even so soon as he perceived that his Father had prepared his body for such an end, then, without delay. This speed implieth forwardness and readiness ; he would lose no opportunity. (2.) His profession in this word, ' said I ;' he did not closely, secretly, timorously, as being ashamed thereof, but he maketh profession beforehand. (3.) This note of observation, ' Lo ;' this is a kind of calling angels and men to witness, and a desire that all might know his inward intention, and the disposition of his heart ; wherein was as great a willingness as any could have to anything. (4.) An offering of himself without any enforcement or compulsion ; this he manifesteth in this word, ' I come.' (5.) That very instant set out in the present tense, ' I come ;' he puts it not off to a future and uncertain time, but even in that moment, he saith, ' I come.' (6.) The first person twice expressed, thus, ' I said,' ' I come.' He sendeth not another person, nor substituteth any in his room ; but he, even he himself in his own person, cometh. All which do abundantly evidence Christ's singular readiness and willingness, as our surety, to do his Father's will, though it were by suffering, and by being made a sacrifice for our sins. God's will was the rule of Christ's active and passive obedience. Jesus Christ, our only mediator and surety, by free and ready obedience and death, did make a proper, real, and full satisfaction to God's justice for the sins of all the elect. Christ hath, by his death and blood, as an invaluable price of our redemption, made sure the favour of God, the pardon of our sins, and the salvation of our souls. Christ hath freed his chosen from all temporal, spiritual, and eternal punishments, properly so called ; so that now the mercy of God may embrace the sinner without the least of wrong to his truth or justice. But,

[5.] Fifthly, Observe that *Jesus Christ, our surety, does not only agree with his Father about the price that he was to lay down for our redemption, but also agrees with his Father about the persons that were to be redeemed, and their sanctification :* Heb. x. 10, ' By the which will '—that is, by the execution of which will, by the obedience of Christ to his heavenly Father—' we are sanctified, through the offering of the body of Jesus Christ, once for all.' Jesus Christ agrees with the Father that all those shall be sanctified for whom he has suffered and satisfied. The virtue, efficacy, and benefit of that which ariseth from the aforesaid will of the Father and of the Son is expressed under this word, 'sanctified.' To pass by the notation and divers acceptations of this word 'sanctified,' let it suffice to tell you it is not here to be taken, as distinguished from justification or glorification, as it is elsewhere taken, 1 Cor. i. 30, and vi. 11 ; but so as comprising under it all the benefits of Christ's sacrifice, Heb. x. 14, and ii. 11; Acts xxvi. 18. In this general and large extent it is sometimes taken ; only this word, sanctified, here gives us to understand that perfection consisteth especially in holiness ; for he expresseth the perfection of Christ's sacrifice under the word 'sanctified,' which implieth 'a making holy.' This was that special part of perfection wherein man was made at first, Eccles. vii. 31 ; and whereunto the apostle alludeth, where he exhorteth, 'To put on that new man, which after God is created in righteousness and true holiness,' Eph. iv. 24; for this end, Christ gave himself even unto death, for his church, 'that he might sanctifiy it,' Eph. v. 25. The principal thing under this word 'sanctified' in this place is, that Christ's sacrifice maketh perfect. In this respect, Christ's sacrifice is here opposed to the legal sacrifices, which could not make perfect ; so that Christ's sacrifice was offered up to do that which they could not do ; for this end was Christ's sacrifice surrogated in the room of the legal sacrifices. Now this surrogation had been in vain, if Christ's sacrifice had not made us perfect. If the dignity of his person that was offered up, and his almighty power, and unsearchable wisdom, and other divine excellencies of his, be duly weighed, we cannot but acknowledge, that as his sacrifice is perfect in itself, so it is sufficient to make us perfect also. Christ's body was given up as a price and ransom, and offered up as a sacrifice for our sins ; and that we might be sanctified and made holy, Christ, by the offering of his body once for all, has purchased of his Father grace and holiness for all his redeemed ones. Christ agrees with his Father that he will lay down an incomparable price for his chosen ones ; and then he further agrees with his Father that all those shall be sanctified for whom he has laid down an invaluable price. The will of God the Father was, that Jesus Christ should have a body, and that that body of his should be offered up, that his elect might be sanctified and saved. Now to this Christ readily answers, 'Lo, I come to do thy will.' From what hath been said from Ps. xl., compared with Heb. x., we may very safely and roundly conclude that it is most clear and evident that there was a covenant, compact, or agreement, between God the Father and Jesus Christ, concerning the redemption of fallen man. This I shall more abundantly clear up before I have said all I have to say about the covenant of redemption that is under our present consideration. But,

(9.) The ninth scripture is that, Ps. lxxxix. 28, 'My mercy will I keep for him for evermore, and my covenant shall stand fast with him.' With whom ? why, with our dear Lord Jesus, of whom David was a singular type. There are many passages in this psalm which do clearly evidence that it is to be interpreted of Christ ; yea,

there are many things in this psalm that can never be clearly, pertinently, and appositely applied to any but Jesus Christ.   For a taste,
see ver. 19, ' I have laid help upon one that is mighty,' mighty to pardon, to reconcile, to justify, to save, to bring to glory; suitable to that
of the apostle, Heb. vii. 25, ' He is able to save unto the uttermost '—
that is, to all ends and purposes, perfectly, completely, fully, continually, perpetually.[1]   Christ is a thorough Saviour, a mighty Saviour :
Isa. lxiii. 1, ' Mighty to save.'   There needs none to come after him to
finish the work which he hath begun: ver. 19, ' I have exalted one, chosen
out of the people,' which is the very title given to our Lord Jesus :
Isa. xlii. 1, ' Behold my servant whom I uphold, mine elect,' or chosen
one, ' in whom my soul delighteth : ver. 20, ' I have found David my
servant.'   Christ is very frequently called by that name, as being
most dearly beloved of God, and most highly esteemed and valued by
God, and as being typified by him both as king and prophet of his
church : ver. 10, ' With my holy oil have I anointed him ;' suitable to
that of Christ : Luke iv. 18, ' The Spirit of the Lord is upon me, because he hath anointed me to preach the gospel to the poor ;' and
therefore we need not doubt of the excellency, authority, certainty,
and sufficiency of the gospel : ver. 27, ' I will make him my firstborn,
higher than the kings of the earth.'[2]   Christ is the firstborn of every
creature, and in all things hath the pre-eminence : ver. 29, ' His seed
also will I make to endure for ever, and his throne as the days of
heaven.'[3]   This is chiefly spoken of Christ and his kingdom.   The
aspectable heaven is corruptible, but the kingdom of heaven is
eternal ; and such shall be Christ's seed, throne and kingdom : ver.
36, ' His seed shall endure for ever, and his throne as the sun before
me.'   ' Christ shall see his seed, he shall prolong his days, and the
pleasure of the Lord shall prosper in his hands,' Isa. liii. 10.   ' And
his throne as the sun before me ;' that is, perpetual and glorious, as
the Chaldee explaineth it, ' shall shine as the sun.'   Other kingdoms
and thrones have their times and their turns, their rise and their ruins,
but so hath not the kingdom and throne of Jesus Christ.   Christ's
dominion is 'an everlasting dominion,' which shall not pass away; 'and
his kingdom that which shall not be destroyed,' Dan. vii. 13, 14.   I
might give further instances out of this Psalm, but enough is as good
as a feast.   Now saith God, ' I have made a covenant with him ;' so
then there is a covenant that God the Father hath made with Christ
the mediator ; which covenant, the Father engages to the Son, shall
stand fast, there shall be no cancelling or disannulling of it.   God the
Father hath not only made a covenant of grace with the saints in
Christ, of which before ; but he has also made a covenant of redemption, as we call it for distinction sake, with Jesus Christ himself, ' My
covenant shall stand fast with him ;' that is, with Christ, as we have
fully and clearly demonstrated.   But,

(10.) The tenth scripture is that, Zech. ix. 11, ' As for thee also,
by the blood of thy covenant,' or whose covenant is by blood, ' I have

---

[1] Ad plenum, *Erasmus ;* ad perfectum, [*Faber*] *Stapulensis.*
[2] See Jer. **xxx.** 9 ; Hosea iii. 5 ; Ezek. **xxxiv.** 23.
     cannot be understood of David's seed, for Solomon's throne was overthrown.

sent forth thy prisoners out of the pit, wherein is no water.'[1] Here God the Father speaks to Christ, with relation to some covenant between them both; and what covenant can that be but the covenant of redemption? All the temporal, spiritual, and eternal deliverances which we enjoy, they swim to us through the blood of that covenant that is passed between the Father and the Son. By virtue of the same blood of the covenant, wherewith we are reconciled, justified, and saved, were the Jews delivered from their Babylonish captivity. The Babylonish captivity, thraldom, and dispersion, was that waterless pit, that dirty dungeon, that uncomfortable and forlorn condition, out of which they were delivered by virtue of the blood of the covenant; that is, by virtue of the blood of Christ, figured by the blood that was sprinkled upon the people, and by virtue of the covenant confirmed thereby, Exod. xxiv. 8; Ps. lxxiv. 20; Heb. xiii. 20. Look, as all the choice mercies, the high favours, the noble blessings that the saints enjoy, are purchased by the blood of Christ; so they are made sure to the saints by the same blood; by the blood of thy covenant 'I have sent forth thy prisoners.' Whatever desperate distresses, and deadly dangers, the people of God may fall into, yet they are 'prisoners of hope,' and may look for deliverance by the blood of the covenant.

By these ten scriptures it is most clear and evident that there was a covenant, a compact, and agreement between God the Father and our Lord Jesus Christ, concerning the work of our redemption. Christ's being called 'the surety of the better covenant,' Heb. vii. 21, shews that there was a covenant between God the Father and him, as there is between a creditor and a surety. Christ gave bonds, as it were, to God the Father, and paid down the debt upon the nail, that breaches might be made up between God and us, and we restored to divine favour for ever. But for the further clearing up of the covenant of redemption, I shall, in the second place, lay down these propositions. And,

(1.) The first is this, *That the covenant of redemption differs from the covenant of grace.* It is true, the covenant of redemption is a covenant of grace, but it is not properly that covenant of grace which the Scripture holds out in opposition to the covenant of works; which I shall thus evidence:—

[1.] The covenant of redemption differs from the covenant of grace in regard of the federates. In the covenant of redemption, it is God the Father and Jesus Christ that mutually covenant; but in the covenant of grace the confederates are God and believers.

[2.] In the covenant of redemption, God the Father requires of Jesus Christ that he should suffer, shed his blood, die, and make himself an offering for our sins. In the covenant of grace, God requires of us that we should believe and embrace the Lord Jesus.

[3.] In the covenant of redemption, God the Father has made many great, precious, and glorious promises to Jesus Christ. As, 'Sit on my right hand, till I make thine enemies thy footstool,' Heb. i. 13; and, 'He shall see his seed, he shall prolong his days, the pleasure of the Lord shall prosper in his hands,' Isa. liii. 10; and, 'Ask of me, and I

---

[1] And thou also died with the blood of thy covenant, when I have sent out thy prisoners out of the cistern in which there are no waters.—*Tremellius.*

will give thee the heathen for thine inheritance, and the uttermost parts of the earth for thy possession,' Ps. ii. 8; and, 'I will be to him a Father, and he shall be to me a Son,' Heb. i. 5. But in the covenant of grace, God promises to us grace and glory, holiness and happiness, both the upper and the lower springs, Ps. lxxxiv. 11; Ezek. xxxvi. 26, 27.

[4.] The covenant of redemption betwixt God and Christ secures the covenant of grace betwixt God and believers; for what God promises to us, he did, before the foundation of the world, promise to Jesus Christ, Titus i. 2; and therefore, if God the Father should not make good his promises to his saints, he would not make good his promises to his dearest Son, which for any to imagine would be high blasphemy. God will be sure to keep touch with Jesus Christ; and therefore we may rest fully assured that he will not fail to keep touch with us.

[5.] The covenant of redemption is the very basis or bottom of the covenant of grace. God made a covenant with Christ, the spiritual David, that he might make a covenant with all his elect in him, Ps. lxxxix. 3, 4; Rom. xi. 26, 27. He made this agreement with Christ, as the head, and on this is reared up the whole frame of precious promises comprised in the covenant of grace, as a goodly building upon a sure foundation. But,

(2.) The second proposition is this, *God the Father, in order to man's redemption and salvation, stands stiffly and peremptorily upon complete satisfaction.* Without full satisfaction, no remission, no salvation. Satisfaction God will have to the utmost, though it cost Christ his life and blood. Man is fallen from his primitive purity, glory, and excellency, and by his fall he hath provoked divine justice, transgressed God's righteous law, and cast a deep dishonour upon his name, Rom. viii. 32. The case standing thus, God is resolved to have ample satisfaction in the reparation of his honour, in the manifestation of his truth, and in the vindication of his holiness and justice. All the attributes of God are alike dear to him, and he stands as much upon the advance of his justice as he does upon the glory of his grace; and therefore he will not remit one sin, yea, not the least sin, without entire satisfaction. In this God the Father is fixed, that he will have 'an offering for sin,' in an expiatory and propitiatory way; 'a price and a ransom' he will have paid down upon the nail, or else the captive sinner shall never be released, pardoned, saved, Isa. liii. 10; 1 Tim. ii. 6. Now lost man being wholly incapable of giving such a satisfaction to divine justice, Christ must give it, or fallen man must perish for ever. Sin and sorrow, iniquity and misery, always go hand in hand. 'The wages of sin is death,' Rom. vi. 23. Every sinner is worthy of death. 'They which commit such things are worthy of death,' Rom. i. 32. If God be a just and righteous God, then sin cannot absolutely escape unpunished; for it is but 'a just and righteous thing with God' to punish the sinner, who is worthy of punishment. 'It is a righteous thing with God,' saith the apostle, 'to recompense tribulation to them that trouble you,' 2 Thes. i. 6. And as God cannot but be just, so he cannot but be true; and if he cannot but be true, then he cannot but make good his threatenings against sin and sinners. The word is gone out of his mouth, 'In the day that thou eatest thereof thou shalt surely die; and the soul which sins shall die,' Gen. ii. 17. Look, as there is not a promise of God but shall take place in time, so there is not a threatening of God but shall take place in time, Ezek. xviii. 4. The faithfulness of God, and the honour of God, is as much concerned in making good of terrible threatenings, as they are concerned in making good of precious promises, 2 Pet. i. 4. God has given it under his own hand, that 'he will by no means clear the guilty;' and that 'the soul that sinneth shall surely die;' and that 'the wickedness of the wicked shall be upon him;' and that 'he will render to every man according to his deeds,' Exod. xxxiv. 7; Ezek. xviii. 20; Rom. ii. 6. And will God abrogate his own laws, or will he dare men to sport and play with his threatenings? Will not every wise and prudent prince look to the execution of their own laws? and shall not that God, who is wonderful in wisdom, and whose understanding is infinite, see all his laws put in execution against offenders? Isa. xl. 28; Ps. cxlvii. 5. Surely yes. Thus you see that God stands upon full satisfaction, and will admit of no treaty of peace with fallen man without it. Now sorry man is never able, either by doing or suffering, to compensate and make God amends for the wrong and injury that he has done to God by his sin; and therefore one that is able, by doing and suffering, to give complete satisfaction, must undertake it, or else we are lost, cast, and undone in both worlds. Concerning that full and complete satisfaction that Jesus Christ has given to God's enraged justice, I have in part discovered already, and shall say no more to it before I close up the covenant of redemption. But,

(3.) The third proposition is this, *The business transacted between those two great and glorious persons, God the Father,* 'whose greatness is unsearchable,' Ps. cxlv. 3, *and Jesus Christ,* 'who is the prince of the kings of the earth,' Rev. i. 5, *was the redemption and salvation of the elect.* Our everlasting blessedness was now fresh in their eyes, and warm upon their hearts. How lost man might be found, and how fallen man might be restored, and how miserable man might be made happy, how slaves might be made sons, and how enemies might be made friends, Luke xv. 30, and how those that 'were afar off might be made nigh,' Eph. ii. 12–17, without the least prejudice to the honour, holiness, justice, wisdom, and truth of God, was the grand business, the thing of things, that lay before them. Upon the account of the covenant, compact, and agreement that was between the Father and the Son, it is that Christ is called 'the second Adam,' 1 Cor. xv. 25; for as with the first Adam God plighted a covenant concerning him and his posterity, so also he did indent with Jesus Christ, concerning that eternal redemption, that he was to obtain and secure for his seed, Heb. ix. 12. For the clearing of this, let us a little consider of the excellent properties of that redemption that we have by Jesus Christ.

[1.] First, *It is a great redemption.* The work of redemption was a great work. The greatness of the person employed in this work speaks out the work to be a great work. This was a work too high, too hard, too great for all the angels in heaven, and all the men on earth to undertake. None but that Jesus who is 'mighty to save,'

Isa. lxiii. 1, was ever able to bring about the redemption of man. Hence Christ is called the Deliverer, Rom. xi. 26 : ' And their redeemer is mighty,' Prov. xxiii. 11 ; Isa. xliv. 6, ' And his redeemer, the Lord of hosts ; ' Isa. xlvii. 4, ' As for our redeemer, the Lord of hosts is his name ; ' Isa. xlix. 26, ' And thy redeemer, the mighty one of Jacob ; ' Jer. l. 34, ' Their redeemer is strong, the Lord of hosts is his name.' Again, the great and invaluable price that was paid down for our redemption speaks it out to be a great redemption. The price that we are bought with is a price beyond all compute. 1 Pet. i. 18, 19, ' Forasmuch as ye know that ye were not redeemed with corruptible things, as silver and gold, from your vain conversation ; but with the precious blood of Christ, as of a lamb without blemish and without spot,' 1 Cor. vi. 19, 20, and vii. 23. Christ was a lamb (1.) for harmlessness ; (2.) for patience and silence in afflictions ; (3.) for meekness and humility ; (4.) for sacrifice. This lamb was ' without blemish,' Isa. liii. 7, that is, free from actual sin, and 'without spot,' that is, free from original sin, Jer. xi. 19, [Aquinas.] That the most absolute and perfect purity of Christ—prefigured in the lambs of the Old Testament, that were to be sacrificed—might be better expressed, the apostle calls him ' a lamb without blemish, and without spot,' Eph. v. 27. The price that this lamb without a spot has laid down is sufficient to pay all our debts ; it is a price beyond all compute. All the silver, gold, pearls, jewels in the world, are of no value, in respect of this price ; a price in itself infinite, and of infinite value. Among the Romans, the goods and estates which men had gotten in the wars, with hazard of their lives, were called *peculium castrense*, or a field-purchase.[1] Oh how well then may the elect be called Christ's *peculium castrense*, his purchase, gotten not only by the jeopardy of his life, but with the loss of his life and blood, John x. 11, 15, 17, 18, and Acts xx. 28. Again, if you compare the work of redemption with other great works, you must necessarily conclude that the work of redemption is a great work. The making of the world was a great work of God, but yet that did but cost him a word of his mouth, a ' let it be ; ' he spake the word, and it was done ; ' He said, Let there be light, and there was light,' &c., Gen. i. 3-6, 9, 11, 14, 20, 24 ; but the work of redemption cost Christ's dearest blood. Much matter of admiration doth the work of redemption afford us. The work of creation is many ways admirable, yet not to be compared with the work of redemption, wherein the power, wisdom, justice, mercy, and other divine attributes of God do much more shine forth ; and wherein the redeemed reap much more good than Adam did by his creation, which will evidently appear by observing these particular differences :

First, In the creation God brought something out of nothing ; but in the work of redemption, out of one contrary he brought another ; out of death he brought life. This was a work of far greater power, wisdom, mercy. Death must first be destroyed, and then life brought forth.

Secondly, In creation there was but a word ; and thereupon the

[1] Neither God nor Christ could lay down a greater price. All things in heaven and earth are not to be compared to this blood, to this price.

work followed; in redemption there was doing and dying. The work of redemption could be brought about by none but God. God must come down from heaven, God must be made man, God must be made sin, God must be made a curse, 2 Cor. v. 21 ; Gal. iii. 13.

Thirdly, In the creation God arrayed himself with majesty, power, and other like properties, fit for a great work ; in the work of redemption he put on weakness, he assumed a nature subject to infirmities, and the infirmities of that nature. He did as David did when he fought against Goliath, he ' put off all armour, and took his staff in his hand, and drew near to the Philistine,' 1 Sam. xvii. 39, 40.

Fourthly, In the work of creation there was nothing to withstand God, to make opposition against God; but in the work of redemption there was justice against mercy, wrath against pity ; death, and he that had the power of death, was vanquished, Heb. ii. 14, 15 ; Col. ii. 14, 15.

Fifthly, By creation man was made after God's image, like him, Gen. i. 26, 27 ; by redemption man was made a member of the same mystical body ' whereof Christ is the head,' Eph. i. 22, 23.

Sixthly, By creation man received a natural being, by redemption a spiritual.

Seventhly, By creation man received a possibility to stand, by redemption a certainty of standing and impossibility of falling, John x. 28–31 ; 1 Pet. i. 5 ; Jer. xxxii. 40, 41.

Eighthly, By creation man was placed in an earthly paradise, but by redemption he is advanced to an heavenly paradise.

Thus you see how the work of redemption transcends the work of creation. Again, the works of providence are great, very great, in the eye of God, of angels, of men ; but what are the works of providence to the works of redemption ? For in order to the accomplishment of that great work, Christ must put off his royal robes, take a journey from heaven to earth, assume our nature, do and die, &c. Again, the work of redemption by Christ will be found a great work, if you will but compare it with those redemptions that were but types of this. Israel's redemption from their Egyptian bondage, and from their Babylonish bondage, were very great redemptions, that were brought about by a strong hand, a mighty hand, and an out-stretched arm, as the Scripture speaks; but, alas! what were those redemptions to our being redeemed from the love of sin, the guilt of sin, the dominion of sin, the damnatory power of sin, and to our being redeemed from the power of Satan, the curse of the law, hell and wrath to come? 1 Thes. i. 10. Lastly, the great things that are wrapped up in the womb, in the belly, of redemption, speak out our redemption by Christ to be a very great redemption. In the womb of this redemption you shall find reconciliation, justification, adoption, eternal salvation, &c. ; and are not these great, very great, things ? Surely yes. But,

[2.] A second excellent property of that redemption that we have by Christ is this, that it is *a free and gracious redemption*. All the rounds in this ladder of redemption are made up of free, rich, and sovereign grace. Though our redemption cost Christ dear, as has been before hinted, yet as to us it is most free: Eph. i. 7, 'In whom we have redemption through his blood, the forgiveness of sins, accord-

ing to the riches of his grace;' that is, according to his exceeding
great and abundant grace: 'Being justified freely by his grace,
through the redemption that is in Christ Jesus.'[1] Our redemption is
from the free love and favour of God. It was free grace that put God
the Father upon finding out a way for the redemption of lost sinners.
It was free grace that put God upon providing of such a surety, as
should undertake the work of redemption, as should carry on the
work of redemption, and as should accomplish and complete the work
of redemption; and it was free grace that moved God the Father to
accept of what Christ did and suffered, in order to the bringing about
of our redemption; and it is free grace that moves God to make an
application of this redemption to the souls of his people. Ah, poor
souls! the Lord looks not, neither for money nor money's worth from
you, towards the purchase of your redemption, and therefore always
look upon your redemption as the mere fruit of rich grace, Isa. lii. 3.
But,

[3.] The third excellent property of that redemption that we have
by Jesus Christ is this, it is *a full and plenteous redemption*: Ps.
cxxx. 7, 'Let Israel hope in the Lord; for with the Lord there is
mercy, and with him is plenteous redemption.' Christ redeems us
from all sin, and from all the consequences of sin. He redeems from
death, and from the power of the grave; he redeems us from the law,
and from the malediction of the law. Christ took that off; he was
made a curse for all that believe on him.[2] He did not only stand in
the room of eminent believers, but he stood in the room of all believers,
and endured the wrath of God to the uttermost for every one that
believeth on him. Every believer is freed from a cursed estate by the
least faith. Every degree of true faith makes the condition to be a
state of life, and passeth us from death and condemnation: 'There is
no condemnation to them that are in Christ Jesus.' And Christ
redeems us from this present evil world, and from the earth, and from
among men, and from wrath to come, and from 'the hands of all our
enemies.'[3] Jesus Christ hath gone thorough-stitch[4] with the work of
our redemption. Christ does not his work by halves; all his works
are perfect; there is no defect or flaw in them at all. Christ does not
redeem us from some of our sins, and leave us to grapple with the rest;
he doth not work out some part of our redemption, and leave us to
work out the rest; he doth not bear the heat and burden of divine
wrath in part, and leave us to wrestle with other parts of divine wrath.
Oh, no; Christ makes most complete work of it. He redeems us from
'all our iniquities; he delivers us out of the hands of all our enemies,'
Heb. vii. 25. He pays all debts, he cuts all scores, he delivers from
all wrath, he takes off the whole curse, he saves to the uttermost, and
will settle us in a state of full and perfect freedom, when grace shall
be turned into glory. In heaven our redemption shall be entire and
perfect.

[4.] The fourth excellent property of that redemption that we have

[1] ἀπολύτρωσιν. This word properly signifies a deliverance, which is brought to pass
by paying of a ransom and price. See Mat. xx. 28; 1 Cor. vi. 20; 1 Pet. i. 18.
[2] Hosea xiii. 14; Titus ii. 14; Rom. vii. 6; Gal. iv. 5, and iii. 13.
[3] Rom. viii. 1; Gal. i. 4; Rev. xiv. 3, 4; 1 Thes. i. 10; Luke i. 71, 74.
[4] 'Completely.'—G.

by Jesus Christ, is this, it is *an eternal, a permanent, a lasting, yea, an everlasting redemption:* Heb. ix. 12, 'Neither by the blood of goats and calves, but by his own blood, he entered in once into the holy place, having obtained eternal redemption for us.' Redemption is in general a freeing one out of thraldom, Exod. vi. 6. Now this is done three ways—(1.) By interceding and pacifying wrath. Thus the prophet Oded, 2 Chron. xxviii. 9, &c., procured redemption for the captives of Judah by his intercession. (2.) By force and might. Thus Abraham redeemed his brother Lot, and the people that were captives with him, by overcoming their enemies, Gen. xiv. 16. (3.) By ransom, or paying a price. Thus a Hebrew that was sold a slave to a stranger might be redeemed by one of his brethren, Lev. xxv. 48, 49. The last of these is most agreeable to the notation of the several words, which in the three learned languages do signify to redeem, though the last be especially intended. In that, mention is made of a price, namely, Christ's blood; yet the other two are not altogether exempted, for Christ hath all those three ways redeemed his people. This will more clearly appear if we duly weigh the distinct kinds of bondage in which we were by reason of sin—(1.) We were debtors to divine justice, Mat. vi. 12; (2.) We were children of wrath, Eph. ii. 3; (3.) We were slaves to Satan, Heb. ii. 14, 15. (1.) As debtors, Christ hath paid a ransom for us; (2.) As children of wrath, Christ makes intercession for us; (3.) But though divine justice be satisfied and divine wrath pacified, yet the devil will not let his captives go; therefore Christ by a strong hand wrests us out of Satan's power, 'and destroys him that had the power of death, that is, the devil,' Heb. ii. 14, 15. The ransom which Christ paid was the ground of man's full and eternal redemption, for by satisfaction of justice way was made to pacify wrath; both which being accomplished, the devil lost his right and power over such as he held in bondage. This redemption is a full freedom from all misery, and compriseth under it reconciliation, justification, sanctification, and salvation. By this redemption divine justice is satisfied, wrath pacified, grace procured, and all spiritual enemies vanquished. The perfection of this redemption is hinted in this word *eternal.* The eternity here meant hath a special respect to the continual duration thereof without end, yet also it respecteth the time past, so as it looks backward and forward. It implieth a virtue and efficacy from the beginning of the world, for Christ was 'a lamb slain from the foundation of the world,' Rev. xiii. 8. Christ himself is, Rev. i. 8, 'Alpha and Omega, the beginning and the ending, which is, and which was, and which is to come.' Now that which is spoken of the person of Christ may very well be applied to our redemption by Christ. This epithet *eternal* is here added to redemption, in opposition to the legal purifications, which were momentary and temporary. They had a day, and endured no longer than the 'time of reformation.' On this ground, by just and necessary consequence, it followeth that the redemption wrought by Christ is absolutely perfect, and that there is no need of any other. This being eternal, all that have been, all that shall be redeemed, have been and shall be redeemed by it; and they who are redeemed by it need no other means. The liberty whereinto Christ Jesus brings the elect is permanent and lasting, it abides irremoveable and unchangeable to all eternity. The Jews which had sold themselves to be servants were to be set free at the jubilee, yet the jubilee lasted but for one year; therefore the same persons might afterwards become bondmen again, Lev. xxv. But this 'acceptable year of the Lord's redeemed,' Isa. lxi. 2, and lxiii. 4, is an everlasting year, it shall never end; therefore they shall never be subject to bondage any more. It is observable that when the Lord would comfort the Jews with hopes of a return from Babylon, he usually annexed evangelical promises respecting the deliverance of poor sinners from the slavery of Satan, whereof that captivity was a type, some of which promises do plainly express the perpetuity of that spiritual freedom which they shall enjoy. Take a taste: [1] Isa. xxxv. 10, 'And the ransomed of the Lord shall return, and come to Zion with songs and everlasting joy upon their heads: they shall obtain joy and gladness, and sorrow and sighing shall flee away.' Isa. li. 6, 'Lift up your eyes to the heavens, and look upon the earth beneath; for the heavens shall vanish away like smoke, and the earth shall wax old like a garment, and they that dwell therein shall die in like manner: but my salvation shall be for ever, and my righteousness shall not be abolished.' Isa. lx. 19, 20, 'The sun shall be no more thy light by day; neither for brightness shall the moon give light unto thee: but the Lord shall be unto thee an everlasting light, and thy God thy glory. Thy sun shall no more go down; neither shall thy moon withdraw itself: for the Lord shall be thine everlasting light, and the days of thy mourning shall be ended.' Jer. xxxi. 11, 12, 'For the Lord hath redeemed Jacob, and ransomed him from the hand of him that was stronger than he. Therefore they shall come and sing in the height of Zion, and their soul shall be as a watered garden, and they shall not sorrow any more at all.' But,

[5.] The fifth excellent property of that redemption that we have by Jesus Christ is this—viz., it is *an enriching redemption ;* it is a redemption that makes men rich in ' spiritual blessings in heavenly places,' Eph. i. 3. There are many choice and rare spiritual benefits that wait and attend on redemption, that go hand in hand with redemption: as reconciliation, remission of our sins, justification of our persons, adoption, sanctification, full glorification, Rom. v. 1, and iii. 24, 25. We have some foretastes of it in this life. Here we have the 'first-fruits of the Spirit,' Rom. viii. 23, 30; but in the morning of the resurrection we shall reap the whole harvest of glory. It is called, by way of eminency, ' the salvation of our souls,' 1 Pet. i. 9. Redemption, and the noble benefits attending on it, are salvation begun; but in heaven this shall be salvation consummate. Redemption is a rich mine, containing a mass of treasure that cannot be valued. Could we dig into it, could we pry into it, we might find variety of the choicest jewels and pearls, in comparison whereof all the riches of the Indies, all the gold of Ophir, and all the precious jewels and most orient pearls that are in the world, are no better than dross. I have read of Tiberius the emperor, that passing by a place where he saw a cross lying in the ground upon a marble stone, and causing the stone to be digged up, he found a great treasure under

[1] See also Jer. xxxii. 39; Ezek. xxxvii. 25-28, and xxxix. 29.

the cross: but what was this treasure but a great nothing to that treasure that is wrapped up in our redemption by Christ! What the Lord said once to his anointed Cyrus, a temporal deliverer of his people, the same he hath spoken, and much more, to his anointed Jesus, the greater Saviour and Redeemer of his church: 'I will give thee the treasures of darkness, the hidden riches of secret places,' Isa. xliii. 3. There are 'unsearchable riches' in Jesus Christ.[1] In him are riches of grace, of all grace; in him are riches of justification, and riches of sanctification, and riches of consolation, and riches of glorification. Would you share in the best of riches, would you share in the most durable riches, would you share in soul riches, would you share in heavenly riches? Oh, then, secure your interest in the redemption that is by Jesus Christ. But,

[6.] The sixth, and last, excellent property of that redemption that we have by Jesus Christ is this—viz., it is a *redemption-sweetening redemption;* it is such a redemption as sweetens all other redemptions. It is redemption by Christ that sweetens our redemption out of this trouble and that, out of this affliction and that, out of this danger and that, out of this sickness and that, out of this bondage and that. Redemption by Christ is like that tree which Moses cast into the bitter waters of Marah, that made them sweet, Exod. xv. 23. This water became sweet for the use and service of the Israelites for a time only, and remained not always sweet after, as appears by Pliny's Natural History, who makes mention of those bitter waters in his time.[2] But the redemption that we have by Jesus Christ does for ever sweeten all the bitter trials and afflictions that we meet with in this world. The Jewish doctors say that this tree was bitter, and they give us this note upon it, 'that it is the manner of the blessed God to sweeten that which is bitter by that which is bitter.' I shall not dispute about the truth of their notion; but this I may safely say, that it is the manner of the blessed God to sweeten our greatest troubles, and our sharpest trials, by that redemption that we have by Jesus Christ. And thus you see the excellent properties of that redemption that Jesus Christ, by covenant or compact with his Father, was engaged to work for us. But,

(4.) The fourth proposition is this—viz., *That the blessed and glorious titles that are given to Jesus Christ, in the Holy Scriptures, do clearly and strongly evidence that there was a covenant of redemption passed between God the Father and Jesus Christ.* He is called a 'mediator of the covenant' of reconciliation, interceding for and procuring of it; and that not by a simple entreaty, but by giving himself over to the Father, calling for satisfaction to justice, that reconciliation might go on, for paying a compensatory price sufficient to satisfy divine justice for the elect. 'There is one God, and one mediator between God and men'—to wit, God incarnate—'the man Christ Jesus, who gave himself a ransom for all'—to wit, his elect children—'to be testified in due time,' 1 Tim. ii. 5, 6. Let me glance a little upon the words, 'one mediator between God and men.' In the Greek, it is one mediator of God and men; which may

---

[1] See my treatise called 'The Unsearchable Riches of Christ.'—[Vol. iii. p. 1, *seq.*—G.]   [2] Plin. Natural History, lib. vi., cap. 29.

refer either to the two parties betwixt which he deals, pleading for God to men and for men to God, or to the two natures, mediator of God, having the divine nature, and of men, having the human nature upon him; one mediator, not of redemption only, as the papists grant, but of intercession too. We need no other master of requests in heaven, but the man Christ Jesus, who being so near us, in the matter of his incarnation, will never be strange to us in the business of intercession. 'A ransom,' the Greek ἀντίλυτρον, is a *counter-price* such as we could never have paid, but must have remained and even rotted in prison, but for our all-sufficient surety and Saviour. The ransom that Christ paid was a real testimony of his mediatorship betwixt God and men, whereby he reconciled both. 'The man Christ Jesus.' Paul speaks not this to exclude his divinity from this office of mediatorship, for he is 'God manifested in the flesh,' 1 Tim. iii. 16, and 'God hath purchased his church by his own blood,' Acts xx. 28; but to shew that, in his human nature, he paid the ransom for us, and that, as man, he is like unto us, Heb. ii. 10; and therefore all sorts and ranks of men have a free access by faith unto him, and to his sacrifice. He is also called a Redeemer, 'I know that my Redeemer liveth,' Job xix. 25. The word redeemer in the Hebrew is very emphatical, *Goel;* for it signifieth a kinsman, near allied unto him; one that was bone of his bone, and flesh of his flesh.[1] Christ is of our kindred by incarnation, and redeems us by his passion. The words are an allusion to the ceremonial law, where the nearest kinsman was to take the wife and buy the land, Ruth iii. 9, 12, 13, and iv. 4, 5. We were Satan's by nature, but Christ our brother, our kinsman, hath redeemed us by the price of his own blood, and will deliver us from hell, and bring us 'to the inheritance of the saints in light,' John xx. 17; and therefore deserves the name of a redeemer, 1 Pet. i. 3, 4; Col. i. 12. Jesus Christ is near, very near, yea, nearest of kin to us, Eph. v. 30; he is flesh of our flesh, and bone of our bone, and blood of our blood: 'Forasmuch as the children are partakers of flesh and blood, he also himself took part of the same,' Heb. ii. 14. Now it is evident, by the old law of redemption, that the nearest kinsman was under a special obligation to redeem; as you may see by comparing Ruth iii. 12, 13 with iv. 4, 5. Boaz was a kinsman, and had right to redeem; yet because there was a nearer kinsman, he would not engage himself, but upon his refusal: 'If thou wilt redeem it, redeem it; but if thou wilt not redeem it, then tell me, that I may know; for there is none to redeem it besides thee, and I am after thee.' Now Jesus Christ is nearest of kin to us, and therefore, upon the strictest terms and laws of redemption, he is *Goel*, our Redeemer. If we consider Jesus Christ as a kinsman, a brother, we must say, that he had not only a right to redeem us; but that he was also under the highest obligation to redeem us. There is a double way of redeeming persons:—(1.) By force and power: thus when Lot was taken prisoner by those four kings that came against Sodom, 'Abraham armed his servants,' and by force and power redeemed them, Gen. xiv. 14, 16. We were all Satan's prisoners, Satan's captives, but Christ our nearest

---

[1] Some read the words thus, 'I know that my kinsman, or he that is near to me, liveth.'

kinsman, our brother, ' by spoiling principalities and powers,' Col. ii. 15, rescues us out of that tyrant's hand. (2.) There is a redemption by price or ransom ; to redeem is to buy again, 1 Cor. vi. 20, ' Ye are bought with a price ;' vii. 23, ' Ye are bought with a price.' The word price is added, not by a *pleonasmus*, but κατ᾽ ἐξοχὴν, to intimate the excellency and dignity of the price wherewith they were bought, which was not ' silver or gold ; but the precious blood of Christ, as of a lamb without blemish, and without spot,' 1 Pet. i. 18, 19. ' Ye are bought with a price;' that is, ye are dearly bought, by a price of inestimable value ; but of this before. Again, sometimes Christ is called ' the surety of a better covenant.' Heb. vii. 22, ' By so much was Jesus made a surety of a better testament,' so called from the manner of the confirmation of it—viz., by the death of Christ. Look, as Christ was our surety to God, for the discharge of our debt—the surety and debtor, in law, are reputed as one person—so he is God's surety to us, for the performance of his promises. The office of a surety being applied to Christ sheweth that he hath so far engaged himself for us, as that he neither can nor will start from his engagement. You shall as soon remove the earth, stop the sun in his course, empty the sea with a cockle-shell, make a world, and unmake yourselves, as any power on earth, or in hell, shall ever be able to hinder Christ from the performance of the office of a surety. A perfect fulfilling of all righteousness, according to the tenor of the law, is required of man. Now Christ our surety, by a voluntary subjection of himself to the law, and by being made under the law, he hath fulfilled all righteousness, Gal. iv. 4 ; Mat. iii. 15 ; and that he did this for us is evident by that phrase of the apostle, Rom. v. 19, ' By the obedience of one shall many be made righteous.' The contents of the law must be accomplished by our surety, or else we can never escape the curse of the law, Gal. iii. 10, 13 ; there must be a translation of the law from us in our persons, unto the person of our surety, or we are undone, and that for ever. Christ is the end of the law for righteousness, and hath made us just by his obedience ; ' We are made the righteousness of God in him,' Rom. x. 4. Our surety became subject to the law, that he might redeem us that were obnoxious to the law, 2 Cor. v. 21. Again, full satisfaction for every transgression is required of man. Now Christ our surety hath made satisfaction for all our sins, he was made a curse for us,' Gal. iii. 13 ; and by that means he hath redeemed us from the curse of the law. To exact a debt which is fully satisfied, is a point of injustice. Now Christ our surety having made full satisfaction for all our sins, we need not fear to stand before the face of God's justice. A debtor that hath a surety that is able and willing to pay his debt, yea, who hath fully paid it, need fear no colours. This title, ' a surety of a better covenant,' does necessarily import a blessed covenant between Jesus Christ and his dear Father, to whom he freely and readily becomes surety for us ; for what is suretyship but a voluntary transferring of another's debt upon the surety, he obliging to pay the debt for which he engageth as surety ? Thus you see, by the blessed and glorious titles that are given to Jesus Christ in the Scriptures, that there was a covenant of redemption passed between God the Father and Jesus Christ. But,

(5.) The fifth proposition is this, *That the work of our redemption and salvation, was transacted between God the Father and Jesus Christ, before the foundation of the world.* This federal transaction between the Father and the Son was from eternity. Upon this account the Lord Jesus is said to be ' the Lamb slain from the foundation of the world,' Rev. xiii. 8, because that it was agreed and covenanted between God the Father and Jesus Christ, that he should, in the fulness of time, be made flesh and die for sinners; and therefore it was said to be done from the foundation of the world.[1] Though Christ was not actually slain, but when he suffered for us upon the cross, yet he was slain from the beginning in God's purpose, in God's decrees, in God's promises, in the sacrifices, in the faith of the elect, and in the martyrs; for Abel, the first that ever died, died a martyr, he died for religion. This compact betwixt the Father and the Son bears date from eternity. This the apostle asserts: 2 Tim. i. 9, ' Who hath saved us and called us with an holy calling; not according to our works, but according to his own purpose and grace, which was given us in Christ Jesus, before the world began.'[2] Here is grace given us in Christ Jesus before the world began. But what grace was that which was given us in Christ Jesus before the world began? Doubtless it was the grace of redemption, which God, in his purpose and decree, had given us in Christ Jesus, before the world began. The scripture last cited does clearly shew that God the Father and Jesus Christ dealt together about the redemption of souls before the world began; and that all our everlasting concernments were agreed on and made sure between them: so that Titus i. 2 gives the same sound, ' In hope of eternal life; which God, that cannot lie, promised before the world began.' How was this life promised before the world began, but in this covenant of redemption, wherein God the Father promised and engaged to Jesus Christ that he would give eternal life to all his seed? So the apostle tells us, ' He hath chosen us in him,' that is, in Christ, 'before the foundation of the world.' There was an eternal contrivance, compact, covenant, or agreement between God the Father and Jesus Christ, concerning the sanctification, holiness, and salvation of the elect. God agrees with Christ about the everlasting happiness of his chosen before the world began.[3] So John x. 16, ' And other sheep I have, which are not of this fold; them also I must bring.' Why must he bring them home? how was he bound, how was he engaged to bring home his other sheep, that he puts a *must* upon it? ' Them also I *must* bring.' Doubtless it was from this covenant and agreement which he had made with God the Father, wherein he had engaged himself to bring home all his elect. Christ takes a great deal of pains to bring home his sheep; being bound in the covenant of redemption, to present all that are given him by charter blameless

---

[1] God loved his people and provided for them, and contrived all their happiness before they were, yea, before the world was.

[2] The grace here spoken of cannot be understood of infused grace, unless we will say that it could be infused into us before either the world was, or we were in it.

[3] The whole business of our salvation was first transacted between the Father and Christ before it was revealed to us, John vi. 27. The Apostle Peter, speaking of our redemption by the precious blood of Christ, saith that ' Christ was foreordained, thereunto, before the foundation of the world,' 1 Pet. i. 20.

before the Father; therefore, saith he, I bring them, and ' I *must* bring them;' the matter not being left arbitrary, even in respect of his obligation to God the Father, Col. i. 22. Certainly the decree, covenant, and agreement between God the Father and Jesus Christ about the whole way of redemption, about all things belonging to the salvation of the elect, to be brought about in due time, was fixed and settled before the world began.[1] Ponder seriously on this, it may be a loadstone to draw out your hearts more than ever, to love the Father and the Son, and to delight in the Father and the Son, and to act faith upon the Father and the Son, and to long to be with the Father and the Son, and all your days to admire at the love of the Father and the Son, who have from eternity, by compact and agreement, secured your souls and your everlasting concernments. But,

(6.) The sixth proposition is this, *That God the Father had the first and chief hand in this great work of saving sinners, by virtue of this covenant of redemption, wherein he and his Son had agreed to bring ' many sons to glory,'* Heb. ii. 10. Weak Christians many times have their thoughts and apprehensions more busied and taken up with the love of the Son, than with the love of the Father; but they must remember, that in the great and glorious work of redemption, God the Father had a great hand, an eminent hand, yea, the first and chief hand. God the Father first laid the foundation-stone of all our happiness and blessedness. His head and heart was first taken up about that heaven-born project, the salvation of sinners: Isa. xxviii. 16, ' Therefore thus saith the Lord God, Behold, I lay in Zion for a foundation a stone, a tried stone, a precious corner-stone, a sure foundation;' Heb., ' I am he that foundeth a stone in Zion.' It is God the Father that hath long since laid Christ as a sure foundation, for all his people to build their hopes of happiness upon; it is he that first laid Christ, the true corner-stone, whereby Zion is for ever secured against death, hell, and wrath. Hence it is said, ' The pleasure of the Lord shall prosper in his hand,' that is, God's eternal decree about the work of our redemption and salvation, shall be powerfully, faithfully, and completely executed by Jesus Christ; who, by his word and Spirit, shall communicate unto all his elect the fruit of his death, to life and salvation, Rom. ix. 33; 1 Pet. ii. 6; Isa. liii. 10. Again: Job xxxiii. 24,[2] ' Deliver him from going down into the pit, for I have found a ransom.' The Hebrew word signifies a price paid to redeem a man's life or liberty, ' I have found a ransom,' or an atonement, a cover for man's sin. Angels and men could never have found a ransom, but by my deep, infinite, and unsearchable wisdom, saith God the Father, ' I have found a ransom,' I have found out a way, a means for the redeeming of mankind, from going down to the infernal pit, viz., the death and passion of my dearest Son. But where, O blessed God, didst thou find a ransom? Not in angels, not in men, not in

---

[1] Ps. ii. 7; Acts xv. 18, and ii. 23; Eph. i. 9; Prov. viii. 22–32.

[2] This is a full place against all Socinians, who boldly assert that God removes the curse of the law, by a free and absolute pardon, without satisfaction. Grotius's exposition on the place is but flat and dull. When God saith, ' I have found a ransom,' we are to understand it of a real ransom, of full pay or satisfaction, and not of a ransom by favour and acceptation.

legal sacrifices, not in gold or silver, not in tears, humblings, and melt-ings of my people ; but in my own bosom. That Jesus, that Son of my love, who has lain in my bosom from all eternity, John i. 18, he is that ransom, that by my own matchless wisdom and singular goodness, ' I have found.' I have not called a council to inquire where to find a ransom, that fallen man might be preserved from falling into the fatal pit of destruction ; but I have ' found a ransom' in my own heart, my own breasts, my own bosom ; without advising or consulting with others, I have found out a way how to save sinners with a salvo to my honour, justice, holiness, and truth. Had all the angels in heaven, from the first day of their creation, to this very day, sat in serious council, to invent, contrive, or find out a way, a means, where-by lost man might be secured against the curse of the law, hell, con-demnation, and wrath to come, and whereby he might have been made happy, and blessed for ever ; and all this without the least wrong or prejudice to the justice and righteousness of God, they could never have found out any way or means to have effected those great things. Our redemption, by a ransom, is God's own invention, and God's only invention. The blessed ransom which the Lord has found out for poor sinners, is the blood of his own dearest Son—a ransom which never entered into the thoughts or hearts of angels and men, till God had revealed it—which is called ' the blood of the covenant,' Heb. x. 29, because thereby the covenant is confirmed, and all covenant-mercies assured to us. Again,—' God so loved the world, that he gave his only-begotten Son,' John iii. 16 ; Hosea xiv. 4. Here is a *sic*, without a *sicut*, that *sic*, *so*, signifies the firstness of the Father's love, and the freeness of the Father's love, and the vehemency of the Father's love, and the admirableness of the Father's love, and the matchless-ness of the Father's love. Oh ! what manner of love is this, for God to give his Son, not his servant ; his begotten Son, not his adopted Son, his only Son, and not one son of many ; his only Son by eternal gene-ration, and communication of the same essence ; to be a ransom and mediator for sinners ! God the Father loving lost man, sent his Son to suffer and to do the office of a mediator, that through his mediation, he might communicate the effects of his love, in a way agreeable to his justice ! for God loved the world, and that antecedently to his giving Christ, and as a cause of it. The design, the project of saving sinners, was first contrived and laid by God the Father ; there-fore Christ says, ' The Son can do nothing of himself, but what he sees the Father do.' God the Father sent his Son, and God the Father sealed his Son a commission to give life to lost sinners. ' Him hath God the Father sealed ;' that is, made his commission authentical, as men do their deeds by their seals. It is a metaphor taken from them who ratify their authority whom they send ; that is, approve of them, as it were, by setting to their seal. Christ is to be acknowledged to be he whom the Father hath authorised and furnished to be the Saviour and Redeemer of lost sinners, and the storehouse from whence they are to expect all spiritual supplies. Look, as kings give sealed warrants and commissions to their ministers of state, who are sent out or employed in great affairs, 1 Kings xxi. 8 ; Eph. iii. 12, and viii. 8, so Christ is the Father's great 'ambassador, authorised and sent out by him to bring about the redemption and salvation of lost man. And look, as a seal represents in wax that which is engraven on it, so the Father hath communicated to him his divine essence and properties, and stamped upon him all divine perfection, for carrying on the work of redemption. And look, as a seal annexed to a commission is a public evidence of the person's authority, so Christ's endowments are visible marks whereby to know him, and clear evidences that he was the true Messiah, and of the Father's installing him into that office of a Redeemer. So John vi. 38, ' I came down from heaven, not to do mine own will, but the will of him that sent me.'[1] In this verse Christ declares in the general that his errand into the world is to do his Father's will who sent him, and not his own ; which is not to be understood that, as God, he hath a different and contrary will to the Father's, though, as man, he hath a distinct and subordinate will to his ; but the meaning is, he came not to do his own will only, as the Jews alleged against him, but the Father's also ; and that in this work he was the Father's commissioner, sent to do what he had intrusted him with, and not, as the Jews gave out, that he was one who did that for which he had no warrant. Christ, in entertaining them that come to him, as in ver. 37, is not only led thereunto by his own mercy, and bounty, and love towards them, as the reward of all his sufferings, but doth also stand obliged thereunto by virtue of a commission and trust laid upon him by the Father, and accepted and undertaken by him ; therefore he doth mention ' the will of him that sent him' as a reason of his fidelity in this matter. By what has been said, it is most evident that God the Father had the first and chief hand in the great work of our redemption. It is good to look upon God the Father as the first projector of our happiness and blessedness, that we may honour the Father as we honour the Son, and love the Father as we love the Son, and value the Father as we value the Son, and admire the Father as we admire the Son, and exalt the Father as we exalt the Son, and cleave to the Father as we cleave to the Son, &c. I have a little the longer insisted on this proposition, because commonly we are more apprehensive of the love of the Son than we are of the love of the Father, and that I may the more heighten your apprehensions of the Father's love in the great work of redemption. Ah ! what amazing love is this, that the thoughts of the Father, that the eye of the Father, that the heart of the Father, should be first fixed upon us, that he should begin the treaty with his Son, that he should make the first motion of love, that he should first propose the covenant of redemption, and thereby lay such a sure foundation for man's recovery out of his slavery and misery. To speak after the manner of men, the business from eternity lay thus : Here is man, saith God the Father to his Son, fallen from his primitive purity, glory, and excellency, into a most woeful gulf of sin and misery ; he that was once a son is now become a slave ; he that was once a friend is now become an enemy, Eph. ii. 12, 13 ; he that was once near us is now afar off ; he that was once in favour is now cast off ; he that was once made in our image has now the image of Satan stamped upon him, Gen. i. 26, 27 ; he who had once sweet communion with us has now fellowship

[1] See John x. 17, and xvi. 27.

with the devil and his angels. Now out of this forlorn estate he can never deliver himself, neither can all the angels in heaven deliver him. Now this being his present case and state, I make this offer to thee, O my Son: If, in the fulness of time, Phil. ii. 7, 8, thou wilt assume the nature of man, 'tread the winepress of my wrath alone,' Isa. lxiii. 3, bear the curse, Gal. iii. 13, shed thy blood, die, suffer, satisfy my justice, fulfil my royal law, then I can, upon the most honourable terms imaginable, save fallen man, and put him into a safer and happier condition than ever that was from whence Adam fell, and give thee a noble reward for all thy sufferings. Upon this Jesus Christ replies: O my Father! I am very ready and willing to do, to suffer, to die, to satisfy thy justice, to comply with thee in all thy noble motions, and in all thy gracious and favourable inclinations, that poor sinners may be sanctified and saved, made gracious and glorious, holy and happy; that poor sinners may never perish, that poor sinners may be secured from wrath to come, and be brought into a state of light, life, and love, 1 Thes. i. 10; Heb. x. 10, 14; I am willing to make myself an offering; and, 'Lo, I am come to do thy will, O God,' Ps. xl. 6, 7. Thus you see how firstly, and greatly, and graciously, the thoughts of God have been set at work, that poor sinners may be for ever secured and saved. But,

(7.) The seventh proposition is this, *It was agreed between the Father and the Son that Jesus Christ should be incarnate, that he should take on him the nature of those whom he was to save, and for whom he was to satisfy, and to bring to glory.*[1] Christ's incarnation was very necessary in respect of that work of redemption, that he, by agreement with the Father, had undertaken. He had engaged himself to his Father that he would redeem lost sinners, and, as their surety, make full satisfaction. By the fall of Adam, God and man was fallen out, they were at variance, at enmity, at open hostility, Rom. viii. 7; so that by this means all intercourse between heaven and earth was stopped, and all trading between God and us ceased. Now to redress all this, and to make an atonement, a mediator was necessary; now this office belonged unto Jesus Christ, both by his Father's ordination and his own voluntary susception, Heb. x. 5–7; and for discharge of it a human nature was very requisite. There was an absolute necessity that Christ should suffer, partly because he was pleased to substitute himself in the sinner's stead, and partly because his sufferings only could be satisfactory. But now, unless Christ be incarnate, how can he suffer? The whole lies thus: without satisfaction no redemption, without suffering no satisfaction, without flesh no suffering; *ergo*, Christ must be incarnate. The Word must be made flesh, John i. 14: and so Heb. ii. 14, 16, 'Forasmuch then as the children are partakers of flesh and blood, he also himself likewise took part of the same; that through death he might destroy him that had the power of death, that is, the devil; for verily he took not on him the nature of angels; but he took on him the seed of Abraham:' 1 Tim. iii. 16, 'Without controversy, great is the mystery of godliness: God was manifested in the flesh, justified in the Spirit, seen of angels, preached unto the Gentiles,

[1] Gen. iii. 15; 1 John iii. 8; Acts ii. 30, and iii. 22; Isa. vii. 14, and ix. 6; Deut. xviii. 15–18; Gal. iv. 4 Rom. viii. 3.

believed on in the world, received up into glory.' This is only applicable to the person of Christ. He that by his office is to be Emmanuel, God with us, he must, in regard of his person, be Emmanuel also, that is, God-man in one person. He that by office is to make peace between God and man, he must be God-man ; he that by office is to stand and minister between God and men, he must be God and man, that so he might not be only zealously faithful towards God's justice, but also tenderly merciful towards men's errors, Heb. ii. 17, 18, and iv. 15, 16. Look, as he must be more than man that he may be able so to suffer, that his sufferings may be meritorious, that he may go through-stitch with the work of redemption, and triumph over death, devils, difficulties, discouragements, curse, hell, wrath, &c., all which Christ could never have done had he been but a mere man, so it was requisite that he should be man, that he might be in a capacity to suffer, die, and obey ; for these are not works for one who is only God. A God only cannot suffer, a man only cannot merit. God cannot obey, man is bound to obey. Wherefore Christ, that he might obey and suffer, he was man ; and that he might merit by his obedience and suffering, he was God-man. Now such a person, and only such a person, did the work of redemption call for. That is a mighty scripture, Phil. ii. 6, 7, ' Who being in the form of God thought it no robbery to be equal with God '—here's Christ's preexisting in the nature of the Godhead, and then after comes his manhood—' but made himself of no reputation :' Greek, he ' emptied himself,' as it were, of his divine dignity and majesty ; he did disrobe himself of his glory, and became a sinner, both by imputation and reputation, for our sakes, for our salvation—' and took upon him the form of a servant, and was made in the likeness of men,' Isa. liii. 6, 9. All this Christ did upon his Father's prescription, and in pursuit of the great work of redemption. The blessed Spirit fitted the man Christ Jesus to be a meet mediator and redeemer for poor sinners. The Spirit formed the nature of man, of the substance of the virgin, after an extraordinary manner for the service of the Lord Christ, Luke i. 35 ; he sanctified the human nature which Christ assumed, after such a perfect manner, that it was free from all sin, Gal. iv. 4 ; Luke i. 35 ; in the very moment of conception he united this pure human nature with the divine in the same person, the person of the Son of God, that he might be a fit head, mediator, and redeemer for us, Heb. x. 5. But,

(8.) The eighth proposition is this,—viz., *That there were commandments from the Father to the Son which he must obey and submit to.* God the Father did put forth his paternal authority, and lay his commands upon his Son, to engage in this great work of redeeming and saving poor sinners' souls. He had a command from the Father what to teach his people, as the prophet of the church : ' For I have not spoken of myself,' saith Christ ; ' but the Father which sent me, he gave me a commandment, what I should say, and what I should speak,' John xii. 49. Christ declares that he had received a commission from the Father, who sent him, concerning his doctrine, and what to say and speak ; and that he was persuaded that this doctrine delivered to him by the Father points out the true way to eternal life ; and that he had exactly followed this commission in preaching, both for matter and manner. The two words of saying and speaking may be taken comprehensively, pointing out all the ways of delivering his commission, by set and solemn preaching, or occasional conferences, and the whole subject-matter of his preaching, in precepts, promises, and threatenings; and so it will import that his commission from the Father was full, both for matter and manner, and his discharge thereof answerable.[1] Christ is a true prophet, who speaks neither more or less in the doctrine of the gospel than what was the Father's will should be delivered to us: 'For whatsoever I speak, even as the Father said unto me, so I speak.' Christ keeps close to his commission, without adding or diminishing; and herein Christ's practice should be every faithful minister's pattern. Again, Christ had a command to lay down his life for those that were given him: 'No man taketh it from me, but I lay it down of myself; I have power to lay it down, and I have power to take it again; this commandment have I received of my Father,' John x. 18. The Father is so well pleased with the reconciliation of lost sinners, that he loveth Christ for the undertaking thereof, and is fully satisfied with his suffering for attaining that end. In both these respects it holds good: 'Therefore doth my Father love me, because I lay down my life,' ver. 17. The Father is pleased with him that he undertook this service, and is content with his death as a sufficient ransom. Christ having laid down his life for the redemption of lost man, did take it again, as a testimony that the Father was satisfied with his sufferings. Now the way of the accomplishment of our redemption was agreed on betwixt the Father and the Son before the accomplishment thereof; therefore saith he, 'This commandment have I received of my Father,' which makes it clear that he came into the world fully instructed about carrying on the work of redemption, [Ps. xl. 6, 7 with Heb. x. 6–8.] It pleased Christ to suffer death, not only voluntarily, but in a way of subjection to his Father's command, that so the merit thereof might every way be full and acceptable to the Father: 'For this commandment have *I received.*' He was content to be a servant by paction, that so his sufferings might be accepted for his people. And so when Christ was going to die, he saith, 'That the world may know that I love the Father; and as the Father gave me commandment, even so I do: arise, let us go hence,' John xiv. 31. As if he had said, Power is permitted to Satan and his accomplices to persecute me to death, that dying for man's redemption, the world may see the obedience and love I bear to the Father, who hath thus determined. All that Christ suffered for the redemption of sinners was by the order, and at the command, of the Father, who did covenant with him concerning this work: 'For as the Father gave me a commandment, even so do I.' In this scripture, as in a crystal glass, you may see that Christ did enter the lists in his sufferings with much willingness and alacrity, with much courage and resolution, that so he might commend his love to us, and encourage us to do the like through him. Therefore, saith he, 'Arise, and let us go hence.' I am very free and ready, by my death and sufferings, to complete the work of man's redemption, according to the covenant and agreement that long since was made

---

[1] Between saying and speaking there is this difference, saith à Lapide: that to say, is to teach and publish a thing gravely; to speak, is familiarly to utter a thing.

between the Father and myself. If Christ should fail in complying with his Father's commands about suffering and dying for us, then not only the breach of articles, but high disobedience too, might be justly charged upon him; but from all such charges Christ has bravely quitted himself. There was a special law laid upon Christ as he was our mediator, which law he was willing and ready to obey, in order to our redemption. That Christ should die was no part of the moral law, but it was a positive special law laid upon Christ. Well, this law he obeys, he complies with: 'I lay down my life for my sheep; this commandment have I received of my Father,' John x. 11, 15, 17, 18. Christ, as mediator, had a command from his Father to die, and he observes it; hence God calls him his servant: 'Behold my servant whom I uphold,' Isa. xlii. 1. And in pursuance of God's royal law, will, and pleasure, he takes upon him the form of a servant; and frequently proclaims before all the world, that he 'came to do the will of him that sent him,' Phil. ii. 6, 7. Again, God the Father lays a special command upon Jesus Christ, to preserve and bring to glory all those that come unto him. Jesus Christ has not only leave to save the elect, but a charge to save the elect: 'All that the Father giveth me, shall come to me; and him that cometh to me, I will in no wise cast out'—where the doubled negatives, in the original, serve to make the assertion strong, and to carry their faith over all their doubts and fears—'for I came down from heaven, not to do mine own will, but the will of him that sent me. And this is the Father's will which hath sent me, that of all which he hath given me, I should lose nothing, but should raise it up again at the last day. And this is the will of him that sent me, that every one which seeth the Son, and believeth on him, may have everlasting life; and I will raise him up at the last day.' [1] Christ is to be answerable for all those that are given to him, at the last day, and therefore we need not doubt but that he will certainly employ all the power of his Godhead to secure and save all those that he must be accountable for. In this blessed scripture there are several special things that we may take notice of, that are pat to our present purpose:—

[I.] As *first*, that it is the great dignity and happiness of the elect, that they are, *from eternity, given to Christ in the covenant of redemption, as the reward of his sufferings, to come to him in due time ;* and that they are given to him in trust, and that he must be accountable for them, as being given by the Father to him, Ps. xxiv. 1. They were the Father's first, not only by the right of creation, but by particular election also; and being thus the Father's, they are given to Christ from eternity, to be redeemed by him, and as the reward of his sufferings. Again, such as are elected and given to Christ, will certainly, in due time, come to him. Their being given from eternity, produceth their being given and coming in time; for God is faithful, who will not frustrate Christ of what he hath purchased; and the power that draweth them is invincible and irresistible; therefore, saith he, 'All that the Father giveth me, shall come to me.' Again, Christ in entertaining them that come to him is not only led thereunto by his own mercy, and bounty, and love towards them as the reward of

---

[1] John vi. 37-40. Here you have Christ's commission to save the elect, &c.

his sufferings, but doth also stand obliged thereunto by virtue of a commission and trust laid upon him by the Father, and accepted and undertaken by him ; therefore doth he mention ' the will of him that sent me,' as a reason of his fidelity in this matter. Further, from ver. 39, we may observe that the gospel contains an extract of the deep counsels of God, and of the eternal transactions betwixt the Father and the Son concerning lost man, so far as is for our good ; for he brings out and reads in the gospel his very commission, and some articles of the covenant, passed betwixt the Father and him. Again, the first fountain and rise of the salvation of any of lost mankind, is in the absolute and sovereign will and pleasure of God; for here he mentions the will of him that sent him, as the first original of all ; from whence their giving to Christ, their coming and safety, do flow. Again, these, whose salvation the Father willeth, are given over to Christ in his eternal purpose, to be brought to him in due time ; for so it is here held out. Again, such as are given to Christ by the Father, and do in time come to him, are put in his keeping, and he hath a care of them, not to lose the least of them, ' For this is the will of him that sent me, that of all he hath given me, I should lose nothing,' John x. 28, 29 ; wherein the Father doth so commit the trust to him, as that he still keeps them in his own hand also. Again, Christ's charge and care of these that are given to him, extends even to the very day of their resurrection, that there he may make a good account of them, when all perils and hazards are now over, and that he may not so much as lose their dust, but gather it together again, and raise it up in glory, to be a proof of his fidelity ; for, saith he, ' I should lose nothing, but raise it up again at the last day ;' and so death and dissolution proves no loss.

[2.] Again, from ver. 40, we may observe, *that such as are given to Christ, to be under his charge, and to participate of his benefits, are drawn to believe on him : and it is the Father's will, and a part of the transaction betwixt him and his Son, that faith be the way to partake of these benefits, and not the fulfilling of the impossible condition of the works of the law ;* for they who are given to Christ, are expounded to be they who believe on him ; and it is the Father's will that such partake of these benefits here mentioned, as of the rest of his purchase. Albeit mortification, holiness, &c., do prepare for the possession of these benefits, and do evidence a right thereunto, and the begun possession thereof ; yet it is only faith in Christ that giveth the right and title, that so it may be of grace, Eph. ii. 6–8. Again, it is covenanted betwixt the Father and the Son, that believers shall be made partakers of everlasting life ; for it is explained, that not to lose them, ver. 39, is ' that they may have everlasting life.' For the further assurance of believers of their eternal happiness, it is also covenanted that they shall have this life in present possession, in the earnest, and firstfruits thereof ; for they have everlasting life even here, and before their raising up. They have everlasting life—(1.) *In promisso;* (2.) *In pretio;* (3.) *In primitiis.* He stands already on the battlements of heaven, he hath one foot in the porch of paradise. Again, Christ having given an earnest-penny of salvation, will not suffer it to be lost, by any difficulty or impediment in the way, but will carry believers through all difficulties, till he destroy death and the grave, and raise up their very dust, that in body and soul they may partake of that bliss ; and that he may make it manifest, that death and rotting in the grave doth not make void his interest, nor cause his affection to cease. Therefore it is added, ' And I will raise him up at the last day.' Thus you see that God the Father did lay his commands upon his Son, to engage in this great work of redeeming and saving poor sinners' souls, &c.

[3.] In the third place, I shall shew you that *the manner or quality of the transaction between God the Father and Jesus Christ, was by mutual engagements and stipulations; each person undertaking to perform his part in order to our recovery and eternal felicity.* We find each person undertaking for himself by solemn promise. The Father promiseth that he will hold Christ's hand and keep him, Isa. xlii. 6. God the Father engages himself to direct and assist Christ, and to keep him from miscarrying ; and that he will give him all necessary strength and ability for the execution of his mediatory office, and work wonders by him and with him, according to that word, ' My Father hitherto worketh, and I work,' John v. 17. And the Son engages himself that he will obey the Father's call, and not be rebellious : Isa. l. 5, ' I was not rebellious, neither turned away back ;' that is, I did not hang back, as Moses once and again did, Exod. iii. 11, 13, and iv. 1, 10, 13 ; nor refuse to go when God sent me, as once Jonah did, chap. i. 3 ; but I offered myself freely and readily to my Father's call. There was no affliction, no opposition, no persecution, no evil usage that I met with in carrying on the work of redemption that did ever startle me or discourage me, or make me flinch or shrink back from that great and blessed work that I had undertaken. I was dutiful and obedient to the calls and commands of my Father, in all things that he required of me or set me about. Now the Father and the Son being thus mutually engaged by promise one to another in honour and faithfulness, it highly concerned them to keep one another close to the terms of the covenant that was made between them, and accordingly they did ; for God the Father peremptorily stands upon that complete and full satisfaction that Christ had promised to give to his justice ; and therefore, when the day of payment came, he would not abate Jesus Christ one penny, one farthing of the many ten thousand talents that he was to pay down upon the nail for us, Mat. xviii. 24 : Rom. viii. 32, ' God spared not his own Son ;' that is, he abated nothing of that full price that, by agreement with his Father, he was to lay down for us. Other fathers give their all to spare and redeem their children ; but the heart of God the Father is so fully and strongly set upon satisfaction that he will not spare his Son, his own Son, his only Son, but give him up to death, yea, to an accursed death, that we might be spared and saved for ever. I have read of a Roman emperor—Mauricius, who died most miserably [1]—who chose rather to spare his money than to redeem his soldiers being taken prisoners. But to redeem us God would not spare, no, not his own Son ; because

---

[1] Rather Mauricius, [Μαυρίκιος.] He was murdered in the church of St Autonomus, Chalcedon, A.D. 602—a commonplace of history.—G.

no money nor treasure would serve the turn, but only the blood, yea, the heart-blood of his dear Son, 1 Pet. i. 18, 19.

And as God the Father keeps Christ close to the terms of the covenant, so Jesus Christ keeps his Father close to the terms of the covenant also: John xvii. 4, 5, 'I have glorified thee on the earth,' saith Christ to his Father, 'I have finished the work which thou gavest me to do. And now, O Father, glorify thou me with thine own self, with the glory which I had with thee before the world was.' O my Father, I have finished the work of redemption; but where is the wages, where is the glory, where is the reward that thou hast promised me? There was nothing committed to Christ by the Father, to be done on earth for the purchasing of our redemption, but he did finish it; so that the debt is paid, justice satisfied, and sin, Satan, and death spoiled; so that nothing remains but that Christ be glorified, according to the promise of the Father to him. The sum of Christ's petition is this, that since he had finished the work of redemption, that therefore the Father, according to his engagement, would advance him to the possession of that glory that he enjoyed from all eternity. Now for the clearing of this we must consider, that as Christ was from eternity the glorious God, so we are not to conceive of any real change in this glory of his godhead; as if by his estate of humiliation he had suffered any diminution; or by his state of exaltation any real accession were made to his glory as God. But the true meaning is this, that Christ having, according to the paction passed betwixt the Father and him, obscured the glory of his godhead for a time, under the veil of the form of a servant, and our sinless infirmities, Phil. ii. 5-8, doth now expect, according to the tenor of the same paction, after he had done his work, to be exalted and glorified, and 'openly declared to be the Son of God,' Rom. i. 4; the veil of his estate of humiliation, though not of our nature, being taken away. It is further to be considered that however this eternal glory be proper to him as God, yet he prays to be glorified in his whole person. 'Glorify me,' because not only his human nature was to be exalted to what glory finite nature was capable of, but the glory of his godhead was to shine in the person of Christ, God-man, and in the man Christ, though without confusion of his natures and properties. Christ did so faithfully discharge his trust, and perfect the work of redemption, as that the Father was engaged by paction to glorify him; and accordingly Christ, God incarnate, is exalted with the Father in glory and majesty; so that believers may be as sure that all things necessary for their redemption are done, as it is sure that Christ is glorified. But,

[4.] In the fourth place, let us seriously consider of the *articles agreed on between the Father and the Son*,—let us weigh well the promises that God the Father makes to Jesus Christ, and the promises that Jesus Christ makes to the Father, for the bringing about our reconciliation and redemption, that so we may the more clearly see how greatly both the heart of the Father and the heart of the Son is engaged in the salvation of poor sinners' souls. Now there are seven things which God the Father promiseth to do for Jesus Christ, upon his undertaking the work of our redemption.

First, That he will give him the Spirit in an abundant measure

' The Spirit of the Lord shall rest upon him, the spirit of wisdom and understanding, the spirit of counsel and might, the spirit of knowledge and of the fear of the Lord,' Isa. xi. 2. God the Father fits Jesus Christ for the work of redemption by a large effusion of the graces and gifts of the Spirit upon him. The Spirit of the Lord shall not only come upon Christ, but rest and abide with him. The Holy Spirit shall take up in a more special, yea, singular, manner its perpetual and never-interrupted or eclipsed residence with him and in him. God the Father promises that Christ shall, in his human nature, be filled with all the gifts and graces of the Holy Ghost, that he may be as an everlasting treasure, and as an overflowing fountain, to all his people. So Isa. xlii. 1, ' Behold my servant, whom I uphold; mine elect, in whom my soul delighteth : I have put my Spirit upon him, he shall bring forth judgment to the Gentiles.' So Isa. lxi. 1, ' The Spirit of the Lord is upon me.' So John iii. 34, ' God giveth not the Spirit by measure unto him.' Christ, as mediator, is endued with the Spirit for the discharge of that office; and though Christ as man hath not an infinite measure of the Spirit, though indeed in that person the fulness of the Godhead dwells, as being God also, for that were to be no more man, but God, yet the gifts and graces of the Spirit are poured out upon the man Christ in a measure far above all creatures, Col. ii. 10; for though every believer be complete in him, yet, for what is inherent in him, they have but some gifts of the Spirit, 1 Cor. xii. 4; Eph. iv. 7; but Jesus Christ had all sorts of gifts. They had gifts for some particular uses, but he had gifts for all uses; they have a measure of gifts which are capable of increase, he above measure, so much as the human nature is capable of, which, though it be finite in itself, yet it cannot be measured nor comprehended by us. So much is imported in that, ' God giveth not the Spirit by measure to him,' being understood of his manhood; though, as we said, if we speak of his person, he hath the Spirit infinitely and without measure, Col. i. 19, and ii. 3, 9. This fulness became Christ as man, that he might be a fit temple for the Godhead, and as a mediator, that he might be the universal head of his church and storehouse of his people, that from him, as from a common person, spiritual root or principle, the Holy Ghost with his gifts and graces might be communicated to us. ' He received gifts for men, yea, for the rebellious also, that the Lord God might dwell among them,' Ps. lxviii. 18; ' Of his fulness we receive grace for grace,' John i. 16; ' The first Adam was a living soul, but the second Adam is a quickening spirit,' 1 Cor. xv. 45. In the man Christ Jesus there is a treasury and fulness of grace and glory for us; he is the lord-keeper of all our lives, of all our souls, of all our comforts, and of all our graces; and he is the lord-treasurer of all our spiritual, durable, and eternal riches, 2 Tim. i. 12. We lost our first stock by the fall of Adam, Prov. viii. 18. God put a stock into our own hands, and we soon proved bankrupts and run out of stock and block. Now since that fatal fall, God will trust us no more; but he hath out of his great love and noble bounty put a new stock of grace and glory for us into the hands of Jesus Christ, who is mighty, who is able to save to the uttermost, and in whom are hid all the treasures of wisdom and knowledge, Isa. ix. 6; Heb. vii. 25; Col.

ii. 3. Christ was more capable, by infinite degrees, of the fulness of the Holy Ghost than mere men were or could be; and his employment being also infinitely beyond the employment of men, the measure of the Holy Ghost's fulness in him must needs be accordingly beyond all measure. Hence, by way of emphasis, Christ is called ' the anointed one of God,' John xii. 15; Acts iii. 22, 23. The kings, priests, and prophets among the Jews, who were anointed, were in their unction but types of Christ, who is the great king, priest, and prophet of his church, and anointed above them all, yea, and above all the apostles, prophets, evangelists, pastors, teachers, and believers under the new testament ministration. In Christ there is all kind of grace, and it is in him in the highest and utmost degree, that he might be able to manage all his offices, and finish ' that work which God gave him to do,' John xvii. 4; and God hath filled him with his Spirit, that he might successfully bring about the redemption and salvation of sinners. But,

Secondly, God the Father promiseth to invest Jesus Christ with a threefold office, and to anoint him and furnish him with whatever was requisite for the discharge of those three offices—viz., his prophetical, priestly, and kingly offices, Isa. lxi. 1–3, and xxxiii. 22. Christ never forced himself into any of these offices, he never intruded himself into any one office, he never run before he was sent, he never assumed any office till his Father had signed and sealed his commission, John vi. 17. Whatever Jesus Christ had acted without a commission under his Father's hand had been invalid and lost, and God would one day have said to him, ' Who hath required this at thy hand?'[1] Isa. i. 12. In order to our spiritual and eternal recovery out of sin and misery, it was absolutely necessary that whatever Christ did act as a priest, prophet, or king, he should act by the authority of his Father, by a commission under the broad seal of heaven: Heb. v. 5, ' So also Christ glorified not himself to be made an high-priest; but he that said unto him, Thou art my Son.' These two conjunctions, οὕτω καὶ, ' so also,' being joined together, are notes of a reddition, or later part of a comparison, which is the application thereof. This application may have reference either to the general proposition, thus, ' As no man taketh this honour unto himself,' so also, nor Christ; or to the particular instance of Aaron, thus, ' As Aaron took not to himself that honour; so, nor Christ.' Both tend to the same end. The high-priesthood was an honour; for Christ to have taken that to himself, without a commission from his Father, had been to glorify himself, by conferring glory and honour upon himself. This negative, that ' Christ glorified not himself,' is a clear evidence that Christ arrogated no honour to himself. Christ would not arrogate honour to himself, but rather wait upon his Father, that he might confer upon him what honour he saw meet. Christ glorified not himself to be made a high-priest; but his Father glorified him, in ordaining or commissionating him to be the high-priest. In short, to be made a high-priest is to be deputed or appointed

---

[1] Melchizedek was a king and a priest; Christ was more—a priest, a prophet, and a king; Samuel was a priest and a prophet; David was a king and a prophet: but never met all three in any but in Christ alone.

and set apart to that function; and thus was our Lord Jesus Christ made a high-priest. He had never undertaken that office had he not been ordained to it by his Father. But, that you may see Christ's threefold commission to his threefold office, consider,

[1.] First, that God the Father promiseth to Jesus Christ *an excellent, royal and eternal priesthood:* Heb. vii. 21, 'For those priests were made without an oath; but this with an oath by him that said unto him, The Lord sware and will not repent, Thou art a priest for ever after the order of Melchisedec;' Heb. ii. 17, 18; Ps. cx. 4. Among the Jews, in the times of the old testament, they had a high-priest, that was in all things to stand between God and them; and in case any sinned, to make an atonement for them. Now look, as the Jews had their high-priest, so the Lord Jesus Christ, he was to be, and he is, the apostle and the high-priest of our Christian profession, as Aaron was of the Jews' profession. The priestly office of Jesus Christ is erected and set up, on purpose for the relief of poor distressed sinners.[1] The work of the high-priest, is to make reconciliation for the sins of the people. In the times of the old testament, the high-priest made an atonement for the people. In case any man had sinned, he brought a sacrifice, and his sins were laid upon the head of the sacrifice. Once every year, the high-priest did enter into the Holy of holies, and with the blood of the sacrifice, did sprinkle the mercy-seat, and laid the sins of the people upon the head of the scape-goat, and so made an atonement for the people, as is clear in that, Lev. xvi. 14, ' He shall take of the blood of the bullock, and sprinkle it with his finger, upon the mercy-seat eastward: and before the mercy-seat shall he sprinkle of the blood with his finger seven times;' and at ver. 21, ' Aaron shall lay both his hands upon the head of the live goat, and confess over him all the iniquities of the children of Israel, and all their transgressions, and all their sins, putting them upon the head of the goat, and shall send him away by the hand of a fit man into the wilderness; and so he shall make an atonement.' This was the work of the high-priest, in case any had sinned, to make an atonement and satisfaction, by the way of type, for the sins of the people The main scope of the apostle in that, Heb. vii., is to advance Christ his priesthood above the Levitical priesthood, in order to which he premiseth this, that those 'priests were made without an oath,' ver. 20. The apostle's third argument to prove the excellency of Christ's priesthood above the Levitical, is taken from the different manner of instituting the one and the other. Christ's institution was more solemn than the

---

[1] Heb. iii. 1. By the way, you may take notice that the whole body of Antichristianism is but an invasion upon the priestly office of Christ. What is the popish mass, that unbloody sacrifice, but a derogation from the sacrifice of Jesus Christ, once upon the cross; and so a derogation from his priestly office? What are all those popish penances and satisfactions enjoined, but a derogation unto the satisfaction of Christ; and so unto the priestly office of Christ? What is all their praying to saints and angels, but a derogation unto the intercession of Christ; and so unto the priestly office? God deputes Christ to his priestly office, as God and man; yet papists say that Christ is a priest only in his human nature. God saith to his Son, 'Thou art a priest;' yet they make many priests. God makes his Son a priest for ever; yet they substitute others in his room. God gave Christ to offer up but one sacrifice, and that but once; but they every day offer up many sacrifices in the mass. God gave Christ to offer up himself; but they offer up bread and wine, upon pretence that it is the body and blood of Christ. Christ's sacrifice was a bloody sacrifice; but they style theirs an unbloody sacrifice.

Levites'; their institution was without an oath, Christ's institution was with an oath. The argument may be thus framed: that priesthood which is established by an oath, is more excellent than that which is without an oath; but Christ's priesthood is with an oath, and theirs without, *ergo*. . . . It is here taken for granted that Christ was most solemnly instituted a priest, even by an oath; yea, by the oath of God himself, which is the greatest and most solemn manner of institution that can be. God's oath imports two things:—(1.) An infallible certainty of that which he sweareth; (2.) A solemn authority and dignity conferred upon that which he instituted by oath. Great and weighty matters of much concernment use to be established by oath. Hereby it appeareth that Christ's priesthood is a matter of great moment, and of much concernment. This will appear the more evident, if we consider the person who was made priest, viz., our Lord Jesus Christ, who was the greatest person that could be; Heb. vii. 28; therefore he is fitly called 'a great high-priest,' Heb. iv. 14. Or if we consider the ends of Christ's priesthood, which were very weighty, and that in reference both to God and man; to God, for the manifestation of his perfect justice, infinite mercy, almighty power, unsearchable wisdom, and other divine attributes, which never were, nor ever can be so manifested, as in and by Christ's priesthood; to man, that God's wrath might be averted, his favour procured, man's sin purged, and he freed from all evil, and brought to eternal happiness. Or if we consider the benefits of Christ's priesthood, which are answerable to the foresaid ends. Jesus Christ was appointed and made by the Father, ' The apostle and high-priest of the church's profession:' Heb. iii. 1, 2, 'Wherefore, holy brethren, partakers of the heavenly calling, consider the apostle and high-priest of our profession, Christ Jesus, who was faithful to him that appointed him.' Christ had a divine call to the execution of all those offices, which he sustained as our mediator, he did not run before he was sent, he did not act without a commission and warrant, he was lawfully constituted by him who had power to undertake that great charge he hath over the church; this we shall find asserted of all his three offices. As for his priestly office, he was made a priest by an immediate call and ordination from God, Heb. v. 4–6. The scope of the apostle is to set out the excellency of Christ's priesthood, by comparing it with the Levitical. His priesthood had a concurrence of all things necessary to the Levitical; and it had many excellencies above that. Now among other things required in the priesthood of Aaron, this was one, there must be a divine regular call. This was in the priesthood of Christ; 'He was called of God, a high-priest, after the order of Melchisedec.'[1] That Ps. cx. 4, is God's sure and irrevocable promise to Christ, touching that excellent and eternal priesthood, whereby the recovery of his seed was to be meritoriously obtained. This priestly office of Christ is sure, because it is confirmed by God's oath, of which before as well as his promise. The promise makes it sure, the oath doubly sure, irrevocable; and certainly the Lord neither can nor will

---

[1] Ps. cx. 4. The Hebrew is, 'Thou a priest,' &c., *i.e.*, 'Thou shalt be a priest for ever;' it being the manner of the Hebrew tongue, sometimes for brevity sake, to leave out a word, which is to be understood and supplied.

ever repent himself of this promise and oath. The priesthood of Christ is the most noble part of all his mediation. In the priesthood of Christ, and in that especially, lies the latitude and longitude, the profundity and sublimity of God's love towards us; and in respect of this especially, is the whole mystery of our redemption by Christ called μεγαλεῖα τοῦ θεοῦ, the magnificent works of God. Christ as man, and as mediator between God and man, was, by his Father, deputed unto his priestly office. Concerning the dignity and excellency of Christ's priestly office, above the Levitical priesthood, I have spoken elsewhere. But,

[2.] Secondly, God the Father promises to Jesus Christ *to make him a prophet, a great prophet, yea, the prince of prophets.* Christ is a prophet, in way of eminency and excellency, above all other prophets; he was the chief, the head of them all. Christ was made a prophet by an immediate call and ordination from God. Christ, in respect of his prophetical office, can plead the authority of his Father; he can shew a commission for this office, under his Father's own hand. Deut. xviii. 18, ' I will raise them a prophet from among their brethren like unto thee, and will put my words in his mouth; and he shall speak unto them all that I shall command them.'[1] Christ does not raise himself up to the prophetical office, but God the Father raises him up to this great office. He was anointed of God to preach glad tidings. Weigh that, Isa. xlii. 6, ' I will give thee for a light to the Gentiles; to open the blind eyes, to bring out the prisoners from their prison, and them that sit in darkness out of the prison-house.' ' The Spirit of the Lord God is upon me, because the Lord hath anointed me, to preach good tidings unto the meek; he hath sent me to bind up the broken-hearted,' &c., Luke iv. 18. Thus you see that this prophetical dignity of Christ, that he is the grand doctor of the church, is built upon the authority of his Father, who hath authorised and commissionated him to that great office: Isa. l. 4, ' The Lord hath given me the tongue of the learned, that I should know how to speak a word in season to him that is weary: he wakeneth morning by morning; he wakeneth mine ear to hear as the learned.'[2] Thus you see that God the Father promiseth to invest Christ with a prophetic office for the opening the eyes of the blind, &c. This great prophet is richly furnished with all kinds of knowledge; ' In him are hid all the treasures of wisdom and knowledge.' They are hid in him as gold and silver are *in suo loco*, as the philosopher speaks, hid in the veins of the earth. ' Treasures of *knowledge*,' that is, precious knowledge, saving knowledge; ' *Treasures* of knowledge,' that is, plentiful knowledge, abundance of knowledge; ' Treasures,' that is, hidden and stored knowledge, was laid up in him. All the angels in heaven, and all the men on earth, do not know all that is in the heart of God; but now Jesus Christ, ' who lies in the bosom of the Father,' John i. 18, he knows all that is in his Father's heart. All those secret mysteries, that were laid up in the bosom of eternity, are fully known to this great prophet of the church; John v. 20, ' The Father loveth the Son,

---

[1] See Acts iii. 22, and vii. 37; Deut. xviii. 15; Isa. lxi. 1.

[2] Christ displaces all Rabbis, by assuming this title to himself, ' one is your doctor and master, even Christ,' Mat. xxiii. 8–10.

and sheweth him all things that himself doth,' by a divine and unspeakable communication. God the Father shews to Jesus Christ all
things that he doth. God's love is communicative, and will manifest
itself in effects, according to the capacity of the party beloved; so
much appeareth in that unspeakable love of the Father to the Son,
'The Father loveth the Son, and sheweth him all things,' &c., or com-
municateth his nature, wisdom, and power, for operation with him;
which is expressed in terms taken from among men, because of our
weakness: and ought to be spiritually, and not carnally conceived of.
And therefore these terms of the Father's ' shewing,' and the Son's
'seeing,' are made use of to prevent all carnal and gross conceptions
of this inexpressible communication from the Father, and participation
by the Son. In the blessed Scripture, Jesus Christ is sometimes called
' the' prophet, and 'that' prophet; because he is one that came from
the bosom of the Father, and lives and lies in the bosom of the Father,
and understands the whole mind, will, heart, counsels, designs, ways,
and workings of the Father. Jesus Christ is anointed by God the
Father to be the great prophet and teacher of his elect; and accordingly Jesus Christ has taken that office upon himself. God the
Father has laid a charge upon Jesus Christ, to teach and instruct all
those that he has given him, in his whole mind and will, so far as is
necessary to their salvation, edification, consolation, &c. 'Moses was
faithful as a servant, but Christ as a Son.' Heb. iii. 2, 5, 6. Christ
cannot be unfaithful in his prophetical office. Those that God the
Father hath charged him to teach and instruct, he will teach and instruct, in the great things of their peace; and no wonder, for the
knowledge that is communicated to Jesus Christ, the great prophet of
his church, is not by dreams, or visions, or revelations of angels, as to
the prophets of old, but by a clear, full, intimate view, and beholding
of the Godhead, the fountain of all sacred knowledge; Rev. v. 6,
' And I beheld, and, lo, in the midst of the throne and of the four
beasts, and in the midst of the elders, stood a lamb as it had been
slain, having seven horns and seven eyes, which are the seven spirits
of God sent forth into all the earth.' [1] The lamb slain opens the prophecies, and foretells what shall befall the church, to the end of the
world. The discovery of the secrets of God in his word, are the fruit
of Christ slain, ascended, and anointed as the great prophet of the
church. The lamb wanted neither power nor wisdom to open the
seven seals, and therefore he is said to have ' seven horns and seven
eyes.' Seven is a number of perfection. Horns signify power, eyes
signify knowledge or wisdom; [2] both joined together, argue a fulness
and perfection of power and wisdom in Christ; so that we have here
a lively representation of the threefold office of Christ: his sacerdotal
or priestly office in the lamb as slain, his royal or princely office in
the horns, and his prophetical office in the eyes. But,

[3.] Thirdly, God the Father promises to make him *a king, yea,
a mighty king also.* The kingly office speaks might and power.
Christ is a king above all other kings; he is a king 'higher than the

---

[1] The Lamb stands, because (1.) prepared to perfect the work of redemption; (2.) to
help; (3.) to judge; (4.) to intercede.
[2] Dan. vii. 24; Isa. xxxv. 5; Mat. xxviii. 18; Col. ii. 3, 9.

kings of the earth; he is the prince of the kings of the earth; he is Lord of lords, and King of kings,' Ps. lxxxix. 27; Rev. i. 5, and xvii. 14. I remember Theodosius the emperor and another emperor did use to call themselves the vassals of Christ; and it is most certain that all the emperors, kings, and princes of the world are but the vassals of this great king. Christ is not only 'King of saints,' but he is also 'King of nations.' 'There was given him dominion and glory, and a kingdom; that all people, nations, and languages should serve him,' Rev. xv. 3, 4, and xii. 5; Dan. vii. 17. God, by promise, hath 'given him the heathen for his inheritance, and the utmost parts of the earth for his possession,' Ps. ii. 8. The monarchs of the world have stretched their empires far. Nebuchadnezzar's kingdom in Strabo reached as far as Spain; the Persians reached farther, Alexander farther than they, and the Romans farther than them all; but none of all these has subdued the whole habitable world, as Christ has and will. 'All power is given unto him both in heaven and in earth. The Father loveth the Son, and hath given all things into his hand, and the Father also hath put all things under his feet,' Rom. x. 18; Rev. xi. 15; Mat. xxviii. 18; John iii. 35; 1 Cor. xv. 27. The government of all the world is given to Jesus Christ as God-man. All the nations of the earth are under the government of Christ. He is to govern them, and rule them, and judge them, and make what use he pleases of them, as may make most for his own glory, and the good of his chosen. Now God the Father promiseth to invest Jesus Christ with his kingly office: Ps. ii. 6, 'Yet have I set my king upon my holy hill of Zion.' [1] These words are spoken by God the Father, of his Son Jesus Christ. In a promissory way, God the Father anoints Jesus Christ as Zion's king; and therefore it cannot but be the highest madness, folly, and vanity, for any sort or number of men under heaven to seek or attempt to pull that king of saints down, whom God the Father hath set up. Christ rules for his Father, and from his Father, and will so rule in despite of all the rage and wrath, malice and madness, of men and devils: 'yet have I set my king'—*Heb.*, 'I have anointed'—where the sign of Christ's inauguration, or entrance into his kingdom, is put for the possession and enjoying thereof. Christ was anointed and appointed by his Father to the office and work of a mediator, and is therefore here called his king. There is an emphasis in the word 'I,' 'Yet have I set my king upon my holy hill of Zion:' 'I,' before whom all the nations of the earth are but as a drop of a bucket, and as the small dust of the balance, Isa. xl. 15, 17; I, before whom all nations are as nothing, yea, less than nothing; I, by whom princes rule, and nobles, even all the judges of the earth, Prov. viii. 16; I, that rule the kingdoms of men, and give them to whomsoever I will, and who set over them the basest of men, Dan. iv. 17; I, that change times and seasons, and that remove kings and set up kings, Dan. ii. 21; I, that can kill and make alive, save and damn, bring to heaven and throw down to hell, Deut. xxxii. 39; I am he that hath set up Christ as king, and therefore let me see the nation, the council, the princes, the nobles, the judges, the family, the person, that dare oppose or run counter-cross

---

[1] ' My king,' in a peculiar way, *Decretum, Scriptum, Promulgatum.*

to what I have done. Again, the Lord, in a promissory way, approves and establisheth this king by a firm decree: Ps. ii. 7, 'I will declare the decree,' not the secret decree, but the decree manifested in the word. I, the Son of God, will, by my everlasting gospel, proclaim my Father's counsel, concerning the establishment of my kingdom. I will declare that irrevocable decree of the Father, for the setting up of his Son's sceptre, *contra gentes*, point-blank, opposite to that decree of theirs, ver. 3. The decree of God, concerning the kingly office and authority of Christ, is immutable, and in effect as irrevocable—so much may be collected out of the propriety of the word פח—as those things are that are most irrevocable in the course of nature. Again, the Lord, in a promissory way, extends the dominion of Christ to the Gentiles, and to the uttermost parts of the earth, ver. 8. So far should the enemies of Christ be from ruining his kingdom, that God the Father promiseth that all the inhabitants of the earth should be his, and brought into subjection to him, not only the Jews, but all the inhabitants of the earth shall be subjected to Christ's kingdom, the elect he shall save, and the refractory he shall destroy. 'He shall have dominion from sea to sea, and from the river even to the ends of the earth.' Again, the Lord, in a promissory way, declares the power, prevalency, and victory of Christ over all his enemies: ver. 9, 'Thou shalt break them with a rod of iron: thou shalt dash them in pieces like a potter's vessel.' This signifies their utter destruction, so that there is no hope of recovery. A potter's vessel, when it is once broken, cannot be made up again. This proverb also signifies facility in destroying them. As for such that plot, bandy, and combine together against the Lord Jesus Christ, he shall as easily and as irrecoverably by his almighty, eternal, and unresistible power, dash them in pieces, as a potter breaks his vessels in pieces: Jer. xix. 11, 'I will break this people and this city, as one breaketh a potter's vessel, that cannot be made whole again:' so Isa. xxx. 14, 'And he shall break it, as the breaking of the potter's vessel, that is broken in pieces, he shall not spare; so that there shall not be found in the burstings of it, a sherd to take fire from the hearth, or to take water withal out of the pit.' The Jews, you know, were Christ's obstinate enemies; and he hath so dashed them in pieces, that they are scattered abroad all the world over. The Lord hath made another promise, that Christ shall king it, Ps. cx. 1–6. And no wonder, when we consider that God the Father hath called Christ to the kingly office. The sceptre is given into his hand, and the crown is put upon his head, and the key of government is laid upon his shoulder by God himself. Isa. xxii. 22, it is written thus of Eliakim, 'The key of the house of David will I lay upon his shoulder; so he shall open, and none shall shut; and he shall shut, and none shall open.' Now herein was this precious soul a lively figure and type of Christ. The words of the prophecy are applied to Christ, in his advertisement to Philadelphia, Rev. iii. 7; and the sense is this, that look, as Eliakim was made steward or treasurer under Hezekiah, that is, the next under the king in government all over the land, to command, to forbid, to permit, to reward, to punish, to do justice, and to repress all disorder; of which authority the bearing of a key on the shoulder was a badge; so Christ, as mediator under his Father, hath regal power and authority over his Church, where he commands in chief, as I may say, and no man may lift up his hand or foot without him ; he hath the key of the house of David upon his shoulder, to prescribe, to inhibit, to call, to harden, to save, and to destroy at his pleasure. Such a monarch and king is Christ, neither hath any such rule and sovereignty beside him. And if you look into Dan. vii. 13, 14, you may observe, that after the abolishing of the four monarchies, Christ's monarchy is established by the Ancient of days, giving to Jesus Christ dominion, and glory, and a kingdom, that all people, nations, and languages should serve him ; and his dominion is an everlasting dominion, which shall not pass away, and his kingdom that which shall not be destroyed. Christ did not thrust himself into the throne, as some have done ; neither did he swim to his crown through a sea of blood, as others have done ; nor yet swam he through a sea of sorrow to this crown, as Queen Elizabeth is said to do ; no, he stayed till authority was given him by his Father. But,

Thirdly, God the Father hath promised, that he will give to Jesus Christ assistance, support, protection, help, and strength to carry on the great work of redemption. God the Father promises and covenants with Jesus Christ, to carry him through all dangers, difficulties, perplexities, trials, and oppositions, &c., that he should meet with in the accomplishing our redemption ; upon which accounts Jesus Christ undertakes to go through a sea of trouble, a sea of sorrow, a sea of blood, and a sea of wrath : Isa. xlii. 1, ' Behold my servant whom I uphold, mine elect in whom my soul delighteth ;' ver. 4, ' He shall not fail nor be discouraged, till he have set judgment in the earth ; and the isles shall wait for his law ;' ver. 6, ' I, the Lord, have called thee in righteousness, and will hold thine hand, and will keep thee.' [1] What is that ? Why, I will support, strengthen, and preserve thee with my glorious power ; I will so hold thy hand, that thou shalt not be discouraged, but finish that great work of redemption, which, by agreement with me, thou hast undertaken. God the Father agreed with Jesus Christ about the power, strength, success, and assistance that he should have to carry on the work of redemption, all which God the Father made good to him till he had sent forth judgment unto victory ; as Christ himself acknowledgeth, saying, ' Listen, O isles, unto me ; and hearken, ye people, from far ; the Lord hath called me from the womb ; from the bowels of my mother hath he made mention of my name ; and he hath made my mouth like a sharp sword ; in the shadow of his hand hath he hid me, and made me a polished shaft ; in his quiver hath he hid me ; and said unto me, Thou art my servant, O Israel, in whom I will be glorified,' Isa. xlix. 1-3. The work of redemption was so high, so hard, so great, so difficult a work, that it would have broken the hearts, backs, and necks of all the glorious angels in heaven, and mighty men on earth, had they engaged in it ; and therefore God the Father engages himself to stand close to Jesus Christ, and mightily to assist him, and to be singularly present with him, and wonderfully to strengthen him in all his mediatory administrations, John xvii. 2 ; upon which accounts Jesus Christ despises his

[1] Christ is our Lord, but in the work of redemption he was the Father's servant.

enemies, bears up bravely under all his sore temptations and trials, and 'triumphs over principalities and powers,' Mat. iv. 11; Luke xxii. 43; Col. ii. 15. And certainly if Christ ·had not had singular support, and an almighty strength from the Godhead, he could never have been able to have bore up under that mighty wrath, and to have drunk of that bloody cup that he did drink of. Now upon the account of God the Father's engaging himself to own Christ, and stand by him in the great work of our redemption, Jesus Christ acts faith against all his deepest discouragements, which he should meet with in the discharge of his mediatory office, as the prophet tells us: 'The Lord God will help me; therefore shall I not be confounded; therefore have I set my face like a flint, and I know that I shall not be ashamed. He is near that justifieth me, who will contend with me?' Isa. l. 7, 8. From the consideration of God's help, Jesus Christ strengthens and encourages himself, in the execution of his office, against all oppositions. God's presence and assistance made Jesus Christ victorious over all wrongs and injuries. Jesus Christ knew that God the Father would clear up his innocency and integrity, and this made him patient and constant to the last. But,

Fourthly, God the Father promiseth to Jesus Christ that he shall not labour in vain, and that the work of redemption shall prosper in his hand, and that he will give a blessed success to all his undertakings, and crown all his endeavours.[1] 'He shall see his seed, and he shall see the travail of his soul.' Another promise of the Father to the Son you have in that, Isa. lv. 5, 'Nations that know thee not, shall run unto thee.' The Gentiles, that never heard of Christ, nor ever were acquainted with Christ, nor ever had any notice of Christ; when Christ calls, they shall readily and speedily repair unto him and submit unto him. Christ shall one day see and reap the sweet and happy fruit of his blood, sufferings, and undertakings; 'The pleasure of the Lord shall,' certainly, 'prosper in his hand.' Christ's sufferings were as a woman's travail, sharp though short. Now though a woman suffers many grievous pains and pangs, yet, when she sees a man-child brought into the world, she joys and is satisfied. So when nations shall run to Christ, he shall see his seed and be satisfied. God the Father promiseth that Jesus Christ shall have a numerous spiritual posterity, begetting and bringing many thousands to the obedience of his Father; 'Nations shall run unto thee;' and this shall fill the heart of Jesus Christ with abundance of joy and comfort, contentment and satisfaction, when he shall see the fruit of his bitter sufferings, when he shall see abundance of poor, filthy, guilty, condemned sinners pardoned, justified, and accepted with his Father, 'his soul shall be satisfied as with marrow and fatness,' Ps. lxiii. 5. The numerous body of believers, past, present, and to come, that God the Father had promised to Jesus Christ, was the life of his life. That is a sweet promise, Ps. cx. 2, 'Rule thou in the midst of thine enemies.' They that will not bend must break; those that will not stoop to his government shall feel his power. 'Thy people' —the people of God are Christ's five ways: (1.) By donation; (2.) By purchase; (3.) By conquest; (4.) By covenant; (5.) By com-

[1] See Isa. liii. 10, and xlix. 6-12; Micah iv. 3.

munication —'shall be willing in the day of thy power'— Heb., *willingnesses* in the abstract and in the plural number, as if the Holy Ghost could not sufficiently set forth their exceeding great willingness to submit to all the royal commands of the Lord; John xvii. 6; 1 Pet. ii. 9; Luke i. 57; 1 Cor. iii. 23. All Christ's subjects are volunteers, free-hearted, like those isles that wait for God's law, Isa. xlii. 4, and lvi. 6; Zech. viii. 21, 'And the inhabitants of one city shall go to another, saying, Let us go speedily to pray before the Lord, and to seek the Lord of hosts: I will go also;' 'From the womb of the morning, thou hast the dew of thy youth,' Ps. cx. 3. Here is the success of Christ's office promised, both in the victorious subduing of his enemies, and in the cheerful willingness of his subjects, and in the wonderful numerousness of his people brought over to him, even like the innumerable drops of the morning dew. Another promise of that great and complete success that God the Father hath made for Jesus Christ in his mediatory office, you have in that Isa. xlix. from the 6th verse to the 14th verse: Christ shall have a people gathered to him, and a seed to serve him, 'because he hath made his soul an offering for their sins.' The multitude of sinners brought over to Jesus Christ, is the product of the satisfaction which he hath made for them, and the trophies of the victory that he hath got by dying the death of the cross. Thus you see that God the Father hath not only engaged himself by compact to preserve Jesus Christ in his work, but he hath also made to him several precious promises of preservation, protection, and success, so that the work of redemption shall be sure to prosper in his hand. And, to make these glorious promises the more valid and binding, God confirms them solemnly by an oath: Heb. vii. 21, 'This priest,' Christ, 'was made with an oath by him that said unto him, The Lord sware, and will not repent, Thou art a priest for ever.' God the Father foresaw from everlasting that Jesus Christ would so infinitely satisfy him and please him by his incarnation, obedience, and death, that thereupon he swears. But,

Fifthly, God the Father promiseth to Jesus Christ rule, dominion, and sovereignty, Ps. ii. 8, 9. This sovereignty and rule is promised to Jesus Christ in Isa. xl. 10, 'His arm shall rule for him.' ' He shall sit in judgment in the earth, and the isles shall wait for his law,' Isa. xlii. 4—not the Jews only, but the Gentiles also, the people of divers countries and nations shall willingly and readily receive and embrace his doctrine, and submit to his laws, and give up themselves to his rule. Micah iv. 3,, He shall judge among many nations,' that is, rule, order, command, and direct as a judge and a ruler among many nations. The conquests that Christ shall gain over the nations shall not be by swords and arms, but he shall bring them to a voluntary obedience and spiritual subjection by his Spirit and Gospel: John iii. 35, 'The Father loveth the Son, and hath given all things into his hand,' that is, God the Father hath given the rule and power over all things in heaven and earth to Jesus Christ. In carrying on the redemption of sinners, as the matter is accorded betwixt the Father and the Son, so the redeemed are not left to themselves, but are put under Christ's charge and custody, who has ' purchased them with his blood,' God the Father having given him dominion over all that may contribute to help or hinder his people's happiness, that he may order them so as may be for their good. And this power he hath as God with the Father, and as man and mediator by donation and gift from the Father, Mat. xxviii. 18, and ii. 3; and thus every believer's happiness is most firm and sure, all things being wisely and faithfully transacted between the Father and the Son. As long as Jesus Christ has all power to defend his people, and all wisdom and knowledge to guide and govern his people, and all dominion to curb the enemies of his people, and a commission and charge to be answerable for them, we may roundly conclude of their eternal safety, security, and felicity, Col. i. 19, and ii. 1. But,

Sixthly, God the Father promiseth to accept of Jesus Christ, in his mediatory office, according to that of Isaiah, ' Though Israel be not gathered, yet shall I be glorious in the eyes of the Lord,' Isa. xlix. 5; that is as if he had said, notwithstanding the infidelity, obstinacy, and impenitency of the greatest part of the Jews, yet my faithful labour and diligence in the execution of my mediatory office is, and shall be, greatly accepted, and highly esteemed of by my heavenly Father. Artaxerxes, the king of Persia, lovingly accepted of the poor man's present of water, because his good will was in it, and put it into a golden vessel, and gave him the vessel of gold, accounting it the part of a truly noble and generous spirit to take in good part small presents offered with a hearty affection. Oh, how much more will God the Father kindly accept of Jesus Christ in his mediatory office: ver. 7, ' Thus saith the Lord, the Redeemer of Israel, and his Holy One, to him whom man despiseth, to him whom the nation abhorreth, to a servant of rulers, Kings shall see and arise, princes also shall worship, because of the Lord that is faithful, and the Holy One of Israel, and he shall choose thee.'[1] God the Father, comforting of Christ, tells him that though he were contemptible to many, yea, to the nation of the Jews, and used basely, like a servant, by their princes, Herod, Annas, Caiaphas, and Pontius Pilate, yet other kings and princes should see his dignity and glory, and submit to him, and honour him as the Saviour and Redeemer of the world. God the Father chose Jesus Christ to be his servant, and to be a mediator for his elect; he designed him to that office of being a Saviour, both to the Jew and Gentile, and accordingly he accepted of him, ' Thus saith the Lord, In an acceptable time have I heard thee, and in a day of salvation have I helped thee; and I will preserve thee, and give thee for a covenant of the people, to establish the earth, to cause to inherit the desolate heritage.' Here you see that God the Father still goes on to speak more and more comfortably and encouragingly to Jesus Christ; for he tells him that he will be at hand to hear, and help, and assist him; and he tells him that he will preserve him, both in his person, and in the execution of his office; and he tells him that he will accept of his person, and of his services, and of his suits and intercession for himself and his people. So Mat. iii. 17, ' And, lo, a

---

[1] Jerome saith that the Jews cursed Christ in their synagogues three times a day. They so greatly abhorred the name *Jesus* that they would not pronounce it; but if they did unawares happen to pronounce it, then they would punish themselves with a blow on their faces, &c.

voice from heaven, saying, This is my beloved Son, in whom I am well pleased.' The voice from heaven was doubtless the voice of his Father, in that he saith, ' This is my beloved Son,' my natural Son, by eternal and incomprehensible generation, and therefore dearest to me, and most acceptable with me; my judgment is satisfied in him, my love is settled upon him, and I have an inestimable value for him; and therefore I cannot but declare my approbation and acceptation both of him and his work. I am well pleased in him, I am infinitely pleased in him, I am only pleased in him, I am at all times pleased in him, I am for ever pleased in him; I am so well pleased in him, that, for his sake, I am fully appeased with all them whom ' I have given him, and who come unto him,' John vi. 37-40.[1] But,

Seventhly, God the Father promiseth highly to exalt Jesus Christ, and nobly to reward him, and everlastingly to glorify him. ' And nations that knew not thee shall run unto thee, because of the Lord thy God, and for the Holy One of Israel; for he hath glorified thee,' Isa. xlix. 4-6, and xl. 10. These are the words of God the Father to his Son, promising of him to set such a crown of glory upon his head as should make the nations of the world run unto him. God the Father made Christ glorious in his birth, by the angels' doxology, ' Glory be to God on high;' in his baptism, by his speaking of him from heaven, ' as his beloved Son;' in his transfiguration on the mount, in his resurrection, and in his ascension into heaven.[2] So Isa. liii. 12, ' Therefore will I divide him a portion with the great, and he shall divide the spoil with the strong, because he hath poured out his soul unto death; and he was numbered with the transgressors, and he bare the sin of many, and made intercession for the transgressors.' The meaning is this: I will impart, saith God the Father, to my Son, such honour, glory, renown, and riches, after his sufferings, as conquerors use to have; and he shall have them as a glorious reward of all his conflicts with my wrath, with temptations, with persecutions, with reproach, with contempt, with death, yea, and with hell itself. The words are a plain allusion to conquerors in war, who are commonly exalted and greatly rewarded by their princes for venturing of their lives, and obtaining of conquests, as all histories will tell you. And, indeed, should not God the Father reward Jesus Christ for all his hard services, and his matchless sufferings, he would express less kindness to him than he has done to heathen princes; for he gave Egypt to Nebuchadnezzar as his hire, for his service at Tyre; and to Cyrus he gave hidden treasure, Ezek. xxix. 18, 19; Isa. xlv. 1-3. But, alas, what were their services to Christ's services, or their sufferings to Christ's sufferings? I have read of Cyrus, how that in a great expedition against his enemies, the better to encourage his soldiers to fight, in an oration that he made at the head of his army, he promised, upon the victory, to make every foot soldier a horseman, and every horseman a commander, and that no officer that did vali-

---

[1] This Jerome applies to the time of Christ's hanging on the cross. He cried out, ' My God, my God, why hast thou forsaken me?' for God made it appear that he heard him, and forsook him not, in that he raised him from the dead, &c. See Heb. v. 7.
[2] Luke ii. 13, 14; Mat. iii. 17, and xvii. 1-5; Rom. i. 4; Acts i. 9-11.

antly should be unrewarded. And will God the Father let the Son of his dearest love, who has fought against all infernal powers, and conquered them, go without his reward? Surely no! Col. ii. 14, 15. So in Ps. ii. 7, ' I will declare the decree; the Lord hath said unto me, Thou art my Son, this day have I begotten thee.' David was God's son by adoption and acceptation; but Christ was his Son, Ps. lxxxix. 26, 27, Prov. viii., and Heb. i. 5, (1.) By eternal generation; (2.) By hypostatical union; and so God had one only Son, as Abraham had one only Isaac, though otherwise he was the father of many nations. Some by ' this day' do understand the day of eternity, where there is no time past nor to come, no beginning nor ending, but always one present day. Others by ' this day' do understand it of the day of Christ's incarnation, and coming into the world. Some again do understand it of the whole time of his manifestation in the world, when he was sent forth as a prophet to teach them, and was declared evidently to be the Son of God, both by his miracles and ministry, John i. 14, and by that voice that was heard from heaven, ' This is my beloved Son, in whom I am well pleased.' Others do understand it of the day of Christ's resurrection, and with them I close, for this seems to be chiefly intended; partly because it seems to be spoken of some solemn time of Christ's manifestation to be the Son of God, and ' he was declared to be the Son of God with power, according to the Spirit of holiness, by the resurrection from the dead,' Rom. i. 4 ; that is, by the power and force of the Deity, sanctifying and quickening the flesh, he was raised from the dead, and so declared mightily to be the Son of God; but mainly because the apostle doth clearly affirm that this was in Christ's resurrection : ' He hath raised up Jesus again, as it is also written in the second psalm, Thou art my Son, this day have I begotten thee,' Acts xiii. 33. In the day of Christ's resurrection he seems to tell all the world, that though from the beginning he had been hid in the bosom of his Father, John i. 18, and that though in the law he had been but darkly shadowed out; yet in the day of his resurrection they might plainly see that he had fully satisfied divine justice, finished his sufferings, and completed the redemption of his elect; and that accordingly his Father had arrayed him with that glory that was suitable to him. Before the resurrection the godhead was veiled under the infirmity of the flesh; but in the resurrection, and after the resurrection, the godhead did sparkle and shine forth very gloriously and wonderfully, 2 Cor. xiii. 4. Lest the human nature of Christ, upon its assumption, should shrink at the approach of sufferings, God the Father engages himself to give Jesus Christ a full and ample reward, ' and to exalt him far above all principality and power, and to put all things under his feet, and to make him head over all things to the church:' and to ' give him a name above every name; that at the name of Jesus every knee should bow ;' and all because, to give satisfaction to his Father, he ' made himself of no reputation, and became obedient unto death, even the death of the cross ;' that is, to his dying day, Eph. i. 21, 22 ; Phil. ii. 9.[1] He went through many a little death, all his life long, and at length underwent that cursed and pain-

---

[1] Name is put for person, and bowing of the knee, a bodily ceremony, to express inward subjection.—*Estius, Beza.*

ful death of the cross; upon which account the Father rewards him highly by exalting him to singular glory and transcendent honour. Look, that as the assumption of the human nature is the highest instance of free mercy, so is the rewarding thereof in its state of exaltation the highest instance of remunerative justice. Oh, how highly is the human nature of Christ honoured by being exalted to a personal union with the Godhead! Though vain men may dishonour Christ, yet the Father hath conferred honour upon him as mediator, that it may be a testimony to us that he is infinitely pleased with the redemption of lost man. Although Christ be, in himself, God all-sufficient, 'God blessed for ever,' and so is not capable of any access of glory; yet it pleased him to condescend so far as to obscure his own glory under the veil of his flesh, and state of humiliation, till he had perfected the work of redemption; and to account of his office of mediator, and the dignity accompanying it, as great honour conferred upon him by the Father, John viii. 54: and it is observable that Christ having finished our redemption on earth, he petitions his Father to advance him to the possession of that glory that he enjoyed from all eternity; 'And now, O Father, glorify thou me with thine own self; with the glory which I had with thee before the world was,' John xvii. 5. Now for the clearing up of this text we are to consider, that as Christ was from all eternity the glorious God, the God of glory; so we are not to conceive of any real change in this glory of his godhead; as if by his estate of humiliation he had suffered any diminution, or by his state of exaltation any real accession were made to his glory as God. But the meaning is this, that Christ having, according to the paction passed betwixt the Father and him, obscured the glory of his godhead for a time, under the veil of the form of a servant, and our sinless infirmities, doth now expect, according to the tenor of the same paction, that, after he hath done his work as mediator, he be highly exalted and glorified in his whole person; that his human nature be exalted to what glory finite nature is capable of, and that the glory of his godhead might shine in the person of Christ, God-man, and in the man Christ Jesus.[1] Thus you see the promises, the encouragements, and rewards that God the Father sets before Jesus Christ. And let thus much suffice concerning the articles of the covenant on God's part.

In the last place, Let us seriously consider of *the articles of the covenant on Christ's part; and let us weigh well the promises that Jesus Christ has made to the Father for the bringing about the great work of our redemption*, that so we may see what infinite cause we have to love the Son as we love the Father, and to honour the Son as we honour the Father, and to trust in the Son as we trust in the Father, and to glorify the Son as we glorify the Father, &c. Now there are six observable things on Christ's part, on Christ's side, that we are to take special notice of, &c.

[1.] First, Christ having consented and agreed with the Father about our redemption, accordingly *he applies himself to the discharge*

---

[1] Jesus Christ is true God, and was infinitely glorious from all eternity, for he had glory with his Father before the world was; and therefore he was no upstart God, and of a later standing, as the Arians and Mohammedans make of him.

of that great and glorious work by taking a body, by assuming our nature: Heb. ii. 14, 'Forasmuch then as the children are partakers of flesh and blood, he also himself likewise took part of the same.' He who was equal with God did so far abase himself as to take on him the nature of man, and subjected himself to all manner of human frailties, so far as they are freed from sin, even such as accompany flesh and blood; and this is one of the wonders of mercy and love, that Christ our head should stoop so low, who was himself full of glory, as to take part of flesh and blood, that he might suffer for flesh and blood: ver. 16, 'For verily he took not on him the nature of angels; but he took on him the seed of Abraham.' Christ assumed the common nature of man, and not of any particular person. The apostle doth here purposely use this word 'seed,' to shew that Christ came out of the loins of man, as Jacob's children and their children are said to come out of his loins, Gen. xlvi. 26, and as all the Jews are said to come out of the loins of Abraham, Exod. i. 5; Heb. vii. 5; and as Solomon is said to come out of the loins of David, 1 Kings viii. 19. In a man's loins his seed is, and it is a part of his substance Thus it sheweth that Christ's human nature was of the very substance of man, and that Christ was the very same that was promised to be the Redeemer of man; for of old he was foretold under this word *seed*, as 'the seed of the woman,' 'the seed of Abraham,' 'the seed of Isaac,' 'the seed of David.'[1] This word, 'he took on him,' as it setteth out the human nature of Christ, so it gives us a hint of his divine nature; for it presupposeth that Christ was before he took on him the seed of Abraham. He that taketh anything on him must needs be before he do so. Is it possible for him that is not, to take anything on him? Now Christ, in regard of his human nature, was not before he assumed that nature; therefore that former being must needs be in regard of his divine nature. In that respect he ever was even the eternal God. Being God, he took on him a human nature. Christ's eternal deity shines in this 16th verse, and so does his true humanity; in that he took upon him the seed of man, it is most evident that he was a true man. Seed is the matter of man's nature, and the very substance thereof. The seed of man is the root, out of which Christ assumed his human nature, Isa. xi. 1. The human nature was not created of nothing, nor was it brought from heaven, but assumed out of the seed of man, Luke i. 35. The human nature of Christ never had a subsistence in itself. At or in the very first framing or making it, it was united to the divine nature; and at or in the first uniting it, it was framed or made. Philosophers say of the uniting of the soul to the body, in creating it it is infused, and in infusing it it is created, *Creando infunditur, et infundendo creatur*. Much more is this true, concerning the human nature of Christ, united to his divine. Fitly therefore is it here said, that he 'took on him the seed of Abraham.' So John i. 14, 'The Word was made flesh, and dwelt among us.' The evangelist having proved the divinity of Jesus Christ, comes now to speak of his humanity, incarnation, and manifestation in the flesh, whereby he became God and man in one person. 'Flesh' here signifies the whole man in Scrip-

[1] Gen. iii. 15; Rom. ix. 7; Heb. xi. 18; John viii. 58.

ture. Ye all know that man consisteth of two parts, which are sometimes called flesh and spirit, and sometimes called soul and body. Now by a synecdoche, either of these parts may be put for the whole: and so sometimes the soul is put for the whole man, and sometimes the body is put for the whole man, as you may see by comparing the scriptures in the margin together.[1] Christ did assume the whole man, he did assume the soul as well as the body, and both under the term *flesh*. And indeed, unless he had assumed the whole man, the whole man could not have been saved. If Christ had not taken the whole man, he could not have saved the whole man. Christ took the nature of man that he might be a fit mediator. If he had not been man, he could not have died; and if he had not been God, he could not have satisfied. So great was the difficulty of restoring the image of God in lost man, and of restoring him to God's favour, and the dignity of sonship, that no less could do it than the natural Son of God his becoming the Son of man, to suffer in our nature; and so great was the Father's love and the Son's love to fallen man, as to lay a foundation of reconciliation betwixt God and man in the personal union of the divine and human nature of Christ. So much is imported in those words, ' the Word was made flesh.'[2] The person of the godhead that was incarnate was neither the Father nor the Holy Ghost, but the Son, the second person, for ' the *Word* was made flesh.' There being a real distinction of the persons, that one of them is not another; and each of them having their proper manner of subsistence, the one of them might be incarnate, and not the other; and it is the Godhead, not simply considered, but the person of the Son subsisting in that Godhead, that was incarnate. And it was very convenient that the second or middle person, in order of subsistence of the blessed Trinity, should be the reconciler of God and man; and that ' he, by whom all things were made,' Col. i. 16, 17, should be the restorer and maker of the new world; and that he who was ' the express image of his Father,' Heb. i. 2, 3, should be the repairer of the image of God in us. Oh the admirable love and wisdom of God that shines in this, that the second person in the Trinity is set on work to procure our redemption! Though reason could never have found out such a way, yet when God hath revealed it, reason, though but shallow, can see a fitness in it; because there being a necessity that the Saviour of man should be man, and an impossibility that any but God should save him, and one person in the Trinity being to be incarnate, it agrees to reason that the first person in the Trinity should not be the mediator; for who should send him? he is of none, and therefore could not be sent. There must be one sent to reconcile the enmity, and another to give gifts to friends; two proceeding persons, the Son from the Father, and the Holy Ghost from the Father and the Son. Accordingly the second person, which is the Son, he is sent upon the first errand, to reconcile man to God; and the third person, the Holy Ghost, he is sent to give gifts to men so reconciled; so as to reason it

---

[1] Acts xxvii. 37; Gen. xlvi. 27; Rom. xii. 1, and iii. 20.

[2] Christ put himself into a lousy, leprous suit of ours, to expiate our pride and robbery in reaching after the Deity, and to heal us of our spiritual leprosy; for if he had not assumed our flesh he had not saved us.—[*Gregory*] *Nazianzen.*

is suitable, and a very great congruity, that God, having made all
things by his Son, should now repair all things by his Son ; that
he that was the middle person in the Trinity should become the
mediator between God and man ; that he that was 'the express image
of the Father's person' should restore the image of God, defaced
in man by his sins. Ah, Christians, how well does it become you
to lose yourselves in the admiration of the wisdom of God in the contrivance of the work of our redemption ! For the Son of God to take
on him the nature of man, with all the essential properties thereof,
and all the sinless infirmities and frailties thereof, is a wonder that
may well take up our thoughts to all eternity. And Christ took the
infirmities of our nature as well as the nature itself. To shew the truth
of his humanity he had a nature that could hunger and thirst even as
ours do, and to sanctify them to us ; and that so he might sympathise
with us as 'a merciful and faithful high priest,' Heb. ii. 16–18, and
iv. 15, 16 ; and that we might confide the more in him, and. have
access to him with boldness. By reason of the personal union of the
two natures in Christ, he is a fit mediator betwixt God and man. His
sufferings are of infinite value, being the sufferings of one who is God,
Acts xx. 28, and who is mighty to carry on the work of redemption,
and to apply his own purchase, and repair all our losses, Isa. lxiii. 1 ;
Heb. vii. 25. Oh, what an honour has Jesus Christ put upon fallen
man by taking the nature of man on him ! What is so near and dear
to us as our own nature ? and lo, our nature is highly preferred
by Jesus Christ to a union in the Godhead. Christ now sits in heaven
with our nature, and the same flesh that we have upon us, only glorified, Acts i. 9–11. It is that which all the world cannot give a
sufficient reason, why the same word in the Hebrew, *Basher*, should
signify both 'flesh' and 'good tidings.' Divinity will give you a
reason, though grammar cannot. Christ's taking of flesh upon him
was good tidings to all the whole world, therefore no wonder if one
word signify both. Abundance of comfort may be taken from hence
to poor souls, when they think God hath forgotten them, to consider, is
it likely that Christ, who is man, should forget man, now he is at
the right hand of the Father, clothed in that nature that we have ?
When we are troubled to think it is impossible God and man should
ever be reconciled, let us consider that God and man did meet in
Christ, therefore it is possible we may meet. What hath been may be
again. The two natures met in Christ, therefore God may be reconciled to man ; yea, they therefore met, that God might be reconciled to
man. He was made Emmanuel, 'God with us,' that he might bring
God and us together. When a man is troubled to think of the
corruptions of his nature, that is so full of defilements, that it cannot
be sanctified perfectly, let him withal think that his nature is capable
of sanctification to the full. Christ received human nature which was
not polluted, his nature is the same, therefore that nature is capable of
sanctification to the uttermost. O sirs ! if Christ, the second person in
the Trinity, did put on man, how careful should men be to put on
Christ ! 'Put you on the Lord Jesus,' saith the apostle, Rom. xiii. 14.
If Christ assumed our human nature, how should we wrestle with God
to be made partakers of the divine nature : 2 Pet. i. 4, 'Whereby are

given unto us exceeding great and precious promises; that by these we may be made partakers of the divine nature.' If Christ became thus one flesh with us, how zealous should we be to become one spirit with Christ, 1 Cor. vi. 17. Even as man and wife is one flesh, so ' he that is joined to the Lord is one spirit.' Was the Word made flesh? did Christ take our nature? yea, did he take our nature at the worst, after the fall? What high cause have we to bless his name for ever for this condescension of his! Should all the princes of the world have come from their thrones, and have gone a-begging from door to door, it would not amount to so much as for Christ to become man for our sakes. Christ took our nature, not in the integrity of it, as in Adam before his fall, but in the infirmities of it, which came to it by the fall. What amazing love was this! For Christ to have taken our nature as it was in Adam, while he stood clothed in his integrity, and stood right in the sight of God, had not been so much as when Adam was fallen and proclaimed traitor; as Bernard saith, *Quo pro me vilior, eò mihi carior, Domine*, Lord, thou shalt be so much the more dear to me, by how much the more thou hast been vile for me. Here is condescension indeed, that Christ should stoop so low to take flesh, and flesh with infirmities. But,

[2.] Secondly, Jesus Christ *promiseth to God the Father that he will freely, readily, and cheerfully accept, undertake, and faithfully discharge his mediatory office, to which he was designed by him, in order to the redemption and salvation of all his chosen ones.* Consult the scriptures in the margin,[1] they having been formerly opened, and in them you will find that Christ did not take the office of mediatorship upon himself, but first the Father calls him to it, and then the Son accepts it: ' Christ glorified not himself, to be made a high-priest; but he that said unto him, Thou art my Son, this day have I begotten thee,' Heb. x. 12, 14, he called him, and then the Son answered him, ' Lo, I come.' God the Father promiseth that upon the payment of such a price by his Son, such and such souls should be ransomed and set free from the curse, from wrath, from hell, &c. Jesus Christ readily consents to the price, and pays it down upon the nail at once, and so makes good his mediatory office. It pleased the glorious Son of God, in obedience to the Father, to humble himself and obscure the glory of his godhead, that he might be like his brethren, and a fit mediator for sympathy and suffering, and that he might engage his life and glory for the redeeming of the elect, and lay by his robes of majesty, and not be reassumed till he gave a good account of that work, till he was able to say, ' I have finished the work that thou gavest me to do.' Christ very freely and cheerfully undertakes to do and suffer whatever was the will of his Father that he should do or suffer, for the bringing about the redemption of mankind. Christ willingly undertakes to be his Father's servant in this great work, and accordingly he looks upon his Father as his Lord, ' Thou art my Lord,' Isa. l. 5–7; Ps. xvi. 2—that is, thou art he to whom I have engaged myself that I will satisfy all thy demands, I will fulfil thy royal law, I will bear the curse, I will satisfy thy justice, I will

---

[1] Compare Ps. xl. 6–11 with Heb. x. 5–11, and Isa. lxi. 1–3; Luke iv. 18–20; Acts xiii. 23, and vii. 22.

humble myself to the death of the cross, Phil. li. 8, I will 'tread the wine-press of my Father's wrath,' Isa. lxiii. 3, I will fully discharge all the bonds, bills, and obligations that lie in open court against any of those whom by compact thou hast given me, Col. ii. 13–15, let their debts be never so many or never so great, or of never so long continuance, I will pay them all. There is no work so high, nor no work so hard, nor no work so hot, nor no work so bloody, nor no work so low, in which I am not ready to engage upon the account of my chosen: 'Lo, I come, I delight to do thy will; yea, thy law is in my heart.' Christ freely submits, not only to the duty of the law, but also to the penalty of the law,—not only to do what the law enjoins, but also to suffer what the law threatens; the former he makes good by his active obedience, and the latter by his passive obedience, Gal. iv. 4, 5. This was the way wherein the Father, by an eternal agreement with his Son, would have the salvation of lost sinners brought about, and accordingly Jesus Christ very readily complies with his Father's will and way, Titus i. 2. Christ, as mediator, had a command from his Father to die, which command he readily closes with: John x. 11, 'I am the good shepherd: the good shepherd layeth down his life for the sheep;' ver. 15, 'I lay down my life for the sheep;' ver. 17, 'I lay down my life, that I might take it again;' ver. 18, 'No man taketh it from me, but I lay it down of myself; this commandment have I received of my Father.' Christ was content to be a servant by paction, that so his sufferings might be accepted for his people; and certainly whatever God the Father put Jesus Christ upon in his whole mediatory work, that Jesus Christ did freely, fully, and heartily comply with: 'Lo, I come; and I have finished the work that thou gavest me to do,' John xvii. 4. And had not Christ been free and voluntary in his active and passive obedience, his active and passive obedience would never have been acceptable, satisfactory, or meritorious. To go further to prove it, would be to light a candle to see the sun at noon. But,

[3.] Thirdly, Jesus Christ *promises and engages himself that he will confide, depend, rely, and trust upon his Father for help and for assistance to go through with his work a-notwithstanding all the wrath and rage, all the malice and oppositions, that he should meet with from men and devils:* Heb. ii. 13, 'And again, I will put my trust in him.' Christ's confidence in his Father was one great encouragement to him to hold out in the execution of his office; and his confidence in God speaks him out to be a true man, in that, as other men, he stood in need of God's aid and assistance; and thereupon, as others of the sons of men, his brethren, he puts his trust in God. The Greek phrase used by the apostle carrieth emphasis; it implieth trust on a good persuasion that he shall not be disappointed. It is translated 'confidence,' Phil. i. 6; word for word it may be here thus translated, 'I will be confident in him.'[1] The relative 'him' hath apparent reference to God, so as Christ himself, being man, rested on God to be supported in his works, and to be carried through all his undertakings, till the top-stone was laid, and the work of redemption accomplished. Christ had many great and potent enemies, and was brought to very

---

[1] ἔσομαι πεποιθὼς ἐπ' αὐτῷ, Ps. xviii. 2; Isa. viii. 18.

great straits; yea, he and his were 'for signs and wonders in Israel;' yet he fainted not, but put his trust in the Lord; yea, his greatest enemies gave him this testimony, that 'he trusted in God;' and though they spoke it in scorn and derision, yet it was a real truth, Ps. xviii. 3-5; Isa. viii. 18; Mat. xxvii. 43. Christ's confidence in his Father was further manifested by the many prayers which, time after time, he made to his Father, Heb. v. 7. Another proof of Christ's confidence in God's assistance, even in his greatest plunges and his sharpest sufferings, the prophet Isaiah will furnish us with: 'The Lord God hath opened mine ear,' saith the prophet, 'and I was not rebellious, neither turned away back. I gave my back to the smiters, and my cheeks to them that plucked off the hair: I hid not my face from shame and spitting. For the Lord God will help me; therefore shall I not be confounded: therefore have I set my face like a flint, and I know that I shall not be ashamed. He is near that justifieth me; who will contend with me? let us stand together; who is mine adversary? let him come near to me. Behold, the Lord God will help me; who is he that shall condemn me? lo, they all shall wax old as a garment; the moth shall eat them up,' Isa. l. 5-9. Christ, as mediator, trusted God the Father to carry him through all difficulties and oppositions, till he had completed the great work of his mediation. Christ strengthens and encourages himself in the execution of his office against all hardships and oppositions, from his confidence and assurance of God's aid and assistance; and by the same eye of faith, he looks upon all his opposites as worn out and weathered by him. Christ's faith, patience, and constancy gave him victory over all wrongs and injuries; so Isa. xlix. 5, 'My God shall be my strength.' Christ is very confident of his Father's assistance to carry him through that work that he had assigned him to. Christ, in the want of comfort, never wanted faith to hang upon God, and to call him his God: 'My God, my God, why hast thou forsaken me?' Mat. xxvii. 46. Christ was never forsaken in regard of the hypostatical union; the union was not dissolved, but the beams, the influence, was restrained.[1] Nor in regard of his faith; for though now he was sweltering under the wrath of God, as our surety, and left in the hands of his enemies, and deserted by his disciples and dearest friends, and under the loss of the comforting and solacing presence of his Father, yet, in the midst of all, such was the strength and power of his faith, that he could say, 'My God, my God.' Christ, before the world began, having promised and engaged to the Father that, in the fulness of time, he would come into the world, assume our nature, be made under the law, tread the winepress of the Father's wrath, bear the curse, and give satisfaction to his justice;[2] now upon the credit of this promise, upon this undertaking of Christ, God the Father takes up the patriarchs and all the old testament believers to glory. God the Father, resting upon the promise and engagement of his Son, admits many thousands into those mansions above, before Christ took flesh upon him, John xiv. 2, 3.

[1] As man he cries out, 'My God, my God,' &c., when as God he promiseth paradise to the penitent thief.—*Hilary.*

[2] Titus i. 2; Gal. iv. 4; Isa. lxiii. 3; Gal. iii. 13; Rom. viii. 3, 4.

Now as the Father of old hath rested and relied on the promise and engagement of Christ, so Jesus Christ doth, to this very day, rest and stay himself upon the promise of his Father, that he shall, in due time, ' see all his seed,' Isa. liii. 10, and reap the full benefit of that full ransom that he has paid down upon the nail for all that have believed on him, that do believe on him, and that shall believe on him. Christ knew God's infinite love, his tender compassions, and his matchless bowels, to all those for whom he died; and he knew very well the covenant, the compact, the agreement that passed between the Father and himself; and so trusted the Father fully in the great business of their everlasting happiness and blessedness, relying upon the love and faithfulness of God, his love to the elect, and his faithfulness to keep covenant with him. As the elect are committed to Christ's charge, to give an account of them, so also is the Father engaged for their conversion, and for their preservation, being converted; as being not only his own, given to Christ out of his love to them, but as being engaged to Christ, that he shall not be frustrate of the reward of his sufferings, but have a seed to glorify him for ever, John vi. 37; Isa. liii. 11. Therefore doth Christ not only constantly preserve them by his Spirit, but doth leave also that burden on the Father: ' Father, keep those whom thou hast given me,' John xvii. 11. But,

[4.] Fourthly, Jesus Christ *promises and engages himself to his Father that he would bear all and suffer all that should be laid upon him, and that he would ransom poor sinners, and fully satisfy divine justice by his blood and death*, as you may see by comparing the scriptures in the margin together.[1] The work of redemption could never have been effected by ' silver or gold,' or by prayers or tears, or by the ' blood of bulls or goats,' but by the second Adam's obedience, even to the death of the cross. Remission of sin, the favour of God, the heavenly inheritance, could never have been obtained but by the precious blood of the Son of God. The innocent Lamb of God was slain in typical prefigurations from the beginning of the world, and slain in real performance in the fulness of time, or else fallen man had lain under guilt and wrath for ever. The heart of Jesus Christ was strongly set upon all those that his Father had given him, and he was fully resolved to secure them from hell and the curse, whatever it cost him; and seeing no price would satisfy his Father's justice below his blood, he lays down his life at his Father's feet, according to the covenant and agreement of old that had passed between his Father and himself. But,

[5.] Fifthly, *The Lord Jesus Christ was very free, ready, willing, and careful to make good all the articles of the covenant on his side, and to discharge all the works agreed on for the redemption and salvation of the elect:* John xvii. 4, ' I have finished the work that thou gavest me to do,' John xii. 49, 50, and xvii. 6. There was nothing committed to Christ by the Father to be done on earth, for the purchasing of our redemption, but he did finish it; so that the debt is paid, justice satisfied, and sin, Satan, and death spoiled of all their

---

[1] Isa. l. 5, 6; John x. 17, 18, and xv. 10; Luke xxiv. 46; Heb. x. 5-7, 10. I have opened these scriptures already.

hurting and destroying power, Col. ii. 14, 15, and Heb. ii. 14. By the covenant of redemption Christ was under an obligation to die, to satisfy to divine justice, to pay our debts, to bring in an everlasting righteousness, Dan. ix. 24, to purchase our pardon, and to obtain eternal redemption for us, Heb. ix. 12; all which he completed and finished before he ascended up to glory: and, without a peradventure, had not Jesus Christ kept touch with his Father, had not he made good the covenant, the compact, the agreement on his part, his Father would never have given him such a welcome to heaven as he did, nor he would never have admitted him to have ' sat down on the right hand of the Majesty on high,' as he did,[1] Acts i. 9–11. The right hand is a place of the greatest honour, dignity, and safety that any can be advanced to. But had not Jesus Christ ' first purged away our sins,' he had never ' sat down on the right hand of his Father.' Christ's advancement is properly of his human nature. That nature wherein Christ was crucified was exalted; for God, being the Most High, needs not be exalted; yet the human nature in this exaltation, is not singly and simply considered in itself, but as united to the deity; so that it is the person, consisting of two natures, even God-man, which is thus dignified, Mat. xxvi. 64; Acts vii. 56. For as the human nature of Christ is inferior to God, and is capable of advancement, so also is the person consisting of a divine and human nature. Christ, as the Son of God, the second person of the sacred Trinity, is, in regard of his deity, no whit inferior to his Father, but every way equal; yet he assumed our nature, and became a mediator betwixt God and man; he humbled himself, and made himself inferior to his Father; his Father therefore hath highly exalted him, and set him down on his right hand, Phil. ii. 8, 9; Eph. i. 20. If Christ had not expiated our sins, and completed the work of our redemption, he could never have sat down on the right hand of God: Heb. x. 12, ' But this man, after he had offered one sacrifice for sins, for ever sat down on the right hand of God.' This verse is added in opposition to the former, as is evident by the first particle, δέ. But in the former verse it was proved that the sacrifices which were offered under the law could not take away sins. This verse proveth that there is a sacrifice which hath done that that they could not do. The argument is taken from that priest's ceasing to offer any more sacrifices after he had offered one; whereby is implied that there needed no other, because that one had done it to the full. Sin was taken away by Christ's sacrifice, for thereby a ransom was paid, and satisfaction made to the justice of God for man's sin, and thereupon sin taken away. Now sin being taken away, Christ ' sits down on the right hand of his Father.' Look, as the humiliation of Christ was manifested in offering a sacrifice, so his exaltation, in sitting at God's right hand, was manifested after that he had offered that sacrifice. This phrase, ' set down,' is a note of dignity and authority; and this dignity and authority is amplified by the place where he is said to sit down—viz., on ' the right hand of God;' and this honour and dignity is much illustrated by the continuance thereof, which is without date, ' For ever sat down on the right hand of God.' It

---

[1] Heb. i. 3; Rom. viii. 34; Col. iii. 1; Heb. viii. 1, and x. 12; 1 Pet. iii. 22.

is an eclipse of the lustre of any glory to have a date and a period. The very thought that such a glory shall one day cease, will cast a damp upon the spirit of him that enjoys that glory. Christ's constant sitting at the right hand of his Father is a clear evidence that he has finished and completed the work of our redemption. Christ could never have gone to his Father, nor never have sat down at the right hand of his Father, if he had not first fulfilled all righteousness, and fully acquitted us of all our iniquities : John xvi. 10, ' Of righteousness, because I go to my Father.' The strength of the argument lies in this, Christ took upon him to be our surety, and he must acquit us of all our sins, and satisfy his Father's justice, before he can go to his Father, and be accepted of his Father, and sit down on the right hand of his Father. If God had not been fully satisfied, or if any part of righteousness had been to be fulfilled, Christ should have been still in the grave, and not gone to heaven ; his very going to his Father argues all is done, all is finished and completed. But,

[6.] Sixthly, *Christ having performed all the conditions of the covenant on his part, he now peremptorily insists upon it, that his Father should make good to him and his the conditions of the covenant on his part.* Christ having finished his work, looks for his reward : ' Father,' says he, ' I have glorified thee on earth, I have finished the work which thou gavest me to do. And now, O Father, glorify thou me with thine own self, with the glory which I had with thee before the world was,' John xvii. 4, 5. There was a most blessed transaction between God the Father and God the Son before the world began, for the everlasting good of the elect ; and upon that transaction depends all the good, and all the happiness, and all the salvation of God's chosen ; [1] and upon this ground pleads with his Father, that all his members may behold his glory : John xvii. 24, ' Father, I will that they also which thou hast given me be with me where I am, that they may behold my glory ;' ' Father, *I will,*' not only I pray, I beseech, but ' I will ;' I ask this as my right, by virtue of the covenant betwixt us ; I have done thus and thus, and I have suffered thus and thus, and therefore I cannot but peremptorily insist upon it, that those that I have undertaken for, ' be where I am, that they may behold my glory ;' for though glory be a gift to us, yet it is a debt due to Christ. It is a part of Christ's joy that we should be where he is. Christ will not be happy alone. As a tender father, he can enjoy nothing if his children may not have part with him. The greatest part of our happiness that we shall have in heaven lies in this, that then we shall be with Christ, and have immediate communion with him. O sirs ! the great end of our being in heaven is to behold and enjoy the glory of Christ. Christ is very desirous, and much taken up with his people's fellowship and company, so that before he removes his bodily presence from them, his heart is upon meeting and fellowship again, as here we see in his prayer before his departure ; and this he makes evident from day to day, in that until that time of meeting come, two or three are not gathered in his name but he is in the midst of them, Mat. xviii. 20, to eye their behaviour, to hear their suits, to guide their way, to pro-

---

[1] This transaction between the Father and the Son is worthy of our most deep, serious, and frequent meditation.

tect their persons, to cheer their spirits, and to delight in their presence. He delights to 'walk in the midst of the seven golden candlesticks,' Rev. ii. 1. The golden candlesticks are the churches, which are 'the light of the world,' Mat. v. 14, 16, and excel all other societies as much as gold doth other metals. And he desires to dwell in the low and little hill of Zion, Ps. lxviii. 16. Zion is his resting-place, his chosen place, his dwelling-place : Ps. cxxxii. 13, 'For the Lord hath chosen Zion, he hath desired it for his habitation;' ver. 14, 'This is my rest for ever : here will I dwell, for I have desired it.' Christ chose Zion for his love, and loves it for his choice ; and accordingly he delights to dwell there. The Lamb stands on mount Zion, Rev. xiv. 1. Christ is ready prest for action ; and in the midst of all antichrist's persecutions he hath always a watchful eye over mount Zion, and will be a sure life-guard to mount Zion, Isa. iv. 5, 6 ; he stands readily prepared to assist mount Zion, to fight for mount Zion, to communicate to mount Zion, and to be a refuge to mount Zion ; and no wonder, for he 'dwells in mount Zion,' Isa. viii. 18. Now if Christ take so much delight to have spiritual communion with his people in this world, no wonder that he can never rest satisfied till their gracious communion with him here issue in their perfect and glorious communion with him in heaven.[1] And certainly the glory and happiness of heaven to the elect will consist much in being in Christ's company, in whom they delight so much on earth. To follow the Lamb whithersoever he goes, to enjoy him fully, and to be always in his presence, is the heaven of heaven, the glory of glory ; it is the sparkling diamond in the ring of glory. The day is coming wherein believers shall be completely happy in a sight of Christ's glory, when he shall be conspicuously glorified and admired in all his saints, and glorified by them ; and when all veils being laid aside, and they fitted for a more full fruition, shall visibly and immediately behold and enjoy him ; therefore is their condition in heaven described, as consisting in this, that they 'may behold my glory which thou hast given me.' Thus I have glanced at Christ's solemn demand on earth for the full accomplishment of that blessed compact, covenant, agreement, and promises that were made to him when he undertook the office of a mediator ; and now in heaven he appears 'in the presence of God for us,' Heb. ix. 25, as a lawyer appears in open court for his client, opens the case, pleads the cause, and carries the day. The verb, ἐμφανισθῆναι, translated 'to appear,' signifieth conspicuously 'to manifest.' It is sometimes taken in a good sense, viz., to appear for one as a favourite before a prince, or as an advocate or an attorney before a judge, or as the high-priests appeared once a year in the holy of holies, to make atonement for the people, Exod. xxx. 10. Christ is the great favourite in the court of glory, and is always at God's right hand, ready on all occasions to present our petitions to his Father, to pacify his anger, and to obtain all noble and needful favours for us, Rom. viii. 34. And Christ is our great advocate to plead our cause effectually for us, 1 John ii. 1. Look, as in human courts there is the

---

[1] 2 Cor. vi. 16, 'I will dwell in them.' The words are very significant in the original, ἐνοικήσω ἐν αὐτοῖς, ·'I will in-dwell in them.' So the words are. There are two *ins* in the original, as if God could never have enough communion with them, 2 Thes. i. 10.

guilty, the accuser, the court, the judge, and the advocate ; so it is here. Heaven is the court, man is the guilty person, Satan is the accuser, God is the judge, and Christ is the advocate. Now look, as the advocate appeareth in the court before the judge to plead for the guilty against the accuser, so doth Christ appear before God in heaven, to answer all Satan's objections and accusations that he may make in the court of heaven against us. ' He ever lives to make intercession for us,' Heb. vii. 25. The verb, ἐντυγχάνειν, translated ' intercession,' is a compound, and signifies ' to call upon one ' It is a judicial word, and importeth a calling upon a judge to be heard in this or that, against another or for another ; so here Christ maketh intercession for them, Acts xxv. 24; Rom. xi. 2, and viii. 34. The metaphor is taken from attorneys or advocates who appear for men in courts of justice ; from counsellors, who plead their client's cause, answer the adversary, supplicate the judge, and procure sentence to pass on their client's side. This act of making intercession may also be taken from kings' favourites, who are much in the king's presence, and ever ready to make request for their friends. But remember, though this be thus attributed to Christ, yet we may not think that in heaven Christ prostrateth himself before him, or maketh actual prayers ; that was a part of his humiliation which he did in the days of his flesh ; but it implieth a presenting of himself a sacrifice, a surety, and one that hath made satisfaction for all our sins, together with manifesting of his will and desires, that such and such should partake of the virtue and benefit of his sacrifice, Heb. v. 7, so as Christ's intercession consisteth rather in the perpetual vigour of his sacrifice and continual application thereof, than in any actual supplication. The intendment of this phrase applied to Christ, ' to make intercession,' is to shew that Christ, being God's favourite, and our advocate, continually appeareth before God, to make application of that sacrifice which once he offered up for our sins. Christ appears in the presence of God for us ; (1.) To present unto his Father himself, who is the price of our redemption ; (2.) To make application of his sacrifice to his church time after time, according to the need of the several members thereof ; (3.) To make our persons, prayers, services, and all good things acceptable to God. But,

[7.] Seventhly and lastly, *The whole compact and agreement between God the Father and our Lord Jesus Christ, about the redemption of poor sinners' souls, was really and solemnly transacted in open court; or, as I may say, in the high court of justice above, in the presence of the great public notary of heaven—viz., the Holy Ghost;* who being a third person of the glorious Trinity, of the same divine essence, and of equal power and glory, makes up a third legal witness with the Father and the Son. They being, after the manner of kings,[1] their own witnesses also: 1 John v. 7, ' For there be three that bear record in heaven, the Father, the Word, and the Holy Ghost, and these three are one.' Three, (1.) In the true and real distinction of their per-

---

[1] So the king writes, *Teste meipso.* This, 1 John v. 7, is a very clear proof and testimony of the Trinity of persons; in the unity of the divine essence ; they are all one in essence and will. As if three lamps were lighted in one chamber, albeit the lamps be divers, yet the lights cannot be severed ; so in the Godhead, as there is a distinction of persons, so a simplicity of nature.

sons; (2.) In their inward properties, as to beget, to be begotten, and to proceed; (3.) In their several offices one to another, as to send and to be sent: 'And these three are one,' one in nature and essence, one in power and will, one in the act of producing all such actions as, without themselves, any of them is said to act; and one in their testimony concerning the covenant of redemption that was agreed on between the Father and the Son Consent of all parties, the allowance of the judge, and public record, is as much as can be desired to make all public contracts authentic in courts of justice; and what can we desire more, to settle, satisfy, and assure our own souls that all the articles of the covenant of redemption shall, on all hands, be certainly made good, than this, that these three heavenly witnesses, God the Father, God the Son, and God the Holy Ghost, do all agree to the articles of the covenant, and are all witnesses to the same covenant? Thus you see that there was a covenant of redemption made with Christ; upon the terms whereof he is constituted to be a Redeemer; ' to say to the prisoners, go forth, to bring deliverance to the captives, and to proclaim the year of release (or jubilee) the acceptable year of the Lord,' as it is, Isa. lxi. 1, 2. I have been the longer in opening the covenant of redemption, partly because of its grand importance to all our souls, and partly because others have spoken so little to it, to the best of my observation, and partly because I have never before handled this subject, either in the pulpit or the press, &c.

Now from the serious consideration of this compact, covenant, and agreement, that was solemnly made between God and Christ, touching the whole business of man's salvation or redemption, I may form up this tenth plea as to the ten scriptures that are in the margin,[1] that refer to the great day of account, or to a man's particular day of account. *O blessed God! I have read over the articles of the covenant of redemption that were agreed on between thyself and thy dearest Son; and I find by those articles that dear Jesus has died, and satisfied thy justice, and pacified thy wrath, and bore the curse, and purchased my pardon, and procured thy everlasting favour: and I find by the same articles that whatever Jesus Christ acted or suffered, he did act or suffer as my surety, and in my stead and room.* O Lord! when I look upon my manifold weaknesses and imperfections, though under a covenant of grace, yet I am many times not only grieved, but also stumbled and staggered; but when I look up to the covenant of redemption, I am cheered, raised, and quieted; for I am abundantly satisfied that both thyself and thy dear Son are infinitely ready, able, willing, and faithful to perform whatever in that covenant is comprised, Isa. xxxviii. 16, 17; by these things men live, and in these is the life of my spirit. Men may fail, and friends may fail, and relations may fail, and trade may fail, and natural strength may fail, and my heart may fail, but the covenant of redemption can never fail, nor the federates, who are mutually engaged in that covenant, can never fail, Ps. lxxiii. 24, 25; and therefore I am safe and happy for ever. What though my sins have been great and heinous, yet they are not greater than Christ's satisfaction; he did bear the curse

---

[1] Eccles. xi. 9, and xii. 14; Mat. xii. 14, and xviii. 23; Luke xvi. 2; Rom. xiv. 10; 2 Cor. v. 10; Heb. ix. 27, and xiii. 17; 1 Pet. iv. 5; Isa. liii. 6; Rom. v. 6, 8; Gal. ii. 20.

for great sins as well as small, for sins against the gospel as well as for sins against the law, for omissions as well as for commissions. Assuredly the covenant of redemption is a mighty thing, and there are no mighty sins that can stand before that covenant. If we look upon Manasseh, in those black and ugly colours that the Holy Ghost paints him out in, we must needs conclude that he was a mighty sinner, a monstrous sinner, 1 Kings xxi. 1–16; and yet his mighty sins, his monstrous sins, could not stand before the covenant of redemption. The greatest sins are finite, but the merit of Christ's redemption is infinite. All the Egyptians were drowned in the Red Sea. There remained not so much as one of them; there was not one of them left alive to carry the news; the high and the low, the great and the small, the rich and the poor, the honourable and the base, were all drowned, Exod. xiv. 28; Ps. cvi. 11. The red sea of Christ's blood drowns all our sins, whether they are great or small, high or low, &c., ' Though my sins be as scarlet, my Redeemer will make them as white as snow; though they be as red as crimson, they shall be as wool,' Isa. i. 18. There is not one of my sins for which Jesus Christ hath not suffered and satisfied, Eph. i. 7; Col. i. 14; nor there is not one of my sins for which Jesus Christ hath not purchased a pardon, and for which he hath not made my peace. Though my sins are innumerable, though they are more than the hairs of my head, Ps. xl. 12, or the sands on the sea-shore, yet they are not to be named in the day wherein the merits of Christ, the satisfaction of Christ, and the covenant of redemption, is mentioned and pleaded. Be my sins ever so many; yea, though they might fill a roll that might reach from east to west, from north to south, from earth to heaven, yet they could but bring me under the curse. Now Christ my surety, that he might redeem me from the curse, hath taken upon him the whole curse, Gal. iii. 13. I know there is no summing up of my debts, but Christ has paid them all. Woe had been to me for ever, had Christ left but one penny upon the score for me to pay. As I have multiplied my sins, so he has multiplied his pardons, Isa. lv. 7. Christ has cancelled all bonds, and therefore it is but justice in God to give me a full acquittance, and to throw down all bonds as cancelled, saying, ' Deliver him, I have found a ransom,' Col. ii. 13–15; Job xxxiii. 24. O God, though my sins are very many, and very great, yet if thou dost not pardon them, the innocent blood of thy dearest Son will lie upon thee, and cry out against thee; for he therefore died, that my sins might be pardoned; so that now, in honour and justice, thou art obliged to ' pardon all my transgressions, and remember mine iniquities no more,' Isa. xliii. 25; Dan. ix. 24. Now this is my plea, O holy God, which I make to all those scriptures that respect my last account, and by this plea I shall stand. Well, saith God the Father, I accept of this plea, I am pleased with this plea, thy sins shall not be mentioned, Ezek. xviii. 22; ' Enter thou into the joy of thy Lord.'

I shall now make a little improvement of what has been said as to the covenant of redemption, and so draw to a conclusion.

First, [1.] This covenant of redemption, as we have opened it, looks sadly and sourly upon those that *make so great a noise about the doctrine of universal redemption.* The covenant of redemption extends itself, not to every man in the world, but only to those that are ' given by God the Father to Jesus Christ.'[1] [2.] It looks sadly and sourly upon those that *make so great a noise about God's choosing or electing of men, upon the account of God's foreseeing their faith, good works, obedience, holiness, when our election is merely of grace and favour, and flows only from* 'the good will of him that dwelt in the bush;' and faith, good works, holiness, sanctification, are the fruits and effects of election, as the Scripture everywhere tells us,[2] and as has been made evident in my opening the gracious terms of the covenant of redemption. But because I have, in another place, treated of these things more largely, a touch here may suffice. But,

(2.) Secondly, *How should this covenant of redemption spirit animate and encourage all the redeemed of God, to do anything for Christ, to suffer anything for Christ, to venture anything for Christ, to part with anything for Christ, to give up anything to Christ, who, according to the covenant of redemption, hath done and suffered such great and grievous things, that he might bring us to glory, that are above all apprehensions, and beyond all expressions,* Mark viii. 34, 35, 38; Heb. x. 34, and xi. Who can tell me what is fully wrapped up in that one expression—viz., ' That he poured out his soul unto death,' Heb. ii. 10, 11. Let us not shrink, nor faint, nor grow weary under our greatest sufferings for Christ. When sufferings multiply, when they are sharp, when they are more bitter than gall or wormwood, yea, more bitter than death itself, then remember the covenant of redemption, and how punctually Christ made good all the articles of it on his side, and then faint and give out if you can. Well may I be afraid, but I do not therefore despair, for I think upon and remember the wounds of the Lord, saith one, [Austin.] *Nolo vivere sine vulnere, cum te video vulneratum ;* O my God, as long as I see thy wounds, I will never live without wound, saith another, [Bonaventura.] *Crux Christi clavis paradisi ;* The cross of Christ is the golden key that opens paradise to us, saith one, [Damascene.] I had rather, with the martyrs and confessors, have my Saviour's cross, than, with their persecutors, the world's crown. The harder we are put to it, the greater shall be our reward in heaven, saith another, [Tertullian.] Gordius the martyr hit the nail, when he said, it is to my loss if you abate me anything in my sufferings, [Chrysostom.] If you suffer not for religion, you will suffer for a worse thing, saith one. Never did any man serve me better than you serve me, said another to his persecutors, [Vincentius.] *Adversus gentes, gratias agimus quod à molestis dominis liberemur ;* We thank you for delivering us from hard task-masters, that we may enjoy more sweetly the bosom of our Lord Jesus, said the martyr. It was a notable saying of Luther, *Ecclesia totum mundum convertit sanguine et oratione ;* The church converteth the whole world by blood and prayers. They may kill me, said Socrates of his enemies, but they cannot hurt me. So may the redeemed of the Lord say, they may take away my head, but they cannot take away my crown of life, of righteousness, of glory, of immortality, Rev. ii. 10; 2

---

[1] Mat. xxiv. 16 ; Luke xii. 32 ; Rom. ix. 11, 12, and xi. 5-8 ; Rom. viii. 39, 40.
[2] Deut. vii. 6-8, and xxxiii. 11 ; Rom. ix. 14 ; 2 Tim. i. 9 ; Eph. i. 4 ; Rom. viii. 29 30 ; 2 Thes. ii. 13 ; 1 Pet. i. 2.

Tim. iv. 8; 1 Pet. v. 4, 5. The Lacedemonians were wont to say, it is a shame for any man to fly in time of danger; but for a Lacedemonian, it is a shame for him to deliberate. Oh, what a shame is it for Christians, when they look upon the covenant of redemption, so much as to deliberate whether they were best to suffer for Christ or no. *Petrus Blesensis* has long since observed, that the courtiers of his time suffered as great trouble, and as many vexations, for vanity, as good Christians did for the truth. The courtiers suffered weariness and painfulness, hunger and thirst, with all the catalogue of Paul's afflictions; and what can the best saints suffer more? Now shall men that are strangers to the covenant of redemption, suffer such hard and great things for their lusts, for very vanity; and will not you, who are acquainted with the covenant of redemption, and who are interested in the covenant of redemption, be ready and willing to suffer anything for that Jesus, who, according to the covenant of redemption, has suffered such dreadful things for you, and merited such glorious things for you? But,

(3.) Thirdly, From this covenant of redemption, as we have opened it, you may see *what infinite cause we have to be swallowed up in the admiration of the Father's love in entering into this covenant, and in making good all the articles of this covenant on his side.* When man was fallen from his primitive purity and glory, from his holiness and happiness, from his freedom and liberty, into a most woeful gulf of sin and misery; when angels and men were all at a loss, and knew no way or means, whereby fallen man might be raised, restored and saved; that then God should firstly and freely propose this covenant, and enter into this covenant, that miserable man might be saved from wrath to come, and raised and settled in a more safe, high and happy estate than that was from which he was fallen in Adam,—oh, what wonderful, what amazing love is this![1] Abraham manifested a great deal of love to God in offering up of his only Isaac, Gen. xxii. 12; but God has shewed far greater love to poor sinners, in making his only Son an offering for their sins: for [1.] God loved Christ with a more transcendent love than Abraham could love Isaac; [2.] God was not bound by the commandment of a superior to do it, as Abraham was, John x. 18; [3.] God freely and voluntarily did it, which Abraham would never have done without a commandment, Heb. x. 10, 12; [4.] Isaac was to be offered after the manner of holy sacrifices, but Christ suffered an ignominious death, after the manner of thieves; [5.] Isaac was all along in the hands of a tender father, but Christ was all along in the hands of barbarous enemies; [6.] Isaac was offered but in show, but Christ was offered indeed and in very good earnest. Is not this an excess, yea, a miracle of love? It is good to be always a-musing upon this love, and delighting ourselves in this love. But,

(4.) Fourthly, From this covenant of redemption, as we have opened it, you may see *what signal cause we have to be deeply affected with the love of Jesus Christ, who roundly and readily falls in with this covenant, and who has faithfully performed all the articles of this covenant.* Had not Jesus Christ kept touch with his Father as to every article

[1] God so loved his Son, that he gave him all the world for his possession, Ps. ii. 8; but he so loved the world that he gave Son and all for its redemption.—*Bernard.*

of the covenant of redemption, he could never have saved us, nor have satisfied divine justice, nor have been admitted into heaven. That Jesus Christ might make full satisfaction for all our sins, ' he was made a curse for us, whereby he hath redeemed us from the curse of the law,' Gal. iii. 13. All his sufferings were for us. All that can be desired of God by man is mercy and truth; mercy in regard of our misery, truth in reference to God's promises. That which moved Christ to engage himself as a surety for us was his respect to God and man: to God, for the honour of his name. Neither the mercy nor the truth nor the justice of God had been so conspicuously manifested, if Jesus Christ had not been our surety, to man, and that to help us in our succourless and desperate estate. No creature either would or could discharge that debt, wherein man stood obliged to the justice of God. This is a mighty evidence of the endless love of Christ, this is an evidence of the endless and matchless love of Christ. We count it a great evidence of love for a friend to be surety for us when we intend no damage to him thereupon; but if a man be surety for that which he knoweth the principal debtor is not able to pay, and there-upon purposeth to pay it himself, this we look upon as an extraordinary evidence of love. But what amazing love, what matchless love is this, for a man to engage his person and life for his friend ! whenas 'skin for skin, and all that a man hath, will he give for his life,' Job ii. 4; and yet, according to the covenant of redemption, Jesus Christ has done all this and much more for us, as is evident, if you will but cast your eye back upon the articles of the covenant, or consult the scriptures in the margin.[1] If a friend, to free a captive, or one con-demned to death, should put himself into the state and condition of him whom he freeth, that would be an evidence of love beyond all com-parison. But now, if the dignity of Christ's person and our unworthi-ness, if the greatness of the debt and kind of payment, and if the benefit which we reap thereby, be duly weighed, we shall find these evidences of love to come as much behind the love of Christ, as the light of a candle cometh short of the light of the sun. Christ's surety-ship, according to the covenant of redemption, is and ought to be a prop of props to our faith. It is as sure a ground of confidence that all is well, and shall be for ever well between God and us, as any the Scriptures does afford. By virtue hereof we have a right to appeal to God's justice, for this surety hath made full satisfaction; and to exact a debt which is fully satisfied is a point of injustice. Christ knew very well what the redemption of fallen man would cost him, *Solus amor nescit difficultates;* he knew that his life and blood must go for it; he knew that he must lay by his robes of majesty, and be clothed with flesh; he knew that he must encounter men and devils; he knew that he must tread the wine-press of his Father's wrath, bear the curse, and make himself an offering for our sins, for our sakes, for our salvation; yet, for all this, he is very ready and willing to bind himself by covenant, that he will redeem us, whatever it cost him. Oh, what tongue can express, what heart can conceive, what soul can comprehend, ' the heights, depths, breadths, and lengths of this love' ?

[1] John x. 11, 15, 17, 18, 28; Rom. v. 6, &c.; Eph. i. 5-7, &c.; Col. ii. 13-15; Heb. ii. 13-15.

Eph. iii. 18, 19.[1] O blessed Jesus, what manner of love is this! that thou shouldst wash away my scarlet sins in thine own blood! that thou shouldst die that I may live! that thou shouldst be cursed that I might be blessed! that thou shouldst undergo the pains of hell that I might enjoy the joys of heaven! that the face of God should be clouded from thee, that his everlasting favour might rest upon me! that thou shouldst be an everlasting screen betwixt the wrath of God and my immortal soul! that thou shouldst do for me beyond all expression, and suffer for me beyond all conception, and gloriously provide for me beyond all expectation! and all this according to the covenant of redemption! What shall I say, what can I say to all this, but fall down before thy grace, and spend my days in wondering at that matchless, bottomless love, that can never be fathomed by angels or men! O Lord Jesus, saith one, *plusquam mea, plusquam meos, plusquam me;* I love thee more than all my goods, and I love thee more than all my friends, yea, I love thee more than my very self, [Bernard.] It is good to write after this copy. But,

XI. The eleventh and last plea that a believer may form up as to the ten scriptures that are in the margin,[2] that refer to the great day of account, or to a man's particular account, may be drawn up from *the consideration of the book of life, out of which all the saints shall be judged in the great day of our Lord:* Rev. xx. 11, ' And I saw a great white throne, and him that sat on it, from whose face the earth and the heaven fled away; and there was found no place for them:' ver. 12, ' And I saw the dead, small and great, stand before God: and the books were opened; and another book was opened, which is the book of life: and the dead were judged out of those things which were written in the books, according to their works:' ver. 13, ' And the sea gave up the dead which were in it; and death and hell delivered up the dead which were in them: and they were judged every man according to their works:' ver. 14, ' And death and hell were cast into the lake of fire. This is the second death. And whosoever was not found written in the book of life was cast into the lake of fire.' In the 11th verse John describes the judge with his preparation; in the 12th verse he describes the persons that should be judged; and then he describes the process and sentence; and lastly, he describes the execution of the sentence, viz., the casting of the reprobates into the lake of fire, and the placing and fixing of the elect in the heavenly Jerusalem, ver. 13-15.

In the five last verses cited you have a clear and full description of the last general judgment, as is evident by the native [3] context and series of this chapter, Rev. xx. 1-3. For having spoken of the devil's last judgment, which, by Jude, is called ' The judgment of the great day,' Jude 6; it is consentaneous, therefore, to understand this of such a judgment whereby he is judged. And, indeed, the expressions are so full, and the matter and circumstances so satisfying and convincing, that they leave no place for fears, doubts, or disputes. This

---

[1] Look where thou wilt, thou art surrounded with flames of his love; and it were strange if thou shouldst not be set on fire; if not, sure thou must needs be a diabolical salamander, says Cusanus.

[2] Eccles. x. 9, and xii. 14; Mat. xii. 14, and xviii. 23; Luke xvi. 2; Rom. xiv. 10; 2 Cor. v. 10; Heb. ix. 27, and xiii. 17; 1 Pet. iv. 5. [3] ' Neighbouring.'—G.

scripture that is under our present consideration runs parallel with that Dan. xii. 1-3, and several other places of Scripture where the day of judgment is spoken of ; and let him that can, shew me at what other judgment all the dead are raised and judged, and all reprobates sent to hell, and all the elect brought to heaven, and death and hell cast into the lake ; all which are plainly expressed here. He shall be an Apollo to me that can make these things that are here spoken of to agree with any other judgment than the last judgment. Let me give a little light into this scripture, before I improve it to that purpose for which I have cited it.

' And I saw a great white throne, and him that sat on it :' a lively description of the last judgment, ' a great throne.' ' Great,' because it is set up for the general judgment of all, for the universal judgment of the whole world. Before this throne all the great ones of the world must stand,—popes, emperors, kings, princes, nobles, judges, prelates, without their mitres, crowns, sceptres, royal robes, gold chains, &c.,— and before this throne all other sorts and ranks of men must stand. And he that sits upon this throne is a great King, and a great God above all gods ; he is ' Prince of the kings of the earth, who is King of kings, and Lord of lords,'[1] Rev. i. 5, xvii. 14, and xix. 16. Upon all which accounts this throne may well be called a great throne; and it is called ' a white throne,' because of its celestial splendour and majesty, and to shew the uprightness and glory of the judge. The white colour in Scripture is used to represent purity and glory. Here it signifies that Christ, the judge, shall give most just and righteous judgment, free from all spot of partiality.

' From whose face the heaven and the earth fled away.' The splendour and majesty of the judge is such, as neither heaven nor earth is able to behold or abide the same; how then shall the wicked be able to stand before him ? Augustine understands it, for the future renovation of heaven and earth ; and here he acknowledgeth an ὑστέρο-σις,[2] for the heaven and the earth fled not before, but after the judgment; to wit, saith he, the judgment being finished, then shall this heaven and earth cease to be, ' when the new heaven and earth shall begin ;' for this world shall pass away by a change of things, not by an utter destruction. ' The heaven and the earth shall flee away ;' that is, this shape of heaven and earth shall pass away ; because they shall be changed from vanity, through fire, that so they may be transformed into a much better and more beautiful estate ; according to that which the apostle Peter writeth, ' The heaven shall pass away with a great noise, and the elements melt with heat; but we expect new heavens and a new earth, wherein dwelleth righteousness,' 1 Pet. iii. 12. How this passing away, or perishing of heaven and earth, shall come to pass, there are divers opinions of learned men. Some think that the substance or essence itself of the world shall wholly perish and be annihilated. Others are of opinion, that only the corruptible qualities thereof shall perish and be changed, and the substance or essence re-

[1] All the thrones of the kings of the earth, with Solomon's golden throne, are but petty thrones to this throne ; yea, they are but footstools to this throne ; and therefore upon this single ground it may well be called a great throne.

[2] *Hysterosis* is, when a thing is before put down, which should come after, or contrariwise. Aug. lib. xx., de C. D., c. 14 ; 1 Pet. iii. 12.

main. There shall be a renovation of all things, say most, and that only the fashion of the world, that is, the outward form and corruptible qualities, shall be destroyed; and so the earth shall be found no more as it was, but shall be made most beautiful and glorious, being to be 'delivered into the glorious liberty,' as far as it is capable, 'of the sons of God,' Rom. viii. 19–22; being to be freed from corruption and bondage; and with these I close. The sum of the 21st verse is, that the creature shall not be always subject to vanity, but shall have a manumission from bondage; of the which deliverance, three things are declared; *First*, Who the creature [is], that is, 'the world;' *Secondly*, From what, from 'corruption,' which is a bondage; *Thirdly*, Into what estate, into 'the glorious liberty of the sons of God.' Some here note the time of the deliverance of the creature, namely, when the children of God shall be wholly set free; for though they have here a freedom unto righteousness, from the bondage of sin, yet they have not a freedom of glory, which is from the bondage of misery. But others take it for the state itself which shall be glorious, not the same with the children of God, but proportioned according to its kind with them; for it is most suitable to the liberty of the faithful, that as they are renewed, so also should their habitation. And as when a nobleman mourneth, his servants are all clad in black; so it is for the greater glory of man, that the creatures, his servants, should in their kind partake of his glory. And whereas some say that it is deliverance enough for the creature, if it cease to serve man, and have an end of vanity, by annihilation, I affirm, it is not enough, because this 21st verse notes, not only such deliverance, but also a further estate which it shall have after such deliverance—namely, to communicate in some degree, with the children of God in glory. Certainly the creatures, in their kind and manner, shall be made partakers of a far better estate than they had while the world endured; because that God shall fully and wholly restore the world, being fallen into corruption through the transgression and sin of mankind. And this doth more plainly appear by the apostle's opposing subsequent liberty against former bondage; which, that he might more enlarge, he calleth it not simply freedom or liberty, but liberty of glory, as it is in the Greek text,[1] meaning thereby, according to the phrase and propriety of the Hebrew tongue, glorious liberty, or liberty that bringeth glory with it; under which term of glory, he compriseth the excellent estate that they shall be in after their delivery from their former baseness and servitude. As for those words, of the 'sons of God,' to which we must refer the glorious liberty before mentioned, they must be understood by a certain proportion or similitude thus; that as in that great day, and not before, God's children shall be graciously freed from all dangers and distresses of this life whatsoever, either in body or soul, and on the other side, made perfect partakers of eternal blessedness; so the creatures then, and not before, shall be delivered from the vanity of man, and their own corruption, and restored to a far

---

[1] ἐλευθερίαν τῆς δόξης. If any shall inquire what shall be the particular properties, works, and uses of all and every creature after the last judgment, I answer, (1.) That as to these things the word is silent, and it is not safe to be wise above what is written; (2.) Here is place for that which Tertullian calls a learned ignorance.

better estate than at present they enjoy; which also may further appear by the words the apostle useth, setting glorious liberty, deliverance and freedom, against servile bondage and slavery. Chrysostom reads διὰ, *for* the glorious liberty of the sons of God: as if the end or final cause of their deliverance were pointed at, namely, that as God made the world for man, and for man's sin subdued it to vanity; so he would deliver it and restore it for men, even to illustrate and enlarge the glory of God's children. I could, by variety of arguments, prove that this deliverance of the creature that our apostle speaks of, shall not be by a reduction into nothing, but by an alteration into a better estate. But I must hasten to a close.

Ver. 12, 'And I saw the dead, small and great, stand before God.' The judge, before whom all do appear, is our dear Lord Jesus, 'who hath the keys of hell and death in his hands,' Rev. i. 18; Acts xvii. 30, 31, and who is designed and appointed by God the Father to be the judge of quick and dead. He hath authority, and a commission under his Father's hand, to sit and act as judge. Here you see that John calleth the judge absolutely God, but Christ is the judge; therefore Christ is God absolutely; and he will appear to be God in our nature in that great day.

The parties judged, who stand before the throne, are, (1.) Generally 'the dead,' all who had died from Adam to the last day. He calls them 'the dead,' after the common law of nature, but then raised from death to life by the power of God, Eph. ii. 5; Col. ii. 13. He speaks not of men dead in sins and trespasses, but of such as died corporally, and now were raised up to judgment. But shall not the living then be judged? Oh, yes! 'For we must all appear before the judgment-seat of Christ: that he may be judge of the quick and the dead, and be Lord both of the dead and the living,' 2 Cor. v. 10; Rom. xiv. 9, 10. Under this phrase, 'the dead,' are comprehended all those that then shall be found alive. By 'the dead' we are to understand the living also, by an argument from the lesser. If the dead shall appear before the judgment-seat, how much more the living! But the dead alone are named, either because the number of the dead, from Adam to the last day, shall be far greater than those that shall be found alive on earth in that day, or because those that remain alive shall be accounted as dead, because 'they shall be changed in the twinkling of an eye,' 1 Cor. xv. 52. Secondly, He describes them from their age and condition, for the words may be understood of both 'great and small,' which takes in all sorts of men, tyrants, emperors, kings, princes, dukes, lords, &c., as well as subjects, vassals, slaves, beggars; rich and poor, strong and weak, bond and free, old and young. All and every one, without exception, are to be judged; for the judgment shall be universal. No man shall be so great as to escape the same, nor none so small as to be excluded; but every one shall have justice done him, without respect of persons, as that great apostle Paul tells us, 'We must all appear before the judgment-seat of Christ, that every one may receive the things done in his body, according to that he hath done, whether it be good or bad,' 2 Cor. v. 10. I am no admirer of the schoolmen's notion, who suppose that all shall be raised about the age of thirty-three, which was Christ's age; but do judge that that perfection, which consisteth in the conforming them to Christ's glorious body, is of another kind than to respect either age, stature, or the like.[1]

'Stand before God,' that is, brought to judgment. The guilty standing ready to be condemned, and the saints standing ready in Christ's presence to be absolved and pronounced blessed, John iii. 18.

'And the books were opened.' Christ the judge being set on his throne, and having all the world before him, 'the books are opened.' (1.) In the general the books are said to be open. (2.) Here is a special book for the elect, 'The book of life was opened.' (3.) Here you have sentence passed and pronounced, 'according to what was written in these books, and according to their works: and the dead were judged out of those things which were written in the books, according to their works.' Here the judicial process is noted by imitation of human courts, in which the whole process is wont to be drawn up, and laid before the judge, from whence the judge determineth for or against the person, according to the acts and proofs that lie open before him. The equity, justice, and righteousness of Christ the judge, that sits on his white throne, is set forth by a metaphor taken from human courts, where the judge pronounceth sentence according to the written law, and the acts and proofs agreeing thereunto. 'All things are naked and bare before him, whose eyes are as a flame of fire,' Heb. iv. 13; Rev. i. 14. But to shew that the judgment shall be as accurate and particular in the trial, and just and righteous in the close, as if all were registered and put on record, nothing shall escape or be mistaken in its circumstances, but all things shall be so cleared and issued beyond all doubts and disputes, as if an exact register of them had been kept and published; in all which there is a plain allusion unto the words of Daniel, speaking thus of this judgment, 'The judgment was set, and the books were opened,' Dan. vii. 10. We find six several books mentioned in the Scripture.

[1.] *The book of nature*, that is mentioned by David, 'Thine eyes did see my substance, yet being unperfect; and in thy book all my members were written, which in continuance were fashioned, when as yet there was none of them,' Ps. cxxxix. 16.[2] It is a metaphor from curious workmen, that do all by the book, or by a model set before them, that nothing may be deficient or done amiss. Had God left out an eye in his commonplace-book, saith one, thou hadst wanted it. 'The heavens declare the glory of God, and the firmament sheweth his handiwork.' The psalmist looks upon that great volume of heaven and earth, and there reads in capital letters the prints and characters of God's glory. This book, saith one, was imprinted at the New Jerusalem by the finger of Jehovah; and is not to be sold, but to be seen, at the sign of glory, of every one that lifts up his eyes to heaven. In this book of nature, which is made up of three great leaves, heaven, earth, and sea, God hath made himself visible, yea, legible, 'even his eternal power and godhead,' Rom. i. 20. So that

---

[1] See General Index, under ' Resurrection,' for more on this point.—G.

[2] The world, saith Clemens Alexandrinus, is, *Dei Scriptura*, the first Bible that God made for the instruction of man.

all men are left without excuse. Out of this book the poor blind Gentiles might have learned many choice lessons, as, *first*, that they had a maker; *secondly*, that this maker, being before the things made, is eternal, without beginning or ending; *thirdly*, that he must needs be almighty, which made all things out of nothing, and sustained such a mass of creatures; *fourthly*, the order, variety, and distinction of creatures declare his marvellous wisdom; *fifthly*, in this book they might run and read the great goodness, and the admirable kindness of God to the sons of men, in making all the creatures for their good, for their service, and benefit; *sixthly* and lastly, in this book they might run and read what a most excellent, what a most admirable, what a most transcendent workman God was. What are the heavens, the earth, the sea, but a sheet of royal paper, written all over with the wisdom and power of God? Now, in the great day of account, this book shall be produced to witness against the heathen world, because they did not live up to the light that was held forth to them in this book, but crucified that light and knowledge by false ways of worship, and by their wicked manners, whereof the apostle gives you a bead-roll or catalogue, from verse 21st to the end of that 1st of the Romans. But,

[2.] Secondly, There is *the book of providence*, wherein all particulars are registered, even such as atheists may count trivial and inconsiderable: Mat. x. 30, ' But the very hairs of your head are all numbered.' And where is their number summed up? Even in the book of providence. The three worthies were taken out of the fiery furnace, with their hairs in full number, not one of them singed, Dan. iii. 27. Paul, encouraging the passengers to eat, who were in fear and danger of death, tells them that ' there should not a hair fall from the head of any of them,' Acts xxvii. 34. And when Saul would have put Jonathan to death, the people told him ' that there should not a hair of his head fall to the ground,' 1 Sam. xiv. 45. Christ doth not say that the hairs of your eyelids are numbered, but the hairs of your head, where there is the greatest plenty, and the least use. Though hair is but an excrement, and the most contemptible part of man, yet every hair of an elect person is observed and registered down in God's books, and not one of them shall be lost. Nor the Holy Ghost doth not say the hairs of your heads *shall be* numbered, but the hairs of your head *are* all numbered. God has already booked them all down, and all to shew us that special, that singular care that God takes of the smallest and least concernments of his chosen ones. This book of providence God will produce in the great day, to confute and condemn the atheists of the world, who have denied a divine providence, and whose hearts have swelled against his government of the world, ' according to the counsels of his own heart.' But,

[3.] Thirdly, There is *the book of men's afflictions*. This some account an entire book of itself: Ps. lvi. 8, ' Thou tellest my wanderings; put thou my tears into thy bottle; are they not in thy book?'[1] God told all those weary steps that David took in passing over those

---

[1] The Septuagint, for my wanderings or flittings, have Ζωὴν, ' my life,' to teach us, saith one, that our life is but a flitting.

two great forests, when he fled from Saul, or thou cipherest up my flittings, as the words may be read.   Whilst David was hunted up and down like a partridge, and hushed[1] out of every bush, and had no certain dwelling-place, but driven from post to pillar, from one country to another, God was all this while a-noting down and a-numbering of his flittings, and a-bottling up his tears, and a-booking down his sighs: 'Put thou my tears into thy bottle;' *Heb.*, 'my tear,' that is, every tear of mine; let not one of them be lost, but kept safe with thee, as so much sweet water.   God is said in Scripture to have a bag and a bottle: a bag for our sins, and a bottle for our tears.   And oh that we would all labour to fill his bottle with our tears, as we have filled his bag with our sins; and certainly if the white tears of his servants be bottled up, the red tears of their blood shall not be cast away.   If God keeps the tears of the saints in store, much more will he remember their blood, to avenge it; and though tyrants burn the bones of the saints,[2] yet they cannot blot out their tears and blood out of God's register: 'Are they not in thy book?' are they not in thy register, or book of accounts, where they cannot be blotted out by any time or tyrants? *i.e.*, yes, certainly they are; thou dost assuredly book them down, and wilt never forget one of them, according to the usual interrogatory that was used among the Hebrews when they affirmed a thing past all doubt.   Let the great Nimrods and oppressors of the saints look to themselves, for God books down all the afflictions, sufferings, and persecutions of his servants; and in the great day he will bring in this book, this register, to witness against them.   Ah, sinners, sinners! look to yourselves.   In the great day of account, the Lord will reckon with you for every rod that he hath spent upon you; he will reckon with you, not only for all your mercies, but also for all your crosses; not only for all your sweets, but also for all your bitters; not only for all your cordials, but also for all your corrosives.   In this book of afflictions there is not only *item* for this mercy and that, but *item* also for this affliction and that, this sickness and that, this cross and that, this loss and that.   And will not the opening of this book of the saints' afflictions and sufferings, and of sinners' afflictions and sufferings, be as the handwriting upon the wall, to all the wicked of the earth, in the great day of account? Dan. v. 5, 6.   Surely yes; for as they cannot answer for one mercy of ten thousand that they have enjoyed, so they cannot answer for one affliction of ten thousand that they have been exercised with.   But,

[4.] Fourthly, There is *the book of conscience.*   Conscience, saith Philo, is the little consistory of the soul.   Conscience is *mille testes*, a thousand witnesses, for or against a man, Rom. ii. 14, 15.   Conscience is God's preacher in the bosom.   Conscience hath a good memory, saith one.   The chief butler forgot the promise that he had made to Joseph, but conscience told him of it, Gen. xli. 9.   *Fama propter homines, conscientia propter Deum*, saith Augustine: a good name will carry it amongst men, but it is a good conscience only that can acquit

---

[1] 'Startled,' as birds by a cry or shout.—G.
[2] Cf. Sibbes, ii., 370, and note *m*, 434.—G.
[3] The conscience is a domestic and true tribunal, saith [Gregory] Nazianzen.

us before God. In this great day the book of every man's conscience shall be opened for their conviction, wherein they shall read their guilt in legible characters; for that is a book of record, wherein men's actions are entered. And although now it be shut up close, and sinners will by no means be brought to look into it, and though many things that are written in this book seem to be so greatly obliterated and blotted that they can hardly be read, yet in that great day of accounts God will refresh and recover the lustre of those ancient writings; and sinners, in that day, shall find that conscience hath an iron memory. In the last day God will bring the book of conscience out of the rubbish, as they did the book of the law in Josiah's time; and the very laying open of this book before sinners will even put them beside their wits, and fill them with unspeakable horror and terror, and be a hell on this side hell unto them. In this book they shall find an exact account of every vain thought they have had, and of every idle word they have spoken, and of every evil action they have done; and oh, what amazement and astonishment will this fill them with! By the *books* in this Rev. xx. 12, Origen does understand the books of conscience, which now are hid, not from God, but from most men; for the hidden things of the heart are not now known, but then they shall be opened, and manifested to the consciences of every sinner, so as there shall be no place, no room left for any excuse or plea.[1] Ambrose saith that the books that are here said to be opened are the books of men's consciences and God's omniscience.[2] Oh, what dreadful challenges and accusations will every sinner be forced to read out of this book of conscience in the great day! Oh, how in that great day will all wicked men wish that they had followed the counsel of the heathen orator when he said, *A recta conscientia ne latum quidem unguem discedendum;* A man may not depart an hair's-breadth all his life long from the dictates of a good conscience.[3] The book of God's omniscience takes in all things past, present, and to come, as if he had kept a diary of every man's thoughts, words, and actions. But,

[5.] Fifthly, There is the *book of Scripture;* and of all books this book is the most precious book. The book of the creature is but as the inventory of the goods; the book of the Scripture is the evidence, and conveyance, and assurance of all good to us. The book of Scripture is the book of the statutes and ordinances of the King of heaven, which must be opened and consulted, and by which all must be judged in the great day: James ii. 12, 'So speak ye, and so do, as they that shall be judged by the law of liberty;' *i.e.*, by the gospel of Jesus Christ, by the whole word of God, registered in the blessed Scriptures, James i. 23–25. Now the whole word of God is called the law of liberty; because thereby we are born again to a new spiritual life, and so freed from the bondage and slavery of sin and Satan.[4] Our Lord Jesus Christ, in his proceedings in the great day of account, will judge us by

---

[1] Comm. ad Rom. xiv.   [2] Ambrose in Ps. i.   [3] Cic. in Offic.
[4] Let the word be president in all assemblies and judgments, saith Beza. In the Nicene Council, Constantine caused the Bible to be set upon the desk as judge of all controversies. The word shall be the judge of all men's estates at last; every man shall stand or fall according as he holds weight in the balance of the sanctuary.

the Scriptures, and pass everlasting sentence upon us according to the tenor of the Scriptures. At the great and general assizes Christ will try all causes by the word of God, and pass judgment upon all sorts of persons according to the word: John xii. 48, 'He that rejecteth me, and receiveth not my words, hath one that judgeth him: the word that I have spoken, the same shall judge him in the last day.' The persons that are to be judged in the great day are not believers in Christ, they are not receivers of Christ, but such as reject his person, and receive not his doctrine. 'He that rejecteth me, and receiveth not my words, hath one that judgeth him,' &c. However the rejecters of Christ may escape judgment for a time, yet they shall never be able to escape the judgment of the last day; they shall assuredly, they shall unavoidably, be judged in the last day. Though the rejecters of Christ had none to witness against them, yet the word of the Lord shall be more than a thousand witnesses against them in the great day, 'The word that I have spoken, the same shall judge him in the last day.' The word of the Lord is so sure and infallible a word, that Christ's sentence in the great day, when heaven and earth shall pass away, 2 Pet. iii. 7, 10–12, shall proceed according to the verdict and testimony thereof, 'For the word that I have spoken shall judge him in the last day.' Christ will pronounce then according to what it saith now; and that as well in favour of believers as against unbelievers. Look, as Christ himself is 'ordained to be the judge of quick and dead,' Acts xvii. 31; so the word, the doctrines which he hath delivered, will be the rule of all his judicial proceedings, both in acquitting the righteous, and condemning the wicked. By the *books* in this Rev. xx. 12, Augustine understands the books of the Old and New Testament, which shall then be opened; because, according to them, the judge will pronounce sentence: [1] Rom. ii. 16, 'When God shall judge the secrets of men by Jesus Christ, according to my gospel,' which promiseth heaven and happiness to all believers. The sentence of the last day shall be but a more manifest declaration of that judgment, that the Lord, in this life, most-an-end [2] hath passed upon men. Heathens shall be judged by the law of nature; profligate professors by the written law, and the word preached; believers by the gospel, which saith, 'He that believeth shall be saved; he that believes shall not perish, but have eternal life; he that believeth on the Son hath everlasting life; he that believeth shall not come into condemnation, but is passed from death to life,' Mark xvi. 16; John iii. 15, 16, 36, and v. 24. Christ shall, in the great day, give sentence according to the doctrine of the gospel, which saith, 'If there be first a willing mind, it is accepted according to that a man hath, and not according to that he hath not.' The Jesuits report of a student at Paris who, coming to confession, and not being able, for tears and sobbings, to speak, was willed by his confessor to write down his sins, which he did; and when the confessor received it, the writing vanished, and there remained nothing but the white and clean paper; this, say they, was by a miracle, because of his great contrition. Let the credit of this

---

[1] Lib. xx. De C. Dei. c. 14; and Bede saith the same with Austin.
[2] 'Continually,' 'generally.'—G.

story be upon the reporter; but upon the credit of the word of God, if we believe, really, savingly, and repent unfeignedly, all our sins shall be blotted out; and a book of clean paper, in respect of sin, shall be presented to the judge. But,

[6.] Sixthly and lastly, There is *a book of life*: Rev. xx. 12, 'And another book was opened, which is the book of life.' The book of life is the book of all those that were elected and redeemed to life through Christ Jesus.[1] This book of life containeth a register of such particular persons in whose salvation God from all eternity determined to have his mercy glorified, and for whom Christ merited faith, repentance, and perseverance, that they should repent, believe, and be finally saved. 'The book of life shall be opened;' that is to say, the decrees of God will be then published and made known, which now are sealed up in his breast and locked up in his archives. Then it will be seen who are appointed to life for the glorifying of God's free, rich, and sovereign grace, and whom he purposed to leave in their sins, and to perish for ever, for the exaltation of his justice. It is called 'a book of life,' not that God hath need of a book, but to note the certainty of predestination—viz., that God knows all and every of the elect, even as men know a thing which, for memory's sake, they set down in writing. This book of life shall be opened in the great day, because then it shall appear who were elect, who reprobates; who truly believed in Christ, who not; who worshipped God in spirit and in truth, and who not; who walked with God as Noah, and who not; who set up God as the object of their fear, who not; who followed the Lamb whither ever he went, and who not; who were sincere, and who not; who preferred Christ above ten thousand worlds, and who preferred Barabbas before Jesus, and their farms, and their oxen, and their swine, yea, their very lusts, before a Saviour, a Redeemer; who are sheep, and who are goats, Mat. xxv. 32; who are sons, and who are slaves; who have mourned for their own sins and the sins of the time, and who they are that have made a sport of sin, Ezek. ix. 4, 6, &c. Of this book of life you read often in Scripture: Phil. iv. 3, 'And I entreat thee also, true yoke-fellow, help those women which laboured with me in the gospel, with Clement also, and with other my fellow-labourers, whose names are in the book of life.' Vorsitus thinks it a speech taken from the custom of soldiers or cities, in which the chosen soldiers or citizens are by name written in a certain book or roll. This book or roll is called here 'the book of life,' because therein are written all the elect who are ordained to eternal life: Rev. iii. 5, 'He that overcometh, the same shall be clothed in white raiment, and I will not blot out his name out of the book of life.' In this book of life all 'the just, that live by faith,' are written. The elect are certain of eternal life, they shall never perish, nor none can ever pluck them out of the Father's hand, nor out of Christ's hand, John x. 28–31. God is said to have books metaphorically; he needs no books to help

---

[1] God neither needeth nor useth books to judge by, but this is spoken after the manner of men. Mordecai's name was registered in the chronicles of Persia, Esth. vi. 1–3; and Tamerlane had always by him a catalogue of his best servants and their good deserts, which he daily perused.

his memory; he does all things by his infinite wisdom, eternal fore-knowledge, counsel, government, and judgment. But thus men cannot do; for whatsoever is done in their councils, cities, families, contracts, &c., for memory's sake, is set down in writing, that so, as there is occasion, they may look it over, and call to mind such things as they desire.[1] Mark, not to have our names blotted out of the book of life is to have them always remain therein; that is, to enjoy eternal glory; and what can the soul desire more? The names of the elect are written in the book of life. They do not obtain salvation by chance, but were elected of God to life and happiness before the foundation of the world. Now their names being once written in the book of life, they shall never, never be blotted out of that book. In the book of predestination there is not one blot to be found—the salvation of the elect is most sure and certain: Rev. xiii. 8, 'And all that dwell on the earth shall worship him, whose names are not written in the book of life of the Lamb slain from the foundation of the world.' The names of the elect are said to be written in the book of life by a usual metaphor; for we commonly write down the names of such as are dear unto us, that we may continually remember them. So God having in his eternal counsel elected some to salvation, hath written their names in the book of life; as our Saviour tells us, 'Rejoice, because your names are written in heaven,' Luke x. 20. Some understand the metaphor of the sonship of the elect; so that to be written in the book of life shews that they are heirs of glory; for we know that such are to inherit whose names are written in the last will and testament of men. Of this book of life you may further read, Rev. xvii. 8, xx. 15, xxi. 27, and xxii. 19.

Now from this book of life, that shall be opened in the great day, when the other books shall be opened, as hath been shewed, every sincere Christian may form up this eleventh plea as to the ten scriptures that are in the margin,[2] that refer to the great day of account, or to a man's particular account. *Most holy and blessed Lord, cast thine eye upon the book of election, and there thou wilt find my name written.* Now my name being written in that book, I am exempt from all condemnation, and interested in the great salvation; my name being written in the book of life, I am secured from coming into the judgment of reprobation or condemnation, John v. 14; Rev. xxi. 27. Jesus Christ, who hath written my name in the book of life, hath made up my accounts for me; he hath satisfied thy justice, and pacified thy wrath, and borne the curse, and purchased my pardon, and put upon me an everlasting righteousness, and given me my *quietus est;* he has crossed out the black lines of my sins with the red lines of his blood; he has cancelled all the bonds wherein I stood obliged to divine justice. I further plead, O blessed Lord, that there is an immutable connexion betwixt being written in this book of life and the obtaining of eternal life; and if the connexion betwixt being

---

[1] The holy God, by an *anthropopatheia*, speaketh to our capacity; for he doth all things without the help of books.

[2] Eccles. xi. 9, and xii. 14; Mat. xii. 14, and xviii. 23; Luke xvi. 2; Rom. xiv. 10; 2 Cor. v. 10; Heb. ix. 27, and xiii. 17; 1 Pet. iv. 5; Dan. ix. 24; Col. ii. 14.

written in this book of life and the obtaining of eternal life were not peremptory, what reason could there be of opening this book in the day of judgment? The book of life is a book of sovereign grace, upon which lies the weight of my salvation, my happiness, my all; and therefore by that book I desire to stand or fall. Well, saith the Lord, I cannot but accept of this plea as holy, honourable, just, and righteous; and therefore 'enter thou into the joy of thy Lord, inherit the kingdom prepared for thee,' Mat. xxv. 21, 34. Thus, by divine assistance, and by a special and a gracious hand of providence upon me, I have finished those select and important cases of conscience which I designed to speak to.

Soli Deo Gloria in Aeternum.

NOTE.

* By the general title-page (See page 264, *ante*) it will be seen that the 'Word in Season' is included in the 'Golden Key;' but nevertheless it forms a separate treatise, of which the title-page will be found below.*—G.

* A WORD IN SEASON
To this Present
GENERATION.

OR

A SOBER AND SERIOUS
DISCOURSE

About the favorable, Signal and eminent Presence of the LORD with his PEOPLE, in their greatest Troubles, deepest Distresses, and most deadly Dangers.

WITH THE

Resolution of several Questions, concerning the DIVINE PRESENCE, as also the Reasons and improvements of this great and glorious Truth.

All tending to encourage Christians in the way of their Duty, in the face of all Afflictions, Oppositions, and Sufferings that they may meet with for Righteousness sake from the Serpents seed, or from Wolves in Sheeps-cloathing.

By *THOMAS BROOKS*, the Author of the *Golden Key* to open hidden Treasures.

But will God indeed dwell on the Earth? Behold the Heaven, and the Heaven of Heavens cannot contain thee, how much less this House that I have builded. 1 Kings 8. 27.

Deus unus est, & ubique totus diffusus. Cyprian.

Maximilian the Emperour was so delighted with that Sentence of PAUL, *Si Deus nobiscum, If God be with us, who shall be against us*, that he caused it to be written upon the Walls in most rooms of his Palace.

LONDON,

Printed for *Dorman Newman*, at the Sign of the Kings Arms in the *Poultrie*. [1675. 4to.]

A GENERAL EPISTLE TO ALL SUFFERING SAINTS.

To all afflicted and distressed Christians all the world over, especially to those that are in bonds for the testimony of Christ in Bristol; and to those that are sufferers there, or in any other city, town, country, or kingdom whatsoever; and to all that have been deep sufferers in their names, persons, estates, or liberties, upon the account of their faithfulness to God, to their light, to their consciences, to their principles, to their profession, and to Christ the king and head of his church; and to all that have been long prisoners to their beds or chambers by reason of age, and the common infirmities that do attend it, or that are under any other afflictive dispensation: and more particularly to my ancient dear and honoured friend, Mrs Elizabeth Drinkwater, who has been many years the Lord's prisoner, and upon the matter, kept wholly from public ordinances, by reason of her bodily weaknesses and infirmities; though in the want of a greater sanctuary, God has been 'a little sanctuary' to her soul, Ezek. xi. 16,—Grace, Mercy, and Peace be multiplied.

DEAR AND HONOURED FRIENDS,—The ensuing treatise about the signal presence of God with his people, in their greatest troubles, deepest distresses and most deadly dangers, I present to the service of all your souls. There has not been any treatise on this subject, that hath ever fallen under mine eye; which hath been one great reason to encourage me in this present undertaking. I know several holy and learned men have written singularly well upon the gracious presence of God with his people, in ordinances and in the worship of his house; but I know that none have made it their business, their work, to handle this subject that I have been discoursing on: though a more excellent, noble, spiritual, seasonable, and necessary subject can rarely be treated on.

There are ten things that I am very well satisfied in, and to me they are things of great importance in this present day. And the first is this—viz.,

1. *That there is no engagement from God upon any of his people, to run themselves into sufferings wilfully, causelessly, groundlessly.* Christians must not be prodigal of their blood, for their blood is Christ's. Their estates, their names, their liberties, their all, is his;

they are not their own, they are bought with a price, 1 Cor. vi. 20, and vii. 23; and therefore to him they must be accountable for their lives, liberties, &c., and therefore they had need be very wary how they part with them. We must not step out of our way to take up a cross. The three worthies were passive,[1] Dan. iii. 20, 21, 28. They did not rush into the fiery furnace, but yielded themselves to be cast into the fiery furnace; they did not stubbornly oppose nor struggle against their enemies, but patiently and quietly yielded their bodies to the flames: neither did the prophets or apostles step over God's hedge, to make way to their own sufferings or martyrdom. No men may, with the Donatists, destroy themselves, rather than they would conform to this or that religion. No man may have a hand in his own destruction, no man may cut his throat with his own hands to avoid a prison, a dungeon, a den, a fiery furnace. Cyprian tells the Christians in his time, that were ambitious of martyrdom, *Non est in tua potestate, sed in Dei dignatione, martyrium.* We may not run ourselves into prison without a *mittimus* from heaven. If righteousness lead me into prison, a righteous God will stand by me in prison, and in the issue, give me a gracious or a glorious deliverance out of prison. But if I wilfully, causelessly run myself into prison, it will be a righteous thing with God, to leave me to shift for myself in prison. If God should meet a man in prison, and say to him—as he did once to Elijah, 'What dost thou here, Elijah?'[2] 1 King xix. 9— What dost thou here, O man? is this a fit place for truth's champion? if a man cannot readily answer, Lord, I have not run myself into a prison—but it is thyself, it is thy truth, it is thy interest, it is thy honour, it is my conscience, it is duty that has brought me hither— what confusion would attend him! Philustrius (?) and Theodoret speak of some that would compel men to kill them out of an affectation of martyrdom; but this was a mad ambition, but no true zeal. It was an error in Tertullian, to say that afflictions, that sufferings were to be sought. No man is to make his own cross, nor scourges to whip himself; nor to cast himself into a suffering state, so long as God hath left him a plain open way to escape suffering without sinning: not but that most men are more apt and prone to sin themselves out of smart sufferings, than unwarrantably to run themselves into sufferings; but it is good for every Christian to be upon his guard, and not run till God sends him, Acts ix. 23-25; John xx. 19, 26. As a Christian must not shun sufferings, so he must not seek them.

(2.) Secondly, *That afflictions, sufferings, persecutions, hath been the common lot and portion of the people of God in all the ages of the world.*[3] Witness the sufferings of the patriarchs, prophets, apostles, the primitive Christians, and the martyrs of a later date. Abel was persecuted by Cain, 1 John iii. 12; and Isaac by Ishmael, Gal. iv. 29; and Jacob by Esau. That seems to be a standing law, 'All that will live godly in Christ Jesus must suffer persecution,' 2 Tim.

---

[1] What sad sufferings do many blind papists run themselves into, out of a superstitious opinion of merit or satisfaction; but under all their penances they cannot say, 'We bear in our bodies the marks of our Lord Jesus Christ,' Gal. vi. 17.

[2] Here he is secretly taxed for leaving his station out of too much fear of Jezebel.

[3] Mat. x. 22, and xvi. 24; Luke xxi. 12; John xv. 20; Heb. xi. The common cry of persecutors hath been *Christianos ad Leones.*

iii. 12. A man may have many faint wishes and cold desires after godliness, and yet escape persecution; yea, he may make some essays and attempts as if he would be godly, and yet escape persecution; but when a man is thoroughly resolved to be godly, and sets himself in good earnest upon pursuing after holiness, upon living a life of holiness, upon growing up in holiness, then he must expect to meet with afflictions and persecutions. The history of the ten persecutions, and that little Book of Martyrs, the eleventh of the Hebrews, and Mr Foxe his Acts and Monuments, with many other histories that are extant, do abundantly evidence that from age to age, and from one generation to another, they that have been 'born after the flesh have persecuted them that have been born after the Spirit,' Gal. iv. 29; and that 'the seed of the serpent hath been still a-multiplying of troubles upon the seed of the woman,' Gen. iii. 15. As there was no way to paradise but by a flaming sword, nor no way to Canaan but through a howling wilderness, so there is no way to heaven but by the gates of hell; there is no way to a glorious exaltation but through a sea of tribulation, of persecution, Acts xiv. 21, 22. The way to heaven is not strewed with roses, but full of thorns and briars, as those 'of whom this world is not worthy' have always experienced, Heb. xi. The serpentine brood takes a very great pleasure to be still a-representing the people of God as foolish, hypocritical, precise, proud, schismatical, seditious, factious, and as persons against order and government, against good laws and customs, as disturbers and troublers of the peace. Thus Ahab accounts Elijah 'the troubler of Israel,' 1 Kings xviii. 17; and Haman laid it to the charge of the Jews, that 'they were disobedient to the king's laws,' Esth. iii. 8; and the adversaries of the Jews told Artaxerxes the king that 'Jerusalem was a rebellious city, hurtful unto kings and princes,' Ezra iv. 15; and the unbelieving Jews at Thessalonica did as much for the apostles, they said they were the men 'that turned the world upside down,' Acts xvii. 6. So Luther was called 'the trumpet of rebellion;' and Tertullus calls Paul 'a pestilent fellow, and a mover of sedition,' Acts xxiv. 5; Λοιμὸν, a pestilence, a botch. Foolish Tertullus mistook the antidote for the poison, the remedy for the disease. Now if so precious a man as Paul, than whom, saith Chrysostom, the earth never bare a better since it bore Christ, were accounted and called a pest, a botch, let us think[1] much if the choicest saints in our days are accounted and esteemed as so many pests and botches. This is the reward the ungrateful world gives the servants of Christ for their zeal and faithfulness in the cause of Christ; instead of encouraging them, they load them with ignominious and hateful terms of rebellion and turbulency, &c., labouring thereby to make them odious, and to enrage the people against them, as the persecutors of old used to wrap the Christians up in bears' skins, and lions' skins, &c., and then to bait them with dogs. It is a very great vanity to think of passing to heaven without suffering. The saints in all ages have found the way thither paved with troubles, and it would be a foolish, childish thing for any of us to think of finding it otherwise now. Constantine the Great, as piously as wittily, told Acesius the Novatian, that if he would not take up with persecution, and such like dealing, he must

---

[1] Query, 'not think'?—ED.

provide him a ladder and climb alone to heaven.[1] We must go to heaven some other way than the saints have done of old, except we resolve of going thither through much tribulation, Acts xiv. 22.

3. Thirdly, *That no person or persons on earth may sinfully shift off sufferings, or avoid sufferings.* There being infinitely more evil in the least sin than there can be in the greatest sufferings that can befall us in this world, it is best, it is safest to choose suffering rather than sinning, as Moses did. So Daniel chose rather to be cast among lions than that his conscience should be a lion within him, Dan. vi.; and the three children, or champions rather, who were holily wilful, chose rather to burn in the fiery furnace than to bow to the image that the king had set up, Dan. iii. He that values peace with God, and peace with conscience, and the honour of God, and the credit of religion, the silencing of sinners, and the rejoicing of the saints, must choose to suffer rather than to sin.[2] When storms arise, and troubles and dangers approach, many begin to consult, not how they may glorify God by suffering, but how they may provide for their own safety by sinning. Plato knew much of God, but, as Josephus shews, durst not set it down for fear of the people; and Lactantius charges the same upon Tully: 'Thou darest not,' saith he, 'undertake the patronage of the truth, for fear of the prison of Socrates;' and Augustine doth as much for Seneca; he spends a whole chapter in shewing how he held the truth in unrighteousness, telling us how he reverenced that which he reproved, did that which he condemned, and worshipped that which he found fault with.[3] Though these wise men saw the vanity of the heathenish deities, and the worship that was given to them, and looked upon them as utterly unworthy of respect from wise and sober men, nay, secretly scorned and derided them; yet would they not openly declare against them, and that for fear of the people who so much doted upon them. But Daniel's three young worthies were men of that heavenly gallantry, that they peremptorily resolved upon this, that though they should not be delivered by their God, yet they would not sin against their God, nor so much as demur, deliberate, or take time to consider whether they should suffer or sin; it was past dispute with them, brave and noble souls that they were. It is observable that when Paul speaks of his afflictions, his sufferings, he calls them 'light,' 2 Cor. iv. 17; but when he speaks of his sin, he speaks of it as a burden that pressed him down, and made him cry out, 'O wretched man that I am!' and to cry out again, 'we groan, being burdened,' Rom. vii. 23; 2 Cor. v. 2, 4. Moses his choice is famous, and celebrated all the world over; for it was not made when he was a child, but when he came to forty years of age, Heb. xi. 25-27; then he preferred suffering, not only before sinning, but before all the honours, riches, and pleasures of Egypt, accounting the worst of Christ, viz., reproaches, better than the best of the world. When Eleazar was promised to be saved from torments and death if he would but make show of yielding, he courageously answered, 'It becometh not our age in anywise to dissemble,' 2 Mac.

---

[1] Socrat. Hist. Eccl., lib. i. cap. 10.

[2] Judas and Spira will rather sin than suffer; but who ever suffered more on this side hell than they suffered?   [3] De Civit., lib. vi. c. 10.

vi. 24; whereby many young persons might think that Eleazar, being fourscore and ten years old, were now gone to a strange religion. Thus also one of the seven brethren, in the name of the rest, 'We are ready to die, rather than transgress the laws of our fathers,' chap. vii. 2; meaning such laws as God of old had given to their fathers, to be observed by them, and by their posterity age after age. Polycarpus,[1] when the governor promised to let him go free if he would deny Christ, answered, I have served him fourscore and six years, and he never hurt me in anything; how shall I curse him who hath saved me? And the governor adding one while promises, another while threatenings, Polycarpus thus cuts off all, Why dost thou make delays? inflict what thou lists.[2] So Galeacius, [Carraciolus,] a gentleman of great estate, who suffered martyrdom at St Angelo in Italy, being much pressed by his friends to recant, and save his life, he replied, that death was much more sweet to him with the testimony of verity, than life with the least denial of truth. Hooper desired rather to be discharged of his bishopric, than yield to certain ceremonies. A man were better displease all his friends, all his relations, yea, all the world, than to displease his God, and displease his own conscience. So Cyprian,—Augustine relates the story,—when the emperor, as he was going to execution, told him that he would give him space to consider whether he were not better cast in a grain into the fire,[3] than be so miserably slain; to which he replied, *In re tam sancta deliberatio non habet locum*, There needs no deliberation in this case. The like we read in the history of France, in the year 1572, presently after that tragical and perfidious slaughter and massacre of so many thousands of protestants by treacherous bloody papists, Charles the Ninth, king of France, called the Prince of Conde, and proposed to him this choice, either to go to mass, or to die presently, or to suffer perpetual imprisonment; to which he returned this noble answer, That by God's help he would never choose the first; and for either of the two latter, he left it to the king's pleasure, and God's providence. Thus you see that the people of God have, when put to it, chose rather to suffer than to sin. But,

4. Fourthly, *That they shall be sure to suffer with a witness, that refuse to suffer, or are afraid to suffer, when Christ calls them to a suffering state.* No men can suffer so much for Christ, as they shall be sure to suffer from Christ, if through weakness or wickedness they either disdain or refuse to suffer for Christ: Mark viii. 35, 'For whosoever will save his life shall lose it; but whosoever shall lose his life for my sake and the gospel's, the same shall save it.' There is no loss, but gain, in losing for Christ. It is a very dangerous thing for men to prefer the safety of their natural lives before the glory of Christ, the cause of Christ, the gospel of Christ, and the profession of his name. It is certain that the glory of Christ ought to be more dear and precious to us than our very lives. Christ, for our redemption and salvation, freely and readily lays down his life, ' I lay down my life for my sheep,' John x. 15; and shall we stand with him for ours, when our call is clear, to lay them down for his sake and

---

[1] Eccles. Hist., lib. iv. 15. [As before.—G.]   [2] ' Choosest.'—G.

[3] A ' grain' of incense into the heathen altar-fire, a frequent demand and test.—G.

the gospel's sake ? He that shall attempt to save his life by crossing his light, by shifting of the truth, or by forsaking of Christ, shall lose it. It is a gainful loss to suffer for the truth ; it is a lossful gain, by time-serving and base complying with the times, the lusts, the wills, the humours of the men of this age, in whom the spirit of Cain and Esau works so furiously, to provide for our present safety, security, plenty, peace, and ease, &c., either by denying the truth, or by betraying the truth, or by exchanging the truth, or by forsaking the truth : Mat. x. 39, ' He that findeth his life shall lose it.' This is a strange expression, a riddle to the world, a seeming contradiction, such as natural reason can never reconcile. ' He that findeth his life;' that is, redeemeth it with the forfeiture of his faith, with the shipwreck of his conscience, 1 Tim. i. 19, 20, makes a loser's bargain; he makes more haste than good speed, whilst in running from death as far as he can, he runs to it as fast as he can. See it in some great instances. When Henry the Fourth of France had conquered his enemies, he turned papist, and gave this reason of it, that he might settle himself in peace and safety. Ravaillac, who slew him as he was riding abroad in his coach to refresh himself, confessed that the reason why he stabbed him was because he was of two religions ; and thus, by his sinful endeavours to save his life, he lost it.[1] There was one Philbert Hamlin in France, having converted a priest to the profession of the truth, was, together with the priest, apprehended, and cast into prison at Bourdeaux ; but after a while, the priest, being terrified with the prison and fear of death, renounced Christ, and was set at liberty. Whereupon Philbert said unto him, O unhappy and more than miserable man ! is it possible that, to save your life for a few days, you should so deny the truth ? Know, therefore, though you have avoided the corporal fire, yet your life shall not be prolonged; for you shall die before me, and you shall not have the honour to die for the cause of Christ ; but you shall be an example to apostates ; and accordingly, as he went out of the prison, two gentlemen, that had a former quarrel with him, met him, and slew him ; and thus, also, he lost his life by endeavouring sinfully to save it.[2] The Angrognians that yielded to the papists, and complied with them, that they might sleep quietly in a whole skin, were more sadly and cruelly handled by the papists than those that continued stout, courageous, and resolute for the truth.[3] Under the fourth persecution there were some Christians who, for fear of torments and death, denied their faith, and sacrificed to idols, yet did not their bloody persecutors spare them ; and it was observed that, being full of guilt, they went to their deaths with dejected and ill-favoured countenances, so that the very Gentiles took notice of it, and reproached them as base apostates, and as such who were worthy to suffer as evil-doers. West, that was chaplain to Bishop Ridley, refusing to die in Christ's cause with his master, said mass against his conscience, and soon after pined away with sorrow and grief. A smith in King Edward the Sixth's days, called Richard Denton, was a forward professor of religion, and, by his Christian instruction, the happy

[1] French History. [As before.—G.]
[2] Non potest, qui pati timet, ejus esse qui passus est.—Tertul.
[3] [Foxe] Acts and Mon., fol. 885.

instrument of the conversion of a young man to the faith. Afterwards, in the reign of Queen Mary, this young man was cast in prison for his religion; who, remembering his old friend and spiritual father, the smith, to whom he always carried a reverent respect for the good he had received by him, sent to know whether he was imprisoned also, and finding that he was not, desired to speak with him; and when he came he asked his advice, whether he thought it best for him to remain in prison, and whether he would encourage him to burn at a stake for his religion. To whom the smith answered, that his cause was good, and that he might with comfort suffer for it; but for my part, said the smith, I cannot burn. But shortly after, he that could not burn for religion, by God's just judgment was burned for his apostasy; for his shop and house being set on fire, and he overbusy to save his goods, was burnt in the flames.[1] They that will not burn for Christ when he calls them to it, shall burn whether they will or no. He that will not suffer for Christ, shall be sure to suffer worse things from Christ than ever he could have suffered for Christ. And therefore Dr Taylor, the martyr, hit the nail when he said, If I shrink from God's truth, said he, I am sure of another manner of death than Judge Hales had, who being drawn, for fear of death, to do things against his light and conscience, did afterwards drown himself.[2] Cyprian, in his sermon, *De Lapsis*, makes mention of divers who, forsaking the profession of their faith, were given over by God to be possessed by evil spirits, and so died fearfully and miserably, making good that word that is more worth than a world, John xii. 25, ' He that loveth his life shall lose it; and he that hateth his life in this world shall keep it unto life eternal.'[3] A man that is sparing of his life when Christ calls for it, doth take the ready way to lose it; and he that doth hazard it for him at his call, is sure to live eternally. Christ approves of no followers who are not resolved on the loss of what is dearest to them, yea, even of life, for his sake; therefore doth he mention our life to be hated, which is not to be understood absolutely, as if it were a sin to love life, as it is the gift of God, or that they should be weary of it, but comparatively, that they should not love it more than Christ, his word, his worship, his ways. He that resolves to save his temporal life upon any terms, he takes the shortest cut to lose both temporal and eternal life also. ' He that loveth his life shall lose it.' He that prefers the honour and service of Christ above his own life, he takes the surest way to preserve both body and soul into eternal life; for ' he that hates his life in this world shall keep it unto life eternal.' Though life be sweet, and every creature makes much of it, from the highest angel to the lowest worm, yet woe, woe to him that is set upon saving of it when Christ calls upon him to lay it down for his sake, or the gospel's sake. No fool to him that thinks to avoid a less danger by running himself into a greater danger, who thinks to save his body by losing his soul, and to save his temporal life by losing eternal life. There is no loser to him

---

[1] [Foxe] Acts and Mon., vol. iii. p. 960.   [2] *Ibid.*, 1382.

[3] Φιλεῖν is here used of excessive and preposterous love. He that so loveth his life, that, out of a desire to save it, he denieth me and my gospel: so this Greek word is used, Mat. x. 37.

who, by sinful attempts to save his life, shall lose a better life than ever he can save. But,

5. Fifthly, Consider, *That of old there had been a very great willingness, readiness, forwardness, and resoluteness in the people of God, cheerfully to suffer for Christ, his truth, his gospel, his worship, his ways, his ordinances, his interest, his honour.* Consult the scriptures in the margin, and many others of the like import, which all knowing Christians can turn to at pleasure.[1] To these I shall add a few examples amongst a multitude of those blessed souls, who willingly, readily, cheerfully, resolutely hazarded all for Christ while they were on earth, and are now a-receiving their reward with him in heaven. Oh, how my heart leapeth for joy, said Mr Philpot, the martyr, that I am so near the apprehension of eternal life! I with my fellows were carried to the coal-house, where we do rouse together in the straw as cheerfully, we thank God, as others do in their beds of down.[2] Mr Glover, the martyr, wept for joy of his imprisonment: and Mr Bradford put off his cap and thanked the Lord when his keeper's wife brought him word that he was to be burnt the next day: and Mr Taylor fetched a pleasant delightful frisk when he was come near to the place where he was to suffer. Mr Rogers, the first that was burnt in Queen Mary's days, did sing in the flames: Vincentius, laughing at his torments, said that death and tortures were to Christians *jocularia et ludicra*, matters of sport and pastime; and he joyed and gloried when he went upon hot burning coals, as if he had trod upon roses. Fire, sword, death, prison, famine, are all pleasures, they are all delightful to me, saith Basil; and in his oration for Barlaam that famous martyr, saith that he delighted in the close prison as in a pleasant green meadow; and he took pleasure in the several inventions of tortures, as in several sweet flowers. William Tims, martyr, in a letter to a friend of his a little before his death, writeth thus, ' Now I take my leave of you till we meet in heaven, and hie you after. I have tarried a great while for you; and seeing you are so long in making ready, I will tarry no longer for you! you shall find me merrily singing, Holy, holy, holy, Lord God of Sabbath, at my journey's end,' &c. And when they kindled the fire at the feet of James Bainham, Methinks, said he, you strew roses before me.[3] When the prefect urged Basil to comply with the emperor, and threatened him with death if he denied, he gave him this resolute and stout answer, ' Thou threatenest me with death,' saith he, ' and I would that it would fall out so well on my side, that I might lay down this carcase of mine in the quarrel of Christ, and in defence of the truth, who is my head and captain:' and when the prefect pressed him to remember himself, and obey the emperor; he, rejecting all, told him, What I am to-day the same thou shalt find me to-morrow.[4]

---

[1] Dan. iii. 16, 17; Rom. viii. 36; Ps. xliv.; Phil. ii. 17; Acts xx. 22–44, and xxi. 13, &c.; Dan. vi.; 1 Pet. iv. 16; Acts v. 41, and vii. 55, 56; 2 Cor. i. 3–5.

[2] Acts and Mon., fol. 867. Modestus, lieutenant to Julian the emperor, told him that when the Christians suffered they did but deride them; and the torments, said he, with which Christians are tormented are more terrible to the tormentors than they are to the tormented.

[3] Foxe and Clarke, as before, under the preceding names.—G.

[4] Socrat. Eccl. Hist., lib. iv. c. 26, Gr.

When Chrysostom was greatly threatened by the cruel empress and others, he made this answer, ' If they keep me poor, I know Christ had not a house to put his head in: if they silence me, and put me out of the synagogue; so was that poor man that confessed Christ, and the apostles enjoined not to speak in the name of Jesus: if they cast me into prison, so was Jeremiah, St Peter, and St Paul, and many more: if I am forced to flee my country, I have that beloved John, and that Atlas-like Athanasius, for precedents of the like nature: or whatsoever else should be done unto me, I have the holy martyrs for my fellow-sufferers; and I will never count my life dear unto me, so I may finish my course with joy; but I will, by God's help be every ready, with all my heart, to suffer anything for the name of Jesus Christ, and for the least jot of his truth,' John ix. 22, 24; Acts v. 40, &c., and xii.; Eph. vi. 20; Rev. i.

Neither were they only a few choice persons who willingly, readily, cheerfully, and resolutely endured martyrdom in Christ's cause; but such multitudes, year after year, month after month, week after week, and day after day, as that one of the ancients testifieth that there was never a day in the year, except the first of January, whereunto the number of five hundred martyrs at least might not be ascribed.[1] So many, one after another, in one day suffered, as the executioner blunted his sword, and, with the pains he took, fainted.[2] That which many of them endured, though to flesh and blood it seemed intolerable, yet with much patience, excellent cheerfulness, and divine courage, they endured it.   They were not like bears hauled to the stake; but while persecutors were sitting on their judgment-seats, and condemning some Christians, others leaped in and professed themselves Christians, and suffered the uttermost that could be inflicted, with joyfulness and a kind of pleasantness, singing psalms as long as their breath lasted.[3]

Bucer, in an epistle to Calvin, tells him that there were some that would willingly redeem to the commonwealth the ancient liberty of worshipping Christ with their very lives.   True grace makes a Christian of a very heroic nature.   Holy zeal will make a Christian very ready to endure anything, or to suffer anything for Christ, his worship, his ways, his truth.

It is a high vanity for any man to think of getting to heaven without suffering.   In all the ages of the world the saints have found the way to happiness paved with troubles, and we must not think of finding it strewed with rosebuds.

When Paul and Silas were in prison, their hearts were so full of joy that they could not hold; but at midnight, when others were sleeping, they must fall a-singing out the praises of the Most High, Acts xvi. 25.   They found more pleasure than pain, more joy than sorrow, more comfort than torment in their bonds.[4]   The consolations of the Spirit rose so high in their souls that their prison was turned into a palace, yea, into a paradise.   Paul was a man that took a great

[1] Jerome, *ad Heliod.*   [2] Euseb. Eccl. Hist., lib. viii. c. 9.
[3] Euseb., *loc citat.*
[4] Paul rattles his chain which he did bear for the gospel's sake, and was as proud of it as a woman of her ornaments, saith Chrysostom.

deal of pleasure in his sufferings for Christ: 2 Cor. xii. 10, ' Therefore I take pleasure in infirmities, in reproaches, in necessities, in persecutions, in distresses, for Christ's sake.' He did not only bear his sufferings patiently, but cheerfully also ; he often sings it sweetly out, ' I Paul, a prisoner of Jesus Christ,' Col. iv. 3, 10 ; Rom. xvi. 7 ; Eph. vi. 20 ; 2 Tim. i. 16, &c. ; not I Paul an apostle, nor I Paul rapt up into the third heaven, nor I Paul that have more gifts, parts, and learning, than others ; but ' I Paul a prisoner,' to shew how much he rejoiced in his bonds and sufferings for Christ. Chrysostom did not hold Paul so happy for his rapture into paradise as he did for his imprisonment for Christ.

Oh, the sweet looks, the sweet words, the sweet hints, the sweet in-comes, the sweet joggings, the sweet embraces, the sweet influences, the sweet discoveries, the sweet love-letters, the sweet love-tokens, and the sweet comforts that Christians experience in their sufferings for Christ! In all their troubles and persecutions they may truly say, We have sweetmeats to eat, and waters of life to drink, and heavenly honeycombs to suck that the world knows not of ; and, indeed, when should the torch be lighted but in a dark night ; and when should the fire be made but when the weather is cold ; and when should the cordial be given but when the patient is weak ; and when should the God of comfort, the God of all kinds of comfort, and the God of all degrees of comfort, comfort his people, but under their troubles and persecutions ; for then comfort is most proper, necessary, seasonable, and suitable, and then God will be sure to pour in the oil of joy into their hearts? 2 Cor. i. 3-5. But,

6. Sixthly, Consider, *That there is a great truth in that old maxim, Non pœna, sed causa facit martyrem ; It is not the punishment, but the cause, that makes a martyr.* Let every man look that his cause be good. It is not the blood, but the cause, that makes a martyr. It is no ways meet that I should engage to suffer in every cause. Every cause will no more bear a man out in suffering than every shoulder will bear every burden, or than every little river will bear every ship that is of the greatest burden. One man suffers as a murderer, another suffers as a thief, another suffers as an evil-doer, and another suffers as a busybody in other men's matters ; but all such sufferers are rather malefactors than Christ's martyrs. ' Let none of you suffer as a murderer, or as a thief, or as an evil-doer, or as a busybody in other men's matters,' 1 Pet. iv. 15. It is but one word in the original, ἀλλοτριοε-πίσκοπος, as bishops in another's diocese, as pryers into other men's matters, as pragmatical persons that meddle with other men's concernments, without cause or call. It is not suffering for evil-doing, but suffering for well-doing that carries the crown, 2 Tim. ii. 12. It is not just, but unjust suffering that hath the recompense of reward annexed to it, 1 Pet. iii. 14, and iv. 14. It is not sufferers for the evil of sin, nor sufferers of the evil of sin ; but sufferers of the evil of punishment, for the avoiding of the evil of sin, whose cause is good. When I consider the cause of my condemnation, said Mr Bradford, I cannot but lament that I do no more rejoice than I do ; for it is for God's verity and truth.[1] So that the condemnation is not a con-

---

[1] Mr Bradford, to all that profess the gospel in Lancashire.

demnation of Bradford simply, but rather a condemnation of Christ and of his truth. Bradford is nothing but an instrument in which Christ and his doctrine is condemned. Christ and the thieves were in the same condemnation; Samson and the Philistines in the same destruction by the downfall of the house. *Similis pœna, dissimilis causa*, saith Augustine. Martyrdom is a crown, as old age, if it be found in a way of righteousness. Though life be a poor little thing to lay down for that Christ that has done such great things for us, and that has suffered such grievous things, and that has prepared such glorious things for us; yet, it is too precious to lay down in any cause but what is honourable, just, and good, Isa. liii.; John xiv. Luther professed to Spalatine that he rejoiced with all his heart, that God called him to suffer for so good a cause, acknowledging himself unworthy of such a favour.[1] It is the goodness of a man's cause that makes him divinely merry with the martyrs, and to sing in a prison with Paul and Silas, Col. ii. 24. When a man's cause is good he may call his sufferings the sufferings of Christ, and his scars and marks, στίγματα, brands and marks of the Lord Jesus, Gal. vi. 17. The Jews have been hated and persecuted for many ages; first by the Romans, and since by all other nations, but not for any just or righteous cause, but for their impiety, obstinacy, and contempt of Christ and his gospel, and for killing the prophets, and stoning them that were sent amongst them, Mat. xxii. 2–8, and xxiii. 30, 34, 37, 38. But gracious persons are endued, not only with reason, but also with spiritual understanding and divine wisdom, which makes them well weigh what they do, and what they suffer. Sincere Christians advisedly endure what they endure for the faith's sake, ' So fight I, not as one that beateth the air,' 1 Cor. ix. 26; that is, not as a madman that fighteth with a shadow, not weighing what he doth, but as a man of understanding, that doth very well know that I have good cause to do what I do. Persecutors commonly judge suffering saints to be no better than sots, idiots, frantics, mad, &c., not knowing the goodness of the cause for which they suffer, nor the noble ends which they aim at in suffering, nor the blessed fruits that attend their sufferings.

But when may a man safely and groundedly conclude that his cause is good, or that he suffers for well-doing, or for a good cause, and as a Christian? Now to this question I shall give these following answers:—

[1.] First, *When a man suffers for doing that which Christ commands*, then he suffers for well-doing, then he suffers as a Christian, and then his cause is good, 1 Pet. iv. 15, 16. You know there is nothing in all the Scripture that God stands more upon than purity of religion, than purity of worship, than purity of ordinances, in opposition to all mixtures and corruptions whatsoever, James i. 27; Phil. iii. 3; John iv. 23, 24. O sirs! the great God stands upon nothing more in all the world than upon purity in his worship. There is nothing that does so provoke and exasperate God against a people as mixtures in his worship and service, Mat. xxi. 12, 13; John ii. 15–17. And no wonder, for mixtures in his worship are expressly cross to his

[1] Ep. ad Spalat., fol. 287.

commands, and pollutions in worship do sadly reflect upon the name of God, the honour of God, the truth of God; and therefore his heart rises against them. Defilements in worship do sorely reflect upon the wisdom of Christ and the faithfulness of Christ, as if he were not faithful enough, nor wise enough, nor prudent, nor understanding enough, to order, direct, and guide his people in the matters of his worship; but must be beholden to the wisdom, prudence, and care of man, of vain man, of sinful man, of vile and unworthy man, to complete, perfect, and make up something that was wanting in his worship and service, &c., Heb. iii. 4–6. Now if a man suffers for owning pure worship and ordinances, for standing for pure worship and ordinances, and for being found in the practice of pure worship and ordinances, his cause is good, and he suffers as a Christian. But,

[2.] Secondly, *When a man suffers for refusing, or for not doing, that which Christ comdemns in his word*, then his cause is good, and he suffers as a Christian for well-doing. Now in matters of divine worship, God condemns all mixtures, all inventions and devices of men. The very spirit, life, and soul of the second commandment lies in these words, 'Thou shalt not make to thyself any graven image.' God abhors that men should mix their water with his wine, their dross with his gold, their chaff with his wheat, &c. When men will venture to be so hardy and bold with God as to defile his worship with their mixtures, then God is fully resolved to be a swift and terrible witness against them, as you may clearly see by comparing those notable places of Scripture together in the margin.[1] There is no sin that does so greatly incense and provoke God to jealousy and wrath against a people, as mixtures in his worship. God can bear with defilements anywhere rather than in worship and service. God did bear much and bear long with the Jews; but when they had defiled and corrupted his worship, then God gave them a bill of divorce, and scattered them as dung among the nations. Now when a man suffers for refusing to worship God with a mixed worship, or with an invented or devised worship, which Christ in his word doth everywhere condemn, then his cause is good, and he suffers as a Christian. But,

[3.] Thirdly, *They that stoutly and resolutely assert that the blessed Scriptures are a sufficient rule to order, guide, and direct them in all matters of worship*, they have a good cause, Luke x. 25, 26; and they that suffer upon this account suffer as Christians for well-doing. Such vain men greatly detract from the sufficiency of the Scripture, who mingle their own or other men's inventions with divine institutions; and who set their posts by God's posts, and their thresholds by God's thresholds, Ezek. xliii. 9. The precepts and traditions of men, with their inventions and additions to the worship of God, are styled posts and thresholds, because the authors of them do lean and stand so much upon them, and set them in the way to hinder others from the enjoyment of temple-privileges, unless they will own and comply with them in their way and mode of worship; but upon all such posts and thresholds, that are of men's setting up in the worship of God, you may run and read folly, weakness, rottenness, and madness. It is only God's

[3] Lev. x. 1, 2; Ezek. v. 11, 12, and xxiii. 38, 39; Jer. vii. 29, 30; Ezek. viii. 17, 18; Rev. ii. 22, 23; Deut. iv. 2, and xii. 32, &c.

posts, God's thresholds, God's institutions, God's appointments, that have- wisdom and holiness, beauty and glory, written upon them.[1] For men to set up their posts by God's posts, and to give their posts equal honour and authority with God's posts, this is a defiling of the worship of God, and a profaning of the name of God, which he will certainly avenge; for he will admit no rival or proprietary in the things of his worship. O sirs! the blessed Scriptures are sufficient to direct us fully in everything that belongs to the worship and service of God, so as that we need not depend upon the wisdom, prudence, care, and authority of any man under heaven to direct us in matters of worship: 2 Tim. iii. 16, 17, 'All scripture is given by inspiration of God, and is profitable for doctrine, for reproof, for correction, for instruction in righteousness: that the man of God may be perfect, thoroughly furnished unto all good works.' The Scriptures are sufficient to inform the ignorant, to confute the erroneous, to reform the vicious, and to guide and direct, support and comfort, those that are gracious.[2] Here a lamb may wade, and an elephant may swim; here is milk for babes, and meat for strong men; here is comfort for the afflicted, and succour for the tempted, and ease for the troubled, and light for the clouded, and enlargement for the straitened, &c. Oh, how full of light, how full of life, how full of love, how full of sweetness, how full of goodness, how full of righteousness and holiness, &c., is every chapter, and every verse in every chapter, yea, and every line in every verse! The Rabbins say that a mountain of matter hangs upon every word of Scripture, yea, upon every tittle of Scripture. When the people of God have been in any outward or inward distresses or troubles, God never sends them to the shop of men's traditions and inventions, but he still sends them to the blessed Scriptures: Isa. viii. 20, 'To the law, and to the testimony; if they speak not according to this word, it is because there is no light' (שׁחר, no morning) 'in them:' chap. xxxiv. 16, 'Seek ye out of the book of the Lord, and read; no one of these shall fail, none shall want her mate; for my mouth it hath commanded, and my Spirit it hath gathered them:'[3] And in the New Testament, Christ sends his hearers to the Scriptures: John v. 39, 'Search the Scriptures, for in them ye think ye have eternal life, and they are they which testify of me.' The Greek word, ἐρευνᾶτε, that is here rendered 'search,' signifies a strict, narrow, curious, diligent search. We must search the Scriptures as we would search for gold, or for some precious stones, which we would fain find; we must search the Scriptures as hunters seek and search out their game. The Scripture is so perfect a rule that the most specious observances, the most glorious performances, the most exact worship, is no way acceptable unto God if not directed in his word. They may have λόγον σοφίας ἐν ἐθελοθρησκείᾳ, 'a show of wisdom in will-worship,' to the pleasing of men, not to the honour

---

[1] It is very remarkable that of old they were to be cut off that made anything like the institutions and appointments of God, Exod. xxx. 32, 33, 37, 38; and if some were so served, would not the world be in more love, peace, and quietness than now it is?

[2] *Adoro plenitudinem Scripturarum*, I adore the fulness of the Scriptures.—*Tertullian.*

[3] No histories are comparable to the histories of the Scripture—(1.) for antiquity; (2.) rarity; (3.) variety; (4.) brevity; (5.) perspicuity; (6.) harmony; (7.) verity; all which should greatly encourage Christians to a serious perusal of them.

of God,' Col. ii. 23.   God gave Moses a pattern for the making of the tabernacle, Exod. xxv. 9, and David for the temple, Heb. viii. 5, and all things were to be ordered and regulated according to this pattern. God hath set us a perfect rule of worship in his word, and no service pleaseth him but what is according to this rule.   As our Saviour told the woman of Samaria concerning the Samaritan worship at Mount Gerizim, and the Jewish worship at Jerusalem, that the Samaritans worshipped they knew not what, John iv. 20–22; the Jews knew what they worshipped, for salvation was of the Jews.   Why so?   Because the Jews had God's special direction and appointment of God's word for their worship and service, which the Samaritans had not.   All our worship must be regulated by God's will, not our own: *Non ex arbitrio Deo serviendum, sed ex imperio;* Not according to our own fancy, but God's command and prescription.   I say of all human-invented will-worship of God, as Tertullian of the heathen worship, *Ex religione superstitio compingitur, et eo irreligiosior, quanto Ethnicus paratior;* Men in this are no better than laboriously superstitious, taking pains to be irreligious.   And so the apostle, 2 Pet. i. 19–21, sends his hearers to the Scriptures, as to a surer word than that of the revelation, all which speaks out the sufficiency of the Scripture, to direct us in all matters of divine worship, and in whatever else may help on the internal and eternal welfare of our precious and immortal souls.

That which bred the popish religion, superstition, idolatry, and pompous worship, was men's departing from the word, and not cleaving to the word as a sufficient rule to direct them in all matters of worship; and what woeful mischiefs and miseries have been brought upon the people of the Lord in this land and elsewhere by men that make not the word the rule of their worship, but cry up an outward pompous worship, I have no mind to enumerate at this time.   But how will these vain men, that accuse the holy Scriptures of insufficiency, blush, be ashamed, and confounded, when in the great day the Lord shall plead the excellency and vindicate the sufficiency and authority of his blessed book, in opposition to all the mixtures of men's traditions with divine institutions!   Now they that suffer for asserting the holy Scriptures to be a sufficient rule to order, guide, and direct them in all matters of worship, they have a good cause, and they suffer as Christians for well-doing.   But,

[4.] *They that are assertors of the true God, in opposition to the idols of the nations,* have a good cause; and they that suffer upon this account suffer as Christians for well-doing.   Upon this foot the Christians under the heathen emperors in the primitive times suffered great things; and are there none that suffer this day upon this account by the Romish powers?   But,

[5.] Fifthly, *They who assert that God will not bear with mixtures in his worship and service, but revenge himself upon the corrupters of his worship,* they have a good cause; and they that suffer upon that account suffer as Christians for well-doing.   All mixtures debase the worship and service of God, and makes the worship a vain worship, Isa. xxix. 13, 14; Mat. xv. 3, 6, 8, 9.   As the mixing of water with wine is the debasing of the wine, and the mixing of tin with silver, or brass with gold, is debasing of the silver and gold, so for men to mix and mingle their traditions and inventions with God's institutions is to debase the worship and service of God, and to detract from the excellency and glory of it. You know that the kings and princes of the world have most severely punished such who by their base mixtures have imbased their coin; and assuredly there is a day a-coming when the King of kings will most severely punish all such who have imbased his worship and service, by mixing human inventions and Romish traditions with his holy institutions: Rev. xxii. 18, ' For I testify unto every man that heareth the words of the prophecy of this book, If any man shall add unto these things, God shall add unto him the plagues that are written in this book.'[1] And no wonder; for what horrible pride, presumption, stoutness, and baseness is it in foolish man to be so bold with the great God, as to dare to mix anything of his own with his worship and service, which, according to divine institution, is so perfect and complete. God will never bear it to see men lay their dirt upon his gold, and to put their rags upon his royal robes. Ah, Christians, it is best to stand up for holy ordinances and pure worship, in opposition to all mixtures whatsoever. Oh, do not touch a polluted worship, do not plead and contend for a polluted worship, but let Baal plead for Baal, 1 Kings xviii. 21; and though all the world should wonder[2] after the beast, yet do not you wonder[2] after the beast, Rev. xiii. 3, 4, 6, 17; and though every forehead should have the mark of the beast upon it, yet do you abhor his mark, and whatever else it be that does but smell and savour of the beast, Rev. xiv. 9, 11. It is a very dangerous thing for any mortals to be adding to God's worship and word; there is a horrible curse that hangs over the heads of all such that add or detract from the blessed Scriptures. If falsifiers of coin are liable unto the civil curse of the law, how much more shall the anathema of eternal damnation be inflicted upon the corrupters of God's word and worship. ' To them that add thereto, God will add all the plagues of this book ' —to wit, the seven last plagues—' and cast them into the lake of fire and brimstone, with the dragon, the beast, and the false prophet,' Rev. xix. Now they that suffer for asserting that God will not bear with mixtures in his worship and service, but revenge himself upon the corrupters of his worship and service, they have a good cause, and they suffer as Christians for well-doing. But,

[6.] Sixthly, *They who are hated, scorned, despised, reproached, opposed, persecuted, imprisoned, ruined for their non-compliance with the times, and with the wills and lusts of men, and with the worship of the world and the ways of the world,* they have a good cause, and they suffer as Christians for well-doing, 1 Pet. iv. 4, 5; Jude 15; Rev. iii. 4; 1 Cor. vii. 23; Gal. i. 10. And is not this the very case of the people of God this day? for would they, or durst they, comply with the times, and with the wills and lusts of men, and with the worship of the world and the ways of the world, they should be white-boys,[3] and instead of prisons might stand in princes' palaces as well as

---

[1] There will come a day when Jews, Turks, and Papists shall pay dear for adding to the Scriptures.

[2] Spelled ' wander.'—G.

[3] A term of endearment, *e.g.* Ford. ' I know, quoth I, I am his white-boy.'—'*Tis Pity,* &c., i. 3. Subsequently applied polemically.—G.

others, and might eat the fat and drink the sweet, and live at ease, and grow rich as well as others. But some do not love that we should either harp hard or long upon this string; and therefore,

[7.] Seventhly, *They that are assertors of Christ, of the true Messiah, and his glorious gospel and gospel ordinances, in opposition to all such as either deny him or his gospel, or that make head against him or gospel ordinances, gospel administrations,* they have a good cause, and if they suffer upon that account, they suffer as Christians for well-doing. The sufferings of the people of God for the first three hundred years, were clearly stated for Christ and the gospel in common. It was the administration of the gospel in the whole and in every part of it, and Gentilism advanced instead thereof, that brought on a warm persecution. Seeing serious Christians are for pure ordinances and pure administrations, and what they have suffered and do daily suffer upon that account, all that do not wilfully shut their eyes may easily discern. It is sad when such men's mouths must be stopped who are qualified, gifted, graced, and called, both by God and men, to preach the glorious, the everlasting gospel, 2 Cor. iv. 4. But when the devil and his factors have done their worst, the gospel will get ground by all the opposition that is made against it, Rev. xiv. 6. Among many other visions that John had, ' he saw an angel fly in the midst of heaven, having the everlasting gospel to preach unto them that dwell on the earth; and to every nation, and kindred, and tongue, and people; saying with a loud voice, Fear God, and give glory to him,' &c., Rev. xiv. 7, 8. Now mark what next follows: ' Another angel, saying, Babylon is fallen, is fallen; Babylon the Great is fallen.' Now behold the efficacy and power of gospel-preaching. Let but the gospel be sincerely preached, and Babylon must down. The devil and Dagon must fall before the ark of God's presence; whatsoever the purposes, projects, pretences, policies, conspiracies, combinations, and confederacies of lewd, superstitious, atheistical, wicked wretches be, yet they shall never be able to stop the stream of God's word, dam up the wells of salvation, or hinder the free passage of the gospel, no more than they are able to bind up the wind in their fists, or stop the sun from running its race, or hinder the clouds from watering the earth.[1] It is true that the faithful ministers of the gospel may, by the instruments of Satan, be stocked, stoned, sawn asunder, burned with fire, slain with the sword, clapped up in prison, fettered in chains, plundered, &c., yet the gospel may be, nay is, in lively operation, a light that cannot be put out, a heat that cannot be smothered, a power that cannot be broken; for even then the courageous and constant sufferings of God's faithful ministers, and their cheerful and patient bearing of the cross, doth, as by a lively voice, publish and proclaim the truth of the gospel for which they suffer, and serves to win many to the faith of Christ. Paul's bonds fell out to the furtherance of the gospel, Phil. i. 7, 12–14, 17. Paul's iron chain was more famous and glorious all the world over, than all the golden chains in Nero's palace. Whatsoever persecuting popes and persecuting emperors have attempted against the gospel, Christ

[1] The more wicked men rage, the more the gospel spreads, as you may see, Acts v. 40–42, and viii. 1, 3–6, 12, and xi. 19–21, 26, and xii. 1–4, 23, 24; Heb. xi. 34–36; Rev. ii. 10; Acts xvi. 23–25.

has turned it all to the furtherance of the gospel.[1] The pope's bulls, and the emperor's thunderbolts, did not amaze and discourage men, but did exceedingly animate and encourage them to own the gospel, to embrace the gospel, and to stand up in the defence of the gospel. Cæsar sending the Protestants' confession abroad to other Christian princes, as desiring their advice about it, dispersed and spread it more in all parts than all the Lutheran preachers could have done; for which cause Luther laughs not a little at the foolish wisdom of the papists, in a certain epistle of his to the elector of Saxony.[2] Julian, observing that the more ministers and Christians were persecuted the more they increased, he gave over persecution, and spared those whom he could have wished out of the world. And would it not be the wisdom and the interest of the persecutors in our days to write after Julian's copy? and if they will not, then let them remember that it is the most effectual way under heaven to propagate those truths, opinions, ways, principles, and practices, which their hearts rise and swell against, by laying them in bonds which stand up most eminently in the defence of those truths, opinions, ways, principles, and practices. The nature of man is very curious and inquisitive. Men, as men, are led by common compassion to desire to understand the grounds of men's sufferings. By this means the sufferings, especially the imprisonment of the apostles, carried the doctrine of the gospel to many places where the apostles themselves never came, nor perhaps could come; no doubt but the fame of their suffering went faster and farther too than they could go. But,

[8.] Eighthly, *They that are assertors of any one fundamental truth, in opposition to error and heresy truly so called,* have a good cause; and if they suffer upon that account, they suffer as Christians for well-doing, Acts xxiv. 14; 1 Cor. xi. 9; 2 Pet. ii. 1; Gal. v. 20. Such were those Christians that suffered under the Arian emperors, Constantius, Valens, and others, who suffered for maintaining that Christ was co-essential, co-equal, and co-eternal with the Father; and such were Wickliffe, John Huss, and Jerome of Prague, &c. Are there none this day among us that suffer in their names, in their estates, in their persons, in their liberties, for asserting and maintaining the great truths of the gospel, in opposition to Socinianism, Arianism, Popery, will-worship, &c.? Are there no Socinian atheists among us who deny with open face the godhead of Christ, and of the Holy Ghost, as if Christ were a constituted God, and not of the same substance with the Father from all eternity; not a God by nature, but by donation in time? And though God hath raised up several champions in this his Israel, to disarm them of all their subtilties, and to beat them out of all their trenches, though they were dug as low as hell; yet, how have they put on a brow of brass, and do all they can to bring on a warm persecution upon their opposers? Prov. xxvii. 22. But,

[9.] Ninthly, *They that plead for the reduction of all ordinances, worship, church-government, and discipline, to the primitive pattern and institution, in opposition to all human and antichristian inventions, traditions, and innovations in the worship of God,* they have a

[1] Scultet. Annal.   [2] Scultet. Annal., 274.

good cause; and they that suffer upon that account, suffer as Christians for well-doing. Surely this is a truth we must live and die by, viz., That no ordinance, worship, government, or discipline, is to be held up or maintained in the church but what has the stamp of a divine institution upon it. The worshipping of God in spirit and in truth is that worship which God commands, commends, accepts, and rewards; and therefore let us make it our business, our work, our heaven, to keep close to this kind of worship, John iv. 23, 24; Rom. i. 9; Phil. iii. 3. Christ will shortly come in flames of fire, and vindicate this kind of worship against all opposers, 2 Thes. i. 7–10. Hold out faith and patience a little, and Christ will call all the troublers of his church and people into the valley of decision, Joel iii. 14; and there, with a strong hand, and with an outstretched arm, he will plead with them, and with all such as have muddied the waters of his sanctuary, and polluted those silver streams; and then it will appear whether the outward ceremonious worshipping of God, or the worshipping him in spirit and in truth, be the true worship, Isa. xl. 10; Jer. xxi. 5; Ezek. xxxii. 2. Judicious Hooker determines, that in God's service to do that which we are not to do is a greater fault than not to do that which we are commanded. Amongst other reasons, he gives this to our purpose, because in the one we seem to charge the law of God with hardness only, and in the other, with foolishness and insufficiency, which God gave us as a perfect rule of his worship and service.[1] But,

[10.] Tenthly and lastly, *They that are assertors of those precious privileges that are the purchase of the blood of Christ,* they have a good cause; and if they suffer upon that account, they suffer as Christians for well-doing, Eph. i. 22, 23; Col. i. 18; Phil. ii. 6–10. As for instance,

First, Christ as mediator hath purchased for himself a headship and supremacy over his church. Now such as stand up for the headship of the Lamb, against all those that would rob him of his headship, either at Rome or elsewhere, they have a righteous cause; and if they suffer upon that account, they suffer as Christians for welldoing.

Secondly, He has purchased for his people a liberty to serve and worship him without fear, in holiness and righteousness all the days of their life, Luke i. 69, 70, 74, 75. He has purchased for his people a liberty from the ceremonies of Moses' law, which were originally the commands of God himself; how much more then from all Paganish and Antichristian ceremonies! Gal. v. 1. The imposition of traditional observances and ceremonies, is to reduce us under the Jewish yoke, which neither we nor our fathers were able to bear, Acts xv. 10; or to impose them as equally obligatory to conscience, as divine commands; or to impose them as the immediate worship of God, or as duties essentially necessary in order to salvation: Christians justly abhor, as the tyranny of Rome, as the infringement of Christian liberty, and as a violation and making void the commandment of God; as our Saviour told the Pharisees of old, that 'they made the commandment

---

[1] Ecclesiastical Polity, book ii. c. vi. [2.]: Works by Keble, vol. i. p. 311, 2d ed., 1841.—G.

of God of none effect,' Mat. xv. 6. The Greek word ἠκυρώσατε, signifies ' to deprive of all rule and authority.' They had such a superstitious
esteem of their traditions, ceremonies, &c., that they sought to shoulder
God out of his throne, to divest and spoil him of his rule and authority,
to ungod him, as it were, by making his commandment void and
invalid. Christ reprehends three things in the Jewish traditions; (1.)
That they obtruded outward cleanness on God, instead of the purity
of the heart; (2.) That by their human traditions, they made void
the worship of God; (3.) That they preferred human traditions before the divine precepts; and were so taken with their traditions, that
they neglected the divine precepts; yea, made them altogether vain,
as the papists, and others that are popishly affected, do this day.[1]
They that are the most zealous for the introducing of useless ceremonies in the church, are usually the most negligent to preach the
cautions in using them; and simple people, like children in eating of
fish, swallow bones and all, to the danger of choking. Besides, what
is observed of horse-hairs, that lying nine days in water, they turn to
snakes; so some ceremonies, though dead at first, in continuance of
time quicken, get stings, and may do much mischief; especially in
such an age, wherein the meddling of some have justly awakened the
jealousy of all.[2]   Now, whoever shall suffer for asserting of any of the
precious privileges, that are the purchase of Christ's blood, they suffer
in a righteous cause, they suffer as Christians, for well-doing. And
thus you see how a man may know when his cause is good, just, and
righteous, and when he suffers as a Christian for well-doing. But,

7. Seventhly, Consider, *That it is not enough for a man to have a
good cause, but he must have a clear call ; else he may be a sufferer,
but no martyr.* Some may have a good cause, and yet want a clear
call. Some may suffer for the cause of God, and yet sin in suffering,
for want of a call.[3] Christ calls not all to suffer; to some it is given,
to others it is not given. When a man's call is clear, his peace will
be sweet, his courage will be high, and his comforts will be strong,
though his sufferings be never so great, nor never so long. Though it
be a high honour to suffer for the gospel, yet ' no man ought to take
this honour upon himself, but he that is called of God.' Christians
must take as much heed how they espouse a suffering state, as how
they shun a suffering state. I am not to go to prison upon choice,
but upon a call, but upon a warrant under God's own hand; though
it be an argument of a gracious spirit, to be always of a ready and
forward mind to suffer for Christ. And when he demands, Who will
go with me? who will bear my cross? cheerfully to answer, I will go,
Lord, let me bear it: yet should we take heed, that as we hang not
back when he says go; so that we run not before he sends us, before
he calls us.

Quest. But how shall I know when I am called to suffer, when I
am called to lay down life, liberty, and all, for the profession of Christ
and the gospel? To this I answer :—

[1] Chemnitius.
[2] Dr [Thomas] Fuller, Serm. [and cf. Spencer, as before under ' ceremonies.'—G.]
[3] Phil. i. 29. A priest might enter into a leper's house without danger, because he
had a calling from God so to do. And we may follow God dry-shod through the Red
Sea when God gives a call.

[1.] First, *When the truth will suffer, and the name of God suffer, and the gospel will suffer, should we decline suffering,* then we are called to suffer. It is our duty to suffer anything, to suffer the worst of things that the worst of men can inflict, rather than that the truth should suffer, or the name of God suffer, or the gospel suffer.

[2.] Secondly, *When the case stands so with us, that we cannot keep life, estate, liberty, &c., without denying of Christ or the gospel, or without concealing this precious truth or that, or without turning our backs upon this ordinance or that, &c.,* then we are called to suffer. When we cannot preserve our lives, our liberties, our estates, without denying of Christ, or the concerns of Christ, in one degree or another, in one kind or another, then we are called to lay down our lives, our liberties, our estates, &c., at the feet of Christ, as the saints and martyrs of old have done before us.

[3.] Thirdly, *When our way is so hedged up with thorns,* Hosea ii. 6, *that we must either sin or suffer, when sin and sufferings surround us, so that we cannot get out or come off, but we must either sin or suffer,* then I must, with the three champions, choose rather to burn than to bow; and with Daniel to the lion's den, than to omit my duty, Dan. iii. 17; and with Moses, choose to suffer afflictions with the people of God, than to enjoy the pleasures of sin, which are but for a season, Heb. xi. 24–26. I may safely and groundedly conclude, that Christ calls me to suffer, when I must either sin or suffer. When the case stands thus, then I may be confident of the singular presence of God with me, the special blessing of God upon me, and a gracious or a glorious deliverance out of all my sufferings. But,

[4.] Fourthly and lastly, *When a Christian, to the best of his understanding, has seriously weighed all things and circumstances, and is well satisfied in his mind and conscience that his sufferings will be the exaltation of Christ, the furtherance of the gospel, the stopping of the mouths of the wicked, the confirmation of those that are strong, and the strengthening and encouraging of those that are weak,* then he may safely conclude that Christ calls him to suffer. But,

8. Eighthly, Consider, *That the sufferings of the saints in these days are light and easy to the sufferings that were inflicted upon the Jews in the days of Antiochus, and on Christians in the times of the ten notorious persecutions under the Roman emperors, and to those that have been inflicted upon the martyrs since.*[1] So cruel was the sight of those tortures which persecutors inflicted, as exceeds all expression.[2] Constant Christians had their flesh torn from their backs with rods, scourges, whips, and cords, so as their bones lay bare; and the raw parts of their bodies were washed with vinegar and salt. They were stretched on racks, their legs were broken, and so left miserably to perish; they were gored with sharp pricks under the lowest parts of their nails; their bodies were scraped with shells to death; their backs were flayed; their skins were pulled over their heads, from the brow to the chin; their noses, lips, ears, hands, and feet were cut off, and

[1] Mac. vi. 9, 10, vii. 1–4. Euseb. Eccles. Hist., lib. viii. c. 6.
[2] Hym. 10, de Rom. Anno. Mart. Laddelacorda computeth forty-four several kinds of torments wherewith the primitive Christians were tried. Adv. Sacr., cap. 128. [As before. See Index, Maurice de la Corde.—G.]

they, as sacrifices, cut in gobbets; their tongues were cut out by the roots, and pulled out of their jaws; their eyes were bored, and digged out; their bodies were rent and pulled in pieces by strong boughs forced together by instruments, and let loose when the limbs of the bodies of martyrs were tied fast unto them; their limbs were also pulled to pieces with wild horses; their brains were knocked out with fuller's clubs; their legs were broken in pieces; they were burnt with fire; they were a long while together parched with hot burning coals; being hanged by the heels, and their heads downward over a soft fire, they were choked with smoke; they were roasted at the fire, as flesh to be eaten used to be roasted; they were leisurely broiled on gridirons over the fire; they were fried in red-hot iron chairs, as in a frying-pan, which annoyed the standers-by with a stench; hot boiling lead was poured down their throats; they clapped fiery plates of brass upon the most tender parts of their bodies.[1] A persecuting tyrant, considering the nature of the country, that it was terrible cold, and the time of the year, that it was winter, and a night wherein the cold extremely increased, and that the north wind then blew there, commanded forty Christians to be set stark naked under the open air in the midst of the city to freeze to death. Then, when they heard that charge, with joy casting away even their innermost vestment, they went on to their death by cold.[2] They endured the violence of leopards, bears, wild boars, and bulls. Attalus and Alexander were twice baited with wild beasts, to be torn in pieces by them, as Eusebius reports.[3] Attalus, escaping the beasts, was reserved to other torments, to be burnt to death in an iron chair, heated red fire hot. Macedonius, Theodulus, and Tatianus were laid upon a gridiron, and broiled to death.[4] There were many Christians together stopped up in lakes or caves, artificially made close, which lakes or ditches were filled with a company of dormice, kept hungry, to gnaw and feed upon the poor Christians, they being all the while bound hand and foot, that they could not keep off those hunger-starved creatures, which were kept without meat also, purposely that they might fasten with the more eagerness upon the bodies of those precious Christians. They were destroyed with hunger, thirst, and cold.[5] Such as were stifled in prisons, they cast to dogs, setting watchmen night and day, lest any of them should be buried. And such remainders as were left both of beasts and fire, in part torn, and in part burnt, together with the heads and bodies of others, they cast out in like manner, unburied, and committed them some days to the custody of soldiers.[6] Thus the barbarous cruelty of persecutors extended itself as far as it could beyond the temporal lives of the martyrs. Ecclesiastical histories tell us that all the apostles died violent deaths.[7] Peter was crucified with his heels upwards. Christ was crucified with his head upwards, but Peter thought this was too great an honour for him to be crucified as his Lord, and therefore he chose to be crucified with his heels upward;

---

[1] Brooks is enumerating the engravings of his favourite folio. Clarke, as before.—G.
[2] Basil in xl. Mart. Conc. *Item* Greg. Nyssen de iisdem, Orat. 2.
[3] Eccles. Hist., lib. v. c. 1.   [4] Socrat. Hist., lib. iii. c. 13.
[5] Mag. Cent. iv. c. 3, ex *Theodoreto.*
[6] Euseb. Eccles. Hist., lib. v. c. 1, lib. viii. c. 6, 7, &c. Niceph., lib. vii. c. 11, 12.
[7] See my 'Beauty of Holiness,' pp. 413-415. [Vol. iv.—G.]

and Andrew was crucified by Egeus, king of Edessa; and James, the son of Zebedee, was slain by Herod with the sword, Acts xii. 2; and Philip was crucified at Hierapolis, in Asia; and while Bartholomew was preaching the glad tiddings of salvation, multitudes fell upon him, and beat him down with staves, and then crucified him; and after all this, his skin was flayed off, and he beheaded; Thomas was slain with a dart at Calumina, in India; and Matthew was slain with a spear, say some; others say he was run through with a sword; and James, the son of Alpheus, who was called the Just, was thrown down from off a pinnacle of the temple; and yet having some life left in him, he was brained with a fuller's club. Lebbeus was slain by Agbarus, king of Edessa, and Paul was beheaded at Rome by Nero; and Simon the Canaanite was crucified in Egypt, say some; others say that he and Jude were slain in a tumult of the people; and Matthias was stoned to death, and John was banished into Patmos, Rev. i. 9.; and afterwards, as some histories tell us, he was by that cruel tyrant Domitian cast into a tub of scalding oil, and yet delivered by a miracle. Thus all these worthies, 'of whom this world was not worthy,' Heb. xi. 38, except John, died violent deaths, and so, through sufferings, entered into glory. To conclude, Lactantius saith, not only the men among the Christians, and those of stronger years and hearts, but even our women and little children, saith he, have endured all torments, and been too hard for their tormentors. No rack, no fire could fetch so much as a groan from them, which the stoutest thieves and malefactors among their persecutors could not undergo, but they would roar and cry out through impatience and disability to endure them.[1] I suppose that more cruel torments cannot be invented than of old have been inflicted on Christians. Persecutors have acknowledged that they were overcome, and had no more to inflict.[2] Such torture and torments so courageously and manfully have sundry Christians in all ages suffered as to them who only heard thereof they seemed incredible; and to many who were eye-witnesses thereof they seemed so strange, and beyond admiration, as they thought the martyrs to be mad, witless, and senseless: but the martyrs had peace and rest and quiet within, and the favourable presence of God so shining upon their souls, that they were encouraged and enabled with a holy and heavenly bravery of spirit to bid defiance to their most cruel persecutors.

Now, Christians, if you compare your most cruel sufferings with the sufferings of the saints of old, how easy and light will they be found to be! What are molehills to mountains, scratches upon the hand to stabs at the heart? No more are your greatest sufferings to those that the saints have met with in former ages. And therefore, though men frown upon you, and threaten you with censures, imprisonment, banishment, confiscation, and all the evil human might and cruelty can do unto you, yet be not moved, but account yourselves happy that you have any opportunity to do or suffer anything whereby you may testify that Christ and his concerns do lie near your hearts, and whereby you may further his opposed interest, and bear witness to his despised truth, 1 Pet. iv. 14, 15. But,

9. Ninthly, Consider, *That the saints and martyrs of old have made*

[1] Lact., lib. v. c. 13.　　　　　[2] Euseb. Eccl. Hist., lib. v. c. 1.

*little reckoning or account of their lives, liberties, relations, or estates,
when they stood in competition with Christ, or his truth, worship, ways,
ordinances, interest, or with their profession of the Christian faith.*
Witness that glorious testimony that the apostle gives of them, 'They
would not accept deliverance.'[1] He means deliverance from death, or
preservation of life. This, though offered, they would not accept—
namely, on persecutors' terms or conditions, which was to deny the
truth of God, or renounce their faith in him. They scorned deliverance upon base terms, and would rather die than deny Christ or his
truth. This phrase, 'Not accepting deliverance,' presupposeth that
deliverance was offered to them, otherwise they could not have rejected it, for their not accepting was a rejecting. Their persecutors
offered them deliverance upon their compliance with their wills, lusts,
ways, worship, &c. This is evident by that which Nebuchadnezzar
said to Daniel's three champions when they were accused for not
worshipping his idol, which was this, 'If ye be ready to fall down
and worship the image,' Dan. iii. 15. He hereby implies that they
should be spared; for he addeth, 'If you worship not, you shall
be cast into a fiery furnace.' And this is further evident in those
to whom the apostle hath reference—viz., the Maccabees, 2 Mac. vi.
18–31. And this was the common practice of the persecuting emperors in the ten persecutions; and after them, with the Antichristian
persecutors; and more particularly, with the high persecutors in
Queen Mary's days. But the Christians in those several ages had such
a mighty presence of God with them, that they chose rather to
suffer the worst of deaths than to preserve their lives by complying
with the wills, lusts, ways, and worship of their persecutors. For
ever remember this, that the envy and malice of persecutors is more
against the glorious truth the saints profess than it is against their
persons; for let but Christians relinquish the truth, deny the truth,
reproach the truth, or oppose the truth, and presently they shall be
white-boys,[2] great favourites, good sons of the church, and what
not. That the envy and malice of persecutors is more against the
truth than the professors of it, is most evident, in that they persecute
strangers whom they never knew before. It is said of Paul, that
'if he found any such, he brought them bound,' Acts ix. 2. All was
fish that was caught in his net. If father or mother, brother or sister,
child or cousin profess the truth, plead for the truth, stand up for
the truth, men of persecuting spirits will prosecute and persecute
them to the death: 'The brother shall deliver up the brother to death,
and the father the child; and the children shall rise up against their
parents, and cause them to be put to death,' Mat. x. 21; Luke xxi.
16. Alphonsus Diarius delivered up his own brother John at Neu-
berg in Germany into his enemies' hands.[3] So Dr London[4] made
Filmer the martyr's own brother witness against him, by supplying of
him with meat and money, and by telling of him he should never
want. So one Woodman was delivered by his own brother into his
enemies' hands.[5] And in the civil wars of France, not to mention
that of England, the sons fought against their fathers, and brothers

---

[1] Heb. xi. 35, *vide* Estius.   [2] As before.—G.   [3] Sleidan, lib. i. 17.
[4] *Sic.*—G.   [5] [Foxe,] Acts and Mon., fol. 1112 and 1801.

against brothers; and even women took up arms on both sides for defence of their religion.[1] And Philip, king of Spain, could frequently say that he had rather have no subjects than heretics, as he called the Protestants; and out of a blind, bloody zeal he suffered his eldest son Charles to be murdered by the cruel Inquisition, because he seemed to favour the Protestant side, [Jerome.] Truth is a glorious, shining light, that discovers the ignorance and darkness, the wickedness and baseness, the unsoundness and hypocrisy, the superstition and vain conversation, of persecutors; and therefore they cannot endure this light, they hate this light, and will do all they can to suppress this light, and those that hold out this light to the world, John iii. 19. The saints and martyrs of old were as willing to die as to dine. Pliny, writing to Trajan the emperor, declares to him that such was their zeal and courage in behalf of their God, that nothing could stir them from it.[2] Neither the imperious checks of the potent emperors, nor the soft language of the eloquent orators, could draw them from the faith; but they steadfastly owned it, and constantly persevered in the defence of it, and were ready and willing to lay down their lives for it. When Ignatius was to suffer, It is better for me, saith he, to be a martyr than to be a monarch. It was a notable saying of a French martyr, when the rope was about his fellow, Give me, said he, that golden chain, and dub me knight of that noble order. Let, saith Ignatius, fire and cross, invasion of beasts, breaking of bones, pulling asunder of members, grinding of my whole body, and what else the devil can inflict, come, so I may hold Jesus Christ.[3] Lucius thanked him that brought him forth to suffer, and said that he should be free from those evil masters, and go to God, a good Father and King.[4] Germanicus, when he was brought forth to be torn in pieces and devoured by wild beasts, the governor, persuading him to be mindful of his youth, that he might be spared, of his own accord incited the beasts against himself. Sanctus, being under tortures for professing himself to be a Christian, unto every question propounded to him, he answered, I am a Christian; whereby he occasioned his torments to be continued to death.[5] Can we think that St Laurence would have accepted of deliverance, who, lying on a red-hot gridiron, over burning coals, with an invincible spirit thus said to the tyrants: Turn the side broiled enough, and see what thy burning fire hath done; and being turned, and thoroughly broiled on the other side, saith thus again: Eat that which is broiled, and try whether raw or broiled be the sweeter. Hippolytus, when he was tied to wild horses to be pulled asunder, thus prayed: Let them rend my limbs; do thou, O Christ, wrap up my soul. To omit other particulars of the ancient martyrs in the primitive times, with whose courageous speeches, manifesting a contempt of death, of which volumes might be filled, it is indefinitely recorded of many, who were famous for their wealth, nobility, glory, eloquence, and learning, that nevertheless they preferred true piety and faith in our Lord Jesus Christ before all those.[6] And though they were entreated by many of their kindred and friends otherwise,

---

[1] Hist. of Council of Trent, fol. 647. [2] Epist. lib. x. ep. 97, p. 316.
[3] Euseb. Hist. Eccl., lib. iii. cap. 36. [4] Ibid., lib. iv. cap. 15.
[5] Ibid., lib. v. cap. 2. [6] Ibid., lib viii. cap. 9.

yea, and by others in great place, and by the judge himself, that they would take pity of themselves, their wives, and children; yet would they not be induced and entreated by so many, and great ones, so to be affected with the love of this life as to forbear the confession of our Saviour, and to set light by the denial of him. Thus you see what little reckoning or account the Christians of old have made of their lives, liberties, and estates, or whatever else was near or dear unto them, when these things stood in competition with Christ, his truth, his worship, his ways, his interest, or with their profession of the Christian faith.

Take a few instances of a later date. John Huss being at the stake, a pardon was offered him if he would recant; to which he answered, I am here ready to suffer death. So Jerome of Prague: If I had feared the fire, said he, I had not come hither. Francis Camba, a martyr, in the diocese of Milan, being much assailed by his friends, and terrified by his foes, by no means could be overcome; but gave thanks to God that he was accounted worthy to suffer a cruel death for the testimony of his Son; and such were his expressions of joy in his sufferings, that his persecutors caused his tongue to be bored through, that he might speak no more to the people. Another [Mrs Anne Askew] being offered the king's pardon if she would recant, gave this resolute answer: I came not here to deny my Lord and Master. By that which she with admirable courage and constancy endured, she verified that which of old Julitta spake concerning their sex, viz., We women ought to be as constant as men in Christ's cause. Another [Walter Mill] who suffered martyrdom in Scotland, being solicited to recant, made this reply: Ye shall know that I will not recant the truth, for I am corn, I am no chaff; I will not be blown away with the wind, nor burst with the flail; but I will abide both. Another, [Mr John Rogers,] being the first martyr in Queen Mary's days, being solicited to recant, that so he might save his life, boldly replied, That which I have preached I will seal with my blood. Another, [Hooper, bishop of Gloucester,] when a pardon was set before him in a box, cried out, If you love my soul, away with it; if you love my soul, away with it. Another [Mr Thos. Hawks, a gentleman in Essex] on the like occasion, gave this resolute answer, If I had a hundred bodies I would suffer them all to be torn in pieces, rather than abjure or recant. So another [Bishop Ridley] spake to the like purpose. So long, said he, as the breath is in my body, I will never deny my Lord Christ and his known truth. Another [Father Latimer] used such a speech to one that advised him to spare himself, as Christ did to Peter on the like occasion, ' Get thee behind me, Satan.' There are a world of other instances of the like nature, but enough is as good as a feast.[1] By all these instances, you may see that blessed word verified, ' They loved not their lives unto the death,' Rev. xii. 11. They were willing to lay down their lives for the glory of Christ, and for the truth of Christ; so that οὐκ ἠγάπησαν, ' They loved not,' is put for ὠλιγόπησαν, ' they neglected or contemned ' their life, as Brightman hath well observed.[2] They slighted, yea, despised their lives, and rather exposed them to hazard and loss, than to deny Christ,

---

[1] Foxe and Clarke, as before.—G.
[2] Works, 1644, ' Revelation of the Apocalypse.'—G.

or their holy profession. It is a paraphrase of the constancy of their faith, even unto martyrdom for the name of Christ. But,

10. Tenthly, Consider, *That God puts a great deal of honour upon suffering saints.* To suffer for Christ is honourable, Phil. i. 29. God will not put this honour upon every one, he puts this honour only upon those that are vessels of honour. By grace God makes men vessels of silver and vessels of gold, and then casts them into the fire to melt and suffer for his name, 2 Tim. ii. 20, 21 ; and a higher glory he cannot put upon them on this side glory. The crown of martyrdom is a crown that the blessed angels, those princes of glory, are not capable of winning or wearing ; and oh,, who art thou ? and what art thou, O man, that God should set this crown upon thy head ? Mark at what a rate Peter speaks : 1 Pet. iv. 14, ' If ye be reproached for the name of Christ, happy are ye ; for the Spirit of glory and of God resteth upon you : on their part he is evil spoken of, but on your part he is glorified.' The very suffering condition of the people of God is at the present a glorious condition, ' for the Spirit of glory rests upon them ;' and therefore they must needs be glorious, yea, very glorious, upon whom the Spirit of glory falls, and in whom the Spirit of glory dwells, Rom. viii. 9, 11. What a glorious mould and metal were the three children made up of, that were cast into the fiery furnace, Dan. iii. ; and what a deal of honour and glory did God put upon them in the eyes of all the world ! The apostles all along accounted their own sufferings, and the sufferings of the saints for Christ, to be the highest honour and glory that God could put upon them in this world, as will be evident by our comparing the scriptures in the margin together.[1] To suffer for Christ is the greatest honour and promotion that God gives in this world, said old Father Latimer ; and, therefore, when sentence was pronounced against him, he cried out, I thank God most heartily for this great honour. So Saunders, ' I am the unmeetest man for this high office that ever was appointed to it.' So Careless, the martyr, ' This is such an honour,' said he, ' as the greatest angel in heaven is not permitted to have.' God forgive me mine unthankfulness,[2] &c. John Noyes took up a fagot at the fire, and kissed it, saying, ' Blessed be the time that ever I was born to come to this preferment.' So when they had fastened Alice Driver with a chain to the stake to be burnt, ' Never,' said she, ' did neckerchief become me so well as this chain.' So Balilus,[3] the martyr, when he was to die, requested this favour of his persecutors, viz., that he might have his chains buried with him as the ensigns of his honour. ' What are we, poor worms, full of vanities and lies,' said Calvin, ' that we should be called to be maintainers of the truth ; for sufferings for Christ are the ensigns of heavenly nobility.' To die for Christ is the greatest promotion that God can bring any in this vale of misery unto, said Mr Philpot, the martyr. A French soldier, for his zealous profession of the Reformed religion, was condemned to the fire with others, only he should have the favour of going to the stake without a wyth ; but he desired that he might wear such a

---

[1] Heb. xi. 36–38 ; 2 Cor. xi. 23–28 ; Heb. x. 23–26.
[2] Acts and Mon., 1361. *Ibid.*, 1744.
[3] Query, ' Babilas ' ? Bishop of Antioch : Clarke, 37.—G.

chain as his fellows did, esteeming this rebuke of Christ more glorious than the ensigns of St Michael's order.[1] It was an excellent saying of Prudentius, ' Their names,' saith he, ' that are written in red letters of blood in the church's calendar, are written in golden letters in Christ's register, the book of life.' The passion-days of the martyrs were anciently called the *Natalitia salutis*, the birthdays of salvation, the daybreak of eternal brightness. We count it a great honour to have princes to be our companions ; Christ, the Prince of peace, and the angels, those princes of glory, are our companions in all our sufferings.[2] Such is the honour that God puts upon his suffering saints, that nothing shall hinder him from being their companion in all their sufferings, in all their afflictions, in all their temptations ; and this, believe it, is no small honour. I have read [3] how that, in the primitive times, when some good people came to comfort some of the martyrs that were in prison and ready to suffer, they called them blessed martyrs ; Oh no, said they, we are not worthy of the name of martyrs ! These holy humble hearts thought martyrdom too high an honour for them. And Luther, writing to those which were condemned to death, saith, The Lord will not do me that honour after all that bustle I have made in the world. In the primitive times they were wont to call martyrdom by the name of *Corona Martyrii*, the crown of martyrdom. We read of a woman-martyr who, having her child in her hand, gave it to another, and offered herself to martyrdom. Crowns, said she, are to be dealt out this day, and I mean to have one. You see what high and honourable thoughts the saints had of their sufferings in those days ; and oh that all suffering saints would labour to write after that noble copy that they have left upon record ! But,

11. Eleventhly, Consider, *That suffering saints do put a great deal of honour and glory upon God, Christ, religion, and upon God's truth, worship, and ways.* What a spreading fame and glory of God did the sufferings of the three worthies scatter all the world over ! Dan. iii. 28, 29. God is acknowledged and adored by Nebuchadnezzar : a decree is made that ' Every people, nation, and language, which speak amiss against the God of Shadrach, Meshach, and Abed-nego, shall be cut in pieces, and their houses shall be made a dunghill,' &c. Here God's glory wonderfully shines out of their sufferings ; here this poor, blind, idolatrous heathen prince is forced to confess that there is no God like Israel's God. Basil and Tertullian do well observe of the primitive martyrs, that divers of the heathen, seeing their zeal, courage, and constancy, glorified God, and turned Christians. Religion is that phœnix which hath always revived and flourished in the ashes of holy men ; and truth hath never been so honoured and gloriously dispersed as when it hath been sealed by the blood of the saints. This made Julian to forbear to persecute ; *non ex clementia, sed invidia*, not out of piety, but envy ; because the church grew so fast, and multiplied, as Nazianzen well observes. We read that sometimes the sufferings of one saint have begot many to the love of the truth. We read that Cecilia,[4] a poor captive virgin, by

---

[1] Thuan. Hist., lib. xi. Anno 1553.
[2] Isa. ix. 6, 7 ; Dan. iii. 24, 25 ; Isa. xliii. 2, and lxiii. 9.
[3] Euseb. Eccles. Hist., lib. v.   [4] Clarke, as before.—G.

her gracious behaviour in her martyrdom, was the means of converting four hundred to Christ. Justin Martyr was also converted by
observing the cheerful and gracious carriage of the saints in their
sufferings. And so Adrianus, seeing the martyrs suffer readily and
joyfully such grievous torments, asked why they would endure such
misery, when they might, by retracting, free themselves. Upon which
one of them cited that text: 'Eye hath not seen, nor ear heard,
neither have entered into the heart of man, the things which God
hath prepared for them that love him,' 1 Cor. ii. 9. Upon the
naming of this scripture, and seeing of them suffer so willingly,
cheerfully, and resolutely, such a divine power took hold of his heart,
that he was converted, and afterwards became a martyr. Now God,
and Christ, and truth, and religion are never more honoured than
when poor souls are soundly converted.[1] Surely the crown of martyrdom is a glorious crown ; and every soul won over to God by a
dying martyr will be as an Orient pearl and precious diamond in his
crown, of far more value than that adamant found about Charles
Duke of Burgundy, slain by the Switzers at the battle of Nantz, sold
for twenty thousand ducats, and placed, as it is said, in the pope's
triple crown.[2] Oh, what foretastes of glory, what ravishments of
soul have many of the blessed martyrs had in their sufferings for
Christ ! Holy Lord, stay thy hand, I can bear no more, said one of
the martyrs ; like weak eyes, that cannot bear too great a light. Is it
not a high honour to a king to have such captains and champions as
will not yield to their sovereign's enemies, but stand it out to the
uttermost till they get the victory, though it cost them their lives to
get it ? yet no mortal king can, as Christ doth, put spirit, courage,
and strength into a subject ; only we may well conceive and conclude that such valorous soldiers as are ready to hazard their lives for
their sovereign serve a good master. Thus do suffering Christians
and martyrs give persecutors to understand that they serve a good
Master, and that they highly prize him, who hath done more, and
suffered more for them, than their dearest blood is worth ; and who
enables them, with courage, constancy, and comfort, to endure whatsoever, for his name's sake, can be inflicted on them ; and therein to
be ($ὑπερνικῶμεν$) more than conquerors, or above conquerors, Rom.
viii. 37. How can that be ? Can a man get more than the victory ?
The meaning is, 'we do over-overcome,' *supersuperamus*—that is,
triumph or overcome before we fight. We are famous and renowned
conquerors, we easily conquer, we conquer by those things which are
used to conquer us, we beat our enemies with their own swords, as
Julian sometime said, being confuted by heathen learning, 2 Cor. ii.
14. Martyr and Piscator expound it thus, We do more than overcome—that is, we obtain a noble, a famous victory. And is not this
a great honour to Christ, the captain of our salvation ? The invincible courage of suffering Christians puts life and spirit into others.
In an army valorous leaders much animate the rest of the soldiers,
and embolden them to follow their leaders, Heb. ii. 10. Now you
know the church is an army with banners, Cant. vi. 4, and suffering

[1] All the preceding names in Foxe and Clarke, as before.—G.
[2] [Foxe,] Acts and Mon., vii. 55-57.

ministers and suffering saints are as leaders; they courageously and victoriously make the onset, and other Christians, by their pious examples, are pricked on to follow them so far as they are followers of the Lamb. But,

12. Twelfthly, Consider, *That all the sufferings and persecutions that you meet with on earth shall advance your glory in heaven.* The more saints are persecuted on earth, the greater shall be their reward in heaven.[1] Look, as persecutions do increase a Christian's grace, so they do advance a Christian's glory. In heaven the martyrs shall have the highest degree of glory; for though God doth not reward men simply for their works, namely, for the merit of them, yet he rewards according to their works, and proportions the degree or measure thereof according to the kind of work which on earth is done, and according to the measure of grace whereby he enables men to do it. Now martyrdom is the most difficult, the most honourable, and the most acceptable work that on earth can be done, and therefore in heaven martyrdom shall be crowned with the highest degree of glory. On this ground, they who set down the different degrees of celestial glory by the different fruits which the good ground brought forth, some thirty, some sixty, and some a hundredfold, Mat. xiii. 8; apply the hundredfold, which is the highest and greatest degree of glory, to martyrdom. Doubtless God's suffering servants, and amongst them especially his martyrs, shall sit down in the chiefest mansions and in the highest rooms in the kingdom of glory.[2] According to the degrees of our sufferings for Christ will be the degrees of our glory. 'What shall we have,' says Peter, that have suffered so many great and grievous things for thy name, 'that have forsaken all, and followed thee?' 'Verily,' says our Saviour, 'every one that hath forsaken houses, &c., shall receive a hundredfold, and shall inherit everlasting life; but ye shall sit upon twelve thrones, judging the twelve tribes of Israel,' Mat. xix. 27–29. A Christian will never repent of all the hard things that he has suffered for Christ or his truth, whenas every one of his sufferings shall be a sparkling jewel to give a lustre to his crown of glory. Suffering for Christ and religion is the most gainful kind of merchandise. Christ is so well pleased with the sufferings of his saints, that he has engaged himself to make up whatever they lose upon his account, yea, to repay all with interest upon interest to a hundred times over. Oh, who would not then turn spiritual purchaser! Christ is a noble, a liberal paymaster, and no small things can fall from so great a hand as his is: Mat. v. 10–12, 'Blessed are they which are persecuted for righteousness' sake: for theirs is the kingdom of heaven. Blessed are ye, when men shall revile you, and persecute you, and shall say all manner of evil against you falsely for my sake. Rejoice, and be ex-

[1] *Quis quisvolens detrahit famœ meœ, nolens addit mercedi meœ,* saith Augustine— The more we suffer with and for Christ, the more glory we shall have with and from Christ, Rom. ii. 6.

[2] Keep your eye upon the recompense of reward, as Moses did, Heb. xi. 26, and as Christ did, chap. xii. 2; as Paul did, Rom. viii. 18. This will work you—(1.) To walk more holily, humbly, thankfully; (2.) To live more cheerfully and comfortably; (3.) To suffer more patiently, freely, resolutely; (4.) To fight against the world, the flesh, and the devil more stoutly and valiantly; (5.) To withstand temptations more steadfastly and strongly; (6.) To be contented with a little; (7.) To leave the world, relations, and friends more willingly; (8.) And to embrace death more joyfully.

ceeding glad; for great is your reward in heaven: for so persecuted they the prophets which were before you:' Luke vi. 22, 23, 'Blessed are ye when men shall hate you, and when they shall separate you from their company, and shall reproach you, and cast out your name as evil, for the Son of man's sake. Rejoice ye in that day, and leap for joy; for, behold, your reward is in heaven: for in the like manner did their fathers unto the prophets.' They that are now excommunicated and anathematised as notorious, shameful, and abominable offenders,—they that are now opposed and persecuted by men, shall at last be owned and crowned by God; yea, and the more afflictions and persecutions are multiplied upon them in this world, the greater shall be their recompense in another world. The original words ἀγαλλιᾶσθε in Matthew, and σκιρτήσατε in Luke, signify 'exceeding great joy,' such as men usually express by skipping and dancing. Let your hearts leap, and let your bodies leap for joy, for great is your reward in heaven. A Dutch martyr, seeing the flame to come to his beard, said he, What a small pain is this, to be compared to the glory to come. Helen Stirk,[1] a Scotch woman, when her husband was at the place of execution, she said to him, Husband, rejoice; for we have lived together many joyful days; but this day, in which we must die, ought to be the most joyful to us both, because we must have joy for ever; therefore I will not bid you good-night, for we shall suddenly meet within the kingdom of heaven. The subscription of Mrs Anne Askew to her confession was this, Written by me, Anne Askew, that neither wisheth for death nor feareth his might, and as merry as one that is bound toward heaven. Oh, how my heart leapeth for joy, said Mr Philpot, that I am so near the apprehension of eternal life! God forgive me mine unthankfulness and unworthiness of so great glory. I have so much joy of the reward prepared for me most wretched sinner, that though I be in a place of darkness and mourning, yet I cannot lament, but both night and day am so joyful as though under no cross at all; yea, in all the days of my life I was never so merry; the name of the Lord be praised therefore for ever and ever! · The same author, in a letter to the congregation, saith, Though I tell you that I am in hell in the judgment of this world, yet assuredly I feel in the same the consolation of heaven; and this loathsome and horrible prison is as pleasant to me as the walks in the garden in the King's Bench.[2] Thus you see that suffering saints have had a heaven beforehand,—they have had an exuberancy of joy such as no good could match nor no evil overmatch, 1 Pet. i. 8. Bernard, speaking of persecutors, saith, That they are but his Father's goldsmiths, who are working to add pearls to the saint's crown. It is to my loss, saith Gordius the martyr, if you abate me anything of my present sufferings. Sufferings for Christ are the saints' greatest glory. *Crudelitas vestra, gloria nostra*, your cruelty is our glory, say they in Tertullian, and the harder we are put to it, the greater shall be our reward in heaven. Chrysostom hit the nail when he said, If one man should suffer all the sorrows of all the saints in the world, yet are they not worth one hour's glory in heaven. By the consent of the schoolmen, all the martyrs shall appear in the church triumphant, bearing the signs of their Christian

[1] Query, 'Stark'?—G.   [2] [Foxe,] Acts and Mon, fol. 613, 1154, 1130, 1670, 1663.

wounds about with them, as so many speaking testimonies of their holy courage, that what here they endured in the behalf of their Saviour, may be there an addition to their glory. O Christians, all your sufferings will certainly increase your future glory; every affliction, every persecution, will be a grain put into the scale of your heavenly glory, to make it more weighty in that day, wherein he will richly reward you for every tear, for every sigh, for every groan, for every hazard, and for every hardship that you have met in the way of your duty, 2 Cor. iv. 16–18. For light afflictions you shall have a weight of glory; and for a few afflictions you shall have as many joys, pleasures, delights, and contents, as there be stars in heaven, or sands on the sea-shore; and for momentary afflictions you shall have an eternal crown of glory. If you have suffering for suffering with Christ on earth, you shall have glory for glory with Christ in heaven. Ah, Christians, your present sufferings are but the seeds of your future glory; and the more plentiful you sow in tears, the more abundant will be your harvest of glory, Ps. cxxvi. 5, 6. Christ our general, the captain of our salvation, promises a crown, Rev. ii. 10, and a throne, chap. iii. 21, to all his afflicted and persecuted ones, which are the greatest rewards that a God can give, or that man can crave. It troubled one of the martyrs when he was at the stake that he was going to a place where he should be for ever a-receiving of wages for a little work. But,

13. Thirteenthly and lastly, *Afflictions, sufferings, persecutions, will discover what metal men are made of.* All is not gold that glisters.[1] Many there be that glister, and look like golden Christians; but when they come to the fire they prove but dross. He is a Christian more worth than the gold of Ophir, who remains gold when under fiery trials. The stony ground did glister and shine very gloriously, for it received the word with joy for a season, Mat. xiii. 20, 21; but when the sun of persecution arose upon it, it fell away. Men that in times of liberty and prosperity embrace the word, will, in times of persecution, distrust the word, reject the word, and turn their backs upon the word, if it be not rooted in their understandings, judgments, wills, affections, and consciences. Men may court the word, and compliment the word, and applaud the word, and seemingly rejoice in the word, but they will never suffer persecution for the word, if it be only received into their heads, and not fast rooted in their hearts. The house built upon the sand, Mat. vii. 26, 27, was as lovely, as comely, as goodly, and as glorious a house to look upon as that which was built upon a rock; but when the rain of affliction descended, and the floods of tribulation came, and the winds of persecution blew and beat upon the house, it fell, and great was the fall of it. No professors will be able to stand it out in all winds and weathers, but such as are built upon a rock; all others will sink, shatter, and fall when the wind of persecution blows upon them. As sure as the rain will fall, the floods flow, and the winds blow, so sure will an unsound heart give out when trials come. No heart but a sound heart will hold out bravely when sufferings come; no heart but a sincere heart will bear the brunt of persecution. The three worthies, Dan. iii. 17, 18, Shadrach, Meshach,

[1] Mat. xiii. ; 2 Tim. i. 15, 16; 1 Tim. i. 19, 20 ; 2 Tim. iv. 10, 14–16.

and Abed-nego, would rather burn than bow, they would rather suffer than sin, which was an evident proof of their sincerity and ingenuity ; they would be Nonconformists, though court, city, and country cried up conformity, which was a sure argument of their integrity. Hypocrites have heart enough for themselves, but none for God. If they see their names, estates, or carnal interest any way touched, they are all on fire, and ready to be burnt up with the flames of their own zeal; but they can see the name, truth, and interest of God, assaulted and torn in pieces, and never stir. In their own concerns, they are as if they were all heart ; but in the cause of God, they are as if, with Ephraim, they had no heart at all, Hosea vii. 11. Oh, it is sad that men should have a heart for themselves, and none for God ; that they should have courage in their own cause, and none in his. As the soul is the glory of the body, so integrity is the glory of the soul. A sincere Christian, with Job, will rather let all go than let his integrity go, Job xxvii. 5 ; he will sooner let the blood be pressed out of his veins, and his soul out of his body, than his integrity out of his soul. Oh, how bravely did the primitive Christians carry themselves as to this matter. Pliny, writing to Trajan,[1] declares to him that such was their zeal and courage in the behalf of their God, that nothing could stir them from it; neither the imperious checks of the potent emperors, nor the soft language of the eloquent orators, could draw them from the faith; but they steadfastly owned it, and constantly persevered in the defence of it. But now base unsound hearts will exceedingly shuffle and shift to shake off persecution. Witness those false teachers, Gal. vi. 12, ' As many as desire to make a fair show,' or, as the Greek has it, to set a good face on it, in the flesh, they constrain you to be circumcised, only lest they should suffer persecution for the cross of Christ.' Mark, at this time the Jews, out of zeal to their law, did sorely persecute those that did either preach or practise anything contrary to their law. Now these false teachers set a good face on it, and make a fair show, as if they were all for carnal rites and ceremonies ; and they pressed circumcision upon the Galatians, but not out of any true affection or zeal that they did bear to the law, but only to procure favour on the one hand, and to avoid and escape the malice and persecution of the Jews on the other hand. They that were no Jews, to avoid persecution, would comply with them that were ; they would seem to be very earnest for Judaism, but not for Christianism, that so they might escape the fury of the Jews. Unsound hearts will say anything, and do anything, and be anything, to avoid persecution, and to ingratiate themselves with persecutors. The Samaritans, so long as the Jewish religion flourished, and was in honour, caused a temple to be built on Mount Gerizim, that therein they might not be inferior to the Jews ; and they boasted themselves to be of the progeny of Joseph, and worshippers of God with them. But when they perceived that the Jews were cruelly afflicted and persecuted by Antiochus Epiphanes for worshipping of the true God, and fearing lest they should be handled in the like manner, they changed both their coat and their note, affirming that they were not Israelites, but Sidonians, and that they had built their temple, not unto God, but unto Jupiter.[2] Thus

[1] Epist. xcvii. p. 316. [2] Joseph. Hist., lib. xiii. [As before.—G.]

you see that times of affliction and persecution will distinguish the precious from the vile, Jer. xv. 19. It will difference the counterfeit professor from the true. Persecution is a Christian's touchstone; it is a *Lapis Lydius* that will try what metal men are made of, whether they be silver or tin, gold or dross, wheat or chaff, shadow or substance, carnal or spiritual, sincere or hypocritical. Nothing speaks out more soundness and uprightness than keeping close to Christ, his worship, truth, and ways, in a day of warm persecution. To stand close and fast to God and his interest in fiery trials, argues much integrity within.

These thirteen particulars are so great truths, written with the beams of the sun, that no man or devil can deny, and therefore I shall make no apology to the persecutors of the day to excuse my writing of.this general epistle; but shall beg hard of God that it may be so owned and crowned and blessed from on high, that it may really and fully answer to all those holy and gracious aims and ends that the author had in his eye and upon his heart when he writ it. And thus much for this general epistle.

SOME WORDS OF COUNSEL TO A DEAR FRIEND.

DEAR LADY AND SISTER IN THE LORD,[1]—I shall now address myself to you in a few lines, and so conclude. I know you have for many years been the Lord's prisoner. Great have been your trials, and many have been your trials, and long have been your trials; but to all these I have spoken at large in my treatise called ' The Mute Christian under the Smarting Rod,' which you have in your hand, which you have read, and which God has greatly blessed to the support, comfort, quiet, and refreshment of your soul under all your trials; and therefore I shall say no more as to those particulars. But knowing that the many weaknesses that hang upon you, and the decays of nature that daily do attend you, seem to point out an approaching dissolution, I shall at this time give you this one word of counsel, viz., that every day you would look upon death in a scripture glass, in a scripture dress, or under a scripture notion; that is,

1. First, *Look upon death as that which is best for a believer:* Phil. i. 23, ' For I am in a strait betwixt two, having a desire to depart, and to be with Christ, which is far better.' The Greek is very significant, ' far, far the better,' or far much better, or much more better. It is a most transcendent expression.[2] Eccles. vii. 1, ' Better is the day of death than the day of one's birth.' A saint's dying day is the daybreak of eternal righteousness. In respect of pleasure, peace, safety, company, glory, a believer's dying day is his best day. I have read of one Trophonius, that when he had built and dedicated that stately temple at Delphos, he asked of Apollo, for his recompense, that thing which was best for man. The oracle wished him to go home, and within three days he should have it; and within that time he died. It was an excellent saying of one of the ancients, ' That is not a death, but life, which joins the dying man to Christ; and that is not a life, but death, which separates a living man from Christ.' But,

2. Secondly, *Look upon death as a remedy, as a cure.* Death will perfectly cure you of all corporeal and spiritual diseases at once: the

---

[1] This second Epistle is headed ' Some Words of Counsel to a Dear Friend,' viz., Mrs Drinkwater, named on page 1. Cf. the General Epistle prefixed.—G.

[2] Πολλῷ μᾶλλον κρεῖσσον. *Nec Christus, nec cœlum patitur hyperbolen,* saith one; here it is hard to hyperbolize.

crazy body and the defiled soul, the aching head and the unbelieving heart: *ultimus morborum medicus mors.* Death will cure you of all your ails, aches, diseases, and distempers. At Stratford-Bow, in Queen Mary's days, there was burned a lame man and a blind man at one stake. The lame man, after he was chained, casting away his crutch, bade the blind man be of good comfort; For death, saith he, will cure us both; thee of thy blindness, and me of my lameness.[1] And as death will cure all your bodily diseases, so it will cure all your soul distempers also. Death is not *mors hominis,* but *mors peccati;* not the death of the man, but the death of his sin. Death will work such a cure as all your duties, graces, experiences, ordinances, assurances, could never do; for it will at once free you fully, perfectly, and perpetually from all sin; yea, from all possibility of ever sinning more. Sin was the midwife that brought death into the world, and death shall be the grave to bury sin.[2] And why, then, should a Christian be afraid to die, unwilling to die, seeing death gives him a writ of ease from infirmities and weaknesses, from all aches and pains, griefs and gripings, distempers and diseases, both of body and soul? When Samson died, the Philistines also died together with him; so when a saint dies, his sins die with him. Death came in by sin, and sin goeth out by death; as the worm kills the worm that bred it, so death kills sin that bred it. But,

3. Thirdly, *Look upon death as a rest, a full rest.* A believer's dying day is his resting day. It is a resting day from sin, sorrow, afflictions, temptations, desertions, dissensions, vexations, oppositions, and persecutions.[3] This world was never made to be the saints' rest. Arise, for this is not your resting-place. They are like Noah's dove, they can rest nowhere but in the ark and in the grave. 'In the grave,' saith Job, 'the weary are at rest.' Upon this very ground some of the most refined heathens have accounted mortality to be a mercy, for they brought their friends into the world with mournful obsequies, but carried them out of the world with all joyful sports and pastimes, because then they conceived they were at rest, and out of gunshot. Death brings the saints to a full rest, to a pleasant rest, to a matchless rest, to an eternal rest. But,

4. Fourthly, *Look upon your dying day as a reaping day:* 2 Cor. ix. 2; Gal. vi. 7–9; Isa. xxxviii. 3; Mat. xxv. 31, 41. Now you shall reap the fruit of all the prayers that ever you have made, and of all the tears that ever you have shed, and of all the sighs and groans that ever you have fetched, and of all the good words that ever you have spoken, and of all the good works that ever you have done, and of all the great things that ever you have suffered. When mortality shall put on immortality, you shall then reap a plentiful crop, a glorious crop, as the fruit of that good seed that for a time hath seemed to be buried and lost, Eccles. xi. 1, 6. As Christ hath a tender heart and a soft hand, so he hath an iron memory; he punctually remembers all the sorrows, and all the services, and all the sufferings of his people, to reward them and crown them, Rev. xxii. 12. But,

5. Fifthly, *Look upon your dying day as a gainful day.* There is

---

[1] [Foxe,] Acts and Mon., fol. 1733.

[2] Peccatum erat obstetrix mortis, et mors sepulchrum peccati.—*Ambrose, De Bono Mortis,* cap. 4.   [3] Rev. xiv. 13; Job iii. 13–17; 2 Thes. i. 7; Micah ii. 10; Jer. l. 6.

no gain to that which comes in by death: Phil. i. 21, 'For me to live is Christ, and to die is gain.' A Christian gets more by death than he doth by life, Eccles. vii. 1; to be in Christ is very good, but to be with Christ is best of all, Phil. i. 23. It was a mighty blessing for Christ to be with Paul on earth, but it was the top of blessings for Paul to be with Christ in heaven. Seriously consider of a few things:—

[1.] First, That by death you shall gain *incomparable crowns*. (1.) A crown of life, Rev. ii. 10; James i. 12; (2.) A crown of righteousness, 2 Tim. iv. 8; (3.) An incorruptible crown, 1 Cor. ix. 24, 25; (4.) A crown of glory, 1 Pet. v. 4. Now there are no crowns to these crowns, as I have fully discovered in my discourse on 'The Divine Presence,' to which I refer you.[1] But,

[2.] Secondly, You shall gain *a glorious kingdom:* Luke xii. 32, 'It is your Father's pleasure to give you a kingdom.' But death is the young prophet that anointeth them to it, and giveth them actual possession of it. They must put off their rags of mortality, that they may put on their robes of glory. Israel must first die in Egypt before he can be carried into Canaan. There is no entering into paradise but under the flaming sword of this angel death, who standeth at the gate. Death is the dirty lane through which the saint passeth to a kingdom, to a great kingdom, to a glorious kingdom, to a quiet kingdom, to an unshaken kingdom, to a durable kingdom, to a lasting kingdom, yea, to an everlasting kingdom. Death is a dark, short way, through which the saints pass to the marriage-supper of the Lamb, Heb. xii. 28; Dan. ii. 44, and iv. 3; Rev. xix. 7. But,

[3.] Thirdly, You shall gain *a safe and honourable convoy into that other world*, Luke xvi. 22. Oh, in what pomp and triumph did Lazarus ride to heaven on the wings of angels! The angels conduct the saints at death through the air, the devil's region; every gracious soul is carried into Christ's presence by these heavenly courtiers. Oh, what a sudden change does death make! behold, he that even now was scorned by men, is all on a sudden, carried by angels into Abraham's bosom. But,

[4.] Fourthly, You shall gain *a glorious welcome, a joyful welcome, a wonderful welcome into heaven*. By general consent of all antiquity, the holy angels and blessed Trinity rejoice at the sinner's conversion; but oh, what inexpressible, what transcendent joy is there, when a saint is landed upon the shore of eternity, Rev. iv. 8–11; Luke xv. 7, 10; Heb. xii. 23. God and Christ, angels and archangels, all stand ready to welcome the believer as soon as his feet are upon the threshold of glory. God the Father welcomes the saints as his elect and chosen ones, Jesus Christ welcomes them as his redeemed and purchased ones, and the Holy Spirit welcomes them as his sanctified and renewed ones, and the blessed angels welcome them as those they have guarded and attended on, Heb. i. 14. When the saints enter upon the suburbs of glory, the glorious angels welcome them with harps in their hands, and ditties in their mouths. But,

[5.] Fifthly, You shall gain *full freedom and liberty from all your enemies within and without*—viz., sin, Satan, and the world, Luke i.

---

[1] Viz., the Treatise to which this Epistle is prefixed.—G.

70, 71, 74, 75. (1.) Death will free you from the indwelling power of sin, Rom. vii. 23. In heaven there is no complaints. As in hell there is nothing but wickedness, so in heaven there is nothing but holiness. (2.) Death will free you from the power and prevalency of sin. Here sin plays the tyrant, but in heaven there is no tyranny, but perfect felicity. (3.) Death will free you from all provocations, temptations, and suggestions to sin. Now you shall be above all Satan's batteries. Now God will make good the promise of treading Satan under your feet, Rom. xvi. 20. Some say serpents will not live in Ireland. The old serpent is cast out, and shall be for ever kept out of the new Jerusalem above, Rev. xii. 8, 9, and xxi. 27. (4.) Death will free you from all the effects and consequents of sin—viz., losses, crosses, sicknesses, diseases, disgraces, sufferings, &c. When the cause is taken away, the effect ceases; when the fountain of sin is dried up, the streams of afflictions, of sufferings, must be dried up; the fuel being taken away, the fire will go out of itself. Sin and sorrow were born together, do live together, and shall die together. To open this fourth particular a little more fully to you, consider these four things:

First, That death will free you from *all reproach and ignominy on your names.* Now Elijah is accounted the troubler of Israel, Nehemiah a rebel against his king, and David the song of the drunkards, and Jeremiah a man of contention, and Paul a pestilent fellow.[1] Heaven wipes away all blots, as well as all tears; as no sins, so no blots are to be found in that upper world. The names of all the saints in a state of glory are written, as I may say, in characters of gold. But,

Secondly, Death will free you from *all bodily infirmities and diseases.* We carry about in our bodies the matter of a thousand deaths, and may die a thousand several ways each several hour. As many senses, as many members, nay, as many pores as there are in the body, so many windows there are for death to enter at.[2] Death needs not spend all its arrows upon us; a worm, a gnat, a fly, a hair, the stone of a raisin, the kernel of a grape, the fall of a horse, the stumbling of a foot, the prick of a pin, the paring of a nail, the cutting of a corn; all these have been to others, and any one of them may be to us, the means of our death, within the space of a few days, nay, of a few hours. Here Job had his blotches, and Hezekiah had his boil, and David his wounds, and Lazarus his sores, and the poor widow her issue of blood, Job ii. 6, 7; Isa. xxxvii. 21; Ps. xxxviii. 5; Luke xvi. 20; Mat. ix. 20. Now the fever burns up some, and the dropsy drowns others, and the vapours stifle others; one dies of an apoplexy in the head, another of a struma in the neck, a third of a squinancy[3] in the throat, and a fourth of a cough and consumption of the lungs; others of obstructions, inflammations, pleurisies, gouts, &c. We are commonly full of complaints; one complains of this distemper, and another of that; one of this disease, and another of that; but death will cure us of all diseases and distempers at once. But,

Thirdly, Death will free you from *all your sorrows, whether inward or outward, whether for your own sins or the sins of others, whether*

---

[1] 1 Kings xviii. 17; Neh. vi. 6; Ps. lxix. 12; Jer. xv. 10; Acts xxiv. 10.
[2] Above all things, let us every day think of our last day, saith Pachomius.
[3] Squinzy or quinsy.—G.

for your own sufferings or the sufferings of others, Ps. xxxviii. 18 ; 2 Cor. vii. 11 ; Ps. cxix. 136 ; Neh. i. 3, 4. Now, it may be, one shall seldom find you but with tears in your eyes, or sorrow in your heart; Oh, but now death will be the funeral of all your sorrows, death will wipe all tears from your eyes, ' and sorrow and mourning shall flee away,' Isa. li. 11. But,

Fourthly, Death will free you from *all those troubles, calamities, miseries, mischiefs, and desolations, that are a-coming upon the earth, or upon this place or that*, Isa. lvii. 1 ; Micah vii. 1–7. A year after Methuselah's death, the flood came and carried away the old world. Augustine died a little before the sacking of Hippo. Luther observes that all the apostles died before the destruction of Jerusalem; and Luther himself died a little before the wars brake forth in Germany. Dear lady, death shall do that for you, which all your physicians could never do for you, which all your relations could never do for you, which all ordinances could never do for you, nor which all your faithful ministers could never do for you. It shall both instantly and perfectly cure you of all sorts of maladies and weaknesses, both inward and outward, or that respects either your body or your soul, or both. O my dear friend, is it not better to die, and be rid of all sin ; to die, and be rid of all temptations and desertions ; to die, and be rid of all sorts of miseries ; than to live, and still carry about with us our sins, our burdens, and such constant ailments, as takes away all the pleasure and comfort of life ? Here both our outward and inward conditions are very various ; sometimes heaven is open, and sometimes heaven is shut ; sometimes we see the face of God, and rejoice, and at other times he hides his face, and we are troubled, Lam. iii. 8, 44, 54–57 ; Ps. xxx. 7 ; 1 Thes. iv. 17, 18 ; Isa. xxxv. 10. Oh, but now death will bring us to an invariable eternity. It is always day in heaven, and joy in heaven.

[6.] Sixthly and lastly, You shall gain *a clear, distinct, and full knowledge of all great and deep mysteries*, 1 Cor. xiii. 10, 12. The mystery of the Trinity, the mystery of Christ's incarnation, the mystery of man's redemption, the mysteries of providences, the mysteries of prophecies, and all those mysteries that relate to the nature, substances, offices, orders, and excellencies of the angels. If you please to consult my ' String of Pearls, or the Best Things Reserved till Last,' with my sermon on Eccles. vii. 1, ' Better is the day of death than the day of one's birth ;' which is at the end of my ' Treatise on Assurance'—both which treatises you have by you—there you will find many more great and glorious things laid open that we gain by death ; and to them I refer you.[1] But,

6. Sixthly, Look upon death *as a sleep*. The Holy Ghost hath phrased it so above twenty times in Scripture, to shew that this is the true, proper, and genuine notion of death.[2] When the saints die, they do but sleep: Mat. ix. 24, ' The maid is not dead but sleepeth.' The same phrase he also used to his disciples concerning Lazarus, ' Our friend Lazarus sleepeth,' John xi. 11. The death of the godly is as a

---

[1] For the ' String of Pearls,' see Vol i. : for the other Sermon, Vol. vi.— G.

[2] 1 Cor. xi. 30, and xv. 51 ; John xi. 12 ; Mark v. 39. The Greeks call their church-yards *dormitories*, sleeping-places; and the Hebrews *Beth-chaiim*, the house of the living.

sleep; Stephen fell asleep, Acts vii. 60; and 'David fell asleep,' Acts xiii. 36; and 'Christ is the firstfruits of them that sleep,' 1 Cor. xv. 20; 'Them that sleep in Jesus, will God bring with him,' 1 Thes. iv. 14. The saints of God do but sleep when they lie down in the grave. That which we call death in such, is not death indeed; it is but the image of death, the shadow and metaphor of death, death's younger brother, a mere sleep, and no more. I may not follow the analogy that is between death and sleep in the latitude of it, the printer calling upon me to conclude. Sleep is the nurse of nature, the sweet *paren-thesis* of all a man's griefs and cares. But,

7. Seventhly, Look upon death *as a departure:* 2 Tim. iv. 6, 'For I am now ready to be offered, and the time of my departure is at hand.' He makes nothing of death. It was no more betwixt God and Moses, but go up and die, Deut. xxxii. 49, 50; and so betwixt Christ and Paul, but launch out, and land immediately at the fair haven of heaven: Phil. i. 23, 'For I am in a strait betwixt two, having a desire to depart, and to be with Christ; which is far better.' Paul longed for that hour wherein he should loose anchor, and sail to Christ, as the Greek word ἀναλῦσαι imports. It is a metaphor from a ship at anchor, importing a sailing from this present life to another port. Paul had a desire to loose from the shore of life, and to launch out into the main of immortality. The apostle, in this phrase, ἀναλῦσαι, hath a reference both to his bonds and to his death; and his meaning is, I desire to be discharged and released, as out of a common jail, so also out of the prison of my body, that I may presently be with Christ my Saviour in heaven, in rest and bliss.[1] After Paul had been in the third heaven, his constant song was, 'I desire to be with Christ.' Nature teacheth that death is the end of misery; but grace will teach us that death is the beginning of our felicity. But,

8. Eighthly and lastly, Look upon death as *a going to bed.* The grave is a bed wherein the body is laid to rest, with its curtains close drawn about it, that it may not be disturbed in its repose: so the Holy Ghost is pleased to phrase it, 'He shall enter into peace, they shall rest in their beds, every one walking in their uprightness,' Isa. lvii. 2. As the souls of the saints pass to a place of rest and bliss, so their bodies are laid down to rest in the grave, as in a bed or bed-chamber, there to sleep quietly until the morning of the resurrection. Death is nothing else but a writ-of-ease to the weary saints; it is a total cessation from all their labour of nature, sin, and affliction, 'Blessed are the dead that die in the Lord, that they may rest from their labours,' Rev. xiv. 13, &c. Whilst the souls of the saints do rest in Abraham's bosom, their bodies do sweetly sleep in their beds of dust, as in a safe and consecrated dormitory. Every sincere Christian may, like the weary child, call and cry to be laid to bed, knowing that death would send him to his everlasting rest. Now you should always look upon death under scripture notions, and this will take off the terror of death; yea, it will make the king of terrors to be the

---

[1] 'Αναλῦσαι, *solvere anchoram.* Or it may be rendered, to return home, or to change rooms. It is a similitude taken from those that depart out of an inn to take their journey towards their own country.

king of desires; it will make you not only willing to die, but even long to die, and to cry out, ' Oh that I had the wings of a dove, to fly away, and be at rest!' At death you shall have an eternal jubilee, and be freed from all incumbrances. Now sin shall be no more, nor trouble shall be no more, nor pain nor ailments shall be no more. Now you shall have your *quietus est*, now ' the wicked shall cease from troubling, and now the weary shall be at rest,' Job iii. 17, now ' all tears shall be wiped from your eyes,' Rev. vii. 17, now death shall be the way to bliss, the gate of life, and the portal to paradise. It was well said of one, so far as we tremble at death, so far we want love. It is sad, when the contract is made between Christ and a Christian, to see a Christian afraid of the making up the marriage. Lord, saith one, [Austin,] I will die that I may enjoy thee; I will not live, but I will die, I desire to die, that I may see Christ; and refuse to live, that I may live with Christ. The broken rings,[1] contracts, and espousals contents not the true lover, but he longs for the marriage day. It is no credit to your heavenly Father for you to be loath to go home. The Turks tell us that surely Christians do not believe heaven to be such a glorious place as they talk of; for if they did, they would not be so unwilling to go thither. The world may well think that the child hath but cold welcome at his father's house, that he lingers so much by the way, and that he does not look and long to be at home. Such children bring an ill report upon their father's house, upon the holy land; but I know you have not so learned Christ, I know you long with Paul, ' to be dissolved, and to be with Christ,' Phil. i. 23; and with old Simeon, to cry out, ' Lord, let thy servant depart in peace,' Luke ii. 29. That God whom you have long sought and served will make your passage into that other world safe, sweet, and easy. Now to the everlasting arms of divine protection, and to the constant guidance and leadings of the Spirit, and to the rich influences of Christ's sovereign grace, and to the lively hopes of the inheritance of the saints in light, he commends you, who is, dear sister, yours in the strongest bonds,

THO. BROOKS.

---

[1] An old English betrothal custom.—G.

THE SIGNAL PRESENCE OF GOD
WITH HIS PEOPLE,

IN THEIR GREATEST TROUBLES, DEEPEST DISTRESSES, AND MOST DEADLY DANGERS.

' Notwithstanding the Lord stood with me, and strengthened me ; that by me the preaching might be fully known, and that all the Gentiles might hear : and I was delivered out of the mouth of the lion.' —2 Tim. iv. 17.[1]

In my text you have three things that are most remarkable :—

First, You have Paul's commemoration of that singular experience that he had of the favourable presence of Christ with him, and of his strengthening of him, ' Nothwithstanding the Lord stood with me,' or παρέστη, ' by me, and assisted me,' Acts xxiii. 11 ; though I was deserted by men, yet I was aided and assisted by Christ, 2 Tim. iv. 16 ; though all men left me to shift for myself, yet the Lord stood by me, and strengthened me with wisdom, prudence, courage, and constancy, in the want of all outward encouragements, and in the face of all outward discouragements, 2 Tim. i. 15.

Secondly, Here is the end for which the Lord stood by him, assisted, strengthened, and delivered him, viz., that he might preach the gospel to the nations, Rom. xi. 13 ; Phil. iv. 22, that he might have more time, and further opportunity, to spread abroad the everlasting gospel among the Gentiles, whose apostle he was. Rome, at this time, was the queen of the world, and in its most flourishing condition; people from all parts of the world flocked to Rome. Now when they should hear and see Paul's prudence, courage, constancy, and boldness, in professing of Christ, and in preaching and professing the gospel, even before that grand tyrant, that monster of mankind, Nero, they could not but be wrought upon, and the fame of the glorious gospel could not but by this means be spread all the world over.

Thirdly, Here is the greatness of the danger from which he was delivered, viz., ' from the mouth of the lion.' Some authors [Calvin, Estius, &c.] do conceive these words, ' and I was delivered from the mouth of the lion,' to be a proverbial speech, noting some eminent,

[1] Preached in March and April 1675.

present, devouring danger; 'I was delivered from the extremest hazard of death,' even as a man rescued out of a lion's mouth, and pulled from between his teeth. Others[1] more genuinely and properly, by 'the mouth of the lion,' do understand Nero's rage and cruelty, who, for his potency in preying on the flock of Christ, is here fitly compared to a lion, which devoured and destroyed the flock of Christ. This cruel lion Nero put a world of Christians to death, and made a bloody decree, that whosoever confessed himself a Christian, he should, without any more ado, be put to death as a convicted enemy of mankind. Tertullian calleth him the dedicator of the condemnation of Christians.[2] This bloody monster, Nero, raised the first bloody persecution. To pick a quarrel with the Christians he set the city of Rome on fire, and then charged it upon the Christians, under which pretence he exposed them to the fury of the people, who cruelly tormented them as if they had been common burners and destroyers of cities, and the deadly enemies of mankind; yea, Nero himself caused them to be apprehended and clad in wild beasts' skins and torn in pieces with dogs; others were crucified; some he made bonfires of to light him in his night-sports. To be short, such horrid cruelty he used towards them as caused many of their enemies to pity them. But God found out this bloody persecutor at last, for being adjudged by the senate an enemy to mankind, he was condemned to be whipped to death, for the prevention whereof he cut his own throat.

The words being thus briefly opened, the main point I shall insist upon is this—viz.,

That when the people of God are in their greatest troubles, deepest distresses, and most deadly dangers, then the Lord will be most favourably, most signally, and most eminenly present with them.

The schoolmen say that God is five ways present—(1.) In the humanity of Christ, by hypostatical union; (2.) In the saints, by knowledge and love; (3.) In the church, by his essence and direction; (4.) In heaven, by his majesty and glory; (5.) In hell, by his vindictive justice.

Hemingius saith, There is a fourfold presence of God:—(1.) There is a presence of power in all men, even in the reprobates; (2.) A presence of grace, only in the elect; (3.) A presence of glory, in the angels, and saints departed; (4.) A hypostatical presence of the Father with the Son. But, if you please, you may take notice that there is a sixfold presence of the Lord:—

1. First, *There is a general presence of God*, and thus he is present with all creatures: 'Whither shall I flee from thy presence?'[3] Ps. cxxxix. 7. Empedocles, the philosopher, said well, That God is a circle, whose centre is everywhere, and whose circumference is nowhere. God is included in no place, and excluded from no place, saith another: *Non est ubi, ubi non est Deus.* They could tell us that God is the soul of the world; and that as the soul is *Tota in toto, et tota in qualibet parte*, so is he; his eye is in every corner, &c. To which purpose they so pourtrayed their goddess Minerva, that which

---

[1] Beza and A-Lapide. *Vide* Euseb. Hist., lib. ii. cap. 22. [Cf. Sibbes i. 315, and note *h* 334.—G.]   [2] Dedicator damnationis Christianorum.—*Tertullian.*
[3] Nusquam est Deus, et ubique est.—*Chrysost.* in Col. ii. hom. v.

way soever one cast his eye, she always beheld him. Though heaven
be God's palace, yet it is not his prison. Diana's temple was burned
down when she was busy at Alexander's birth, and could not be at
two places together, but God is present both in paradise and in
the wilderness at the same time: 1 Kings viii. 27, 'But will God
indeed dwell on the earth? behold, the heaven and heaven of heavens
cannot contain thee; how much less this house that I have builded?'[1]
By the heaven of heavens is meant that which is by the learned called
the empyreal heaven, where the angels and the saints departed do
enjoy the glorious and beatifical vision of God; and it is called the
heaven of heavens, both because it is the highest and doth contain the
other heavens within its orb, and also by way of excellency, as the
'most holy place' in the temple is called the 'holy of holies,' because
it far surpasseth all the rest in splendour and glory, Isa. lxvi. 1;
Prov. v. 21; Heb. iv. 13; Job xxvi. 6. Jer. xxiii. 24, 'Can any hide
himself in secret places that I should not see him? saith the Lord.
Do not I fill heaven and earth? saith the Lord.' Prov. xv. 3, 'The
eyes of the Lord are in every place, beholding the evil and the good.'
God is πανόφθαλμος, all eye. The poor heathen could say, *Deus
intimior nobis intimo nostro:* God is nearer to us than we are to
ourselves. Repletively he is everywhere, though inclusively nowhere:
Job xxxiv. 21, 'For his eyes are upon the ways of man, and he seeth
all his goings;' ver. 22, 'There is no darkness, nor shadow of death
where the workers of iniquity may hide themselves.' Sinners shall
never be able to shroud themselves nor their actions from God's all-
seeing eye. The Rabbins put *Makom,* which signifies *place,* among
the names of God. Bythner brings them in expounding that text in
Esther iv. 14, 'Deliverance shall arise from another place;' that is,
from God. They called him Place, because he is in every place,
though in the assemblies of his saints more eminently and gloriously.
God is present with all his creatures—(1.) *Viâ productionis,* by raising them up; (2.) *Viâ sustentationis,* by staying of them up; they
are his family, and he feeds and clothes them, Mat. v. 45; Acts xvii.
27, 28; Ps. xxxiii. 13, 14; (3.) *Viâ inclinationis,* by giving unto
them power of motion; man could neither live nor move unless the
Lord were with him; (4.) *Viâ observationis,* by taking notice of them;
he observeth and marks both their persons and their actions—he sees
who they are, and how they are employed; (5.) *Viâ ordinationis,* by
governing and ruling of them and all their actions, to the service of
his glory and the good of his poor people, Acts iv. 25-29. But this
is not that presence that we are to discourse of.

2. Secondly, There is *a miraculous presence of Christ,* and this
some of the prophets of old had, and the apostles and others had in
Christ's time; and by virtue of this miraculous presence of Christ
with them, they cast out devils, healed diseases, and did many wonderful things, Mat. vii. 22; Mark iii. 15. But this is not the presence that falls within the compass of that main point we purpose to
speak to.

3. Thirdly, There is *a relative presence of Christ,* and that is his

---

[1] God is higher than the heaven, deeper than hell, broader than the earth, and more
diffuse than the sea.—*Bernard.*

presence in his ordinances, and with his churches.[1] Of this presence
the Scripture speaks very largely : Exod. xx. 24, ' In all places where
I record my name, I will come unto thee, and I will bless thee ; '
Exod. xxv. 8, ' And let them make me a sanctuary, that I may dwell
amongst them ; ' Exod. xxix. 45, ' And I will dwell among the children of Israel, and will be their God ; ' Lev. xxvi. 11, ' And I will set
my tabernacle amongst you, and my soul shall not abhor you ; ' ver.
12, ' And I will walk among you, and will be your God, and ye shall
be my people ; ' Ps. lxxvi. 1, ' In Judah is God known : his name is
great in Israel ; ' ver. 2, ' In Salem also is his tabernacle, and his
dwelling-place in Zion ; ' Isa. viii. 18, ' From the Lord of hosts which
dwelleth in mount Zion ; ' Ps. ix. 11, ' Sing praises to the Lord which
dwelleth in Zion.' The churches are said to be the temples in which
the Lord doth dwell, and the house of the living God, and the golden
candlesticks amongst which he doth walk.[2] Oh, how much does it
concern all the churches to prize their church state, and to keep close
together, and to walk suitable to that gracious presence of God, that
shines in the midst of them ! But this is not that presence that falls
under our present consideration. But,

4. Fourthly, There is *a majestical and glorious presence of Christ*,
and thus he is said to be in heaven : Ps. ii. 4, ' He that sitteth in the
heavens will laugh ; the Lord shall have them in derision ; ' Heb. i. 13,
' But to which of the angels said he at any time, Sit thou on my right
hand until I make thine enemies thy footstool ? ' chap. ix. 24, ' For
Christ is not entered into the holy places made with hands, which
are the figure of the true, but into heaven itself, now to appear in the
presence of God for us.' Not that heaven is *circulus concludens*, a place
wherein Christ is shut up, but, *palatium resplendens*, the court, as
it were, where his majesty, in acts of wisdom, and power, and mercy,
and conjunction of grace and glory, doth most of all appear.[3] As
the soul of man, though it be in every part of man, yet it doth principally appear and manifest itself in the heart and brain ; so here, &c.
Monica, Austin's mother, standing one day and seeing the sun shine,
raised this meditation, ' Oh, if the sun be so bright, what is the light
of Christ's presence in glory ! ' But this is not the presence we design
now to discourse of.

5. Fifthly, There is *a judicial or wrathful presence of the Lord;*
and thus he is present with wicked men, sometimes blinding of them,
sometimes hardening of them, sometimes leaving of them to their own
heart's lusts, sometimes giving them up to their own heart's lusts,
sometimes filling their faces with shame, and their consciences with
terrors.[4] He is judicially present with wicked men by a particular
observation of their persons and ways, Ps. xxxiii. 13, 14 ; Job xxxiv.
21, 22. He sees who they are, and how they are employed against
his honour, his interest, his saints, his ways, and by a special detestation of their persons and ways, &c. But this is not that presence that
at this time falls under our consideration ; and therefore,

[1] See Ps. xlvi. 4, 5 ; Cant. vii. 5 ; Joel iii. 21 ; Zech. ii. 10, 11, and viii. 3 ; Ps. cxxxv. 21.
[2] 1 Cor. iii. 16, 17 ; 2 Cor. vi. 16 ; Heb. iii. 6 ; 1 Pet. ii. 5 ; Rev. ii. 1.
[3] Job xvi. 19 ; 2 Thes. i. 9 ; Ps. xvi. 11; 1 Tim. vi. 14–16 ; Rev. iii. 21.
[4] See Exod. ix. 14 ; Isa. vi. 9, 10, and lxiv. 1–4; Ps. lxxxi. 12 ; 2 Thes. ii. 11, 12 ; Ps.
lxviii. 2 ; Jer. iv. 26 ; Ezek. xxxviii. 20 ; Hab. i. 12.

6. Sixthly and lastly, There is *a gracious, a favourable, a signal, or eminent presence of the Lord with his faithful people in their greatest troubles, deepest distresses, and most deadly dangers,* as the Scriptures do everywhere evidence.[1] Take a taste of some : Gen. xxxix. 20, 'And Joseph's master took him, and put him into the prison, a place where the king's prisoners were bound, and he was there in the prison ;' ver. 21, 'But the Lord was with Joseph, and shewed him mercy, and gave him favour in the sight of the keeper of the prison.' A prison keeps not God from his. Witness the apostles and martyrs, whose prisons, by God's presence, became palaces, and their stocks a music-school, Acts xvi. 25. Bradford, after he was put in prison, had better health than before, and found great favour with his keeper, who suffered him to go whither he would upon his promise to return by such an hour to his prison again.[2] If men knew by experience the sweet that is in suffering for Christ, they would desire with Chrysostom, if it were put to their choice, rather to be Paul a prisoner of Jesus Christ than Paul rapt up in the third heaven. Basil, in his oration for Barlaam,[3] that famous martyr, saith, 'He delighted in the close prison as in a pleasant green meadow, and he took pleasure in the several inventions of tortures, as in several sweet flowers.' Luther reports of that martyr, St Agatha, that as she went to prisons and tortures, she said she went to banquets and nuptials. The sun enlightens the world, saith Cyprian, but he that made the sun is a greater light to you in prison, &c. Fire, sword, prisons, famines, are pleasure, they are all delightful to me, saith Basil. Paul rattles his chain which he bears for the gospel, and was as proud of it as a woman of her ornaments, saith Chrysostom.[4] Paul and Silas in a prison found more pleasure than pain, more joy than sorrow, and when they were whipped, it was with rosemary branches, as I may say. Paul greatly rejoiced in his sufferings for Christ, and therefore often sings out, 'I, Paul, a prisoner of Jesus Christ,' not I, Paul, rapt up in the third heaven. Christ shewed his great love to him in rapping him up in the third heaven, and he shewed his great love to Christ in a cheerful suffering for him. Eusebius tells of one that writ to his friend from a stinking dungeon, and dated his letter 'From my delicate orchard.' Mr Glover the martyr wept for joy of his imprisonment ; and God forgive me, said Mr Bradford when a prisoner, my unthankfulness for this exceeding great mercy, that among so many thousands he chooseth me to be one in whom he will suffer. I was carried to the coal-house, saith Mr Philpot, the martyr, where I with my fellows do rouse together in the straw as cheerfully, we thank God, as others do in their beds of down.[5] Philip, landgrave of Hesse, being a long time prisoner under Charles the Fifth, was asked what upheld him in his long imprisonment. He answered that he felt the divine consolations of the martyrs: Gen. xlix. 23, 'The archers,' or, as the Hebrew here hath it, the arrow-masters, 'have sorely grieved him, and shot at him, and hated him.' These arrow-masters were his barbarous brethren that sold him, his adulterous

[1] The compassionate parent is most with the sick child ; so here.
[2] [Foxe,] Acts and Mon., fol. 1489, and 1457.
[3] Clarke, as before, 56.—G.
[4] Eph. vi. 20 ; 2 Tim. i. 16 ; Acts xv. 26, 29 ; Phil. i. 7, 13, 14, 16 ; Col. iv. 3, 18 ; 2 Tim. ii. 9, &c.   [5] [Foxe,] Acts and Mon., fol. 1633.

mistress that, harlot-like, 'hunted for his precious life,' his injurious master that, without any desert of his, imprisoned him, the tumultuating Egyptians, that pined with hunger, perhaps spake of stoning of him, and the envious courtiers and enchanters that spake evil of him before Pharaoh, to bring him out of favour; but by divine assistance, and God's favourable preference, 1 Sam. xxx. 6, he proved too strong for them all. Ver. 24, 'But his bow abode in strength, and the arms of his hands were made strong by the hands of the mighty God of Jacob,' &c. Joseph is likened to a strong archer, that, as his other enemies as archers shot at him, so his bow was steadfast, and his arms strong by the signal presence of God with him.[1] Such an eminent presence of God had Joseph with him, that he never wanted courage, comfort, or counsel when he was at the worst. The divine presence will make a man stand fast and firm under the greatest pressures. It made Joseph use his bow against his adversaries, as David did his sling against Goliath. He slung, saith one, as if he had wrapped up God in his sling. Ps. xxiii. 4, 'Yea, though I walk through the valley of the shadow of death, I will fear no evil; for thou art with me; thy rod and thy staff they comfort me.' The presence of the Lord with his people in the most deadly dangers fills their souls full of courage, confidence, and comfort. That darkness which comes upon a dying man, a little before he gives up the ghost, is the greatest darkness; and yet let a Christian then have but God by the hand, and he will not fear the most hideous and horrid representations of death: Dan. iii. 24, 'Then Nebuchadnezzar the king was astonied, and rose up in haste, and spake and said unto his counsellors, Did not we cast three men bound into the midst of the fire? They answered and said unto the king, True, O king;' ver. 25, 'He answered and said, Lo, I see four men loose, walking in the midst of the fire, and they have no hurt; and the form of the fourth is like the Son of God.' The presence of the Son of God turned the fiery furnace into a garden of delights, a gallery of pleasure. This divine presence in the midst of fire and flame kept them from fainting, sinning, and shrinking, and filled their souls with comfort, peace, ease, and heavenly refreshing. One of the ancients [Augustine] rhetorically speaking to Nebuchadnezzar, who said, 'he saw one like the Son of God,' ' Whence came this?' saith he. ' Who told thee that this was the Son of God, what law, what prophet? He is not yet born into the world, and the similitude of him that was to be born is known to thee. Whence came this? Who told thee this, but the divine fire enlightening thee within, that whilst thou beholdest these three as thine enemies in the fire, thou mightest give testimony to the Son of God?' This heathenish prince looked upon the fourth person as one like a son of the gods, or like some young god, most bright and glorious, exceeding fair, and excelling in beauty, as if he were not of human, but of divine offspring. But whatever notions or apprehensions Nebuchadnezzar had, we may very safely understand this fourth to be, as the words do literally bear, the very true Son of God, our Lord and Saviour, who is signally present with his people in their greatest extremities and most deadly dangers:

[1] Junius, Mercer. Not that his arms were adorned with bracelets and gold, as the Chaldee saith, &c.

Zech. i. 8, 'I saw by night, and behold a man riding upon a red horse, and he stood amongst the myrtle-trees that were in the bottom; and behind him were three red horses, speckled, and white.' The man riding upon the red horse is the man Christ Jesus; it is the captain of the Lord's host, and the captain of our salvation.[1] Christ is here represented in his kingly state, under the type of a man riding on a red horse, and having his royal attendants; for under the type of red horses, speckled, and white, behind him, is represented his having angels for ministers, and all creatures ready for every dispensation; whether sad, represented by red; or comfortable, represented by white; or mixed of mercy and judgment, represented by speckled horses. Christ is here represented as a man on horseback, ready to make out or sally forth for the good of his people when they are at the lowest. The low, afflicted, and suffering state of the church is fitly compared to myrtle-trees that grow in a shady grove, in valleys, and bottoms, and by water-sides. Now, when his people are in a very low condition, then Christ appears on horseback, for his people's protection, and their enemies' confusion. Christ will be sure to lodge with his people when they are at lowest. When the church is in danger Christ is not asleep; he is always ready upon his red horse, watching all opportunities and advantages, to shew his zeal and courage for his people, and his severity and fury against their enemies. The man that stood amongst the myrtle-trees, ver. 10, is that man Christ Jesus, whose special residence is with his people when they are in the most low, dangerous, and forlorn condition. No troubles, no distresses, no dangers, can banish Christ from his people, or make him seek another lodging: Isa. xliii. 2, 'When thou passest through the waters, I will be with thee; and through the rivers, they shall not overflow thee: when thou walkest through the fire, thou shalt not be burnt; neither shall the flame kindle upon thee.' The Israelites went through the Red Sea, and were not drowned; and the three children walked up and down in the fiery furnace, and were not so much as singed, Dan. iii. 27. By 'fire and water' we may well understand the various troubles, distresses, and dangers that may attend the people of God. Now in all these various troubles, &c., the Lord will be signally present with them, to protect and defend, to secure and deliver them out of all their various troubles, their deepest distresses, and most deadly dangers. 2 Cor. iv. 9, 'Persecuted, but not forsaken; cast down, but not destroyed.' Persecuted by men, but not forsaken by God. The saints may be shaken, not shivered; persecuted, not conquered; cast down, but not cast off. Luther, speaking of his enemies, saith, They may thrust me, but not throw me; shew their teeth, but not devour me; kill me, but not hurt me, &c., because of that favourable and signal presence of Christ that is with me. Now this is that presence of the Lord that falls under our present consideration.

But for the further opening of this important point, let us a little inquire how the Lord does manifest his favourable, his signal, his eminent presence to his people in their greatest troubles, deepest dis-

---

[1] 1 Tim. ii. 5; Josh. iv. 14; Heb. ii. 10. Among the Romans the crown or garland of those that did shout for victory, or ride in triumph, was made of myrtle, Plin., lib. xv. c. 29.

tresses, and most deadly dangers. Now to this question I shall give these twelve answers :—

(1.) First, The Lord does manifest his favourable, signal, and eminent presence with his people in their greatest troubles, deepest distresses, and most deadly dangers, *by raising their faith to more than an ordinary pitch at such a time:* Exod. xiv. 10, 'And when Pharaoh drew nigh, the children of Israel lift up their eyes, and, behold, the Egyptians marched after them, and they were sore afraid: and the children of Israel cried out unto the Lord;' ver. 11, 'And they said unto Moses, Because there were no graves in Egypt, hast thou taken us away to die in the wilderness? wherefore hast thou dealt thus with us, to carry us forth of Egypt?' ver. 12, 'Is not this the word that we did tell thee in Egypt, saying, Let us alone, that we may serve the Egyptians? for it had been better for us to serve the Egyptians, than that we should die in the wilderness.' [1] Thus you see their great troubles, deep distresses, and most deadly dangers, they having a Red Sea before them, and a cruel, bloody, and enraged enemy just at the heels of them. Now in this extremity, see to what a high pitch Moses his faith rises: ver. 13, 'And Moses said unto the people, Fear ye not, stand still, and see the salvation of the Lord, which he will shew to you to-day: for the Egyptians whom ye have seen to-day, ye shall see them again no more for ever.' [2] He saith they shall never see the Egyptians again, that is, in that manner as they saw them that day insulting against them and pursuing after them, as the Septuagint do well interpret it, ὃν τρόπον ἑωράκατε, 'after what sort ye have seen them,' for they saw them afterward, but drowned, and lying dead upon the shore, Exod. xiv. 30: ver. 14, 'The Lord shall fight for you, and ye shall hold your peace.' A strong faith will help a Christian at a dead lift. Though Moses had received no particular promise how the Israelites should be delivered, yet he rested upon God's general promise before, that he would get himself honour upon Pharaoh and his host: 'The Lord shall fight for you, and ye shall be still.' As if he had said, Ye shall be merely passive, and do nothing at all towards the subduing of your enemies, neither in words nor deeds; the Lord shall fight against your enemies, and defeat them himself by a strong hand and an outstretched arm ; compose yourselves, act faith and hope in God, without doubting, murmuring, grudging, fainting, or fretting; for God deferreth his chiefest aid until man's greatest need. When the enemy is highest, salvation is nearest; when the danger is greatest, the help of God is readiest, as at this time they found it.

2 Chron. xiii. 3, 'Abijah set the battle in array, with an army of valiant men of war, even four hundred thousand chosen men: Jeroboam also set the battle in array against him, with eight hundred thousand chosen men, being mighty men of valour.' Jeroboam had two to one: ver. 7, 'And there are gathered unto him vain men, the children of Belial, and have strengthened themselves against Rehoboam the son of Solomon, when Rehoboam was young and tender-

---

[1] The faithful cry unto God in their extremities, but the unbelievers become mad.— *Pellican.* [Qu., Pellicanus (Conrad)?—G.]

[2] Vide Josephus, lib. ii. cap. 6.

hearted, and could not withstand them.' Rehoboam was no warrior, he was no expert prince in the use of arms ; he was but young, not in age, but in experience, policy, and valour ; he was hen-hearted, he had no courage, no mettle.[1] Jeroboam takes hold of these advantages, and gathers eight hundred thousand *Racas,* brainless fellows, light and empty, yokeless and masterless persons ; men of no piety, civility, ingenuity, or common honesty. Now see what a mighty spirit of faith God raised in the children of Judah : ver. 17, 'And Abijah and his people slew them with a great slaughter : so there fell down slain of Israel five hundred thousand chosen men.' A monstrous and matchless slaughter, the greatest number that ever we read slain in any battle ; far beyond that of Tamerlane when he took Bajazet, or Atius the Roman prefect, when he fought with Attila and his Huns in the fields of Catalonia, where were slain on both sides one hundred sixty-five thousand : ver. 18, 'Thus the children of Israel were brought under at that time, and the children of Judah prevailed,' because they relied upon the Lord God of their fathers. Faith at a dead lift never miscarrieth. God never has, nor never will, fail those that place their confidence upon him in their greatest dangers.

Esth. iv. 14, ' For if thou altogether hold thy peace at this time, then shall there enlargement and deliverance arise to the Jews from another place ; but thou and thy father's house shall be destroyed : and who knoweth whether thou art come to the kingdom for such a time as this ?' Their great trouble, their deep distress, and their most deadly danger you have in that, Esth. iii. 13, 'And the letters were sent by the posts into all the king's provinces, to destroy, to kill, and to cause to perish, all Jews, both young and old, little children and women, in one day, even upon the thirteenth day of the twelfth month, (which is the month Adar,) and to take the spoil of them for a prey.'[2] Haman, that grand informer, with his wicked crew, would have spoiled them of their lives and goods, but that they were prevented by a miraculous providence, as you know. Now in this deep distress and most deadly danger, at what rate doth Mordecai believe ? ' For if thou altogether holdest thy peace at this time, then shall there enlargement'—[*Heb.,* respiration]—'and deliverance arise'—[*Heb.,* stand up, as on its basis or bottom, so as none shall be able to withstand it.] This Mordecai speaketh not by a spirit of prophecy, but by the power and force of his faith, grounded upon the precious promises of God's defending his church, hearing the cries of his people, arising for their relief and succour, and grounded upon all the glorious attributes of God, viz., his power, love, wisdom, goodness, and all-sufficiency, &c., all which are engaged in the covenant of grace, to save, protect, and secure his people in their greatest troubles and most deadly dangers. Mordecai's faith in this black, dark, dismal day, was a notable faith indeed, and worthy of highest commendation. Faith can look through the perspective of the promises, and see deliverance at a great distance, salvation at the door. What though sense saith, Deliverance will not come ; and what though reason saith, Deliverance cannot come ; yet a raised

---

[1] 2 Chron. xii. 13. He was one-and-forty years old when he came to the crown.

[2] Here are great aggravations of his cruelty, in that neither sex nor age are spared ; rage and malice knows no bounds.

faith gets above all fears, and disputes, and says, Deliverance will certainly come, redemption is at hand.

Num. xiii. 30, ' And Caleb stilled the people before Moses, and said, Let us go up at once, and possess it, for we are well able to overcome it ;' chap. xiv. 9, ' Only rebel not ye against the Lord, neither fear ye the people of the land, for they are bread before us; their defence is departed from them, and the Lord is with us: fear them not.' The spies by their lies did what they could to daunt and discourage the people, by crying up the strength of the Anakims, and the impossibility of the conquest, Num. xiii. 32, 33. These hollow-hearted hypocritical spies blow hot and cold almost in a breath, Num. xiii. 23–28. First, they make a narrative of the fruitfulness of the land, and presently they conclude that it was a land that was not sufficient to nourish the inhabitants, yea, a land that did devour the inhabitants, ver. 32. Liars have no iron memories. But now behold to what a mighty pitch Caleb's faith is raised. ' Let us go up at once, and possess it, for we are able to overcome it.' Or, nearer the Hebrew, ' Marching up, march up, subduing, subdue.' Let us, saith believing Caleb, march up to the land of Canaan courageously, resolutely, undauntedly, for the day is our own, the land is our own, all is our own. ' They are bread for us,' we shall make but a breakfast of them, we shall as easily and as surely root them out, and cut them down with our swords, as we cut the bread we eat. ' Their defence is departed from them.' In the Hebrew it is, ' Their shadow is departed from them.' The shadow you know guards a man from the scorching heat of the sun, Ps. xci. 1, and cxxi. 5, 6. Caleb, by faith, saw God withdrawn from them ; by the eye of his faith he looked upon them as a people without a fence, a shadow, a guard, a covert, a protection ; and therefore, as a people that might easily be subdued and destroyed. His faith told him that it was not their strong cities, nor their high walls, nor their sons of Anak, that could preserve, shelter, secure, or defend them, seeing the Lord had forsaken them, and would be no longer as a shadow or a shelter to them. ' And the Lord is with us,' to make us victorious, to tread down our enemies, and to give us a quiet possession of the good land.

So Dan. iii. 16, ' Shadrach, Meshach, and Abed-nego, answered and said to the king, O Nebuchadnezzar, we are not careful to answer thee in this matter.' Ver. 17, ' If it be so, our God, whom we serve, is able to deliver us from the burning fiery furnace, and he will deliver us out of thy hand, O king.' In the fiery furnace they are protected by a divine providence, they escape death beyond all men's expectations, for the fire touched them not, neither could it burn during their abode in the furnace, for God so fortified their bodies that they could not be consumed by fire,[1] which accident[2] made them in great estimation with the king, for that he saw that they were virtuous, and beloved of God, and for that cause they were highly honoured by him. Here is a fiery furnace before them, and a proud, boasting, tyrannical, enraged prince domineering over them, for not obeying his idolatrous will. Now to what a mighty pitch is their faith raised ! ' Our God, whom we serve, is able to deliver us, and he will deliver us.' Their

---

[1] Josephus, Antiq., pp. 259, 260.   [2] ' Occurrence.'—G.

faith was bottomed upon their propriety in God: ' *Our* God;' and upon the power, providence, and all-sufficiency of God: ' Is able to deliver us;' and upon the gracious readiness and willingness of God: ' And he will deliver us out of thy hand, O king.' When dangers are greatest, then God commonly raises the faith of his people highest; faith doth most and best for us, when we are at a dead lift. It quenches the violence of fire, Heb. xi. 34 ; as the apostle speaks, pointing at the faith of these three children, or rather champions. Though now the fiery furnace was heat[ed] seven times hotter than it used to be at other times, yet such was the strength, and might, and power of their faith, that it so quenched the flames, that they had not one hair of their heads singed, nor their coats changed, nor the smell of fire found upon them, Dan. iii. 27 ; and thus the blessed martyrs may be said by their faith, patience, and constancy to quench the violence of the fire, though their bodies were consumed to ashes in the fire. So Dan. vi. 16. Daniel is cast into the den of hungry, enraged lions; innocent Daniel is exposed to the cruel paws and hungry jaws of lions. This kind of capital punishment was not unusual among the Babylonians, the Medes and Persians, and among the Romans also, with whom it was a common saying in Tertullian's time, Let the Christians be cast to the lions. The faces of the lions are stern, and their voices are terrible, Amos iii. 8 ; they are roaring and ravening, they are greedy of their prey. They are vigilant and subtle. Lying in wait to get their prey, they sleep little, and when they sleep, it is *apertis oculis*, with open eyes. They mind their prey much, and are cunning to catch it, Ps. xvii. 12. The lion hides himself, and when the prey comes near he suddenly surprises it. They are proud and stately, they go alone, they eat not with the lioness, much less with other creatures, they will not stoop to any, or turn away from any, they do what they list; they are most cruel, bloody, devouring creatures; they have terrible claws, sharp teeth, and are strong and mighty to crush and break the bones; and it is very dangerous to meddle with lions.[1] Num. xxiv. 9, ' He lieth down as a lion, as a great lion: who shall stir him up?' Lions if offended and provoked are very revengeful. In the hunting or taking of lions, the lion observes who wounds him, and on him if possible he will be revenged. Ælian tells of a bear that came into a lion's den, and bit the whelps she found there. The lion returning, the bear to shift for herself got up into a high tree. The lioness watched at the foot of the tree. The lion ranged abroad in the woods, and meets with a man that had an axe, and used to fell trees; this man the lion brings to the den, shewed him the wounded whelps, directs him to the tree where the bear was, which he cut down; the bear being torn in pieces, the man was safely dismissed. By these hints we may guess at the deadly danger that Daniel was in. Some writers tell us, that if a cloth be cast upon the eyes of a lion to cover them, he will not hurt a man ;[2] or if he be full. —Josephus, to illustrate the history, saith, that these princes pleaded before the king, saying that the lions were full and gorged, and therefore they would not touch Daniel ;[3] which he hearing, being displeased

---

[1] Prov. xxx. 3; Neh. ii. 12; 2 Kings xvii. 6; Prov. xxviii. 15; 1 Pet. v. 8.
[2] Aristot., Pliny, Pereriue.   [3] Josephus, Antiq., pp. 262, 263.

with their injurious malice, said, that the lions should now be fed, and then they cast in to see when they were gorged, whether they could likewise escape: but this being done, they were suddenly destroyed, before they came to the bottom of the den, Dan. vi. 24. To what a fatal end came these informers! As to their wives and children that were cast into the den of lions, it is most probable that they were accessary to that wicked conspiracy against Daniel, by stirring up and provoking their husbands and fathers, to engage all their power, interest, and policy against him, and never to suffer a poor captive to be advanced in honour and dignity above them; and how just and righteous a thing was it with God, that they who had plotted together, and contrived together, the ruin and destruction of a holy innocent person, that these should suffer together, and go to the den together, and be torn in pieces together. Sinners, look to yourselves; if you will sin with others, you must expect to suffer with others.—Or if a man hath been beneficial to him; or if a man lieth prostrate before him, in the manner of a supplicant. But Daniel was not safe, he was not secured by any of these means, but God secured him in the midst of these dreadful dangers by the ministry of an angel. ' My God hath sent his angel, and hath shut the lions' mouths, that they have not hurt me,' Dan. vi. 22. Others say, that God secured Daniel,· by taking away the lions' hunger from them at that time, and by causing in them a satiety. And some tell us, that God secured him, by raising such a fantasy in the lions that they looked upon Daniel, not as a prey, but as on one that was a friend unto them. But now in the midst of this dreadful danger, how doth Daniel's faith sparkle and shine: ver. 23, ' Then was the king exceeding glad for him, and commanded that they should take Daniel up out of the den; so Daniel was taken up out of the den, and no manner of hurt was found upon him, because he believed in his God.' Daniel in a fiery furnace looks upon God as his God, in the midst of the flames he acts faith upon the power of God, the promises of God, &c. Of all living creatures lions are most fierce, cruel, and irresistible, and yet such was the strength and force of Daniel's faith, that it stopped their mouths, see Heb. xi. 33; Judges xiv. 6; 1 Sam. xvii. 34. Though Daniel was but one man, yet such was the power of his faith, that it stopped the mouths of many lions. As Luther says of prayer, so may I say of faith; it hath a kind of omnipotency in it; it is able to do all things, *est quædam omnipotentia precum.* Thus you see by these famous instances to what a mighty pitch the Lord has raised the faith of his people, when they have been in the greatest troubles, deepest distresses, and most deadly dangers; and this is the first way wherein the Lord doth manifest his favourable, his signal, his eminent presence with his people, in their greatest troubles, deepest distresses, and most deadly dangers. But,

(2.) Secondly, The Lord doth manifest his favourable, his signal, his eminent presence with his people in their greatest troubles, deepest distresses, and most deadly dangers, *by his teaching and instructing of them;* Ps. xciv. 12, ' Blessed is the man whom thou chastenest, O Lord, and teachest him out of thy law.'[1] This divine presence turns

---

[1] *Feri Domine, feri,* said Luther: Strike while thou pleasest, Lord! only to thy correction add instruction, *ut quod noceat, doceat.*

every lash into a happy lesson. In this psalm the Holy Ghost useth six arguments to prove that a man is blessed who is chastened. [1.] Because he is instructed by being afflicted, as here. [2.] Because the end why God lays affliction on his people is to give them rest from the days of adversity, ver. 13. [3.] Until the pit be digged for the wicked, in the same verse, until the cold grave hold his body, and hot hell hold his soul. [4.] Because God will support them under all their afflictions. When God casteth his people into the furnace of afflictions, his everlasting arms shall be underneath them. Though God may cast down his people, yet he will never cast off his people. [5.] Because there shall be a glorious restoration: ver. 15, 'Judgment shall return unto righteousness.' [6.] Because all the upright in heart shall follow it, in the same verse—viz., in their affections they are carried out after it, earnestly desiring that dear day when God will unriddle his providences, and clear up his proceedings with the sons of men. Jerome, writing to a sick friend, hath this expression: 'I account it a part of unhappiness not to know adversity; I judge you to be miserable, because you have not been miserable.' Demetrius saith, Nothing seems more unhappy to me than he to whom no adversity hath happened. *Impunitas, securitatis mater, virtutum noverca, religionis virus, tinea sanctitatis:* Freedom from punishment is the mother of security, the stepmother of virtue, the poison of religion, the moth of holiness, [Bernard.] It was a speech of a German divine, [Gaspar Olevianus,] in his sickness: In this disease, saith he, I have learned how great God is, and what the evil of sin is. I never knew to purpose what God was before, nor what sin meant before. God's corrections are our instructions, his lashes our lessons, his scourges our schoolmasters, his chastisements our advertisements.[1] And to note this, the Hebrews and Greeks both express chastening and teaching by one and the same word, מוּסָר, *musar*, παιδεία; because the latter is the true end of the former, according to that in the proverb, 'Smart makes wit, and vexation gives understanding.' Job xxxvi. 8, 'And if they be bound in fetters, and be holden in cords of affliction;' ver. 9, 'Then he sheweth them their work, and their transgressions that they have exceeded;' ver. 10, 'He openeth also their ear to discipline, and commandeth that they return from iniquity.' Sanctified afflictions open men's ears to discipline, and turn them from iniquity, which is a piece of learning that a Christian can never pay too dear for. Affliction is *verus Scripturæ commentarius:* An excellent comment upon the Scriptures. Afflictions make way for the word of the Lord to come to the heart. Affliction sanctified is *Lex practica*, a practical law. Bernard had a brother of his, who was a riotous and profane soldier; Bernard gives him many good instructions and admonitions, &c., but his brother slighted them, and made nothing of them. Bernard comes to him, and puts his hand to his side. One day, saith he, God will make way to this heart of yours by some spear or lance. And so it fell out; for, going into the wars, he was wounded, and then he remembers his brother's instructions and admonitions, and then they got to his heart, and lay upon it to some purpose: Job xxxiii. 16, 'Then he openeth the ears of men, and

[1] *Schola crucis, schola lucis,* Isa. xxvi. 9; Prov. iii. 12, 13, and vi. 23.

sealeth their instruction.' *Oculos quos peccatum claudit, pœna aperit:*
The eye that sin shuts, afflictions open, [Gregory.]   The cross opens
men's eyes, as the tasting of honey did Jonathan's.·   By correction
God seals up instruction; God sets on the one by the other; as when
a schoolmaster would have a lesson learned indeed, he sets it on with
a whipping.   As Gideon taught the elders of the city and the men of
Succoth with the thorns and briars of the wilderness, so God teaches
his people by affliction many a holy and happy lesson, Judges viii. 16.
By afflictions, troubles, distresses, and dangers, the Lord teaches his
people to look upon sin as the most loathsome thing in the world, and
to look upon holiness as the most lovely thing in the world.   Sin is
never so bitter, and holiness is never so sweet, as when our troubles
are greatest and our dangers highest.   By afflictions the Lord teaches
his people to sit loose from this world, and to make sure the great
things of that other world.   By affliction God shews his people the
vanity, vexation, emptiness, weakness, and nothingness of the creatures, and the choiceness, preciousness, and sweetness of communion
with himself, and of interest in himself.   Christ, though he knew,
' yet learned he obedience by the things which he suffered,' Heb. v. 8;
that is, he shewed obedience more than before; not as if Christ were
to go to school to learn, or as if by certain acts he were to fit himself
for obedience; he did not learn that which he knew not before, but
did that which he did not before.   He that was put upon the trial of
his obedience, he came to know by experience what a hard matter it
was thus to obey God.[1]   By God's favourable presence a man comes to
learn many lessons in a time of adversity which he never learned in a
day of prosperity; for we are like idle boys and bad scholars, that
learn best when the rod is over us.   Hezekiah was better upon his
sick-bed than when he was shewing of his treasures to the ambassadors of the king of Babylon, Isa. xxxix. 1–5; and David was a better
man when he was in his wilderness-condition than when he sat upon
his royal throne, Ps. xxx. 6, 7.   The Jews are ever best when in the
worst condition; the Athenians would never mend till they were in
mourning.   When Munster lay sick, and his friends asked him how
he did, and how he felt himself; he pointed to his sores and ulcers,
whereof he was full, and said, These are God's gems and jewels
wherewith he decketh his best friends, and to me they are more precious than all the gold and silver in the world.   Here, as that martyr
phrased it, we are but learning our A B C, and our lesson is never
past Christ's cross, and our walking is still home by Weeping-Cross.
Usually men are worst in a prosperous condition.   In a prosperous
condition God speaks to us, and we mind him not: ' I spoke to thee
in thy prosperity, but thou wouldest not hear: and this hath been
thy manner from thy youth upwards,' Jer. ii. 21.   Pope Martin reported of himself that, whilst he was a monk and lived in the cloister,
he had some evidences for heaven; when he was a cardinal, he began
to fear and doubt; but after he came to be pope, he utterly despaired.
The Lord never shews more of his favourable, signal, and eminent presence, than by teaching of his people many gracious and gospel lessons
by their great troubles, deep distresses, and most deadly dangers.   But

---

[1] παθήματα μαθήματα, *Nocumenta documenta.*

(3.) Thirdly, The Lord doth manifest his favourable, his signal, his eminent presence with his people, in their greatest troubles, deepest distresses, and most deadly dangers, *by raising, strengthening, and acting,*[1] *their suffering graces*—viz., their faith, hope, love, patience, prudence, courage, boldness, zeal, constancy. Thus in the text, 'The Lord stood by me, and strengthened me.' He put new life, and strength, and vigour into all my graces. Although there are habits of grace always resident in the hearts of the saints, yet those habits are not always in exercise. The habits of grace cannot act of themselves, there must be renewed strength imparted to set them on work. 'Make me to go in the path of thy commandments, for therein do I delight,' Ps. cxix. 35. Though David had a spirit of new life within him, yet he could not actually walk in the path of God's precepts, till by an additional force he was set agoing: Cant. iv. 16, 'Awake, O north wind, and come thou south wind, blow upon my garden, that the spices thereof may flow out.'[2] By the garden we may safely understand a sanctified soul, and by the spices in this garden we may understand the several graces planted in the soul. Now these spices can never flow out, and send forth their fragrant smell, till the north and south wind blows upon them. Habitual grace cannot operate, and dilate, and put forth itself into exercise, till by the concurrent presence and assistance of Christ it is educed into act. No saint can act that grace he hath received, by his own strength, without the presence and assistance of Christ: 1 Cor. xv. 16, 'But by the grace of God, I am what I am; and his grace, which was bestowed upon me, was not in vain, but I labour more abundantly than they all, yet not I, but the grace of God, which was with me.' He does not say, the grace of God which was in me, that habitual grace which I had; but the grace of God which was with me. So then it is not the strength of habitual grace that will carry a man through doing or suffering work, but the auxiliary, the assisting, the conquering grace of Jesus Christ. It is his grace with us, more than his grace in us. So John xv. 5, 'Without me ye can do nothing.' Ye that are my disciples, ye that have the Spirit of Jesus Christ, 'Without me ye can do nothing.'[3] The habits of grace, the actings of grace, and the perfecting of grace, are all from Jesus Christ. It is more emphatical in the original, for there you have two negatives, 'cannot do nothing.' He does not say, 'Without me ye cannot do many things,' but, 'Without me ye can do *nothing;*' nor he does not say, 'Without me ye can do no great thing,' but, 'Without me ye can do *nothing;*' nor he does not say, 'Without me ye can do no difficult thing,' but, 'Without me ye can do *nothing;*' nor he does not say, 'Without me ye can do no spiritual thing,' but, 'Without me ye can do *nothing.*' Whatever a saint may do by the power of gifts, or habits of grace received, yet he can do nothing in a lively spiritual acceptable way without the presence of Christ, without a constant dependence upon Christ, without a sweet and special communion and fellowship with Christ. If we cannot put forth a natural action

---

[1] 'Causing to act,' as, on a little, 'actuated.'—G.

[2] Christ is the divers winds, both cold and hot, moist and dry, binding and opening, north and south; and therefore what wind soever blows, it shall blow good to his people.

[3] χωρὶς ἐμοῦ, separate from me, or apart from me. Erasmus, *sine me.* Beza, *seorsim a me.* Members divided from the head cannot live; so here.

without him—for in him we live, move, and have our being, Acts xvii. 28—how much less can we perform a spiritual action, in a spiritual manner, without his presence and assistance? Let the king sit but at his table, and then our spikenard will send forth a sweet smell, Cant. i. 12; that is, let Jesus Christ be but present with us, and then our graces, which are compared to spikenard, will send forth a sweet smell. Sitting at the table with King Jesus intimates the sweetest friendship and fellowship with him. It was held a great honour and happiness to stand before Solomon, 1 Kings x. 8; what is it then to sit with Christ at his table? 'My spikenard sendeth forth the smell thereof;' that is, My faith is actuated, and all my other graces are exercised and increased. Christ's presence puts life into all our graces: Isa. xli. 10; Luke xxi. 14, 15, 'Fear thou not, for I am with thee; be not dismayed, for I am thy God; I will strengthen thee, yea, I will uphold thee with the right hand of my righteousness:' 2 Cor. xii. 10, 'When I am weak, then am I strong.' When I am weak in myself, then am I strong in Christ. If the sun shine upon the marigold, how soon does the marigold open; so when the Sun of righteousness does but shine upon a Christian's graces, how do they open and act! Mal. iv. 2. To shew how the presence of Christ has acted the faith, love, courage, boldness, and patience, &c., of the saints in the Old and New Testament, the primitive Christians and the martyrs, in the latter ages of the world, when they have been in their greatest troubles, deepest distresses, and most deadly dangers, would take up more than a little time; besides, in my other writings I have opened these things more fully to you, and to them I must refer you. And therefore,

(4.) Fourthly, The Lord doth manifest his favourable, signal, and eminent presence with his people, in their greatest troubles, deepest distresses, and most deadly dangers, *by laying a law of restraint upon every wicked man, and by bridling and checking their fury and insolency, that they shall not add afflictions to the afflicted, as otherwise they would;* as he did upon Laban: Gen. xxxi. 24, 'And God came to Laban the Syrian in a dream by night, and said unto him, Take heed that thou speak not to Jacob, either good or bad.' Ver. 29, 'It is in the power of my hand to do you hurt; but the God of your fathers spake unto me yesternight, saying, Take thou heed that thou speak not to Jacob, either good or bad.' See what a law of restraint God laid upon Esau, Gen. xxxiii. 1–4; and upon Abimelech, Gen. xx. 6–8, 17, 18; and upon Benhadad, 1 Kings xx. 1, 10, 29, 30; and upon Haman, as you may see by comparing the 3d and 6th chapters of Esther together; and upon Pharaoh, Exod. xv. 9, 10; and upon Sennacherib, Isa. xxxvii. 28, 29, 33–36; and upon Herod, Acts xii. Maximinus set forth a proclamation engraven in brass for the utter abolishing of Christ and religion: he was eaten up of lice. Valens being to subscribe an order for the banishment of Basil, was smitten with a sudden trembling of his hand that he could not subscribe the order; afterwards he was burned to death by the Goths.[1]

Domitian, the author of the second persecution against the Christians, having drawn a catalogue of the names of such as he was to kill, in which was the name of his own wife and other friends; upon which

[1] History of the Council of Trent, page 417.

he was, by the consent of his wife, slain by his own household servants with daggers in his privy-chamber. His body was buried without honour, his memory cursed to posterity, and his arms and ensigns were thrown down and defaced. Julian vowed to make a sacrifice of the Christians upon his return from the wars; but, in a battle against the Persians, he was deadly wounded, and throwing his blood in the air, in a high contempt of Christ, he died with that desperate blasphemous expression in his mouth, *Vicisti tandem, Galilœe,* 'Thou Galilean hast overcome me.'

Felix, Earl of Wurtemberg, was a great persecutor of the saints, and did swear that ere he died he would ride up to the spurs in the blood of the Lutherans; but the very same night, wherein he had thus sworn and vowed, he was choked in his own blood.

The judgments of God were so famous and frequent upon the persecutors of the saints in Bohemia, that it was used as a proverb among the adversaries themselves, that if any man were weary of his life let him but attempt against the Piccardines—so they called the Christians—and he should not live a year to an end. By these short hints you may see that all along God has made good that word that is more worth than a world, 'Surely the wrath of man shall praise thee; and the remainder of wrath shalt thou restrain'—Hebrew, 'Shalt thou gird,' that is, curb, and keep within compass; or as the Greek hath it, 'It shall keep holiday to thee,' that is, cease from working or acting outwardly, how restless soever it be within.[1] 'The remainder of wrath shalt thou restrain,' that is, those that are left alive of thy wrathful enemies, that have still any malice against thy people, thou wilt curb and restrain, and not suffer their wrath to be so great as formerly; or if they go about to recruit their forces, and to set again upon thy people, thou wilt set such bounds to their wrath that they shall not accomplish their desires, nor shall they proceed one step further than shall make signally for thy glory and thy people's good; so some carry the words. The more eager and furious the enemies are against God's people, the more honour and glory will God get in protecting and securing his people, and in girding, binding, and tying up their enemies. Were it not for this favourable, signal, and eminent presence of God with his people in their greatest troubles, deepest distresses, and most deadly dangers, wicked men would still be a-multiplying of their sorrows, increasing their troubles, and adding of burden to burden. It is this favourable presence of God that binds wicked men over to their good behaviour, and that chains them up from doing that mischief that they design and intend. But,

(5.) Fifthly, The Lord does manifest his favourable, signal, and eminent presence with his people, in their greatest troubles, deepest distresses, and most deadly dangers, *by guiding and leading them into those paths and waves which make most for their own peace and quiet, safety and security, contentation and satisfaction, happiness here, and blessedness hereafter,* Exod. xii. 21, 22; Isa. lxiii. 12–14; Ps. v. 8. Deut. xxxii. 10, 'He found me in a desert land, and in the waste howling wilderness; he led him about, he instructed him, he kept him

[1] Ps. lxxvi. 10—Hebrew, 'Gird,' that is, keep it within compass as with a girdle.

as the apple of his eye.' [1] A wilderness-condition is, you know, a condition of straits, wants, deep distresses, and most deadly dangers. Now when his people were in this condition he instructs them by his words and works, and he takes them by the hand, as I may say, and leads them with all care, tenderness, gentleness, and sweetness, as a man would do a poor helpless infant, which he should find in a desert, in a waste howling wilderness. God never left leading of his people till he had brought them at last through the wilderness to the land of Canaan. Ah! this leading presence of God turns a wilderness into a paradise, a desert into a Canaan. Let a Christian's troubles, distresses, and dangers, be never so many or never so great, yet as long as he has the guiding presence of God with him, he is safe from dangers in the midst of dangers. 'The fire shall not burn him, nor the waters overflow him,' Isa. xliii. 2: Ps. cvii. 4, 'They wandered in the wilderness in a solitary way; they found no city to dwell in:' ver. 5, 'Hungry and thirsty, their soul fainted in them:' ver. 6, 'Then they cried unto the Lord in their troubles, and he delivered them out of their distresses.' Here you see their great troubles, deep distresses, and most deadly dangers; and now God gives them his hand, ver. 7, 'And he led them forth by the right way, that they might go to a city of habitation;' that is, to a state of settlement, say some, to Jerusalem, say others, or to that 'city which hath foundations, whose builder and maker is God,' saith another, Heb. xi. 10. In that 32d Psalm you may see David's great troubles, deep distresses, and most deadly dangers: ver. 3, 'When I kept silence, my bones waxed old, through my roaring all the day long:' ver. 4, 'For day and night thy hand was heavy upon me: my moisture is turned into the drought of summer. Selah.' But will God be his guide now? Oh yes, ver. 8, 'I will instruct thee, and teach thee in the way which thou shalt go: I will guide thee with mine eye.' Let the hand of the Lord be never so heavy upon a person, yet the presence of God guiding and instructing of him will keep him from utter fainting and sinking under that hand, Isa. xxx. 21; Ps. lxxiii. 24. When the people of God are in their greatest troubles, deepest distresses, and most deadly dangers, he leads and guides them, Ps. xxv. 9, 12, and v. 8. [1.] Into supernatural ways: Prov. xv. 24, 'The way of life is above to the wise.' He hath his feet where other men's heads are, and, like a heavenly eagle, delights himself in flying high. [2.] Into good ways, Jer. vi. 16. [3.] Into strait and strict ways, Mat. vii. 14. Hence they are called right or straight paths which lie betwixt two extremes; or, if you will, which directly lead you to the view of heaven. They are paths which lie level with the rule and with the end. A man may see salvation and heaven at the end of them. [4.] Into pleasant ways: Prov. iii. 17, 'Her ways are ways of pleasantness, and all her paths are peace.' Such as were those of Adam before his fall, strowed with roses and paved with peace. Some degree of comfort, pleasantness, and peace, follows every good action, as heat accompanies fire, as

[1] The apple of the eye is the tenderest piece of the tenderest part. Hebrew, *Ishon* of *Ish*, as *pupilla* of *pupa*, because therein appears the likeness of a little man, or because a man is to be prized above all other creatures, as so God esteemeth his people above all the world, Heb. xi. 38.

beams and influences issue from the sun. [5.] Into right paths: Prov. iv. 11, ' I have taught thee in the way of wisdom ; I have led thee in right paths :' Hosea i. 9, ' The ways of the Lord are right, and the righteous shall walk in them.' The ways of his will, the ways of his word, and the ways of his worship, are all right ways, they carry us on in a straight line unto a right end. [6.] Into old and ancient ways : Jer. vi. 16, ' Ask for the old paths, where is the good way, and walk therein, and ye shall find rest to your souls:' Jer. xviii. 15, ' They have caused them to stumble in their way from the ancient paths.' The ways of holiness are of the greatest, highest, and ancientest antiquity. The first ways of Adam were ways of holiness. The ways of sin are of a later edition than the ways of holiness. God stamped his image of holiness upon man before ever Satan assayed to tempt him. Holiness is of the ancientest house, of the greatest antiquity. Sin is but an upstart, holiness is the. firstborn. The way of holiness is the eldest way, the way of holiness is gray-headed and of ancientest institution. All other ways are but of yesterday, they are but new ways to the ways of holiness. The stamp of antiquity upon many things is a praise and an honour to them, as old gold, old friends, old manuscripts, old monuments, old scars, and old holiness. The stamp of antiquity upon the ways of holiness is the praise and honour of the ways of holiness. [7.] Into paths of righteousness: Ps. xxiii. 3, ' He leads me in paths of righteousness for his name's sake ;' or in plain, smooth, easy paths, or in sheep-tracks, wherein I may walk unweariedly and unblamably. Herein he alludes to the shepherd's care in leading his sheep gently in fair and plain ways, and not through deep mire, brambles, and briars, or over craggy ways that must needs be hard and troublesome for them to go in. The word here used is metaphorical ; sometimes respecting the blind, who cannot walk without a guide ; sometimes little or weak children, who cannot go without a leader ; and here the weak and wandering sheep, which stand in need of the shepherd to go in and out before them. [8.] Into paths of salvation : Acts xvi. 17, ' These men are the servants of the most high God, which shew unto us the way of salvation.' [9.] Into ways of truth : 2 Pet. ii. 2, ' And many shall follow their pernicious ways, by reason of whom the way of truth shall be evil spoken of.' ' The way of truth,' that is, the true Christian religion revealed from heaven, which shews. the way to true happiness, to eternal salvation. [10.] Into ways of uprightness: Prov. ii. 13, ' Who leave the paths of uprightness, to walk in the ways of darkness.' Now when the people of God are in their greatest troubles, deepest distresses, and most deadly dangers, the Lord by leading them [1.] into supernatural ways, [2.] into good ways, [3.] into strict and straight ways, [4.] into pleasant ways, [5.] into right ways, [6.] into old and ancient ways, [7.] into righteous ways, [8.] into ways of salvation, [9.] into ways of truth, and [10.] into ways of uprightness, does gloriously manifest his favourable, his signal, and his eminent presence with them. There is nothing below a mighty presence of God that can enable a Christian— especially when he is under great troubles, and in deep distresses, and most deadly dangers—to do these five things:—[1.] To approve of the ways of God; [2.] To choose the ways of the Lord; [3.] Highly to prize them; [4.] To delight and take pleasure in them; [5.] To walk in them and to keep close to them; and yet in all these five things the Lord doth greatly and graciously help his poor people, when they are, as it were, in the very mouth of the lion. But,

(6.) Sixthly, The Lord doth manifest his favourable presence, his signal and eminent presence with his people, in their greatest troubles, deepest distresses, and most deadly dangers, *by encouraging, imbold-ening, animating and heartening up his people in the midst of all their troubles, distresses, and dangers, and by putting new life, spirit, and mettle into them, when they are even in the very mouth of the lion:* Josh. i. 6, ' Be strong and of a good courage.' Ver. 7, ' Only be thou strong and very courageous.' Ver. 9, ' Be strong and of a good courage; be not afraid, neither be thou dismayed: for the Lord thy God is with thee whithersoever thou goest.' 2 Chron. xiii. 12; Num. xiii. 32, 33, compared with xiv. 9. Joshua was a sword-man as well as a book-man; he had his name changed from Oshea to Joshua, from *Let God save,* to *God shall save,* Num. xiii. 16. Christ will never want a champion to stand up for his church. If Moses dies, Joshua shall stand up. There shall be a succession of sword-men and book-men, of rulers and teachers, to carry on Christ's work in the world till the top-stone be laid with grace unto it, Zech. iv. 7; Mal. ii. 15. The residue of the Spirit is with the Lord, and therefore he can and will put such an anointing of his Spirit upon one and another as shall fit them to carry on his works in the world. Joshua was very valiant, and a man of singular good mettle, yet because he was sure to meet with such troubles, deep distresses, and deadly dangers, as would put him to it, therefore he is pressed so frequently to be courageous: ver. 6, ' Be strong and of good courage.' Ver. 7, ' Only be thou strong and very courageous.' Ver. 9, ' Be strong and of a good. courage.' Ver. 18, ' Only be strong and of a good courage.' Deut. xxxi. 7, ' And Moses called unto Joshua, and said unto him in the sight of all Israel, Be strong and of a good courage,' &c.[1] And why all this? Not because Joshua had discovered any fainthearted-ness or cowardice, but because the work he was to undertake was so weighty and perilous, in regard of those many and mighty nations whom he was to destroy, and plant the Israelites in their room. The work that Joshua was to undertake was attended with many great diffi-culties and dangers, in respect of the enemies he was to encounter, as being men of vast and giant-like statures and strength, and dwelling in cities with high walls and strongly fortified. Now the main argument to raise his courage and mettle is drawn from God's special presence and assistance: Josh. i. 9, ' For the Lord thy God is with thee whithersoever thou goest.' We are not to understand it of God's general presence in all places, but of his special, favourable, signal, and eminent presence, which God would manifest in his preserva-tion, and protection, notwithstanding all the difficulties, enterprises, dangers, and enemies that he was to encounter with. So 2 Chron. xxxii. 7, ' Be strong and courageous, be not afraid nor dismayed for the king of Assyria, nor for all the multitude that is with him: for

---

[1] Moses had a special command from God to charge Joshua to be courageous, Deut. i. 38, and iii. 28. God himself also lays the same command upon him, Deut. xxxi. 23.

there be more with us than with him.' Ver. 8, 'With him is an arm of flesh; but with us is the Lord our God to help us, and to fight our battles,' &c. At this time the king of Assyria was the greatest monarch in the world, and the most formidable enemy Israel had. He had a mighty army, for there was a hundred fourscore and five thousand of them slain in one night, ver. 21. Now the great thing they were to mind and attend was to look narrowly to it, that the favourable, signal, and eminent presence of God with them, did raise all their hearts above all discouragements, fears, and dismayedness. What is the chaff to the whirlwind? what are thorns and briars to a consuming fire? what is an arm of flesh to the arm, strength, and power of a God? what is weakness to strength, and the nothing-creature to the Lord of hosts? Now if the special signal presence of God with his people in their greatest troubles and most deadly dangers won't put singular courage, life, and mettle into them, what will? Acts xxiii. 10, 'And when there arose a great dissension, the chief captain, fearing lest Paul should have been pulled in pieces of them, commanded the soldiers to go down, and take him by force from among them, and to bring him into the castle.' Ver. 11, 'And the night following the Lord stood by him, [namely, in a vision, or in a dream, or in an ecstasy,] and said, Be of good cheer, Paul: for as thou hast testified of me in Jerusalem, so must thou bear witness also at Rome.' The favourable, signal presence of the Lord with him turned his prison into a palace. Mr Philpot, being a prisoner for the testimony of Jesus, writes thus to his friends :[1] 'Though I tell·you that I am in hell in the judgment of this world, yet assuredly I feel in the same the consolation of heaven, I praise God; and this loathsome and horrible prison is as pleasant to me as the walks in the garden of the King's Bench.' When Paul was in great danger the Lord stood by him, to cheer, comfort, and encourage him, see Acts xxvii. 23, 24. Now God claps him on the back, and puts new life and mettle into him.

When Dionysius was given up by the executioner to be beheaded, he remained constant and courageous, saying, Come life, come death, I will worship none but the God of heaven and earth.[2]

When Chrysostom had told Eudoxia the empress that for her covetousness she would be called a second Jezebel, she thereupon sent him a threatening message, to which he gave this stout and resolute answer, 'Go tell her, *nil nisi peccatum timeo,* I fear nothing but sin.'

When the executioner had kindled the fire behind Jerome of Prague, he bade him kindle it before his face; For, said he, if I had been afraid of it, I had not come to this place, having had so many opportunities offered me to escape it. At the giving up of the ghost he said, *Hanc animam in flammis offero, Christe, tibi,* This soul of mine, in flames of fire, O Christ, I offer thee.

The emperor, coming into Germany, sent for Luther to Worms; but many of his friends, from the danger they apprehended hanging over his head, dissuaded him from going; to whom he gave this prudent, courageous, and resolute answer, 'That these discouragements were cast in his way by Satan, who knew that by his profession of the

[1] [Foxe,] Acts and Mon., 1663.   [2] Clarke, as before.—G.

truth in so illustrious a place, his kingdom would be shaken; and that, therefore, if he knew that there were as many devils in Worms as there were tiles on the houses, yet he would go.'

The German knight, in his apologetical letter for Luther against the pontifical clergy, saith, 'I will go through with what I have under-taken against you, and will stir up men to seek their freedom. I neither care nor fear what may befall me, being prepared for either event, either to ruin you to the great benefit of my country, or myself to fall with a good conscience,' &c.

William Flower the martyr said, 'That the heavens should as soon fall as I will forsake my profession, or budge in the least degree from it.'

Apollonius being asked, 'If he did not tremble at the sight of the tyrant,' made this answer, 'God, which gave him a terrible counte-nance, hath given also unto me an undaunted heart.'

When Gardiner asked Rowland Taylor if he did not know him, &c., to whom he answered, 'Yea, I know you, and all your greatness, yet you are but a mortal man; and if I should be afraid of your lordly looks, why fear ye not God the Lord of us all?'

Basil affirms of the primitive Christians, that they had so much courage and magnanimity of spirit in their sufferings, that many heathens, seeing their heroic zeal, resoluteness, and undauntedness, turned Christians.

When one of the ancient martyrs was terrified with the threatenings of his persecutors, he replied, 'There is nothing of things visible, nor nothing of things invisible, that I fear; I will stand to my profession of the name of Christ, and contend earnestly for the faith once delivered to the saints, come on it what will.'[1]

By these instances, which may be of great use in this trying day, you may clearly see how the Lord has manifested his favourable, signal, and eminent presence to his people in their greatest troubles, deepest distresses, and most deadly dangers, by raising up in them a spirit of courage, magnanimity, and holy gallantry. But,

(7.) Seventhly, The Lord doth manifest his favourable, signal, and eminent presence to his people in their greatest troubles, deepest dis-tresses, and most deadly dangers, *by preserving them from troubles in the midst of troubles, from dangers in the midst of dangers:* Dan. iii. 25, 'He answered, and said, Lo, I see four men loose, walking in the midst of the fire, and they have no hurt, and the form of the fourth is like the Son of God.' The presence of the Son of God preserves these three valiant champions from dangers in the midst of dangers. 'They fell down bound in the fiery furnace,' saith my author, [Polanus,] 'and they walked loose in the midst of the fire without any hurt, for the angel of the Lord descended together with them in the same moment, who shook the flames of the fire forth out of the furnace, and pre-served the servants of God safe without any trouble, being cooled, as it were, with a dew coming upon them in a pleasant manner.' But give me leave to say, that these words, 'One like the Son of God,' doth not argue that in this vision there was not a representation of the Son of God to come afterwards in the flesh, but rather that this great mys-

[1] Foxe and Clarke for all these names, as before.—G.

tery was here shewed for the greater comfort of the faithful, that they might courageously bear all their sufferings, having the Prince and Head both of angels and men present with them herein to mitigate their pains, and carry them through with joy; this being a greater wonder of grace and love than to have the protection of a mere angel, concerning whose power also, whether he can change the nature of fire, that it shall not burn, is very doubtful and questionable, seeing this argueth omnipotency, which is in God alone, and not communicable to any creature. Where, by the way, you may observe a strong and solid argument to prove that Jesus is the Son of God against all gainsayers, thus: he whom Nebuchadnezzar saw in the fiery furnace was the Son of God in a human shape; but he was typically Jesus, *ergo,* &c. The major is proved, because he did that which none but God could do, viz., he qualified the most fierce and raging fire, which burned up some coming but near it, and had no power, at the same instant of time, so much as to singe a hair of the heads of others. The minor is proved also, because God, appearing in a glorious human shape at any time, was not God the Father or Holy Ghost, but God the Son; for 'no man hath seen God at any time,' John i. 18; 1 Tim. vi. 16; 1 John iv. 12; but the Son hath revealed him, both when in him appearing in a human shape under the law, and when, under the Gospel, shewing himself in the man Jesus, born of the Virgin Mary, and hypostatically united unto him: Exod. iii. 2, 'And the angel of the Lord,' that is, Christ, the angel of the covenant, 'appeared unto him in a flame of fire out of the midst of a bush; and he looked, and, behold, the bush burned with fire, and the bush was not consumed;' ver. 3, 'And Moses said, I will now turn aside, and see this great sight, why the bush is not burned.'[1] The Hebrew word *Seneh* which is here used signifies a dry bush, a bramble bush, whence the mount and wilderness is called *Sinai*, of the store of brambles that grew there, or of this bush or vision. Now for a bush, a dry bush, a bramble bush, to be all on fire and yet not consumed, this must be a wonder of wonders; but all this is from the good will 'of him that dwelt in the bush.' Out of these two verses we may briefly observe these few things:—

[1.] First, *The low, and weak, and brittle estate of the church,* represented by a bush, a dry bush, a bramble bush. What more brittle, weak, base, low, and despicable than a dry bush, a bramble bush? What is such a bush good for but the fire, or to stop a gap, or some such inferior use? A bush is a black, deformed, and uncomely thing. Corruption and affliction, sin and suffering, renders the saints very uncomely. The church is compared not to a strong, sturdy oak, but to a weak, brittle bush; and elsewhere to a vine, a dove, a lamb, a sheep, &c., all frail, weak creatures. It is good for all saints to have low and mean thoughts of themselves, for here they are resembled to a dry bush, a bramble bush. But,

[2.] Secondly, A dry bush, a bramble bush, *pricks, wounds, and vexes them that handle it roughly.* This bush is in Hebrew called *Seneh,* as I have hinted before, which the Hebrews describe to be a shrub full of pricks, and without fruit, and so thick that a bird cannot

---

[1] Christ is called the Messenger or Angel of the Covenant, Mal. iii. 1.

enter without the ruffling and pulling off her feathers.   Let the proud enemies of the church look to themselves, for this bramble bush will vex, prick, wound, tear, and put them to the worst, when they have done their worst.   In all the ages of the world this bramble bush, the church, hath been a cup of trembling unto all the people round about, and a burdensome stone; so that all that burden themselves with it shall be cut in pieces, though all the people of the earth be gathered together against it, Zech. xii. 2, 3.   But,

[3.] Thirdly, Consider *the cruelties of the church's enemies is signified and represented by a fire.*   The bush burns with fire.   In this resemblance is shadowed out the oppressed, afflicted, and persecuted estate of the Israelites in the Egyptian furnace; and by fire here is meant the most painful, terrifying, and tormenting afflictions and miseries that should attend them.   Great afflictions and persecutions are in Scripture commonly set out by fire, as the fiery trial, the fire of affliction, 1 Pet. iv. 12; Lam. ii. 3, 4; Hab. ii, 13.   Fire is very painful and tormenting, in which respects hell torments are compared to fire; so are great afflictions, miseries, and sufferings; they are very painful and tormenting; they put persons into sore pain and travail.   Next to the pangs of conscience, and the pains of hell, there are none to these pains and pangs that are bred and fed by sore afflictions, by terrible trials.   It has been the lot and portion of God's dearest children, to be exercised with very great and grievous afflictions, and that in order to the discovery of sin, to the embittering of sin, to the preventing of sin, and to the purging away of sin, and in order to the trial of grace, the discovery of grace, the exercise of grace, and the increase of grace; and in order to the weaning of them from this world, and to the completing their conformity to Christ, the captain of their salvation, ' who was made perfect through sufferings,' Heb. ii. 10; and to ripen them for heaven, and to work in them more bowels of pity and compassion to those that are in misery, and that sigh and groan under their Egyptian taskmasters.

[4.] Fourthly, Consider *the eminence of their preservation, though in the fire, yet unconsumed.*   The church of God was hot, yea, all in flames, and yet not consumed.[1]   Let the fire be never so hot, so fierce, so furious, so spreading, the church shall have a being, and live and bear up in the midst of the flames.   If the church like the sea lose in one place, it gets ground in another.   When the worst of men, and devils, and informers have done their worst, the Lord will have a name among his people on earth.   The church, with the lamp in the story, laughs at all those winds, that would blow it out.   Well may we stand amazed and wonder, that so flaming and terrible a fire, falling upon so contemptible a bush, and so dry and despicable a shrub, should not presently turn it into ashes; for why, is the fire too weak?   Oh no!   Is the bush so strong, as to defend and secure itself against devouring flames?   Oh no!   Or is the bush not apt to burn and consume by so fierce a fire?   Oh no.   It is not from the impotency of the fire, nor from the strength or constitution of the bush; for a dry

---

[1] This fire was a supernatural fire, (1.) It continued without fuel to feed upon.   (2.) It kept below and ascended not.   (3.) It burned and consumed not.   All which shews it to be a supernatural work.

bramble bush, in the matter of it is as combustible as any chaff, and as easily destroyed as any stubble; but because the natural force thereof was restrained by the glorious power of God: for if God concur not with the nature of things, they cannot work nor shew their kind. There are two inseparable qualites of fire: (1.) To give light. (2.) To burn; and yet divine power divides and separates these two: for this fire giveth light, but burneth not. Oh, what a mighty, what an astonishing preservation is here! The afflictions and sufferings of the church are not a consuming fire, but a trying fire, as the fire in a furnace consumes the dross, but tries the gold, and puts a new lustre, beauty, and glory upon it. Hesiod speaks of thirty thousand demigods, that were keepers of men; but what are so many thousand gods to that one God that neither slumbers nor sleeps, but day and night keeps his people as his jewels, as the apple of his eye, that keeps them in his pavilion, as a prince his favourite?[1] There is a dialogue between a heathen and a Jew; after the Jews returned from captivity—all nations round about them being enemies unto them—the heathen asked the Jew, how he and his countrymen could hope for any safety, because, saith he, every one of you is as a silly sheep compassed about with fifty wolves. Ay, but, saith the Jew, we are kept by such a shepherd, as can kill all these wolves when he pleases, and by that means preserve his sheep. But,

[5.] Fifthly, Consider how this eminent preservation of his people from dangers in the midst of dangers *is effected and brought about, and that is by the presence of the Lord Jesus Christ, the great angel of the covenant;* for Moses saith expressly of this vision, that 'The Lord appeared unto Moses, and God calleth unto him out of the midst of the bush, and said, Moses, Moses,' &c., ver. 4. This calling of Moses by his name, and the doubling of his name, in such a familiar and loving manner, was a sign of God's singular favour to Moses. Choice favourites God frequently called by name, as you may see in those instances of Abraham, Isaac, and Jacob, &c., and so our Lord Jesus Christ called Peter by his name, and Nathanael by his name, and Mary by her name, &c.[2] The same presence of the Son of God, that preserved the three children, or rather champions, in that furious furnace of Nebuchadnezzar from burning or singeing, preserved the bush, though not from burning, yet from consuming, by restraining the natural force of the fire, and strengthening the bush against it. The bush, the church in the fire, came forth of the hottest furnace that ever was kindled, not blacker nor worser, but brighter and better, and more glorious than the sun in his strength; and all this from the presence of the angel of the covenant that dwelt in the bush. Divine presence can preserve a flaming bush from being consumed. Witness our preservation to this day, though we have been as a burning bush. ' God is in the midst of her, she shall not be moved, God shall help her, and that right early,' Ps. xlvi. 5. *Heb.,* 'When the morning appeareth,' that is, in the nick of time, when help shall be most seasonable and best welcome. The presence of the Lord in the midst

---

[1] Ps. cxxi. 4; Isa. xxvii. 3; Mal. iii. 17; Zech. ii. 8; Ps. xxxi. 20.
[2] Scipio by way of favour called the citizens by their names, and so Cyrus upon the same ground called his soldiers by their names.

of his church, will secure her from being greatly moved in the midst
of all those great dreadful confusions that are abroad in the world.
Hence the church is called, *Jehovah shammah*, ' The Lord is there,'
Ezek. xlviii. 35.   His presence in heaven, makes it heaven, and
his presence in the church, makes it happy and safe.   Nothing
shall disturb or harm them that have the presence of God in the
midst of them.[1]   The church is built upon a rock, she is invincible,
Mat. xvi. 18.   Jer. i. 8, ' Be not afraid of their faces, for I am with
thee, to deliver thee, saith the Lord.'   Ver. 17, ' Thou therefore
gird up thy loins, and arise, and speak unto them all that I command
thee ; be not dismayed at their faces, lest I confound thee before them.'
Ver. 18, ' For behold, I have made thee this day a defenced city,
and an iron pillar and brazen wall against the whole land ; against
the kings of Judah, against the princes thereof, against the priests
thereof, and against the people of the land.'   Ver. 19, ' And they shall
fight against thee, but they shall not prevail against thee ; for I am
with thee, saith the Lord, to deliver thee.'   God's presence with his
messengers is a guard, and a safeguard, all-sufficient against all opposition whatsoever.   Earthly princes and sovereigns are not wont to
go with those whom they send on embassage, but God always goes
along with those whom he sends, and will, by his powerful presence,
protect and defend them against opposers, at all times and in all
places, when all others fail and forsake us.   Christ's presence is security
sufficient, for ' if he be with us, who can be against us ? '   They must
first prevail against him before they can prevail against them that
withstand and oppose those whom he standeth by to back and protect.
How comes this to pass, that Jeremiah, a man, a man alone, should
bear up so stoutly, and stand so strong against kings, princes,
priests, and people ?   It is from the signal presence of God with him.
' I am with thee.'[2]   And what can all the great ones of the world,
and all the wicked ones of the world, do against one messenger of the
Lord, that is armed with his glorious power ?   The ambassadors of
the King of kings, and Lord of lords, must not be terrified with the
multitude of opposers, nor with the grandeur or greatness of opposers ;
but set the presence of the Lord against them all, and say as that
noble soldier, Pædarelus, in Erasmus, did to them that told him of
that numerous and mighty army which came against him, *Tanto plus
gloriæ referemus, quoniam eo plures superabimus,* The number of
opposers makes the Christian conquests the more illustrious.   The
more the Pharisees of old, and their successors of late time, have opposed the truth, the more it hath prevailed ; and it is observable that
the reformation in Germany was much furthered by the papists' opposition, yea, when two kings, amongst many others, wrote against
Luther, viz., Henry the Eighth of England, and Ludovicus of Hungary ;
this kingly title being entered into the controversy, making men more
curious to examine the matter, stirred up a general inclination towards Luther's opinion.   So Jer. xv. 20, ' And I will make thee

---

[1] Opposition is, as Calvin writes to the French king, *Evangelii genius*, the black angel
that dogs the gospel at the heels.
[2] In some cases a man were better lose his life than be cowardly.   Aristotle, eth. iii.
cap. 1.

unto this people a fenced brazen wall; and they shall fight against thee, but they shall not prevail against thee: for I am with thee to save thee, and to deliver thee, saith the Lord.' When the messengers of the Lord go on constantly and courageously in the faithful discharge of their duties, not relenting, or yielding, or complying with their greatest opposers, then they shall have such a signal presence of the Lord with them, as shall sufficiently protect them against all their enemies' might and malice, wrath and rage: ver. 21, 'And I will deliver thee out of the hand of the wicked, and I will redeem thee out of the hand of the terrible or violent ones.' Though thou shouldst fall into the hand of the wicked, *id est,* power, and into the hand of the terrible and violent ones, yet they shall not hurt thee, nor harm thee; they shall not have their wills upon thee. When thou art in their hands, I will lay a law of restraint upon their hearts, that they shall not mischief thee, nor triumph over thee; I will be sure to secure thee, and rescue thee from dangers in the midst of dangers. A gracious messenger of the Lord in the midst of all oppositions, as Chrysostom said of Peter, is a man made all of fire walking in stubble, he overcomes and consumes all opposition; all difficulties are but whetstones to his fortitude. The moon will run her course though the dogs bark at it; so does the traveller, and so will the faithful messengers of the Lord hold on in their way and work, let men and devils bark and do their worst.

Moulin, speaking of the French Protestants, said, 'When papists hurt us for reading the Scriptures, we burn with zeal to be reading of them.' He is a fool, we say, that will be laughed out of his coat, but he is a fool in folio that will be laughed out of his skin, out of his profession, out of his religion, out of his principles, out of the ways of God, nay, out of his soul, out of his salvation, because he can't endure to be opposed, derided, or laughed at by lewd and wicked men. The divine presence will make a man set light by such paper-shot.

A gracious spirit is raised by opposition. The more opposition it meets with in a way of duty, the more resolute he is for it. So far is he from being afraid of the threatenings of men, of the frowns of men, or of losing this man's favour, or of incurring such a man's displeasure, that his spirit riseth far more for it. It is with such a man as it is with the fire in winter. The fire burns the hotter because of the coldness of the air; so it is with all the messengers of the Lord, who are inflamed in the way of their duty. Come to David, and tell him, Oh, there is a Goliath, and he is come out with a spear like a weaver's beam, and there is one that bears his target goes before him! Where is he? saith David; I will fight with him, saith he, [1 Sam. xvii. 4–11, compared with ver. 26, 27.] Difficulties and dangers do but whet and raise his spirit; he is not afraid of any uncircumcised Philistine. Ah, my friends, this is a true noble spirit! Holy greatness of mind lies in this, when a man's spirit is borne up upon the greatness of his God, and the goodness of his cause; and if that will not bear me out, saith such a soul, let me sink in it, I am content to perish. That is a good word, more worth than a world in a faithful minister's eye: Ezek. iii. 8, 'Behold, I have made thy face strong against their faces, and thy forehead strong against their foreheads;' ver. 9, 'As an adamant, harder than a flint, have I made thy forehead; fear them not, neither be dismayed at their looks, though they be a rebellious house.' The adamant is the hardest of stones, it is *lapis servabilis*, because it keeps itself by its hardness from all injuries ; no weather, no violence of hammer or fire will break it or conquer it. God engages himself to give the prophet such undaunted boldness, and invincible courage and constancy, as neither shame nor fear should prevail against. Divine presence, divine assistance, does always accompany a divine call. Such whom God sends he seconds, such whom he calls he encourages against all difficulties and discouragements ; such as are called by Christ, and sent by Christ, shall never want the strengthening, comforting, corroborating, animating, and preserving presence of Christ. It is this divine presence that makes them stand it out, and shew themselves like men—like men of courage, like men of God, and that secures them from dangers in the midst of dangers. In the greatest storms the adamant shrinks not, it fears not, it changeth not its hue, no, not in the least. Divine presence will keep gracious men from shrinking, fearing, and changing their way, their work, their Lord, and Master, in the worst of storms that can beat upon them. In all winds and weather the adamant is still the same, and so will all the faithful messengers of the Lord be, whatever wind may blow upon them. The signal presence of God with them will keep them from fearing, fainting, flying, and preserve them from dangers in the midst of dangers. But,

(8.) Eighthly, The Lord doth manifest his favourable, signal, and eminent presence with his people in their greatest troubles, deepest distresses, and most deadly dangers, *by frustrating and disappointing the plots, designs, counsels, and contrivances of their powerful, subtle, secret, and malicious adversaries, who would fain be multiplying of their troubles, sorrows, sufferings, and miseries upon them :* Neh. iv. 8, 'And conspired all of them together to come and fight against Jerusalem, and to hinder it.' Ver. 11, 'And our adversaries said, They shall not know, neither see, till we come in the midst amongst them, and slay them, and cause the work to cease.' Ver. 15, 'And it came to pass, when our enemies knew that it was known unto us, and God had brought their counsels to nought,' &c.[1] The craft of the church's enemies is never but accompanied with cruelty, and their cruelty is seldom without craft. The devil lends them his seven heads to plot, and his seven horns to push ; but in the things wherein they deal proudly, God is above them, and by his presence with his people he brings all their plots, counsels, and enterprises to nought. The gunpowder traitors betrayed themselves, and all came to light, though they had digged as low as hell to hide their counsels from the Lord. The enemies of the Jews, in Nehemiah's time, made great brags at first what they would do ; but when they saw their plots discovered, and their purposes defeated, they are presently crestfallen, and have no mind nor courage to advance at all ; so that to these plotters may be fitly applied that which Guicciardini saith of Charles the Eighth, king of France, in his expedition against Naples, ' That he came into the field like thunder and lightning, but went out like a

---

[1] The Thebans had a band of men they called *sacra cohors*, consisting of such only as were joined in bonds of love, and resolved to live and die together. These Jews under Nehemiah's command were such, and were therefore insuperable.

snuff; more thán a man at first, and less than a woman at last.' In all the ages of the world, the heads, the wits, the hands, the hearts, and the tongues of the wicked have been engaged against the just; they have been still a-plotting and devising mischief against the favourites of heaven, as if rebels could meddle with none but the children of a king, and yet God's signal presence with his people, in point of affection and protection, has blasted all their designs, and frustrated all their counsels. As the rage of wicked men against the saints have been endless, so it has been fruitless, because God has been in the midst of them. Haman plots against the lives, liberties, and estates of the Jews, Esth. iii. 8, *seq.*, but his plot was timely discovered and seasonably prevented, and the grand plotter and informer detected, debased, condemned, and executed: Esth. vii. 10, ' So they hanged Haman on the gallows that he had prepared for Mordecai. Then was the king's wrath pacified.' The kings of Persia had absolute and unquestionable power to do whatsoever they listed. *Quicquid libuit, licuit:* all their subjects, except their queens, were no better than slaves,—' whom they would they slew, and whom they would they kept alive; whom they would they set up, and whom they would they put down,' Dan. v. 19; Esth. vii. 9. Haman is here without order of law, more than the king's command, adjudged to be hanged. The truth is, it was a clear case, and the malefactor was self-condemned. 'Hang him, therefore,' saith the king; a short and a just sentence, and soon executed. Ah, how soon is Haman fallen from the palace to the gallows, from the highest stage of honour to the lowest stair of disgrace; from feasting with the king to be made a feast for crows, and so lies wrapped up in the sheet of perpetual infamy. ' So let all thine enemies perish, O Lord.' It is a good observation of Josephus upon Esth. vii. 10: ' I cannot,' saith he, ' but admire the Lord's wisdom, and acknowledge his justice, in that he not only punished him for his malice to the church, but, by turning his own mischief upon himself, hath made him an example to all posterity; hanging him up in gibbets that others may take warning.'[1] Let all plotters and informers beware of making a match with mischief, they may have enough of it in the end. Haman was a main stickler for the devil, who paid him his wages at last, with a witness, or, if you will, with a halter. Let all the enemies of·the saints tremble at such ends, and be careful to avoid them by flying such like foul and flagitious practices. The bloody plot being thus laid by Haman, the king's minion, behold the footsteps of God's favourable, signal, and eminent presence for his people and with his people in their deadly dangers, and that in raising up in them a very great spirit of faith, prayer, and mourning, and by raising an undaunted courage and resolution in Esther: ' And so I will go in unto the king, and if I perish, I perish,' Esth. iv. 16. This she speaks not rashly or desperately, as prodigal of her life, but as one willing to sacrifice the same for the honour of God, his cause and people, saying, as that martyr, ' Can I die but once for Christ?' Esther had rather die than shrink from her duty. She thought it better to do worthily and perish for a kingdom, than unworthily and perish with a kingdom.

[1] Unde mihi contigit mirari nomen Dei, et sapientiam, et justitiam ejus agnoscere, &c. —*Joseph. Ant.*, lib. i. c. 6.

Here was a mighty preference of God in raising Esther's heroical courage and resolution above all those visible dangers that did attend her attempt of going in to the king against the known law of the land. And the king held out to Esther the golden sceptre, chap. v. 2. He did not kick her out of his presence, as some Cambyses would have done; neither did he command her to the block, as Henry the Eighth did his Anne Boleyne, upon a mere misprision of disloyalty; neither yet did he cashier her, as he had Vashti for a less offence, but by holding out his sceptre, shews his gracious respects unto her. This was the Lord's own work, and a great demonstration of his signal presence with her, in giving her favour in the eyes of the great king. ' So Esther drew near, and touched the top of the sceptre' with her hand, saith the Chaldee, with her mouth, saith the Vulgar translation. This she did either in token of submission, or as a sign of reverence and subjection, or for the avoiding of danger; for, as Josephus saith, ' He that touched the king's sceptre was out of the reach of evil,' or, according to the custom of the times, God's favourable presence is transparent, in the king's extended favour to her. ' On that night could not the king sleep,' *Heb.*, ' the king's sleep fled away,' Esth. vi. 1; and like a shadow it fled away so much the faster, as it was more followed. Crowns have their cares, thistles in their arms, and thorns in their sides. Lo! he that commanded one hundred and twenty-seven provinces cannot command one hour's sleep. The king's head might perhaps be troubled with thinking what great request it should be that Esther had to make, that was so hardly drawn from her; but herein appeared the signal presence of God in keeping the king awake; for Mordecai might have been hanged before Esther had known anything of it—Haman being come early the next morning, ver. 4, to beg this of the king—had not God kept him from sleep, and directed him to read in that place of the Chronicles where Mordecai's service was recorded, and so made way to his advancement and Haman's ruin. God's favourable presence shined upon his people in keeping the king from sleep, for excellent ends, and in putting small thoughts into his heart for great purposes. God will appear for his poor people, $\dot{\epsilon}\nu \ \tau\hat{\omega} \ \kappa\alpha\iota\rho\hat{\omega}$, in the nick and opportunity of time, when there is but a step between them and death; and further, the power, providence, presence, and goodness of God was made evident, in the behalf of his people, in directing the reader to that very place where Mordecai's singular service, in discovering the barbarous and murderous plot that was laid against the king's life and crown, was recorded, Esth. vi. 2. That Mordecai should have no present reward, but that it should be deferred till a fitter opportunity, when God might be more glorified in the signal preservation of his people, and in the famous overthrow of their enemies, was from that mighty hand of God, that was stretched out for the good of his people. In this great story we may, as in a mirror, see how the Lord, by his wisdom, providence, presence, and grace, brings about and overrules the wills of men, the affairs of men, the counsels of men, the designs of men, the words and speeches of men, to the fulfilling of his own will and decree, and the promoting of his own honour and glory, and the good of his people, when vain men think least of doing his will, or serving his providence. Here you may see the wisdom, prudence, and courage of Esther, striking whilst the iron was hot, charging the bloody decree upon Haman to his face, and that before the king, that things might the better stick and work, and painting him out in his own proper colours. 'The adversary,' *Heb.*, 'the man adversary,' the *Lycanthropos*, the man of might that distresseth us. 'And enemy,' that is, the cruel enemy, the bloody enemy, the utter enemy, the worst enemy, that sworn swordman of Satan, from whom Haman hath drawn his ancient enmity, Gen. iii. 15. 'Is this wicked Haman,' that is, as wicked a wretch as goes on two legs, a man of blood, a man made up of mischief and malice, a sink of wickedness, a very mystery of iniquity, a breathing devil. Tiberius was rightly characterised by his tutor Theodorus Gadareus,[1] dirt knead[2] with blood. Haman was such another, if not worse. And now Queen Esther is plain and round with him, and calls a spade a spade. Though others styled him noble, great, serene, magnificent, &c., Esther gives him his own with a witness. 'The adversary and enemy is this wicked Haman.' But what a mighty courage had Esther to speak at this rate before the king, and of his grand favourite, and before his face. Surely all this was from the signal presence of God with her soul. This was a great work of faith, and a singular fruit of prayer. 'And now Haman stood up to make request for his life.' Oh, what a strange turn of things is here all upon a sudden! He that a little before was bowed unto by all men, is now upon his knees before a woman; he that was, the very day before, a professed enemy of the Jews, is now suppliant to a Jewess; he that a few weeks before had contrived the death and ruin of the Jews, is now begging hard for his own life; he that had provided a gallows for Mordecai, fears nothing more now than that himself should be hanged on it. Yesterday, oh the caps, knees, and bows that Haman had, and now the same man covers his face, in token of his irrecoverable ruin, Esth. vii. 8. The Turks cast a black gown upon such as they sit at supper with the great Turk, and presently strangle them. Many of their viziers or greatest favourites die in this sort, which makes them use this proverb, 'He that is greatest in office, is but a statue of glass.' Plutarch wittily compareth great men to counters, which now stand for a thousand pounds, and anon for a farthing. This was Haman's case.[3] And so Sejanus, the same senators who accompanied him to the senate, conducted him to prison; they which sacrificed to him as to their god, which kneeled down to adore him, scoffed at him, seeing him dragged from the temple to the gaol, from supreme honour to extreme ignominy. When once the emperor frowned upon him, they shewed themselves most passionate against him, saying that if Cæsar had clemency, he ought to reserve it for men, and not to use it toward monsters. This is courtier's custom, to adore the rising sun, and

---

[1] Θεόδωρος Γαδαρεύς: on his connexion with Tiberius, see Quint: Instit. Orat., lib. iii. c. 1, §§ 17, 18. Seneca, *Suasoria* iii., *sub fin.* The particular saying quoted by Brooks is found in Suetonius, (Tiber., c. 57,) and is as follows: πηλὸν αἵματι πεφυρμένον, 'clay tempered with blood.'—G.   [2] Spelled 'knod.'—G.
[3] Courtiers shift their sails to the fitting of every wind. A cubit was half a yard at least. In those parts they had trees very small, or they might piece one to another; but why so high a gallows, but for the greater disgrace to Mordecai, and terror to all that should slight the king's grand favourite.

when great favourites fall into disgrace, all about princes will be ready to pluck them up by the roots, if the season be fair to clear the court or land of such noisome weeds.   The king's indignation being up, the courtiers point at the gallows fifty cubits high, that Haman had set up for Mordecai.   All are now for Mordecai, there is not a courtier that has one good word for Haman.   Ah, what a rare hand of God was there in all these things, for the good of his people, and the utter overthrow of their grand enemy !   To sum all up in a little room, the breaking of the king's sleep, was the breaking of one of the most bloody designs that ever was laid against the people of God.   Well, what though the king could not sleep, could he not lie still in his bed ?   No, he must have a book, and that book must be the Book of Chronicles, and that book must be opened where accidentally—not by turning to that place purposely—yet surely by God's providence directing him that read, to that very story concerning Mordecai, where was registered his faithfulness, in discovering and disappointing of a murder intended against the king; whereupon God sets this act of faithfulness so close upon the king's heart, that he could not rest till Mordecai was nobly rewarded for it, and this reward must be Haman's ruin ; his advancement, Haman's abatement; and this was the rise of Haman's disappointment.   In this famous instance you may run and read the favourable, signal, and eminent presence of the Lord, in the miraculous preservation of his church from a total ruin and destruction, and in the disappointing the plots, designs, and counsels of their greatest enemies, and in taking of them in the very snares that they had laid for others ; suitable to that of the psalmist, ' He made a pit and digged it, and is fallen into the ditch which he made ; his mischief shall return upon his own head, and his violent dealing upon his own pate,' Ps. vii. 16, 17.   Henry the Third of France was stabbed in the same chamber where he had helped to contrive the French massacre ; and his brother, Charles the Ninth, had blood given him to drink, for he was worthy.   There is no end of stories of this nature.   So Ps. ix. 15, ' The heathen are sunk down in the pit that they made : in the net which they hid, is their own foot taken.'   The wicked are compared to hunters for their cruelty, and to fowlers for their craft ; but see their success, they are sunk down in their own pit, caught in their own net. Thus it befell Pharaoh, Jabin, and Sisera, Sennacherib, Antiochus Epiphanes, Maxentius the tyrant, who fell into the Tiber, from his own false bridge laid for Constantine; the Spanish armada, and our powder-plotters :[1] ver. 16, ' The wicked is snared in the work of his own hands. Higgajon, Selah.' Goliath was killed with his own sword. Christ's justice hath two acclamatory notes, ' Higgajon, Selah ;' the like is not found in all the Scripture, as worthy of present admiration, and of deep and perpetual meditation.   I have been the longer a-glancing at this famous story of Esther, because of its seasonableness and suitableness to the days and times wherein we live.

A further proof of this eighth particular, that is under our present consideration, you have in Isa. viii. 9, ' Associate yourselves, O ye people, and ye shall be broken in pieces ; and give ear, all ye of far countries : gird yourselves, and ye shall be broken in pieces ; gird

[1] Exod. ix. 15 ; Judges x. 4 ; 2 Chron. xxxii. ; Euseb., lib. ix. c. 9.

conduce much to a right understanding of God's covenant.[1]   The derivation of the Hebrew word, and of the Greek, may give us great light, and is of special use to shew the nature of the covenant which they principally signify, and what special things are therein required.   (1.) The Hebrew word, ברית, *Berith*, a covenant, is by learned men derived from several roots :

[1.] First, Some derive it from ברר, *Barar*, to purify, make clear, and to purge out dross, chaff, and all uncleanness; and to select, and choose out, and separate the pure from the impure, the gold and silver from the dross, and the pure wheat from the chaff. The reasons of this derivation are these two :—(1.) Because by covenants open and clear amity is confirmed, and faithfulness is plainly and clearly declared and ratified, without deceit or sophistication, betwixt covenanters ; and things are made plain and clear betwixt them in every point and article.   (2.) Because God, in the covenant of works, did choose out man especially, with whom he made the covenant; and because in the covenant of grace he chooseth out of the multitude his elect, even his church and faithful people, whom he did separate by predestination and election from all eternity, to be a holy people to himself in Christ, Eph. i. 4.   (3.) Some derive it from ברה, and verily, the Lord, when he makes a covenant with any, he doth separate them from others, he looks on them, and takes them, and owns them for his ' peculiar people,' 1 Pet. ii. 9, for his ' peculiar treasure,' Exod. xix. 5, and agrees with them as the chosen and choicest of all others.   The first staff in Zech. xi. 10, is called ' Beauty,' and this was the covenant ; and certainly it must be a high honour for a people to be in covenant with God ; for by this means God becomes ours, and we are made nigh unto him, Jer. xxxi. 38, 40, 41. He is ours, and we are his, in a very peculiar way of relation ; and by this means God opens his love and all his treasures of grace unto us. In his covenant he tells us of his special care, love, kindness, and great intentions of good to us ; and by this means his faithfulness comes to be obliged to make good all his covenant relations and engagements to us, Deut. vii. 9.   Now in all this God puts a great favour and honour upon his people.   Hence, when the Lord told Abraham that he would make a covenant with him, Abraham fell upon his face ; he was amazed at so great a love and honour, Gen. xvii. 2, 3.

[2.] Secondly, Some derive the word from ברה, *Barah, comedit*, to eat, because usually they had a feast at the making of covenants.   In the Eastern countries they commonly established their covenants by eating and drinking together.   Herodotus tells us that the Persians were wont to contract leagues and friendship, *inter vinum et epulas*, in a full feast, whereat their wives, children, and friends, were present. The like, Tacitus reports of the Germans.   Amongst the Greeks and other nations, the covenanters ate bread and salt together.   The Emperor of Russia, at this day, when he would shew extraordinary

---

[1] The word *covenant* in our English tongue, signifies, as we all know, a mutual promise, bargain, and obligation, between two persons ; and so likewise doth the Hebrew *Berith*, and the Greek διαθηκη.   A covenant is a solemn compact or agreement between two chosen parties, or more ; whereby, with mutual, free, and full consent, they bind and oblige themselves one to another. A covenant is *Amicus status inter fœderatos :* so Martin [Luther ?] ' A friendly state between allies.'

resemble God his Father, or because he appeareth before the face or in the presence of God for us. This angel took to heart their afflictions, he was himself grieved for them and with them. This angel secured and safeguarded them all the way through the wilderness, from Egypt to Canaan. This angel did not only lead them, but he also lifted them up and took them in his arms, as parents or nurses are wont to do with such children that are young and weakly and in danger. And this angel carried them, as the eagle doth her young ones, that are not fully fledged, or that are unable yet to fly, on her wings. Oh the pity, the clemency, the sympathy, and admirable compassion of Christ to his people in their suffering state! Zech. ii. 8, 'He that toucheth you, toucheth the apple of his eye.' The eye is the tenderest piece of the tenderest part. The eye is kept most diligently, and strongly guarded by nature with five tunicles. A man can better bear a thump on the back, the biting of his finger, the cutting of his hand, the pricking of his leg, or a blow upon his arm, than a touch on the eye. Oh that persecutors would be quiet, and let God's people alone, and take heed how they meddle with God's eyes.[1] There is no touching of them, to wrong or injure them, but you wrong and injure the Holy One of Israel, who will certainly revenge himself upon you. They that strike at God's eyes, do through them strike at God himself, which he will never put up. It is a dangerous thing to molest and trouble, to afflict or annoy the people of God; for God himself is very sensible of it, and accordingly he will certainly requite it. Acts ix. 4, 'Saul, Saul, why persecutest thou me?' They that persecute the servants of Christ, they persecute Christ himself, who liveth in them, and is mystically united to them. Look, as there is by virtue of the natural union a mutual sympathy betwixt the head and the members, the husband and the wife, so it is here betwixt Christ and his saints, for he is a most sympathising, compassionate, tender-hearted Saviour, Heb. iv. 15, and v. 2; Col. i. 24; Heb. xiii. 13; Isa. liii. 4. Those that shoot at the saints, hit Christ; their sufferings are held his, and their reproaches are counted his. He that bore the saints' griefs when he was on earth, really and properly, he bears them still now he is in heaven, in a way of sympathy. Christ in his glorified state hath a very tender sense of all the evil that is done to his children, his members, his spouse, and looks upon it as done to himself. A great lord said to another great lord of the council, in king Henry the Eighth's days, concerning Cranmer, 'Let him alone, for the king will not suffer his finger to ache.' So say I to the persecutors of the day, Let the people of God alone, for if you do but make their finger ache, God will make your heads and hearts ache for it before he has done with you.[2] But,

(10.) Tenthly, The Lord doth manifest his favourable, signal, and eminent presence with his people in their greatest troubles, deepest distresses, and most deadly dangers, *by pouring out upon them a greater spirit of prayer and supplication in their greatest troubles,*

[1] *Ishon of Ish;* it is here called *Bath*, the daughter of the eye, because it is as dear to a man as an only daughter. *Oculus et fama non patiuntur jocos,* The eye and the good name will endure no jests.

[2] See the first part of my 'Golden Key,' pp. 277–279, more of this. [The present volume, pp. 193–195.—G.]

deepest distresses, and most deadly dangers, than formerly they have had. Isa. xxvi. 16, 'Lord, in trouble have they visited thee; they poured out a prayer when thy chastening was upon them.' 'They poured out their still prayer.'[1] The Hebrew word *Lachus* signifieth properly a soft or low kind of muttering which can hardly be heard. The prophet hereby would intimate to us, that in their great troubles and deepest distresses they sighed or groaned unto God, and prayed in a still and silent manner. Saints never visit God more with their prayers, than when he visits them most with his rod. Saints never pray with that seriousness, that spiritualness, that heavenliness, that humbleness, that brokenness, that fervency, that frequency, as they do when they are under the mighty hand of God; and all this is from that signal presence of God, that it is with them in their greatest troubles, deepest distresses, &c. When it was a day of great trouble, of great distress, of great danger to the people of God in Germany, God poured out a very great spirit of prayer upon Luther; at length he comes out of his closet triumphantly, saying to his fellow-labourers and friends, '*Vicimus, vicimus,* We have overcome, we have overcome;' at which time it is observed that there came out a proclamation from Charles the Fifth that none should be further molested for the profession of the gospel. In days of troubles and distress Luther was so warm, zealous, and powerful in prayer, that made one of his best friends say, *Iste vir potuit, quod voluit,* That man could have of God what he pleased. Being once very warm in prayer, he let fall this transcendent rapture of a daring faith, *Fiat mea voluntas,* Let my will be done; and then falls off sweetly, *Mea voluntas, Domine, quia tua,* My will, Lord, because thy will. It is reported in the life of Luther, that when he prayed it was *tantâ reverentiâ ut si Deo, et tantâ fiduciâ ut si amico,* It was with so much reverence as if he were praying to God, and with so much boldness as if he had been speaking to his friend. I have read of a fountain that at noonday is cold, and at midnight it grows warm; so many Christians are cold in praying, in hearing, &c., in the day of prosperity, but yet are warm and lively in praying and wrestling with God in the day of adversity.[2] Manasseh got more by prayer in his iron chains than ever he got by his golden crown. Afflictions are like the prick at the nightingale's breast that awakens her, and that puts her upon her sweet and delightful singing. A sincere Christian never prays so sweetly as when under the rod. One reports of Joachim, the father of the Virgin Mary, that he would often say, *Cibus et potus mihi erit oratio,* Prayer is my meat and drink. When a Christian is in trouble, then prayer is his meat and drink. Oh, what a spirit of prayer was upon Jonah when he was in the whale's belly; and upon Daniel when he was among the lions; and upon David in his wilderness-state; and upon the thief when he was on the cross; and upon Jehoshaphat, when Moab and Ammon and others came against him to battle; and upon Hezekiah, when Sennacherib had invaded Judah;

---

[1] Before they would say a prayer, but now they poured out a prayer.

[2] 2 Chron. xxxiii. 11–13; Jonah ii.; Dan. vi.; Ps. viii. 4; Luke xxiii. 42; 2 Chron xx. 1–13; Isa. xxxvii. 14–22; Gen. xxxii. 6–13, and ver. 24–31. Now he oils the key of prayers with tears, Hosea xii. 4.

and upon Jacob, when his brother Esau came to meet him with four hundred bloody cut-throats at his heels! As there be two kinds of antidotes against poison—viz., hot and cold ; so there are two kinds of antidotes against all the troubles of this life—viz., fervent prayer and holy patience, the one hot, the other cold ; the one quenching, the other quickening. When a Christian under great troubles, deep distresses, and most deadly dangers, prays more for the sanctification of affliction than the removal of affliction ; when he prays more to get off his sins than to get off his chains ; when he prays more to get good by the rod than to get free from the rod ; when he prays more that his afflictions may be a refining fire than a consuming fire, and that his heart may be low and his graces high, and that all his troubles may wean him more from this world, and ripen him the more for the glory of that upper world,—it is a great demonstration of the signal presence of God with him in all his troubles and deep distresses. But,

(11.) Eleventhly, The Lord doth manifest his favourable, signal, and eminent presence with his people in their greatest troubles, deepest distresses, and most deadly dangers, *by drawing the hearts of his people nearer and closer to himself, by all the afflictions, troubles, distresses, and dangers that do attend them in this world :* Ps. cxix. 67, 'Before I was afflicted I went astray, but now have I kept thy word.' God brought David nearer to himself by Weeping-Cross, [Chrysostom.] Affliction is a fire to purge out our dross, and to make virtue shine. It is a potion to carry away ill humours, better than all the *benedicta medicamenta,* as physicians call them. Master Ascham was a good schoolmaster to Queen Elizabeth, but affliction was a better, &c. By afflictions God humbles the hearts of his people, and betters the hearts of his people, and draws the hearts of his people nearer and closer to himself : ver. 71, 'It is good for me that I have been afflicted.' The Lacedemonians of old grew rich by war, and were bettered by it, when all other kingdoms were undone by it. The saints gain by their crosses, troubles, and distresses. Their graces are more raised, their experiences are more multiplied, and their comforts are more augmented, and their communion with God is more heightened, Rom. v. 3, 4 ; 2 Cor. i. 3-5 ; Hosea ii. 14. The waves did but lift Noah's ark nearer to heaven, and the higher the waters grew the more the ark was lifted up to heaven. The troubles and distresses that the saints meet with do but raise them in their fellowship with the Father, Son, and Spirit, Ps. lxxiii. 13, 14, 28. When Tiribazus, a noble Persian, was arrested, at first he drew out his sword to defend himself ; but when they charged him in the king's name, and informed him that they came from the king to carry him to the king, he yielded willingly. So when afflictions arrest a noble Christian, he may murmur and struggle at the first ; but when he considers it is sent from God, to bring him to the sight of God, the King of glory, he willingly and readily submits to the rod, and kisses the rod. All the stones that came thick about Stephen's ears did but knock him the closer to Christ the corner-stone, Acts vii. 55, 60. Tiburtius saw paradise when he walked upon burning coals.[1] If there be any way to heaven

---

[1] Clarke, as before, p. 35.—G.

on horseback, it is by the cross, said Bradford.   Hosea ii. 6, 'Therefore, behold, I will hedge up thy way with thorns, and make a wall,
that she shall not find her paths.'   By afflictions, difficulties, and distresses God hedges up his people's way.   Well, what then?   Mark, ver.
7, 'I will go and return to my first husband;' that is, to God : I have
run away from him by my sins, and now I will return to him again
by repentance.   The grand design of God in all the afflictions that
befall his people, is to bring them nearer and closer to himself.   The
church could have no rest at home, nor no comfort abroad, till by
affliction she was brought into the presence and company of her first
husband: Hosea vi. 1, 'Come and let us return unto the Lord, for he
hath torn, and he will heal us ; he hath smitten, and he will bind us
up.'   The great design of God in playing the lion's part with his
people, Hosea v. 14, is to bring them nearer and closer to himself.
And, behold, how sweetly this blessed design of God did take : 'Come
and let us return unto the Lord,' &c.   The power of God, the presence
of God, and the grace of God, is most gloriously manifested by bringing the hearts of his people nearer and closer to himself by all the
troubles, distresses, and dangers that do attend them.   In the winter
season all the sap of the tree runs down to the root, and when a man
is sick all the blood goes to the heart ; so in the winter of affliction,
when the soul is running out more and more to God, and a-getting
closer and nearer to God, it is a most sure evidence of the signal
presence of God with that soul.   But,

(12.) Twelfthly and lastly, The Lord doth manifest his favourable,
signal, and eminent presence with his people in their greatest troubles,
deepest distresses, and most deadly dangers, *by rendering them invincible and unconquerable under all their troubles, distresses, and dangers:* Rev. xii. 11, 'And they overcame him by the blood of the
Lamb, and by the word of their testimony, and they loved not their
lives unto the death:' Rev. xiv. 1–4 ; 2 Chron. xxxii. 7, 8, 21, 22.
By virtue of Christ's blood the saints are made victorious both over
Satan and all his instruments ; they set little by their lives in respect
of Christ and his truth ; yea, they despised them in comparison of
God's glory and the great things of the gospel.   They made so little
account of them that they exposed them to all hazards and dangers
for the cause of Christ.   In the days of that bloody persecutor, Diocletian, the Christians shewed as glorious power in the faith of martyrdom as in the faith of miracles.[1]   The valour of the patients, and
the savageness of the persecutors, striving together, till both exceeding nature and belief, bred wonder and astonishment in beholders
and readers.   It was a good saying of Cyprian, speaking of the saints
and martyrs in those days, *Occidi poterant sed vinci non poterant:*
They may kill them, but they cannot overcome them.   Rev. xvii. 14,
'These shall make war with the Lamb, and the Lamb shall overcome
them : for he is the Lord of lords, and King of kings ; and they that
are with him are called, and chosen, and faithful.'   The presence of
the Lamb has and will make the saints victorious in all the ages of

---

[1] Sulpicius. Rupertus saith that God did more gloriously triumph in St Lawrence
his patience and constancy, when he was broiled on the gridiron, than if he had saved
his body from burning by a miracle. His faith and patience made him invincible.

the world. Modestus, lieutenant to Julian the emperor, said to Julian, While they suffer they deride us, saith he; and the torments are more fearful to them that stand by than to the tormented. There is no end in instances of this nature. There is nothing more clear in Scripture and in history than this, that the signal presence of the Lord with his people, in all their great troubles, deep distresses, and most deadly dangers, hath made them invincible and unconquerable. But now others, that have been destitute of this favourable, signal, and eminent presence of the Lord, in times of great troubles, deep distresses, and most deadly dangers, how have they fled when none have pursued them! How faint-hearted, how greatly daunted, and how sadly discouraged have they been! How have they turned their backs, and quitted the field, and run from their colours, without striking one stroke! Many in Cyprian's time were overcome before the encounter, for they revolted to idolatry before any persecution once assailed them. In the Palatinate, when there was a warm persecution, scarce one professor of twenty stood out, but fell to popery as fast as leaves fall from the trees in autumn. And so in the persecution under Decius many professors that were rich and great in the world, they soon shrunk from Christ, and turned their backs upon his ways. It is God's favourable, signal, and eminent presence with his people that makes them stand to it in an evil day: Rom. viii. 31, 'If God be for us, who can be against us?' that is, none; but this is a more forcible denying, 'Who can?' Dost thou Paul ask, 'Who can?' I will tell thee. The devil can, and tyrants can, and informers can, and persecutors can, and the whole world can; but *ridendus est furor inanis:* They are as nothing, and can do nothing against us. Wicked men may set themselves against the saints, but they shall not prevail against the saints. What if all the world should strive to hinder the sun from rising or shining, or the wind from blowing, or the rain from falling; or, like those pigmies which went with their arrows and bows to repress the flowing of the sea. Ludibrious acts, and mere follies! All that wicked men can do against the people of God will be but as throwing stones against the wind. 'If God be with us, who can be against us?' Methinks these are words of great resolution; as if he should say, We have many enemies, and powerful enemies, and daring enemies, and malicious enemies, and designing enemies, and enraged enemies, yet let the proudest of them shew their faces, and lift up their banners, I fear them not, I regard them not: 'Who can?' who dare be against us? Let me give a little light into this precious scripture, 'If God be for us, who can be against us?' That is, none.

[1.] First, None can be so against us *as to hurt us or harm us;* therefore Aquinas well expounds that *Quis contra nos? i.e., Quis efficaciter?* and others, *Quis læsivè et prevalenter?* Who can be against us, so as to hurt us? Dan. iii. 25, 27, and vi. 22. Acts xviii. 9, 'Then spoke the Lord to Paul in the night by a vision, Be not afraid, but speak, and hold not thy peace;' ver. 10, 'For I am with thee, and no man shall set on thee, to hurt thee, for I have much people in this city.' God had many souls in this city to convert and to bring in to Christ, and therefore he animates and encourages Paul to preach boldly, and to go on in his work undauntedly.[1] Ay, but, Lord, there be many in the city, that will set themselves against me. Ay, but I am with thee. Ay, but, Lord, there be many in the city that will hate me. Ay, but there is no man that shall set on thee to hurt thee. They may kill me, said Socrates of his enemies, but they cannot hurt me. It was the speech of Anaxarchus, a heathen, whenas he by the tyrant was commanded to be put in a mortar, and be beaten to pieces with an iron pestle, he cries out to the persecutors, You do but beat the vessel of Anaxarchus; you do not beat me, nor hurt me; you do but beat the case, the husk, the vessel that contains another thing. His body was to him but as a case, a husk; he counted his soul himself, which his persecutors could not reach nor hurt. Though there were many in the city of Corinth that would be ready furiously to set on Paul, yet there should not be a man that should be able to hurt Paul. God would be his lifeguard to protect him, and he would make void all the mischievous designs and endeavours of his adversaries against him. When in a city the Lord hath those that are ordained to salvation, he will bless the labours of his faithful servants with happy success; so that faithful ministers may not, yea, must not, for fear of the invincible malice of some, neglect the salvation of others. All the arrows that men of might and malice should shoot at Paul in the city of Corinth, should never reach him, they should never hurt him, nor harm him: 1 Pet. iii. 13, 'And who is he that will harm you, if ye be followers of that which is good?' They may oppose you, but they cannot harm you; they may hate you, but they cannot harm you; they may plot and devise mischief against you, but they cannot harm you; they may persecute you, but they cannot harm you. I know Cæsar told Metellus that he could as easily take away his life as bid it be done; but these were only bravadoes, for that is a royalty which belongs to God only, 'to whom belong the issues of death,' Ps. lxviii. 20, or the goings out from death; that is, deliverances from death and deadly dangers. It is an allusion to one that keepeth a passage or a door; that is, God hath all the ways which lead out from death in his own keeping. Christ hath the keys of death, the sole dominion and disposal of it, Rev. i. 18; 2 Pet. ii. 9. The Lord knows how to deliver his people from the most desperate and deadly dangers; he can deliver them out of the mouth of the lion, he can pull them out of the jaws of death, and so secure them from all harm or hurt. None can be so against the people of God as to harm their souls, as to hurt their happiness. But,

'If God be with us, who can be against us?' I answer,

[2.] Secondly, None can be so against us as *to prevail over us*. The gates of hell may fight against us, but the gates of hell cannot prevail against us. Christ is the captain of your salvation, God hath made him general of the field, and therefore you may be sure that he will stand by you and bring you off with honour, Mat. xvi. 18; Heb. ii. 10; Jer. i. 19, and xx. 11. You need never fear having the day, who have Christ your captain for your second. Though your persecutors are as so many roaring lions, yet Christ, who is the lion of the tribe of Judah, will make you victorious over them all, Rev. v. 5. In all storms and

---

[1] What said Justin Martyr to his murderers in the behalf of himself and his fellow-martyrs? You may kill us, but you can never hurt us.

tempests the church will stand fast, because it stands upon a rock, Ps. cxxix. 2. God is on Zion's side, and the enemies of Zion must first prevail against Zion's God before they can prevail over Zion herself. Zion's God will be a wall of fire about her, and therefore Zion's enemies shall never prevail over her, Zech. ii. 5; Deut. xxxiii. 26–29. Were Zion's shelter stones, these might be battered; were it walls of lead, these might be melted; were it a defence of waters, these might be dried up; were it garrisons of mighty men, these might be scattered; were it engines of war, these might be defeated; were it trenches, these might be stopped; were it bulwarks, these might be overthrown; but Zion is guarded with a wall of fire round about her, and therefore all her opposers can never prevail over her. The enemies of Zion are weak enemies, they are infatuated enemies, they are conquered enemies, they are limited enemies, they are chained enemies, they are cursed enemies, and they are naked enemies, and therefore they shall never be prevalent enemies over Zion, 2 Chron. xxxii. 7, 8; Rom. viii. 37; Gen. iii. 12; Num. xiv. 9. Pharaoh followed the Israelites, but he and his mighty men were drowned, and Israel delivered, for God was with them, Exod. xiv. Saul hunted David as a partridge in the mountains, 1 Sam. xxvi. 20, but Saul perisheth, and David was crowned, for God was with him. Haman hated Mordecai and plotted against Mordecai, but Haman is hanged and Mordecai advanced, for God was with him, Esth. vi. 7. The presidents and princes inform against Daniel and plot against Daniel, but they are by the lions torn and devoured, and Daniel is delivered and exalted, for God was with him, Dan. vi. Herod kills James with the sword and imprisons Peter, but Herod is devoured by worms, and Peter is delivered out of prison by an angel, for God was with him, Acts xii. Let atheists, papists, and persecutors cease from plotting against Zion, from persecuting of Zion, for it is utterly impossible to prevail against Zion. Let all Zion's adversaries remember once for all that if any policy, counsel, lying, cursing, strength, or cruelty could have prevailed against Zion, Zion had been rooted out of the world long ago. If Balaam was at our enemies' elbows he would tell them roundly and plainly, that it is 'in vain to curse those whom God blesseth,' Num. xxiii. 8. 'It is hard to kick against the pricks,' Acts ix. 5. It is high madness for men to run their naked bodies against a sword's point. Let Zion's enemies remember that God, who takes pleasure in Zion, sits upon the circle of the earth, and all the inhabitants are as grasshoppers; yea, all the nations as a drop of a bucket, and less than the dust of the balance, Isa. xl. 12, 15, 17, and therefore he can easily revenge all the wrongs and injuries that is done to Zion by those that would fain prevail over her, and triumph in her ruin.[1]   But,

[3.] Thirdly, 'If God be with us, who can be against us?' I answer, None can be so against us as *to be able to separate us from the love of God and the love of Christ:* Rom. viii. 35, 'Who shall separate us from the love of Christ? shall tribulation, or distresses, or perse-

---

[1] Some observe that Paul's style is so beautified with wonderful eloquence and rhetoric, that not Tully nor Demosthenes could ever have so spoken.—*Augustine, Erasmus.* Some report of Augustine that he wished for three things: (1.) To see Christ in the flesh; (2.) To see Rome in the pride of it; (3.) To have heard Paul preach.

cution, or famine, or nakedness, or peril, or sword?' Ver. 36, 'As it is written, For thy sake are we killed all the day long: we are accounted as sheep for the slaughter.' Ver. 37, 'Nay, in all these things we are more than conquerors through him that loved us.' Ver. 38, 'For I am persuaded that neither death, nor life, nor angels, nor principalities, nor powers, nor things present, nor things to come,'—ver. 39,—'nor height, nor depth, nor any other creature, shall separate us from the love of God, which is in Christ Jesus.' It is not the pleasures of life nor the pains of death, it is not evils felt nor evils feared, it is not the height of prosperity nor the depth of adversity, it is not bonds nor banishment, it is not power nor policy, honour nor baseness, it is not violent persecutions nor multiplied tribulations, it is not the scorns of men, nor reproaches of men, nor revilings of men, nor designs of men, nor anything else, that can separate us from the love of the Father or the love of the Son. In the 35th ver. is a position that no crosses nor creatures can deprive us of the love of God, which is set down in a double interrogation, that he might add the more force and life to it and ravish the readers: 'Who shall separate us?' That is, none can. But he speaks with contempt; 'Who shall? shall tribulation?' as if he should say, I scorn it. As Goliath defied David, saying, 'Dost thou come to me with a staff?' so Paul with a better spirit defies all crosses, sufferings, trials, &c., as things not able to deprive sincere Christians of Christ's love; 'shall tribulation,' &c. He had before spoken of persons, now here he speaks of things, because Satan and his sworn slaves think by such things to separate between God and his people. Chrysostom observes Paul's wisdom in three things. (1.) That he saith not, Shall the love of riches, pleasures, honours, &c., which have a mighty force in them to bewitch us; but 'shall tribulation, distress,' &c. (2.) That he begins with the lighter, and so riseth to greater troubles, placing them in this order, not casually, but by singular art. (3.) That though these which he here rehearseth consist of a certain number, yet every one as a general hath special troops under it: as when he saith tribulation, he saith imprisonments, bonds, slanders, banishments, &c. 'Shall tribulation, distress, persecution,' &c.? No. They are 'blessed which endure these things,' Mat. v. 10, 11. Shall famine? He which feeds on Christ shall never perish for hunger. Shall nakedness? Christ's righteousness is my clothing; I shall willingly follow him even naked; who when he was clothed with infinite glory as with a garment was content to be born naked and to be stripped on the cross for my sake. Shall peril? I know the hardest. Shall the sword? Christ is to me in life and death advantage. But,

[4.] Fourthly, 'If God be for us, who can be against us?' I answer, None can be against us so, *as to bring us to their bow, their beck, their will, their humour, their lusts:* 1 Kings xix. 18, 'Yet I have left me seven thousand in Israel, all the knees which have not bowed unto Baal, and every mouth which hath not kissed him;'[1] that is, I have many thousands that have not worshipped Baal. Here a set number is put for an indefinite number; he means a very great number.

[1] Kissing was an outward token—(1.) Of great and entire affection; (2.) Of submissive reverence; (3.) Of willing and ready subjection.

Idolaters used not only to bow and kneel before their idols, but also to kiss them, according to that Hosea xiii. 2, 'Let the men that sacrifice kiss the calves.' Cicero saith that the chin of the image of Hercules was much worn with the kisses of them that adored him. Now God had several thousands of true Israelites indeed that had not in the least kind polluted themselves with the idolatry of Baal. The denial of bowing the knee and kissing with the mouth shews that God's faithful servants were so far from setting their hearts upon Baal, as that they would not make the least show of any affection or subjection to him. These good souls had too great spirits to be conformable to the idolatry of the times. Jeroboam with his eight hundred thousand chosen men, his popish priests, and his golden calves, could not bring Judah to his bow, 2 Chron. xiii. 3, 20. Nebuchadnezzar, nor his princely informers, nor his fiery furnace, could never bring the three children to his bow; the three champions would be Nonconformists, though court, city, and country were violent for conformity, Dan. iii. Neither Darius, his presidents, nor princes, could ever bring Daniel to their bow, Dan. vi.; Daniel would keep off from idolatry, and keep close to his God, and close to his duty, let all his enemies do their worst. The rulers and elders of Israel charged the apostles, and threatened the apostles, and beat the apostles, and commanded the apostles, that they should not speak in the name of Jesus; but they could never bring them to their bow, Acts iii., iv., v. For 'they departed from the presence of the council, rejoicing that they were counted worthy to suffer shame for his name, and daily in the temple, and in every house they ceased not to teach and preach Jesus Christ,' Acts v. 41, 42. Pharaoh by all his oppressions could never bring Israel to his bow; nor Saul by all his persecutions could never bring David to his bow; nor Haman by all his plots and designs could never bring Mordecai to his bow; and Paul will rather die upon the spot than be brought to his enemies' bow, Acts xx. 21–24, and xxi. 13. The ten persecuting emperors could never bring the primitive Christians to their bow; nor the bloody, fierce, and fiery papists could never bring the martyrs to their bow, as you may see throughout the books of martyrs. Among the many hundred instances that are there, I shall only refresh your memory with this one: There were endeavours to bring Hawkes to their bow, but all in vain. At last some of his Christian friends desired him, for their encouragement and confirmation, to give some token when he was in the flames; a strange time one would think to attend upon signs by friends, whether the pains were tolerable or no. He was bound to the stake, fire put to the wood, it burns, it flames, it consumes his flesh, his eyes start out of his head, his fingers are consumed with the fire; and when every one thought him dead, expecting the fall of his body: lo, suddenly he lifts up his stumps, and thrice as a famous conqueror he claps them over his head. In this he was more than conqueror.[1]

In former times the sense of the love of God made the martyrs esteem tyrants as gnats and fleas, and torments as fleabitings. Tertullian, speaking of his times, saith, That to be accused was the wish

[1] [Foxe,] Acts and Mon., page 1447.

of Christians, and punishment for Christ they counted felicity.[1] A certain woman, running in all haste with her child in her arms, being asked the cause, Oh, saith she, I hear a great sort of Christians are appointed to be martyred, and I am afraid lest I and my little one come too late. When the Emperor Valens banished Basil, and the tribune threatened his death, I would, said Basil, I had anything of worth, I would bestow it on him that should cut Basil's windpipe. And when he had that night given him to deliberate, he answered, That he would be the same man to-morrow, and wished that the tribune should not be changed. Chrysostom, being in banishment by the means of Eudoxia the empress, wrote to a bishop called Cyriacus, and, upon occasion, tells of his resolution before he was banished: I thought with myself, saith he, that if she will banish me, the earth is the Lord's; if she will saw me asunder, I remembered the prophet Isaiah; if drown me, Jonas came to my mind; if stone me, I thought of Stephen; if behead me, of John Baptist; if take away my goods, 'Naked came I out of my mother's womb.' By all which you may clearly see, that let the wicked do their worst, they can never bring the saints to their bow. But,

[5.] Fifthly, 'If God be with us, who can be against us?' I answer, None, so as *to hinder the operation of all things for our good.* When men and devils have done their worst, all the great troubles, deep distresses, and most deadly dangers, that do attend the saints, shall work for their good: Rom. viii. 28, 'And we know that all things work together for good to them that love God, to them that are called according to his purpose.'[2] In this verse there are two things observable: *First,* A proposition, or a glorious privilege: 'All things work together for good.' This word, συνεργεῖ εἰς, 'work together,' is a physical expression. Several poisonful ingredients put together, being tempered by the skilful apothecary, make a sovereign medicine, and work together for the good of the patient. They work together, not *invicem,* between themselves, but together with God; not of their own nature, for so they do not co-operate, but contra-operate, but being sanctified by God. And therefore one takes the verb passively, are 'wrought;' for, indeed, take away God, and afflictions work for our hurt; but all God's providences, being divinely tempered and sanctified, do work together for the best to the people of God. When the worst of men have done their worst against the saints, all things shall sweetly concur, yea, conspire for their good. *Second,* The proof, which is double. (1.) From the experience of all saints, 'We know;' it is not a matter pendulous or doubtful. The apostle doth not say, 'We think,' but 'We know.' Nor he doth not say, 'We hope,' but 'We know.' Nor he doth not say, 'We guess,' 'we conjecture,' but 'We know.' Nor he doth not say, 'We desire' that all things may work together for good, but 'We know all things work together for good.' Nor he doth not say, 'We pray' that all things may work together for good, but 'We know all things work

---

[1] Accusatio votum est, et pœna felicitas.—*Tert. advers. Gent.*

[2] I have read of a Jewish rabbin, who would still say it was good whatever befell him. When he met with a cross, he would say it was good; when he met with a loss, he would say it is good.

together for good.' The wicked know not this secret, as the Philistines understood not Samson's riddles, Judg. xiv. 12–14; but we know that all the world shall not hinder the cross from working for our good. (2.) From a description of them that love God, they are ' called according to God's purpose;' that is, God hath purposed the salvation of his people, he hath chosen them to salvation, and called them to it; and therefore it must needs be that all these afflictions that befall his people must work together for their internal and eternal good, otherwise he should do that which should cross his own purpose, which wise men will not do; and oh, how much less will the most wise God act counter-cross to his own purpose! So Jer. xxiv. 5, ' Thus saith the Lord, the God of Israel, Like these good figs, so will I acknowledge them that are carried away captive of Judah, whom I have sent out of this place into the land of the Chaldeans for their good.' To be carried captive to Babylon was doubtless a very sore and matchless affliction: Dan. ix. 12, 'And he hath confirmed his words which he spake against us, and against our judges that judged us, by bringing upon us a great evil; for under the whole heaven hath not been done, as hath been done upon Jerusalem.' This may be the abridgment of Jeremiah's Lamentations: Lam. i. 12, ' Is it nothing to you, all ye that pass by? Behold, and see if there be any sorrow like unto my sorrow, which is done unto me, wherewith the Lord hath afflicted me in the day of his fierce anger;' chap. iv. 16, ' For the punishment of the iniquity of the daughter of my people is greater than the punishment of the sin of Sodom, that was overthrown as in a moment, and no hands stayed on her.' Sodom sustained not any siege from foreign forces, they were not vexed and plagued with the armies of the Chaldeans; there was no hand of man in the destruction of Sodom, but a hand of heaven only. Sodom was not kept long in pains and misery as I and my people have been, but was suddenly overwhelmed, and in an instant despatched; all which shews that their miseries and sufferings were incomparable and matchless; and that they were so indeed will evidently appear, if you please but seriously to consider either the antecedents of it or the consequents of it. The antecedents of it: what went before their captivity—viz., blood, and slaughter, and dreadful devastations. Or if you consider the consequents of it: as, (1.) The enslaving of their persons under a fierce and most cruel enemy; (2.) The loss of their estates; (3.) The leaving of their country and the land of their nativity; (4.) A deprivation of the ordinances and worship of God; (5.) The scorns and reproaches, the exultations and triumphs of their adversaries, that pleased and delighted themselves in their captivity and misery.[1] These were the woeful consequences of that captivity, and yet all the power and malice of men in the world could not hinder these amazing and astonishing trials from working together for the spiritual and everlasting good of his captive people. That God will do his people good by the most terrible dispensations that they are under, you may see more and more evident by comparing the scriptures in the margin together.[2] As the apothecary of poison makes treacle to drive out

---

[1] See Ps. cxxxvii. 7; Obad. xii. 13–16; Ezek. xxv. 6; Ps. xliv. 13, 14.
[2] Deut. viii. 15, 16; Ps. cxix. 71, 75; Heb. xii. 10.

poison, so can God make the poison of afflictions, which in themselves are the curse of the law, to drive out the poison of sin. All the world can never hinder the affliction, troubles, and evils that befall the people of God, from working for their good; for God does and will by these means, (1.) Discover sin; (2.) Prevent sin; (3.) Imbitter sin; (4.) Mortify sin. And God will by afflictions, troubles, &c., (1.) Revive, quicken, and recover his children's decayed graces; (2.) Exercise his children's graces; (3.) Increase his children's graces; (4.) Make a further trial and discovery of his children's graces.[1] Let the enemies of Sion storm and rage, plot and combine, &c., yet they shall never be able to hinder the greatest troubles, the deepest distresses, and most deadly dangers, from working for the internal and eternal good of all the sincere lovers of God. I have read a story of one Pereus, who, running at another with a sword to kill him, by·accident the sword only run into his imposthume and broke that; and so he was instrumental to save him whom he designed to have killed: and so all the afflictions and troubles that the righteous meet with, they do but serve to cure them of the imposthume of pride, or of the imposthume of earthly-mindedness, or of the imposthume of self-love, or of the imposthume of hypocrisy. Look upon the revolution of the heavens, how every planet moves in its proper orb. Their motions are not alike, but various, nay, opposite each unto the other. Hence those different conjunctions, oppositions, and aspects of the planets, yet by the wheeling round of the *primum mobile*, they are brought about to one determinate point. The people of God have many enemies in the world, whose course and scope, whose aims and ends and actions are not the same, yea diverse, nay adverse, one thwarting and crossing the other, yet the overruling providence so sways all subordinate and inferior instruments and enemies, that in the midst of their mutual jars they conspire in a sacred harmony, as if they were entered into a holy league, or some sacred combination for the good of his chosen. Wherever our enemies be in respect of their places, whosoever they be in regard of their persons, and however they are disjoined in regard of their affections, yet all their projects and practices shall tend and end in the good of those that love God. But,

[6] Sixthly, 'If God be with us, who can be against us?' I answer, None, so as *to hinder our communion and fellowship with the Father, Son, and Spirit:* 1 John i. 3, ' That which we have seen and heard, declare we unto you, that ye may have fellowship with us: and truly our fellowship is with the Father, and with his Son Jesus Christ.' Man's *summum bonum* stands in his communion with God, as Scripture and experience evidences. A man whose soul is conversant with God, shall find more pleasure in a desert, in a den, in a dungeon, in a fiery furnace, yea, and in the valley of the shadow of death, than in the palace of a prince.[2] There is a sweet and intimate communion which believers have with God; hence they are said to ' walk with God,' Gen. v. 24, and vi. 9; and to ' talk with God,' as

[1] See my ' London's Lamentations,' pp. 34–53. See also my ' Mute Christian under the Smarting Rod.' [Former in vol. vi. and the latter in vol. i.—G.]

[2] *Nunquam minus solus, quam cum solus,* never less alone than when alone, said the heathen; and may not a saint say so much more, that has communion with Father, Son, and Spirit? My God and I are good company, said famous Dr Sibbes.

Moses frequently did; and to 'dwell in God,' 1 John iv. 15; and to 'sup with God,' Rev. iii. 20; and to 'lodge with God,' Cant. vii. 11. The nearness of this fellowship which we have with the Father, is represented by a gradation of allusions in Scripture, all which do excellently illustrate this truth. There is some kind of participation that a servant hath with his master; yet greater is that which one friend hath with another; but yet greater is that which a son hath with the father; but greatest of all is that which the bride hath with the bridegroom. Now in all·these relations we stand to the Father; we are his servants and he is our Lord, Exod. xii. 7; we are his friends, John xv. 14, 15; James ii. 23; and he is our friend, Cant. v. 1; an able friend, a sure friend, a faithful friend, a close friend, a constant friend. Plutarch's reasoning is good, τὰ τῶν φιλῶν πάντα κοινὰ, friends have all things in common. But God is our friend : *ergo* we cannot want; a most rare speech from a poor heathen ! He is our Father, Isa. lxiii. 16, and lxiv. 8; and we are his children, Isa. lxiii. 8. He is our bridegroom, and we are his bride, Isa. lxi. 10; Hosea ii. 19, 20; Isa. lxii. 5. And therefore it is no pride nor presumption for believers to say, ' Our fellowship is with the Father.' Our fellowship with Jesus Christ is set forth by the parable of the wedding-feast, and by·the entertainment of the prodigal son, and by such relations or various similitudes, as carry communion in their bosoms, as of the head and the members, root and branches, foundation and building, husband and wife, Mat. xxii. 1–3; Luke xv. The head hath communion with the body by sense, influence, motion. The root with the branches, by leaf, sap, and juice. The foundation with the building, by support and strength. The husband with the wife, by love and consent. Thus it is betwixt Christ and the believers : 1 Cor. i. 9, ' God is faithful, by whom ye are called to the fellowship of his Son Jesus Christ.' All believers have fellowship with Christ, whether they be strong or weak, rich or poor, high or low, ripe and well grown, or new-born babes, and very tender, Gal. iii. 28; 1 Pet. ii. 2; John xvii. 20–23. The head hath conjunction with all the members, and an influence into all the members, even the little toes, as well as into the strongest arms; and the root, in the virtue of it, extends to the weakest branches, as well as to the strongest limbs of the tree. Communion is as large as union. All believers are united to Christ, and all believers have communion with Christ. Though one star exceeds another in magnitude, yet all are alike seated in the heavenly orb; and though one member be larger in the body than another, yet every one hath an equal conjunction with the head: and as believers have fellowship with the Father and the Son, so they have fellowship with the Spirit also. Every believer's communion extends to all the persons in the Trinity : 2 Cor. xiii. 14, ' The grace of our Lord Jesus Christ, and the love of God, and the communion of the Holy. Ghost be with you all. Amen.' Now no men, no devils, no wrath, no rage, no malice, no enmity, no afflictions, no oppositions, no persecutions, no troubles, no trials, no bonds, no banishment, can interrupt or hinder a believer's communion with the three persons in Trinity. But,

[7.] Seventhly, ' If God be with us, who can be against us?' I answer, None, so as to *hinder our private trade to heaven.* All the world can never hinder a sincere Christian from driving a secret trade with heaven, as you may see by comparing the scriptures in the margin together.[1] A Christian can as well hear without ears, and live without food, and fight without hands, and walk without feet, as he is able to live without secret prayer. Secret prayer is the life of our lives, the soul, the sweet, the heaven of all our enjoyments. Of all the duties of religion, secret prayer is the most soul-sweetening, soul-strengthening, soul-nourishing, soul-fattening, soul-refreshing, soul-satisfying, and soul-encouraging duty. In all the ages of the world, the saints have kept the trade. In spite of all opposers and perse-cutors, in prisons, in dungeons, in dens, in bonds, in banishments, on racks, and in the very flames, the saints have still kept up this secret trade ; as you may see at large in my treatise on closet prayer, called 'The Privy Key of Heaven,' to which I refer you.[2] But,

[8.] Eighthly, 'If God be with us, who can be against us?' I answer, None, so as *to deprive us of the sweet testimony of our renewed consciences:* 2 Cor. i. 12, 'For our rejoicing,' or boasting,[3] 'is this, the testimony of our conscience, that in simplicity and godly sincerity, not with fleshly wisdom, but by the grace of God, we have had our con-versation in the world, and more abundantly to you-ward.' They were in great and pressing troubles in Asia, ver. 8, and yet they boasted in the testimony of their consciences; they were under a sen-tence of death in themselves, ver. 9, and yet gloried in the testimony of their consciences. Joy of conscience is the greatest joy, as trouble of conscience is the greatest trouble; when conscience bears its testi-mony with us, and for us, how full of joy is the soul, even in the midst of the deepest sorrows and greatest sufferings ! *Conscientia pura semper secura,* a good conscience hath sure confidence, and he that hath it, sits Noah-like—

————mediis tranquillus in undis—

quiet in the greatest combustions; freed, if not from the common de-struction, yet from the common distraction. A good conscience is an impregnable fort. It fears no colours; it will enable a man to stand against the fiercest batteries of men and devils. A good conscience will fill a man with courage and comfort in the midst of all his troubles and distresses. Paul had enough to say for himself when standing before the council; he could say, 'Men and brethren, I have lived in all good conscience before God until this day,' Acts xxiii. 1, 2. And though as soon as he had said so, Ananias commanded to smite him on the mouth, yet he bears up bravely, because his conscience did not smite him, but acquit him. That man can never want music, whose conscience speaks in consort, and is harmonious with himself. A good conscience is a paradise in a wilderness, it is riches in poverty, and health in sickness, and strength in weakness, and liberty in bonds, and life in death, Isa. xxxviii. 3. A good conscience will enable a man to triumph over innumerable evils, yea, over death itself. Death to such a person is not the king of terrors, but the king of desires, Phil. i. 23. A good conscience will be a Christian's best friend in the

---

[1] Ps. iii. 2–4 ; Ps. vi. 8–10 ; Ps. cxxxviii. 3 ; Lam. iii. 55–59.
[2] Vol. ii. pp. 137, *seq.*—G.
[3] καύχησις, boasting or glorying.

worst times; it will be a sword to defend him, a staff to support him, a pillar of fire to lead him, a Joseph to nourish him, a Dorcas to clothe him, a Canaan to refresh him, and a feast to delight him: 'He that is of a merry heart hath a continual feast,' Prov. xv. 15. Now there ·is nothing that can make a man divinely merry below a good conscience. A good conscience, saith one,[1] is *thalamus Dei, palatium Christi, habitaculum Spiritus Sancti, paradisus deliciarum,* The bed of God, the palace of Christ, the habitation of the Holy Ghost, the paradise of delights, and wherein every tree yieldeth a feast. *Tranquillitas conscientiæ, et securitas innocentiæ, quæcunque mundus bona judicat, excellunt,* The tranquillity of conscience, and the security of innocence, excel all the things which the world counteth good.[2] He that hath a good conscience enjoys a continual serenity, and sits continually at that blessed feast, whereat the blessed angels are cooks and butlers, as Luther hath it, and the three persons in Trinity glad guests. All other feasts to this of a good conscience are stark hunger. The feast of a good conscience is a full feast, a noble feast, a lasting feast; not for a day, as that of Nabal's; nor for seven days, as that of Samson's; nor of nine score days, as that of Ahasuerus; but a durable, continual feast, without intermission of solace, or interruption of society. The best way in this world for a man to turn his whole life into a merry festival, is to get and keep a good conscience. The heathen philosopher could say, ὁ ἀγαθὸς αἰεὶ ἑορτάζει, a good man keeps holiday all the year about. It was the testimony of a good conscience that made the apostles rejoice when they were beaten and abused by the council. It was the testimony of a good conscience that made Paul and Silas to sing in the prison, Acts v. 40–42, and xvi. 25, 26. It was the testimony of a good conscience that made Moses prefer Christ's cross before Egypt's crown, and Christ's reproaches before Egypt's treasures. It was the testimony of a good conscience that made those worthies in that 11th of the Hebrews more willing to die than to live, to die than to dine, Heb. xi. 35. It was the testimony of a good conscience that made the martyrs to kiss the stake, to hug their executioners, to clap their hands in the flames, and to tread upon burning coals as upon beds of roses. Now it is not in the power or policy of men or devils to deprive a Christian of the testimony of his conscience; and as long as that bird in the bosom sings, no troubles, no trials, no oppositions, no persecutions, no dangers, no death can make a Christian miserable. The testimony of a good conscience will make a man triumph over the worst of men, and the worst of sufferings. But,

[9.] Ninthly, 'If God be with us, who can be against us?' I answer, None, so as *to hinder the help, assistance, and succour of God at a dead lift.* Heb. xiii. 5, 'Let your conversation be without covetousness,'—or 'without the love of silver,' as the Greek word signifies—'and be content with such things as you have.' *Contenti præsentibus,* so Beza, ' Be content with present things.'[3] The Hebrews had been plundered of all they had; though they had nothing they must be content, Heb. x. 34. If men cannot bring their means to

---

[1] Augustine, ser. x. ad Fratres in Erem.   [2] Ambrose, Offic. lib. ii. cap. 1.
[3] ἀρκούμενοι τοῖς παροῦσιν.

their minds, let them bring their minds to their means; a little will serve our turn till we get to heaven, till we come to our Father's house: 'For he hath said, I will never leave thee, nor forsake thee.' There are five negatives in the Greek;[1] I read not the like throughout the New Testament. In that this promise is set down negatively, 'I will never leave thee,' this makes the promise to be of a larger extent; for it includes all times, all places, all estates, all dangers, all needs, all distresses whatsoever; as if he had more largely said, thou shalt never stand in need of any of my help and protection, but thou shalt be sure to find it. Affirmative promises are not of that extent as negative promises are; for if a man should promise to assist, help, succour, or counsel me, if he do it now and then, or upon some special occasions, he has kept his promise; but negatively for a man to say, I will not fail thee, I will never leave thee, though he should help, assist, succour, or stand by me, a hundred, yea, a thousand times, and yet fail me but once, that negative promise is not punctually kept, it is not perfectly kept. It is further considerable that there is a great emphasis in doubling and trebling a negative particle in Greek. Doubling and trebling negatives in Greek makes them much the stronger. The doubling of the negative particle doth in this place carry the greater emphasis, because, in setting down the same thing, it is not only twice doubled, but in the latter place it is trebled; so as there are in all five negatives, as I have already hinted. These two phrases, 'Never leave nor forsake,' are so general as they include all the wants, all dangers, all distresses, all necessities, all calamities, all miseries, that can befall us in this world.[2] These two phrases, God's not leaving, God's not forsaking, imply all needful succours. It is more than if he had said, I will supply all thy wants, I will heal all thy diseases, I will secure thee against all sorts of dangers, I will ease thee of all thy pains, I will free thee of all thy oppressors, I will break all thy bonds, I will bring thee out of prison, I will vanquish all thine enemies, I will knock off all thy chains, and I will make thee triumph over all thy sufferings; for these generals comprise all manner of particulars under them: Heb. xiii. 6, 'So that we may boldly say, The Lord is my helper, and I will not fear what man shall do unto me.' In this verse there is an inference made upon the former promise of God's not leaving nor forsaking his; the conjunction, 'so that,' implieth an inference, and such an inference in this place as teacheth us to make a good use of the forenamed promise. The use here set down is double: the first is confidence in God, 'The Lord is my helper;' secondly, courage against man, 'I will not fear what man shall do unto me.' Assurance of God's presence to help at a dead lift should raise us up above all base and slavish fears of the power of men, of the spoilings of men, of the designs of men, &c. God being with us, and for us, and on our side, we may boldly, safely, and confidently, rest upon it, that he will freely, readily, graciously, afford all needful help, assistance, and succour, when we are in the greatest troubles, deepest distresses, and most deadly dangers. The Greek word βοηθος, 'helper,' according to the notation of it, signifies one that is ready to run at the cry of another. This notation implies

---

[1] οὐ μὴ οὐδ' οὐ μὴ.　　　[2] A general promise compriseth all particulars of that kind.

a willing readiness, and a ready willingness in God, to help and succour his people when they are at a dead lift. You know the tender father, the indulgent mother, the careful nurse, they presently run when any of them hears the child cry, or sees the child in any danger or distress; so when God sees his poor children in any danger or distress, when he hears them complain and cry out of their sufferings, their bonds, their burdens, their oppressions, their dangers, &c., he presently runs to their relief and succour, Exod. ii. 23–25, and iii. 7–10. Ps. xxxiii. 20, ' Our soul waiteth for the Lord : he is our help and our shield :' Ps. xlix. 17, ' Thou art my deliverer : God is the Lord of hosts, with him alone is strength and power to deliver Israel out of all his troubles.' He may do it, he can do it, he will do it, he is wise in heart and mighty in strength; besides him there is no Saviour, no deliverer ; he is a shield to the righteous, strength to the weak, a refuge to the oppressed ; he is *Instar omnium*, all in all.[1] Who is like him in all the world to help his people at a dead lift ? when friends cannot help, when power cannot help, when policy cannot help, when riches cannot help, when princes cannot help, when parliaments cannot help, yet then God can and will help his people when all human help fails. ' For the Lord shall judge his people, and repent himself for his servants, when he seeth that their power,' or hand, ' is gone, and there is none shut up, or left,' Deut. xxxii. 36. When God's people are at the very brink of ruin, then God will come in seasonably to their help ; their extremity shall be his opportunity, to succour his people, and to judge their enemies. No men, no devils, no power, no policy, can hinder God from helping, aiding, assisting, and succouring of his people when they are at a dead lift. But,

[10.] Tenthly, ' If God be with us, who can be against us ?' I answer, None, so as to *hinder the springs of joy and comfort from rising and flowing in their souls:* Ps. lxxi. 20, ' Thou which hast shewed me great and sore troubles shalt quicken me again, and shalt bring me up again from the depths of the earth;' ver. 21, ' Thou shalt increase my greatness, and comfort me on every side.' The psalmist was in those desperate dangers, that he seemed to be as a man that was dead and buried, and yet he had faith enough to believe that God would surround him with cordials, and supply him with comforts from all sides. There is no true comfort to be drawn out of the standing pools of outward sufficiencies, but out of the living fountains of the all-sufficiencies of the Lord Almighty. ' Thou shalt comfort me on every side.' Ps. xciv. 19, ' In the multitude of my thoughts within me,' or of my careful, troubled, perplexed thoughts, as the word properly signifies, ' thy comforts delight mv soul.' As the psalmist always found God a present help, so he always found him a present comfort in the day of troubles. God never did, nor never will want a cordial to revive and keep up the spirits of his people from fainting and sinking in an evil day. When the psalmist was under many griefs, cares, fears, and perplexities of spirit, God came in with those comforts that did delight his soul, and cheer up his spirits, Ps. cxix. 49, 50. The word of the Lord is never more a word of comfort, nor the Spirit of the Lord is never more a Spirit of com-

[1] Ps. ix. 7, 8; Isa. xliii. 11 ; Ps. v. 12, and xxii. 12 ; 2 Kings vi. 26, 27.

fort, than when the saints are in their deepest distresses and sorest perplexities: John xiv. 16, 'And I will pray the Father, and he shall give you another comforter, that he may abide with you for ever;' ver. 26, 'But the comforter, which is the Holy Ghost, whom the Father will send in my name.' Hudson, the martyr, being at the stake, he went from under his chain, and having prayed earnestly, he was so comforted and refreshed by the Holy Spirit that he suffered valiantly and cheerfully. The Holy Ghost is called again and again the comforter, because his office is to work consolation in the hearts of God's people in all their troubles and distresses. Spiritual comfort is therefore called 'joy in the Holy Ghost,' because the Holy Ghost doth create it in the soul, Rom. xiv. 17. When a man suffers for righteousness' sake, God comes with his cordials in the very nick of time, 1 Pet. iv. 13. When a man's suffering is upon the account of Christ, God seldom fails to send the comforter for the refreshing and relieving of his spirit. When a man is under bodily confinement for the cause of Christ, God will never fail to be a spring of life, a well of salvation, and breast of consolation to him, Isa. xii. 3, and lxvi. 11. When a Christian is brought to 'a piece of bread,' then is the season for God to feed him with heavenly manna. I have told you of Mr Glover, who found no comfort in the time of his imprisonment, but when he was going to the stake, he cried out to his friend, ' He is come, he is come,' meaning the comforter. Hab. iii. 17, 'Although the fig-tree shall not blossom, neither shall fruit be in the vines ; the labour of the olive shall fail, and the fields shall yield no meat ; the flock shall be cut off from the fold, and there shall be no herd in the stalls;' ver. 18, ' Yet I will rejoice in the Lord, I will joy in the God of my salvation.' In these words you have these two parts: (1.) A sad supposition, ' Although the fig-tree shall not blossom,' &c. ; (2.) A noble and comfortable resolution, ' Yet I will rejoice in the Lord, I will joy in the God of my salvation.' Let me first hint a little at the sad supposition, ' Although the fig-tree should not blossom,' &c.

[1.] First, Though there should be *a famine in that land, that of all lands was the most plentiful and fruitful land,* yet Habakkuk would ' rejoice in the Lord, and joy in the God of his salvation.' The land of Canaan, of all lands, was the fruitfullest. It was as the garden of God. It was a land that ' flowed with milk and honey,' a land of vineyards, the best of all lands, as Moses describes it; a land that brought forth to Isaac no less than a hundredfold. It was so rich a land that it was the granary of other neighbouring cities and countries. It had not only plenty for itself, but bounty for others. Yet now, when God shall turn a paradise into a wilderness, Habakkuk will rejoice in the Lord, and joy in the God of his salvation, Deut. viii. 7-9, and xxxii. 13, 14 ; Gen. xxvi. 12 ; 1 Kings v. 11 ; Acts xii. 20. But,

[2.] Secondly, When *the anger and wrath of God shall cause a dearth in those fruits that naturally are most yielding and pleasant,* yet then Habakkuk would rejoice in the Lord, and joy in the God of his salvation. The fig-tree, of all trees, is most fruitful, bringing forth of its own accord, with the least care and culture, fructifying in the most barren and stony places, bearing twice a year, soonest ripening, and rarely failing. So the vine, that is a fruitful plant, is made the emblem of plenty and fruitfulness. Now when there shall be a dearth upon these pleasant fruits, yet then Habakkuk will ' rejoice in the Lord, and joy in the God of his salvation.' But,

[3.] Thirdly, Another print of divine displeasure in the scarcity threatened is, that it is *a national famine, a general famine, an overspreading famine.* Usually, if one part of the land suffers scarcity, other parts abound with plenty; but when God calls for a famine, he turns a whole land into a desert, into a barren wilderness. ' Bashan languisheth, and Carmel, and the flower of Lebanon languisheth,' Ps. cvii. 33, 34; Nah. i. 4. These were the richest soil of all the country, yet these were parched up and fruitless by his displeasure, and yet for all this Habakkuk will ' rejoice in the Lord, and joy in the God of his salvation.' But,

[4.] Fourthly, Another print of divine displeasure is this, that the Lord makes it *a universal scarcity upon all kind of foods and supports of life.* Here is the ' staff of bread' broken, and ' the herds and flocks fail,' and the refreshing of the wine-press, ' the seed and the vine, and the fig-tree and the olive-tree,' all become fruitless. Such a desolation is more than ordinary. Usually, when one commodity fails, another abounds. If corn be dear, cattle will be cheap. That weather ofttimes that hinders one kind of grain, helps another; but here God blasts all the helps of nature. Therefore God compares his judgments to a fire that burns all before it : Joel ii. 3, ' The land is as the garden of Eden before it, and behind it a desolate wilderness,' and this the Lord points at as a wonder : Joel i. 2, ' Hear this, ye old men'—who can talk of dear years—' hath this been in your days, or even in the days of your fathers ? that which the palmer-worm hath left, hath the caterpillers eaten.' When God begins in a way of judgment, he makes an end, he makes the decays of nature excessive and violent ; and yet Habakkuk will ' rejoice in the Lord, and joy in the God of his salvation.' In his resolution you have the first particle, ' although,' ver. 17. Now this particle is an act of forecast ; these miseries may befall us ; and in the 18th verse you have the particle ' yet,' and that is an act of preparation against these miseries. That particle ' although' forecasts the misery, and that particle ' yet' forelays the remedy. He foresees sorrows in the first, and he provides against them in the second, ' Yet I will rejoice in the Lord, and joy in the God of my salvation.'

So Paul comes with a *benedictus* in his mouth—and surely it was in his heart before it was in his mouth : 2 Cor. i. 3, ' Blessed be God, even the God of our Lord Jesus Christ, the Father of mercies, and the God of all comfort :' ver. 4, ' Who comforteth us in all our tribulations, that we may be able to comfort them which are in any trouble, by the comfort wherewith we ourselves are comforted of God :' ver. 5, ' For as the sufferings of Christ abound in us, so our consolation aboundeth by Christ.'[1] The apostle begins here with thanksgiving, according to his accustomed manner in all his epistles ; but contrary to his custom doth he apply this thanksgiving wholly to himself. The reason was, saith Beza, because the Corinthians did begin to despise

---

[1] εὐλόγητος ; that is, word for word, ' Let God be well spoken of.' God blesseth us really, signally, greatly ; and we bless him verbally, mentally, practically.

him for his afflictions—it being the common course of the world to despise the people of God when they are under sufferings; therefore he answered confidently for himself, that though he had been much afflicted, yet he had been much comforted; and rejoiced the more in his comforts, because God had comforted him for that very cause, that he might be able and willing to comfort others. God is the God of all sorts and degrees of comfort, who hath all comforts at his disposal. This phrase, 'The God of all comforts,' intimates to us; (1.) That no comfort can be found anywhere else; he hath the sole gift of comfort. (2.) Not only some, but all comfort; no imaginable comfort is wanting in him, nor to be found out of him. Look, as the air lights not without the sun, and as fuel heats not without fire, so neither can anything soundly comfort us without God. (3.) All degrees of comfort are to be found in him, in our greatest troubles, deepest distresses, and most deadly dangers. The lower the ebb, the higher the tide; the deeper the distress, the greater the comforts. Though the apostle was greatly afflicted, yet his comforts did exceed his afflictions: 2 Cor. vii. 6, 'Nevertheless God, that comforteth those that are cast down, comforted us by the coming of Titus.' When the Corinthians were in a very low condition, when they were even spent with grief and swallowed up in sorrows, when they were destitute of all relief and comfort, then the God of all comforts did comfort them.[1] No tribulations, no persecutions, no grievances, no prison doors, no bolts, no bars, can keep out the consolations of God from flowing in upon his people. God loves to comfort his people when all their outward comforts fail them. God's comforts are not only sweet, but seasonable; he never comes too soon, nor never stays too long. If one drop of the joy of the Holy Ghost should fall into hell, it would swallow up all the torments of hell, saith Austin. 'The joy of the Holy Ghost' will certainly swallow up all the troubles and sufferings that we meet with in a way of righteousness. None have been more divinely cheerful and merry than the saints have been under their greatest sufferings, 1 Pet. iv. 12–14. John Noyes took up a faggot at the fire and kissed it, saying, 'Blessed be the time that ever I was born to come to this preferment.' When they fastened Alice Driver to the stake to be burnt, 'Never did neckerchief,' said she, with a cheerful countenance, 'become me so well as this chain.' Mr Bradford put off his cap and thanked God when the keeper's wife brought him word that he was to be burnt on the morrow. Mr Taylor fetched a frisk when he was come near the place where he was to suffer. Henry and John, two Augustine monks, being the first that were burnt in Germany, and Mr Rogers, the first that was burnt in Queen Mary's days, did all sing in the flames. Thus you see that it is not the greatest troubles, nor the deepest distresses, nor the most deadly dangers, that can hinder the joy of the Lord from overflowing the soul. But,

[11.] Eleventhly, 'If God be with us, who can be against us?' I answer, None, so as *to deprive us of our graces, which next to Christ are our choicest jewels.* 1 John iii. 9, 'Whosoever is born of God doth not commit sin.' That is, doth not give himself over to a voluntary serving of sin; he does not make a trade of sin; he sins not totally, finally,

---

[1] This is a most sweet attribute of God; a breast that we should be still sucking at.

maliciously, habitually, studiously, resolutely, wilfully, delightfully, deadly, ἁμαρτίαν οὐ ποιεῖ, 'He does not make it his work to sin,' he cannot follow his lusts, as a workman follows his trade, 'for his seed remaineth in him.' 'The seed of God,' the seed of grace, is an abiding seed. Grace in itself is certain and unchangeable, though the feeling thereof be uncertain. Grace hath an abiding excellency in it; grace hath eternity stamped upon it. It is durable riches. Other riches 'make themselves wings, and fly from us,' Prov. viii. 18, and xxvii. 24; but grace will keep us company till we get to heaven. Our last step in holiness will be into happiness. Grace is a blossom of eternity. It is an anointing that abides, 1 John ii. 27; John iv. 14, and vii. 38. That is, the principle of grace infused into you, which was typified by the unctions or anointings in the ceremonial law, which was signified by the precious ointment poured upon the head of Aaron, that ran down to the skirts of his garments—this principle will prove durable and lasting. Grace is 'a well of water, springing up into ever-lasting life.' Grace is a river of living water. Now this river can never be dried up, because the Spirit of God is the constant spring that feeds it and maintains it. Grace is not a stream or a pond that may run dry, but a well, yea, a springing well of inexhaustible fulness, sweetness, virtue, and refreshment. Grace will still be springing up and flowing out in all the carriages and deportments of a Christian. Grace will be flowing out in all a Christian's duties and services, in his outward calling and employments, in his trials and sufferings. Grace will break out at a Christian's eyes, ears, tongue, hands, feet. Where grace is a well of water, a river of living water, there that Christian will see for Christ, and hear for Christ, and talk for Christ, and do for Christ, and walk with Christ. Grace is a well, a river, that will be springing up to everlasting life. Grace and glory differ, *non specie sed gradu*, in degree, not in kind. Grace differs very little from glory. The one is the seed, the other the flower. Grace is glory mili-tant, and glory is grace triumphant. Grace is a beginning of glory. It may be compared to the golden chain in Homer, whose top was fastened to the chair of Jupiter.[1] Grace and glory are individual, and inseparable. The psalmist joins them together, 'The Lord will give grace and glory,' Ps. lxxxiv. 11. Grace is a living spring that never faileth, a seed that never dieth, a jewel which never consumeth, a sun that never setteth. All other gifts of whatsoever kind, worth, or excellency, are but like a cloud soon dispelled, a vessel of clay soon broken, a sandy foundation soon sunk. Grace is more excellent than gold. Gold draws the heart from God, grace draws the heart to God; gold doth but enrich the mortal part, the ignoble part, but grace en-riches the angelical part, the noble part; gold perishes, but grace per-severes, 1 Peter i. 7. If grace were not permanent, it could not be excellent; if grace were not durable, it could not be pleasurable; if grace were not lasting, yea everlasting, it could not be a Christian's comfort in life, his support in death, and his glorious crown in the great day of account. Grace in itself is permanent, incorruptible; it fadeth not away; it is a birth that shall never die; it is a plant of re-nown that shall never wither, but grow up more and more till grace be

---

[1] Iliad, book viii. line 18, *seq.*—G.

turned into glory : upon which account one of the ancients [Jerome] had rather have St Paul's coat with his heavenly graces, than the purple of kings with their kingdoms. No troubles, no distresses, no dangers can deprive us of our graces, can rob us of our spiritual treasure. But,

[12.] Twelfthly, ' If God be with us, who can be against us ?' I answer, None, so as *to deprive us of our inward peace, rest, and quiet.* Though it thunder, and lighten, and rain, and blow abroad, yet a man may be at peace and rest and quiet at home. A man may have much trouble in the world, and yet rest and quiet in his own spirit : John xiv. 27, ' Peace I leave with you, my peace I give unto you, not as the world giveth give I unto you,' [*as bonum hœreditarium ;*] 'let not your heart be troubled, neither let it be afraid.' No men nor devils, no troubles nor distresses, can deprive a Christian of that inward and blessed peace that Christ hath purchased and paid so dear for. Peace with God, and peace of conscience, are rare jewels, that none can strip us of. The world may wish you peace, but it is only Christ can give you peace, Rom. v. 1, and 2 Cor. i. 12. The world's peace is commonly a dear-bought peace ; but Christ's peace is a cheap peace, a free peace. ' My peace I give unto you.' The world's peace is commonly a sinful peace, but Christ's peace is a holy peace ; the world's peace is a cursed peace, but Christ's peace is a blessed peace ; the world's peace is but an earthly peace, but Christ's peace is a heavenly peace, Rom. xiv. 17 ; Heb. xii. 14, and Ps. xxix. 11. Some Christians thought that others could not come to heaven if they did not eat such meats as they ; but Paul tells them that the kingdom of God consists not in meat or drink, but ' in righteousness, and peace, and joy of the Holy Ghost.' The world's peace is but an imaginary peace, but Christ's peace is a real peace. The world's peace is but a superficial peace, but Christ's peace is a solid and substantial peace. The world's peace is but a transient peace, but Christ's peace is a permanent peace. The world's peace is but a temporary peace, but Christ's peace is an eternal peace. It is a peace that all the world can't give to a Christian, and it is a peace that all the world can't take from a Christian, 1 Thes. v. 3 ; 1 Pet. iii. 11 ; James iii. 21 ; Isa. ix. 6, 7 ; Ps. xxxvii. ; Isa. xxvi. 3, and xxvii. 5. When the tyrant threatened one of the ancients that he would ' take away his house,' he answered, ' Yet thou canst not take away my peace.' ' I will break up thy school ; ' ' yet shall I keep whole my peace.' I will ' confiscate all thy goods ; ' ' yet there is no *premunire* against my peace.' ' I will banish thee thy country : ' ' yet I shall carry my peace with me.' All above a believer is at peace ; the controversy betwixt God and him is ended. Christ takes up the quarrel betwixt God and a believer. ' We have peace with God,' Rom. v. 1. All within a believer is at peace. A peaceable God makes all at peace. When our peace is made in the court of heaven, which is upon the first act of believing, then follows peace in the court of conscience, ' peace which passeth all understanding,' Phil. iv. 7. And all below a believer is at peace with him. He has peace with all the creatures. When we are friends with God, then all the creatures are our friends. ' The stones of the field shall be at league with thee, the beasts of the field shall be at peace with thee,' &c., Job v. 23. The peace that Christ gives is the inheritance of saints only. It was all the legacy which the prince of peace left to his subjects, and this legacy none can take from them. Persecutors may take away my goods, but they cannot take away my peace; they may take away my estate, but they cannot take away my peace; they may take away my liberty, but they cannot take away my peace; they may take away my good name, but they cannot take away my peace; they may take away my relations, but they cannot take away my peace; they may take away my life, but they cannot take away my peace. I grant that the best have no perfection of peace, because they have no perfection of grace. If there were a perfection of grace, then there might be a perfection of peace; but the perfection of both is reserved for another world; and it must be granted that though sometimes a believer may want the sense of peace, the sweet of peace, yet the grounds of his peace are still fixed, certain, and constant; they are 'like mount Zion, that cannot be removed.' Now the grounds of a Christian's peace are these—viz., interest in Christ, reconciliation with God, justification, remission of sin, adoption, the covenant of grace and peace, &c. Now these are always sure and everlasting, though the sense of peace may ebb and flow, rise and fall, in a believer's breast, especially when he is a-combating with strong corruptions, or high temptations, or under sad desertions, or when unbelief has got the throne, or when their hearts are quarrelsome—for commonly a quarrelsome heart is a troublesome heart, or when they have blotted their evidences for heaven, or when they are fallen from their first love, or when they have contracted eminent guilt upon their souls, or when they are declined in their communion with God, &c. Now in these cases, though a believer may lose the sense of peace, yet the grounds of his peace remain firm and sure; and though he may lose the sense of his peace, yet in all these sad and dark conditions his soul is day and night in the pursuit of peace, and he will never leave the chase till he has recovered his peace, knowing that God will first or last speak peace to his soul; yea, though he has lost the sense of peace, yet he has that abiding seed of grace in his soul that will in time recover his peace, Ps. lxxxv. 8. Do your enemies threaten to take away this or that from you, you may throw up your caps at them, and bid them do their worst, for they can never take that peace from you that Christ has given as a legacy to you, 1 John iii. 9. When there are never so great storms within or without, yet then a believer may find peace in the prince of peace, Isa. ix. 6. When his imperfections are many, a perfect Saviour can keep him in perfect peace in the midst of them all, Isa. xxvi. 3, 4. Though his sacrifices are imperfect, yet Christ a perfect priest can speak peace to his soul, Heb. vii. Peace is that never-fading garland which Christ will so set and settle upon the heads of the upright, that none shall be able to take it off. A Christian can never lose his inward peace, either totally or finally. It is true by sin, Satan, and the world, a Christian's peace may be somewhat interrupted, but it can never be finally lost. The greatest storms in this world that beat upon a believer will in time blow over, and the Sun of righteousness, the prince of peace, will shine as gloriously upon him as ever. Under this word שׁלוֹם, *Shalom*, the Jews comprehend all peace, prosperity, and happy success. When the worst of men have done their worst against the people of God, yet the issue shall be peace, prosperity, and happy success. ' My peace I give unto you; ' that is, that ' peace with God and peace with conscience that I have purchased with my blood, I give unto you.' And what power or policy is there that can deprive us of this legacy? surely none. The peace that Christ gives is bottomed upon his blood, upon his righteousness, upon his satisfaction, upon his intercession, and upon a covenant of peace, and therefore it must needs be a lasting peace, an abiding peace. But,

[13.] Thirteenthly, ' If God be with us, who can be against us?' I answer, None, so as to *hinder us from being hid, secured, guarded, and protected by God in an evil day, or in a day of greatest trouble, distress, or danger:* Jer. xxxix. 11, ' Now Nebuchadrezzar king of Babylon gave charge concerning Jeremiah to Nebuzar-adan the captain of the guard, saying,' ver. 12, ' Take him, and look well to him,'—*Heb.*, ' set thine eyes upon him,'—' and do him no harm ; but do unto him even as he shall say unto thee.' Here you shall see the admirable power, wisdom, and goodness of God inclining the heart of this great monarch and conqueror to provide for the prophet's safety and security. He that was a dreadful scourge to punish the wicked, is made by God the deliverer and preserver of the prophet. In the 12th verse you have the king's royal commission to the captain of his guard to be as kind to him, as tender of him, and to carry it as courteously to him even as the prophet himself should desire : ' Look well to him, do him no harm ; but do unto him even as he shall say unto thee.' Let him have all the content, all the satisfaction, and all the accommodation that himself shall require. Jer. xv. 11, ' The Lord said, Verily I will cause the enemy to entreat thee well in the time of evil, and in the time of affliction,'—*Heb.*, ' If I do not cause,' &c. A defective speech in the nature of an oath, as if God had said, ' Let me not be deemed a God of my word, let me not be accounted true, let none reckon me faithful in my promise, if I don't turn his sufferings into his advantage, and save him from danger in the midst of danger.' If in the time of the enemies' invasion I be not ' a wall of fire about him,' Zech. ii. 5, if in the time of public calamity I don't secure him, never trust me for a God more. If he don't find more favour at the hand of his enemies than he hath formerly found among his own people, never own me for a God more. Ver. 20, ' I am with thee to save thee, and to deliver thee, saith the Lord ; ' ver. 21. ' And I will deliver thee out of the hand of the wicked, and I will redeem thee out of the hand of the terrible,' Jer. xl. 1-5, xxvi. 23, 24, and xlv. 4. God engages himself to protect him against all the might and malice of his most terrible enemies; and though he should fall into their hands, yet he would deliver him out of their hands. Ps. xxxiii. 3, ' They have consulted against thy hidden ones.' The saints are (1.) hid in God's decree, (2.) hid in Christ's wounds, (3.) hid in the chambers of divine providence, (4.) hid in common dangers, as Noah was hid in his ark, and as Lot was hid in Zoar, and as Daniel was hid in the lions' den, and as the three children were hid in the fiery furnace, and as Jonah was hid in the whale's belly, Isa. xxvi. 20; (5.) hid 'with Christ in God,' Col. iii. 3.   In times of greatest trouble the saints are hid under the hollow of God's hand, under the shadow of God's wing, Ps. xci. 1, 4.   Ps. xxvii. 5, 'For in the time of trouble he shall hide me in his pavilion.'   The Hebrew *Succoh* is written with a little *samech*, to shew, say some, that a little pavilion or cottage where God is shall be sufficient to safeguard the saints in the day of adversity. 'He shall hide me in his hut, as a shepherd doth his sheep in a stormy day.'   'In the secret of his tabernacle shall he hide me.'   I shall be as safe as if I were shut up in his holy ark, tabernacle, or temple,— whither they use to flee for shelter to the horns of the altar, yea, as if a man were hid in the most holy place, where none might enter but only the high-priest once a year, which is therefore called 'God's secret place.'   A shepherd should not be more careful to shelter his sheep in a tent or tabernacle from the heat of the sun, nor a king should not be more ready to protect a favourite in his pavilion, whence none durst venture to take him, than God would be careful and ready to shroud and shelter his people from the rage, madness, and malice of their enemies, Ezek. vii. 22.   How did God hide his church in Egypt? the bush was still burning, and yet was not consumed, Exod. iii. 2, 3; and how did he hide seven thousand in Elijah's time, that had not bowed their knees to Baal? 1 Kings xix. 18.   Though 'the woman,' the church, 'be driven to flee into the wilderness, yet there she is hid, and there she had a place prepared of God, that they should feed her there a thousand two hundred and threescore days,' Rev. xii. 6.   Let our enemies do their worst, they shall not hinder us of divine protection.   No power nor policy can hinder our being pre- served and secured by God in the greatest troubles, deepest distresses, and most deadly dangers that can attend us.   But,

[14.] Fourteenthly, 'If God be with us, who can be against us?' I answer, None, so as *to deprive us of our union with Christ, as to dissolve that blessed union that is between Christ and our souls,* John xv. 1–5.   When men and devils have done their worst, our marriage- union with Christ holds good.   This union is indissoluble.   This union between Christ and believers is not capable of any separation. They are so one, that all the violence of the world, nor all the power of darkness, can never be able to make them two again.   Hence the apostle's triumphant challenge, 'Who shall separate us from the love of Christ?' Rom. viii. 35.   If the question did not imply a strong negation, the apostle himself doth give us a negation in words at length, 'Neither death, nor life, nor angels, nor powers, nor things present, nor things to come, nor height, nor depth, nor any other creature, shall be able to separate us,' &c., ver. 38, 39.   Here you have a long catalogue, consisting of a large induction of various par- ticulars; but none of all these can dissolve the union between Christ and believers.   None can untie that knot that is tied by the Spirit on Christ's part, and by faith on ours.   Christ and believers are so firmly joined together, that all the powers on earth, and all the united strength of hell, shall never be able to put them asunder, or to separate them one from another.   Look, as no distance of place can hinder this union, so no force or violence from devils or men shall ever be able to dissolve this union; and herein lies the peculiar transcendent blessedness of this union above all other unions. They all may cease, be broken, and come to nothing; every one of them is soluble: the head may be separated from the members, and the members from the head; the husband must be separated from the wife, and the wife from the husband; the parents must be separated from the children, and the children from the parents, and bosom friends must be separated one from another. The foundation and the house may be separated, and the branches may be cut off from the vine—yea, the soul and body may be disunited by death, but the mystical union stands fast for ever. Christ and a gracious soul can never be separated; God hath joined them together, and no mortal shall ever be able to put them asunder, Mat. xix. 6. There is not only a continuation of it all our life, but also in death itself. Our very bodies sleeping in the dust are even then in union with Christ. There are two abiding things in the saints, their unction and their union. Their unction abides, 'But the anointing which ye have received of him abideth in you,' 1 John ii. 27; and their union abides, for it follows, 'and ye shall abide in him.' Christ earnestly prays that we might be one, as he and his Father are one, John xvii. 20-23; not essentially, nor personally, but spiritually, so as no other creature is united to Christ. There can be no divorce between Christ and the believing soul. Christ hates putting away, Mal. ii. 16. Sin may for a time seemingly separate between Christ and the believer, but it can never finally separate between Christ and the believer. Look, as it is impossible for the leaven that is in the dough to be separated from the dough after it is once mixed, for it turneth the nature of the dough into itself; so it is impossible for the saints ever to be separated from Christ: for Christ is in the saints as nearly and as really as the leaven is in the dough. Christ and believers are so incorporated as if Christ and they were one lump, Rom. viii. 10; Col. i. 27; 1 John iii. 21; John xvii. 23. Our nature is now joined to God by the indissoluble tie of the hypostatical union in the second person; and we in our persons are joined to God by the mystical indissoluble bond of the Spirit, the third person. Our union with the Lord Jesus is so near, so close, and so glorious, that it makes us one spirit with him. In this blessed union the saints are not only joined to the graces and benefits which flow from Christ, but to the person of Christ, to Christ himself, 1 Cor. vi. 17. All the powers on earth, and all the powers in hell, can never separate Christ from the believer, nor the believer from Christ. When all other unions are dissolved, this union holds good, John i. 16; Rom. viii. 32; 1 Cor. iii. 21-23.

I readily grant that the sense and apprehension of this union may in this life be much interrupted, and many times greatly darkened, but the substance of the union still remains. And I readily grant that a believer may be much assaulted and tempted to doubt of his union with Christ, and to question his union with Christ, and yet nevertheless a believer's union with Christ continues and abides for ever. And I readily grant that the influences of it for some time may be suspended, but yet the union itself is not—nay, cannot be dissolved. As it was in the hypostatical union; for a time there was a suspending of the comforting influences of the divine nature in the human, insomuch that our Saviour cried out, ' My God, my God, why hast thou forsaken me?' Mat. xxvii. 46; yet for all this the union between the two natures was not in the least abolished. So here in the mystical union the sensible effects, comforts, and benefits of our union with Christ may sometimes be kept in and not appear, but yet the union itself abides, and' shall abide firm and inviolable for ever; it is an inseparable and insuperable union. Look, as no power on earth is sufficient to overpower the Spirit of Christ, which on Christ's part makes the union, so no power on earth shall be able to conquer faith, which on our part also makes the union, John x. 27-31; 1 John iv. 4; 1 Pet. i. 5; Luke xxii. 31, 32. Satan and the world may make attempts upon this union, but they will never be able to break this union, to dissolve this union; yea, though death be the bane of all natural unions, yet death can never be the bane of this mystical union. Though death puts a period to all other unions, yet death can never put a period to this union. When the believer is in his grave his union with Christ holds good. But,

[15.] Fifteenthly, ' If God be with us, who can be against us?' I answer, None, so as *to deprive us of our crowns.* There is no power nor policy on earth or in hell that can deprive a Christian,

First, Of his crown of righteousness: 2 Tim. iv. 8, ' Henceforth there is laid up for me a crown of righteousness, which the Lord, the righteous judge, shall give me at that day; and not to me only, but unto all them also that love his appearing.' It is a metaphor, say several, [Estius, Scultetus, &c.,] from the custom in war, who used to crown the conquerors with honour, &c. It is a similitude taken from fighters or combatants, who for a prize received a crown when they had contended lawfully. The reward of eternal life here is called ' a crown of righteousness,' (1.) Because it is purchased for us by the righteousness of Christ. By his perfect and complete righteousness and obedience, dear Jesus hath merited this for us, and so in Christ it is due to us by way of merit, though in respect of us it is of mere grace, of rich grace, of sovereign grace, of infinite grace, of glorious grace. (2.) Because he is righteous that hath promised this crown. Though every promise that God makes is of free and rich grace, yet when once they are made, the truth and justice of God obligeth him to keep touch with his people; for as he cannot deny himself, so he cannot do anything unworthy of himself, Rev. ii. 10, and iii. 21; 1 John ii. 25; 2 Thes. i. 5-7, 10. Men say and unsay, they promise one thing and mean another. Men many times eat their words as soon as they have spoken them; but thus God can never, thus God will never, do. God can never repent of his promises; he can never waver, he can never go back from his word: ' God is not a man, that he should lie; neither the son of man, that he should repent: hath he said, and shall he not do it? or hath he spoken, and shall he not make it good?' Num. xxiii. 19. All the promises that refer to this life and a better are sure, firm, faithful, unchangeable, immutable. All the promises are the word of a God, and given upon the honour of a God, that they shall be made good. O my friends, the all-sufficiency of God, the omniscience of God, the omnipotency of God, the loving-kindness and faithfulness of

God, yea, and the oath of God, may fully, yea, abundantly, satisfy us, and secure us, that God will certainly make good all his precious promises to us.[1] We commonly say, when an honest man passeth his word for a little money, Oh, it is as sure as if it were in our purse; but God's word of promise is abundantly more sure, for as his nature is eternal, so his word of promise is unchangeable. The promises are a firm foundation to build our hopes and happiness upon; they are an anchor both sure and steadfast, Hab. ii. 3; Jer. xxxii. 41; Ps. lxxxix. 34. Memorable is that saying of David, Ps. cxxxviii. 2, 'For thou hast magnified thy word above all thy name;' which words are to be understood, as David Kimchi saith, *hysteron proteron*, that thou hast by thy word, that is, by performing thy word and promises, magnified thy name above all things. (3.) Because it is a just and righteous thing with God to crown them with glory at last, who have been crowned with shame, reproach, and dishonour for his name and interest in this world; so that eternal life is a crown of righteousness, *ex parte Dei*, God hath promised it to such as overcome; and, *ex parte rei*, it is just with God to give unto his suffering servants rest and peace. (4.) Because it is given only to righteous men. All that wear this crown come to it in a way of righteousness. A righteous crown cannot be had but in the use of righteous means. The Chaldean, the Persian, the Grecian, and the Roman princes commonly gained their crowns by fraud, flattery, policy, blood, &c.; so that their crowns were bloody crowns, and not righteous crowns. (5.) And lastly, the apostle calls it 'a crown of righteousness, which the righteous judge shall give him,' the more fitly to follow the metaphor taken from runners and wrestlers for prizes at their solemn exercises or games in Greece, in which there were certain judges appointed to observe those that proved masters, and gave just sentence on the conqueror's side, if he strove lawfully, and fairly won the prize. Now this crown is 'laid up;' the Greek word ἀπόκειται imports two things: (1.) A designation of that which is laid up to some peculiar person; (2.) A reservation and safe keeping of it, to the use of those it is designed to. Earthly crowns have been often pulled off from princes' heads, but this crown of righteousness is so safely laid up, that none can reach it, none can touch it, none can pull it from a believer's head. Xerxes crowned his steersman in the morning, and beheaded him in the evening of the same day. And Andronicus the Greek emperor crowned his admiral in the morning, and then took off his head in the afternoon. Roffensis had a cardinal's hat sent him, but his head was cut off before it came to him. 'Doth the crown,' saith Solomon, 'endure to every generation?' Prov. xxvii. 24. It is a question which implieth a strong negation: oh, no! there is nothing more uncertain than earthly crowns. Henry the Sixth was honoured with the crowns of two kingdoms, France and England; the first was lost by the faction of his nobles, the other was twice pulled from his head. Princes' crowns are withering things. Earthly crowns may be soon put on, and as soon be pulled off. Most princes' crowns do but hang on one side of their heads. All the powers on earth, and all the devils in hell, can never reach this crown of righteousness.

---

[1] Promissa hæc tua sunt, Domine, saith Austin, et quis falli timet, cum promittit ipsa veritas?

Though wicked men have long reaches, yet they can never reach a believer's crown, which is his joy and comfort in the midst of all his sorrows and sufferings. Thus Basil speaketh of some martyrs that were cast out all night naked in a bitter cold frosty season, and were to be burned the next day, how they comforted themselves in this manner: ' The winter is sharp, but paradise is sweet; here we shiver for cold, but the bosom of Abraham will make amends for all.' [1] The philosopher could say to the tyrant's face: You may kill me, but you cannot hurt me; you may take away my head, but you cannot take away my crown. O Christians! let this be your joy and triumph, that the crown of righteousness is laid up safe for you; no tyrant's arm is long enough to reach that crown. But,

Secondly, There is no power nor policy on earth or in hell that can deprive a Christian of his *crown of life:* James i. 12, ' Blessed is the man that endureth temptation, for when he is tried he shall receive the crown of life, which the Lord hath promised to them that love him.' ' The crown of life,' that is eternal life, whereby after the fight and conquest he shall be glorified as with a crown; as there was a crown to him that overcame in their exercises among the Grecians, [Piscator.] Blessedness is the general reward, the crown of life is the particular reward. In these words, as Chrysostom observes, there is a great emphasis, they are both emphatical; for life is the best of all natural things, and a crown is the best of all civil things. Here is the best and the best. Words are too weak to express what a rare blessing a crown of life is. The crown of life is in the other world, saith Gregory. This life is the life of conflict; that, of crowns and wreaths. But you will say, What doth this crown of life signify? I answer,

(1.) First, The crown of life signifies *solid and substantial honour and glory;* as a crown is a solid and substantial thing. Heaven admits of no honour and glory but what is solid and substantial. The crown of life is a massy crown, a ponderous crown, to shew that the glory above is a massy glory, substantial glory. That you may see it is massy and substantial, observe what a word the apostle useth: ' The weight of glory,' ' the exceeding eternal weight of glory,' 2 Cor. iv. 17. Such a weight as infinitely over-poiseth all afflictions. The apostle alludeth to the Hebrew and Chaldee words which signify both weight and glory.[2] The Arabic version renders it, ' Worketh for us a weight of glory in the most eminent and largest degree and measure.' [3] The Syriac reads it, ' *Infinitam gloriam,*' An infinite glory. Haymo reads it, ' *Magnitudinem gloriæ supra omnem modum et mensuram,*' A greatness of glory, beyond all bounds and measure. Beza reads it, '*Excellenter excellens,*' Exceedingly excellent. Yet none of these reach the height of the apostle's rhetoric, neither is any translation able to express it. Glory is so great a weight that if the saints were not upheld by the infinite power and strength of God, it were impossible they should be able to bear it. To gold and precious things the weight addeth to the value; as the more massy and weighty a crown is, the more it is worth. The glory of heaven is not only eternal glory, but it

[1] Basil, ad 40, Martyr, &c.
[2] יקר, כבוד
[3] Modo eminentissimo et largissimo.

is a weight of glory; yea, such a weight as exceeds all expressions, all comparisons. The honour and glory of this world is but like the cracking of thorns under a pot; it is but like a blaze, a shadow, a dream, a vapour; it is but like a fading flower, or the picture of a prince drawn upon the ice, with his purple robes and his glorious crown, &c., which melts away as soon as the sun riseth; the consideration of which made one prince say of his crown: 'O crown! more noble than happy!' A crown is the choicest and chiefest of all human rewards. Amongst all terrene gifts none more honourable and glorious than a crown. This is the height of human excellencies, and for the attainment of which many have made most sad, desperate, and dangerous adventures; but, alas! what are all earthly crowns, for honour and dignity, to the crown of life? No more than shadows to substances, pebbles to pearls, or dross to gold. But,

(2.) Secondly, The crown of life signifies *the greatest honour and glory.* There is nothing higher in the estimation and in the admiration of men than a crown; it is the highest appendant of majesty. A crown is the emblem of majesty, and so it notes that imperial and kingly dignity to which believers are advanced by Christ, Ps. viii. 7. There is nothing that men esteem of above a crown, or admire than a crown, or are ambitious of than a crown, Eph. i. 3. The crown is the top of royalty. All earthly crowns have crosses hanging upon them; all earthly crowns are stuffed with thorns: which made a great prince [Xerxes] say, ' You look upon my crown and my purple robes, but did you but know how they are lined with thorns, you would not stoop to take them up.' Queen Elizabeth is said to swim to her crown through a sea of sorrow: and so many of the princes of this world have swam to their crowns through a sea of sin, a sea of trouble, a sea of sorrow, and a sea of blood. The crown of life is an honourable crown, and that is the reason why the heavenly glory is expressed by a crown, Rev. iii. 21. The saints are heirs, not only of Christ's cross, but also of his crown; that is, of his honour and glory. The honour and glory of all earthly crowns are greatly darkened and obscured by the cares and troubles, the temptations and dangers that are inseparably annexed to them; but no cares, no troubles, attend the crown of life, the crown of glory. Eternal life is a coronation day. But,

(3.) Thirdly, The crown of life signifies *the reward of victory.* A crown is the honour of those that strive; crowns were always the rewards of conquerors: Rev. ii. 10, ' Be thou faithful to the death, and I will give thee a crown of life.' A crown without cares, corrivals, envy, end; a crown not of gold, silver, pearls, laurels, or such like fading, perishing, corruptible things, but a crown of life, an ever-living crown, an everlasting crown, a never-fading crown. It is an allusion to a custom that was amongst the Grecians, for such as got the mastery in their games of wrestling, or running, or the like, were crowned with a garland in token of victory. It is not he that fights, but he that conquers, that carries the crown.[1] The crown of life is for that man, and that man is for the crown of life, who holds on conquering and to conquer, as Christ his head has done before him. The hea-

---

[1] Dr Rainolds against Hart, page 482.

thens in their Olympics had their cups, and garments, and crowns that were the rewards of the conquerors; yea, if a horse did but run a race and won, he had a cup or a crown; and thereupon Theocritus saith, ' See what poor things the world glories in, that brute beasts are taken with; their conquerors are crowned, and so are their horses'.[1] But what were all their cups, garments, and crowns of ivy and laurel, &c., to this crown of life that is promised to the overcoming Christian? You must first be conquering Christians before you shall be crowned Christians. Why do you require that in one place, saith one of the ancients, [Ambrose,] which is due in another? why would you preposterously have the crown before you overcome? Whilst we are in our warring state fighting against the world, the flesh and the devil, a crown does not become us. I have read how that upon a triumph all the Emperor Severus his soldiers, for the greater pomp, were to put on crowns of bays, but there was one Christian among them that wore it on his arm, and being asked the reason of it he boldly answered, *Non decet Christianum in hac vita coronari*, It becomes not a Christian to wear his crown in this life. That crown that is made out of the tree of life is a wreath of laurel that never withers, a crown that never fades, a crown that will sit fast on no head but the conqueror's. But,

(4.) Fourthly, The crown of life signifies *a lasting crown, a living crown*. To say the crown of life, is to say a living crown; and living crowns are only to be found in heaven, Prov. xxvii. 24; Ezek. xxi. 25–27. The word crown notes the perpetuity of glory. A crown is round, and hath neither beginning nor ending; and therefore the glory of the saints in heaven is called an immortal, an immarcessible,[2] incorruptible, and never-fading crown, 2 Pet. i. 4; 1 Cor. ix. 24. The crown of life signifies the lasting honour and glory of the saints in heaven. I have read of an emperor that had three crowns, one on his sword, another on his head, and then cries out, *Tertiam in cœlis*, ' The third is in heaven, and my hope,' saith he, ' shall be in the everlasting crown.'[3] The life to come is only the true life, the happy life, the safe life, the honourable life, the lasting, yea, the everlasting life, and therefore the crown is reserved for that life. King William the Conqueror was crowned three times every year all his reign, at three several places—viz., Gloucester, Winchester, and Westminster—but death hath long since put a period to his crown. The crowns of the greatest monarchs in the world, though they last long, yet are corruptible, subject to wearing, cracking, stealing : they will be taken from them, or they from their crowns, suddenly. Witness that pile of crowns, as the historian speaks, [Hakewill,] that was piled up, as it were, at Alexander's gates, when he sat down and wept because there were no more worlds to conquer. All scripture and histories do abundantly tell us that there is nothing more fading than princes' crowns. But,

(5.) Fifthly, The crown of life notes *a well-entitled crown ;* a crown that comes by a true and noble title. A Christian has the best title imaginable to the crown of life. (1.) He has a title by Christ's blood ;

---

[1] Idyll. xvi, line 46, *seq.*—G.   [2] ' Unfading.'—G.
[3] See my ' String of Pearls.' [Vol. i. p. 398, *seq.*—G.]

(2.) By the new birth ; (3.) By free and precious promises ; (4.) By donation ; (5.) By marriage union and communion with Christ, who is heir-apparent to all the glory of heaven ; (6.) By a sure and ever-lasting covenant.[1] King Henry the Seventh of England pretended a sixfold title to the crown ; (1.) By conquest ; (2.) By the election of the soldiers in the field ; (3.) By parliament ; (4.) By birth ; (5) By donation ; (6.) By marriage. But what was his pretended title to that real and full title that a believer has to the crown of life? But,

(6.) Sixthly, and lastly, The crown of life notes *the perfection of the glory of the saints in heaven.* As the crown compasseth the head on every side, so in heaven there is an aggregation of all internal and eternal good. One of the ancients,[2] speaking concerning what we can say of the glory of heaven, saith, ' It is but a little drop of the sea, and a little spark of the great furnace ; for those good things of eternal life are so many that they exceed number, so great that they exceed measure, so precious that they are above all estimation.' *Nec Christus nec cœlum patitur hyperbolem,* Neither Christ nor heaven can be hyperbolised. *Nescio quid erit, quod ista vita non erit.* And, saith one of the fathers, ' What will that life be, or rather, what will not that life be, since all good either is not at all, or is in such a life ? Light which place cannot comprehend, voices and music which time cannot ravish away, odours which are never dissipated, a feast which is never consumed, a blessing which eternity bestoweth, but eternity shall never see at an end !' Do you ask me what heaven is? saith one: when I meet you there I will tell you. The world to come, say the Rabbins, is the world where all is well. I have read of one that would willingly swim through a sea of brimstone to get to heaven ; for there, and only there, is perfection of happiness. What are the silks of Persia, the spices of Egypt, the gold of Ophir, and the treasures of both Indies, to the glory of another world ? Augustine tells us that one day, when he was about to write something upon the eighth verse of the thirty-sixth Psalm, ' Thou shalt make them drink of the rivers of thy pleasures ;' and being almost swallowed up with the contemplation of heavenly joys, one called unto him very loud by his name ; and, inquiring who it was, he answered, I am Jerome, with whom in my lifetime thou hadst so much conference concerning doubts in Scripture, and am now best experienced to resolve thee of any doubts concerning the joys of heaven ; but only let me first ask thee this question, Art thou able to put the whole earth, and all the waters of the sea, into a little pot ? Canst thou measure the waters in thy fist, and mete out heaven with thy span ? or weigh the mountains in scales, and the hills in a balance ? If not, no more is it possible that thy understanding should comprehend the least of the joys of heaven ; and certainly the least of the joys of heaven are unconceivable and inexpressible. But,

Thirdly, There is no power nor policy on earth or in hell, that can deprive a believer of *an incorruptible crown :* Ps. xxi. 3 ; 1 Cor. ix. 25, ' And every man that striveth for the mastery is temperate in all things ; now they do it to obtain a corruptible crown, but we an in-

[1] Eph. i. 7 ; 1 Pet. i. 3, 4 ; 2 Pet. i. 4 ; Luke xii. 32 ; 2 Cor. xi. 2 ; Heb. i. 2 ; 2 Sam. xxiii. 5 Jer. xxxii. 40, 41. [2] August. de Triplic. Habitu, c. 4.

corruptible.' He alludes to the Olympic exercises ; now running and wrestling were two of the Olympic games. Now in these Olympic games the reward was only a corruptible crown, a crown made up of laurels, or olive-branches, or oaken-leaves, or of flowers and herbs, or at the highest of silver and gold, which soon faded ; but we run for an incorruptible crown of glory. A man, saith Chrysostom, would dwell in this contemplation of heaven, and be loath to come out of it. Nay, saith Augustine, a man might age himself in it, and sooner grow old than weary : 1 Pet. i. 4, ' To an inheritance incorruptible and undefiled, that fadeth not away, reserved in heaven for you.' Here are superexcellent properties of the heavenly inheritance.

(1.) First, It is κληρονομίαν ἄφθαρτον, an 'incorruptible inheritance.'[1] All earthly inheritances are liable to corruption ; they are true gardens of Adonis, where we can gather nothing but trivial flowers, surrounded with many briars, thorns, and thistles. Oh, the hands, the hearts, the thoughts, the lives that have been corrupted by earthly inheritances ! Oh, the impure love, the carnal confidence, the vain boastings, the sensual joys, that have been the products of earthly inheritances. If a man's estates lies in money, that may rust, or the thieves may break through and steal it ; if in cattle, they may die, or fall into the hands of the Sabeans and Chaldeans ; if in houses, they may be burnt. Witness the late dreadful fire that turned London into a ruinous heap. If in lands, a foreign enemy may invade them and conquer them.[2] All earthly inheritances are no better than the cities which Solomon gave to Hiram, which he called *Cabul*, that is to say, displeasing or dirty, 1 Kings ix. 13. Earthly inheritances they do but dirt, daub, and dust the children of men ; it is only the heavenly inheritance that is incorruptible.

(2.) Secondly, It is κληρονομία ἀμίαντος, an 'inheritance undefiled.' There are few earthly inheritances, but some defilement or other sticks close to them. Many times they are got by fraud, oppression, violence, injustice, &c., and as they are often wickedly got, so they are as often wickedly kept. They that will but go to Westminster Hall may every term understand enough of these things. The heavenly inheritance is the only undefiled inheritance. There is no sin, no sinner, no devil, to defile or pollute the heavenly inheritance, the incorruptible crown. The Greek word, ἀμίαντος, signifies a precious stone, which though it be never so much soiled, yet it cannot be blemished nor defiled, yea the oftener you cast it into the fire and take it out, the more clear, bright, and shining it is. The apostle may probably allude to this stone : and it is as if he should say, ' The incorruptible crown that you shall receive shall be studded with the stone *amiantos*, which cannot be defiled. No unclean thing shall enter into heaven to defile this crown, this inheritance, Rev. xxi. 27. The serpent got into the earthly paradise, and defiled Adam's crown, yea he robbed him of his crown, but the subtle serpent can never enter into the heavenly paradise. But,

(3.) Thirdly, It is κληρονομίαν ἀμάραντον, an 'inheritance that

---

[1] An incorruptible inheritance. Gen. iii. 18 ; Isa. xxiii. 9.
[2] James v. 2-5 ; Mat. vi. 19, 20 ; Job i. 14, 15, 17. See my ' London's Lamentation.'
[Vol. vi.—G.]

fadeth not away:' a metaphor taken from flowers. The beauty of flowers, and the sweetness of flowers, withers in a moment, and is quickly gone, and then they are good for nothing but to be cast upon the dunghill; so it is with all earthly inheritances, they soon lose their glory and fragrancy. Where is the glory of the Chaldean, Persian, Grecian, and Roman kingdoms? Dan. vii. 3-8. *Sic transit gloria mundi* hath been long since written upon them all; yea, all the glory of the world is like the flower of the field that soon fadeth away, Isa. xl. 6; 1 Pet. i. 24. How many great men and great kingdoms have for a time shined in great glory, even like so many suns in the firmament, but are now vanished away like so many blazing comets! How hath the moon of great men's honours been eclipsed at the full, and the sun of their pomp gone down at noon! How soon is the courtier's glory eclipsed if his prince do but frown upon him! and how soon does the prince become a peasant if God does but frown upon him! The Greek word *amarantos*, say some, is the proper name of a flower which is still fresh and green after it hath hung up in the house a long time. It is as if the apostle had said, 'Your incorruptible crown shall be garnished or adorned with the precious flower *amarantos*, which is always fresh and green and flourishing. And indeed this is the excellency of the heavenly inheritance, that it fadeth not away, that it is a flower that never withereth. All the glory of that upper world is like God himself, lasting, yea, everlasting. This never-fading crown is like the flower we call *Semper vivens*, it keeps always fresh and splendent. The glory of believers shall never fade nor wither, it shall never grow old nor rusty. Thrice happy are those souls that have a share in this incorruptible crown. When Alexander heard the philosopher's discourse of another world in which he had no part, he wept, to speak with the apostle, as 'one without hope,' 1 Thes. iv. 13. None on earth have such cause to weep, as those that have no interest in that inheritance that fadeth not away. But,

(4.) Fourthly and lastly, There is no power nor policy on earth or in hell that can deprive a sincere Christian of *a crown of glory*. 1 Pet. v. 4, 'And when the chief shepherd shall appear, ye shall receive a crown of glory which fadeth not away,'—as the garlands did wherewith the conquerors at games, races, and combats were crowned, which were made of herbs, leaves, and flowers. A crown imports perpetuity, plenty, dignity. It is the height of human ambition. The Greek word *amarantinon* cometh from *amarantus*, which is a flower that fadeth not, of which garlands were made in former times, and wherewith they crowned the images of the heathen gods. A believer's crown, his inheritance, his glory, his happiness, his blessedness shall be as fresh and flourishing after he hath been many millions of years in heaven as it was at his first entrance into it. Earthly crowns are like tennis-balls, which are bandied up and down from one to another, and in time wear out. When time shall be no more, when earthly crowns and kingdoms shall be no more, yea, when the world shall be no more, a Christian's crown of glory shall be fresh, flourishing, and continuing. All the devils in hell shall never wrangle a believer out of his heavenly inheritance, nor deprive him of his crown of glory. The least thing in heaven is better than the greatest

things in this world.   All things on earth are fading, but the crown
of glory never fadeth away.   Thus you see why heaven and the glory
above is expressed by a crown.   Sometimes it is called a crown of
righteousness, to note the grounds and rise of it; sometimes it is
called a crown of life, because it is only to be enjoyed in everlasting
life; sometimes it is called an incorruptible crown, to note the duration and continuance of it; and sometimes it is called a crown of
glory, to note the honour, splendour, and eternity of it.   Now let
devils, let oppressors, let persecutors do their worst, they shall never
be able to deprive the saints of their blessed and glorious crowns.
But,

[16.] Sixteenthly, 'If God be with us, who can be against us?' I
answer, None, so as to *make void our covenant-relation, or our covenant-interest;* as you may see by comparing the scriptures in the
margin together.[1]   The covenant of grace is bottomed upon God's free
love, upon God's everlasting love, upon God's special and peculiar love,
upon God's unchangeable love, so that God can as soon cease to be, as
he can cease to love those whom he has taken into covenant with himself, or cease to keep covenant with them.   Those whom free grace
hath brought into covenant shall continue in covenant for ever and
ever.   Once in covenant and for ever in covenant.   The covenant of
grace is bottomed upon God's immutable counsel and purpose.   'The
foundation of God standeth sure,' Heb. vi. 17; 2 Tim. ii. 19, that is,
the degree and purpose of God's election stands firm and sure.   Now
the purpose of God's election is compared to a foundation, because it is
that upon which all our happiness and blessedness is built and bottomed,
and because as a foundation it abides firm and sure, John x. 28–32; 1
Pet. i. 5; Jude i.   The covenant of grace is bottomed upon God's glorious power, upon God's infinite power, upon God's supreme power, upon
God's invincible power, upon God's independent power, upon God's
incomparable power, and till you can find a power that can overmatch
this divine power, the saints' covenant-relation holds good.   The covenant
of grace is bottomed upon the oath of God; 'To perform the mercy
promised to our fathers, and to remember his holy covenant, the oath
which he sware to our fathers,' Luke i. 72, 73.   Now to think that
God will break his oath, or be perjured, is an intolerable blasphemy.
The covenant of grace is bottomed upon the precious blood of Christ.
The blood of Christ is called 'The blood of the everlasting covenant.'
'Now the God of peace, that brought again from the dead our Lord
Jesus, that great Shepherd of the sheep, through the blood of the everlasting covenant,' Mat. xxvi. 28; Heb. ix. 15, and xiii. 20.   Now by
these hints it is most evident that the saints' covenant-relation, their
covenant-interest, holds good at all times, in all cases, and in all conditions.   It is not the indwelling power of sin, nor spiritual desertions,
nor violent temptations, nor heavy afflictions, nor divine delays, that
can dissolve our covenant-relation.   Though sin may work, and Satan
may tempt, and fears may be high, and God may hide his face from
his people, and stop his ears at the prayers of his people, Isa. viii. 17;
Lam. iii. 44, yet God will still maintain his interest in his people, and
his people's relation to himself.   'God hath not cast away his people,

[1] Ps. lxxxix. 30, 35; Jer. xxxi. 31, and xxxii. 38–41; Isa. liv. 10; Heb. viii. 8, 10.

whom he foreknew,' Rom. xi. 2 ; ' I am the Lord, I change not,' Mal. iii. 6 ; ' I will betroth thee unto me for ever,' Hosea ii. 19 ; ' I will never leave thee, nor forsake thee,' Heb. xiii. 5.   It is not all the powers of hell, nor all the powers on earth, that can make null or void our covenant-relation, our covenant-interest.   But,

(17.) Seventeenthly and lastly, ' If God be with us, who can be against us ?' I answer, None, so as to *hinder our growth in grace, or the thriving and flourishing estate of our precious and immortal souls.* The troubles, afflictions, persecutions, and sufferings that the saints meet with in a way of holiness shall but further the increase and growth of their graces.   Grace never rises to so great a height as it does in times of persecution.   Suffering times are a Christian's harvest times, Ps. lx. 7–9, 12.   Let me instance in that grace of zeal : I remember Moulin, speaking of the French Protestants, saith, When papists hurt us, and persecute us for reading the Scripture, we burn with zeal to be reading of them, but now persecution is over, our Bibles are like old almanacks.   Michal's scoffing at David did but inflame and raise his zeal ; ' If this be to be vile, I will be more vile,' 2 Sam. vi. 20–22.   Look, as fire in the winter burns the hotter, by an *antiperistasis,* because of the coldness of the air, so in the winter of persecution, that divine fire, the zeal of a Christian, burns so much the hotter, and flames forth so much the more vehemently and strongly. When one desired to know what kind of man Basil was, there was presented to him in a dream, saith the historian, a pillar of fire, with this motto, *Talis est Basilius,* Basil is such a one, he is all on a-light-fire for God.   Warm persecutions will but set Christians all on a-light-fire for God, as you may see among the apostles, primitive Christians, and the martyrs of a later date.   Grace usually is in the greatest flourish when the saints are under the greatest trials.   The snuffing of the candle makes it burn the brighter.   God suffers wicked men to beat and bruise his links, to make them burn the brighter ; and to pound and bruise his spices to make them send forth the greater aromatical flavour.   Fiery trials are like the teazle, which though it be sharp and scratching, it is to make the cloth more pure and fine.   Stars shine brightest in the darkest nights, and so do the graces of the saints shine brightest in the darkest nights of affliction and tribulation.   God does sometimes more carry on the growth of grace by a cross than by an ordinance ; yea, the Lord will first or last turn all fiery trials into ordinances, for the helping on the growth of grace in his people's souls.   Commonly the saints' spiritual growth in grace is carried on by such divine methods, and in such ways as might seem to deaden grace, and weaken it, rather than any ways to augment and increase it.   We know that winter is as necessary to bring on harvest as the spring, and so fiery trials are as necessary to bring on the harvest of grace as the spring of mercy is.   Though fiery trials are grievous, yet they shall make the saints more gracious. God usually, by smart sufferings, turns his people's sparks of grace into a mighty flame, their mites into millions, their drops into seas. All the devils in hell, and all the sinners on earth, cannot hinder the Lord from carrying on the growth of grace in his people's souls. When men and devils have done their worst, God will, by all sorts of ordinances, and by all sorts of providences, and all sorts of changes, make his people more and more holy, and more and more humble, and more and more meek and lowly, and more and more heavenly, wise, faithful, fruitful, sincere, courageous, &c. Though the church of Smyrna was outwardly poor, yet she was inwardly rich, rich in grace, and rich towards God, Rev. ii. 9. I think he hit the mark who said, It is far better to be a poor man and a rich Christian, than to be a rich man and a poor Christian. Though the Corinthians were under great trials and sufferings, yet they did abound in everything, in faith, and utterance, and knowledge, and diligence, and in their love to gospel ministers, 2 Cor. viii. 7. The storm beat hard upon the Romans, and yet you see what a singular testimony the apostle gives of them, 'I myself also am persuaded of you, my brethren, that ye also are full of goodness, filled with all knowledge, able to admonish one another,' Rom. xv. 14. The Thessalonians were under great persecutions and troubles, and yet were strong in the grace that was in Christ Jesus; they were very growing and flourishing Christians. Singular prophecies speak out the saints' growth and flourishing in grace. 'The Lord is exalted; for he dwelleth on high: he hath filled Zion with judgment and righteousness.' 'The Spirit shall be poured upon us from on high, and the wilderness shall be a fruitful field.' [1] 'The desert shall rejoice, and blossom as the rose: it shall blossom abundantly:' 'the glory of Lebanon shall be given unto it, the excellency of Carmel and Sharon;' 'they shall see the glory of the Lord, and the excellency of our God.' And as singular prophecies, so choice and precious promises, speak out the saints' growth in grace. Take a taste of some of them. 'But the path of the just is as the shining light, that shineth more and more unto the perfect day.' 'The righteous shall hold on his way; and he that hath clean hands shall be stronger and stronger.' 'They shall go from strength to strength; every one of them in Zion appeareth before God.' 'The righteous shall flourish like the palm-tree; he shall grow like a cedar in Lebanon.' 'Those that be planted in the house of the Lord shall flourish in the courts of our God; in old age they shall be fat and flourishing,' Prov. iv. 18; Job xvii. 9; Ps. lxxxiv. 7, and xcii. 12–14. I have read of an old man who, being asked whether he grew in grace? answered, I believe I do, for God hath promised that in old age his children should be fat and flourishing. So Isa. xlvi. 3, 'Hearken unto me, O house of Jacob, and all the remnant of the house of Israel, which are borne by me from the belly, which are carried from the womb:' ver. 4, 'And even to your old age I am he; and even to hoar hairs will I carry you: I have made, and I will bear; even I will carry, and will deliver you:' Zech. xii. 8, 'And he that is feeble among them at that day shall be as David; and the house of David shall be as God, as the angel of the Lord before them:' Hosea xiv. 5, 'I will be as the dew unto Israel: he shall grow as the lily, and cast forth his roots as Lebanon:' ver. 6, 'His branches shall spread, and his beauty shall be as the olive-tree, and his smell as Lebanon:' ver. 7, 'They that dwell under his shadow shall return; they shall revive as the corn, and grow as the vine: the scent thereof shall be as

[1] 2 Thes. i. 3, 8; Isa. xxxiii. 5, xxxii. 15, xxxv. 1.

the wine of Lebanon:' Mal. iv. 2, 'But unto you that fear my name shall the Sun of righteousness arise with healing under his wings; and ye shall go forth, and grow up as the calves of the stall:' Ps. i. 3, 'He shall be like a tree planted by the rivers of water, that bringeth forth his fruit in his season : his leaf also shall not wither ; and whatsoever he doeth shall prosper:' John iv. 14, 'Whosoever drinketh of the water that I shall give him shall never thirst; but the water that I shall give him shall be in him a well of water springing up to eternal life.' The light and glory of the church rises by degrees ; (1.) Looking forth as the morning ; with a little light ; (2.) Fair as the moon ; more light; (3.) Clear as the sun ; that is, come up to a higher degree of spiritual light, life, and glory, Cant. vi. 10. By all which it is most evident that all the powers of hell, nor all the powers on earth, cannot hinder the saints' growth in grace, nor the thriving and flourishing estate of their precious and immortal souls.

But you will say, What are the reasons why God will be favourably, signally, and eminently present with his people in their greatest troubles, deepest distresses, and most deadly dangers? I answer there are these ten great reasons for it :—

[1.] First, *To awaken and convince the enemies of his people, and to render his suffering children glorious in the very eyes and consciences both of sinners and saints:* Dan. iii. 24, 'Then Nebuchadnezzar the king was astonied, and rose up in haste, and spake and said unto his counsellors, Did we not cast three men into the fire ? They answered and said unto the king, True, O king.' Ver. 25, 'He answered and said, ' Lo, I see four men loose, walking in the midst of the fire, and they have no hurt, and the form of the fourth is like the Son of God.'[1] Now see what a majesty there is in this presence of Christ with his people in the fire, to convince Nebuchadnezzar, and to render the three champions very glorious in his eyes. Ver. 28, 'Then Nebuchadnezzar spake and said, Blessed be the God of Shadrach, Meshach, and Abednego, who hath sent his angel, and delivered his servants that trusted in him, and have changed the king's word, and yielded their bodies, that they might not serve nor worship any God except their own God.' Ver. 29, 'Therefore I make a decree, that every people, nation, and language which speak anything amiss against the God of Shadrach, Meshach, and Abednego, shall be cut in pieces, and their houses shall be made a dunghill, because there is no other God that can deliver after this sort.' Ver. 30, 'Then the king promoted Shadrach, Meshach, and Abednego in the province of Babylon.' The presence of the Lord with the three children commanded favour, respect, reverence, and honour from this great monarch, Nebuchadnezzar. The presence of God with his people is very majestical; the greatest monarchs have fallen down before it; not only Nebuchadnezzar, but also Darius, falls down before the signal presence of God with Daniel when he was in the lions' den, Dan. vi. 20 *seq.* And Herod falls down before the presence of God with John, Mark vi. 20. And King Joash falls down before the presence of God with Jehoiada, 2 Kings xi. 1, 2. And Saul falls down before

---

[1] Ponder upon these scriptures :—Micah vii. 8–10, 16, 17; Ps. cxxvi. 1, 2; Exod. viii. 19; Isa. lx. 13, 14; Rev. iii. 8, 9; Acts iv. 13, and vi. 15; John vii. 44–46, &c.

the presence of God with David : ' Thou art more righteous than I,'
1 Sam. xxiv. 17, &c.   And Alexander the emperor falls down before
the presence of God in Jaddua, the high-priest.[1]   In the signal
presence of God with his people in their affliction there is such a
sparkling lustre, that none can behold it but must admire it, and bow
before the graceful majesty of it.   Such has been the signal presence
of God with the martyrs in their fiery trials, that many have been
convinced and converted.   I have read of a citizen of Paris who was
burned for Protestantism, how the presence of God did so shine in
his courage and constancy, that many did curiously inquire into that
religion for which he so stoutly and resolutely suffered, so that the
number of sufferers was much increased thereby.[2]   I read that Cecilia,
a poor virgin, by her gracious behaviour in her martyrdom, was the
means of converting four hundred to Christ.   It was the observation
of Mr John Lindsay, that the very smoke of Mr [Patrick] Hamilton
converted as many as it blew upon.[3]   Alexandrinus cites Plato,
expressing himself thus : ' Although a righteous man be tormented,
although his eyes be digged out, yet he remains a blessed man '[4]   The
same Plato could say, ' That no gold or precious stone doth glister so
gloriously as the prudent spirit of a good man.'   And the very
Hittites could say of Abraham, who had a very signal presence of
God with him, ' Thou art a prince of God among us,' Gen. xxiii. 6 ;
not that he was a king or had any authority over them, as the Septuagint reads, ' Thou art a king from God among us ;' but he is
called a prince of God, say some, [Lyra and Tostatus,] because he was
as God's oracle—the Lord speaking to him by visions and dreams—
unto whom they had recourse for counsel in difficult matters.   Others
say, he is called Prince of God, because God prospered him, and
made him famous for his virtue and godliness.   But the Hebrews
commonly speak so of all things that are notable and excellent,
because all excellency cometh from God ; as the angel of God, the
mount of God, the city of God, the wrestlings of God, Exod. iii. 2,
and iv. 37 ; Ps. xxvi. 4 ; Gen. xxx. 8, &c.   ' Thou art a prince of
God ;' that is, Thou art a most excellent person.   Seneca saw so
much excellency that morality put upon a man, that he could say,
Ipse aspectus boni viri delectat: The very looks of a good man
delights one.   And why then may not the sons of Heth call him a
prince of God, from that majesty and glory that they saw shine forth
in his graces, and in his gracious behaviour and conversation, and
because they did observe a signal presence of God with him in all he
did, it being no higher observation than what Abimelech had made
before them ? Gen. xxi. 22.   Chrysostom, speaking of Babilas the
martyr, saith, *Magnus atque admirabilis vir,* &c. : He was an excellent and admirable man, &c.[5]   Tertullian, writing to some of the
martyrs, who had a mighty presence of God with them, saith, *Non
tantus sum ut vos alloquar,* &c. ; I am not good enough to speak unto
you.   Oh that my life and a thousand more such wretches might

---

[1] Misprinted Jaddus : Josephus, A. J. xi. 8, sec. 7, and cf. Prideaux, Coun. i. 545.—G.
[2] History of the Council of Trent, p. 418, 2d edit.
[3] Clemens Alex. Strom. lib. iv. p. 495.
[4] As before.—G.   [5] Clarke, as before.—G.

go for yours, &c. In Queen Mary's days,[1] not of blessed but of abhorred memory, the people of God met—sometimes forty, sometimes a hundred, sometimes two hundred—together. The fiery persecutors of that day sent in one among them to spy out their practices and to give information of their names, that they might be brought to Smithfield shambles; but there was such a presence of God in the assembly of his people, that this informer was convinced and converted, and cried them all mercy: 1 Cor. xiv. 24, ' But if all prophesy, and there come in one that believeth not, or one unlearned, he is convinced of all, he is judged of all;' ver. 25, ' And thus are the secrets of his heart made manifest, and so falling down on his face, he will worship God, and report that God is in you of a truth.' It may be before they came to the assembly of the saints, they had hard thoughts of the people of God: they thought that folly was in them, or that disloyalty was in them, or that madness and rebellion was in them, or that plots and designs against the government was in them, or that the devil was in them. Oh, but now such a majestical presence of God appears in the midst of his people, that the unbeliever is convinced, and confesses ' that God is in them of a truth.' Blessed Bradford had such a signal presence of God with him in his sufferings, as begot great reverence and admiration, not only in the hearts of his friends, but in the very hearts of very many papists also. Henry the Second, king of France, being present at the martyrdom of a poor tailor, who was burnt by him for his religion ; the poor man had such a signal presence of God with him in his sufferings, that his courage and boldness, his holy and gracious behaviour, did so amaze and terrify the king, that he swore, at his going away, that he never would be present at such a sight more.[2] As the presence of God is the greatest ornament of the church triumphant, so the presence of God is the greatest ornament of the church militant. The redness of the rose, the whiteness of the lily, and all the beauties of sun, moon, and stars, are but deformities to that beauty and glory that the presence of God puts upon his people, in all their troubles and trials. There is nothing in the world that will render the saints so amiable and lovely, so eminent and excellent in the eyes of their enemies, as the signal presence of God with them in their greatest trials. Demetrius[3] was so passing fair of face and countenance, that no painter was able to draw him. The presence of God with his people in their greatest troubles, deepest distresses, and most deadly dangers, puts so rare a beauty and glory upon them, that no painter can ever be able to draw them. But,

[2.] A second reason why God will be signally present with his people in their greatest troubles, deepest distresses, and most deadly dangers, is drawn from *the covenant of grace, and those precious promises that God has made to be with his people.* God's covenant is, that he will be with his people for ever, and that he will never turn away from them to do them good, Jer. xxxii. 40, 41. That is a branch of the covenant: ' I will never leave thee, nor forsake thee,' Heb. xiii. 5. And that is a branch of the covenant: ' I am thy shield, and thy

---

[1] Foxe, Acts and Mon., 1881.
[2] [Foxe,] Acts and Mon., p. 1458. Epist. Hist. Gal., 82.
[3] Plutarch in the Life of Demetrius.

exceeding great reward,' Gen. xv. 1; see Ps. cxv. 9–11. The shield is between the body and the thrust. So saith God, I will put in betwixt thee and harm. Though those kings whom thou hast even now vanquished, may rant high and threaten revenge, yet I will shield off all dangers that thou mayest be incident to. Though God's people be in the waters and in the fires, yet his promise is to be with them; so the psalmist, ' I will be with him in trouble, I will deliver him, and honour him,' Isa. xliii. 2; Ps. xci. 15, and l. 15; Job v. 19; Hosea ii. 14. God will not fail to keep his people company in all their troubles. No storm, no danger, no distress, no fiery trial, can keep God and his people asunder. God is immutable in his nature, in his counsels, in his covenant, and in all his promises, Mal. iii. 6. Though all creatures are subject to change, yet God is unchangeable; though angels and men, and all inferior creatures are dependent, yet God is independent. He is as the schoolmen say, *Omnino immutabilis*, altogether immutable, and therefore he will be sure to keep touch with his people. Precious promises are *Pabulum fidei, et anima fidei*, The food of faith, and the very soul of faith. They are a mine of rich treasures, a garden full of choice flowers, able to enrich a suffering Christian with all celestial contentments, and to sweeten the deepest distresses. God has deeply engaged himself, both by covenant and promises, that he will be with his people in their greatest troubles, deepest distresses, and most deadly dangers; and therefore he will not fail them: Deut. vii. 9, ' Know therefore that the Lord thy God, he is God, the faithful God, which keepeth covenant,' &c., or 'the God of amen.' God will never suffer his faithfulness to fail, nor alter the thing that is gone out of his mouth, Ps. lxxxix. 33. All his precepts, menaces, predictions, and promises are the issue of a most wise, holy, faithful, and righteous will, and therefore they shall certainly be made good to his people. But,

[3.] Thirdly, The Lord will be signally present with his people in their greatest troubles, deepest distresses, and most deadly dangers, because it *makes most eminently for the advancement of his own honour and glory in the world.* God never gets more honour than by helping his people when they are at a dead lift. God's signal presence with Israel at the Red Sea, makes Moses sing a song of praise, Exod. xv. A great part of the revenue of divine glory arises from the special presence of God with his people in their deepest distresses and most deadly dangers, as you may see by comparing the scriptures in the margin together.[1] It is the honour of a husband to be most present with his wife in her greatest troubles, and the honour of a father to be most present with his children in their deepest distresses, and the honour of commanders to be present with their soldiers in the heat of battle, when many fall on their right hand and on their left: Exod. xv. 3, ' The Lord is a man of war,' that is, an excellent warrior, ' the Lord is his name;' according to the Septuagint, συντρίβων πολέμους, ' He breaketh battles, and subdueth war.' God, like a brave commander, stands upon his honour, and therefore he will stand by his soldiers in the greatest dangers. The word *ish*, here used for man, signifies an eminent man, a mighty man, a famous warrior, or, as

---

[1] Exod. xv.; Judges v.; Ps. xxiii. 4, 6; Isa. xliii. 2, 5, 7.

the Chaldee paraphrast hath it, *Victor bellorum*, an overcomer of battles. Now eminent warriors, mighty warriors, famous warriors, they always stick closest to their soldiers in their greatest dangers, as all know that have read either Scripture or history. Now the Lord is such a man of wars, such a famous warrior, as that he will be sure to stick closest to his people in the greatest dangers. God is both in the van and in the rear, Isa. lii. 12. And as there is nothing that more raises the honour, fame, and renown of great warriors in the world than their presence with their soldiers when the bullets fly thickest; so there is nothing by which God gets himself a greater name, fame, and honour in the world, than by his signal presence with his people in their greatest troubles, deepest distresses, and most deadly dangers. But,

[4.] Fourthly, The Lord will be signally present with his people in their greatest troubles, deepest distresses, and most deadly dangers, because then *his people stands in most need of his presence.* A believer needs the presence of God at all times, but never so much as in great troubles, deep distresses, and most deadly dangers; for now Satan will be stirring. He loves to fish in troubled waters. Now earthly friends and earthly comforts and earthly succours will commonly fail us; now cares and fears will be multiplied upon us; now unbelief, which is virtually all evil, will be raising doubts and cavils and objections in the soul,[1] so that if God does not stand by us now, what can we say? what can we do? how can we bear up? how can we stand fast? What was Samson, that man of strength, when his hair was gone, but as weak as water? Judges xvi. 19, 20; and what is the strongest Christian when his God is gone, but as weak as weakness itself? All our doing strength, and all our suffering strength, and all our bearing strength, and all our witnessing strength, lies in the special presence of God with our souls. All our comforts, and all our supports, and all our ease, and all our refreshments, flow from the presence of God with our souls in our greatest troubles and deepest distresses; and therefore, if God should leave us in a day of trouble, what would become of us? and whither should we go? and where should we find rest? When doth a man need a brother or friend, but in a day of adversity? 'A brother is born for adversity,' Prov. xvii. 17. Though at other times brethren may jar and jangle and quarrel, yet in a day of adversity, in a strait, in a stress, birth and good blood and good nature will be working. Adversity breeds love and unity. Ridley and Hooper differed very much about ceremonies in the day of their liberty; but when they were both prisoners in the Tower, then they could agree well enough, and then they could be mutual comforts one to another. And when does a Christian most need the strength of God, the consolations of God, the supports of God, the teachings and quickenings of God, and the signal singular presence of God, but when they are in the greatest troubles, deepest distresses, and most deadly dangers? When the people of God are in a low and afflicted condition, then the Lord knows that that is the season of seasons for him to grace them with his gracious presence, Isa. xxxiii. 9, 10. When calamities and dangers break in upon us,

---

[1] Job ii. 9, and xix. 13-17; Ps. lxxxviii. 18; Isa. xli. 17, 18.

and when all heads and hands and hearts and counsels are set against us, now is the time for God to help us, for God to succour us, for God to stand by us. But,

[5.] Fifthly, The Lord will be signally present with his people in their greatest troubles, deepest distresses, and most deadly dangers, because *he dearly loves them.* God entirely loves his people, and therefore he will not leave his people. Persons whom we entirely love we cannot leave, especially when they are in a distressed condition. 'A friend loves at all times,' saith Solomon, and God is such a friend, Prov. xvii. 17. God loves not by fits and starts, as many do, but his love is like himself, sincere and steadfast. Because he loves them, he won't forsake them when they are in the greatest troubles and most terrible dangers, 1 Sam. xii. 22, 'For the Lord will not forsake his people for his great name's sake: because it hath pleased the Lord to make you his people.' He chose you for his love, and he still loveth you for his choice, and therefore he won't forsake you.[1] Chide you he may, but forsake you he won't; for it will not stand with the glory of God to leave a people, to forsake a people of his love. Should I cast you off whom I love, the heathen nations would say that I was mutable in my purposes, or unfaithful in my promises. Though David's parents forsook him, yet God did not forsake him, but took him up into his care and keeping, Ps. xxvii. 10. It is the deriding question which the enemies of the saints put to them in the time of their greatest troubles, deep distresses, and most deadly dangers, *Ubi Deus?* Where is now your God? Ps. lxxix. 10. But they may safely and groundedly return this answer when they are at lowest, *Hic Deus*, Our God is here; he is nigh unto us, he is round about us, and he is in the midst of us, Isa. lii. 12. Witness that golden promise, that is more worth than a world, 'I will never leave thee, nor forsake thee,' Heb. xiii. 5, 11. God is a God of bowels, a God of great pity, a God of tender compassion, and therefore he will not leave his people in a time of distress, Hosea viii. 9; Mic. vii. 19; Jer. xxxi. 18–20. Parents' bowels do most yearn towards their children when they are sick, and weak, and most in danger. It goes to the very heart of a man to leave a friend in misery. But what are the bowels of men to the bowels of God! or the compassions of men to the compassions of God! There is an ocean of love in the hearts of parents towards their children when they are in distress, 2 Sam. xix. 6; and this love makes them sit by their children, and sit up with their children, and not stir from their children. God's love does so link his heart to his people in their deep distresses, that he cannot leave them, he cannot stir from them, Ps. xci. 15: Isa. xliii. 4, 'Since thou wast precious in my sight, thou hast been honourable, and I have loved thee.' Well, and what then? This love so endears and unites God to his people, that he cannot leave them, he cannot stir one foot from them: ver. 2, 'When thou passest through the waters, I will be with thee; and through the rivers, they shall not overflow thee: when thou walkest through the fire, thou shalt not be burnt; neither shall the flame kindle upon thee.' The Lord dearly loves his people, and he highly prizes his people, and he greatly

[1] Deut. vii. 6-8. Amat quia amat.—*Bernard.*

delights in his people, and therefore he will be signally present with his people, both in the fire and in the water, both in the fire of persecution, and in the waters of affliction. God loves the persons of his people, and he loves the presence of his people, and he loves the graces of his people, and he loves the services of his people, and he loves the fellowship of his people; and therefore he will never leave his people, but stand by them, and be signally present with them, in their greatest troubles and deepest distresses. Such is God's singular love to his covenant-people, that he will neither forsake them nor forget them in their greatest troubles, deepest distresses, and most deadly dangers. The Jews were low—yea, very low, in Babylon; their distresses were great, and their dangers many; they looked upon themselves as so many dead men, 'Our bones are dry, our hope is lost, and we are cut off for our parts,' Ezek. xxxvii. 1–15. They looked upon themselves both as forsaken and forgotten by God. Behold, captive Zion lamentingly saith, 'The Lord hath forsaken me, and my Lord hath forgotten me,' Isa. xlix. 13–18; Ps. lxxxiv. 7; Isa. i. 27; Heb. xii. 22. *Zion* is taken several ways in Scripture: (1.) For the place properly so called, where they were wont to meet to worship the Lord; but this place was long ago destroyed. (2.) For the blessed angels, 'Ye are come to mount Zion, to the heavenly Jerusalem, to an innumerable company of angels.' (3.) For the congregation of saints, of believers, of which it is said, 'The Lord loves the gates of Zion more than all the habitations of Jacob,' Ps. lxxxvii. 2. The believing Jews being sorely oppressed and afflicted by a long captivity, Dan. ix. 22; Lam. iv. 6, and by many great and matchless miseries that did befall them in their captive state, they look upon God as one that had quite forsaken them and forgotten them; but they were under a very high mistake, and very erroneous in their complaint, as appears by God's answer to Zion: ver. 15, 'Can a woman forget her sucking child, that she should not have compassion on the son of her womb? yea, they may forget, yet will I not forget thee.' Ver. 16, 'Behold, I have graven thee upon the palms of my hands, thy walls are continually before me.' In these words, as in a crystal glass, you may see how pathetically, how sweetly, how graciously, how readily, how resolutely God doth engage himself that he will neither forsake Zion, nor yet forget Zion in her captive state. Now let us a little observe how this singular promise is amplified, and that, (1.) By an emphatical illustration; God's compassionate remembering of Zion far transcends the most compassionate remembrance of the tenderest mother to her dear sucking babe. Now this is laid down—

First, Interrogatively, 'Can a woman,' the most affectionate sex, 'forget a sucking child, for having compassion on the son of her womb?' Can a woman, can a mother so forget as not to compassionate a child, which she naturally inclines to pity? A sucking child that hangeth on her breast, such as mothers are wont to be most chary of, and to be most tenderly affected towards? her sucking child, which, together with the milk from the breast, draws love from her heart? her sucking child of her own womb, which her bowels do more yearn over than they do over any sucking nurse-child in the world? And this is the '*son* of her womb,' which the mother usually embraceth with more warm affections than the daughter of her womb. Can a woman, yea, can a mother forget to exercise love, pity, and compassion to such a poor babe ? Surely very rarely.

Second, Affirmatively, 'Yea, they may forget.' It is possible that a woman may be so unwomanly, and that a mother may be so unmotherly in some cases, and in some extremities, as to forget her sucking child, yea, as to eat the fruit of her womb, as the pitiful women did boil and eat their own children in the siege of Samaria and Jerusalem, 2 Kings vi. 24–30; Lam. iv. 10. Extremity of hunger overmastered natural affections, and made the pitiful mothers require of their children those lives which not long before they had given them, laying children not in their bosoms, but in their bowels.

Thirdly, Negatively, 'Yet will I not forget thee.' God will be more constantly, unmovably, and unchangeably mindful of Zion, and tender of Zion, and compassionate of Zion, and watchful over Zion, than any mother could be over her youngling; yea, he would be more motherly to his poor captives in Babylon than any mother could be to her sucking babe. This precious promise is amplified by a convincing argumentation, and that partly from his 'engraving of them upon the palms of his hands.' This is an allusion, say some, to those that carry about with them, engraven on some tablet, or on the stone of some ring which they wear on their finger, the mark, name, or picture of some person they entirely affect. Their portraiture, their memorial, was like a signet graven upon his hand. God will as soon blot out of mind, and forget his own hands, as his Zion; and partly from his placing their walls still in his sight. The ruined demolished walls of Jerusalem were still before him as to their commiseration, and to their reparation, God being fully resolved in the fittest season to raise and re-edify them. Look, as the workman hath his model or pattern constantly either before his eye, or in his thoughts, or in his brain, that he is for to work by, so, saith God, Zion is continually in my eye, Zion is still in my thoughts; I shall never forsake her, I shall never forget her. But,

[6.] Sixthly, The Lord will be signally present with his people in their greatest troubles, deepest distresses, and most deadly dangers, because of *his propriety and interest in them, and his near and dear relation to them:* Isa. xliii. 1, 'But now thus saith the Lord that created thee, O Jacob, and he that formed thee, O Israel, Fear not: for I have redeemed thee, I have called thee by thy name; thou art mine.' Thou art mine, for I have made thee; thou art mine, for I have chosen thee; thou art mine, for I have bought thee, I have purchased thee; thou art mine, for I have called thee; thou art mine, for I have redeemed thee; thou art mine, for I have stamped mine image upon thee; thou art mine, for I have put my Spirit into thee, Isa. xv. 16; 1 Cor. vi. 20; 1 Pet. i. 18; Phil. iv. 23, 24, xxxvi. 26, 27. Now mark what follows: ver. 2, 'When thou passest through the waters, I will be with thee; and through the rivers, they shall not overflow thee; when thou walkest through the fire, thou shalt not be burnt; neither shall the flame kindle upon thee.' God will certainly keep his own people, his own children, company, both in the fire and in the water; that is, in those various trials and troubles that they are incident to in this world, Isa. liv. 5; Ps. ciii. 13, 14; Exod. xv. 3; Mal. iv. 2; Mat. ix. 12; Ps. xxiii. 1.   When should a husband be with his wife, but when she is in greatest troubles? and a father with his child, but when he is in deep distresses? and a general with his army, but when they are in greatest dangers?   When should the physician be most with his patient, but when he is most desperately sick? and when should the shepherd be nearest his sheep, but when they are diseased, and the wolf is at hand?   Now God, you know, stands in all these relations to his people, and therefore he will not fail to be near them when troubles, distresses, and dangers are growing upon them.   But,

[7.] Seventhly, The Lord will be signally present with his people in their greatest troubles, deepest distresses, and most deadly dangers, because *such times are commonly times of great and sore temptations.* When God's hand is heaviest, then Satan will be busiest, Job ii. 7, 8; Mat. ix. 4; Heb. ii. 18.   The devil is never more violent in his temptations than when the saints are under afflictions: James i. 2, ' My brethren, count it all joy, when ye fall into divers temptations,' that is, ' afflictions;' ver. 12, ' Blessed is the man that endureth temptation,' that is, affliction; 2 Pet. ii. 9, ' The Lord knoweth how to deliver the godly out of temptation,' that is, out of affliction.   Now affliction is called temptation, not in the vulgar sense, as temptation is put for an occasion or inducement to sin, but in its proper and native signification, as it is taken for probation and trial.   Thus God is said to tempt Abraham, Gen. xxii. 1, that is, he did try and prove the faith, the fear, the love, the obedience of Abraham.   Afflictions are called temptations, partly because as afflictions will try what mettle we are made off, so will temptations; and partly because as afflictions are burdensome and grievous to us, so are temptations.   But mainly afflictions are called temptations, because in time of affliction Satan will be sifting and winnowing of the saints.   Now he will make use of all his devices, methods, depths, darts, yea, fiery darts, that he may vex, afflict, trouble, grieve, wound, torture, and torment those dear hearts that God would not have grieved and wounded; and therefore now the Lord steps in and stands by his people, and by his favourable, signal, and refreshing presence, he bears up their heads above water, and keeps their hearts from fainting and sinking under Satan's most dangerous and desperate temptations, Luke xxii. 31; 2 Cor. xii. 7; 2 Cor. ii. 11; Eph. vi. 11; Rev. ii. 24; Eph. vi. 16.   When a city is besieged, and the enemies have raised their batteries, and have made breaches upon their walls, and their provisions grow low, oh, then, if ever, there is need of succour and relief!   So here.   But,

[8.] Eighthly, The Lord will be signally present with his people in their greatest troubles, deepest distresses, and most deadly dangers, because *he highly prizes them, and sets an honourable value and esteem upon them:* Isa. xliii. 4, ' Since thou wast precious in my sight, thou hast been honourable, and I have loved thee, therefore will I give men for thee,' [*Heb.,* ' In thy room, or in thy stead,] ' and people for thy life,' that is, for thy preservation and protection.   God sets such a mighty price upon his people, that to preserve them from ruin and

destruction, he makes nothing of giving up to the sword and destruction, the most rich, strong, populous, and warlike nations in the world.
Now the high price and value that he sets upon them, engages him
to be present with them: ver. 2, ' When thou passest through the
waters, I will be with thee ; and through the rivers, they shall not overflow thee: when thou walkest through the fire, thou shalt not be
burnt ; neither shall the flame kindle upon thee.'   Them we highly
prize, we won't leave in a day of distress ; no more won't God.   God
prizes his people as his peculiar treasure: Exod. xix. 5, as his
' portion ;' Deut. xxxii. 9, as his ' pleasant portion ;' Jer. xii. 10, as
his ' jewels ;' Mal. iii. 17, as his ' glory ;' Isa. iv. 5, as his ' crown
and royal diadem.'   Yea, he prizes the poorest, the meanest, and the
weakest saint in the world above a multitude, yea, above a world of
sinners.   Heb. xi. 37, 38, ' Of whom the world was not worthy.'
Though they did not rustle in silks and velvets, but were clad ' in
sheep-skins and goat-skins ;' yet they had that inward excellency, as
that the world was not worthy of their company : and though they
did not dwell in ceiled houses, nor in stately palaces, but ' in deserts
and mountains, and in dens and caves of the earth ;' yet the vile sinful
persecuting world was not worthy of their presence, or prayers, or of
their prudent counsels, or pious examples, &c.   God sets a higher
value upon a Job, though on a dunghill, than upon an Ahab, though
on his royal throne, Job i. 1, and ii. 3.   God values men by their inward excellencies, and not by their outward dignities and worldly
glories.   He sets a higher price upon a Lazarus in his tattered rags,
than upon a rich Dives in his purple robes.   Such persons have most
of our company whom we prize most, Job ii. 11–13.   Job's three
friends did highly value him, and therefore in his deepest distresses,
they own him, they pity him, they weep over him, they accompany
him, and they keep close unto him.   Because God highly prizes his
people, he will be signally present with them in their greatest troubles
and deepest distresses.   But,
     [9.] Ninthly, The Lord will be signally present with his people
in their greatest troubles, deepest distresses, and most deadly dangers,
because *they won't leave him, but stick close to him, and to his
interest, gospel, and glory ; and will cleave fast to his word, worship, and ways, in their greatest troubles, deepest distresses, and
most deadly dangers, come what will on it,* Josh. xxiv. ; Jer. xiii.
11 ; Acts xi. 23.   You may take away my life, said Basil, but you
cannot take away my comfort ; my head, but not my crown ; yea,
saith he, had I a thousand lives, I would lay them all down for my
Saviour's sake, who hath done abundantly more for me.   John Ardley
professed to Bonner, when he told him of burning, and how ill he could
endure it, that if he had as many lives as he had hairs on his head, he
would lose them all in the fire before he would lose his Christ or part
with his Christ.   It was a common thing among the martyrs to make all
haste to the fire, lest they should miss of that noble entertainment.
Gordius the martyr said, It is to my loss if ye bate me anything of my
sufferings.   The sooner I die, said another, the sooner I shall be happy.
Ps. lxiii. 1, ' O God, thou art my God, early will I seek thee ; my soul
thirsteth for thee in a dry and thirsty land, where no water is ;' ver. 8,

'My soul followeth hard after thee,' &c. This notes, (1.) The strength of his intention; (2.) The strength of his affection; (3.) The constancy of his pursuit; and all this in a dry and barren wilderness, and in the face of all discouragements, and in the want of all outward encouragements, Dan. ix. 3; Ps. cxix. 20. Whatever the danger or distress be, the psalmist is peremptorily resolved to cleave close to the Lord, and to follow hard after the Lord: Ps. xliv. 17, 'All this is come upon us, yet have we not forgotten thee, neither have we dealt falsely in thy covenant;' ver. 18, 'Our heart is not turned back, neither have our steps declined from thy way;' ver. 19, 'Though thou hast sore broken us in the place of dragons, and covered us with the shadow of death;' see 2 Tim. i. 11, 12, and ii. 8–10; Eph. vi. 19, 20; Col. iv. 3, 18. In the face of all dangers, deaths, distresses, miseries, &c., God's faithful servants will own the Lord, and cleave to his ways, and keep close to his worship and service, let persecutors do their worst: ver. 22, 'Yea, for thy sake are we killed all the day long, we are accounted as sheep for the slaughter,' Rom. viii. 36. It is a question when, and upon what occasion, this psalm was written. Some think that it was written upon occasion of the seventy years' captivity in Babylon; but this cannot be, because that captivity was the fruit and product of their high iniquities, as the Scriptures do everywhere evidence, Dan. ix. 11–14. They could not say in Babylon, 'For thy sake we are killed all the day long;' but for sin's sake, for our wickedness' sake, we are killed all the day long. It is more probable that this psalm was penned upon the occasion of the horrible persecution of the church under Antiochus Epiphanes, unto which I guess Paul hath reference towards the latter end of that 11th to the Hebrews. In this 22d verse you have three things observable, (1.) The greatness of their sufferings: 'they were killed,' amplified by a similitude, 'as sheep to the slaughter.' (2.) The cause: not for their sin, but 'for thy sake.' (3.) The continuance: how long, even 'all the day long.' Their sufferings are great and long. That tyrant Antiochus made no more reckoning of taking away of their lives, than a butcher doth of cutting the throats of the poor sheep, Dan. xi.; and as butchers kill the sheep without making conscience of the effusion of their blood, even so did that tyrant Antiochus destroy the saints of the Most High, without making the least conscience of shedding innocent blood. And as butchers think well of their work, and are glad when they have butchered the poor sheep, so did this tyrant Antiochus; he thought he did God good service in butchering of the holy people, and rejoiced in that bloody service; and yet notwithstanding all the dreadful things that these blessed souls suffered, they still kept close to God, and close to his covenant, and close to his ways, and close to his worship. And Austin observes,[1] that though the heathen sought to suppress the growth of Christianity by binding, butchering, racking, stoning, burning, &c., yet still they increased and multiplied, Exod. i. 12, and still they kept close to God and his ways. The church was at first founded in blood, and it has thriven best when it has been moistened with blood. It was at first founded in the blood of Christ, and ever since it has been moistened or watered, as it were,

[1] Aug. de Civit. Dei, lib. xxii. cap. 6.

with the blood of the martyrs. The church of Christ in all ages hath been like the oak, which liveth by his own wounds; and the more limbs are cut off, the more new sprouts. Oh, how close to God, his ways and worship, did the saints keep in the ten persecutions! 'They have followed the Lamb whithersoever he went,' Rev. xiv. 4, 5. If they would have complied with the ways of the world, and the worship of the world, and the customs of the world, they might have had ease, honour, riches, preferments, &c., Heb. xi. 35; but nothing could work them off from God or his ways; and therefore he will certainly stand by them, and cleave to them, and be signally present with them in their greatest troubles, deepest distresses, and most deadly dangers. But,

[10.] Tenthly, The Lord will be signally present with his people in their greatest troubles, deepest distresses, and most deadly dangers, *that they may be joyful and cheerful under all their troubles, and that they may glory in all their tribulations*, Mat. v. 12; Luke vi. 23. It is good to have a patient spirit, but it is better to have a joyful spirit in all our sufferings, troubles, distresses, &c., that we meet with in a way of well-doing, 2 Cor. xii. 10. Acts v. 40, 'And to him they agreed: and when they had called the apostles, and beaten them, they commanded that they should not speak in the name of Jesus, and let them go;' ver. 41, 'And they departed from the presence of the council, rejoicing' [*Gr.*, 'rejoice and leap for joy,'] 'that they were counted worthy to suffer shame for his name.' In the original, ὅτι κατηξιώθησαν ἀτιμασθῆναι, 'that they were honoured to be dishonoured for Christ.' They looked upon it as a high honour to be dishonoured for Christ, and as a grace to be disgraced for Christ. It was the divine presence that made Paul and Silas to sing when they were accounted trouble-towns, and when they were beaten with many stripes, and cast into prison, into the inner prison, and laid neck and heels together, as the word τό ξύλον notes, Acts xvi. 20, 22-24, [Beza.] The divine presence made Paul and Silas to glory in all their stripes, sores, and wounds, as old soldiers glory in their scars and wounds which they receive in battle for their prince and country, Eph. vi. 17; Rom. v. 3. The divine presence might well make Paul and Silas to say of their stripes and sores, as Munster once said of his ulcers, *Hæ sunt gemmæ et pretiosa ornamenta Dei*, These are the jewels and the precious ornaments with which God adorns his dearest servants. It was the divine presence that made Ignatius say in the midst of all his sufferings, τά δεσμά περιφέρω τοὺς πνευματικοὺς μαργαρίτας, I bear my bonds as so many spiritual pearls. So 2 Cor. vii. 4, 'I am filled with comfort, I am exceeding joyful in all our tribulations.' *Gr.* ὑπερπερισσεύομαι, 'I do overabound with joy.' Ver. 5, 'For, when we were come into Macedonia, our flesh had no rest, but we were troubled on every side: without were fightings, within were fears;' ver. 6, 'Nevertheless God, that comforteth those that are cast down, comforted us.' It was the divine presence that filled the Corinthians with exceeding comfort and joy when their flesh had no rest, and when they were troubled on every side. This signal presence of God with them in all their tribulations filled their souls with such an exuberancy of joy, that no good could match it nor no evil over-

match it It was the divine presence that made the martyrs, both
ancient and modern, so comfortable and cheerful under all their
hideous sufferings. It was the divine presence that made Francisco
Soyit (?) say to his adversaries, 'You deprive me of this life and promote me to a better, which is as if you should rob me of counters and
furnish me with gold.' Oh, how my heart leapeth for joy, said one,
that I am so near the apprehension of eternal bliss ! God forgive me
mine unthankfulness and unworthiness of so great glory. In all the
days of my life I was never so merry as now I am in this dark dungeon.
Believe me, there is no such joy in the world as the people of Christ
have under the cross, said blessed Philpot, that went to heaven in
flames of fire.[1] Let God but withdraw this signal presence from his
people in their sufferings, and you will quickly find their hearts to
droop, their spirits to fail, and they overwhelmed in a sea of sorrows,
as you see in Mr Glover the martyr, and many others. It was this
divine presence that made the primitive Christians to rejoice more
when they were condemned than absolved,[2] and to kiss the stake, and
to thank the executioner, and to sing in the flames, and to desire to
be with Christ. So Justin Martyr, Apol. i., Adv. Gent, *Gratias
agimus quod à molestis dominis liberemur,* We thank you for delivering us from hard taskmasters, that we may more sweetly enjoy the bosom of Jesus Christ. The bee gathers the best honey of
the bitterest herbs, and Christ made the best wine of water. Certainly the best, the purest, the strongest, and the sweetest joys spring
from the signal presence of God with his people in their greatest
troubles and deepest distresses. Only remember this, that that joy
that flows from the divine presence in times of troubles and distress, it
is an inward joy, a spiritual joy, a joy that lies remote from a carnal
eye. 'The heart knoweth his own bitterness ; and a stranger doth not
intermeddle with his joy,' Prov. xiv. 10. The joy of the saints in
sufferings is a jewel that falls not under a stranger's eye. The joy of
a Christian lies deep, it cannot be expressed, it cannot be painted.
Look, as no man can paint the sweetness of the honeycomb, nor the
sweetness of a cluster of grapes, nor the fragrancy of the rose of
Sharon ; so no man can paint out the sweetness and spiritualness of
that joy that the divine presence raises in the soul when a Christian
is under the greatest troubles, deepest distresses, and most deadly
dangers. Holy joy is a treasure that lies deep ; and it is not every
man that has a golden key to search into this treasury. Look, as a
man standing on the sea-shore sees a great heap of waters, one wave
riding upon the back of another, and making a dreadful noise, but all
this while, though he sees the water rolling, and hears it raging and
roaring, yet he sees not the wealth, the gold, the silver, the jewels, and
incredible treasures that lie buried there : so wicked men they see
the wants of the saints, but not their wealth ; they see their poverty,
but not their riches ; their miseries, but not their mercies ;. their conflicts, but not their comforts ; their sorrows, but not their joys. Oh,
this blind world cannot see the joys, the comforts, the consolations
that the divine presence raises in the souls of the saints when they

[1] [Foxe,] Act. and Mon., fol. 1668-1670.
[2] Magis damnati quam absoluti gaudemus.— *Tert. in Apol.*

are at worst! Holy joy and cheerfulness under great troubles and deep distresses is an honour to God, a glory to Christ, and a credit to religion; it stops the mouths of sinners, and it encourages and strengthens weak saints; and therefore the Lord will be signally present with his people in their greatest troubles, &c., that they may grace their suffering condition with joy and cheerfulness. And let thus much suffice for the reasons of the point.

But before I come to the useful application, to prevent the objections, and to allay the fears and doubts and disputes that may arise in the hearts of weak Christians concerning this signal presence of God, I shall briefly lay down these following propositions:—

1. First, *That Christ is many times really present when he is seemingly absent:* Gen. xxviii. 16, 'And Jacob said, Surely the Lord is in this place, and I knew it not.' Choice Christians may have the presence of Christ really with them when yet they may not be kindly sensible of his presence, nor yet affected with it, Ps. cxxxix. God is present everywhere, but especially with his saints; and not only then when they are apprehensive of him, but when they perceive no evidence of his presence. Being awakened, he perceived that God had very graciously and gloriously appeared to him; and therefore he falls admiring and extolling the singular goodness and the special kindness of God towards him: as if he had said, I thought that such strange and blessed apparitions were peculiar to the family of the faithful; I thought that God had only in this manner revealed himself in my father's house: I did not in the least think or imagine that such an apparition, such a divine revelation should happen to me in such a place; but now I find that that God, who is everywhere in respect of his general presence, he hath, by the special testimonies of his presence, manifested himself to me also in this place. So Job, 'Lo, he goeth by me, and I see him not: he passeth on also, but I perceive him not,'[1] Job ix. 11. So Jonah, chap. ii. 4, 'Then I said, I am cast out of thy sight; yet I will look again toward thy holy temple.' In times of sore afflictions God's children are very prone to have hard conceits of God, and heavy conceits of themselves. Unbelief raises fears, doubts, despondency, despair, and works a Christian many times, when he is under deep distresses, to draw very sad conclusions against his own soul, 'I am cast out of thy sight.' But this was but an hour of temptation, and therefore he soon recollects and recovers himself again; 'yet I will look again toward thine holy temple.' Here now faith has got the upper hand of unbelief. In the former part of the verse you have Jonah doubting and despairing, 'I am cast out of thy sight;' but in the latter part of the verse you have Jonah conquering and triumphing, 'yet I will look again toward thine holy temple.' When sense saith a thing will never be, and when reason saith such a thing can never be, faith gets above sense and reason, and saith, ay, but it shall be. What do you tell me of a roaring, raging sea, of the belly of hell, of the weeds about my head, of the billows and waves passing over my head; for yet as low as I am, and as forlorn as I am, 'I will yet look towards God's holy temple,' I will

[1] Consult those scriptures, Luke xxiv. 32; John xx. 13-15; Ps. xxxi. 22; Cant. iii. 1-5, and v. 6-8.

eye God in the covenant of grace; though I am in the sea, though I am in the belly of hell, yet by faith 'I will look toward thy holy temple,'—toward which they were to pray, 1 Kings viii.—and triumph over all those difficulties which formerly I looked upon as insuperable; I will pray and look, and look and pray; all which does clearly evidence a singular presence of God with him, even then when he peremptorily concludes that he was cast out of God's presence, out of his sight, out of his favour, out of his care, out of his heart. The Lord is many times really present with his people when he is not sensibly present with his people: Judges vi. 12, 'And the angel of the Lord appeared to him, and said unto him, The Lord is with thee, thou mighty man of valour.' Ver. 13, 'And Gideon said unto him, O my Lord; if the Lord be with us, why then is all this befallen us? and where be all his miracles, which our fathers told us of, saying, Did not the Lord bring us up from Egypt? but now the Lord hath forsaken us, and delivered us into the hands of the Midianites.'[1] God may be really present with his people, they may have his favourable presence with their inward man, when it goes very ill with their outward man. Certainly we must frame a new Bible ere we can find any colour out of God's afflicting us to prove that he doth not love us, or that he hath withdrawn his presence from us. Christ had never more of the real presence of his Father than when he had least of his sensible presence, of his comfortable presence: 'My God, my God, why hast thou forsaken me?' Mat. xxvii. 46. Here is first a compellation or invocation of God twice repeated: 'My God, my God.' Secondly, the complaint itself, or matter complained of, touching God's forsaking of him. Christ was forsaken of God in some sort, and he was very sensible of his Father's withdrawing, though it was but in part and for a time, 'Why hast thou forsaken me?' This forsaking is not to be understood of his whole person, but of his human nature only, according to which and in the which he now suffered on the cross. Though the person of Christ suffered, and was forsaken, yet he was not forsaken in, or according to his whole person, but in respect of his human nature only. The godhead of Christ could not be forsaken, for then God should have forsaken himself, which is impossible. The personal union of the godhead with the manhood of Christ continued all the time of his passion and death, it was never dissolved, nor ever shall be: yea, the godhead did uphold the manhood all the time of Christ's sufferings, so that he was not forsaken when he was forsaken; he was not forsaken wholly when he was forsaken in part. The love and favour of God the Father towards Jesus Christ did not ebb and flow, rise and fall; for God never loved Jesus Christ more or better than at the time of his passion, when he was most obedient to his Father's will. 'Therefore doth my Father love me, because I lay down my life for my sheep,' John x. 17. Christ had never more of the supporting presence of his Father than when he had least of his comfortable presence. When Christ was in his grievous agony and distress of body and mind, the godhead did withdraw the comfortable presence from the manhood; and so far, and so far only, was Christ forsaken. Though the union was not dissolved, yet there was a suspension of

---

[1] God may sometimes appear terribly to those whom he loves entirely, Job ix. 34.

vision for the time, so as the human nature did neither see nor feel any present comfort from God. Now so far as the godhead did withdraw its comfortable presence, so far our Saviour was forsaken, and no further; that was but in part, and therefore he was but in part forsaken. God was really present with Christ when in respect of his comfortable presence he was withdrawn from him. So here. The husband may be in the house and the wife not know it; the sun may shine and I not see it; there may be fire in the room and I not feel it; so God may be really present with his people when he is not sensibly present with his people. But,

2. The second proposition is this, *That the favourable, signal, and eminent presence of God with his people in their greatest troubles, deepest distresses, and most deadly dangers, is only to be extended to his covenant-people, to those that are his people by special grace :* Jer. xxxii. 38, 'And they shall be my people, and I will be their God:' ver. 40, 'And I will make an everlasting covenant with them, that I will not turn away from them, to do them good ; but I will put my fear in their hearts, that they shall not depart from me:' ver. 41, 'Yea, I will rejoice over them to do them good.' There are many precious promises of the divine presence, as I have already shewed; but they are all entailed upon God's covenant-people. We are all the people of God by creation, both good and bad, sinners and saints, bond and free, rich and poor, high and low ; and we are all the people of God by outward profession. All that do make an outward profession of God, and perform external worship to God, they are all the people of God in this sense. All the carnal Israelites are frequently called the people of God, as well as the spiritual seed. Thus Cain was one of God's people as well as Abel, and Esau as well as Jacob. Now such as are only the people of God by creation, or by profession, these are strangers to God, these are enemies to God, Eph. ii. 12 ; and will he be favourably present with these ? Such as are only the people of God by creation and outward profession, they are dead in trespasses and sins ; and can the living God take pleasure in being among the dead ? Eph. ii. 1; Col. ii. 13. Such are under all the threatenings of the law, and under all the curses of the law, Gal. iii. 10, even to the uttermost extent of them ; such are not one moment secure ; the threatenings of God and the curses of the law may light upon them, when in the house, when in the field, when waking, when sleeping, when alone, when in company, when rejoicing, when lamenting, when sick, when well, when boasting, when despairing, when upon the throne, when upon a sick-bed ; and will God grace these with his presence ? Lev. xxvi.; Deut. xxviii. Surely no. Such say to God, 'Depart from us; for we desire not the knowledge of thy ways. What is the Almighty, that we should serve him ? and what profit should we have, if we pray unto him ?' Job xxi. 14, 15. Such queryings as this carry greatest contempt in them, and would lay the Almighty quite below the required duty as if Almighty were but an empty title ; and will God ever honour such with his favourable presence, who bid him be packing, who reject his acquaintance, and are willing to be rid of his company ? Surely no. Such as are only his people by creation, and an outward profession, such are under

the wrath and displeasure of God. 'God is angry with the wicked every day,' Ps. vii. 11 ; not with a paternal, but with a judicial anger, even to hatred and abhorment. 'The wicked is an abomination to him, and he hates all workers of iniquity,' Prov. iii. 32, and xv. 9. And therefore to these he will never vouchsafe his signal presence. Such may well expect that God will pour on them the fierceness of that wrath and indignation, that they can neither decline nor withstand. Such wrath is like the tempest and whirlwind that breaks down all before it. It is like burning fire, and devouring flames, that consumes all. This wrath will break down all the sinner's arrogancies, and strangle all his vain hopes, and mar all his sensual joys, and fill him with amazing distractions, and make him drunk with the wine of astonishment. And will God dwell with these ? will he keep house with these ? Surely no. By these short hints it is most evident that the special presence of God is entailed upon none out of covenant, John xiv. 21, 23. God loves to keep house with none but his covenant-people. He will grace none with his gracious presence, but those that are his people by special grace, 1 Cor. i. 16-18. When wicked men are in great troubles, deep distresses, and most deadly dangers, God either leaves them, as he did Saul, 1 Sam. xxviii. 15, 16, &c.; or else pursues them to an utter overthrow, as he did Pharaoh, Exod. xiv. ; or else cuts them off by an invisible hand, as he did Sennacherib's mighty hosts, Isa. xxxvii. 36, and proud king Herod, Acts xii. 23 ; or else he leaves them to be their own executioners, as he did Ahithophel and Judas, &c. But,

3. The third proposition is this, *That a sincere Christian may enjoy the presence of the Lord in great troubles, deep distresses, and most deadly dangers, supporting and upholding of him when he has not the presence of God quickening, comforting, and joying of him,* Ps. cxix. 117: Ps. xxxvii. 24, 'Though he fall, he shall not be utterly cast down; for the Lord upholdeth him with his hand,' סוֹמֵךְ יָדוֹ, 'upholding with his hand.' This is the upholding psalm. There is not one moment wherein the Lord doth not uphold his people by the hand. The root *samach* signifies to sustain and bear up, as the nurse or tender mother does the little child, the weak child, the sick child. God's hand is still under his, so that they can never fall below supporting grace: Ps. lxiii. 8, 'Thy right hand upholdeth me ; ' or, 'Thy right hand underprops me.' God never did, nor never will, want a hand to uphold, a hand to underprop his poor people in their greatest troubles and deepest distresses. Though the saints have not always the comforting presence of God in their afflictions, yet they have always the supporting presence of God in their afflictions, as Christ in his bitter and bloody agony had much of the supporting presence of his Father, when he had none of the comforting presence of his Father with him : Mat. xxvii. 46, 'My God, my God,' &c. ; so, the saints in their deep distresses have many times much of the supporting presence of God. His left hand is under their heads, and his right hand doth embrace them, Cant. ii. 6, when, in respect of his comforting presence, they may say with the weeping prophet, 'The comforter that should relieve my soul is far from me,' Lam. i. 16., When the love-sick spouse

was ready to faint, Christ circleth her with amiable embracements; ' His left hand is under her head, and his right hand doth embrace her.' It is an allusion to their conjugal and mensal beds, on which the guests are so bestowed, that the first laid his left hand under the head of him that was next, and put him so in his bosom, that with his other hand he might also, if he pleased, embrace him, which was a posture and sign of the greatest love, which the sick fainting spouse here glories in.   Christ's two hands are testimonies and witnesses of his great power and might, who is able to preserve his people, though lame cripples, from falling, and also to lift them up again when they are fallen never so low, and likewise to support and uphold them, that they shall never finally and utterly be cast down. When the hearts of the saints are ready to faint and sink, then the Lord will employ all his power for their support, bearing them up as it were with both hands. He hath put his left hand under my head, as a pillow to rest upon, and with his right hand he hath embraced me, as a loving husband cherisheth his sick wife, and doth her all the help he can, Eph. v. 29.   The best of saints would fail and faint in a day of trouble, if Christ did not put to both his hands to keep them up.   In days of sorrow God's people stands in need of a whole Christ to support them and uphold them.   My head sinks, O my beloved, put thy left hand, softer than pillows of roses, firmer than pillars of marble, under it ; my heart faileth and dieth—oh let thy right hand embrace me.   But,

4. The fourth proposition is this, *That all saints have not a like measure of the presence of the Lord in their troubles and trials, in their sorrows and sufferings.*   Some have more, and others have less of this presence of God in an evil day. (1.) All saints have not alike work to do in an evil day. (2.) All saints have not alike temptations to withstand in an evil day. (3.) All saints have not alike testimony to give on an evil day. (4.) All saints have not alike burdens to bear in an evil day. (5.) All saints have not alike things to suffer in an evil day.   There are greater and there are lesser troubles, distresses, and dangers; and there are ordinary troubles, distresses, and dangers; and there are extraordinary troubles, distresses, and dangers.[1]   Now, where the trouble, the distress, the danger, is ordinary, there an ordinary presence of God may suffice ; but where the trouble, the distress, the danger, is extraordinary, there the people of God shall have an extraordinary presence of God with them, as you may see in the three children, Daniel, the apostles, the primitive Christians, and the Book of Martyrs.   Some troubles, distresses, and dangers, are but of a short continuance, as Athanasius said of his banishment, *Nubecula est, citò transibit*, It is but a little cloud, and will quickly be gone.   Others are of a longer continuance, and accordingly God suits his presence. All saints have not alike outward succours, supplies, reliefs, comforts, &c., in their troubles, distresses, and dangers.   Some have a shelter, a friend at hand, others have not ; some have many friends, and others may cry out with him, O my friends, I have never a friend ! some are surrounded with outward comforts, and others have not one, not

[1] Lam. i. 12, and iv. 6 ; Dan. ix. 12, 13 ; 2 Cor. xi. 21 to the end ; Heb. xi. 25 to the end.

one penny, not one friend, not one day's work, &c.; in a storm some have good harbours at hand, others are near the rocks, and in danger of being swallowed up in the sands. So here, and accordingly God lets out more or less of his presence among his people; some need more of his presence than others do, and accordingly God dispenseth it among his saints. But,

5. The fifth proposition is this, *That none of the saints have at all times, in all afflictions, distresses, and dangers, the same measure and degree of the presence of the Lord; but in one affliction they have more, in another less, of the divine presence.*[1] In one affliction a Christian may have more of the enlightening presence of God than in another; and in another affliction a Christian may have more of the comforting presence of God than in another. In this trouble a Christian may have more of the awakening presence of God than in another, and in that trouble a Christian may have more of the sanctifying presence of God than in another; and in this distress a Christian may have more of the supporting presence of God than in that. No one saint doth at all times, nor in all troubles, need a like measure of the divine presence. The primitive Christians and the martyrs had sometimes more and sometimes less of the divine presence with them, as their condition did require. God, who is infinitely wise, does always suit the measures and degrees of his gracious, favourable, signal presence to the necessities of his saints. This is so clear and great a truth, that there are many thousands that can seal to it from their own experience; and therefore I need not enlarge upon it. But,

6. The sixth and the last proposition is this, *That many precious Christians, in their great troubles, deep distresses, and most deadly dangers, may have this favourable, signal, and eminent presence of God with them, and yet fear and doubt, yea, peremptorily conclude that they have not this presence of God with them,*[2] Ps. lxxvii. 7–10. These sad interrogatories argues much fear and diffidence; but let me evidence the truth of this proposition by an induction of particulars. Thus, first: If Christ be not signally with you, why are you in your troubles so fearful of offending of him, and so careful and studious in pleasing of him? Gen. xxxix. 9, 10; Ps. xvii. 3–5; Dan. iii. 16, 17, and vi. 10–13. Secondly, If Christ be not signally with you, how comes it to pass that under all your troubles, deep distresses, and most deadly dangers, you are still a-justifying of God, a-clearing of God, a-speaking well of God, a-giving a good report of God? Ps. cxix. 75; Ezra ix. 13; Neh. ix. 32, 33; Dan. ix. 12, 14. Thirdly, If God be not signally with you, how come you to bear up so believingly, sweetly, stoutly, cheerfully, and patiently under your troubles, deep distresses, and greatest dangers? Gen. xlix. 23, 24; 1 Sam. xxx. 6; Hab. iii. 17, 18; Acts v. 40–42, xvi. 25, 26, and xxvii. 22–26; Heb. x. 34. Fourthly, If Christ be not signally present with you, how comes it to pass that your thoughts, desires, hearts, thirstings and longings of soul, are so earnestly, so seriously, so frequently, and so constantly carried out after more and more of Christ,

---

[1] Some scores of Psalms do evidence the truth of this proposition.
[2] Jonah ii. 4; Cant. v. 6–10; Ps. lxxxviii.

and after more and more of the presence of Christ, and after more and more communion with Christ? Ps. cxxxix. 17, 18, lxiii. 1, 8, xxvii. 4, and xlii. 1-3; Exod. xxxiii. 13-16; Cant. i. 2. Fifthly, If Christ be not signally present with you, why are you so affected and afflicted with the dishonours and indignities, wrongs and injuries, that are done to the Lord by others? Ps. lxix. 9, and cxix. 53, 136, 158; Jer. ix. 1, 2; Ezek. ix. 4, 6; 2 Pet. ii. 7, 8. None but such that have the presence of the Lord signally with them can seriously and sincerely lament over the high dishonours that are done to the Lord by others. Sixthly, If the Lord be not signally present with you under all your troubles and deep distresses, why do you not cast off prayer, and neglect hearing, and forsake the assembling of yourselves together, and turn your backs upon the table of the Lord, and take your leaves of closet duties? Job xv. 4; Heb. x. 25. But, seventhly, If the Lord be not signally present with you under your great troubles and deep distresses, why don't you say with Pharaoh, 'Who is the Lord, that I should obey his voice?' And with the king of Israel, 'Behold, this evil is of the Lord, and why should I wait for the Lord any longer?' Or with that noble pagan, 'If the Lord would make windows in heaven, might this thing be?' Or with Saul, Why don't you run to a witch? Or with Ahab, Why don't you sell yourselves to work evil in the sight of the Lord? Or with Ahaz, Trespass most when you are distressed most?[1] Why don't you fret, and faint, and lie in the streets as a wild bull, full of the fury of the Lord? Why don't you grope for the wall, and stumble at noonday, and roar all like bears? But, eighthly, If the Lord be not signally present with you in your greatest troubles and deepest distresses, why do you, with Moses, prefer suffering before sinning, and Christ's reproaches before Egypt's treasures? Heb. xi. 25, 26. Why do you scruple the sinning of yourselves out of your sorrows? Ps. xxxviii. 4; Gen. xxxix. 9, 10. Why do you look upon sin as your greatest burden? Why are you so tender in the point of transgression, and so stout in resistance of the most pleasing temptation? But, ninthly, If the Lord be not signally with you in your great troubles and deep distresses, why do you set so high a price upon those that have much of the presence of God with them in their troubles and trials? Ps. xvi. 3, 4; Prov. xii. 26; Heb. xi. 38. Why do you look upon them as more excellent than their neighbours? yea, as such worthies of whom this world is noways worthy? But, tenthly and lastly, If the Lord be not signally present with you in your greatest troubles and deepest distresses, how comes it to pass that you are somewhat bettered, somewhat amended, somewhat reformed by the rod—by the afflictions that have been, and still are, upon you? Ps. cxix. 67, 71; Hosea v. 14, 15, and vi. 1, 2; Hosea ii. 6, 7. When the heart is more awakened, humbled, and softened by the rod, when the will is more compliant with the will of God in doing or suffering, when the mind is more raised and spiritualised, when the conscience is more quick and tender, and when the life is more strict and circumspect,—then we may safely and roundly conclude that such persons do undoubtedly enjoy the

---

[1] Exod. v. 2; 2 Kings vi. 32, and vii. 2; 1 Sam. xviii. 15, 16; 1 Kings xxi. 20; 2 Chron. xxviii. 22; Isa. li. 20, and lix. 10, 11.

signal and singular presence of God with them in their greatest troubles, deepest distresses, and most deadly dangers, Eph. v. 15. And thus I have laid down these six propositions; which, if well weighed and improved, may many ways be of singular use to sincere Christians.

We shall now come to the application or useful improvement of this great and seasonable truth. Explication is the drawing of the bow, but application is the hitting of the mark, the white. Is it so, that when the people of the Lord are in great troubles, deep distresses, and most deadly dangers, that then the Lord will be favourably, signally, and eminently present with them? Then let me briefly infer these ten things.

[1.] First, *That the saints are a people of Christ's special care:* 2 Chron. xvi. 9, ' For the eyes of the Lord run to and fro through the whole earth, to shew himself strong in the behalf of them, whose heart is perfect towards him.' The words contain, (1.) *The universality of God's providence.* His eyes walk the rounds, they run to and fro through the whole earth, to defend and secure the sincere in heart. Diana's temple was burnt down when she was busied at Alexander's birth, and could not be at two places together; but God is present at all times, in all places, and among all persons, and therefore his church, which is his temple, can never suffer through his absence, 1 Cor. iii. 16, and vi. 19. The Egyptians had an idol called Baal-Zephon, which is by interpretation, *Dominus speculæ*, Lord of the watch-tower, Exod. xiv. 2; his office was to fright such fugitive Jews as should offer to steal out of the country; but when Moses and the people of Israel passed that way, and pitched their camp there, this drowsy god was surely fast asleep, for they all marched on their way without let or molestation; whereas he that keepeth Israel ' neither slumbereth nor sleepeth;' he kept his Israel then, and he hath kept his Israel ever since: he made good his title then, and will make good his title still; he ever was, and he ever will be, watchful over his people for their good, Ps. cxxi. 3–5; Isa. xxvii. 3, 4. (2.) *The efficacy of his providence,* to shew himself strong. God fights with his eyes as well as his hands; he doth not only see his people's dangers, but saves them from dangers in the midst of dangers, Zech. ii. 5. When the philosopher in a starry night was in danger of drowning, he cried out, Surely I shall not perish; there are so many eyes of providence over me. King Philip said he could sleep safely because his friend Antipater watched for him. Oh, how much more may the saints sleep safely, who have always a God that keeps watch and ward about them! Ps. iii. 5, 6. God is so strong a tower that no cannon can pierce it, Prov. xviii. 10, and he is so high a tower that no ladder can scale it, and he is so deep a tower that no pioneer can undermine it; and therefore they must needs be safe and secure who lodge within a tower so impregnable, so inexpugnable. Now this is the case of all the saints. The fatherly care and providence of God is still exercised for the good of his people: Deut. xxxii. 10, ' He found him in a desert land, and in the waste howling wilderness; he led him about, he instructed him, he kept him as the apple of his eye:' ver. 11, ' As an eagle stirreth up her nest, fluttereth over her young, spreadeth abroad her wings, taketh them, beareth them on her wings:' ver. 12, ' So the Lord alone did lead him,' &c.[1] The eagle carries her young ones upon her wings, and not between her talons, as other birds do, openly, safely, swiftly ; and so did God his Israel, being choice and chary of them all the way, securing them also from their enemies, who could do them as little hurt as any do the eagle's young, which cannot be shot but through the body of the old one, Isa. lxiii. 4–6, and lix. 15. See at what a rate God speaks in that, Isa. xl. 27, 28. Observe how God comes on with his high interrogatories, ' Hast thou not known ?' What an ignorant people ! ' Hast thou not heard ?' What a deaf people ! What ! keep no intelligence with heaven ? 1 Pet. v. 7, ' Casting all your care upon him, for he careth for you.' I will now with you sing away care, said John Careless, martyr, in his letter to Mr Philpot,[2] for now my soul is turned to her old rest again, and hath taken a sweet nap in Christ's lap. I have cast my care upon the Lord, which careth for me, and will be *careless* according to my *name*. It was a strange speech of Socrates, a heathen, Since God is so careful of you, saith he, what need you be careful for anything yourselves ? God's providence extendeth to all his creatures; it is like the sun, of universal influence, but in a special manner it is operative for the safety of his saints. In common dangers men take special care of their jewels, and will not God ; will not God take special care of his jewels? Mal. iii. 17; Heb. iii. 6; 1 Pet. ii. 5. Surely, yes. The church of God is the house of God, and will not God take care of his house ? Surely that shall be well guarded, whatsoever be neglected. His house is every moment within the view of his favourable eye, and under the guard of his almighty arm ; his thoughts and heart is much upon his house. God hath a peculiar and paternal care over his saints. That distich of Musculus cometh in fitly :—

> Est Deus in cælis, qui providus omnia curat,
> Credentes nunquam deseruisse potest.

> A God there is, whose providence doth take
> Care for his saints, whom he will not forsake.

' His eyes run,' implying the celerity and swiftness of God in hastening relief to his people ; ' His eyes run through the whole earth,' implying the universality of help. There is not a saint in any dark corner of the world, under any straits or troubles, but God eyes him, and will take singular care of him. God will always suit his care to his people's conditions, to which his eminent appearances for them in days of distress and trouble give signal testimony. It is our work to cast care ; it is God's work to take care. Let not us, then, by soul-dividing thoughts, take the Lord's work out of his hand. But,

[2.] Secondly, Will the Lord be signally present with his people in their greatest troubles, deepest distresses, and most deadly dangers ? Then here you may see *the true reason why the saints are so comfortable, cheerful, and joyful in their greatest troubles, deepest distresses, and most deadly dangers.* It is because of that signal presence of

---

[1] Isa. xlix. 16, xxxi. 5, and xxxii. 1, 2. See my ' Heavenly Cordial after a Wasting Plague,' much of the special care of God. [Vol. vi.—G.]
[2] [Foxe,] Acts and Mon., fol. 1743.

God with them.[1] It was this signal presence of God with the martyrs' that made them rejoice in the midst of their greatest sufferings, and that made them endure great sufferings without any sensible feeling of their sufferings : as that young child in Josephus, who, when his flesh was pulled in pieces with pincers, by the command of Antiochus, said, with a smiling countenance, Tyrant, thou losest time. Where are those smarting pains with which thou threatenedst me? make me to shrink and cry out if thou canst! And Bainham, an English martyr, when the fire was flaming about him, said, You papists talk of miracles ; behold here a miracle. I feel no more pain than if I were in a bed of down; it is as sweet to me as a bed of roses.[2] Surely their strength was not the strength of stones, nor their flesh of brass, Job vi. 12, that they should not be sensible of so great sufferings ; but this was only from that signal presence of God, that made them endure grievous pains without pain, and most exquisite torments without torment, and sore sufferings without feeling of their sufferings, Heb. xi. 33–39. And other choice souls there were, who, though they were sensible of their sufferings, yet by the divine presence they were filled with unspeakable courage, comfort, and alacrity. Laurence, when his body was roasted upon a burning gridiron, cried out, This side is roasted enough ; turn the other. Marcus of Arethusa, a worthy minister, when his body was cut and lanced and anointed with honey, and hung up aloft in a basket to be stung to death by wasps and bees ; he, looking down cheerfully upon the spectators, said, I am advanced, despising you that are below. And when we shall see poor, weak, feeble creatures like ourselves defying their tormentors and their torments, conquering in the midst of their greatest sufferings, and rejoicing and triumphing in the midst of their fiery trials ; singing in prison, as Paul and Silas did ; kissing the stake, as Henry Voes did ; clapping their hands when they were half consumed in the flames, as John Noyes did ; calling their execution-day their wedding-day, as Bishop Ridley did ; we cannot but conclude that they had a singular presence of God with them, that made all their sufferings seem so easy and so light unto them. Cæsar cheered up his drooping mariners in a storm by minding them of his presence ; but, alas! alas! what was Cæsar's presence to this divine, this signal presence that the saints have enjoyed in their greatest troubles and deepest distresses? But,

[3.] Thirdly, Will the Lord be signally present with his people in their greatest troubles, deepest distresses, and most deadly dangers? Then from hence you may see *the weakness, madness, sottishness, and folly of all such as make opposition against the saints; that affront, injure, and make head against those that have the presence of the great God in the midst of them*, Isa. viii. 9, 10, and xxvii. 4 ; 1 Cor. i. 25. O sirs! the weakness of God is stronger than men. What then is the strength of God? 1 Cor. x. 22, 'Do we provoke the Lord to jealousy? are we stronger than he?' Ah, who knows the power of his anger! Ps. xc. 11. It is such that none of the potentates of the

[1] Acts v. 40, 41, and xvi. 25; Rom. v. 3; 2 Cor. vii. 4, and xii. 10; 1 Pet. iv. 12–14. These scriptures are already opened and improved.

[2] Clarke, as before, p. 397. See Clarke and Foxe for the names that follow.—G.

world, who set themselves against the saints, can avert or avoid, avoid or abide. That God is a mighty God the Scriptures do abundantly evidence, and it appears also in the epithet, that is added unto *El-*, which is *Gibbor*, importing that he is a God of prevailing might. By Daniel he is called *El-Elim*, ' the mighty of mighties.' Now what folly and madness is it for dust and ashes, for crawling worms, to make head against a mighty God; yea, an Almighty God, who can curse them, and crush them with a word of his mouth: 2 Chron. xxxii. 7, ' Be strong and courageous, be not afraid nor dismayed for the king of Assyria, nor for all the multitude that is with him, for there be more with us than with him;' ver. 8, ' With him is an arm of flesh, but with us is the Lord our God, to help us, and to fight our battles;' Gen. xlix. 25; Num. xxiv. 4, 16; Ruth i. 20, 21. The king of Assyria was at that time the greatest monarch in the world, and the most formidable enemy the church had, yet the divine presence was a sovereign antidote to expel all base slavish fears that might arise in any of their hearts concerning his greatness, power, or multitude. What was that great multitude that was with the king of Assyria, to that innumerable company of angels that was with Hezekiah?[1] And what was an arm of flesh to God's supreme sovereignty, that had this proud prince in chains, and that put a hook in his nose, and a bridle in his lips, and cut off his great army by the hand of an angel in one night, and left him to fall by the sword of his own sons? The Lord of hosts can crush the greatest armies in the world into atoms at pleasure. When the emperor Heraclius sent ambassadors to Chosroes, king of Persia, to desire peace of him, he received this threatening answer: I will not spare you, till I have made you curse your crucified God, and adore the sun. He was afterwards, like another Sennacherib, deposed and murdered by his own siroes.[2] When the divine presence is armed against the great ones of the world they must certainly fall. In Dioclesian's time, under whom was the last and worst of the ten persecutions, though then Christian religion was more desperately opposed than ever, yet such was the presence of God with his people in those times, that religion prospered and prevailed more than ever; so that Dioclesian himself, observing that the more he sought to blot out the name of Christ it became the more legible, and to block up the way of Christ it became the more passable; and whatever of Christ he thought to root out, it rooted the deeper and rose the higher, thereupon he resolved to engage himself no further, but retired to a private life, [Ruffinus.] This is a good copy for the persecutors of the day to write after. O sirs! what folly and madness is it for weakness to engage against strength, the creature against the Creator, an arm of flesh against the Rock of Ages! What is the chaff to the whirlwind, stubble and straw to the devouring flames? No more are all the enemies of Zion to the great and glorious God, that is signally present with his people in their greatest troubles and deepest distresses, &c., Acts v. 38–40; Ps. lxxvi. 12, and cx. 5, 6; Rev. vi. 14–16. There was not one of those persecuting emperors that carried on the ten

---

[1] 2 Kings vi. 17; Ps. xxxiv. 7, &c., and xci. 11; Heb. xii. 22, and i. 14; Isa. xxxvii. 29, 36–38.

[2] Diac. Cedren. [Chosroes II. or Khosru. Query, 'siroes' a misprint for 'sons'?—G.

bloody persecutions against the saints, but came to miserable ends ; yea, histories tell us of three and forty persecuting emperors that fell by the hand' of revenging justice ; first or last the presence of God with his people will undo all the persecutors in the world. But,

[4.] Fourthly, Will the Lord be signally present with his people in their greatest troubles, deepest distresses, and most deadly dangers ? Then from hence you may see *the Lord's singular love and admirable kindness to his people in gracing them with his presence in their greatest troubles*, Isa. xliii. 2, 4. That is a friend indeed that will stick close to a man in the day of his troubles, as Job's friend did stick close to him in the day of his troubles, and as Jonathan did stick close to David in his greatest dangers, and as the primitive Christians did stick close one to another, though with the hazard of their lives, and to the amzement of their enemies, Job ii. 11–13 ; 1 Sam. xx. 30–33. 'Behold,' said they, 'how the Christians love one another,' and stand by one another. The people of God, in their greatest troubles, are a people of his special love. When they are in distress, he lays them in his very bosom, and his ' banner over them is love,' Cant. ii. 4. The love of God to his people is engraven upon the most afflictive dispensation they are under. When he smartly rebukes them, even then he dearly loves them, Rev. iii. 19. 'Hear ye the rod,' Mic. vi. 9. Oh, the rod speaks love. Many of the saints have read much of the Lord's love, written in letters of their own blood. They have read love in prisons, and love in flames, and love in banishment, and love in the cruellest torments their enemies could invent. When a Christian's wounds are bleeding, then God comes in with a healing plaster, Mal. iv. 2. When a Christian is in a storm, then the presence of the Lord makes all calm and quiet within, Mat. viii. 26. The presence of the Lord with his people in their troubles and distresses speaks out the reality of his love, the cordialness of his love, the greatness of his love, and the transcendency of his love. The truth and strength of relations' love one to another doth best appear by their presence one with another, when either of them are in the iron furnace, or in bonds, or in great straits or wants, or deep distresses. The parents shew most of their love to their sick and weak children by their daily presence with them ; and the husband shews most of his dear and tender love by keeping his wife company when she is in greatest straits and dangers. So here. But,

[5.] Fifthly, Will the Lord be signally present with his people in their greatest troubles, deepest distresses, and most deadly dangers ? Then this may serve to *justify the saints, and to encourage the saints to write after this fair copy that Christ has set them.* Oh visit them ! oh stand by them ! oh stick close to them in all their troubles, distresses, and dangers. Let the same mind be in you, one towards another, as is in Christ towards you all. Are there any Jobs upon the dunghill ? visit them. Are there any Pauls in chains ? find them out, and be not ashamed of their chains : 2 Tim. i. 16, 'The Lord give mercy to the house of Onesiphorus ; for he oft refreshed me, and was not ashamed of my chain ;' ver. 17, ' But when he was in Rome, he sought me out diligently, and found me ;' ver. 18, ' The Lord grant unto him that he may find mercy of the Lord in that day ; and in how many things he ministered unto me at Ephesus, thou knowest very well.' 'He oft refreshed me.' Greek, [ἀνέψυξε,] 'Poured cold water upon me ;' as that angel did upon the racked limbs of Theodorus the martyr, mentioned by Socrates and Ruffinus, in the days of Julian the apostate. It is a metaphor taken from those who, being almost overcome with heat, are refreshed by cooling. 'And was not ashamed of my chain.' Learned antiquaries observe that the apostle at this time was not in prison with fetters, but in the custody of a soldier, with whom he might go abroad, having a chain on his right arm, which was tied to the soldier's left arm. Paul at this time was not in prison, much less a close prisoner; for then Onesiphorus needed not to have made any great search to find him; but was a prisoner at large, going up and down with his keeper to despatch his affairs; and therefore he speaks not of chains in the plural number, but of a chain in the singular, with which he was tied to the soldier that kept him. It noways becomes the saints to be ashamed of the bonds or chains that may be found upon the ambassadors of Christ in an evil day. The primitive Christians were not ashamed of the martyrs' chains, but owned them in their chains, and stood by them in their chains, and frequently visited them in their chains, and freely and nobly relieved them and refreshed them in their chains: and will you, will you be ashamed to visit the saints in bonds? 'Oh let not this be told in Gath, nor published in the streets of Askelon,' 2 Sam. i. 20, that the high-flown professors and Christians of these times are ashamed to own, relieve, and stand by the saints in bonds. So Mat. xxv. 36, 'I was sick, and ye visited me: I was in prison, and ye came unto me.'[1] It is very remarkable that the last definitive sentence shall pass upon men, according to those acts of favour and kindness that have been shewed to the saints in their suffering state; and that the sentence of absolution shall contain a manifestation of all their good works. In this great day Christ sees no iniquity in his people, he objects nothing against them, and he only makes honourable mention of the good that has been done by them. O sirs, all the visits you give to sick saints, and all the visits you give to imprisoned saints, Christ takes as visits given to himself: suffering saints and you are brethren; and will you not visit your own brethren? suffering saints and Christ are brethren; and will you not visit Christ's brethren? suffering saints and you are companions; and will you not visit your own companions? suffering saints and you are travelling heaven-wards; and will you not visit your fellow-travellers? suffering saints and you are fellow-citizens; and will you not visit your fellow-citizens? suffering saints and you are fellow-soldiers; and will you not visit your fellow-soldiers? suffering saints and you are fellow-heirs; and will you not visit your fellow-heirs?[2] Oh, never be ashamed of those that Christ is not ashamed of! Oh, never fail to visit those whom Christ daily visits in their suffering state! Oh, never turn your backs upon those to whom Christ hath given the right hand of fellowship! Oh, be not shy of them, nor

---

[1] See Exod. ii. 11, 12, compared with Acts vii. 23-29, only remember the case was extraordinary, and his call was extraodinary.

[2] Mat. xxv. 40 ; John xx. 17; Ps. cxix. 63; 2 Cor. viii. 19 ; Eph. ii. 19 ; Phil. ii. 25; Rom. viii. 17.

strange to them whom Christ lays daily in his bosom! Oh, be not unkind to them with whom one day you must live for ever! But,

[6.] Sixthly, Will the Lord be signally present with his people in their greatest troubles, deepest distresses, and most deadly dangers? Then *never give way to base slavish fears*, Ps. li. 12, 13, and xlvi. 1–3; Mat. x. 28, &c. There are as many *fear nots* in Scripture as there are *fears*. Take a taste of some of them:—Heb. xiii. 5, 'He hath said, I will never leave thee, nor forsake thee.' Ver. 6, 'So that we may boldly say, The Lord is my helper, and I will not fear what man shall do unto me.' This text is taken out of Ps. cxviii. 6, 'The Lord is on my side, I will not fear what man can do unto me.' Some read it by way of interrogation, 'What can man do unto me?'[1] There is some difference in the apostle's quoting the text betwixt the Hebrew and the Greek. The Hebrew thus reads·it, 'The Lord is with me,' or for me; or as our English hath translated it, 'The Lord is on my side.' The Greek thus, 'The Lord is my helper.' But the sense being the same with the Hebrew, the apostle would not alter that translation. The alteration which is in the Greek serves for an exposition of the mind and meaning of the psalmist; for God being with us, or for us, or on our side, presupposeth that he is our helper. So as there is no contradiction betwixt the psalmist and the apostle, but a clear interpretation of the psalmist's mind; and a choice instruction thence ariseth —viz., that God's signal presence with us, for us, or on our side, may abundantly satisfy us, and assure us that he will afford all needful help and succour to us. The consideration of which should abundantly arm us against all base slavish fears. God is not present with his saints in their troubles and distresses as a stranger, but as a father; and therefore he cannot but take such special care of them, as to help them, as to succour them, and as to secure them from dangers in the midst of dangers, and therefore why should they be afraid? Isa. xliii. 2. The Greek word βοηθὸς, that is translated helper in that Heb. xiii. 6, according to the notation of it, signifieth one that is ready to run at the cry of another. Now this notation implieth a willing readiness and a ready willingness in God to afford all succour and relief to his people in their greatest troubles and deepest distresses. Herein God shews himself like a tender father, mother, or nurse, who presently runs when any of them hear the child cry, or see danger near: Isa. viii. 10, 'God is with us.' Ver. 12, 'Fear ye not their fear, nor be afraid.' The divine presence should arm us against all base slavish fears of men's power, policy, wrath, or rage. Kings and princes, compared with God, or with the signal presence of God, are but as so many grasshoppers, skipping and leaping up and down the field; and does it become Christians that enjoy this divine presence to be afraid of grasshoppers? Isa. xl. 22: Isa. xli. 10, 'Fear thou not; for I am with thee: be not dismayed; for I am thy God: I will strengthen thee; yea, I will help thee; yea, I will uphold thee with the right hand of my righteousness.' God expects that his signal presence with us should arm us against all base fear and dismayedness: Ps. xxiii. 4, 'Yea, though I walk through the valley of the shadow of death, I will fear no evil: for

[1] The Earl of Murray, speaking of Mr. John Knox, said, Here lies the body of him who in his lifetime never feared the face of any man.

thou art with me.' The divine presence raised David above all his fears: Ps. xxvii. 1, 'The Lord is my light and my salvation; whom shall I fear? the Lord is the strength of my life, of whom shall I be afraid?' Who is the enemy that I should be afraid of? where is the enemy that I should be afraid of? by what name or title is the enemy dignified or distinguished that I should be afraid of? I look before me and behind me, I look round about me and I look at a distance from me, and I cannot see the man, the devil, the informer that I should fear or be afraid of, for God is with me. Where God is, said king Herod in a speech to his army,[1] there neither wants multitude nor fortitude. We may safely, readily, and cheerfully set the divine presence against all our enemies in the world. When Antigonus his admiral told him that the enemies number far exceeded his: But how many do ye set me against? said the king. Look about you and see who is with you. Ah, Christians, Christians, look about you, look about you, and see who is signally present with you, and then be afraid if you can. But,

[7.] Seventhly, Will the Lord be signally present with his people in their greatest troubles, deepest distresses, and most deadly dangers? Then certainly *there is no such great evil in troubles, distresses, sufferings, &c., as many conceive, fear, dream, think, judge.* Many men look upon troubles, afflictions, sufferings, in a multiplying glass, and then they cry out, There is a lion in the way, a lion in the streets, Prov. xxii. 13, and xxvi. 13. But, sirs, the lion is not always so fierce as he is painted, nor afflictions are not always so grievous as men apprehend. There are many who have been very fearful of prisons, and have looked upon a prison as a hell on this side hell, who when they have been there for righteousness' sake, and the gospel's sake, have found prisons to be palaces, and the imaginary hell to be a little heaven unto them. Many fear afflictions, and flee from afflictions as from toads and serpents, as from enemies and devils; and yet certainly there is no such great evil in affliction as they apprehend, for the Lord is signally present with his people in their greatest troubles and deepest distresses. Now what evil can there be in that condition wherein a man enjoys the divine presence, that makes every bitter sweet, and every burden light, and that turns winter nights into summer days, &c.? yea, many times the saints enjoy more of the singular presence of God in their afflictions, in their day of adversity, than ever they did in the day of prosperity, or in the day of their worldly glory. What bride is afraid to meet her bridegroom in a dark entry, or in a dirty lane, or in a narrow passage, or in a solitary wood; and why then should a Christian be afraid of this or that afflicted condition, who is sure to meet his blessed bridegroom, the Lord Jesus Christ, in every state, in every condition, who is sure to enjoy the presence of Christ with him in every turn or change that may pass upon him? How many martyrs have ventured into the very flames to meet with Christ, Heb. xi. 34, and that have many other ways made a sacrifice of their dearest lives, and all to meet with Christ! Oh the cruel mockings, the scourgings, the bonds, the imprisonments, the stoning, the sawing asunder that many of the Lord's worthies have ventured upon, and all to meet with the presence

---

[1] Josephus, lib. **xv.**

of the Lord; and why then should any of you be afraid to enter into
an afflicted condition, where you shall be sure to meet the singular
presence of the Lord, that will certainly turn your afflicted condition
into a comfortable condition to you? Rev. xii. 11, and Heb. xi. 36–38.
The great design of the Lord in afflicting his people is to meet with
them, and to draw them into a nearer communion with himself. It
is that they may see more of him than ever, and taste more of him
than ever, and enjoy more of him than ever; in order to which he
subdues their corruptions by afflictions, and strengthens their graces,
and heightens their holiness by all their troubles and trials, Isa. i. 25,
xxvii. 8, 9; Heb. xii. 10, 11; Hosea ii. 14. Whenever he leads his
spouse into a wilderness, it is that he may speak friendly and comfortably to her, or that he may speak to her heart, as the Hebrew runs.
The great design of the Lord in bringing her into a wilderness was
that he might make such discoveries of himself, of his love, and of his
sovereign grace, as might cheer up her heart, yea, as might even make
her heart leap and dance within her. Or, as some sense it, ' I will
take her alone for the purpose, even into a solitary wilderness,
where I may more freely impart my mind to her,' that she having
her whole desire she may come up from the wilderness leaning upon
her beloved, Cant. viii. 5, and so be brought into the bride-house with
all solemnity. By all which it is most evident that there is no such
evil in a wilderness estate, in an afflicted condition, as many imagine.
But,

[8.] Eighthly, Will the Lord be signally present with his people in
their greatest troubles, deepest distresses, and most deadly dangers?
Then *what a high encouragement should this be to poor sinners to
study Christ, to acquaint themselves with Christ, to embrace Christ,
to choose Christ, to close with Christ, to submit to Christ, and to make
a resignation of themselves to Christ, and to secure their interest in
Christ*, that so they may enjoy his signal presence in their greatest
troubles, deepest distresses, and most deadly dangers, John i. 12; Ps.
cxii. 2, 3, and ii. 12; 2 Cor. viii. 5. Oh, how many mercies are wrapt up
in this mercy of enjoying the singular presence of the Lord in all the
troubles and trials of this life! Ps. xxiii. 4. It is a mercy to have the
presence of a friend, it is a greater to have the presence of a near and
dear relation with us in a day of distress, in a day of darkness; but
what a mercy is it then to have the presence of the Lord with one in
a dark day! That is excellent counsel that the wisest prince that ever
swayed a sceptre gives in that Eccles. xi. 8, ' Remember the days of
darkness, for they shall be many.' When light shall be turned into
darkness, pleasure into pain, delights into wearisomeness, calms into
storms, summer days into winter nights, and the lightsome days of
life into the dark days of old age and death; oh, now the singular
presence of the Lord with a man in these days of darkness will be
a mercy more worth than ten thousand worlds! To have a wise, a
loving, a powerful, a faithful friend to own us in the dark, to stand
by us in the dark, to uphold us in the dark, to refresh us in the
dark, to encourage us in the dark, &c., is a very choice and singular
mercy, Ps. lxxi. 20, 21. Oh then, what is it to have the presence of
the Lord with us in all those dark days that are to pass over our

heads! What David said of the sword of Goliath in another case, ' There is none like that,' 1 Sam. xxi. 8, 9, that I may say of the divine presence with a man in the dark, ' There is none like that.' The psalmist hit the mark, the white, when he said, ' My flesh and my heart faileth: but God is the strength of my heart, and my portion for ever.'[1] When his ' flesh,' that is his outward man, and when his ' heart,' his courage, that is his inward man, failed him, then God was 'the strength of his heart,' or 'the rock of his heart,' as the Hebrew runs. At the very last gasp God came in with his sovereign cordial, and revived him and recovered him, and brought new life and strength into him. When a saint is at worst, when he is at lowest, when he is even overwhelmed with troubles and sorrows, and when the days of darkness so multiply upon him that he seems past all hope of recovery, then the divine presence does most gloriously manifest itself and display itself in supporting, strengthening, comforting, and encouraging of him. In the Rev. iv. 6, you read that the world is like a sea of glass, ' I saw before the throne a sea of glass.' The world is transitory, very frail and brittle as glass, and it is unstable, tumultuous, and troublesome as the sea. ·Here the world is shadowed out to us by a sea of glass; and how can we stand on this sea, how can we live on this sea, how can we walk on this sea, if Christ don't take us by the hand, and lead us and support us and secure us? O sirs, we cannot uphold ourselves on this sea of glass, nor others cannot uphold us on this sea of glass; it is none but dear Jesus, it is no presence but his singular presence that can make us to stand or go on this sea of glass. And if this world be a sea of glass, oh what infinite cause have we to secure our interest in Christ, who alone can pilot us safe over this troublesome, dangerous, and tempestuous sea! Oh that I could prevail with poor sinners to take Christ into the ship of their souls, that so he may pilot them safe into the heavenly harbour, the heavenly Canaan. No pilot in heaven or earth can land you on the shore of a happy eternity, from off this sea of glass, but Jesus. When on this sea of glass the winds blow high, storms arise, and the bold waves beat into the ship, oh then the sinner cries, ' A kingdom for a Christ,' a world for a pilot to save us from eternal drowning! Oh that before eternal storms and tempests do beat upon poor sinners, they would be prevailed with to close with Christ, to accept of Christ, and to enter into a marriage-covenant, a marriage-union with Christ; that so they may enjoy his singular presence with them whilst they are on this sea of glass, Ps. xi. 6, and ix. 17; Hosea ii. 19, 20; 2 Cor. xi. 2. There is no presence so greatly desirable, so absolutely necessary, and so exceeding sweet and comfortable, as the presence of Christ; and therefore, before all and above all, secure this presence of Christ by matching with the person of Christ, and then you will be safe and happy on a sea of glass. But,

[9.] Ninthly, Will the Lord be signally present with his people in their greatest troubles, deepest distresses, and most deadly dangers? Then let me infer *that unbelief, infidelity, and despondency of spirit in an evil day, does very ill become the people of God.* Is the Lord present with you in your greatest troubles, and will you flag in your

---

[1] Ps. lxxiii. 26. The Greek saith, The God of my heart, &c.

faith, and be crestfallen in your courage, when the blast of the terrible ones is as a storm against the wall? Isa. xxv. 4; what is this but to tell all the world that there is more power in your troubles to sink and daunt you, than there is in the presence of the Lord to support and encourage you? When a Christian is upon the very banks of the Red Sea, yet then the divine presence should encourage him 'to stand still, and see the salvation of the Lord,' Exod. xiv. 13. It would be good for timorous Christians in an evil day to dwell much upon the prophet's commission: Isa. xxxv. 3, 'Strengthen ye the weak hands, and confirm the feeble knees. Say to them that are of a fearful heart, Be strong, fear not.' Ah, but how shall weak hands be strong, and a timorous heart cease to fear and faint? Why, 'Behold, your God will come with vengeance, even God with a recompense; he will come and save you;' he is on his way, he will be suddenly with you, yea, he is already in the midst of you, and he will save you. If you cast but your eye upon precious promises, if you cast but your eye upon the new covenant, which is God's great storehouse, there you will find all supports, all supplies, all helps, and all comforts, laid up, and laid in for you; and therefore never despond, never faint, never be discouraged in an evil day, in a dark time.[1] As Joseph had his storehouses to give a full supply to the Egyptians in time of famine, so dear Jesus, of whom Joseph was but a type, has his storehouses of mercy, of goodness, of power, of plenty, of bounty, out of which in the worst of times he is able to give his people a full supply according to all their needs; and therefore be not discouraged, do not despond in a day of trouble. O my friends, how often has the Lord hid you in the secret of his presence from the pride of men, and kept you secretly in his pavilion from the strife of tongues! Ps. xxvii. 5, and xxxi. 20. And therefore ' be strong, and lift up the hands that hang down, and the feeble knees,' Heb. xii. 12. When David was in a very great distress, he does not despond nor give way to unbelief, but encourages himself in the Lord his God, 1 Sam. xxx. 6. The Hebrew word is derived from *Chazack*, which notes a laying hold on God with all his strength, as men do when they are in danger of drowning, who will suffer anything rather than let go their hold. When David was almost under water, when he was in danger of drowning, then, by a hand of faith, he lays hold on the Rock of Ages, and encourages himself in the Lord his God. What heavenly gallantry of spirit did good Nehemiah shew from that divine presence that was with him in that great day of trouble and distress, when ' the remnant of the captivity were in great affliction and reproach: and the wall of Jerusalem broken down, and the gates thereof burnt with fire!' Neh. i. 3. You know Shemaiah advises him to take sanctuary in the temple, because the enemy had designed to fall upon him by night and slay him, and cause the work to cease; but Nehemiah, having a signal presence of God with him, gives this heroic and resolute answer, ' Should such a man as I flee? and who is there, being as I am, would go into the temple to save his life?' Neh. vi. 10, 11. I will not go in. Should I flee into the temple like a malefactor to take

---

[1] Isa. xli. 10, and xliii. 2; Heb. xiii. 5; Jer. xxxii. 40, 41, xxxi. 31-38; Gen. xli. 35, 36, 48, 49; Col. i. 19, and ii. 3.

sanctuary there, how would God be dishonoured, religion reproached, the people discouraged, the weak scandalised, and the wicked emboldened to insult and triumph over me ! saying, Is this the man that is called by God, and qualified by God, for this work and service ? Is this the man that is countenanced and encouraged by the king to build the walls, and gates, and city of Jerusalem ? Neh. ii. 5-10. Is this the man that is the chief magistrate and governor of the city ? Is this the man that is sent and set for the defence of the people, and that should encourage them in their work? Oh what a mouth of blasphemy would be opened, should I make a base retreat into the temple to save my life ! This is a work that I will rather die than do. I have found the face of God, the presence of God, in bowing the heart of king Artaxerxes, to contribute his royal aid, and commission me to the work; and in the bending of the hearts of the elders of the Jews to own my authority, and to rise up as one man to build ; and therefore I will rather die upon the spot than go into the temple to save my life. O my friends, it becomes not those that have the presence of God with them in their greatest troubles, deepest distresses, and most deadly dangers, to sink so low in their faith and confidence, as to cry out with the prophet's servant, ' Alas, master ! what shall we do ?' or, with the disciples when in a storm, ' We perish ;' or, with the whole house of Israel, ' Our bones are dried, and our hope is lost : we are cut off for our parts ;' or, with weeping Jeremiah, ' My strength and my hope is perished from the Lord ;' or, with Zion, ' The Lord hath forsaken me, and my Lord hath forgotten me,' 2 Kings vi. 15 ; Mat. viii. 25 ; Ezek. xxxvii. 11 ; Lam. iii. 18 ; Isa. xlix. 14. Oh, it is for a lamentation when God's dearest children shall bewray their infidelity by a fainting, sinking, discouraged spirit in an evil day. But,

[10.] Tenthly and lastly, Will the Lord be signally present with his people in their greatest troubles, deepest distresses, and most deadly dangers? Then let *the people of the Lord be very thankful for his presence with them in their greatest troubles*, &c., Exod. xxxiii. 13-16 ; 2 Tim. iv. 22 ; Ps. xvi. 11. O sirs ! this divine presence is a great mercy. It is a peculiar mercy, it is a distinguishing mercy, it is a big-bellied mercy, it is a mercy that hath many mercies in the womb of it. It is a mercy-greatening mercy ; it greatens all the mercies we do enjoy. It is a mercy-sweetening mercy ; it sweetens health, strength, riches, honours, trade, relations, liberty, &c. It is a soul-mercy, a mercy that reaches the soul, that cheers the soul, that lifts up the soul, that quiets the soul, that satisfies the soul, and that will go to heaven with the soul, Eph. i. 3. And will you not be thankful for such a mercy ? Will you be thankful for temporal mercies, and will you not be thankful for spiritual mercies ? Will you be thankful for left-handed mercies, and will you not be thankful for right-handed mercies? Will you be thankful for the mercies of the footstool, and will you not be thankful for the mercies of the throne ? Will you be thankful for the mercies of this lower world, and will you not be thankful for the mercies of the upper world? Ps. ciii. 1-4. To enjoy the presence of God when we most need it, is a mercy that deserves perpetual praises. Oh, it is infinite mercy not to be left alone in a day of trouble. It is very uncomfortable to be left alone: 'Woe to him that is alone,' Eccles. iv. 10, 11. If a man fall, and be left alone, who shall help him up? If a man be in danger and alone, how miserable is his case! But this is the support and comfort of a Christian in all his difficulties, that he is never left alone; but his God is with him when he is at the lowest ebb, Heb. xiii. 5; Ps. xxxvii. 24, xxxi. 3, lxxiii. 24; Exod. xxxiii. 2, 14–16. For God to afford us the presence of our friends in a day of trouble is a very great mercy; but what is it, then, to enjoy the presence of God in a day of trouble? What is the presence of a friend, a favourite, in a day of distress, to the presence of a prince? yea, what is the presence of an angel to the presence of God in an evil day? To enjoy the presence of God in an afflicted condition is a more transcendent mercy than to enjoy the presence of twelve legions of angels in an afflicted condition. The divine presence is the greatest good in the world. It is life eternal; it is the bosom of God, the gate of glory, the beginning of heaven, the suburbs of happiness; and therefore be much in blessing of God, in admiring of God, for his presence with you in a dark and trying day. There is no gall, no wormwood, no affliction, no judgment to that of God's departing from a people, Lam. iii. 19, 20: Jer. vi. 8, 'Be thou instructed, O Jerusalem, lest my soul depart from thee, lest I make thee desolate, a land not inhabited.' When God departs, nothing followeth but desolation upon desolation; desolation of persons, desolation of peace, of prosperity, of trade, and of all that is near and dear unto us: Hosea ix. 12, 'Though they bring up their children, yet will I bereave them, that there shall not be a man left; yea, woe also to them when I depart from them.' All terrible threatenings are summed up in this, 'Woe unto them when I depart from them.' Surely even woe to them; he put a sureness upon this 'woe to them when I depart from them.' As if the Holy Ghost should say, What, do I threaten this or the other evil? the great evil of all, the rise of all evils, is God's forsaking of them. Hell itself is nothing else but a separation from God's presence, with the ill consequents thereof. And were hell as full of tears as the sea is full of water, yet all would not be sufficient to bewail the loss of that beatifical vision. How miserable was Cain when cast off by God! Gen. iv.; and Saul, when the Lord departed from him! It was a most dreadful speech of Saul, 'I am sore distressed, for the Philistines make war against me, and God is departed from me,' 1 Sam. xxviii. 15, 16.[1] When God left the Israelites, though for a little while, the Holy Ghost saith they were naked, Exod. xxxii. 25. How naked? *Non veste, sed gratia et præsidio Dei,* Not for want of raiment, or weapons of war, but for want of God's presence and protection.[2] When God departs from a people, that people lies naked; that is, they lie open for all storms, tempests, and dangers. Now if it be the greatest evil in the world to be shut out from the gracious presence of Christ, then it must be the greatest mercy in this world to enjoy the gracious presence of God in our great troubles and desperate dangers. And therefore let all sincere Christians be much in thankfulness to the Lord, and in blessing and praising the Lord, for his signal presence with them in their low and afflicted estate. Oh, the light, the life, the love, the

---

[1] They that are out of God's care are under his curse.　　　　[2] Junius *in loc.*

holiness, the peace, the grace, the comforts, the supports that always attends the gracious presence of the Lord with his people in their deep distresses, &c.   Therefore let the high praises of God for ever be in their mouths, who enjoy this signal presence of God.   The 46th Psalm is called by some Luther's psalm; that is a psalm that Luther was wont to call to his friends to sing when any danger, trouble, or distress was near.   When the clouds began to gather, Come, saith Luther, let us sing the 46th Psalm, and then let our enemies do their worst.[1]   Observe the confidence and triumph of the church in the face of the greatest dangers : ver. 1, ' God is our refuge and strength, a very present help in trouble :' ver. 2, ' Therefore will not we fear, though the earth be removed, and though the mountains be carried into the midst of the sea ;' ver. 3, ' Though the waters thereof roar and be troubled, though the mountains shake with the swelling thereof. Selah.' Ver. 6, ' Though the heathen rage, and the kingdoms were moved,' to remove and root out the church with great force and fury.   Now mark, by the change of the earth and removing of the mountains, are often meant the greatest alterations and concussions of states and polities, Hag. ii. 22, 23 ; Jer. li. 25 ; Rev. vi. 14.   Now, saith the psalmist, all these dreadful turns, changes, shakings, and concussions of states and kingdoms shall never trouble us, nor daunt us ; they shall never make us fret, faint, or fear. Why, what is the ground ? .' The Lord of hosts is with us ; the God of Jacob is our refuge,' ver. 7 ; and so, ver. 11, the same words are repeated again. ' God is not gone, God is not withdrawn, God is not departed from us.' Oh no ! ' The Lord of hosts is with us, the Lord of hosts is with us ; the God of Jacob is our refuge, the God of Jacob is our refuge ;' and therefore we are divinely fearless and divinely careless.   Though hell and earth should combine against us, yet we will bear up, and be bold to believe that all shall go well with us ; for God is in the midst of us, ' The Lord of hosts is with us,' even the Lord, who commandeth far other hosts and armies than the enemy hath any. ' The God of Jacob is our refuge ;' *Heb.*, ' Our high tower.'   God is a tower, so high, so strong, so inaccessible, so invincible, that all our enemies, yea, all the powers of darkness, can never hurt, reach, storm, or take ; and therefore we that are sheltered in this high tower may well cast the gauntlet to our proudest, strongest, and subtlest enemies.   And let thus much suffice for the inferences.

The next use is a use of exhortation, to exhort all the people of God *so to order and demean themselves as to keep the divine presence, as to keep the signal, the singular presence of God, with them in their greatest troubles, deepest distresses, and most deadly dangers.*   Now that this may stick in power upon your souls, consider seriously of these following motives :—

[1.] First, The signal presence of God with his people puts *the greatest honour, dignity, and glory upon a people imaginable ; vide* Isa. xliii. 2, 4 ; Jer. xiii. 11 ; Ezek. xlviii. 35.   There are many titles of honour amongst men ; but this, above all, is the truly honourable

[1] We may translate it, ' He is found ;' that is, God is present, at hand; as, Gen. xix. 15, ' God is a present help.' The Hebrew word, in a secondary sense, signifies ' to be sufficient,' Num. xi. 22. A sufficient help : you need no other.

title, that we have God so near unto us: Deut. iv. 7, 'What nation is there so great, who hath God so nigh unto them, as the Lord our God is to us?' Whilst he vouchsafed his presence amongst them, how honourable, how renowned were they all the world over ! But when he departed from them they became the scorn and contempt of all nations. It may be said of some men, they have large estates, but not the presence of God with them ; they are highly honoured and dignified in the world, but no presence of God with them ; they have great trades and vast riches, but no presence of God with them ; they are nobly related, but no presence of God with them ; they have singular parts and natural accomplishments, but no presence of God with them. The want of the divine presence gives a dash, casts a blot upon all their grandeurs and worldly glory, and, like coprice,[1] turns all their wine, be it never so rich, into ink and blackness. What a deal of honour and glory did the presence of God cast upon Joseph in prison, Gen. xxxix. 19, 20; and upon Daniel in the den ; and upon the three children in the fiery furnace ; and upon David, when a persecuting Saul could cry out, 'Thou art more righteous than I,' 1 Sam. xxiv. 17 ; and upon John, when a bloody Herod feared him and observed him, Mark vi. 20 ; and upon Paul, when a tyrannical Felix trembled before him, Acts xxiv. 25 ; as if Paul had been the judge, and Felix the prisoner at the bar. Some write of the crystal, that what stone soever it toucheth, it puts a lustre and loveliness upon it. The presence of God puts the greatest lustre, beauty, glory, and loveliness that can be put upon a person. Now because the witness of an adversary is a double testimony, let Balaam—who, as some write of a toad, had a pearl in his head, though his heart was naught, very naught, stark naught—give in his evidence. 'How goodly are thy tents, O Jacob, and thy tabernacles, O Israel,' Num. xxiv. 5. He speaks both by way of interrogation and admiration : their tents are so comely, and their tabernacles so lovely, that their grand enemy was affected and ravished with them. But whence is it that Israel is so formidable and terrible in his eye ? How comes this about, that he who came to fight against them thinks them beyond all compare ; nay, doth himself admire their postures and order, their great glory and brave gallantry ? Why, all is from the presence of their Lord-General with them : 'The Lord their God is with them ; the shout of a king is amongst them,' Num. xxiii. 21. It is the highest honour, renown, and dignity of a people to have God in the midst of them, to have God near unto them. Thus Moses sets out the honour and dignity of the Jews: Deut. xxvi. 18, 'The Lord hath avouched thee this day to be his peculiar people :' ver. 19, 'To make thee high, above all nations which he hath made, in praise, and in name, and in honour.' When God reckons up the dignities of his people, this is the main, the top, of all : Ps. lxxxvii. 5, 'And of Zion it shall be said, This and that man was born in her ; and the Highest himself shall establish her.' If you would keep your honour and dignity, keep the presence of God in the midst of you. When God is departed from Israel, then you may write *Ichabod* upon Israel ; 'The glory is departed from Israel,' 1 Sam. iv. 21, 22. But,

---

[1] 'Copperas.'—G.

[2.] Secondly, To move you so to order, demean, and carry your-selves as you may enjoy the gracious presence of God with you in your greatest troubles and deepest distresses, consider *that nothing can make up the want of this signal presence of God.* It is not the pre-sence of friends, of relations, of ministers, of ordinances, of outward comforts, that can make up the want of this presence. It is not candle-light, or torchlight, or starlight, nor moonlight, that can make up the light of the sun. When the sun is set in a cloud, all the world cannot make it day; and when the presence of God is withdrawn, nothing can make up that dismal loss. ' Thou didst hide thy face and I was troubled,' Ps. xxx. 6, 7, that is, thou didst suspend the actual influence and communication of thy grace and favour. The Chaldee calleth it ' Shechinah, the divine presence:' and I was all-amort.[1] It was not his crown, his kingdom, his riches, his dignities, his royal attendance, &c., that could make up the loss of the face of God; neither is it the presence of an angel that can make up the want of the presence of God: Exod. xxxiii. 2, 'And I will send an angel before thee.' God here promiseth Moses that he would send an angel before them, but withal adds that he would not go up himself in the midst of them : ay, but such a guide, such a guardian, such a nurse, such a companion, such a captain-general would not satisfy Moses, Exod. xxxiii. 3. Ver. 14, 'And he said, My presence shall go with thee, and I will give thee rest.' Ver. 15, ' And he said unto him, If thy presence go not with me, carry us not up hence.' Nothing would satisfy Moses below the presence of God, because he knew that they were as good never move a foot farther, as to go on without God's favourable presence. God engages himself that he will drive out the Canaanite, the Amorite, and Hittite, and the Perizzite, and the Hivite, and the Jebusite out of the land. Oh, but ' if thy presence go not with me, carry us up not hence.' I will bring the necks of all thy proud, stout, strong, and subtle enemies under thy feet. Oh, but ' if thy presence go not with me, carry us not up hence.' Ay, but, Deut. xxxii. 13-16, ' I will bring thee to a land flowing with milk and honey : I will make thee to ride on the high places of the earth, and I will make thee to suck honey out of the rock, and oil out of the flinty rock ; and thou shalt drink the pure blood of the grape.' Oh, but ' if thy presence go not with me, carry us not up hence.' I will bring thee to the paradise of the world, to a place of pleasure and delight, to Canaan, a type of heaven ! Oh, but ' if thy presence go not with me, carry us not up hence.' O Lord, if I might have my wish, my desire, my choice, I had infinitely rather to live in a barren, howling wilderness with thy presence, than in Canaan without it ! It is a mercy to have an angel to guard us, it is a mercy to have our enemies sprawling under our feet, it is a mercy to be brought into a pleasant land: oh, but ' if thy presence go not with me, carry us not up hence.' Lord, nothing will please us, nothing will profit us, nothing will secure us, nothing will satisfy us, without thy presence ; and therefore ' if thy presence go not with us, carry us not up hence.' I have read of the Tyrians, that they bound their gods with chains, that they might not in their greatest need pass over to the enemy ; and among the rest they

---

[1] ' Dead:' also ' stunned,' ' confused.'—G.

chained and nailed their god Apollo to a post, that they might be sure
to keep their idol, because they thought their safety was in it. I am
sure our safety, our comfort, our all, lies in the signal presence of God
with us; and therefore let us by faith and prayer chain God to us; if
we let him go, a thousand worlds cannot make up his absence. I suppose you have heard of the *palladium* of the heathens in Troy; they
imagined that so long as that idol was kept safe, they were unconquerable; all the strength and power of Greece were never able to
prevail against them. Wherefore the Grecians sought by all the
means they could to get it from them. O my friends, so long as you
keep the presence of God with you, I am sure you are unconquerable !
but if God withdraw his presence, the weakest enemy will be too hard
for you, yea, wounded men will prevail over you: Jer. xxxvii. 10,
'For though ye had smitten the whole army of the Chaldeans that
fight against you, and there remained but wounded men among them,
yet should they rise up and burn this city with fire.' The bush, which
was a type of the church, consumed not while it burned with fire,
because God was in the midst of it. Oh, do but keep God in the
midst of you, and nothing shall hurt you, nothing shall burn you ! but
if God depart, nothing can secure you, nor nothing can make up his
withdrawing from you. But,

[3.] Thirdly, To move you so to order, demean, and carry yourselves
as that you may enjoy the gracious presence of God with you in the
greatest troubles and deepest distresses, consider that if you do not
labour to demean, order, and carry yourselves so as that you may enjoy
the favourable, signal, and eminent presence of God with you in your
greatest troubles, deepest distresses, and most deadly dangers, *you have
high reason to question whether ever you have really enjoyed this
favourable, this signal presence of God with you or no;* for there are
always four things to be found in him that has really tasted, and in
good earnest experienced, the sweet, the life, the power, the virtue, that
is in the favourable signal presence of God—(1.) Such a person sets the
highest price and value imaginable upon it, he prizes it above all the
honours, riches, dignities, delights, comforts, and contents of this world,
Ps. iv. 6, 7; yea, he prizes it above life itself: Ps. lxiii. 3, 'Thy
loving-kindness is better than life.' The Hebrew is plural, *Chajim,
lives.* The loving-kindness of God, the presence of God in a wilderness, is better than lives, than many lives, than all lives with the ap-
purtenances. There is a greater excellency in the favour of God, in
the presence of God, than in all lives put together. There have been
many persons that have been weary of their lives, but there never was
any man that has been weary of the favour of God, of the presence of
God, 1 Kings xix. 4; Job vii. 15; Jonah iv. 8; Prov. xxviii. 14.
(2.) Such a person keeps up in his soul a humble fear of losing of it.
The divine presence is a jewel more worth than all the world, and he
that has experienced the sweetness of it had rather lose all he hath in
this world than lose it. I have read of a religious woman, that having
born nine children, professed that she had rather endure all the pains
of those nine travails at once, than endure the misery of the loss of
God's presence. (3.) Such a person keeps up in his soul a diligent
care to maintain this presence; his head, his heart is still a-contriving

how he may keep his God with him: Jer. xiv. 9, 'Why shouldest thou be as a man astonied, as a mighty man that cannot save? yet thou, O Lord, art in the midst of us, and we are called by thy name; leave us not.' This person had rather that his dearest friends should leave him, that his nearest relations should leave him, yea, that all the world should leave him, than that his God should leave him. The daily, yea, the hourly language of the soul is, Lord, leave me not; though all the world should leave me, yet don't thou leave me! (4.) Such a person will do all he can that all under his care and charge may partake of this signal presence of God; he will do his utmost that children, yoke-fellow, kindred, servants, may taste the sweetness of the divine presence, John i. 40 to the end, and iv. 28–43; Acts x. 24–36. When Samson had found honey in the carcase of the lion, he did not only eat himself, but he gave of the honey to his father and mother, and they did eat also, Judg. xiv. 8, 9. Of all sweets the presence of God is the greatest sweet; and whenever a poor soul comes to taste of this heavenly honey, he will do his best that all others, especially those that are near and dear to him, may taste of the same honey. But,

[4.] Fourthly, To move you so to order, demean, and carry yourselves as that you may enjoy the gracious presence of God with you in your greatest troubles and deepest distresses, consider *the excellent properties or qualities of this favourable, this signal presence of God with his people.* This I can but hint at, because I must hasten all I can to a close. (1.) It is the best presence, Ps. lxiii. 3. It is better than the presence of friends, of relations, of saints, of angels, &c. (2.) It is the greatest presence, it is the presence of the great King, it is the presence of the King of kings and Lord of lords, it is the presence not only of a mighty but of an almighty God, 1 Kings viii. 27; Rev. xvii. 14, and xix. 16; Num. xxiv. 4, 16; Ruth i. 20, 24. (3.) It is the happiest presence. It is a presence that makes a man really happy, presently happy, totally happy, eminently happy, and eternally happy, Ps. cxliv. 15; 1 Kings x. 8; Deut. xxxiii. 29; Prov. iii. 18. He can never be truly happy that wants this presence; he can never be truly miserable that enjoys this presence. True happiness is too great a thing to be found in anything below this favourable, this signal presence of God. He that enjoys this presence enjoys all; he that wants this presence enjoys nothing at all; he that wants this presence may write *nothing* or *nought* upon his honours, riches, pleasures, dignities, offices, relations, friends, &c., Amos vi. 13. All a man has are but ciphers without a figure if he be not blessed with this divine presence. This divine presence was Jacob's 'enough,' yea, Jacob's 'all:' Gen. xxxiii. 11, 'I have all,' Esau had much, *Li-zab*, 'I have much, my brother;' ver. 9, 'But Jacob had all.' *Habet omnia, qui habet habentem omnia,* 'He hath all who hath him that is all in all.' *Omne bonum in summo bono,* 'All good is in the chiefest good,' [Augustine.] Secure this divine presence, and you secure all, Col. iii. 11. (4.) It is the most desirable presence. Consult these scriptures in the margin.[1] Job xxiii. 3, 'Oh that I knew where I might find him! that I might come even to his seat.' Exod. xxxiii. 15, 'If thy presence go not

[1] Ps. xlii. 1, 2, lxiii. 1, 2, 8, and xxvii. 4; Gen. xxviii. 20; Ps. lxxxiv.

with me, carry us not up hence;' ver. 16, 'For wherein shall it be known here, that I and my people have found grace in thy sight, is it not in that thou goest with us?' Cant. iii. 1, 'By night on my bed I sought him whom my soul loveth, I sought him, but I found him not.' The presence of bad men is never desirable; the presence of good men is not always desirable, for there are cases wherein their presence may be a burden to us, as Job and others have experienced, Jer. ix. 1, 2; Job xvi. 1–4, and xix. 3–5. Job xvi. 2, 'Miserable comforters are ye all;' chap. xix. 2; 'How long will you vex my soul, and break me in pieces with words?' But the presence of the Lord is very desirable, most desirable, and always desirable, and the more any man has of this divine presence, the more his heart will be inflamed after more and more of it. A sound sincere Christian can never have enough power against sin, nor never enough strength against temptation, nor never enough weanedness from this world, nor never enough ripeness for heaven, nor never enough of the presence of the Lord. Enough of the divine presence he may have to quiet him, and cheer him, and encourage him, but whilst he is out of heaven he can never have enough of the divine presence to satisfy him, so as not to cry out, Lord, more of thy presence! oh, a little more of thy presence! Prov. xxx. 15, 16. (5.) It is the most joyful, refreshing, and delightful presence, Ps. xvi. 11; Acts v. 40, 41, and xvi. 25. This Vincentius and many thousand martyrs and suffering Christians have experienced in all the ages of the world, but of this before, Isa. lx. 1, 2; Ps. xlvi. 7. (6.) It is a peculiar and distinguishing presence, Exod. xxxiii. 16. This favourable signal presence of God is a choice jewel that he hangs on no breasts, a bracelet that he puts upon no arms, a crown that he sets upon no heads, but such whom he loves with a peculiar love, with an everlasting love. The general presence of God extends and reaches to all sinners and saints, angels and devils; to all, both in that upper and this lower world; but this favourable signal presence of God is peculiar to those that are the purchase of Christ's blood, and the travail of his soul, Jer. xxxi. 3; John xiii. 1; Ps. cxxxix. 7–10; 1 Pet. i. 18, 19; Isa. liii. 11; Ruth i. 4–18. (7.) It is an inflaming presence. Oh, how does it, [1.] Inflame the heart to duty! Ps. lxiii. 1–3. [2.] How does it inflame the heart against sin! Job xxxi. 4–7; Gen. xxxix. 9, 10; Rom. viii. 10. [3.] To long for the majestical and glorious presence of God in heaven, Cant. viii. 14; Luke ii. 28–30; 2 Cor. v. 8; Phil. i. 23; Rev. xxii. 20. [4.] How does it inflame their love to the Lord, his ways, his worship, his interest, his glory! Cant. i. 3, 4, ii. 3–6, and viii. 1–3, 5–7. [5.] It inflames against temptations, ver. 10, 11. It was this divine presence that did steel and strengthen Basil, Luther, and a world of others, against the worst of temptations, Heb. xi. [6.] It inflames the hearts of the saints into great freeness, readiness, and willingness to suffer many things, to suffer great things, to suffer anything for Christ, his gospel, his interest, &c. Oh, how did this divine presence make many martyrs hasten to the flames! &c. [8.] It is a soul-quieting, a soul-silencing, and a soul-stilling presence, Ps. iii. 5, iv. 8; Cant. ii. 3, iii. 4, 5. When friends can't quiet us, when relations can't quiet us, when ministers can't quiet us, when duties can't quiet us, when ordinances can't quiet us, when outward comforts can't quiet us, yet then this divine presence will quiet us. When babies[1] and rattles can't quiet the child, yet then the breasts can. So here. [9.] This divine presence is a sweetening presence: (1.) It sweetens all duties and services, public and private, ordinary and extraordinary. (2.) It sweetens all personal afflictions and trials. (3.) It sweetens all our sufferings for righteousness' sake. (4.) It sweetens all gospel ordinances, Exod. xx. 24. (5.) It sweetens all a man's outward mercies and blessings ; it sweetens health, strength, riches, trade, &c. (6.) It sweetens all interchangeable providences. Here providence smiles, and there it frowns ; here it lifts up, and there it casts down ; this providence is sweet, and that is bitter ; this providence kills, and that providence makes alive. Oh, but this divine presence sweetens every providence ! (7.) It sweetens all other presences ; it sweetens the presence of friends, it sweetens the presence of relations, it sweetens the presence of strangers, it sweetens all civil societies, it sweetens all religious societies. (8.) It sweetens the thoughts of death, the arrests of death ; it turns the king of terrors into the king of desires, Job xiv. 5, 14, xxx. 23, and xvii. 13, 14. How does Job court the worms, as if he were of a family with them, and near of kin to them ! How does he look upon the grave as his bed, and makes no more to die than to go to bed ! It was this divine presence that made the martyrs as willing to die as to dine. But,

[5.] Fifthly, To move you so to order, demean, and carry yourselves, as that you may enjoy the gracious presence of God with you in your greatest troubles and deepest distresses, consider that in great troubles, deep distresses, and most deadly dangers, *you will most need the favourable signal presence of God with you.* We always stand in need of the divine presence, but never so much as when we are under great troubles and deep distresses. For, (1,) In days of trouble and distress, men's affections are most apt to be greatly disordered, and their hearts discomposed, as you see in Job and Jonah, Job iii. ; Jonah iv. (2.) Now their fears, doubts, and disputes are apt to rise highest. When the wind rises high, and the sea roars, men are most apt to be afraid, Jonah ii. 2–7. (3.) Now Satan commonly is busiest. Satan loves to fish in troubled waters. When the hand of God is heaviest upon us, then Satan will shoot his most deadly darts at us, Job ii. 9 ; James i. 12. The sons of Jacob fell upon the Shechemites when they were sore, Gen. xxxiv. 25 ; and Amalek fell upon God's Israel and smote them, when they were weak, and feeble, and faint, and weary, Deut. xxv. 17–19 ; and Satan falls foul upon Christ, when he was in the wilderness, and when he had fasted forty days and forty nights, and was a-hungry, Mat. iv. 1–11 ; and as he dealt with the head, so he still deals with the members. (4.) Now unbelief is most turbulent, strong, and mighty in operation, as you may see in the spies, Num. xiii. 31–33, ' We be not able to go up against the people, for they are stronger than we. The land through which we have gone to search it, is a land that eateth up the inhabitants thereof; and all the people that we saw in it are men of great stature; and there we saw the giants, the sons of Anak, which come of the giants; and we were in our own sight as grasshoppers, and so we were in their sight:' so 2 Kings vi. 33, ' This evil is of the Lord ; what should I wait for the

[1] ' Dolls.'—G.

Lord any longer?' *Vide* 2 Kings vii. 1, 2, 19, 20 : so David, Ps. cxvi. 11, 'I said in my haste, all men are liars.' The prophets have all deceived me, and Samuel has deluded me, they have told me of a kingdom, a crown, but I shall never wear the one, nor possess the other : so 1 Sam. xxvii. 1, 'I shall now perish one day by the hand of Saul.' Thus his fear is got above his faith, and his soul wherried about with unbelief, to the scandal of the weak, and the scorn of the wicked, besides his own particular disadvantage. (5.) Now fainting-fits will be most strengthened, increased, and multiplied. Now faint-ing-fits, like Job's messengers, or like the rolling waves, will come thick one upon another, Prov. xxiv. 10 ; Job iv. 5 ; Lam. i. 12, 13. (6.) Now conscience will be most startled and disquieted, Gen. xlii. 21, and l. 15 ; 1 Kings xvii. 18. Great troubles and deep distresses are many times like strong physic, which stirs the humours and makes the patient sick, very sick, yea, heart-sick. Conscience commonly never reads the soul such sad and serious lectures as when the rod lies heaviest upon the back. By all which you see, what high cause the people of God have so to order, demean, and carry themselves, as that they may find the gracious presence of God with them in their greatest troubles, and deepest distresses, for then they will certainly need most of the divine presence. But,

[6.] Sixthly, To move you so to order, demean, and carry your-selves, as that you may enjoy the gracious presence of God with you in your greatest troubles and deepest distresses, consider *this divine presence will make you divinely fearless in the midst of your greatest troubles and deepest distresses :* Ps. xxiii. 4, 'Though I walk through the valley of the shadow of death, I will fear no evil; for thou art with me, thy rod and thy staff they comfort me :' Ps. xlvi. 2, 'We will not fear though the earth be removed, and though the mountains be carried into the midst of the sea :' ver. 3, 'Though the waters thereof roar,' &c, Why ? 'God is in the midst of her, she shall not be moved; God shall help her, and that right early,' ver. 5 ; 'The Lord of hosts is with us, the God of Jacob is our refuge. Selah,' ver. 7 : Num. xiv. 9, 'Neither fear ye the people, for they are bread for us, their defence is departed from them, and the Lord is with us; fear them not :' Deut. vii. 21, 'Thou shalt not be affrighted at them, for the Lord thy God is among you, a mighty God and terrible :' so Heb. xiii. 5, 'I will never leave thee, nor forsake thee;' ver. 6, 'I will not fear what man shall do unto me.' There is no such way to keep down all base slavish fears of men, as to keep up the presence of God in the midst of you. You will not fear the power of men, nor the policy of men, nor the threats of men, nor the wrath of men, if you do but enjoy this gracious, this signal presence of God that is under our present consideration. Men's fears are never so rampant as when God withdraws his presence from them, 1 Sam. xxviii. 15, 20. But,

[7.] Seventhly, To move you so to order, demean, and carry your-selves, as that you may enjoy the gracious presence of God with you in your greatest troubles and deepest distresses, consider *that there is in God a very great unwillingness to withdraw his presence from his people when they are in great troubles and deep distresses :* Ezek. viii. 6, 'Son of man, seest thou what they do ? even the great abominations that the house of Israel committeth here, that I should go far off from my sanctuary?' Isa. i. 2-4, 16, 18; Ezek. xviii. 31, and xxxiii. 11; Jer. iii. 13, 14. Of all sins, the sin of idolatry drives God farthest off from his sanctuary. When God goes off from a people, he goes not off rashly, he goes not off suddenly, but he goes off gradually; he removes not at once, but by degrees; now a step, and then a step, as Lot did when he lingered in Sodom, Gen. xix. 16. Lot was not more loath to depart out of Sodom than God is loath to leave his people.[1] He goes first to the threshold: Ezek. ix. 3, 'And the glory of the God of Israel was gone up from the cherub whereupon he was to the threshold of the house.' Then over the threshold: x. 4, 'Then the glory of the Lord went up from the cherub, and stood over the threshold of the house.' Here is a second step. This is the second time of resting before God departs. The Lord had his ordinary dwelling-place in the holy of holies. Now God's first remove was from the most holy place; his second remove was from the holy place; his third remove was higher towards heaven: ver. 19, 'And the cherubims lift up their wings, and mounted up from the earth in my sight, then to the door of the east gate,' or foremost gate, 'of the Lord's house,' to note God's total remove from his house. Then to the midst of the city: Ezek. xi. 23, 'And the glory of the Lord went up from the midst of the city, and then he stood upon the mountain which is on the east side of the city.' This is God's last stop in his departure, by which is signified that he was willing to make one trial more, to see if the people would, in this present danger, call him back by invitation and lively repentance. God is greatly troubled when it comes to parting: Hosea xi. 8, 'How shall I give thee up, Ephraim? how shall I deliver thee, Israel? how shall I make thee as Admah? how shall I set thee as Zeboim? Mine heart is turned within me, my repentings are kindled together.' This is spoken *per anthropopatheian* and not properly, because diverse thoughts and repentance are not incident to God, 'who is without all variableness, or shadow of change,' James i. 17. The Lord seemeth here to be at a stand, or at strife with himself, about the destruction of this people. Howbeit God, in the bowels of his mercy, yearning, and taking pity of his elect amongst them, spareth to lay upon them the extremity of his wrath, and is ready to save them for his mercy's sake. Observe how fatherlike he melts and mourns over them, and how mercy interposeth her four several ' hows!' Here are four such pathetical interrogations as the like are not to be found in the whole book of God, and not to be answered by any but God himself, as indeed he doth to each particular in the following words: 'My heart is turned within me;' that is the first answer. The second is, 'My repentings are kindled together.' The third is, 'I will not execute the fierceness of my wrath.' The fourth is, 'I will not destroy Ephraim.' And why? First, 'I am God, and not man;' secondly, 'The Holy One in the midst of thee.' God is mighty unwilling to break up house, and to leave his people desolate. Now is God so unwilling to withdraw his presence; and shall not we do all what we can to retain him in the midst of us? When dear friends are unwilling to leave us, we are

---

[1] 1 Sam. iv. 4; Ps. viii. 20; Isa. xxxvii. 16.

the more earnest in pressing them to stay and abide with us. God is marvellously unwilling to go, and therefore let us, with the church, cry out, 'Leave us not,' Jer. xiv. 9. But,

[8.] Eighthly, To move you so to order, demean, and carry yourselves, as that you may enjoy the gracious presence of God with you in your greatest troubles and deepest distresses, consider *that troubles will be no troubles, distresses will be no distresses, dangers will be no dangers, if you can but secure the presence of God with you.* Mountains will be molehills, stabs at the heart will be but as scratches upon the hand, if the divine presence be with you. God's signal presence will turn storms into calms, winter nights into summer days, prisons into palaces, banishments into enlargements. The favourable presence of God will turn sickness into health, weakness into strength, poverty into plenty, and death into life. It can never be night so long as the sun shines. No afflictions, no trials, can make it night with a Christian, so long as he enjoys the presence of God with his spirit, 2 Tim. iv. 22. That courtier need not complain that this man slights him, and that the other neglects him, who enjoys the delightful presence of his prince. When Samson had the presence of God with him, he made nothing of carrying the gates of the city, with the posts and bars, to the top of a hill, Judges xvi. 3. So whilst a Christian enjoys the singular presence of God with him, he will make nothing of this affliction and that, of this trouble and that, of this loss and that. This presence makes heavy afflictions light, and long afflictions short, and bitter afflictions sweet, 2 Cor. iv. 16, 17. It was this presence that made the martyrs set light by all the great and grievous things that they suffered for Christ's sake and the gospel's sake, Heb. xi. 33–39. God's gracious presence makes every condition to be a little heaven to the believing soul. A man in misery, without this gracious presence of God, is in a very hell on this side hell. There is nothing, there can be nothing, but heaven, where God is signally present. But,

[9.] Ninthly, To move you so to order, demean, and carry yourselves, as that you may enjoy the gracious presence of God with you in your greatest troubles and deepest distresses, consider *that the worst of men cannot fasten a curse upon you whilst you keep the presence of God with you*: Num. xxiii. 21, 'The Lord his God is with him, and the shout of a king is among them.' There could be no enchantment against them, for the Lord their God was with them, and the shout of a king was among them, that is, God reigneth as a king among them. Hereby also is meant the faith, joy, boldness, courage, and confidence of God's people in their king. As when a king comes amongst the armies of his people, he is received with joyful shoutings and acclamations, and when he goes forth to battle with them, he goes accompanied with the sound of trumpets and shouts of the people, signs of their joy and courage; so it fared with the Israelites, because of that signal presence of God that was amongst them, which was evident by his protecting and defending of them: 1 Sam. iv. 5, 'And when the ark of the covenant of the Lord came into the camp, all Israel shouted with a great shout, so that the earth rang again.' Here is a valorous shout of a puissant people, encouraging each other to the battle, and a victorious shout as having obtained the victory in the battle. So 2 Chron. xiii.

12, 'And behold, God himself is with us for our captain, and his priests with sounding trumpets to cry alarm against you, O children of Israel.' Num. xxiii. 23, 'Surely there is no enchantment against Jacob, neither is there any divination against Israel;' that is, there is none against Israel that shall be of force, or that shall take any effect to do the posterity of Jacob or Israel any hurt, any harm, any prejudice. But why? Because the Lord his God is with him, and the shout of a king is among them. The presence of God with his Israel blasts all Balaam's enchantments, and makes null and void all his divinations. God is with his people to counsel them in all doubtful and difficult cases, and to defend them, and secure them against all their enemies and opposers. Balaam had a month's mind to curse the people of God, as his unwearied endeavours to that purpose do abundantly evidence, Num. xxiii. 1, 13, 28, 29, and xxiv. 1; but the presence of God with his people prevented all his mischievous designs. Shimei curses David, but his curses could not hurt him, for God was with him, 2 Sam. xvi. 7, 9, 11, 12. The people generally cursed Jeremiah, chap. xv. 10, and i. 17–19; but all their curses could not harm him, for God was with him. The Jews in their prayers daily curse the Christian churches, but all their curses can't prejudice them, because God is in the midst of them, Exod. xx. 24. And who will say that the reformed churches are one pin the worse for all the pope's excommunications and execrations with bell, book, and candle? The signal presence of God with his people is a most sovereign antidote against all the curses and cursings of cursed men, and therefore whatever you part with, be sure you don't part with your God; let him be but in the midst of you, and then no curses shall be prevalent against you. This age abounds with such monsters, whose mouths are full of curses; but if every curse should stick a visible blister on the curser's tongue, as it doth insensible ones on the curser's soul, their tongues would quickly be too big for their mouths, and they would soon grow weary of cursing the people of God, the things of God, the ways of God, the providences of God, and the faithful dispensers of the mysteries of God. But the best of it is, when they have done their worst, and spat out all their curses, 'the curse causeless will not come,' Prov. xxvi. 2, for the ever-blessed God is in his people, and with his people, and among his people, and 'a wall of fire always about his people,' Zech. ii. 5, and therefore they are safe and secure enough when men and devils have done their worst. But,

[10.] Tenthly and lastly, To move you so to order, demean, and carry yourselves, as that you may enjoy the gracious presence of God with you in your greatest troubles and deepest distresses, consider *that the divine presence will make up the absence of all outward comforts.* This gracious presence will supply and fill up the place of a friend, a child, a father, a husband. Some of the rabbis write that manna had all sorts of tastes and all sorts of sweets in it. Sure I am that the favourable presence of God has all sorts of sweets in it, Ps. iv. 6, 7; Prov. iv. 23. It has the sweet of all ordinances in it, it has the sweet of all duties in, it has the sweet of all church privileges in it, it has the sweet of all relations in it, it has the sweet of all your outward comforts in it; and therefore, above all keeping, keep the presence of

God with you. Many in their distresses and miseries are full of complaints. One cries out, he wants a faithful friend; another cries out, he wants an active relation; a third cries out that he wants necessaries both for back and belly; a fourth cries out he wants the means that others enjoy; but he that enjoys the gracious presence of God finds all these wants made up to him—yea, he finds the divine presence to be infinitely better than the presence of all outward comforts. As Elkanah said to Hannah, ' Am not I better than ten sons ?' 1 Sam. i. 8, so assuredly the presence of the Lord is wonderfully better than all other things to every soul that has tasted the sweetness of it. You know that one sun is more glorious, delightful, useful, and comfortable than ten thousand stars; so here. Seneca tells a courtier that had lost his son, *Fas tibi non est, salvo Cæsare, de fortuna tua queri,* &c., That he had no cause to mourn, either for that or aught else, so long as his sovereign was in safety, and he in favour with his sovereign; he had all things in· him, and he should be unthankful to his good fortune if he were not cheerful both in heart and look, so long as things stood so with him as they did. How much more may we. say to every sincere Christian that enjoys the gracious presence of God with him, let thy wants and thy crosses be never so great, thy afflictions never so pressing, thy necessities never so biting, thou hast no just cause to be troubled or dejected, so long as thou art in favour with God, and enjoyest the presence of God. All mercies, all comforts, all contentments, all enjoyments, they meet and centre in the gracious presence of God, as all lights meet in the sun, and as all waters meet in the sea; and therefore let not that soul mourn or complain of the want of anything, who enjoys that gracious presence of God that is better than every terrene thing. Thus much for the motives.

· But some may say, O sir, what means should we use that we may enjoy the gracious presence of the Lord with us in our greatest troubles, deepest distresses, and most deadly dangers ? I answer,

1. *First, There are some things that you must carefully shun and take heed of;* as,

[1.] First, Take heed *of high sinnings, take heed of scandalous sins.* High sinnings do greatly dishonour God, wound conscience, reproach religion, stagger the weak, grieve the strong, open the mouths of the wicked, and provoke God to withdraw his gracious presence, Ps. li. 11, 12; Exod. xxxii. 8, and xxxiii. 3; Isa. lxiii. 10. Turn to these scriptures, and seriously ponder upon them. Great transgressions do eclipse the favour of God as well as the honour of God. In great transgressions we turn our backs upon God, and God turns away his face from us. Gross sins will provoke God to withdraw his presence, both in respect of vigour and strength, as also in respect of peace and comfort. But,

[2.] Secondly, Take heed *of impenitency.* Next to our being preserved from sin, it is the greatest mercy in the world, when we are fallen by our transgressions, to make a quick and speedy return to God. When by your sins you have made work for repentance, for hell, or for the physician, souls, immediately make up the breach, take up the controversy between God and your souls, humble yourselves, judge yourselves, and speedily return to the Most High, Hosea vi. 1 ; Exod. xxxii. 9–15.   Thus Peter did, and recovered the favourable presence of God presently, Mat. xxvi. 75 ; Mark xvi. 7.   But if men will commit sin and lie in it, if they will fall and have no mind to rise, God will certainly withdraw his favourable presence from them, as you see in David and Solomon, Ps. li. 11, 12 ; 1 Kings xi. 9 ; Josh. vii. 1–5.   This is further evident in that case of Achan, Josh. vii., ' The Israelites they came to fight with the men of Ai, and fled before them, for the Lord was not with them.'   Why, what was the cause of God's withdrawing himself ?   See ver. 11, ' Israel hath sinned.'   And ver. 12, ' Therefore the children of Israel could not stand before their enemies, but turned their backs.'   Their sins having betrayed them into the hand of divine justice, and into their enemies' hands also ; mark what follows, ' Neither will I be with you any more, except ye destroy the accursed from amongst you.'   If we will not stone our Achans, our sins, by the lively exercise of faith and repentance ; if we will keep up our lusts in despite of all that God does against us, we must never expect to retain the gracious presence of God with us. But,

[3.] Thirdly, Take heed either of *neglecting gospel-worship, or of corrupting gospel-worship.*   Omissions will damn as well as commissions, and omissions will provoke God to withdraw his presence, as well as commissions.   When persons are careless in their attendance on gospel ordinances, no wonder if God withdraw his presence from them in their distresses, Cant. v. 2, 3, 6, and iv. 1–3.   Cain went off from ordinances, and the Lord set a mark upon him, Gen. iv. 15, 16.   Oh, the black and dismal marks of misery, that God has set upon many that have neglected gospel-worship, and for profit's sake, and for Diana's sake, are fallen roundly in with the worship of the world !   2 Tim. iv. 10 ; Acts xix. 24, 36.   O sirs, the great God stands upon nothing more in all the world than upon purity in his worship.   There is nothing that doth so provoke and exasperate God against a people as corrupt worship.   Corrupt worship sadly reflects upon the name of God, the honour of God, the truth of God, and the wisdom of God ; and therefore his heart rises against such worship and worshippers, and he will certainly withdraw from them, and be a swift and terrible witness against them, as you may see by comparing the scriptures in the margin together.[1]   Corrupt worship is contrary to the unity of God.   Now deny his unity, and you deny his deity, ' For the Lord is one, and his name is one,' Zech. xiv. 9.   It is contrary to the sovereignty of God, ' He is the only ruler, the only potentate,' 1 Tim. vi. 15.   It is contrary to the all-sufficiency of God. The heathen worshipped several gods, as thinking that several gods did bestow several blessings.   They begged health of one god, wealth of another god, and victory of a third god, thus imagining to themselves several deities for several supplies.   Their god was but a Jupiter, a partial helper, an auxiliary god, but ' our God is Jehovah,' who is abundantly able to supply all our wants, Eph. iii. 20.   Now, if either we neglect his true instituted worship, or fall in with a false worship,

[1] Ps. cvi. 39–43; Ps. lxxviii. 58–64 ; 2 Chron. vii. 19–22, and xxxii. 16–21; Deut. xxix. 22–29.

he was, by the consent of his wife, slain by his own household servants with daggers in his privy-chamber. His body was buried without honour, his memory cursed to posterity, and his arms and ensigns were thrown down and defaced. Julian vowed to make a sacrifice of the Christians upon his return from the wars ; but, in a battle against the Persians, he was deadly wounded, and throwing his blood in the air, in a high contempt of Christ, he died with that desperate blasphemous expression in his mouth, *Vicisti tandem, Galilœe*, ' Thou Galilean hast overcome me.'

Felix, Earl of Wurtemberg, was a great persecutor of the saints, and did swear that ere he died he would ride up to the spurs in the blood of the Lutherans ; but the very same night, wherein he had thus sworn and vowed, he was choked in his own blood.

The judgments of God were so famous and frequent upon the persecutors of the saints in Bohemia, that it was used as a proverb among the adversaries themselves, that if any man were weary of his life let him but attempt against the Piccardines—so they called the Christians—and he should not live a year to an end. By these short hints you may see that all along God has made good that word that is more worth than a world, ' Surely the wrath of man shall praise thee ; and the remainder of wrath shalt thou restrain '—Hebrew, ' Shalt thou gird,' that is, curb, and keep within compass ; or as the Greek hath it, ' It shall keep holiday to thee,' that is, cease from working or acting outwardly, how restless soever it be within.[1] ' The remainder of wrath shalt thou restrain,' that is, those that are left alive of thy wrathful enemies, that have still any malice against thy people, thou wilt curb and restrain, and not suffer their wrath to be so great as formerly ; or if they go about to recruit their forces, and to set again upon thy people, thou wilt set such bounds to their wrath that they shall not accomplish their desires, nor shall they proceed one step further than shall make signally for thy glory and thy people's good ; so some carry the words. The more eager and furious the enemies are against God's people, the more honour and glory will God get in protecting and securing his people, and in girding, binding, and tying up their enemies. Were it not for this favourable, signal, and eminent presence of God with his people in their greatest troubles, deepest distresses, and most deadly dangers, wicked men would still be a-multiplying of their sorrows, increasing their troubles, and adding of burden to burden. It is this favourable presence of God that binds wicked men over to their good behaviour, and that chains them up from doing that mischief that they design and intend. But,

(5.) Fifthly, The Lord does manifest his favourable, signal, and eminent presence with his people, in their greatest troubles, deepest distresses, and most deadly dangers, *by guiding and leading them into those paths and waves which make most for their own peace and quiet, safety and security, contentation and satisfaction, happiness here, and blessedness hereafter*, Exod. xii. 21, 22 ; Isa. lxiii. 12–14 ; Ps. v. 8. Deut. xxxii. 10, ' He found me in a desert land, and in the waste howling wilderness ; he led him about, he instructed him, he kept him

---

[1] Ps. lxxvi. 10—Hebrew, ' Gird,' that is, keep it within compass as with a girdle.

hazard of honour! Oh the 'damage of dignity! how soon are we broken upon the soft pillow of ease! Flies settle upon the sweetest perfumes when cold; and so does sin on the best hearts, when they are dissolved and dispirited by prosperity. Oh how apt are the holiest of men to be proud and secure, and promise themselves more than ever God promised them—viz., immunity from the cross. He thought that his kingdom and all prosperity was tied unto him with cords of adamant; he sitting quietly at Jerusalem, and free from fear of all his enemies, 2 Sam. xi. 1; but God quickly confutes his carnal confidence by giving him to know that he could as easily blast the strongest oak as he could trample the smallest worm under his feet. Ver. 7, 'Thou didst hide thy face, and I was troubled.' God will quickly suspend his favour and withdraw his presence when his children begin to be proud and carnally confident. Look, as at the eclipse of the sun the whole frame of nature droops; so when God hides his face, when he withdraws his presence, the best of saints cannot but droop and hang down their heads. So Jer. xvii. 5, 'Cursed be the man that trusteth in man, and maketh flesh his arm, and whose heart departeth from the Lord.' Ver. 6, 'For he shall be like the heath in the desert, and shall not see when good cometh.' But,

[6.] Sixthly, Take heed *of barrenness and unfruitfulness under gospel ordinances.* Turn to these scriptures, Isa. v. 1-8; Mat. xxxi. 34-42; 2 Chron. xxxii. 16, to the last. Of all spiritual judgments, barrenness is the greatest; and when men are given up to this judgment, God withdraws; he has no pleasure to dwell in a barren soil. What are barren grounds and barren wombs to barren hearts? He that remains wholly barren under gospel ordinances, may well question his marriage-union with Christ, Ezek. xlvii. 11; Mat. xiii. 19; Hosea ix. 14; John xv. 3; Heb. ii. 6-8; Jude 12: for, Rom. vii. 4, We are said to be 'married to Christ, that we may bring forth fruit to God.' There is a double end of marriage—viz., cohabitation and propagation; and therefore there cannot be a greater and clearer evidence that thou art not yet taken into a married union with Christ, than a total barrenness under gospel enjoyments. Christ's spouse is fruitful: Cant. i. 16, 'Our bed is green;' chap. iv. 1, 'Behold, thou art fair, my love, behold, thou art fair: thou hast doves' eyes within thy locks: thy hair is as a flock of goats, that appear from mount Gilead;' ver. 2, 'Thy teeth are like a flock of sheep that are even shorn, which come up from the washing: whereof every one bears twins, and none is barren among them.' Christ hath no further delight in his people, nor will no further grace his people with his special presence, than they make conscience of weeping over their barrenness, and of bringing forth fruit to him, Cant. vii. 11-13. 'Now my husband will love me, now he will be joined to me, now I have born him this son also,' Gen. xxix. 34, said Leah. So may the fruit-bearing soul reason it out with Christ: Now I know dear Jesus will love me, now I know he will delight in me, now I know he will dwell with me, now I know he will honour me with his presence, for now I bring forth fruit unto him. Barrenness under the means of grace drives God from us, and the gospel from us, and trade, and peace, and prosperity from us, and one Christian from another. Ursinus observes, that the sins and barrenness of the Protestants under the gospel in king Edward's days, brought in the persecution in queen Mary's days; and he tells us, that those who fled out of England in queen Mary's days acknowledged that that calamity befell them for their great unprofitableness under the means of grace in king Edward's days. Among other prodigies, which were about the time that Julian came to the empire, there were wild grapes appeared upon the vines, with which many wise men in that day were much affected, looking upon it as ominous. Ah, England! England! I look upon nothing to be so ominous to thee as the barrenness of the professors of the day! No wonder if God leave his house, when the trees that are planted in it and about it are all barren. The nutmeg-tree makes barren all the ground about it; so doth the spice of worldly love make the hearts of Christians barren under the means of grace. But I must hasten.

[7.] Seventhly, Take heed *of pride and haughtiness of spirit:*[1] Hosea v. 5, 'And the pride of Israel doth testify to his face: therefore shall Israel and Ephraim fall in their iniquity: Judah also shall fall with them;' ver. 6, 'They shall go with their flocks, and with their herds to seek the Lord,' but they shall not find him, he hath withdrawn himself from them.' Pride is the great master-pock of the soul; it will bud and blossom, it cannot be hid; it is the leprosy of the soul, that breaks forth in the very forehead, and so testifieth to his face, Ezek. vii. 10; Isa. iii. 16-25. Some have called Rome, *Epitomen universi,* An epitome, or abridgment of the whole world: so it may be said of pride, that it is the sum of all naughtiness, a sea of sin, a complicated sin, a mother sin, a breeding sin, a sin that has all sorts of sin in the womb of it. Consult the scriptures in the margin.[2] Aristotle, speaking of justice, saith, That in justice all virtues are couched, συλλήβδην, summarily; so it may be truly said of pride, that in it all vices are as it were in a bundle lapped up together; and therefore no wonder if God withdraw his presence from proud persons, 'He hath withdrawn himself from them'—*Heb.,* 'Hath snatched away himself;' hath thrown himself out of their company, as Peter threw himself out from the rude soldiers into a by-corner to weep bitterly, Mark xiv. 72. God will have nothing to do with proud persons, he will never dwell with them, he will never keep house with them. He that dwells in the highest heavens will never dwell in a haughty heart. 'The proud he knoweth afar off,' Isa. lvii. 15;. Ps. cxxxviii. 6. He won't vouchsafe to come so near such loathsome lepers; he stands off from such as [are] odious and abominable; he cannot abide the sight of them, yea, his very heart rises against them, Prov. xv. 25, and xvi. 5: James iv. 6, 'God resisteth the proud,'—ἀντιτάσσεται, 'He sets himself in battle array against him,' as the Greek word emphatically signifies. Above all sorts of sinners, God sets himself against proud persons, as invaders of his territories and foragers or plunderers of his chief treasures. God defieth such as deify themselves. God will arm himself against them, he will never vouchsafe his gracious presence to them; and therefore as ever you would enjoy the divine presence, arm against pride, watch against pride, and pray hard against pride. But,

[8.] Eighthly, Take heed *of a slothful, lazy, trifling spirit in the*

---

[1] See my 'Unsearchable Riches' of Christ, pp. 49-58. [Vol. iii. pp. 41-48.—G.]

[2] Hab. i. 16; Isa. xlviii. 9, and xxvi. 12; Hab. ii. 5, &c.

things of God: Cant. v. 2, 'I sleep, but my heart waketh; it is the voice of my beloved that knocketh, saying, Open to me, my sister, my love, my dove, my undefiled; for my head is filled with dew, and my locks with the drops of the night;' ver. 3, 'I have put off my coat, how shall I put it on? I have washed my feet, how shall I defile them?' Christ's head is filled with dew; *i.e.*, Christ came to his spouse full of the dew of spiritual and heavenly blessings. Christ always brings meat in his mouth, and a reward in his hand, Eph. i. 3, 4; Rev. xxii. 12. Christ never visits his people empty handed. He is no beggarly or niggardly guest. When he comes, he brings everything that heart can wish or need require. And now stand and wonder at the silly excuse that the spouse makes for herself: ver. 3, Trouble me not, for I am in bed; my clothes are off, my feet are washed, and I am composed to a settled rest! But are you so indeed? might Christ have replied. Is this your kindness to your friend? 2 Sam. xvi. 17. Is this the part and posture of a vigilant Christian? Would it not have been much better for you to have had your loins girt, your lamp burning, and you waiting for your Lord's return? Is it so great a trouble? Is it such a mighty business for you to rise out of your bed, to put on your clothes, and to let in such a guest, as comes not to take anything from you, but to enrich you with the best and noblest of favours? Now mark how severely Christ punishes his spouse's sluggishness, laziness, slothfulness, and delays to entertain him when he knocked: ver. 6, 'I opened to my beloved, but my beloved had withdrawn himself, and was gone: my soul failed when he spake: I sought him, but I could not find him; I called him, but he gave no answer;' or he was gone, he was gone, a most passionate complaint for his departure; or my best-beloved was departed, he was gone away. By the iteration or doubling of this sentence, wherein the spouse complains of the departure of her bridegroom, is signified her great trouble, her hearty sorrow, her inexpressible grief, that lay as a heavy load upon her spirit; because, by her unworthy usage of him, she had foolishly occasioned him to withdraw his presence from her. Spiritual desertions are of three sorts: (1.) Cautional, for preventing of sin, as Paul's seems to be, 1 Cor. i. 2, 8, 9; (2.) Probational, for trial and exercise of grace; (3.) Penal, for chastisement of spiritual sloth and sluggishness, as here in the spouse. Now this last is far the saddest and heaviest; and therefore as ever you would enjoy the gracious presence of the Lord, take heed of a lazy, slothful, sluggish spirit in the things of God, in the concernments of your souls. That man must needs be miserable that is lazy and slothful, and had rather go sleeping to hell than sweating to heaven. But,

[9.] Ninthly, Take heed *of a covetous worldly spirit under the smarting rod, under the severe rebukes of God:* Isa. lvii. 17, 'For the iniquity of his covetousness I was wroth, and smote him: I hid me, and was wroth, and he went on frowardly in the way of his heart.' Covetousness was the common sin of the Jews. This disease had infected all sorts and ranks of men; this leprosy did spread itself over princes, prophets, and people, as you may see in comparing the scriptures in the margin together.[1] Now 'covetousness being the root of

---

[1] Isa. lvi. 11; Jer. vi. 13, and viii. 10; 1 Tim. vi. 10.

all evil,' as the apostle speaks, and the darling sin of the nation, God
is so provoked by it that he first smites, and then hides himself, as one
that in displeasure, having left one to the evil and harsh usage of
some other, withdraweth himself out of the way, and having shut himself up in his closet, will not be seen or spoken with. A worldly man
makes the world his god. Covetousness is flat idolatry : Col. iii. 5,
'Mortify therefore your members which are upon the earth ; fornication, uncleanness, inordinate affection, evil concupiscence, and covetousness, which is idolatry.' Now though it be true that whatever a man
loves most and best, that is his god, be it his belly or his back ;
yet, in a special manner, covetousness is idolatry, so as no other sin is,
Phil. iii. 19 ; Isa. iii. 16–25. Three things especially make a god ;
First, our judgment, when we esteem it in our serious thoughts to be
our chiefest good, and that in which we place our happiness. Now
the covetous man looks upon the riches of the world as his heaven,
his happiness, his great all. Pope Sylvester placed so much happiness
in riches, that, to enjoy the popedom for seven years, he sold his soul
to the devil. The people of Constantinople placed so much of their
happiness in riches, and were so excessively covetous, that they were
buying and selling in their shops, even three days after the Turks
were within the walls of the city, and that was the reason that the
streets run down with the blood of them, their wives, and children.
Secondly, our confidence. That is a homage which makes a god,
when we place our trust in anything make it our rock, our fortress,
our all-sufficient good. This the covetous man doth, ' He saith to the
wedge of gold, thou art my confidence,' Job xxi. 34. The rich man's
heart dances about his golden calf, saying to his ' wedge of gold, thou
art my confidence ;' and yet his wedge of gold shall prove but as
Achan's wedge, a wedge to cleave his soul in sunder, and, as that
Babylonish garment, to be his winding-sheet, Josh. vii. 21 to end. ' The
rich man's wealth is his strong city,' Prov. x. 15 ; 1 Tim. vi. 27.
Covetous persons do really think themselves simply the better and the
safer for their hoards and heaps of riches ; but they may one day find
themselves greatly mistaken. Famous is that story of Crœsus among
the heathens.[1]   He was a great king, and tumbled up and down
in his gold and silver ; and Solon, that wise man of Greece, coming
into his country, he desired to speak with him, and when he saw him,
after Solon had seen and viewed all his wealth and glory, he asked
him whom he thought to be the happiest man in the world, imagining
that Solon would have said Crœsus. But Solon answered, I think
Tellus was the most happy man. Tellus, saith he ; why Tellus ?
Because, said Solon, though he was poor, yet he was a good man, and
content with that which he had ; and having governed the commonwealth well, and brought up his child honestly and religiously, he
died honourably. Well, then, said Crœsus, but who dost thou think
the second happy man in the world ? I think, said he, those two brothers
that, instead of horses, drew their mother in a chariot to the temple.
Whereupon, said Crœsus, what thinkest thou of me ? I think, says
he, thou art a very rich man ; but a man may be happy though he be
poor, and a man may be unhappy though he be rich, for he may lose

[1] Herodot., lib. i.

all his riches before he die; and therefore, *Ante obitum nemo, &c.*, I think none truly happy but he that lives well and dies well. Whereupon that wise man Solon was dismissed the court with neglect. But afterward this Crœsus, making war against Cyrus, he was overcome by Cyrus; and being taken captive, he was laid upon a pile of wood to be burned to death, then lying on the pile of wood he cried out and said, O Solon! Solon! Solon! Cyrus inquiring what he meant, he answered, This Solon was a wise man of Greece, that told me that happiness did not consist in riches, for they might all be lost, and a rich man might die miserable; whose words, said he, I then neglected, but now I find true; and therefore now I cry out, O Solon, Solon, Solon! Let us now tell the covetous man, the worldly man, that his happiness lies not in riches, though he looks upon his riches as his strong city; he won't mind us, he won't regard. Oh but there is a time a-coming wherein the worldling will cry out, O Solon, Solon, Solon! *Thirdly,* Our service, Mat. vi. 24. That is a homage which makes a god. When we devote all our pains, labour, and service to it, be it this or that, that makes a god. Now the covetous man, his heart is most upon the world, his thoughts are most upon the world, his affections are most upon the world, and his discourse is most about the world. He that hath his mind taken up with the world, and chiefly delighted with the world's music, he hath also his tongue tuned to the same key, and taketh his joy and comfort in speaking of nothing else but the world and worldly things. If the world be in the heart, it will break out at the lips. A worldly-minded man speaketh of nothing but worldly things. 'They are of the world, therefore they speak of the world,' John iv. 5. The water riseth not above the fountain. Out of the warehouse the shop is furnished. The love of this world makes men forget God, neglect Christ, slight ordinances, refuse heaven, despise holiness, and oils the tongue for worldly discourses, Mat. xix. 21, 22. Ah the time, the thoughts, the strength, the spirits, the words that are spent upon the world, and the things of the world, whilst sinners' souls lie a-bleeding, and eternity is posting on upon them! I have read of a griping usurer, who was always best when he was most in talking of the world. Being near his end, he was much pressed to make his will. At last he was overcome, and then he dictates to the scrivener after this manner:—First, I bequeath my own soul to the devil, for being so greedy of the muck of this world; item, next I give my wife's soul to the devil, for persuading me to this course of life; item, I give the parson of our parish's soul to the devil, because he did not shew me the danger I lived in, nor reprove me for it. Oh, the danger of making the world our god, when we come to die and to make up our accounts with God! Now when men make the world their god, and set up their riches, pleasures, and profits in the place of God, no wonder if God withdraws his presence from them; and therefore, as ever you would retain the gracious presence of God with you, take heed of a covetous spirit, a worldly spirit. But,

[10.] Tenthly and lastly, As ever you would enjoy the gracious presence of God with you in your greatest troubles, deepest distresses, and most deadly dangers, take heed *of a cross, froward, and inflexible spirit under the rod.*[1]   When the child is froward under the rod, the father withdraws; so here, Isa. lvii. 17, 'I was wroth, I smote him; I hid me, and was wroth, and he went on frowardly in the way of his heart;' Isa. xlvii. 6.   Though I manifested my displeasure by giving them up to their enemies, and by laying them under the tokens of my anger, they persisted in their own cross, crooked, and rebellious courses, refusing to repent and turn to the Most High; and therefore God changes his countenance, hides his face, and withdraws his presence from them: Deut. xxxii. 20, 'And he said, I will hide my face from them, for they are a very froward generation.' *Heb.*, A generation of perversenesses. When the sick man is froward, friends withdraw and leave him alone: Ps. xviii. 26, 'With the froward thou wilt shew thyself froward.' God will meet with froward persons in their own way, and make them reap the fruits of their own doings.   God will walk cross and contrary to the froward, opposing and crossing them in all they do.   God has no delight to grace froward persons with his presence.   When men begin to be froward under a divine hand, God commonly hides his face, and turns his back upon them.   Men sick of impatiency are no fit company for the God of all patience.   Men that are peevish and pettish under the rod will always see a cloud upon the face of God; and thus you see that there are ten things that you must carefully take heed of, as you would enjoy the gracious presence of God with you in your greatest troubles, deepest distresses, and most deadly dangers, Rom. xv. 5; Prov. xi. 20.   But,

2. Secondly, As there are many things to be avoided, so there are several things *to be put in practice*, as you would enjoy the gracious presence of God with you, in your greatest troubles, deepest distresses, and most deadly dangers.   Let me glance at a few:—

[1.] First, Be sure that *you are brought under the bond of the covenant*.   This gracious signal presence of God with his people, under their greatest troubles, and deepest distresses, is peculiar to those that are in covenant with God.[2]   Noah was in covenant with God, and God was with him, providing an ark for him, and preserving of him from drowning in the midst of drowning.   Lot was in covenant with God, and God was with him, and secures him in Zoar, when he rained hell out of heaven upon Sodom and Gomorrah.   Joseph was in covenant with God, and God was with Joseph in prison.   Jeremiah was in covenant with God, and God kept him company in the dungeon. The three children, or rather champions, were in covenant with God, and God was signally present with them in the fiery furnace.   Daniel was in covenant with God, and God was wonderfully with him in the lions' den.   Job was in covenant with God, and God was with him in six troubles, and in seven, Job iii. 18, 19.   David was in covenant with God, and God was with him in the valley of the shadow of death, Ps. lxxxix. 33, 34, and xxiii. 4.   Take not up in a name to live, nor in a form of godliness, nor in common convictions, nor in an outward reformation; take up in nothing below a covenant-relation, as you would enjoy the precious presence of the Lord with you in your greatest

---

[1] See my 'Mute Christian under the Smarting Rod.' [Vol. i. p. 285, *seq.*—G.]

[2] Ezek. xx. 37; Ps. xxv. 14, and l. 5; Jer. xxxii. 40, 41; Gen. vi. 8, 18, xix. 20-26 and xxxix. 20-22; Jer. i. 17-19, and xxxvii. 15, *seq.*; Dan. iii. 23-25, and vi. 22, 23.

troubles, and deepest distresses, Deut. xxvi. 17–19. If you choose him for your God, you shall then assuredly find him to be your God; if he be the God of our love and fear, he will be the God of our comfort and safety; if God be your God in covenant, then in distress the cities of refuge are open to you; he will stick close to you, he will never leave you nor forsake you, Heb. xiii. 5–7; you have a Father to go to, a God to flee to, a God that will take care of you: ' Come my people, enter thou into thy chambers, and shut thy doors about thee, hide thyself, as it were for a little moment, until the indignation be overpassed.' Here are chambers, with drawing-rooms provided, not open chambers, but with doors, and doors shut round about, intimating that guard of protection, which the people of God shall find from him, even in a common inundation.   But,

[2.] Secondly, If you would enjoy the gracious presence of God with you, in your greatest troubles, deepest distresses, and most deadly dangers, then *look to the practical part of holiness, keep up the power of godliness in your hearts and lives:* 2 Chron. xv. 2; John xiv. 21, ' He that hath my commandments, and keepeth them, he it is that loveth me; and he that loveth me, shall be loved of my Father, and I will love him, and will manifest myself to him:' ver. 23, ' If a man love me, he will keep my words, and my Father will love him, and we will come unto him, and make our abode with him.' He that frames his heart and life according to Christ's rule, shall be sure of Christ's presence. Ezekiel was a man that kept up the power of holiness and godliness in his heart and life.[1] And oh! the glorious visions, and deep mysteries, and rare discoveries of God, and of his presence, and of the great things that should be brought about in the latter days, that was discovered to him! Daniel kept up the power of holiness and godliness in his heart and life; and oh, what secrets and mysteries did God reveal to him! Many of those great and glorious things, which concerns the destruction of the four last monarchies, and the growth, increase, exaltation, flourishing, durable, invincible and unconquerable estate of his own kingdom, was discovered to him. Paul was a person that kept up the power of holiness and godliness in his heart and life; and oh, what a mighty presence of God had he with him, in all his doing, suffering, and witnessing work! And oh, what glorious revelations and discoveries of God had he, when he was caught up into the third heaven, into paradise, and heard unspeakable words, or wordless words, such as words were too weak to utter, such ' as was not possible for man to utter,' and that either because they transcended man's capacity in this life, or else because the apostle was forbid to utter them, they being revealed to him not for the public use of the church, but only for his particular encouragement, that he might be the better able to encounter with all hardships, difficulties, dangers, and deaths that did or might attend him in his ministerial work, 2 Cor. i. 7–10. Some of the ancients are of opinion that he saw God's essence, for, say they, other things in heaven might have been uttered, but the essence of God is so great and so glorious a thing that no man or angel can utter it. But here I must crave leave to enter my dissent from these learned men, for the scripture is express in this, ' that no

[1] This is evident throughout the whole book of the prophet Ezekiel. See ii. 4, 7–12.

man hath thus ever seen the Lord at any time, and that no man can thus see the Lord, and live,' John i. 18; 1 Tim. vi. 16; 1 John iv. 12; Exod. xxxiii. 20–23. And as great a favourite of Heaven as Moses was, yet he could only see the back parts of God, he could only behold some lower representations of God. Some say that he heard the heavenly singing of angels and blessed spirits, which was so sweet, so excellent and glorious, that no mortal man was able to utter it; and this of the two is most probable. But no man is bound to make this opinion an article of his faith. This, I think, we may safely conclude, that in this rapture, besides the contemplation of celestial mysteries, he felt such unspeakable delight and pleasure, that was either like to that, or exceeded that, which Adam took in the terrestrial paradise. Doubtless the apostle did see and hear such excellent things as was impossible for the tongue of any mortal man to express or utter. John was 'a burning and a shining light,'[1] John v. 35, both in life and doctrine. He was a man that kept up in his heart and life the power of holiness and godliness; and Christ reveals to him the general estate of his church and all that should befall his people, and that from John's time unto his second coming. Christ gives John a true representation of all the troubles, trials, changes, mercies, and glories that in all times and in all ages and places should attend his church until he came in all his glory. About sixty years after Christ's ascension,[2] Christ comes to John, and opens his heart, and unbosoms his soul, and makes known to him all that care, that love, that tenderness, that kindness, and that sweetness that he would exercise towards his church from that very time to the end of the world. Christ tells John, that though he had been absent, and seemingly silent for about threescore years, that yet he was not so taken up with the delights, contents, and glory of heaven, as that he did not care what became of his church on earth. Oh no! and therefore he opens his choicest secrets, and makes known the most hidden and glorious mysteries to John that ever was made known to any man. As there was none that had so much of the heart of Christ as John, so there was none had so much of the ear of Christ as John. Christ singles out his servant John from all the men in the world, and makes known to him all the happy providences and all the sad occurrences that were to come upon the followers of the Lamb, that so they might know what to fit for, and what to pray for, and what to wait for. Also he declares to John all that wrath and vengeance, all that desolation and destruction that should come upon the false prophet and the beast, and upon all that wandered after them, and that were worshippers of them, and that had received their marks either in their foreheads or in their hands. Thus you see that they which keep up the power of holiness in their hearts and lives, they shall be sure to enjoy the choicest presence of God, and the clearest, fullest, and sweetest discoveries of God, and of these great things that concern the internal and eternal good of their souls. Nothing wins upon God like

[1] This is the second time wherein Brooks confounds John the Baptist with John the Apostle.—G.

[2] It is the general opinion of the learned that this Book of the Revelation was penned about the latter end of the reign of Domitian the emperor, which was about sixty years after Christ's ascension.

holiness, nothing delights God like holiness, nothing engages the presence of God like holiness, Ps. l. 23.[1]   He shews his salvation to him that ordereth his conversation aright.   He that puts every piece of his conversation in the right order, he shall see and know that he shall be saved.   He that walks accurately and exactly, that walks as in a frame, treading gingerly, stepping warily, he shall have a prospect of heaven here, and a full fruition of heaven hereafter, ' Thou meetest him that rejoiceth, and worketh righteousness, those that remember thee in thy ways,' Isa. lxiv. 5.   He that works righteousness and walks in righteousness shall be sure to meet with God, and to enjoy the precious presence of God in his greatest troubles and deepest distresses.   But,

[3.] Thirdly, If you would enjoy the gracious presence of God with you in your greatest troubles, deepest distresses, and most deadly dangers, then *keep close to instituted worship, keep close to gospel ordinances, keep close to your church state:* Exod. xx. 24, ' In all places where I record my name, I will come unto thee and bless thee, Isa. lxiv. 5; Rev. ii. i; Cant. vii. 5; Ezek. xlviii. 35.   Where God fixeth his solemn worship for the memorial and honour of his name, there he will vouchsafe his gracious presence: Mat. xviii. 20, ' For where two or three are gathered together in my name, there am I in the midst of them.'   The promise of God's gracious assistance, presence, and acceptance is annexed to his church, whether it be great or small, numerous or few: Mat. xxviii. 20, ' Lo, I am with you alway,' according to my godhead, majesty, grace, and Spirit.   Lo, I am with you, to own you!   Lo, I am with you, to counsel and direct you!   Lo, I am with you, to cheer and comfort you!   Lo, I am with you, to assist and strengthen you!   Lo, I am with you, to shelter you and protect you!   Lo, I am with you, to do all your works in you and for you!   Lo, I am with you, to strengthen your graces and to weaken your sins!   Lo, I am with you, to scatter your fears and answer your doubts!   Lo, I am with you, to better your hearts and to mend your lives!   Lo, I am with you, to bless you and crown you with immortality and glory![3]   And what can the soul desire more?   Such as have low thoughts of gospel ordinances, such as slight gospel ordinances, such as neglect gospel ordinances, such as vilify gospel ordinances, such as decry gospel ordinances, such as oppose gospel ordinances,—such may talk of the presence of Christ, and such may boast of the presence of Christ, but all such are out of the way of enjoying the presence of Christ.   Christ is only to be met with in his own worship, and in his own ways.   Ah, how many in these days are there that are like to old Barzillai, that had lost his taste and hearing, and so cared not for David's feasts and music! 2 Sam. xix. 35.   How many are there that formerly were very zealous for ordinances, but now are as zealous against them!   How many formerly have made many great, hard, and dangerous ventures to enjoy gospel ordinances, who now won't venture a broken shin for an ordinance,

---

[1] *Vide, Muis* in loc.

[2] Christ in his ordinances doth, as Mary, open a box of ointments, which diffuseth a spiritual savour among the saints, and this makes the ordinances precious in their eyes.

no, nor stir out of doors to enjoy an ordinance, &c. ! How many in our days, upon neglecting and despising gospel ordinances, have grown from naught to be very naught, and from very naught to be stark naught. He shall be an Apollo to me that can shew me one man in the world that ever grew better or holier by neglecting or slighting gospel ordinances. Many come to the ordinances, too, like the Egyptian dog, which laps a little as he runs by the side of Nylus,[2] but stays not to drink. How many in this great city run every Sabbath to hear this man and that; and here they lap a little and there a little, but never stay to drink—never fix in this congregation or that, this way or that. These persons are neither wise, serious, lovely, nor lively in the ways of God. I think they are judicially blinded and hardened, that are indifferent whether they enjoy ordinances or not, or that can part with ordinances with dry eyes. Surely the child is either very sullen or very sick that cries not for the breast, Zeph. iii. 18. As ever you would enjoy the gracious presence of God with you in all your troubles and distresses, make conscience of sticking close to gospel ordinances. But,

[4.] Fourthly, If you would enjoy the gracious presence of God with you in your greatest troubles, deepest distresses, and most deadly dangers, then, *when you are not in troubles, distresses, dangers, &c., be sure you make much conscience of five things*, (1.) Of prizing his presence above all other things; so Moses did, Exod. xxxiii. 13-17; so Augustine would willingly go through hell to Christ; and Luther had- rather be in hell with Christ than in heaven without him; and Bernard had rather have Christ in a chimney corner than be in heaven without him. (2.) Of improving this gracious presence against sin, the world, the flesh, oppositions and temptations, &c. (3.) Of walking suitable to this gracious presence. (4.) Of lamenting and mourning over those that want this gracious presence. (5.) Of holding any secret intelligence or correspondence with the profest and known enemies of Christ. Princes will never vouchsafe their favourable presence to such subjects as hold any secret intelligence with their profest and known enemies, either at home or abroad; so here. But,

[5.] Fifthly, If you would enjoy the gracious presence of God with you in your greatest troubles, deepest distresses, and most deadly dangers, then, in all your troubles and distresses, &c., *maintain uprightness and integrity of spirit with God*, Ps. v. 12: 2 Chron. xvi. 9, ' For the eyes of the Lord run to and fro throughout the whole earth, to shew himself strong in the behalf of them whose heart is perfect towards him.' Ps. lxxxiv. 11, ' For the Lord God is a sun and shield: the Lord will give grace and glory; no good thing will be withhold from them that walk uprightly.' This is the largest promise we find in the whole book of God. The creature stands in need of two things, provision and protection; for the first, the Lord is a sun, as full of goodness as the sun is of light. He is a sun, in that he doth enlighten and enliven his church, whenas all the world besides lie under darkness and the shadow of death; and in that he doth cheer, and warm, and comfort the hearts of his people by his presence and lightsome countenance, and is the fountain from whence all external, internal,

and eternal blessings are derived to them.   For the second, a shield,
Ps. xviii. 2.   Among all inanimate creatures the sun is the most
excellent, and among all artificial creatures a shield is chiefest, and
was of greatest use in those days.   The sun notes all manner of excellency and prosperity, and the shield notes all manner of protection
whatsoever, Isa. lxii. 20 ; Ps. iii. 4.   Under the name of ' grace,' all
spiritual good things are to be understood ; and under the name of
' glory,' all eternal good things are to be understood ; and under that
phrase of ' No good thing will he withhold,' all temporal good things
are to be understood, so far as they make for his glory, and his people's
real good.   Now this choice, this sweet, this full, this large promise,
is made over only to the upright, and therefore, as you would have
any share in it, maintain your uprightness : Ps. xi. 7, ' His countenance doth behold the upright ; ' *Heb.*, His faces.   Every gracious
discovery of God to the upright is his face.   God will all manner of
ways make gracious discoveries of his love and delight to upright
ones.   No father can so much delight to behold the countenance of
his child, as God delights to behold the countenance of the upright :
Ps. cxii. 4, ' Unto the upright there ariseth light in darkness.'   Light
commonly signifies joy, comfort, peace, help, deliverance, Job xxx.
26 ; Esther viii. 16 ; 2 Cor. vi. 10.   The upright man shall have joy
in tribulation, plenty in penury, liberty in bonds, life in death, as the
martyrs have frequently and gloriously experienced.   Sometimes God
turns the upright man's adversity into prosperity, his sickness into
health, his weakness into strength, his night into day, his storms into
calms, his long winter nights into pleasant summer days.   Sometimes
God hides his upright ones in the hollow of his hand, in his pavilion,
in his presence-chamber, Isa. xxvi. 9, 20 ; Mal. iii. 17.   When his judgments are abroad in the earth he takes special care of his jewels, and
many times, when the upright are in darkness and in great distress,
God cheers their hearts with the consolations of his Spirit and the
light of his countenance, Ps. xciv. 19, and lxxi. 20, 21.   By all which
it is most evident that ' Unto the upright there ariseth light in darkness.'   O sirs, do but maintain your uprightness in all your troubles
and distresses, and then you will be sure of the gracious presence of
God with you in all your troubles and distresses.   God values an
upright Job upon a dunghill before a deceitful Jehu upon his royal
throne, Job i. 8, and ii. 3, 7-9 ; he sets a higher price upon an upright
Lazarus in rags than upon a rich Dives in his purple robes, Luke xvi.
And therefore when an upright man is in troubles and distresses, God
will be sure to keep him company.   The upright man's motto is
semper idem; he is like the philosopher's die, cast him which way
you will, and into what condition you will, he is still upright ; and
therefore, of all persons, God loves to grace the upright man with his
gracious presence.   But,

[6.] Sixthly, If you would enjoy the gracious presence of God with
you in all your troubles, deep distresses, and most deadly dangers, then
you must *be very earnest and importunate with God not to leave you,
but to stay with you, to abide with you, and to dwell in the midst of you,*
Ps. cxlviii. 18, ' The Lord is nigh unto all that call upon him ; ' but,
to prevent mistakes, I mean, ' to all that call upon him in truth.'

There are many that call upon God, but not in truth; from these God stands at a distance, Prov. i. 28; Isa. i. 11–17; Deut. iv. 4; 2 John 4. There are others that call upon God in truth, in plainness and singleness of heart; and these God are [1] near, not only in regard of his essence, which is everywhere, but also in regard of the effects of his power, and the readiness of his will in granting their requests. Abijah prays, and finds an admirable presence of God with him, giving him a mighty victory over his most powerful enemy, 2 Chron. xiii. 3, 10, 11, 17, 18. Asa prays, and finds such a singular presence of God with him as made him victorious over a host of a thousand thousand and three hundred chariots, a huger host than that of Xerxes. Josephus saith it consisted of nine hundred thousand foot, and one hundred thousand horse, 2 Chron. xiv. 9 to the end. Jehoshaphat prays, and had such a signal presence of God with him that those numerous forces that were combined against him fall by their own swords, 2 Chron. xx. 1–11, with ver. 22–25. The wrath of God wrought their ruin, as by an ambuscade, unexpectedly and irresistibly. Some understand this ambushment of the holy angels sent suddenly in upon them to slay them; whereupon they, mistaking the matter, and supposing it had been their own companions, flew upon them, and so sheathed their swords in one another's bowels. [2] Others say that the Lord did suddenly and unexpectedly cut them off, as when men are cut off by enemies that lie in ambush against them, and that by sending some unexpected strife among those nations, whereupon they fell out among themselves, and slew one another, and so accomplished that which the Levite had foretold, ver. 17, ' Ye shall not need to fight in this battle: set yourselves, stand ye still, and see the salvation of the Lord with you, O Judah and Jerusalem: fear not, nor be dismayed; to-morrow go out against them: for the Lord will be with you.' It was the presence of God with his people that was their preservation, and their enemies' destruction. There is no power, no force, no strength, no combinations that can stand before the powerful presence of God with his people, and a spirit of prayer upon his people. Hezekiah prays, and finds such a powerful presence of God with him as bears up his heart, and as strengthens his faith, and as cuts off his enemies, Isa. xxxvii. 14–21, with ver. 36. Oh, beg hard of the Lord that he will stay with you, do as they did when Christ made as though he would have gone from them: Luke xxiv. 29, ' But they constrained him, saying, Abide with us, for it is towards evening, and the day is far spent; and he went in to tarry with them.' [3] By prayer and importunity lay hold on Christ; say, Lord, night is near, the night of trouble, the night of distress, the night of danger, the night of death is near; stay with us, depart not from us. They over-entreated him by their importunity, they compelled him by entreaty. ' Night is near, and the day is far spent.' Some conjecture that Cleophas, observing

[1] Query, 'and to these God is'?—ED.
[2] They were carried by such a spirit of rage and fury that no man spared his neighbour, but each one destroyed him that was next him.
[3] Luke xxiv. 28. Equivocators abuse this place greatly, but they must know that Christ did not pretend one thing, and intend another, but as he made an offer to depart, so without question he would have gone farther, if the importunity of the disciples had not staid him.

Christ to be very expert in the prophets, and to discourse so admirable well of Christ's person, sufferings, and glory, his heart burning in him with musing who this should be, he is marvellous importunate with him to stay at his house, and at last prevails. Oh, lay a hand of holy violence upon God, as Jacob did, and say, as he, ' I will not let thee go.' Jacob, though lamed and hard laid at, yet will not let Christ go. Jacob holds fast with both hands when his joints were out of joint, being fully resolved that whatever he did let go, he would not let go his Lord till he had blessed him, Gen. xxxii. 25, 26; Hosea iv. 12. Oh, be often a-crying out with Jeremiah, ' Leave us not, Lord,' Jer. xiv. 9. Though in our great troubles and deep distresses friends should leave us, and relations leave us, and all the world leave us, yet don't thou leave us. Oh, don't thou leave us, Lord ! Though all creatures should desert us, yet, if thou wilt but stand by us, we shall do well enough ; but woe, woe unto us if God depart from us. Oh, leave us not ! But,

[7.] Seventhly, *Keep humble, and walk humbly with your God,* Micah vi. 8 ; Ps. xxv. 9: The highest heavens and the lowest hearts, are the habitation of God's glorious presence: Isa. lvii. 15, ' For saith the high and lofty One that inhabiteth eternity, whose name is Holy ; I dwell in the high and holy place, with him also that is of a contrite and humble spirit, to revive the spirit of the humble, and to revive the heart of the contrite ones.' He that would in good earnest enjoy the gracious presence of God with him in his great troubles, deep distresses, and most deadly dangers, he must keep humble, and walk humbly with his God. God will keep house with none but humble souls. There are none that feel so great a need of the divine presence as humble souls, there are none that so prize the divine presence as humble souls, there are none that so love the divine presence, and that are so enamoured with the divine presence as humble souls, there are none that so thirst and long for much of the divine presence as humble souls, there are none that so lament and bewail the loss of the divine presence as humble souls, there are none that make such a singular and thorough improvement of the divine presence as humble souls; and therefore no wonder that of all the men in the world God singles out the humble Christian, to make his heart the habitation where his honour delights to dwell. Abraham is but dust and ashes in his own eyes, Gen. xviii. 27 ; and what man on earth had ever more of the divine presence of God with him than he ? Gen xv. 12-19, xvii. 1-10, and xviii. 17-19, &c. Jacob was less than the least of all mercies in his own eyes, Gen. xxxii. 10 ; and he had a mighty presence of God with him, Gen. xxxii. 24-31, &c. David in his own eyes was but a worm and no man, Ps. xxii. 6. The word in the original, *tolagnath,* signifieth a very little worm, which breedeth in scarlet. It is so little, that no man can hardly see it or perceive it ; and yet what a mighty presence of God had David with him in the many battles he fought, and in the many dangers he was in, and in the many miraculous deliverances he had ! See them all summed up in that 18th Psalm. It is his triumphant song after many victories won, deliverances vouchsafed, and mercies obtained ; and therefore worthy of frequent perusal. Paul was the least of all saints in his own eyes ; yea, he was less than the least of all saints, Eph. iii. 8, ἐλαχιστοτέρῳ. This is a double diminutive, and signifies 'lesser than the least,' if lesser might be. Here you have the greatest apostle descending down to the lowest step of humility, 1 Cor. xv. 8, iv. 9 ; 1 Tim. i. 15. Great Paul is least of saints, least of the apostles, and greatest of sinners in his own eyes, and never had any mortal more of the gracious presence of God with him in all his services and in all his sufferings, in all his afflictions and in all his temptations, in all his trials and in all his troubles, which were many and great. See Acts xvi. 23–25, xxiii. 10, 11, xxvii. 23–25; 2 Cor. i. 8–10, iv. 8–11, vii. 4–7, xi. 21, *seq.*, xii. 7–10. Is your condition low, then let your hearts be low. He that is little in his own account, is great in God's esteem, and shall be sure to enjoy most of his presence. God can dwell, God will dwell with none but those that are lowly in heart ; and therefore as ever you would enjoy the signal presence of God with you in your greatest troubles and deepest distresses, be sure you walk humbly with your God. Many may talk much of God, and many may profess much of God, and many may boast much of God ; but he only enjoys much of God who makes conscience of walking humbly with God. But,

[8.] Eighthly, and lastly, If you would enjoy the signal presence of God with you in your greatest troubles, deepest distresses, and most deadly dangers, then *labour every day more and more after greater measures of holiness.* The more holiness you reach to, the more you shall have of the presence of a holy God with you in all your straits and trials.[1] If the Scriptures be narrowly searched, you will find that men of the greatest measures and degrees of holiness have always enjoyed the greatest measures of the divine presence : witness Enoch, Gen. v. 24 ; Noah, Gen. vi. 8, 9, 17, 18. So Abraham, Jacob, Joseph, Job, David, Daniel, John, Paul, &c. They were all famous for holiness ; and accordingly they had a famous presence of God with them, as hath been shewed in part, and might more fully have been discovered, but that the press calls upon me to hasten to a conclusion ; and therefore I shall now but hint at things. Consider,

[1.] First, *That the more holy any person is, the more excellent that person is.* All corruptions are diminutions of excellency. The more mixed anything is, the more abased it is. The more you mix your wine with water, the more you abase your wine ; and the more you mix your gold with tin, the more you abase your gold : but the purer your wine is, the richer and better your wine is ; and the purer your gold is, the more glorious and excellent it is. So the purer and holier any person is, the more excellent and glorious that person is. Now the more divinely excellent and glorious any person is, the more he is beloved of God, Dan. ix. 23 ; and the more he is the delight of God, and the more he shall have of the presence of God. Consider,

[2.] Secondly, The more holy any person is, *the more that person pleases the Lord.* Fruitfulness in holiness fills heaven with joy. The husbandman is not so much pleased with the fruitfulness of his fields, nor the wife with the fruitfulness of her womb, as God is

[1] Ponder upon these scriptures, Isa. lviii. 8–11; 2 Cor. vi. 16–18, and vii. 1 ; Deut. xxiii. 13, 14.

pleased with the fruitfulness of his people in grace and holiness. Now certainly, the more God is pleased with any person, the more he will be present with that person. They commonly have most of our presence that most please us. Enoch had this testimony, before his translation, that he pleased God, or gave God content, as the original word, εὐηρεστηκέναι, imports. Enoch eyed God at all times, in all places, and in all companies ; and this pleased God. Whereever Enoch was, his eye was still upon God.[1] Enoch walked constantly with God ; his whole life was but one continued day of walking with God ; and this pleased God. Enoch kept himself from the corruptions and pollutions of the times, which were very great ; he was not carried away with the stream of the times ; he kept a constant counter-motion to the corrupt courses of the times ; and this pleased God. Enoch maintained and kept up a clear, choice, and standing communion with God ; and this pleased God. Enoch made it his business, his work, his heaven, to approve his heart to God, and his ways to God ; and this pleased God. Enoch was very serious and studious to avoid everything that might be a dishonour to God, or displeasing to God ; and this pleased God. Enoch had great, and high, and honourable thoughts of God ; and this pleased God. God was so pleased and taken with Enoch that he translates him from earth to heaven, from a gracious to a glorious presence.[2] It was a singular mercy for God to be with Enoch on earth, but it was a far more glorious mercy for Enoch to be with God in heaven. The gracious presence of God is very desirable, but the glorious presence of God is most comfortable. Enoch pleases God, and God translates Enoch. We can never have those friends near enough to us who take a pleasure and delight to please us : so here Enoch was a bright morning star, a rising sun, for virtue and holiness ; and therefore God could not satisfy himself, to speak after the manner of men, that he should live at so great a distance from him, and therefore translates him from earth to heaven. Well, my friends, the greater measures of holiness you reach to, the more you will please God ; and the more you please God, the more you shall be sure to enjoy of the presence of God. Consider,

[3.] Thirdly, The more holy any person is, *the more like to God he is ; and the more like to God he is, doubtless the more he is beloved of God.* It is likeness both in nature and grace that always draws the strongest love, 1 Pet. i. 15, 16 ; Lev. xi. 44, and xix. 2, and xx. 7. Though every child is the father multiplied, the father of a second edition ; yet the father loves him best, and delights in him most who is most like him, and who in feature, spirit, and action does most resemble him to the life ; and so does the Father of spirits also ; he always loves them best who in holiness resemble him most, Heb. xii. 9. There are four remarkable things in the beloved disciple above all the rest, John xiii. 23, and xviii. 16, and xix. 26, 27, and Mark xiv. 50: (1.) That he lay nearest to Christ's bosom at the table ; (2.) That he followed

---

[1] Heb. xi. 5 ; Gen. v. 24. The Hebrew word ויתהלך from הלך is in Hithpael, and notes a continual walking with God without ceasing.

[2] God took him up in a whirlwind, say the Hebrew doctors, as Elias was. He changed his place, but not his company, for he still walked with God ; as on earth, so in heaven.

Christ closest to the high-priest's palace; (3.) That he stood close to Christ when he was on the cross, though others had basely deserted him and turned their backs upon him; (4.) That Christ commended the care of his virgin mother to him. Now why did Christ's desire, love, and delight run out with a stronger and a fuller tide towards John than to the rest of the disciples? doubtless it was because John did more resemble Christ than the rest, it was because John was a more exact picture and lively representation than the others were of Christ. Now the more any man in holiness is like to Christ, the more any man in holiness resembles Christ, the more that man shall enjoy of the presence of Christ, the more that man shall lie in the bosom of Christ. The Father loves to be most with that child that is like him most: so here, as ever you would enjoy the presence of God in your greatest troubles, deepest distresses, and most deadly dangers, be sure that you keep up holiness in your hearts and lives, be sure that you grow in holiness, and flourish in holiness, and then you shall be sure of the presence of God with you in all your troubles and deep distresses; a holy God will never leave the holy Christian. And thus much for this use of exhortation.

The last use of all is a use of comfort and consolation to all the people of God, in their greatest troubles and deepest distresses. Now here consider,

(1.) First of all, That God himself hands out this as a rare comfort to his people in all their troubles, distresses, and dangers—viz., *That he will be graciously present with them in the midst of all their sorrows and sufferings:* Gen. xxvi. 3, 'Sojourn in this land, and I will be with thee, and will bless thee;' xxviii. 15, 'And behold I am with thee, and will keep thee in all places whither thou goest, and will bring thee again into this land; for I will not leave thee,' &c., Isa. xliii. 2; Ps. xci. 15; Josh. i. 5; Heb. xiii. 5; Exod. iii. 12. Don't talk of thy loss of friends, for I will be with thee; nor don't talk of thy country, for I will give thee this land, which is the paradise of the world; nor don't talk of thy poverty, for thou shalt spread abroad to the west, and to the east, and to the north, and to the south, ver. 14. Nor don't talk of thy solitariness and aloneness, 'for I will not leave thee.' Isa. xli. 10, 'Fear thou not; for I am with thee: be not dismayed; for I am thy God: I will strengthen thee; yea, I will help thee; yea, I will uphold thee with the right hand of my righteousness.' Suppose a man was injuriously dealt with by this man or that, would it not be a comfort to him that a just and righteous judge stood by and was an eye-witness of all the violences that were offered to him? Suppose a man were in exile with David, or in prison with Joseph, or in a dungeon with Jeremiah, or in the stocks with Paul and Silas, or in banishment for the testimony of Jesus, with John, yet would it not be a singular comfort to him to have the presence of a kind father, a bosom friend, a wise counsellor, an able physician with him? O Christian, be thou in what place thou wilt, and with what company thou wilt, and in what condition thou wilt, yet thy loving God, thy kind father, thy bosom friend, &c., will be still with thee, he will never leave thee, nor forsake thee; and oh what a spring of comfort should this be to thee! But,

(2.) Secondly, Know for your comfort, *that there is always some special favours and blessings annexed to this signal presence of God,* as ' I will be with thee, and bless thee :' Gen. xxvi. 3, ' I am with thee, and will keep thee in all places whither thou goest:' xxviii. 15, ' I will be with him in trouble, and honour him :' Ps. xci. 15, ' I will be with him, and strengthen him :' Isa. xli. 10, ' I will be with thee, and the flames shall not kindle upon thee:' xliii. 2, ' I will be with thee, and there shall not a man be able to stand before thee :' Josh. i. 5, ' I will be with thee, to deliver thee:' Jer. i. 19, ' I am with thee, to save thee, and to deliver thee out of the hand of the wicked, and out of the hand of the terrible,' xv. 20, 21.   Hushai's presence with David was a burden : Job's wife's presence was but a vexation unto him, and Christ's presence among the Gergesenes was a terror to them, and the presence of talkative friends is many times a trouble to us, 2 Sam. xv. 33; Job ii. 9, 10; Mat. viii. 28, 34.   Oh, but this signal, this favourable presence of the Lord with his people, in their greatest troubles and deepest distresses, is a sweet presence, a comfortable presence, a delightful presence, a blessed presence, yea, such a presence as has many singular blessings annexed to it.   But,

(3.) Thirdly, Know for your comfort, *that you shall have mercy and kindness, and whatever good you need in due season, at that very instant, at that very nick of time wherein you most need mercy.* God will time your mercies, and your blessings for you ; he is nigh, and will not fail you at a dead lift, Ps. cxlv. 18; Deut. iv. 7 ; Gen. xxii. 10–13. When Abraham had bound his son, and bent his sword, and the knife was up, then comes a voice from heaven, ' Abraham, Abraham, hold thy hand.'   At that very nick of time, when the four hundred and thirty years were expired, Israel was delivered out of their captivity and slavery, Exod. xii. 41, 51 : Deut. xi. 14, ' I will give you the rain of your land in his due season, the first rain, and the latter rain, that thou mayest gather in thy corn, and thy wine, and thine oil.'   God gives rain to all by a providence, but he gives rain to his Israel by virtue of a promise, Acts xiv. 18 ; Job xxxviii. 26.   God engages himself not only to give rain, but to give it in due season ; he will give the first rain after the sowing of the seed, that it might take rooting in the earth; and he will give the latter rain a little before harvest, that the ears might be full.   O my friends ! it is wonderful mercy, that God will time our mercies for us.   When Jehoshaphat was put to a hard pinch, at that very nick of time God owns him, stands by him, and gives him a great victory, 2 Chron. xx. 12, 22–26. When David was at a great plunge, Saul being at his very heels, at that very nick of time, tidings were brought to Saul, that the Philistines had invaded the land, and so David escapes, 1 Sam. xxiii. 26– 28.   When all human help failed, God came in and helped at a dead-lift.[1]   So Julian was cut off by the Persian war, at that very nick of time when he had vowed at his return, to make a sacrifice of the Christians' lives.   And so Charles the Fifth was diverted from persecuting of the Protestants by the Turks breaking into Hungary, at that very nick of time when his heart was set upon a warm persecution.

---

[1] Let him, saith Augustine, choose his own opportunity, that so freely grants the mercy.

And so Justice Gilford,[1] a violent papist in Queen Mary's days, going up the stairs to Mrs Roberts her chamber, to compel her, will she or will she not, to go to mass, at that very nick of time he was suddenly taken with his old disease the gout, and so grievously tormented, that he swore he would never trouble her more.[2] When Faux was giving fire to the match, that should have given fire to the powder that should have blown up king, lords, and commons, at that very nick of time, he that never slumbers nor sleeps prevented him; and so turned our intended funeral into a festival, Ps. cxxi. 3–5. O Christian! are thy troubles many in number, strange in nature, heavy in measure, much in burthen, and long in continuance, yet remember that thy God is near, whose mercies are numerous, whose wisdom is wondrous, and whose power is miraculous. The nearness or remoteness of a friend is very material and considerable in our troubles, distresses, wants, dangers, &c. I have such a friend, and he would help me, but he lives so far off; and I have another friend that has a great love for me, that is able to counsel me, and to speak a word in season to me, and that in my distress would stand close to me, but he is so remote. I have a special friend, that did he know how things stand with me, would make my burdens his, and my wants his, and my sorrows his; but he is in a far country, he is at the Indies, and I may be undone before I can hear from him. But it is not thus with you, O Christians! who have a God so nigh unto you, who have the signal presence of God in the midst of you, yea who have a God always standing by you, 'The Lord stood by me,' &c. O my friends, how can you want comfort, that have the God of all consolation present with you? How can you want counsel, that have the wonderful counseller so near unto you? How can you want grace, who have the God of all grace standing by you? How can you want peace, who have always the presence of the prince of peace with you? 2 Cor. i. 3; Isa. ix. 6; 1 Pet. v. 10; Isa. ix. 6. But,

(4.) Fourthly, Know for your comfort, *that if God be with you, there is nothing, there can be nothing but weakness against you.*[3] Isa. xxvii. 4, 'Who would set the briars and thorns against me in battle, I would go through them, I would burn them together?' What are briars and thorns to a devouring fire, to the consuming flames? no more are all the enemies of the church to the presence of God with his people. God will be a burning and destroying fire to all the enemies of Zion. Wicked men are chaff: Ps. i. 4, 'And what is that to the wind, to the whirlwind? they are stubble.' Job xxi. 18, 'They are as driven stubble to his bow.' Isa. xli. 2, 'They are as stubble fully dry.' Nah. i. 10. 'They are as stubble before the flame.' Joel ii. 5, 'They are like dust.' 2 Kings xiii. 7, 'Yea, like small dust.' Isa. xxix. 5, 'They are like a morning cloud, an early dew, a little smoke.' Hosea xiii. 3. The morning cloud is soon dispelled, the early dew is soon dried up, the rolling smoke out of the chimney is presently scattered.' Oh, the weakness of man! Oh, the power of God! No people on

---

[1] *Sic:* query, Gifford?—G.   [2] [Foxe,] Acts and Mon., 1880.
[3] God holdeth the church's enemies in chains, having his hook in their nose, and his bridle in their lips, Isa. xxxvii. 29; he can easily rule and over-rule his proudest enemies.

earth have such a power on their sides as the saints have. Consult these scriptures, 2 Kings vi. 16; 2 Chron. xxxii. 6, 7; Isa. viii. 9, 10; Num. xiii. 28, 30–33, and xiv. 9. No Christian can look upon the strong and mighty enemies of Zion in a scripture glass, but must behold them as weak and impotent persons. Who could but smile to see weak children to attempt to besiege a wall of brass, or a wall of fire? Zech. ii. 5; as great a folly and weakness it is for wicked men to make attempts upon the saints, who have been to this day, and will be to the end, a trembling and a burdensome stone to all that gather together against them, Zech. xii. 2, 3. Sense looks upon the powers of the world as strong, mighty, and invincible; but faith looks upon them as poor, weak, contemptible, gasping, dying men. Thus heroical Luther looked upon them, *Contemptus est a me Romanus et favor et furor*, I care neither for Rome's favour nor fury; I am neither fond of the one, nor afraid of the other. It is dangerous to look upon the powers of the world in the devil's multiplying glass; it is best and safest to look upon them in a scripture glass, and then we shall never fear them, nor sinfully shift them. But,

(5.) Fifthly, If God be signally present with his people, in their greatest troubles, deepest distresses, and most deadly dangers, then know for your comfort, *that none can be against you but they must be against God himself*, Acts ix. 4–6; for God is with you in all your troubles, as a father is with his child, a husband with his wife, a general with his army, and as a confederate with his allies, who is with them offensively and defensively. Hence they are said to rage against God, Isa. xxxvii. 28, 29; and to blaspheme God, 2 Kings xix. 3, 6; and to fight against God, Acts v. 38, 39, and xxiii. 9; Prov. xxi. 30. To fight against God is labour in vain. Who ever fought against God and prospered? Some think that this phrase of fighting against God is drawn from the fable of the giants, which were said to make war with the gods. The church of Christ always flourisheth most, and increaseth most, when the tyrants of the earth oppose it most, and persecute it most. Diocletian laid down the empire in great discontent, because he could not by any persecution suppress the true Christian religion. The more violent he was against the people of God, the more they increased and multiplied, and the more they were emboldened and encouraged; and therefore in a rage he throws up all. But,

[1.] *First*, It is the presence of an *Almighty* God: Gen. xvii. 1, 'I am the Almighty God; walk before me, and be thou perfect,' Gen. xlix. 25, and Num. xxiv. 4. Some derive the word *Shaddai*, here used from *dai*, that signifieth *sufficiency*. God is an all-sufficient good, and a self-sufficient good; he is an independent good, an absolute good, an original good, a universal good. Some derive the word Shaddai from *Shad*, that signifieth *a breast, a dug*, because God feedeth his children with sufficiency of all good things, as the loving mother doth the child with the milk of her breasts. God is the only satisfactory good, and proportionable good, and suitable good to our souls; as the breast, the dug is the most suitable good to the child's stomach. And others derive the word Shaddai from *Shaddad*, which signifieth *to spoil, conquer, or overcome*, and so they say that God did here invert or overcome the order of nature, in causing the barren to bear. But most authors do translate it *omnipotent*. God, then, is called Shaddai, that is omnipotent and all-sufficient, for his omnipotency includeth also all-sufficiency.

[2.] *Secondly*, You have the presence of *a loving God* with you: Isa. xliii. 4, 'Since thou wast precious in my sight, thou hast been honourable, and I have loved thee.' But that this may the better stick and work, you must remember, *First*, That God loves you with a first love, see Deut. vii. 7, 8 : 1 John iv. 19, 'We love him because he first loved us.' Our love is but a reflex of his. God first cast an eye of love upon us before we cast an eye of love on him, and therefore God is no way indebted to us for our love. Mary answers not Rabboni till Christ first said unto her *Mary*, John xx. 16. The pure nature of love is more seen in God's first love to us than in ours to him. By nature we were without God, and afar off from God ; we were strangers to God, and enemies to God, yea, haters of God ; and therefore if God had not loved us firstly, we had been done everlastingly, Eph. ii. 12, 19 ; Rom. v. 10, and i. 30. *Secondly*, As God loves you with a first love, so he loves you with a free love : Hosea xiv. 4, 'I will heal their backsliding, I will love them freely.' I know they are backslidden, but I will heal their backslidings. I know they have broken their bones by their fall, but I will make those broken bones to rejoice. I know there is nothing at all in them that is excellent or eminent, that is honourable or acceptable, that is laudable or lovely, yet 'I will love them freely,' *Ex mero motu*, of mine own, - free, rich, absolute, sovereign, and independent grace. *Thirdly*, As he loves you with a free love, so he loves you with an everlasting love : Jer. xxxi. 3, 'I have loved thee with an everlasting love; therefore, with loving-kindness have I drawn thee.' *Heb.*, I love thee with the love of perpetuity, or with the love of eternity. My love and my affections continue still the same to thee, and shall do for ever ; or, as others carry the words, I love thee with an ancient love, or with the love of antiquity ; I love thee still with the same affection that in former ages I bare towards thee. *Fourthly*, As he loves you with an everlasting love, so he loves you with an unchangeable love : Mal. iii. 6, 'I am the Lord, I change not ; therefore ye sons of Jacob are not consumed.' Men change, and counsels change, and occurrences change, and friends change, and relations change, and kingdoms change, and commonwealths change, but God never changes, as Balaam confesses, who was the devil's hackney, and who had a mind to dance with the devil all day, and then sup with Christ at night, Num. xxiii. 10. God is neither false nor fickle ; he cannot, like men, say and unsay ; he cannot alter his mind nor eat his words. 'The eternity of Israel cannot lie nor repent, for he is not a man that he should repent,' Ps. lxxxix. 34 ; 1 Sam. xv. 29. Men are so mutable and changeable, that there is no hold to be taken of what they say ; but God is immutable in his nature, in his essence, in his counsels, in his attributes, in his decrees, in his promises, &c. He is, as the school-men say, *Omninò immutabilis*, Altogether immutable. *Fifthly*, As he loves you with an unchangeable love, so he loves you with a special love, with a peculiar love, with a distinguishing love, with a superlative love, Ps. cxlvi. 7, 8. The Lord executes judgment for the oppressed;

he gives food to the hungry, he looseth the prisoners, he opens the eyes of the blind, he raises them that are bowed down, he loveth the righteous, and this is more than all the rest. *Sixthly* and lastly, As he loves his people with a special love, with a peculiar love, so he loves them with the greatest love, with a matchless love. 'O Daniel greatly beloved:' John iii. 16, 'God so loved the world,' &c. Here is a *sic* without a *sicut*, there being nothing in nature wherewith to parallel it. This *sic* without a *sicut* signifies the greatness of God's love, the vehemency of his love, and the admirableness of his love. Now, what an unspeakable comfort must this be to his saints, to have the presence of a loving God, to have the presence of such a loving God with them in all their troubles and deep distresses! If the presence of a loving friend, a loving relation in our troubles and distresses, be such a mercy, oh, what then is the presence of a loving God!

[3.] *Thirdly*, It is the presence of an *active God*, who will be a defence to you, a shield to you, a sword to you, a buckler to you, a sun to you, a strong tower to you, a salvation to you. None can withstand him, none can equal him, none can out-act him, Ps. xviii. 2; 2 Chron. xvi. 9; Prov. xviii. 10; Jer. xxxii. 40, 41; Isa. xxx. 18, 19, and xxvii. 3; Jer. xxxi. 28.

[4.] *Fourthly*, It is the presence of *a wakeful God, of a watchful God, of a God that never, no never, slumbers or sleeps*. God will be so far from sleeping, that he will not so much as slumber, Ps. cxxi. 3-5. The phrase is taken from watchmen, who stand on the walls in time of war to discover the approaches of enemies, and accordingly give warning. Now watchmen have been treacherous and sleepy. The capitol of Rome had been taken by the Gauls, if the geese had not been more wakeful than the watchmen of the walls. Iphicrates, the Athenian captain, visiting the guards on the walls of Corinth, found one of the watch asleep, and presently thrust him through with his sword, saying, Dead I found him, and dead I left him. Though watchmen slumber and sleep, yet that God that is present with his people doth neither; his seven eyes are always open.

[5.] *Fifthly*, It is the presence of a *wise God, of an omniscient God*. God fills all things, he encompasseth all things, and he sustaineth all things, and therefore he must needs know all things, Ezek. iii. 9; Ps. xxxiii. 10, 11; Isa. xlvi. 10, and xl. 28; Rom. xi. 33; 2 Pet. ii. 9; Jonah i. 5; 2 Kings xiv. 6; Mat. xxvi. 24, 25. God can find Jonah in the bottom of the ship; and Jeroboam's wife in her disguises; and Judas in his treason; and Demas in his apostasy; and the scribes and Pharisees in their hypocrisy, 2 Tim. iv. 10; Mat. xxiii.; Rev. iv. 6. The whole world is to him as a sea of glass: *corpus diaphanum;* a clear transparent body. There is nothing hid from his eyes; so that he that can but find out a place where God sees not, there let that man sin and spare not: 'All things are naked and opened unto the eyes of him with whom we have to do,' Heb. iv. 13: γυμνά, 'naked,' as when the skin is pulled off, and τετραχηλισμένα, 'opened as the entrails of a sacrifice,' cut down the back. The apostle, say some, useth a metaphor taken from a sheep, whose skin is taken off, and he hanged up by the neck, with his back towards the wall, and all his entrails laid bare and exposed to open view. He alludes, say others, to the anatomising of a creature, wherein men are very cautious to find out every little vein or muscle, though they be never so close. They are naked, therefore God sees their outside; and opened, dissected, quartered, and cleft asunder through the backbone, so that he sees their inside also. *Opened* is more than *naked: naked* is that which is not clothed or covered; *opened* is that whose inwards are discovered and made conspicuous. Some make it a metaphor from those that lie with their faces upwards, that all passengers may see who they are. Is it such a comfort to have the presence of a wise and knowing friend with us in our greatest troubles and deepest distresses? what a transcendent comfort must it be then to enjoy the presence of an all-seeing and an all-knowing God in all our troubles and distresses! The eye of heaven sees all, and knows all, and writes down all thy troubles and trials, thy sorrows and sufferings, thy losses and crosses, Mat. vi. 32; and accordingly will an all-knowing God act for his own glory and his people's good.

[6.] *Sixthly* and lastly, It is the presence of *a God of mercy, a God of bowels, a God of compassions*, Exod. xxxiii. 7, 8; Jer. xxxi. 18–20; Hosea xi. 8, 9; Lam. iii. 22. 'His compassions fail not.' Mercy is as essential to God as light is to the sun, Micah vii. 18, 19, or as heat is to the fire. He delights in mercy, as the senses and faculties of the soul do in their several actions. Patience, and clemency, and mercy, and compassion, and peace are the fruits of his bowels—the offspring which the divine nature doth produce. God's compassions are fatherly compassions, Ps. ciii. 13; they are motherly compassions, Isa. xlix. 15; they are brotherly compassions, Heb. ii. 12; they are friendly compassions, Cant. v. 1, 2. Oh, how sweet must the presence of a God of mercy, a God of compassion, be to the saints in a day of trouble! The presence of a compassionate friend in a day of distress is very desirable and comfortable; what then is the presence of a compassionate God! Thus you see that there is no presence to the divine presence—no presence to the signal presence of God with his people in their greatest troubles and deepest distresses. But,

(7.) Seventhly and lastly, If God be signally present with his people in their greatest troubles and deepest distresses, then let them all know for their comfort, *that this presence will make up the want or oss of all outward comforts, this presence will make up the loss of a husband, a child, a friend, an estate*, &c., 1 Sam. i. 8. Look, as all light meets in the sun, and as all water meets in the sea, so all our outward comforts meets in the God of all comfort, 2 Cor. i. 3. When Alexander asked king Porus, being then his prisoner, how he would be used? He answered in one word, Βασιλικῶς, *i.e.*, like a king. Alexander again replying, Do you desire nothing else? No, saith Porus, all things are in Βασιλικῶς, in this one word, like a king; so all things, all comforts are to be found in this signal presence of God with his people, in their greatest troubles and deepest distresses. Certainly the gracious presence of the Lord is infinitely better than the presence of all outward comforts, as you know one sun is more glorious and comfortable than ten thousand stars.

Question. But how may a person that has lost this gracious presence of God, recover it again?

Response 1. First, *Observe how you lost this presence of God, and labour to recover it by a contrary course.* Did you lose it by sinful omissions? then be more active in a way of duty. Didst thou lose the presence of God by neglecting thy watch, or by not walking with God, or by an eager pursuit of the world, or by closing with this or that temptation, or by letting fall thy communion with God? take a contrary course. Now keep up thy watch, walk close with God, keep up a daily converse with lively Christians, let thy heart and affections be set upon things above, keep thy ground in the face of all temptations, maintain a standing communion with God, Ps. cxix. 63; Col. iii. 1, 2. After Christ had stood knocking and calling to his spouse—'Open to me, my sister, my love, my dove, my undefiled; for my head is filled with dew, and my locks with the drops of the night,' Cant. v. 2, 3, 6 —but found no entrance, he retired and withdrew himself, because she would not arise and put on her coat; but when she bestirs herself, 'she finds him whom her soul loved,' chap. iii. 1-4. Then Christ comes into his garden again, and returns to his spouse again, and forgets all former unkindness, chap. vi. 1, 2. But,

Response 2. Secondly, *Inquire where, when, and why God has withdrawn himself;* as we do when dear friends absent themselves from us. 'O the Hope of Israel, the Saviour thereof in time of trouble, why shouldest thou be as a stranger in the land, and as a wayfaring man that turneth aside to tarry for a night?' Jer. xiv. 8. Ver. 9, 'Why shouldest thou be as a man astonied, as a mighty man that cannot save? Yet thou, O Lord, art in the midst of us, and we are called by thy name; leave us not.'

Response 3. Thirdly, *Stand not with Christ for anything, not for a right eye, or a right hand, nor for an Isaac or a Benjamin.* Don't say this work is too high, and that too hard, and the other too hot, and the other too dangerous, in order to the recovery of God's countenance and presence. Thou must not think anything in the world too much to do for Christ, or to suffer for Christ. Thou wilt be a happy man if thou canst recover Christ's lost presence; though it be upon the hardest terms imaginable. But,

Response 4. Fourthly, *Let your hearts lie humble and low under the loss of God's gracious presence,* Ps. li. 8-12; 1 Pet. 5, 6. For, (1.) It is the greatest loss. (2.) It is a loss-embittering loss; it is a loss that will greatly embitter all your worldly losses. I have lost my health, I have lost a hopeful child, I have lost a gracious yoke-fellow, which was the delight of mine eyes and the joy of my heart; I have lost a fair estate, I have lost an intimate friend, I have lost a brave trade. Oh, but that which embitters all my losses, and puts a sting into them, is this, that I have lost the gracious presence of God that once I enjoyed. (3.) It is a loss that all outward comforts can never make up. When the sun is down, nothing can make it day with us. (4.) It is an invisible loss; and no losses to invisible losses. As there are no mercies to invisible mercies, so there are no losses to invisible losses. (5.) It is a loss that will cost a man dear before it will be made up again. Oh the sighs, the groans, the strong cries, the earnest prayers, the bottles of tears that the recovery of the divine presence will cost a Christian; upon all which accounts, how well does it become a Christian to lie humble at the foot of God!

Response 5. Fifthly, *Lift up a mighty cry to heaven.* Thus the saints of old have done. Consult these scriptures, Ps. li. 6–13; Lam. iii. 56, 57; Ps. iv. 6, 7; xxvii. 9, xxxviii. 21, 22, cxxxviii. 3, and cxix. 8, 'O forsake me not utterly.' Christ was forsaken for a few hours, David for a few months, and Job for a few years, for the trial and exercise of his faith and patience; but then they all sent up a mighty cry to heaven. Leave them God did, to their thinking; forsake them he did in regard of vision, but not in regard of union.[1] The promise is, that 'God will draw near to us if we draw near to him,' James iv. 8. Draw nigh to God in duty, and he will draw nigh to you in mercy: sanctify him, and he will satisfy you. Prayer is the only means to supply all defects, it gets all, and makes up the loss of all; as a gracious poor woman said in her distress, I have no friend, but I have prayer; that will get favour with my God; so long as I can find a praying heart, God will, I am sure of that, find a pitying heart and a helping hand. It is not the length, but the strength of prayer; it is not the labour of the lip, but the travail of the heart that prevails with God, Jer. xxix. 12–14. It is not the arithmetic of our prayers, how many they are; nor the rhetoric of our prayers, how eloquent they be; nor the geometry of our prayers, how long they be; nor the music of our prayers, how sweet they be; nor the logic of our prayers, how methodical they be, that will carry the day with God. It is only fervency, importunity in prayer, that will make a man prevalent with God. * Fervent prayer hits the mark, carries the day, and pierceth the walls of heaven, though like those of Gaza, made of brass and iron, James v. 16, 17; Luke xviii.; Isa. xlv. 2. The child has got many a kiss and many a hug by crying. If God has withdrawn his presence, the best, the surest, and the readiest way to recover it is to send up a mighty cry to heaven. But,

Response 6. Sixthly, *Be sure you don't take up your rest in any creature, in any comfort, in any contentment, in any worldly enjoyment,* Jer. l. 6. When the presence of God is withdrawn from you, say as Absalom, 'What is all this to me, so long as I am banished my father's presence, so long as I can't see the king's face?' 2 Sam. xiv. 24, 28, 32, 33. When the mother sees that the child is taken with the baby, the rattle, the fiddle, she comes not in sight. If you take up your rest in any of the babies, in any of the poor things of this world, God will certainly keep out of sight. He will never honour them with his countenance and presence, who take up in anything below himself, below his favour, below his presence. I have read of a devout pilgrim, who going up to Jerusalem was very kindly and nobly entertained in several places, but still he cried out, Oh, but this is not Jerusalem! this is not Jerusalem! So when you cast your eye upon this creature or that, oh then cry out, This is not the presence of God, this is not the presence of God; and when you begin to be tickled and taken with this and that enjoyment, with this or that content-

---

[1] Suidas saith Job was clouded and to his sense and feeling forsaken seven years; but you are not bound to make this an article of your faith.

ment, oh then remember this is not the presence of God, this is not the presence of God! Here is a gracious yoke-fellow, here are hopeful children, here is a pleasant habitation, here is brave air, here is a gainful trade, &c., but what are all these to me, so long as my sun is set in a cloud, and God has withdrawn his presence from me? Remember this once for all, that the whole world is but a barren wilderness without the countenance and presence of God, Ps. lxiii. 1–3. But,

Response 7. Seventhly and lastly, *Patiently and quietly wait upon him in the way of his ordinances for the recovery of his presence.* Consult the scriptures in the margin.[1] Here God dwells, here he walks, here he makes known his glory, here he gives forth his love, here he vouchsafes his presence. When God is withdrawn, your great business is to prize ordinances, and to keep close to ordinances, till God shall be pleased to lift up the light of his countenance and vouchsafe his presence to you. You will never recover the divine presence by neglecting ordinances, nor by slighting ordinances, nor by turning your back upon ordinances, nor by entertaining low thoughts of ordinances. He that thinks ordinances to be needless things, concludes—(1.) That the taking away of the kingdom of heaven from the Jews was no great judgment, Mat. xxi. 43. (2.) That the bestowing of it upon other people is no great mercy. If God be gone, it is good to lie at the pool till he returns, John v. 2–10. There are many dear Christians who have lost their God for a time, but after a time they have found him again in the way of his ordinances; and therefore let no temptation draw thee off from ordinances; say, Here I will live, here I will lie, here I will wait at the pool of ordinances, till the Lord shall return in mercy to my soul.

I shall follow this discourse of the divine presence with my earnest prayers that it may from on high be so signally blest, as that it may issue in the furtherance of the internal and eternal good, both of Writer, Reader, and Hearer.[2]

Soli Deo Gloria in Aeternum.

---

[1] Exod. xx. 24; Mat. xviii. 20; Isa. lxiv. 5; Ps. xxvii. 4, and lxv. 4; Rev. ii. 1; Ps. xl. 1–3; Isa. viii. 17; Mic. vii. 7–9; Isa. xxvi. 8, 9.

[2] Here follows this notice, 'Thus ends the second part of the Golden Key;' but see Note prefixed to this second half of the volume.—G.

END OF VOL. V.

BALLANTYNE AND COMPANY, PRINTERS EDINBURGH.

www.ingramcontent.com/pod-product-compliance
Lightning Source LLC
Chambersburg PA
CBHW060447100426
42812CB00025B/2721